Film Theory and Criticism

FILM THEORY
AND
CRITICISM

Introductory Readings

SEVENTH EDITION

Edited by

LEO BRAUDY
MARSHALL COHEN

New York   Oxford
OXFORD UNIVERSITY PRESS
2009

Oxford University Press, Inc., publishes works that further
Oxford University's objective of excellence
in research, scholarship, and education.

Oxford   New York
Auckland   Cape Town   Dar es Salaam   Hong Kong   Karachi
Kuala Lumpur   Madrid   Melbourne   Mexico City   Nairobi
New Delhi   Shanghai   Taipei   Toronto

With offices in
Argentina   Austria   Brazil   Chile   Czech Republic   France   Greece
Guatemala   Hungary   Italy   Japan   Poland   Portugal   Singapore
South Korea   Switzerland   Thailand   Turkey   Ukraine   Vietnam

Published by Oxford University Press, Inc.,
198 Madison Avenue, New York, New York 10016
www.oup.com

Oxford is a registered trademark of Oxford University Press

Library of Congress Cataloging-in-Publication Data
Film theory and criticism : introductory readings / edited by Leo Braudy, Marshall Cohen. —7th ed.
   p. cm.
 Includes bibliographical references and index.
 ISBN 978–0–19–536562–7
 1. Motion pictures. I. Braudy, Leo. II. Cohen, Marshall.
 PN1994.M364 2008
 791.43—dc22
                    2008045137

MANTHIA DIAWARA "Black Spectatorship: Problems of Identification and Resistance," *Screen 29*, 4 (1988). Reprinted by permission.

WIMAL DISSANAYAKE "Issues in World Cinema," from World Cinema: Critical Approaches, Edited by John Hill and Pamela Church Gibson; this essay was also printed in The Oxford Guid to Film Studies, Edited by John Hill and Pamela Church Gibson. Reprinted by permission of Oxford University Press, Inc.

MARY ANN DOANE "The Voice in the Cinema: The Articulation of Body and Space," *Yale French Studies* (1980). Reprinted by permission.

RICHARD DYER *Stars*, Revised Edition. Copyright © 2008. Reprinted by permission of Palgrave Macmillan.

SERGEI EISENSTEIN *Selected Works*, ed. and trans. Richard Taylor. © 1988 BFI Publishing and Indiana University Press. Reprinted by permission.

S. M. EISENSTEIN, V. I. PUDOVKIN, G. V. ALEXANDROV *Selected Works*, ed. and trans. Richard Taylor. © 1988 BFI Publishing and Indiana University Press. Reprinted by permission.

CYNTHIA A. FREELAND "Feminist Frameworks for Horror Films," pp. 195-218. From *Post-Theory: Reconstructing Film Studies*. Ed. by David Bordwell and Noel Carroll. © 1996 by the Board of Regents of the University of Wisconsin System. Reprinted by permission of The University of Wisconsin Press.

ANNE FRIEDBERG From *Reinventing Film Studies*, Edited by Christine Gledhill and Linda Williams. Copyright © 2000 by Oxford University Press, Inc. Reprinted by permission.

TOM GUNNING Selections from Chapter 1, "Theory and History: Narrative Discourse and the Narrative System," from *D. W. Griffith and the Origins of American Narrative Film:The Early Yeats at Biograph*. Copyright 1991 by the Board of Trustees of the University of Illinois. Used with permission of the author and the University of Illinois Press. "An Aesthetic of Astonishment: Early Film and the (In)credulous Spectator," *Art and Text, 34* (Spring 1989). Reprinted by permission of the author.

GILBERT HARMAN "Semiotics and the Cinema: Metz and Wollen," *Quarterly Review of Film Studies*, February 1977. Reprinted by permission from Harwood Academic Publishers.

MOLLY HASKELL *From Reverence to Rape: The Treatment of Women in the Movies*. Penguin Books. Copyright © 1973, 1974, 1987 by Molly Haskell. Reprinted by permission of Georges Borchardt, Inc. for the author.

BRIAN HENDERSON "Toward a Non-Bourgeois Camera Style," © 1970 by The Regents of the University of California. Reprinted from *Film Quarterly*, 24, no. 2, (December 1970), 2–14, by permission.

RICHARD B. JEWELL "How Howard Hawks Brought Baby Up: An Apologia for the Studio System," in *Journal of Popular Film and Television* (Washington, D.C.), Winter 1984. © Richard B. Jewell.

SIEGFRIED KRACAUER "Basic Concepts," and "The Establishment of Physical Existence," from *Theory of Film: The Redemption of Physical Reality*, copyright © 1960 by Oxford University Press. Reprinted by permission.

JERROLD LEVINSON 'Film Music and Narrative Agency', in D. Bordwell and N. Carroll (eds.), *Post-Theory: Reconstructing Film Studies* (Madison: University of Wisconsin Press, 1996), 254–88. Reprinted with permission.

LEV MANOVITCH *The Language of New Media*, pp. 185-191, 293-302, © 2001 Massachusetts Institute of Technology, by permission of The MIT Press.

GERALD MAST *Film/Cinema/Movie: A Theory of Experience*. Copyright © 1977 by Gerald Mast. Reprinted by permission of Harper & Row, Publishers, Inc.

BRIAN MCFARLANE *Novel to Film: An Introduction to the Theory of Adaptation*, copyright © 1996 by Oxford University Press. Reprinted with permission.

CHRISTIAN METZ *Film Language: A Semiotics of the Cinema*, translated by Michael Taylor. Translation copyright © 1974 by Oxford University Press, Inc. Reprinted by permission. "Identification, Mirror," "The Passion for Perceiving," and "Disavowel/Fetishism" from *The Imaginary Signifier*. Reprinted from *Screen*, Volume 16, Number 2 (1975), by permission of Society for Education in Film and Television and the author.

TANIA MODLESKI "The Terror of Pleasure: The Contemporary Horror Film and Postmodern Theory," *Studies in Entertainment*, Tania Modleski, ed., Indiana University Press, 1986. Reprinted by permission of Indiana University Press. *The Women Who Knew Too Much: Hitchcock and Feminist Theory*. Copyright © 1988 by Tania Modleski by permission of Taylor & Francis.

LAURA MULVEY "Visual Pleasure and Narrative Cinema." Reprinted from *Screen*, Volume 16, Number 3 (1975), by permission of *Screen* and the author.

JAMES NAREMORE *Acting in the Cinema* © 1988 Regeants of the University of California. Published by the University of California Press.

ERWIN PANOFSKY *Bulletin of the Department of Art and Archaeology*. Princeton University, 1934. Reprinted by permission of Dr. Gerda Panofsky.

GILBERTO PEREZ *The Material Ghost: Films and Their Medium*. pp. 114–122. © 1997 The Johns Hopkins University Press.

STEPHEN PRINCE "The Discourse of Pictures: Iconicity and Film Studies," © 1993 by The Regents of the University of California. Reprinted from *Film Quarterly*, 47:1, Fall 1993, pp. 16–28, by permission.

VSEVOLOD PUDOVKIN *Film Acting and Film Technique*, trans. Ivor Montagu, 1958. Reprinted by permission of Vision Press Ltd., London.

PHILIP ROSEN *from Change Mummified: Cinema, Historicity, Theory* Minneappolis, MN: University of Minnesota Press, 2001, pp. 314–326. Reprinted by permission of University of Minnesota Press.

WILLIAM ROTHMAN © 1975 by The Regents of the University of California. Reprinted from *Film Quarterly*, Volume 29 no. 1 (October 1975), pp. 45–50, by permission.

ANDREW SARRIS *Film Culture*, Winter 1962–63. Reprinted by permission of the author.

THOMAS SCHATZ *The Genius of the System*. Copyright © 1988 by Thomas Schatz. Reprinted by permission of Pantheon Books, a division of Random House, Inc. Selections from chapter 2, "Film Genre and the Genre Film," from *Hollywood Genres*, 1981. Reprinted by permission of The McGraw-Hill Companies.

PAUL SCHRADER "Notes on Film Noir, "Film Comment (Spring, 1972), p. 8. Reprinted by permission of Film Society of Lincoln Center.

ROBERT STAM and LOUISE SPENCE "Colonialism, Racism, and Representation: An Introduction," *Screen, 24*, 2 (1983). Reprinted by permission of Screen and the authors.

ROBERT WARSHOW *The Immediate Experience*, 1962. Reprinted by permission of Paul Warshow.

KRISTEN WHISSEL © Regents of the University of California. Published by University of California Press. "Tales of Upward Mobility," *Film Quarterly* 59, no. 4 (June 2006), 23-34.

LINDA WILLIAMS In Doane, Mellencamp, Williams, ed.: *Re-Vision: Essays in Feminist Film Criticism*, 1984. Reprinted by permission of University Publications of America, Inc. and the American Film Institute. "Film Bodies: Gender, Genre, and Excess," © 1991 by The Reagent of the University of California. Reprinted from *Film Quarterly*, 44, no. 4, (July 1991), 2–12, by permission.

PETER WOLLEN "Godard and Counter Cinema: *Vent d'Est*," *Afterimage* (Fall 1972), New Left Books. "The Auteur Theory" from *Signs and Meaning in the Cinema*. Copyright © 1972 by Indiana University Press. Reprinted by permission of Indiana University Press and the British Film Institute.

ROBIN WOOD *Film Comment*, Volume 13, Number 1 (January–February 1977). Copyright © 1977 by the Film Society of Lincoln Center. All rights reserved.

MITSUHIRO YOSHIMOTO "The Difficulty of Being Radical: The Discipline of Film Studies and the Postcolonial World Order," in *boundary 2*, Volume 18, no. 3, pp. 242-257. Copyright, 1991, Duke University Press. All rights reserved. Used by permission of the publisher.

CONTENTS

CONTENTS xi

VII ❑ Film: Spectator and Audience   659

PREFACE

In the thirty-five years since the first edition of this collection appeared in 1974—
let alone the more than one hundred years since the first films were shown—the academic study of film has changed enormously, and the journalistic and popular
criticism of film has been deeply affected as well. Yet many of the same issues that
preoccupied and stimulated writers from the very beginning of film theory and criticism are still puzzling later generations: Is the filmed world realistic or artificial? Is
film a language? Is its world best expressed in silence? in sound? through stories that
may be derived from other arts? through stories that can be told only on film?

Many of these questions were first formulated in critical language indebted to the
methods and terminology of such humanistic disciplines as literary criticism, art history,
and aesthetics. But early on, theorists began to emphasize the obligation to appreciate
what was different, even unique, about film in comparison with the other arts: its formal
qualities, its need for enormous capital investment, and its relation to a mass audience.

In the light both of continuing issues and evolving ideas, we might roughly divide
the history of film theory into three somewhat overlapping phases. The first, which
generally corresponds to the silent period, was formalist. From the early 1920s to the
mid-1930s, theorists such as V. I. Pudovkin, Rudolf Arnheim, and Sergei Eisenstein
attempted to demonstrate that film was indeed an art, not just a direct recording of
nature. The coming of synchronized sound then brought on a realist reaction to the
formalist argument. Siegfried Kracauer and André Bazin among others argued that
film was not an art in contrast to nature but an art *of* nature.

By the 1960s and 1970s, this classical phase of film theory was being challenged
by writers responding both to historical conditions (the Viet Nam war, the student
riots in France and America) and to new developments in the academic conception of
"knowledge," as defined by literature and the social sciences. Just at the time that film
study itself was gaining an academic status separate from the departments of literature and art in which it had often first appeared, these writers questioned the confidence with which classical film theory had used such terms as art, nature, society,
reality, illusion, self, performance, work, author, and artist—and in the process

claimed to unearth hidden assumptions about race, class, gender, and language itself that could be best addressed through an analysis of film.

Especially beginning in the 1970s an explosion of new interpretive approaches derived from a broad range of disciplines began to have a tremendous influence on humanistic studies generally and—in part because of the relative youth of the field— on film study in particular. One powerful early inspiration came from linguistics. Here, drawing upon the work of C. S. Peirce, Ferdinand de Saussure, Roman Jakobson, Louis Hjelmslev, and Noam Chomsky, film theorists and critics explored the structures of meaning that allow communication of all kinds to exist. A formal consideration of the meaning of individual films, or the special nature of film among the arts, became a less significant question than the place of both in more general systems of communication and meaning.

In this fertile and energetic period—perhaps the richest in new explorations of film since the invention of the medium itself—the most salient avenues of interpretation first followed semiotic and structuralist models, derived from the structural anthropology of Claude Lévi-Strauss as well as the demystified cultural history of Roland Barthes and Michel Foucault, often augmented with Marxist historical and Freudian psychoanalytic analysis. Somewhat later came the influence of Jacques Lacan's revisionary view of Freud (itself responsive to linguistic issues), the feminist interrogation of the power structures of vision (in which Marx and Freud were often married), and the deconstructive views of Jacques Derrida (where efforts to pierce the surface of the text and discover its "contradictions" often employed Marxist and psychoanalytic tools).

None of these new approaches appeared without controversy or has maintained its relevance without polemic. Each in its own way has contributed to such classical issues of film theory as the relation of film to reality and how film may (or may not) be considered a language. In addition, they have introduced such fresh considerations as the way that films reveal the underlying social attitudes and ideologies of the cultures that produce them, the ways films manipulate audience beliefs, and the ways they raise, exploit, and seek to satisfy audience desires.

In the 1990s and into the twenty-first century, film study still maintains its earliest concerns with discovering the general terms and assumptions required for understanding film. However, since the mid-1980s, we have entered a fourth, more eclectic, period. One significant aspect of this new phase seeks to merge insights owed to history, psychology, and linguistics into larger perspectives suitable for understanding individual films as well as film in general. These approaches sometimes draw upon feminism, neoformalism, cognitive psychology, analytic philosophy, or phenomenology. They may assert the shaping activity of the audience on film meaning (as opposed to the passive audience often postulated in earlier approaches). Or they may emphasize the resistance of the performer, especially the star, to the meaning imposed by the film narrative; the ability of the independent filmmaker to construct a personal statement despite the supposedly totalitarian necessities of the medium; and the web of financial, political, and artistic decisions that constitute film production. In order to register these crucial arenas of new critical and theoretical work, we have expanded our previous final section, "Psychology, Ideology, and Technology" into two new sections: "Spectator and Audience" and "Digitization and Globalization."

Surveys of how earlier editions of *Film Theory and Criticism* were being used in the classroom have indicated that courses are most often structured around an interplay between classical and contemporary answers to basic issues, along with an acute awareness of the new avenues that have been opened by the willingness to venture beyond disciplinary barriers. With this new phase already demonstrating its potential to reveal important aspects of film, we have maintained the historical perspective of this collection as a broad survey of thinking about film over the past century. In revising, we have therefore retained a good number of "classical" works that have set the agenda of even some of the most advanced recent theory and criticism. We have maintained an emphasis on such major theorists as Sergei Eisenstein, André Bazin and Christian Metz. At the same time we have tried to illustrate the crucial new directions theory has taken over the last thirty and more years. In the process of opening space for new essays, we have regretted the need to drop old favorites, if only to keep the collection to a manageable size (and price). But we encourage readers to seek out the books and essays from which these excerpts have been taken to enrich their own understanding of the ideas presented here.

Perhaps because so many of these questions about film have turned out to be perennially interwoven, our division of the complexity of theory into now eight major topics more than ever indicates general emphasis rather than exclusive argument. The new sections VII and VIII most obviously carry the banners of important current approaches: how film shapes or reflects cultural attitudes, reinforces or rejects the dominant modes of cultural thinking, and stimulates or frustrates the needs and drives of the psyche; the challenge of digitization and new forms of media; and the changing sense of what constitutes a "national cinema" in an age of globalization.

But the impact of new thinking is visible in each section. Every teacher will have his or her own way of organizing these essays into a course, and every reader will discover connections and ramifications that go beyond the confines of a particular section. To help those echoes be heard more clearly, we have continued to include an index of proper names, marking especially those places where individual films are discussed at length by different authors. We have also for this edition included headnotes to the essays, which place the authors biographically and critically.

New essays have been added to many of the sections. Section I treats basic issues of "Film Language." Section II discusses "Film and Reality." Section III focuses on "The Film Medium: Image and Sound." Section IV emphasizes the connections between film and the other arts in particular through the issues of adaptation and film narration. A consideration of "The Film Artist" takes up Section V, while issues of "Film Genre" are stressed in Section VI, with a particular focus on the genres of horror and film noir, which still attract so much attention from critics and theorists (as well as audiences). Each section begins with a brief essay discussing the arguments of the different authors and comparing their approaches to those of authors included elsewhere.

Our deep thanks to all those friends and colleagues whose suggestions and criticism helped us formulate this new edition, as well as the teachers of film who took the time to respond in such useful detail to Oxford's queries about their use of the sixth edition. We would also like to express our gratitude to Amaranth Borsuk, who drafted the headnotes, and also prepared the index for the present edition.

Los Angeles; May 2008   L. B.
M. C.

Film Theory and Criticism

I

Film Language

Because films embody, communicate, enforce, and suggest meanings, film theorists often suggested that film constitutes a language, a "visual esperanto." They have spoken of film's grammar, its vocabulary, and even of its jargon. The poet Vachel Lindsay spoke of film as a kind of "hieroglyphic" language while the theorist Béla Balász thought of it as a new "form-language." Russian formalists have similarly talked of "semantic signs" and investigated film's relation to "inner speech." In what sense, then, is film a language? Is the claim a suggestive metaphorical one or one that can, as the semioticians think, be subjected to systematic, scientific analysis? And, more generally, by what procedures does film generate meaning?

Those who consider film to be a language often rely on the analogy between the word and the shot. But simply stringing words together does not produce intelligible discourse, and most theorists agree that simply stringing separate photographic shots together will not produce intelligible works of visual art.

The great Soviet filmmakers Sergei M. Eisenstein and Vsevolod Pudovkin asked what more than mere ability to photograph reality was required to transform the new technical resources into a great new art. Their answer was montage, the art of combining pieces of film or shots into larger units—first, the scene, then the sequence, and, finally the complete film. D. W. Griffith, the great American director of *The Birth of a Nation* and *Intolerance*, to whom the Soviet directors acknowledged a great debt, was not important because he took better pictures than anybody else. He was important for having discovered montage, the fluid integration of the camera's total range of shots, from extreme close-up to distant panorama, so as to produce the most coherent narrative sequence, the most systematic meaning, and the most effective rhythmic pattern. In doing so, Griffith had, they thought, contributed to the development of a cinematic language and invented the distinctive art of the film.

1

Eisenstein viewed montage as a kind of collision or conflict, especially between a shot and its successor. He sees each shot as having a kind of potential energy that can display itself in purely visual terms: the direction of its movements, the volume of its shapes, the intensity of its light, and so forth. This potential energy becomes kinetic when the first shot collides with the succeeding one. The two shots can produce a conflict in their emotional content (happy versus sad), in their use of illumination (dark versus light), in their rhythms (slow versus fast), in their objects (large versus small), in their directions of movement (right versus left), in their distances (close-up versus far shot), or in any combination thereof. In his films, this conflict produced the tense, violent rhythms that became an Eisenstein trademark. Conflict was also important to Eisenstein because he took it to be an expression, in the realm of images, of the Marxist dialectical principle. Indeed, Eisenstein maintained that just as the meaning of a sentence arises from the interaction of its individual words, cinematic meaning is the result of the dialectical interplay of shots. His emphasis on the conflict of shots, as distinct from a mere linking of shots, distinguishes his concept from that of his colleague, Pudovkin. Pudovkin's view of montage as a method of building, of adding one thing to another, is not merely of theoretical interest. His theory produced more realistic narratives, with their more deliberate, calmer pace.

Eisenstein, like many theorists who emerged in the era of silent films, was uncomfortable with the addition of synchronized dialogue. Because "silent" films had always used asynchronous sound effects and music, Eisenstein believed that the sound film could use these tools with even greater precision and complexity. But he rejected dialogue as being incompatible with the proper use of montage (see Section III). By contrast, André Bazin, while agreeing that dialogue and montage are incompatible, regards synchronized speech as a necessary and proper development. For Bazin, dialogue returns film to the rightful path from which montage and silence diverted it. According to him, the film image ought to reveal reality whole, not cut it into tiny bits. The cinematic method Bazin endorses, which combines composing with the camera and staging an action in front of it, has, like montage, come to be known by a French term, *mise-en-scène*.

In Bazin's view the montage theorists did not in fact speak for all of the silent film. He discerns in the work of Erich von Stroheim, F. W. Murnau, and Robert Flaherty an alternative, *mise-en-scène* tradition, which emphasizes not the ordering, but the content of images. The film's effect and meaning are not the product of a juxtaposition of images, but are inherent in the visual images themselves. For Bazin, the montage theorists' emphasis on the analogy between word and shot is false, and he rejects it along with their reluctance to employ sound as a source of cinematic meaning. Bazin argues that the *mise-en-scène* tradition within silent film actually looked toward the incorporation of synchronous sound as a fulfillment, not as a violation, of the film's destiny.

Bazin considers German expressionism and Russian symbolism to have been superseded in the 1930s and 1940s by a form of editing more appropriate to the dialogue film. This "analytic" editing, which characteristically manifests itself in the dramatic technique of shot/reverse shot, was an important innovation. Still more important, however, was the development of the depth of field shot by Orson Welles and William Wyler in the early 1940s (anticipated in the 1930s by Jean Renoir), which made even the use of "analytic" montage unnecessary. Entire scenes could now be covered in one take, the camera sometimes remaining motionless. For Bazin, the shot-in-depth, like the use of synchronous sound, constituted a crucial advance toward total cinema and an important stage in the evolution of the language of cinema. It allowed for greater realism and encouraged a more active mental attitude on the part of the viewer, who could now explore more fully the interpretive and moral ambiguity inherent in the film image.

Bazin's composition-in-depth is one kind of long take, but Brian Henderson calls attention to a quite different type developed by Jean-Luc Godard. Godard's long, slow tracking shot avoids depth. Cinema is a two-dimensional art that creates the illusion of a third dimension through its "walk-around" capability. Indeed, both montage and composition-in-depth are techniques that reach for that third dimension, although in different ways: montage through a succession of shots from different angles and at different ranges, composition-in-depth through movements of the camera or of the actors. Bazin's shot can thus be regarded as a long take, in which the camera pauses before a scene rich with interpretive possibilities. In his analysis of the films of Godard, Henderson calls attention to a quite different kind of long take: Godard's slow tracking shot that (perhaps in polemical opposition to the views of Bazin) concertedly avoids and even excludes the impression of depth, to adhere to the single-point perspective of painting.

In Henderson's view, Godard does so for ideological reasons. Composition-in-depth presents an infinitely deep, rich, complex, ambiguous and mysterious bourgeois world. Godard's reversion to one plane demystifies this world and its pretenses. Godard's style of presentation is intimately related to the critical point of view he insists upon. The viewer is presented visually and ideologically with a single flat picture of the bourgeois world not to be unthinkingly accepted as transparent and easy to understand, but to be examined, criticized, and (Godard might conclude) rejected.

Eisenstein and Bazin, for all their differences, were both intrigued by the idea that film was a language, and we might view Godard as adding to the resources of that language. But it is only with the rise of structuralism and semiotics that writers such as Christian Metz and Umberto Eco subjected the topic to more precise analysis. Metz particularly brought this issue to the center of film studies and attempted to put the discussion on a firm scientific basis. He did so by invoking the analysis of language provided by linguists in the semiotic tradition of Ferdinand de Saussure, a tradition that attempted to develop a science of "signs." Saussure distinguished sharply between signs which constitute a *langue* and those that constitute a *langage*. It is Metz's contention that film does not constitute a *langue* in the strict sense of constituting a language system, but that it nevertheless qualifies as a *langage* in the looser sense of being a signifying practice characterized by recognizable ordering procedures ("cinematographic grammar"). Cinema lacks the double articulation characteristic of natural language. The phonemes of natural language are basic, distinctive units of sound which do not themselves signify. It is only when they are articulated at the second level by combining them into monemes (morphemes) or words that they signify. By contrast, the basic unit of cinema, the shot, conveys meaning because of the iconic or isomorphic relation it bears to the world it photographs. The shot is motivated, and is unlike the basic units of language which are arbitrary, conventional and unmotivated.

If Metz rejects the assimilation of film language to natural language, he also rejects the common analogy between shot and word. In Metz's view the shot is equivalent not to the word but to the sentence or statement, and it is the organization of shots in the film chain that invites and supports the claim that film constitutes a language. In the beginning film was purely iconic—it signified exclusively by means of the resemblance of its imagery to objects in the visible world. But reality does not tell stories. It is only when shots are organized according to repeatable, recognizable codes that they become discourse and are capable of telling a story. Cinematic language comprises a number of cinematic codes and sub-codes, but the code which Metz analyses in detail (the code which was more or less established by the time of D. W. Griffith) is the *grande syntagmatique* of the image track. This code, a sub-code of the montage code, permits us to account for the procedures by which cinema denotes such narrative phenomena as succession, priority, temporal breaks, and spatial continuity. As he shows in his analysis of what he calls the alternate syntagma (one of the eight he describes) the order in which signifying images occur may or may not be the same as that in which the realities they signify occur. The student of the language of cinema must therefore account for the processes and mechanisms that make it possible for the viewer to interpret them correctly. For Metz film does not simply reveal reality; it describes it in a language whose features we are only beginning to understand.

Gilbert Harman, in his essay on Metz and Wollen, raises many questions about the entire semiotic approach to film study. He questions Metz's emphasis on plot and on the denotative codes that Metz considers to be primary. Wollen attributes this emphasis to Metz's reliance on the linguistic analogy in developing his version of film semiotics. In Wollen's view the basic linguistic codes are needed for determining literal significance, but the codes of cinema are primarily poetic rather than literal and are best understood through C. S. Pierce's categories of signs. Harman, however, criticizes the basic concept of the code, which Metz and Wollen share. He points out the ambiguous uses to which the concept of code is put and concludes that the proposed science of semiotics has little to contribute to the study of film.

Despite Metz's critique of the claim that film constitutes a *langue*, many theorists in the tradition of Saussure, Louis Althusser, and Jacques Lacan maintain that all cinematic meaning is essentially linguistic and that the relation between signifier and signified is arbitrary, conventional, and both culturally determined and culturally relative. The meanings of signifiers are determined by their relation to other signifiers rather than by their reference to any extra-linguistic reality. Films are texts to be "read" and reading them requires our initiation into the specific conventions and ideological biases of cinematic discourse. As Stephen Heath argues, "the match of film and world is a matter of representation, and representation is in turn a matter of discourse. . . . [I]n this sense at least, film is a series of languages, a history of codes."

Against this influential view Stephen Prince argues that cinematic coding is not linguistic but is largely iconic and mimetic, that film images are typically understood because they resemble the realities to which they refer. The capacity to understand these signs has a biological basis (even animals manifest it). Interpreting iconic signs is more a matter of recognizing similarities by transferring real world skills to the cinematic situation than it is a matter of mastering arbitrary, unmotivated, cultural conventions. Indeed, the capacity to understand iconic signs is shared cross-culturally and this ability helps to explain the intelligibility and global popularity of cinema (recall the early description of it as a verbal Esperanto). Pictorial meaning cannot be explained as a kind of linguistic meaning.

Daniel Dayan views film language from a post-structuralist perspective which goes beyond Metz's earlier, structuralist concept. Using a term drawn from the psychoanalytic theories of Lacan, Dayan describes the system of the suture which negotiates the viewer's access to the film. In Dayan's view this system, which relates to classical narrative cinema as verbal language does to literature, is ideologically charged. Bazin prizes the depth-of-field shot, while Henderson analyzes the meaning of Godard's parallel tracking shot. Essential to Dayan's system is his revaluation of the shot/reverse shot sequence. The viewer's pleasurable possession of the image, his seeing of the image in shot one, is disrupted by his discovery of the frame and his sense of being dispossessed of what he is prevented from seeing. In the first step of reading the film he discovers that he is authorized to see only what happens to be in the axis of the glance of another spectator, called by Jean-Pierre Oudart "the absent-one." The second shot, the reverse shot of the first, represents the fictional owner of the glance corresponding to the first shot. The reverse shot "sutures" the hole opened in the spectator's imaginary relationship with the filmic field by the perception of the absent one.

The absent one stands for that which any shot necessarily lacks if it is to attain meaning—another shot. For, within the system of the suture, the meaning of a shot depends on the next shot and the pair constitute a cinematic statement. The meaning of the shot is given retrospectively and only in the memory of the spectator. Thus, the system encroaches on the spectator's freedom by interpreting, indeed, by remodeling his memory. According to this deconstructive analysis, the system imposes an ideology and the spectator loses his access to the present. The system of the suture is not, however, the only cinematographic system, and Dayan describes how Godard has explored an alternative in his later films.

William Rothman rejects Dayan's assumption of a prior relation in which the viewer "sees" the film image as an unmediated view of reality. He also questions the assumption that classical narrative continuity is illusionistic or necessarily the vehicle of bourgeois ideology. Rothman especially critiques Dayan's contention that the "system of suture" is based on a two-shot (view/viewer) figure: a pair of shots that together constitute a complete cinematographic statement. He argues instead that the point-of-view shot is ordinarily part of a three-shot sequence (viewer/view/viewer), typically initiated when a character visibly attends to something outside the frame. Therefore no ghostly sovereign need be invoked to authorize the point-of-view sequence. It ordinarily manifests the film's power by appropriating a character's gaze, but it does *not* present a figure and then force the viewer to accept that figure as the source of the power. Thus the point-of-view sequence does not lie about its real origin. Indeed, it makes no statement about reality–because it makes no statement at all. The sequence is analogous to a sentence, not a statement, and therefore does not assert whether it is true or false. The film, not the sequence, constitutes the statement–if, indeed, the film makes any statement at all. According to Rothman, we need a critical history of the way cinematic forms have been used, not an a priori assertion that certain cinematic forms are destined by their nature to serve bourgeois ideology.

Like Rothman, Nick Browne rejects the adequacy of the shot/reverse shot sequence to account for the operation and effects of classic film style. But his more complex rhetorical analysis is meant to contribute to the semiotic study of filmic texts. According to him the system of suture establishes the origin of film imagery by reference to the agency of character (the absent-one) but, surprisingly, does not consider the final agency, the authority of the narrator. The traces of the narrator's action may seem to be effaced by the system as the suture theorists suggest but, in Browne's opinion, such an effect can only be the result of a more general rhetoric. He therefore proposes an account in which the structure of the imagery, whatever its apparent forms of presentation, refers jointly to the action of an implied narrator (who defines his position with respect to the tale by his judgments, including his moral judgments) as well as to the imaginative action occasioned by his placing or being placed by the spectator. The point-of-view of the spectator, in turn, and contrary to the ideas of Jean-Luc Comolli and Jean Narboni (see Section VII), is not centered at a single point of view or at the center of any simply optical system. The way in which we, as spectators, are implicated in the action is as much a function of our position with respect to the unfolding of events as it is in their representation from a point in space. In Browne's analysis of Ford's *Stagecoach* he shows that, although we see the action with Lucy's eyes and are invited by a set of structures to experience the force and character of that view, we are put in a position finally of having to reject it as a view either that is right or that we must assent to. Even though we have been sutured into that point of view, we are not thereby committed to the ideology enforced by the system of the suture.

VSEVOLOD PUDOVKIN
FROM FILM TECHNIQUE

[ON EDITING]

A soldier in the Russian army in World War I, Pudovkin (1893–1953) returned home from a German prisoner-of-war camp to find that government financing of film and film study was a high priority due to Lenin's belief in the medium's potential as a propaganda tool. Pudovkin enrolled in the State Cinema School where he learned the essentials of filmmaking and was soon working on communist agitprop. In Lev Kuleshov's experimental film studio his fascination with montage was inspired by a viewing of D.W. Griffith's *Intolerance* (1914). By recutting found footage, Kuleshov and his cohort later theorized that emotional connection and narrative could be propelled through juxtaposition, believing that the real character development in a film took place in the cutting room rather than before the camera. In films such as *Mother* (1926) and *The End of St. Petersburg* (1927), Pudovkin also frequently cast non-professional actors to enhance their realism, using montage to reveal the psychological turmoil of his characters.

METHODS OF TREATMENT OF THE MATERIAL

(Structural Editing)

A cinematograph film, and consequently also a scenario, is always divided into a great number of separate pieces (more correctly, it is built out of these pieces). The sum of the shooting-script is divided into sequences, each sequence into scenes, and, finally, the scenes themselves are constructed from a whole series of pieces (script-scenes) shot from various angles. An actual scenario, ready for use in shooting, must take into account this basic property of the film. The scenarist must be able to write his material on paper exactly as it will appear upon the screen, thus giving exactly the content of each shot as well as its position in sequence. The construction of a scene from pieces, a sequence from scenes, and reel from sequences, and so forth, is called *editing*. Editing is one of the most significant instruments of effect possessed by the film technician and, therefore, by the scenarist also. Let us now become acquainted with its methods one by one.

Editing of the Scene

Everyone familiar with a film is familiar with the expression "close-up." The alternating representation of the faces of the characters during a dialogue; the

7

representation of hands, or feet, filling the whole screen—all this is familiar to every-one. But in order to know how properly to use the close-up, one must understand its significance, which is as follows: the close-up directs the attention of the spec-tator to that detail which is, at the moment, important to the course of the action. For instance, three persons are taking part in a scene. Suppose the significance of this scene consist in the *general* course of the action (if, for example, all three are lifting some heavy object), then they are taken simultaneously in a *general* view, the so-called long-shot. But suppose any one of them change to an independent action having significance in the scenario (for example, separating himself from the others, he draws a revolver cautiously from his pocket), then the camera is directed on him alone. His action is recorded separately.

What is said above applies not only to persons, but also to separate parts of a per-son, and objects. Let us suppose a man is to be taken apparently listening calmly to the conversation of someone else, but actually restraining his anger with diffi-culty. The man crushes the cigarette he holds in his hand, a gesture unnoticed by the other. This hand will always be shown on the screen separately, in close-up, otherwise the spectator will not notice it and a characteristic detail will be missed. The view formerly obtained (and is still held by some) that the close-up is an "inter-ruption" of the long-shot. This idea is entirely false. It is no sort of interruption. It represents a proper form of construction.

In order to make clear to oneself the nature of the process of editing a scene, one may draw the following analogy. Imagine yourself observing a scene unfolded in front of you, thus: a man stands near the wall of a house and turns his head to the left; there appears another man slinking cautiously through the gate. The two are fairly widely distant from one another—they stop. The first takes some object and shows it to the other, mocking him. The latter clenches his fists in a rage and throws himself at the former. At this moment a woman looks out of a window on the third floor and calls, "Police!" The antagonists run off in opposite directions. Now, how would this have been observed?

1. The observer looks at the first man. He turns his head.

2. What is he looking at? The observer turns his glance in the same direction and sees the man entering the gate. The latter stops.

3. How does the first react to the appearance on the scene of the second? A new turn by the observer; the first takes out an object and mocks the second.

4. How does the second react? Another turn; he clenches his fists and throws him-self on his opponent.

5. The observer draws aside to watch how both opponents roll about fighting.

6. A shout from above. The observer raises his head and sees the woman shout-ing at the window.

7. The observer lowers his head and sees the result of her warning—the antago-nists running off in opposite directions.

The observer happened to be standing near and saw every detail, saw it clearly, but to do so he had to turn his head, first left, then right, then upwards, whitherso-ever his attention was attracted by the interest of observation and the sequence of the developing scene. Suppose he had been standing farther away from the action, taking in the two persons and the window on the third floor simultaneously, he would have received only a general impression, without being able to look separately at the first, the second, or the woman. Here we have approached closely the basic significance of editing. Its object is the showing of the development of the scene in relief, as it were, by guiding the attention of the spectator now to one, now to the other separate element. The lens of the camera replaces the eye of the observer, and the changes of angle of the camera—directed now on one person, now on another, now on one detail, now on another—must be subject to the same conditions as those of the eyes of the observer. The film technician, in order to secure the greatest clarity, emphasis, and vividness, shoots the scene in separate pieces and, joining them and showing them, directs the attention of the spectator to the separate elements, compelling him to see as the attentive observer saw. From the above is clear the manner in which editing can even work upon the emotions. Imagine to yourself the excited observer of some rapidly developing scene. His agitated glance is thrown rapidly from one spot to another. If we imitate this glance with the camera we get a series of pictures, rapidly alternating pieces, creating a *stirring scenario editing-construction*. The reverse would be long pieces changing by mixes, conditioning a calm and slow editing-construction (as one may shoot, for example, a herd of cattle wandering along a road, taken from the viewpoint of a pedestrian on the same road).

We have established, by these instances, the basic significance of the constructive editing of scenes. It builds the scenes from separate pieces, of which each concentrates the attention of the spectator only on that element important to the action. The sequence of these pieces must not be uncontrolled, but must correspond to the natural transference of attention of an imaginary observer (who, in the end, is represented by the spectator). In this sequence must be expressed a special logic that will be apparent only if each shot contain an impulse towards transference of the attention to the next. For example: (1) A man turns his head and looks; (2) What he looks at is shown.

Editing of the Sequence

The guidance of the attention of the spectator to different elements of the developing action in succession is, in general, characteristic of the film. It is its basic method. We have seen that the separate scene, and often even the movement of one man, is built up upon the screen from separate pieces. Now, the film is not simply a collection of different scenes. Just as the pieces are built up into scenes endowed, as it were, with a connected action, so the separate scenes are assembled into groups forming whole sequences.The sequence is constructed (edited) from scenes. Let us suppose ourselves faced with the task of constructing the following sequence: two spies are creeping forward to blow up a powder magazine; on the way one of them loses a letter with instructions. Someone else finds the letter and warns the guard, who appears in time to arrest the spies and save the magazine. Here the scenarist has to deal with simultaneity of various actions in several different places. While the spies are crawling towards the magazine, someone else finds the letter and hastens to warn the guard. The spies have nearly reached their objective; the guards are warned and rushing towards the magazine. The spies have completed their preparations; the guard arrives in time. If we pursue the previous analogy between the camera and an observer, we now not only have to turn it from side to side, but also to move it from place to place. The observer (the camera) is now on the road shadowing the spies, now in the guardroom recording the confusion, now back at the magazine showing the spies at work, and so forth. But, in combination of the separate scenes (editing), the former law of sequence succession remains in force. A consecutive sequence will appear upon the screen only if the attention of the spectator be transferred correctly from scene to scene. And this correctness is conditioned as follows: the spectator sees the creeping spies, the loss of the letter, and finally the person who finds the letter. The person with the letter rushes for help. The spectator is seized with inevitable excitement—Will the man who found the letter be able to forestall the explosion? The scenarist immediately answers by showing the spies nearing the magazine—his answer has the effect of a warning "Time is short." The excitement of the spectator—Will they be in time?—continues; the scenarist shows the guard turning out. Time is very short—the spies are shown beginning their work. Thus, transferring attention now to the rescuers, now to the spies, the scenarist answers with actual impulses to increase of the spectator's interest, and the construction (editing) of the sequence is correctly achieved.

There is a law in psychology that lays it down that if an emotion give birth to a certain movement, by imitation of this movement the corresponding emotion can be called forth. If the scenarist can effect in even rhythm the transference of interest of the intent spectator, if he can so construct the elements of increasing interest that the question, "What is happening at the other place?" arises and at the same moment the spectator is transferred whither he wishes to go, then the editing thus created can really excite the spectator. One must learn to understand that editing is in actual fact a compulsory and deliberate guidance of the thoughts and associations of the spectator. If the editing be merely an uncontrolled combination of the various pieces, the spectator will understand (apprehend) nothing from it; but if it be co-ordinated according to a definitely selected course of events or conceptual line, either agitated or calm, it will either excite or soothe the spectator.

Editing of the Scenario

The film is divided into reels. The reels are usually equal in length, on an average from 900 to 1,200 feet long. The combination of the reels forms the picture. The usual length of a picture should not be more than from 6,500 to 7,500 feet. This length, as yet, involves no unnecessary exhaustion of the spectator. The film is usually divided into from six to eight reels. It should be noted here, as a practical hint, that the average length of a piece (remember the editing of scenes) is from 6 to 10 feet, and consequently from 100 to 150 pieces go to a reel. By orientating himself on these figures, the scenarist can visualise how much material can be fitted into the scenario. The scenario is composed of a series of sequences. In discussing the construction (editing) of the scenario from sequences, we introduce a new element into the scenarist's work—the element of so-called dramatic continuity of action that was discussed at the beginning of this sketch. The continuity of the separate sequences when joined together depends not merely upon the simple transference of attention from one place to another, but is conditioned by the development of the action forming the foundation of the scenario. It is important, however, to remind the scenarist of the following point: a scenario has always in its development a moment of greatest tension, found nearly always at the end of the film. To prepare the spectator, or, more correctly, preserve him, for this final tension, it is especially important to see that he is not affected by unnecessary exhaustion during the course of the film. A method . . . that the scenarist can employ to this end is the careful distribution of the titles (which always distract the spectator), securing compression of the greater quantity of them into the first reels, and leaving the last one for uninterrupted action.

Thus, first is worked out the action of the scenario, the action is then worked out into sequences, the sequences into scenes, and these constructed by editing from the pieces, each corresponding to a camera angle.

EDITING AS AN INSTRUMENT OF IMPRESSION

(Relational Editing)

We have already mentioned, in the section on editing of sequences, that editing is not merely a method of the junction of separate scenes or pieces, but is a method that controls the "psychological guidance" of the spectator. We should now acquaint ourselves with the main special editing methods having as their aim the impression of the spectator.

Contrast. Suppose it be our task to tell of the miserable situation of a starving man; the story will impress the more vividly if associated with mention of the senseless gluttony of a well-to-do man.

On just such a simple contrast relation is based the corresponding editing method. On the screen the impression of this contrast is yet increased, for it is possible not only to relate the starving sequence to the gluttony sequence, but also to relate separate scenes and even separate shots of the scenes to one another, thus, as it were, forcing the spectator to compare the two actions all the time, one strengthening the other. The editing of contrast is one of the most effective, but also one of the commonest and most standardised, of methods, and so care should be taken not to overdo it.

Parallelism. This method resembles contrast, but is considerably wider. Its substance can be explained more clearly by an example. In a scenario as yet unproduced a section occurs as follows: a working man, one of the leaders of a strike, is condemned to death; the execution is fixed for 5 A.M. The sequence is edited thus: a factory-owner, employer of the condemned man, is leaving a restaurant drunk, he looks at his wrist-watch: 4 o'clock. The accused is shown—he is being made ready to be led out. Again the manufacturer, he rings a door-bell to ask the time: 4.30. The prison waggon drives along the street under heavy guard. The maid who opens the door—the wife of the condemned—is subjected to a sudden senseless assault. The drunken factory-owner snores on a bed, his leg with trouser-end upturned, his hand hanging down with wrist-watch visible, the hands of the watch crawl slowly to 5 o'clock. The workman is being hanged. In this instance two thematically unconnected incidents develop in parallel by means of the watch that tells of the approaching execution. The watch on the wrist of the callous brute, as it were connects him with the chief protagonist of the approaching tragic *dénouement*, thus ever present in the consciousness of the spectator. This is undoubtedly an interesting method, capable of considerable development.

Symbolism. In the final scenes of the film *Strike* the shooting down of workmen is punctuated by shots of the slaughter of a bull in a stockyard. The scenarist, as it were, desires to say: just as a butcher fells a bull with the swing of a pole-axe, so, cruelly and in cold blood, were shot down the workers. This method is especially interesting because, by means of editing, it introduces an abstract concept into the consciousness of the spectator without use of a title.

Simultaneity. In American films the final section is constructed from the simultaneous rapid development of two actions, in which the outcome of one depends on the outcome of the other. The end of the present-day section of *Intolerance* . . . is thus constructed. The whole aim of this method is to create in the spectator a maximum tension of excitement by the constant forcing of a question, such as, in this case: Will they be in time? will they be in time?

The method is a purely emotional one, and nowadays overdone almost to the point of boredom, but it cannot be denied that of all the methods of constructing the end hitherto devised it is the most effective.

Leit-motif (reiteration of theme). Often it is interesting for the scenarist especially to emphasise the basic theme of the scenario. For this purpose exists the method of reiteration. Its nature can easily be demonstrated by an example. In an anti-religious scenario that aimed at exposing the cruelty and hypocrisy of the Church in employ of the Tsarist régime the same shot was several times repeated: a church-bell slowly ringing and, superimposed on it, the title: "The sound of bells sends into the world a message of patience and love." This piece appeared whenever the scenarist desired to emphasise the stupidity of patience, or the hypocrisy of the love thus preached.

The little that has been said above of relational editing naturally by no means exhausts the whole abundance of its methods. It has merely been important to show that constructional editing, a method specifically and peculiarly filmic, is, in the hands of the scenarist, an important instrument of impression. Careful study of its use in pictures, combined with talent, will undoubtedly lead to the discovery of new possibilities and, in conjunction with them, to the creation of new forms.

1926

SERGEI EISENSTEIN
FROM FILM FORM

BEYOND THE SHOT [THE CINEMATOGRAPHIC PRINCIPLE AND THE IDEOGRAM]

Trained as a civil engineer, Eisenstein (1898–1948) gained much of his early film experience on the stage, in the acting troupe he founded as a boy, in the Proletkult Theater, which he joined in 1920, and at Vsevolod Meyerhold's avant-garde theater workshop, where he staged circus-like plays aimed at captivating a mass audience. In 1924 Eisenstein shifted his attention to film, hoping to find an art form capable of a more thorough-going realism. His first films, *Strike* (1924) and *Potemkin* (1925), established the use of expressionistic camera angles, visual metaphors, non-professional actors, and rapid montage that would mark much of his later career. Unlike Pudovkin's stress on the narrative and emotional flow possible with montage, Eisenstein emphasizes its disjunctive and colliding effect, akin to the Marxist idea of dialectic. Eisenstein also had a more tumultuous relationship with the Soviet government and believed filmmakers should work independently and pursue art above all else. His devotion to avant-garde techniques over more straightforward visual styles and propagandistic subjects brought him into conflict with officials in the 1930s. When he was prohibited from making films, he turned to teaching and writing about cinema, publishing a number of essays outlining the psychological impact of montage and other cinematic techniques. After an abortive attempt to make a film in Mexico with American backing, Eisenstein returned to Russia, tried to make his peace with the government, and directed *Alexander Nevsky* (1938) and *Ivan The Terrible* (1944), which was approved by Stalin, while its second part (of a projected trilogy) was condemned and not released until ten years after his death.

(Other selections from works by Eisenstein appear in Sections III and IV.)

It is a weird and wonderful feeling to write a booklet about something that does not in fact exist.

There is, for example, no such thing as cinema without cinematography.

Nevertheless the author of the present book has managed to write a book about the *cinema* of a country that has no *cinematography*, about the cinema of a country that has an infinite multiplicity of cinematic characteristics but which are scattered all over the place—with the sole exception of its cinema.

This article is devoted to the cinematic features of Japanese culture that lie outside Japanese cinema and it lies outside the book in the same way as these features lie outside Japanese cinema.

Cinema is: so many firms, so much working capital, such and such a 'star', so many dramas.

Cinema is, first and foremost, montage.

Japanese cinema is well provided with firms, actors and plots.

And Japanese cinema is quite unaware of montage.

Nevertheless the principle of montage may be considered to be an element of Japanese representational culture.

The script, for their script is primarily representational.

The hieroglyph.

The naturalistic representation of an object through the skilled hands of Ts'ang Chieh in 2650 B.C. became slightly formalised and, with its 539 fellows, constituted the first 'contingent' of hieroglyphs.

The portrait of an object, scratched with a stylus on a strip of bamboo, still resembled the original in every way.

But then, at the end of the third century, the brush was invented.

In the first century after the "happy event" (A.D.) there was paper

and in the year 220 indian ink.

A complete transformation. A revolution in draughtsmanship. The hieroglyph, which has in the course of history undergone no fewer than fourteen different styles of script, has crystallised in its present form.

The means of production (the brush and indian ink) determine the form. The fourteen reforms have had their effect.

In short, it is already impossible to recognise in the enthusiastically cavorting hieroglyph *ma* (a horse) the image of the little horse settling pathetically on its hind legs in the calligraphy of Ts'ang Chieh, the horse that is so well known from ancient Chinese sculpture.

But to hell with the horse and with the 607 remaining symbols of the *hsiang-cheng*, the first *representational* category of hieroglyphs.

It is with the second category of hieroglyphs—the *huei-i*, or 'copulative'—that our real interest begins.

The point is that the copulation—perhaps we had better say the combination—of two hieroglyphs of the simplest series is regarded not as their sum total but as their product, i.e. as a value of another dimension, another degree: each taken separately corresponds to an object but their combination corresponds to a *concept*. The combination of two 'representable' objects achieves the representation of something that cannot be graphically represented.

For example: the representation of water and of an eye signifies 'to weep',
the representation of an ear next to a drawing of a door means 'to listen',
a dog and a mouth mean 'to bark'
a mouth and a baby mean to 'scream'
a mouth and a bird mean 'to sing'
a knife and a heart mean 'sorrow', and so on

But—this is montage!!

Yes. It is precisely what we do in cinema, juxtaposing representational shots that have, as far as possible, the same meaning, that are neutral in terms of their meaning, in meaningful contexts and series.

It is an essential method and device in any cinematographic exposition. And, in a condensed and purified form, it is the starting-point for 'intellectual cinema',

a cinema that seeks the maximum laconicism in the visual exposition of abstract concepts.

We hail the method of the (long since) dead Ts'ang Chieh as a pioneering step along this path.

I have mentioned laconicism. Laconicism provides us with a stepping-stone to another point. Japan possesses the most laconic forms of poetry, the *hai-kai* (that appeared at the beginning of the 12th century) and the *tanka*.

They are virtually hieroglyphics transposed into phrases. So much so that half their value is judged by their calligraphic quality. The method by which they are resolved is quite analogous.

This method, which in hieroglyphics provides a means for the laconic imprinting of an abstract concept, gives rise, when transposed into semantic exposition, to a similarly laconic printed imagery.

The method, reduced to a stock combination of images, carves out a dry definition of the concept from the collision between them.

The same method, expanded into a wealth of recognised semantic combinations, becomes a profusion of *figurative* effect.

The formula, the concept, is embellished and developed on the basis of the material, it is transformed into an image, which is the form.

In exactly the same way as the primitive thought form—thinking in images—is displaced at a certain stage and replaced by conceptual thought.

But let us pass on to examples:

The *hai-kai* is a concentrated Impressionist sketch:

> Two splendid spots
> on the stove.
> The cat sits on them.
>   (GE-DAI)

> Ancient monastery.
> Cold moon.
> Wolf howling.
>   (KIKKO)

> Quiet field.
> Butterfly flying.
> Sleeping.
>   (GO-SIN)

The *tanka* is a little longer (by two lines).

> Mountain pheasant
> moving quietly, trailing
> his tail behind.
> Oh, shall I pass
> endless night alone.
>   (HITOMASO)

We see these as montage phrases, montage lists.

The simplest juxtaposition of two or three details of a material series produces a perfectly finished representation of another order, the psychological.

Whereas the finely honed edges of the intellectual formulation of the concept produced by the juxtaposition of hieroglyphs are here blurred, the concept blossoms forth immeasurably in *emotional* terms.

In Japanese script you do not know whether it is the inscription of a character or the independent product of graphics.

Born from a cross between the figurative mode and the denotative purpose, the hieroglyphic method has continued its tradition not just in literature but also, as we have indicated, in the *tanka* (not *historically* consistent but consistent *in principle* in the minds of those who have created this method).

Precisely the same method operates in the most perfect examples of Japanese figurative art.

Sharaku was the creator of the finest prints of the 18th century and, in particular, of an immortal gallery of actors' portraits. He was the Japanese Daumier. That same Daumier whom Balzac (himself the Bonaparte of literature) in turn called the 'Michelangelo of caricature'.

Despite all this Sharaku is almost unknown in our country.

The characteristic features of his works have been noted by Julius Kurth. Examining the question of the influence of sculpture on Sharaku, he draws a parallel

The expression on the mask, also created in Sharaku's day, is the same as that in the portrait of Tomisaburo. The facial expression and the arrangement of masses are very similar to one another even though the mask represents an old man and the print a young woman (Tomisaburo in the role of a woman). The similarity is striking but nevertheless the two have nothing in common. Here we find a characteristic feature of Sharaku's work: whereas the anatomical proportions of the carved wooden mask are almost correct, the proportions of the face in the print are quite simply impossible. The distance between the eyes is so great as to make a mockery of common sense. The nose, in comparison with the eyes at least, is twice as long as a normal nose could possibly be, the chin is on the whole out of all proportion to the mouth: the relationships between the eyebrows, the mouth, the details in general are quite unthinkable. We can observe the same thing in all Sharaku's large heads. It is just not possible that the great master was unaware that these proportions were wrong. He quite deliberately repudiated naturalism and, *while each detail taken separately is constructed on the principles of concentrated naturalism, their general compositional juxtaposition is subjugated to a purely semantic purpose. He took as the norm for the proportions the quintessence of psychological expressiveness. . . .*

between the portrait of the actor Nakayama Tomisaburo and an antique mask of the semi-religious No theatre, the mask of Rozo, the old bonze.

Is this not the same as the hieroglyph that juxtaposes the independent 'mouth' and the dissociated 'child' for the semantic expression 'scream'?

Just as Sharaku does by stopping time so we too do in time by provoking a monstrous disproportion between the parts of a normally occurring phenomenon, when we suddenly divide it into 'close-up of hands clasped', 'medium shots of battle' and 'big close-ups of staring eyes' and produce a montage division of the phenomenon into the types of shot! We make an eye twice as large as a fully grown man! From the juxtaposition of these monstrous incongruities we reassemble the disintegrated phenomena into a single whole but from our own perspective, in the light of our own orientation towards the phenomenon.

The disproportionate representation of a phenomenon is organically inherent in us from the very beginning. A. R. Luria has shown me a child's drawing of 'lighting a stove'. Everything is depicted in tolerable proportions and with great care: firewood, stove, chimney. But, in the middle of the room space, there is an enormous rectangle crossed with zigzags. What are they? The turn out to be 'matches'. Bearing in mind the crucial importance of these matches for the process depicted, the child gives them the appropriate scale.

The representation of an object in the actual (absolute) proportions proper to it is, of course, merely a tribute to orthodox formal logic, a subordination to the inviolable order of things.

This returns periodically and unfailingly in periods when absolutism is in the ascendancy, replacing the expressiveness of antiquated disproportion with a regular 'ranking table' of officially designated harmony.

Positivist realism is by no means the correct form of perception. It is simply a function of a particular form of social structure, following on from an autocratic state that has propagated a state uniformity of thought.

It is an ideological uniformity that makes its visual appearance in the ranks of uniforms of the Life Guard regiments. . . .

Thus, we have seen how the principle of the hieroglyph—'denotation through representation'—split into two.

Following the line of its purpose (the principle of 'denotation') to the principles of the creation of literary imagery.

Following the line of the methods of achieving this purpose (the principle of 'representation') to the striking methods of expressiveness used by Sharaku.

Just as we say that the two diverging arms of a hyperbola meet at infinity (although no one has ever been such a long way away!), so the principle of hieroglyphics, splitting endlessly into two (in accordance with the dynamic of the signs), unexpectedly joins together again from this dual divergence in yet a fourth sphere—theatre.

Estranged from one another for so long, they are once again—the theatre is still in its cradle—present in *parallel* form, in a curious dualism.

The denotation of the action, the representation of the action, is carried out by the so-called Joruri, a silent puppet on the stage.

This antiquated practice, together with a specific style of movement, passes into the early Kabuki theatre as well. It is preserved to this day, as a partial method, in the classical repertoire.

But let us pass on. This is not the point. The hieroglyphic (montage) method has penetrated the very technique of acting in the most curious ways.

However, before we move on to this, since we have already mentioned the representational aspect, let us dwell on the problem of the shot so that we settle the matter once and for all.

The shot.

A tiny rectangle with some fragment of an event organised within it.

Glued together, these shots form montage. (*Of course*, if this is done in the appropriate rhythm!)

That, roughly, is the teaching of the old school of film-making.

Screw by screw,
Brick by brick. . . .

Kuleshov, for instance, even writes with a brick: 'If you have an idea-phrase, a particle of the story, a link in the whole dramaturgical chain, then that idea is expressed and built up from shot-signs, just like bricks. . . .

> Screw by screw,
> Brick by brick . . .

as they used to say.

The shot is an element of montage.

Montage is the assembling of these elements.

This is a most pernicious mode of analysis, in which the understanding of any process as a whole (the link: shot—montage) derives purely from the external indications of the course it takes (one piece glued to another).

You might, for instance, come to the notorious conclusion that trams exist merely to block streets. This is an entirely logical conclusion if you confine yourself to the functions that they performed, for example, in February 1917. But the Moscow municipal authorities see things in a different light.

The worst of the matter is that an approach like this does really, like an insurmountable tram, block the possibilities of formal development. An approach like this condemns us not to dialectical development but to [the process of] mere evolutionary 'perfection', in so far as it does not penetrate to the dialectical essence of the phenomenon.

In the final analysis this kind of evolutionising leads either through its own refinement to decadence or, vice versa, to straightforward weakness caused by a blockage in the blood supply. However odd it may seem, there is an eloquent, nay melodious, witness to both these eventualities simultaneously in Kuleshov's *The Happy Canary*.

The shot is by no means a montage *element*.

The shot is a montage cell. Beyond the dialectical jump in the *single* series: shot—montage.

What then characterises montage and, consequently, its embryo, the shot? Collision. Conflict between two neighbouring fragments. Conflict. Collision.

Before me lies a crumpled yellowing sheet of paper.

On it there is a mysterious note:

'Series—P' and 'Collision—E'.

This is a material trace of the heated battle on the subject of montage between E (myself) and P (Pudovkin) six months ago.

We have already got into a habit: at regular intervals he comes to see me late at night and, behind closed doors, we wrangle over matters of principle.

So it is in this instance. A graduate of the Kuleshov school, he zealously defends the concepts of montage as a *series* of fragments. In a chain. 'Bricks'. Bricks that *expound* an idea serially.

I opposed him with my view of montage as a *collision*, my view that the collision of two factors gives rise to an idea.

In my view a *series* is merely one possible *particular* case.

Remember that physics is aware of an infinite number of combinations arising from the impact (collision) between spheres. Depending on whether they are elastic, non-elastic or a mixture of the two. Among these combinations is one where the collision is reduced to a uniform movement of both in the same direction.

That corresponds to Pudovkin's view.

Not long ago we had another discussion. Now he holds the view that I held then. In the meantime he has of course had the chance to familiarise himself with the set of lectures that I have given at the GTK since then.

So, montage is conflict.

Conflict lies at the basis of every art. (A unique 'figurative' transformation of the dialectic.)

The shot is then a montage cell. Consequently we must also examine it from the point of view of *conflict*.

Conflict within the shot is:

potential montage that, in its growing intensity, breaks through its four-sided cage and pushes its conflict out into montage impulses between the montage fragments;

just as a zigzag of mimicry flows over, making those *same* breaks, into a zigzag of spatial staging,

just as the slogan, 'Russians know no obstacles', breaks out in the many volumes of peripeteia in the novel *War and Peace*.

If we are to compare montage with anything, then we should compare a phalanx of montage fragments—'shots'—with the series of explosions of the internal combustion engine, as these fragments multiply into a montage dynamic through "impulses" like those that drive a car or a tractor.

Conflict within the shot. It can take many forms: it can even be part of . . . the story. Then it becomes the 'Golden Series'. A fragment 120 metres long. Neither the analysis nor the questions of film form apply in this instance.

But these are 'cinematographic':

the conflict of graphic directions (lines)

the conflict of shot levels (between one another)

the conflict of volumes

the conflict of masses (of volumes filled with varying intensities of light)

the conflict of spaces, etc.

Conflicts that are waiting only for a single intensifying impulse to break up into antagonistic pairs of fragments. Close-ups and long shots. Fragments travelling graphically in different directions. Fragments resolved in volumes and fragments resolved in planes. Fragments of darkness and light . . . etc.

Lastly, there are such unexpected conflicts as:

the conflict between an object and its spatial nature and the conflict between an event and its temporal nature.

However strange it may seem, these are things that have long been familiar to us. The first is achieved through optical distortion by the lens and the second through animation or *Zeitlupe* [slow motion].

The reduction of all the properties of cinema to a single formula of conflict and of cinematographic indicators to the dialectical series of one *single indicator* is no empty rhetorical pastime.

We are now searching for a single system of methods of cinematographic expression that will cover all its elements.

The reduction of these to a series of general indicators will solve the problem as a whole.

Our experience of the various elements of cinema is quite variable.

Whereas we know a very great deal about montage, we are floundering about, as far as the theory of the shot is concerned, between the Tretyakov Gallery, the Shchukin Museum and geometricisations that set your teeth on edge.

If we regard the shot as a particular molecular instance of montage and shatter the dualism 'shot—montage', then we can apply our experience of montage directly to the problem of the theory of the shot.

The same applies to the theory of lighting. If we think of lighting as the collision between a beam of light and an obstacle, like a stream of water from a fire hose striking an object, or the wind buffeting a figure, this will give us a quite differently conceived use of light from the play of 'haze' or 'spots'.

Thus far only the principle of conflict acts as this kind of denominator:

the principle of optical counterpoint.

We should not forget now that we must resolve a counterpoint of a different order, *the conflict between the acoustic and the optical in sound cinema.*

But let us for the moment return to one of the most interesting optical conflicts: the conflict between the frame of the shot and the object.

The position of the cinema represents the materialisation of the conflict between the organising logic of the director and the inert logic of the phenomenon in collision, producing the dialectic of the camera angle.

In this field we are still sickeningly impressionistic and unprincipled.

Nevertheless there is a clear principle even in this technique.

A mundane rectangle that cuts across the accident of nature's randomness. . . .

Once again we are in Japan! Because one of the methods of teaching drawing used in Japanese schools is so cinematographic.

Our method of teaching drawing is to: take an ordinary sheet of Russian paper with four corners. In the majority of cases you then squeeze on to it, ignoring the edges (which are greasy with sweat!), a bored caryatid, a conceited Corinthian capital or a plaster Dante (not the magician, the other one—Alighieri, the man who writes comedies).

The Japanese do it the other way round. You have a branch of a cherry tree or a landscape with a sailing boat.

From this whole the pupil cuts out compositional units: a square, a circle, a rectangle.

He creates a shot!

These two schools (theirs and ours) precisely characterise the two basic tendencies that are fighting one another in contemporary cinema!

Our school: the dying method of spatial organisation of the phenomenon in front of the lens:

from the 'staging' of a scene to the erection literally of a Tower of Babel in front of the lens.

The other method, used by the Japanese, is that of 'capturing' with the camera, using it to organise. Cutting out a fragment of reality by means of the lens.

Now, however, at a time when the centre of attention in intellectual cinema is at last beginning to move from the raw material of cinema as it is to 'deductions and conclusions', to 'slogans' based on the raw material, the differences are becoming less important to both schools and they can quietly blend into a synthesis.

Eight or so pages back, the question of theatre slipped from our grasp, like a pair of galoshes on a traum, slipped from our grasp.

Let us go back to the question of the methods of montage in Japanese theatre, particularly in acting.

The first and most striking example, of course, is the purely cinematographic method of 'transitionless acting'. Together with extremely refined mime transitions the Japanese actor also makes use of the direct opposite. At a certain moment in his performance he halts. The 'black men' obligingly conceal him from the audience. So, he emerges in new make-up, a new sign: these characterise a new stage (step) in his emotional state.

Thus, for instance, the play *Narukami* is resolved by Sadanji's transition from drunkenness to madness. Through a mechanical cut. And a change in the range (arsenal) of coloured stripes on his face, emphasising those whose duty it is to demonstrate that the intensity is greater than in the first make-up.

This method is organic to film. The forced introduction into film of the European acting tradition of fragments of 'emotional transitions' once more compels cinema to make time. At the same time, the method of 'cut' acting provides the opportunity to devise entirely new methods. If you replace a single changing face by a whole gamut of faces of varying dispositions—typage—the expression is always more intense than that on the surface of the face of a professional actor, which is too receptive and devoid of any organic resistance.

I have utilised the distinction between the polar stages of facial expression in a pointed juxtaposition in our new film about the countryside [*Old and New*]. This results in a more pointed 'play of doubt' around the separator. Will the milk thicken or not? Deception? Money? Here the psychological process of the play of motives—faith and doubt—resolves into the two extreme states of joy (cer-

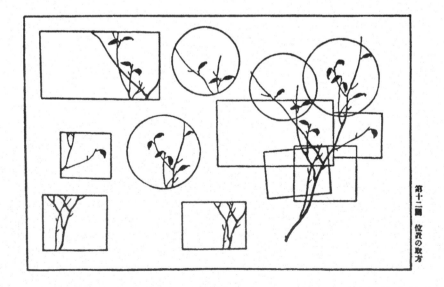

tainty) and gloom (disillusionment). In addition, this is heavily underlined by light (which by no means conforms to real life). This leads to a significant heightening of tension.

Another remarkable feature of the Kabuki theatre is the principle of 'decomposed acting'. Shocho, who played the leading female roles when the Kabuki troupe visited Moscow, portrayed the dying girl in *The Mask Maker* through quite disconnected fragments of acting.

Acting with just the right arm. Acting with one leg. Acting merely with the neck and head. The whole process of the death agony was decomposed into solo performances by each 'party' separately: the legs, the arms, the head. Decomposition into shot levels. And each successive fragment became shorter as the unhappy ending—death—approached.

Freed from primitive naturalism and using this method, the actor wins the audience over completely 'with his rhythm', which makes a scene based on its general composition on the most consistent and detailed naturalism (blood, etc.) not only acceptable but extremely attractive.

Since we are no longer distinguishing in principle between montage and what happens within the shot, we can cite here a third method.

The Japanese actor in his work utilises slow tempo to a degree that is unknown in our theatre. Take the famous hara-kiri scene in *The Forty-Seven Samurai*. That degree of slowing down is unknown on our stage. Whereas in our previous example we observed the decomposition of the links between movements, here we see the decomposition of the process of movement, i.e. *Zeitlupe* [slow motion]. I know of only one case of the consistent application of this method, which is technically acceptable in cinema, on a compositionally meaningful level. (It is usually deployed either for visual effect, as in the 'underwater kingdom' in *The Thief of Bagdad*, or for a dream, as in *Zvenigora*. Even more frequently it is used simply for formal trifles and pointless mischief with the camera, as in Vertov's *The Man with the Movie Camera*.) I have in mind Epstein's *The Fall of the House of Usher*. Judging by press reports, normally acted states [of mind], shot with a speeded-up camera and played back in slow motion on the screen, produced unusual emotional tension. If you bear in mind that the attraction exerted by the actor's performance on the audience is based on the audience's identification with it, you can easily attribute both examples to one and the same casual explanation. The intensity of our perception increases because the process of identification is easier when the movement is decomposed.

Even instruction is handling a rifle can be drummed into the heads of the densest raw recruit if the instructor uses the method of 'decomposition'.

The most interesting link is of course the one between Japanese theatre and sound film which can and must learn from the Japanese what to it is fundamental: the reduction of visual and aural sensations to a single physiological denominator.

Thus, it has been possible to establish briefly the fact that the most varied branches of Japanese culture are permeated by a purely cinematic element and by its basic nerve—montage.

And it is only cinema that falls into the same trap as the 'left-inclining' Kabuki. Instead of learning how to isolate the principles and techniques of their unique acting from the traditional feudal forms of what they are acting, the progressive theatrical people of Japan rush to borrow the loose formlessness of the acting of our 'intuitivists'. The result is lamentable and saddening. In its cinema Japan also strives to imitate the most appalling examples of the most saleable mediocre American and European commercial trash.

Understand and apply its specific cultural quality to its own cinema—that is what Japan must do!

Japanese comrades, are you really going to leave this to us?

THE DRAMATURGY OF FILM FORM
[THE DIALECTICAL APPROACH TO FILM FORM]

According to Marx and Engels the system of the dialectic is only the conscious reproduction of the dialectical course (essence) of the external events of the world.

RAZUMOVSKY, *The Theory of Historical Materialism*, Moscow, 1928

Thus:
the projection of the dialectical system of objects into the brain
—*into abstract creation*—
—*into thought*—
produces dialectical modes of thought—dialectical materialism—PHILOSOPHY.
Similarly:
the projection of the same system of objects—in concrete creation—in form—produces ART.

The basis of this philosophy is the *dynamic* conception of objects: being as a constant evolution from the interaction between two contradictory opposites.

Synthesis that *evolves* from the opposition between thesis and antithesis.

It is equally of basic importance for the correct conception of art and all art forms.

In the realm of art this dialectical principle of the dynamic is embodied in CONFLICT as the essential basic principle of the existence of every work of art and every form. FOR ART IS ALWAYS CONFLICT:

1. because of its social mission.
2. because of its nature,
3. because of its methodology.

1. *Because of its social mission, since*: it is the task of art to reveal the contradictions of being. To forge the correct intellectual concept, to form the right view by sitting up contradictions in the observer's mind and through the dynamic clash of opposing passions.

2. *Because of its nature, since*: because of its nature it consists in the conflict between natural being and creative tendentiousness. Between organic inertia and purposeful initiative.

The hypertrophy of purposeful initiative—of the principle of rational logic—leaves art frozen in mathematical technicism. (Landscape becomes topography, a

From *Potemkin* (1925). "Representation of a spontaneous action. Woman with pince-nez. Followed immediately—without a transition—by the same woman with shattered pince-nez and bleeding eye. Sensation of a shot hitting the eye" (EISENSTEIN, p. 35).

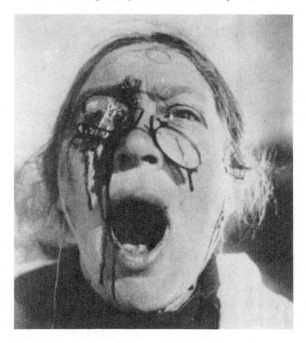

painting of St. Sebastian becomes an anatomical chart.) Hypertrophy of organic naturalness—of organic logic—dissolves art into formlessness. (Malevich becomes
Kaulbach, Archipenko a waxworks show.)

Because: the limit of organic form (the passive principle of being) is NATURE.
The limit of rational form (the active principle of production) is INDUSTRY *and*:
at the intersection of nature and industry stands ART.

1. The logic of organic form versus 2. the logic of rational form produces in collision the dialectic of the art form.

The interaction between the two produces and determines the dynamic. (Not
just in the sense of space-time, but also in the field of pure thought. I similarly
regard the evolution of new concepts and attitudes in the conflict between normal conceptions and particular representations as a dynamic—a dynamisation of
the inertia of perception—a dynamisation of the 'traditional view' into a new
one.)

The basis of distance determines the intensity of the tension: (viz., for instance,
in music the concept of intervals. In it there can be cases where the gap is so wide
that it can lead to a break, to a disintegration of the homogeneous concept of art.
The 'inaudibility' of certain intervals.)

*The spatial form of this dynamic is the expression of the phases in its tension—
rhythm.* This applies to every art form and, all the more so, to every form of its
expression. Thus human expression is a conflict between conditioned and unconditioned reflex.

(I do not agree on this point with Klages who
1. considers human expression not dynamically as process but statically as result and
2. attributes everything that moves to the field of the 'soul' and, by contrast, only
that which restrains to 'reason', in the idealistic concept of 'reason' and 'soul' which
here corresponds indirectly with the ideas of conditioned and unconditioned reflex.)

The same is equally true for every field, in so far as it can be understood as art.
Thus, for instance, logical thought, viewed as art, also produces the same dynamic
mechanism: 'The intellectual lives of Plato or Dante . . . were largely guided and
sustained by their delight in the sheer beauty of the *rhythmic relation* between law
and instance, species and individual, or cause and effect.'

This also applies in other fields, e.g. in language, where the strength, vitality and
dynamism derive from the irregularity of the particular in relation to the rule governing the system as a whole.

In contrast to this we can see the sterility of expression in artificial, totally regulated languages like Esperanto. It is from this same principle that the whole charm
of poetry derives: its rhythm emerges as conflict between the metric measure adopted
and the distribution of sounds that ambushes that measure.

The concept of even a formally static phenomenon as a dynamic function dialectically symbolises the wise words of Goethe that

'Architecture is frozen music.'

We shall employ this concept further. And, just as in homogeneous thought
(a monistic attitude), both the whole and the minutest detail must be permeated by
a *single principle*, so, together with the conflict of *social conditionality* and the conflict of *reality*, that same principle of conflict serves as the foundation stone for the

methodology of art. As the basic principle of the rhythm that is to be created and of the derivation of the art form.

3. *Because of its methodology*: shot and montage are the basic elements of film.

MONTAGE

Soviet film has stipulated this as the nerve of film.

To determine the essence of montage is to solve the problem of film as such.

The old film-makers, including the theoretically quite outmoded Lev Kuleshov, regarded montage as a means of producing something by describing it, adding individual shots to one another like building blocks.

Movement within these shots and the resulting length of the pieces were thus to be regarded as rhythm.

A fundamentally false notion! It would mean defining an object exclusively in terms of its external course. Regarding the mechanical process of sticking the pieces together as a principle. We cannot characterise this kind of relationship between lengths as rhythm.

It would give rise to a metre that was as opposed to rhythm as such as the mechanical-metric Mesendick system is opposed to the organic-rhythmic Bode school in the case of bodily expression.

According to this definition (which Pudovkin also shares as a theorist) montage is the means of *unrolling* an idea through single shots (the "epic" principle).

But in my view montage is not an idea composed of successive shots stuck together but an idea that DERIVES *from the collision between two shots that are independent of one another* (the 'dramatic' principle). ('Epic' and 'dramatic' in relation to the methodology of form and not content or plot!!) As in Japanese hieroglyphics in which two independent ideographic characters ('shots') are juxtaposed and *explode* into a concept.

Sophistry? Not at all! Because we are trying here to derive the whole essence, the stylistic principle and the character of film from its technical (-optical) foundations.

We know that the phenomenon of movement in film resides in the fact that still pictures of a moved body blend into movement when they are shown in quick succession one after the other.

The vulgar description of what happens—as a *blending*—has also led to the vulgar notion of montage mentioned above.

Let us describe the course of the said phenomenon more precisely, just as it really is, and draw our conclusions accordingly.

Is that correct? In pictorial-phraseological terms, yes.

But not in mechanical terms.

For in fact each sequential element is arrayed, not *next* to the one it follows, but on *top* of it. *For*: the idea (sensation) of movement arises in the process of superimposing on the retained impression of the object's first position the object's newly visible second position.

That is how, on the other hand, the phenomenon of spatial depth as the optical superimposition of two planes in stereoscopy arises. The superimposition of two dimensions of the same mass gives rise to a completely new higher dimension.

In this instance, in the case of stereoscopy, the superimposition of two non-identical two-dimensionalities gives rise to stereoscopic three-dimensionality. In another field: concrete word (denotation) set against concrete word produces abstract concept.

As in Japanese (see above), in which *material* ideogram set against *material* ideogram produces *transcendental result* (concept).

The incongruity in contour between the first picture that has been imprinted on the mind and the subsequently perceived second picture—the conflict between the two—gives birth to the sensation of movement, the idea that movement has taken place.

The degree of incongruity determines the intensity of impression, determines the tension that, in combination with what follows, will become the real element of authentic rhythm.

Here we have, in the temporal sense, what we see emerging spatially on the graphic or painted surface.

What does the dynamic effect of a picture consist of?

The eye follows the direction of an element. It retains a visual impression which then collides with the impression derived from following the direction of a second element. The conflict between these directions creates the dynamic effect in the apprehension of the whole.

I. It may be purely linear: Fernand Léger, Suprematism.

II. It may be 'anecdotal'. The secret of the fabulous mobility of the figures of Daumier and Lautrec consists in the fact that various parts of the bodies of their figures are depicted in spatial situations (positions) that vary temporally. See, for instance, Lautrec's 'Miss Cissy Loftus':

A logical development of position A for the foot leads to the elaboration of a corresponding position A for the body. But from the knee up the body is already represented in position A + a. The cinematic effect of the still picture is already visible here: from hips to shoulders we already have A + a + a. The figure seems alive and kicking!

III. Primitive Italian Futurism lies somewhere between I and II: the man with six legs in six positions. (Between I and II because II achieves its effects by retaining natural unity and anatomical cohesion, whereas I achieves this through purely elementary elements, while III, although undermining nature, is not yet pushed as far as abstraction.)

IV. It can be of ideographic kind. Like the pregnant characterisation of a Sharaku (eighteenth-century Japan). The secret of his extremely clever power of expression lies in the anatomical *spatial disproportion* of the parts. (You might term I above *temporal disproportion*.)

The spatial calculation of the corresponding size of one detail in relation to another and the collision between that and the dimension determined for it by the artist produces the characterisation: the resolution of the representation.

Finally, colour. A colour shade conveys a particular rhythm of vibration to our vision. (This is not perceived visually, but purely physiologically, because colours are distinguished from one another by the frequency of their light vibrations.) The nearest shade has a different frequency of vibration.

The counterpoint (conflict) between the two—the retained and the still emerging—frequency produces the dynamic of our perceptions and of the interplay of colour.

From here we have only to make one step from visual vibration to acoustic vibration and we find ourselves in the field of music. We move from the realm of the spatial-pictorial to the realm of the temporal-pictorial.

Here the same law rules. Because for music counterpoint is not just a form of composition but the basic rationale for the possibility of sound perception and differentiation. One might also say that in all the cases cited here the same *principle of comparison* operates: it makes possible for us discovery and observation in every field. With the moving image (film) we have, as it were, the synthesis of these two counterpoints: the spatial counterpoint of the image and the temporal counterpoint of music. Characterised in film through what we might describe as:

VISUAL COUNTERPOINT

This concept, when applied to film, allows us to designate various approaches to the problem, to a kind of film grammar. Similarly with a syntax of film expressions in which the visual counterpoint can determine a completely new system of forms of expression. (Experiments in this direction will be illustrated by extracts from my films.) In all this:

The *basic presupposition* is:

The shot is not a montage element—the shot is a montage cell (a molecule). This formulation explodes the dualistic division in the analysis:

of: title and shot

and: shot and montage.

Instead it is viewed dialectically as three different *phases in the formation of a homogeneous expressive task.* With homogeneous characteristics that determine the homogeneity of their structural laws.

The relationship between the three: conflict within a thesis (an abstract idea):

1. is *formulated* in the dialectic of the *title,*
2. is *formed* spatially in the *conflict within* the shot—and
3. *explodes* with the growing intensity of the *conflict montage between the shots.*

Once again this is quite analogous to human psychological expression. This is a conflict of motives. Conceivable, likewise, in three phases:

1. Purely verbal utterance. Without intonation: spoken expression.
2. Gesticulative (mimic-intentional) expression. Projection of conflict on to the entire expressive body-system of man. ("Gesture" and "sound gesture"—intonation).

3. Projection of conflict into the spatial. With the growing intensity (of motives) the zigzag of mimic expression is catapulted into the surrounding space according to the same distorting formula. A zigzag of expression deriving from the spatial disposition of man in space.

Herein lies the basis for a quite new conception of the problems of film form. We cite as examples of conflict:

1. Graphic conflict
2. Conflict between planes
3. Conflict between volumes
4. Spatial conflict
5. Conflict in lighting.
6. Conflict in tempo, etc., etc.

(N.B.: Here they are characterised by their principal feature, by their *dominant*. It is obvious that they occur mainly as complexes, grouped together. That applies to both the shot and to montage.)

For montage transition it is sufficient to imagine any example as being divided into two independent primary pieces

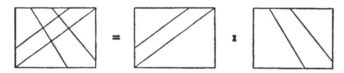

N.B. The graphic case. It applies also to all other cases. The extent to which the conflict concept extends in the treatment of film form is illustrated by the following further examples:

7. Conflict between matter and shot (achieved by *spatial distortion* using camera angle).
8. Conflict between matter and its spatiality (achieved by *optical distortion* using the lens).
9. Conflict between an event and its temporality (achieved by slowing down and speeding up [*Multiplikator*]) and lastly:
10. Conflict between the entire *optical* complex and a quite different sphere.

That is how the conflict between optical and acoustic experience produces:

SOUND FILM

which is realisable as

AUDIO-VISUAL COUNTERPOINT.

The formulation and observation of the phenomenon of film in the form of conflict provides the first opportunity to devise a homogeneous system of *visual dramaturgy* for every special and particular case of the problem of film.

To create a *dramaturgy of visual film form* that is determined in the same way as the existing *dramaturgy of film material* is determined. . . .

The same standpoint—viewed as an outcome for film composition—produces the following stylistic forms and possibilities and this could constitute a

Ten shots from the montage sequence on the "Odessa Steps" from *Potemkin* (1925). "The gradual succession continues in a process of comparing each new image with its common designation and *unleashes a process that, in terms of its form, is identical to a process of logical deduction*" (EISENSTEIN, p. 40). "The creation of a sense or meaning not proper to the images themselves but derived exclusively from their juxtaposition" (BAZIN, p. 44).

(continued)

(continued)

FILM SYNTAX
A TENTATIVE FILM SYNTAX

We shall list here:

A series of compositional possibilities that develop dialectically from the thesis that the concept of filmic movement (time lapse) derives from the superimposition of—the counterpoint between—two different stills.

I. *Each moving piece of montage in its own right*. Each photographed piece. The technical determination of the phenomenon of movement. *Not yet composition* (a man running, a gun firing, water splashing).

II. *Artificially produced representation of movement*. The basic optical sign is used for arbitrary composition:

A. *Logical*

Example 1. *Ten Days That Shook the World (October)*.

Montage: repetition of a machine-gun firing by cross-cutting the relevant details of the firing.

Combination a):

Brightly lit machine-gun. Dark one.
Different shot. Double burst:
Graphic burst and light burst.

Combination b):

Machine-gun.
Close up of the machine-gunner
Effect almost of double exposure with rattling montage effect.
Length of the pieces—two frames.

Example 2. *Potemkin* (1925)

Representation of a spontaneous action, *Potemkin*. Woman with pince-nez. Followed immediately—without a transition—by the same woman with shattered pince-nez and bleeding eye. Sensation of a shot hitting the eye.

B. *Alogical*

Example 3. *Potemkin.*

This device used for symbolic pictorial expression. *Potemkin*. The marble lion leaps us, surrounded by the thunder of *Potemkin*'s guns firing in protest against the bloodbath on the Odessa Steps.

Cut together from three immobile marble lions at Alupka Castle (Crimea). One sleeping. One waking. One rising. The effect was achieved because the length of the middle piece was correctly calculated. Superimposition on the first piece produced the first jump. Time for the second position to sink in. Superimposition of the third position on the second—the second jump. Finally the lion is standing.

Example 4. *Ten Days.*

The firing in Example 1 is symbolically produced from elements that do not belong to the actual firing. To illustrate General Kornilov's attempted monarchist *putsch* it occurred to me that his militarist *tendency* could be shown in the cutting (montage), but creating the montage material itself out of religious details. Because Kornilov had betrayed his tsarist tendency in the form of a curious "crusade" of Mohammedans (!) (his "Wild Division" from the Caucases) and Christians (all the others) against the . . . Bolsheviks. To this end a Baroque Christ with beams streaming (exploding) from its halo was briefly intercut with a self-contained egg-shaped Uzume mask. The temporal conflict between the self-contained egg shape and the graphic star produced the effect of a simultaneous explosion (a bomb, a shot).

Example 5. *Ten Days*.

A similar combination of a Chinese sacred statue and a madonna with a halo. (NB As we see, this already provides the opportunity for tendentious (ideological) expression.)

Another example of more primitive effect from the same place: in the simple cross-cutting between church towers leaning in opposite directions.

So far the examples have shown *primitive-psychological* cases—using *only* the optical superimposition of movement.

III. The case of emotional combinations not merely of the visible elements of the pieces but principally of the chains of psychological association. *Associational montage (1923–4)*. As a means of sharpening (heightening) a situation emotionally.

In Case I we had the following: two pieces A and B following one another area materially identical. According to the position of the material in the shot they are, however, not identical:

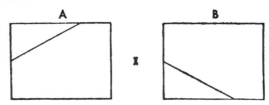

These two combined produced dynamisation in space—the impression of spatial dynamic:

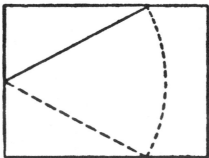

The degree of difference between positions A and B determines the tension of the movement. But let us take a new case:

Shot A and Shot B are, in terms of material, *not identical*. The associations of the two shots are identical: associatively identical. By analogy this *dynamisation of the material* produces, not in the spatial but in the *psychological, i.e. the emotional, field*:

EMOTIONAL DYNAMISATION

Example 1. *The Strike* (1923–4).

The shooting down of the workers is cut in such a way that the massacre is intercut with the slaughter of a cow. (Difference in material. But the slaughter is employed as an appropriate association.) This produces a powerful emotional intensification of the scene.

N.B.: In this case the homogeneity of gesture plays a very great role in generally achieving the effect (the homogeneity of the dynamic gesture: movement within the shot—or of the static gesture: the graphic attitude of the shot). Here is an excerpt from the first version of this scene in the montage list (1923):

1. The head of a bull.
2. The butcher's knife strikes a downward blow.
3. Five hundred workers fall down a hill.
4. Fifty men get up. Hands.
5. A soldier's face. He aims.
6. Shots.
7. The bull standing. It twitches and falls.
8. Close-up. Convulsions of the hind legs. A hoof kicks into the blood.
9. Rifles.
10. Semi-close-up. People get up. Wounded.
11. Imploring hands raised towards the camera.
12. Butcher with blood-stained rope approaches the camera.
13. Hands.
14. The butcher approaches, etc.

This principle was subsequently also used by Pudovkin in *The End of St Petersburg* (1927) when he intercut shots of stock exchange and battlefield. And, in *The Mother* (1926), the ice breaking and the workers' demonstration.

This method may decay pathologically if the essential viewpoint—the emotional dynamisation of the material—gets lost. Then it ossifies into lifeless literary symbolism and stylistic mannerism. We may cite the following as an example:

Example 2: *Ten Days.*

The mellifluous peace overtures of the Mensheviks at the Second Congress of the Soviets (during the storming of the Winter Palace) are intercut with harp-playing hands. A purely literary parallelism that does nothing to enliven the material.

Similarly in Otsep's *The Living Corpse*, with the intercutting (in imitation of *Ten Days*) of church cupolas or lyrical landscapes into the speeches of the prosecution and the defence counsels in the court. The same mistake as that above.

On the other hand, the predominance of purely dynamic effects may have a positive result:

Example 3: *Ten Days*.

The pathos of the adherence of the cycle battalion to the Second Congress of the Soviets is dynamised by the fact that, when their delegates enter, abstractly spinning cycle wheels (association with the battalion) were intercut. These resolved the pathetic content of the event as such into a perceptible dynamic. The same principle—the emergence of a concept, of a sensation from the juxtaposition of two disparate events—led on to:

IV. *The emancipation of closed action from its conditioning by time and space.* The first attempts at this were made in the *Ten Days* film.

Example 1. (*Ten Days*)

A trench packed with soldiers seems to be crushed by the weight of an enormous cannonball descending on the whole thing. Thesis brought to expression. In material terms the effect is achieved through the apparently chance intercutting between an independently existing trench and a metal object with a similarly military character. In reality they have absolutely no spatial relationship with one another.

Example 2: *Ten Days*.

Similarly in the scene of Kornilov's *putsch* attempt, which puts an end to Kerensky's Bonapartist plans. In this sequence one of Kornilov's tanks, emerging from the trench, shatters the plaster figure of Napoleon that stands on Kerensky's desk in the palace of Petrograd and has purely symbolic meaning.

This method of making whole sequences in this way is now mainly being employed by Dovzhenko: *The Arsenal* (1929). Also by Esfir Shub on her Tolstoy film (1928). In addition to this method of dissolving the accepted forms of handling film material I should like to cite another example, which has, however, not been realised in practice.

In 1924–5 I was very concerned with the idea of the filmic representation of real (actual) man. At that time the prevailing trend was that living man could only be shown in film in *long* dramatic scenes. And that cutting (montage) would destroy the idea of real man.

Abram Room established the record in this respect in *The Bay of Death* by using eighty metre-long uncut dramatic scenes. I felt (and feel) that such a concept is utterly unfilmic.

For what really is, in linguistic terms, a precise characterisation of man?

His raven-black hair . . .

The waves in his hair . . .

His flashing, bright blue eyes . . .

His steely muscles . . .

Even when it is not so exaggeratedly phrased, every description, every verbal representation of a man (see above!) becomes an accumulation of waterfalls, lightning conductors, landscapes, birds, etc.

Why then should cinema in its forms follow theatre and painting rather than the methodology of language, which gives rise, through the combination of concrete descriptions and concrete objects, to quite new concepts and ideas? It is much closer to film than, for instance, painting, where form derives from *abstract* elements (line, colour). In film, by contrast, it is precisely the material *concreteness* of the shot as an element that is the most difficult aspect of the process of formation. Why not then lean rather more towards the system of language, where the same mechanism exists in the use of words and word complexes?

Why is it, on the other hand, that montage cannot be avoided even in the orthodox feature film?

The differentiation in montage pieces is determined by the fact that each piece has in itself no reality at all. But each piece is itself in a position to evoke a certain association. The accumulation of associations then achieves the same effect as that provoked in the audience by purely physiological means by a theatrical play that is unfolding in reality.

E.g. Murder on stage has a purely physiological effect. Perceived in a *single* montage sequence it acts like an item of *information*, a title. It only begins to work *emotionally* when it is presented in montage fragments. In montage pieces, each of which provokes a certain association, the sum of which amounts to a composite complex of emotional feeling. In traditional terms:

1. A hand raises a knife.
2. The eyes of the victim open wide.
3. His hands clutch the table.
4. The knife jerks.
5. The eyes close.
6. Blood spurts out.
7. A mouth shrieks.
8. Drops fall on to a shoe . . .

and all that kitsch! In any event each *individual piece* is already almost *abstract* in relation to the *action as a whole*. The more differentiated they are, the more abstract they become, aiming only at provoking a certain association. Now the following thought arises quite logically: could one not achieve the same effect more productively if one did not adhere so slavishly to plot but materialised the notion of *murder* in a free accumulation of associative material? Because the most important thing is to convey the representation of murder, the feeling of murder as such. Plot is only one of the means without which we still do not know how to communicate something to the audience. At any rate an attempt of this sort would produce the most interesting variety of forms. Let someone try it! Since 1923–4, when this thought occurred to me, I have unfortunately not had the time to carry out this experiment. Now I have turned to quite different problems.

But, *revenons à nos moutons*, which will bring us closer to these tasks. Whereas, with 1, 2 and 3 the suspense was calculated to achieve purely physiological effects, from the purely optical to the emotional, we must also mention here the case in which the same conflict tension serves to achieve new concepts, new points of view, in other words, serves purely intellectual ends.

Example 1: *Ten Days*.

Kerensky's rise to (untrammelled) power and dictatorship after July 1917. Comic effect is achieved by *intercutting titles denoting ever higher rank* ('Dictator', 'Generalissimo', 'Minister of the Navy and the Army', etc.) with five or six sequences of the staircase in the Winter Palace with Kerensky ascending the *same* flight each time.

Here the conflict between the kitsch of the ascending staircase and Kerensky treading the same ground produces an intellectual resultant: the satirical degradation of these titles in relation to Kerensky's nonentity.

Here we have a counterpoint between a verbally expressed, conventional idea and a pictorial representation of an individual who is unequal to that idea.

The incongruity between these two produces a purely *intellectual* resolution at the expense of this individual. Intellectual dynamisation.

Example 2: *Ten Days.*

Kornilov's march on Petrograd took place under the slogan 'In the Name of God and the Fatherland'. Here we have an attempt to use the representation for anti-religious ends. A number of images of the divine were shown in succession. From a magnificent Baroque Christ to an Eskimo idol.

Here a conflict arises between the concept 'God' and its symbolisation. Whereas idea and image are completely synonymous in the first Baroque image, they grow further apart with each subsequent image. We retain the description 'God' and show idols that in no way correspond with our own image of this concept. From this we are to draw anti-religious conclusions as to what the divine as such really is.

Similarly, there is here an attempt to draw a purely intellectual conclusion as a resultant of the conflict between a preconception and its *gradual tendentious discrediting by degrees* through pure illustration.

The gradual succession continues in a process of comparing each new image with its common designation and *unleashes a process that, in terms of its form, is identical to a process of logical deduction*. Everything here is already intellectually conceived, not just in terms of the resolution but also of the method of expressing ideas.

The conventional *descriptive* form of the film becomes a kind of reasoning (as a formal possibility).

Whereas the conventional film directs and develops the *emotions*, here we have a hint of the possibility of likewise developing and directing the entire *thought process*.

These two attempts were received in a very hostile fashion by the majority of the critics. Because they were understood in purely political terms, I willingly concede that it is precisely *this form that is best suited to express ideologically critical theses*. But it is a pity that the critics completely overlooked the filmic opportunities that could be derived from it. In both these attempts we find the first, still embryonic attempts to construct a really quite new form of filmic expression.

A purely intellectual film which, freed from traditional limitations, will achieve direct forms for thoughts, systems and concepts without any transitions or paraphrases. And which can therefore become a SYNTHESIS OF ART AND SCIENCE. That will become the really new watchword for our epoch in the field of art. And really justify Lenin's statement that 'of all the arts . . . cinema is the most important.'

One of my next films, which is intended to embody the Marxist world-view, will be devoted to an experiment in this direction.

1929

ANDRÉ BAZIN
FROM WHAT IS CINEMA?

THE EVOLUTION OF THE LANGUAGE OF CINEMA

André Bazin (1918–1958) was instrumental in founding two influential French film periodicals: in 1947 *La Revue du Cinéma* and in 1951 the groundbreaking *Cahiers du Cinéma*. Responding to the wave of cinephilia which swept France after World War II, *Cahiers* became the most influential forum for critical discussion of film history and contemporary international film of the fifties and sixties. Bazin's stress on mise-en-scène, or the content of filmic images, shifted film criticism away from montage and toward elements of composition that reveal the filmmaker's vision, emphasizing the way films re-present reality rather than manipulate it through elaborate cutting. Bazin's criticism especially focuses on those directors whose artistic choices permeated each frame of their films: Orson Welles, Jean Renoir, Charles Chaplin, Erich von Stroheim, Alfred Hitchcock, Vittorio DeSica, William Wyler, and Akira Kurosawa among others. Although Bazin never made a film himself, he was highly influential in the lives of many of the filmmakers associated with the New Wave that emerged at the end of *Cahiers'* first decade, including Jean-Luc Godard, Claude Chabrol, and Francois Truffaut, all of whom wrote for the journal in their early years.

(Other selections from works by Bazin appear in Sections II and IV.)

By 1928 the silent film had reached its artistic peak. The despair of its elite as they witnessed the dismantling of this ideal city, while it may not have been justified, is at least understandable. As they followed their chosen aesthetic path it seemed to them that the cinema had developed into an art most perfectly accommodated to the "exquisite embarrassment" of silence and that the realism that sound would bring could only mean a surrender to chaos.

In point of fact, now that sound has given proof that it came not to destroy but to fulfill the Old Testament of the cinema, we may most properly ask if the technical revolution created by the sound track was in any sense an aesthetic revolution. In other words, did the years from 1928 to 1930 actually witness the birth of a new cinema? Certainly, as regards editing, history does not actually show as wide a breach as might be expected between the silent and the sound film. On the contrary there is discernible evidence of a close relationship between certain directors of 1925 and 1935 and especially of the 1940s through the 1950s. Compare for example Erich von Stroheim and Jean Renoir or Orson Welles, or again Carl Theodore

Dreyer and Robert Bresson. These more or less clear-cut affinities demonstrate first of all that the gap separating the 1920s and the 1930s can be bridged, and secondly that certain cinematic values actually carry over from the silent to the sound film and, above all, that it is less a matter of setting silence over against sound than of contrasting certain families of styles, certain basically different concepts of cinematographic expression.

Aware as I am that the limitations imposed on this study restrict me to a simplified and to that extent enfeebled presentation of my argument, and holding it to be less an objective statement than a working hypothesis, I will distinguish, in the cinema between 1920 and 1940, between two broad and opposing trends: those directors who put their faith in the image and those who put their faith in reality. By "image" I here mean, very broadly speaking, everything that the representation on the screen adds to the object there represented. This is a complex inheritance but it can be reduced essentially to two categories: those that relate to the plastics of the image and those that relate to the resources of montage, which after all, is simply the ordering of images in time.

Under the heading "plastics" must be included the style of the sets, of the make-up, and, up to a point, even of the performance, to which we naturally add the lighting and, finally, the framing of the shot which gives us its composition. As regards montage, derived initially as we all know from the masterpieces of Griffith, we have the statement of Malraux in his *Psychologie du cinéma* that it was montage that gave birth to film as an art, setting it apart from mere animated photography, in short, creating a language.

The use of montage can be "invisible" and this was generally the case in the prewar classics of the American screen. Scenes were broken down just for one purpose, namely, to analyze an episode according to the material or dramatic logic of the scene. It is this logic which conceals the fact of the analysis, the mind of the spectator quite naturally accepting the viewpoints of the director which are justified by the geography of the action or the shifting emphasis of dramatic interest.

But the neutral quality of this "invisible" editing fails to make use of the full potential of montage. On the other hand these potentialities are clearly evident from the three processes generally known as parallel montage, accelerated montage, montage by attraction. In creating parallel montage, Griffith succeeded in conveying a sense of the simultaneity of two actions taking place at a geographical distance by means of alternating shots from each. In *La Roue* Abel Gance created the illusion of the steadily increasing speed of a locomotive without actually using any images of speed (indeed the wheel could have been turning on one spot) simply by a multiplicity of shots of ever-decreasing length.

Finally there is "montage by attraction," the creation of S. M. Eisenstein, and not so easily described as the others, but which may be roughly defined as the reenforcing of the meaning of one image by association with another image not necessarily part of the same episode—for example the fireworks display in *The General Line* following the image of the bull. In this extreme form, montage by attraction was rarely used even by its creator but one may consider as very near to it in principle the more commonly used ellipsis, comparison, or metaphor, examples of which are the throwing of stockings onto a chair at the foot of a bed, or the milk overflowing

Above: McTeague (Gibson Gowland) confronting Marcus Schouler (Jean Hersholt) in the wastes of Death Valley in *Greed* (1923). *Below*: Nanook building his igloo in *Nanook of the North* (1922). Von Stroheim and Flaherty were two of "those who put their faith in reality" (BAZIN, p. 42).

in H. G. Clouzot's *Quai des orfèvres*. There are of course a variety of possible combinations of these three processes.

Whatever these may be, one can say that they share that trait in common which constitutes the very definition of montage, namely, the creation of a sense or meaning not proper to the images themselves but derived exclusively from their juxtaposition. The well-known experiment of Kuleshov with the shot of Mozhukhin in which a smile was seen to change its significance according to the image that preceded it, sums up perfectly the properties of montage.

Montage as used by Kuleshov, Eisenstein, or Gance did not give us the event; it alluded to it. Undoubtedly they derived at least the greater part of the constituent elements from the reality they were describing but the final significance of the film was found to reside in the ordering of these elements much more than in their objective content.

The matter under recital, whatever the realism of the individual image, is born essentially from these relationships—Mozhukhin plus dead child equal pity—that is to say an abstract result, none of the concrete elements of which are to be found in the premises; maidens plus appletrees in bloom equal hope. The combinations are infinite. But the only thing they have in common is the fact that they suggest an idea by means of a metaphor or by an association of ideas. Thus between the scenario properly so-called, the ultimate object of the recital, and the image pure and simple, there is a relay station, a sort of aesthetic "transformer." The meaning is not in the image, it is in the shadow of the image projected by montage onto the field of consciousness of the spectator.

Let us sum up. Through the contents of the image and the resources of montage, the cinema has at its disposal a whole arsenal of means whereby to impose its interpretation of an event on the spectator. By the end of the silent film we can consider this arsenal to have been full. On the one side the Soviet cinema carried to its ultimate consequences the theory and practice of montage while the German school did every kind of violence to the plastics of the image by way of sets and lighting. Other cinemas count too besides the Russian and German, but whether in France or Sweden or the United States, it does not appear that the language of cinema was at a loss for ways of saying what it wanted to say.

If the art of cinema consists in everything that plastics and montage can add to a given reality, the silent film was an art on its own. Sound could only play at best a subordinate and supplementary role: a counterpoint to the visual image. But this possible enhancement—at best only a minor one—is likely not to weigh much in comparison with the additional bargain-rate reality introduced at the same time by sound.

Thus far we have put forward the view that expressionism of montage and image constitute the essence of cinema. And it is precisely on this generally accepted notion that directors from silent days, such as Erich von Stroheim, F. W. Murnau, and Robert Flaherty, have by implication cast a doubt. In their films, montage plays no part, unless it be the negative one of inevitable elimination where reality superabounds. The camera cannot see everything at once but it makes sure not to lose any part of what it chooses to see. What matters to Flaherty, confronted with Nanook hunting the seal, is the relation between Nanook and the animal; the actual length of the waiting period. Montage could suggest the time involved. Flaherty however confines himself to showing the actual waiting period; the length of the hunt is the very substance of the image, its true object. Thus in the film this episode requires one set-up. Will anyone deny that it is thereby much more moving than a montage by attraction?

Murnau is interested not so much in time as in the reality of dramatic space. Montage plays no more of a decisive part in *Nosferatu* than in *Sunrise*. One might be inclined to think that the plastics of his image are impressionistic. But this would be a superficial view. The composition of his image is in no sense pictorial. It adds nothing to the reality, it does not deform it, it forces it to reveal its structural depth, to bring out the preexisting relations which become constitutive of the drama. For example, in *Tabu*, the arrival of a ship from left screen gives an immediate sense of destiny at work so that Murnau has no need to cheat in any way on the uncompromising realism of a film whose settings are completely natural.

But it is most of all Stroheim who rejects photographic expressionism and the tricks of montage. In his films reality lays itself bare like a suspect confessing under the relentless examination of the commissioner of police. He has one simple rule for direction. Take a close look at the world, keep on doing so, and in the end it will lay bare for you all its cruelty and its ugliness. One could easily imagine as a matter of fact a film by Stroheim composed of a single shot as long-lasting and as close-up as you like. These three directors do not exhaust the possibilities. We would undoubtedly find scattered among the works of others elements of nonexpressionistic cinema in which montage plays no part—even including Griffith. But these examples suffice to reveal, at the very heart of the silent film, a cinematographic art the very opposite of that which has been identified as *cinéma par excellence*, a language the semantic and syntactical unit of which is in no sense the Shot; in which the image is evaluated not according to what it adds to reality but what it reveals of it. In the latter art the silence of the screen was a drawback, that is to say, it deprived reality of one of its elements. *Greed*, like Dreyer's *Jeanne d' Arc*, is already virtually a talking film. The moment that you cease to maintain that montage and the plastic composition of the image are the very essence of the language of cinema, sound is no longer the aesthetic crevasse dividing two radically different aspects of the seventh art. The cinema that is believed to have died of the soundtrack is in no sense "*the* cinema." The real dividing line is elsewhere. It was operative in the past and continues to be through thirty-five years of the history of the language of the film.

Having challenged the aesthetic unity of the silent film and divided it off into two opposing tendencies, now let us take a look at the history of the last twenty years.

From 1930 to 1940 there seems to have grown up in the world, originating largely in the United States, a common form of cinematic language. It was the triumph in Hollywood, during that time, of five or six major kinds of film that gave it its overwhelming superiority: (1) American comedy (*Mr. Smith Goes to Washington*, 1936); (2) The burlesque film (The Marx Brothers); (3) The dance and vaudeville film (Fred Astaire and Ginger Rogers, and the Ziegfield Follies); (4) The crime and gangster film (*Scarface, I Am a Fugitive from a Chain Gang, The Informer*); (5) Psychological and social dramas. (*Back Street, Jezebel*); (6) Horror or fantasy films (*Dr. Jekyll and Mr. Hyde, The Invisible Man, Frankenstein*); (7) The western

(*Stagecoach*, 1939). During that time the French cinema undoubtedly ranked next. Its superiority was gradually manifested by way of a trend towards what might be roughly called stark somber realism, or poetic realism, in which four names stand out: Jacques Feyder, Jean Renoir, Marcel Carné, and Julien Duvivier. My intention not being to draw up a list of prize-winners, there is little use in dwelling on the Soviet, British, German, or Italian films for which these years were less significant than the ten that were to follow. In any case, American and French production sufficiently clearly indicate that the sound film, prior to World War II, had reached a well-balanced stage of maturity.

First as to content: Major varieties with clearly defined rules capable of pleasing a worldwide public, as well as a cultured elite, provided it was not inherently hostile to the cinema.

Secondly as to form: well-defined styles of photography and editing perfectly adapted to their subject matter; a complete harmony of image and sound. In seeing again today such films as *Jezebel* by Willian Wyler, *Stagecoach* by John Ford, or *Le Jour se lève* by Marcel Carné, one has the feeling that in them an art has found its perfect balance, its ideal form of expression, and reciprocally one admires them for dramatic and moral themes to which the cinema, while it may not have created them, has given a grandeur, an artistic effectiveness, that they would not otherwise have had. In short, here are all the characteristics of the ripeness of a classical art.

I am quite aware that one can justifiably argue that the originality of the postwar cinema as compared with that of 1938 derives from the growth of certain national schools, in particular the dazzling display of the Italian cinema and of a native English cinema freed from the influence of Hollywood. From this one might conclude that the really important phenomenon of the years 1940–1950 is the introduction of new blood, of hitherto unexplored themes. That is to say, the real revolution took place more on the level of subject matter than of style. Is not neorealism primarily a kind of humanism and only secondarily a style of filmmaking? Then as to the style itself, is it not essentially a form of self-effacement before reality?

Our intention is certainly not to preach the glory of form over content. Art for art's sake is just as heretical in cinema as elsewhere, probably more so. On the other hand, a new subject matter demands new form, and as good a way as any towards understanding what a film is trying to say to us is to know how it is saying it.

Thus by 1938 or 1939 the talking film, particularly in France and in the United States, had reached a level of classical perfection as a result, on the one hand, of the maturing of different kinds of drama developed in part over the past ten years and in part inherited from the silent film, and, on the other, of the stabilization of technical progress. The 1930's were the years, at once, of sound and of panchromatic film. Undoubtedly studio equipment had continued to improve but only in matters of detail, none of them opening up new, radical possibilities for direction. The only changes in this situation since 1940 have been in photography, thanks to the increased sensitivity of the film stock. Panchromatic stock turned visual values upside down, ultrasensitive emulsions have made a modification in their structure possible. Free to shoot in the studio with a much smaller aperture, the operator could, when necessary, eliminate the soft-focus background once considered essential. Still there are a number of examples of the prior use of deep focus, for example in the work of Jean Renoir. This had always been possible on exteriors, and given a measure of skill, even in the studios. Anyone could do it who really wanted to. So that it is less a question basically of a technical problem, the solution of which has admittedly been made easier, than of a search after a style—a point to which we will come back. In short, with panchromatic stock in common use, with an understanding of the potentials of the microphone, and with the crane as standard studio equipment, one can really say that since 1930 all the technical requirements for the art of cinema have been available.

Since the determining technical factors were practically eliminated, we must look elsewhere for the signs and principles of the evolution of film language, that is to say by challenging the subject matter and as a consequence the styles necessary for its expression.

By 1939 the cinema had arrived at what geographers call the equilibrium-profile of a river. By this is meant that ideal mathematical curve which results from the requisite amount of erosion. Having reached this equilibrium-profile, the river flows effortlessly from its source to its mouth without further deepening of its bed. But if any geological movement occurs which raises the erosion level and modifies the height of the source, the water sets to work again, seeps into the surrounding land, goes deeper, burrowing and digging. Sometimes when it is a chalk bed, a new pattern is dug across the plain, almost invisible but found to be complex and winding, if one follows the flow of the water.

THE EVOLUTION OF EDITING SINCE THE ADVENT OF SOUND

In 1938 there was an almost universal standard pattern of editing. If, somewhat conventionally, we call the kind of silent films based on the plastics of the image and the artifices of montage, "expressionist" or "symbolistic," we can describe the new form of storytelling "analytic" and "dramatic." Let us suppose, by way of reviewing one of the elements of the experiment of Kuleshov, that we have a table covered with food and a hungry tramp. One can imagine that in 1936 it would have been edited as follows:

1. Full shot of the actor and the table.
2. Camera moves forward into a close-up of a face expressing a mixture of amazement and longing.
3. Series of close-ups of food.
4. Back to full shot of person who starts slowly towards the camera.
5. Camera pulls slowly back to a three-quarter shot of the actor seizing a chicken wing.

Whatever variants one could think of for this scene, they would all have certain points in common:

1. The verisimilitude of space in which the position of the actor is always determined, even when a close-up eliminates the decor.
2. The purpose and the effects of the cutting are exclusively dramatic or psychological.

In other words, if the scene were played on a stage and seen from a seat in the orchestra, it would have the same meaning, the episode would continue to exist objectively. The changes of point of view provided by the camera would add nothing. They would present the reality a little more forcefully, first by allowing a better view and then by putting the emphasis where it belongs.

It is true that the stage director like the film director has at his disposal a margin within which he is free to vary the interpretation of the action but it is only a margin and allows for no modification of the inner logic of the event. Now, by way of contrast, let us take the montage of the stone lions in *The End of St. Petersburg*. By skillful juxtaposition a group of sculptured lions are made to look like a single lion getting to its feet, a symbol of the aroused masses. This clever device would be unthinkable in any film after 1932. As late as 1935 Fritz Lang, in *Fury*, followed a series of shots of women dancing the can-can with shots of clucking chickens in a farmyard. This relic of associative montage came as a shock even at the time, and today seems entirely out of keeping with the rest of the film. However decisive the art of Marcel Carné, for example, in our estimate of the respective values of *Quai des Brumes* or of *Le Jour se lève* his editing remains on the level of the reality he is analyzing. There is only one proper way of looking at it. That is why we are witnessing the almost complete disappearance of optical effects such as superimpositions, and even, especially in the United States, of the close-up, the too violent impact of which would make the audience conscious of the cutting. In the typical American comedy the director returns as often as he can to a shot of the characters from the knees up, which is said to be best suited to catch the spontaneous attention of the viewer—the natural point of balance of his mental adjustment.

Actually this use of montage originated with the silent movies. This is more or less the part it plays in Griffith's films, for example in *Broken Blossoms*, because with *Intolerance* he had already introduced that synthetic concept of montage which the Soviet cinema was to carry to its ultimate conclusion and which is to be found again, although less exclusively, at the end of the silent era. It is understandable, as a matter of fact, that the sound image, far less flexible than the visual image, would carry montage in the direction of realism, increasingly eliminating both plastic impressionism and the symbolic relation between images.

Thus around 1938 films were edited, almost without exception, according to the same principle. The story was unfolded in a series of set-ups numbering as a rule about 600. The characteristic procedure was by shot-reverse-shot, that is to say, in a dialogue scene, the camera followed the order of the text, alternating the character shown with each speech.

It was this fashion of editing, so admirably suitable for the best films made between 1930 and 1939, that was challenged by the shot in depth introduced by Orson Welles and William Wyler. *Citizen Kane* can never be too highly praised. Thanks to the depth of field, whole scenes are covered in one take, the camera remaining motionless. Dramatic effects for which we had formerly relied on montage were created out of the movements of the actors within a fixed framework. Of course Welles did not invent the in-depth shot any more than Griffith invented the close-up. All the pioneers used it and for a very good reason. Soft focus only appeared with montage. It was not only a technical must consequent upon the use of images in juxtaposition, it was a logical consequence of montage, its plastic equivalent. If at a given moment in the action the director, as in the scene imagined above, goes to a close-up of a bowl of fruit, it follows naturally that he also isolates it in space through the focusing of the lens. The soft focus of the background confirms therefore the effect of montage, that is to say, while it is of the essence of the storytelling, it is only an accessory of the style of the photography. Jean Renoir had already clearly understood this, as we see from a statement of his made in 1938 just after he had made *La Bête humaine* and *La Grande illusion* and just prior to *La Règle du jeu*: "The more I learn about my trade the more I incline to direction in depth relative to the screen. The better it works, the less I use the kind of set-up that shows two actors facing the camera, like two well-behaved subjects posing for a still portrait." The truth of the matter is, that if you are looking for the precursor of Orson Welles, it is not Louis Lumière or Zecca, but rather Jean Renoir. In his films, the search after composition in depth is, in effect, a partial replacement of montage by frequent panning shots and entrances. It is based on a respect for the continuity of dramatic space and, of course, of its duration.

To anybody with eyes in his head, it is quite evident that the sequence of shots used by Welles in *The Magnificent Ambersons* is in no sense the purely passive recording of an action shot within the same framing. On the contrary, his refusal to break up the action, to analyze the dramatic field in time, is a positive action the results of which are far superior to anything that could be achieved by the classical "cut."

All you need to do is compare two frames shot in depth, one from 1910, the other from a film by Wyler or Welles, to understand just by looking at the image, even apart from the context of the film, how different their functions are. The framing in the 1910 film is intended, to all intents and purposes, as a substitute for the missing fourth wall of the theatrical stage, or at least in exterior shots, for the best vantage point to view the action, whereas in the second case the setting, the lighting, and the camera angles give an entirely different reading. Between them, director and cameraman have converted the screen into a dramatic checkerboard, planned down to the last detail. The clearest if not the most original examples of this are to be found in *The Little Foxes* where the *mise-en-scène* takes on the severity of a working drawing. Welles' pictures are more difficult to analyze because of his overfondness for the baroque. Objects and characters are related in such a fashion that it is impossible for the spectator to miss the significance of the scene. To get the same results by way of montage would have necessitated a detailed succession of shots.

What we are saying then is that the sequence of shots "in depth" of the contemporary director does not exclude the use of montage—how could he, without reverting to a primitive babbling?—he makes it an integral part of his "plastic." The storytelling of Welles or Wyler is no less explicit than John Ford's but theirs has the advantage over his that it does not sacrifice the specific effects that can be derived from unity of image in space and time. Whether an episode is analyzed bit by bit or presented in its physical entirety cannot surely remain a matter of indifference, at least in a work with some pretensions to style. It would obviously be absurd to deny that montage had added considerably to the progress of film language, but this has happened at the cost of other values, no less definitely cinematic.

This is why depth of field is not just a stock in trade of the cameraman like the use of a series of filters or of such-and-such style of lighting, it is a capital gain in the field of direction—a dialectical step forward in the history of film language.

Nor is it just a formal step forward. Well used, shooting in depth is not just a more economical, a simpler, and at the same time a more subtle way of getting the most out of a scene. In addition to affecting the structure of film language, it also affects the relationships of the minds of the spectators to the image, and in consequence it influences the interpretation of the spectacle.

It would lie outside the scope of this article to analyze the psychological modalities of these relations, as also their aesthetic consequences, but it might be enough here to note, in general terms:

(1) That depth of focus brings the spectator into a relation with the image closer to that which he enjoys with reality. Therefore it is correct to say that, independently of the contents of the image, its structure is more realistic;

(2) That it implies, consequently, both a more active mental attitude on the part of the spectator and a more positive contribution on his part to the action in progress. While analytical montage only calls for him to follow his guide, to let his attention follow along smoothly with that of the director who will choose what he should see, here he is called upon to exercise at least a minimum of personal choice. It is from his attention and his will that the meaning of the image in part derives.

(3) From the two preceding propositions, which belong to the realm of psychology, there follows a third which may be described as metaphysical. In analyzing reality, montage presupposes of its very nature the unity of meaning of the dramatic event. Some other form of analysis is undoubtedly possible but then it would be another film. In short, montage by its very nature rules out ambiguity of expression. Kuleshov's experiment proves this *per absurdum* in giving on each occasion a precise meaning to the expression on a face, the ambiguity of which alone makes the three successively exclusive expressions possible.

On the other hand, depth of focus reintroduced ambiguity into the structure of the image if not of necessity—Wyler's films are never ambiguous—at least as a possibility. Hence it is no exaggeration to say that *Citizen Kane* is unthinkable shot in any other way but in depth. The uncertainty in which we find ourselves as to the spiritual key or the interpretation we should put on the film is built into the very design of the image.

It is not that Welles denies himself any recourse whatsoever to the expressionistic procedures of montage, but just that their use from time to time in between sequences of shots in depth gives them a new meaning. Formerly montage was the very stuff of cinema, the texture of the scenario. In *Citizen Kane* a series of superimpositions is contrasted with a scene presented in a single take, constituting another and deliberately abstract mode of story-telling. Accelerated montage played tricks with time and space while that of Welles, on the other hand, is not trying to deceive us; it offers us a contrast, condensing time, and hence is the equivalent for example of the French imperfect or the English frequentative tense. Like accelerated montage and montage of attractions these superimpositions, which the talking film had not used for ten years, rediscovered a possible use related to temporal realism in a film without montage.

The shot-in-depth from *Citizen Kane* (1941). "Thanks to the depth of field, whole scenes are covered in one take, the camera remaining motionless. . . . Director and cameraman have converted the screen into a dramatic checkerboard, planned down to the last detail" (Bazin, pp. 48, 49).

Herbert Marshall and Bette Davis in *The Little Foxes*: ". . . the *mise-en-scène* takes on the severity of a working drawing. . . . Objects and characters are related in such a fashion that it is impossible for the spectator to miss the significance of the scene." (BAZIN, p. 49).

If we have dwelt at some length on Orson Welles it is because the date of his appearance in the filmic firmament (1941) marks more or less the beginning of a new period and also because his case is the most spectacular and, by virtue of his very excesses, the most significant.

Yet *Citizen Kane* is part of a general movement, of a vast stirring of the geological bed of cinema, confirming that everywhere up to a point there had been a revolution in the language of the screen.

I could show the same to be true, although by different methods, of the Italian cinema. In Roberto Rossellini's *Paisà* and *Allemania Anno Zero* and Vittorio de Sica's *Ladri de Biciclette*, Italian neorealism contrasts with previous forms of film realism in its stripping away of all expressionism and in particular in the total absence of the effects of montage. As in the films of Welles and in spite of conflicts of style, neorealism tends to give back to the cinema a sense of the ambiguity of reality. The preoccupation of Rossellini when dealing with the face of the child in *Allemania Anno Zero* is the exact opposite of that of Kuleshov with the close-up of Mozhukhin. Rossellini is concerned to preserve its mystery. We should not be misled by the fact that the evolution of neorealism is not manifest, as in the United States, in any form of revolution in editing. They are both aiming at the same results by different methods. The means used by Rossellini and de Sica are less spectacular but they are no less determined to do away with montage and to transfer to the screen the *continuum* of reality. The dream of Zavattini is just to make a ninety-minute film of the life of a man to whom nothing ever happens. The most "aesthetic" of the neorealists, Luchino Visconti, gives just as clear a picture as Welles of the basic aim of his directorial art in *La Terra Trema*, a film almost entirely composed of one-shot sequences, thus clearly showing his concern to cover the entire action in interminable deep-focus panning shots.

However we cannot pass in review all the films that have shared in this revolution in film language since 1940. Now is the moment to attempt a synthesis of our reflections on the subject.

It seems to us that the decade from 1940 to 1950 marks a decisive step forward in the development of the language of the film. If we have appeared since 1930 to have lost sight of the trend of the silent film as illustrated particularly by Stroheim, F. W. Murnau, Robert Flaherty, and Dreyer, it is for a purpose. It is not that this trend seems to us to have been halted by the talking film. On the contrary, we believe that it represented the richest vein of the so-called silent film and, precisely because it was not aesthetically tied to montage, but was indeed the only tendency that looked to the realism of sound as a natural development. On the other hand it is a fact that the talking film between 1930 and 1940 owes it virtually nothing save for the glorious and retrospectively prophetic exception of Jean Renoir. He alone in his searchings as a director prior to *La Règle du jeu* forced himself to look back beyond the resources provided by montage and so uncovered the secret of a film form that would permit everything to be said without chopping the world up into little fragments, that would reveal the hidden meanings in people and things without disturbing the unity natural to them.

It is not a question of thereby belittling the films of 1930 to 1940, a criticism that would not stand up in the face of the number of masterpieces, it is simply an attempt to establish the notion of a dialectic progress, the highest expression of which was found in the films of the 1940s. Undoubtedly, the talkie sounded the knell of a certain aesthetic of the language of film, but only wherever it had turned its back on its vocation in the service of realism. The sound film nevertheless did preserve the essentials of montage, namely discontinuous description and the dramatic analysis of action. What it turned its back on was metaphor and symbol in exchange for the illusion of objective presentation. The expressionism of montage has virtually disppeared but the relative realism of the kind of cutting that flourished around 1937 implied a congenital limitation which escaped us so long as it was perfectly suited to its subject matter. Thus American comedy reached its peak within the framework of a form of editing in which the realism of the time played no part. Dependent on logic for its effects, like vaudeville and plays on words, entirely conventional in its moral and sociological content, American comedy had everything to gain, in strict line-by-line progression, from the rhythmic resources of classical editing.

Undoubtedly it is primarily with the Stroheim-Murnau trend—almost totally eclipsed from 1930 to 1940—that the cinema has more or less consciously linked up once more over the last ten years. But it has no intention of limiting itself simply to keeping this trend alive. It draws from it the secret of the regeneration of realism in storytelling and thus of becoming capable once more of bringing together real time, in which things exist, along with the duration of the action, for which classical editing had insidiously substituted mental and abstract time. On the other hand, so far from wiping out once and for all the conquests of montage, this reborn realism gives them a body of reference and a meaning. It is only an increased realism of the image that can support the abstraction of montage. The stylistic repertory of a director such as Hitchcock, for example, ranged from the power inherent in the basic document as such, to superimpositions, to large close-ups. But the close-ups of Hitchcock are not the same as those of C. B. de Mille in *The Cheat* [1915]. They are just one type of figure, among others, of his style. In other words, in the silent days, montage evoked what the director wanted to say; in the editing of 1938, it described it. Today we can say that at last the director writes in film. The image— its plastic composition and the way it is set in time, because it is founded on a much higher degree of realism—has at its disposal more means of manipulating reality and of modifying it from within. The film maker is no longer the competitor of the painter and the playwright, he is, at last, the equal of the novelist.

1950–55

BRIAN HENDERSON
TOWARD A NON-BOURGEOIS CAMERA STYLE

Brian Henderson has been a member of the editorial board at *Film Quarterly* since 1973. Together with the journal's editor, Ann Martin, he published *Film Quarterly: Forty Years, a Selection* (1999), which brings together seminal essays on film theory and analysis, specific films and directors, and the techniques and technologies of filmmaking. *A Critique of Film Theory* (1980) collects Henderson's essays from *Film Quarterly* and *Film Comment*, including work on Christian Metz, André Bazin's film theory and emphasis on the long take, Eisenstein's montage theory, and the work of Jean-Luc Godard. These early essays played a central role in the debates about constructing a theoretical approach to film analysis in the late 1970s and early 1980s, a debate in which Henderson's stance was pluralistic and anti-auteurist. He has also edited and introduced two volumes of screenplays by Preston Sturges, on whose life and films he has published extensively. He is currently professor of media studies at the State University of New York at Buffalo.

Godard has developed a new camera style in his later period.[1] Its prime element is a long, slow tracking shot that moves purely laterally—usually in one direction only (left to right or right to left), sometimes doubling back (left to right then right to left, right to left then left to right)—over a scene that does not itself move, or strictly speaking, that does not move in any relation to the camera's movement. Examples of this shot are the automobile trilogy or triptych: the backed-up highway of cars in *Weekend*, the wrecked cars piled up in *One Plus One*, and the auto assembly line in *British Sounds*; most of the studio scenes with the Stones in *One Plus One*; several of the guerrilla scenes in *Weekend* ("I salute you, old ocean"); and the shot of the University of Nanterre and environs in *La Chinoise*. Before we consider this shot as part of a stylistic complex and in the various contexts in which it appears, we must consider the shot in itself—its structure and implications as shot.

First we must distinguish Godard's tracking shot from other such shots in the history of cinema. It is not, first of all, forward camera movement, proving the depth of space, as in Murnau. Godard's tracking shot moves neither forward nor backward in space, nor in any diagonal or arc, nor at any angle but 90° to the scene it is shooting. That is, Godard's track lies exactly along the 0°/180° line. The scenes or subjects which these shots address lie also along a 0°/180° line, which, further-

---

[1]This article is part of a longer critical study, "*Weekend* and History," which considers that film in its various historical contexts—cinema and dramatic history, history of the bourgeoisie, human history.

more, is exactly parallel to the camera line. This extreme stylization, wherein a plane or planes of subject are paralleled exactly by the plane of art, is unusual in cinema and gives the shot very much the form of a planimetric painting. A partial exception to the rule is the camera's sinuosity in the traffic jam shot in *Weekend*, its slight "angling" to left and right as it moves laterally, getting slightly behind or ahead of the scene it is filming, a kind of warp in the shot's even, continuous space-time. The base line of the camera's movement remains exactly straight, however, and exactly parallel to the scene. More fundamental departures from the lateral track are the Action Musicale sequence-shot in *Weekend*, in which the camera remains in the center of the scene and *turns* 360°, and the shot in *One Plus One*, in which the camera *tracks* 360° around the studio in which the Stones are playing. In the first the camera is at the center of a circle, in the second at the periphery, but in both there is the sense of a circular subject rendered flat and linear: these shots look like the lateral tracking shot and fit easily into formats which align them end-to-end with such shots.

The shot, secondly, is not like Ophuls's tracking shots which—though often lateral and hence formally like Godard's—are essentially following shots. Ophuls tracks in order to follow his characters, to give them movement or to attend their movement. His tracks center on, are filled with, derive life and motion from his characters, that is, from individuals. Godard, like Eisenstein, repudiates "the individualist conception of the bourgeois hero" and his tracking shots reflect this. His camera serves no individual and prefers none to another. It never initiates movement to follow a character and if it picks one up as it moves it leaves him behind as haphazardly (the workers and Wiazemsky in the Action Musicale and the shot with Juliet Berto in and out, in *Weekend*). Also—though some may dispute this—Ophuls's tracks are essentially uncritical of their subjects, whereas the essence of Godard's tracking shot is its critical distance from what it surveys. Also, Ophuls frequently uses the composition-in-depth technique of interposing objects in the foreground, between character and camera. Godard never does this.

Thirdly, the shot is not like Fellini's pans and short tracks, though the latter also survey persons fixed in space rather than moving ones, that is, "discover" them in place as the camera moves. There are two chief differences. First, Fellini's camera *affects* his characters, calls them into life or bestows life upon them. Godard's camera does not affect the reality it unfolds and is not affected by it. There is a different camera dialectic in each: Fellini's camera interacts with reality, touches and is touched, causes as well as registers effects; Godard's camera assumes a position over against reality, outside, detached. Secondly, Fellini's tracks are frequently subjective—in the sense that the camera eye is a character's eye. In *8 1/2* the reactions of characters to the camera are their reaction to Guido; the pain we feel when we see them is Guido's pain. Because subjective, Fellini's tracks are most often in medium close or close-up range, sometimes with only faces coming into view; Godard's tracks, which are never subjective, are usually in long shot, taking in as much of an event and its context as possible. Also, Fellini introduces depth by arraying characters and objects in multiple planes, some very close to the camera, others at a distance, making for surprise and variety as the camera moves over them. Godard avoids depth: he arranges his characters in a single plane only—none is ever closer to the camera than another. The resulting flatness of Godard's shots, particularly in *Weekend*, is discussed below.

Godard's tracking shot is a species of long take,[2] very often of sequence shot,[3] but it has few or none of the characteristics in terms of which André Bazin discussed and defended the shot and cinematic styles based upon it. In Godard's shot there is continuity of dramatic space and time, the irreducibles of the long take (indeed its very definition); but there is strict avoidance of composition-in-depth, for Bazin the essence of the shot—or that of greatest value in its use. As mentioned, Godard's frames are flat, composed in relation to the plane occupied by his characters. Other planes, where present, are used merely as backdrop to this one. Not only composition-in-depth but the *values* which Bazin found in composition-in-depth are missing in Godard's version of the long take (and in late Godard generally): greater realism, greater participation on the part of the viewer, and a reintroduction of ambiguity into the structure of the film image. It is clear that Godard is no realist; in *La Chinoise* he specifically repudiates the realist aesthetic (of Bazin and others): "Art is not the reflection of a reality; it is the reality of that reflection." Godard's later style does require the active participation of the viewer, but not in Bazin's sense of choosing what to see within a multilayered image and, presumably, making his own moral connections within it also. Godard presents instead an admittedly synthetic, single-layered construct, which the viewer must examine critically, accept or reject. The viewer is not drawn *into* the image, nor does he make choices within it; he stands outside the image and judges it *as a whole*. It is clear also that Godard of the later films is not interested in ambiguity—through flatness of frame and transparency of action, he seeks to eliminate ambiguity. Thus Godard uses the long take for none of the traditional reasons; in fact he reinvents the long take, and the tracking shot, for his own purposes.

A camera moves slowly, sideways to the scene it is filming. It tracks. But what is the result when its contents are projected on a screen? It is a band or ribbon of reality that slowly unfolds itself. It is a mural or scroll that unrolls before the viewer and rolls up after him. To understand the nature of this visual band we must go beyond the tracking shot itself. We encounter here the aesthetic problem of parts and wholes: Godard's tracking shot is but one element in a remarkably rich and complete stylistic complex or repertoire. It appears not in isolation, but in formal combinations with other kinds of shots, and with sounds. In short, the tracking shot cannot be understood apart from the varying contexts in which it appears—it has

---

[2]A single piece of unedited film; of course "long" is relative to "short"—the cut-off would seem to be a shot used for wholly independent effect rather than as part of a montage pattern. None of Eisenstein's early films contains a single long take—such was the theoretical purity of his practice; no Godard film is without several long takes.

[3]A sequence filmed in one take; a one-shot sequence. A sequence is a series of closely related scenes; a scene is a shot or shots that cover a single and continuous dramatic action. We must bear in mind that Godard's "sequences" are not those of conventional narrative cinema, hence the concepts "sequence" and "sequence shot" lose the reasonably clear meaning they had for Bazin. What meanings will take their place, we do not yet know. See André Bazin, "The Evolution of the Language of Cinema," trans. Hugh Gray, in *What Is Cinema?* (Berkeley: University of California Press, 1967); also contained in *The New Wave*, ed. by Peter Graham (New York: Doubleday, 1968). [And reprinted on pp. 41–53 in this volume.

a different meaning and formal function in *La Chinoise*, in *Weekend*, in *One Plus One*, and in *British Sounds*, and even at different places within the same film. Moreover, the matter of "context" is not as simple as it might appear. Each of the latter films is built upon a complex camera/sound conception or donnée, and no two of these are alike. Our principal concern is the formal construction of *Weekend* and the specific role of the tracking shot in that construction; that is, the relation of formal part and whole. We will not understand either aspect of *Weekend*, however, until we see that film's characteristic shot in the alternative contexts of the other late films and understand the formal principles of those works themselves. The use of the tracking shot in the other films clarifies its use in *Weekend* and the formal principles of the other films put into perspective the formal principle of *Weekend* itself.

La Chinoise contains some interesting instances of the tracking shot even though the film is in no sense built upon this shot, as both *Weekend* and *One Plus One* are. (In the latter films, the whole is chiefly a relation among tracking shots; in *La Chinoise* the whole is a relation among many kinds of shots, relatively few of which are tracking shots.) There are, first of all, the remarkable shots from the balcony, in which the action within the apartment is carefully orchestrated in relation to the camera's passage, in various mathematical variations, along the apartment's three windows and two walls, and back. There is, secondly, a usage of the shot as a special kind of documentation. As Véronique describes her awakening to social contradictions at Nanterre, the camera tracks slowly (from right to left) across the shabby, overcrowded dwellings of the Algerian workers who live near the university, coming to rest at last on the modern, efficient buildings of the university complex. The workers' shacks are flat and horizontal, the university buildings high and vertical, but the shot is set up so that the camera does not have to move back to take in the tall, commanding structures—it takes in everything within a single perspective. Eisenstein would have cut from a shot of the one to a shot of the other, making the juxtaposition for the viewer, obliterating time and space relations to make a clearcut social relation. Godard observes the time and space relations and lets the viewer make the social relation. His shot establishes the true proportions of extreme contrast and close proximity. He does this by virtue of the long take's continuity of dramatic space and time, which this usage reveals as itself a form of argumentation or demonstration; the shot has its own internal relations, its own logic. This instance of the shot seems Bazinian but, far from fidelity to the real, Godard rips this bit of footage from its grounding in the real and puts it down in the midst of a highly abstract film essay. Goddard impresses the real into his own service—ignoring the form of the real itself, he subjects it firmly to his own formal construct. Besides the tracking shots, *La Chinoise* also includes several static long takes—the two dialogues between Véronique and Guillaume, the assassination scene—as well as montage (or collage) constructions. (It has become a commonplace that modern film-makers fall between Eisenstein and Bazin, that they combine editing techniques and long takes in various, distinctive styles.) The overall formal principle of *La Chinoise* would seem to be collage, which is also the formal principle of *The Married Woman*, portions of *Le Gai Savoir*, and, in certain senses, or *Pravda*.

The difference between montage and collage is a complex question. Film critics generally use the term collage without elucidating its meaning nor even its difference from montage. There is sometimes the suggestion that the pieces of a collage are shorter or more fragmented than those of a montage, but this does not hold up. Modern filmmakers rarely use any shorter than Eisenstein's average shot in *Potemkin*. Moreover, collage as practiced by moderns allows long takes and tracking shots; montage as practiced by Eisenstein did not. It seems clear that the difference between montage and collage is to be found in the divergent ways in which they associate and order images, not in the length or nature of the images themselves. Montage fragments reality in order to reconstitute it in highly organized, synthetic emotional and intellectual patterns. Collage does not do this; it collects or sticks its fragments together in a way that does not entirely overcome their fragmentation. It seeks to recover its fragments *as fragments*. In regard to overall form, it seeks to bring out the internal relations of its pieces, whereas montage imposes a set of relations upon them and indeed collects or creates its pieces to fill out a preexistent plan. (This point is discussed further in the comparison of the collage principle to the visual organization of *Weekend* and *One Plus One* below.)

In *Weekend* the collage principle all but disappears. Intercut titles—showing the day and the hour, the car speedometer, names of sequences such as "Action Musicale," "Scenes from Provincial Life"—serve as breaks within takes and between scenes, but all within the film's single-image continuum. They do not interact with the pictorial images to form montage patterns, as in *La Chinoise*. Conversely: whereas in *La Chinoise* the tracking shot is incidental, in *Weekend* it is the master shot: the entire film aspires to the condition of this shot. The cuts are merely connective; once outside the Paris apartment, the film might as well be a single, fixed-distance travelling shot along the highway and across the provincial landscape. *Weekend* indeed approximates this ideal form by its remarkable adherence to a single camera range—it is filmed almost entirely in long shot. Thus *Weekend* is the film in which the structure of the tracking shot and the formal principle of the whole very nearly coincide. Not just its characteristic shot but the whole of *Weekend* itself is a continuous visual band that unfolds itself along a linear axis.[4]

We have found that *Weekend* is the one film among the later works in which the structure of the tracking shot and the formal principle of the whole are nearly identical. Because the shots of *Weekend* deal with a single situation (rather than two or more), they are not juxtaposed (as in *One Plus One*), but merely linked—as though to form one long composite tracking shot. This continuity is emphasized by the near-constant camera range of long shot, which renders the entire film, even static shots, into a single band of reality. In our discussion of the tracking shot as long take we distinguished it from composition-in-depth shots and thereby characterized the tracking shot in terms of a certain kind of flatness. If the overall structure of *Weekend* parallels that of the tracking shot, then the film as a whole must exhibit flatness

---

[4]Omitted from this reprinting is a passage that extends the discussion of the tracking shot and of part-whole relations to the films that Godard made after *Weekend*—*One Plus One*, *British Sounds*, *Le Gai Savoir*, *Pravda*, and *Wind From the East*. In these films, more than in *Weekend* and *La Chinoise*, the organization of sound-image relation (at levels of part and whole) is fundamental.—B.H.

also. In light of our distinction between parts and wholes, it must also be that flatness of the whole is something different from flatness of the part; and in *Weekend* this is found to be true. Nevertheless—flatness seems an odd category in which to discuss the formal organization of a work, partly because it seems a negative concept, partly because "flatness" has no meaning except in relation to "depth." In fact, however, *Weekend* itself is negative—regarding its subject, the bourgeoisie—in several important respects. And, as we shall see also, the "flatness" of *Weekend* has specific relation to a previous "depth"—composition-in-depth, the principal mode of bourgeois self-presentment in cinema.

If we now propose to discuss the formal organization of *Weekend*, part and whole, in terms of flatness, the effect may well be one of anticlimax and disappointment. If this is so, it is due in large measure to the imprecision that such terms, and especially this term, carry in film analysis. What this means, since the category of flatness comes up inescapably here and elsewhere, is that some theoretical clarification needs to be done. This task cannot be undertaken here but minimal clarification must be done to permit our analysis of *Weekend*. There is no single sense of flatness in cinema but in fact several senses, not only in regard to different films but often in regard to the same film. A single work may be flat in several senses, or now in one sense and now in another; so we must ask not simply which films and scenes are "more flat" than others but in precisely which senses they are flat. An equally great problem area is how critics use the judgment of flatness—the correlations they make between flatness and other matters, particularly those of subject and meaning. Clearly an undifferentiated judgment of flatness cannot be the basis for an adequate interpretation or discussion of subject. A correlation between the "flatness" of *Made in USA* or *Weekend* and Herbert Marcuse's theory of a one-dimensional society is too general—in regard to both elements—to be of much use. Criticism must cut finer than this or it is not helpful. Rather we must ask in each case which of several kinds of flatness has/have been achieved and what is its/their specific relation to the subject of the part and/or whole to which it relates.

Cinema, like painting, is a two-dimensional art which creates the illusion of a third dimension. Painting is limited to its two dimensions; cinema is not. Cinema escapes the limits of two dimensions through its own third dimension, time. It does this by varying its range and perspective, by taking different views of its subject (through montage and/or camera movement). Cinema overcomes two-dimensionality through its "walk-around" capability, which is also a prime feature of ordinary human perception. E. H. Gombrich says: "While (one) turns, in other words, he is aware of a succession of aspects which swing round with him. What we call 'appearance' is always composed of such a succession of aspects, a melody, as it were, which allows us to estimate distance and size; it is obvious that this melody can be imitated by the movie camera but not by the painter with his easel." [5] Cinema can take several views of a subject, go from one camera angle to a reverse angle or other angle, from long shot to close-up, etc. It can take the measure of a character or object from many sides, in short, in three dimensions. Both montage and composition-in-depth

---

[5] E.H. Gombrich, *Art and Illusion*, pp. 256–57.

accomplish this walk-around project, both create and explore three dimensions, though in two-dimensional steps or segments, so to speak. It is obvious how montage accomplishes this—through a succession of shots from different angles and at different ranges. It is equally clear that a moving camera can accomplish the same succession of aspects within a single shot. Even in those long takes which do not involve a moving camera, the actors themselves may move with respect to the camera; that is, they walk back-and-forth, or at diagonals, changing in relative size, etc. In short, the actors *turn themselves* around for us, creating different angles and perspectives on themselves. Instead of the camera's walking around, they walk around in relation to the camera. This also is well beyond the two dimensions of painting, whereby we see only one side of a figure, which must stand for and suggest his entirety.

It is precisely cinema's capacity for depth which Godard excludes in *Weekend*. His moving camera, by adhering rigidly to the single-perspective, one-sided view of painting, eliminates the succession of aspects. The tracking shot's lateral motion *extends* this single perspective rather than alters it, very much as a mural does. The movement of Godard's camera creates not a succession of aspects, but a single aspect upon an unfolding subject matter. Both montage and the usual moving camera multiply aspects or perspectives *in regard to a single subject*. To borrow a term from music, the succession of aspects is a kind of *elaboration*. The subject in question is put through multiple variations (or views), toward some *exhaustion* of its nature, meaning, or appearance. Godard's tracking shot does not elaborate in this sense. Its variations through time open up ever new subject matter; they do not elaborate or take multiple views of the same subject, as both montage and composition-in-depth (nearly) always do. Throughout the duration of a tracking shot, a one-to-one relation is maintained: a single perspective per stretch or segment of subject matter, with never a doubling or curving of perspective on a single subject.

It should be emphasized that this flatness of the single aspect is a formal quality of the whole, not of the part. We cannot judge aspect succession or constancy on the basis of the part alone since the succession of aspects is often a succession *of shots*. It is true that each tracking shot in *Weekend* is flat in this sense of singleness of perspective, but what is done in one shot may be undone, or complemented, by another. This is the method of montage, whereby the angle and range of one shot give way to those of another and another, until a totality of aspects is accumulated. Even with lateral long takes, a subsequent tracking shot may provide a different view of the subject of a previous tracking shot. Thus we do not know until a film is over whether a given subject is elaborated multiply or not. We must look at *all* the shots of a sequence or film before we can say whether they present a succession of aspects on a single subject or, as in *Weekend*, a single aspect on a single, unfolding subject. Thus the flatness of the mural effect is an attribute or quality of the whole.

We have argued that *Weekend* is flat in an overall or structural sense in that it eliminates the succession of aspects, by which cinema approximates the third dimension. This is an absolute flatness—a sequence, a film either varies aspects or it does not. Generally speaking, the frames of *Weekend* are also relatively flat in several painterly respects, and this is always a relative flatness, a question of more or less. The clearest case of this kind of flatness is achieved by posing a character or characters against a short wall or background, as Godard does in *Masculin Feminin, Made in USA*, and other films, and as Skolimowski does in all his films. *Weekend* has certain of these shots, but it also has others with considerable depth—the camera follows its subjects, the bourgeois couple, across a continuous background/landscape that is sometimes flat (thick foliage behind the pair), sometimes deep (the highway backup).

But there are other kinds of flatness. The shallow wall shot achieves flatness simply by eliminating the long shot range, and perhaps also the medium-shot range. Godard's tracking shot achieves a converse flatness by eliminating the close-up, medium-close, and often medium shot ranges—by arranging his subject(s) and background all within the long shot range. The point may be clarified by a comparison with composition-in-depth, which aims for maximum visual and expressive use of depth, in that both a close-up and a long shot can be included within the same shot. Composition-in-depth achieves its illusion of great depth by arranging its subject through all possible ranges of the deep-focus shot and, of course, by making dramatic relations among these subject ranges. Godard achieves flatness using only a portion of the depth which deep-focus lenses permit—he uses the long-shot range and leaves the shorter ranges "blank," so to speak. Thus, even where there are several planes in a *Weekend* shot—highway, countryside, tree-line, etc.—they are all relatively flattened together, because all lie within the long-shot range. (Moreover, Godard does not achieve this flattening by using telephoto lenses, as Kurosawa did in *Red Beard*.)

Secondly, Godard's planes, even where multiple, are strictly parallel—they do not intersect or interrelate. Consequently the eye is not led back into the depth of the frame nor forward to its surfaces. How we have to "read" a painting or frame is one aspect of its depth; to read the frames of *Weekend*, the eye moves strictly from left to right (sometimes from right to left), never from front to back or back to front. What is true in a compositional sense is also true of the subject of these frames: the film's action. The characters, their movements and activities, never take us into or out of the frame but always from side to side. Neither in a compositional sense nor a narrative sense are we ever required to relate foreground and background in *Weekend*. Strictly speaking, there is no foreground and background, only background, just as in the shallow wall shot there is only foreground. In another sense, foreground and background are here merged into a single plane. Again, composition-in-depth provides a definitive contrast. Like the baroque in painting, composition-in-depth makes a great deal of foreground/background relations, or foreshortening, of huge objects in the foreground, etc. It is not too much to say that foreground/background relation is the axis of composition-in-depth expressivity. As we have seen, it is its moral base also.

Thirdly, the non-intersection of planes in *Weekend* is the result not only of their strict parallelism but also of the fixed, 90° camera angle, which arranges all planes in parallel to the borders of the frame itself. Of these planes, all are inert or non-operative in both a narrative and a compositional sense, except that occupied by the characters. All interest and movement reside in the characters and they occupy (or constitute) always the same plane; they do not move between planes. *Weekend* is single-planed in the sense that the camera and the viewer's eye fix upon only one plane, that occupied by the characters, and follow it out, in one direction only, at infinite length. The frame may contain several planes, but the film as a whole is constructed in relation to only one of these.

Weekend's single-plane construction sets it apart from either school of film aesthetics, montage or composition-in-depth; comparing *Weekend* to them will help us understand the various senses of the film's flatness historically. It is clear that montage editing (and overall film construction) involves or results in a series of planes or planar perspectives. Cutting among close-ups, medium close-ups, medium shots, and long shots, in any order or combination, is obviously an alternation of the planes of a scene, and the result when assembled a sequence of planes.[6] The scene or event is broken into its component parts or planes, then these are reconstructed in various patterns, in accord with a structural montage principle—rhythmic, emotional, or intellectual. Besides changes of camera range, there are also changes of angle, which can alternate planar perspectives rather than particular planes. Cutting to a different angle on the same scene, however, is also a rearrangement or reordering of the planes bearing upon the action. This ordering or sequence of planes is the very texture of Eisenstein's art. Composition-in-depth is not fundamentally different in principle and overall purpose. Composition-in-depth internalizes the sequence of planes within the shot; its ideal, as Bazin presents it, is the inclusion of all planes bearing upon an action within a single camera set-up. With all the planes of a situation before or available to the camera, the entire action of the scene may be worked out within a single shot. As with montage cinema, dramatic action is advanced by way of the alternation and interaction of planes, but now this is done by camera movement and/or by the movement of actors, themselves planes or parts of planes, through or in relation to the planes of the scene. At the same time the camera must organize these planes in terms of importance, dramatic interest, etc. By composition-in-depth the succession of planes is greatly fluidized, proceeding in a smooth flow rather than in jumps, but the right solution to a given scene becomes more difficult and complex. Implicit in the shot's first image, or accessible to it, must be all the scene's action and the full exploitability of its planes. Shots must be worked out carefully and carefully rehearsed. An example of the way that composition-in-depth orders planes within the frame is given by Bazin—the scene in *The Little Foxes* in which the steel box sought by several characters occupies the extreme foreground of the frame while its seekers are arrayed in multiple planes behind it. A more extreme case is the scene in *Citizen Kane* in which Mrs. Kane learns about her son's inheritance. Shot with a static camera, the shot is very narrow and very deep, virtually a visual corridor. Within the squeezed cabin room we

---

[6]As it happens, this phrase also appears in Stuart Gilbert's translation of André Malraux's *Museum Without Walls* (Garden City: Doubleday, 1967, p. 75): "The means of reproduction in the cinema is the moving photograph, but its means of expression is the sequence of planes. (The planes change when the camera is moved; it is their sequence that constitutes cutting.)" A similar mistranslation of the French *plan* (shot) as plane occurs in Gilbert's translations of Malraux's variants of this passage in *The Psychology of Art: I: Museum Without Walls* (New York: Pantheon, 1949–51, p. 112) and in *The Voices of Silence* (New York: Doubleday, 1953, p. 122), in which Malraux is made to assert that "the average duration of each [plane] is ten seconds." But Malraux was simply expounding the classical view that cutting, the sequence of shots, is the source of expressivity in cinema.

see the mother huge in the foreground, the banker from the East behind her, the window in the wall of the cabin behind them, and in the far distance, young Kane playing with his sled. Not only the composition of the shot but its dramatic action requires the eye to move continually back and forth. It is clear that Godard's treatment of planes in *Weekend* is directly opposed to that of this shot, an extreme in the opposite direction. Godard's visual field has little or no depth and has—or aspires to—infinite length; that is, it exists in a single lateral plane.

Consideration of *Weekend* points up underlying similarities between montage and composition-in-depth and serves to set Godard's film apart from either school of film aesthetics: both montage and composition-in-depth define cinema in terms of a multiplicity of planes and both see the problem of form or technique as the inclusion or relation of planes in a meaningful format. Godard in *Weekend* renounces the multiplicity of planes as a project of cinema and hence rejects both schools.

What are the implications of these shifts from three dimensions to two, from depth to flatness? An ideological interpretation suggests itself—composition-in-depth projects a bourgeois world infinitely deep, rich, complex, ambiguous, mysterious. Godard's flat frames collapse this world into two-dimensional actuality; thus reversion to a cinema of one plane is a demystification, an assault on the bourgeois world-view and self-image.[7] *Weekend*'s bourgeois figures scurry along without mystery toward mundane goals of money and pornographic fulfillment. There is no ambiguity and no moral complexity. That space in which the viewer could lose himself, make distinctions and alliances, comparisons and judgments, has been abrogated—the viewer is presented with a single flat picture of the world that he must examine, criticize, accept or reject. Thus the flatness of *Weekend* must not be analyzed only in itself but in regard to the previous modes of bourgeois self-presentment, particularly of composition-in-depth. The subject of *Weekend* is the historical bourgeoisie, the bourgeoisie in history; the film's flatness must not be seen statistically, as a single moment, but dialectically, as a *flattening*. Given this overall correlation, the specific correlations of the several senses of flatness fall into place. The succession of aspects not only multiplies viewpoints on the bourgeois world so that final judgment and any kind of certainty become impossible, it projects a bourgeois world infinitely inexhaustible and elaborable. Godard's tracking shot format insists on a single perspective and on the sufficiency of a single comprehensive survey for understanding of the transparent, easy-to-understand bourgeois world. Whereas in montage and composition-in-depth, complex form works on simple material, working it up as complex also, in Godard simple form works on simple material.

---

[7]This transition is more than a formal one. The practitioners and advocates of composition-in-depth genuinely believed in this moral depth and ambiguity. Bazin points out that the conception and interpretation of *Citizen Kane* depend on the composition of the image. It could hardly be otherwise in a great masterpiece. William Wyler's composition-in-depth films, which (as Bazin says) have little or no ambiguity, are not masterpieces. In such a case composition-in-depth becomes merely an imposed format, a style without internal correlates. (Wyler's better films, such as *The Letter*, are not structured around composition-in-depth.) Welles, the greatest composition-in-depth director, is also the director who has made the most of the theme of inexhaustible mystery. Not only *Kane* but many or most of Welles's other films center on impenetrable mystery and several, also like *Kane*, proceed through a multiplicity of viewpoints and perspectives which nevertheless fail to yield certainty concerning the underlying questions.

The tracking shot and single-plane construction suggest an infinitely thin, absolutely flat bourgeois substance that cannot be elaborated but only surveyed. Finally, the single camera range represents not only a refusal to participate in bourgeois space, through forward camera movement, intercutting camera ranges, etc., it also has to do with the maintenance of critical perspective. Given that the film's subject is the historical bourgeoisie, Godard keeps his subject before him at all times. He refuses to pick and choose within the bourgeois world or to prefer any part of it to any other—even for a moment—because that involves partial eclipse of the whole. The nature of the bourgeois totality and the project of criticizing it require that it never be lost from view, or broken up into parts and aspects, but always be kept before the viewer as single and whole. Obviously the long-shot range is the range of the totality and the tracking shot the instrument of its critical survey. For this reason also Godard does not allow the close-up and medium-close ranges to be filled, for a face or figure huge in the foreground literally obstructs the whole and distracts attention from it in an emotional and intellectual sense also. Flatness in *Weekend*, in its various senses, is in fact the result of a formal totality that refuses to relinquish total perspective on the socio-historical totality that is its subject.

1970

CHRISTIAN METZ
FROM FILM LANGUAGE

SOME POINTS IN THE SEMIOTICS OF THE CINEMA

One of the most influential theorists of the 1970s and 80s, Christian Metz (1931–1993) in *Film Language: A Semiotics of the Cinema* applied the categories of structural linguistics to film. He emphasized that although film is not a *langue* or language system (like Latin, French, or English), it is nevertheless a *langage* whose codes of expression can be analyzed and organized to show how film mobilizes its structure and resources to signify meaning. Through a system of shot and scene classification, *la grand syntagmatique*, Metz outlines a possible grammar of cinema. He taught psychoanalysis and film at the École des Hautes Études en Sciences Sociales in Paris and the Centre Universitaire Américain du Cinéma. A selection from one of his later works, *The Imaginary Signifier* (1977) is included in Part VII of this anthology. Drawing on the work of Freud and Lacan, that book also examines the spectator experience of film, in which Metz posits that we identify with the camera, rather than the protagonists of a given movie.

CINEMA AND NARRATIVITY

A first choice confronts the film semiologist: Is the corpus to be made up of feature films (*narrative films*) or, on the contrary, of short films, documentaries, technological, pedagogical, or advertising films, etc.? It could be answered that it depends simply on what one wants to study—that the cinema possesses various dialects, and that each one of these dialects can become the subject of a specific analysis. This is undoubtedly true. Nevertheless, there is a hierarchy of concerns (or, better yet, a methodological urgency) that favors—in the beginning at least—the study of the narrative film. We know that, in the few years immediately before and after the Lumière brothers' invention in 1895, critics, journalists, and the pioneer cinematographers disagreed considerably among themselves as to the *social function* that they attributed to, or predicted for, the new machine: whether it was a means of preservation or of making archives, whether it was an auxiliary technography for research and teaching in sciences like botany or surgery, whether it was a new form of journalism, or an instrument of sentimental devotion, either private or public, that could perpetuate the living image of the dear departed one, and so on. That, over all these possibilities, the cinema could evolve into a machine for telling stories had never been really considered. From the very beginnings of the cinematograph, there were various indications and statements that suggested such

65

an evolution, but they had no common measure with the magnitude that the narrative phenomenon was to assume. The merging of the cinema and of narrativity was a great fact, which was by no means predestined—nor was it strictly fortuitous. It was a historical and social fact, a fact of civilization, . . . a fact that in turn conditioned the later evolution of the film as a semiological reality, somewhat in the same way—indirect and general, though effective—that "external" linguistic events (conquests, colonizations, transformations of language) influence the "internal" functioning of idioms. In the realm of the cinema, all nonnarrative genres—the documentary, the technical film, etc.—have become marginal provinces, border regions so to speak, while the *feature-length film of novelistic fiction*, which is simply called a "film"—the usage is significant—has traced more and more clearly the king's highway of filmic expression.

This purely numerical and social superiority is not the only fact concerned. Added to it is a more internal consideration: Nonnarrative films for the most part are distinguished from "real" films by their social purpose and by their content much more than by their "language processes." The basic figures of the semiotics of the cinema—montage, camera movements, scale of the shots, relationships between the image and speech, sequences, and other large syntagmatic units—are on the whole the same in "small" films and in "big" films. It is by no means certain that an independent semiotics of the various nonnarrative genres is possible other than in the form of a series of discontinuous remarks on the points of difference between these films and "ordinary" films. To examine fiction films is to proceed more directly and more rapidly to the heart of the problem.

There is, moreover, an encouraging diachronic consideration. We know, since the observations of Béla Balázs, André Malraux, Edgar Morin, Jean Mitry, and many others, that the cinema was not a specific "language" from its inception. Before becoming the means of expression familiar to us, it was a simple means of mechanical recording, preserving, and reproducing moving visual spectacles—whether of life, of the theater, or even of small *mises-en-scène*, which were specially prepared and which, in the final analysis, remained theatrical—in short, a "means of reproduction," to use André Malraux's term. Now, *it was precisely to the extent that the cinema confronted the problems of narration* that, in the course of successive groupings, it came to produce a body of specific signifying procedures. Historians of the cinema generally agree in dating the beginning of the cinema as we know it in the period 1910–15. Films like *Enoch Arden, Life for the Czar, Quo Vadis?, Fantômas, Cabiria, The Golem, The Battle of Gettysburg*, and above all *Birth of a Nation* were among the first films, in the acceptation we now give this word when we use it without a determinant: Narration of a certain magnitude based on procedures that are supposed to be specifically cinematographic. It so happens that these procedures were perfected in the wake of the narrative endeavor. The pioneers of "cinematographic language"—Méliès, Porter, Griffith—couldn't care less about "formal" research conducted for its own sake; what is more (except for occasional naïve and confused attempts), they cared little about the symbolic, philosophical, or human "message" of their films. Men of denotation rather than of connotation, they wanted above all to tell a story; they were not content unless they could subject the continuous, analogical material of photographic duplication to the *articulations*—

however rudimentary—of a narrative discourse. Georges Sadoul has indeed shown how Méliès, in his storyteller's naïveté, was led to invent double-exposure, the device of multiple exposures with a mask and a dark backdrop, the dissolve and the fade-in, and the pan shot. Jean Mitry, who has written a very precise synthesis of these problems, examines the first occurrences of a certain number of procedures of filmic language—the close-up, the pan shot, the tracking shot, parallel montage, and inter-laced, or alternative, montage—among the film primitives. I will summarize the conclusions he reaches: The principal inventions are credited to the Frenchmen Méliès and Promio, to the Englishmen G. A. Smith and J. Williamson, and to the American E. S. Porter; it was Griffith's role to define and to stabilize—we would say, to codify—the *function* of these different procedures in relation to the filmic narrative, and thereby unify them up to a certain point in a coherent "syntax" (note that it would be better to use the term *syntagmatic category*; Jean Mitry himself avoids the word "syntax"). Between 1911 and 1915, Griffith made a whole series of films having, more or less consciously, the value of experimental probings, and *Birth of a Nation*, released in 1915, appears as the crowning work, the sum and the public demonstration of investigations that, however naïve they may have been, were nonetheless systematic and fundamental. Thus, it was in a single motion that the cinema became narrative and took over some of the attributes of a language.

Today, still, the so-called filmic procedures are in fact filmic narrative. This, to my mind, justifies the priority of the narrative film in the filmosemiological enter-prise—a priority that must not of course become an exclusivity.

STUDIES OF DENOTATION AND STUDIES OF CONNOTATION IN THE SEMIOTICS OF THE CINEMA

The facts I have just reviewed lead to another consequence. The semiotics of the cinema can be conceived of either as a semiotics of connotation or as a semiotics of denotation. Both directions are interesting, and it is obvious that on the day when the semiological study of film makes some progress and begins to form a body of knowledge, it will have considered connotative and denotative significations together. The study of connotation brings us closer to the notion of the cinema as an art (the "seventh art"). . . . [T]he art of film is located on the same semiological "plane" as literary art: The properly aesthetic orderings and constraints—versification, composition, and tropes in the first case; framing, camera movements, and light "effects" in the second—serve as the connoted instance, which is super-imposed over the denoted meaning. In literature, the latter appears as the purely lin-guistic signification, which is linked, in the employed idiom, to the units used by the author. In the cinema, it is represented by the literal (that is, perceptual) mean-ing of the spectacle reproduced in the image, or of the sounds duplicated by the soundtrack. As for connotation, which plays a major role in all aesthetic languages, its significate is the literary or cinematographic "style," "genre" (the epic, the west-ern, etc.), "symbol" (philosophical, humanitarian, ideological, and so on), or "poetic atmosphere"—and its signifier is the whole denotated semiological material, whether signified or signifying. In American gangster movies where, for example, the slick pavement of the waterfront distills an impression of anxiety and hardness (significate of the connotation), the scene represented (dimly lit, deserted wharves, with stacks of crates and overhead cranes, the significate of denotation), and the technique of the shooting, which is dependent on the effects of lighting in order to produce a certain *picture* of the docks (signifier of denotation), converge to form the signifier of connotation. The same scene filmed in a different light would produce a different impression; and so would the same technique used on a different subject (for example, a child's smiling face). Film aestheticians have often remarked that filmic effects must not be "gratuitous," but must remain "subordinate to the plot." This is another way of saying that the significate of connotation can establish itself only when the corresponding signifier brings into play *both* the signifier and the significate of denotation.

The study of the cinema as an art—the study of cinematographic expressiveness—can therefore be conducted according to methods derived from linguistics. . . . But there is another task that requires the careful attention of the film semiologist. For also, and even first of all, through its procedures of *denotation*, the cinema is a specific language. The concept of *diegesis* is as important for the film semiologist as the idea of art. The word is derived from the Greek διηγησις, "narration," and was used particularly to designate one of the obligatory parts of judiciary discourse, the recital of facts. The term was introduced into the framework of the cinema by Étienne Souriau. It designates the film's *represented* instance (which Mikel Dufrenne contrasts to the expressed, properly aesthetic, instance)—that is to say, the sum of a film's denotation: the narration itself, but also the fictional space and time dimensions implied in and by the narrative, and consequently the characters, the landscapes, the events, and other narrative elements, in so far as they are considered in their denoted aspect. How does the cinema indicate successivity, precession, temporal breaks, causality, adversative relationships, consequence, spatial proximity, or distance, etc.? These are central questions to the semiotics of the cinema.

One must not indeed forget that, from the semiological point of view, the cinema is very different from still photography whence its technique is derived. In photography, as Roland Barthes has clearly shown, the denoted meaning is secured entirely through the automatic process of photochemical reproduction; denotation is a visual transfer, which is not codified and has no inherent organization. Human intervention, which carries some elements of a proper semiotics, affects only the level of connotation (lighting, camera angle, "photographic effects," and so on). And, in point of fact, there is no specifically photographic procedure for designating the significate "house" in its denoted aspect, unless it is by showing a house. In the cinema, on the other hand, a whole semiotics of denotation is possible and necessary, for a film is composed of *many* photographs (the concept of montage, with its myriad consequences)—photographs that give us mostly only partial views of the diegetic referent. In film a "house" would be shot of a staircase, a shot of one of the walls taken from the outside, a close-up of a window, a brief establishing shot of the building, etc. Thus a kind of filmic *articulation* appears, which has no equivalent in photography: It is the denotation itself that is being constructed, organized, and to a certain extent codified (*codified*, not necessarily *encoded*). Lacking absolute laws, filmic intelligibility nevertheless depends on a certain number of dominant habits: A film put together haphazardly would not be understood.

I return to my initial observations: "Cinematographic language" is first of all the literalness of a plot. Artistic effects, even when they are substantially inseparable from the semic act by which the film tells us its story, nevertheless constitute another level of signification, which from the methodological point of view must come "later."

PARADIGMATIC AND SYNTAGMATIC CATEGORIES

. . . In the cinema, where the number of images is indefinite. Several times indefinite, one should say. For the pro-filmic spectacles are themselves unlimited in number; the exact nature of lighting can be varied infinitely and by quantities that are nondiscrete; the same applies to the axial distance between the subject and the camera (in variations which are said to be scalar—that is, scale of the shot), to the camera angle, to the properties of the film and the focal length of the lens, and to the exact trajectory of the camera movements (including the stationary shot, which represents zero degree in this case). It suffices to vary one of these elements by a perceptible quantity to obtain *another* image. The shot is therefore not comparable to the word in a lexicon; rather it resembles a complete statement (of one or more sentences), in that it is already the result of an essentially free combination, a "speech" arrangement. . . . The image is almost always assertive—and assertion is one of the great "modalities" of actualization, of the semic act. It appears therefore that the paradigmatic category in film is condemned to remain partial and fragmentary, at least as long as one tries to isolate it on the level of the *image*. This is naturally derived from the fact that *creation* plays a larger role in cinematographic language than it does in the handling of idioms: To "speak" a language is to use it, but to "speak" cinematographic language is to a certain extent to invent it. The speakers of ordinary language consitute a group of users; filmmakers are a group of creators. On the other hand, movie *spectators* in turn constitute a group of users. That is why the semiotics of the cinema must frequently consider things from the point of view of spectator rather than of the filmmaker. Étienne Souriau's distinction between the filmic point of view and the *cinéastique*, or filmmaking, point of view is a very useful concept; film semiotics is mainly a *filmic* study. The situation has a rough equivalent in linguistics: Some linguists connect the speaker with the message, while the listener in some way "represents" the code, since he requires it to understand what is being said to him, whereas the speaker is presumed to know beforehand what he wants to say.

But, more than paradigmatic studies, it is the syntagmatic considerations that are at the center of the problems of filmic denotation. Although each image is a free creation, the arrangement of these images into an intelligible sequence—cutting and montage—brings us to the heart of the semiological dimension of film. It is a rather paradoxical situation: Those proliferating (and not very discrete!) units—the *images*—when it is a matter of composing a film, suddenly accept with reasonably good grace the constraint of a few large syntagmatic structures. Although no image ever entirely resembles another image, the great majority of narrative films resemble each other in their principal syntagmatic figures. *Filmic narrativity*—since it has again crossed our path—by becoming stable through convention and repetition over innumerable films, has gradually shaped itself into forms that are more or less fixed, but certainly not immutable. These forms represent a synchronic "state" (that of the

present cinema), but if they were to change, it could only be through a complete positive evolution, liable to be challenged—like those that, in spoken languages, produce
diachronic transformations in the distribution of aspects and tenses. Applying de
Saussure's thought to the cinema, one could say that the large syntagmatic category
of the narrative film *can change*, but that no single person can make it change over
night. A failure of intellection among the viewers would be the automatic sanc-
tioning of a purely individual innovation, which the system would refuse to confirm.
The originality of creative artists consists, here as elsewhere, in tricking the code,
or at least in using it ingeniously, rather than in attacking it directly or in violating
it—and still less in ignoring it. . . .

OTHER PROBLEMS

These very brief remarks provided an example of what the syntagmatic study of
filmic denotation could be. There are important differences between the semiotics
of the cinema and linguistics itself. Without repeating those mentioned elsewhere,
let me recall some of the main points: Film contains nothing corresponding to the
purely distinctive units of the second articulation; all of its units—even the simplest,
like the dissolve and the wipe—are directly significant (and moreover, as I have
already pointed out, they only occur in the actualized state). The commutations and
other manipulations by which the semiotics of the cinema proceeds therefore affect
the large significatory units. The "laws" of cinematographic language call for *statements* within a narrative, and not monemes within a statement, or still less phonemes
within a moneme.

Contrary to what many of the theoreticians of the silent film declared or suggested (*Ciné langue*, "visual Esperanto," etc.), the cinema is certainly not a language system (*langue*). It can, however, be considered as a *language*, to the extent
that it orders signifying elements within ordered arrangements different from those
of spoken idioms—and to the extent that these elements are not traced on the perceptual configurations of reality itself (which does not tell stories). Filmic manipulation transforms what might have been a mere visual transfer of reality into
discourse. Derived from a kind of signification that is purely analogous and continuous—animated photography, cinematography—the cinema gradually shaped,
in the course of its diachronic maturation, some elements of a proper semiotics,
which remain scattered and fragmentary within the open field of simple visual
duplication.

The "shot"—an already complex unit, which must be studied—remains an indispensable reference for the time being, in somewhat the same way that the "word"
was during a period of linguistic research. It might be somewhat adventurous to
compare the shot to the *taxeme*, in Louis Hjelmslev's sense, but one can consider
that it constitutes the largest *minimum segment* (the expression is borrowed from
André Martinet), since at least one shot is required to make a film, or part of a
film—in the same way, a linguistic statement must be made up of at least one
phoneme. To isolate several shots from a sequence is still, perhaps, to analyze the
sequence; to remove several frames from a shot is to destroy the shot. If the shot

is not the smallest unit of filmic *signification* (for a single shot may convey several informational elements), it is at least the smallest unit of the filmic chain.

One cannot conclude, however, that every minimum filmic segment is a shot. Besides shots, there are other minimum segments, *optical devices*—various dissolves, wipes, and so on—that can be defined as visual but not photographic elements. Whereas images have the objects of reality as referents, optical procedures, which do not represent anything, have images as referents (those contiguous in the syntagma). The relationship of these procedures to the actual shooting of the film is somewhat like that of morphemes to lexemes; depending on the context, they have two main functions: as "trick" devices (in this instance, they are sorts of semiological exponents influencing contiguous images), or as "punctuation." The expression "filmic punctuation," which use has ratified, must not make us forget that optical procedures separate large, complex statements and thus correspond to the articulations of the literary narrative (with its pages and paragraphs, for example), whereas actual punctuation—that is to say, typographical punctuation—separates sentences (period, exclamation mark, question mark, semicolon), and clauses (comma, semicolon, dash), possibly even "verbal bases," with or without characteristics (apostrophe, or dash, between two "words," and so on).

IN CONCLUSION

The concepts of linguistics can be applied to the semiotics of the cinema only with the greatest caution. On the other hand, the methods of linguistics—commutation, analytical breakdown, strict distinction between the significate and the signifier, between substance and form, between the relevant and the irrelevant, etc.—provide the semiotics of the cinema with a constant and precious aid in establishing units that, though they are still very approximate, are liable over time (and, one hopes, through the work of many scholars) to become progressively refined.

PROBLEMS OF DENOTATION IN THE FICTION FILM

The film semiologist tends, naturally, to approach his subject with methods derived from linguistics. Consequently wherever the language of cinematography differs from language itself, film semiology encounters its greatest obstacles. Let us begin immediately with the points of *maximum difference*. There are two of them: There is the problem of the *motivation* of signs and that of the *continuity* of meanings. Or, if one prefers, the question of the arbitrariness of signs (in the Saussurian sense) and the question of discrete units.

CINEMATOGRAPHIC SIGNIFICATION IS ALWAYS MORE OR LESS MOTIVATED, NEVER ARBITRARY

Motivation occurs on two levels: on that of the relationship between the denotative signifiers and significates, and on that of the relations between the connotative signifiers and significates.

Denotation: The motivation is furnished by analogy—that is to say, by the perceptual similarity between the signifier and of the significate. This is equally true for the soundtrack (the sound of a cannon on film resembles a real cannon sound) as for the image track (the image of a dog is like the dog).

We therefore have visual analogy and auditory analogy; for the cinema is derived from photography and from the phonograph, which are both modern technologies of *mechanical duplication*. Of course the duplication is never perfect; between the object and its image there are many perceptible differences, which film psychologists have studied. But, from the point of view of semiotics, it is not necessary that the signifier and the significate be *identical*. Simple analogy provides sufficient motivation.

For, even when it partially distorts its model, mechanical duplication does not *analyze* into specific units. There is no actual transformation of the object, but a simple partial *distortion*, which is purely perceptual.

Connotation: Connotative meanings are motivated, too, in the cinema. But in this case the motivation is not necessarily based on a relationship of perceptual analogy. . . .

We will not insist upon the problems of cinematographic connotation here, for this is a study of denotation. Suffice it to say that cinematographic connotation is always symbolic in nature: The significate motivates the signifier but goes beyond it. The notion of *motivated overtaking* (*depassement motivé*) may be used to define almost all filmic connotations. Similarly, one says that the cross is the symbol of Christianity because, although Christ died on a cross (the motivation), there are many more things in Christianity than there are in a cross (the "overtaking").

The *partial motivation* of filmic connotations does not prevent them from giving rise quite often to codifications or to conventions, which are more or less extended according to the case. Here is a simple example: In a talking film in which the hero has, among other diegetic peculiarities, the habit of whistling the first bars of a certain tune—and provided that this fact has been clearly impressed upon the spectator from the beginning of the film—the mere appearance of the tune on the sound track (in the visual absence of the hero himself) will be sufficient to suggest the totality of the character later in the film after the hero has gone on a long journey or even vanished. It is not without powerful connotations that the character may have been thus designated. In this simplified example we see that the hero has not been symbolized by some arbitrary characteristic, but by a feature entirely his own (thus, lack of *total* arbitrariness). Yet in the whole character there was more than just the familiar tune; other features, which belong to him also, could have been chosen to symbolize him (and would have involved other connotations). There is, then, some arbitrariness in the relationship between the connotative signifier (the melody) and the connotative significate (the character).

Even the subtlest and most ingenious cinematographic connotations are based then on this simple principle, which we might state as follows: A visual or an auditory theme—or an arrangement of visual and auditory themes—once it has been placed in its correct syntagmatic position within the discourse that constitutes the whole film, takes on a value greater than its own and is increased by the additional meaning it receives. But this addition itself is never entirely arbitrary, for what the theme symbolizes in this manner is an integral situation or whole process, *a part of which in fact it is,* within the story told by the film (or which the spectator knows to be an actual part of life). In short, the connotative meaning *extends over* the denotative meaning, but without *contradicting* or *ignoring* it. Thus the partial arbitrariness; thus the absence of total arbitrariness.... Many of the misunderstandings and arguments about these subjects derive from the fact that no one has yet attempted to draw up a half-way complete list of the different heterogeneous and superimposed codes co-present in any cultural activity of some importance, and no one has yet tried to clarify the precise organization of their interactions.

In any event, it seems to me that one can distinguish at least two main types of signifying organization: *cultural* codes and *specialized* codes. The first define the culture of each social group; they are so ubiquitous and well assimilated that the viewers generally consider them to be natural—basic constituents of the humankind itself (although they are clearly *products*, since they vary in space and time). The handling of these codes requires no special training—that is to say, no training other than that of living, and having been raised, in a society. On the other hand the codes I have called "specialized" concern more specific and restricted social activities. They appear more explicitly as codes, and they require a special training—to a large or small extent depending on the case (relatively "small" in the cinema)—that is to say, a training even the "native" person, possessing the culture of his group, cannot dispense with....

A Frenchman, born and raised in France, does not need to be specially taught the gestures expressing anger, refusal, resigned acceptance, or the gesture that stands for "Come here!"—but, though he is French, he will need to be specially taught the sign language of the deaf and dumb (in his own language), otherwise he will never know it.

The purely cinematographic signifying figures studied here (montage, camera movements, optical effects, "rhetoric of the screen," interaction of visual and auditory elements, and so on) constitute specialized codes—although relatively easy ones, as we will see later—that function above and beyond photographic and phonographic analogy. The iconological, perceptual, and other codes are cultural codes, and they function in good part *within* photographic and phonographic analogy, as Umberto Eco, to whom the hypothesis advanced in these pages owes much, has rightly pointed out.

So far, I have been speaking about denotation (the literal sense of the film). But, among the large body of connoted significations in the cinema (the symbolic sense of all varieties), there are a certain number that, outside of the specifically cinematographic codifications, intrude into the film by means of perceptual analogy each time an object or an ordering of objects (visual or auditory) symbolizes within the film what it would have symbolized outside of the film—that is to say, within culture (with the chance that it will carry *in addition*, and only in the film, symbolic significations that will then derive from its location within the cinematographic discourse proper). Objects (and characters must also be included)—that is to say, the different basic elements of filmic discourse—do not enter the film in a virgin state; they carry with them, before even cinematographic language can intervene, a great deal more than their simple literal identity—which does not prevent the spectator

belonging to a given culture from deciphering this "increment" at the same time
that he identifies the object. . . .

THE CINEMA AS SUCH HAS NOTHING CORRESPONDING TO THE DOUBLE ARTICULATION OF VERBAL LANGUAGES

Let us note first that the cinema has no *distinctive* units (I mean distinctive units
of its own). It does not have anything corresponding to the phoneme or to the relevant phonic feature on the level of expression, nor, on the level of content, does it
have anything equivalent to the seme in A. J. Greimas's sense, or in Bernard Pottier's
sense.

Even with respect to the signifying units, the cinema is initially deprived of discrete elements. It proceeds by whole "blocks of reality," which are actualized with
their total meaning in the discourse. These blocks are the "shots." The discrete units
identifiable in the filmic discourse on another level—for, as we shall see, there is
another level—are not equivalent to the first articulation of spoken languages.

Certainly, it is true that montage is in a sense an analysis, a sort of articulation
of the reality shown on the screen. Instead of showing us an entire landscape, a
filmmaker will show us successively a number of partial views, which are broken
down and ordered according to a very precise intention. It is well known that the
nature of the cinema is to transform the world into discourse.

But this kind of articulation is not a true articulation in the linguistic sense. Even
the most partial and fragmentary shot (what film people call the close-up) still presents a complete segment of reality. The close-up is only a shot taken closer than
other shots.

It is true that the film *sequence* is a real unit—that is to say, a sort of coherent
syntagma within which the shots react (semantically) to each other. This phenomenon recalls up to a certain point the manner in which words react to each other
within a sentence, and that is why the first theoreticians of the cinema often spoke
of the shot as a word, and the sequence as a sentence. But these were highly erroneous identifications, and one can easily list five radical differences between the
filmic shot and the linguistic word:

(1) Shots are infinite in number, contrary to words, but like statements, which
can be formulated in a verbal language.
(2) Shots are the creations of the filmmaker, unlike words (which preexist in lexicons), but similar to statements (which are in principal the invention of the
speaker).
(3) The shot presents the receiver with a quantity of undefined information, contrary to the word. From this point of view, the shot is not even equivalent to the
sentence. Rather, it is like the complex statement of undefined length. (How is
one to describe a film shot completely by means of natural language?)
(4) The shot is an actualized unit, a unit of discourse, an assertion, unlike the
word (which is a purely virtual lexical unit), but like the statement, which always
refers to reality or a reality (even when it is interrogative or jussive). The image

of a house does not signify "house," but "Here is a house"; the image contains a sort of index of actualization, by the mere fact that it occurs in a film.

(5) Only to a small extent does a shot assume its meaning in paradigmatic contrast to the other shots that might have occurred at the same point along the filmic chain (since the other possible shots are infinite in number), whereas a word is always a part of at least one more or less organized semantic field. The important linguistic phenomenon of the clarification of present units by absent units hardly comes into play in the cinema. Semiologically, this confirms what the aestheticians of the cinema have frequently observed: namely, that the cinema is an "art of presence" (the dominance of the image, which "shuts out" everything external to itself).

The filmic shot therefore resembles the statement rather than the word. Nevertheless, it would be wrong to say that it is equivalent to the statement, for there are still great differences between the shot and the linguistic statement. Even the most complex statement is reducible, in the final analysis, to discrete elements (words, morphemes, phonemes, relevant features), which are fixed in number and in nature. To be sure, the filmic shot is also the result of an ordering of several elements (for example, the different visual elements in the image—what is sometimes called the *interior montage*), but these elements are indefinite in number and undefined in nature, like the shot itself. The analysis of a shot consists in progressing from a nondiscrete whole to smaller nondiscrete wholes: One can decompose a shot, but one cannot reduce it.

All that can be affirmed, therefore, is that a shot is less unlike a statement than a word, but it does not necessarily resemble a statement. . . .

REMARK ON THE DIACHRONIC EVOLUTION OF CINEMATOGRAPHIC CODES

The large syntagmatic category of the cinema is not immutable; it has a diachronic aspect. It evolves distinctly *faster* than languages do, a circumstance derived from the fact that art and language are more closely interrelated in film than in the verbal field. The creative filmmaker exerts more influence on the diachronic evolution of cinematographic language than the imaginative writer on the evolution of his idiom, for idiom may exist in the absence of art, whereas the cinema must be an art to become a language with a partial denotative code. Remember, also, that filmmakers constitute a limited social group (creative group), whereas the users of language are coextensive as a group with society itself (user group).

Nevertheless the large syntagmatic category of the cinema ensures a codification that is coherent for every diachronic state. Too great a deviation from this codification at any given moment results in the inability to understand—for the mass of the spectators—the film's literal meaning (example: certain avant-garde films). . . .

FILM AND DIEGESIS: THE SEMIOTICS OF THE CINEMA AND THE SEMIOTICS OF THE NARRATIVE

The reader will perhaps have observed in the course of this article (and especially in the definition of the different types of autonomous segment) that it is no easy matter to decide whether the large syntagmatic category in film involves the *cinema* or the cinematographic *narrative*. For all the units I have isolated are located *in* the film but in *relation* to the plot. This perpetual see-saw between the screen instance (which signifies) and the diegetic instance (which is signified) must be accepted and even erected into a methodological principle, for it, and only it, renders commutation possible, and thus identification of the units (in this case, the autonomous segments).

One will never be able to analyze film by speaking *directly* about the diegesis (as in some of the film societies, *ciné clubs*, in France and elsewhere, where the discussion is centered around the plot and the human problems it implies), because that is equivalent to examining the significates without taking the signifiers into consideration. On the other hand, isolating the units without considering the diegesis as a *whole* (as in the "montage tables" of some of the theoreticians of the silent cinema) is to study the signifiers without the significates—since the nature of narrative film is to narrate. . . .

The necessity of this see-sawing I have just described is nothing other than the consequence of an underlying cultural and social fact: The cinema, which could have served a variety of uses, in fact is most often used to *tell stories*—to the extent that even supposedly nonnarrative films (short documentary films, educational films, etc.) are governed essentially by the same semiological mechanisms that govern the feature films.

Had the cinema not become thoroughly narrative, its grammar would undoubtedly be entirely different (and would perhaps not even exist). The reverse of this coin, however, is that a given narrative receives a very different semiological treatment in the cinema than it would in a novel, in classical ballet, in a cartoon, and so on.

There are therefore two distinct enterprises, neither of which can replace the other: On the one hand, there is the semiotics of the narrative film, such as the one I am attempting to develop; on the other hand, there is the structural analysis of actual narrativity—that is to say, of the narrative taken *independently from the vehicles carrying it* (the film, the book, etc.). . . . The *narrated event*, which is a significate in the semiotics of narrative vehicles (and notably of the cinema), becomes a signifier in the semiotics of narrativity.

CONCLUSION

The concept of a cinematographic grammar is very much out of favor today; one has the impression, indeed, that such a thing cannot exist. But that is only because it has not been looked for in the right place. Students have always implicitly referred themselves to the *normative grammar of particular languages* (namely, their maternal languages), but the linguistic and grammatical phenomenon is much vaster than any single language and is concerned with the *great and fundamental figures of the transmission of all information*. Only a general linguistics and a general semiotics (both nonnormative and simply analytical disciplines) can provide the study of cinematographic language with the appropriate methodological models. It does not suffice merely to observe that there is nothing in the cinema corresponding to the consecutive clause in French, or to the Latin adverb, which are extremely particular linguistic phenomena, are not necessary, and are not universal. The dialogue between the film theoretician and the semiologist can commence only beyond the level of such idiomatic specifications or such restrictive prescriptions. *The fact that must be understood is that films are understood.* Iconic analogy alone cannot account for the intelligibility of the cooccurrences in filmic discourse. That is the function of the large syntagmatic category.

1968

GILBERT HARMAN
SEMIOTICS AND THE CINEMA:
METZ AND WOLLEN

In addition to his work on semiotics and cinema in response to Christian Metz, included here, Gilbert Harman had published widely on ethics, epistemology, metaphysics, and the philosophy of language and mind. Harman shares the belief of W.V. Quine that philosophy and science are continuous, as well as Quine's skepticism about conceptual analysis. As a moral philosopher he is best known for his explanatory argument for antirealism and for his defense of ethical relativism, most recently expounded in *Moral Relativism and Moral Objectivity* (1996), in which he debates the issue with Judith Jarvis Thomson. Among his major publications are *Thought* (1973); *The Nature of Morality* (1977); *Reasoning, Meaning and Mind* (1990); and, with S. Kulkarni, *Reliable Reasoning: Induction and Statistical Learning Theory* (2007). Harman, who was awarded the Jean Nicod Prize (2005), is currently Stuart professor of philosophy at Princeton University.

Some film theorists advocate what they call a semiotics or semiology of the cinema. I will discuss two somewhat different proposals of this sort here, one by Christian Metz[1] and another by Peter Wollen.[2]

The term *semiotics* (and, equivalently, the term *semiology*) means theory of signs. Linguistics is one such theory, since it is the theory of language-as-a-system-of-signs. The semiotics of the cinema is, similarly, the theory of film-as-a-system-of-signs. The idea is that we are to think of film as a kind of language and are to try to develop a linguistics of this language of film.

This means, according to Christian Metz, that we will only be interested in certain aspects of film. We will be concerned only with the various ways in which particular films can have meaning and significance for normal spectators. We will be directly concerned with the nature of the film image, the relation between sound and image, and the effect of various kinds of editing. We will not be directly concerned with such things as camera mechanisms, the process of developing and printing films, or the technological structure of the film industry.

There are, of course, very different kinds of films: narrative feature films, documentaries, travel films, advertising films, instructional films, abstract underground

---

[1]*Film Language: A Semiotics of the Cinéma* (New York: Oxford University Press, 1974), a translation of *Essais sur la Signification au Cinema*, Tome I. (Paris: Klinksieck, 1968, 2nd ed. 1971). *Language and Cinema* (The Hague: Mouton, 1974), a translation of *Language et Cinéma* (Paris: Larousse, 1971).
[2]*Signs and Meaning in the Cinema* (London: Indiana University Press, 3rd rev. ed. 1972).

films, and so forth. Metz argues, however, that in the first instance we should restrict our study to narrative feature films and ignore the other type of film. According to Metz, before the narrative film existed, the cinema was conceived as a mere technological resource, a recorder of events, and "it was precisely to the extent that the cinema confronted the problems of narration that . . . it came to produce a body of specific signifying procedures." Narrative feature films are, furthermore, what we first think of as films. Shorts of various kinds inhabit "border regions"; their signifying procedures are, for the most part, derived from those in narrative films. We will therefore not go wrong, Metz thinks, if we restrict our attention to the signifying procedures that are used in feature length narrative films.

Moreover, Metz says, we should study denotation before connotation. We should study, that is, the ways in which various aspects of plot are presented before we study how symbolic, philosophical, and human messages are presented and before we study such things as style, genre, and poetic mood. Denotation is basic, according to Metz, because, in the first instance, the basic materials of the film—its sounds and images—present a series of events that constitute the plot or story. That is what is denoted. In other words, the basic material of the film is directly a sign of the denotation, according to Metz. Connotation is secondary in the sense that it is not directly presented by the basic materials of the film in the way that the denotation or plot is. Connotation is, in fact, partly indicated by the denotation. What happens in the film has a certain significance, given the way in which it is presented. This significance is connotation. The connotation is what is signified by a sign when the sign combines aspects of the basic materials of the film and the story that those aspects denote.

We are, therefore, to ask first how narrative films present their plots. In particular, "How does the cinema indicate successivity, precession, temporal breaks, casuality, adversative relationships, consequence, spatial proximity or distance, etc.? These are central questions to the semiotics of the cinema."

A similar group of questions can be raised about language. How does language indicate one or another state of affairs or series of events? Linguistics seeks in the first instance to answer that question. Only after considerable progress has been made on that front in understanding linguistic denotation could linguistics hope to be able to investigate style, atmosphere, and other aspects of linguistic connotation. The same thing is true in the semiotics of the cinema, according to Metz.

One big difference, though, as Metz observes, is that linguistic denotation is largely conventional. The word *horse* denotes horses and *man* denotes men; but it could have been otherwise. The word *man* could have denoted horses and *horse* could have denoted men. The sentence *the man is on the horse* has a conventional meaning which depends on its grammatical structure and the meanings of its words. It denotes a situation in which a man is on a horse. If different conventions were in force it might denote a situation in which a horse is on a man. The sentence by itself has no natural meaning, apart from convention, and it can be understood only by someone who is acquainted with the relevant conventions. In the case of film, the situation is quite different. A shot of a man on a horse has an immediate and natural interpretation that does not depend on any filmic conventions.

There is, furthermore, according to Metz, an important sense in which film does not have a syntax. No significant unit in film corresponds to the word in language.

The smallest unit of film—the image—is already at the level of the sentence or paragraph. A shot of a revolver does not correspond to the word *revolver* but to the sentence *here is a revolver* or even to a description of the revolver. There cannot be an ungrammatical shot, in the way that there can be an ungrammatical sequence of words.

There are, nevertheless, certain rules and conventions, or "codes," which narrative feature films exploit in order to indicate their denotations, and it is the task of film semiotics, as Metz conceives it, to specify these codes and say how they work. There are certain conventions of filmic punctuation, concerning the interpretation of a fade as opposed to a dissolve, for example. Or, to take another example, Metz suggests that films are made up of a series of minimal sequences that he calls "syntagmas." Syntagmas can be distinguished on the basis of montage and what that montage signifies. A series of different views of a house, for example, might constitute what Metz calls a "descriptive syntagma"—showing what the house is like and not presenting an event unfolding in time. Another series of shots showing various effects of war would constitute what he calls a "bracket syntagma"—in which a number of things are grouped together because of a certain association among those things. A third series might show alternating shots of two different actions, indicating that they are happening simultaneously, for example, alternating shots of the two parties at the opposite ends of a telephone conversation—or alternating shots of pursuer and pursued. And so on. According to Metz, there are only a small number of other possible syntagmas.

Having gone this far, Metz sees the following tasks on the immediate horizon. First, we must attempt to discover the various denotative codes that are exploited in films; and we must classify these codes in terms of their generality. Some of them are relevant to narration in general; some to any sort of depiction, including painting; some only to photographic images; some only to sequences of images, as in comic strips; some only to sequences of moving photographic images correlated with sound; and so forth. As film semioticists, we are to be particularly concerned with codes that are specific to film. These, as previously indicated, will concern mainly such things as filmic punctuation, the various syntagmas, and the meanings of close-ups, zoom shots, and so on.

Second, having carried out that part of our study, we can then begin to investigate questions of style and genre by seeing what subcodes out of the codes available are used in works of that style or genre. We might consider, for example, the codes of dress, behavior, and landscape, that define the western. Or we can study the sorts of codes a particular director or group of directors tends to use.

This summarizes Metz's proposal. What can we say about it? One immediate difficulty is that his order of priorities depends to a considerable extent on his distinction between denotation and connotation. We are to study denotation first, ignoring connotation for the time being. The difficulty is that Metz's definition of the denotation-connotation distinction does not work and it is unclear that there is any way to fix up his definition so as to support his program. He says that the denotation—the series of events of plot portrayed—is what is signified directly by the raw material—images and sound—of the film, whereas connotation is what is signified by the events portrayed plus the way they are signified. But, typically, in order to understand what is happening in the film even at the level of plot, you need to have some understanding of what else has been happening at that level. Most aspects of the plot—who a depicted person is, where the person is going, whom he loves, whom he is betraying, etc.—are indicated not just by image and sound but by other aspects of plot as well. Metz's definition would make these aspects part of connotation rather than denotation. These are, moreover, central aspects of plot, in Metz's own terms, not just aspects suggested or hinted at. Consider, for example, how we are to identify one or another of Metz's syntagmas. A simple scene depicting a conversation with alternating shots of whoever is speaking, coheres as a simple scene rather than as one of Metz's bracket syntagmas, say, not because of aspects of image and sound alone but because the denotation of the various shots allows us to suppose that we are seeing shots of a single event. In order to determine what sort of syntagma is occurring, you need to know not only how many shots there are and what sorts of characteristics the shots have as visual and auditory images but also what the denotations of the shots are. So Metz's definition of the connotation denotation distinction cannot be used for his purposes.

Nor can he say simply that he wants, first, to restrict himself to examining the semiotic mechanisms by which the story of the film is indicated. That is arbitrary unless there is a clear distinction between the ways in which plot is indicated and the ways in which other aspects of meaning are indicated. Metz's own limited investigations cast doubt on this, since, for example, one of his syntagmas, the bracket syntagma, is a series of shots showing things between which some relationship holds and not showing something that would normally be considered part of plot. The relation presented in this way cannot clearly be distinguished from the sorts of suggestions and human and philosophical messages that Metz counts as part of connotation.

Nor is this criticism of Metz merely theoretical. For, in fact, although Metz has been developing his account of "film language" for over a decade in many articles and in three large books, his analysis remains almost entirely programmatic. The only substantive results that he has achieved concern his classification of syntagmas, a classification that is in my opinion of minimal interest. A theoretical program that leads to so little in practice is clearly suspect.

This suggests that there are practical as well as theoretical reasons for the film semioticist to study exactly those aspects of film signification that Metz assigns to connotation, and this is what Peter Wollen proposes to do. Wollen believes, as Metz does, that the study of film should take the form of a semiotics of the cinema. But he disagrees with Metz's priorities. He suggests that Metz's emphasis on how plot is presented is due to a commitment to realism in the cinema and, furthermore, that this commitment reflects a mistake in semiotics. In order to bring out the nature of this error, we must, according to Wollen, develop semiotics in accordance with the theory of signs envisioned by the American philosopher C. S. Peirce. In particular, we must recall Peirce's distinction between three aspects of a sign: iconic, indexical, and symbolic.

A sign is an *icon* to the extent that its significance depends on the inner nature of the sign—typically, some sort of qualitative or structural resemblance between the sign and what it signifies. Paintings, diagrams, and color samples are predominantly icons. A sign is an *index* to the extent that its significance depends on a real connection between the sign and what it signifies. Proper names, demonstrative pronouns, evidence at the scene of a crime, and symptoms of a disease are predominantly indices. Finally, a sign is a *symbol*, in Peirce's special sense of this term, to the extent that its significance depends on human convention or an arbitrary decision. Labels on diagrams, Chinese ideograms, and English words are predominently symbols in this sense.

Most signs have more than one aspect. A sentence of English will have a symbolic aspect because of the conventions on which the meanings of its word depend. It will have an indexical aspect if it contains proper nouns, which have the significance they do because of a real connection between name and thing named. And, according to Peirce, the sentence will have an iconic aspect since its significance depends in part on its logical-grammatical structure, which is an internal property of the sentence and is relevant to what other sentences logically imply or are implied by it.

A photograph has an indexical aspect; what it pictures depends to a large extent on a real connection between the picture and the object photographed. It also has an iconic aspect because of the resemblance between the picture and what is pictured. There may also be a symbolic aspect to the photograph if, for example, the subject matter is identifiable by appeal to some sort of convention or stipulation.

So far, this is simply Peirce's classification of signs. Given this classification Wollen observes, "In the cinema, it is quite clear, indexical and iconic aspects are by far the most powerful. The symbolic is limited and secondary." But, it is, according to Wollen, exactly the "submerged" secondary aspects of signs that assume importance in art. Since in the cinema "it is the symbolic which is the submerged dimension, we should therefore expect that in the 'poetry' of the cinema, this aspect will be manifested more palpably."

Metz's error, according to Wollen, is to take the linguistic analogy too seriously, thus overlooking the fact that film is primarily iconic and indexical rather than symbolic. Metz looks for conventions in film that bear some resemblance to the conventions of language. But that is to miss the point that the role of conventional symbols or codes in film is different from its role in language. The basic linguistic codes are needed for literal significance. The relevant codes in cinema primarily concern the poetic rather than the literal.

Wollen's first conclusion is, therefore, the opposite of Metz's. As film semioticists, our primary task must be to uncover the codes exploited in films in producing the sort of poetry that films can produce. We must do this, moreover, remembering that signs combine all three of Peirce's aspects of significance, iconic, indexical, and symbolic.

Wollen's next point is that although signs are often used to communicate messages, they are not always used in that way and are not used that way in films. A scientist working out the implications of a theory, a mathematician doing a calculation, and a traveller planning an itinerary are all using signs, but not to communicate with anyone. They are, as it were, seeing the implications of certain signs. Similarly, a poet, an artist, and a film director are using signs but not to communicate any sort of message. To suppose that they are is simply to make a mistake about what they are doing. They, like the mathematician, scientist, and traveller, are using signs for a different purpose. Like them, they are constructing signs in order to see what the implications of those signs are.

Wollen therefore rejects Metz's idea that the purpose of film semiotics is "to study the ordering and functionings of the main signifying units used in the filmic message." Metz's proposal is due to his linguistic analogy. Language is often used to communicate messages but film is not normally used in that way. Films have meaning and significance but they do not carry messages—any more than other works of art.

According to Wollen, works of art exploit and call attention to various codes. The greatest works "interrogate" their own codes by pitting them against each other. "We know that *Don Quixote* was destructive of the chivalric romance . . . that *Ulysses* or *Finnegans Wake* are destructive of the nineteenth century novel. . . . A valuable work, a powerful work, at least, is one which challenges codes, overthrows established ways of reading or looking, not simply to establish new ones, but to compel an unending dialogue, not at random but productively." Wollen goes on to argue that an analysis along these lines can enable us to see what is great about a director like Godard.

Both Metz and Wollen believe, then, that the theory of film must become part of semiotics, although they disagree slightly about the nature of semiotics. For Metz, "the methods of linguistics . . . provide the semiotics of the cinema with a constant and precious aid in establishing units that, although they are still very approximate, are liable over time (and, one hopes, through the work of many scholars) to become progressively refined." For Wollen, this appeal to linguistics is an error. We must rely, rather, on Peirce's general theory of signs, which allows us to see that filmic significance is very different from linguistic signification, and allows us to understand why the role of codes in films is different from the primary role that linguistic codes play in the everyday use of language. Still, Wollen endorses the idea that we ought "to dissolve cinema criticism and cinema aesthetics into a special province of the general science of signs." The differences between Wollen and Metz are then really matters of emphasis rather than anything else. Their first priorities are different. But Metz would agree with Wollen that it is important to discover the various symbolic codes that give film its importance as a work of art; and Wollen can agree that there is *some* point to specifying the significance of close-ups, zoom shots, filmic punctuation, and Metz's syntagmas.

I now want to look more closely at the idea, endorsed by both Metz and Wollen, that films exploit certain codes. What do they mean by codes?

The word *code* as it is ordinarily used is ambiguous. It can mean either cipher or standards. We speak in one sense of messages in code and in another sense of the military code and of codes of dress. Metz and Wollen use the term in a way that appears to combine both of these senses. On the one hand, they speak of decoding works of art and they take codes to be systems of signs with meanings. Here *code* would seem to mean cipher. To decode is to decipher. What would it mean to decode (in this sense) actions done in accordance with the military code? On the other hand, Metz and Wollen also speak, without any sign that they are using the term in a different sense, of codes of dress and even musical codes.

Now, in what sense are there musical codes? Certainly not in the sense of ciphers. Instrumental music does not encode messages. A piano solo does not in any obvious way have meaning. It does not represent, indicate, or signify anything. There are various musical structures, of course, and we might speak of these or of the principles of structure as codes, but that is certainly stretching a point. We would not normally speak of symphonic or fugal codes.

But then what counts as decoding music? Apparently that is supposed to be figuring out what the structure of a piece of music is, hearing it as having a certain structure, hearing what there is to hear in the music. Similarly, to decode a style of dress—the style of dress in westerns, for example—is first to uncover the dress code that is involved and then, perhaps, to indicate the meaning or significance of that code.

In this usage, then, any sort of system or structure might be called a code; to decode a work is to uncover the various structures that are relevant to it and appreciate their significance for the work in question. Furthermore, any system of assumptions, beliefs, ideology, or stereotypes that is relied on or alluded to in a film or other work of art can be called a code. For, to "decode" the work is also to see how its significance is affected by such things.

What is the point of this usage? Why call all these different things codes, especially when they are not all codes in the same sense of the term and some are not codes at all in any ordinary sense of the term? The answer is that Metz and Wollen are cheating. Their usage disguises the fact that much of aesthetics and criticism is properly concerned with something other than the significance of signs. Instrumental music is not a language, a system of signs. It has no meaning. It does not represent or signify anything. An understanding of musical structure plays a role in our appreciation of music, but that is not to say that an understanding of the significance of musical signs plays a role in our appreciation of music.

Much the same is true of our understanding and appreciation of films. To appreciate something about the structure of a film is not necessarily to appreciate something that functions as a sign. To say, for example, that the love triangle functions as a specific code in the films of Max Ophuls[3] is to say no more than that the love triangle is a feature of many of Max Ophuls's films and to say it in a way that wrongly suggests that you are saying something semiotic. Once this is clear, it is obvious that neither Metz nor Wollen has given any reason at all for identifying film theory with film semiotics—indeed it is or should be clear that there is nothing to be said for such an identification.

Of course, even if film theory cannot be *identified* with the semiotics of the cinema, the semiotics of the cinema might be a useful subject in its own right. But there are ample reasons for skepticism about this. Both Metz and Wollen envision a science of signs. What makes them think that there is such a science or could be one? What are its laws? Its principles? To be sure, there is Peirce's distinction between the iconic, indexical, and symbolic aspects of signs. You can spend a con-

---

[3]E.g., Dudley Andrew "Semiology and Film: A Discussion of Metz," *University Film Study Center Newsletter Supplement* 5, no. 3, p. 4 (Cambridge, MA).

siderable amount of time separating out the relevant components in various cases. That can be fun, for a while, but it does not constitute a science.

Part of the problem is that Peirce's use of the term *sign* is a technical one, which counts as signs rather different sorts of things. Words are not normally signs in any ordinary sense of the term *sign*, nor are pictures or diagrams; and the sense in which road signs are signs is different from the sense in which smoke is a sign of fire. It is by no means obvious that there is a unitary phenomenon to be captured in a theory of signs in Peirce's sense.

Smoke means fire and the word *combustion* means fire, but not in the same sense of *means*. The word *mean* is ambiguous. To say smoke means fire is to say that smoke is a symptom, sign, indication, or evidence of fire. To say that the word *combustion* means fire is to say that people use the word to mean fire. The word is not normally a symptom, sign, indication, or evidence of fire; on the other hand, people do not normally use smoke to mean fire. Furthermore, there is no ordinary sense of the word *mean* in which a picture of a man means a man or means that man. This suggests that Peirce's theory of signs would comprise at least three rather different subjects: a theory of intended meaning, a theory of evidence, and a theory of pictorial depiction. There is no reason to think that these theories must contain common principles.

A fourth and different subject is also relevant—the study of representation. In our scientific, practical, and aesthetic thinking, we often let certain things stand for or represent others, so that relations among the first things can represent corresponding relations among the others. We do this for several reasons—to see the implications of a theory, to see how a battle went, or might go, and so forth. This sort of representation may seem to be exactly what Peirce had in mind when he spoke of signs, since the relation that leads us to let one thing stand for another might be iconic, indexical, conventional, or just arbitrary choice. But, in fact, this sort of representation is a much narrower phenomenon than what Peirce had in mind. Pictures do not ordinarily in this sense "stand for" what they depict; words do not "stand for" their meanings; and evidence does not "stand for" what it indicates.

Metz observes that in the film *M*, a loose balloon caught in overhead wires symbolizes the death of a girl whom we earlier saw always holding a balloon. Now, the earlier photographic images of the girl holding a balloon *depict* a girl holding a balloon but do not stand for or represent a girl with a balloon. The loose balloon by itself, without the wires, would be evidence of her capture and therefore her death, given the filmic context, but the balloon would not in that case stand for or represent her, her capture, or her death. The capturing of the balloon by the wires does stand for the capturing of the girl. The balloon stands for the girl in this context. It is not clear whether the wires stand for the man who captures her; I am inclined to think not. The capturing of the balloon by the wires does not directly stand for the death of the girl. It symbolizes the death because it represents the capture which leads to her death.

Sometimes we arbitrarily let one thing stand for another; sometimes, as in the example just described, we find that it is "natural" to take a particular thing to stand for another. We might try to discover under what conditions such representation seems "natural," although there is, in fact, no reason to suppose that we will ever be able to do this.

In conclusion, let me summarize briefly. Metz and Wollen advocate replacing film theory and criticism with a semiotics of the cinema. I have tried to suggest several reasons for being doubtful about this. Many aspects of film aesthetics appear to be part of semiotics only because of an equivocation in the use of the word *code*. The theory of signs, in Peirce's sense, contains no laws or general principles; at best it contains a few categories of classification. Semiotics is really a collection of three or four disparate subjects. It is not obvious that a close study of any of these subjects will be particularly fruitful for the study of film.

1975

STEPHEN PRINCE
THE DISCOURSE OF PICTURES: ICONICITY AND FILM STUDIES

Stephen Prince is currently professor of communication and film studies at Virginia Tech. He has published numerous books on film aesthetics and history including monographs on the work of directors Sam Peckinpah and Akira Kurosawa. His essays on film violence, cinematic iconicity, pornographic film, and CGI emphasize viewer experience and interpretation. He questions the linguistic and psychoanalytic methodologies on which much film analysis is founded, urging a more empirical approach that accounts for the changing technologies of film production and reception.

In its analysis of images, film theory since the 1970s has been deeply indebted to structuralist and Saussurean-derived linguistic models. Indeed, it would be difficult to overstate the depth and importance of this relationship. As Robert Stam has noted, "Semiotics in general, and film semiotics in particular, must be seen . . . as local manifestations of a more widespread linguistic turn."[1] To speak, for example, about "reading" a film, as many film analysts now do, irrespective of the critical methodology employed to generate the reading, is to index and emphasize this lineage. Like books, films are regarded as texts for reading by viewers or critics, with the concomitant implication that such reading activates similar processes of semiotic decoding.

But does it? To what extent are linguistic models appropriate for an understanding of how images communicate? Film theory since the 1970s has tended to place great emphasis upon what is regarded as the arbitrary nature of the signifier-signified relationship, that is, upon the purely conventional and symbolic aspect of signs. What this focus has tended to displace is an appreciation of the iconic and mimetic aspect of certain categories of signs, namely pictorial signs, those most relevant to an understanding of the cinema. This stress upon the arbitrary nature of semiotic coding has had enormous consequences for the way film studies as a discipline has tended to frame questions about visual meaning and communication.

Our purpose here is to examine some of these consequences and to see how well they square with the observable evidence about how viewers perceive and comprehend cinematic sequences. We will see that current film theory, tracing its lineage

My thanks to Carl Plantinga for reading an earlier version of this essay and offering helpful suggestions.

[1] Robert Stam, "Film and Language: From Metz to Bakhtin," in *The Cinematic Text: Methods and Approaches*, ed. R. Barton Palmer (New York: AMS Press, 1989), p. 277.

from Saussure, Althusser, and Lacan, has constructed accounts of the ways in which film transmits meaning that are, in certain important respects, counter to the observable skills, abilities, and reactions of real-world viewers. The viewer, as theorized in these accounts, differs substantially from his/her real-world counterpart. We shall emphasize some of these discrepancies in order to suggest a reorientation of theoretical focus. In short, a renewed attention to the iconic, mimetic nature of pictorial signs is warranted, so that our theories might become more sensitive to the unique, constitutive features of pictorial—as opposed to linguistic—modes of communication. (It is important to note that other currents exist in contemporary film theory. Pier Paolo Pasolini and Peter Wollen, for example, have offered analyses of cinematic signs that are inflected rather differently than the Saussurean-inspired accounts that this essay examines.[2] More than twenty years ago, Wollen stressed the importance of paying attention to the iconic aspect of pictorial signs. Borrowing from Charles Peirce's triadic model of the sign, he argued that in cinema, iconic and indexical aspects are more powerful than symbolic, and he pointed out that semiologists have neglected the subject of iconic signs because they are biased in favor of conceptions of signs as arbitrary and symbolic.)

Let me state very clearly at the outset that this suggested reorientation is not intended as a substitute for the very real and necessary work on the role that culture plays in film spectatorship and interpretation. Culture-bound attitudes do indeed inflect the content of film narratives, along with their stylistic visualization, at the point of production and, again, through the inferences viewers draw from those narratives. The position this essay takes is not intended as a replacement either for the critical work of ideological analysis and interpretation, or for inquiries into how viewers' judgements about the nature of a social world depicted in film may be shaped by elements of cinematic structure. But, in the interest of conducting this kind of interpretive work, it is important to have a clear sense of where cultural variables do and do not enter into the production of meaning by the cinematic image. Only when we have a good understanding of those aspects of visual signification where culture plays a less determinative role are we likely to be able to construct a clear portrait of where it does play a role. Thus, this essay certainly does not argue against the role of cultural analysis in film interpretation, but it does attempt to suggest some reasons for caution when employing linguistic categories and models of cultural relativism in film analysis. It is not that there are no cases in which they might profitably be applied, but rather that there are some significant aspects of visual communication to which they probably *should not* be applied.

THE LINGUISTIC TURN IN CONTEMPORARY FILM STUDIES

To begin, it will help to briefly trace the linguistic influence on contemporary film theory, after which we may question whether it supplies an adequate account

---

[2]See Pier Paolo Pasolini, *Heretical Empiricism*, ed. Louise K. Barnett, trans. Ben Lawton and Louise K. Barnett (Bloomington: Indiana University Press, 1988); and Peter Wollen, *Signs and Meaning in the Cinema* (Bloomington: Indiana University Press, 1976), especially pp. 116–54.

of images or even, in certain crucial respects, of language itself. It is well known that Saussure's account of the sign as having an arbitrary and unmotivated connection between its structural components has been directly taken over by many film theorists. As Philip Rosen has pointed out, "One effect of the argument for the basic conventionality of cinematic images was to open the way for a utilization of the ideal of difference in cinematic signification."[3] Stressing the signifier as a differential construction enabled film theory to emphasize communication as discourse, as a culture-bound activity, relative to and differentially patterned by the unique social worlds of diverse groups of interactants. Signs, whether linguistic or cinematic, were viewed as culturally instantiated: "Sign systems don't produce meaning outside of the social and cultural context from which they have developed."[4]

This concept of the sign enabled theorists to explicate many aspects of cinematic coding, from discrete optical devices like dissolves or wipes to more complex structures such as shot/reverse-shot cutting, subjective images, and other aspects of point-of-view editing. Viewing these devices as symbolic codes permitted theorists to emphasize the construction of cinematic discourse, that is, the deployment in film of an elaborate semiotic system whose address, and effects, could be comprehensible in Althusserian-Lacanian terms as the interpellation of subjects. Using a symbol system like language, in this view, entails being positioned—socially, ideologically— in and by the categories which that system has helped create. Thus film, like language, could be comprehensible as discourse, as the creation of apparent meaning where only true relations of difference prevail (due to the arbitrary nature of the sign and the consequent need for it to receive definition only in relation to what it is not, i.e., to all other signs). As Althusser and Lacan (and the film theory they inspired) emphasized, these deceptively real constellations of apparently fixed meaning could be an excellent site for ideology and for imaginary conceptions of the self to take root. Viewed as discourse, cinema assumed a symbiotic relationship with ideology, becoming an effective vehicle for its transmission. The work of film theory became increasingly focused on deciphering the ideology at work inside the cinema's deceptive and transparent appearance of reality. That appearance of reality was, furthermore, suspect for having ideological effects (e.g., naturalizing that which is historical or cultural, etc.) and for creating ideal and false subject unities.[5] Viewed in these terms, film history is the history of discourse, and the relation between film and the world is a matter of representational convention. As Stephen Heath has written, "That reality, the match of film and world, is a matter of representation, and representation is in turn a matter of discourse. . . . [I]n this sense at least, film is a series of languages, a history of codes."[6]

---

[3]Philip Rosen, ed., *Narrative, Apparatus, Ideology* (New York: Columbia University Press, 1986), p. 3.

[4]"Introduction," in *Explorations in Film Theory: Selected Essays from Cine-Tracts*, ed. Ron Burnett (Bloomington: Indiana University Press, 1991), p. xv.

[5]In the influential analyses of Jean-Louis Baudry, these functions are a consequence of the machinery of camera and projector, irrespective of the content and subjects that are filmed. See "Ideological Effects of the Basic Cinematographic Apparatus" and "The Apparatus: Metapsychological Approaches to the Impression of Reality in the Cinema," in Rosen, ed., *Narrative, Apparatus, Ideology*, pp. 286–318. [See also pp. 171–188 in this volume.]

[6]Stephen Heath, *Questions of Cinema* (New York: Macmillan, 1981), p. 26.

Furthermore, an emphasis upon differential and relational signifiers has entailed a denial, or, at best a suspicion, of reference. If signs are arbitrarily related to what they represent, then meaning is at best provisional, at worst illusory or ideological. Representation which is non-arbitrary tends to be construed by film theory in terms of a relationship of identity between sign and referent, thus generating a dichotomy of arbitrariness/identity. Semiotic representation is either a matter of arbitrary coding or of identity and transparence, with the latter condition being construed negatively in terms of illusion and error. Identity is regarded as a deceptively false universal, as a part of what is sometimes called the ideology of the visual. "Reading encounters the text as a relation of difference not identity."[7] Taken a step further, this view regards empirical knowledge about the world as being thoroughly mediated by signs, as itself discourse. "The empirical . . . is not 'the real' but the product of the discourses of the dominant ideology."[8] Since the "real" embodies the false universals of ideology, the relations among cinematic signifiers tend to be seen as cultural (and therefore symbolic), rather than as iconic or mimetic. The spectator's understanding of the cinema is therefore explained as a matter of cultural conditioning and learning. "The spectator chains together the film's signifiers on a cultural grid of intelligibility—an ensemble of assumptions and presuppositions about the 'real'—into an account that makes the film socially intelligible."[9]

Note the assumptions here. Language imposes a system of relational distinctions upon the world, creating culture from the real. One makes entry into language, or, in Lacanian terms, into the Symbolic order, learning the culturally patterned distinctions and, in the process, being interpellated as a subject. Film is akin to language by virtue of employing relational, differential signifiers. Comprehension of the cinema, then, should likewise be predicated upon cultural conditioning, upon the apprehension of "cultural grids of intelligibility." But, as we will see, the spectator's understanding of cinematic images seems more immediately explicable in terms of mimetic, referential coding rather than via the chains of displaced, arbitrary, and relational meaning in prevailing theories. In other words, this understanding is more a matter of recognition than translation. We will return to this point. Moreover, iconic representation is appropriately understood in terms of degrees of resemblance rather than the all-or-nothing terms of arbitrariness or identicality. A photograph, for example, exhibits a higher degree of iconicity than a line drawing.

Transposed in film theory to units of cinematic structure, the Saussurean view of the sign as an arbitrary and, taken in isolation, meaningless unit has allowed current theory to construct an extended analogy with language. Although no one any longer searches for the filmic equivalent of such linguistic features as the period or the comma, the debt to Saussurean linguistics is apparent in the axioms that the connections between cinematic representation and the world are, in all important

---

[7]D. N. Rodowick, *The Difficulty of Difference: Psychoanalysis, Sexual Difference and Film Theory* (New York: Routledge, 1991), p. 138.

[8]Mas'ud Zavarzadeh, *Seeing Films Politically* (Albany: State University of New York Press, 1991), p. x.

[9]Ibid., p. 11.

respects, a matter of historical or cultural coding and convention, that is, that filmic representation is a matter of symbolic rather than iconic coding and that a viewer, rather than perceiving a film, "reads" it.

PROBLEMS WITH LINGUISTIC RELATIVITY

We shall explore some discrepancies between these axioms and the observable evidence about how viewers perceive and process cinematic images. First, however, it will be helpful to discuss some reservations regarding the alleged arbitrariness of the linguistic sign and the uses to which film studies has put this concept. As Devitt and Sterelny have recently pointed out, emphasizing the sign as a relational entity, defined through relations of difference, presents a problem for meaning.[10] This emphasis fails to specify how meaning may arise or even how lexical borrowing from other language systems may occur. When speakers borrow terms from another language, they are often doing so in response to a perception that some thing or condition exists that needs a name, although at present it has none or is insufficiently labeled. In such a case, linguistic skills are deployed in response to non- or extra-linguistic perceptions, a condition which models of linguistic determinism have a hard time accounting for. Furthermore, rejecting reference, as Saussurean models do, mystifies language acquisition.

In a Saussurean view, where meaning is defined through relations of difference (e.g., Jonathan Culler's well-known view that understanding the color brown entails grasping the relation between brown and what it is not, i.e., all other colors), it is difficult to see how a child ever learns a language. As Devitt and Sterelny note, "We want to say that a child begins by learning a minimal vocabulary and a few rudimentary syntactic rules. The child continues by extending these rules. On a structuralist picture of language, we cannot say this. Vocabulary does not remain constant across changes in the system. Each time the child changes the system, *everything changes*. Language learning cannot be represented as a cumulative process."[11]

Part of the problem here is that to specify meaning, one at times has to step outside the language system, and poststructural methodologies have been most unwilling to posit the possibility of doing this. In many accounts, one cannot get outside representation at all because it is, by definition, determinative of human thought and experience. It is commonly maintained that "there is no absolute moment without signs, without language, without, in other words, a whole host of mediations between seeing, experience, and knowledge."[12] Stephen Heath has noted that the referents of cinematic images exist only in discourse, as representations already constituted by history and culture. "The represented a discourse produces is grasped, realized, exists as such in the particular discursive process of representation, and it is this that needs first and foremost to be interrogated."[13]

---

[10]Michael Devitt and Kim Sterelny, *Language and Reality* (Cambridge, MA: MIT Press, 1987), pp. 215–18.

[11]Ibid., p. 216.

[12]Burnett, *Explorations in Film Theory*, p. xvii.

[13]Heath, *Questions of Cinema*, p. 191.

This view—that pictorial representations and, beyond them, patterns of human and social organization are the expressions of discursive relations and positions— is a reformulation of the famous Whorf-Sapir hypothesis which suggested that radically different language systems might organize the world in unique ways for their users. The Whorf-Sapir hypothesis is a statement of extreme linguistic relativity, arguing for the influence of features of linguistic organization upon the perceptual habits of a community. It is a relativistic view because it argues against the possibility of semantic or perceptual universals. As languages vary, so do the realities they construct. The Whorf-Sapir hypothesis has been a very seductive and influential one for film studies. Bill Nichols has noted the relevance of this hypothesis for poststructural film theory. "Post-structuralist work does not regard language or, by extension, film as the neutral means by which we understand ourselves, others, and our world. Rather, it draws on versions of the Whorf-Sapir hypothesis, which describes a world constructed in, by, and through language."[14]

Benjamin Lee Whorf's study of Indian languages led him to emphasize how different languages may segment the world for their community of speakers in divergent ways.[15] There are some data to support a limited view of this hypothesis.[16] Language undoubtedly does modulate our experience of the world. Yet there is little evidence to support the extreme relativity of the Whorfian view (i.e., that language determines both thought and perception) and some clear evidence to counter it.[17] Advocates of linguistic relativity, or discourse relativity, often support their position with reference to color terminology, i.e., to the fact that different cultures have varying numbers of color terms to designate locally important attributes, such as snow for an arctic community. In suggesting that representational images, like other texts, rely upon culturally determined codes. Nichols, for example, has employed this notion of linguistic relativity, writing that "to not know the perceptual codes maintained by a given culture is tantamount to being an illiterate infant wandering through an unintelligible world. (An example would be the utter inability of most members of non-Eskimo cultures to distinguish the dozens of different kinds of snow for which the Eskimo has separate words.)"[18] Analogously, Mas'ud Zavarzadeh has asserted that "we understand colors not because we respond to them directly through our sensory organs, but because the responses of our sensory organs are made meaningful for us by the language. Different languages make sense of this physical continuum in startlingly different and dissimilar ways. . . ."[19]

---

[14]"Introduction," in *Movies and Methods*, vol. 2, ed. Bill Nichols (Berkeley: University of California Press, 1986), p. 16.

[15]The relevant essays explicating this position can be found in *Language, Thought and Reality: Selected Writings of Benjamin Lee Whorf*, ed. John B. Carroll (Cambridge, MA: MIT Press, 1984).

[16]See, for example, John B. Carroll and Joseph B. Casagrande, "The Function of Language Classifications in Behavior," in *Readings in Social Psychology*, ed. Eleanor E. Maccoby, Theodore M. Newcomb, and Eugene L. Hartley (New York: Holt, Rinehart and Winston, 1958), pp. 18–31. It should be noted, however, that the results of this study, while offering some support of the Whorfian view, are nevertheless mixed and somewhat inconsistent.

[17]For a review of evidence bearing on strong and weak versions of Whorfian hypothesis, see Earl Hunt and Franca Agnoli, "The Whorfian Hypothesis: A Cognitive Psychology Perspective," *Psychological Review* 98, no. 3 (1991): 377–89.

[18]Bill Nichols, *Ideology and the Image* (Bloomington: Indiana University Press, 1981), p. 26.

[19]Zavarzadeh, *Seeing Films Politically*, p. 102.

In contrast to the Whorf-Sapir hypothesis, however, a classic crosscultural study of color terminology found respondents plotting the same range of basic colors on a Munsell color chart irrespective of the labels furnished by their culture.[20] Experimental data were obtained from speakers of 20 languages and were supplemented with historical information on 78 additional languages. The researchers found a universal inventory of eleven basic color categories across all languages studied and a fixed evolutionary sequence governing the order in which languages added new basic color categories. Writing that the allegation of arbitrariness in the way languages segment the color spectrum is "a gross overstatement," the researchers concluded that "the referents for the basic color terms of all languages appear to be drawn from a set of eleven universal perceptual categories, and these categories become encoded in the history of a given language in a partially fixed order. There appears to be no evidence to indicate that differences in complexity of basic color lexicons between one language and another reflect perceptual differences between the speakers of those languages."[21] Different languages can make more or fewer distinctions according to environmental or cultural needs but cannot override the biological basis of color perception.

The evidence furnished by Berlin and Kay on color terminology fails to support the extreme linguistic relativity hypothesis that has been so influential for film studies, and suggests instead the importance of retaining a concept of referentiality outside language to which language may respond. This example can be a heuristic one for film theory. Reopening a space for principles of referentiality and iconicity could be a very useful development, enabling our theories to move closer to observable real-world evidence about how viewers understand the cinema. Thus, with respect to pictures, film theory might ask if there is a nonlinguistic, even biological, basis on which visual communication might rest. Investigation of this question may help provide a more secure sense of the methodological limits constraining the equation of cinema with discourse. Julian Hochberg has recently made this point, noting, "only when we know where the line lies that separates . . . lower, mandatory cognitive processes from the higher, elective functions, can we sensibly formulate explanations—linguistic, psychoanalytic, and so on—that rest on cultural determination."[22]

One final point to note about the concepts of linguistic relativity and arbitrariness operative in current film theory is the extent to which accounts of the cinema as discourse, analogized with language, construct the analogy based on limited features rather than seeing language in more comprehensive terms. The linguist Charles Hockett, for example, seeking to distinguish human language from animal systems of communication, formulated a set of thirteen design features uniquely characterizing human language.[23] Arbitrariness of the sign was only one of them, and many of the others, such as prevarication, displacement, and abstractness, point to clear

[20]Brent Berlin and Paul Kay, *Basic Color Terms: Their Universality and Evolution* (Berkeley: University of California Press, 1969).

[21]Ibid., pp. 4–5.

[22]Julian Hochberg, "The Perception of Moving Images," *Iris*, no. 9 (Spring, 1989): 41.

[23]See Charles F. Hockett, "Logical Considerations in the Study of Animal Communication," in *The View from Language: Selected Essays 1948–1974* (Athens: University of Georgia Press, 1977), pp. 124–62.

differences between the communicational capabilities of language and pictures, suggesting that analogies with language may not be the best way of explicating pictorial communication. The design feature of displacement, for example, denotes the capability of the language-system to create messages that refer to a time and space outside of the immediate communicational situation. Pictures, by contrast, lack tense and other aspects of syntax that can be used to establish remote temporal or spatial conditions (the dissolves, wipes, and odd music used to signal flashbacks in Hollywood narratives are a less powerful and flexible means of approximating this ability). Furthermore, as several scholars have pointed out, pictures cannot express negatives.[24] These and other differences between pictorial and linguistic messages point toward distinctly different communicational modalities. Interestingly, Christian Metz also noted some of these fundamental distinctions between linguistic and pictorial modes of communication. He pointed out that cinema lacks the double level of structure in language (i.e., the morphemic and phonemic levels) and is a one-way system of communication, unlike language, where senders and receivers are interchangeable, and he concluded, therefore, that the concept of a language is probably inapplicable to film. Despite these objections, Metz nevertheless went on to explore film structure as *parole*, in terms of a taxonomy of segment types.

If cinematic meaning is to be developed from a theoretical basis originating with a Saussurean conception of the relativity of the sign, film theory sometimes seems a little imprecise about the functional and at times invariant nature of communicational rules. As noted, film theory tends to view cutting patterns, camera positions, even perspectively based images as culturally relative yet syntactically precise conventions. But, with respect to language (and perceptual images), Noam Chomsky points out that "having acquired the system of language, the person can (in principle) choose to use it or not, as he can choose to keep to or disregard his judgements concerning the position of objects in space. He cannot choose to have sentences mean other than what they do, any more than he can choose to have objects distributed in perceptual space otherwise than the way they are."[25] In other words, if the assumptions of the Saussurian view, as applied to pictures, are correct, we should find more crosscultural variation on basic picture recognition tasks than we in fact do. We will explore this point in more detail shortly.

VISUAL GRAMMAR OR NARRATIVE CONTEXT?

Chomsky's observation raises the issue of grammaticality, which should be central to questions about whether film structure operates like a language. As noted, Metz's presentation is somewhat ambiguous with respect to grammaticality, but this is an issue that cannot easily be avoided for accounts that seek to analogize film and language. Film theory has identified a number of syntactic elements (e.g., point-of-view editing employing perspectively based images, suture) which are thought

---

[24]Sol Worth, "Pictures Can't Say Ain't," in *Film/Culture*, ed. Sari Thomas (Metuchen, NJ: Scarecrow Press, 1982), pp. 97–109; and Edward Branigan, "Here Is a Picture of No Revolver," *Wide Angle* 8, no. 34 (1986): 8–17.

[25]Noam Chomsky, *Reflections on Language* (New York: Pantheon, 1975), p. 71.

to operate as codes with discernible effects across a range of individual films, thus constituting a kind of cinematic grammar. But the test of ungrammaticality is not often applied (that is, judgements about the syntactic correctness of given filmic constructions). The most thorough and complete exploration of the application of linguistic principles to problems of film structure is found in the work of John Carroll, who has sought to apply Chomskian transformational-generative grammar to the cinema.[26]

Carroll identifies a series of principles underlying cinema grammar violations of which ostensibly constitute cinematic equivalents of grammatical errors and allegedly give rise to sequences that viewers will judge to be confusing or unfilmic. These are essentially continuity editing rules, such as the injunction that if an actor looks and reacts to anything off-frame, the next shot will be interpreted by viewers as a subjective shot. Carroll describes a sequence from *The Birds* where Hitchcock seems to violate this principle, and he remarks that viewers will find this confusing. It is the scene showing Tippi Hedren waiting outside the schoolhouse while, behind her, the birds gather en masse on the playground jungle gym. Hitchcock cuts between a shot of Hedren looking off-frame and a shot of the gathering flock, as if to imply (by virtue of the cutting pattern) that she must see it.

In a recent and thorough review of the issue of visual literacy in film and television, Messaris points out that, while Carroll is technically correct, the salient point is that the confusion (not shared by all viewers) is only momentary, because the surrounding contextual-narrative information makes it clear that the subsequent shot is not a subjective one.[27] In other words, given the narrative context, it would be implausible to assume the character sees the birds without reacting because their deadly nature has already been established in the story. Messaris points out that one reason why notions of grammaticality are difficult to apply to film is that narrative context often overrules code. "The role of formal conventions in conveying a movie's meaning is generally subordinate to conventional standards of plausibility or probability ('conventional' in the sense that the film-maker must be able to assume them of her/his audience). . . . [T]he viewer's interpretation of edited sequences is largely a matter of cross-referencing possible interpretations against a broader context (i.e., the larger story in the movie itself, together with corresponding situations from real life and other movies), rather than a matter of 'decoding' formal devices (e.g., an off-screen look followed by a cut to a new shot). . . . Interpretation is driven by the narrative context, not the code."[28]

Another example should make this clear, although this instance does not involve an alleged violation of grammar. In *The Searchers*, after Ethan and Marty discover that Lucy has been killed by her Indian abductors and Brad, her lover, is killed while charging into the Indian camp, the searchers ride into a snowy landscape where Marty despairs of ever finding Debbie. Ethan, in reply, makes his famous speech about being a critter that just keeps coming. Fade out and fade in on the Jorgensens' ranch as Ethan and Mary ride up. As a symbolic pictorial device that has no clear

[26]See John M. Carroll, *Toward a Structural Psychology of Cinema* (New York: Mouton, 1980).
[27]Paul Messaris, *Visual Literacy: Image, Mind, and Reality* (Boulder, CO: Westview Press, 1994).
[28]Ibid.,

analogy in real-life visual experience, the fade operates in accord with its conventional usage to bracket and separate sections of the narrative, assisting the viewer's parsing operations. But it is the contextual narrative information that provides the salient cues about the precise nature of the narrative shift. At the Jorgensens', Ethan and Marty inhabit a different landscape. The absence of snow indicates a seasonal shift, and Jorgensen tells Ethan that his letter about Brad's death arrived the previous year. The viewers' extra-filmic knowledge of seasonal patterns and, most importantly, the dialogue between Ethan and Jorgensen establish the precise nature of the time shift in a way that the purely visual code—the fade—cannot. The dominance of narrative context over code explains why it would be equally permissible—though not in a film of the 1950s—to signal the temporal shift with a straight cut. With redundant informational cues available in the narrative, the viewer should be able to follow the flow of events, permitting a degree of interchangeability in the use of codes. Thus, image patterns may not need to be as rigidly sequenced as the concept of a "grammar" might imply, and the ostensive violation of grammatical rules may carry less significance (for the viewer's interpretational abilities) than is sometimes thought, as the violations of the 180-degree rule in contemporary productions should indicate.

EMPIRICAL EVIDENCE ABOUT IMAGE COMPREHENSION

The foregoing discussion has suggested that the linguistic orientation of film theory may not be the most efficacious for dealing with visual meaning or cinema structure. Currently, the discipline is undergoing some profound shifts as the Saussurean and Lacanian accounts are contested by alternative formulations advocating perceptually or cognitively based approaches. The cognitive turn in contemporary theory has opened a space for renewed appraisal of perceptual evidence that runs counter to notions of film as language and their logical consequence—that viewers must learn to interpret pictorial displays. Reviewing the results of empirical research on the perceptual and cognitive processing of visual images and narratives will help clarify some of the problems inherent in using concepts of arbitrary or relational signifiers to explain principles of cinematic meaning and communication.

Contemporary notions that film is analogous to a language are consistent with the speculations of film theorists dating from virtually the beginning of cinema history. Boris Eichenbaum, for example, noted that "Film language is no less conventional than any other language. . . . Cinema has not only its 'language,' but also its 'jargon,' rather inaccessible to the uninitiated."[29] Béla Balázs suggested that, to be comprehended, the new "form-language" of cinema required of its viewers a new sensibility and understanding, without which novice viewers would be baffled.[30] However, to posit language-based modes of cinematic communication is to implicitly raise the issue of visual literacy by implying that a period of tutoring would be logically necessary in order to gain interpretive mastery of the cinematic vocabu-

---

[29]Boris Eichenbaum, "Cinema Stylistics," in *Russian Formalist Film Theory*, ed. Herbert Eagle (Ann Arbor: University of Michigan Press, 1981), p. 77.

[30]Béla Balázs, *Theory of the Film* (New York: Dover, 1970), p. 34.

lary (learning, for example, that a subjective shot represents the view of the absent character or that the portions of an event elided by continuity editing nevertheless still occurred within the narrative). The assumption that untutored or inexperienced viewers would encounter difficulties making sense of unfamiliar images finds some apparent confirmation in the existing anecdotal reports of viewers' bewildering first-time encounters with motion and still pictures.[31] However, these difficulties are often due less to an inherent inability of naïve viewers to see the pictorial objects than to a first-time encounter with a novel recording surface (e.g., paper in the case of still pictures) or a culturally unfamiliar depth cue used to render an object in abstract terms (e.g., linear perspective suggesting a straight road in a line drawing). Moreover, even where anthropologists and field workers report difficulties with picture perception, respondents typically are able to integrate figure-ground relations rather quickly, resulting in correct picture perception.[32] Viewers who find picture perception completely impossible under any condition are quite rare and probably anomalous.

Convincing evidence about inherent human abilities to perceive pictures is available from a classic experiment in which the researchers prevented a child (their own) from birth from seeing pictures until the age of nineteen months, when it began to actively seek them out.[33] The child learned his vocabulary solely through the use of objects and received no training regarding pictorial meaning or content. He was nevertheless able to recognize, when tested with a series of 21 two-dimensional line drawings and photographs, the series of pictured objects (people and things familiar in his environment). The researchers concluded that the results indicate the existence of innate picture perception abilities and that, if there are allegations of cultures or viewers lacking these, it cannot be a matter of not yet having learned the language of pictures.

Empirical research indicates that one basis for these innate abilities probably lies in the activation by pictures of perceptual skills (object recognition, depth perspective, etc.) developed in real-world experience, skills which are then transferred to pictures. Scholars have commonly emphasized that pictures replicate a series of monocular depth cues used in real-world experience for inferring information about the positioning of objects in physical space (e.g., overlap, texture density gradients, shading, and, in motion pictures, motion parallax).[34] Picture perception, then, seems clearly based on 3D spatial skills transferred to the 2D representation, and one would expect that the more complete the set of cues employed by the picture regarding the spatial layout of the depicted scene, and the more culturally familiar the depicted objects, the greater the ease of recognition. If naïve viewers can perceive still pictures, there is no logical reason for inferring that they would have difficulty doing

---

[31]See the accounts in Balázs, *Theory of the Film*, pp. 34–35, and J. B. Deregowski, "Real Space and Represented Space: Cross-Cultural Perspectives," in *Behavioral and Brain Sciences* 12 (1989): 56–59.

[32]Messaris also makes this point.

[33]Julian Hochberg and Virginia Brooks, "Picture Perception as an Unlearned Ability: A Study of One Child's Performance," *American Journal of Psychology* 74, no. 4 (December 1962): 624–28.

[34]Discussing these cues, David Bordwell points out that cinematic images also routinely distort or alter them (e.g., through the effects of different focal length lenses, etc.). David Bordwell, *Narration in the Fiction Film* (Madison: University of Wisconsin Press, 1985), pp. 107–10.

so with moving pictures, especially since movies will supply the additional real-world depth cue of motion parallax.

But what about the role of culture in visual perception? As we have seen, culture-bound determinations are very important in language-based film theories which rely on arbitrary, relational signifiers. The move to empirical, perceptually based evidence might be unwelcome for linguistically based accounts of pictorial meaning because it can be seen as replacing cultural categories with biological (and therefore ideologically suspect) ones, and because it may suggest that pictorial and linguistic modalities are distinct from each other. With respect to the role of culture in picture perception, some evidence does exist for varying cultural susceptibilities to different visual illusions (the Mueller-Lyer illusion and the Sander parallelogram), perhaps due to variations in the physical environments of different cultures, but these do not seem to impact basic picture perception abilities.[35]

In a recent summary of the existing crosscultural research on picture perception, Deregowski suggests that relationships of culture, perception, and viewing abilities be conceptualized in terms of sets of contiguous and, at times, overlapping skills.[36] Real-world spatial experience may utilize 3D skills that 2D representations do not exploit, such as binocular disparity (using the differences in the images recorded by each eye as a means of inferring information about depth and distance). Many real-world perceptual skills, by contrast, do overlap with visual skills relevant for picture perception, and some may be influenced by varying patterns of cultural organization (e.g., as Segall et al. point out, respondents from plains or dense jungle environments may demonstrate less sensitivity to linear perspective when used as a pictorial depth code). Finally, some pictures employ purely representational codes with no overlap in real-life experience (e.g., wipes in film or streaky lines used to represent speed in comics). Obviously, with this last category one might expect greater interpretational difficulties for naïve viewers, but not inevitably. As our example from *The Searchers* indicated, narrative contextual information may be used to connect separate images or events even when the optical transition employed is a more symbolic one.

What, then, does all of this imply about the need for a period of tutoring implicit in the film-as-language model? Quite simply, such a period should not be necessary for inferring narrative relations in standard movies (i.e., movies that do not create deliberate narrative enigmas, in contrast to movies like *Last Year at Marienbad*). Empirical research with naïve viewers (in most cases young children and, in one unique study, inexperienced adults) offers evidence that the use of specifically cinematic devices (or, as the film-as-language paradigm might term them, symbolic codes), such as montage, camera movement, or subjective shots, do not pose substantial interpretational obstacles for naïve viewers provided developmental requisites are met (i.e., that the viewers have developed sufficient real-world conceptual and cognitive skills that can be applied to the film or television medium). A brief

---

[35]See Marshall H. Segall, Donald T. Campbell, and Melville J. Herskovits, *The Influence of Culture on Visual Perception* (Indianapolis, IN: Bobbs-Merrill, 1966).

[36]Deregowski, "Real Space," pp. 69–72.

review of some of this evidence will help clarify these points and will provide further evidence from which to question the theoretical and methodological efficacy of grounding film theory in conceptions of cinematic relationships involving arbitrary, unmotivated signs.

Young children's comprehension of an array of cinematic techniques was explored in a recent study by Smith, Anderson, and Fisher.[37] In one experiment, they showed three- and five-year-old children brief stop-animation video sequences that employed pans, zooms, and cuts to present a simply story. Another group of children saw the same stories in sequences with no editing or camera movement. When the children were invited to recreate the stories using the dolls and sets seen in the films, no differences in story comprehension were observed between the two groups, indicating that these film techniques seemed to pose few cognitive or interpretational problems for these young viewers. These were viewers who had seen television before. It is, however, the absence of age-related differences in their performance that is striking, especially in light of the hypothesis that these techniques should require medium-specific learning in order to be understood.

Because these sequences were relatively simple in structure (featuring only one pan, zoom, and cut), the researchers ran a second experiment with more complex visual presentations and longer visual narratives. Cinematic manipulations this time consisted of parallel editing to imply simultaneity of action, subjective shots representing a character's literal viewpoint, ellipses achieved through editing that deletion portions of a continuous event or action, and editing to imply a layout of contiguous spaces (e.g., cutting from an establishing shot of two buildings to a shot of a character looking out of a window, then to a reverse-angle interior shot of the character at the window). This time the children were four and seven years old.

As before, they were asked to recreate character perspectives and spatial layouts using the dolls and sets that had appeared in the films. Comparisons across all classes of montage indicated that clear majorities in both age groups made correct inferences of space, ellipsis, and character perspective. Inferences of simultaneity proved difficult for the four-year-olds, but not for the seven-year-olds. Both groups proved especially skilled at reconstructing implied actions omitted in the edited narratives.

This study indicates good comprehension by young children of basic montage techniques, which is what one would expect if interpretation of the visual displays draws on a child's developing real-world visual skills and experience. Emphasizing the status of cinematic images as iconic signs having a clear referential basis and inviting a transfer of real-world visual skills to the pictorial display does not deny the existence of medium-specific skills relevant for making sense of a motion picture, but it does reserve a more modest space for them than would the arbitrary-relational signifier model. Clearly, some film techniques are more symbolic than iconic and may be coded in a more arbitrary fashion. Such techniques would invite the viewer's application of specific, medium-based competencies. For example, the Smith et al study employed parallel editing as one category of montage. Drawing the correct

---

[37]Robin Smith, Daniel R. Anderson, and Catherine Fischer, "Young Children's Comprehension of Montage," *Child Development* 56 (1985): 962–71.

inference from parallel editing is arguably a medium-specific skill, and, as one would expect, the largest age differences in the average percentage of correct responses showed up there. But, rather than needing to become proficient at manipulating an arbitrarily symbolic set of cinematic signifiers, children can generally interpret visual displays involving point-of-view editing by transferring to the display their developing real-world visual skills and experience. Evidence supporting a developmental view of the application of real-world cognitive and perceptual skills to film and television displays involving point-of-view editing is found in Comuntzis-Page's study of the relationship between children's evolving real-world perspective-taking skills and their ability to infer meaning from an edited video sequence.[38] She found that children who successfully demonstrated a knowledge of visual perspectives in actual three-dimensional situations (e.g., children who knew that observers situated in different places can see different sides of a common object) were better able to understand the changing camera viewpoints of a television presentation. In fact, she found that skill at inferring character relationships in a three-dimensional layout seemed to be a prerequisite for making the proper analogous inferences from the two-dimensional video display. Only children who did well at the former task also did well on the latter, and clear age-related differences between perspective takers and nonperspective takers were found, supporting a developmental view.

The research cited thus far has used children to represent a population of relatively unskilled viewers. However, one unique study of motion picture perception and interpretation exists using adult viewers who had little familiarity with any mass media.[39] Working with a seminomadic, nonliterate, pastoral tribe in Kenya, a community whose aesthetic expressions concentrated on personal adornment and performance arts, the researchers showed adult villagers two videotapes of a culturally familiar story. One version was unedited, the other featured 14 cuts with frequent alterations of close-ups, medium shots, long shots, and zooms. No significant differences in ability to recall story information were found between respondents who viewed the edited and unedited versions. Fragmentation of the visual scene through point-of-view editing did not hinder comprehension, nor did it seem to require the use of any medium-specific skills. The researchers concluded that, on the contrary, continuity editing codes that manipulate point of view seem to function as "analogs of perceptual processes."[40]

LEVELS OF ICONICITY

The evidence reviewed thus far bears on the capability of pictures to furnish cues regarding the spatial layout of a scene or situation that are analogous to sources of information commonly found in real-world visual experience. It also bears mentioning, however, that another level of iconic information typically exists in pictures which

---

[38]Georgette Comuntzis-Page, "Changing Viewpoints in Visual Presentations: A Young Child's Point of View," paper presented at Eastern Communication Association Convention, Baltimore, 1988.

[39]Renee Hobbs, Richard Frost, Arthur Davis, and John Stauffer, "How First-Time Viewers Comprehend Editing Conventions," *Journal of Communication* 38 (1988): 50–60.

[40]Ibid., p. 58.

is central to a consideration of the comprehensibility and emotional effects of the cinema. Photographic images of people necessarily reproduce that information about facial expression and gesture which Ray Birdwhistell has called "kinesics." Birdwhistell and his colleagues studied the systematic patterning of body motion within cultures and designed an elaborate notational system to transcribe and study the distinctively patterned strings of body motion cues (called "kines") that are situationally articulated as a communicative form in everyday life. Birdwhistell explicitly rejected the notion that language was the most important channel of communication, arguing instead for a conception of communication as a multi-model, multi-sensory process which included visual and gestural as well as auditory channels.[41] He demonstrated how body motions are culturally patterned in symbolically significant ways that are understood by members of a given community whose socialization processes have sensitized them to coded kinesic displays. While Birdwhistell emphasized the importance of cultural context in determining the encoding of specific kinesic patterns, other researchers have argued that some gestural expressions—those on the face, for example—may function as biologically based pancultural signals for emotion. While all cultures mandate display rules governing who may display which emotions and when, experimental evidence furnished by Paul Ekman and his colleagues has indicated that certain facial displays seem correlated with basic categories of human emotion and are capable of being recognized crossculturally.[42]

The obvious point to be made from this brief discussion of the work on facial and body motion communication is that the motion picture camera furnishes an excellent means of recording the expressive meanings carried by these channels. Birdwhistell, in fact, employed still photographs and motion picture footage to record and store the data used in his analyses. It should be an assertion of the obvious to point out that a major source of the appeal and power of the movies lies here, in film's ability to capture the subtleties and nuances of socially resonant streams of kinesic expressions, and not just to passively capture them but, via close-ups and other expressive devices, to intensify and emphasize the most salient cues for the viewer's understanding in cognitive and affective terms of the meaning of the scenes depicted on screen. (Recent studies of acting by James Naremore and Roberta Pearson have emphasized the way that different performance traditions code expressive behavior and how film technique may be used to frame and emphasize this coding.[43]) The relational-arbitrary signifier hypothesis has tended to draw attention

---

[41]See Ray L. Birdwhistell, *Kinesics and Context* (Philadelphia: University of Pennsylvania Press, 1970).

[42]See Paul Ekman and Wallace V. Friesen, "Constants Across Cultures in the Face and Emotion," *Journal of Personality and Social Psychology* 17, no. 2 (1971): 124–29; and Paul Ekman, "Expression and the Nature of Emotion," in *Approaches to Emotion*, ed. Klaus R. Scherer and Paul Ekman (Hillsdale, NJ: Lawrence Erlbaum Association, 1984), pp. 319–43. The latter volume is especially useful for containing a range of theoretical positions, often competing, on the nature and expression of emotion and the ways it may be culturally coded.

[43]See James Naremore, *Acting in the Cinema* (Berkeley: University of California Press, 1988), and Roberta Pearson, *Eloquent Gestures: The Transformation of Performance Style in the Griffith Biograph Films* (Berkeley: University of California Press, 1992).

away from this clear source of iconic meaning in motion pictures, despite its obvious importance in helping to explicate the crosscultural appeal and power of the movies.

THE DISCOURSE OF PICTURES

What do these studies and avenues of research tell us about cinematic codes and the appropriateness of defining them, as current film theory does, as a series of relational differences among arbitrary signs? The empirical evidence clearly suggests that pictorial identification skills do not develop from an extended period of exposure to signification and consequent learning, as do language skills, and that this is probably due to the fact that most realistic pictures are isomorphic with corresponding real-world visual displays, unlike symbolic signs, which have a more arbitrary relationship to what they represent. Furthermore, via the technologies of motion picture recording, the camera is able to reproduce in clearly recognizable and even intensified form the familiar streams of facial and body motion cues which symbolically encode the meanings of the social situations portrayed on screen. These cues should be readily understood by cinema viewers, just as they are in real-world visual experience. If the distinctions between iconic and symbolic modes that we have been emphasizing are really relevant to differences between pictures and language, then one would expect iconic modes to be processed more readily than symbolic ones, especially by young children, and existing research lends support to this idea.[44]

Thus, it is not clear how the concept of the relational, arbitrary signifier might apply to cinematic images or, for that matter, to any iconic image. Certainly, as Hockett indicated, few communicational signs are completely iconic, since a state of total iconicity would imply that the sign was completely indistinguishable from its referent.[45] Nevertheless, pictorial signs do bear clear structural similarities to their referents, with the attendant consequences for perception and comprehension that we have just reviewed. The linguistic model has proven to be a very powerful paradigm for the analysis of images and larger film structures (e.g., dramatic scenes) in part because that analysis is typically conducted via words. When film scholars analyze images, visual information is translated into verbal description, one modality is substituted for another. But, as Branigan has noted, one must be cautious in speaking about the discourse of pictures: "The analyst must recognize that the very fact of talking about narration requires a re-presentation of it by verbal or other means which may capture only some of its features."[46] The concept of the relational, arbitrary signifier would seem most applicable to pictures here, in the language of analysis which is employed to intellectually manipulate pictorial representations. Furthermore, while empirical evidence indicates that viewers easily and readily make the required inferences necessary to sequence a series of pictures into a coherent

---

[44]See S. L. Calvert, A. C. Huston, B. A. Watkins, and J. C. Wright, "The Effects of Selective Attention to Television Forms on Children's Comprehension of Content," *Child Development* 53 (1982): 601–10; and D. S. Hayes and D. W. Birnbaum, "Preschoolers' Retention of Televised Events: Is a Picture Worth a Thousand Words?" *Developmental Psychology* 16 (1980): 410–16.

[45]Hockett, "Logical Considerations in the Study of Animal Communication," p. 143.

[46]Branigan, "Here Is a Picture of No Revolver," p. 11.

narrative, even to the extent of inferring information about situations not directly pictured,[47] several scholars have argued that these inferences are organized on a conceptual and propositional—but not necessarily a linguistic—basis. Pylyshyn, for example, suggested that

"Such concepts and predicates may be perceptually well defined without having any explicit natural language label.

Thus we may have a concept corresponding to the equivalence class of certain sounds or visual patterns without an explicit verbal label for it. Such a view implies that we can have mental concepts or ways of abstracting from our sense data which are beyond the reach of our current stock of words, but for which we could develop a vocabulary if communicating such concepts became important."[48] Linguistic models, in other words, are not requisite for explaining how we respond to and make sense out of pictorial information, nor even for describing how we encode visual information for longterm memory storage such that it can be subsequently reaccessed.[49]

As noted, arbitrary-relational signifier models are most applicable where the discourse being examined is language-based rather than strictly pictorial. In his respect, it follows that theories about ideology and ideological effects are best formulated not with regard to pictures sui generis (e.g., as has been done with perspective-based images) or with such machines for seeing as the camera and projector, but rather as a matter of the content of a given film and its modulation via techniques of cinematic style. As Noël Carroll has remarked, ideological design needs to be examined film by film, on an individual case-by-case basis. Because theories about linguistic structure do not seem to be directly applicable to pictures, they therefore form an insufficient basis for grounding a critique of cinematic discourse or the place of ideology in pictorial images.

Proponents of the application of the Saussurean lineage to cinema studies might reply that the poststructural attention to textuality and discourse as culturally relative constructs provides a framework for investigating ideology and the cultural or political polyvalence of a given text. That the poststructural methodology works in this way is undoubtedly true. But, unfortunately, what tends to be displaced are issues of how cinema is able to communicate crossculturally (i.e., attain global popularity) and the even more basic questions of what makes the cinema intelligible to its viewers. Not all cultures organize libidinal and psychic energy in the same way, and one would not therefore wish to posit Lacanian categories as basic mechanisms explicating the means of cinematic communication. Yet all cultures currently studied do demonstrate clear pictorial and cinematic perception abilities. Moreover, these

---

[47]See Patricia Baggett, "Memory for Explicit and Implicit Information in Picture Stories," *Journal of Verbal Learning and Verbal Behavior* 14 (1975): 538–48.

[48]Zenon W. Pylyshyn, "What the Mind's Eye Tells the Mind's Brain: A Critique of Mental Imagery," *Psychological Bulletin* 80, no. 1 (July 1973): 7.

[49]However, with regard to certain categories of pictures—namely, relatively ambiguous ones—some evidence exists to indicate that linguistic cues may influence the recollection of details of pictorial form. See the classic study by L. Carmichael, H. P. Hogan, and A. A. Walter, "An Experimental Study of the Effect of Language on the Reproduction of Visually Perceived Form," *Journal of Experimental Psychology* 15 (1932): 73–86; and the replication by W. C. H. Prentice, "Visual Recognition of Verbally Labelled Figures," *American Journal of Psychology* 67 (1954): 315–20.

abilities are shared with a variety of animals.[50] Picture recognition abilities have been demonstrated across a wide range of nonhuman subjects—primates, birds, fish, reptiles, even insects. These include unlearned, spontaneous responses to still and motion pictures as well as responses that are the result of conditioning. Recognition of objects by nonhuman subjects has been demonstrated across different classes of pictorial media—black-and-white and color photographs, high-contrast photographs, film and videotape, even line drawings. Comprehension of filmed events has been elicited, as well as the formation and pickup of object-class concepts from pictures (e.g., as in the ability of pigeons, trained to recognize human figures in slides of various environments, to transfer this ability and the class concept of "human being" to sets of slides they had never seen before).

Positing arbitrary signifiers and unconscious processes of the mind seems to deflect the ability of cinema studies to grapple with some of the most basic questions about cinema, namely, how are viewers crossculturally able to make sense of the medium and what is the necessary biological basis of pictorial communication that makes it so effective for human and nonhuman subjects alike. As Noël Carroll has recently suggested, emphasizing the way that film structure works to secure the cognitive clarity of the experience for the viewer can give us a basis for explaining the attractiveness and appeal, and perhaps even the emotional power, of the medium.[51]

Furthermore, emphasizing the cinematic code as an arbitrary, unmotivated sign places film theory in the uncomfortable position of implying certain consequences for the real-world viewer that are contrary to the observable evidence, namely, that cinematic images should not function in ways that are isomorphic with their real-world counterparts, that viewers should have to learn the symbolic meanings of basic cinematic structure, and that, logically, because discourse is culture-bound, the appeal of the medium should be too. Film theory has dealt with these problems by pointing to the transparency effect of the cinema or to the illusionism of the photographic image based on what are regarded as the culture-bound and symbolic conventions of perspective. But, as this article has suggested, some important gaps and contradictions are found between these formulations, the Saussurean lineage, and the empirical evidence regarding pictorial recognition and visual communication. Unless film theory can reconceptualize the cinema as an iconic, rather than as a purely symbolic, mode of communication, it is difficult to see how these serious theoretical gaps may be closed. We need to recover a recognition of the analogical component of pictorial signs. Rather than dealing with this component in metaphorical terms (e.g., via transparency effects, subject positioning in the discourse of the Imaginary, or illusionism), an appreciation of the isomorphic relations between pictorial signs and their referents, and attention to the *differences* between pictorial and linguistic modes of communication, can help invigorate film theory by reconnecting it to the observable experiences of real viewers.

---

[50]For a review of picture-perception research involving animals, see Patrick A. Cabe, "Picture Perception in Nonhuman Subjects," in *The Perception of Pictures*, vol. 2, ed. Margaret A. Hagen (New York: Academic Press, 1980), pp. 305–43.

[51]Noël Carroll, *Mystifying Movies* (New York: Columbia University Press, 1988).

As noted at the beginning of this essay, the intention here is not to remove cultural considerations from questions about film viewing and interpretation. Culture clearly enters into the inferences viewers draw from cinematic images and narratives where meaning may be constructed in terms of the intellectual horizons provided by class, race, gender, and similar variables. But it has been the contention of this essay that culture plays a less decisive role at the level of comprehension discussed herein. Furthermore, only by knowing where cultural considerations shade off into what may be more properly termed physiological or cognitive capabilities are we likely to be able to apply cultural analyses in fruitful and relevant ways. This approach can help theory explicate the intelligibility and power of the movies in ways that are responsive to, and grounded in, the observable experiences of actual viewers.

1993

DANIEL DAYAN
THE TUTOR-CODE OF CLASSICAL CINEMA

Daniel Dayan's work focuses on the way audiences receive and are in turn influenced by film, television, and new media. He is co-author with Elihu Katz of *Media Events; The Live Broadcasting of History* (2007), which examines the performance, ritualization, and reception of live broadcasts of spectacular "historical" events. Dayan has also written about the Beijing Olympics, televisual representations of terrorism, and media morality. He is currently professor of media studies at the École des Hautes Études en Sciences Sociales in Paris.

Semiology deals with film in two ways. On the one hand it studies the level of fiction, that is, the organization of film content. On the other hand, it studies the problem of "film language," the level of enunciation. Structuralist critics such as Barthes and the *Cahiers du Cinéma* of "*Young Mr. Lincoln*" have shown that the level of fiction is organized into a language of sorts, a mythical organization through which ideology is produced and expressed. Equally important, however, and far less studied, is filmic enunciation, the system that negotiates the viewer's access to the film—the system that "speaks" the fiction. This study argues that this level is itself far from ideology-free. It does not merely convey neutrally the ideology of the fictional level. As we will see, it is built so as to mask the ideological origin and nature of cinematographic statements. Fundamentally, the enunciation system analyzed below—the system of the *suture*—functions as a "tutor-code." It speaks the codes on which the fiction depends. It is the necessary intermediary between them and us. The system of the suture is to classical cinema what verbal language is to literature. Linguistic studies stop when one reaches the level of the sentence. In the same way, the system analyzed below leads only from the shot to the cinematographic statement. Beyond the statement, the level of enunciation stops. The level of fiction begins.

Our inquiry is rooted in the theoretical work of a particular time and place, which must be specified. The political events of May 1968 transformed reflection on cinema in France. After an idealist period dominated by André Bazin, a phenomenologist period influenced by Cohen-Séat and Jean Mitry, and a structuralist period initiated by the writings of Christian Metz, several film critics and theorists adopted a perspective bringing together semiology and Marxism. This tendency is best

---

Brian Henderson collaborated in writing this article from a previous text.

represented by three groups, strongly influenced by the literary review *Tel Quel*; the cinematographic collective *Dziga Vertov*, headed by Jean-Pierre Gorin and Jean-Luc Godard: the review *Cinéthique*; the new and profoundly transformed *Cahiers du Cinéma*.

After a relatively short period of hesitation and polemics, *Cahiers* established a sort of common front with *Tel Quel* and *Cinéthique*. Their program, during the period which culminated between 1969 and 1971, was to establish the foundations of a science of cinema. Defined by Althusser, this required an "epistemological break" with previous, ideological discourses on cinema. In the post-1968 view of *Cahiers*, ideological discourses included structuralist systems of an empiricist sort. In seeking to effect such a break within discourse on cinema, *Cahiers* concentrated on authors of the second structuralist generation (Kristeva, Derrida, Schefer) and on those of the first generation who opposed any empiricist interpretation of Lévi-Strauss's work.

The point was to avoid any interpretion of a structure that would make it appear as its own cause, thus liberating it from the determinations of the *subject* and of *history*. As Alain Badiou put it,

> The structuralist activity was defined a few years ago as the construction of a "simulacrum of the object," this simulacrum being in itself nothing but intellect added to the object. Recent theoretical work conducted both in the Marxist field and in the psychoanalytic field shows that such a conception of structure should be completely rejected. Such a conception pretends to find inside of the real, a knowledge of which the real can only be the object. Supposedly, this knowledge is already there, just waiting to be revealed.[1]

Unable to understand the causes of a structure, what they are and how they function, such a conception considers the structure as a cause in itself. The effect is substituted for the cause; the cause remains unknown or becomes mythical (the "theological" author). The structuralism of *Cahiers* holds, on the other hand, that there is more to the whole than to the sum of its parts. The structure is not only a result to be described, but the trace of a structuring *function*. The critic's task is to locate the invisible agent of this function. The whole of the structure thus becomes the sum of its parts plus the cause of the structure plus the relationship betwen them, through which the structure is linked to the context that produced it. To study a structure is therefore *not* to search for latent meanings, but to look for that which causes or determines the structure.

Given the *Cahiers* project of a search for causes, what means were available to realize it? As Badiou points out, two systems of thought propose a structural conception of causality, Louis Althusser's Marxism and Jacques Lacan's psychoanalysis. Althusser's theses massively influenced the *Cahiers* theoretical production during the period in question. His influence was constantly commented on and made explicit, both within the *Cahiers* texts and by those who commented on them. Less well understood is the influence on *Cahiers* of Lacanian psychoanalysis, that *other* system from which a science of cinema could be expected to emerge by means of a critique of empiricist structuralism.

---

[1]Cited by Jean Narboni in an article on Jancsó, *Cahiers du Cinéma*, no. 219 (April, 1970).

For Lacan, psychoanalysis is a science.

Lacan's first word is to say: in principle, Freud founded a *science*. A new science which was the science of a new object: the unconscious. . . . If psychoanalysis is a science because it is the science of a distinct object, it is also a science with the structure of all sciences: it has a *theory* and a *technique* (method) that makes possible the knowledge and transformation of its object in a specific *practice*. As in every authentically constituted science, the practice is not the absolute of the science but a theoretically subordinate moment; the moment in which the theory, having become method (technique), comes into theoretical contact (knowledge) or practical contact (cure) with its specific object (the unconscious).[2]

Like Claude Lévi-Strauss, Lacan distinguishes three levels within human reality. The first level is nature, the third is culture. The intermediate is that in which nature is transformed into culture. This particular level gives its structure to human reality—it is the level of the symbolic. The symbolic level, or order, includes both language and other systems which produce signification, but it is fundamentally structured by language.

Lacanian psychoanalysis is a theory of intersubjectivity, in the sense that it addresses the relationship(s) between "self " and "other" independently of the subjects who finally occupy these places. The symbolic order is a net of relationships. Any "self" is definable by its position within this net. From the moment a "self" belongs to culture its fundamental relationships to the "other" are taken in charge by this net. In this way, the laws of the symbolic order give their shape to originally physical drives by assigning the compulsory itineraries through which they can be satisfied. The symbolic order is in turn structured by language. This structuring power of language explains the therapeutic function of speech in psychoanalysis. The psychoanalyst's task is, through the patient's speech, to re-link the patient to the symbolic order, from which he has received his particular mental configuration.

Thus for Lacan, unlike Descartes, the subject is *not* the fundamental basis of cognitive processes. First, it is only one of many psychological functions. Second, it is not an innate function. It appears at a certain time in the development of the child and has to be constituted in a certain way. It can also be altered, stop functioning, and disappear. Being at the very center of what we perceive as our self, this function is invisible and unquestioned. To avoid the encrusted connotations of the term "subjectivity," Lacan calls this function "the imaginary." It must be understood in a literal way—it is the domain of images.

The imaginary can be characterized through the circumstances of its genesis or through the consequences of its disappearance.

The imaginary is constituted through a process which Lacan calls the mirror-phase. It occurs when the infant is six to eighteen months old and occupies a contradictory situation. On the one hand, it does not possess mastery of its body; the various segments of the nervous system are not coordinated yet. The child cannot move or control the whole of its body, but only isolated discrete parts. On the other hand, the child enjoys from its first days a precocious visual maturity. During this stage, the child identifies itself with the visual image of the mother or the person playing

---

[2]Louis Althusser, *Lenin and Philosophy* (New York: Monthly Review Press, 1971), pp. 198–199.

the part of the mother. Through this identification, the child perceives its own body as a unified whole by analogy with the mother's body. The notion of a unified body is thus fantasy before being a reality. It is an image that the child receives from outside.

Through the imaginary function, the respective parts of the body are united so as to constitute one body, and therefore to constitute somebody: one self. Identity is thus a formal structure which fundamentally depends upon an identification. Identity is one effect, among others, of the structure through which images are formed: the imaginary. Lacan thus operates a radical desacralization of the subject: the "I," the "ego," the "subject" are nothing but images, reflections. The imaginary constitutes the subject through a "speculary" effect common to the constitution of all images. A mirror on a wall organizes the various objects of a room into a unified, finite image. So also the "subject" is no more than a unifying reflection.

The disappearance of the imaginary results in schizophrenia. On the one hand, the schizophrenic loses the notion of his "ego" and, more generally, the very notion of ego, of person. He loses both the notion of his identity and the faculty of identification. On the other hand, he loses the notion of the unity of his body. His fantasies are inhabited by horrible visions of dismantled bodies, as in the paintings of Hieronymus Bosch. Finally, the schizophrenic loses his mastery of language. The instance of schizophrenia illuminates the role of language in the functioning of the imaginary in general. Because this relationship language-imaginary is highly important for our subject, the role of the imaginary in cinema, we will pursue this point in some detail.

The role of the imaginary in the utilization of language points to an entire realm of inadequacy, indeed absence, in traditional accounts of language. Saussure merely repressed or avoided the problem of the role of the subject in language utilization. The subject is eliminated from the whole field of Saussurian linguistics. This elimination commands the famous oppositions between code and message, paradigm and syntagm, language system and speech. In each case, Saussure grants linguistic relevance to one of the terms and denies it to the other. (The syntagm term is not eliminated, but is put under the paradigms of syntagms, i.e., syntax). In this way, Saussure distinguishes a deep level of linguistic structures from a superficial one where these structures empirically manifest themselves. The superficial level belongs to the domain of subjectivity, that is, to psychology. "The language system equals language less speech." Speech, however, represents the utilization of language. The entity which Saussure defines is language less its utilization. In the converse way, traditional psychology ignores language by defining thought as prior to it. Despite this mutual exclusion, however, the world of the subject and the universe of language do meet. The subject speaks, understands what he is told, reads, and so on.

To be complete, the structuralist discourse must explain the relationship language/subject. (Note the relevance of Badiou's critique of empiricist structuralism to Saussure.) Here Lacan's definition of the subject as an imaginary function is useful. Schizophrenic regression shows that language cannot function without a subject. This is not the subject of traditional psychology: what Lacan shows is that language cannot function outside of the imaginary. The conjunction of the language system and the imaginary produces the effect of reality: the referential dimension of language. What we perceive as "reality" is definable as the intersection of two functions, either of which may be lacking. In that language is a system of differences, the meaning of a statement is produced negatively, that is, by elimination of the other possibilities formally allowed by the system. The domain of the imaginary translates this negative meaning into a positive one. By organizing the statement into a whole, by giving limits to it, the imaginary transforms the statement into an image, a reflection. By conferring its own unity and continuity upon the statement, the subject organizes it into a body, giving it a fantasmatic identity. This identity, which may be called the "being" or the "ego" of the statement, is its meaning, in the same way that "I" am the meaning of my body's unity.

The imaginary function is not limited to the syntagmatic aspect of language utilization. It commands the paradigms also. A famous passage by Borges, quoted by Foucault in *The Order of Things*, illustrates this point. An imaginary Chinese encyclopedia classified animals by this scheme: (a) belonging to the emperor; (b) embalmed; (c) tamed; (d) guinea-pigs; (e) sirens; (f) fabulous; (g) dogs without a leash; (h) included in the present classification. According to Foucault, such a scheme is "impossible to think" because the sites where things are laid are so different from each other that it becomes impossible to find any surface that would accept all the things mentioned. It is impossible to find a space common to all the animals, a common ground under them. The common place lacking here is that which holds together words and things. The paradigms of language and culture hold together thanks to the perception of a common place, of a "topos" common to its elements. This common place can be defined at the level of history or society as "episteme" or "ideology." This common place is what the schizophrenic lacks.

Thus, in summary, the speculary, unifying, imaginary function constitutes, on the one hand, the proper body of the subject and, on the other, the limits and the common ground without which linguistic syntagms and paradigms would be dissolved in an infinite sea of differences. Without the imaginary and the limit it imposes on any statement, statements would not function as mirrors of the referent.

The imaginary is an essential constituent in the functioning of language. What is its role in the functioning of language? What is its role in *other* semiotic systems? Semiotic systems do not follow the same patterns. Each makes a specific use of the imaginary; that is, each confers a distinctive function upon the subject. We move now from the role of the subject in language use to the role of the subject in classical painting and in classical cinema. Here the writings of Jean-Pierre Oudart, Jean Louis Schefer, and others will serve as a guide in establishing the foundations of our inquiry.[3]

---

[3]See Jean-Louis Schefer, *Scénographie d'un tableau* (Paris: Seuil, 1969); and articles by Jean-Pierre Oudart, "La Suture, I and II," *Cahiers du Cinéma*, nos. 211, 212 (April–May, 1969), "Travail, Lecture, Jouissance," *Cahiers du Cinéma*, no. 222 (with S. Daney, July 1970), "Un discours en defaut," *Cahiers du Cinéma*, no. 232 (October 1971).

We meet at the outset a fundamental difference between language and other semiotic systems. A famous Stalinian judgment established the theoretical status of language: language is neither part of science nor part of ideology. It represents some sort of a third power, appearing to function—to some extent—free of historical influences. The functioning of semiotic systems such as painting and cinema, however, clearly manifests a direct dependency upon ideology and history. Cinema and painting are historical products of human activity. If their functioning assigns certain roles to the imaginary, one must consider these roles as resulting from choices (conscious or unconscious) and seek to determine the rationale of such choices. Oudart therefore asks a double question: What is the semiological functioning of the classical painting? Why did the classical painters develop it?

Oudart advances the following answers. (1) Classical figurative painting is a discourse. This discourse is produced according to figurative codes. These codes are directly produced by ideology and are therefore subjected to historical transformations. (2) This discourse defines in advance the role of the subject, and therefore predetermines the reading of the painting. The imaginary (the subject) is used by the painting to mask the presence of the figurative codes. Functioning without being perceived, the codes reinforce the ideology which they embody while the painting produces "an impression of reality" (*effet-de-réel*). This invisible functioning of the figurative codes can be defined as a "naturalization": the impression of reality produced testifies that the figurative codes are "natural" (instead of being ideological products). It imposes as "truth" the vision of the world entertained by a certain class. (3) This exploitation of the imaginary, this utilization of the subject is made possibly by the presence of a system which Oudart calls "representation." This system englobes the painting, the subject, and their relationship upon which it exerts a tight control.

Oudart's position here is largely influenced by Schefer's *Scénographie d'un tableau.* For Schefer, the image of an object must be understood to be the pretext that the painter uses to illustrate the system through which he translates ideology into perceptual schemes. The object represented is a "pretext" for the painting as a "text" to be produced. The object hides the painting's textuality by preventing the viewer from focusing on it. However, the text of the painting is totally offered to view. It is, as it were, hidden *outside* the object. It is here but we do not see it. We see through it to the imaginary object. Ideology is hidden in our very eyes.

How this codification and its hiding process work Oudart explains by analyzing *Las Meninas* by Velasquez.[4] In this painting, members of the court and the painter himself look out at the spectator. By virtue of a mirror in the back of the room (depicted at the center of the painting), we see what they are looking at: the king and queen, whose portrait Velasquez is painting. Foucault calls this the representation of classical representation, because the spectator—usually invisible—is here inscribed into the painting itself. Thus the painting represents its own functioning, but in a paradoxical, contradictory way. The painter is staring at us, the spectators who pass in front of the canvas; but the mirror reflects only one, unchanging thing, the royal couple. Through

---

[4]Oudart borrows here from ch. 1 of Michel Foucault's *The Order of Things* (London: Tavistock, 1970).

this contradiction, the system of "representation" points toward its own functioning. In cinematographic terms the mirror represents the reverse shot of the painting. In theatrical terms, the painting represents the stage while the mirror represents its audience. Oudart concludes that the text of the painting must not be reduced to its visible part; it does not stop where the canvas stops. The text of the painting is a system which Oudart defines as a double-stage. On one stage, the show is enacted; on the other, the spectator looks at it. In classical representation, the visible is only the first part of a system which always includes an invisible second part (the "reverse shot").

Historically speaking, the system of classical representation may be placed in the following way. The figurative techniques of the quattrocento constituted a figurative system which permitted a certain type of pictorial utterance. Classical representation produces the same type of utterances but submits them to a characteristic transformation—by presenting them as the embodiment of the glance of a subject. The pictorial discourse is not only a discourse which uses figurative codes. It is that which somebody sees.

Thus, even without the mirror in *Las Meninas*, the other stage would be part of the text of the painting. One would still notice the attention in the eyes of the painting's figures, etc. But even such psychological clues only reinforce a structure which could function without them. Classical representation as a system does not depend upon the subject of the painting. The Romantic landscapes of the nineteenth century submit nature to a remodeling which imposes on them a monocular perspective, transforming the landscape into that which is seen by a given subject. This type of landscape is very different from the Japanese landscape with its multiple perspective. The latter is *not* the visible part of a two-stage system.

While it uses figurative codes and techniques, the distinctive feature of representaiton as a semiological system is that it transforms the painted object into a sign. The object which is figured on the canvas in a certain way is the signifier of the presence of a subject who is looking at it. The paradox of *Las Meninas* proves that the presence of the subject must be signified but empty, defined but left free. Reading the signifers of the presence of the subject, the spectator occupies this place. His own subjectivity fills the empty spot predefined by the painting. Lacan stresses the unifying function of the imaginary, through which the act of reading is made possible. The representational painting is *already unified*. The painting proposes not only itself, but its own reading. The specator's imaginary can only coincide with the painting's built-in subjectivity. The receptive freedom of the spectator is reduced to the minimum—he has to accept or reject the painting as a whole. This has important consequences, ideologically speaking.

When I occupy the place of the subject, the codes which led me to occupy this place become invisible to me. The signifiers of the presence of the subject disappear from my consciousness because they are the signifiers of my presence. What I perceive is their signified: myself. If I want to understand the painting and not just be instrumental in it as a catalyst to its ideological operation, I must avoid the empirical relationship it imposes on me. To understand the ideology which the painting conveys, I must avoid providing my own imaginary as a support for that ideology. I must refuse that identification which the painting so imperiously proposes to me.

Oudart stresses that the initial relationship between a subject and any ideological object is set up by ideology as a trap which prevents any real knowledge concerning the object. This trap is built upon the properties of the imaginary and must be deconstructed through a critique of these properties. On this critique depends the possibility of a real knowledge. Oudart's study of classical painting provides the analyst of cinema with two important tools for such a critique: the concept of a double-stage and the concept of the entrapment of the subject.

We note first that the filmic image considered in isolation, the single frame or the perfectly static shot, is (for purposes of our analysis) equivalent to the classical painting. Its codes, even though "analogic" rather than figurative, are organized by the system of representation: it is an image designed and organized not merely as an object that is seen, but as the glance of a subject. Can there be a cinematography not based upon the system of representation? This is an interesting and important question which cannot be explored here. It would seem that there has not been such a cinematography. Certainly the classical narrative cinema, which is our present concern, is founded upon the representation system. The case for blanket assimilation of cinema to the system of representation is most strongly put by Jean-Louis Baudry, who argues that the perceptual system and ideology of representation are built into the cinematographic apparatus itself.[5] Camera lenses organize their visual field according to the laws of perspective, which thereby operate to render it as the perception of a subject. Baudry traces this system to the sixteenth and seventeenth centuries, during which the lens technology which still governs photography was developed.

Of course cinema cannot be reduced to its still frames and the semiotic system of cinema cannot be reduced to the systems of painting or of photography. Indeed, the cinematic succession of images threatens to interrupt or even to expose and to deconstruct the representation system which commands static paintings or photos. For its succession of shots is, by that very system, a succession of views. The viewer's identification with the subjective function proposed by the painting or photograph is broken again and again during the viewing of a film. Thus cinema regularly and systematically raises the question which is exceptional in painting (*Las Meninas*): "Who is watching this?" The point of attack of Oudart's analysis is precisely here—what happens to the spectator-image relation by virtue of the shot-change peculiar to cinema?

The ideological question is hardly less important than the semiological one and, indeed, is indispensable to its solution. From the standpoint of the imaginary and of ideology, the problem is that cinema threatens to expose its own functioning as a semiotic system, as well as that of painting and photography. If cinema consists in a series of shots which have been produced, selected, and ordered in a certain way, then these operations will serve, project, and realize a certain ideological position. The viewer's question, cued by the system of representation itself—"Who is watching this?" and "Who is ordering these images?"—tends, however, to expose this ideological operation and its mechanics. Thus the viewer will be aware (1) of

---

[5]"Ideological Effects of the Basic Cinematographic Apparatus," *Cinéthique* 7–8 (1970).

the cinematographic system for producing ideology and (2) therefore of specific ideological messages produced by this system. We know that ideology cannot work in this way. It must hide its operations, "naturalizing" its functioning and its messages in some way. Specifically, the cinematographic system for producing ideology must be hidden and the relation of the filmic message to this system must be hidden. As with classical painting, the code must be hidden by the message. The message must appear to be complete in itself, coherent and readable entirely on its own terms. In order to do this, the filmic message must account *within itself* for those elements of the code which it seeks to hide—changes of shot and, above all, what lies behind these changes, the questions "Who is viewing this?" and "Who is ordering these images?" and "For what purpose are they doing so?" In this way, the viewer's attention will be restricted to the message itself and the codes will not be noticed. That system by which the filmic message provides answers to the viewer's questions—imaginary answers—is the object of Oudart's analysis.

Narrative cinema presents itself as a "subjective" cinema. Oudart refers here not to avant-garde experiments with subjective cameras, but to the vast majority of fiction films. These films propose images which are subtly designated and intuitively perceived as corresponding to the point of view of one character or another. The point of view varies. There are also moments when the image does not represent anyone's point of view; but in the classical narrative cinema, these are relatively exceptional. Soon enough, the image is reasserted as somebody's point of view. In this cinema, the image is only "objective" or "impersonal" during the intervals between its acting as the actors' glances. Structurally, this cinema passes constantly from the personal to the impersonal form. Note, however, that when this cinema adopts the personal form, it does so somewhat obliquely, rather like novelistic descriptions which use "he" rather than "I" for descriptions of the central character's experience. According to Oudart, this obliqueness is typical of the narrative cinema: it gives the impression of being subjective while never or almost never being strictly so. When the camera *does* occupy the very place of a protagonist, the normal functioning of the film is impeded. Here Oudart agrees with traditional film grammars. Unlike them, however, Oudart can justify this taboo, by showing that this necessary obliquity of the camera is part of a coherent system. This system is that of the suture. It has the function of transforming a vision or seeing of the film into a reading of it. It introduces the film (irreducible to its frames) into the realm of signification.

Oudart contrasts the seeing and the reading of a film by comparing the experiences associated with each. To *see* the film is *not* to perceive the frame, the camera angle and distance, etc. The space between planes or objects on the screen is perceived as real, hence the viewer may perceive himself (in relation to this space) as fluidity, expansion, elasticity.

When the viewer discovers the frame—the first step in reading the film—the triumph of his former *possession* of the image fades out. The viewer discovers that the camera is hiding things, and therefore distrusts it and the frame itself, which he now understands to be arbitrary. He wonders why the frame is what it is. This radically transforms his mode of participation—the unreal space between characters and/or objects is no longer perceived as pleasurable. It is now the space which separates the camera from the characters. The latter have lost their quality of presence.

Space puts them between parentheses so as to assert its own presence. The spectator discovers that his possession of space was only partial, illusory. He feels dispossessed of what he is prevented from seeing. He discovers that he is only authorized to see what happens to be in the axis of the glance of another spectator, who is ghostly or absent. This ghost, who rules over the frame and robs the spectator of his pleasure, Oudart proposes to call "the absent-one" (*l'absent*).

The description above is not contingent or impressionistic—the experiences outlined are the effects of a system. The system of the absent-one distinguishes cinematography, a system producing meaning, from any impressed strip of film (mere footage). This system depends, like that of classical painting, upon the fundamental opposition between two fields: (1) what I see on the screen, (2) that complementary field which can be defined as the place from which the absent-one is looking. Thus: any filmic field defined by the camera corresponds to *another* field from which an absence emanates.

So far we have remained at the level of the shot. Oudart now considers that common cinematographic utterance which is composed of a shot and a reverse shot. In the first, the missing field imposes itself upon our consciousness under the form of the absent-one who is looking at what we see. In the second shot, the reverse shot of the first, the missing field is abolished by the presence of somebody or something occupying the absent-one's field. The reverse shot represents the fictional owner of the glance corresponding to shot one.

This shot/reverse shot system orders the experience of the viewer in this way. The spectator's pleasure, dependent upon his identification with the visual field, is interrupted when he perceives the frame. From this perception he infers the presence of the absent-one and that other field from which the absent-one is looking. Shot two reveals a character who is presented as the owner of the glance corresponding to shot one. That is, the character in shot two occupies the place of the absent-one corresponding to shot one. This character retrospectively transforms the absence emanating from shot one's other stage into a presence.

What happens in *systemic* terms is this: the absent-one of shot one is an element of the code that is attracted into the message by means of shot two. When shot two replaces shot one, the absent-one is transferred from the level of enunciation to the level of fiction. As a result of this, the code effectively disappears and the ideological effect of the film is thereby secured. The code, which *produces* an imaginary, ideological effect, is hidden by the message. Unable to see the workings of the code, the spectator is at its mercy. His imaginary is sealed into the film; the spectator thus absorbs an ideological effect without being aware of it, as in the very different system of classical painting.

The consequences of this system deserve careful attention. The absent-one's glance is that of a nobody, which becomes (with the reverse shot) the glance of a somebody (a character present on the screen). Being on screen he can no longer compete with the spectator for the screen's possession. The spectator can resume his previous relationship with the film. The reverse shot has "sutured" the hole opened in the spectator's imaginary relationship with the filmic field by his perception of the absent-one. This effect and the system which produces it liberates the imaginary of the spectator, in order to manipulate if for its own ends.

Besides a *liberation of the imaginary*, the system of the suture also commands a *production of meaning*. The spectator's inference of the absent-one and the other field must be described more precisely: it is a *reading*. For the spectator who becomes frame-conscious, the visual field *means* the presence of the absent-one as the owner of the glance that constitutes the image. The filmic field thus simultaneously belongs to representation and to signification. Like the classical painting, on the one hand it represents objects or beings, on the other hand it signifies the presence of a spectator. When the spectator ceases to identify with the image, the image necessarily signifies to him the presence of another spectator. The filmic image presents itself here not as a simple image but as a show, that is, it structurally asserts the presence of an audience. The filmic field is then a signifier; the absent-one is its signified. Since it represents another field from which a fictional character looks at the field corresponding to shot one, the reverse shot is offered to the film audience as being the other field, the field of the absent-one. In this way, shot two establishes itself as the signified of shot one. By substituting for the other field, shot two becomes the meaning of shot one.

Within the system of the suture, the absent-one can therefore be defined as the intersubjective "trick" by means of which the second part of a given representative statement is no longer simply what comes after the first part, but what is *signified* by it. The absent-one makes the different parts of a given statement the signifiers of each other. His stratagem: Break the statement into shots. Occupy the space between shots.

Oudart thus defines the basic statement of classical cinematography as a unit composed of two terms: the filmic field and the field of the absent-one. The sum of these two terms, stages, and fields realizes the meaning of the statement. Robert Bresson once spoke of an exchange between shots. For Oudart such an exchange is impossible—the exchange between shot one and shot two cannot take place directly. Between shot one and shot two the other stage corresponding to shot one is a necessary intermediary. The absent-one represents the exchangability between shots. More precisely, within the system of the suture, the absent-one represents the fact that no shot can constitute by itself a complete statement. The absent-one stands for that which any shot necessarily lacks in order to attain meaning: another shot. This brings us to the dynamics of meaning in the system of the suture.

Within this system, the meaning of a shot depends on the next shot. At the level of the signifier, the absent-one continually destroys the balance of a filmic statement by making it the incomplete part of a whole yet to come. On the contrary, at the level of the signified, the effect of the suture system is a retroactive one. The character presented in shot two does not replace the absent-one corresponding to shot two, but the absent-one corresponding to shot one. The suture is always chronologically posterior to the corresponding shot, that is, when we finally know what the other field was, the filmic field is no longer on the screen. The meaning of a shot is given retrospectively, it does not meet the shot on the screen, but only in the memory of the spectator.

The process of reading the film (perceiving its meaning) is therefore a retroactive one, wherein the present modifies the past. The system of the suture systematically encroaches upon the spectator's freedom by interpreting, indeed by remodeling his memory. The spectator is torn to pieces, pulled in opposite directions. On the one hand, a retroactive process organizes the *signified*. On the other hand, an anticipatory process organizes the *signifier*. Falling under the control of the cinematographic system, the spectator loses access to the present. When the absent-one points toward it, the signification belongs to the future. When the suture realizes it, the signification belongs to the past. Oudart insists on the brutality, on the tyranny with which this signification imposes itself on the spectator or, as he puts it, "transits through him."

Oudart's analysis of classical cinema is a deconstruction not a destruction of it. To deconstruct a system implies that one inhabits it, studies its functioning very carefully, and locates its basic articulations, both external and internal. Of course there are other cinematographic systems besides that of the suture.[6] One of many such others is that of Godard's late films such as *Wind from the East*. Within this system, (1) the shot tends to constitute a complete statement, and (2) the absent-one is continuously perceived by the spectator. Since the shot constitutes a whole statement, the reading of the film is no longer suspended. The spectator is not kept waiting for the remaining-part-of-the statement-which-is-yet-to-come. The reading of the shot is contemporary to the shot itself. It is immediate, its temporality is the present.

Thus the absent-one's functional definition does not change. Within the Godardian system as well as within the suture system the absent-one is what ties the shot (filmic level) to the statement (cinematographic level). However, in Godard's case, the two levels are not disjoined. Cinematography does not hide the filmicity of the shot. It stands in a clear relationship to it.

The system of the suture represents exactly the opposite choice. The absent-one is masked, replaced by a character, hence the real origin of the image—the conditions of its production represented by the absent-one—is replaced with a false origin and this false origin is situated inside the fiction. The cinematographic level fools the spectator by connecting him to the fictional level rather than to the filmic level.

But the difference between the two origins of the image is not only that one (filmic) is true and the other (fictional) false. The true origin represents the cause of the image. The false origin suppresses that cause and does not offer anything in exchange. The character whose glance takes possession of the image did not produce it. He is only somebody who sees, a spectator. The image therefore exists independently. It has no cause. It is.

In other terms, it is its own cause. By means of the suture, the film-discourse presents itself as a product without a producer, a discourse without an origin. It speaks. Who speaks? Things speak for themselves and, of course, they tell the truth. Classical cinema establishes itself as the ventriloquist of ideology.

1974

---

[6]Indeed, shot/reverse shot is itself merely one figure in the system(s) of classical cinema. In this initial moment of enunciation in film, we have chosen it as a privileged example of the way in which the origin of the glance is displaced in order to hide the film's production of meaning.

WILLIAM ROTHMAN
AGAINST "THE SYSTEM OF THE SUTURE"

William Rothman received a Ph.D. in Philosophy from Harvard University, where he studied with Stanley Cavell, whose work he has analyzed with Marian Keane in *Reading Cavell's "The World Viewed": A Philosophical Perspective on Film* (2001). His writing on film is largely concerned with questions of authorship, a subject he deals with extensively in *Hitchcock: The Murderous Gaze* (1982) and *The "I" of the Camera* (1988). He has written on the films of D. W. Griffith, Billy Wilder, Yasujiro Ozu, and the documentary films of the 1970s, in addition to writing screenplays. He is currently professor of motion pictures at the University of Miami.

Dayan is interested in what he calls the "system of enunciation" basic to "classical" cinema.

He writes, "Structuralist critics such as Barthes and the *Cahiers du Cinéma of 'Young Mr. Lincoln'* have shown that the level of fiction is organized into a language of sorts, a mythical organization through which ideology is produced and expressed. Equally important, however, and far less studied, is filmic enunciation, the system that negotiates the viewer's access to the film—the system that 'speaks' the fiction."[1]

The system of enunciation of classical cinema, the "tutor-code" which "speaks the codes on which the fiction depends," is, according to Dayan (here as elsewhere in the article in large part summarizing the ideas of Jean-Pierre Oudart, who in turn draws on many sources) *the system of the suture.*

This is not the forum for a detailed criticism of Dayan's position from a theoretical point of view. Such a criticism might well systematically investigate his use of terms such as "ideology," "system," "codes," "classical cinema," "fiction," "enunciation," "de-construction" and so on—each of which is used in a way loaded with theoretical implications which could be challenged. Nor for a thorough analysis of the prose strategy of invoking—and assuming the authority of—a body of writing that is only partially explained and yet unavailable to the ordinary reader's independent criticism. Nor for a critical account of the interpenetration of structuralism, semiology, modernism, and Marxism which find expression in Oudart and the other writers Dayan cites.

I will rather concentrate on what I take to be clear-cut flaws in Dayan's argument.

According to Oudart/Dayan, the system of the suture is grounded in a two-shot figure. This figure causes the viewer's experience to conform to a certain scenario.

---

[1] Daniel Dayan, "The Tutor-code of Classical Cinema," *Film Quarterly*, vol.28, no.1 (Fall 1974), 22–31. All subsequent references are to this article.

In the first shot, the viewer discovers the frame.

> When the viewer discovers the frame—the first step in reading the film—the triumph of his former *possession* of the image fades out. The viewer discovers that the camera is hiding things, and therefore distrusts it and the frame itself, which he now understands to be arbitrary. He wonders why the frame is what it is. This radically transforms his mode of participation—the unreal space between characters and/or objects is no longer perceived as pleasurable. . . . He feels dispossessed of what he is prevented from seeing. He discovers that he is only authorized to see what happens to be in the axis of the glance of another spectator, who is ghostly or absent. This ghost, who rules over the frame and robs the spectator of his pleasure, Oudart proposed to call "the absent-one."

In the second shot, the reverse field shot of the first, "the missing field is abolished by the presence of somebody or something occupying the absent-one's field. The reverse shot represents the fictional owner of the glance corresponding to shot one."

The first shot as it were opens a hole in the spectator's imaginary relationship with the filmic field. This hole is "sutured" by the shot of the character presented as the absent-one of the preceding shot. Then "the spectator can resume his previous relationship with the film."

At the same time, the second shot constitutes the meaning of the first shot, and the system of the suture makes a "cinematographic statement" out of the pair of shots. The first shot presents, say, a view looking across Bodega Bay to the Brenner home, and as it were raises the question, "Whose view is this?"[2] The second shot presents itself as answering that question, thereby revealing the meaning of the first shot. It is *Melanie Daniels*' view.

It is Oudart's and Dayan's central contention that this system is an intrinsically tyrannical one. "It does not merely convey neutrally the ideology of the fictional level. . . . It is built so as to mask the ideological origin and nature of cinematographic statements." The first shot raises a question as to the source of the image. The second shot identifies that source as a character within the fiction. The two-shot figure constitutes a statement about itself. This statement is a *lie*.

Dayan argues that this sequence of "experiences" (the viewer's discomforting discovery of the frame; his uncertainty as to why the frame is what it is; his realization that he is only authorized to see what is contained in the glance of an "absent-one" who rules over that frame; his acceptance of the figure shown in the subsequent reverse shot *as* that sovereign "absent-one") is not contingent: it is the effect of a system.

But *what* is the "system" of which the above outlined experiences are effects? Studying Dayan's article, it becomes clear that he has not in fact described any mechanism which could cause a viewer to "discover the frame," and so on.

I see this failure as linked to a general uncertainty as to the actual role of the "system of the suture" in classical film. At times, Dayan writes as if it were *the* "system of enunciation" of classical cinema ("the system of the suture is to classical cinema what verbal language is to literature," etc.). But at other times (for example, in a footnote that appears added as an afterthought, despite the apparent centrality of

---

[2]Throughout, I will use this example from *The Birds*. The sequence is analyzed in detail, shot by shot, by Raymond Bellour in *Cahiers du Cinéma*, no. 216 (October 1969): 24–38.

the point it registers) he modifies the claim: it is *one* of the central enunciation systems of classical cinema (although still a "privileged" one).

The Oudart/Dayan scenario is predicated on a "previous" relationship which the viewer is said to enjoy with the film—an initial relationship that is supposedly disrupted by the viewer's discovery of the frame, and to which he returns when that disruption is "sutured." Dayan understands this to be a relationship in which the viewer "sees" rather than "reads" the film. This relationship is comparable to the relationship between spectator and representational painting, as Oudart analyses it.

Then how and why is this relationship disrupted?

Is it that film "naturally" disrupts this relationship? If that were the case, there would be no need for an explanation of the *means* by which classical cinema effects such a disruption, nor for an account of its (historical) motivation. Is it that this disruption is the necessary consequence of cutting from shot to shot in a film (as Dayan seems to suggest at one point)? But then it would need to be explained why shot changes were ever instituted.

In fact, the natural suggestion is that the strategies and "rules" of *continuity cutting* developed by Griffith and his contemporaries and followers (crystallized in the "30° rule," the "180° rule," and others) constituted precisely a system for sustaining *across shot changes* just that relationship between the viewer and the film that Dayan takes to be disrupted by the viewer's discovery of the frame. This means that the "system of the suture" was—for some reason, and in some manner—instituted despite the priority of a system which would appear to have satisfied the demands of *bourgeois* "illusionism." Given the system of continuity cutting (which would seem to have made film an extension of painting's system of representation), the viewer had to be *made* aware of the frame for the "system of the suture" to be instituted. How this awareness was effected, and what motivated the institution of this system, then become questions crucial to our understanding of "classical cinema" and its history.

Although I cannot argue this claim here, I would wish to assert that once the relationship between continuity cutting and the "system of the suture" (that is to say, *point-of-view cutting*)[3] is opened up to serious investigation, Dayan's assumption of a "previous relationship" in which the viewer "sees" the film image as an unmediated image of reality will have to be challenged. The time has come for a re-examination of the whole idea that classical narrative continuity is "illusionistic." I will here only suggest that Dayan's avoidance of a serious consideration of the historical

---

[3]Dayan avoids the term "point-of-view shot." I see no reason to follow him in this. The kind of shot whose frame is discovered in his scenario is what everyone knows is called a point-of-view shot. Dayan's terminology gives us no way of referring to the "figure" of which the point-of-view shot is part. If we call it a "shot/reverse shot pair," that does not differentiate it from the shot/reverse shot forms which do *not* contain point-of-view shots. In *The Birds*, the dialogue between Melanie and the mother is an example of this non-point-of-view shot/reverse shot form. Characteristically used in the filming of dialogues, it is logically and historically distinct from the kind of point-of-view sequence Dayan is describing. Then again, point-of-view sequences must also be differentiated from "subjective" sequences which attempt to render directly non-objective states of consciousness (rather than a view objectively seen by a fictional viewer). Hitchcock uses subjective rather than point-of-view form in *Notorious*, for example, to convey Ingrid Bergman's experience of poisoning.

motivation of the "system of the suture" and his avoidance of a serious consideration of continuity cutting, in general, are aspects of a single strategy.

Once we address ourselves to the question of how the viewer actually reads a
point-of-view shot, a fundamental error in the Oudart/Dayan scenario becomes
apparent.

The scenario presumes that the "system of the suture" is based on a two-shot
[view/viewer] figure: a pair of shots which together constitute a complete cinematographic statement.

But in fact, the point-of-view shot is ordinarily (that is to say, *always*, except in
special cases) part of a three shot [viewer/view/viewer] sequence.

Typically, such a sequence is initiated when, within an "objective" shot, a character visibly attends to something outside the borders of the frame. For example,
Melanie looks out from her boat to something we cannot see. This constitutes a
cue that the next shot may be a point-of-view shot presenting that "absent-view"
to the viewer. Sure enough, we get the shot looking across the Bay, as if in response
to the question, "What is she looking at?" (or "What does she see?"). Then we get
a "reaction shot," which shows us Melanie's reaction to what she has seen, and at
the same time confirms that the previous shot *was* from her point of view. (As is
usual with Hitchcock, no particular identifiable emotion is registered in the reaction shot.)[4]

Thus the point-of-view shot is ordinarily introduced by a shot which calls attention to its own frame by indicating (by a *cue*) that there is something about to be
shown that lies outside the boundaries of that frame. This cue is a condition of the
viewer's discovery of the frame of the point-of-view shot itself. The viewer recognizes this as a point-of-view shot from Melanie's point of view in part because the
cue establishes the significance of Melanie's absence from the following frame. The
viewer perceives Melanie as significantly absented from that frame, and hence indirectly perceives the frame. This perception is a condition of the viewer's reading of
the shot as one from Melanie's point of view.

Note that this specifically reverses the Oudart/Dayan scenario. It is not that the
viewer discovers the frame of the shot looking out across Bodega Bay (unaccount-
ably), infers a sovereign "absent-one," and falls prey to a tyrannical system, which
makes him take Melanie, shown in the reverse shot, to be that absent-one. Rather,
following on the first shot of the sequence with its conventional cue that asserts its

---

[4]Two points. (a) The third shot can double as the initial shot of a second point-of-view sequence. The
shot that presents Melanie's reaction to what she has just seen also shows her continuing to look. Thus
it contains a cue that prepares the viewer for another point-of-view shot. An extended series of tele-
scoped point-of-view sequences can be constructed in this way. (This is in fact the case at this point in
The Birds.) Dayan's model cannot easily accommodate this possibility. (b) A general distinction can be
drawn between point-of-view sequences which attribute a particular (psychological) reaction to the character whose view is presented, and sequences which provide no psychologically unambiguous reaction
shot. The Hitchcock point-of-view sequence ordinarily authorizes the viewer to accept with no possibility of doubt that the character has seen what the point-of-view shot has just shown. The meaning of
that view is not revealed by the character's "reaction," but in the actions he proceeds to take which
acknowledge, or withhold acknowledgment of, what he has witnessed.

frame, the viewer perceives Melanie's absence from the next frame. Perception of this specific absence is a condition of the viewer's reading of it as a shot from her point of view. This reading is confirmed by the third shot of the sequence, with its return to Melanie.

No ghostly sovereign is invoked by the point-of-view sequence.

According to the Oudart/Dayan scenario, the viewer discovers that he is "only authorized to see what happens to be in the axis of the glance of another spectator, who is ghostly or absent." *This ghost rules over the frame and robs the spectator of his pleasure.* The implication is that it is this ghost who "authorizes" the shot we are presented, who is *responsible* for the film, who *produces* the image. Thus when we accept as that "absent-one" the figure shown in the reverse shot, we are accepting what is in reality a fictional character created by the film as the creator of the film. We accept a lying statement as to the film's real source or production.

But when the viewer takes Melanie to be the "owner" of the glance corresponding to the point-of-view shot, he in no way regards Melanie as *authorizing* that shot. On the contrary, the point-of-view shot is read as an *appropriation* of her gaze. It is read as *unauthorized* by her.

The point-of-view sequence, then, ordinarily manifests the film's power of appropriating a character's gaze without authorization. It does *not* then present a figure and force the viewer to accept it as the source of that power.

Thus the point-of-view sequence in itself does not constitute a lying statement about its own real origin. Melanie is *not* presented as the real source of the image we read as "hers." The image of Melanie is manifestly derived from the same source as the image that we read as an appropriation of her gaze. Again, the sequence in itself does not constitute a statement about that source. (But the possiblity cannot be ruled out a priori that the film as a whole inscribes a statement about that source, which may truthfully acknowledge that this is a film and its world is not present.)

Dayan writes as if viewers did not know what point-of-view shots *were*, as if they did not possess the *category* of the point-of-view shot. But, of course, films that use point-of-view shots are designed for viewers who are familiar with their logic, who know how to recognize and read them.

I have spoken of the viewer's perception of "cues" that lead him to read the subsequent shot as a point-of-view shot. It is perfectly possible for a viewer to recognize such a cue and to read the point-of-view sequence correctly whether or not he has had any particular "experiences" at all. A point-of-view sequence does not depend for its reading on its "effects." It is an error to suppose that point-of-view sequences simply correspond to some "system" that can be defined by its "effects."

Not only is a point-of-view sequence not dependent for its reading on any particular effects, but its reading also does not depend on the viewer's acceptance of the *reality* of the world projected in the film. The viewer can "read" a point-of-view sequence whether or not he takes the film's world to correspond to "reality."

Dayan has given no argument that counters the commonsense position that the "effects" of a point-of-view sequence depend on the sequence, its context within the particular film, and also on the viewer's stance toward it. So, too, whether a point-of-view sequence is integral to an ideological project of a particular kind depends on the sequence and on the film. And whether a film's ideological project is *successful*—whether a viewer will actually submit to a film designed to tyrannize—depends in part on the attitude of the viewer.

Part of what I am saying is that the point-of-view sequence in itself makes no statement about reality—that is, makes no statement—at all.

Christian Metz erred in his supposition that a single shot in a "classical" film is equivalent to a *sentence*. As Dayan shows, a single shot is ordinarily incomplete ("grammatically"). But Dayan in turn is wrong in concluding that a "sutured" sequence of shots in itself constitutes a *statement*. The point-of-view sequence, with its syntactical structure, is analogous to a *sentence*, not a statement. In itself, it makes no claim that is true or false.

Films have been used in many ways. The making of various kinds of statements is, historically, among the uses of "classical" films. In order to make its statement, a film may require that a particular point-of-view sequence be placed in a specific setting within it.

Again, it seems to me that it is the film and not the sequence that constitutes the statement (if the film *makes* a statement). The statement thus made by a film may be, at one level, a statement—lying or truthful—about itself. Whether a film makes a false statement about itself, or about the world, cannot be settled merely by determining whether the film incorporates point-of-view sequences into its form.[5]

I think it is clear that Dayan has not succeeded in demonstrating that a point-of-view sequence as such, by its very nature, necessarily turns any film that depends on it (and thus the whole body of "classical" films) into a system of *bourgeois* ideology. *Distinctions have to be made*, grounded in serious acts of criticism, and integrated into a serious history.

But Dayan's argument was designed as a demonstration that such distinctions do not have to be made. If classical cinema depends on a system of enunciation that is by its very nature ideological (*bourgeois*), then criticism and history can be reduced to (replaced by) "de-construction."

Dayan begins from the assumption that he already knows what "classical cinema" *is*: a *bourgeois* ideological system. Of course, he also assumes that he already knows what "*bourgeois* ideology" is. Dayan's writing reveals the attitude that "*bourgeois* ideology" and "classical cinema" are a-historical absolutes, linked by their essences which may be abstracted from history. Throughout Dayan's article, there is an unacknowledged tension between the Marxist trappings he adopts and the fundamentally anti-Marxist idea that point-of-view sequences and hence "classical"

---

[5]Dayan is clearly wrong as well in suggesting that the shot of the "owner" constitutes the *meaning* of the point-of-view shot. If that were so, what is contained within the frame of the point-of-view shot itself would be irrelevant to its meaning. That is hardly plausible. The point-of-view shot has significance within the film, which arises in part from the identity of the character whose view it is, in part from the occasion of his act of viewing, and in part from what is contained in the view itself. In the same way, the meaning of an utterance "in the real world" is determined by the identity of the person who utters it, by the specific circumstances of his act of uttering these words, and also by the meanings of the words he utters.

films are *by their very nature* (regardless of history) reflections of a timeless *bourgeois* ideology.

The commonsense position would appear to be that "classical cinema" has through its complex history served a variety of masters. "Classical" films, to be sure, have in countless cases served many different forms of *bourgeois* ideology. But they have also been instrumental in concrete attacks on particular ideological forms. Nor has Dayan said anything which would rule out the possiblity that there have been "classical" films that were their *own* masters.

We ought not to let ourselves feel constrained from the outset to deny on a priori grounds that there are fundamental differences among point-of-view sequences and the films that use them.

Dayan argues that *Wind from the East* resorts to an alternative system of enunciation in formulating its anti-*bourgeois* acknowledgment of its own form and production. But *Man with a Movie Camera* would appear to be no less anti-*bourgeois* for its systematic use of point-of-view technique (Vertov can be said to use point-of-view sequences in this film as a tool for his de-construction of conventional narrative forms).[6] And I have been working on a critical analysis of late Hitchcock films which attempts to demonstrate that Hitchcock attacks conventional uses of point-of-view form by taking its logic absolutely seriously. Hitchcock does not "de-construct" the fundamental forms of "classical cinema": he acknowledges the meanings his films have accorded them.

Again: what we need is a serious history of cinematic forms, grounded in critical analyses of the significant uses to which these forms were put. Dayan proposes in place of such a concrete history an a priori demonstration that certain forms of cinema are destined by their nature to serve *bourgeois* ideology, and thus do not stand in need of serious critical acknowledgment.

1975

---

[6]Linda Podheiser has analyzed Vertov's use of point-of-view technique in an unpublished paper.

NICK BROWNE
THE SPECTATOR-IN-THE-TEXT: THE RHETORIC OF *STAGECOACH*

Nick Browne's *Rhetoric of Filmic Narration* (1982) explores through semiotic analysis the way the points of view of narrator, characters, and spectator are organized by the visual structure in the films of three prominent directors: John Ford, Alfred Hitchcock, and Robert Bresson. Browne's recent work has focused on depictions of violence in contemporary American film with emphasis on the public health repercussions of such representations. He has edited the anthologies *Chinese Cinemas: Forms, Identities, Politics* (1994), *Refiguring American Film Genres: History and Theory* (1998), and *Francis Ford Coppola's Godfather Trilogy* (2000), as well as co-edited the English translation of *Cahiers du Cinéma* (1990). He is currently professor of film studies in the department of film, television, and digital media at the University of California, Los Angeles.

The sequence from John Ford's *Stagecoach*, shown in the accompanying stills, raises the problem of accounting for the organization of images in an instance of the "classical" fiction film and of proposing the critical terms appropriate for that account. The formal features of these images—the framing of shots and their sequencing, the repetition of setups, the position of characters, the direction of their glances—can be taken together as a complex structure and understood as a characteristic answer to the rhetorical problem of telling a story, of showing an action to a spectator. Because the significant relations have to do with seeing—both in the ways the characters "see" each other and the way those relations are shown to the spectator—and because their complexity and coherence can be considered as a matter of "point of view," I call the object of this study the "specular text."

Explanations of the imagery of the classical narrative film are offered by technical manuals and various theories of editing. Here, though, I wish to examine the connection between the act of narration and the imagery, specifically in the matter of the framing and the angle of view determined by setups, by characterizing the narrating agency or authority which can be taken to rationalize the presentation of shots. An explanation of this kind necessarily involves clarifying in some detail the notion of the "position of the spectator." Thus we must characterize the spectator's implied position with respect to the action, the way it is structured, and the specific features of the process of "reading" (though not in the sense of interpretation). Doing so entails a description (within the terms of the narrative) of the relation of literal

and fictional space that comprehends what seems, ambiguously, like the double origin of the filmic images.

An inquiry into the forms of authority for the imagery and the corresponding
strategies which implicate the viewer in the action has few precedents, yet it raises
general but basic questions about filmic narration that begin to clarify existing
accounts of the relation of narrative to image. The sequence from *Stagecoach* is
interesting as a structure precisely because, in spite of its simplicity (it has no narrative or formal eccentricity), it challenges the traditional premises of critical efforts
to account for the operation and effects of "classical" film style.

The traditional rationale for the presentation of imagery is often stated by the
camera's relation to the spectator. For instance, a basically dramatic account has it
that the shots should show essentially what a spectator would see if the action were
played on a stage, and if at each moment he had the best view of the action (thus
the changing angles only supply "accents"). Editing would follow the spectator's
natural course of attention as it is implied by the action of the *mise-en-scène*. In
such a mode the question of agency—that is, who is "staging" and making these
events appear in this way—is referred not to the author or narrator but to the action
itself, fully embodied in the characters. Everything that happens must be exhibited
clearly for the eye of the spectator. On this theory, all the structures of the presentation are directed to a place external to the scene of the action—to the final authority, the ideal spectator. Oudart's account proposes that imagery is paradigmatically
referred to the authority of the glance of the "absent one," the offscreen character
within the story who in the countershot is depicted within the frame; the spectator
"identifies" with the visual field of the "owner" of the glance. The "system of the
suture" is an explanation that establishes the origin of the imagery by reference to
the agency of character, but, surprisingly, it does not consider (indeed it seems to
deny) the final agency, the authority of the narrator. The traces of the action of the
narrator may seem to be effaced by this sytem, but such an effect can only be the
result of a certain more general rhetoric. Thus I am proposing an account in which
the structure of the imagery, whatever its apparent forms of presentation, refers
jointly to the action of an implied narrator (who defines his position with respect to
the tale by his judgments) and to the imaginative action occasioned by his placing
and being placed by the spectator. Neither the traditional nor the more recent theories seem fully adequate to this problematic.

Thus the problem that arises from *Stagecoach* is to explain the functioning of the
narrator and the nature and effects of spectator placement; specifically, describing and
accounting for in detail a filmic rhetoric in which the agency of the narrator in his
relation to the spectator is enacted jointly by the characters and the particular sequence
of shots that show them. To describe this rhetoric in a rigorous and illuminating way
means clarifying in filmic terms the notions of "narrative authority," "point of view,"
and "reading," and showing that these concepts are of use precisely because they arise
naturally from the effort to account for the concrete structures of the text.

The moment in the story that the sequence depicts is the taking of a meal at the
Dry Fork station on the stage's way to Lordsburg. Earlier in the film, the prostitute
Dallas (the woman in the dark hat) has been run out of town by the Ladies' Law
and Order League and has been put aboard the stagecoach. There she joined, among

others, a cavalry officer's wife named Lucy (in the white hat) and Hatfield, her chivalrous but distant escort. Just before the present scene, the Ringo Kid (John Wayne), who has broken out of jail to avenge his brother's murder, has been ordered aboard by the sheriff when discovered by the side of the road. The sequence begins immediately after a vote among the members of the group to decide whether to go on to Lordsburg and ends shortly before the end of the scene when the group exits the station. For purposes of convenience, I have called shots 4, 8, and 10, which are from the same setup, series A, and shots 3, 7, 9, and 11, series B.

One of the rationales that might be proposed to account for the setups, the spatial fields they show, the sequence of shots, is their relation to the "psychology" of the characters. How, if at all, are the setups linked to the visual attention, as with the glance, or say the interests of a character in the story? In the shot/reverse shot pattern which is sometimes, wrongly I think, taken as an exclusive paradigm of the "classical" style, the presence of the shot on the screen is "explained" or read as the depiction of the glance of the offscreen character, who, a moment later, is shown in the reverse shot. But because only a few shots of this sequence (or of most films) follow this pattern, we shall be pressed to a different formulation. The general question is how the two setups of the two major series of shots—series A from the head of the table and series B from the left side—are to be explained.

Series A is related to the visual attention of the woman at the head of the table, Lucy. The connection between the shots and her view, especially in the modulation of the force and meaning of that view, must, however, be established. These shots from A are readable as the depiction of Lucy's glance only retrospectively, after series B has shown her at the head of the table and after the animation conveyed in the dolly forward has implied its significance. The point remains, however, that the shots of series A are finally clearly authorized by a certain disposition of attention of one of the characters.

In contrast to series A, the series B shots from the left of the table are like the opening and closing shots (1, 12) in not being associated with or justified spatially as the depiction of anyone's glance. Can the placement of these shots be justified either as the "best angle" for the spectator or as the depiction of some other more complex conception of "psychology" of character than an act of attention in a glance? Persons to whom these shots might be attributed as mental disposition, ensemble of attitude, judgment and intention, is this framing significant of? Whose disposition? On what basis would such an attribution be effected? If establishing the interpretation of the framing depended on or was referred to as a character's "state of mind," which in fact changes significantly over the course of the sequence for each of the major characters (Dallas, Ringo, and Lucy), how would it be possible to accommodate those changing feelings to the fixity of setup? The fact of the fixity of setup denies that the explanation for camera placement can as a principle be referred to a psychology of character(s) based on the kind of emotional changes—surprise, repudiation, naiveté, humiliation—that eventuate in the sequence.

As another hypothesis we could say that the particular compositional features of series B are a presentation not of the "mind" of any single character but of a state of affairs within the group, a relationship among the parties. What is the state of affairs within this society that the framing depicts? There are two significant features

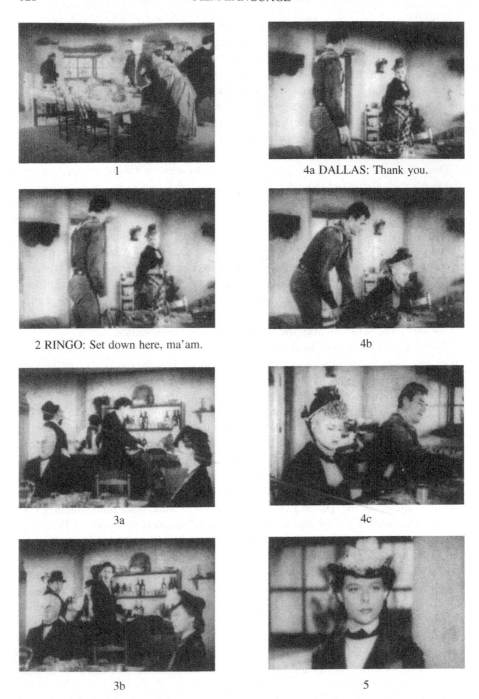

A sequence from John Ford's *Stagecoach* (1939). "The formal features of these images—the framing of shots and their sequencing, the repetition of setups, the position of characters, the direction of their glances—can be taken as a complex structure and understood as a characteristic answer to the rhetorical problem of telling a story, of showing an action to a spectator" (BROWN, p. 125).

6a

8a

6b

8b

7a

9 HATFIELD: May I find you another place, Mrs. Mallory? It's cooler by the window

7b

10

11a LUCY: Thank you.

12a

11b

12b

11c

of the compostion from setup B: the relation of Lucy in the immediate foreground to the group behind her, a group whose responsiveness to events repeats the direction of her own attention, and her relation, spatially, to Dallas and Ringo, who, excluded by the left edge of the frame, are outside. The permanent and underlying fact about the *mise-en-scène* which justifies the fixity of camera placement is its status as a social drama of alliance and antagonism between two social roles—Lucy, an insider, a married woman and defender of custom; and Dallas, outsider and prostitute who violates the code of the table. The camera setups and the spatial fields they reveal, the compositional exclusion of the outlaw couple and their isolation in a separate space, with the implied assertion of Lucy's custodial relation to the body of legitimate society, respond to and depict in formal terms the social "positions" of the characters. In the kind of dramatic presentation they effect, the features of the framing are not justified as the depiction of personal psychology considered as changes of feeling; instead, by their emphasis on social positions, or types, they declare a psychology of intractable situations.

The framing of series B from the left of the table does not represent literally or figuratively any single person's view; rather, it might be said, it depicts, by what it excludes and includes, the interplay of social positions within a group. This asymmetry of social position of Lucy over Dallas extends as well to formal and compositional features of the sequence. Though setup B represents both positions, Dallas's negatively, it makes Lucy's position privileged in the formal mechanism of narrative exposition. The fundamental narrative feature of the sequence is a modification and inflection of the logic of shot/countershot. Here it is an alternation of series A and B around, not two characters, but either Lucy's eye or body. That is, in series A Lucy is present as an eye, as the formal beholder of the scene. Alternately, in B, Lucy is shown bodily dominating the foreground, and as the eye to which the views of series A are referred. Formally the narration proceeds by alternatingly shifting Lucy's presence from the level of the depicted action, as body (B), to the level of representation, as the invisible eye (A), making Lucy's presence the central point of spatial orientation and legibility. In shots 5 and 6, the closeup of the exchange of looks between the two women, the formal asymmetry is the difference of their frontality, and the shot of Lucy is from a place that Dallas could not literally occupy. Lucy's frontality (5) marks a dispossession, a displacement, that corresponds to Dallas's social "absence" in the entire sequence—to her exclusion from the frame in B, to her isolation as the object of Lucy's scornful glance in A. By contrast to Lucy's presence everywhere, as body and eye, Dallas's eye is never taken as the source of authority for a shot. Her eye is averted. She is always, in both A and B, the object of another's gaze—a condition that corresponds to the inferiority of her social position, and to her formal invisibility—she cannot authorize a view.

The shots of setup B, which might be called "objective," or perhaps "nobody's" shots, in fact refer to or are a representation of Lucy's social dominance and formal privilege. B shows a field of vision that closely matches Lucy's *conception* of her own place in that social world: its framing corresponds to her alliance with the group and to her intention to exclude the outsiders, to deny their claim to recognition. It is, in other words, not exactly a description of Lucy's subjectivity but an objectification of her social self-conception. Though Lucy is visible in the frame, series B might be said, metaphorically, to embody her point of view.

This explanation seems cogent as far as it goes. But there are some further issues that arise from the passage, in the way it is experienced, that suggests that the foregoing analysis of the justification of these formal features is incomplete as an account of the grounds for the effects the passage produces and theoretically limited in terms of explaining the strategies of framing and other premises of the narration.

Simply put, the experience of the passage is a feeling of empathy for Dallas's exclusion and humiliation, and a repudiation of Lucy's prejudice as unjust, two feelings brought together by a sense of inevitability of the conflict. There is, in other words, a curious opposition between the empathetic response of a spectator toward Dallas and the underlying premises of the mechanism of the narrative which are so closely related, formally, to Lucy's presence, point of view, and interests. It is this sense of incongruity between feeling and formal structure that occasions the following effort to consider the sequence in terms of the ways it produces its effects, that is, rhetorically.

One question about a formal matter which draws attention to the limitations of a structural account based on a conception of the social order is why the outsiders are seen from a position that is associated with Lucy's place at the table, her gaze. This fact, and the action of the audience within the film, casts doubt on two theories of agency. Our attention as spectators, in the shots of series B, does not follow the visual attention of any depicted characters. These shots might perhaps be read as statements of the "interests" of characters, the nature of their social positions, but that is already a kind of commentary or interpretation that needs explanation. The actions of the men at the bar, the audience within the film, disprove the traditional rationale for editing stated by reference to an ideal spectator: as "placed" spectators we anticipate, not follow, the movements of their attention (2, 3); the object of their attention is sometimes out of the frame we see (3b) and what they see is shown only from a view significantly different from any simply "accented" or "best view," indeed from a place they could not occupy; and sometimes (7b, 8) they have turned away, uninterested, but the screen doesn't go black. In general, an adequate account of the formal choices of the passage must be quite different from an account of the event as if it were staged for the natural attention of a spectator, depicted or real. To ask why the spectator sees in the way he does refers to a set of premises distinguishable from an account based on the attention of either a character or an ideal spectator. It refers to the concrete logic of the placement of the implied spectator and to the theory of presentation that accounts for the shaping of his response. Such an account makes the "position" of the spectator, the way in which he is implicated in the scene, the manner and location of his presence, his point of view, problematical.

It is this notion of the "position of the spectator" that I wish to clarify insofar as that notion illuminates the rhetorical strategies, particularly choice of setup (implying scale and framing) that depicts the action. In contemporary French film theory, particularly in the work of Comolli and Baudry, the notion of the "place" of the spectator is derived from the central position of the eye in perspective and photographic representation. By literally substituting the epistemological subject, the spectator, for the eye, in an argument about filmic representation, the filmic spectator is said to be "theological," and "centered" with respect to filmic images. Thus the theory of the filmic spectator is treated as if subject to the Derridean critique of center, presence, etc. French theory is wrong to enforce this analogy, based on the position of the eye in photographic perspective, because what is optical and literal in that case corresponds only to the literal place of the spectator in the projection hall, and not at all to his figurative place in the film, nor to his place as subject to the rhetoric of the film, or reader or producer of the sense of the discourse. Outside of a French ideological project which fails to discriminate literal and figurative space, the notion of "place" of the spectator, and of "center," is an altogether problematic notion whose significance and function in critical discussion has yet to be explicated.

The sequence from *Stagecoach* provides the terms in which the notion of the position of the spectator might be clarified, provided we distinguish, without yet expecting full clarification, the different senses of "position." A spectator is (a) seated physically in the space of the projection hall and (b) placed by the camera in a certain fictional position with respect to the depicted action; moreover (c), insofar as we see from what we might take to be the eye of a character, we are invited to occupy the place allied to the place he holds, for example, in the social system; and finally (d), in another figurative sense of place, it is the only way that our response can be accounted for, that we can identify with a character's position in a certain situation.

In terms of the passage at hand, the question is then: how can I describe my "position" as spectator in identifying with the humiliated position of one of the depicted characters, Dallas, when my views of her belong to those of another, fictional character, Lucy, who is in the act of rejecting her? What is the spectator's "position" in identifying with Dallas in the role of the passive character? Dallas in averting her eyes from Lucy's in shot 6 accepts a view of herself in this encounter as "prostitute" and is shamed. However, in identifying with Dallas in the role of outcast, presumably the basis for the evocation of our sympathy and pity, our response as spectator is not one of shame, or anything even analogous. We do not suffer or repeat the humiliation. I understand Dallas's feeling but I am not so identified with her that I reenact it. One of the reasons for this restraint is that though I identify with Dallas's abject position of being seen as an unworthy object by someone whose judgment she accepts, I identify with her as the object of another's action. Indeed, in a remarkable strategy, I am asked to see Dallas through Lucy's eyes. That as spectator I am sharing Lucy's view and, just as important, her manner of viewing, is insisted on most emphatically by the dolly forward (4) and by disclosures effected by shot/countershot, thus placing me in a lively and implicated way in a position fully associated with Lucy's place at the head of the table.

Insofar as I identify with Dallas, it is not by repeating her shame, but by imagining myself in her position (situation). The early scenes of the film have carefully prepared us to believe that this exclusion is an unjust act. When the climactic moment arrives, our identification with Dallas as an object of view is simultaneously established as the ground for repudiating the one whose view we share and are implicated in. Though I share Lucy's literal geographical position of viewing at this moment in the film, I am not committed to her figurative point of view. I can, in other words, repudiate Lucy's view of or judgment on Dallas, without negating it as a view, in a way that Dallas herself, captive of the other's image, cannot. Because our feelings as spectators are not "analogous" to their interests and feelings of the characters, we are not bound to accept their views either of themselves or of others. Our "position" as spectator then is very different from the previous senses of "position"; it is defined neither in terms of orientation within the constructed geography of the fiction nor in terms of social position of the viewing character. On the contrary, our point of view on the sequence is tied more closely to our attitude of approval or disapproval and is very different from any literal viewing angle or character's point of view.

Identification asks us as spectators to be two places at once, where the camera is and "with" the depicted person—thus its double structure of viewer/viewed. As a powerful emotional process it thus throws into question any account of the position of the spectator as centered at a single point or at the center of any simply optical system. Identification, this passage shows, necessarily has a double structure in the way it implicates the spectator in the position of both the one seeing and the one seen. This sequence, however, does establish a certain kind of "center" in the person of Lucy. Each of the shots is referred alternatingly to the scene before her eye or the scene of her body, but it is a "center" that functions as a principle of spatial legibility, and is associated with a literal point within the constructed space of the fiction. This center stands, though, as I have suggested, in a very complicated relation to our "position" as spectator. That is, the experience of the passage shows that our identification, in the Freudian sense of an emotional investment, is not with the center, either Lucy or the camera. Rather, if, cautiously, we can describe our figurative relation to a film in geographical terms, of "in," "there," "here," "distance" (and this sequence, as part of its strategy as a fiction, explicitly asks us to by presenting action to us from the literal view of a character), then as spectators, we might be said to formally occupy someone else's place, to be "in" the film, all the while being "outside" it in our seats. We can identify with a character and share her "point of view" even if the logic of the framing and selection of shots of the sequence deny that she has a view or a place within the society that the *mise-en-scène* depicts. There are significant differences between structures of shots, views, and identification: indeed, this sequence has shown, as a principle, that we do not "identify" with the camera but with the characters, and hence do not feel dispossessed by a change in shots. For a spectator, as distinct perhaps from a character, point of view is not definitively or summarily stated by any single shot or even set of shots from a given spatial location.

The way in which we as spectators are implicated in the action is as much a matter of our position with respect to the unfolding of those events in time as in their representation from a point in space. The effect of the mode of sequencing, the regular opposition of insiders and outsiders, is modulated in ways that shape the attitudes of the spectator/reader toward the action. This durational aspect emphasizes the process of inhabiting a text with its rhythms of involvement and disengagement in the action, and suggests that the spectator's position, his being in time, might appropriately be designated the "reader-in-the-text." His doubly structured position of identification with the features and force of the act of viewing and with the object in the field of vision are the visual terms of the dialectic of spectator placement. The rhetorical effort of shots 2–6 is directed to establishing the connection between shots and a "view," to endowing the position at the head of the table with a particular sense of a personalized glance. Shot 2, like 4, cannot at the moment it appears on the screen be associated with Lucy's glance. The shot/countershot sequencing discloses Lucy's location, and the turn of the head (3b) establishes a spatial relation between A and B; the animation, or gesture, implied by the dolly forward, combined with the emotional intensity implied by the choice of scale (5, 6) is read in terms of a personalized agency and clarified by what is shown in the visible field, Lucy's stern face (5). It is a rhetoric that unites the unfolding shots and gives meaning to this depicted glance—affront. It creates with the discrete shots (2, 3, 4) the impression of a coherent act of viewing, a mental unity whose meaning must make itself felt by the viewer at the moment of confrontation (5, 6) to effect the sense of repudiation of Lucy's view and the abjectness of Dallas. It takes time—a sequence of shots, in other words—to convey and specify the meaning of an act of viewing.

Reading, as this instance shows, is in part a process of retrospection, situating what could not be "placed" at the moment of its origin and bringing it forward to an interpretation of the meaning of the present moment. As such it has a complex relation to the action and to the spatial location of viewing. But the process of reading also depends on forgetting. After the climactic moment (5, 6) signaling Dallas's averting her eyes, a different temporal strategy is in effect. Lucy has looked away in 7b, and in subsequent shots from the head of the table, our attention is directed not so much to the act of showing, and what it means—unawareness (2), recognition (4), rejection (6)—but rather in 8 and 10 is directed at the action within the frame. The spectator's forgetting of what the dramatic impact depended on just a few moments before (here the personalized force that accompanied the act of showing the shot as a glance) is an effect of placement that depends on an experience of duration which occludes a previous significance and replaces it with another, a process we might call fading.

The modulation of the effects of fading is what, to take another example, is at issue in the interpretation of the shots of both series A and B. I have argued above that the setup and field of B correspond to Lucy's understanding of her place in the social system—to her point of view in the metaphorical sense. This interpretation corresponds to the general impression of the first six shots, taken together, as representing Lucy's manner of seeing. Shot 7 initiates a new line of dramatic action that poses the question of what Lucy will do now, and also begins a process not exactly of rereading, but a search for a new reading of the meaning of the setups. At this moment (7b), Lucy has turned her attention away from Dallas and is now turned toward Hatfield; and Ringo, previously occupied with his table etiquette (2, 4) is looking (8b, 10) intently out of frame right. The initial sense of the setup B is partially replaced by but coexists with another: that the depicted action in the frame is now being viewed by someone looking from outside the frame, namely Ringo, who is waiting expectantly for something to happen. The view from the left of the table is readable, not exactly as Lucy's self-conceptions as before, and not as a depiction of Ringo's glance, but as a representation of his interest in the scene, his point of view (again, in the metaphorical sense). Similarly, shots 8 and 10, showing Dallas and Ringo, no longer seem to characterize Lucy as the one doing the seeing, as in 4 and 6; they have become impersonal. The rigidity and opposition of setups A and B correspond to the rigidity of social position, but our reading of the

changing secondary significances of the framing is an effect of fading that is responsive to acts of attention and seeing depicted within the frame.

Our anticipation, our waiting to see what will happen, is provoked and represented
on the level of the action by the turning around of the audience-in-the-film (Billy
and Doc Boone in 3b, 9). Our own feeling, because of our visual place to the left of
the table, is closer to Ringo's than to theirs. Certainly the distention and delay of the
climactic moment by a virtual repetition (9, 11a) of those shots of a hestitating Lucy
(unnecessary for simple exposition) produce a sense of our temporal identification
with Ringo (8b, 10), necessary for the success of the moment as drama—its uncertainty and resolution. The drama depends for the lesson it demonstrates not on Lucy's
self-regard before a general public as previously, but on being watched by the parties to be affected. It is Ringo's increasingly involved presence as an authority for a
view, even though he mistakenly thinks he is being ostracized, that makes the absent
place left by Lucy's departure so evidently intended as a lesson in manners, so accus-
ingly empty. By these strategies and effects of duration—retrospection, fading, delay,
and anticipation—the reading of emphasis on the act of showing or what is shown,
the significance of angle and framing, can be modulated. Together these means define
features of a rhetoric which, though different from the placement effected by visual
structures, also locate and implicate the reader/spectator in the text.

The spectator's place, the locus around which the spatiotemporal structures of
presentation are organized, is a construction of the text which is ultimately the product of the narrator's disposition toward the tale. Such structures, which in shaping
and presenting the action prompt a manner and indeed a path of reading, convey
and are closely allied to the guiding moral commentary of the film. In this sequence
the author has effaced himself, as in other instances of indirect discourse, for the
sake of the characters and the action. Certainly he is nowhere visible in the same
manner as the characters. Rather he is visible only through the materialization of
the scene and in certain masked traces of his action. The indirect presence to his
audience that the narrator enacts, the particular form of self-effacement, could be
described as the masked displacement of his narrative authority as the producer of
imagery from himself to the agency of his characters. That is, the film makes it
appear as though it were the depicted characters to whom the authority for the presentation of shots can be referred—most evidently in the case of a depiction of a
glance, but also, in more complex fashion, in the reading of shots as depictions of
a "state of mind." The explanation of the presence of the imagery is referred by the
film not to the originating authority who stands invisible, behind the action, but to
his masks within the depicted space.

In accord with the narrator's efforts to direct attention away from his own activity, to mask and displace it, the narrator of *Stagecoach* has a visible persona, Lucy,
perform a significant formal function in the narration: to constitute and to make legible and continuous the depicted space, by referring shots on the screen alternately
to the authority of her eye or the place of her body. The literal place of the spectator in the projection hall, where in a sense all the shots are directed, is a "center"
that has a figurative correspondence on the level of the discourse in the "place" that
Lucy occupies in the depicted space. But because Lucy performs her integrative
function not exactly by her being at a place, the head of the table, but by enacting

a kind of central consciousness that corresponds to a social and formal role, a role which for narrative purposes can be exploited by shifting the views representing the manner of her presence, the notion of "center" might be thought of not as a geographical place but as a structure or function. As such, this locus makes it possible for the reader himself to occupy that role and himself to make the depicted space coherent and readable. For the spectator, the "center" is not just a point either in the projection hall or in the depicted geography, but is the result of the impression produced by the functioning of the narrative and of his being able to fictionally occupy the absent place.

Locating this function, "inscribing" the spectator's place on the level of the depicted action, has the effect of making the story seem to tell itself by reference not to an outside author but to a continuously visible, internal narrative authority. This governing strategy, of seeming to internalize the source of the exposition in characters, and thus of directing the spectator's attention to the depicted action, is supported by other features of the style: shot/countershot, matching of glances, continuity.

Consequently, the place of the spectator in his relation to the narrator is established by, though not limited to, identifications with characters and the views they have of each other. More specifically his "place" is defined through the variable force of identification with the one viewing and the one viewed—as illustrated in the encounter between Lucy and Dallas. Though the spectator may be placed in the "center" by the formal function Lucy performs, he is not committed to her view of things. On the contrary, in the context of the film, that view is instantly regarded as insupportable. Our response to Dallas supports the sense that the spectator's figurative position is not stated by a description of where the camera is in the geography of the scene. On the contrary, though the spectator's position is closely tied to the fortunes and views of characters, our analysis suggests that identification, in the original sense of an emotional bond, need not be with the character whose view he shares, even less with the disembodied camera. Evidently, a spectator is several places at once—with the fictional viewer, with the viewed, and at the same time in a position to evaluate and respond to the claims of each. This fact suggests that like the dreamer, the filmic spectator is a plural subject: in his reading he is and is not himself.

In a film, imagining ourselves in a character's place by identification, in respect to the actual situation, is a different process, indeed a different order of fiction than taking a shot as originating from a certain point within the fictional geography. The relation though between the literal space of the projection hall and the depicted space of the film image is continuously problematic for a definition of the "thatness" of the screen and for an account of the place of the spectator. If a discourse carries a certain impression of reality, it is an effect not exactly of the image but rather of the way the image is placed by the narrative or argument. My relation to an image on the screen is literal because it can be taken as being directed to a physical point, my seat (changing that seat doesn't alter my viewing angle on the action), as though I were the fixed origin of the view. On the other hand, the image can also be taken as originating from a point in a different kind of space, recognizably different in terms of habitability from that of the projection hall: it is from a fictional and changeable place implied by an origin contained in the image. The filmic image thus implies the ambiguity of a double origin—both from my literal place as spectator and from the place where the camera is within the imaginative space.

One structural result of the ambiguous relation of literal and depicted space and of the seemingly contradictory efforts of the text to both place and displace the spectator is the prohibition against the "meeting," though no such act is literally possible, of actor's and spectator's glances, a prohibition that is an integral feature of the sequence as a "specular text." In its effect on the spectator, the prohibition defines the different spaces he simultaneously inhabits before the screen. By denying his presence in one sense, the prohibition establishes a boundary at the screen that underscores the fact that the spectator can have no actual physical exchange with the depicted world, that he can do nothing relevant to change the course of the action. It places him irretrievably outside the action.

At the same time, the prohibition is the initial premise of a narrative system for the representation of fictional space and the means of introducing the spectator imaginatively into it. The prohibition effects this construction and engagement by creating an obliquity between our angle of viewing and that of the characters which works to make differences of angle and scale readable as representations of different points of view. As such it plays a central part in our process of identification or nonidentification with the camera and depicted characters. It provides the author an ensemble of narrative forms—an imaginary currency consisting of temporary exchange, substitution, and identification—that enables us, fictionally, to take the place of another, to inhabit the text as a reader.

Establishing agency by either the authority of character or of spectator corresponds in its alternative rhetorical forms to the articulation of the ambiguity of the double origin of the image. In a particular text it is the narration that establishes and arbitrates the spectator's placement between these two spaces. *Stagecoach* makes definite efforts to imply that not only is the spectator not there, not present in his seat, but that the film-object originates from an authority within the fictional space. The narration seems to insist that the film is a free-standing entity which a spectator, irrelevant finally to its construction, could only look on from the outside. On the other hand, in the ways that I have described, the film is directed in all its structures of presentation toward the narrator's construction of a commentary on the story and toward placing the spectator at a certain "angle" to it. The film has tried not just to direct the attention but to place the eye of the spectator inside the fictional space, to make his presence integral and constitutive of the structure of views. The explanation the film seems to give of the action of narrative authority is a denial of the existence of a narrator different from character and an affirmation of the dominating role of fictional space. It is a spatial mode not determined by the ontology of the image as such but is in the last instance an effect of the narration.

Masking and displacement of narrative authority are thus integral to establishing the sense of the spectator "in" the text, and the prohibition to establishing the film as an independent fiction, different from dream in being the product of another, that can nevertheless be inhabited. Fascination by identification with character is a way the integrity of fictional space is validated, and because the spectator occupies a fictional role, is a way too that the film can efface the spectator's consciousness of his position. As a production of the spectator's reading, the sense of reality that the film enacts, the "impression of the real," protects the account the text seems to give of the absent narrator.

The cumulative effect of the narrator's strategy of placement of the spectator from moment to moment is his introduction into what might be called the moral order of the text. That is, the presentational structures which shape the action both convey a point of view and define the course of the reading, and are fundamental to the exposition of moral idea—specifically a discussion about the relation of insiders to outsiders. The effect of the distinction between pure and impure is the point of the sequence, though as a theme it is just a part of the total exposition. The sequence thus assists in the construction of attitudes toward law and custom and to those who live outside their strictures. It introduces the question of the exercise of social and customary (as distinguished from legal) authority. To the extent we identify with Ringo and Dallas—and the film continuously invites us to by providing multiple grounds: the couple's bravery, competence, and sincerity—the conventional order and the morality it enforces is put in doubt. Without offering a full interpretation of the theme of *Stagecoach*, which would I think be connected with the unorthodox nature of their love and the issue of Ringo's revenge and final exemption from the law by the sheriff, I can still characterize the spectator's position at this particular moment in the film.

It amounts to this: that though we see the action from Lucy's eyes and are invited by a set of structures and strategies to experience the force and character of that view, we are put in the position finally of having to reject it as a view that is right or that we could be committed to. The sequence engages us on this point through effecting an identification with a situation in which the outsider is wronged and thus that challenges Lucy's position as the agent of an intolerant authority. We are asked, by the manner in which we must read, by the posture we must adopt, to repudiate Lucy's view, to see behind the moral convention that supports intolerance, to break out of a role that may be confining us. As such, the importance of the sequence in the entire film is the way it allies us emotionally with the interests and fortunes of the outsiders as against social custom, an identification and theme that, modulated in subsequent events, continues to the end of the film. The passage, lifted out of its context, but drawing on dispositions established in prevous sequences, is an illustration of the process of constructing a spectator's attitudes in the film as a whole through the control of point of view. Whether or not the western genre can in general be characterized by a certain mode of identification, as, for example, in the disposition or wish to see the right done, and whether *Stagecoach* has a particularly significant place in the history of the genre by virtue of its treatment of outsiders, is an open question. In any case the reader's position is constituted by a set of views, identifications, and judgments that establish his place in the moral order of the text.

Like the absent narrator who discloses himself and makes his judgments from a position inseparable from the sequence of depicted events that constitute the narrative, the spectator, in following the story, in being subject of and to the spatial and temporal placement and effects of exposition, is in the process of realizing an identity we have called his position. Following the trajectory of identifications that establishes the structure of values of a text, "reading" as a temporal process could be said to continuously reconstruct the place of the narrator and his implied commentary on the scene. In this light, reading, as distinct from interpretation, might be characterized as a guided and prompted performance that (to the extent a text allows it, and I believe *Stagecoach* does) recreates the point of view enacted in a scene. As a correlative of narration, reading could be said to be the process of reenactment by fictionally occupying the place of the narrator.

Certain formal features of the imagery—framing, sequencing, the prohibition, and "invisibility" of the narrator—I have suggested, can be explained as the ensemble of ways authority implicitly positions the spectator/reader. As a method, this analysis of *Stagecoach* points to a largely unexplored body of critical problems associated with describing and accounting for narrative and rhetorical signifying structures. The "specular text" and the allied critical concepts of "authority," "reading," "point of view," and "position of the spectator," however provisional, might be taken then as a methodological initiative for a semiotic study of filmic texts.

1975

II

Film and Reality

The main tradition of Western aesthetics, deriving from Aristotle's *Poetics*, adopts the view that art "imitates" nature or, in Hamlet's phrase, holds "the mirror up to nature." Painting, from the early Renaissance to the late nineteenth century, from Giotto to Manet and the Impressionists, pursued this ideal with ever-increasing success. Later the novels of Balzac and Tolstoy provided a more detailed representation of nature and society than anything literature had previously known, and the plays of Ibsen and Chekhov seemed to carry Hamlet's ideal of the theater to its limit. All these achievements were eclipsed, however, by the invention of photography, for the camera, and especially the motion picture camera, was unique in its ability to represent nature. If the ideal of art is to create an illusion of reality, the motion picture made it possible to achieve this ideal in an unprecedented way.

But is the primary aim of art to imitate nature? And if it is, what role remains for the other arts when film achieves it so simply and perfectly? An anti-realist tradition therefore denies that the goal of art is the imitation of nature. Some anti-realists have argued that to create a work of art is not simply to copy the world but to add another, and very special, object to the world. This object may be valuable because it offers an interpretation or an idealization of the world, or even because it creates another, wholly autonomous, world. Others in this anti-realist tradition argue that the value of such an object may be that it expresses the feelings and emotions of its creator, or that the artist manages to impose a beautiful or a significant form on the materials with which he works. The artist's feelings may be expressed abstractly, and the resulting form may be purely imaginative. The work of art may not allude to nature at all.

Theorists of modern painting, for example, have argued that painting should not even attempt to provide a three-dimensional representation of reality but acknowledge, instead, that it is essentially the application of pigments to a two-dimensional

141

surface. This modernist view assumes that painting cannot and should not compete with film in attempting to mirror reality. Painting must renounce that task altogether. Other critics have countered, however, that film cannot reproduce reality either. Even if it could, it ought not to try. According to this anti-realist view, film, like any other art form, must offer an interpretation of the world or, by the manipulation of the camera, create an alternative world. Just as painting must acknowledge that it is not really a mirror but pigments on canvas, cinema must acknowledge that it is simply projected images on a screen. To claim that these images ought to be images of physical reality—as opposed to any other kinds of images—is pure dogma. Why should these images not liberate the imagination from the tedium of reality, introducing us to the world of abstractions or of dreams instead?

Siegfried Kracauer is a leading exponent of the realist view of cinema. In his book, *Theory of Film*, Kracauer argues that because film literally photographs reality it alone is capable of holding the mirror up to nature. Film actually reproduces the raw material of the physical world within the work of art. This makes it impossible for a film to be an expression of the artist's formative intentions or an abstract, imaginative expression of his emotions. Kracauer insists that it is the clear obligation and the special privilege of film (a descendant of still photography) to record and reveal, and thereby redeem, physical reality.

Kracauer's attitude is a response to the common complaint that the abstractions and categorizations of modern science and technology make it impossible for us to appreciate the concrete world in which we live—what John Crowe Ransom called "the world's body." The distinct function of art (especially of poetic imagery) might therefore well be to help us possess the concrete world once more. Kracauer believes that film art actually does this; it "literally redeems this world from its dormant state, its state of virtual nonexistence, by endeavoring to experience it through the camera." For Kracauer film delivers us from technology by technology.

André Bazin also insists on the unique realism of cinema, but from a markedly different viewpoint. Bazin, a French critic who founded the influential journal *Cahiers du Cinéma* in the late 1940s and whose disciples include Jean-Luc Godard, François Truffaut, and Claude Chabrol, is perhaps the first important theorist for whom the experience of silent film is no longer decisive. In "The Ontology of the Photographic Image" Bazin argues that photography and cinema are discoveries that finally satisfy the obsession with realism (long manifested in our obsession with realism in painting). The photographic image is a mechanical reproduction of reality and we therefore accept as real the object reproduced or *re*-presented. The cinematic image similarly shares the being of the model, whose reality is transferred to it. For the first time, an image of the world is formed automatically, without the creative intervention of man. Alone among the arts, photography derives an advantage from man's absence. Despite his celebration of the mechanical nature of photography Bazin points out in "The Myth of Total Cinema" that any account of cinema that relied merely on the technical inventions that made it possible would be wholly inadequate. These very inventions were born of the converging of various obsessions based on a "myth of total cinema" that preceded and motivated them. The myth expressed a nonaesthetic, psychological need to recreate the world in its own image, an image unburdened by the artist's desire to interpret.

Bazin's commitment to the realist aesthetic manifested itself in his admiration for the realist style of the French director Jean Renoir, the American directors Orson Welles and William Wyler, and the major works of Italian neorealism. In contrast both to the chief schools of realism that preceded it and to Soviet cinema, neo-realism never makes reality the servant of some pre-existing point of view. And in contrast to expressionism it asks the actor, often the man in the street rather than the professional actor, to *be* rather than to act or pretend to be; it prefers an open, natural setting to an expressionistic *mise-en-scène* that imposes meaning on action. Above all, it requires the narrative to respect the actual qualities and duration of the event in preference to the artificial, abstract, or dramatic duration favored in classic montage. Bazin's admiration for these characteristics of neorealism is based on an ontological position as much as a stylistic preference. Like the films of Vittorio de Sica, it expresses a love for creation itself.

Rudolf Arnheim, who has also written extensively on the psychology of perception, is a leading early exponent of the anti-realist tradition in film theory. For Arnheim, if cinema were the mere mechanical reproduction of real life it could not be an art at all. Arnheim acknowledges the existence of a primitive desire to get material objects into one's power by creating them afresh, but he believes that this primitive impulse must be distinguished from the impulse to create art. The "wax museum" ideal may satisfy our primitive impulse, but it fails to satisfy the true artistic urge—not simply to copy, but to originate, to interpret, and to mold. The very properties that keep photography from reproducing reality perfectly must be exploited by the film artist, for they alone provide the possibilities for a film art. Bazin's myth of "total" cinema is nothing more than Arnheim's fallacy of the "complete" film. The pursuit of an ever more complete realism through the use of sound, color, and stereoscopic vision is simply a prescription for undermining the achievement of film art, which must respect, even welcome, the inherent limitations of the art.

Jean-Louis Baudry compares the experience of film to that of dream. He attempts, in doing so, to account for the "impression of reality," that "more than real" experience created by film. Baudry observes that many features of the film spectator's situation—features, that is, of the cinematic apparatus—resemble the dream. According to psychoanalytic theory, the dream is endowed with this quality of heightened reality because it occasions a regression to the stage of primitive narcissism. The spectator's movements are inhibited; he sits in a darkened room and is unable to engage in reality testing. The distinction between perception and representation does not operate. The intense, "more-than-real" images he views are projected on a screen (in the dreamer's case the mother's breast, what Bertram Lewin calls the dream screen). Given the many similarities between the film experience and the dream experience, argues Baudry, we can infer that the more-than-real experience of the film spectator is attributable to a similar regression. The desire for this regressive experience explains the history and creation of the cinematic apparatus and was already expressed in Plato's myth of the cave. According to Baudry, the prisoner in Plato's cave bears a striking analogy to both to dreamer and the film spectator.

Noël Carroll challenges every significant feature of Baudry's analogy between the film spectator and the dreamer. In his view, the film spectator does not suffer motor inhibition but can get up and even have a smoke. Unlike dreams, film images are publicly accessible, but reality testing in Baudry's sense is in fact inapplicable to them. The dreamer may be (or may not be) in a darkened room, but this is not, in any case, part of the dream experience. Dreams are not, in fact, typically projected on (white) breasts, and, insofar as one can work with the vague concept of the "more-than-real," this notion applies more typically to dreams than to film. Carroll agrees that some films provide a heightened experience of this sort but, when they do, this effect should be attributed more to particular features of their internal structure than to the projection situation or to the cinematic apparatus itself. Carroll doubts the utility of the dream analogy to the understanding of film since we understand film better than we understand dreams. And he is highly critical of what he regards as a literary and impressionistic approach to questions that require scientific evidence and analytic precision.

For Baudry cinema is the satisfaction of a desire inherent in our psyches. He is, therefore, critical of the attempt to trace cinema's history from the magic lantern and the camera obscura. Bazin, by contrast, invokes this tradition and for him the decisive moment comes with the first scientific system of reproduction in the Renaissance—perspective. Da Vinci's camera obscura thus foreshadows the camera of the early French photographer Niepce and finally the invention of cinema proper, when the mechanical reproduction of reality became possible. Jonathan Crary examines the assumed continuity of this tradition and its assumption that observation leads to truthful inferences about an external world. He argues that this view was displaced in the 1820s and 1830s by radically different notions of what an observer is and what constitutes vision. The collapse of the camera obscura model of the observer's objective status, in other words, is part of a much larger process of modernization. In the early 1800s the rigidity of the camera obscura, its linear optical system, its fixed positions, its categorical distinction between inside and outside, and its identification of perception and object were too inflexible for the needs of the new century

One crucial development was physiology's discovery that knowledge is conditioned by the functioning of the body, in particular the eyes. The doctrine of specific nerve energies redefines vision as a capacity for being affected by sensations that have no necessary link to an actual object outside the self, thus undermining any assumption about the coherence of visual meaning. This growing awareness that vision was not an objective witness to the world was a necessary precondition for the artistic experiments of modernism and for new forms of aesthetic structure and spectacle that are inseparable from the advancing technologies of photography and film. Paradoxically, the increasing pervasiveness of these two techniques helped re-establish earlier myths that vision was incorporeal, veridical, and "realistic." But if cinema and photography seemed to reincarnate the camera obscura, it was only a mirage of transparency that modernity continued to dissipate.

Like Bazin, the French philosopher Gilles Deleuze views Italian neo-realism as marking a fundamental break in the historical development of the film image. In contrast to those who defined neo-realism by its social context, however, Bazin argued that its crucial feature was the exhibition of a new form of reality, which he characterized as dispersive, elliptical, errant, or wavering, with deliberately weak connections between floating events. Instead of representing an already deciphered reality, neo-realism aimed at an always ambiguous reality that resisted deciphering. Deleuze admires the richness of Bazin's conception but believes that the introduction of an "additional reality" is insufficient. For Deleuze the crucial change in the nature of film arises at the level of the mental and displays itself in terms of thought. Hollywood films before World War II, he argues, are dominated by the movement-image in its various forms: the perception-image, affection-image, and action-image. After the war Italian neo-realism loosens this sensory-motor scheme and thereby opens the way to the regime of the time-image, which for Deleuze is more significant than the transition from silents to talkies.

In classical Hollywood cinema, Deleuze claims, situations typically occasion actions that in turn create new situations (the SAS structure). All these elements are governed by the intelligible causal relations that make traditional narrative possible. By contrast, modern cinema emphasizes situations in which the characters no longer know how to react, in spaces we no longer know how to describe with any precision. These conditions disrupt the orderly narrative procedures of the commercial Hollywood film and inaugurate a more difficult cinema whose images are no longer linked by rational cuts, whose spaces are empty, fragmentary, and discontinuous, and whose characters are seers rather than doers, visionaries rather than agents. Actions create situations that in turn generate new actions (the ASA structure).

These features enable but do not yet establish the time-image. In the time-image, the subordination of time to movement is reversed, and a direct, rather than an indirect, image of time is revealed on the surface of the screen. The time-image presents a purely optical and sound situation that replaces the faltering sensory-motor system and its control of action. Into the world of continuous space-time where practical action occurs, the modern cinema brings the emancipated senses into direct relation with thought and time, where the audience may grasp something too powerful, too unjust, or too beautiful, something that outstrips its sensory-motor capacities. To the extent that optical and visual description replaces motor action in this new regime of opsigns and sonsigns, a new principle of indeterminacy governs. We no longer know the difference between subjective and objective, imaginary and real, physical and mental—not because we are confused but because there is no longer a secure place from which to ask the questions.

SIEGFRIED KRACAUER
FROM THEORY OF FILM

BASIC CONCEPTS

Although he made his mark in cultural studies, Siegfried Kracauer (1889–1966) trained and worked as an engineer, publishing numerous articles on architecture before becoming editor of the influential newspaper *Frankfurter Zeitung* in 1920. Between 1920 and 1933 he published articles on mass culture and the white-collar class that would form the backbone of his first two books, uniting his interests in film and in sociology. In 1933, after Hitler became chancellor, he left Germany for Paris in order to escape the rising Nazi threat. In 1941, he immigrated to the United States, where he began research for *From Caligari to Hitler*. In it, he traces the use of expressionist cinematic techniques to instill nationalist sentiment and totalitarian politics by distracting the masses from social and political realities. His later emphasis on the necessity for cinematic realism (see section III of this anthology) stems from this distrust of the political misuse of expressionist film. In America, Kracauer continued to write and publish cultural criticism while working at the Bureau for Applied Social Research at Columbia University.

Like the embryo in the womb, photographic film developed from distinctly separate components. Its birth came about from a combination of instantaneous photography, as used by Muybridge and Marey, with the older devices of the magic lantern and the phenakistoscope. Added to this later were the contributions of other nonphotographic elements, such as editing and sound. Nevertheless photography, especially instantaneous photography, has a legitimate claim to top priority among these elements, for it undeniably is and remains the decisive factor in establishing film content. The nature of photography survives in that of film.

Originally, film was expected to bring the evolution of photography to an end—satisfying at last the age-old desire to picture things moving. This desire already accounted for major developments within the photographic medium itself. As far back as 1839, when the first daguerreotypes and talbotypes appeared, admiration mingled with disappointment about their deserted streets and blurred landscapes. And in the 'fifties, long before the innovation of the hand camera, successful attempts were made to photograph subjects in motion. The very impulses which thus led from time exposure to snapshot engendered dreams of a further extension of photography in the same direction—dreams, that is, of film. Abut 1860, Cook and Bonnelli, who had developed a device called a photobioscope, predicted a "complete revolution of photographic art. . . . We will see . . . landscapes," they announced, "in which the trees bow to the whims of the wind, the leaves ripple and glitter in the rays of the sun."

Along with the familiar photographic leitmotif of the leaves, such kindred subjects as undulating waves, moving clouds, and changing facial expressions ranked high in early prophecies. All of them conveyed the longing for an instrument which would capture the slightest incidents of the world about us—scenes that often would involve crowds, whose incalculable movements resemble, somehow, those of waves or leaves. In a memorable statement published before the emergence of instantaneous photography, Sir John Herschel not only predicted the basic features of the film camera but assigned to it a task which it has never since disowned: "the vivid and lifelike reproduction and handing down to the latest posterity of any transaction in real life—a battle, a debate, a public solemnity, a pugilistic conflict." Ducos du Hauron and other forerunners also looked forward to what we have come to label newsreels and documentaries—films devoted to the rendering of real-life events. This insistence on recording went hand in hand with the expectation that motion pictures could acquaint us with normally imperceptible or otherwise induplicable movements—flashlike transformations of matter, the slow growth of plants, etc. All in all, it was taken for granted that film would continue along the lines of photography. . . .

PROPERTIES OF THE MEDIUM

The properties of film can be divided into basic and technical properties.

The basic properties are identical with the properties of photography. Film, in other words, is uniquely equipped to record and reveal physical reality and, hence, gravitates toward it.

Now there are different visible worlds. Take a stage performance or a painting: they too are real and can be perceived. But the only reality we are concerned with is actually existing physical reality—the transitory world we live in. (Physical reality will also be called "material reality," or "physical existence," or "actuality," or loosely just "nature." Another fitting term might be "camera-reality.") . . . The other visible worlds reach into this world without, however, really forming a part of it. A theatrical play, for instance, suggests a universe of its own which would immediately crumble were it related to its real-life environment.

As a reproductive medium, film is of course justified in reproducing memorable ballets, operas, and the like. Yet even assuming that such reproductions try to do justice to the specific requirements of the screen, they basically amount to little more than "canning," and are of no interest to us here. Preservation of performances which lie outside physical reality proper is at best a sideline of a medium so particularly suited to explore that reality. This is not to deny that reproductions, say, of stage production numbers may be put to good cinematic use in certain feature films and film genres.

Of all the technical properties of film the most general and indispensable is editing. It serves to establish a meaningful continuity of shots and is therefore unthinkable in photography. (Photomontage is a graphic art rather than a specifically photographic genre.) Among the more special cinematic techniques are some which have been taken over from photography—e.g., the close-up, soft-focus pictures, the use of negatives, double or multiple exposure, etc. Others, such as the lap-dissolve, slow and quick motion, the reversal of time, certain "special effects," and so forth, are for obvious reasons exclusively peculiar to film.

These scanty hints will suffice. It is not necessary to elaborate on technical matters which have been dealt with in most previous theoretical writings on film. Unlike these, which invariably devote a great deal of space to editing devices, modes of lighting, various effects of the close-up, etc., the present book concerns itself with cinematic techniques only to the extent to which they bear on the nature of film, as defined by its basic properties and their various implications. The interest lies not with editing in itself, regardless of the purposes it serves, but with editing as a means of implementing—or defying, which amounts to the same—such potentialities of the medium as are in accordance with its substantive characteristics. In other words, the task is not to survey all possible methods of editing for their own sake; rather, it is to determine the contributions which editing may make to cinematically significant achievements. Problems of film technique will not be neglected; however, they will be discussed only if issues going beyond technical considerations call for their investigation.

This remark on procedures implies what is fairly obvious anyway: that the basic and technical properties differ substantially from each other. As a rule the former take precedence over the latter in the sense that they are responsible for the cinematic quality of a film. Imagine a film which, in keeping with the basic properties, records interesting aspects of physical reality but does so in a technically imperfect manner; perhaps the lighting is awkward or the editing uninspired. Nevertheless such a film is more specifically a film than one which utilizes brilliantly all the cinematic devices and tricks to produce a statement disregarding camera-reality. Yet this should not lead one to underestimate the influence of the technical properties. It will be seen that in certain cases the knowing use of a variety of techniques may endow otherwise nonrealistic films with a cinematic flavor.

THE TWO MAIN TENDENCIES

If film grows out of photography, the realistic and formative tendencies must be operative in it also. Is it by sheer accident that the two tendencies manifested themselves side by side immediately after the rise of the medium? As if to encompass the whole range of cinematic endeavors at the outset, each went the limit in exhausting its own possibilities. Their prototypes were Lumière, a strict realist, and Méliès, who gave free rein to his artistic imagination. The films they made embody, so to speak, thesis and antithesis in a Hegelian sense.

Lumière and Méliès

Lumiére's films contained a true innovation, as compared with the repertoire of the zootropes or Edison's peep boxes: they pictured everyday life after the manner of photographs. Some of his early pictures, such as *Baby's Breakfast* (*Le Déjeuner de bébé*) or *The Card Players* (*La Partie d'écarté*), testify to the amateur photographer's delight in family idyls and genre scenes. And there was *Teasing the Gardener* (*L'Arroseur arrosé*), which enjoyed immense popularity because it elicited from the flow of every-day life a proper story with a funny climax to boot. A gardener is watering flowers and, as he unsuspectingly proceeds, an impish boy steps on the hose, releasing it at the very moment when his perplexed victim examines the dried-up nozzle. Water squirts out and hits the gardener smack in the face. The denouement is true to style, with the gardener chasing and spanking the boy. This film, the germ cell and arche-type of all film comedies to come, represented an imaginative attempt on the part of Lumière to develop photography into a means of story telling. Yet the story was just a real-life incident. And it was precisely its photographic veracity which made Maxim Gorki undergo a shock-like experience. "You think," he wrote about *Teasing the Gardener*, "the spray is going to hit you too, and instinctively shrink back."

On the whole, Lumière seems to have realized that story telling was none of his business; it involved problems with which he apparently did not care to cope. Whatever story-telling films he, or his company, made—some more comedies in the vein of his first one, tiny historical scenes, etc.—are not characeristic of his pro-duction. The bulk of his films recorded the world about us for no other purpsoe than to present it. This is in any case what Mesguich, one of Lumière's "ace" camera-men, felt to be their message. At a time when the talkies were already in full swing he epitomized the work of the master as follows: "As I see it, the Lumière Brothers had established the true domain of the cinema in the right manner. The novel, the theater, suffice for the study of the human heart. The cinema is the dynamism of life, of nature and its manifestations, of the crowd and its eddies. All that asserts itself through movement depends on it. Its lens opens on the world."

Lumière's lens did open on the world in this sense. Take his immortal first reels *Workers Leaving the Lumière Factory* (*Sortie des usines Lumière*), *Arrival of a Train* (*L'Arrivée d'un train*), *La Place des Cordeliers à Lyon*: their themes were public places, with throngs of people moving in diverse directions. The crowded streets captured by the stereographic photographs of the late 'fifties thus reappeared on the primitive screen. It was life at its least controllable and most unconscious moments, a jumble of transient, forever dissolving patterns accessible only to the camera. The much-imitated shot of the railway station, with its emphasis on the con-fusion of arrival and departure, effectively illustrated the fortuity of these patterns; and their fragmentary character was exemplifed by the clouds of smoke which leisurely drifted upward. Significantly, Lumière used the motif of smoke on several occasions. And he seemd anxious to avoid any personal interference with the given data. Detached records, his shots resembled the imaginary shot of the grandmother which Proust contrasts with the memory image of her.

Contemporaries praised these films for the very qualities which the prophets and forerunners had singled out in their visions of the medium. It is inevitable that, in the comments on Lumière, "the ripple of leaves stirred by the wind" should be referred to enthusiastically. The Paris journalist Henri de Parville, who used the image of the trembling leaves, also identified Lumière's over-all theme as "nature caught in the act." Others pointed to the benefits which science would derive from Lumière's invention. In America his camera-realism defeated Edison's kinetoscope with its staged subjects.

Lumière's hold on the masses was ephemeral. In 1897, not more than two years after he had begun to make films, his popularity subsided. The sensation had worn off; the heyday was over. Lack of interest caused Lumière to reduce his production.

Georges Méliès took over where Lumière left off, renewing and intensifying the medium's waning appeal. This is not to say that he did not occasionally follow the latter's example. In his beginnings he too treated the audience to sightseeing tours; or he dramatized, in the fashion of the period, realistically staged topical events. But his main contribution to the cinema lay in substituting staged illusion for unstaged reality, and contrived plots for everyday incidents.

The Two Tendencies: Lumière's *Workers Leaving the Lumière Factory* (1895) and Méliès's *The Witch* (1900). "Lumière's lens did open on the world . . . Méliès ignored the workings of nature out of the artist's delight in sheer fantasy" (KRACAUER, pp. 150, 152).

The two pioneers were aware of the radical differences in their approach. Lumière told Méliès that he considered film nothing more than a "scientific curiosity," thereby implying that his cinematograph could not possibly serve artistic purposes. In 1897, Méliès on his part published a prospectus which took issue with Lumière: "Messrs. Méliès and Reulos specialize mainly in fantastic or artistic scenes, reproductions of theatrical scenes, etc. . . . thus creating a special genre which differs entirely from the customary views supplied by the cinematograph—street scenes or scenes of everyday life."

Méliès's tremendous success would seem to indicate that he catered to demands left unsatisfied by Lumière's photographic realism. Lumière appealed to the sense of observation, the curiosity about "nature caught in the act"; Méliès ignored the workings of nature out of the artist's delight in sheer fantasy. The train in *Arrival of a Train* is the real thing, whereas its counterpart in Méliès's *An Impossible Voyage* (*Voyage à travers l'impossible*) is a toy train as unreal as the scenery through which it is moving. Instead of picturing the random movements of phenomena, Méliès freely interlinked imagined events according to the requirements of his charming fairy-tale plots. Had not media very close to film offered similar gratifications? The artist-photographers preferred what they considered aesthetically attractive compositions to searching explorations of nature. And immediately before the arrival of the motion picture camera, magic lantern performances indulged in the projection of religious themes, Walter Scott novels, and Shakespearean dramas.

Yet even though Méliès did not take advantage of the camera's ability to record and reveal the physical world, he increasingly created his illusions with the aid of techniques peculiar to the medium. Some he found by accident. When taking shots of the Paris Place de l'Opéra, he had to discontinue the shooting because the celluloid strip did not move as it should; the surprising result was a film in which, for no reason at all, a bus abruptly transformed itself into a hearse. True, Lumière also was not disinclined to have a sequence of events unfold in reverse, but Méliès was the first to exploit cinematic devices systematically. Drawing on both photography and the stage, he innovated many techniques which were to play an enormous role in the future—among them the use of masks, multiple exposure, superimposition as a means of summoning ghosts, the lap-dissolve, etc. And through his ingenuity in using these techniques he added a touch of cinema to his playful narratives and magic tricks. Stage traps ceased to be indispensable; sleights-of-hand yielded to incredible metamorphoses which film alone was able to accomplish. Illusion produced in this climate depended on another kind of craftsmanship than the magician's. It was cinematic illusion, and as such went far beyond theatrical make-believe. Méliès's *The Haunted Castle* (*Le Manoir du diable*) "is conceivable only in the cinema and due to the cinema," says Henri Langlois, one of the best connoisseurs of the primitive era.

Notwithstanding his film sense, however, Méliès still remained the theater director he had been. He used photography in a pre-photographic spirit—for the reproduction of a papier-maché universe inspired by stage traditions. In one of his greatest films, *A Trip to the Moon* (*Le Voyage dans la lune*), the moon harbors a grimacing man in the moon and the stars are bull's-eyes studded with the pretty faces of music hall girls. By the same token, his actors bowed to the audience, as if they performed on the stage. Much as his films differed from the theater on a technical plane, they failed to transcend its scope by incorporating genuinely cinematic subjects. This also explains why Méliès, for all his inventiveness, never thought of moving his camera; the stationary camera perpetuated the spectator's relation to the stage. His ideal spectator was the traditional theatergoer, child or adult. There seems to be some truth in the observation that, as people grow older, they instinctively withdraw to the positions from which they set out to struggle and conquer. In his later years Méliès more and more turned from theatrical film to filmed theater, producing *féeries* which recalled the Paris Châtelet pageants.

The Realistic Tendency

In following the realistic tendency, films go beyond photography in two respects. First, they picture movement itself, not only one or another of its phases. But what kinds of movements do they picture? In the primitive era when the camera was fixed to the ground, it was natural for film makers to concentrate on moving material phenomena; life on the screen was life only if it manifested itself through external, or "objective," motion. As cinematic techniques developed, films increasingly drew on camera mobility and editing devices to deliver their messages. Although their strength still lay in the rendering of movements inaccessible to other media, these movements were no longer necessarily objective. In the technically mature film "subjective" movements—movements, that is, which the spectator is invited to execute—constantly compete with objective ones. The spectator may have to identify himself with a tilting, panning, or traveling camera which insists on bringing motionless as well as moving objects to his attention. Or an appropriate arrangement of shots may rush the audience through vast expanses of time and/or space so as to make it witness, almost simultaneously, events in different periods and places.

Nevertheless the emphasis is now as before on objective movement; the medium seems to be partial to it. As René Clair puts it: "If there is an aesthetics of the cinema . . . it can be summarized in one word: 'movement.' The external movement of the objects perceived by the eye, to which we are today adding the inner movement of the action." The fact that he assigns a dominant role to external movement reflects, on a theoretical plane, a marked feature of his own earlier films—the ballet-like evolutions of their characters.

Second, films may seize upon physical reality with all its manifold movements by means of an intermediary procedure which would seem to be less indispensable in photography—staging. In order to narrate an intrigue, the film maker is often obliged to stage not only the action but the surroundings as well. Now this recourse to staging is most certainly legitimate if the staged world is made to appear as a faithful reproduction of the real one. The important thing is that studio-built settings convey the impression of actuality, so that the spectator feels he is watching events which might have occurred in real life and have been photographed on the spot.

Falling prey to an interesting misconception, Emile Vuillermoz champions, for the sake of "realism," settings which represent reality as seen by a perceptive painter. To his mind they are more real than real-life shots because they impart the essence of what such shots are showing. Yet from the cinematic point of view these allegedly realistic settings are no less stagy than would be, say, a cubist or abstract composition. Instead of staging the given raw material itself, they offer, so to speak, the gist of it. In other words, they suppress the very camera-reality which film aims at incorporating. For this reason, the sensitive moviegoer will feel disturbed by them. (The problems posed by films of fantasy which, as such, show little concern for physical reality will be considered later on.)

Strangely enough, it is entirely possible that a staged real-life event evokes a stronger illusion of reality on the screen than would the original event if it had been captured directly by the camera. The late Ernö Metzner who devised the settings for the studio-made mining disaster in Pabst's *Kameradschaft*—an episode with the ring of stark authenticity—insisted that candid shots of a real mining disaster would hardly have produced the same convincing effect.

One may ask, on the other hand, whether reality can be staged so accurately that the camera-eye will not detect any difference between the original and the copy. Blaise Cendrars touches on this issue in a neat hypothetical experiment. He imagines two film scenes which are completely identical except for the fact that one has been shot on the Mont Blanc (the highest mountain of Europe) while the other was staged in the studio. His contention is that the former has a quality not found in the latter. There are on the mountain, says he, certain "emanations, luminous or otherwise, which have worked on the film and given it a soul." Presumably large parts of our environment, natural or man-made, resist duplication.

The Formative Tendency

The film maker's formative faculties are offered opportunities far exceeding those offered the photographer. The reason is that film extends into dimensions which photography does not cover. These differ from each other according to area and composition. With respect to areas, film makers have never confined themselves to exploring only physical reality in front of the camera but, from the outset, persistently tried to penetrate the realms of history and fantasy. Remember Méliès. Even the realistic-minded Lumière yielded to the popular demand for historical scenes. As for composition, the two most general types are the story film and the nonstory film. The latter can be broken down into the experimental film and the film of fact, which on its part comprises, partially or totally, such subgenres as the film on art, the newsreel, and the documentary proper.

It is easy to see that some of these dimensions are more likely than others to prompt the film maker to express his formative aspirations at the expense of the realistic tendency. As for areas, consider that of fantasy: movie directors have at all times rendered dreams or visions with the aid of settings which are anything but∞realistic. Thus in *Red Shoes* Moira Shearer dances, in a somnambulistic trance, through fantastic worlds avowedly intended to project her conscious mind—agglomerates of landscape-like forms, near-abstract shapes, and luscious color schemes which have all the traits of stage imagery. Disengaged creativity thus drifts away from the basic concerns of the medium. Several dimensions of composition favor the same preferences. Most experimental films are not even designed to focus on physical existence; and practically all films following the lines of a theatrical story evolve narratives whose significance overshadows that of the raw material of nature used for their implementation. For the rest, the film maker's formative endeavors may also impinge on his realistic loyalities in dimensions which, because of their emphasis on physical reality, do not normally invite such encroachments; there are enough documentaries with real-life shots which merely serve to illustrate some self-contained oral commentary.

Clashes Between the Two Tendencies

Films which combine two or more dimensions are very frequent; for instance, many a movie featuring an everyday-life incident includes a dream sequence or a documentary passage. Some such combinations may lead to overt clashes between the realistic and formative tendencies. This happens whenever a film maker bent on creating an imaginary universe from freely staged material also feels under an obligation to draw on camera-reality. In his *Hamlet* Laurence Olivier has the cast move about in a studio-built, conspicuously stagy Elsinore, whose labyrinthine architecture seems calculated to reflect Hamlet's unfathomable being. Shut off from our real-life environment, this bizarre structure would spread over the whole of the film were it not for a small, otherwise insignificant scene in which the real ocean outside that dream orbit is shown. But no sooner does the photographed ocean appear than the spectator experiences something like a shock. He cannot help recognizing that this little scene is an outright intrusion; that it abruptly introduces an element incompatible with the rest of the imagery. How he then reacts to it depends upon his sensibilities. Those indifferent to the peculiarities of the medium, and therefore unquestioningly accepting the staged Elsinore, are likely to resent the unexpected emergence of crude nature as a letdown, while those more sensitive to the properties of film will in a flash realize the make-believe character of the castle's mythical splendor. Another case in point is Renato Castellani's *Romeo and Juliet*. This attempt to stage Shakespeare in natural surroundings obviously rests upon the belief that camera-reality and the poetic reality of Shakespeare verse can be made to fuse into each other. Yet the dialogue as well as the intrigue establish a universe so remote from the chance world of real Verona streets and ramparts that all the scenes in which the two disparate worlds are seen merging tend to affect one as an unnatural alliance between conflicting forces.

Actually collisions of this kind are by no means the rule. Rather, there is ample evidence to suggest that the two tendencies which sway the medium may be interrelated in various other ways. Since some of these relationships between realistic and formative efforts can be assumed to be aesthetically more gratifying than the rest, the next step is to try to define them.

THE CINEMATIC APPROACH

It follows from what has been said . . . that films may claim aesthetic validity if they build from their basic properties; like photographs, that is, they must record and reveal physical reality. . . . One might argue that too exclusive an emphasis on the medium's primary relation to physical reality tends to put film in a strait jacket. This objection finds support in the many existing films which are completely unconcerned about the representation of nature. There is the abstract experimental film. There is an unending succession of "photoplays" or theatrical films which do not picture real-life material for its own sake but use it to build up action after the manner of the stage. And there are the many films of fantasy which neglect the external world in freely composed dreams or visions. The old German expressionist films went far in this direction; one of their champions, the German art critic Herman G. Scheffauer, even eulogizes expressionism on the screen for its remoteness from photographic life.

Why, then, should these genres be called less "cinematic" than films concentrating on physical existence? The answer is of course that it is the latter alone which afford insight and enjoyment otherwise unattainable. True, in view of all the genres which do not cultivate outer reality and yet are here to stay, this answer sounds somewhat dogmatic. But perhaps it will be found more justifiable in the light of the following two considerations.

First, favorable response to a genre need not depend upon its adequacy to the medium from which it issues. As a matter of fact, many a genre has a hold on the audience because it caters to widespread social and cultural demands; it is and remains popular for reasons which do not involve questions of aesthetic legitimacy. Thus the photoplay has succeeded in perpetuating itself even though most responsible critics are agreed that it goes against the grain of film. Yet the public which feels attracted, for instance, by the screen version of *Death of a Salesman*, likes this version for the very virtues which made the Broadway play a hit and does not in the least care whether or not it has any specifically cinematic merits.

Second, let us for the sake of argument assume that my definition of aesthetic validity is actually one-sided; that it results from a bias for one particular, if important, type of cinematic activities and hence is unlikely to take into account, say, the possibility of hybrid genres or the influence of the medium's nonphotographic components. But this does not necessarily speak against the propriety of that definition. In a strategic interest it is often more advisable to loosen up initial one-sidedness—provided it is well founded—than to start from all too catholic premises and then try to make them specific. The latter alternative runs the risk of blurring differences between the media because it rarely leads far enough away from the generalities postulated at the outset; its danger is that it tends to entail a confusion of the arts. When Eisenstein, the theoretician, began to stress the similarities between the cinema and the traditional art media, identifying film as their ultimate fulfillment, Eisenstein, the artist, increasingly trespassed the boundaries that separate film from elaborate theatrical spectacles: think of his *Alexander Nevsky* and the operatic aspects of his *Ivan the Terrible*.

In strict analogy to the term "photographic approach" the film maker's approach is called "cinematic" if it acknowledges the basic aesthetic principle. It is evident that the cinematic approach materializes in all films which follow the realistic tendency. This implies that even films almost devoid of creative aspirations, such as newsreels, scientific or educational films, artless documentaries, etc., are tenable propositions from an aesthetic point of view—presumably more so than films which for all their artistry pay little attention to the given outer world. But as with photographic reportage, newsreels and the like meet only the minimum requirement.

What is of the essence in film no less than photography is the intervention of the film maker's formative energies in all the dimensions which the medium has come to cover. He may feature his impressions of this or that segment of physical existence in documentary fashion, transfer hallucinations and mental images to the screen, indulge in the rendering of rhythmical patterns, narrate a human-interest story, etc. All these creative efforts are in keeping with the cinematic approach as long as they benefit, in some way or other, the medium's substantive concern with our visible world. As in photography, everything depends on the "right" balance between the realistic tendency and the formative tendency; and the two tendencies are well balanced if the latter does not try to overwhelm the former but eventually follows its lead.

THE ISSUE OF ART

When calling the cinema an art medium, people usually think of films which resemble the traditional works of art in that they are free creations rather than explorations of nature. These films organize the raw material to which they resort into some self-sufficient composition instead of accepting it as an element in its own right. In other words, their underlying formative impulses are so strong that they defeat the cinematic approach with its concern for camera-reality. Among the film types customarily considered art are, for instance, the above-mentioned German expressionist films of the years after World War I; conceived in a painterly spirit, they seem to implement the formula of Hermann Warm, one of the designers of *The Cabinet of Dr. Caligari* settings, who claimed that "films must be drawings brought to life." Here also belongs many an experimental film; all in all, films of this type are not only intended as autonomous wholes but frequently ignore physical reality or exploit it for purposes alien to photographic veracity. By the same token, there is an inclination to classify as works of art feature films which combine forceful artistic composition with devotion to significant subjects and values. This would apply to a number of adaptations of great stage plays and other literary works.

Yet such a usage of the term "art" in the traditional sense is misleading. It lends support to the belief that artistic qualities must be attributed precisely to films which neglect the medium's recording obligations in an attempt to rival achievements in the fields of the fine arts, the theater, or literature. In consequence, this usage tends to obscure the aesthetic value of films which are really true to the medium. If the term "art" is reserved for productions like *Hamlet* or *Death of a Salesman*, one will find it difficult indeed to appreciate properly the large amount of creativity that goes into many a documentary capturing material phenomena for their own sake. Take Ivens's *Rain* or Flaherty's *Nanook*, documentaries saturated with formative intentions: like any selective photographer, their creators have all the traits of the imaginative reader and curious explorer; and their readings and discoveries result from full absorption in the given material and significant choices. Add to this that some of the crafts needed in the cinematic process—especially editing—represent tasks with which the photographer is not confronted. And they too lay claim to the film maker's creative powers.

This leads straight to a terminological dilemma. Due to its fixed meaning, the concept of art does not, and cannot, cover truly "cinematic" films—films, that is, which incorporate aspects of physical reality with a view to making us experience them. And yet it is they, not the films reminiscent of traditional art works, which are valid aesthetically. If film is an art at all, it certainly should not be confused with the established arts. There may be some justification in loosely applying this fragile concept to such films as *Nanook*, or *Paisan*, or *Potemkin* which are deeply steeped in camera-life. But in defining them as art, it must always be kept in mind that even the most creative film maker is much less independent of nature in the raw than the painter or poet; that his creativity manifests itself in letting nature in and penetrating it.

1960

ANDRÉ BAZIN
FROM WHAT IS CINEMA?

THE ONTOLOGY OF THE PHOTOGRAPHIC IMAGE

If the plastic arts were put under psychoanalysis, the practice of embalming the dead might turn out to be a fundamental factor in their creation. The process might reveal that at the origin of painting and sculpture there lies a mummy complex. The religion of ancient Egypt, aimed against death, saw survival as depending on the continued existence of the corporeal body. Thus, by providing a defense against the passage of time it satisfied a basic psychological need in man, for death is but the victory of time. To preserve, artificially, his bodily appearance is to snatch it from the flow of time, to stow it away neatly, so to speak, in the hold of life. It was natural, therefore, to keep up appearances in the face of the reality of death by preserving flesh and bone. The first Egyptian statue, then, was a mummy, tanned and petrified in sodium. But pyramids and labyrinthine corridors offered no certain guarantee against ultimate pillage.

Other forms of insurance were therefore sought. So, near the sarcophagus, alongside the corn that was to feed the dead, the Egyptians placed terra cotta statuettes, as substitute mummies which might replace the bodies if these were destroyed. It is this religious use, then, that lays bare the primordial function of statuary, namely, the preservation of life by a representation of life. Another manifestation of the same kind of thing is the arrow-pierced clay bear to be found in prehistoric caves, a magic identity-substitute for the living animal, that will ensure a successful hunt. The evolution, side by side, of art and civilization has relieved the plastic arts of their magic role. Louis XIV did not have himself embalmed. He was content to survive in his portrait by Le Brun. Civilization cannot, however, entirely cast out the bogy of time. It can only sublimate our concern with it to the level of rational thinking. No one believes any longer in the ontological identity of model and image, but all are agreed that the image helps us to remember the subject and to preserve him from a second spiritual death. Today the making of images no longer shares an anthropocentric, utilitarian purpose. It is no longer a question of survival after death, but of a larger concept, the creation of an ideal world in the likeness of the real, with its own temporal destiny. "How vain a thing is painting" if underneath our fond admiration for its works we do not discern man's primitive need to have the last word in the argument with death by means of the form that endures. If the history of the plastic arts is less a matter of their aesthetic than of their psychology then it will be seen to be essentially the story of resemblance, or, if you will, of realism.

Seen in this sociological perspective photography and cinema would provide a natural explanation for the great spiritual and technical crisis that overtook modern painting around the middle of the last century. André Malraux has described the cinema as the furthermost evolution to date of plastic realism, the beginnings of which were first manifest at the Renaissance and which found a limited expression in baroque painting.

It is true that painting, the world over, has struck a varied balance between the symbolic and realism. However, in the fifteenth century Western painting began to turn from its age-old concern with spiritual realities expressed in the form proper to it, towards an effort to combine this spiritual expression with as complete an imitation as possible of the outside world.

The decisive moment undoubtedly came with the discovery of the first scientific and already, in a sense, mechanical system of reproduction, namely, perspective: the camera obscura of Da Vinci foreshadowed the camera of Niepce. The artist was now in a position to create the illusion of three-dimensional space within which things appeared to exist as our eyes in reality see them.

Thenceforth painting was torn between two ambitions: one, primarily aesthetic, namely the expression of spiritual reality wherein the symbol transcended its model; the other, purely psychological, namely the duplication of the world outside. The satisfaction of this appetite for illusion merely served to increase it till, bit by bit, it consumed the plastic arts. However, since perspective had only solved the problem of form and not of movement, realism was forced to continue the search for some way of giving dramatic expression to the moment, a kind of psychic fourth dimension that could suggest life in the tortured immobility of baroque art.[1]

The great artists, of course, have always been able to combine the two tendencies. They have allotted to each its proper place in the hierarchy of things, holding reality at their command and molding it at will into the fabric of their art. Nevertheless, the fact remains that we are faced with two essentially different phenomena and these any objective critic must view separately if he is to understand the evolution of the pictorial. The need for illusion has not ceased to trouble the heart of painting since the sixteenth century. It is a purely mental need, of itself nonaesthetic, the origins of which must be sought in the proclivity of the mind towards magic. However, it is a need the pull of which has been strong enough to have seriously upset the equilibrium of the plastic arts.

---

[1] It would be interesting from this point of view to study, in the illustrated magazines of 1890–1910, the rivalry between photographic reporting and the use of drawings. The latter, in particular, satisfied the baroque need for the dramatic. A feeling for the photographic document developed only gradually.

The quarrel over realism in art stems from a misunderstanding, from a confusion between the aesthetic and the psychological; between true realism, the need that is to give significant expression to the world both concretely and its essence, and the pseudorealism of a deception aimed at fooling the eye (or for that matter the mind); a pseudorealism content in other words with illusory appearances.[2] That is why medieval art never passed through this crisis; simultaneously vividly realistic and highly spiritual, it knew nothing of the drama that came to light as a consequence of technical developments. Perspective was the original sin of Western painting.

It was redeemed from sin by Niepce and Lumière. In achieving the aims of baroque art, photography has freed the plastic arts from their obsession with likeness. Painting was forced, as it turned out, to offer us illusion and this illusion was reckoned sufficient unto art. Photography and the cinema on the other hand are discoveries that satisfy, once and for all and in its very essence, our obsession with realism.

No matter how skillful the painter, his work was always in fee to an inescapable subjectivity. The fact that a human hand intervened cast a shadow of doubt over the image. Again, the essential factor in the transition from the baroque to photography is not the perfecting of a physical process (photography will long remain the inferior of painting in the reproduction of color); rather does it lie in a psychological fact, to wit, in completely satisfying our appetite for illusion by a mechanical reproduction in the making of which man plays no part. The solution is not to be found in the result achieved but in the way of achieving it.[3]

This is why the conflict between style and likeness is a relatively modern phenomenon of which there is no trace before the invention of the sensitized plate. Clearly the fascinating objectivity of Chardin is in no sense that of the photographer. The nineteenth century saw the real beginnings of the crisis of realism of which Picasso is now the mythical central figure and which put to the test at one and the same time the conditions determining the formal existence of the plastic arts and their sociological roots. Freed from the "resemblance complex," the modern painter abandons it to the masses who, henceforth, identify resemblance on the one hand with photography and on the other with the kind of painting which is related to photography.

Originality in photography as distinct from originality in painting lies in the essentially objective character of photography. [Bazin here makes a point of the fact that the lens, the basis of photography, is in French called the "objectif," a nuance that is lost in English.—TR.] For the first time, between the originating object and its reproduction there intervenes only the instrumentality of a nonliving agent. For the first time an image of the world is formed automatically, without the creative intervention of man. The personality of the photographer enters into the proceedings only in his selection of the object to be photographed and by way of the purpose he has in mind. Although the final result may reflect something of his personality, this does not play

---

[2]Perhaps the Communists, before they attach too much importance to expressionist realism, should stop talking about it in a way more suitable to the eighteenth century, before there were such things as photography or cinema. Maybe it does not really matter if Russian painting is second-rate provided Russia gives us first-rate cinema. Eisenstein is her Tintoretto.

[3]There is room, nevertheless, for a study of the psychology of the lesser plastic arts, the molding of death masks for example, which likewise involves a certain automatic process. One might consider photography in this sense as a molding, the taking of an impression, by the manipulation of light.

the same role as is played by that of the painter. All the arts are based on the presence of man, only photography derives an advantage from his absence. Photography affects us like a phenomenon in nature, like a flower or a snowflake whose vegetable or earthly origins are an inseparable part of their beauty.

This production by automatic means has radically affected our psychology of the image. The objective nature of photography confers on it a quality of credibility absent from all other picture-making. In spite of any objections our critical spirit may offer, we are forced to accept as real the existence of the object reproduced, actually *re*-presented, set before us, that is to say, in time and space. Photography enjoys a certain advantage in virtue of this transference of reality from the thing to its reproduction.[4]

A very faithful drawing may actually tell us more about the model but despite the promptings of our critical intelligence it will never have the irrational power of the photograph to bear away our faith.

Besides, painting is, after all, an inferior way of making likenesses, an *ersatz* of the processes of reproduction. Only a photographic lens can give us the kind of image of the object that is capable of satisfying the deep need man has to substitute for it something more than a mere approximation, a kind of decal or transfer. The photographic image is the object itself, the object freed from the conditions of time and space that govern it. No matter how fuzzy, distorted, or discolored, no matter how lacking in documentary value the image may be, it shares, by virtue of the very process of its becoming, the being of the model of which it is the reproduction; it *is* the model.

Hence the charm of family albums. Those grey or sepia shadows, phantomlike and almost undecipherable, are no longer traditional family portraits but rather the disturbing presence of lifes halted at a set moment in their duration, freed from their destiny; not, however, by the prestige of art but by the power of an impassive mechanical process: for photography does not create eternity, as art does, it embalms time, rescuing it simply from its proper corruption.

Viewed in this perspective, the cinema is objectivity in time. The film is no longer content to preserve the object, enshrouded as it were in an instant, as the bodies of insects are preserved intact, out of the distant past, in amber. The film delivers baroque art from its convulsive catalepsy. Now, for the first time, the image of things is likewise the image of their duration, change mummified as it were. Those categories of *resemblance* which determine the species *photographic* image likewise, then, determine the character of its aesthetic as distinct from that of painting.[5]

The aesthetic qualities of photography are to be sought in its power to lay bare the realities. It is not for me to separate off, in the complex fabric of the objective world, here a reflection on a damp sidewalk, there the gesture of a child. Only the impassive lens, stripping its object of all those ways of seeing it, those piled-up

---

[4]Here one should really examine the psychology of relics and souvenirs which likewise enjoy the advantages of a transfer of reality stemming from the "mummy-complex." Let us merely note in passing that the Holy Shroud of Turin combines the features alike of relic and photograph.

[5]I use the term *category* here in the sense attached to it by M. Gouhier in his book on the theater in which he distinguishes between the dramatic and the aesthetic categories. Just as dramatic tension has no artistic value, the perfection of a reproduction is not to be identified with beauty. It constitutes rather the prime matter, so to speak, on which the artistic fact is recorded.

preconceptions, that spiritual dust and grime with which my eyes have covered it, is able to present it in all its virginal purity to my attention and consequently to my love. By the power of photography, the natural image of a world that we neither know nor can know, nature at last does more than imitate art: she imitates the artist.

Photography can even surpass art in creative power. The aesthetic world of the painter is of a different kind from that of the world about him. Its boundaries enclose a substantially and essentially different microcosm. The photograph as such and the object in itself share a common being, after the fashion of a fingerprint. Wherefore, photography actually contributes something to the order of natural creation instead of providing a substitute for it. The surrealists had an inkling of this when they looked to the photographic plate to provide them with their monstrosities and for this reason: the surrealist does not consider his aesthetic purpose and the mechanical effect of the image on our imaginations as things apart. For him, the logical distinction between what is imaginary and what is real tends to disappear. Every image is to be seen as an object and every object as an image. Hence photography ranks high in the order of surrealist creativity because it produces an image that is a reality of nature, namely, an hallucination that is also a fact. The fact that surrealist painting combines tricks of visual deception with meticulous attention to detail substantiates this.

So, photography is clearly the most important event in the history of plastic arts. Simultaneously a liberation and an accomplishment, it has freed Western painting, once and for all, from its obsession with realism and allowed it to recover its aesthetic autonomy. Impressionist realism, offering science as an alibi, is at the opposite extreme from eye-deceiving trickery. Only when form ceases to have any imitative value can it be swallowed up in color. So, when form, in the person of Cézanne, once more regains possession of the canvas there is no longer any question of the illusions of the geometry of perspective. The painting, being confronted in the mechanically produced image with a competitor able to reach out beyond baroque resemblance to the very identity of the model, was compelled into the category of object. Henceforth Pascal's condemnation of painting is itself rendered vain since the photograph allows us on the one hand to admire in reproduction something that our eyes alone could not have taught us to love, and on the other, to admire the painting as a thing in itself whose relation to something in nature has ceased to be the justification for its existence.

On the other hand, of course, cinema is also a language.

1945

THE MYTH OF TOTAL CINEMA

Paradoxically enough, the impression left on the reader by Georges Sadoul's admirable book on the origins of the cinema is of a reversal, in spite of the author's Marxist views, of the relations between an economic and technical evolution and the imagination of those carrying on the search. The way things happened seems to call for a reversal of the historical order of causality, which goes from the economic infrastructure to the ideological superstructure, and for us to consider the basic technical discoveries as fortunate accidents but essentially second in importance to the preconceived ideas of the inventors. The cinema is an idealistic phenomenon. The concept men had of it existed so to speak fully armed in their minds, as if in some platonic heaven, and what strikes us most of all is the obstinate resistance of matter to ideas rather than of any help offered by techniques to the imagination of the researchers.

Furthermore, the cinema owes virtually nothing to the scientific spirit. Its begetters are in no sense savants, except for Marey, but it is significant that he was only interested in analyzing movement and not in reconstructing it. Even Edison is basically only a do-it-yourself man of genius, a giant of the *concours Lépine*. Niepce, Muybridge, Leroy, Joly, Demeny, even Louis Lumière himself, are all monomaniacs, men driven by an impulse, do-it-yourself men or at best ingenious industrialists. As for the wonderful, the sublime E. Reynaud, who can deny that his animated drawings are the result of an unremitting pursuit of an *idée fixe*? Any account of the cinema that was drawn merely from the technical inventions that made it possible would be a poor one indeed. On the contrary, an approximate and complicated visualization of an idea invariably precedes the industrial discovery which alone can open the way to its practical use. Thus if it is evident to us today that the cinema even at its most elementary stage needed a transparent, flexible, and resistant base and a dry sensitive emulsion capable of receiving an image instantly—everything else being a matter of setting in order a mechanism far less complicated than an eighteenth-century clock—it is clear that all the definitive stages of the invention of the cinema had been reached before the requisite conditions had been fulfilled. In 1877 and 1880, Muybridge, thanks to the imaginative generosity of a horse-lover, managed to construct a large complex device which enabled him to make from the image of a galloping horse the first series of cinematographic pictures. However to get this result he had to be satisfied with wet collodion on a glass plate, that is to say, with just one of the three necessary elements— namely instantaneity, dry emulsion, flexible base. After the discovery of gelatino-bromide of silver but before the appearance on the market of the first celluloid reels, Marey had made a genuine camera which used glass plates. Even after the appearance of celluloid strips Lumière tried to use paper film.

Once more let us consider here only the final and complete form of the photographic cinema. The synthesis of simple movements studied scientifically by Plateau had no need to wait upon the industrial and economic developments of the nineteenth century. As Sadoul correctly points out, nothing had stood in the way, from antiquity, of the manufacture of a phenakistoscope or a zoötrope. It is true that here the labors of that genuine savant Plateau were at the origin of the many inventions that made the popular use of his discovery possible. But while, with the photographic cinema, we have cause for some astonishment that the discovery somehow precedes the technical conditions necessary to its existence, we must here explain, on the other hand, how it was that the invention took so long to emerge, since all the prerequisites had been assembled and the persistence of the image on the retina had been known for a long time. It might be of some use to point out that although the two were not necessarily connected scientifically, the efforts of Plateau are pretty well contemporary with those of Nicéphore Niepce, as if the attention of researchers had waited to concern itself with synthesizing movement until chemistry quite independently of optics had become concerned, on its part, with the automatic fixing of the image.

I emphasize the fact that this historical coincidence can apparently in no way be explained on grounds of scientific, economic, or industrial evolution. The photographic cinema could just as well have grafted itself onto a phenakistoscope foreseen as long ago as the sixteenth century. The delay in the invention of the latter is as disturbing a phenomenon as the existence of the precursors of the former.

But if we examine their work more closely, the direction of their research is manifest in the instruments themselves, and, even more undeniably, in their writings and commentaries we see that these precursors were indeed more like prophets. Hurrying past the various stopping places, the very first of which materially speaking should have halted them, it was at the very height and summit that most of them were aiming. In their imaginations they saw the cinema as a total and complete representation of reality; they saw in a trice the reconstruction of a perfect illusion of the the outside world in sound, color, and relief.

As for the latter, the film historian P. Potoniée has even felt justified in maintaining that it was not the discovery of photography but of stereoscopy, which came onto the market just slightly before the first attempts at animated photography in 1851, that opened the eyes of the researchers. Seeing people immobile in space, the photographers realized that what they needed was movement if their photographs were to become a picture of life and a faithful copy of nature. In any case, there was not a single inventor who did not try to combine sound and relief with animation of the image—whether it be Edison with his kinetoscope made to be attached to a phonograph, or Demenay and his talking portraits, or even Nadar who shortly before producing the first photographic interview, on Chevreul, had written, "My dream is to see the photograph register the bodily movements and the facial expressions of a speaker while the phonograph is recording his speech" (February, 1887). If color had not yet appeared it was because the first experiments with the three-color process were slower in coming. But E. Reynaud had been painting his little figurines for some time and the first films of Méliès are colored by stencilling. There are numberless writings, all of them more or less wildly enthusiastic, in which inventors conjure up nothing less than a total cinema that is to provide that complete illusion of life which is still a long way away. Many are familiar with that passage from *L'Éve Future* in which Villiers de l'Isle-Adam, two years before Edison had begun his researches on animated photography, puts into the inventor's mouth the following description of a fantastic achievement: ". . . the vision, its transparent flesh miraculously photographed in color and wearing a spangled costume, danced a kind of popular Mexican dance. Her movements had the flow of life itself, thanks to the process of successive photography which can retain six minutes of movement on microscopic glass, which is subsequently reflected by means of a powerful lampascope. Suddenly was heard a flat and unnatural voice, dull-ounding and harsh. The dancer was singing the *alza* and the *olé* that went with her *fandango*."

The guiding myth, then, inspiring the invention of cinema, is the accomplishment of that which dominated in a more or less vague fashion all the techniques of the mechanical reproduction of reality in the nineteenth century, from photography to the phonograph, namely an integral realism, a recreation of the world in its own image, an image unburdened by the freedom of interpretation of the artist or the irreversibilty of time. If cinema in its cradle lacked all the attributes of the cinema to come, it was with reluctance and because its fairy guardians were unable to provide them however much they would have liked to.

If the origins of an art reveal something of its nature, then one may legitimately consider the silent and the sound film as stages of a technical development that little by little made a reality out of the original "myth." It is understandable from this point of view that it would be absurd to take the silent film as a state of primal perfection which has gradually been forsaken by the realism of sound and color. The primacy of the image is both historically and technically accidental. The nostalgia that some still feel for the silent screen does not go far enough back into the childhood of the seventh art. The real primitives of the cinema, existing only in the imaginations of a few men of the nineteenth century, are in complete imitation of nature. Every new development added to the cinema must, paradoxically, take it nearer and nearer to its origins. In short, cinema has not yet been invented!

It would be a reversal then of the concrete order of causality, at least psychologically, to place the scientific discoveries or the industrial techniques that have loomed so large in its development at the source of the cinema's invention. Those who had the least confidence in the future of the cinema were precisely the two industrialists Edison and Lumière. Edison was satisfied with just his kinetoscope and if Lumière judiciously refused to sell his patent to Méliès it was undoubtedly because he hoped to make a large profit out of it for himself, but only as a plaything of which the public would soon tire. As for the real savants such as Marey, they were only of indirect assistance to the cinema. They had a specific purpose in mind and were satisfied when they had accomplished it. The fanatics, the madmen, the disinterested pioneers, capable, as was Berard Palissy, of burning their furniture for a few seconds of shaky images, are neither industrialists nor savants, just men obsessed by their own imaginings. The cinema was born from the converging of these various obsessions, that is to say, out of a myth, the myth of total cinema. This likewise adequately explains the delay of Plateau in applying the optical principle of the persistence of the image on the retina, as also the continuous progress of the syntheses of movement as compared with the state of photographic techniques. The fact is that each alike was dominated by the imagination of the century. Undoubtedly there are other examples in the history of techniques and inventions of the convergence of research, but one must distinguish between those which come as a result precisely of scientific evolution and industrial or military requirements and those which quite clearly precede them. Thus, the myth of Icarus had to wait on the internal combustion engine before descending from the platonic heavens. But it had dwelt in the soul of everyman since he first thought about birds. To some extent one could say the same thing about the myth of cinema, but its forerunners prior to the nineteenth century have only a remote connection with the myth which we share today and which has prompted the appearance of the mechanical arts that characterize today's world.

1946

RUDOLF ARNHEIM
FROM FILM AS ART

THE COMPLETE FILM

Psychologist and theorist of visual art, Rudolf Arnheim (1904–2007) studied with gestalt psychologists Wolfgang Köhler and Max Wertheimer,
whose theories he drew upon to create his own emphasis on the role of
sense perception in thought. As a student, he wrote film reviews for several Berlin publications and upon graduating, became an editor at the
weekly *Die Weltbühne* and in the 1920s explored the burgeoning art movements of the Weimar republic including Brechtian theater, Bauhaus art and
architecture, German expressionism, and international avant-garde film,
which he covered in his cultural column for the newspaper. His first book,
Film as Art, defended film as an art form for its ability to defamiliarize
reality. Due to Hitler's rise to power, the book was subsequently banned
and *Die Weltbühne* was forced to stop publishing. Arnheim left Germany
for Italy, where he continued to write about film and published a book on
radio as an art form. Sensing the growing fascism of the country under
Mussolini's racial laws, Arnheim left, first for England and finally America
in 1940, where he became professor of psychology at the New School for
Social Research, and later at Sarah Lawrence College, Harvard University,
and the University of Michigan. A pioneer of gestalt theory, he held that
visual perception, rather than language, is our primary means of thinking
about and understanding our world, an idea he argued most elaborately in
Visual Thinking (1969).

(Another selection from Arnheim's work appears in Part III.)

The technical development of the motion picture will soon carry the mechanical imitation of nature to an extreme. The addition of sound was the first obvious
step in this direction. The introduction of sound film must be considered as the
imposition of a technical novelty that did not lie on the path the best film artists
were pursuing. They were engaged in working out an explicit and pure style of
silent film, using its restrictions to transform the peep show into an art. The introduction of sound film smashed many of the forms that the film artists were using
in favor of the inartistic demand for the greatest possible "naturalness" (in the most
superficial sense of the word). By sheer good luck, sound film is not only destructive but also offers artistic potentialities of its own. Owing to this accident alone
the majority of art-lovers still do not realize the pitfalls in the road pursued by the

movie producers. They do not see that the film is on its way to the victory of wax museum ideals over creative art.

The development of the silent film was arrested possibly forever when it had hardly begun to produce good results; but it has left us with a few splendidly mature films. In the future, no doubt, "progress" will be faster. We shall have color films and stereoscopic films, and the artistic potentialities of the sound film will be crushed at an even earlier stage of their development.

What will the color film have to offer when it reaches technical perfection? We know what we shall lose artistically by abandoning the black-and-white film. Will color ever allow us to achieve a similar compositional precision, a similar independence of "reality"?

The masterpieces of painting prove that color provides wider possibilities than black-and-white and at the same time permits of a very exact and genuine style. But can painting and color photography be compared? Whereas the painter has a perfectly free hand with color and form in presenting nature, photography is obliged to record mechanically the light values of physical reality. In achromatic photography the reduction of everything to the gray scale resulted in an art medium that was sufficiently independent and divergent from nature. There is not much likelihood of any such transposition of reality into a qualitatively different range of colors in color film. To be sure, one can eliminate individual colors—one may, for example, cut out all blues, or, vice versa, one may cut out everything except the blues. Probably it is possible also to change one or more color tones qualitatively—for example, give all reds a cast of orange or make all the yellows greenish—or let colors change places with one another—turn all blues to red and all reds to blue—but all this would be, so to speak, only transposition of reality, mechanical shifts, whose usefulness as a formative medium may be doubted. Hence there remains only the possibility of controlling the color by clever choice of what is to be photographed. All kinds of fine procedures are conceivable, especially in the montage of colored pictures, but it must not be overlooked that in this way the subjective formative virtues of the camera, which are so distinctive a characteristic of film, will be more and more restricted, and the artistic part of the work will be more and more focused upon what is set up and enacted *before* the camera. The camera is thereby increasingly related to the position of a mere mechanical recording machine.

Above all, it is hardly realistic to speculate on the artistic possibilities of the color film without keeping in mind that at the same time we are likely to be presented with the three-dimensional film and the wide screen. Efforts in these directions are in progress. The illusion of reality will thereby have been increased to such a degree that the spectator will not be able to appreciate certain artistic color effects even if they should be feasible technically. It is quite conceivable that by a careful choice and arrangement of objects it might be possible to use the color on the projection surface artistically and harmoniously. But if the film image becomes stereoscopic there is no longer a plane surface within the confines of the screen, and therefore there can be no composition of that surface; what remains will be effects that are also possible on the stage. The increased size of the screen will render any two-dimensional or three-dimensional composition less compelling; and formative devices such as montage and changing camera angles will become unusable if the illusion of reality is so enormously strengthened. Obviously, montage will seem an intolerable accumulation of heterogeneous settings if the illusion of reality is very strong. Obviously also a change in the position of the camera will now be felt as an actual displacement within the space of the picture. The camera will have to become an immobile recording machine, every cut in the film strip will be mutilation. Scenes will have to be taken in their entire length and with a stationary camera, and they will have to be shown as they are. The artistic potentialities of this form of film will be exactly those of the stage. Film will no longer be able in any sense to be considered as a separate art. It will be thrown back to before its first beginnings—for it was with a fixed camera and an uncut strip that film started. The only difference will be that instead of having all before it film will have nothing to look forward to.

This curious development signifies to some extent the climax of that striving after likeness to nature which has hitherto permeated the whole history of the visual arts. Among the strivings that make human beings create faithful images is the primitive desire to get material objects into one's power by creating them afresh. Imitation also permits people to cope with significant experiences; it provides release, and makes for a kind of reciprocity between the self and the world. At the same time a reproduction that is true to nature provides the thrill that by the hand of man an image has been created which is astoundingly like some natural object. Nevertheless, various countertendencies—some of them purely perceptual—have prevented mechanically faithful imitation from being achieved hundreds of years ago. Apart from rare exceptions, only our modern age has succeeded in approaching this dangerous goal. In practice, there has always been the artistic urge not simply to copy but to originate, to interpret, to mold. We may, however, say that aesthetic theory has rarely sanctioned such activities. Even for artists like Leonardo da Vinci the demand for being as true to nature as possible was a matter of course when he talked theory, and Plato's attack on artists, in which he charged them with achieving nothing but reproductions of physical objects, is far from the general attitude.

To this very day some artists cherish this doctrine, and the general public does so to an even greater extent. In painting and sculpture it is only in recent decades that works have been appearing which show that their creators have broken with this principle intellectually and not merely practically. If a man considers that the artist should imitate nature, he may possibly paint like Van Gogh, but certainly not like Paul Klee. We know that the very powerful and widespread rejection of modern art is almost entirely supported by the argument that it is not true to nature. The development of film shows clearly how all powerful this ideal still is.

Photography and its offspring, film, are art media so near to nature that the general public looks upon them as superior to such old-fashioned and imperfect imitative techniques as drawing and painting. Since on economic grounds film is much more dependent on the general public than any other form of art, the "artistic" preferences of the public sweep everything before them. Some work of good quality can be smuggled in but it does not compensate for the more fundamental defeats of film art. The complete film is the fulfillment of the age-old striving for the complete illusion. The attempt to make the two-dimensional picture as nearly as possible like its old model succeeds; original and copy become practically indistinguishable.

Thereby all formative potentialities which were based on the differences between model and copy are eliminated and only what is inherent in the original in the way of significant form remains to art.

H. Baer in a remarkable little essay in the *Kunstblatt* has pointed out that color film represents the accomplishment of tendencies which have long been present in graphic art. "Graphic art [he says]—of which photography is one branch—has always striven after color. The oldest woodcuts, the blockbooks, were finished off by being handpainted. Later, a second, colored, plate was added to the black-and-white—as in Dürer's portrait of 'Ulrich Varnbühler.' A magnificent picture of a knight in armor in black, silver, and gold, exists by Burgmair. In the eighteenth century multicolored etchings were produced. In the nineteenth the lithographs of Daumier and Gavarni are colored in mass production. . . . Color invaded the graphic arts as an increased attraction for the eye. Uncivilized man is not as a rule satisfied with black-and-white. Children, peasants and primitive peoples demand the highest degree of bright coloring. It is the primitives of the great cities who congregate before the film screen. Therefore film calls in the aid of bright colors. It is a fresh stimulus."

In itself, the perfection of the "complete" film need not be a catastrophe—if silent film, sound film, and colored sound film were allowed to exist alongside it. There is no objection to the "complete" film as an alternative to the stage—it might help to take into remote places fine performances of good works, as also of operas, musical comedies, ballets, the dance. Moreover, by its very existence it would probably have an excellent influence on the other—the real—film forms, by forcing them to advance along their own lines. Silent film, for example, would no longer provide dialogue in its titles, because then the absence of the spoken word would be felt as artificial and disturbing. In sound film, too, any vague intermediate form between it and the stage would be avoided. Just as the stage will feel itself obliged by the very existence of film to emphasize its own characteristic—the predominance of dramatic speech—so the "complete" film could relegate the true film forms to their own sphere.

The fact is, however, that whereas aesthetically these categories of film could and should exist along with mechanically complete reproduction, they are inferior to it in the capacity to imitate nature. Therefore the "complete" film is certain to be considered an advance upon the preceding film forms, and will supplant them all.

1933

JEAN-LOUIS BAUDRY

THE APPARATUS: METAPSYCHOLOGICAL APPROACHES TO THE IMPRESSION OF REALITY IN CINEMA

Jean-Louis Baudry began his career as one of the prime members of the so-called *Tel Quel* group, named after the journal founded in 1960 by Philippe Sollers and published from 1960 to 1982, which featured articles on literature, culture, semiotics, psychoanalysis, and linguistic theory. Drawing upon the psychoanalytic theories of Jacques Lacan, Baudry's essays on the structure and ideological function of film technologies consider the way film constructs the viewing subject. His work ushered in a shift to a psychoanalytically-oriented film theory grounded in the ideas of Freud and Lacan, along with the neo-Marxist ideas of Louis Althusser. In addition to his work on the cinematic "apparatus," Baudry has written on creativity and writing, sound technologies, and changing theories of perception and perspective from the Renaissance to the present.

One constantly returns to the scene of the cave: real effect or impression of reality. Copy, simulacrum, and even simulacrum of simulacrum. Impression of the real, more-than-the-real? From Plato to Freud, the perspective is reversed; the procedure is inverted—so it seems. The former comes out of the cave, examines what is intelligible, contemplates its source, and, when he goes back, it is to denounce to the prisoners the apparatus which oppresses them, and to persuade them to leave, to get out of that dim space. The latter (on the contrary—no, for it is not a matter of simple opposition, or of a simplifying symmetry) is more interested in making them go back there precisely where they are; where they didn't know how to find themselves, for they thought themselves outside, and it is true they had been contemplating the good, the true, and the beautiful for a long time. But at what price and as a result of what ignorance; failure to recognize or repress, compromise, defense, sublimation? Like Plato, he urges them to consider the apparatus to overcome their resistances, to look a little more closely at what is coming into focus on the screen, the other scene. The other scene? What brings the two together and separates them? For both, as in the theater, a left side, a right side, the master's lodge, the valet's orchestra. But the first scene would seem to be the second's other scene. It is a question of truth in the final analysis, or else: "the failure to recognize has moved to the other side." Both distinguish between two scenes, or two places, opposing or confronting one another, one dominating the other. These aren't the same places; they don't respond point by point, although, in many respects, we who come after Freud would not be unjustified in superimposing more or less grossly the solar scene where the philosopher is at first dazzled, blinded by the good, on the scene of the conscious and its well-meaning exploits—we who, as a result of this very discovery of the unconscious, or of the other scene, could be induced to interpret the move, the exit, ascension, an initial blinding of the philosopher in a totally different manner. "Suppose one of them were set free and forced suddenly to stand up, turn his head, and walk with eyes lifted to the light; all these movements would be painful, and he would be too dazzled to make out the objects. . . . And if he were forced to look at the firelight itself, would not his eyes ache, so that he would try to escape and turn back to the things which he could see distinctly?" But the philosopher's cave could certainly not be superimposed onto that other scene, the scene of the unconscious! That remains to be seen. For we are dealing here with an apparatus, with a metaphorical relationship between places or a relationship between metaphorical places, with a topography, the knowledge of which defines for both philosopher and analyst the degree of relationship to truth or to description, or to illusion, and the need for an ethical point of view.

So you see, we return to the real or, for the experiencing subject (I could say, for the subject who is felt or who is acted), the impression of reality. And one could naively wonder why, some two and half thousand years later, it is by means of an optical metaphor—of an optical construct which signals term for term the cinematographic apparatus—that the philosopher exposes man's condition and the distance that separates him from "true reality"; and why it is again precisely by means of an optical metaphor that Freud, at the beginning and at the end of his writings, tries to account for the arrangement of the physical apparatus, for the functioning of the Unconscious and for the rapport/rupture Conscious-Unconscious. Chapter 7 of the *Traumdeutung*:

> What is presented to us in these words is the idea of a *psychical locality*. I shall entirely disregard the fact that the mental apparatus with which we are concerned is also known to us in the form of an anatomical preparation, and I shall carefully avoid the temptation to determine psychical locality in an anatomical fashion. I shall remain upon psychological ground, and I propose simply to follow the suggestion that we should picture the instrument which carries out our mental functions as resembling a compound microscope or a photographic apparatus, or something of the kind. On that basis, psychical locality will correspond to a point inside the apparatus at which one of the preliminary stages of an image comes into being. In the microscope and telescope, as we know, these occur in part at ideal points, regions in which no tangible component to the apparatus is situated. I see no necessity to apologize for the imperfections of this or of any similar imagery.[1]

However imperfect this comparison may be, Freud takes it up again forty years later at the very beginning of the *Abriss*: "We admit that psychical life is the function of an apparatus to which we attribute a spatial extension which is made up of several parts. We imagine it like a kind of telescope, or microscope or some similar device." Freud doesn't mention cinema. But this is because cinema is already too technologically determined an apparatus for describing the psychical apparatus as a whole. In 1913, however, Lou Andréas Salomé remarked: "Why is it that cinema has been of no use to us [analysts]? To the numerous arguments that could be advanced to save face for this Cinderella of the artistic conception of art, several psychological

---

[1]Sigmund Freud, *The Interpretation of Dreams* (New York: Avon, 1965), pp. 574–75.

considerations should be added. First, that the cinematographic technique is the only one that makes possible a succession of images rapid enough to roughly correspond to our faculty for producing mental images. Furthermore," she concludes "this provides food for reflection about the impact film could have in the future for our psychical make-up." Clearly Salomé seems to envision a very enigmatic track, unless we have misunderstood her. Does she mean that film may bear some sort of likeness to the psychical apparatus, that, for this reason, it could be of interest to those who, because of its direct relation to their practice, are immediately affected by a theorization of psychical operation linked to the discovery of the Unconscious? And is it not the apparatus, the cinematographic process itself rather than the content of images— that is, the film—which is under scrutiny here? She only points out that there might be correspondences between cinematographic technique and our ability to produce mental images. But there are many aspects of film technique, many different connections, from the recording of the images to their reproduction—an entire process which we have named elsewhere the *basic cinematographic apparatus*. And certainly such a technical construct—if only as examples and metaphor—should have interested Freud, since the major purpose of metapsychological research is to comprehend and to theoretically construct devices capable of recording traces, memory traces, and of restoring them in the form of representation. He admits: the concept of the "magic writing pad" (which he substitutes for the optical metaphor to which he later returns) is missing something: the possibility of restoring inscribed traces by using specific memory mechanisms which are exclusively constituted by living matter but which a certain number of technical inventions of the time already mimic: the phonograph and cinema, precisely. The advantage of the magic writing pad is that since the external surface doesn't retain any trace of the inscriptions, it is best suited to illustrate the system Perception-Conscious; in addition, the waxy substance inside preserves, superimposed and to some extent associated, the different traces which have inscribed themselves throughout time, preserves them from what could be called historical accidents. Obviously, nothing prevents the same thing from applying to the material of the record or to the film stock of the film if not that such reproduction would be confusing and indecipherable to us: the inscription follows other tracks, which are organized according to other principles than those of inanimate matter.

Yet, there is something there which should capture our attention: the double place of the subject (constituted on the one hand by the system perception = Conscious characterized by the transience, successiveness, and mobility of perceptions and representations; on the other by Unconscious system traces/inscriptions characterized by permanence) finds itself once more within an idealist perspective considerably displaced with respect to the unconscious in Plato. But as we have learned from Marx, there is often a truth hidden from or in idealism, a truth which belongs to materialism, but which materialism can only discover after many detours and delays—a hidden or disguised truth. In Plato, something haunts the subject; something belabors him and determines his condition (could it be the pressure of the "Ideas"?) As for Freud, the subject which Plato describes, the prisoner in the cave, is deceived (this whole theme of the mistaken subject which runs through the history of philosophy!); he is the prey of illusions, and, as for Freud, these illusions are but distortions and symptoms (gradations, the idealist would say—and admit this changes everything) of what is happening somewhere else. Even though Ideas take the place of the

Unconscious for him, Plato confronts a problem equivalent to that which at first preoccupies Freud in his metapsychological research and which, precisely, the cave myth is presumed to resolve: the transfer, the access from one place to another, along with the ensuing distortions. Plato's prisoner is the victim of an illusion of reality, that is, of precisely what is known as a hallucination, if one is awake, as a dream, if asleep; he is the prey of an impression, of *an impression of reality*. As I have said, Plato's *topos* does not and could not possibly correspond exactly to Freud's and surely, although it may be interesting to show what displacement occurs from one *topos* to the other (the location of reality for Plato obviously doesn't correspond to what is real for Freud), it is still more important to determine what is at work on the idealist philosopher's discourse unknown to him, the truth which proclaims, very different yet contained within the one he consciously articulates.

As a matter of fact, isn't it curious that Plato, in order to explain the transfer, the access from one place to another and to demonstrate, reveal, and make understood what sort of illusion underlies our direct contact with the real, would imagine or resort to an apparatus that doesn't merely evoke, but quite precisely describes in its mode of operation the cinematographic apparatus[2] and the spectator's place in relation to it.

It is worth rereading the description of the cave from this perspective.

First, the space: "a kind of cavernous underground chamber with an entrance open to the light" but too small to light it up. As Plato points out farther on: "a dim space." He emphasizes the effect of the surrounding darkness on the philosopher after his sojourn in the outside world. To his companions he will at first appear blind, his eyesight ruined; and his clumsiness will make them laugh. They will not be able to have confidence in him. In the cave, the prisoner-spectators are seated, still, prisoners because immobilized: unable to move—constraint or paralysis? It is true that they are chained, but, freed, they would still refuse to leave the place where they are; and so obstinately would they resist that they might put to death anyone trying to lead them out. In other words, this first constraint, against their will, this deprivation of movement which was imposed on them initially, this motor inhibition which affected so much their future dispositions, conditions them to the point that they prefer to stay where they are and to perpetuate this immobility rather than leave. Initial constraint which seems in this way to turn itself into a kind of spite or at least to inscribe the compulsion to repeat, the return to a former condition. There are things like that in Plato? It is not unnecessary to insist on this point as we reread the Platonic myth from the special perspective of the cinematographic apparatus. Forced immobility is undoubtedly a valuable argument for the demonstration/description that Plato makes of the human condition: the coincidence of religious and idealist conceptions; but the initial immobility was not invented by Plato; it can also refer to the forced immobility of the child who is without motor resources at birth, and to the forced immobility

---

[2]In a general way, we distinguish the *basic cinematographic apparatus* [*l'appareil de base*], which concerns the ensemble of the equipment and operations necessary to the production of a film and its projection, from the apparatus [*le dispositif*] discussed in this article, which solely concerns projection and which includes the subject to whom the projection is addressed. Thus the *basic cinematographic apparatus* involves the film stock, the camera, developing, montage considered in its technical aspects, etc., as well as the apparatus [*dispositif*] of projection. The basic cinematographic apparatus is a long way from being the camera by itself, to which some have wanted to say I limit it (one wonders what bad arguments this can serve).

of the sleeper who we know repeats the postnatal state and even interuterine existence; but this is also the immobility that the visitor to the dim space rediscovers, leaning back into his chair. It might even be added that the spectators' immobility is characteristic of the filmic apparatus as a whole. The prisoner's shackles correspond to an actual reality in the individual's evolution, and Plato even draws the conclusion that it could have an influence on his future behavior, and would be a determining factor in the prisoner's resistance to breaking away from the state of illusion. "He might be required once more to deliver his opinion on those shadows, in competition with the prisoners who had never been released. . . . If they could lay hands on the man who was trying to set them free and lead them up, they would kill him." Does he mean that immobility constitutes a necessary if not sufficient condition for the prisoner's credulity, that it constitutes one of the causes of the state of confusion into which they have been thrown and which makes them take images and shadows for the real? I don't want to stretch Plato's argument too far, even if I am trying to make his myth mean more than it actually says. But note: "In this underground chamber they have been *from childhood*, chained by the leg and also by the neck, so that they cannot move and can see only what is in front of them, because the chains will not let them turn their heads" [my emphasis]. Thus it is their motor paralysis, their inability to move about that, making the reality test impractical for them, reinforces their error and makes them inclined to take for real that which takes its place, perhaps its figuration or its projection onto the wall/screen of the cavern in front of them and from which they cannot detach their eyes and turn away. They are bound, shackled to the screen, tied and related—relation, extension between it and them due to their inability to move in relation to it, the last sight before falling asleep.

Plato says nothing about the quality of the images: is two dimensional space suited to the representation of depth produced by the images of objects? Admittedly, they are flat shadows, but their movements, crossings over, superimpositions, and displacements allow us perhaps to assume that they are moving along different planes. However, Plato calls the projector to mind. He doesn't feel a need for making use of natural light; but it is also important to him to preserve and protect that light from an impure usage: idealism makes the technician. Plato is satisfied with a fire burning behind them "at some distance higher up." As a necessary precaution, let us examine Plato's accuracy in assembling his apparatus. He is well aware that, placed otherwise, the fire would transmit the reflections of the prisoners themselves most prominently onto the screen. The "operators," the "machinists" are similarly kept out of the prisoners' sight, hidden by "a parapet, like the screen at a puppet-show, which hides the performers while they show their puppets over the top." For, undoubtedly, by associating themselves with the objects that they are moving back and forth before the fire, they would project a heterogeneous image capable of canceling the reality effect they want to produce: they would awake the prisoner's suspicions; they would awake the prisoners.

Here is the strangest thing about the whole apparatus. Instead of projecting images of natural/real objects, of living people, etc. onto the wall/screen of the cave as it would seem only natural to do for simple shadow plays, Plato feels the need, by creating a kind of conversion in the reference to reality, to show the prisoners not direct images and shadows of reality but, even at this point, a simulacrum of it. One might easily recognize the idealist's prudence, the calculated progress of the philosopher who prefers pushing the real back another notch and multiplying the steps leading to it, lest excessive haste lead his listener again to trust his senses too much. In any case, for this reason (or for another), he is led to place and to suppose between the projector, the fire, and the screen something which is itself a mere prop of reality, which is merely its image, its copy, its simulacrum: "figures of men and animals in wood or stone or other materials" suggestive of studio objects of papier mâché decor, were it not for the more striking impression created by their passing in front of the fire like a film.

All that is missing is the sound, in effect much more difficult to reproduce. Not only this: more difficult to copy, to employ like an image in the visible world; as if hearing, as opposed to sight, resisted being caught up in simulacra. Real voices, then, they would emanate from the bearers, the machinists, and the marionette players (a step is skipped in the reference to reality) but nevertheless, given over to the apparatus, integrated with it since it requires a total effect for fear of exposing the illusion. But voice that does not allow representation as do artificial objects—stone and wooden animals, and statues—will still give itself over to the apparatus thanks to its reverberation. "And suppose their prison had an echo from the wall facing them?" "When one of the people crossing behind them spoke, they could only suppose that the sound came from the shadow passing before their eyes." If a link is missing in the chain that connects us back to reality, the apparatus corrects this, by taking over the voice's echo, by integrating into itself these excessively real voices. And it is true that in cinema—as in the case of all talking machines—one does not hear an image of the sounds but the sounds themselves. Even if the procedures for recording the sounds and playing them back deforms them, they are reproduced and not copied. Only their source of emission may partake of illusion; their reality cannot. Hence, no doubt one of the basic reasons for the privileged status of voice in idealist philosophy and in religion: voice does not lend itself to games of illusion, or confusion, between the real and its figurativity (because voice cannot be represented figuratively) to which sight seems particularly liable. Music and singing differ qualitatively from painting in their relation to reality.

As we have seen, Plato constructs an apparatus very much like sound cinema. But, precisely because he has to resort to sound, he anticipates an ambiguity which was to be characteristic of cinema. This ambiguity has to do with the impression of reality: with the means used to create it, and with the confusion and lack of awareness surrounding its origin, from which result the inventions which mark the history of cinema. Plato effectively helps us to recognize this ambiguity. For, on the one hand, he is careful to emphasize the artificial aspect of reproduced reality. It is the apparatus that creates the illusion, and not the degree of fidelity with the Real: here *the prisoners have been chained since childhood*, and it will therefore not be the reproduction of this or that specific aspect of that reality, which they do not know, which will lead them to attribute a greater degree of reality to the illusion to which they are subject (and we have seen that Plato was already careful to insert artifice, and that already what was projected was deception). On the other hand, by introducing voice, by reconstructing a talking machine, by complementing the projection with sound, by illustrating, as it were, the need to affect as many sense faculties as possible, at any rate the two most important, he certainly seems to comply

with a necessity to duplicate reality in the most exact manner and to make his artifice as good a likeness as can be made. Plato's myth evidently functions as a
metaphor for an analogy on which he himself insists before dealing with the myth:
namely, that what can be known through the senses is in the same relationship to
that which can be known through the intellect as projection in the cave is to experience (that is, to ordinary reality). Besides that, isn't it remarkable that Plato should
have been forced to resort to such a procedure and that, in his attempt to explain
the position, the locus of that which can be known through the intellect, he was led
to take off, so to speak, toward "illusion"; he was led to construct an apparatus
which will make it possible, that it is capable of producing a special effect through
the impression of reality it communicates to the spectator.

Here I must add something which may be of importance: in the scene taking place
inside the cave, voices, words, "[these echoes which] they could only suppose that
the sound came from the shadow passing before their eyes," do not have a discursive or conceptual role; they do not communicate a message; they belong to ordinary reality which is as immediate to the prisoners as are images; they cannot be
separated from the latter; they are characterized according to the same mode of existence and in effect treated in the same way as words in a dream "fragments of discourse *really* spoken or heard, *detached from their context*" (my emphasis), and
functioning like other kinds of dream representation.

But there is another way to state the problem. What desire was aroused, more
than two thousand years before the actual invention of cinema, what urge in need
of fulfillment would be satisfed by *a montage, rationalized into an idealist perspective precisely in order to show that it rests primarily on an impression of reality?* The impression of reality is central to Plato's demonstration. That his entire
argument is developed in order to prove that this impression is deceptive abundantly
demonstrates its existence. As we have already noted, something haunts Plato's text:
the prisoners' fascination (how better to convey the condition that keeps them
chained up, those fetters that prevent them from moving their heads and necks),
their reluctance to leave, and even their willingness to resort to violence. But isn't
it principally the need to construct another scene apart from the world, underground,
in short to construct it as if it existed, or as if this construction also satisfied a desire
to objectify a similar scene—an apparatus capable precisely of fabricating an impression of reality. This would appear to satisfy and replace the nostalgia for a lost
impression which can be seen as running through the idealist movement and eating
away at it from inside, and setting it in motion. That the real in Plato's text is at an
equal distance from or in a homologous relationship to the "intelligibly real"—the
world of Ideas—and "reality-subject"—"the impression of reality" produced by the
apparatus in the cave should moreover be sufficient to make us aware of the real
meaning of the world of Ideas and of the field of desire on which it has been built
(a world which, as we know, "exists outside of time," and which, after numerous
encounters, the conscious subject can rediscover in himself).

Cave, grotto, "sort of cavernous chamber underground," people have not failed
to see in it a representation of the maternal womb, of the matrix into which we are
supposed to wish to return. Granted, but only the place is taken into account by this
interpretation and not the apparatus as a whole; and if this apparatus really produces

images, it first of all produces an effect of specific subjects—to the extent that a subject is intrinsically part of the apparatus; once the cinema has been technically perfected, it produces this same effect defined by the words "impression of reality" (words that may be confusing but which nevertheless need to be clarified). This impression of reality appears as if—just as if—it were known to Plato. At the very least, it seems that Plato ingeniously attempts and succeeds in fixing up a machine capable of reproducing "something" that he must have known, and that has less to do with its capacity for repeating the real (and this is where the Idealist is of great help to us by sufficiently emphasizing the artifice he employs to make his machine work) than with reproduction and repetition of a particular condition, and the representation of a particular place on which this condition depends.

Of course, from the analytic perspective we have chosen, by asking cinema about the wish it expresses, we are aware of having distorted the allegory of the cave by making it reveal, from a considerable historic distance, the approximate construct of the cinematographic apparatus. In other words, a same apparatus was responsible for the invention of the cinema and was already present in Plato. The text of the cave may well express a desire inherent to a participatory effect deliberately produced, sought for, and expressed by cinema (and the philosopher is first of all a spokesman of desire before becoming its great "channeler," which shows why it is far from useless to bring an analytic ear to bear on him despite or because of his rationalizations, even though he would deny it as tolerable suspicion, even and especially though he complains, rightly from his point of view, of our having distorted his text). We can thus propose that the allegory of the cave is the text of a signifier of desire which haunts the invention of cinema and the history of its invention.

You see why historians of cinema, in order to unearth its first ancestor, never leave off dredging a prehistory which is becoming increasingly cluttered. From the magic lantern to the praxinoscope and the optical theater up to the *camera obscura*, as the booty piles up, the excavations grow: new objects and all kinds of inventions—one can feel the disarray increasing. But if cinema was really the answer to a desire inherent in our psychical structure, how can we date its first beginnings? Would it be too risky to propose that painting, like theater, for lack of suitable technological and economic conditions, were dry runs in the approximation not only of the world of representation but of what might result from a certain aspect of its functioning and which only the cinema is in a position to implement? These attempts have obviously produced their own specificity and their own history, but their existence has at its origin a psychical source equivalent to the one which stimulated the invention of cinema.

It is very possible that there was never any first invention of cinema. Before being the outcome of technical considerations and of a certain state of society's development (necessary to its realization and to its completion), it was primarily the target of a desire which, moreover, its immediate success as well as the interest which its ancestors had aroused has demonstrated clearly enough. A desire, to be sure, a form of lost satisfaction which its apparatus would be aimed at rediscovering in one way or another (even to the point of simulation) and to which the impression of reality would seem to be the key.

I would now like to look more closely at what the impression of reality and the desire objectified in its entails by surveying certain analytical texts.

And since I have already mentioned the cave, "a kind of cavernous underground chamber," as Plato says, I went back to the *Interpretation of Dreams* and discovered a remark of Freud's that could guide our search. This remark is to be found in the passage dedicated to examples of dream work. Freud examines the kinds of figuration that occur during analysis. After having shown how the treatment gets itself represented, Freud comes to the unconscious, "If the unconscious, insofar as it belongs to waking thought, needs to be represented in dreams, it is represented in them in underground places." Freud adds the following which, because of the above, is very interesting: "Outside of analytic treatment, these representations would have symbolized the woman's body or the womb." If the world of Ideas offers numerous concepts which correspond to those which Freud discovered in the Unconscious (the permanence of traces, the ignorance of time), that is, if the philosophical edifice can be envisaged as a rationalization of the Unconscious's thrust, of its suspected but rejected existence, then we can ask whether it is not the Unconscious or certain of its mechanisms that are figured, that represent themselves in the apparatus of the cave. In any case, paraphrasing Fechner, we could propose that the scene of the cave (and of cinema) is perhaps quite different from that of the activity of representation in a state of wakefulness. In order to learn a little more about that other scene, it might be useful to linger a while before the dream scene.

A parallel between dream and cinema had often been noticed: common sense perceived it right away. The cinematographic projection is reminiscent of dream, would appear to be a kind of dream, really a dream,[3] a parallelism often noticed by the dreamer when, about to describe his dream, he is compelled to say "It was like in a movie . . ." At this point, it seems useful to follow Freud closely in his metapsychological analysis of dream. Once the role and function of dream as a protector of sleep and as fulfillment of a wish has been recognized as well as its nature and the elaboration of which it is the result, and after the material, the translation of the manifest content into dream thoughts, has been studied, one must still determine the conditions of dream formation, the reasons that give dream a specific qualitative nature in the whole of the psychical life, the specific "dream effect" that it determines. This is the subject of chapter 7 of *The Interpretations of Dreams* and the *Supplement to the Theory of Dreams* fifteen years later. In the latter text, Freud at first seems concerned with understanding why dream manifests itself to the dreamer's consciousness in the form of what might be called the "specific mode of dream," a feature of reality which should more properly belong to the perception of

---

[3]A close relationship which has led filmmakers to believe that cinema was the instrument finally suited for the representation of dreams. The failure of their attempt still remains to be understood. Is it not that the representation of dreams in cinema would not function like the representation of dreams in dreams, precisely destroying the impression of reality in the same way as the thought that one is dreaming intervenes in dream as a defense mechanism against the "mashing" desire of dream. The displacement of dream in the projection results unavoidably in sending the spectator back to his consciousness; it imposes a distance which denounces the artifice (and is there anything more ridiculous than those soft focus clouds, supposedly dreamlike representations) and it destroys completely the *impression of reality* which precisely also defines dream.

the external world. What are the determining factors of a necessarily metapsychological order, that is, involving the construction and operation of the psychical apparatus, which makes it possible for dream to pass itself off for reality to the dreamer. Freud begins with sleep: dream is the psychical activity of the dreamer. Sleep, he tells us, "from a somatic viewpoint is *a revivescence of one's stay in the body of the mother, certain conditions of which it recreates: the rest position, warmth, and isolation which protects him from excitement*" [emphasis added]. This makes possible a first form of regression: *temporal regression*, which follows two paths—regression of the libido back to a previous period of hallucinatory satisfaction of desire; and regression in the development of the self back to a primitive narcissism which results in what has been defined as the totally egotistical nature of dream: "*the person who plays the main part in dream scenes is always the dreamer himself.*" Sleep favors the appearance of another form of regression which is extremely important for the manifestation of the dream effect: by deactivating equally the Cs, Pcs, and Ucs systems, that is, by allowing an easier communication between them, sleep leaves open the regressive path which the cathetic representations will follow as far as perception. *Topical regression* and *temporal regression* combine to reach the edge of dream.

I do not want to insist excessively on Freud's analysis. We need only note that the dream wish is formed from daytime residues in the Proconscious system which are reinforced by drives emanating from the Unconscious. Topical regression first allows the transformation of the dream thoughts into images. It is through the intermediary of regression that word representations belonging to the Preconscious system are translated into thing representations which dominate the Unconscious system.[4] "Thoughts are transposed into images—mostly visual ones—thus the representations of words are reduced to representations of objects corresponding to them as if, throughout the whole system, considerations of representability overwhelmed the whole process." So much so that a dream wish can be turned into a dream fantasy. Once again, it is regression which gives dream its definitive shape. "The completion of the dream process is also marked by the fact that the content of thought, transformed by regression and reshaped into a fantasy of desire, comes into consciousness as a sensory perception and then undergoes the secondary elaboration which affects any perceptual content. We are saying that the dream wish is hallucinated and finds, in the guise of hallucination a belief in the reality of its fulfillment." Dream is "an hallucinatory psychosis of desire"—that is, a state in which mental perceptions are taken for perceptions of reality. Moreover, Freud hypothesized that the satisfaction resulting from hallucination is a kind of satisfaction which we knew at the beginning of our psychical life when perception and representation could not be differentiated, when the different systems were confused, that is, when the system of Consciousness-Perception had not differentiated itself. The object of desire (the object of need), if it happens to be lacking, can at this point be halluci-

---

[4]In *The Ego and the Id*, Freud adds comments which allow him to assert that "visual thought is closer to the unconscious processes than verbal thought, and older than the latter, from the phylogenetic as well as from the ontogenetic standpoints. Verbal representations all belong to the Pcs, while the unconscious only relies on visual ones."

nated. It is precisely the repeated failure offered by this form of satisfaction which results in the differentiation between perception and representation through the creation of the reality test. A perception which can be eliminated by an action is recognized as exterior. The reality test is dependent on "motoricity." Once "motoricity" has been interrupted, as during sleep, the reality test can no longer function. The suspension of "motoricity," its being set apart, would indeed favor regression. But it is also because sleep determines a withdrawal of cathexis in the Cs, Ucs, and Pcs systems that the fantasies of the dream wish follow the original path which differentiate them from fantasies produced during the waking state.[5] Like daytime fantasies, they could have become conscious without nevertheless being taken for real or completed; but, having taken the path of regression, not only are they capable of taking over consciousness but, because of the subject's inability to rely upon the reality test, they are marked by the very character of perception and appear as reality. The processes of dream formation succeed well in presenting dream as real.

The transformations accomplished by sleep in the psychical apparatus: withdrawal of cathexis, instability of the different systems, return to narcissism, loss of motoricity (because of the impossibility of applying the reality test), contribute to produce features which are specific to dream: its capacity for figuration, translation of thought into images, reality extended to representations. One might even add that we are dealing with a *more-than-real* in order to differentiate it from the impression of the real which reality produces in the normal waking situation: the more-than-real translating the cohesion of the subject with his perceived representations, the submersion of the subject in his representations, the near impossibility for him to escape their influence and which is dissimilar if not incompatible with the impression resulting from any direct relation to reality. There appears to be an ambiguity in the words poorly expressing the difference between the relationship of the subject to his representations experienced as perceived and his relation to reality.

Dream, Freud also tells us, is a projection, and, in the context in which he uses the word, projection evokes at once the analytic use of the defense mechanism which consists in referring and attributing to the exterior representations and affects which the subject refuses to acknowledge as his own, and it also evokes a distinctly cinematographic use since it involves images which, once projected, come back to the subject as a reality perceived from the outside.

That dream is a projection reminiscent of the cinematographic apparatus is indeed what seems to come out of Lewin's discovery of the *dream screen*, the hypothesis for which was suggested to him by his patients' enigmatic dreams. One young woman's dream, for example: "I had my dream all ready for you, but while I was lying here looking at it, it began to move in circles far from me, wrapped up on itself, again and again, like two acrobats." This dream shows that the screen, which

---

[5]This is why it is not by paying attention to the content of images that one is able to account for the impression of reality but by questioning the apparatus. The differentiation between fantasies and dream is due to the transformation of the psychical apparatus during the transition from the state of being awake to sleep. Sleep will make necessary the work of figuration the economy of which can be created by daytime fantasies; in addition, daytime fantasies do not accompany the belief in reality of the fulfillment which characterizes dream. This is why in attempting to understand the cinema effect—the impression of reality—we have to go through the intermediary of dream and not daytime fantasies.

can appear by itself, like a white surface, is not exclusively a representation, a content—in which case it would not be necessary to privilege it among other elements of the dream content; but, rather, it would present itself in all dreams as the indispensable support for the projection of images. It would seem to pertain to the dream apparatus. "The dream screen is a surface on which a dream seems to be projected. It is the 'blank background' (empty basic surface) which is present in dream although it is not necessarily seen; the manifest content of dream ordinarily perceived takes place over it, or in front of it." "Theoretically it can be part of the latent content or of the manifest content, but the distinction is academic. The dream screen is not often noticed by analysts, and, in the practice of dream interpretation, the analyst does not need to deal with it." It is cinema which suggested the term to Lewin because, in the same way as its analog in the cinematographic apparatus, the dream screen is either ignored by the dreamer (the dreaming spectator) or unrelated to the interest resulting from the images and the action.[6] Lewin adds nevertheless (and this remark reminds us of a modern use of the screen in cinema) that in some circumstances, the screen does play a part of its own and becomes discernible. According to Lewin's hypothesis, the dream screen is the dream's hallucinatory representation of the mother's breast on which the child used to fall asleep after nursing. In this way, it expresses a state of complete satisfaction while repeating the original condition of the oral phase in which the body did not have limits of its own, but was extended undifferentiated from the breast. Thus, the dream screen would correspond to the desire to sleep: archetype and prototype of any dream. Lewin adds another hypothesis: the dream itself, the visual representations which are projected upon it, would correspond to the desire to be awake. "A visual dream repeats the child's early impression of being awake. His eyes are open and he sees. For him, to see is to be awake." Actually, Lewin insists on Freud's explanation of the predominance of visual elements in dream: that latent thoughts in a dream are to a large extent shaped by unconscious mnemic traces which can only exist as a visual representation—the repetition of a formal element from the child's earliest experience. It is evident that the dream screen is a residue from the most archaic mnemic traces. But, additionally, and this is at least as important, one might assume that it provides an opening for understanding the dreamer's "primal scene" which establishes itself during the oral phase. The hallucinatory factor, the lack of distinction between representation and perception—representation taken as perception which makes for our belief in the reality of dream—would correspond to the lack of distinction between active and passive, between acting and suffering experience, undifferentiation between the limits of the body (body/breast), between eating and being eaten, etc., characteristics of the oral phase and borne out by the envelopment of the subject by the screen. For the same reasons, we would find ourselves in a position to understand the specific mode in which the dreamer identifies with his dream, a mode which is anterior to the mirror stage, to the formation of the self, and therefore founded on a permeability, a fusion of the interior with the exterior.

---

[6]Bertram Lewin, "Sleep, the Mouth and the Dream Screen," *Psychoanalytic Quarterly* (1946), 15: 419–43, "Inferences from the Dream Screen," *International Journal of Psychoanalysis* (1948). 29: 224–431.

On the other hand, if the dream itself, in its visual content, is likely to represent the desire to stay awake, the combination dream screen/projected images would manifest a conflict between contradictory motions, a state in effect of undistinction between a hallucinatory wish, sign of satisfaction, and desire for perception, of contact with the real. It is therefore conceivable that something of a desire in dream unifying perception and representation—whether representation passes itself for perception, in which case we would be closer to hallucination, or whether perception passes itself for perceived representation, that is, acquires as perception the mode of existence which is proper to hallucination—takes on the character of specific reality which reality does not impart, but which hallucination provokes: *a more-than-real* that dream precisely, considered as apparatus and as the repetition of a particular state which defines the oral phase, would, on its own, be able to bring to it. Dream alone?

Lewin's hypothesis, which complements and extends Freud's ideas on the formation of dream in relation to the feeling of reality which is linked to it, presents, in my opinion, the advantage of offering a kind of formation stage, of dream constitution, which might be construed as operative in the cinema effect. Impression of reality and that which we have defined as the desire of cinema, as cinema in its general apparatus would recall, would mime a form of archaic satisfaction experienced by the subject by reproducing the scene of it.

Of course, there is no question of identifying mental image, filmic image, mental representation, and cinematographic representation. The fact that the same terms are used, however, does reveal the very workings of desire in cinema, that is, at the same time the desire to rediscover archaic forms of desire which in fact structure any form of desire, and the desire to stage for the subject, to put in the form of representation, what might recall its own operation.

In any case, this deviation through the "metapsychological fiction" of dream could enlighten us about the effect specific to cinema, "the impression of reality," which, as is well known, is different from the usual impression which we receive from reality, but which has precisely this characteristic of being more than real which we have detected in dream.

Actually, cinema is a simulation apparatus. This much was immediately recognized, but, from the positivist viewpoint of scientific rationality which was predominant at the time of its invention, the interest was directed toward the simulation of reality inherent to the moving image with the unexpected effects which could be derived from it, without finding it necessary to examine the fact that the cinematographic apparatus was initially directed toward the subject and that *simulation could be applied to states or subject effects before being directed toward the reproduction of the real.* It is nevertheless curious that in spite of the development of analytic theory, the problem should have remained unsolved or barely considered since that period. Almost exclusively, it is the technique and content of film which have retained attention: characteristics of the image, depth of field, offscreen space, shot, single-shot sequence, montage, etc.; the key to the impression of reality has been sought in the structuring of image and movement, in complete ignorance of the fact that the impression of reality is dependent first of all on a subject effect and that it might be necessary to examine the position of the subject facing the image in order to determine the raison d'être for the cinema effect. Instead of considering cinema as an ideologically neutral apparatus, as it has been rather stupidly called, the impact of which would be entirely determined by the content of the film (a consideration which leaves unsolved the whole question of its persuasive power and of the reason for which it revealed itself to be an instrument particularly well suited to exert ideological influence), in order to explain the cinema effect, it is necessary to consider it from the viewpoint of the apparatus that it constitutes, apparatus which in its totality includes the subject. And first of all, the subject of the unconscious. The difficulties met by the theoreticians of cinema in their attempt to account for the impression of reality are proportionate to the persisting resistance to really recognizing the unconscious. Although nominally accepted, its existence has nevertheless been left out of the theoretical research. If psychoanalysis has finally permeated the content of certain films, as a complement to the classic psychology of character's action and as a new type of narrative spring, it has remained practically absent from the problematics raised by the relation of the projection to the subject. The problem is nevertheless to determine the extent to which the cinematographic apparatus plays an important part in this subject which Lacan after Freud defines as an apparatus,[7] and the way in which the structuring of the unconscious, the modalities of the subject's development throughout the different strata deposited by the various phases of drives, the differentiation between the Cs, Pcs, and Ucs systems and their relations, the distinction between primary and secondary processes, make it possible to isolate the effect which is specific to cinema.

Consequently, I will only propose several hypotheses.

First of all, that taking into account the darkness of the movie theater, the relative passivity of the situation, the forced immobility of the cine-subject, and the effects which result from the projection of images, moving images, the cinematographic apparatus brings about a state of artificial regression. It artificially leads back to an anterior phase of his development—a phase which is barely hidden, as dream and certain pathological forms of our mental life have shown. It is the desire, unrecognized as such by the subject, to return to this phase, an early state of development with its own forms of satisfaction which may play a determining role in his desire for cinema and the pleasure he finds in it. Return toward a relative narcissism, and even more toward a mode of relating to reality which could be defined as enveloping and in which the separation between one's own body and the exterior world is not well defined. Following this line of reasoning, one may then be able to understand the reasons for the intensity of the subject's attachment to the images and the process of identification created by cinema. A return to a primitive narcissism by the regression of the libido, Freud tells us, noting that the dreamer occupies the entire field of the dream scene; the absence of delimitation of the body; the transfusion of the interior out into the exterior, added Lewin (other works, notably Melanie Klein's could also be mentioned); without excluding other processes of identification which derive from the specular regime of the ego, from its constitu-

---

[7]"The subject is an apparatus. This apparatus is lacunary, and it is within this lacuna that the subject sets up the function of an object as lost object." Jacques Lacan, *Les Quatres Concepts fondamenteux de la psychanalyse* (Paris: Le Seuil, 1973).

tion as "Imaginary." These do not, however, strictly pertain to the cinema effect, although the screen, the focalization produced by the basic apparatus, as I indicated in my earlier paper,[8] could effectively produce mirror effects and cause specular phenomena to intervene directly in the viewing experience. In any case, the usual forms of identification, already supported by the apparatus, would be reinforced by a more archaic mode of identification, which has to do with the lack of differentiation between the subject and his environment, a dream scene model which we find in the baby/breast-screen relationship.

In order to understand the particular status of cinema, it is necessary to underline the partial elimination of the reality test. Undoubtedly, the means of cinematographic projection would keep the reality test intact when compared to dreams and hallucination. The subject has always the choice to close his eyes, to withdraw from the spectacle, or to leave, but no more than in dream does he have means to act in any way upon the object of his perception, change his viewpoint as he would like. There is no doubt that in dealing with images, and the unfolding of images, the rhythm of vision and movement are imposed on him in the same way as images in dream and hallucination. His relative motor inhibition which brings him closer to the state of the dreamer, in the same way as the particular status of the reality he perceives (a reality made up of images) would seem to favor the simulation of the regressive state, and would play a determining role in the subject effect of the impression of reality, this more-than-real of the impression of reality, which as we have seen is characteristic not of the relation of the subject to reality, but precisely of dreams and hallucinations.

One must therefore start to analyze the impression of reality by differentiating between perception and representation. The cinematographic apparatus is unique in that *it offers the subject perceptions "of a reality" whose status seems similar to that of representations experienced as perception.* It should also be noted in this connection that if the confusion between representation and perception is characteristic of the primary process which is governed by the pleasure principle, and which is the basic condition for the satisfaction produced by hallucination, the cinematographic apparatus appears to succeed in suspending the secondary process and anything having to do with the principle of reality without eliminating it completely. This would then lead us to propose the following paradoxical formula: the more-than-real, that is, the specific characteristic (whatever is specific) of what is meant by the expression "impression of reality," consists in keeping apart (toning down, so that they remain present but as background) the secondary process and the reality principle. Perception of the image passing for perception: one might assume that it is precisely here that one might find the key to the impression of reality, that which would at once approximate and differentiate the cinematographic effect and the dream. Return effect, repetition of a phase of the subject's development during which representation and perception were not yet differentiated, and the desire to return to that state along with the kind of satisfaction associated to it, undoubtedly

---

[8]Jean-Louis Baudry, "Cinéma: Effets idéologiques produits par l'appareil de base," *Cinéthique*, nos. 7–8 (1970): 1–8. Published in an English translation by Alan Williams in *Film Quarterly* (Winter 1974–75), 28(2): 39–47.

an archetype for all that which seeks to connect with the multiple paths of the subject's desire. It is indeed desire as such, that is, desire of desire, the nostalgia for a state in which desire has been satisfied through the transfer of a perception to a formation resembling hallucination, which seems to be activated by the cinematographic apparatus. According to Freud: "To desire initially must have been a hallucinatory cathexis of the memory of satisfaction."[9] Survival and insistence of bygone periods, an irrepressible backward movement. Freud never ceased to remind us that in its formal constitution, dream was a vestige of the subject's phylogenetic past, and the expression of a wish to have again the very form of existence associated with this experience. "Dream which fulfills its wish by the short-cut of regression does nothing but conserve a type of primary operation of the psychical apparatus which had been eliminated because of its inefficiency." It is also the same survival and the same wish which are at work in some hallucinatory psychoses. Cinema, like dream, would seem to correspond to a temporary form of regression, but whereas dream, according to Freud, is merely a "normal hallucinatory psychosis," cinema offers an artificial psychosis without offering the dreamer the possibility of exercising any kind of immediate control. What I am really saying is that for such a regression to be possible, it is necessary for anterior phases to survive, but that it be cathected by a wish, as is proven by the existence of dream. This wish is remarkably precise, and consists in obtaining, from reality a position, a condition in which what is perceived would no longer be distinguished from representations. It can be assumed that it is this wish which prepares the long history of cinema: the wish to construct a simulation machine capable of offering the subject perceptions which are really representations mistaken for perceptions. Cinema offers a simulation of regressive movement which is characteristic of dream—the transformation of thoughts by means of figuration. The withdrawal of cathexis of all the systems Cs, Pcs, Ucs during sleep causes the representations cathected by dream during the dream work to determine a sensory activity; the operation of dream can be crudely represented by a diagram.

The simulation apparatus therefore consists in transforming a perception into a quasi-hallucination endowed with a reality effect which cannot be compared to that which results from ordinary perception. The cinematographic apparatus reproduces the psychical apparatus during sleep: separation from the outside world, inhibition of motoricity; in sleep, these conditions causing an overcathexis of representation can penetrate the system of perception as sensory stimuli; in cinema, the images perceived (very likely reinforced by the setup of the psychical apparatus) will be

---

[9]It may seem peculiar that desire which constituted the cine-effect is rooted in the oral structure of the subject. The conditions of projection do evoke the dialectics internal/external, swallowing/swallowed, eating/being eaten, which is characteristic of what is being structured during the oral phase. But, in the case of the cinematographic situation, the visual orifice has replaced the buccal orifice: the absorption of images is at the same time the absorption of the subject in the image, prepared, predigested by his very entering the dark theater. The relationship visual orifice/buccal orifice acts at the same time as analogy and differentiation, but also points to the relation of consecution between oral satisfaction, sleep, white screen of the dream on which dream images will be projected, beginning of the dream. On the importance of sight during the oral phase, see Spitz's remarks in *The Yes and the No*. In the same order of ideas, it may be useful to reintroduce Melanie Klein's hypothesis on the oral phase, her extremely complex dialectics between the inside and the outside which refer to reciprocal forms of development.

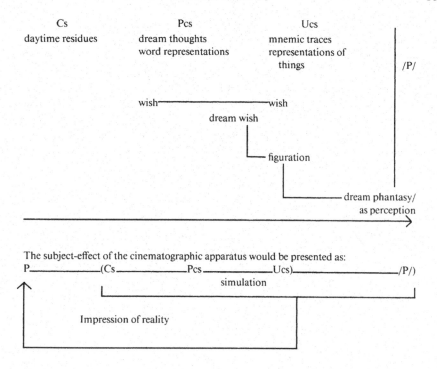

The subject-effect of the cinematographic apparatus would be presented as:

over-cathected and thus acquire a status which will be the same as that of the sensory images of dream.

One cannot hesitate to insist on the *artificial* character of the cine-subject. It is precisely this artificiality which differentiates it from dream or hallucinations. There is, between cinema and these psychical states, the same distance as between a real object and its simulacrum, with this additional factor that dream and hallucination are already states of simulation (something passing itself off for something else, representation for perception). One might even argue that it is this embedded structure which makes it so difficult to deal with the subject effect. While, in dreams and hallucinations, representations appear in the guise of perceived reality, a real perception takes place in cinema, if not an ordinary perception of reality. It would appear that it is this slight displacement which has misled the theoreticians of cinema, when analyzing the impression of reality. In dream and hallucination, representations are taken as reality in the absence of perception; in cinema, images are taken for reality but require the mediation of perception. This is why, on the one hand, for the realists, cinema is thought of as a duplicate of reality—and on the other cinema is taken as an equivalent of dream—but the comparison stops there, leaving unresolved the problem raised by the impression of reality. It is evident that cinema is not dream: but it reproduces an impression of reality, it unlocks, releases a cinema effect which is comparable to the impression of reality caused by dream. The entire cinematographic apparatus is activated in order to provoke this simulation: it is indeed a simulation of a condition of the subject, a position of the subject, a subject and not reality.

Desire for a real that would have the status of hallucination or of a representation taken for a perception—one might wonder whether cinema is not doubled by
another wish, complementary to the one that is at work in the subject and which we
have presumed to be at work in Plato's cave apparatus.

For, if dream really opens onto another scene by way of a regressive track, one
might suppose that the existence of an unconscious where the subject's early mode
of functioning, defined by the primary process, persists, the unconscious, constantly
denied, rejected, excluded, never ceases requiring of the subject and proposing to
him, by multiple detours (even if only through artistic practice), representations of
his own scene. In other words, without his always suspecting it, the subject is induced
to produce machines which would not only complement or supplement the workings of the secondary process but which could represent his own overall functioning to him: he is led to produce mechanisms mimicking, simulating the apparatus
which is no other than himself. The presence of the unconscious also makes itself
felt through the pressure it exerts in seeking to get itself represented by a subject
who is still unaware of the fact that he is representing to himself the very scene of
the unconscious where he is.

1975

NOËL CARROLL
FROM MYSTIFYING MOVIES

JEAN-LOUIS BAUDRY AND "THE APPARATUS"

Noël Carroll's background in analytic philosophy and cognitive psychology informs much of his critical work, and he has been considered an early proponent of cognitivism–the theory that our perception of and emotional response to film are based on the same rational cognitive processes with which we experience and make sense of the world around us. His early books, *Philosophical Problems of Classical Film Theory* and *Mystifying Movies: Fads and Fallacies in Contemporary Film Theory* (both 1988), were tightly argued rebuttals of the structuralist, psychoanalytic, and Marxist film theory popular in the 1970s and 80s, which he criticized as overly dogmatic and inadequate to a rigorous philosophical study of film. The anthology *Post-Theory: Reconstructing Film Studies* (1996), co-edited with David Bordwell, takes a cognitivist and historical approach to specific films, genres, and film-makers. Carroll has also written articles and reviews on the philosophy of horror film, mass art, modern dance, and the films of Buster Keaton. He is currently Distinguished Professor at the Graduate Center of the City University of New York.

(Another selection from Carroll's work appears in Section III.)

A major reason, given by contemporary film theorists, for their shift from a semiological framework of study to a psychoanalytic one, is that the semiological model is too narrow. It concerns itself with the structure of the cinematic sign but does not, according to many contemporary film theorists, pay sufficient attention to the effects of cinema upon the spectator. The semiological model, at least in the ways it was employed in the late sixties and early seventies, was felt to be myopically object-oriented. In order to remedy this putative shortcoming, film theorists resorted to psychoanalysis.

Jean-Louis Baudry's essay "The Apparatus" was a seminal essay in the turn to psychoanalysis. In this essay, he attempts to account for the impression of reality that cinema is said to impart to spectators. He intends to use psychoanalysis, that is, to analyze what he takes to be a paramount effect of cinema on audiences. However, though the phrase "impression of reality" recurs frequently in "The Apparatus," one must be careful in that which one identifies as the phenomenon with which Baudry is concerned. For Baudry does not contend that the impression of reality caused by cinema is equivalent to our everyday encounters with the world; cinema is not a replication of our ordinary impressions of reality. Rather, cinema is said to deliver an impression of reality that is more-than-real. That is, less paradoxically stated, Baudry wishes to deploy psychoanalysis to explain cinema's intense effect on spectators; he wants to analyze the peculiarly charged relationship we have with the screen when we attend movies.

Moreover, Baudry does not search for this effect by scrutinizing the content of the images or the stories of particular films or even of particular kinds of films. Instead he sees this effect as the product of what he calls "the apparatus," a network which includes the screen, the spectator, and the projector. That is, Baudry seeks the origin of the impression-of-reality effect in the projection situation itself, irrespective of what is being screened.

Baudry's basic procedure for discovering the origin of the impression-of-reality effect is to draw a series of analogies between dreams and the projection context, or, as he prefers to call the latter, the apparatus. He is motivated in this by a belief that dreams like film engender an impression of reality that is highly charged, that is, an impression of what Baudry thinks of as the more-than-real effect. Thus, Baudry hopes to extrapolate the psychoanalytic explanation of the charged impression of reality in dreams into an explanation of the impression of reality in cinema.

Though Baudry does not set out his case in a logically rigorous fashion, his analysis implicitly takes the form of an inductive argument by logical analogy. For example, he notes that the film viewer and the dreamer share the property of having their movements inhibited, that both inhabit darkened rooms, and that both film and dream impart an impression of reality. Dream, in turn, is said to have this consequence insofar as it induces regression to an earlier psychosexual stage, that of primitive narcissism where the self is supposedly not differentiated from the other nor is perception differentiated from representation. On the basis of the similar conditions and effects, respectively, of film and dream, Baudry infers that the impression of reality in film is brought about by a regressive mechanism similar to that operative in dream.

Though arguments by analogy are not absolutely conclusive—they are, after all, inductive rather than deductive—and though they are often abused, they are a respectable form of reasoning. We use them all the time. For example, if you have a 1964 Saab and I have a 1964 Saab, and both cars are the same model, both engines are in exactly the same condition and state of repair, both carry the same weight, use the same fuel, and have been serviced in the same way by the same mechanic, and my Saab can go 55 mph, then we infer that (probably) your car can go 55 mph. Stated formally, this type of argument takes the following pattern: If we have items A and B, and they are similar in a number of relevant respects, say in terms of properties $p1$ through $px\text{-}1$, and item B also has property px, then we infer that (probably) A has px. That is,

1. Item A has properties $p1 \ldots px\text{-}1$ (e.g., A is a 1964 Saab).
2. Item B has properties $p1 \ldots px\text{-}1$.
3. Item B also has property px (e.g., B can go 55 mph).
4. Therefore, (probably) Item A also has property px.

Premises 1 and 2 set out the analogy; if more items are being analogized more premises will be added here. Once the analogy is set out, these premises can be combined with premise 3, which states a property known to be possessed by B (but not observed to be a property of A), in order to license the probable conclusion stated in 4. Obviously such arguments gain strength when the number of items and/or the number of relevant properties cited are multiplied. Inversely, the argument loses force as either data base for the analogy is diminished. This can be done by:

A. showing that the analogies cited fail (for example, your car is really a 1921 Ford, not a 1964 Saab).
B. demonstrating that the analogies cited are irrelevant to what is at issue (for example, that both cars are green).
C. noting relevant disanalogies between items A, B . . . in order to challenge the purported similarity of the cases under comparison (for example, that your Saab has no wheels).

With this sketch of the logic of Baudry's approach, we can go on to fill in the details and evaluate the persuasiveness of his account of the psychic mechanism that he believes causes cinema's characteristic impression of reality.

As we have already noted, Baudry holds that the conditions of reception of film and dream are analogous; both involve a darkened room and the inhibition of movement. The film viewer sits in his seat; the dreamer lies abed. Inhibited motoricity is also a feature of the infantile state to which the dreamer is said to regress. Connected to this inhibition of motoricity is another feature: the lack of the means to test reality. Baudry writes:

> In order to understand the particular status of cinema, it is necessary to underline the partial elimination of the reality test. Undoubtedly, the means of cinematographic projection would keep the reality test intact when compared to dreams and hallucination. The subject always has the choice to close his eyes, to withdraw from the spectacle or to leave but no more than dreams does he have means to act in any way upon the object of his perception, change his viewpoint as he would like. . . . His relative motor inhibition which brings him closer to the state of the dreamer, in the same way as the particular status of the reality he perceives (a reality made up of images) would seem to favor the simulation of the regressive state, and would play a determining role in the subject effect of the impression of reality, this more-than-real impression of reality, which as we have seen is characteristic not of the relation of the subject to reality, but precisely of dreams and hallucinations.[1]

Here, Baudry notes that there is only a partial analogy in regard to reality testing between film and dream. But he thinks this similarity is important because along with inhibited motoricity, and perhaps because of it, the lack of reality testing reproduces the conditions of the infantile state of primitive narcissism that explains the impression-of-reality effect that the cinematic apparatus is said to induce. Also, in this passage, Baudry alludes to two other analogies between film and dreams: both traffic in the medium of images and both deliver a more-than-real impression of reality.

---

[1] Jean-Louis Baudry, "The Apparatus: Metapsychological Approaches to the Impression of Reality in the Cinema." [see p. 185 in this volume.]

So far five analogies between film and dream have been noted: inhibited motoricity in the subject; lack of reality testing; darkened rooms; the medium of images; the more-than-real impression of reality. Are there other analogies?

For Baudry, following the psychoanalyst Bertram Lewin, dreams, like the cinematic apparatus, have screens. That is, Baudry argues that dreams are projections onto dream screens in a way that is analogous to film projection. Baudry writes:

> That dream is a projection reminiscent of the cinematographic apparatus is indeed what seems to come out of Lewin's discovery of the *dream screen*, the hypothesis for which was suggested to him by his patients' enigmatic dreams. One young woman's dream, for example: "I had my dream all ready for you, but while I was lying here looking at it, it began to move in circles far from me, wrapped up on itself, again and again like two acrobats." This dream shows that the screen, which can appear by itself, like a white surface, is not exclusively a representation, a content—in which case it would not be necessary to privilege it among other elements of the dream content; but, rather, it would present itself in all dreams as the indispensable support for the projection of images. It would seem to pertain to the dream apparatus. "The dream screen is a surface on which a dream seems to be projected. It is the 'blank background' (empty basic surface) which is present in the dream although it is not necessarily seen; the manifest content of dream ordinarily perceived takes place over it, or in front of it."[2]

Baudry also points out that people often describe their dreams as being like movies.

The dream screen/film screen, dream apparatus/film apparatus analogy is particularly crucial for Baudry. For Lewin has a psychoanalytic account of the dream screen that is pertinent to the effect dreams have upon us. And Baudry intends to extend that account to cinema.

> According to Lewin's hypothesis, the dream screen is the dream's hallucinatory representation of the mother's breast on which the child used to fall asleep after nursing. In this way, it expresses a state of complete satisfaction while repeating the original condition of the oral phase in which the body did not have limits of its own, but was extended undifferentiated from the breast.[3]

Thus, via the dream screen, the dreamer regresses to and relives a stage in our psychosexual development marked by primitive narcissism, a stage where self and environment are said to merge and where perception and representation are believed to be undifferentiated. Moreover, this regression satisfies a desire, a desire to return to that sense of undifferentiated wholeness. It is this desire in turn which gives the dream imagery its special charge and which accounts for the intensity with which we regard it.

Insofar as the cinematic apparatus mirrors relevant aspects of the dream apparatus—inhibited motoricity, lack of reality testing, visual imagery, the more-than-real impression of reality, projection, and a screen support—Baudry feels warranted in adopting Lewin's hypothesis about the causation of dream and the dream effect as an explanation of our animating desire for and our experience of the cinematic apparatus. That is, a regressive mechanism seeking to revive the experience of primitive narcissism in what draws us to movies while satisfaction of that desire is what renders that experience more-than-real. So, by postulating the return to prim-

---

[2]Baudry, pp. 181–182 in this volume.
[3]Ibid, p. 182.

itive narcissism as the operative agency in film spectators, Baudry thinks he has isolated the cause of the cinematic effect while also, in the process, supplying an account of why the movie experience is desirable to us. . . . From Baudry's perspective, the answer seems to be to relive that stage of primitive narcissism where all-is-one, including a conflation of perception and representation. Indeed, for Baudry, the cinematic apparatus incarnates a wish for a simulation machine "capable of offering the subject perceptions which are really representations mistaken for perceptions,"[4] thereby recalling the dream state which itself derives from a regression to an archaic state where perception and representation are not differentiated.

Summarizing Baudry's case so far, his argument looks like this:

1. The dream apparatus has the following features: inhibition of movement; lack of reality testing; an imagistic medium; a dark room; projection; a screen; a more-than-real impression of reality; a tendency to efface the distinction between perception and representation.
2. The cinematic apparatus has exactly the same features noted in premise 1.
3. A significant animating force behind the dream apparatus is the desire for and regression to primitive narcissism which enactment causes the charged experience of dreams.
4. Therefore it is probable that a significant animating force behind the cinematic apparatus is the desire for and regression to primitive narcissism which enactment causes the charged experience of cinema.

Baudry, of course, does not hold that films are mistaken for dreams. He rather construes them as simulations of dreams. For this reason he might want to say that the regression encountered in cinema is less intense than that of dreams. Nevertheless, he would appear to hold that to whatever degree the more-than-real impression of reality of film approximates the analogous effect of dreams, it is a function of the process of some measure of regression to the all-is-one state of primitive oral narcissism.

Because of the emphasis Baudry places on the cinematic apparatus as a simulation of unconscious phenomena, specifically of the hallucinatory aura of dreams, one might offer a slightly different interpretation of Baudry's argument than the one just presented. That is, one might take Baudry to be saying that since film replicates the most significant conditions of dreaming—for example, motor inhibition, lack of reality testing, and so on—it triggers the same effect—regression to primitive narcissism. On this interpretation of Baudry's strategy, the argument rides on the principle: same conditons, same effects. However, whether one chooses this interpretation or the interpretation of the analysis as an inductive argument by analogy is logically indifferent for the purposes of evaluating Baudry's central claims. For in either case Baudry's central assertions stand or fall on the basis of the adequacy of the correlations he draws between cinema and dreams.

Baudry concludes his essay by asserting that the unconscious has an instinctual desire to manifest itself to consciousness. This suggests that cinema is one means

---

[4]Baudry, p. 185 in this volume.

for fulfilling this instinctual desire. For in simulating dream, cinema satisfies the desire of the unconscious for acknowledgment. This somewhat resembles a claim that Metz makes to the effect that by combining elements of night dream and day-dream film causes pleasure by externalizing what is usually experienced as inter-nal. But this claim of Baudry's can only be accepted if cinema is a suitable simulation of dreams, that is, if the analogies Baudry draws between film and dream are fitting and if they are not outweighed by significant disanalogies.

However, before turning to an assessment of Baudry's central thesis, it is impor-tant to take notice of an elaborate complication in the text which has not been remarked upon so far. Baudry not only analogizes film and dream but he also com-pares both with the description of the circumstances of the prisoners in Plato's myth of the cave.[5] Those prisoners are chained in a darkened vault. Behind and above them, fires burn. As passersby walk between the prisoners and the flames, the strollers' ambulating shadows are cast upon the wall of the cave. The prisoners see these moving shadows and take them for reality. Through this allegory, Plato sets forth his disparaging estimation of the ordinary person's "knowledge" of the world. It is based on illusion; it is nought but shadowy deception.

Baudry calls attention to the ways in which Plato's cave resembles the cinematic apparatus. The cave is analogous to the apparatus in obvious respects: the motoric-ity of the prisoners is inhibited as is their capacity to test reality. The cave, like the movie theater, is a dim space. The shadows in Plato's cave might be thought of as projections and the wall of the cave is a screen of sorts. Moreover, the projecting device is above and behind the prisoners and is, so to speak, hidden from them. The imagery in both Plato's cave and the cinema is a matter of shadows or reflections caused by passing something before a light. And in both cases, one can designate the play of "two scenes": first, the scene in the world that gives rise to the "shad-ows" and second, the scene comprised of the shadows themselves. These analogies lead Baudry to conclude that Plato's myth of the cave "doesn't merely evoke, but quite precisely describes in its mode of operation the cinematographic apparatus and the spectator's place in relation to it."[6]

Now the question immediately arises as to what logical purpose the analogies between Plato's cave and the cinematic apparatus serve in the context of Baudry's overall analysis of film in terms of regression to primitive narcissism. For these added cave analogies do not function logically to enhance Baudry's argument con-cerning film and dream. The conclusion of that argument is that regression is the motor of the cinematic apparatus just as it is the motor of the dream apparatus. For the analogies with Plato's cave to film and dream to bolster this conclusion—namely, that regression to primitive narcissism is the motor of the cinematic apparatus—we would have to have reason to claim antecedent knowledge to the effect that Plato's myth was generated by the type of regressive mechanism that the argument wants to attribute to the cinematic apparatus. But we do not have such knowledge. Whether Plato's myth of the cave derives from a regressive desire remains to be proved to the same degree that the cinematic apparatus' origin in such a desire does. That is,

---

[5]Plato, *Republic* 7.514.
[6]Baudry, "The Apparatus," p. 174 in this volume.

the psychoanalytic cause of Plato's myth is not known prior to Baudry's argument and in that sense is logically in the same boat as whatever the animating force behind the cinematic apparatus turns out to be. Thus, adding the analogies of Plato's cave, since the cause of that myth cannot be supplied as a premise of the argument (but, at best, as a corollary conclusion), does not strengthen the argument by analogy between the cinematic apparatus and the dream apparatus. So the question remains as to the point of Baudry's ornate rendition of Plato's myth.

Baudry, of course, has no wish to endorse Plato's epistemological position which he, Baudry, misidentifies as idealism, a label more apt for a post-Cartesian such as Berkeley (that is, Plato does not believe that all that exists is mental and, indeed, the mental/physical distinction relevant to the formation of an idealist philosophy does not appear to have been historically available to Plato). Rather, Baudry tears the myth of the cave out of the context in which it functions as an allegory, and he treats it as a fantasy ripe for psychoanalysis. Among other things, Baudry claims that it is a proto-cinematic wish, that is, a deep-seated wish for something very much like cinema before the invention of cinema. Baudry sees evidence for similar proto-cinematic wishes throughout history: the camera obscura, the magic lantern, the praxinoscope. What Baudry seems to conclude from the existence of a proto-cinema stretching from Plato's cave to the praxinoscope is that it supplies evidence for a transhistorical, psychical, or instinctual source of desire behind the invention of the cinematic apparatus and its prefigurations.[7] And, of course, if the compelling force behind cinema is instinctual, that may supply prima facie grounds for approaching it psychoanalytically. Thus, I take it that the point of Baudry's use of Plato's cave in "The Apparatus" is not to enhance the central argument about the causal relevance of regression to film, but rather to mount a coordinated but independent argument to persuade us that the recent invention of cinema is really a manifestation of a long-standing, transhistorical, or instinctual desire of the sort that psychoanalysis is fitted to examine. That is, the discussion of Plato's cave is meant to convince us of the appropriateness of psychoanalyzing cinema and it is not, properly speaking, part of the argument by analogy that concludes with the assertion of regression as key to the cinematic apparatus.

Of course, in speaking this way I am offering an interpretation of Baudry's essay, one guided by the logical requirements of the type of argument Baudry appears to advance. I admit that at points Baudry himself writes as though the analysis of the allegory of the cave were an essential part of the film/dream argument. Not only does this fly in the face of the logical point made earlier, but it also promotes many extravagant and confusing, free-associative leaps as Baudry attempts to forge connections simultaneously between Plato's cave, film, and dream. For example, Plato's cave correlates with the darkened room of the movie theater. What connection does this have with dreams? Baudry says that the dreamwork often represents the unconscious by means of underground places.[8] Now even if this has some connection with Plato's cave, what is its relevance to the cinematic apparatus? Films are not characteristically viewed in caves or underground places. The effects of such whimsical

---

[7]Baudry, p. 178 in this volume.
[8]Ibid., p. 179.

flights of fancy can be minimized if we restrict our attention to the central argument that analogizes film and dream which, anyway, is the logical fulcrum of Baudry's case. Thus, a sense of interpretive charity leads me to regard the film/dream argument and the analysis of Plato's cave as making separate though coordinated points.

Undoubtedly, Baudry's essay also attempts to show that the "apparatus" of Plato's cave has the same regressive mechanism behind it as does the dream "apparatus." And Baudry's way of showing this is ostensibly an argument by analogy like that concerning the cinematic apparatus. But this is, logically, a parallel argument to the film/dream argument, one that neither supports nor derives support from the speculations on film and dream. That is, the cave/dream argument concluding with regression as the motor behind Plato's myth is an induction to be pursued independently of the film/dream argument. Indeed, Baudry's discussion of Plato is only relevant to film theorists—as opposed to historians of philosophy—insofar as the myth of the cave can be demonstrated to be proto-cinematic. Thus, I will restrict comment upon Baudry's cave/dream analogies to those points that are relevant to establishing the existence of a proto-cinematic wish.

Baudry's "The Apparatus," then, contains at least two major arguments for film theorists: that the apparatus of cinema importantly involves regression to primitive narcissism and that the archaic wish underlying cinema is atavistic, reaching as far back in history as Plato's myth of the cave. Of these two arguments the former seems to me of greater moment because, if it is true, it is what gives the claim about a proto-cinematic wish precise substance, and also because it would supply an interesting and substantial insight even if the claims about proto-cinematic wishes were false, that is, if the invention of cinema responded to a historically recent wish rather than to an ancient longing of the human race.

The argument that the cinematic apparatus involves regression to a period of primitive narcissism where self is not differentiated from the environment is an inductive argument by analogy and, therefore, its conclusions are only probable. This is not problematic for most of what we value as knowledge is at best probable. The degree of warrantability in such an argument, however, depends on the strength of the analogies cited in the premises and on the presumption that there are not significant disanalogies, in this case between film and dream, which would neutralize or outweigh the persuasiveness of the analogies advanced. Thus, to assess Baudry's thesis we must consider whether his analogies are apt and compelling, and whether or not there are profound disanalogies between film and dream which render Baudry's analogies fledgling.

The two analogies that Baudry repeatedly stresses involve the inhibition of movement and the absence of reality testing, features purportedly shared by the cinematic apparatus and dream. Supposing that these are features of dreams, are they also features of film viewing? The dreamer is asleep; insofar as he is not a somnambulist, his literal movement is restricted to tossing and turning. Of course, his movement capacities as a character in his own dream can be quite expansive. But insofar as he is asleep, the movement of his physical body is involuntary. But what of the cinema viewer?

Conventionally we sit in our seats, moving our heads, arms, and so on within a small perimeter of activity. But is our movement inhibited in a way that is significantly analogous to the inertness of sleep? First of all, a key reason for speaking of motor inhibition, both in terms of sleep and in terms of the infantile state of primitive narcissism, is that in those cases the lack of mobility, for different reasons, is involuntary. However, no matter how sedentary our film viewing is, we are not involuntary prisoners in our seats.

Of course, Baudry speaks of this lack of motoricity not only in respect to film viewing and dreaming, but also with reference to Plato's prisoners whose constraint is involuntary. So the dream state and that of the prisoners correlate along the dimension of involuntary motor inhibition. And movie viewers are supposed to resemble the prisoners. But from this one cannot surmise that it is correct to claim corresponding motor inhibition for movie spectators since movie spectators resemble the prisoners only in such respects as being viewers of reflection and not in terms of involuntariness. Unlike Plato's prisoners, the film viewer can move her head voluntarily, attending to this part of the screen and then the next. What she sees comes under her control, unlike the dreamer or the prisoner, in large measure because of her capacity to move her head and her eyes. And, the film viewer, as Baudry admits, can leave the theater, change her seat, or go into the lobby for a smoke.

Though Baudry does not make this move, a proponent of the inhibition analogy might claim that when a film spectator adopts the convention of sitting before the movie screen, she adopts the pretense of having her motor capacities inhibited. But there is no evidence that such a game of make-believe is occurring. A more likely description of what the spectator does when adopting the convention of taking a seat is that she opts for the easiest method of attending to the film. Literally, her motoricity is not inhibited, nor does she feel it or pretend it to be. If we are willing to describe film viewing as involving motor inhibition, we should be equally willing to describe witnessing baseball games and listening to political speeches as involving motor inhibition. And to the extent that such descriptions of baseball and speeches is inaccurate, so is a description of movie viewing as movement inhibited inaccurate. Moreover, even if there is a sense in which we might say that movement in all these cases is "inhibited," it is certainly not a matter of motor inhibition, but a voluntary inhibition promoted by respect for conventional decorum.

Of course, the point that sitting at movies is a social convention is central. Movies can be watched *with no loss of effect* while standing; people frequently walk to the rear of the theater and watch, stand in the aisles while they grab a smoke or relax their bottoms. Nor are such standing filmgoers necessarily stationary; if one watches the film while pacing across a side aisle, the impression the film imparts need not be lost. Baudry connects the putative impression of reality imparted by film to inhibited motoricity. Given this, one would predict that that impression would not occur if the spectator watched while also moving voluntarily. If there is such a phenomenon as the impression of reality, then it should be an empirical matter to establish whether it disappears when the spectator is in movement. In my own case, I have found that I can back out of a movie theater while watching the screen or return to my seat from the beverage bar with no discernible difference in the impressions I derive from the screen than when I am seated. I know I'm walking in one case and sitting in the other, but these are proprioceptive impressions and not screen impressions.

Perhaps Baudry would admit that the film viewer's movement is not literally inhibited, but would attempt to save his analogy by saying that the film viewer *feels* inhibited. Phenomenologically, I have never had such an experience. But even if others do have such experiences, this will not help the analogy that Baudry wishes to draw. Why? Well, if we shift to a phenomenological register, then the dreamer often *feels* in motion when dreaming, for instance, when one dreams one is falling or being pursued by a three-headed ogre. That is, the dreamer often feels in motion when he is not, whereas the film viewer does not ordinarily take himself to be literally in motion when he is not.[9] Of course, Baudry may say that the inhibited movement which is attributed to the movie spectator is really metaphorical. But why should a correlation between his metaphorical description of the film viewer and the literal motor inhibition of the sleeper count as anything more than an entertaining but fanciful piece of equivocation?

Baudry's second key analogy between the cinematic apparatus and dream hinges on the claim that both involve an absence of reality testing. Of course, in one sense, the film viewer is fully capable of indulging in reality testing. He can go up to the screen and touch it; he can shift his view of the screen, noting that the contours around the objects do not alter, and, thereby, he can surmise that the projected array is two dimensional. Also, things like coke bottles and cabbages can be and have been thrown at movies, a dramatic measure for revealing the nature of the screen. Baudry is aware of this; when he speaks of an absence of reality testing in film viewing, his reference is not to an incapacity the viewer has in relation to objects, such as screens, in the actual world; rather Baudry has in mind that the viewer lacks the ability to test reality within the world of the film. That is, the movie viewer cannot enter the visual array onscreen in order to ascertain whether the buildings in *Siegfried* are concrete or merely cardboard.

Baudry also connects lack of reality testing with the inhibition of movement. Plato's prisoners, and the preambulatory infants at the stage of primitive narcissism cannot test reality at a distance because they are immobile. But the same correlation between motor inhibition and absence of reality testing cannot, as Baudry suggests, be extrapolated to film viewing and dreaming. For if there is an absence of reality testing in both these cases, then that is a function of the fact that, *loosely speaking*, there is no reality to be tested *in* the world of the film and the world of the dream (where "reality" is understood as the foil of "representation"). So if the correlation based on absence of reality due to inhibited movement is key to aligning film and dream with the infantile state of primitive narcissism, the analogy is inaccurate.

We may also wish to know whether it is really appropriate to hold that the film viewer has no means for testing reality inside the world of the film. Certainly it is true that we cannot walk into the world of *Casablanca* in order to determine whether

---

[9]"Ordinarily" here is meant to acknowledge that there are certain tricks which, as in Cinerama, can induce the impression of, say, plummeting. But these are extraordinary moments of cinema, and not the sort of evidence to be adduced in an account of the customary effects of film.

the characters are really drinking whiskey. But at the same time, I think that it pays to recall a really overwhelming disanalogy between film viewing and dreaming. Namely, films are publicly accessible; they can be viewed by more than one person. Moreover, they can be repeated; we can see the same film again and again, and we can fall back on all sorts of evidence—production and distribution records, the testimony of other viewers and of the filmmakers, the existence of similar prints, and so on—to warrant the claim that the film we just saw, say *Captain Blood*, is the same film we saw in the past. This is a radical disanalogy with dreaming. Neither the analyst nor anyone but the dreamer has access to the dream. And no one, including the dreamer, can be sure that his report of a dream is accurate; there is no interpersonal validation available. Even with a "recurring" dream, we have little reason to be confident that the dreamer experienced exactly the same dream from night to night. What does this epistemic disanalogy have to do with reality testing? Simply that with films there is a way in which we can "test reality," that is, corroborate our experience of a movie. We can ask someone else if she saw what we saw. Nor is this something we do only after a film is over. During *Lifeforce* I leaned over to my neighbor and asked "Did I really just see a vampire-nun?" to which she replied "I saw her too."

There are, in short, means to test the veracity of our experience of films. We cannot plunge into the image, but we can corroborate what we see there, which is the sort of reality testing that is appropriate to visual fictions (as opposed to what might be called ordinary visual "realities"). Moreover, if we are worried about testing the fidelity of documentaries to their subjects, that is also possible. My point here is simply that it seems to me inappropriate to describe the film viewer as lacking the means for testing reality. And if I am right in this matter, this short-circuits Baudry's second key analogy between film and dream. However, if I am wrong and the analogy is acceptable, the considerations I have just raised present another problem for Baudry. For even if in some sense his analogy works, I have also pointed to a major disanalogy between film and dream: namely, that film experiences are open to interpersonal verification. This appears to me to be important enough to outweigh analogies between film and quasi-solipsistic phenomena, since it establishes that film viewing has an objective dimension and is not purely subjective.

Films are a visual medium and so are dreams. Is this a significant analogy between the external and internal phenomena under comparison? Not really. For memories are also often visual. Why not analogize film to memories as certain film realists might propose? Here, it might be argued that dream is the appropriate analog—that we know to eliminate memory as a viable candidate—because of the earlier analogies that correlate film with dream rather than memory. But as I hope I have shown, those earlier analogies are not so sturdy, nor, I might add, is the film theorist under any imperative to identify *any* mental correlate for film.

However, there is also an important disanalogy between film imagery and dream imagery which indicates that the two are not congruent. The single film image is ordinarily complete, by which I mean that, typically, it is visually articulated throughout. Dream images, on the other hand, tend to be incomplete, foregrounds without backgrounds or figures in a void. This can be simulated in film as can the "noise" of the dreamwork; note Brakhage's films. However, the ordinary film image does not "look like" the ordinary dream image. That is, even if film and dream are imagistic, they are radically dissimilar imagistic media. They are too unlike to be treated as cognate phenomena. . . . Metz notices further, crucial dissimilarities between film and dream,[10] which added to the disanalogies I adduce render Baudry's argument even more unlikely.

Baudry's analogy between film and dream in respect of darkened rooms is also problematic. One can, of course, fall asleep mid-day on the beach. And movies can be viewed in well-lit circumstances. I expect that Baudry is probably right in asserting that most of the time we dream and view films in the dark. But there is still something strange about this correlation. The film viewer is not only objectively in a darkened room; she is experientially aware of being in a darkened room. But even if the dreamer is objectively in a darkened room, she is unaware of it. Indeed, she may believe that she is on a blistering, sun-baked desert. That is, though there is a possible objective analogy between the film viewer and the dreamer, their experiences are disanalogous. Now if a film is supposed to simulate dreams or trigger the same kind of response or mechanism in the subject, wouldn't it seem more likely that what the viewer experiences be key to the dream analogy rather than the objective, physical conditions of reception? That is, the dreamer does not have the same experiential awareness of a darkened room that the film viewer does. So why would the film viewer's awareness of a darkened room remind one of dreaming or simulate dreaming for the unconscious? In this case, Baudry seems to overvalue the significance of correlations between the objective, physical conditions of film viewing and dreaming while forgetting the crucial, phenomenological disanalogies between the film experience and dream experience. We saw that there was a similar problem with his treatment of inhibited motoricity, where he ignored the fact that objectively, physically leaden sleepers often feel in vigorous motion.

Another analogy that Baudry proposes between film and dream is that both impart what he refers to as a more-than-real impression of reality. Part of the problem with evaluating this claim is the vagueness of the notion of a more-than-real impression of reality. That is, even if film and dream impart such broadly describable impressions, are their respective impressions the same in analytically revealing respects? Both quartz and lemurs can be described as matter but they are matter of such different sorts that the observation does not tell us much that is useful. Are the respective more-than-real impressions proffered by film and dream very alike or very unalike?

Answering this question is difficult since Baudry tells us next to nothing about the phenomena to which he wants us to refer. However, if the impressions he has in mind are a matter of imagery charged with affect, we can remark that dream imagery is, if not just more vividly charged, it is at least more invariantly charged than movie imagery. The reason for this, which Metz notes,[11] is that the affect that attaches to dream imagery originates in the dreamer and her personal associations whereas the affect derivable from film imagery comes from an external source—such as the imaginations of screenwriters and directors—which may or may not cor-

---

[10]In Christian Metz, "The Fiction Film and its Spectator," *New Literary History* (Fall 1976).
[11]Ibid.

respond to the film viewer's emotive life. Thus, if the more-than-real impression of reality of films and dreams is identified with a constant correlation of imagery and affect, then the film apparatus and dream are very different. Moreover, if the more-than-real impression of reality is not a matter of a constant coincidence of affect and imagery, what is it? Merely occasionally exciting imagery? But isn't that enough to correlate a televised chess game to dreams?

But there is another way to probe the problems with Baudry's use of the notion of the more-than-real impression of reality. In dream, this impression appears to refer to imagery charged with affect. In film, we are told that this impression is one that diverges from our ordinary encounters with mundane life. And, admittedly, the events we witness on film are most often more exciting, more expressively characterized, and more emotionally arresting than those of quotidian existence. However, it is important to note that films of this sort, though common, are also very special. They are, in the majority of cases, fiction films or they are films otherwise designed explicitly to promote intense affective responses. A film like *Greed*, or *Sunrise*, or *Potemkin*, or *The Passion of Joan of Arc*, may leave an impression that is, as they say, "larger than life." But this sort of impression is not a function of simply throwing an image on the screen. It is the internal structure of these films that accounts for their effect, not the fact that they are projected. Not all films bestow comparable affective results. Home movies, or bank surveillance footage, especially of persons unknown to us, may appear affectless, flat, and lackadaisical. That is, many films are projected, but few are chosen. Now this is an important point against Baudry. For he claims that the more-than-real impression of which he writes is a consequence of the cinematic apparatus, a claim tantamount to predicting that whatever is projected onscreen will be swathed in affect. But this is downright false; just recall Warhol's *Empire*.

Another major analogy between film and dream that Baudry produces asserts that both have screens, or projection supports. It seems reasonable, barring the complications of TV, to agree that films are *normally* projected onto screens. But frankly the claim seems shaky in regard to dreams. The evidence appears to be that some of Lewin's patients reported dream screens in their nightly reveries. I have no reason to question their reports. However, does this amount to evidence that something like a dream screen is an essential or normal element in all dreams? Perhaps Lewin's patients had personal associations with movie screens and this accounts for the appearance of screens in *their* dreams. Why suppose that a screen element is a characteristic feature of all dreams? Were there visions of screens in dreams before there were screened entertainments? Were there visions of screens in cultures without screened entertainments? And, furthermore, what general criteria are there for establishing that phenomena, like the appearance of a screen in a dream, are organic ingredients of dreaming rather than the associative imagery of given dreams? Until these questions can be satisfactorily answered the dream screen/film screen correspondence—and with it the dream/film apparatus analogy—appear extremely dubious. Of course, as I have already admitted, dream imagery is often incomplete; but where the dream "picture" is unarticulated it is not necessarily the case that the dreamer apprehends a screen, white, silver, or otherwise. There is rather just a void.

So far Baudry's argument by analogy has been attacked by showing that his analogies are hardly compelling and by remarking upon salient disanalogies between film and dream. The accumulated force of these objections shows that Baudry's argument by analogy is without substantial warrant. I think the previously cited disanalogies are enough to swamp his case. But also the premises that set out the analogies between film and dream are virtually without support.[12] Thus, Baudry's argument fails to go through.[13]

Of course, questions, as well, might be raised not only about Baudry's analogies but also about the crucial premise that asserts that the underlying mechanism in dream is regression to primitive, oral narcissism. This is a psychoanalytic claim, not a film theoretical one, and, as such, we should probably not pursue this issue in depth here. Yet, it pays to remember that the Lewin-Baudry hypothesis about regression is extremely controversial.

The regression hypothesis appears to ride upon the postulation of a dream screen which, in turn, can be associated with a mother's breast. The evidence for a dream screen as an organic, essential, or merely characteristic element of dreaming has already been challenged. Insofar as the dream screen serves as a linchpin for the inference of regression, and insofar as the dream screen phenomenon is not generic, then there is no evidence for a generic regressive mechanism, of the specificity Baudry claims, in dreaming.

Also one must at least question the purported screen/breast association. What is its basis? And how extensive is it? Maybe some white people envision breasts as white and then go on to associate the latter with white screens. But not everyone is white. And I even wonder if many whites associate breasts and screens. Certainly it is not an intuitively straightforward association like that between guns and penises. For example, screens are flat; and lactating breasts are not. A screen is, ideally, uniform in color and texture; but a breast has a nipple. Nor will the association work if it is put forward by saying that breasts are, for the infant in the state of oral regression, targets of projections as are screens. For according to the theory of primitive narcissism, the mother's breasts are part of an undifferentiated, all-is-one experience, and, therefore, could not have been recognized way back then by the primitive narcissist, and, thus, cannot be recalled now to be targets of projection. For primitive narcissism admits no distinctions between targets of projections, projections, and projectionists.

I do not deny that there may be some people who associate screens and breasts, thereby at least suggesting the hypothesis of oral regression in those cases. After all, it is probably psychologically possible to associate anything with anything else. But even if some people associate breasts and screens, that does not provide enough evidence to claim a general pattern of association between breasts and screens such as might support a theory about all dreaming. And if oral regression is not the general

---

[12]A film/dream analogy of Baudry's that I have not touched upon is the assertion that, in film and dream, representation is taken as perception. I reject the notion that film spectators mistake cinematic representations as perceptions and, therefore, reject the basis of this analogy.

[13]Moreover, if Baudry's analogies between film and dream are groundless, then it is hard to see how film could simulate dream, nor is it easy to see how film could trigger the same sort of regression that dreams do.

causal force energizing the dream, then it cannot be extrapolated by analogy as the causal force behind the cinema apparatus.

Baudry's central argument in "The Apparatus" is beset by problems at every turn. Do his subsidiary arguments fare any better? By analogical reasoning, he links Plato's myth of the cave with dreaming, and also with filmgoing, inferring that all three can be explicated by reference to regression. Plato's cave, furthermore, is identified as proto-cinematic, indicating to Baudry, that the instinctual desire that propels filmgoing is ancient.

The analogies between Plato's prisoners and dreamers are rather weak, often in ways reminiscent of the problems with Baudry's film/dream analogies. Both prisoners and dreamers are said to be immobile, in a darkened place, bombarded with visual imagery, and unable to test reality. Contra Baudry, we must note again, with reference to darkened places, that people can sleep and dream in broad daylight, while the "world of the dream" need not be dark. And, as was pointed out earlier, the dreamer as a character in a dream need not be immobile, while the sleeper, unlike Plato's prisoners, is unaware of being immobile. Also, what Plato's prisoners see differs radically from the dreamer's imagery—that is, Plato's prisoners see uniformly black figures whose only features are shadowy contours rather than internally articulated figures with eyes and moustaches. And, of course, Plato's prisoners are awake while dreamers are not, which reminds us that Plato's prisoners do literally see something—even if they misinterpret it—and this indicates that they can objectively correct each other about the look of the shadows before them, a type of reality testing not available to the dreamer. One could go on at length discounting Baudry's dream analysis of Plato, but this appears to be more of an issue for historians of philosophy, if it is an issue for anyone, than for film theorists. So let the preceding, hurried refutation of Baudry's version of Plato's cave suffice.

Baudry also claims that Plato's myth of the cave is a prefiguration of cinema. Needless to say this ignores the philosophical purposes Plato designed the myth to serve. But Baudry believes that the myth evinces a myth deeper than Plato was aware of. Baudry holds that Plato's cave is proto-cinematic, which leads him to claim that cinema answers a desire of ancient, instinctual origins. Many, more historically minded, film theorists might wish to question the existence of transhistorical, transcultural desires of the sort Baudry postulates. Nor is the existence of such a transcultural desire absolutely integral to the project of psychoanalyzing the cinematic apparatus. For cinema might be the answer to culturally specific desires of the nineteenth and twentieth centuries.

Baudry's analogies between the cinematic apparatus and Plato's cave are underwhelming. Both, purportedly, involve projection from behind the spectator. But films are often rear-projected and early Japanese cinemas positioned their audiences at right angles to the projection apparatus (not to mention the possibility of projecting films via large video screens). Are either of these practices uncinematic or do audiences at, for example, rear-projected movies have different film experiences than those at cinemas with projectors behind the audience. Baudry speaks of the projection in the cave and in cinema as hidden. But film projection is not always hidden. One can set up a projector in one's living room or in a classroom or boardroom, for all to see, and still have a typical film experience. We have already noted the film viewer is not necessarily immobile. Plato's prisoners are shackled at the neck; even the seated film viewer can move her head. Furthermore, the images of film are immensely different than Plato's shadows. The prisoners see solid black blotches on the wall while film viewers see internally articulated pictures. How, for example, could Plato's prisoner see the eyes of one of the people who cast the shadows on their wall? And isn't this disanalogy far more striking than the analogies that Baudry defends?

Plato's prisoners cannot enter the world of the shadows for purposes of reality testing and neither can viewers of *Casablanca* belly up to Rick's bar for a fast Scotch. But, on the other hand, film viewers can touch the screen, and what is more important, they are aware that there is a screen, and that they are watching a movie. Thus, their status, epistemologically, is exactly opposite that of Plato's prisoners. Also, I think we would agree that one could see a film that portrayed the world accurately whereas Plato's shadow representations are putatively always deceptive. There are surely some surface resemblances between Plato's prisoners and film viewers—they both see projections. But this is hardly sufficient for supporting the claim that both film and the myth of the cave address the same psychic need and mobilize the same psychic mechanism.

Baudry believes that Plato's cave is part of the prehistory of cinema. Apart from the inductive weakness of the analogies he draws, there is also something strained in Baudry's use of the notion of the prehistory of cinema. Is every instance and/or report of shadow projection, prior to 1895, to be considered part of the prehistory of cinema? What criteria determine that which we are to count as legitimately and four-squarely part of the prehistory of cinema? The camera obscura, Marey's repeating camera, the praxinoscope, and Muybridge's battery of cameras are clear-cut examples of what people include in the prehistory of cinema. And it is easy to see that what these devices have in common is that they can figure in causal accounts of the invention of cinema. But there is no historical argument in sight to show that Plato's myth of the cave literally played a role in the invention of cinema. Thus, even if Baudry's analogies were more convincing, it is not clear that it would be appropriate to consider Plato's cave as part of the prehistory of cinema.

The central argument, as well as the subsidiary ones, in "The Apparatus" appear, upon scrutiny, to be utterly groundless. Undoubtedly, some readers may complain that my methods of examining Baudry's hypotheses are not suitable and perhaps even boorish. For, in my account, Baudry is making a series of literal, logical, scientific claims about a causal process. Thus, Baudry's conclusions are assessed with the rigor one would apply to any scientific hypothesis. However, many contemporary film theorists might object that Baudry is doing something more "interesting" or "important" than pedestrian science.

Personally, I find it difficult to see why a claim about the isolation of a causal mechanism (in this case, regression as a motor force behind cinema) should not be treated as a scientific hypothesis. And so treated, Baudry's arguments by analogy are woefully inept; he fails to consider significant disanalogies, while the analogies he presents are loose and superficial. But many contemporary film theorists, especially those with backgrounds in literature, may counter that that which I call "loose" and "superficial" is really graceful, imaginative, and ingenious. They admire Baudry, as they admire Barthes, for his supposed expertise in belles lettres. But however seductive to some literary sensibilities "The Apparatus" may be, contemporary belles lettres does not afford the means to defend causal claims about the processes underlying cinema. Film theorists with backgrounds in literature may bewail this fact; but it is unavoidable. Moreover, as we shall see, the confusion of belles lettres, on the one hand, with scientific and philosophical reasoning, on the other, is one of the most egregious problems in contemporary film theory. Indeed, the extremely detailed, literal-minded, and argumentive style of this chapter . . . is mandated by my conviction that contemporary film theorists, with their penchant for belletristic expression, including slippery analogies and metaphors, must be shown that they are using the wrong tools for the tasks at hand.

1988

JONATHAN CRARY
FROM VISION AND VISUALITY

MODERNIZING VISION

Jonathan Crary's study of visual culture began with *Techniques of the Observer: On Vision and Modernity in the Nineteenth Century* (1990), which considers the intersection of philosophy, art, optics, and entertainment technologies in the nineteenth century that led to a redefinition of vision as subjective, fallible, and manipulable. *Suspensions of Perception: Attention, Spectacle and Modern Culture* (2000) closely analyzes paintings by Manet, Seurat, and Cezanne. Co-finder of the nonprofit publishing house Zone Books, which publishes works of art theory, sociology, and philosophy, he is currently Schapiro professor of modern art and theory in the department of art history and archaeology at Columbia University.

My starting point is the various ways in which vision and the techniques and discourses surrounding it have been periodized historically. It is interesting that so many attempts to theorize vision and visuality are wedded to models that emphasize a continuous and overarching Western visual tradition. Obviously at times it is strategically necessary to map out and pose the outlines of a dominant Western speculative or scopic tradition of vision that is continuous or in some sense effective, for instance, from Plato to the present, or from the Quattrocento into the twentieth century, or to whenever. My concern is not so much to argue against these models, which have their own usefulness, but rather to insist there are some important discontinuities that such hegemonic constructions have prevented from coming into view. The specific account that interests me here, one that has become almost ubiquitous and continues to be developed in a variety of forms, is that the emergence of photography and cinema in the nineteenth century is a fulfillment of a long unfolding of technological and/or ideological development in the West in which the camera obscura evolves into the photographic camera. Implied is that at each step in this evolution the same essential presuppositions about an observer's relation to the world are in place. One could name a dozen or more books on the history of film or photography in whose first chapter appears the obligatory seventeenth-century engraving depicting a camera obscura, as a kind of inaugural or incipient form on a long evolutionary ladder.

These models of continuity are used in the service of both, for lack of better terms, the right and the left. On the one hand are those who pose an account of ever-increasing progress toward verisimilitude in representation, in which Renaissance perspective and photography are part of the same quest for a fully objective equivalent of "natural vision." On the other are those who see, for example, the camera obscura and cinema as bound up in a single enduring apparatus of power, elaborated over several centuries, that continues to define and regulate the status of an observer.

What I want to do are essentially two related things: (1) to briefly and very generally articulate the camera obscura model of vision in terms of its historical specificity, and (2) to suggest how that model collapsed in the early nineteenth century—in the 1820s and 1830s—when it was displaced by radically different notions of what an observer was and of what constituted vision. So if later in the nineteenth century cinema or photography seem to invite formal comparisons with the camera obscura, or if Marx, Freud, Bergson, and others refer to it, it is within a social, cultural, and scientific milieu in which there had already been a profound rupture with the conditions of vision presupposed by this device.

For at least two thousand years it has been known that, when light passes through a small hole into a dark, enclosed interior, an inverted image will appear on the wall opposite the hole. Thinkers as remote from each other as Euclid, Aristotle, Roger Bacon, and Leonardo noted this phenomenon and speculated in various ways how it might or might not be analogous to the functioning of human vision.

But it is crucial to make a distinction between the empirical fact that an image can be produced in this way (something that continues to be as true now as it was in antiquity) and the camera obscura as a socially constructed artifact. For the camera obscura was not simply an inert and neutral piece of equipment or a set of technical premises to be tinkered upon and improved over the years; rather, it was embedded in a much larger and denser organization of knowledge and of the observing subject. If we want to be historical about it, we must recognize how for nearly two hundred years, from the late 1500s to the end of the 1700s, the structural and optical principles of the camera obscura coalesced into a dominant paradigm through which were described the status and possibilities of an observer.

It became a model, obviously elaborated in a variety of ways, for how observation leads to truthful inferences about an external world. It was an era when the camera obscura was simultaneously and inseparably a central epistemological figure within a discursive order, as in Descartes's *Dioptrics*, Locke's *Essay on Human Understanding*, and Leibniz's critique of Locke, *and* occupied a major position within an arrangement of technical and cultural practices, for example in the work of Kepler and Newton. As a complex technique of power, it was a means of legislating for an observer what constituted perceptual "truth," and it delineated a fixed set of relations to which an observer was made subject.

What I will argue is that very early on in the nineteenth century the camera obscura collapses as a model for an observer and for the functioning of human vision. There is a profound shift in the way in which an observer is described, figured, and posited in science, in philosophy, and in new techniques and practices of vision. Here I want briefly and very sketchily to indicate a few important features of this shift.

First, a bit more about the camera obscura in the seventeenth and eighteenth centuries. Above all, whether in the work of scientists or artists, empiricists or rationalists, it was an apparatus that guaranteed access to an objective truth about the world. It assumed importance as a model both for the observation of empirical phenomena and for reflective introspection and self-observation. In Locke, for example, the camera is a means of spatially visualizing the position of an observing subject.[1] The image of the room in Locke takes on a special significance, referring to what it meant in the seventeenth century to be *in camera*, that is, within the chambers of a judge or person of title.[2] Thus he adds onto the observer's passive role a more authoritative and juridical function to guarantee and to police the correspondence between exterior world and interior representation and to exclude anything disorderly or unruly.

Richard Rorty has pointed to Locke and Descartes as key figures in establishing this conception of the human mind as "an inner space in which clear and distinct ideas passed in review before an inner Eye . . . an inner space in which perceptual sensations were themselves the objects of quasi-observation."[3] For Descartes, the camera obscura was a demonstration of how an observer can know the world "uniquely by perception of the mind." The secure positioning of the self with this empty interior space was a precondition for knowing the outer world. Its enclosedness, its darkness, its categorical separation from an exterior incarnates Descartes's announcement in the Third Meditation, "I will now shut my eyes, I shall stop my ears, I shall disregard my senses."[4] If part of Descartes's method implied a need to escape the uncertainties of mere human vision, the camera obscura is compatible with his quest to found knowledge on a purely objective view of the world. The aperture of the camera corresponds to a single mathematically definable point from which the world could be logically deduced and re-presented. Founded on laws of nature—that is, geometrical optics—the camera provided an infallible vantage point on the world. Sensory evidence that depended in any way on the body was rejected in favor of the representations of this mechanical and monocular apparatus, whose authenticity was placed beyond doubt.

Monocular, not binocular. A single eye, not two. Until the nineteenth century, binocular disparity, the fact that we see a slightly different image with each eye, was never seriously addressed as a central issue. It was ignored or minimized as a problem, for it implied the inadmissible physiological and anatomical operation of human vision. A monocular model, on the other hand, precluded the difficult problem of having to reconcile the dissimilar and therefore provisional and tentative images presented to each eye. Monocularity, like perspective and geometrical optics, was one of the Renaissance codes through which a visual world is constructed according to systematized constants, and from which any inconsistencies

---

[1]John Locke, *An Essay Concerning Human Understanding* (New York: Dover Publications, 1959), vol. 2, pp. xi, 17.

[2]Ibid., vol. 2, pp. iii, 1.

[3]Richard Rorty, *Philosophy and the Mirror of Nature* (Princeton, Princeton University Press, 1979), pp. 49–50.

[4]René Descartes, *The Philosophical Writings of Descartes*, trans. John Cottingham et al, (Cambridge: Cambridge University Press, 1984), vol. 2, p. 24.

and irregularities are banished to ensure the formation of a homogeneous, unified, and fully legible space.

Finally, to wind up this extremely compressed outline, it should also be suggested how closely the camera obscura is bound up with a metaphysic of interiority. It is a figure for the observer, who is nominally a free sovereign individual but who is also a privatized isolated subject enclosed in a quasi-domestic space separated from a public exterior world. It defined an observer who was subjected to an inflexible set of positions and divisions. The visual world could be appropriated by an autonomous subject but only as a private unitary consciousness detached from any active relation with an exterior. The monadic viewpoint of the individual is legitimized by the camera obscura, but his or her sensory experience is subordinated to an external and pre-given world of objective truth.

What is striking are the suddenness and thoroughness with which this paradigm collapses in the early nineteenth century and gives way to a diverse set of fundamentally different models of human vision. I want to discuss one crucial dimension of this shift, the insertion of a new term into discourses and practices of vision: the human body, a term whose exclusion was one of the foundations of classical theories of vision and optics as I have just suggested. One of the most telling signs of the new centrality of the body in vision is Goethe's *Theory of Colours*, published in 1810, which I have discussed at length elsewhere.[5] This is a work crucial not for its polemic with Newton over the composition of light but for its articulation of a model of subjective vision in which the body is introduced in all its physiological density as the ground on which vision is possible. In Goethe we find an image of a newly productive observer whose body has a range of capacities to generate visual experience; it is a question of visual experience that does not refer or correspond to anything external to the observing subject. Goethe is concerned mainly with the experiences associated with the retinal afterimage and its chromatic transformations. But he is only the first of many researchers who become preoccupied with the afterimage in the 1820s and 1830s throughout Europe. Their collective study defined how vision was an irreducible amalgam of physiological processes and external stimulation, and dramatized the productive role played by the body in vision.

Although we are talking about scientists, what is in question here is the discovery of the "visionary" capacities of the body, and we miss the significance of this research if we don't recall some of its strange intensity and exhilaration. For what was often involved was the experience of staring directly into the sun, of sunlight searing itself onto the body, palpably disturbing it into a proliferation of incandescent color. Three of the most celebrated students of vision of this period went blind or permanently damaged their eyesight by repeatedly staring at the sun: David Brewster, who invented the kaleidoscope and stereoscope; Joseph Plateau, who studied the so-called persistence of vision; and Gustav Fechner, one of the founders of modern quantitative psychology. Fechner's biography provides an account of the

---

[5]Johann Wolfgang von Goethe, *Theory of Colours*, trans. Charles Lock Eastlake (Cambridge, Mass.: Massachusetts Institute of Technology Press, 1970). See my "Techniques of the Observer," *October* 45 (Summer 1988).

almost addictive fascination with which he persisted in this activity. At the same time in the late 1830s and early 1840s, we have the visual expression of these attempts in the late paintings of Turner, in which there is that piercing confrontation of eye and sun, paintings in which the strictures that previously had mediated and regulated vision are abandoned. Nothing now protects or distances the observer from the seductive and sensual brilliance of the sun. The symbolic confines of the camera obscura have crumbled.

Obviously afterimages have been noted and recorded since antiquity, but they had always been outside or on the margins of the domain of optics. They were considered illusions—deceptive, spectral, and unreal. In the early nineteenth century such experiences that previously had been an expression of the frailty and the unreliability of the body now constituted the positivity of vision. But perhaps more important, the privileging of the body as a visual producer began to collapse the distinction between inner and outer upon which the camera obscura depended. Once the objects of vision are coextensive with one's own body, vision becomes dislocated and depositioned onto a single immanent plane. The bipolar setup vanishes. Thirdly, subjective vision is found to be distinctly temporal, an unfolding of processes within the body, thus undoing notions of a direct correspondence between perception and object. By the 1820s, then, we effectively have a model of autonomous vision.

The subjective vision that endowed the observer with a new perceptual autonomy and productivity was simultaneously the result of the observer having been made into a subject of new knowledge, of new techniques of power. And the terrain on which these two interrelated observers emerged in the nineteenth century was the science of physiology. From 1820 through the 1840s it was very unlike the specialized science that it later became; it had then no formal institutional identity and came into being as the accumulated work of disconnected individuals from diverse branches of learning. In common were the excitement and wonderment at the body, which now appeared like a new continent to be mapped, explored, and mastered, with new recesses and mechanisms uncovered for the first time. But the real importance of physiology lay in the fact that it became the arena for new types of epistemological reflection that depended on new knowledge about the eye and processes of vision. Physiology at this moment of the nineteenth century is one of those sciences that stand for the rupture that Foucault poses between the eighteenth and nineteenth centuries, in which man emerges as a being in whom the transcendent is mapped onto the empirical.[6] It was the discovery that knowledge was conditioned by the physical and anatomical structure and functioning of the body, and, in particular, of the eyes. At the same time, as Georges Canguilhem has noted, for the new sciences in the nineteenth century the body was a priori a productive body: it existed to be set to work.[7]

Even in the early 1820s the study of afterimages quickly became the object of a more rigorous and *quantitative* scientific research throughout Europe. Studied were the persistence and modulation of afterimages: how long they lasted, what changes

---

[6]Michel Foucault, *The Order of Things* (New York: Pantheon Books, 1971), pp. 318–20.

[7]Georges Canguilhem, "Qu'est-ce que le psychologie," in his *Études d'histoire et de philosophie des sciences*, 5th ed. (Paris: J. Vrin, 1983), pp. 377–78.

they went through, and under what conditions. But instead of recording afterimages in terms of the lived time of the body, as Goethe had generally done, they were studied as part of a comprehensive quantification of the irritability of the eye. Researchers timed how long it took the eye to become fatigued and how long dilation and contraction of the pupil took, and they measured the strength of eye movements. They examined convergence and accommodation in binocular vision and the relation of image to retinal curvature.

The physical surface of the eye itself became a field of statistical information: the retina was demarcated in terms of how color changes hue depending on where it strikes the eye. Also measured were the extent of the area of visibility and of peripheral vision, the distinction between direct and indirect vision, and the location of the blind spot. Classical optics, which had studied the transparency of mechanical optical systems, gave way to a mapping of the human eye as an opaque territory with varying zones of efficiency and aptitude and specific parameters of normal and pathological vision. Some of the most celebrated of these experiments were Joseph Plateau's calculation, in the 1830s, of the average duration of an afterimage, or persistence of vision, which was about one-third of a second, and later, Helmholtz's measurement of the speed of nerve transmission, which astounded people by how slow it was, about ninety feet per second. Both statistics heightened the sense of a temporal disjunction between perception and its object *and* suggested new possibilities of intervening externally in the process of vision.

Clearly this study of the eye in terms of reaction time and thresholds of fatigue and stimulation was not unrelated to increasing demand for knowledge about the adaptation of a human subject to productive tasks in which optimum attention span was indispensable for the rationalization of human labor. The economic need for rapid coordination of hand and eye in performing repetitive actions required accurate knowledge of human optical and sensory capacities. In the context of new industrial models of factory production the problem of visual in-attention was a serious one. But what developed was a notion of vision that was fundamentally quantitative, in which the terms constituting the relation between perception and object became abstract, interchangeable, and nonvisual. One of the most paradoxical figures of the nineteenth century is Gustav Fechner, whose delirious and even mystical experiences with solar afterimages led to his mathematization of perception, in which he established a functional relation between stimulus and sensation.[8] Sensory perception was given a measurable magnitude solely in terms of the known and controllable magnitudes of external stimulation. Vision became studied in terms of abstract measurable regularities, and Fechner's famous equations were to be one of the foundations of modern stimulus-response psychology.

Another dimension of the collective achievement of physiology in the first half of the nineteenth century was the gradual parcelization and division of the body into increasingly separate and specific systems and functions. Especially important were the localization of brain and nerve functions and the distinction between sensory nerves and motor nerves. Finally, by 1826, it was determined that sensory nerves were of

---

[8]See Gustav Fechner, *Elements of Psychophysics*, trans. Helmut E. Adler (New York: Holt, Rinehart & Winston, 1966).

five distinct types, corresponding to the five senses. All of this produced a new "truth" about the body, which some have linked to the so-called "separation of the senses" in the nineteenth century, and to the idea that the specialization of labor was homologous to a specialization of sight and of a heightened autonomous vision, something that Fredric Jameson develops briefly but provocatively in *The Political Unconscious*.[9] I believe, however, that such a homology doesn't take account of how thoroughly vision was reconceived in the earlier nineteenth century. It still seems to pose observation as the act of a unified subject looking out onto a world that is the object of his or her sight, only that, because the objects of the world have become reified and commodified, vision in a sense becomes conscious of itself as sheer looking.

But in the first major scientific theorization of the separation of the senses, there is a much more decisive break with the classical observer, and what is at stake is not simply the heightening or isolating of the optical but rather a notion of an observer for whom vision is conceived without any necessary connection to the act of looking at all. The work in question is the research of the German physiologist Johannes Müller, the single most important theorist of vision in the first half of the nineteenth century.[10] In his study of the physiology of the senses, Müller makes a comprehensive statement on the subdivision and specialization of the human sensory apparatus; his fame was due to his theorization of that specialization: the so-called doctrine of specific nerve energies. It was a theory in many ways as important to the nineteenth century as the Molyneux problem was to the eighteenth century. It was the foundation of Helmholtz's *Optics*, which dominated the second half of the 1800s; in science, philosophy, and psychology it was widely propounded, debated, and denounced even into the early twentieth century. (Also, I believe Marx was paraphrasing this work when he discussed the separation of the senses in his *1844 Manuscripts*.[11]) In short, this is a major way in which an observer was figured in the nineteenth century, a way in which a certain "truth" about sight was depicted.

The theory was based on the discovery that the nerves of the different senses were physiologically distinct. It asserted quite simply—and this is what marks its epistemological scandal—that a uniform cause (e.g., electricity) would generate utterly different sensations from one kind of nerve to another. Electricity applied to the optic nerve produces the experience of light, applied to the skin the sensation of touch. Conversely, Müller shows that a variety of different causes will produce the *same* sensation in a given sensory nerve; in other words, he describes a fundamentally arbitrary relation between stimulus and sensation. It is a description of a body with an innate capacity, one might even say a transcendental faculty, to *misperceive*, of an eye that renders differences equivalent.

His most exhaustive demonstration concerns the sense of sight, and he concludes that the observer's experience of light has no necessary connection with any actual light. Müller enumerates the agencies capable of producing the sensation of light.

[9]Fredric Jameson, *The Political Unconscious: Narrative as a Socially Symbolic Act* (Ithaca, NY: Cornell University Press, 1981), pp. 62–64.

[10]See Johannes Müller, *Handbuch der Physiologie des Menschen* (Koblenz, Germany: Holscher, 1838); *Elements of Physiologie*, trans. William Baly (London: Taylor & Walton, 1848).

[11]See Karl Marx, *The Economic and Philosophic Manuscripts of 1844*, ed. Dirk J. Struik, trans. Martin Milligan (New York: International Publishers, 1964), pp. 140–41.

"The sensations of light and color are produced wherever parts of the retina are excited (1) by mechanical influences, such as pressure, a blow, or a concussion; (2) by electricity; (3) by chemical agents, such as narcotics, or digitalis; (4) by the stimulus of the blood in a state of congestion."[12] Then, last on his list, almost begrudgingly, he adds that luminous images also can be produced by "the undulations and emanation which by their action on the eye are called light."

Again the camera obscura model is made irrelevant. The experience of light becomes severed from any stable point of reference or from any source or origin around which a world could be constituted and apprehended. And of course the very independent identity of light had already been undermined as a new wave theory of light became part of a science of electromagnetic phenomena.

Sight here has been separated and specialized certainly, but it no longer resembles any classical models. The theory of specific nerve energies presents the outlines of a visual modernity in which the "referential illusion" is unsparingly laid bare. The very absence of referentiality is the ground on which new instrumental techniques will construct for an observer a new "real" world. It is a question of a perceiver whose very empirical nature renders identities unstable and mobile, and for whom sensations are interchangeable. And remember, this is roughly 1830. In effect, the doctrine of specific nerve energies redefines vision as a capacity for being affected by sensations that have no necessary link to a referent, thus threatening any coherent system of meaning. Müller's theory was potentially so nihilistic that it is no wonder that Helmholtz and others, who accepted its empirical premises, were impelled to invent theories of cognition and signification that concealed its uncompromising cultural implications. But what was at stake and seemed so threatening was not just a new form of epistemological skepticism about the unreliability of the senses but a positive reorganization of perception and its objects. The issue was not just how does one know what is real, but that new forms of the real were being fabricated and a new truth about the capacities of a human subject was being articulated in these terms.

The theory of specific nerve energies eradicated distinctions between internal and external sensation, so that interiority was drained of the meanings it once had for a classical observer, or for the model of the cameral obscura. In his supposedly empirical description of the human sensory apparatus, Müller presents the subject not as a unitary "tabula rasa," but as a composite structure on which a wide range of techniques and forces could produce a manifold of experiences that are all equally "reality." If John Ruskin proposed reclaiming the "innocence of the eye," this was about as innocent as one could get. The observer is simultaneously the object of knowledge and the object of procedures of stimulation and normalization, which have the essential capacity *to produce experience for the subject.* Ironically the notions of the reflex arc and reflex action, which in the seventeenth century referred to vision and the optics of reflection, begin to become the centerpiece of an emerging technology of the subject, culminating in the work of Pavlov.

---

[12]Müller, *Hanbuch de Physiologie des Menschen*, p. 1064.

In his account of the relation between stimulus and sensation, Müller suggests not an orderly and legislative functioning of the senses, but rather their receptivity to calculated management and derangement. Émile Dubois-Reymond, a colleague of Helmholtz, seriously pursued the possibility of electrically cross-connecting nerves, enabling the eye to see sounds and the ear to hear colors, well before Rimbaud. It must be emphasized that Müller's research and that of psychophysics in the nineteenth century are inseparable from the resources made available by contemporary work in electricity and chemistry. Some of the empirical evidence by Müller had been available since antiquity, or was in the domain of common-sense knowledge. However, what is new is the extraordinary privilege given to a complex of electro physical techniques. What constitutes "sensation" is dramatically expanded and transformed, and it has little in common with how it was discussed in the eighteenth century. The adjacency of Müller's doctrine of specific nerve energies to the technology of nineteenth-century modernity is made particularly clear by Helmholtz:

> Nerves in the human body have been accurately compared to telegraph wires. Such a wire conducts one single kind of electric current and no other; it may be stronger, it may be weaker, it may move in either direction; it has no other qualitative differences. Nevertheless, according to the different kinds of apparatus with which we provide its terminations, we can send telegraphic dispatches, ring bells, explode mines, decompose water, move magnets, magnetize iron, develop light, and so on. *The same thing with our nerves.* The condition of excitement which can be produced in them, and is conducted by them, is . . . everywhere the same.[13]

Far from the specialization of the senses, Helmholtz is explicit about the body's indifference to the sources of its experience and of its capacity for multiple connections with other agencies and machines. The perceiver here becomes a neutral conduit, one kind of relay among others to allow optimum conditions of circulation and exchangeability, whether it be of commodities, energy, capital, images, or information.

The collapse of the camera obscura as a model for the status of an observer was part of a much larger process of modernization, even as the camera obscura itself was an element of an earlier modernity. By the early 1800s, however, the rigidity of the camera obscura, its linear optical system, its fixed positions, its categorical distinction between inside and outside, its identification of perception and object were all too inflexible and unwieldy for the needs of the new century. A more mobile, usable, and productive observer was needed in both discourse and practice— to be adequate to new uses of the body and to a vast proliferation of equally mobile and exchangeable signs and images. Modernization entailed a decoding and deterritorialization of vision.

What I've been trying to do is give some sense of how radical was the reconfiguration of vision by 1840. If our problem is vision and modernity we must look first at these early decades, not to modernist painting in the 1870s and 1880s. A new type of observer was formed then, and not one that we can see figured in paintings

---

[13]Hermann von Helmholtz, *On the Sensations of Tone as a Physiological Basis for the Theory of Music*, 2nd ed., trans. Alexander J. Ellis (New York: Dover Publications, 1954), pp. 148–49.

or prints. We've been trained to assume that an observer will always leave visible tracks, that is, will be identifiable in terms of images. But here it's a question of an observer who takes shape in other, grayer practices and discourses, and whose immense legacy will be all the industries of the image and the spectacle in the twentieth century. The body, which had been a neutral or invisible term in vision, now was the thickness from which knowledge of vision was derived. This opacity or carnal density of the observer loomed so suddenly into view that its full consequences and effects could not be immediately realized. But it was this ongoing articulation of vision as nonveridical, as lodged in the body, that was a *condition of possibility* both for the artistic experimentation of modernism and for new forms of domination, for what Foucault calls the "technology of individuals."[14] Inseparable from the technologies of domination and of the spectacle in the later nineteenth and twentieth century were of course film and photography. Paradoxically, the increasing hegemony of these two techniques helped re-create the myths that vision was incorporeal, veridical, and "realistic." But if cinema and photography seemed to reincarnate the camera obscura, it was only as a mirage of a transparent set of relations that modernity had already overthrown.

---

[14]Michel Foucault, *Discipline and Punish: The Birth of Prison*, trans. Alan Sheridan (New York: Vintage Books, 1975), p. 225.

GILLES DELEUZE
FROM CINEMA 1 and CINEMA 2

PREFACE TO THE ENGLISH EDITION

Gilles Deleuze's first book, *Nietzsche and Philosophy* (1962) established his interest in non-dialectical philosophy and helped revive an interest in Nietzsche that would later contribute to the emergence of post-structuralist theory. His philosophy celebrates indeterminacy and the free play of signifier and signified, foundational concepts in French thought of the 1960s that would also be developed in the work of Jean-François Lyotard, Michel Foucault, and Jacques Derrida. In addition to considerations of Nietzsche, Kant, Spinoza, and Bergson, Deleuze (1925–1995) wrote extensively on literature and film. Some of his best-known works are those written in collaboration with the psychoanalyst Felix Guattari, *The Anti-Oedipus* (1975), and *Capitalism and Schizophrenia* (1988), in which they critique the inadequacy of psychoanalysis in capitalist society. Deleuze's *Cinema I: The Movement-Image* (1986) and *Cinema 2: The Time-Image* (1989), excerpted here, chart a shift in film narrative from the pre-World War Two "movement-image" to the post-war "time-image" that is especially clear in Italian neo-realism. This shift, he argues, undermines the unified subject and the coherent narrative of classical montage to create a cinema of uncertainty that more accurately mirrors the uncertainty and indeterminancy of reality.

Over several centuries, from the Greeks to Kant, a revolution took place in philosophy: the subordination of time to movement was reversed, time ceases to be the measurement of normal movement, it increasingly appears for itself and creates paradoxical movements. Time is out of joint: Hamlet's words signify that time is no longer subordinated to movement, but rather movement to time. It could be said that, in its own sphere, cinema has repeated the same experience, the same reversal, in more fast-moving circumstances. The movement-image of the so-called classical cinema gave way, in the post-war period, to a direct time-image. Such a general idea must of course be qualified, corrected, adapted to concrete examples.

Why is the Second World War taken as a break? The fact is that, in Europe, the post-war period has greatly increased the situations which we no longer know how to react to, in spaces which we no longer know how to describe. These were 'any spaces whatever', deserted but inhabited, disused warehouses, waste ground, cities in the course of demolition or reconstruction. And in these any-spaces-whatever a new race of characters was stirring, kind of mutant: they saw rather than acted, they were seers. Hence Rossellini's great trilogy, *Europe 51, Stromboli, Germany Year 0:* a child in the destroyed city, a foreign woman on the island, a bourgeoise woman who starts to 'see' what is around her. Situations could be extremes, or, on the contrary, those of everyday banality, or both at once: what tends to collapse, or at least to lose its position, is the sensory-motor schema which constituted the action-image of the old cinema. And thanks to this loosening of the sensory-motor linkage, it is time, 'a little time in the pure state', which rises up to the surface of the screen. Time ceases to be derived from the movement, it appears in itself and itself gives rise to *false movements*. Hence the importance of *false continuity* in modern cinema: the images are no longer linked by rational cuts and continuity, but are relinked by means of false continuity and irrational cuts. Even the body is no longer exactly what moves; subject of movement or the instrument of action, it becomes rather the developer [*révélateur*] of time, it shows time through its tirednesses and waitings (Antonioni).

It is not quite right to say that the cinematographic image is in the present. What is in the present is what the image 'represents', but not the image itself, which, in cinema as in painting, is never to be confused with what it represents. The image itself is the system of the relationships between its elements, that is, a set of relationships of time from which the variable present only flows. It is in this sense, I think, that Tarkovsky challenges the distinction between montage and shot when he defines cinema by the 'pressure of time' in the shot. What is specific to the image, as soon as it is creative, is to make perceptible, to make visible, relationships of time which cannot be seen in the represented object and do not allow themselves to be reduced to the present. Take, for example, a depth of field in Welles, a tracking shot in Visconti: we are plunged into time rather than crossing space. Sandra's car, at the beginning of Visconti's film, is already moving in time, and Welles's characters occupy a giant-sized place in time rather than changing place in space.

This is to say that the time-image has nothing to do with a flashback, or even with a recollection. Recollection is only a former present, whilst the characters who have lost their memories in modern cinema literally sink back into the past, or emerge from it, to make visible what is concealed even from recollection. Flashback is only a signpost and, when it is used by great authors, it is there only to show much more complex temporal structures (for example, in Mankiewicz, 'forking' time: recapturing the moment when time could have taken a different course. . .). In any case, what we call temporal structure, or direct time-image, clearly goes beyond the purely empirical succession of time—past-present-future. It is, for example, a coexistence of distinct durations, or of levels of duration; a single event can belong to several levels: the sheets of past coexist in a non-chronological order. We see this in Welles with his powerful intuition of the earth, then in Resnais with his characters who return from the land of the dead.

There are yet more temporal structures: the whole aim of this book is to release those that the cinematographic image has been able to grasp and reveal, and which can echo the teachings of science, what the other arts uncover for us, or what philosophy makes understandable for us, each in their respective ways. It is foolish to talk about the death of the cinema because cinema is still at the beginning of its investigations: making visible these relationships of time which can only appear in a creation of the image. It is not cinema which needs television—whose image remains so regrettably in the present unless it is enriched by the art of cinema. The relations and disjunctions between visual and sound, between what is seen and what is said, revitalize the problem and endow cinema with new powers for capturing time in the image (in quite different ways, Pierre Perrault, Straub, Syberberg . . .). Yes, if cinema does not die a violent death, it retains the power of a beginning. Conversely, we must look in pre-war cinema, and even in silent cinema, for the workings of a very pure time-image which has always been breaking through, holding back or encompassing the movement-image: an Ozu still life as unchanging form of time?

I would like to thank Robert Galeta and Hugh Tomlinson for the care which they have put into translating this adventure of movement and time.

July 1988

THE ORIGIN OF THE CRISIS: ITALIAN NEO-REALISM AND THE FRENCH NEW WAVE

But can a crisis of the action-image be presented as something new? Was this not the constant state of the cinema? The purest action films have always had value in episodes outside the action, or in idle periods between actions, through a whole set of extra-actions and infra-actions which cannot be cut out in montage without disfiguring the film (hence the formidable power of producers). At all times too, the cinema's potentialities, its vocation for changes of location, have caused directors to wish to limit or even to suppress the unity of action, to undo the action, the drama, the plot or the story and to carry further an ambition with which literature was already permeated. On the one hand, the SAS structure found itself called into question: there was no globalising situation which was able to concentrate itself in a decisive action, but action or plot were only to be a component in a dispersive set, in an open totality. Jean Mitry is right in this sense to show that Delluc, scriptwriter of Germaine Dulac's *La Fête espagnole* already wanted to plunge the drama into a 'multiplicity of facts', none of which would be principal or secondary, so that it could only be reconstituted following a broken line lifted from among all the points and all the lines of the whole of the festival. On the other hand, the structure ASA was subjected to an analogous critique. In the same way as there was no previous history, there was no preformed action whose consequences on a situation could be foreseen, and the cinema could not transcribe events which had already happened, but necessarily devoted itelf to reaching the event in the course of happening, sometimes by cutting across an 'actuality', sometimes by provoking or producing it. Comolli has shown this very well: however far the work of preparation in many directors goes, the cinema cannot avoid the 'detour through the direct'. There is always a moment when the cinema meets the unforeseeable or the improvisation, the irreducibility of a present living under the present of narration, and the camera cannot even begin its work without engendering its own improvisations, both as obstacles and as indispensable means. These two themes, the open totality and the event in the course of happening, are part of the profound Bergsonianism of the cinema in general.

Nevertheless, the crisis which has shaken the action-image has depended on many factors which only had their full effect after the war, some of which were social, economic, political, moral and others more internal to art, to literature and to the cinema in particular. We might mention, in no particular order, the war and its consequences, the unsteadiness of the 'American Dream' in all its aspects, the new consciousness of minorities, the rise and inflation of images both in the external world and in people's minds, the influence on the cinema of the new modes of narrative with which literature had experimented, the crisis of Hollywood and its old genres. . . . Certainly, people continue to make SAS and ASA films: the greatest commercial successes always take that route, but the soul of the cinema no longer does. The soul of the cinema demands increasing thought, even if thought begins by undoing the system of actions, perceptions and affections on which the cinema had fed up to that point. We hardly believe any longer that a global situation can give rise to an action which is capable of modifying it—no more than we believe that an action can force a situation to disclose itself, even partially. The most 'healthy' illusions fall. The first things to be compromised everywhere are the linkages of situation–action, action–reaction, excitation–response, in short, the sensory-motor links which produced the action-image. Realism, despite all its violence—or rather with all its violence which remains sensory-motor—is oblivious to this new state of things where the synsigns disperse and the indices become confused. We need new signs. A new kind of image is born that one can attempt to identify in the post-war American cinema, outside Hollywood.

In the first place, the image no longer refers to a situation which is globalising or synthetic, but rather to one which is dispersive. The characters are multiple, with weak interferences and become principal or revert to being secondary. It is nevertheless not a series of sketches, a succession of short stories, since they are all caught in the same reality which disperse them. Robert Altman explores this direction in *A Wedding* and particularly in *Nashville*, with the multiple sound-tracks and the anamorphic screen which allows several simultaneous stagings. The city and the crowd lose the collective and unanimist character which they have in King Vidor; the city at the same time ceases to be the city above, the upright city, with skyscrapers and low-angle shots, in order to become the recumbent city, the city as horizontal or at human height, where each gets on with his own business, on his own account.

In the second place, the line or the fibre of the universe which prolonged events into one another, or brought about the connection of portions of space, has broken. The small form ASA is therefore no less compromised than the large form SAS. Ellipsis ceases to be a mode of the tale [*récit*], a way in which one goes from an action to a partially disclosed situation: it belongs to the situation itself, and reality is lacunary as much as dispersive. Linkages, connections, or liaisons are deliberately weak. Chance becomes the sole guiding thread, as in Altman's *Quintet*. Sometimes the event delays and is lost in idle periods, sometimes it is there too quickly, but it does not belong to the one to whom it happens (even death . . .). And there are close relationships between these aspects of the event: the dispersive, the direct in the course of happening and the non-belonging. Cassavetes plays on these three aspects in *The Killing of a Chinese Bookie* and in *Too Late Blues*. We could call them white events, events which never truly concern the person who provokes or is subject to them, even when they strike him in his flesh: events whose bearer, a man internally dead, as Lumet says, is in a hurry to extricate himself. In Scorsese's *Taxi Driver,* the driver wavers between killing himself and committing a political murder and, replacing these projects by the final slaughter, is astonished by it himself, as if the carrying out concerned him no more than did the preceding whims. The actuality of the action-image, the virtuality of the affection-image can interchange, all the more easily for having fallen into the same indifference.

In the third place, the sensory-motor action or situation has been replaced by the stroll, the voyage and the continual return journey. The voyage has found in America the formal and material conditions of a renewal. It takes place through internal or external necessity, through the need for flight. But now it loses the initiatory aspect that it had in the German journey (even in Wenders' films) and that it kept, despite everything, in the beat journey (Dennis Hopper and Peter Fonda's *Easy Rider*). It has become urban voyage, and has become detached from the active and affective structure which supported it, directed it, gave it even vague directions. How could there be a nerve fibre or a sensory-motor structure between the driver of *Taxi Driver* and what he sees on the pavement in his driving mirror? And, in Lumet, everything happens in continual trips and in return journeys, at ground level, in aimless movements where characters behave like windscreen wipers (*Dog Day Afternoon, Serpico*). This is in fact the clearest aspect of the modern voyage. It happens in any-space-whatever—marshalling yard, disused warehouse, the undifferentiated fabric of the city—in opposition to action which most often unfolded in the qualified space-time of the old realism. As Cassavetes says, it is a question of undoing space, as well as the story, the plot or the action.

In the fourth place, we ask ourselves what maintains a set [*ensemble*] in this world without totality or linkage. The answer is simple: what forms the set are *clichés*, and nothing else. Nothing but clichés, clichés everywhere. . . . The problem had already been raised by Dos Passos, and the new techniques that he began in the novel, before the cinema had ever dreamed of them: dispersive and lacunary reality, the swarming of characters with weak interferences, their capacity to become principal and revert to being secondary, events which descend on the characters and which do not belong to those who undergo or provoke them. Now, what consolidates all this, are the current clichés of an epoch or a moment, sound and visual slogans, which Dos Passos calls, with names borrowed from the cinema, 'actualities' and 'eye of the camera' (actualities are news interwoven with political or social events, interest items, interviews and light-hearted songs and the eye of the camera is the internal monologue of any third whatever, who is not an identified character). They are these floating images, these anonymous clichés, which circulate in the external world, but which also penetrate each one of us and constitute his internal world, so that everyone possesses only psychic clichés by which he thinks and feels, is thought and is felt, being himself a cliché among the others in the world which surrounds him. Physical, optical and auditory clichés and psychic clichés mutually feed on each other. In order for people to be able to bear themselves and the world, misery has to reach the inside of consciousnesses and the inside has to be like the outside. It is this romantic and pessimist vision that we discover in Altman or Lumet. In *Nashville* the city locations are redoubled by the images to which they give rise—photos, recordings, television—and it is in an old song that the characters are finally brought together. This power of the sound cliché, a little song, is asserted in Altman's *A Perfect Couple:* the voyage/ballad* takes on its second sense here, the sung and danced poem. In Lumet's *Bye Bye Braveman*, which tells the story of the stroll through the city of four Jewish intellectuals going to the burial of a friend, one of the four wanders among the tombs reading to the dead the recent news from the newspapers. In *Taxi Driver* Scorsese makes a catalogue of all the psychic clichés which bustle about in the driver's head, but at the same time of the optical and sound clichés of the neon-city that he sees filing past along the streets: he himself, after his slaughter, will be the national hero of a day, attaining the state of cliché, without the event being his for all that. Finally, it is no longer even possible to distinguish what is physical and psychic in the universal cliché of *King of Comedy,* sucking the interchangeable characters into a single void.

The idea of one single misery, internal and external, in the world and in consciousness, had already been had by English Romanticism in its blackest form, notably in Blake or Coleridge. People would not accept the intolerable if the same 'reasons' which it imposed on them from the outside were not insinuating themselves in them in order to make them adhere, from the inside. According to Blake there was a whole *organisation of misery*, from which the American revolution could perhaps save us. But we can see how America, on the contrary, raised the romantic question again, by giving it a still more radical, still more urgent, still more technical form: the reign of clichés internally as well as externally. How can one not believe in a powerful concerted organisation, a great and powerful plot, which has found the way to make clichés circulate, from outside to inside, from inside to outside? The criminal conspiracy, as organisation of Power, was to take on a new aspect in the modern world, that the cinema would endeavour to follow and to show. It is no longer the case, as in the *film noir* of American realism, of an organisation which related to a distinctive milieu, to assignable actions by which the criminals would be distinguishable (although very successful films of this kind, like *The Godfather*, are still made). There is no longer even a magic centre, from which hypnotic actions could start spreading everywhere as in Lang's first two Mabuse films. We do, it is true, see that Lang evolves in this respect: *The Testament of Dr Mabuse* no longer passes through a production of secret actions, but rather through a monopoly of reproduction. Occult power is confused with its effects, its supports, its media, its radios, its televisions, its microphones: it now only operates through the 'mechanical reproduction of images and of sounds'. And this is the fifth characteristic of the new image, this is the one which inspired post-war American cinema. In Lumet, the conspiracy is the system of reception, surveillance and transmission of *The Anderson Tapes; Network*, also, doubles the city with all the transmissions and reception that it ceaselessly produces, whilst *The Prince of the City* records

---

*'Bal(l)ade': an untranslatable pun on the words '*ballade*' (ballad) and '*balade*' (voyage).

the whole city on magnetic tape. And Altman's *Nashville* fully grasps this operation which doubles the city with all the clichés that it produces, and divides in two
the clichés themselves, internally and externally, whether optical or sound clichés
and psychic clichés.

   These are the five apparent characteristics of the new image: *the dispersive situation, the deliberately weak links, the voyage form, the consciousness of clichés, the
condemnation of the plot*. It is the crisis of both the action-image and the American
Dream. Everywhere there is a re-examination of the sensory-motor schema; and the
Actors Studio becomes the object of severe criticism, at the same time as it undergoes an evolution and internal splits. But how can the cinema attack the dark organisation of clichés, when it participates in their fabrication and propagation, as much
as magazines or television? Perhaps the special conditions under which it produces
and reproduces clichés allow certain directors to attain a critical reflection which
they would not have at their disposal elsewhere. It is the organisation of the cinema
which means that, however great the controls which bear upon him, the creator has
at his disposal at least a certain time to 'commit' the irreversible. He has the chance
to extract an Image from all the clichés and to set it up against them. On the condition, however, of there being an aesthetic and political project capable of constituting a positive enterprise. Now, it is here that the American cinema finds its limits.
All the aesthetic or even political qualities that it can have remain narrowly critical
and in this way even less 'dangerous' than if they were being made use of in a project of positive creation. Then, either the critique swerves abruptly and attacks only
a misuse of apparatuses and institutions, in striving to save the remains of the
American Dream, as in Lumet; or it extends itself, but becomes empty and starts to
grate, as in Altman, content to parody the cliché instead of giving birth to a new
image. As Lawrence said about painting: the rage against clichés does not lead to
much if it is content only to parody them; maltreated, mutilated, destroyed, a cliché
is not slow to be reborn from its ashes. In fact, what gave the American cinema its
advantage, the fact of being born without a previous tradition to suffocate it, now
rebounded against it. For the cinema of the action-image had itself engendered a
tradition from which it could now only, in the majority of cases, extricate itself negatively. The great genres of this cinema, the psycho-social film, the *film noir*, the
Western, the American comedy, collapse and yet maintain their empty frame. For
great creators the path of emigration was thus reversed, for reasons which were not
just related to McCarthyism. In fact, Europe had more freedom in this respect; and
it is first of all in Italy that the great crisis of the action-image took place. The timing is something like: around 1948, Italy; about 1958 France; about 1968, Germany.

TOWARDS A BEYOND OF THE MOVEMENT-IMAGE

   Why Italy first, before France and Germany? It is perhaps for an essential reason, but one which is external to the cinema. Under the impetus of de Gaulle, France
had, at the end of the war, the historical and political ambition to belong fully to
the circle of victors. The Resistance, therefore, even when underground, needed to
appear as the detachment of a regular, perfectly organised army and the life of the
French, even when full of conflict and ambiguities, needed to appear as a contribution

In Vittorio de Sica's *The Bicycle Thief* (1948) Father (Lamberto Maggiorani) and son (Enzo Staiola) search for the father's stolen bicycle, without which he will lose his job. "It is the post-war economic crisis, on the other hand, which inspires De Sica, and leads him to shatter the ASA [action-situation-action] form: there is no longer a vector or line of the universe which extends and links up the events of *The Bicycle Thief*; the rain can always interrupt or deflect the search fortuitously, the voyage of the man and of the child" (DELEUZE, p. 224).

to victory. These conditions were not favourable to a renewal of the cinematographic image, which found itself kept within the framework of a traditional action-image, at the service of a properly French 'dream'. The result of this was that the cinema in France was only able to break with its tradition rather belatedly and by a reflexive or intellectual detour which was that of the New Wave. The situation in Italy was completely different. It could certainly not claim the rank of victor; but, in contrast to Germany, on the one hand it had at its disposal a cinematographic institution which had escaped fascism relatively successfully, on the other hand it could point to a resistance and a popular life underlying oppression, although one without illusion. To grasp these, all that was necessary was a new type of tale [*récit*] capable of including the elliptical and the unorganised, as if the cinema had to begin again from zero, questioning afresh all the accepted facts of the American tradition. The Italians were therefore able to have an intuitive consciousness of the new image in the course of being born. This explains nothing of the genius of Rossellini's first films. But it does at least explain the reaction of certain American critics who saw in them the inordinate pretension of a defeated country, an odious form of blackmail, a way of making the conquerors ashamed. And above all, it is this very special situation of Italy which made possible the enterprise of neo-realism.

It was Italian neo-realism which forged the five preceding characteristics. In the situation at the end of the war, Rossellini discovered a dispersive and lacunary reality—already in *Rome, Open City*, but above all in *Païsa*—a series of fragmentary, chopped up encounters, which call into question the SAS form of the action-image. It is the post-war economic crisis, on the other hand, which inspires De Sica, and leads him to shatter the ASA form: there is no longer a vector or line of the universe which extends and links up the events of *The Bicycle Thief;* the rain can always interrupt or deflect the search fortuitously, the voyage of the man and of the child. The Italian rain becomes the sign of idle periods and of possible interruption. And again the theft of the bicycle, or even the insignificant events of *Umberto D*, have a vital importance for the protagonists. However, Fellini's *I Vitelloni* testifies not only to the insignificance of events, but also to the uncertainty of the links between them and of their non-belonging to those who experience them in this new form of the voyage. In the city which is being demolished or rebuilt, neo-realism makes any-space-whatevers proliferate—urban cancer, undifferentiated fabrics, pieces of waste-ground—which are opposed to the determined spaces of the old realism. And what rises to the horizon, what is outlined on this world, what will be imposed in a third moment, is not even raw reality, but its understudy, the reign of clichés, both internally and externally, in people's heads and hearts as much as in the whole of space. Did not *Païsa* already propose all the possible clichés of the encounters between America and Italy? And in *Voyage in Italy* Rossellini catalogues the clichés of pure Italianness, as seen by a bourgeois woman out walking; volcano, museum statues, Christian sanctuary. . . . In *General della Rovere* he drew out the cliché of the manufacture of a hero. In a very special way, it is Fellini who put his first films under the sign of the manufacture, the detection and the proliferation of external and internal clichés: the photo-novel of *The White Sheikh*, the photo-inquest of *Un' Agenzia matrimoniale*, the nightclubs, music halls and circuses, and all the jingles which console or despair. Should we add the great conspiracy which organised this misery, and for which Italy had a ready-made name, the Mafia? Francesco Rosi set up the faceless portrait of the bandit *Salvatore Giuliano*, by cutting up history according to the prefabricated roles which were imposed on it by a power which cannot be pinned down, which is only known by its effects.

Neo-realism already had a high technical conception of the difficulties that it would encounter and of the means that it invented; it had a no less sure intuitive consciousness of the new image in the course of being born. It is rather by way of an intellectual and reflexive consciousness that the French New Wave was able to take up this mutation on its own account. It is here that the voyage-form is freed from the spatio-temporal co-ordinates which were left over from the old Social Realism and begins to have value for itself or as the expression of a new society, of a new pure present: the return journey from Paris to the provinces and from the provinces to Paris in Chabrol (*Le beau Serge* and *Les Cousins*); wanderings which have become analytic instruments of an analysis of the soul, in Rohmer (the series of *Moral Tales*) and in Truffaut (the trilogy of *L'Amour à vingt ans, Baisers volés* and *Domicile conjugal*); Rivette's investigation-outing [*promenade-enquête*] (*Paris nous appartient*); the flight-outing [*promenade-fuite*] of Truffaut (*Tirez sur le pianiste*) and particularly of Godard (*A bout de souffle, Pierrot le fou*). In these we see the birth of a race of charming, moving characters who are hardly concerned by the events which happen to them—even treason, even death—and experience and act out obscure events which are as poorly linked as the portion of the any-space-whatever which they traverse. Rivette's film title is echoed by Péguy's song-formula, 'Paris belongs to no one.' And, in Rivette's *L'Amour fou*, forms of behaviour are replaced by the postures of the asylum, by explosive acts, which shatter the actions of characters as well as the connexions of the play which they are rehearsing. In this new kind of image the sensory-motor links tend to disappear, a whole sensory-motor continuity which forms the essential nature of the action-image vanishes. It is not only the famous scene in *Pierrot le fou*, 'I dunno what to do', where the voyage/ballad imperceptibly becomes the sung and danced poem; but it is also a whole upsurge of sensory-motor disturbances, which are hardly indicated when necessary, movements which make false [*font faux*], 'slight warping of perspectives, slowing down of time, alteration of gestures' (Godard's *Les Carabiniers, Tirez sur le pianiste*, or *Paris nous appartient*). Making-false [*faire-faux*] becomes the sign of a new realism, in opposition to the making-true of the old. Clumsy fights, badly aimed punches or shots, a whole out-of-phase of action and speech replace the too perfect duels of American Realism. Eustache makes a character in *La Maman et la putain* say, 'The more you appear false like that, the farther you go, the false is the beyond.'

Under this power of the false all images become clichés, sometimes because their clumsiness is shown, sometimes because their apparent perfection is attacked. The gauche gestures of the *Carabiniers* have as a correlate the series of postcards that they bring back of the war. The external, optical and sound clichés have as their correlate internal or psychic clichés. It is perhaps in the perspectives of the new German cinema that this element finds its fullest development: Daniel Schmid invents a slowness which makes possible the dividing in two of characters, as if they were to one side of what they say and do, and chose from among the external clichés the one that they will embody from the inside, in a perpetual interchangeability of inside and outside (already in *La Paloma* but above all in *Schatten der Engel* where 'the Jew could be the fascist, the prostitute could be the pimp . . .', in a game of cards which makes each player himself a card, but a card played by another). If things are like this, how is it possible not to believe in a world-wide, diffuse conspiracy, an enterprise of generalised enslavement which extends to every location of the any-space-whatever, spreading death everywhere? In Godard, *Le petit Soldat, Pierrot le fou, Made in USA, Weekend,* with their maquis of resistance to the end illustrate in different ways a plot from which escape is impossible. And Rivette, from *Paris nous appartient* to *Pont du Nord*, via *La Religieuse,* ceaselessly invokes the world-wide conspiracy which distributes roles and situations in a kind of malevolent game of snakes and ladders.

But, if everything is clichés and a plot to exchange and propagate them, the only result seems to be a cinema of parody or contempt for which Chabrol and Altman are sometimes criticised. What do the neo-realists mean, on the contrary, when they speak of the respect and the love which is necessary for the birth of the new image? Far from being satisfied with a negative or parodic critical consciousness, the cinema is engaged in its highest reflection, and has constantly deepened and developed it. We will find in Godard formulas which express the problem: if images have become clichés, internally as well as externally, how can an Image be extracted from all these clichés, 'just an image', an autonomous mental image? An image *must* emerge from the set of clichés. . . . With what politics and what consequences? What is an image which would not be a cliché? Where does the cliché end and the image begin? But, if the question has no immediate answer, it is precisely because the set of preceding characteristics do not constitute the new mental image which is being sought. The five characteristics form an envelope (including physical and psychic clichés), they are a necessary external condition, but do not constitute the image although they make it possible. And here one can assess the similarities to and the differences from Hitchcock. The New Wave could be called with good reason Hitchcocko-Marxian, rather than 'Hitchcocko-Hawksian'. Like Hitchcock it wanted to reach mental images and figures of thought (thirdness). But, whilst Hitchcock saw there a kind of complement which ought to have extended and realised the traditional 'perception-action-affection' system, it discovered there on the contrary a requirement which was enough to smash the whole system, to cut perception off from its motor extension, action, from the thread which joined it to a situation, affection from adherence or belonging to characters. The new image would therefore not be a bringing to completion of the cinema, but a mutation of it. It was necessary, on the contrary, to want what Hitchcock had constantly refused. The mental image had not to be content with weaving a set of relations, but had to form a new substance. It had to become truly thought and thinking, even if it had to become 'difficult' in order to do this. *There were two conditions.* On the one hand, it would require and presuppose a putting into crisis of the action-image, the perception-image and the affection-image, even if this entailed the discovery of 'clichés' everywhere. But, on the other hand, this crisis would be worthless by itself, it would only be the negative condition of the upsurge of the new thinking image, even if it was necessary to look for it beyond movement.

1983

BEYOND THE MOVEMENT-IMAGE

1

Against those who defined Italian neo-realism by its social content, Bazin put forward the fundamental requirement of formal aesthetic criteria. According to him, it was a matter of a new form of reality, said to be dispersive, elliptical, errant or wavering, working in blocs, with deliberately weak connections and floating events. The real was no longer represented or reproduced but 'aimed at'. Instead of representing an already deciphered real, neo-realism aimed at an always ambiguous, to be deciphered, real; this is why the sequence shot tended to replace the montage of representations. Neo-realism therefore invented a new type of image, which Bazin suggested calling 'fact-image'. This thesis of Bazin's was infinitely richer than the one that he was challenging, and showed that neo-realism did not limit itself to the content of its earliest examples. But what the two theses had in common was the posing of the problem at the level of reality: neo-realism produced a formal or material 'additional reality'. However, we are not sure that the problem arises at the level of the real, whether in relation to form or content. Is it not rather at the level of the 'mental', in terms of thought? If all the movement-images, perceptions, actions and affects underwent such an upheaval, was this not first of all because a new element burst on to the scene which was to prevent perception being extended into action in order to put it in contact with thought, and, gradually, was to subordinate the image to the demands of new signs which would take it beyond movement?

When Zavattini defines neo-realism as an art of encounter—fragmentary, ephemeral, piecemeal, missed encounters—what does he mean? It is true of encounters in Rossellini's *Paisa*, or De Sica's *Bicycle Thief*. And in *Umberto D*, De Sica constructs the famous sequence quoted as an example by Bazin: the young maid going into the kitchen in the morning, making a series of mechanical, weary gestures, cleaning a bit, driving the ants away from a water fountain, picking up the coffee grinder, stretching out her foot to close the door with her toe. And her eyes meet her pregnant woman's belly, and it is as though all the misery in the world were going to be born. This is how, in an ordinary or everyday situation, in the course of a series of gestures, which are insignificant but all the more obedient to simple sensory-motor schemata, what has suddenly been brought about is a *pure optical situation* to which the little maid has no response or reaction. The eyes, the belly, that is what an encounter is . . . Of course, encounters can take very different forms, even achieving the exceptional, but they follow the same formula. Take, for example, Rossellini's great quartet, which, far from marking an abandonment of neo-realism, on the contrary, perfects it. *Germany Year Zero* presents a child who visits a foreign country (this is why the film was criticized for not maintaining the social mooring which was held to be a condition of neo-realism), and who dies from what he sees. *Stromboli* presents a foreign woman whose revelation of the island will be all the more profound because she cannot react in a way that softens or compensates for the violence of what she sees, the intensity and the enormity of the tunny-fishing ('It was awful . . .'), the panic-inducing power of the eruption ('I am finished, I am afraid, what mystery, what beauty, my God . . .'). *Europe 51* shows a bourgeoise woman who, following the death of her child, crosses various spaces and experiences the tenement, the slum and the factory ('I thought I was see-ing convicts'). Her glances relinquish the practical function of a mistress of a house who arranges things and beings, and pass through every state of an internal vision, affliction, compassion, love, happiness, acceptance, extending to the psychiatric hos-pital where she is locked up at the end of a new trial of Joan of Arc: she sees, she has learnt to see. *Voyage in Italy* follows a female tourist struck to the core by the simple unfolding of images or visual clichés in which she discovers something unbearable, beyond the limit of what she can personally bear. This is a cinema of the see-er and no longer of the agent [*de voyant, non plus d'actant*].

What defines neo-realism is this build-up of purely optical situations (and sound ones, although there was no synchronized sound at the start of neo-realism), which are fundamentally distinct from the sensory-motor situations of the action-image in the old realism. It is perhaps as important as the conquering of a purely optical space in painting, with impressionism. It may be objected that the viewer has always found himself in front of 'descriptions', in front of optical and sound-images, and nothing more. But this is not the point. For the characters themselves reacted to situations; even when one of them found himself reduced to helplessness, bound and gagged, as a result of the ups and downs of the action. What the viewer perceived therefore was a sensory-motor image in which he took a greater or lesser part by identification with the characters. Hitchcock had begun the inversion of this point of view by including the viewer in the film. But it is now that the identification is actually inverted: the character has become a kind of viewer. He shifts, runs and becomes animated in vain, the situation he is in outstrips his motor capacities on all sides, and makes him see and hear what is no longer subject to the rules of a response or an action. He records rather than reacts. He is prey to a vision, pursued by it or pursuing it, rather than engaged in an action. Visconti's *Obsession* rightly stands as the forerunner of neo-realism; and what first strikes the viewer is the way in which the black-clad heroine is possessed by an almost hallucinatory sensuality. She is closer to a visionary, a sleep-walker, than to a seductress or a lover (similarly, later, the Countess in *Senso*).

In Volume 1 the crisis of the action-image was defined by a number of charac-teristics: the form of the trip/ballad, the multiplication of clichés, the events that hardly concern those they happen to, in short the slackening of the sensory-motor connections. All these characteristics were important but only in the sense of pre-liminary conditions. They made possible, but did not yet constitute, the new image. What constitutes this is the purely optical and sound situation which takes the place of the faltering sensory-motor situations. The role of the child in neo-realism has been pointed out, notably in De Sica (and later in France with Truffaut); this is because, in the adult world, the child is affected by a certain motor helplessness, but one which makes him all the more capable of seeing and hearing. Similarly, if everyday banality is so important, it is because, being subject to sensory-motor schemata which are automatic and pre-established, it is all the more liable, on the least disturbance of equilibrium between stimulus and response (as in the scene with the little maid in *Umberto D*), suddenly to free itself from the laws of this schema and reveal itself in a visual and sound nakedness, crudeness and brutality which make it unbearable, giving it the pace of a dream or a nightmare. There is, there-fore, a necessary passage from the crisis of image-action to the pure optical-sound image. Sometimes it is an evolution from one aspect to the other: beginning with trip/ballad films [*films de bal(l)ade*] with the sensory-motor connections slackened, and then reaching purely optical and sound situations. Sometimes the two coexist in the same film like two levels, the first of which serves merely as a melodic line for the second.

It is in this sense that Visconti, Antonioni and Fellini are definitely part of neo-realism, in spite of all their differences. *Obsession*, the forerunner, is not merely one of the versions of a famous American thriller, or the transposition of this novel to the plain of the Po. In Visconti's film, we witness a very subtle change, the beginnings of a mutation of the general notion of situation. In the old realism or on the model of the action-image, objects and settings already had a reality of their own, but it was a functional reality, strictly determined by the demands of the situation, even if these demands were as much poetic as dramatic (for instance, the emotional value of objects in Kazan). The situation was, then, directly extended into action and passion. After *Obsession*, however, something appears that continues to develop in Visconti: objects and settings [*milieux*] take on an autonomous, material reality which gives them an importance in themselves. It is therefore essential that not only the viewer but the protagonists invest the settings and the objects with their gaze, that they see and hear the things and the people, in order for action or passion to be born, erupting in a pre-existing daily life. Hence the arrival of the hero of *Obsession*, who takes a kind of visual possession of the inn, or, in *Rocco and his Brothers*, the arrival of the family who, with all their eyes and ears, try to take in the huge station and the unknown city: this will be a constant theme in Visconti's work, this 'inventory' of a setting—its objects, furniture, tools, etc. So the situation is not extended directly into action: it is no longer sensory-motor, as in realism, but primarily optical and of sound, invested by the senses, before action takes shape in it, and uses or confronts its elements. Everything remains real in this neo-realism (whether it is film set or exteriors) but, between the reality of the setting and that of the action, it is no longer a motor extension which is established, but rather a dreamlike connection through the intermediary of the liberated sense organs. It is as if the action floats in the situation, rather than bringing it to a conclusion or strengthening it. This is the source of Visconti's visionary aestheticism. And *La Terra Trema* confirms these new parameters in a singular way. Of course the fishermen's situation, the struggle they are engaged in, and the birth of a class consciousness are revealed in this first episode, the only one that Visconti completed. But this embryonic consciousness' here depends less on a struggle with nature and between men than on a grand vision of man and nature, of their perceptible and sensual unity, from which the 'rich' are excluded and which constitutes the hope of the revolution, beyond the setbacks of the floating action: a Marxist romanticism.

In Antonioni, from his first great work, *Story of a Love Affair*, the police investigation, instead of proceeding by flashback, transforms the actions into optical and sound descriptions, whilst the tale itself is transformed into actions which are dislocated in time (the episode where the maid talks while repeating her tired gestures, or the famous scene with the lifts). And Antonioni's art will continue to evolve in two directions: an astonishing development of the idle periods of everyday banality; then, starting with *The Eclipse*, a treatment of limit-situations which pushes them to the point of dehumanized landscapes, of emptied spaces that might be seen as having absorbed characters and actions, retaining only a geophysical description, an abstract inventory of them. As for Fellini, from his earliest films, it is not simply the spectacle which tends to overflow the real, it is the everyday which continually organizes itself into a travelling spectacle, and the sensory-motor linkages which give way to a succession of *varieties* subject to their own laws of passage. Barthélemy Amengual produces a formula which is true for the first half of this work: 'The real becomes spectacle or spectacular, and fascinates for being the real thing . . . The everyday is identified with the spectacular . . . Fellini achieves the deliberate confusion of the real and the spectacle' by denying the heterogeneity of the two worlds, by effacing not only distance, but the distinction between the spectator and the spectacle.

The optical and sound situations of neo-realism contrast with the strong sensory-motor situations of traditional realism. The space of a sensory-motor situation is a setting which is already specified and presupposes an action which discloses it, or prompts a reaction which adapts to or modifies it. But a purely optical or sound situation becomes established in what we might call 'any-space-whatever', whether disconnected, or emptied (we find the passage from one to the other in *The Eclipse*, where the disconnected bits of space lived by the heroine—stock exchange, Africa, air terminal—are reunited at the end in an empty space which blends into the white surface). In neo-realism, the sensory-motor connections are now valid only by virtue of the upsets that affect, loosen, unbalance, or uncouple them: the crisis of the action-image. No longer being induced by an action, any more than it is extended into one, the optical and sound situation is, therefore, neither an index nor a synsign. There is a new breed of signs, *opsigns* and *sonsigns*. And clearly these new signs refer to very varied images—sometimes everyday banality, sometimes exceptional or limit-circumstances—but, above all, subjective images, memories of childhood, sound and visual dreams or fantasies, where the character does not act without seeing himself acting, complicit viewer of the role he himself is playing, in the style of Fellini. Sometimes, as in Antonioni, they are objective images, in the manner of a *report*, even if this is a report of an accident, defined by a geometrical frame which now allows only the existence of relations of measurement and distance between its elements, persons and objects, this time transforming the action into displacement of figures in space (for instance, the search for the vanished woman in *L'Avventura*). . . .

We can already see in Fellini that a particular image is clearly subjective, mental, a recollection or fantasy—but it is not organized into a spectacle without becoming objective, without going behind the scenes, into 'the reality of the spectacle, of those who make it, who live from it, who are absorbed in it': the mental world of a character is so filled up by other proliferating characters that it becomes inter-mental, and through flattening of perspectives ends 'in a neutral, impersonal vision . . . all our world' (hence the importance of the telepath in *8 $^1/_2$*). Conversely, in Antonioni, it is as if the most objective images are not formed without becoming mental and going into a strange, invisible subjectivity. It is not merely that the method of report has to be applied to feelings as they exist in a society, and to draw from them such consequences as are internally developed in characters: Eros sick is a story of feelings which go from the objective to the subjective, and are internalized in everyone. In this respect,

Antonioni is much closer to Nietzsche than to Marx; he is the only contemporary author to have taken up the Nietzschean project of a real critique of morality, and this thanks to a 'symptomatologist' method. But, from yet another point of view, it is noticeable that Antonioni's objective images, which impersonally follow a becoming, that is, a development of consequences in a story [*récit*], none the less are subject to rapid breaks, interpolations and 'infinitesimal injections of a-temporality': for example, the lift scene in *Story of a Love Affair*. We are returned once more to the first form of the any-space-whatever: disconnected space. The connection of the parts of space is not given, because it can come about only from the subjective point of view of a character who is, nevertheless, absent, or has even disappeared, not simply out of frame, but passed into the void. In *Il Grido*, Irma is not only the obsessive, subjective thought of the hero who runs away to forget, but the imaginary gaze under which this flight takes place and connects its own segments: a gaze which becomes real again at the moment of death. And above all in *The Adventure*, the vanished woman causes an indeterminable gaze to weigh on the couple—which gives them the continual feeling of being spied on, and which explains the lack of co-ordination of their objective movements, when they flee whilst pretending to look for her. Again in *Identification of a Woman*, the whole quest or investigation takes place under the presumed gaze of the departed woman, concerning whom we will not know, in the marvellous images at the end, whether or not she has seen the hero curled up in the lift cage. The imaginary gaze makes the real something imaginary, at the same time as it in turn becomes real and gives us back some reality. It is like a circuit which exchanges, corrects, selects and sends us off again. From *The Eclipse* onwards, the any-space-whatever had achieved a second form: empty or deserted space. What happened is that, from one result to the next, the characters were objectively emptied: they are suffering less from the absence of another than from their absence from themselves (for example, *The Passenger*). Hence, this space refers back again to the lost gaze of the being who is absent from the world as much as from himself, and, as Ollier says in a phrase which is true for the whole of Antonioni's work, replaces 'traditional drama with a kind of *optical drama* lived by the character'.

In short, pure optical and sound situations can have two poles—objective and subjective, real and imaginary, physical and mental. But they give rise to opsigns and sonsigns, which bring the poles into continual contact, and which, in one direction or the other, guarantee passages and conversions, tending towards a point of indiscernibility (and not of confusion). Such a system of exchange between the imaginary and the real appears fully in Visconti's *White Nights*.

The French new wave cannot be defined unless we try to see how it has retraced the path of Italian neo-realism for its own purposes—even if it meant going in other directions as well. In fact, the new wave, on a first approximation, takes up the previous route again: from a loosening of the sensory-motor link (the stroll or wandering, the ballad, the events which concern no one, etc.), to the rise of optical and sound situations. Here again, a cinema of seeing replaces action. If Tati belongs to the new wave, it is because, after two ballad-films, he fully isolates what was taking shape in these—a burlesque whose impetus comes from purely optical and, in particular, sound, situations. Godard begins with some extraordinary ballads, from *Breathless* to *Pierrot le fou*, and tends to draw out of them a whole world of opsigns and sonsigns which already constitute the new image (in *Pierrot le fou*, the passage from the sensory-motor loosening, 'I dunno what to do', to the pure poem sung and danced, 'the line of your hips'). And these images, touching or terrible, take on an ever greater autonomy after *Made in USA;* which may be summed up as follows: 'A witness providing us with a series of reports with neither conclusion nor logical connection . . . without really effective reactions.' Claude Ollier says that, with *Made in USA*, the violently hallucinatory character of Godard's work is affirmed for itself, in an art of description which is always being renewed and always replacing its object. This descriptive objectivism is just as critical and even didactic, sustaining a series of films, from *Two or Three Things I Know about Her*, to *Slow Motion*, where reflection is not simply focused on the content of the image but on its form, its means and functions, its falsifications and creativities, on the relations within it between the sound dimension and the optical. Godard has little patience with or sympathy for fantasies: *Slow Motion* will show us the decomposition of a sexual fantasy into its separate, objective elements, visual, and then of sound. But this objectivism never loses its aesthetic force. Initially serving a politics of the image, the aesthetic force is powerfully brought out for its own sake in *Passion:* the free build-up of pictorial and musical images as *tableaux vivants*, whilst at the other end the sensory-motor linkages are beset by inhibitions (the stuttering of the female worker and the boss's cough). *Passion*, in this sense, brings to its greatest intensity what was already taking shape in *Le Mépris*, when we witnessed the sensory-motor failure of the couple in the traditional drama, at the same time as the optical representation of the drama of Ulysses and the gaze of the gods, with Fritz Lang as the intercessor, was soaring upwards. Throughout all these films, there is a creative evolution which is that of a visionary Godard. . . .

2

Although he was subject, from the outset, to the influence of certain American authors, Ozu built up in a Japanese context a body of work which was the first to develop pure optical and sound situations (even so he came quite late to the talkie, in 1936). The Europeans did not imitate him, but came back to him later via their own methods. He none the less remains the inventor of opsigns and sonsigns. The work borrows a trip/ballad [*bal(l)ade*] form, train journey, taxi ride, bus trip, a journey by bicycle or on foot: the grandparents' return journey from the provinces to Tokyo, the girl's last holiday with her mother, an old man's jaunt . . . But the object is everyday banality taken as family life in the Japanese house. Camera movements take place less and less frequently: tracking shots are slow, low 'blocs of movement'; the always low camera is usually fixed, frontal or at an unchanging angle: dissolves are abandoned in favour of the simple *cut*. What might appear to be a return to 'primitive cinema' is just as much the elaboration of an astonishingly temperate modern style: the montage-cut, which will dominate modern cinema, is a purely optical passage or punctuation between images, working directly, sacrificing all synthetic effects. The sound is also affected, since the montage-cut may culminate in the 'one shot, one line' procedure borrowed from American cinema. But there, for instance, in Lubitsch, it was a matter of an action-image functioning as an index, whereas Ozu modifies the meaning of the procedure, which now shows the absence of plot: the action-image disappears in favour of the purely visual image of what a character *is*, and the sound image of what he *says*, completely banal nature and conservation constituting the essentials of the script (this is why the only things that count are the choice of actors according to their physical and moral appearance, and the establishment of any dialogue whatever, apparently without a precise subject-matter.

It is clear that this method immediately presents idle periods, and leads to their increase in the course of the film. Of course, as the film proceeds, it might be thought that the idle periods are no longer important simply for themselves but recoup the effect of something important: the shot or the line would, on this view, be extended by a quite long silence or emptiness. But it is definitely not the case, with Ozu, that we get the remarkable *and* the ordinary, limit-situations *and* banal ones, the former having an effect on, or purposely insinuating themselves into, the latter. We cannot follow Paul Schrader when he contrasts, like two phases, 'the everyday' on one hand, and, on the other, 'the moment of decision', 'the disparity', which introduce an inexplicable break or emotion into daily banality. This distinction would seem strictly more valid for neo-realism. In Ozu, everything is ordinary or banal, even death and the dead who are the object of a natural forgetting. The famous scenes of sudden tears (that of the father in *An Autumn Afternoon* who starts to weep silently after his daughter's wedding, that of the daughter in *Late Spring* who half smiles as she looks at her sleeping father, then finds herself on the verge of tears, that of the daughter in *Dernier caprice* who makes a sharp comment about her dead father, then bursts into tears) do not mark out a strong period which might be contrasted with the weak periods in the flow of life, and there is no reason to suggest the emergence of a repressed emotion as 'decisive action'. . . .

Daily life allows only weak sensory-motor connections to survive, and replaces the action-image by pure optical and sound images, opsigns and sonsigns. In Ozu, there is no universal line which connects moments of decision, and links the dead to the living, as in Mizoguchi; nor is there any breathing space or encompasser to contain a profound question, as in Kurosawa. Ozu's spaces are raised to the state of any-space-whatevers, whether by disconnection, or vacuity (here again Ozu may be considered one of the first inventors). The false continuity of gaze, of direction and even of the position of objects are constant and systematic. . . .

Between an empty space or landscape and a still life properly so called there are certainly many similarities, shared functions and imperceptible transitions. But it is not the same thing; a still life cannot be confused with a landscape. An empty space owes its importance above all to the absence of a possible content, whilst the still life is defined by the presence and composition of objects which are wrapped up in themselves or become their own container: as in the long shot of the vase almost at the end of *Late Spring*. Such objects are not necessarily surrounded by a void, but may allow characters to live and speak in a certain soft focus, like the still life with vase and fruit in *The Woman of Tokyo*, or the one with fruit and golf-clubs in *What Did the Lady Forget?* It is like Cézanne, the landscapes—empty or with gaps—do not have the same principles of composition as the full still lifes. There comes a point when one hesitates between the two, so completely can their functions overlap each other and so subtle are the transitions that can be made: for instance, in Ozu, the marvellous composition with the bottle and the lighthouse, at the beginning of *A Story of Floating Weeds*. The distinction is none the less that of the empty and the full, which brings into play all the nuances or relations in Chinese and Japanese thought, as two aspects of contemplation. If empty spaces, interiors or exteriors, constitute purely optical (and sound) situations, still lifes are the reverse, the correlate.

The vase in *Late Spring* is interposed between the daughter's half smile and the beginning of her tears. There is becoming, change, passage. But the form of what changes does not itself change, does not pass on. This is time, time itself, 'a little time in its pure state': a direct time-image, which gives what changes the unchanging form in which the change is produced. The night that changes into day, or the reverse, recalls a still life on which light falls, either fading or getting stronger (*That Night's Wife, Passing Fancy*). The still life is time, for everything that changes is in time, but time does not itself change, it could itself change only in another time, indefinitely. At the point where the cinematographic image most directly confronts the photo, it also becomes most radically distinct from it. Ozu's still lifes endure, have a duration, over ten seconds of the vase: this duration of the vase is precisely the representation of that which endures, through the succession of changing states. A bicycle may also endure; that is, represent the unchanging form of that which moves, so long as it is at rest, motionless, stood against the wall (*A Story of Floating Weeds*). The bicycle, the vase and the still lifes are the pure and direct images of time. Each is time, on each occasion, under various conditions of that which changes in time. Time is the full, that is, the unalterable form filled by change. Time is 'the visual reserve of events in their appropriateness'. Antonioni spoke of 'the horizon of events', but noted that in the West the word has a double meaning, man's banal horizon and an inaccessible and always receding cosmological horizon. Hence the division of western cinema into European humanism and American science fiction. He suggested that it is not the same for the Japanese, who are hardly interested in science fiction: one and the same horizon links the cosmic to the everyday, the durable to the changing, one single and identical time as the unchanging form of that which changes. It is in this way that nature or stasis was defined, according to Schrader, as the form that links the everyday in 'something unified and permanent'. There is no need at all to call on a transcendence. In everyday banality, the action-image and even the movement-image tend to disappear in favour of pure optical situations, but these reveal connections of a new type, which are no longer sensory-motor and which bring the emancipated senses into direct relation with time and thought. This is the very special extension of the opsign: to make time and thought perceptible, to make them visible and of sound.

3

A purely optical and sound situation does not extend into action, any more than it is induced by an action. It makes us grasp, it is supposed to make us grasp, something intolerable and unbearable. Not a brutality as nervous aggression, an exaggerated violence that can always be extracted from the sensory-motor relations in the action-image. Nor is it a matter of scenes of terror, although there are sometimes

corpses and blood. It is a matter of something too powerful, or too unjust, but sometimes also too beautiful, and which henceforth outstrips our sensory-motor capacities. *Stromboli:* a beauty which is too great for us, like too strong a pain. It can be
a limit-situation, the eruption of the volcano, but also the most banal, a plain factory,
a wasteland. In Godard's *Les carabiniers* the girl militant recites a few revolutionary slogans, so many clichés; but she is so beautiful, of a beauty which is unbearable for her torturers who have to cover up her face with a handkerchief. And this
handkerchief, lifted again by breath and whisper ('Brothers, brothers, brothers . . .'),
itself becomes unbearable for us the viewers. In any event something has become
too strong in the image. Romanticism had already set out this aim for itself: grasping the intolerable or the unbearable, the empire of poverty, and thereby becoming
visionary, to produce a means of knowledge and action out of pure vision.

Nevertheless, are there not equal amounts of fantasy and dreaming in what we
claim to see as there are of objective apprehending? Moreover, do we not have a
subjective sympathy for the unbearable, an empathy which permeates what we see?
But this means that the unbearable itself is inseparable from a revelation or an illumination, as from a third eye. Fellini has strong sympathies with decadence, only
in so far as he prolongs it, extends its range, 'to the intolerable', and reveals beneath
the movements, faces and gestures a subterranean or extra-terrestrial world, 'the
tracking shot becoming a means of peeling away, proof of the unreality of movement', and the cinema becoming, no longer an undertaking of recognition [*recon-
naisance*], but of knowledge [*connaisance*], 'a science of visual impressions, forcing
us to forget our own logic and retinal habits'. Ozu himself is not the guardian of
traditional or reactionary values, he is the greatest critic of daily life. He picks out
the intolerable from the insignificant itself, provided that he can extend the force of
a contemplation that is full of sympathy or pity across daily life. The important thing
is always that the character or the viewer, and the two together, become visionaries.
The purely optical and sound situation gives rise to a seeing function, at once fantasy and report, criticism and compassion, whilst sensory-motor situations, no matter how violent, are directed to a pragmatic visual function which 'tolerates' or 'puts
up with' practically anything, from the moment it becomes involved in a system of
actions and reactions.

In Japan and Europe, Marxist critics have attacked these films and their characters for being too passive and negative, in turn bourgeois, neurotic or marginal, and
for having replaced modifying action with a 'confused' vision. And it is true that,
in cinema, characters of the trip/ballad are unconcerned, even by what happens to
them: whether in the style of Rossellini, the foreign woman who discovers the island,
the bourgeoise woman who discovers the factory; or in the style of Godard, the
Pierrot-le-fou generation. But it is precisely the weakness of the motor-linkages, the
weak connections, that are capable of releasing huge forces of disintegration. These
are the characters with a strange vibrance in Rossellini, strangely well-informed in
Godard and Rivette. In the west as in Japan, they are in the grip of a mutation, they
are themselves mutants. On the subject of *Two or Three Things* . . . , Godard says
that *to describe* is to observe mutations. Mutation of Europe after the war, mutation of an Americanized Japan, mutation of France in '68: it is not the cinema that
turns away from politics, it becomes completely political, but in another way. One

of the two women strollers in Rivette's *Pont du Nord* has all the characteristics of
an unforeseeable mutant: she has at first the capacity of detecting the Maxes, the
members of the organization for enslaving the world, before going through a metamorphosis inside a cocoon, then being drafted into their ranks. Similarly with the
ambiguity of the *Petit soldat*. A new type of character for a new cinema. It is because
what happens to them does not belong to them and only half concerns them, because
they know how to extract from the event the part that cannot be reduced to what
happens: that part of inexhaustible possibility that constitutes the unbearable, the
intolerable, the visionary's part. A new type of actor was needed: not simply the
non-professional actors that neo-realism had revived at the beginning, but what might
be called professional non-actors, or, better, 'actor-mediums', capable of seeing and
showing rather than acting, and either remaining dumb or undertaking some never-
ending conversation, rather than of replying or following a dialogue (such as, in
France, Bulle Ogier or Jean-Pierre Léaud).

Neither everyday nor limit-situations are marked by anything rare or extraordinary. It is just a volcanic island of poor fishermen. It is just a factory, a school . . .
We mix with all that, even death, even accidents, in our normal life or on holidays.
We see, and we more or less experience, a powerful organization of poverty and
oppression. And we are precisely not without sensory-motor schemata for recognizing such things, for putting up with and approving of them and for behaving ourselves subsequently, taking into account our situation, our capabilities and our tastes.
We have schemata for turning away when it is too unpleasant, for prompting resignation when it is terrible and for assimilating when it is too beautiful. It should
be pointed out here that even metaphors are sensory-motor evasions, and furnish us
with something to say when we no longer know what do to: they are specific
schemata of an affective nature. Now this is what a cliché is. A cliché is a sensory-
motor image of the thing. As Bergson says, we do not perceive the thing or the
image in its entirety, we always perceive less of it, we perceive only what we are
interested in perceiving, or rather what it is in our interest to perceive, by virtue of
our economic interests, ideological beliefs and psychological demands. We therefore normally perceive only clichés. But, if our sensory-motor schemata jam or
break, then a different type of image can appear: a pure optical-sound image, the
whole image without metaphor, brings out the thing in itself, literally, in its excess
of horror or beauty, in its radical or unjustifiable character, because it no longer has
to be 'justified', for better or for worse . . . The factory creature gets up, and we
can no longer say 'Well, people have to work . . .' *I thought I was seeing convicts:*
the factory is a prison, school is a prison, literally, not metaphorically. You do not
have the image of a prison following one of a school: that would simply be pointing out a resemblance, a confused relation between two clear images. On the contrary, it is necessary to discover the separate elements and relations that elude us at
the heart of an unclear image: to show *how and in what sense* school is a prison,
housing estates are examples of prostitution, bankers killers, photographs tricks—
literally, without metaphor. This is the method of Godard's *Comment ça va:* not
being content to enquire if 'things are OK' or if 'things are not OK' between two
photos, but 'how are things' [*comment ça va*] for each one and for the two together.
This was the problem with which Volume 1 ended: tearing a real image from clichés.

On the one hand, the image constantly sinks to the state of cliché: because it is introduced into sensory-motor linkages, because it itself organizes or induces these linkages, because we never perceive everything that is in the image, because it is made for that purpose (so that we do not perceive everything, so that the cliché hides the image from us . . .). Civilization of the image? In fact, it is a civilization of the cliché where all the powers have an interest in hiding images from us, not necessarily in hiding the same thing from us, but in hiding something in the image. On the other hand, at the same time, the image constantly attempts to break through the cliché, to get out of the cliché. There is no knowing how far a real image may lead: the importance of becoming visionary or seer. A change of conscience or of heart is not enough (although there is some of this, as in the heroine's heart in *Europe 51*, but, if there were nothing more, everything would quickly return to the state of cliché, other clichés would simply have been added on). Sometimes it is necessary to restore the lost parts, to rediscover everything that cannot be seen in the image, everything that has been removed to make it 'interesting'. But sometimes, on the contrary, it is necessary to make holes, to introduce voids and white spaces, to rarify the image, by suppressing many things that have been added to make us believe that we were seeing everything. It is necessary to make a division or make emptiness in order to find the whole again.

What is difficult is to know in what respect an optical and sound image is not itself a cliché, at best a photo. We are not thinking simply of the way in which these images provide more cliché as soon as they are repeated by authors who use them as formulas. But is it not the case that the creators themselves sometimes have the idea that the new image has to stand up against the cliché on its own ground, make a higher bid than the postcard, add to it and parody it, as a better way of getting over the problem (Robbe-Grillet, Daniel Schmid)? The creators invent obsessive framings, empty or disconnected spaces, even still lifes: in a certain sense they stop movement and rediscover the power of the fixed shot, but is this not to resuscitate the cliché that they aim to challenge? Enough, for victory, to parody the cliché, not to make holes in it and empty it. It is not enough to disturb the sensory-motor connections. It is necessary to *combine* the optical-sound image with the enormous forces that are not those of a simply intellectual consciousness, nor of the social one, but of a profound, vital intuition.

Pure optical and sound images, the fixed shot and the montage-cut, do define and imply a beyond of movement. But they do not strictly stop it, neither in the characters nor even in the camera. They mean that movement should not be perceived in a sensory-motor image, but grasped and thought in another type of image. The movement-image has not disappeared, but now exists only as the first dimension of an image that never stops growing in dimensions. We are not talking about dimensions of space, since the image may be flat, without depth, and through this very fact assumes all the more dimensions or powers which go beyond space. Three of these growing powers can be briefly summarized. First, while the movement-image and its sensory-motor signs were in a relationship only with an indirect image *of* time (dependent on montage), the pure optical and sound image, its opsigns and sonsigns, are directly connected to a time-image which has subordinated movement. It is this reversal which means that time is no longer the measure of movement but movement is the perspective of time: it constitutes a whole cinema of time, with a new conception and new forms of montage (Welles, Resnais). In the second place, at the same time as the eye takes up a clairvoyant function, the sound as well as visual elements of the image enter into internal relations which means that the whole image has to be 'read', no less than seen, readable as well as visible. For the eye of the seer as of the soothsayer, it is the 'literalness' of the perceptible world which constitutes it like a book. Here again all reference of the image of description to an object assumed to be independent does not disappear, but is now subordinated to the internal elements and relations which tend to replace the object and to delete it where it does appear, continually displacing it. Godard's formula, 'it isn't blood, it's some red', stops being only pictural and takes on a sense specific to the cinema. The cinema is going to become an analytic of the image, implying a new conception of cutting, a whole 'pedagogy' which will operate in different ways; for instance, in Ozu's work, in Rossellini's late period, in Godard's middle period, or in the Straubs. Finally, the fixity of the camera does not represent the only alternative to movement. Even when it is mobile, the camera is no longer content sometimes to follow the characters' movement, sometimes itself to undertake movements of which they are merely the object, but in every case it subordinates description of a space to the functions of thought. This is not the simple distinction between the subjective and the objective, the real and the imaginary, it is on the contrary their indiscernibility which will endow the camera with a rich array of functions, and entail a new conception of the frame and reframings. Hitchcock's premonition will come true: a camera-consciousness which would no longer be defined by the movements it is able to follow or make, but by the mental connections it is able to enter into. And it becomes questioning, responding, objecting, provoking, theorematizing, hypothesizing, experimenting, in accordance with the open list of logical conjunctions ('or', 'therefore', 'if', 'because', 'actually', 'although . . .'), or in accordance with the functions of thought in a *cinéma-vérité*, which, as Rouch says, means rather truth of cinema [*vérité du cinéma*].

This is the triple reversal which defines a beyond of movement. The image had to free itself from sensory-motor links; it had to stop being action-image in order to become a pure optical, sound (and tactile) image. But the latter was not enough: it had to enter into relations with yet other forces, so that it could itself escape from a world of clichés. It had to open up to powerful and direct revelations, those of the time-image, of the readable image and the thinking image. It is in this way that opsigns and sonsigns refer back to 'chronosigns', 'lectosigns' and 'noosigns'.

Antonioni, considering the evolution of neo-realism in relation to *Outcry*, said that he was tending to do without a bicycle—De Sica's bicycle, naturally. Bicycle-less neo-realism replaces the last quest involving movement (the trip) with a specific weight of time operating inside characters and excavating them from within (the chronicle). Antonioni's art is like the intertwining of consequences, of temporal sequences and effects which flow from events out-of-field. Already in *Story of a Love Affair* the investigation has the result, of itself, of provoking the outcome of a first love affair, and the effect of making two oaths of murder ring out in the future and in the past. It is a whole world of chronosigns, which would be enough to cast doubt on the false evidence according to which the cinematographic image is necessarily in the present. If we are sick with Eros, Antonioni said, it is because Eros is himself sick; and he is sick not just because he is old and worn out in his content, but because he is caught in the pure form of a time which is torn between an already determined past and a dead-end future. For Antonioni, there is no other sickness than the chronic. Chronos is sickness itself. This is why chronosigns are inseparable from lectosigns, which force us to read so many symptoms in the image, that is, to treat the optical and sound image like something that is also readable. Not only the optical and the sound, but the present and the past, and the here and the elsewhere, constitute internal elements and relations which must be deciphered, and can be understood only in a progression analogous to that of a reading: from *Story of a Love Affair*, indeterminate spaces are given a scale only later on, in which Burch calls a 'continuity grasped through discrepancy' [*raccord à appréhension décalée*], closer to a reading than to a perception. And later, Antonioni the colourist would be able to treat variations of colours as symptoms, and monochrome as the chronic sign which wins a world, thanks to a whole play of deliberate modifications. But *Story of a Love Affair* already exhibits a 'camera autonomy' when it stops following the movement of the characters or directing its own movement at them, to carry out constant reframings as functions of thought, noosigns expressing the logical conjunctions of sequel, consequence, or even intention.

1985

III

The Film Medium: Image and Sound

Film theory and film criticism have been largely concerned with one central issue: What is "cinematic"? Which paths should the cinema follow? Which should it reject? Attempts to answer this question inevitably take their lead from Lessing's classic essay, *Laocoön*. In it the eighteenth-century German dramatist attempted to demonstrate that the visual arts organize their materials spatially while the poetic arts organize their materials temporally. The materials, procedures, subjects, and effects of these two different forms (or "media") of artistic organization are therefore necessarily different. In this spirit, some film theorists have attempted to discover the essential characteristics of the film medium, declaring those subjects, materials, procedures, and effects that "exploit" the characteristics of the medium truly cinematic and those that "violate" those essential characteristics fundamentally uncinematic.

The concept of a medium is, of course, a difficult one. Is the medium to be defined in purely physical terms (that is, the projection of images at twenty-four frames per second on a screen) or in terms of an artistic language (angle and distance of shots, rhythms and patterns of editing, and so forth)? Does the concept include the main structural features of the art (such as plot) and its main historical conventions (say, its genres)? And how are we to determine which possibilities of the medium are legitimate? Is it legitimate to pursue any possibility inherent in the medium, or only those for which the medium has a special affinity? And how are we to judge what those special affinities are? May two different artistic media share those affinities or must an art confine itself, as certain purists urge, to realizing only those possibilities that it shares with no other art?

Erwin Panofsky, an art historian who was a contemporary of both Arnheim and Kracauer, has written the most influential discussion of the subject. He argues that an art ought to exploit the "unique and specific" possibilities of its medium; and in the film medium these can be defined as the "dynamization of space" and the "spatialization of time." Both these features are visual, and Panofsky's primarily visual concept of the film medium is vulnerable to the objection that it accords an undue priority to the silent film, placing unwise restrictions on the use of speech in films. According to Panofsky's principle of "co-expressibility," "sound, articulate or not, cannot express any more than is expressed, at the same time, by visible movement." Panofsky claims that the dialogue in the film version of Shaw's *Pygmalion* falls flat and suggests that Olivier's monologues in *Henry V* are successful only to the extent that Olivier's face becomes "a huge field of action" in oblique "close-up." But those who admire the brilliant Hollywood "dialogue" comedies of the 30s and early 40s and who recall that Olivier does not deliver the "St. Crispin's Day" speech in *Henry V* in close-up will receive these views with a measure of skepticism. Indeed, Panofsky modified them in the revised version of his essay that appears in this anthology.

Siegfried Kracauer acknowledges the difficulty of defining the film medium but also believes, nevertheless, that cinema has certain "inherent affinities." There are, in particular, certain subjects in the physical world that may be termed "cinematic" because they exert a peculiar attraction for the medium. Kracauer argues that cinema is predestined and even eager to exhibit them. Like Panofsky, Kracauer accepts the use of sound in films only under certain very restrictive conditions, and he especially dislikes the development of the "theatrical" film: "What even the most theatrical minded silent film could not incorporate—pointed controversies, Shavian witticisms, Hamlet's soliloquies—has been annexed to the screen." Kraucauer finds this annexation unfortunate; it in no way proves that such theatrical speeches are legitimate possibilities of the cinematic medium, for "popularity," in Kracauer's view, has no bearing on questions of aesthetic legitimacy.

Kracauer calls the comedies of Frank Capra and Preston Sturges borderline cases, but only on the ground that their witty dialogue is "complemented and compensated for" by "visuals of independent interest" (like slapstick sequences). Just as witty dialogue violates the visual requirements of the medium and requires "compensation," surrealistic projections of inner realities, expressionist dreams and visions, and experimental abstractions violate the realist requirements of the medium. On the other hand, certain types of movement—the chase and dancing—and certain types of objects—those that are normally too big or too small to be seen—are peculiarly appropriate subjects of cinema. But does the dance really have a greater affinity for the film than it does for the stage? Must the film avoid what is normally seen simply because it is the subject matter of other arts? One can agree with Kracauer that the close-up is a peculiarly cinematic technique, and even with the Hungarian filmmaker Béla Balász, that the close-up is responsible for the "discovery of the human face," without supposing that the film must confine itself exclusively to the exploitation of these "unique" potentialities.

Rudolf Arnheim shares Panofsky's and Kracauer's view that the film ought to stress the specific possibilities of the cinematic medium. But he feels obligated to refute the idea that cinema is a mere mechanical reproduction of physical reality. If it were, it would not be an art. Arnheim therefore emphasizes the various discrepancies between the film image and the standard perception of physical reality. The film image suffers a reduction of depth, a distortion of perspective, an accentuation of perspective overlapping, and, in the past, an absence of color and articulate speech. Arnheim asserts that the true task of cinema is to exploit these very "defects" and turn them to an advantage, just as painting exploits the fact that it is a two-dimensional, enclosed object. Perhaps a great art can be devised that confines itself to exploiting these defects (the silent film may have been such an art), but can we accept the suggestion that film must avoid exploiting the affinities with physical reality that Kracauer mentions, just because they conform to, rather than deviate from, reality? Should we regret the development of sound, as all three of these theorists do?

Noël Carroll examines the logic underlying the specificity thesis that is assumed by all three of these early theorists. He challenges the notion that what a medium does best will coincide with what differentiates it from other media. Indeed, he questions whether an art should confine itself either to doing what it does best or to what differentiates it from the other arts. In particular, Carroll's critique of Arnheim's *A New Laocoön* provides a very different view of the possibilities for combining language and visuals in the art of film.

Gerald Mast similarly rejects the idea that what is distinctively cinematic is based on the method of recording moving images—photographic or otherwise. Instead, he regards the projection of images by light as the essential feature of any cinematic work. And the fact of projection permits him to distinguish the experience of cinema from that of theater, television, and painting. He also argues that a careful investigation of the characteristics of projected images undermines a number of commonly held opinions. In particular he questions the assumption that one must project photographic images, upon which Kracauer's theory (and that of all realist cinema theory) is founded, and the view that the projected image is two-dimensional and perceived as flat—claims upon which Arnheim's theory (and that of most "pure" film theory) is based.

Stanley Cavell also places great emphasis on the importance of projection and, more particularly, on the fact of projection onto a screen. For Cavell, the projected image is the image of a world, and of a world which, in contrast to the world of a painting, exists beyond the frame. Indeed, the only difference between the projected world and reality is that the projected world does not exist now. It is simultaneously absent and present. One function of the movie screen, then, is to screen that world from the audience, and the audience from the projected world. Unlike the audience in a theater, which by convention is not present to the actors on stage, the film medium renders the audience absent mechanically and automatically. By this enforced invisibility, movies give expression to a modern experience of privacy and anonymity as well as a longing for invisibility and the absence of responsibility it confers. Film satisfies precisely this wish. In watching a film we view a magically reproduced world while remaining invisible to it. This condition makes the experience of film essentially voyeuristic and even pornographic. It permits the audience a magical-sexual contact with the hypnotic Garbos, Dietrichs, and Gables of the screen.

However, unlike Panofsky and many other theorists, Cavell does not think that the aesthetic possibilities of the movie medium can be deduced from its physical or technical properties. A medium is simply something through which or by means of which something specific gets said or done in particular ways. In his view, only the art itself, and not a mere consideration of its physical medium, can discover its aesthetic possibilities. Cavell further argues that the issues of genre and of medium are inseparable, and that the classical Hollywood world was composed of three such media—stories or structures that revolve about the Military Man, the Dandy, and the Woman. The Military Man conquers evil for the sake of society (James Stewart in *The Man Who Shot Liberty Valance*, Gary Cooper in *Mr. Deeds Goes to Town*); the Dandy pursues his own interests, values, and self-respect (John Wayne in *Red River*, Cary Grant in anything); and the Woman attracts men as flames attract the moth (Garbo, Dietrich, Davis). With the loss of conviction in these genres, film reached (very belatedly in comparison to the other arts of the twentieth century) the condition of modernism, in which the self-conscious artist seeks to produce a new genre, a new medium, rather than simply producing more instances of a familiar one.

As we have seen, many of the classic film theorists considered the cinema an essentially visual medium. Even those who have welcomed, or at least endorsed, the exploitation of sound in cinema have had difficulty in agreeing on the terms of its admission to the film medium. Thus, in their "Statement" on sound, Eisenstein, Pudovkin, and Alexandrov acknowledge the use of sound as an important new resource for film. They believe, however, that the montage principle, to which they attribute the greatest achievement of film, would be undermined if sounds were synchronized with sights. As they see it, every adhesion of sound to a visual montage piece increases its inertia as a montage piece. They therefore endorse only the nonsynchronous use of sound, a use that would eschew "talking films" and propose that sound be used only in orchestral counterpoint to visual images. Avoiding the use of naturalistic "talk," films of this sort would strengthen the possibility of a truly international cinema.

Mary Ann Doane approaches the problem of sound from a psychoanalytic point of view and investigates the relation of sounds to the unified body reconstituted by the technology and practices of cinema. These technologies, which increasingly succeed in concealing the work of Jean-Louis Baudry's apparatus, reduce the distance between the object and its representation, and this reduction of distance, and the attendant loss of "aura" first noticed by Walter Benjamin (see Section VII), is particularly evident in the case of the reproduction of sound. Doane believes that a proper understanding of the relation between sound and image is crucial to explaining the pleasure of the spectator in mainstream cinema. She analyzes such techniques as voice-off, voice-over during a flashback, and the interior monologue and contrasts them with the disembodied voice-over commentary of the documentary. Its radical otherness with respect to the diegesis endows the voice-over with a certain authority. In the history of the documentary this voice has been for the most part male, and its guarantee of knowledge lies in its irreducibility to the spatiotemporal limits of the body on screen. The voice-over commentary speaks more or less directly to the spectator. More frequently, in the fiction film, the use of synchronous dialogue and the voice-off presupposes a spectator who overhears and, overhearing, is unheard and unseen himself. This activity with respect to the sound track is not unlike the voyeurism often exploited by the cinematic image. The use of voice in the cinema appeals to the spectator's desire to hear, what Jacques Lacan calls the invocatory drive.

Memories of the first experience of the voice, of the hallucinatory satisfaction it offered, circumscribe the pleasure of hearing and ground its relation to the "phantasmatic" body. Classical *mise-en-scène* has a stake in perpetuating the image of unity and identity sustained by his body and in staving off the fear of fragmentation. In certain "post-modernist" films, those of Jean-Luc Godard and Jean-Marie Straub come to mind, the image of the body is not one of imaginary cohesion but of dispersal, division, and fragmentation. This approach can be understood as an attempt to forge oppositional political erotics of the voice. But this attempt is problematic, and the voice presents a particular problem for feminist theory. Over and against the theorization of the image as phallic, as the support for voyeurism and fetishism, the voice appears to provide an alternative to the image, as a politically viable means by which the woman can "make herself be heard." Luce Irigaray, for instance, claims that patriarchal culture has a heavier investment in seeing than in hearing. Doane warns, however, that while psychoanalysis delineates a pre-Oedipal scenario in which the voice of the mother dominates, the voice, in psychoanalysis, is also the instrument of the patriarchal order. Contemporary Marxist and psychoanalytic film theory regards technology as an ideological phenomenon that is constituted by socioeconomic determinants. John Belton argues, however, that even though technological evolution performs an ideological function, the work of technology can never efface itself and disappear. It remains visible—or audible—in every film, for in the positioning of the camera or the microphones a consciousness is always present that sees and hears and coexists with what is seen and heard.

ERWIN PANOFSKY
STYLE AND MEDIUM IN THE MOTION PICTURES

Best known for *Studies in Iconology* (1939), Erwin Panofsky (1892–1968) was one of the founders of the study of iconology and iconography in the history of art. From 1920 to 1933, when he taught in several German universities, he developed his theories of symbolism in art, especially focusing on the painting of the Netherlands and Northern Europe. Invited to lecture in the United States in 1931 by New York University, Panofsky later took a permanent position in the Institute for Advanced Study in Princeton, where he remained until his death. Among his other works are important studies of Albrecht Dürer, Titian, and Leonardo da Vinci. His early exposure to film during the silent era led him to see the medium as primarily visual and to emphasize its visual characteristics in his aesthetic analysis.

Film art is the only art the development of which men now living have witnessed from the very beginnings; and this development is all the more interesting as it took place under conditions contrary to precedent. It was not an artistic urge that gave rise to the discovery and gradual perfection of a new technique; it was a technical invention that gave rise to the discovery and gradual perfection of a new art.

From this we understand two fundamental facts. First, that the primordial basis of the enjoyment of moving pictures was not an objective interest in a specific subject matter, much less an aesthetic interest in the formal presentation of subject matter, but the sheer delight in the fact that things seemed to move, no matter what things they were. Second, that films—first exhibited in "kinetoscopes," viz., cinematographic peep shows, but projectable to a screen since as early as 1894—are, originally, a product of genuine folk art (whereas, as a rule, folk art derives from what is known as "higher art"). At the very beginning of things we find the simple recording of movements: galloping horses, railroad trains, fire engines, sporting events, street scenes. And when it had come to the making of narrative films these were produced by photographers who were anything but "producers" or "directors," performed by people who were anything but actors, and enjoyed by people who would have been much offended had anyone called them "art lovers."

The casts of these archaic films were usually collected in a "café" where unemployed supers or ordinary citizens possessed of a suitable exterior were wont to assemble at a given hour. An enterprising photographer would walk in, hire four or five convenient characters and make the picture while carefully instructing them what to do: "Now, you pretend to hit this lady over the head"; and (to the lady): "And you pretend to fall down in a heap." Productions like these were shown, together with those purely factual recordings of "movement for movement's sake," in a few small and dingy cinemas mostly frequented by the "lower classes" and a sprinkling of youngsters in quest of adventure (about 1905, I happen to remember, there was only one obscure and faintly disreptuable *kino* in the whole city of Berlin, bearing, for some unfathomable reason, the English name of "The Meeting Room"). Small wonder that the "better classes," when they slowly began to venture into these early picture theaters, did so, not by way of seeking normal and possibly serious entertainment, but with that characteristic sensation of self-conscious condescension with which we may plunge, in gay company, into the folkloristic depths of Coney Island or a European kermis; even a few years ago it was the regulation attitude of the socially or intellectually prominent that one could confess to enjoying such austerely educational films as *The Sex Life of the Starfish* or films with "beautiful scenery," but never to a serious liking for narratives.

Today there is no denying that narrative films are not only "art"—not often good art, to be sure, but this applies to other media as well—but also, besides architecture, cartooning and "commercial design," the only visual art entirely alive. The "movies" have reestablished that dynamic contact between art production and art consumption which, for reasons too complex to be considered here, is sorely attenuated, if not entirely interrupted, in many other fields of artistic endeavor. Whether we like it or not, it is the movies that mold, more than any other single force, the opinions, the taste, the language, the dress, the behavior, and even the physical appearance of a public comprising more than 60 per cent of the population of the earth. If all the serious lyrical poets, composers, painters and sculptors were forced by law to stop their activities, a rather small fraction of the general public would become aware of the fact and a still smaller fraction would seriously regret it. If the same thing were to happen with the movies the social consequences would be catastrophic.

In the beginning, then, there were the straight recordings of movement no matter what moved, viz., the prehistoric ancestors of our "documentaries"; and, soon after, the early narratives, viz., the prehistoric ancestors of our "feature films." The craving for a narrative element could be satisfied only by borrowing from older arts, and one should expect that the natural thing would have been to borrow from the theater, a theater play being apparently the *genus proximum* to a narrative film in that it consists of a narrative enacted by persons that move. But in reality the imitation of stage performances was a comparatively late and thoroughly frustrated development. What happened at the start was a very different thing. Instead of imitating a theatrical performance already endowed with a certain amount of motion, the earliest films added movement to works of art originally stationary, so that the dazzling technical invention might achieve a triumph of its own without intruding upon the sphere of higher culture. The living language, which is always right, has endorsed this sensible choice when it still speaks of a "moving picture" or, simply, a "picture," instead of accepting the pretentious and fundamentally erroneous "screenplay."

The stationary works enlivened in the earliest movies were indeed pictures: bad nineteenth-century paintings and postcards (or waxworks à la Madame Tussaud's), supplemented by the comic strips—a most important root of cinematic art—and the subject matter of popular songs, pulp magazines and dime novels; and the films descending from this ancestry appealed directly and very intensely to a folk art mentality. They gratified—often simultaneously—first, a primitive sense of justice and decorum when virtue and industry were rewarded while vice and laziness were punished; second, plain sentimentality when "the thin trickle of a fictive love interest" took its course "through somewhat serpentine channels," or when Father, dear Father returned from the saloon to find his child dying of diphtheria; third, a primordial instinct for bloodshed and cruelty when Andreas Hofer faced the firing squad, or when (in a film of 1893–94) the head of Mary Queen of Scots actually came off; fourth, a taste for mild pornography (I remember with great pleasure a French film of ca. 1900 wherein a seemingly but not really well-rounded lady as well as a seemingly but not really slender one were shown changing to bathing suits—an honest, straightforward *porcheria* much less objectionable than the now extinct Betty Boop films and, I am sorry to say, some of the more recent Walt Disney productions); and, finally, that crude sense of humor, graphically described as "slapstick," which feeds upon the sadistic and the pornographic instinct, either singly or in combination.

Not until as late as ca. 1905 was a film adaptation of *Faust* ventured upon (cast still "unknown," characteristically enough), and not until 1911 did Sarah Bernhardt lend her prestige to an unbelievably funny film tragedy, *Queen Elizabeth of England*. These films represent the first conscious attempt at transplanting the movies from the folk art level to that of "real art"; but they also bear witness to the fact that this commendable goal could not be reached in so simple a manner. It was soon realized that the imitation of a theater performance with a set stage, fixed entries and exits, and distinctly literary ambitions is the one thing the film must avoid.

The legitimate paths of evolution were opened, not by running away from the folk art character of the primitive film but by developing it within the limits of its own possibilities. Those primordial archetypes of film productions on the folk art level—success or retribution, sentiment, sensation, pornography, and crude humor—could blossom forth into genuine history, tragedy and romance, crime and adventure, and comedy, as soon as it was realized that they could be transfigured—not by an artificial injection of literary values but by the exploitation of the unique and specific possibilities of the new medium. Significantly, the beginnings of this legitimate development antedate the attempts at endowing the film with higher values of a foreign order (the crucial period being the years from 1902 to ca. 1905), and the decisive steps were taken by people who were laymen or outsiders from the viewpoint of the serious stage.

These unique and specific possibilities can be defined as *dynamization of space* and, accordingly, *spatialization of time*. This statement is self-evident to the point of triviality but it belongs to that kind of truths which, just because of their triviality, are easily forgotten or neglected.

In a theater, space is static, that is, the space represented on the stage, as well as the spatial relation of the beholder to the spectacle, is unalterably fixed. The spectator cannot leave his seat, and the setting of the stage cannot change, during one act (except for such incidentals as rising moons or gathering clouds and such illegitimate reborrowings from the film as turning wings or gliding backdrops). But, in return for this restriction, the theater has the advantage that time, the medium of emotion and thought conveyable by speech, is free and independent of anything that may happen in visible space. Hamlet may deliver his famous monologue lying on a couch in the middle distance, doing nothing and only dimly discernible to the spectator and listener, and yet by his mere words enthrall him with a feeling of intensest emotional action.

With the movies the situation is reversed. Here, too, the spectator occupies a fixed seat, but only physically, not as the subject of an aesthetic experience. Aesthetically, he is in permanent motion as his eye identifies itself with the lens of the camera, which permanently shifts in distance and direction. And as movable as the spectator is, as movable is, for the same reason, the space presented to him. Not only bodies move in space, but space itself does, approaching, receding, turning, dissolving and recrystallizing as it appears through the controlled locomotion and focusing of the camera and through the cutting and editing of the various shots—not to mention such special effects as visions, transformations, disappearances, slow-motion and fast-motion shots, reversals and trick films. This opens up a world of possibilities of which the stage can never dream. Quite apart from such photographic tricks as the participation of disembodied spirits in the action of the *Topper* series, or the more effective wonders wrought by Roland Young in *The Man Who Could Work Miracles*, there is, on the purely factual level, an untold wealth of themes as inaccessible to the "legitimate" stage as a fog or a snowstorm is to the sculptor; all sorts of violent elemental phenomena and, conversely, events too microscopic to be visible under normal conditions (such as the life-saving injection with the serum flown in at the very last moment, or the fatal bite of the yellow-fever mosquito); full-scale battle scenes; all kinds of operations, not only in the surgical sense but also in the sense of any actual construction, destruction or experimentation, as in *Louis Pasteur* or *Madame Curie*; a really grand party, moving through many rooms of a mansion or a palace. Features like these, even the mere shifting of the scene from one place to another by means of a car perilously negotiating heavy traffic or a motorboat steered through a nocturnal harbor, will not only always retain their primitive cinematic appeal but also remain enormously effective as a means of stirring the emotions and creating suspense. In addition, the movies have the power, entirely denied to the theater, to convey psychological experiences by directly projecting their content to the screen, substituting, as it were, the eye of the beholder for the consciousness of the character (as when the imaginings and hallucinations of the drunkard in the otherwise overrated *Lost Weekend* appear as stark realities instead of being described by mere words). But any attempt to convey thought and feelings exclusively, or even primarily, by speech leaves us with a feeling of embarrassment, boredom, or both.

What I mean by thoughts and feelings "conveyed exclusively, or even primarily, by speech" is simply this: Contrary to naïve expectation, the invention of the sound track in 1928 has been unable to change the basic fact that a moving picture, even when it has learned to talk, remains a picture that moves and does not convert itself into a piece of writing that is enacted. Its substance remains a series of visual sequences held together by an uninterrupted flow of movement in space (except, of course, for such checks and pauses as have the same compositional value as a rest in music), and not a sustained study in human character and destiny transmitted by effective, let alone "beautiful," diction. I cannot remember a more misleading statement about the movies than Mr. Eric Russell Bentley's in the spring number of the *Kenyon Review*, 1945: "The potentialities of the talking screen differ from those of the silent screen in adding the dimension of dialogue—which could be poetry." I would suggest: "The potentialities of the talking screen differ form those of the silent screen in integrating visible movement with dialogue which, therefore, had better not be poetry."

All of us, if we are old enough to remember the period prior to 1928, recall the old-time pianist who, with his eyes glued on the screen, would accompany the events with music adapted to their mood and rhythm; and we also recall the weird and spectral feeling overtaking us when this pianist left his post for a few minutes and the film was allowed to run by itself, the darkness haunted by the monotonous rattle of the machinery. Even the silent film, then, was never mute. The visible spectacle always required, and received, an audible accompaniment which, from the very beginning, distinguished the film from simple pantomime and rather classed it—*mutatis mutandis*—with the ballet. The advent of the talkie meant not so much an "addition" as a transformation: the transformation of musical sound into articulate speech and, therefore, of quasi pantomime into an entirely new species of spetacle which differs from the ballet, and agrees with the stage play, in that its acoustic component consists of intelligible words, but differs from the stage play and agrees with the ballet in that this acoustic component is not detachable form the visual. In a film, that which we hear remains, for good or worse, inextricably fused with that which we see; the sound, articulate or not, cannot express any more than is expressed, at the same time, by visible movement; and in a good film it does not even attempt to do so. To put it briefly, the play—or, as it is very properly called, the "script"—of a moving picture is subject to what might be termed the *principle of coexpressibility*.

Empirical proof of this principle is furnished by the fact that, wherever the dialogical or monological element gains temporary prominence, there appears, with the inevitability of a natural law, the "close-up." What does the close-up achieve? In showing us, in magnification, either the face of the speaker or the face of the listeners or both in alternation, the camera transforms the human physiognomy into a huge field of action where—given the qualification of the performers—every subtle movement of the features, almost imperceptible from a natural distance, becomes an expressive event in visible space and thereby completely integrates itself with the expressive content of the spoken word; whereas, on the stage, the spoken word makes a stronger rather than a weaker impression if we are not permitted to count the hairs in Romeo's mustache.

This does not mean that the scenario is a negligible factor in the making of a moving picture. It only means that its artistic intention differs in kind from that of a stage play, and much more from that of a novel or a piece of poetry. As the success of a Gothic jamb figure depends not only upon its quality as a piece of sculpture but also, or even more so, upon its integrability with the architecture of the portal, so does the success of a movie script—not unlike that of an opera libretto—

depend, not only upon its quality as a piece of literature but also, or even more so, upon its integrability with the events on the screen.

As a result—another empirical proof of the coexpressibility principle—good movie scripts are unlikely to make good reading and have seldom been published in book form; whereas, conversely, good stage plays have to be severely altered, cut, and, on the other hand, enriched by interpolations to make good movie scripts. In Shaw's *Pygmalion*, for instance, the actual process of Eliza's phonetic education and, still more important, her final triumph at the grand party, are wisely omitted; we see—or, rather, hear—some samples of her gradual linguistic improvement and finally encounter her, upon her return from the reception, victorious and splendidly arrayed but deeply hurt for want of recognition and sympathy. In the film adaptation, precisely these two scenes are not only supplied but also strongly emphasized; we witness the fascinating activities in the laboratory with its array of spinning disks and mirrors, organ pipes and dancing flames, and we participate in the ambassadorial party, with many moments of impending catastrophe and a little counterintrigue thrown in for suspense. Unquestionably these two scenes, entirely absent from the play, and indeed unachievable upon the stage, were the highlights of the film; whereas the Shavian dialogue, however severely cut, turned out to fall a little flat in certain moments. And wherever, as in so many other films, a poetic emotion, a musical outburst, or a literary conceit (even, I am grieved to say, some of the wisecracks of Groucho Marx) entirely lose contact with visible movement, they strike the sensitive spectator as, literally, out of place. It is certainly terrible when a softboiled he-man, after the suicide of his mistress, casts a twelve-foot glance upon her photograph and says something less-than-coexpressible to the effect that he will never forget her. But when he recites, instead, a piece of poetry as sublimely morethan-coexpressible as Romeo's monologue at the bier of Juliet, it is still worse. Reinhardt's *Midsummer Night's Dream* is probably the most unfortunate major film ever produced; and Olivier's *Henry V* owes its comparative success, apart from the all but providential adaptability of this particular play, to so many *tours de force* that it will, God willing, remain an exception rather than set a pattern. It combines "judicious pruning" with the interpolation of pageantry, nonverbal comedy and melodrama; it uses a device perhaps best designated as "oblique close-up" (Mr. Olivier's beautiful face inwardly listening to but not pronouncing the great soliloquy); and, most notably, it shifts between three levels of archaeological reality: a reconstruction of Elizabethan London, a reconstruction of the events of 1415 as laid down in Shakespeare's play, and the reconstruction of a performance of this play on Shakespeare's own stage. All this is perfectly legitimate; but, even so, the highest praise of the film will always come from those who, like the critic of the *New Yorker*, are not quite in sympathy with either the movies *au naturel* or Shakespeare *au naturel*.

As the writings of Conan Doyle potentially contain all modern mystery stories (except for the tough specimens of the Dashiell Hammett school), so do the films produced between 1900 and 1910 pre-establish the subject matter and methods of the moving picture as we know it. This period produced the incunabula of the Western and the crime film (Edwin S. Porter's amazing *Great Train Robbery* of

1903) from which developed the modern gangster, adventure, and mystery pictures (the latter, if well done, is still one of the most honest and genuine forms of film entertainment, space being doubly charged with time as the beholder asks himself not only "What is going to happen?" but also "What has happened before?"). The same period saw the emergence of the fantastically imaginative film (Méliès) which was to lead to the expressionist and surrealist experiments (*The Cabinet of Dr. Caligari, Sang d'un Poète*, etc.), on the one hand, and to the more superficial and spectacular fairy tales à la Arabian Nights, on the other. Comedy, later to triumph in Charlie Chaplin, the still insufficiently appreciated Buster Keaton, the Marx Brothers and the pre-Hollywood creations of René Clair, reached a respectable level in Max Linder and others. In historical and melodramatic films the foundations were laid for movie iconography and movie symbolism, and in the early work of D. W. Griffith we find, not only remarkable attempts at psychological analysis (*Edgar Allan Poe*) and social criticism (*A Corner in Wheat*) but also such basic technical innovations as the long shot, the flashback and the close-up. And modest trick films and cartoons paved the way to Felix the Cat, Popeye the Sailor, and Felix's prodigious offspring, Mickey Mouse.

Within their self-imposed limitations the earlier Disney films, and certain sequences in the later ones,[1] represent, as it were, a chemically pure distillation of cinematic possibilities. They retain the most important folkloristic elements—sadism, pornography, the humor engendered by both, and moral justice—almost without dilution and often fuse these elements into a variation on the primitive and inexhaustible David-and-Goliath motif, the triumph of the seemingly weak over the seemingly strong; and their fantastic independence of the natural laws gives them the power to integrate space with time to such perfection that the spatial and temporal experiences of sight and hearing come to be almost interconvertible. A series of soap bubbles, successively punctured, emits a series of sounds exactly corresponding in pitch and

---

[1] I make this distinction because it was, in my opinion, a fall from grace when *Snow White* introduced the human figure and when *Fantasia* attempted to picturalize The World's Great Music. The very virtue of the animated cartoon is to animate, that is to say endow lifeless things with life, or living things with a different kind of life. It effects a metamorphosis, and such a metamorphosis is wonderfully present in Disney's animals, plants, thunderclouds and railroad trains. Whereas his dwarfs, glamourized princesses, hillbillies, baseball players, rouged centaurs and *amigos* from South America are not transformations but caricatures at best, and fakes or vulgarities at worst. Concerning music, however, it should be borne in mind that its cinematic use is no less predicated upon the principle of coexpressibility than is the cinematic use of the spoken word. There is music permitting or even requiring the accompaniment of visible action (such as dances, ballet music and any kind of operatic compositions) and music of which the opposite is true; and this is, again, not a question of quality (most of us rightly prefer a waltz by Johann Strauss to a symphony by Sibelius) but one of intention. In *Fantasia* the hippopotamus ballet was wonderful, and the Pastoral Symphony and "Ave Maria" sequences were deplorable, not because the cartooning in the first case was infinitely better than in the two others (*cf.* above), and certainly not because Beethoven and Schubert are too sacred for picturalization, but simply because Ponchielli's "Dance of the Hours" is coexpressible while the Pastoral Symphony and the "Ave Maria" are not. In cases like these even the best imaginable music and the best imaginable cartoon will impair rather than enhance each other's effectiveness.

Experimental proof of all this was furnished by Disney's recent *Make Mine Music* where The World's Great Music was fortunately restricted to Prokofieff. Even among the other sequences the most successful ones were those in which the human element was either absent or reduced to a minimum; Willie the Whale, the Ballad of Johnny Fedora and Alice Blue-Bonnet, and, above all, the truly magnificent Goodman Quartet.

volume to the size of the bubbles; the three uvulae of Willie the Whale—small, large and medium—vibrate in consonance with tenor, bass and baritone notes; and the very concept of stationary existence is completely abolished. No object in creation, whether it be a house, a piano, a tree or an alarm clock, lacks the faculties of organic, in fact anthropomorphic, movement, facial expression and phonetic articulation. Incidentally, even in normal, "realistic" films the inanimate object, provided that it is dynamizable, can play the role of a leading character as do the ancient railroad engines in Buster Keaton's *General* and *Niagara Falls*. How the earlier Russian films exploited the possibility of heroizing all sorts of machinery lives in everybody's memory; and it is perhaps more than an accident that the two films which will go down in history as the great comical and the great serious masterpiece of the silent period bear the names and immortalize the personalities of two big ships: Keaton's *Navigator* (1924) and Eisenstein's *Potemkin* (1925).

The evolution from the jerky beginnings to this grand climax offers the fascinating spectacle of a new artistic medium gradually becoming conscious of its legitimate, that is, exclusive, possibilities and limitations—a spectacle not unlike the development of the mosaic, which started out with transposing illusionistic genre pictures into a more durable material and culminated in the hieratic supernaturalism of Ravenna; or the development of line engraving, which started out as a cheap and handy substitute for book illumination and culminated in the purely "graphic" style of Dürer.

Just so the silent movies developed a definite style of their own, adapted to the specific conditions of the medium. A hitherto unknown language was forced upon a public not yet capable of reading it, and the more proficient the public became the more refinement could develop in the language. For a Saxon peasant of around 800 it was not easy to understand the meaning of a picture showing a man as he pours water over the head of another man, and even later many people found it difficult to grasp the significance of two ladies standing behind the throne of an emperor. For the public of around 1910 it was no less difficult to understand the meaning of the speechless action in a moving picture, and the producers employed means of clarification similar to those we find in medieval art. One of these were printed titles or letters, striking equivalents of the medieval *tituli* and scrolls (at a still earlier date there even used to be explainers who would say, *viva voce*, "Now he thinks his wife is dead but she isn't" or "I don't wish to offend the ladies in the audience but I doubt that any of them would have done that much for her child"). Another, less obtrusive method of explanation was the introduction of a fixed iconography which from the outset informed the spectator about the basic facts and characters, much as the two ladies behind the emperor, when carrying a sword and a cross respectively, were uniquely determined as Fortitude and Faith. There arose, identifiable by standardized appearance, behavior and attributes, the well-remembered types of the Vamp and the Straight Girl (perhaps the most convincing modern equivalents of the medieval personifications of the Vices and Virtues), the Family Man, and the Villain, the latter marked by a black mustache and walking stick. Nocturnal scenes were printed on blue or green film. A checkered tablecloth meant, once for all, a "poor but honest" milieu; a happy marriage, soon to be endangered by the shadows from the past, was symbolized by the young wife's pouring the breakfast coffee for her husband; the first kiss was invariably announced by the lady's gently playing with her partner's necktie and was invariably accompanied by her kicking out with her left foot. The conduct of the characters was predetemined accordingly. The poor but honest laborer who, after leaving his little house with the checkered tablecloth, came upon an abandoned baby could not but take it to his home and bring it up as best he could; the Family Man could not but yield, however temporarily, to the temptations of the Vamp. As a result these early melodramas had a highly gratifying and soothing quality in that events took shape, without the complications of individual psychology, according to a pure Aristotelian logic so badly missed in real life.

Devices like these became gradually less necessary as the public grew accustomed to interpret the action by itself and were virtually abolished by the invention of the talking film. But even now there survive—quite legitimately, I think—the remnants of a "fixed attitude and attribute" principle and, more basic, a primitive or folkloristic concept of plot construction. Even today we take it for granted that the diphtheria of a baby tends to occur when the parents are out and, having occurred, solves all their matrimonial problems. Even today we demand of a decent mystery film that the butler, though he may be anything from an agent of the British Secret Service to the real father of the daughter of the house, must not turn out to be the murderer. Even today we love to see Pasteur, Zola or Ehrlich win out against stupidity and wickedness, with their respective wives trusting and trusting all the time. Even today we much prefer a happy finale to a gloomy one and insist, at the very least, on the observance of the Aristotelian rule that the story have a beginning, a middle and an ending—a rule the abrogation of which has done so much to estrange the general public from the more elevated spheres of modern writing. Primitive symbolism, too, survives in such amusing details as the last sequence of Casablanca where the delightfully crooked and right-minded *préfet de police* casts an empty bottle of Vichy water into the wastepaper basket; and in such telling symbols of the supernatural as Sir Cedric Hardwicke's Death in the guise of a "gentleman in a dust-coat trying" (*On Borrowed Time*) or Claude Rains's Hermes Psychopompos in the striped trousers of an airline manager (*Here Comes Mister Jordan*).

The most conspicuous advances were made in directing, lighting, camera work, cutting and acting proper. But while in most of these fields the evolution proceeded continuously—though, of course, not without detours, breakdowns and archaic relapses—the development of acting suffered a sudden interruption by the invention of the talking film; so that the style of acting in the silents can already be evaluated in retrospect, as a lost art not unlike the painting technique of Jan van Eyck or, to take up our previous simile, the burin technique of Dürer. It was soon realized that acting in a silent film neither meant a pantomimic exaggeration of stage acting (as was generally and erroneously assumed by professional stage actors who more and more frequently condescended to perform in the movies), nor could dispense with stylization altogether; a man photographed while walking down a gangway in ordinary, every-day-life fashion looked like anything but a man walking down a gangway when the result appeared on the screen. If the picture was to look both natural and meaningful the acting had to be done in a manner equally different from the style of the stage and the reality of ordinary life; speech had to be made dispensable by establishing an organic relation between the acting and the technical procedure of cinephotography—much as in Dürer's prints color had been made dispensable by establishing an organic relation between the design and the technical procedure of line engraving.

This was precisely what the great actors of the silent period accomplished, and it is a significant fact that the best of them did not come from the stage, whose crystallized tradition prevented Duse's only film, *Cenere*, from being more than a priceless record of Duse. They came instead from the circus or the variety, as was the case of Chaplin, Keaton and Will Rogers; from nothing in particular, as was the case of Theda Bara, of her greater European parallel, the Danish actress Asta Nielsen, and of Garbo; or from everything under the sun, as was the case of Douglas Fairbanks. The style of these "old masters" was indeed comparable to the style of line engraving in that it was, and had to be, exaggerated in comparison with stage acting (just as the sharply incised and vigorously curved *tailles* of the burin are exaggerated in comparison with pencil strokes or brushwork), but richer, subtler and infinitely more precise. The advent of the talkies, reducing if not abolishing this difference between screen acting and stage acting, thus confronted the actors and actresses of the silent screen with a serious problem. Buster Keaton yielded to temptation and fell. Chaplin first tried to stand his ground and to remain an exquisite archaist but finally gave in, with only moderate success (*The Great Dictator*). Only the glorious Harpo has thus far successfully refused to utter a single articulate sound; and only Greta Garbo succeeded, in a measure, in transforming her style in principle. But even in her case one cannot help feeling that her first talking picture, *Anna Christie*, where she could ensconce herself, most of the time, in mute or monosyllabic sullenness, was better than her later performances; and in the second, talking version of *Anna Karenina*, the weakest moment is certainly when she delivers a big Ibsenian speech to her husband, and the strongest when she silently moves along the platform of the railroad station while her despair takes shape in the consonance of her movement (and expression) with the movement of the nocturnal space around her, filled with the real noises of the trains and the imaginary sound of the "little men with the iron hammers" that drives her, relentlessly and almost without her realizing it, under the wheels.

Small wonder that there is sometimes felt a kind of nostalgia for the silent period and that devices have been worked out to combine the virtues of sound and speech with those of silent acting, such as the "oblique close-up" already mentioned in connection with *Henry V*; the dance behind glass doors in *Sous les Toits de Paris*; or, in the *Histoire d'un Tricheur*, Sacha Guitry's recital of the events of his youth while the events themselves are "silently" enacted on the screen. However, this nostalgic feeling is no argument against the talkies as such. Their evolution has shown that, in art, every gain entails a certain loss on the other side of the ledger; but that the gain remains a gain, provided that the basic nature of the medium is realized and respected. One can imagine that, when the cavemen of Altamira began to paint their buffaloes in natural colors instead of merely incising the contours, the more conservative cavemen foretold the end of paleolithic art. But paleolithic art went on, and so will the movies. New technical inventions always tend to dwarf the values already attained, especially in a medium that owes its very existence to technical experimentation. The earliest talkies were infinitely inferior to the then mature silents, and most of the present technicolor films are still inferior to the now mature talkies in black and white. But even if Aldous Huxley's nightmare should come true and the experiences of taste, smell and touch should be added to those of sight and hearing, even then we may say with the Apostle, as we have said when first confronted with the sound track and the technicolor film, "We are troubled on every side, yet not distressed; we are perplexed, but not in despair."

From the law of time-charged space and space-bound time, there follows the fact that the screenplay, in contrast to the theater play, *has no aesthetic existence independent of its performance, and that its characters have no aesthetic existence outside the actors.*

The playwright writes in the fond hope that his work will be an imperishable jewel in the treasure house of civilization and will be presented in hundreds of performances that are but transient variations on a "work" that is constant. The scriptwriter on the other hand, writes for one producer, one director and one cast. Their work achieves the same degree of permanence as does his; and should the same or a similar scenario ever be filmed by a different director and a different cast there will result in an altogether different "play."

Othello or Nora are definite, substantial figures created by the playwright. They can be played well or badly, and they can be "interpreted" in one way or another; but they most definitely exist, no matter who plays them or even whether they are played at all. The character in a film, however, lives and dies with the actor. It is not the entity "Othello" interpreted by Robeson or the entity "Nora" interpreted by Duse; it is the entity "Greta Garbo" incarnate in a figure called Anna Christie or the entity "Robert Montgomery" incarnate in a murderer who, for all we know or care to know, may forever remain anonymous but will never cease to haunt our memories. Even when the names of the characters happen to be Henry VIII or Anna Karenina, the king who ruled England from 1509 to 1547 and the woman created by Tolstoy, they do not exist outside the being of Garbo and Laughton. They are but empty and incorporeal outlines like the shadows in Homer's Hades, assuming the character of reality only when filled with the lifeblood of an actor. Conversely, if a movie role is badly played there remains literally nothing of it, no matter how interesting the character's psychology or how elaborate the words.

What applies to the actor applies, *mutatis mutandis*, to most of the other artists, or artisans, who contribute to the making of a film: the director, the soundman, the enormously important cameraman, even the make-up man. A stage production is rehearsed until everything is ready, and then it is repeatedly performed in three consecutive hours. At each performance everybody has to be on hand and does his work; and afterward he goes home and to bed. The work of the stage actor may thus be likened to that of a musician, and that of the stage director to that of a conductor. Like these, they have a certain repertoire which they have studied and present in a number of complete but transitory performances, be it *Hamlet* today and *Ghosts* tomorrow, or *Life with Father per saecula saeculorum*. The activites of the film actor and the film director, however, are comparable, respectively, to those of the plastic artist and the architect, rather than to those of the musician and the conductor. Stage work is continuous but transitory; film work is discontinuous but permanent. Individual sequences are done piecemeal and out of order according to the most efficient use of sets and personnel. Each bit is done over and over again until it stands; and when the whole has been cut and composed everyone is through with it forever. Needless to say that this very procedure cannot but emphasize the curious consubstantiality that exists between the person of the movie actor and his role. Coming into existence piece by piece, regardless of the natural sequence of events, the "character" can grow into a unified whole only if the actor manages to be, not merely to play, Henry VIII or Anna Karenina throughout the entire wearisome period of shooting. I have it on the best of authorities that Laughton was really difficult to live with in the particular six or eight weeks during which he was doing—or rather being—Captain Bligh.

It might be said that a film, called into being by a cooperative effort in which all contributions have the same degree of permanence, is the nearest modern equivalent of a medieval cathedral; the role of the producer corresponding, more or less, to that of the bishop or archbishop; that of the director to that of the architect in chief; that of the scenario writers to that of the scholastic advisers establishing the iconographical program; and that of the actors, cameramen, cutters, sound men, make-up men and the diverse technicians to that of those whose work provided the physical entity of the finished product, from the sculptors, glass painters, bronze casters, carpenters and skilled masons down to the quarry men and woodsmen. And if you speak to any

Laurence Olivier in *Henry V* (1944). The film "uses a device perhaps best designated as 'oblique close-up' (Mr. Olivier's beautiful face inwardly listening to but not pronouncing the great soliloquy)." (PANOFSKY, p. 252).

one of these collaborators he will tell you, with perfect *bona fides*, that his is really the most important job—which is quite true to the extent that it is indispensable.

The comparison may seem sacrilegious, not only because there are, proportionally, fewer good films than there are good cathedrals, but also because the movies are commercial. However, if commercial art be defined as all art not primarily produced in order to gratify the creative urge of its maker but primarily intended to meet the requirements of a patron or a buying public, it must be said that noncommercial art is the exception rather than the rule, and a fairly recent and not always felicitous exception at that. While it is true that commercial art is always in danger of ending up as a prostitute, it is equally true that noncommercial art is always in danger of ending up as an old maid. Noncommercial art has given us Seurat's "Grande Jatte" and Shakespeare's sonnets, but also much that is esoteric to the point of incommunicability. Conversely, commercial art has given us much that is vulgar or snobbish (two aspects of the same thing) to the point of loathsomeness, but also Dürer's prints and Shakespeare's plays. For, we must not forget that Dürer's prints were partly made on commission and partly intended to be sold in the open market; and that Shakespeare's plays—in contrast to the earlier masques and intermezzi

Caligari (Werner Krauss) feeding Cesare (Conrad Veidt) in *The Cabinet of Doctor Caligari* (1919). "The expressionist settings . . . could exert but little influence upon the general course of events. To prestylize reality prior to tackling it amounts to dodging the problem" (PANOFSKY, p. 261). "Films of this type are not only intended as autonomous wholes but frequently ignore physical reality or exploit it for purposes alien to photographic veracity" (KRACAUER, p. 157).

which were produced at court by aristocratic amateurs and could afford to be so incomprehensible that even those who described them in printed monographs occasionally failed to grasp their intended significance—were meant to appeal, and did appeal, not only to the select few but also to everyone who was prepared to pay a shilling for admission.

It is this requirement of communicabiilty that makes commercial art more vital than noncommercial, and therefore potentially much more effective for better or for worse. The commercial producer can both educate and pervert the general public, and can allow the general public—or rather his idea of the general public—both to educate and to pervert himself. As is demonstrated by a number of excellent films that proved to be great box office successes, the public does not refuse to accept good products if it gets them. That it does not get them very often is caused not so much by commercialism as such as by too little discernment and, paradoxical though it may seem, too much timidity in its application. Hollywood believes that it must produce "what the public wants" while the public would take whatever Hollywood produces. If Hollywood were to decide for itself what it wants it would get away with it—even if it should decide to "depart from evil and do good." For, to revert to whence we started, in modern life the movies are what most other forms of art have ceased to be, not an adornment but a necessity.

That this should be so is understandable, not only from a sociological but also from an art-historical point of view. The processes of all the earlier representational arts conform, in a higher or lesser degree, to an idealistic conception of the world. These arts operate from top to bottom, so to speak, and not from bottom to top; they start with an idea to be projected into shapeless matter and not with the objects that constitute the physical world. The painter works on a blank wall or canvas which he organizes into a likeness of things and persons according to his idea (however much this idea may have been nourished by reality); he does not work with the things and persons themselves even if he works "from the model." The same is true of the sculptor with his shapeless mass of clay or his untooled block of stone or wood; of the writer with his sheet of paper or his dictaphone; and even of the stage designer with his empty and sorely limited section of space. It is the movies, and only the movies, that do justice to that materialistic interpretation of the universe which, whether we like it or not, pervades contemporary civilization. Excepting the very special case of the animated cartoon, the movies organize material things and persons, not a neutral medium, into a composition that receives its style, and may even become fantastic or pretervoluntarily symbolic, not so much by an interpretation in the artist's mind as by the actual manipulation of physical objects and recording machinery. The medium of the movies is physical reality as such: the physical reality of eighteenth-century Versailles—no matter whether it be the original or a Hollywood facsimile indistinguishable therefrom for all aesthetic intents and purposes—or of a suburban home in Westchester; the physical reality of the Rue de Lappe in Paris or of the Gobi Desert, of Paul Ehrlich's apartment in Frankfurt or of the streets of New York in the rain; the physical reality of engines and animals, of Edward G. Robinson and Jimmy Cagney. All these objects and persons must be organized into a work of art. They can be arranged in all sorts of ways ("arrangement" comprising, of course, such things as make-up, lighting and camera work); but there is no running away from them. From this point of view it becomes evident that an attempt at subjecting the world to artistic prestylization, as in the expressionist settings of *The Cabinet of Dr. Caligari* (1919), could be no more than an exciting experiment that could exert but little influence upon the general course of events. To prestylize reality prior to tackling it amounts to dodging the problem. The problem is to manipulate and shoot unstylized reality in such a way that the result has style. This is a proposition no less legitmate and no less difficult than any proposition in the older arts.

1934; revised 1947

SIEGFRIED KRACAUER
FROM THEORY OF FILM

THE ESTABLISHMENT OF PHYSICAL EXISTENCE

In establishing physical existence, films differ from photographs in two respects: they represent reality as it evolves in time; and they do so with the aid of cinematic techniques and devices.

Consequently, the recording and revealing duties of the two kindred media coincide only in part. And what do they imply for film in particular? The hunting ground of the motion picture camera is in principle unlimited; it is the external world expanding in all directions. Yet there are certain subjects within that world which may be termed "cinematic" because they seem to exert a peculiar attraction on the medium. It is as if the medium were predestined (and eager) to exhibit them. The following pages are devoted to a close examination of these cinematic subjects. Several lie, so to speak, on the surface; they will be dealt with under the title "recording functions." Others would hardly come to our attention or be perceptible were it not for the film camera and/or the intervention of cinematic techniques; they will be discussed in the subsequent section "revealing functions." To be sure, any camera revelation involves recording, but recording on its part need not be revealing.

RECORDING FUNCTIONS

Movement

At least two groups of quite common external phenomena are naturals for the screen. As might be expected, one is made up of all kinds of movements, these being cinematic because only the motion picture camera is able to record them. Among them are three types which can be considered cinematic subjects par excellence.

The Chase

"The chase," says Hitchcock, "seems to me the final expression of the motion picture medium." This complex of interrelated movements is motion at its extreme, one might almost say, motion as such—and of course it is immensely serviceable for establishing a continuity of suspenseful physical action. Hence the fascination the chase has held since the beginning of the century. The primitive French comedies availed themselves of it to frame their space-devouring adventures. Gendarmes pursued a dog who eventually turned the tables on them (*Course des sergeants de ville*); pumpkins gliding from a cart were chased by the grocer, his donkey, and passers-by through sewers and over roofs (*La Course des potirons, 1907*; English title: *The Pumpkin Race*). For any Keystone comedy to forgo the chase would have been an unpardonable crime. It was the climax of the whole, its orgiastic finale— a pandemonium, with onrushing trains telescoping into automobiles and narrow escapes down ropes that dangled above a lion's den.

But perhaps nothing reveals the cinematic significance of the reveling in speed more drastically than D. W. Griffith's determination to transfer, at the end of all his great films, the action from the ideological plane to that of his famous "last-minute rescue," which was a chase pure and simple. Or should one say, a race? In any case, the rescuers rush ahead to overwhelm the villains or free their victims at the very last moment, while simultaneously the inner emotion which the dramatic conflict has aroused yields to a state of acute physiological suspense called forth by exuberant physical motion and its immediate implications. Nor is a genuine Western imaginable without a pursuit or a race on horseback. As Flaherty put it, Westerns are popular "because people never get tired of seeing a horse gallop across the plains." Its gallop seems still to gain momentum by contrast with the immense tranquility of the far-away horizon.

Dancing

The second type of specifically cinematic movement is dancing. This does not apply, of course, to the stage ballet which evolves in a space-time outside actuality proper. Interestingly enough, all attempts at "canning" it adequately have so far failed. Screen reproductions of theatrical dancing either indulge in a completeness which is boring or offer a selection of attractive details which confuse in that they dismember rather than preserve the original. Dancing attains to cinematic eminence only if it is part and parcel of physical reality. René Clair's early sound films have judiciously been called ballets. True, they are, but the performers are real-life Parisians who just cannot help executing dance movements when going about their love adventures and minor quarrels. With infinite subtlety Clair guides them along the divide between the real and unreal. Sometimes it appears as though these delivery boys, taxi drivers, girls, clerks, shopkeepers, and nondescript figures are marionettes banding together and parting from each other according to designs as delicate as lacework; and then again they are made to look and behave like ordinary people in Paris streets and bistros. And the latter impression prevails. For, even granted that they are drawn into an imaginary universe, this universe itself reflects throughout our real world in stylizing it. What dancing there is, seems to occur on the spur of the moment; it is the vicissitudes of life from which these ballets issue.

Fred Astaire too prefers apparent impromptu performances to stage choreography; he is quite aware that this type of performance is appropriate to the medium. "Each dance," says he, "ought to spring somehow out of character or situation, otherwise it is simply a vaudeville act." This does not mean that he would dispense with theatrical production numbers. But no sooner does he perform in vaudeville fashion than he breaks out of the prison of prearranged stage patterns and, with a genius for improvisation, dances over tables and gravel paths into the everyday world. It is a one-way route which invariably leads from the footlights to the heart of camera-reality. Astaire's consummate dancing is meant to belong among the real-life events with which he toys in his musicals; and it is so organized that it imperceptibly emerges from, and disappears, in the flow of these happenings. . . .

Nascent Motion

The third type of motion which offers special interest cinematically is not just another group of interrelated movements but movement as contrasted with motionlessness. In focusing upon this contrast, films strikingly demonstrate that objective movement—any movement, for that matter—is one of their choice subjects. Alexander Dovzhenko in both *Arsenal* and *Earth* frequently stops the action to resume it after a short lull. The first phase of this procedure—characters or parts of them abruptly ceasing to move—produces a shock effect, as if all of a sudden we found ourselves in a vacuum. The immediate consequence is that we acutely realize the significance of movement as an integral element of the external world as well as film.

But this is only part of the story. Even though the moving images on the screen come to a standstill, the thrust of their movement is too powerful to be discontinued simultaneously. Accordingly, when the people in *Arsenal* or *Earth* are shown in the form of stills, the suspended movement nevertheless perpetuates itself by changing from outer motion into inner motion. Dovzhenko has known how to make this metamorphosis benefit his penetrations of reality. The immobile lovers in *Earth* become transparent; the deep happiness which is moving them turns inside out. And the spectator on his part grasps their inward agitation because the cessation of external motion moves him all the more intensely to commune with them. Yet despite these rewarding experiences he cannot help feeling a certain relief when eventually the characters take on life again—an event which marks the second and final phase of the procedure. It is a return to the world of film, whose inherent motion alone renders possible such excursions into the whirlpool of the motionless. . . .

Inanimate Objects

Since the inanimate is featured in many paintings, one might question the legitimacy of characterizing it as a cinematic subject. Yet it is a painter—Fernand Léger—who judiciously insists that only film is equipped to sensitize us, by way of big close-ups, to the possibilities that lie dormant in a hat, a chair, a hand, and a foot. Similarly Cohen-Séat: "And I? says the leaf which is falling.—And we? say the orange peel, the gust of wind. . . . Film, whether intentionally or not, is their mouthpiece." Nor should it be forgotten that the camera's ability to single out and record the orange peel or the hand marks a decisive difference between screen and stage, so close to each other in some respects. Stage imagery inevitably centers on the actor, whereas film is free to dwell on parts of his appearance and detail the objects about him. In using its freedom to bring the inanimate to the fore and make it a carrier of action, film only protests its peculiar requirement to explore all of physical existence, human or nonhuman. Within this context it is of interest that in the early 'twenties, when the French cinema was swamped with theatrical adaptations and stage-minded dramas, Louis Delluc tried to put the medium on its own feet by stressing the tremendous importance of objects. If they are assigned the role due to them, he argued, the actor too "is no more than a detail, a fragment of the matter of the world."

Actually, the urge to raise hats and chairs to the status of full-fledged actors has never completely atrophied. From the malicious escalators, the unruly Murphy beds, and the mad automobiles in silent comedy to the cruiser Potemkin, the oil derrick in *Louisiana Story* and the dilapidated kitchen in *Umberto D.*, a long procession of unforgettable objects has passed across the screen—objects which stand out as protagonists and all but overshadow the rest of the case. Or remember the powerful presence of environmental influences in *The Grapes of Wrath*, the part played by nocturnal Coney Island in *Little Fugitive*, the interaction between the marshland and the guerilla fighters in the last episode of *Paisan*. Of course, the reverse hold true also: films in which the inanimate merely serves as a background to self-contained dialogue and the closed circuit of human relationships are essentially uncinematic.

REVEALING FUNCTIONS

"I ask that a film *discover* something for me" declares Luis Buñuel, who is himself a fiery pathfinder of the screen. And what are films likely to discover? The evidence available suggests that they assume three kinds of revealing functions. They tend to reveal things normally unseen; phenomena overwhelming consciousness; and certain aspects of the outer world which may be called "special modes of reality."

Things Normally Unseen

The many material phenomena which elude observation under normal circumstances can be divided into three groups. The first includes objects too small to be readily noticed or even perceived by the naked eye and objects so big that they will not be fully taken in either.

The Small and the Big

The small. The small is conveyed in the form of close-ups. D. W. Griffith was among the first to realize that they are indispensable for cinematic narration. He initiated their use, as we now know it, in *After Many Years* (1908), an adaptation of Tennyson's *Enoch Arden*. There his memorable first close-up appeared within contexts which Lewis Jacobs describes as follows: "Going further than he had ventured before, in a scene showing Annie Lee brooding and waiting for her husband's return,

Griffith daringly used a large close-up of her face. . . . He had another surprise, even more radical, to offer. Immediately following the close-up of Annie, he inserted a picture of the object of her thoughts—her husband cast away on a desert isle."

On the surface, this succession of shots seems simply designed to lure the spectator into the dimension of her intimate preoccupations. He first watches Annie from a distance and then approaches her so closely that he sees only her face; if he moves on in the same direction, as the film invites him to do, it is logical that he should penetrate Annie's appearance and land inside her mind. Granting the validity of this interpretation, the close-up of her face is not an end in itself; rather, along with the subsequent shots, it serves to suggest what is going on behind that face—Annie's longing for reunion with her husband. A knowingly chosen detail of her physique thus would help establish the whole of her being in a dramatic interest.

The same obviously holds true of another famous Griffith close-up: Mae Marsh's clasped hands in the trial episode of *Intolerance*. It almost looks as if her huge hands with the convulsively moving fingers were inserted for the sole purpose of illustrating eloquently her anguish at the most crucial moment of the trial; as if, generally speaking, the function of any such detail exhausted itself in intensifying our participation in the total situation. This is how Eisenstein conceives of the close-up. Its main function, says he, is "not so much to *show* or to *present* as to *signify*, to *give meaning*, to *designate*." To designate what? Evidently something of importance to the narrative. And montage-minded as he is, he immediately adds that the significance of the close-up for the plot accrues to it less from its own content than from the manner in which it is juxtaposed with the surrounding shots. According to him, the close-up is primarily a montage unit.

But is this really its function? Consider again the combination of shots with the close-up of Annie's face: the place assigned to the latter in the sequence intimates that Griffith wanted us also to absorb the face for its own sake instead of just passing through and beyond it; the face appears before the desires and emotions to which it refers have been completely defined, thus tempting us to get lost in its puzzling indeterminacy. Annie's face is also an end in itself. An so is the image of Mae Marsh's hands. No doubt it is to impress upon us her inner condition, but besides making us experience what we would in a measure have experienced anyway because of our familiarity with the characters involved, this close-up contributes something momentous and unique—it reveals how her hands behave under the impact of utter despair.

Eisenstein criticizes the close-ups in Griffith films precisely for their relative independence of the contexts in which they occur. He calls them isolated units which tend "to show or to present"; and he insists that to the extent that they indulge in isolation they fail to yield the meanings which the interweaving processes of montage may elicit from them. Had Eisenstein been less possessed with the magic powers of montage he would certainly have acknowledged the cinematic superiority of the Griffith close-up. To Griffith such huge images of small material phenomena are not only integral components of the narrative but disclosures of new aspects of physical reality. In representing them the way he does, he seems to have been guided by the conviction that the cinema is all the more cinematic if it acquaints us with the physical origins, ramifications, and connotations of all the emotional and intellectual events which comprise the plot; that it cannot adequately account for these inner developments unless it leads us through the thicket of material life from which they emerge and in which they are embedded. . . .

The big. Among the large objects, such as vast plains or panoramas of any kind, one deserves special attention: the masses. No doubt imperial Rome already teemed with them. But masses of people in the modern sense entered the historical scene only in the wake of the industrial revolution. Then they became a social force of first magnitude. Warring nations resorted to levies on an unheard-of scale and identifiable groups yielded to the anonymous multitude which filled the big cities in the form of amorphous crowds. Walter Benjamin observes that in the period marked by the rise of photography the daily sight of moving crowds was still a spectacle to which eyes and nerves had to get adjusted. The testimony of sensitive contemporaries would seem to corroborate this sagacious observation: The Paris crowds omnipresent in Baudelaire's *Les Fleurs du mal* function as stimuli which call forth irritating kaleidoscopic sensations; the jostling and shoving passers-by who, in Poe's *Man of the Crowd*, throng gas-lit London provoke a succession of electric shocks.

At the time of its emergence the mass, this giant animal, was a new and upsetting experience. As might be expected, the traditional arts proved unable to encompass and render it. Where they failed, photography easily succeeded; it was technically equipped to portray crowds as the accidental agglomerations they are. Yet only film, the fulfillment of photography in a sense, was equal to the task of capturing them in motion. In this case the instrument of reproduction came into being almost simultaneously with one of its main subjects. Hence the attraction which masses exerted on still and motion picture cameras from the outset. It is certainly more than sheer coincidence that the very first Lumière films featured a crowd of workers and the confusion of arrival and departure at a railway station. Early Italian films elaborated upon the theme; and D. W. Griffith, inspired by them, showed how masses can be represented cinematically. The Russians absorbed his lesson, applying it in ways of their own. . . .

The Transient

The second group of things normally unseen comprises the transient. Here belong, first, fleeting impressions—"the shadow of a cloud passing across the plain, a leaf which yields to the wind." Evanescent, like dream elements, such impressions may haunt the moviegoer long after the story they are called upon to implement has sunk into oblivion. The manes of the galloping horses—flying threads or streamers rather than manes—in the chariot race episode of Fred Niblo's *Ben Hur* are as unforgettable as the fiery traces of the projectiles that tear the night in *Desert Victory*. The motion picture camera seems to be partial to the least permanent components of our environment. It may be anticipated that the street in the broadest sense of the word is a place where impressions of this kind are bound to occur. "The cinema," says Aragon, delighting in its snapshot-like predilection for the ephemeral, "has taught us more about man in a few years than centuries of painting have taught: fugitive expressions, attitudes scarcely credible yet real, charm and hideousness."

Second, there are movements of so transitory a nature that they would be imperceptible were it not for two cinematic techniques: accelerated-motion, which condenses extremely slow and, hence, unobservable developments, such as the growth of plants, and slow-motion, which expands movements too fast to be registered. Like the big close-up, these correlated techniques lead straight into "reality of another dimension." Pictures of stalks piercing the soil in the process of growing open up imaginary areas, and racing legs shown in slow-motion do not just slow down but change in appearance and perform bizarre evolutions—patterns remote from reality as we know it. Slow-motion shots parallel the regular close-ups; they are, so to speak, temporal close-ups achieving in time what the close-up proper is achieving in space. That, unlike the latter, they are used rather infrequently, may be traced to the fact that the enlargement of spatial phenomena, as effected by the close-up, seems more "natural" to us than the expansion of a given time interval. (On the other hand, it appears that film makers draw more readily on slow-motion than on the reverse technique—perhaps simply because it does not require so lengthy preparations.)

As contrived-reality pictures, the deviant images gained by both techniques, especially slow-motion, may well figure in nonrealistic experimental films. Yet they live up to the cinematic approach only if they are made to fulfill a revealing function within contexts focusing on physical existence. The late Jean Epstein, who felt so immensely attracted by "reality of another dimension," considered this their true destination. Referring to waves in slow-motion and clouds in accelerated-motion, he declared that for all their "startling physics and strange mechanics" they "are but a portrait—seen in a certain perspective—of the world in which we live."

Blind Spots of the Mind

The third and last group of things normally unseen consists of phenomena which figure among the blind spots of the mind; habit and prejudice prevent us from noticing them. The role which cultural standards and traditions may play in these processes of elimination is drastically illustrated by a report on the reactions of African natives to a film made on the spot. After the screening the spectators, all of them still unacquainted with the medium, talked volubly about a chicken they allegedly had seen picking food in the mud. The film maker himself, entirely unaware of its presence, attended several performances without being able to detect it. Had it been dreamed up by the natives? Only by scanning his film foot by foot did he eventually succeed in tracing the chicken: it appeared for a fleeting moment somewhere in a corner of a picture and then vanished forever.

The following types of objects are cinematic because they stubbornly escape our attention in everyday life.

Unconventional complexes. Film may bare real-life complexes which the conventional figure-ground patterns usually conceal from view. Imagine a man in a room: accustomed as we are to visualize the human figure as a whole, it would take us an enormous effort to perceive instead of the whole man a pictorial unit consisting, say, of his right shoulder and arm, fragments of furniture and a section of the wall. But this is exactly what photography and, more powerfully, film may make us see. The motion picture camera has a way of disintegrating familiar objects and bringing to the fore—often just in moving about—previously invisible interrelationships between parts of them. These newly arising complexes lurk behind the things known and cut across their easily identifiable contexts. *Jazz Dance,* for instance, abounds with shots of ensembles built from human torsos, clothes, scattered legs, and what not—shapes which are almost anonymous. In rendering physical existence, film tends to reveal configurations of semi-abstract phenomena. Sometimes these textures take on an ornamental character. In the Nazi propaganda film *Triumph of the Will* moving banners fuse into a very beautiful pattern at the moment when they begin to fill the screen.

The refuse. Many objects remain unnoticed simply because it never occurs to us to look their way. Most people turn their backs on garbage cans, the dirt underfoot, the waste they leave behind. Films have no such inhibitions; on the contrary, what we ordinarily prefer to ignore proves attractive to them precisely because of this common neglect. Ruttman's *Berlin* includes a wealth of sewer grates, gutters, and streets littered with rubbish; and Cavalcanti in his *Rien que les heures* is hardly less garbage-minded. To be sure, shots in this vein may be required by the action, but intrigues inspired by a sense of the medium are often so devised that they offer the camera ample opportunity to satisfy its inborn curiosity and function as a rag-picker; think of the old silent comedies—e.g., Chaplin's *A Dog's Life*—or pictures which involve crime, war, or misery. Since sights of refuse are particularly impressive after spectacles extolling the joy of living, film makers have repeatedly capitalized on the contrast between glamorous festivities and their dreary aftermath. You see a banquet on the screen and then, when everybody has gone, you are made to linger for a moment and stare at the crumpled tablecloth, the half-emptied glasses, and the unappetizing dishes. The classical American gangster films indulged in this effect. *Scarface* opens on a restaurant at dawn, with the remnants of the nocturnal orgy strewn over floors and tables; and after the gangster's ball in Sternberg's *Underworld* Bancroft totters through a maze of confetti and streamers left over from the feast.

The familiar. Nor do we perceive the familiar. It is not as if we shrank from it, as we do in the case of refuse; we just take it for granted without giving it a thought. Intimate faces, streets we walk day by day, the house we live in—all these things are part of us like our skin, and because we know them by heart we do not know them with the eye. Once integrated into our existence, they cease to be objects of perception, goals to be attained. In fact, we would be immobilized if we focused on them. This is confirmed by a common experience. A man entering his room will immediately feel disturbed if during his absence something has been changed in it. But in order to find out about the cause of his uneasiness he must discontinue his routine occupations; only in deliberately scrutinizing, and thus estranging, the room will be able to discover what it actually is that has been changed. Proust's narrator is acutely aware of this very estrangement when he suddenly sees his grandmother not as he always believed her to be but as she is or at least as she would appear to a stranger—a snapshot likeness severed from his dreams and memories.

Films make us undergo similar experiences a thousand times. They alienate our environment in exposing it. One ever-recurrent film scene runs as follows: Two or more people are conversing with each other. In the middle of their talk the camera, as if entirely indifferent to it, slowly pans through the room, inviting us to watch the faces of the listeners and various furniture pieces in a detached spirit. Whatever this may mean within the given context, it invariably dissolves a well-known total situation and thereby confronts the spectator with isolated phenomena which he previously neglected or overlooked as matter-of-course components of that situation. As the camera pans, curtains become eloquent and eyes tell a story of their own. The way leads toward the unfamiliar in the familiar. How often do we not come across shots of street corners, buildings, and landscapes with which we were acquainted all our life; we naturally recognize them and yet it is as if they were virgin impressions emerging from the abyss of nearness. The opening sequence of Vigo's *Zéro de conduite* shows two boys traveling back to school by train. Is it just an ordinarily night trip? Vigo manages to transform a familiar railway compartment into a magic wigwam in which the two, drunk from their boasts and pranks, are floating through the air.

This transformation is partly achieved with the aid of a device, both photographic and cinematic, which deserves some attention—the use of uncommon camera angles. Vigo occasionally represents the railway compartment slantwise and from below so that the whole room seems to drift along in the haze from the cigars which the high-strung schoolboys are smoking, while little toy balloons hover to and fro before their pale faces. Proust knew about the alienating effect of this device. After having mentioned that certain photographs of scenery and towns are called "admirable," he continues: "If we press for a definition of what their admirers mean by that epithet, we shall find that it is generally applied to some unusual picture of a familiar object, a picture different from those that we are accustomed to see, unusual and yet true to nature, and for that reason doubly impressive because it startles us, makes us emerge from our habits, and at the same time brings us back to ourselves by recalling to us an earlier impression." And to concretize this definition, he refers to the picture of a cathedral which does not render it as it is normally seen—namely, in the middle of the town—but is taken from a point of view from which the building "will appear thirty times the height of the houses." . . .

Phenomena Overwhelming Consciousness

Elemental catastrophes, the atrocities of war, acts of violence and terror, sexual debauchery, and death are events which tend to overwhelm consciousness. In any case, they call forth excitements and agonies bound to thwart detached observation. No one witnessing such an event, let alone playing an active part in it, should therefore be expected accurately to account for what he has seen. Since these manifestations of crude nature, human or otherwise, fall into the area of physical reality, they range all the more among the cinematic subjects. Only the camera is able to represent them without distortion.

Actually the medium has always shown a predilection for events of this type. There is practically no newsreel that would not indulge in the ravages of an inundation, a hurricane, an airplane crash, or whatever catastrophe happens to be at hand. The same applies to feature films. One of the first film strips ever made was *The Execution of Mary Queen of Scots* (1895); the executioner cuts off her head and then holds it in his uplifted hand so that no spectator can possibly avoid looking at the frightful exhibit. Pornographic motifs also emerged at a very early date. The path of the cinema is beset with films reveling in disasters and nightmarish incidents. Suffice it to pick out, at random, the war horrors in Dovzhenko's *Arsenal* and Pabst's *Westfront 1918*; the terrible execution sequence at the end of *Thunder over*

Mexico, a film based on Eisenstein's Mexican material; the earthquake in *San Francisco*; the torture episode in Rossellini's *Open City*; the depiction of a Polish Nazi concentration camp in *The Last Stop*; the scene with the young hoodlums wantonly mistreating a blind man in Buñuel's *Los Olvidados*.

Because of its sustained concern with all that is dreadful and off limits, the medium has frequently been accused of a penchant for cheap sensationalism. What lends support to this verdict is the indisputable fact that films have a habit of dwelling on the sensational much longer than any moral purpose would seem to justify; it often is as if that purpose served merely as a pretext for rendering a savage murder or the like.

In defense of the medium one might argue that it would not be the main medium it is if it failed to provide stunning sensations; and that, in offering them, it only follows a venerable tradition. Since time immemorial, people have craved spectacles permitting them vicariously to experience the fury of conflagrations, the excesses of cruelty and suffering, and unspeakable lusts—spectacles which shock the shuddering and delighted onlooker into unseeing participation.

Yet this argument misses the point. The point is, rather, that the cinema does not simply imitate and continue the ancient gladiator fights or the *Grand Guignol* but adds something new and momentous: it insists on rendering visible what is commonly drowned in inner agitation. Of course, such revelations conform all the more to the cinematic approach if they bear on actual catastrophes and horrors. In deliberately detailing feats of sadism in their films, Rossellini and Buñuel force the spectator to take in these appalling sights and at the same time impress them on him as real-life events recorded by the imperturbable camera. Similarly, besides trying to put across their propaganda messages, the Russian films of the 'twenties convey to us the paroxysmal upheavals of real masses which, because of their emotional *and* spatial enormity, depend doubly upon cinematic treatment to be perceptible.

The cinema, then, aims at transforming the agitated witness into a conscious observer. Nothing could be more legitimate than its lack of inhibitions in picturing spectacles which upset the mind. Thus it keeps us from shutting our eyes to the "blind drive of things."

Special Modes of Reality

Finally films may expose physical reality as it appears to individuals in extreme states of mind generated by such events as we have mentioned, mental disturbances, or any other external or internal causes. Supposing such a state of mind is provoked by an act of violence, then the camera often aspires to render the images which an emotionally upset witness or participant will from of it. These images also belong among the cinematic subjects. They are distorted from the viewpoint of a detached observer; and they differ from each other according to the varying states of mind in which they originate.

In his *Ten Days That Shook the World*, for instance, Eisenstein composes a physical universe reflecting exultation. This episode runs as follows: At the beginning of the October Revolution, worker delegates succeed in bringing a contingent of Cossacks over to their side; the Cossacks put their half-drawn swords with the ornamented pommels back into their sheaths, and then the two groups boisterously fraternize in a state of euphoria. The ensuing dance scene is represented in the form of an accelerated montage sequence which pictures the world as experienced by the overjoyed. In their great joy, dancers and onlookers who constantly mingle cannot help perceiving incoherent pieces of their immediate environment in motion. It is a whirling agglomerate of fragments that surrounds them. And Eisenstein captures this jumble to perfection by having follow each other—in a succession which becomes ever faster with the growing ecstasy—shots of Cossack boots executing the *krakoviak*, worker legs dancing through a puddle, clapping hands, and faces inordinately broadened by laughter.

In the world of a panic-stricken individual laughter yields to grimacing and dazzling confusion to fearful rigidity. At any rate, this is how Ernö Metzner conceived of that world in his *Ueberfall*. Its "hero" is a wretched little fellow who gets a lucky break thanks to a coin he furtively picks up in the street and then stakes in a crap game. As he walks away with his wallet stuffed, a thug follows him at a steadily diminishing distance. The man is scared. No sooner does he take to his heels than all the objects about him make common cause with his pursuer. The dark railway underpass turns into a sinister trap; frozen threats, the dilapidated slum houses close ranks and stare at him. (It is noteworthy that these effects are largely due to accomplished photography.) Temporarily saved by a streetwalker, who puts him up in her room, the man knows that the thug continues to lie in wait for him down in the street. The curtain moves, and he feels that the room itself harbors dangers. There is no escape wherever he looks. He looks into the mirror: what shines out of it are distorted reflections of his mask-like features.

1960

BÉLA BALÁSZ
FROM THEORY OF THE FILM

THE CLOSE-UP

Born Herbert Bauer in Hungary, Béla Balázs (1884–1949) came to film from a background in art and philosophy. In the early part of the twentieth century he worked as a journalist, also writing poems, plays, and, notably, the libretto for Béla Bartók's only opera, *Bluebeard's Castle* (1911). In 1919, he fled to Austria when the Hungarian Communist government was overthrown and widespread pogroms targeted communist sympathizers. Balász eventually moved from Austria to Germany, where he began writing film reviews for the newspaper *Der Tag* and published his first book of film theory *The Visible Man* (1924), which influenced the thought of both Pudovkin and Eisenstein. Like many early theorists, he was fascinated with montage and the close-up and hopeful for the edifying and aesthetic values of this new medium, arguing for its consideration as an art form with its own language. In the 1930s, he worked on films with G.W. Pabst, Bertolt Brecht, and Leni Riefenstahl, but left Germany for the Soviet Union in 1933, where he taught film at Moscow's State Film Institute. When he returned to Hungary in 1945, he worked persistently to reinvigorate the national film industry, publishing *Theory of Film* (1948), one of the first book-length studies of film aesthetics. In 1958 a studio was established in his name in Budapest to continue his efforts to aid aspiring filmmakers.

THE FACE OF THINGS

The first new world discovered by the film camera in the days of the silent film was the world of very small things visible only from very short distances, the hidden life of little things. By this the camera showed us not only hitherto unknown objects and events: the adventures of beetles in a wilderness of blades of grass, the tragedies of day-old chicks in a corner of the poultry-run, the erotic battles of flowers and the poetry of miniature landscapes. It brought us not only new themes. By means of the close-up the camera in the days of the silent film revealed also the hidden mainsprings of a life which we had thought we already knew so well. Blurred outlines are mostly the result of our insensitive short-sightedness and superficiality. We skim over the teeming substance of life. The camera has uncovered that cell-life of the vital issues in which all great events are ultimately conceived; for the greatest landslide is only the aggregate of the movements of single particles. A multitude of close-ups can show us the very instant in which the general is transformed into the particular. The close-up has not only widened our vision of life, it has also deepened it. In the days of the silent film it not only revealed new things, but showed us the meaning of the old.

VISUAL LIFE

The close-up can show us a quality in a gesture of the hand we never noticed before when we saw that hand stroke or strike something, a quality which is often more expressive than any play of the features. The close-up shows your shadow on the wall with which you have lived all your life and which you scarcely knew; it shows the speechless face and fate of the dumb objects that live with you in your room and whose fate is bound up with your own. Before this you looked at your life as a concert-goer ignorant of music listens to an orchestra playing a symphony. All he hears is the leading melody, all the rest is blurred into a general murmur. Only those can really understand and enjoy the music who can hear the contrapuntal architecture of each part in the score. This is how we see life: only its leading melody meets the eye. But a good film with its close-ups reveals the most hidden parts in our polyphonous life, and teaches us to see the intricate visual details of life as one reads an orchestral score.

LYRICAL CHARM OF THE CLOSE-UP

The close-up may sometimes give the impression of a mere naturalist preoccupation with detail. But good close-ups radiate a tender human attitude in the contemplation of hidden things, a delicate solicitude, a gentle bending over the intimacies of life-in-the-miniature, a warm sensibility. Good close-ups are lyrical; it is the heart, not the eye, that has perceived them.

Close-ups are often dramatic revelations of what is really happening under the surface of appearances. You may see a medium shot of someone sitting and conducting a conversation with icy calm. The close-up will show trembling fingers nervously fumbling a small object—sign of an internal storm. Among pictures of a comfortable house breathing a sunny security, we suddenly see the evil grin of a vicious head on the carved mantelpiece or the menacing grimace of a door opening into darkness. Like the leitmotif of impending fate in an opera, the shadow of some impending disaster falls across the cheerful scene.

Close-ups are the pictures expressing the poetic sensibility of the director. They show the faces of things and those expressions on them which are significant because they are reflected expressions of our own subconscious feeling. Herein lies the art of the true cameraman.

In a very old American film I saw this dramatic scene: the bride at the altar suddenly runs away from the bridegroom whom she detests, who is rich and who has been forced on her. As she rushes away she must pass through a large room full of wedding presents. Beautiful things, good things, useful things, things radiating plenty and security smile at her and lean towards her with expressive faces. And there are the presents given by the bridegroom: faces of things radiating touching attention, consideration, tenderness, love—and they all seem to be looking at the fleeing bride, because she looks at them; all seem to stretch out hands towards her, because she feels they do so. There are ever more of them—they crowd the room and block her path—her flight slows down more and more, then she stops and finally turns back. . . .

Having discovered the soul of things in the close-up, the silent film undeniably overrated their importance and sometimes succumbed to the temptation of showing "the hidden little life" as an end in itself, divorced from human destinies; it strayed away from the dramatic plot and presented the "poetry of things" instead of human beings. But what Lessing said in his *Laocoön* about Homer—that he never depicted anything but human actions and always described objects only inasmuch as they took part in the action—should to this day serve as a model for all epic and dramatic art as long as it centers around the presentation of man.

THE FACE OF MAN

Every art deals with human beings, it is a human manifestation and presents human beings. To paraphrase Marx: "The root of all art is man." When the film close-up strips the veil of our imperceptiveness and insensitivity from the hidden little things and shows us the face of objects, it still shows us man, for what makes objects expressive are the human expressions projected on to them. The objects only reflect our own selves, and this is what distinguished art from scientific knowledge (although even the latter is to a great extent subjectively determined). When we see the face of things, we do what the ancients did in creating *gods* in man's image and breathing a human soul into them. The close-ups of the film are the creative instruments of this mighty visual anthropomorphism.

What was more important, however, than the discovery of the physiognomy of things, was the discovery of the human face. Facial expression is the most subjective manifestation of man, more subjective even than speech, for vocabulary and grammar are subject to more or less universally valid rules and conventions, while the play of features, as has already been said, is a manifestation not governed by objective canons, even though it is largely a matter of imitation. This most subjective and individual of human manifestations is rendered objective in the close-up.

A NEW DIMENSION

If the close-up lifts some object or some part of an object out of its surroundings, we nevertheless perceive it as existing in space; we do not for an instant forget that the hand, say, which is shown by the close-up, belongs to some human being. It is precisely this connection which lends meaning to its every movement. But when Griffith's genius and daring first projected gigantic "severed heads" on to the cinema screen, he not only brought the human face closer to us in space, he also transposed it from space into another dimension. We do not mean, of course, the cinema screen and the patches of light and shadow moving across it, which being visible things, can be conceived only in space; we mean the expression on the face as revealed by the close-up. We have said that the isolated hand would lose its meaning, its expression, if we did not know and imagine its connection with some human being. The facial expression on a face is complete and comprehensible in itself and therefore we need not think of it as existing in space and time. Even if we had just seen the same face in the middle of a crowd and the close-up merely separated it from the others, we would still feel that we have suddenly been left alone with this one face to the exclusion of the rest of the world. Even if we have just seen the owner of the face in a long shot, when we look into the eyes in a close-up, we no longer think of that wide space, because the expression and significance of the face has no relation to space and no connection with it. Facing an isolated face takes us out of space, our consciousness of space is cut out and we find ourselves in another dimension: that of physiognomy. The fact that the features of the face can be seen side by side, i.e., in space—that the eyes are at the top, the ears at the sides and the mouth lower down—loses all reference to space when we see, not a figure of flesh and bone, but an expression, or in other words when we see emotions, moods, intentions and thoughts, things which although our eyes can see them, are not in space. For feelings, emotions, moods, intentions, thoughts are not themselves things pertaining to space, even if they are rendered visible by means which are.

MELODY AND PHYSIOGNOMY

We will be helped in understanding this peculiar dimension by Henri Bergson's analysis of time and duration. A melody, said Bergson, is composed of single notes which follow each other in sequence, i.e., in time. Nevertheless a melody has no dimension in time, because the first note is made an element of the melody only because it refers to the next note and because it stands in a definite relation to all other notes down to the last. Hence the last note, which may not be played for some time, is yet already present in the first note as a melody-creating element. And the last note completes the melody only because we hear the first note along with it. The notes sound one after the other in a time-sequence, hence they have a real duration, but the coherent line of melody has no dimension in time; the relation of the notes to each other is not a phenomenon occurring in time. The melody is not born gradually in the course of time but is already in existence as a complete entity as soon as the first note is played. How else would we know that a melody is begun? The single notes have duration in time, but their relation to each other, which gives meaning to the individual sounds, is outside time. A logical deduction also has its sequence, but premise and conclusion do not follow one another in time. The process of thinking as a psychological process may have duration; but the logical forms, like melodies, do not belong to the dimension of time.

Now facial expression, physiognomy, has a relation to space similar to the relation of melody to time. The single features, of course, appear in space; but the significance of their relation to one another is not a phenomenon pertaining to space, no more than are the emotions, thoughts and ideas which are manifested in the facial expressions we see. They are picture-like and yet they seem outside space; such is the psychological effect of facial expression.

SILENT SOLILOQUY

The modern stage no longer uses the spoken soliloquy, although without it the characters are silenced just when they are the most sincere, the least hampered by convention: when they are alone. The public of today will not tolerate the spoken soliloquy, allegedly because it is "unnatural." Now the film has brought us the silent soliloquy, in which a face can speak with the subtlest shades of meaning without appearing unnatural and arousing the distaste of the spectators. In this silent monologue the solitary human soul can find a tongue more candid and uninhibited than in any spoken soliloquy, for it speaks instinctively, subconsciously. The language of the face cannot be suppressed or controlled. However disciplined and practisedly hypocritical a face may be, in the enlarging close-up we see even that it is concealing something, that is looking a lie. For such things have their own specific expressions superimposed on the feigned one. It is much easier to lie in words than with the face and the film has proved it beyond doubt.

In the film the mute soliloquy of the face speaks even when the hero is not alone, and herein lies a new great opportunity for depicting man. The poetic significance of the soliloquy is that it is a manifestation of mental, not physical, loneliness. Nevertheless, on the stage a character can speak a monologue only when there is no one else there, even though a character might feel a thousand times more lonely if alone among a large crowd. The monologue of loneliness may raise its voice within him a hundred times even while he is audibly talking to someone. Hence the most deep-felt human soliloquies could not find such expression, for the close-up can lift a character out of the heart of the greatest crowd and show how solitary it is in reality and what it feels in this crowded solitude.

The film, especially the sound film, can separate the words of a character talking to others from the mute play of features by means of which, in the middle of such a conversation, we are made to overhear a mute soliloquy and realize the difference between this soliloquy and the audible conversation. What a flesh-and-blood actor can show on the real stage is at most that his words are insincere and it is a mere convention that the partner in such a conversation is blinded to what every spectator can see. But in the isolated close-up of the film we can see to the bottom of a soul by means of such tiny movements of facial muscles which even the most observant partner would never perceive.

A novelist can, of course, write a dialogue so as to weave into it what the speakers think to themselves while they are talking. But by so doing he splits up the sometimes comic, sometimes tragic, but always awe-inspiring, unity between spoken word and hidden thought with which this contradiction is rendered manifest in the human face and which the film was the first to show us in all its dazzling variety.

POLYPHONIC PLAY OF FEATURES

The film first made possible what, for lack of better description, I call the polyphonic play of features. By it I mean the appearance on the same face of contradictory expressions. In a sort of physiognomic chord a variety of feelings, passions and thoughts are synthesized in the play of the features as an adequate expression of the multiplicity of the human soul.

Asta Nielsen once played a woman hired to seduce a rich young man. The man who hired her is watching the results from behind a curtain. Knowing that she is under observation, Asta Nielsen feigns love. She does it convincingly: the whole gamut of appropriate emotion is displayed in her face. Nevertheless we are aware that it is only play-acting, that it is a sham, a mask. But in the course of the scene Asta Nielsen really falls in love with the young man. Her facial expression shows little change; she had been "registering" love all the time and done it well. How else could she now show that this time she was really in love? Her expression changes only by a scarcely perceptible and yet immediately obvious nuance—and what a few minutes before was a sham is now the sincere expression of a deep emotion. Then Asta Nielsen suddenly remembers that she is under observation. The man behind the curtain must not be allowed to read her face and learn that she is now no longer feigning, but really feeling love. So Asta now pretends to be pretending. Her face shows a new, by this time threefold, change. First she feigns love, then she genuinely shows love, and as she is not permitted to be in love in good earnest, her face again registers a sham, a pretence of love. But now it is this pretence that is a lie. Now she is lying that she is lying. And we can see all this clearly in her face, over which she has drawn two different masks. At such times an invisible face appears in front of the real one, just as spoken words can by association of ideas conjure up things unspoken and unseen, perceived only by those to whom they are addressed.

In the early days of the silent film Griffith showed a scene of this character. The hero of the film is a Chinese merchant. Lillian Gish, playing a beggar-girl who is being pursued by enemies, collapses at his door. The Chinese merchant finds her, carries her into his house and looks after the sick girl. The girl slowly recovers, but her face remains stone-like in its sorrow. "Can't you smile?" the Chinese asks the frightened child who is only just beginning to trust him. "I'll try," says Lillian Gish, picks up a mirror and goes through the motions of a smile, aiding her face muscles with her fingers. The result is a painful, even horrible mask which the girl now turns towards the Chinese merchant. But his kindly friendly eyes bring a real smile to her face. The face itself does not change; but a warm emotion lights it up from inside and an intangible nuance turns the grimace into a real expression.

In the days of the silent film such a close-up provided an entire scene. A good idea of the director and a fine performance on the part of the actor gave as a result an interesting, moving, new experience for the audience.

MICROPHYSIOGNOMY

In the silent facial expression, isolated from its surroundings, seemed to penetrate to a strange new dimension of the soul. It revealed to us a new world—

the world of microphysiognomy which could not otherwise be seen with the naked eye or in everyday life. In the sound film the part played by this "microphys-iognomy" has greatly diminished because it is now apparently possible to express in words much of what facial expression apparently showed. But it is never the same—many profound emotional experiences can never be expressed in words at all.

Not even the greatest writer, the most consummate artist of the pen, could tell in words what Asta Nielsen tells with her face in close-up as she sits down to her mirror and tries to make up for the last time her aged, wrinkled face, riddled with poverty, misery, disease and prostitution, when she is expecting her lover, released after ten years in jail; a lover who has retained his youth in captivity because life could not touch him there.

ASTA AT THE MIRROR

She looks into the mirror, her face pale and deadly earnest. It expresses anxiety and unspeakable horror. She is like a general who, hopelessly encircled with his whole army, bends once more, for the last time, over this maps to search for a way out and finds there is no escape. Then she begins to work feverishly, attacking that disgustingly riddled face with a trembling hand. She holds her lipstick as Michelangelo might have held his chisel on the last night of his life. It is a life-and-death struggle. The spectator watches with bated breath as this woman paints her face in front of her mirror. The mirror is cracked and dull, and from it the last convulsions of a tortured soul look out on you. She tries to save her life with a little rouge! No good! She wipes it off with a dirty rag. She tries again. And again. Then she shrugs her shoulders and wipes it all off with a movement which clearly shows that she has now wiped off her life. She throws the rag away. A close-up shows the dirty rag falling on the floor and after it has fallen, sinking down a little more. This movement of the rag is also quite easy to understand—it is the last convulsion of a death agony.

In this close-up, microphysiognomy showed a deeply moving human tragedy with the greatest economy of expression. It was a great new form of art. The sound film offers much fewer opportunities for this kind of thing, but by no means excludes it and it would be a pity if such opportunities were to be neglected, unnecessarily making us all the poorer. . . .

MUTE DIALOGUES

In the last years of the silent film the human face had grown more and more visible, that is, more and more expressive. Not only had microphysiognomy developed but together with it the faculty of understanding its meaning. In the last years of the silent film we saw not only masterpieces of silent monologue but of mute dialogue as well. We saw conversations between the facial expressions of two human beings who understood the movements of each others' faces better than each others' words and could perceive shades of meaning too subtle to be conveyed in words.

A necessary result of this was ... that the more space and time in the film was taken up by the inner drama revealed in the microphysiognomic close-up, the less was left of the predetermined 8,000 feet of film for all the external happenings. The silent film could thus dive into the depths—it was given the possibility of presenting a passionate life-and-death struggle almost exclusively by close-ups of faces.

The accusers and Joan (Falconetti) in *The Passion of Joan of Arc* (1928). In "Dreyer's film ... we move in the spiritual dimension of facial expression along" (BALÁSZ, p. 281). "It is a documentary of faces" (BAZIN, p. 354).

Dreyer's film *Jeanne d'Arc* provided a convincing example of this in the powerful, lengthy, moving scene of the Maid's examination. Fifty men are sitting in the same place all the time in this scene. Several hundred feet of film show nothing but big close-ups of heads, of faces. We move in the spiritual dimension of facial expression alone. We neither see nor feel the space in which the scene is in reality enacted. Here no riders gallop, no boxers exchange blows. Fierce passions, thoughts, emotions, convictions battle here, but their struggle is not in space. Nevertheless this series of duels between looks and frowns, duels in which eyes clash instead of swords, can hold the attention of an audience for ninety minutes without flagging. We can follow every attack and riposte of these duels on the faces of the combatants; the play of their features indicates every strategem, every sudden onslaught. The silent film has here brought an attempt to present a drama of the spirit closer to realization than any stage play has ever been able to do. . . .

1945

RUDOLF ARNHEIM
FROM FILM AS ART

FILM AND REALITY

Film resembles painting, music, literature, and the dance in this respect—it is a medium that may, but need not, be used to produce artistic results. Colored picture post cards, for instance, are not art and are not intended to be. Neither are a military march, a true confessions story, or a strip tease. And the movies are not necessarily film art.

There are still many educated people who stoutly deny the possibility that film might be art. They say, in effect: "Film cannot be art, for it does nothing but reproduce reality mechanically." Those who defend this point of view are reasoning from the analogy of painting. In painting, the way from reality to the picture lies via the artist's eye and nervous system, his hand and, finally, the brush that puts strokes on canvas. The process is not mechanical as that of photography, in which the light rays reflected from the object are collected by a system of lenses and are then directed onto a sensitive plate where they produce chemical changes. Does this state of affairs justify our denying photography and film a place in the temple of the Muses?

It is worth while to refute thoroughly and systematically the charge that photography and film are only mechanical reproductions and that they therefore have no connection with art—for this is an excellent method of getting to understand the nature of film art.

With this end in view, the basic elements of the film medium will be examined separately and compared with the corresponding characteristics of what we perceive "in reality." It will be seen how fundamentally different the two kinds of image are; and that it is just these differences that provide film with its artistic resources. We shall thus come at the same time to understand the working principles of film art.

THE PROJECTION OF SOLIDS UPON A PLANE SURFACE

Let us consider the visual reality of some definite object such as a cube. If this cube is standing on a table in front of me, its position determines whether I can realize its shape properly. If I see, for example, merely the four sides of a square, I have no means of knowing that a cube is before me, I see only a square surface. The human eye, and equally the photographic lens, acts from a particular position and from there can take in only such portions of the field of vision as are not hidden by things in front. As the cube is now placed, five of its faces are screened by the sixth, and therefore this last only is visible. But since this face might equally well conceal something quite different—since it might be the base of a pyramid or one side of a sheet of paper, for instance—our view of the cube has not been selected characteristically.

We have, therefore, already established one important principle: If I wish to photograph a cube, it is not enough for me to bring the object within range of my camera. It is rather a question of my position relative to the object, or of where I placed it. The aspect chosen above gives very little information as to the shape of the cube. One, however, that reveals three surfaces of the cube and their relation to one another, shows enough to make it fairly unmistakable what the object is supposed to be. Since our field of vision is full of solid objects, but our eye (like the camera) sees this field from only one station point at any given moment, and since the eye can perceive the rays of light that are reflected from the object only by projecting them onto a plane surface—the retina—the reproduction of even a perfectly simple object is not a mechanical process but can be set about well or badly.

The second aspect gives a much truer picture of the cube than the first. The reason for this is that the second shows more than the first—three faces instead of only one. As a rule, however, truth does not depend on quantity. If it were merely a matter of finding which aspect shows the greatest amount of surface, the best point of view could be arrived at by purely mechanical calculation. There is no formula to help one choose the most characteristic aspect: it is a question of feeling. Whether a particular person is "more himself" in profile than full face, whether the palm or the outside of the hand is more expressive, whether a particular mountain is better taken from the north or the west cannot be ascertained mathematically—they are matters of delicate sensibility.

Thus, as a preliminary, people who contemptuously refer to the camera as an automatic recording machine must be made to realize that even in the simplest photographic reproduction of a perfectly simple object, a feeling for its nature is required which is quite beyond any mechanical operation. We shall see later, by the way, that in artistic photography and film, those aspects that best show the characteristics of a particular object are not by any means always chosen; others are often selected deliberately for the sake of achieving specific effects.

REDUCTION OF DEPTH

How do our eyes succeed in giving us three-dimensional impressions even though the flat retinae can receive only two-dimensional images? Depth perception relies mainly on the distance between the two eyes, which makes for two slightly different images. The fusion of these two pictures into one image gives the three-dimensional impression. As is well known, the same principle is used in the stereoscope, for which two photographs are taken at once, about the same distance apart as the human eyes. This process cannot be used for film without recourse to awkward devices, such as colored spectacles, when more than one person is to watch the projection. For a single spectator it would be easy to make a stereoscopic film. It would only mean taking two simultaneous shots of the same incident a couple of inches apart and then showing one of them to each eye. For display to a larger number of spectators, however, the problem of stereoscopic film has not yet been solved satisfactorily— and hence the sense of depth in film pictures is extraordinarily small. The movement of people or objects from front to back makes a certain depth evident—but it is only necessary to glance into a stereoscope, which makes everything stand out most realistically, to recognize how flat the film picture is. This is another example of the fundamental difference between visual reality and film.

The effect of film is neither absolutely two-dimensional nor absolutely three-dimensional, but something between. Film pictures are at once plane and solid. In Ruttmann's film *Berlin* there is a scene of two subway trains passing each other in opposite directions. The shot is taken looking down from above onto the two trains. Anyone watching this scene realizes, first of all, that one train is coming toward him and the other going away from him (three-dimensional image). He will then also see that one is moving from the lower margin of the screen toward the upper and the other from the upper toward the lower (plane image). This second impression results from the projection of the three-dimensional movement onto the screen surface, which, of course, gives different directions of motion.

The obliteration of the three-dimensional impression has as a second result a stronger accentuation of perspective overlapping. In real life or in a stereoscope, overlapping is accepted as due merely to the accidental arrangement of objects, but very marked cuts result from superimpositions in a plane image. If man is holding up a newspaper so that one corner comes across his face, this corner seems almost to have been cut out of his face, so sharp are the edges. Moreover, when the three-dimensional impression is lost, other phenomena, known to psychologists as the constancies of size and shape, disappear. Physically, the image thrown onto the retina of the eye by any object in the field of vision diminishes in proportion to the square of the distance. If an object a yard distant is moved away another yard, the area of the image on the retina is diminished to one-quarter of that of the first image. Every photographic plate reacts similarly. Hence in a photograph of someone sitting with his feet stretched out far in front of him the subject comes out with enormous feet and much too small a head. Curiously enough, however, we do not in real life get impressions to accord with the images on the retina. If a man is standing three feet away and another equally tall six feet away, the area of the image of the second does not appear to be only a quarter of that of the first. Nor if a man stretches out his hand toward one does it look disproportionately large. One sees the two men as equal in size and the hand as normal. This phenomenon is known as the constancy of size. It is impossible for most people—excepting those accustomed to drawing and painting, that is, artificially trained—to see according to the image on the retina. This fact, incidentally, is one of the reasons the average person has trouble copying things "correctly."

Now an essential for the functioning of the constancy of size is a clear three-dimensional impression; it works excellently in a stereoscope with an ordinary photograph, but hardly at all in a film picture. Thus, in a film picture, if one man is twice as far from the camera as another, the one in front looks very considerably the taller and broader.

It is the same with the constancy of shape. The retinal image of a table top is like the photograph of it; the front edge, being nearer to the spectator, appears much wider than the back; the rectangular surface becomes a trapezoid in the image. As far as the average person is concerned, however, this again does not hold good in practice: he sees the surface as rectangular and draws it that way too. Thus the perspective changes taking place in any object that extends in depth are not observed but are compensated unconsciously. That is what is meant by the constancy of form. In a film picture it is hardly operative at all—a table top, especially if it is near the camera, looks very wide in front and very narrow at the back.

These phenomena, as a matter of fact, are due not only to the reduction of three-dimensionality but also to the unreality of the film picture altogether—an unreality due just as much to the absence of color, the delimitation of the screen, and so forth. The result of all this is that sizes and shapes do not appear on the screen in their true proportions but distorted in perspective. . . .

ABSENCE OF THE NONVISUAL WORLD OF THE SENSES

As regards the other senses: No one who went unprejudiced to watch a silent film missed the noises which would have been heard if the same events had been taking place in real life. No one missed the sound of walking feet, nor the rustling of leaves, nor the ticking of a clock. The lack of such sounds (speech, of course, is also one of them) was hardly ever apparent, although they would have been missed with a desperate shock in real life. People took the silence of the movies for granted because they never quite lost the feeling that what they saw was after all only pictures. This feeling alone, however, would not be sufficient to prevent the lack of sound being felt as an unpleasant violation of the illusion. That this did not happen is again connected with what was explained above: that in order to get a full impression it is not necessary for it to be complete in the naturalistic sense. All kinds of things may be left out which would be present in real life, so long as what is shown contains the essentials. Only after one has known talkies is the lack of sound conspicuous in a silent film. But that proves nothing and is not an argument against the potentialities of silent film, even since the introduction of sound.

It is much the same with the sense of smell. There may be people who if they see a Roman Catholic service on the screen imagine that they can smell incense; but no one will miss the stimulus. Sensations of smell, equilibrium, or touch are, of course, never conveyed in a film through direct stimuli, but are suggested indirectly through sight. Thence arises the important rule that it is improper to make films of occurrences whose central features cannot be expressed visually. Of course a revolver shot might occur as the central point of a silent film; a clever director could afford to dispense with the actual noise of the shot. It is enough for the spectator to see the revolver being fired and possibly to see the wounded man fall. In Josef von Sternberg's *The Docks of New York* a shot is very cleverly made visible by the sudden rising of a flock of scared birds.

THE MAKING OF A FILM

It has been shown above that the images we receive of the physical world differ from those on the movie screen. This was done in order to refute the assertion that film is nothing but the feeble mechanical reproduction of real life. The analysis has furnished us with the data from which we can hope to derive now the principles of film art.

By its very nature, of course, the motion picture tends to satisfy the desire for faithful reports about curious, characteristic, exciting things going on in this world of ours. The first sensation provided by film in its early music-hall days was to depict everyday things in a lifelike fashion on the screen. People were greatly thrilled by the sight of a locomotive approaching at top speed or the emperor in person riding down *Unter den Linden*. In those days, the pleasure given by film derived almost entirely from the subject matter. A film art developed only gradually when the movie makers began consciously or unconsciously to cultivate the peculiar possibilities of cinematographic technique and to apply them toward the creation of artistic productions. To what extent the use of these means of expression affects the large audiences remains a moot question. Certainly box-office success depends even now much more on what is shown than on whether it is shown artistically.

The film producer himself is influenced by the strong resemblance of his photographic material to reality. As distinguished from the tools of the sculptor and the painter, which by themselves produce nothing resembling nature, the camera starts to turn and a likeness of the real world results mechanically. There is serious danger that the filmmaker will rest content with such shapeless reproduction. In order that the film artist may create a work of art it is important that he consciously stress the peculiarities of his medium. This, however, should be done in such a manner that the character of the objects represented should not thereby be destroyed but rather strengthened, concentrated, and interpreted.

Our next task will be to bring examples to show how the various peculiarities of film material can be, and have been, used to achieve artistic effects.

ARTISTIC USE OF PROJECTIONS UPON A PLANE SURFACE

In an earlier section I showed what conditions arise from the fact that in a photographic representation three-dimensional bodies and spaces are projected on a two-dimensional plane, that is, the surface of the picture. It was first demonstrated that an object can be reproduced characteristically or otherwise according to what view of it is chosen. When film art was in its infancy, nobody paid much attention to the subtleties of these problems. The camera was stationed well in front of the people to be photographed in order that their faces and movements might be easily seen. If a house was to be shown, the cameraman placed himself straight in front of it at such a distance that nothing would be left out of the picture. It was only gradually that the particular effects that can be achieved by means of perspective projection were realized.

In Chaplin's film *The Immigrant* the opening scene shows a boat rolling horribly and all the passengers being seasick. They stagger to the side of the ship pressing their hands to their mouths. Then comes the first shot of Charlie Chaplin: he is seen hanging over the side with his back to the audience, his head well down, his legs kicking wildly—everyone thinks the poor devil is paying his toll to the sea. Suddenly Charlie pulls himself up, turns round and shows that he has hooked a large fish with his walking stick. The effect of surprise is achieved by making use of the fact that the spectator will be looking at the situation from a certain definite position. The idea underlying the scene is no longer "a man is doing such and such a thing, for example, he is fishing or being sick," but "a man is doing this and that, and at the same time the spectator is watching him from a particular station point." The element of surprise exists only when the scene is watched from one particular position. If the scene had been taken from the waterside, the audience would have realized at once that Charlie was not being sick but was fishing; and hence the wrong idea would not have first been implanted. The invention is no longer concerned merely with the subject matter but is cinematographic inasmuch as a definite feature of film technique is being used as a means to secure an effect.

ARTISTIC UTILIZATION OF REDUCED DEPTH

Every object reproduced in film appears solid and at the same time flat. This fact contributes greatly to the impressive results achieved by the clever shots discussed in the last section. The worm's-eye view of a man appears as such a great distortion of nature because the depth effect is reduced. The same view looked at in a stereoscope seems much less distorted. The contrast between the vast bulk of the trunk and the disproportionately small head is much less forcible when it is perceived as being due to foreshortening. But if there is only a slight feeling of space and if the three-dimensional volume of the pictured object is flattened out, a huge body and a little head are seen.

The purely formal qualities of the picture come into prominence only because of the lack of depth. Every good film shot is satisfying in a purely formal sense as a linear composition. The lines are harmoniously disposed with reference to one another as well as to the margins. The distribution of light and shade in the shot is evenly balanced. Only because the spatial effect is so slight, the spectator's attention is drawn to the two-dimensional pattern of lines and shadow masses. These, after all, are actually the components of three-dimensional bodies and become elements of the surface composition only through being projected onto a plane. It has already been mentioned above how the skirt of a dancer seen through a pane of glass seemed to open and close like the petals of a flower. This is an entirely anti-functional effect in that it is not a normally characteristic feature of the skirt as a material object. The curious expansion and contraction of the edge of the skirt results only when it is looked at from one particular viewpoint and then projected upon a flat surface. It would be less noticeable in a stereoscopic view. Only when the feeling of depth is reduced does the up-and-down movement of the skirt give the effect of being an in-and-out movement. It is one of the most important formal qualities of film that every object that is reproduced appears simultaneously in two entirely different frames of reference, namely, the two-dimensional and the three-dimensional, and that as one identical object it fulfills two different functions in the two contexts.

The reduction of depth serves, moreover, to emphasize the perspective superposition of objects. In a strongly stereoscopic picture of the manner in which these various objects are placed relative to one another does not impose itself any more than it does in real life. The concealing of certain parts of the various objects by others that come in front seems chance and unimportant. Indeed, the position of the camera in a stereoscopic picture seems itself to be a matter of indifference inasmuch as it is obvious that there is a three-dimensional space which may just as easily, and at the next moment probably will, be looked at from another point of view. If, however, the effect of depth is almost negligible, the perspective is conspicuous and compelling. What is visible and what is hidden strike one as being definitely intentional; one is forced to seek for a reason to be clear in one's own mind as to why the objects are arranged in this particular way and not in some other. There is no leeway between the objects: they are like flat surfaces stuck over one another, and seem almost to lie in the same plane.

Thus the lack of depth brings a very welcome element of unreality into the film picture. Formal qualities, such as the compositional and evocative significance of particular superimpositions, acquire the power to force themselves on the attention of the spectator. A shot like that described above where half of the girl's full face is cut off by the dark silhouette of the man's head, would possess only a fraction of its effectiveness if there were a strong feeling of space. In order to achieve the striking effect it is essential that the division across the face shall not seem accidental but intentional. The two faces must seem to be practically in one plane, with no leeway between them to show that they might easily be moved into different relative positions.

The fact that the lack of depth perception also leads to the almost total disappearance of the phenomena which the psychologist calls the "constancies" of size and form has already been discussed. The film artist takes advantage of their absence to produce remarkable effects. Everyone has seen a railway engine rushing on the scene in a film. It seems to be coming straight at the audience. The effect is most vivid because the dynamic power of the forward-rushing movement is enhanced by another source of dynamics that has no inherent connection with the object itself, that is, with the locomotive, but depends on the position of the spectator, or—in other words—of the camera. The nearer the engine comes the larger it appears, the dark mass on the screen spreads in every direction at tremendous pace (a dynamic dilation toward the margins of the screen), and the actual objective movement of the engine is strengthened by this dilation. Thus the apparent alteration in the size of an object which in reality remains the same size enhances its actual activity, and thus helps the film artist to interpret the impact of that activity visually. . . .

ARTISTIC USE OF THE ABSENCE OF NONVISUAL SENSE EXPERIENCES

People who did not understand anything of the art of film used to cite silence as one of its most serious drawbacks. These people regard the introduction of sound as an improvement or completion of silent film. This opinion is just as senseless as if the invention of three-dimensional oil painting were hailed as an advance on the hitherto known principles of painting.

From its very silence film received the impetus as well as the power to achieve excellent artistic effects. Charles Chaplin wrote somewhere that in all his films there was not a single scene where he "spoke," that is, moved his lips. Hundreds of the most various situations in human relationships are shown in his films, and yet he did not feel the need to make use of such an ordinary faculty as speech. And nobody has missed it. The spoken word in Chaplin's films is as rule replaced by pantomime. He does not say that he is pleased that some pretty girls are coming to see him, but performs the silent dance, in which two bread rolls stuck on forks act as dancing feet on the table (*The Gold Rush*). He does not argue, he fights. He avows his love by smiling, swaying his shoulders, and moving his hat. When he is in the pulpit he does not preach in words, but acts the story of David and Goliath (*The Pilgrim*). When he is sorry for a poor girl, he stuffs money into her handbag. He shows renunciation by simply walking away (finale of *The Circus*). The incredible visual concreteness of every one of his scenes makes for a great part of Chaplin's art; and this should not be forgotten when it is said—as is often done and of course not without foundation—that his films are not really "filmic" (because his camera serves mainly as a recording machine).

Mention has already been made of the scene from Sternberg's *The Docks of New York* in which a revolver shot is illustrated by the rising of a flock of birds. Such an effect is not just a contrivance on the part of a director to deal with the evil of silence by using an indirect visual method of explaining to the audience that there has been a bang. On the contrary, a positive artistic effect results from the paraphrase. Such indirect representation of an event in a material that is strange to it, or giving not the action itself but only its consequences, is a favorite method in all art. To take an example at random: when Francesca da Rimini tells how she fell in love with the man with whom she was in the habit of reading, and only says "We read no more that day," Dante thereby indicates indirectly, simply by giving the consequences, that on this day they kissed each other. And this indirectness is shockingly impressive.

In the same way, the rising of the birds is particularly effective, and probably more so than if the actual sound of the pistol shot were heard. And then another factor comes in: the spectator does not simply *infer* that a shot has been fired, but he actually *sees* something of the quality of the noise—the suddenness, the abruptness of the rising birds, give visually the exact quality that the shot possess acoustically. In Jacques Feyder's *Les Nouveaux Messieurs* a political meeting becomes very uproarious, and in order to calm the rising emotions Suzanne puts a coin into a mechanical piano. Immediately the hall is lit up by hundreds of electric bulbs, and now the music chimes in with the agitative speech. The music is not heard: it is a silent film. But Feyder shows the audience excitedly listening to the speaker; and suddenly the faces soften and relax; all the heads begin quite gently to sway in time to the music. The rhythm grows more pronounced until at last the spirit of the dance has seized them all; and they swing their bodies gaily from side to side as if to an unheard word of command. The speaker has to give way to the music. Much more clearly than if the music were actually heard, this shows the power that suddenly unites all these discontented people, puts them into the same merry mood; and indicates as well the character of the music itself, its sway and rhythm. What is particularly noteworthy in such a scene is not merely how easily and cleverly the director makes visible something that is not visual, but by so doing, actually strengthens its effect. If the music were really heard, the spectator might simply realize that music was sounding, but by this indirect method, the particular point, the important part of this music—its rhythm, its power to unite and "move" men—is conspicuously brought out. Only these special attributes of the music are given, and appear as the music itself. Similarly the fact that a pistol shot is sudden, explosive, startling, becomes doubly impressive by transposition into the visible, because only these particular attributes and not the shot itself are given. Thus silent film derives definite artistic potentialities from its silence. What it wishes particularly to emphasize in an audible occurrence is transposed into something visual; and thus instead of giving the occurrence "itself," it gives only some of its telling characteristics, and thereby shapes and interprets it.

Owing to its insubstantiality silent film does not in any way give the effect of being dumb pantomime. Its silence is not noticed, unless the action happens to culminate in something acoustic for which nothing can be substituted, and which is therefore felt as missing—or unless one is accustomed to sound film. Because of sound film, in the future it will be possible only with great difficulty to show speech in a silent way. Yet this is a most effective artistic device. For if a man is heard speaking, his gestures and facial expression only appear as an accompaniment to underline the sense of what is said. But if one does not hear what is said, the meaning becomes indirectly clear and is artistically interpreted by muscles of the face, of the limbs, of the body. The emotional quality of the conversation is made obvious with a clarity and definiteness which are hardly possible in the medium of actual speech. Moreover, the divergence between reality and dumb show gives the actor and his director plenty of leeway for artistic invention. (The creative power of the artist can only come into play where reality and the medium of representation do not coincide.)

Dialogue in silent film is not simply the visible part of a real spoken dialogue. If a real dialogue is shown without the sound, the spectator will often fail to grasp what it is all about; he will find the facial expression and the gestures unintelligible. In silent film, the lips are no longer word-forming physical organs but a means of visual expression—the distortion of an excited mouth or the fast chatter of lips are not mere by-products of talking; they are communications in their own right. Silent laughter is often more effective than if the sound is actually heard. The gaping of the open mouth gives a vivid, highly artistic interpretation of the phenomenon "laughter." If, however, the sound is also heard, the opening of the mouth appears obvious and its value as a means of expression is almost entirely lost. This opportunity of the silent film was once used by the Russians in a most unusual and effective manner. A shot of a soldier who had gone mad in the course of a battle and was laughing hideously with his mouth wide open was joined with a shot of the body of a soldier who had died of poison gas, and whose mouth was fixed in death in a ghastly, rigid grin.

The absence of the spoken word concentrates the spectator's attention more closely on the visible aspect of behavior, and thus the whole event draws particular interest to itself. Hence it is that very ordinary shots are often so impressive in silent films—such as a documentary shot of an itinerant hawker crying his wares with grandiose gestures. If his words could be heard the effect of the gestures would not be half as great, and the whole episode might attract very little attention. If, however, the words are omitted, the spectator surrenders entirely to the expressive power of the gestures. Thus by merely robbing the real event of something—the sound—the appeal of such an episode is greatly heightened. . . .

1933

NOËL CARROLL
FROM PHILOSOPHICAL PROBLEMS OF CLASSICAL FILM THEORY

THE SPECIFICITY THESIS

The notion that each art form has its own special subject matter that it of all the arts is best suited to represent is an eighteenth-century idea. The idea grew in reaction to an earlier style of art theorizing, represented by words such as Abbé Charles Batteux's 1746 treatise called *The Fine Arts Reduced to the Same Principle*.[1] For Batteux, all the arts were similar because they all had the same subject—the imitation of the beautiful in nature. This tendency to reduce the arts to their common denominator was the dominant trend in pre-Enlightenment art theory. During the eighteenth century, however, thinkers began to oppose this type of theorizing. They began to focus on what differentiated the arts from one another. An important work in this new tendency was Abbé Jean Baptiste Dubos's *Critical Reflections on Painting and Poetry*.[2] Dubos claimed that poetry and painting differ, in that painting imitates the single moment whereas poetry imitates process. Similar analyses were offered in the works of James Harris and Moses Mendelsohn.[3] The best known work of this revisionist sort, entitled *Laocoön*, was published in 1766 by Gotthold Ephraim Lessing. That book contains several important presumptions of Arnheim's *Materialtheorie*: that the arts (1) differ from each other in terms of (2) what each represents (imitates) best, due to (3) the peculiar (specific) structure of its formal/physical medium.

Comparing painting and poetry, Lessing writes:

I argue thus. If it be true that painting employs wholly different signs or means of imitation from poetry—the one using forms and colors in space and the other articulate

---

[1] In Monroe Beardsley, *Aesthetics: From Classical Greece to the Present* (New York: Macmillan, 1966; Tuscaloosa: University of Alabama Press, 1975), 160.
[2] Ibid.
[3] Ibid.

sounds in time—and if signs must unquestionably stand in convenient relation with the thing signified, then signs arranged side by side can represent only objects existing side by side, or whose parts so exist, while consecutive signs can express only objects which succeed each other in time.

Objects which exist side by side, or whose parts so exist, are called bodies. Consequently, bodies with their visible properties are the peculiar subjects of painting.

Objects which succeed each other, or whose parts succeed each other in time, are actions. Consequently, actions are the peculiar subjects of poetry.[4]

Here we see Lessing attempting to extrapolate from the structure of the medium—the structure of what, in advance of semiotics, he calls "signs"—to the appropriate subject matter of the medium. Arnheim, as well, attempts to move from the structural peculiarities of the medium to injunctions about the proper direction of film-making.

Before examining the specificity thesis in terms of truth or falsity, I would like to note that although for many reasons the thesis no longer seems acceptable, in its day it performed a useful service. The specificity thesis served as a corrective to the vagueness of the tendency to reduce all the arts to a common denominator. As a result, theorists began to look more closely at the various art forms. The gain was one of rigor. This does not, of course, entail that the specificity thesis is true. However, theorists like Arnheim who adopt it do tend to give very close, precise accounts of artistic structures. Thus, even if the specificity thesis is false, it has beneficial side effects.

One difference between Lessing and Arnheim is that Lessing focuses on the physical medium, of painting for example, and teases out of that an analysis of what the medium can represent at its best—what is most convenient for its signs to depict—whereas Arnheim, in *Film as Art*, examines cinematic devices to find where they fall short of successful representation. Lessing is concerned to find where a medium excels in representation, whereas Arnheim is most interested in where a medium falters in terms of perfect representation. In and of itself, this contrast does not present a problem for Arnheim. Arnheim, like Lessing, wants to establish a special domain for each medium. Film, he tells us, is the realm of the animated image. But here is a lacuna in this New Laocoön. For how do the various peculiarities that Arnheim points to—the lack of constancy of size and of the spatiotemporal continuum, and so forth—ever add up to or imply that film is concerned with the animated image? The peculiarities or specificities of the medium that Arnheim points to constitute a list of things that cinematic representations do not have. How do these amount to a positive commitment to the animated image? If the peculiar structures of the medium are what entail the medium's commitment to the animated image, it is not clear how Arnheim's examples show this.

Another problem with the specificity thesis is that Arnheim seems to believe that, as a matter of fact, every medium diverges from the referents it represents because of its own peculiar formal/physical structure. Arnheim says "representation never produces a replica of the object but its structural equivalent in a *given* medium.[5]"

---

[4]Gotthold Ephraim Lessing, *Laocoön* (New York: Noonday Press, 1969), 91.
[5]*Art and Visual Perception*, Arnheim, 162.

But if each medium automatically, so to speak, diverges not only from each referent but also from the depiction of such referents in other media, then what point is
there to the specificity thesis stated as an injunction? That is, why urge artists to
make certain that they exploit the peculiarities of their medium if this is unavoidable and bound to happen anyway? Moreover, how can Arnheim rail against sound
films? Sound films will automatically be differentiated from theater because the
media are physically different. If one believes that every medium is automatically
unique in terms of the structure of its symbols, then why fear that media will ille-
gitimately spill over each others' boundaries? It will be impossible.

Arnheim's specificity thesis is not a description; it is a recommendation. Were
the specificity thesis a description, there could be no problems involving the tres-
passing of the sound film in the domain of theater. It would make no sense to use
the specificity thesis to attempt to chide filmmakers if the specificity thesis were a
description—filmmakers would necessarily employ the peculiar (specific) characteristics of their medium.

As a recommendation, the specificity thesis appears to have two components. One
component is the idea that there is something that each medium does best. The other
is that each of the arts should do what differentiates it from the other arts. These
two components can be called the excellence requirement and the differentiation
requirement. The two can be combined in the imperative that each art form should
explore only those avenues of development in which it exclusively excels above all
other arts. The incorporation of "exclusively" in this formula sounds the differentiation requirement while the rest of the formula states the excellence requirement.
Applied to Arnheim's film theory, the specificity thesis states that filmmakers should
stress the differentiating features (the limitations) that enable the medium to portray
animated action (what cinema does best).

Some of the problems with the specificity thesis are the result of the combination of the differentiation and excellence requirements. The assumption is that what
a medium does best will coincide with what differentiates it. But why should this
be so? For example, many media narrate. Film, drama, prose, and epic poetry all
tell stories. For argument's sake, let us say narration is what each does best—that
is, best of all the things each of them does. However, this does not differentiate
these art forms. What does the specificity thesis require in such a situation? If film
and the novel both excel in narration, should (1) neither art form narrate since narration fails to differentiate them? or (2) should film not narrate since narration will
fail to differentiate it from the novel and the novel claimed the domain of narration
first? or (3) should the novel give up narration and let the newcomer have its chance?

The first alternative is simply absurd; it would sacrifice a magnificent cultural
invention—narration—for whatever bizarre satisfaction that could be derived from
adherence to the differentation requirement. I am assuming that excellence is more
important to us than differentiation.

The second alternative is also unattractive. In this case the specificity thesis would
seem to confuse history with ontology. That is, film is to forswear narrating just
because literature already has that turf staked out. But surely this is only an accident of history. What if movies had arisen before writing? Then would literature
have to find some other occupation? Clearly such accidents of history should not

preclude a medium from pursuing an area in which it excels. Nor should accidents of history be palmed off as ontological necessities—another proclivity of the specificity thesis. The special subject matter of each medium supposedly follows from its nature. But the story is more complicated, since a medium specializes in what it excels in only if that area of special achievement differentiates it from other media. The question of differentiation is not simply a question about the nature of the medium; it is a question about the comparison of arts. And it is quite possible that a new art may be invented that excels in an area where an older art already excels. Awarding the domain to the older art just because it is already established seems arbitrary, as does the third alternative—awarding the domain to the younger art just because it is younger. If two arts both excel in domain, it seems natural to allow them both to explore it. That will enrich the culture by multiplying the number of excellent things. This is surely the case with narrative. The world is far richer for having novels *and* fiction films *and* epic poems *and* dramas *and* comic books *and* narrative paintings *and* operas, though the differentiation component of the specificity thesis would block this.

One point should be emphasized in the preceding discussion: narration does seem to be one instance where many arts do share the same pursuit. And yet specificity theorists, especially the major film theorists who champion the specificity thesis, rarely seem to be ruffled by this fact. It seems as though they are so concerned to differentiate film from theater that they fail to notice that film is similar to other narrative arts, such as the short story and the novel. These latter similarities or overlaps seem to be tolerable. Why? The only way I can account for this anomaly is that historical circumstances were such that only the canned theater argument against film vividly presented itself as so threatening that it had to be dealt with. For, of course, in the days when these arguments raged, theater and film could be thought of as directly competing for the same audience. They were locked in economic conflict as well as aesthetic struggle, which meant that more was at issue in the battle between them than in the relation between film and the other narrative arts. Thus, many film theorists who upheld the specificity thesis never noticed that they should have been exercised by the overlap with the other narrative arts, even though such an overlap should call into question the specificity thesis.

The specificity thesis has both an excellence component and a differentiation component. Perhaps one interpretation of the theory is that each art form should pursue those projects that fall in the area of intersection between what the art form excels in and what differentiates it from other art forms. But this does not seem to be an acceptable principle because, among other things, it entails that the reason an art form might not be employed to do what it does best is that some other art form also does it well. *The specificity thesis seems to urge us to sacrifice excellence on principle.* But excellence is, in fact, always the overriding consideration in deciding whether a particular practice or development is acceptable in art.

Indeed, I believe that what could be called the priority of excellence is the central telling point against the specificity thesis. To dramatize this, let us imagine that for some reason the only way that G. B. Shaw could get backing for *Pygmalion* was to make it as a talking picture—since in our possible world Shaw was known only as a successful screenwriter. Let us also suppose that in some sense it is true that theater is a better showcase for aesthetically crafted language. Would we decide that *Pygmalion* should not be made? I think our answer is "no," because our intuitions are that the specificity thesis should not be allowed to stand between us and excellence.

Nor need the excellence in question be a matter of the highest excellence achievable in a given medium. The specificity thesis seems to urge that a medium pursue only what it does best. But if a medium does something well and the occasion arises to do it, why should it be inhibited because there is something it does better? Certain magical transformations—turning weaklings into werewolves for example—can be most vividly executed in cinema. But they can also be done quite efficiently on stage. Should this minor excellence be foregone in a stage adaptation of *Dr. Jekyll and Mr. Hyde*, either because transformation is not what theater does best or because film can do it better?

Another disturbing feature of the specificity thesis is that it appears to envision each art form on the model of a highly specialized tool with a range of determinate functions. A film, play, poem, or painting is thought of, it seems, analogous to something like a Phillips screwdriver. If you wish to turn a screw with a cross-shaped groove on top, use a Phillips screwdriver. If you wish to explore the potentials of aesthetically crafted language, use theater. If your topic is animated action, use film. Likewise, just as you should not use a Phillips screwdriver as a church key (though it can open a beer can), you should not, all things being equal, use cinema to perform theater's task, and vice versa. But I think it is incumbent on us to question whether this underlying metaphor has any applicability when it comes to art forms. Are art forms highly specialized tools? I think not. If art forms are like tools at all, then they are more like sticks than like Phillips screwdrivers. That is, they can be used to do many things; they have not been designed to perform a specific task. In most cases art forms are not designed—that is, they are not invented with a specific task in mind. Moreover, even with self-consciously invented arts like film, it is soon discovered that the form can perform many more tasks than the one it was originally designed for. Indeed, interest in art forms is to a large measure interest in how artists learn or discover new ways of using their medium. The idea of the artist discovering new ways of using the medium would make no sense if the medium were designed for a single purpose.

An artistic medium, including a self-consciously invented one, is such that many of its potentials remain to be discovered. But discovery would not be a relevant expectation to have of artists nor would an interest in it be relevant to an art form, if the task of the art form were as fixed as that of a Phillips screwdriver. A correlative fact against the idea of the fixedness of function of art forms is the fact that they very often continue to exist over time, obviously because they are periodically reinvented and new uses are found for them. But if art forms were as determinately set in their functions as are Phillips screwdrivers, one would expect them, or at least many of them, to pass away as their function becomes archaic. That they are readapted, reinvented, and redirected bodes ill for the metaphor of the art form as a specialized tool—a view that seems strongly suggested by the specificity thesis.

One consideration offered in favor of the specificity thesis proceeds by asking why else there would be *different* media unless they were supposed to pursue different ends? That is, the specificity thesis is, in this light, an inference to the best explanation.

Given the fact that we have a number of arts, we ask "Why?" The answer that seems most reasonable is that each art has, or should have, a different function.

This particular line of thought presupposes that it is legitimate to ask why we have different arts. It also supposes that it is legitimate to expect as an answer to this question something like a rational principle. Perhaps for idealists it is reasonable to expect a rationale or a rationalization here. But for others the issue appears to be a matter of historical accident. I believe that it was Wittgenstein who said that where there is no question, there is no answer. We can use this principle, I think, to rid ourselves of the preceding argument. For its question, when stated nonelliptically, is not "Why are there diverse arts?" but "What is the rationale that explains why we have exactly the diverse arts that we have?" Now there may be no single answer to this question. Rather we may have to settle for a series of answers to the former question—answers of a historical and anthropological variety. For example, we have film because Edison invented it to supplement the phonograph; we have painting because one day a Cro-Magnon splashed some adhesive victuals on a cave wall and it looked strikingly like a bison; and so on. But there is no answer to the second question: "What is the rationale for having exactly the several arts we do have?" Rather, each art arose due to a chain of events that led to its discovery or invention and to its popularization. The result is the *collection* of arts we have, which we only honorifically refer to as a *system*. There is no rationale for the system, for in truth it is only a collection. Thus, we have no need for the specificity thesis, for the question it answers—"Why is there a system of different arts?"—is really not an admissible question at all.[6]

Before concluding this section, some discussion of Arnheim's application of the specificity thesis to sound film is appropriate, for Arnheim's maledictions against the talking picture are undoubtedly the most notorious part of his film theory. Arnheim holds that if there is a truly composite art form, then none of the constituent media can be anything but fully developed. That is, in a truly composite art form none of the media combined would be subservient, nor would any be redundant, that is, merely repetitive of what is already conveyed by another, more dominant, medium. Each must function equally and be fully articulated on its own terms. For Arnheim, opera is not really a composite because music is the dominant constituent medium to which the language and the scenography are subservient. Nor are laconic talking films with functional dialogue acceptable composites, because such dialogue is subservient to the visuals and, for the most part, is redundant to the action. On the other hand, more fully developed dialogue tends to make the film medium subservient to speech, paralyzing the action and thwarting the medium's commitment to animated movement. Dialogue cannot be artistically expanded upon and articulated without interfering with the depiction of action, which will transform the work into a piece of theater, denying the camera the opportunity to represent what it alone portrays best.[7]

---

[6]For expanded and amplified arguments against the specificity thesis, see my "The Specificity of Media in the Arts," *The Journal of Aesthetic Education* 19 (Winter 1984): 5–20; and my "Medium Specificity Arguments and the Self-Consciously Invented Arts: Film, Photography and Video," *Millennium Film Journal*, nos. 14–15 (1984–85): 127–53.

[7]*FAA*, 228–30.

There are two sides to this argument. Either dialogue is made to facilitate action, in which case the medium of speech is short-changed, or dialogue is developed artistically, in which case the action of the film is paralyzed. In neither case is the art truly composite. Instead, the sound film is a mongrel.

Of course, one wonders whether Arnheim's ideal of a truly composite art form is a worthwhile one. Why must a legitimate composite abide by such inflexible standards of equality between the constituent media? Often in nineteenth-century ballet the music was not so distinguished as the dancing, since the point of this form was to direct attention to the movement. Does this imply that ballet, or at least ballet done in this format, is not a truly composite art? But if ballet is not a truly composite art and neither is opera, then one suspects that Arnheim is defining the category of composite art out of existence. Moreover, if the example of nineteenth-century ballet is taken seriously, one horn of Arnheim's dilemma can be neutralized. It may be perfectly acceptable to have composite art forms where one medium is subservient to another. Specifically, there may be many sound films that, although their scripts do not make edifying reading, have perfectly serviceable dialogue supporting the visuals. Films like *Citizen Kane*, *Psycho*, and *Rules of the Game* surely are examples of this sort. Thus, questioning Arnheim's criterion for a truly composite medium dispels half of the dilemma.[8]

The other half can be dispelled by questioning whether it is impossible to combine language and visuals so that each is given full honor. Surely the opening scene of Olivier's *Henry V* fully honors both action and poetry. Other examples also come to mind, Polonsky's *Force of Evil* for one—a film whose highly poetic script was rhythmically integrated with the action.

Furthermore, several objections raised against the specificity thesis in general can be applied to its use in the context of the sound film. Undoubtedly, great moments in dialogue film—for example, Groucho's speech to the ministers in *Duck Soup*—are not begrudged because they were seen on celluloid rather than on stage. If the specificity thesis entails cutting this scene, then so much the worse for the specificity thesis. Of course, it may be held that the specificity theorist is not committed to disparaging this scene. Rather, such a theorist might praise the scene, but as theater rather than film. But this seems wrong. For part of what is excellent about the scene is that it is delivered by that man, Groucho Marx, with that voice, at that period of time (the Depression). These things fit together in a powerful expressive ensemble. Indeed, part of what is valuable about the scene is that it is a *recording* of a performance, exactly the aspect of cinema Arnheim is most disposed to denounce. Moreover, the black and white photography, the cut of the actor's clothing, their diction, their bearing all conspire to evoke a powerful feeling of "thirties-ness" that could not be replicated today on stage or film— not only because many of the actors are dead but also because films don't look and sound that way any more, and, in all likelihood, theater never did. That that specific performance is on film—film of a certain technological vintage—is part and parcel of the scene's power, no matter that it is dominated by speech.

1988

---

[8]Interestingly, Arnheim differs from other specificity theorists like Panofsky who are willing to accept functional dialogue as the proper means of keeping cinema pure while at the same time using sound.

GERALD MAST
FROM FILM/CINEMA/MOVIE

PROJECTION

Gerald Mast's work as a film historian (1940–1988) helped to establish the field. Founder of the University of Chicago's Film Archive and Study Center, in addition to co-editing the first three editions of this anthology, his pioneering books include *A Short History of the Movies* (1971) and *The Comic Mind: Comedy and the Movies* (1973). Among his other books are a guide to Jean Renoir's *Rules of the Game* (1973), *Howard Hawks, Storyteller* (1982), and *Film/Cinema/Movie: A Theory of Experience* (1977), from which the following excerpt is drawn. In it, he proposes a theory of film that lies between formalism and realism, arguing that the shot and not the still image is the fundamental element of film and that, therefore, semiotics is an inadequate tool to analyze the film experience.

An obvious assumption of the preceding chapter is that the *aesthetic event* of cinema is the projection of the finished work—analogous to the reading of the type that is a novel, the attending to the motion and conversation that are a play, the listening to the sound that is a piece of music, or the looking at the color on canvas that is a painting. The creative process of shooting and assembling film is certainly a worthy subject of study—as are the notebooks of Henry James or the Georges Seurat sketches for *A Sunday Afternoon on the Island of La Grande Jatte*. To study this process reveals both the artist's specific choices and the general way he viewed his art and his craft. But it nonetheless studies the means to the end, and that end is experiencing the work of art itself, which remains its own testament and as solid a piece of evidence as any. With the cinema art it is perhaps an even solider piece of evidence than its maker's recollections of the creative process, since the memories of moviemakers are at least as prone to error as any, since the movie business encourages self-congratulation, and since the creative process of moviemaking is such an admittedly collective one.[1]

---

[1]Movie directors are notoriously unreliable. Frank Capra claims he watched Leo McCarey direct Laurel and Hardy at the Hal Roach studio in 1924 (L & H never worked together until 1927); Mack Sennett went to his grave claiming Buster Keaton was one of his Keystone Cops (never); Groucho Marx is under the impression that there are no musical numbers in *A Night at the Opera* (poor Kitty Carlisle and Allan Jones; or rather, poor us—because Groucho is unfortunately wrong). One of the consistent mistakes of film historians is to quote the recollections of moviemakers as gospel; the American Film Institute has invested both time and money in the recording of some four-hundred "oral histories" of their recollections. To preserve these thoughts and voices for posterity is undeniably valuable, but gospel it isn't.

This emphasis on projection necessarily excludes certain interesting kinds of questions, among them some of the classic problems of film, cinema, and movie theory. It denies the notion of "the cinematic" altogether, since it assumes that any finished piece of cinema is indisputably a piece of cinema. The precise meaning of "cinematic" is "of or pertaining to the cinema," and its essence is merely that a succession of frames moves forward through the projector. You can, of course, then discuss whether that succession of frames is interesting or boring, beautiful or ugly, good or bad. True, the primitive film strips of Edison, Lumière, and most of their pre-Griffith contemporaries might properly be called "uncinematic," simply because they had no notion at all of one of the three principles of temporal succession (imagistic succession) and a very clumsy and undeveloped notion of another (structural succession). One of today's experimental, minimal films is certainly not uncinematic in the same way, for its maker was aware of all the possible principles of succession, but deliberately tried to extend or eliminate the use of some of them.

The insistence on projection has certain theoretical advantages. First, it clearly distinguishes cinema from a live theatrical performance, on the one hand, and from television on the other. The fact that film is projected alters its tense (it must necessarily *have been* photographed and processed in the past), whereas the tense of a live theatrical performance (dance, drama, opera) is the now. The fact that film is projected also means that it will be perceived and received differently from a live performance, particularly since projections are perceived and received as a series of different kinds of successions. In a live performance, although plot might parallel structural succession, there are no equivalents to the literal and imagistic successions of cinema; the stage movement is continuous, not successive. The visual power and concentration of cinema's successiveness (coupled with the kinetic power of the individual images) give the force of the spoken word a different (and lighter) "weight" in the cinema than in the drama (as noted and developed by Bazin). Television transmission is not a projection at all; nor is its literal succession identical to cinema's. These differences produce the reduced clarity, sublety, luminosity, density, and (for the present anyway) size of the television image. This reduction also guarantees a different emotional response and reaction to our perception of the weakened kinesis of the television image.

Indeed, the emphasis on projection as the aesthetic event consistently forces our attention on how a work of cinema is received and perceived rather than on what cinema is. Arnheim gets into all kinds of trouble with this problem since he constantly explores the ways in which the cinema image differs physically from natural vision. What he never unscrambles, however, is whether the cinema makes us perceive its differences from nature or whether it fools us by erasing those physical differences so that we perceive the image as apparently quite natural. For example, Arnheim's first principle is that photography converts three-dimensional space into a two-dimensional plane. He then develops the ways that this "fact" can be exploited artistically, some of those exploitations based on the way that the focal lengths of various lenses can alter the way we perceive relative distances between objects. One of his examples is that a newspaper appears to be "cut out" of the face of the person reading it; the converse effect would be the way that a wide-angle lens can make a hand holding a gun in the foreground appear ten times larger than the assailant's face, only an arm's length away.

But do we perceive the projected image as two-dimensional at all? The very fact that we call one object in the projected image apparently close to or far away from another implies that there is some kind of mental translation of the two-dimensional image into three-dimensional terms. In the cinema, when we see large and small, we translate our perception either into close and far (based on our awareness of relative distances and the sizes of objects in life) or into not so close or far but deliberately distorted for some effect by the lens (as in that hand-face example, which we know is based on an impossible relationship of size and distance in nature). We perceive the projected image as a kind of three-dimensional system, once we have learned to translate it (which means that we must learn to watch cinema, just as we must learn any system of translation—and just as we learn to translate sizes into distances in life).

The occasional 3-D movie (or the re-release of one from the Great Flurry of '52) proves that our perception of the projected three-dimensional image is nothing like that of the natural three-dimensional one either. The whole tendency of the 3-D image is to push the action and motion at us; not simply the deliberately hurled objects that sail toward our heads, but even the horizontal movement of walking from left to right feels as if it were thrusting toward us. Even the stationary walls seem to loom out at us, in a way that I do not usually perceive walls to do in life.

The projected cinema image does not appear to be flat; light on a screen is not perceived the same way as paint on canvas. Why not? First, paint is itself a hard, physical material that refracts light. That refraction is the physical stimulus that produces the effect of the painting (since light produces our perception of color by refraction); but it also reminds us of the flatness of the canvas and the material on it (because light bounces off the paint material itself, and that bouncing is perceived as a kind of surface refraction). Those painters who became self-conscious about the flatness of paint on canvas (for example, the evolving rough-textured brush strokes of Van Gogh) simply called attention to the essential flatness of the art by trying to avoid or exploit it. And what else was the development of perspective but a response to the flatness of canvas and paint? It was not the modernist response, however, as was Van Gogh's.

But the "material" of projected images is the immaterial operation of light itself; the images of cinema are produced by light's bouncing off the beaded surface of a screen, a refraction that is not, however, perceived as a refractive bouncing of light off a surface, but as the images themselves. The screen seems more to absorb the images (like a sponge) than to refract and bounce them, although such a refraction is literally what we see (but not perceive). The immateriality of light itself and the perception that the screen is a kind of translucent sponge (yet another cinema illusion) militate against the flatness of the projected image, convincing us that the image has a kind of depth (which it obviously does not).

Second, paintings are still and projected images are not. The two physical forms of cinema succession work upon the eye by keeping the photographed subjects constantly in motion. Not only is this motion a further diversion from any consciousness of the screen's flatness, but it is also a way of defining distance and dimensionality. The enlarging or shrinking of an object over a period of time or the length of time required to travel between two points are two familiar ways of defining terms like "close" and "far." One of the striking effects of halting the cinema's motion—of the "freeze frame"—is the sudden reduction of the screen's apparent depth. Only by freezing the movement that is the essence of cinema's succession does one convert the photographed image into a truly two-dimensional plane.

The projection of successive images does not convert three-dimensional nature into a two-dimensional pattern, but changes three-dimensional nature into a different three-dimensional system using two-dimensional symbols. As always, there are exceptional films that attempt to make the projected image appear as flat as possible (the Zagreb animation films, any experimental films that deliberately use the static flatness of lettering and title cards, the films of Len Lye, Norman McLaren, Robert Breer, or anyone else who uses drawn figures of any kind). Walt Disney's entire career in animation can be chronicled as a progressive war against the flatness of cinema cartooning, as a struggle to make the drawn image as apparently three-dimensional as the photographed one. Like so many valuable cinema experiments, these uses or denials of two-dimensionality are ironic reversals or revelations of traits that seem inherent to cinema.

The insistence on projection also addresses whether cinema is or is not an "automatic" art (is for Bazin, Kracauer, Cavell, and their followers; is not for Arnheim, Eisenstein, and theirs). Projection is obviously automatic, but is the shooting of a film equally automatic? And these theories of film as "automatic" art are all based on the recording, not the projection, process. There is *something* about the shooting of a film that is certainly automatic—the precise moment of etching the light on the film material itself. Other than that moment of recording, however, almost nothing about the shooting of a film is automatic. The creators control the intensity and quality of the light; even outdoor sequences use key lights, floodlights, reflectors, and scrims, as well as selecting the precise type of time of day for shooting—as Antonioni did in *Red Desert* or Mizoguchi did in all his films). They control the action within the shot, the setting, the colors, the objects, the details of décor. They control the specific lens that will be used, and the filters for it (if any), and the speed and type of film itself. To reduce the question to the absurd, could you call the shooting of an animated film automatic? Yes, the film captures the light automatically when the single frame is exposed. But no, the entire world that is so captured is the project of a human imagination.

The primacy of projection also solves the nature-nurture controversy in the cinema, since that controversy is a corollary of considering the shooting process as automatic (i.e., cinema automatically records the integrity of nature) or not (i.e., cinema is the artificial project of human choices, not a mechanical recording of nature). Obviously, the projection of a reel of film has nothing to do with nature—no more than does the reading of a novel or the looking at a painting. There may be a good deal of nature (or human life, or natural experience) in the work's succession of frames, images, and events, but there may also be a good deal of this same kind of nature in the content of a novel or the subject of a painting. To emphasize projection is to reiterate that the work of cinema is necessarily as artificial as any work of any art.

To emphasize projection is also to reiterate that an essential condition of the cinema experience is viewing flickering light in an enveloping darkness. This piercing of darkness by projected light is the source of cinema's hypnotic power, paralleling the way that the professional hypnotist entrances a subject by focusing attention on a bright and rhythmically flickering source of light. This light-in-darkness also generates several paradoxes that infuse and influence our experiencing of cinema: we both sit in darkness and are bathed in light; the experience is both private and public at the same time; the projected images both speak to our personal dreams and fantasies and seem to depict the most public and familiar realities. Projection gives us both the concreteness of visual images and the abstract play of light itself.

1977

STANLEY CAVELL
FROM THE WORLD VIEWED

PHOTOGRAPH AND SCREEN

Stanley Cavell's major interests center on the intersection of the analytical tradition (especially the work of Wittgenstein and Austin) with moments of the continental tradition (Nietzsche and Wittgenstein); with American philosophy (Emerson and Thoreau); with the arts (Shakespeare, film and opera); and with psychoanalysis. His first book on film, *The World Viewed: Reflections on the Ontology of Film* (1971), from which the following excerpts are taken, earned him an important place in the tradition of realist film theorists. His work takes a personal approach to understanding film, often drawing on his own experience and viewing habits. His other works on film include *Pursuits of Happiness: The Hollywood Comedy of Remarriage* (1988), *Contesting Tears: The Hollywood Melodrama of the Unknown Woman* (1996), and the collection, *Cavell on Film* (2005).

Let us notice the specific sense in which photographs are of the world, of reality as a whole. You can always ask, pointing to an object in a photograph—a building, say—what lies behind it, totally obscured by it. This only accidentally makes sense when asked of an object in a painting. You can always ask, of an area photographed, what lies adjacent to thAt area, beyond the frame. This generally makes no sense asked of a painting. You can ask these questions of objects in photographs because they have answers in reality. The world of a painting is not continuous with the world of its frame; at its frame, a world finds its limits. We might say: A painting *is* a world; a photograph is *of* the world. What happens in a photograph is that *it* comes to an end. A photograph is cropped, not necessarily by a paper cutter or by masking but by the camera itself. The camera crops it by predetermining the amount of view it will accept; cutting, masking, enlarging, predetermine the amount after the fact. (Something like this phenomenon shows up in recent painting. In this respect, these paintings have found, at the extremest negation of the photographic, media that achieve the condition of photographs.) The camera, being finite, crops a portion from an indefinitely larger field; continuous portions of that field could be included in the photograph in fact taken; in principle, it could all be taken. Hence objects in photographs that run past the edge do not feel cut; they are aimed at, shot, stopped live. When a photograph is cropped, the rest of the world is cut *out*. The implied presence of the rest of the world, and its explicit rejection, are as essential in the experience of a photograph as what it explicitly presents. A camera is an opening in a box: that is the best emblem of the fact that a camera holding on an object is holding the rest of the world away. The camera has been praised for extending the senses; it may, as the world goes, deserve more praise for confining them, leaving room for thought.

The world of a moving picture is screened. The screen is not a support, not like a canvas; there is nothing to support, that way. It holds a projection, as light as light. A screen is a barrier. What does the silver screen screen? It screens me from the world it holds—that is, makes me invisible. And it screens that world from me—that is, screens its existence from me. That the projected world does not exist (now) is its only difference from reality. (There is no feature, or set of features, in which it differs. Existence is not a predicate.) Because it is the field of a photograph, the screen has no frame; that is to say, no border. Its limits are not so much the edges of a given shape as they are the limitations, or capacity, of a container. The screen is a frame; the frame is the whole field of the screen—as a frame of film is the whole field of a photograph, like the framer of a loom or a house. In this sense, the screen-frame is a mold, or form.

The fact that in moving pictures successive film frames are fit flush into the fixed screen frame results in a phenomenological frame that is indefinitely extendible and contractible, limited in the smallness of the object it can grasp only by the state of its technology, and in largeness only by the span of the world. Drawing the camera back, and panning it, are two ways of extending the frame; a close-up is of a part of the body, or of one object or small set of objects, supported by and reverberating the whole frame of nature. The altering frame is the image of perfect attention. Early in its history the cinema discovered the possibility of *calling* attention to persons and parts of persons and objects; but it is equally a possibility of the medium not to call attention to them but, rather, to let the world happen, to let its parts draw attention to themselves according to their natural weight. This possibility is less explored than its opposite. Dreyer, Flaherty, Vigo, Renoir, and Antonioni are masters of it.

AUDIENCE, ACTOR, AND STAR

The depth of the automatism of photography is to be read not alone in its mechanical production of an image of reality, but in its mechanical defeat of our presence to that reality. The audience in a theater can be defined as those to whom the actors are present while they are not present to the actors. But movies allow the audience to be mechanically absent. The fact that I am invisible and inaudible to the actors, and fixed in position, no longer needs accounting for; it is not part of a convention I have to comply with; the proceedings do not have to make good the fact that I do nothing in the face of tragedy, or that I laugh at the follies of others. In viewing a movie my helplessness is mechanically assured: I am present not at something happening, which I must confirm, but at something that has happened, which I absorb (like a memory). In this, movies resemble novels, a fact mirrored in the sound of narration itself, whose tense is the past.

It might be said: "But surely there is the obvious difference between a movie house and a theater that is not recorded by what has so far been said and that outweighs all this fiddle of differences. The obvious difference is that in a theater we are in the presence of an actor, in a movie house we are not. You have said that in both places the actor is in our presence and in neither are we in his, the difference lying in the mode of our absence. But there is also the plain fact that in a theater a real man is *there*, and in a movie no real man is there. That is obviously essential to the differences between our responses to a play and to a film." What that means must not be denied; but the fact remains to be understood. Bazin meets it head on by simply denying that "the screen is incapable of putting us 'in the presence of' the actor"; it, so to speak, relays his presence to us, as by mirrors. Bazin's idea here really fits the facts of live television, in which the thing we are presented with is happening simultaneously with its presentation. But in live television, what is present to us while it is happening is not the world, but an event standing out from the world. Its point is not to reveal, but to cover (as with a gun), to keep something on view.

It is an incontestable fact that in a motion picture no live human being is up there. But a human *something* is, and something unlike anything else we know. We can stick to our plain description of that human something as "in our presence while we are not in his" (present at him, because looking at him, but not present to him) and still account for the difference between his live presence and his photographed presence to us. We need to consider what is present or, rather, since the topic is the human being, *who* is present.

One's first impulse may be to say that in a play the character is present, whereas in a film the actor is. That sounds phony or false: one wants to say that both are present in both. But there is more to it, ontologically more. Here I think of a fine passage of Panofsky's:

> Othello or Nora are definite, substantial figures created by the playwright. They can be played well or badly, and they can be "interpreted" in one way or another; but they most definitely exist, no matter who plays them or even whether they are played at all. The character in a film, however, lives and dies with the actor. It is not the entity "Othello" interpreted by Robeson or the entity "Nora" interpreted by Duse, it is the entity "Greta Garbo" incarnate in a figure called Anna Christie or the entity "Robert Montgomery" incarnate in a murderer who, for all we know or care to know, may forever remain anonymous but will never cease to haunt our memories.

If the character lives and dies with the actor, that ought to mean that the actor lives and dies with the character. I think that is correct, but it needs clarification. Let us develop it slightly.

For the stage, an actor works himself into a role; for the screen, a performer takes the role onto himself. The stage actor explores his potentialities and the possibilities of his role simultaneously; in performance these meet at a point in spiritual space—the better the performance, the deeper the point. In this respect, a role in a play is like a position in a game, say, third base: various people can play it, but the great third baseman is a man who has accepted and trained his skills and instincts most perfectly and matches them most intimately with his discoveries of the possibilities and necessities of third base. The screen performer explores his role like an attic and takes stock of his physical and temperamental endowment; he lends his being to the role and accepts only what fits; the rest is nonexistent. On the stage there are two beings, and the being of the character assaults the being of the actor; the actor survives only by yielding. A screen performance requires not so much training as planning. Of course, both the actor and the performer require, or can make use of, experience. The actor's role is his subject for study, and there is no end to it. But the screen performer is essentially not an actor at all: he *is* the subject of study, and a study not his own. (That is what the content of a photograph is—its subject.) On a screen the study is projected; on a stage the actor is the projector. An exemplary stage performance is one which, for a time, most fully creates a character. After Paul Scofield's performance in *King Lear*, we know who King Lear is, we have seen him in the flesh. An exemplary screen performance is one in which, at a time, a star is born. After *The Maltese Falcon* we know a new star, only distantly a person. "Bogart" means "the figure created in a given set of films." His presence in those films is who he is, not merely in the sense in which a photograph of an event is that event; but in the sense that if those films did not exist, Bogart would not exist, the name "Bogart" would not mean what it does. The figure it names is not only in our presence, we are in his, in the only sense we could ever be. That is all the "presence" he has.

But it is complicated. A full development of all this would require us to place such facts as these: Humphrey Bogart was a man, and he appeared in movies both before and after the ones that created "Bogart." Some of them did not create a new star (say, the stable groom in *Dark Victory*), some of them defined stars—anyway meteors— that may be incompatible with Bogart (e.g., Duke Mantee and Fred C. Dobbs) but that are related to that figure and may enter into our later experience of it. And Humphrey Bogart was both an accomplished actor and a vivid subject for a camera. Some people are, just as some people are both good pitchers and good hitters; but there are so few that it is surprising that the word "actor" keeps on being used in place of the more beautiful and more accurate word "star"; the stars are only to gaze at, after the fact, and their actions divine our projects. Finally, we must note the sense in which the creation of a (screen) performer is also the creation of a character—not the kind of character an author creates, but the kind that certain real people are: a type.

TYPES; CYCLES AS GENRES

Our attention turns from the physical medium of cinema in general to the specific forms or genres the medium has taken in the course of its history.

Both Panofsky and Bazin begin at the beginning, noting and approving that early movies adapt popular or folk arts and themes and performers and characters: farce, melodrama, circus, music hall, romance, etc. And both are gratifyingly contemptuous of intellectuals who could not come to terms with those facts of life. (Such intellectuals are the alter egos of the film promoters they so heartily despise. Roxy once advertised a movie as "Art, in every sense of the word"; his better half declaims, "This is not art, in any sense of the word.") Our question is, why did such forms and themes and characters lend themselves to film? Bazin, in what I have read of him, is silent on the subject, except to express gratitude to film for revivifying these ancient forms, and to justify in general the legitimacy of adaptation from one art to another. Arnold Hauser, if I understand him, suggests wrong answers, in a passage that includes the remark "Only a young art can be popular," a remark that not only is in itself baffling (did Verdi and Dickens and Shakespeare and Chaplin and Frank Loesser work in young arts?) but suggests that it was only natural for the movies to pick up the forms they did. It *was* natural—anyway it happened fast enough—but not because movies were destined to popularity (they were at first no more popular than other forms of entertainment). In any case, popular arts are likely to pick up the forms and themes of high art for their material—popular theater naturally *burlesques*. And it means next to nothing to say that movies are young, because we do not know what the normal life span of an art is supposed to be, nor what would count as a unit of measure. Panofsky raises the question of the appropriateness of these original forms, but his answer is misleading.

> The legitmate paths of evolution [for the film] were opened, not by running away from the folk art character of the primitive film but by developing it within the limits of its own possibilities. Those primordial archetypes of film productions on the folk art level—success or retribution, sentiment, sensation, pornography, and crude humor—could blossom forth into genuine history, tragedy and romance, crime and adventure, and comedy, as soon as it was realized that they could be transfigured—not by an artifical injection of literary values but by the exploitation of the unique and specific possibilities of the new medium.

The instinct here is sound, but the region is full of traps. What are "the unique and specific possibilities of the new medium"? Panofsky defines them as dynamization of space and spatialization of time—that is, in a movie things move, and you can be moved instantaneously from anywhere to anywhere, and you can witness successively events happening at the same time. He speaks of these properties as "self-evident to the point of triviality" and, because of that, "easily forgotten or neglected." One hardly disputes this, or its importance. But we still do not understand what makes these properties "the possibilities of the medium." I am not now asking how one would know that these are *the* unique and specific possibilities (though I will soon get back to that); I am asking what it means to call them possibilities at all.

Why, for example, didn't the medium begin and remain in the condition of home movies, one shot just physically tacked on to another, cut and edited simply according to subject? (Newsreels essentially did, and they are nevertheless valuable, enough so to have justified the invention of moving pictures.) The answer seems obvious: narrative movies emerged because someone "saw the possibilities" of the medium—cutting and editing and taking shots at different distances from the subject. But again, these are mere actualities of film mechanics: every home movie and newsreel contains them. We could say: to make them "possibilities of the medium" is to realize what will give them *significance*—for example, the narrative and physical rhythms of melodrama, farce, American comedy of the 1930s. It is not as if filmmakers saw these possibilities and then looked for something to apply them to. It is truer to say that someone with the wish to make a movie saw that certain established forms would give point to certain properties of film.

This perhaps sounds like quibbling, but what it means is that the aesthetic possibilities of a medium are not givens. You can no more tell what will give significance to the unique and specific aesthetic possibilities of projecting photographic images by thinking about them or seeing some, than you can tell what will give significance to the possibilities of paint by thinking about paint or by looking some over. You have to think about painting, and paintings; you have to think about motion pictures. What does this "thinking about them" consist in? Whatever the useful criticism of an art consists in. (Painters before Jackson Pollock had dripped paint, even deliberately. Pollock made dripping into a medium of painting.) I feel like saying: The first successful movies—i.e., the first moving pictures accepted as motion pictures—were not applications of a medium that was defined by given possibilities, but the *creation of a medium* by their giving significance to specific possibilities. Only the art itself can discover its possibilities, and the discovery of a new possibility is the discovery of a new medium. A medium is something through which or by means of which something specific gets done or said in particular ways. It provides, one might say, particular ways to get through to someone, to make sense; in art, they are forms, like forms of speech. To discover ways of making sense is always a matter of the relation of an artist to his art, each discovering the other.

Panofsky uncharacteristically skips a step when he describes the early silent films as an "unknown language . . . forced upon a public not yet capable of reading it." His notion is (with good reason, writing when he did) of a few industrialists forcing their productions upon an addicted multitude. But from the beginning the language was not "unknown"; it was known to its creators, those who found themselves speaking it; and in the beginning there was no "public" in question; there were just some curious people. There soon was a public, but that just proves how easy the thing was to know. If we are to say that there was an "unknown" something, it was less like a language than like a fact—in particular, the fact that something is intelligible. So while it may be true, as Panofsky says, that "for a Saxon peasant of around 800 it was not easy to understand the meaning of a picture showing a man as he pours water over the head of another man," this has nothing special to do with the problems of a moviegoer. The meaning of that act of pouring in certain communities is still not easy to understand; it was and is impossible to understand for anyone to whom the practice of baptism is unknown. Why did Panofsky suppose that comparable understanding is essential, or uniquely important, to the reading of movies? Apparently he needed an explanation for the persistence in movies of "fixed iconography"—"the well-remembered types of the Vamp and the Straight Girl . . . the Family Man, and the Villain," characters whose conduct was "predetermined accordingly"—an explanation for the persistence of an obviously primitive or folkloristic element in a rapidly developing medium. For he goes on, otherwise inexplicably, to say that "devices like these became gradually less necessary as the public grew accustomed to interpret the action by itself and were virtually abolished by the invention of the talking film." In fact such devices persist as long as there are still Westerns and gangster films and comedies and musicals and romances. *Which* specific iconography the Villain is given will alter with the times, but that his iconography remains specific (i.e., operates according to a "fixed attitude and attribute" principle) seems undeniable: if Jack Palance in *Shane* is not a Villain, no honest home was ever in danger. Films have changed, but that is not because we don't need such explanations any longer; it is because we can't *accept* them.

These facts are accounted for by the actualities of the film medium itself: types are exactly what carry the forms movies have relied upon. These media created new types, or combinations and ironic reversals of types; but there they were, and stayed. Does this mean that movies can never create individuals, only types? What it means is that this is the movies' way of creating individuals: they create *individualities*. For what makes someone a type is not his similarity with other members of that type but his striking separateness from other people.

Until recently, types of black human beings were not created in film: black people were stereotypes—mammies, shiftless servants, loyal retainers, entertainers. We were not given, and were not in a position to be given, individualities that projected particular ways of inhabiting a social role; we recognized only the role. Occasionally the humanity behind the role would manifest itself; and the result was a revelation not of a human individuality, but of an entire realm of humanity becoming visible. When in *Gone With the Wind* Vivien Leigh, having counted on Butterfly McQueen's professed knowledge of midwifery, and finding her as ignorant as herself, slaps her in rage and terror, the moment can stun us with a question: What was the white girl assuming about blackness when she believed the casual claim of a black girl, younger and duller and more ignorant than herself, to know all about the mysteries of childbirth? The assumption, though apparently complimentary, is dehumanizing—with such creatures knowledge of the body comes from nowhere, and in general they are to be trusted absolutely or not at all, like lions in a cage, with whom you either do or do not know how to deal. After the slap, we are left with two young girls equally frightened in a humanly desperate situation, one limited by a distraction which expects and forgets that it is to be bullied, the other by an energetic resourcefulness which knows only how to bully. At the end of Michael Curtiz' *Breaking Point*, as the wounded John Garfield is carried from his boat to the dock, awaited by his wife and children and, just outside the circle, by the other woman in his life (Patricia Neal), the camera pulls away, holding on the still waiting child of his black partner who only the unconscious Garfield knows has been killed. The poignance of the silent and unnoticed black child overwhelms the yarn we had been shown. Is he supposed to symbolize the fact of general human isolation and abandonment? Or the fact that every action has consequences for innocent bystanders? Or that children are the real sufferers from the entangled efforts of adults to straighten out their lives? The effect here is to rebuke Garfield for attaching so much importance to the loss of his arm, and generally to blot out attention to individual suffering by invoking a massive social evil about which this film has nothing to say.

The general difference between a film type and a stage type is that the individuality captured on film naturally takes precedence over the social role in which that individuality gets expressed. Because on film social role appears arbitrary or incidental, movies have an inherent tendency toward the democratic, or anyway the idea of human equality. (But because of film's equally natural attraction to crowds, it has opposite tendencies toward the fascistic or populistic.) This depends upon recognizing film types as inhabited by figures we have met or may well meet in other circumstances. The recognized recurrence of film performers will become a central idea as we proceed. At the moment I am emphasizing only that in the case of black performers there was until recently no other place for them to recur in, except just the role within which we have already met them. For example, we would not have expected to see them as parents or siblings. I cannot at the moment remember a black person in a film making an ordinary purchase—say of a newspaper, or a ticket to a movie or for a train, let alone writing a check. (*Pinky* and *A Raisin in the Sun* prove the rule: in the former, the making of a purchase is a climactic scene in the film; in the latter, it provides the whole subject and structure.)

One recalls the list of stars of every magnitude who have provided the movie camera with human subjects—individuals capable of filling its need for individualities, whose individualities in turn, whose inflections of demeanor and disposition were given full play in its projection. They provided, and still provide, staples for impersonators: one gesture or syllable of mood, two strides, or a passing mannerism was enough to single them out from all other creatures. They realized the myth of singularity—that we can still be found, behind our disguises of bravado and cowardice, by someone, perhaps a god, capable of defeating our self-defeats. This was always more important than their distinction by beauty. Their singularity made them more like us—anyway, made their difference from us less a matter of metaphysics, to which we must accede, than a matter of responsibility, to which we must bend. But then that made them even more glamorous. That they should be able to stand upon their singularity! If one did that, one might be found, and called out, too soon, or at an inconvenient moment.

What was wrong with type-casting in films was not that it displaced some other, better principle of casting, but that factors irrelevant to film-making often influenced the particular figures chosen. Similarly, the familiar historical fact that there are movie cycles, taken by certain movie theorists as in itself a mark of unscrupulous commercialism, is a possibility internal to the medium; one could even say, it is the best emblem of the fact that a medium had been created. For a cycle is a genre (prison movies, Civil War movies, horror movies, etc.); and a genre is a medium.

As Hollywood developed, the original types ramified into individualities as various and subtle, as far-reaching in their capacities to inflect mood and release fantasy, as any set of characters who inhabited the great theaters of our world. We do not know them by such names of Pulcinella, Crispin, Harlequin, Pantaloon, the Doctor, the Captain, Columbine; we call them the Public Enemy, the Priest, James Cagney, Pat O'Brien, the Confederate Spy, the Army Scout, Randolph Scott, Gary Cooper, Gable, Paul Muni, the Reporter, the Sergeant, the Sheriff, the Deputy, the D.A., the Quack, the Shyster, the Other Woman, the Fallen Woman, the Moll, the Dance Hall Hostess. Hollywood was the theater in which they appeared, because the films of Hollywood constituted a world, with recurrent faces more familiar to me than the faces of the neighbors of all the places I have lived.

The great movie comedians—Chaplin, Keaton, W. C. Fields—form a set of types that could not have been adapted from any other medium. Its creation depended upon two conditions of the film medium mentioned earlier. These conditions seem to be necessities, not merely possibilities, so I will say that two necessities of the medium were discovered or expanded in the creation of these types. First, movie performers cannot project, but are projected. Second, photographs are of the world, in which human beings are not ontologically favored over the rest of nature, in which objects are not props but natural allies (or enemies) of the human character. The first necessity—projected visibility—permits the sublime comprehensibility of Chaplin's natural choreography; the second—ontological equality—permits his Proustian or Jamesian relationships with Murphy beds and flights of stairs and with vases on runners on tables on rollers: the heroism of momentary survival, Nietzsche's man as a tightrope across an abyss. These necessities permit not merely the locales of Keaton's extrications, but the philosophical mood of his countenance and the Olympic resourcefulness of his body; permit him to be perhaps the only constantly beautiful and continuously hilarious man ever seen, as though the ugliness in laughter should be redeemed. They permit Fields to mutter and suffer and curse obsessively, but heard and seen only by us; because his attributes are those of the gentleman (confident swagger and elegant manners, gloves, cane, outer heartiness), he can manifest continuously with the remorselessness of nature, the psychic brutalities of bourgeois civilization.

IDEAS OF ORIGIN

It is inevitable that in theorizing about film one at some point speculate about its origins, because despite its recentness, its origin remains obscure. The facts are well enough known about the invention and the inventors of the camera, and about improvements in fixing and then moving the image it captures. The problem is that the invention of the photographic picture is not the same thing as the creation of photography as a medium for making sense. The historical problem is like any other: a chronicle of the facts preceding the appearance of this technology does not explain why it happened when and as it did. Panofsky opens his study of film by remarking, "It was not an artistic urge that gave rise to the discovery and gradual perfection of a new technique; it was a technical invention that gave rise to the discovery and gradual perfection of a new art." We seem to understand this, but do we understand it? Panofsky assumes we know what it is that at any time has "given rise" to a "new art." He mentions an "artistic urge," but that is hardly a candidate to serve as an explanation; it would be about as useful as explaining the rise of modern science by appealing to "a scientific urge." There may be such urges, but they are themselves rather badly in need of explanation. Panofsky cites an artistic urge explicitly as the occasion for a new "technique." But the motion picture is not a new *technique*, any more than the airplane is. (What did we use to do that such a thing enables us to do better?) Yet some idea of flying, and an urge to do it, preceded the mechanical invention of the airplane. What is "given rise to" by such inventions as movable type or the microscope or the steam engine or the pianoforte?

It would be surprising if the history of the establishment of an artistic medium were less complex a problem for the historical understanding than (say) the rise of modern science. I take Bazin to be suggesting this when he reverses the apparent relation between the relevant technology and the idea of cinema, emphasizing that the idea preceded the technology, parts of it by centuries, and that parts of the technology preceded the invention of movies, some of it by centuries. So what has to be explained is not merely how the feat was technically accomplished but, for example, what stood in the way of its happening earlier. Surprisingly, Bazin, in the selection of essays I have read, does not include the contemporary condition of the related arts as a part of the ideological superstructure that elicited the new material basis of film. But it is certainly relevant that the burning issue during the latter half of the nineteenth century, in painting and in the novel and in the theater, was realism. And unless film captured possibilities opened up by the arts themselves, it is hard to imagine that its possibilities as an artistic medium would have shown up as, and as suddenly as, they did.

The idea of and wish for the world re-created in its own image was satisfied *at last* by cinema. Bazin calls this the myth of total cinema. But it had always been one of the myths of art; each of the arts had satisfied it in its own way. The mirror was in various hands held up to nature. In some ways it was more fully satisfied in theater. (Since theater is on the whole not now a major art for us, it on the whole no longer makes contact with its historical and psychological sources; so we are rarely gripped by the trauma we must once have suffered when the leader of the chorus stopped contributing to a narrative or song and turned to face the others, suffering incarnation.)

What is cinema's way of satisfying the myth? Automatically, we said. But what does that mean—mean mythically, as it were? It means satisfying it without *my* having to do anything, satisfying it *by* wishing. In a word, *magically*. I have found myself asking: How could film be art, since all the major arts arise in some way out of religion? Now I can answer: Because movies arise out of magic; from *below* the world.

The better a film, the more it makes contact with this source of its inspiration; it never wholly loses touch with the magic lantern behind it. This suggests why movies of the fantastic (*The Cabinet of Dr. Caligari, Blood of a Poet*) and filmed scenes of magic (say, materialization and dematerialization), while they have provided moods and devices, have never established themselves as cinematic media, however strongly this "possibility" is suggested by the physical medium of film: they are technically and psychologically trivial compared with the medium of magic itself. It is otherwise if the presented magic is itself made technically or physically interesting (*The Invisible Man, Dr. Jekyll and Mr. Hyde, Frankenstein, 2001: A Space Odyssey*), but then that becomes another way of confirming the physicality of our world. Science presents itself, in movies, as magic, which was indeed one source of science. In particular, projected science retains magic's mystery and forbiddenness. Science-fiction films exploit not merely certain obvious aspects of adventure, and of a physicality that special effects specialize in, but also the terrific mumbo-jumbo of hearsay science: "My God, the thing is impervious to the negative beta ray! We must reverse the atom recalcitration spatter, before it's too late!" The dialogue has the surface of those tinbox-and-lever contraptions that were sufficiently convincing in prime *Flash Gordon*. These films are carried by the immediacy of the fantasy that motivates them (say, destruction by lower or higher forms of life, as though the precariousness of human life is due to its biological stage of development); together with the myth of the one way and last chance in which the (external) danger can be averted. And certainly the beauty of forms and motions in

Frankenstein's laboratory is essential to the success of *Frankenstein*; computers seem primitive in comparison. It always made more sense to steal from God than to try to outwit him.

How do movies reproduce the world magically? Not by literally presenting us with the world, but by permitting us to view it unseen. This is not a wish for power over creation (as Pygmalion's was), but a wish not to need power, not to have to bear its burdens. It is, in this sense, the reverse of the myth of Faust. And the wish for invisibility is old enough. Gods have profited from it, and Plato tells it at the end of the *Republic* as the Myth of the Ring of Gyges. In viewing films, the sense of invisibility is an expression of modern privacy or anonymity. It is as though the world's projection explains our forms of unknownness and of our ability to know. The explanation is not so much that the world is passing us by, as that we are displaced from our natural habitation within it, placed at a distance from it. The screen overcomes our fixed distance; it makes displacement appear as our natural condition.

1971

SERGEI EISENSTEIN, VSEVOLOD PUDOVKIN, AND GRIGORI ALEXANDROV
STATEMENT ON SOUND

Co-author of the following selection with Sergei Eisenstein and V. I. Pudovkin, Grigori Alexandrov (1903–1983) was part of Russian theatre and film from an early age. Road manager of a traveling theatre group during World War I, he later worked with Eisenstein at the Prolekult Theatre and collaborated with him as a writer on *Strike* (1925) and co-director on *October* (1928). His first film as solo director, also working with Eisenstein was *Romance Sentimentale* (1930), after which he made many films, primarily musicals and comedies, replacing Eisenstein as artistic director of Mosfilm in 1944.

Our cherished dreams of a sound cinema are being realised. The Americans, having developed the technique of sound cinema, have embarked on the first stage towards its rapid practical implementation. Germany is working intensively in the same direction. The whole world now speaks of the 'silent' that has found its voice.

We who work in the USSR recognise that, given our technical capabilities, the practical implementation of sound cinema is not feasible in the near future. At the same time we consider it opportune to make a statement on a number of prerequisite theoretical principles, particularly as, according to reports reaching us, attempts are being made to use this new improvement in cinema for the wrong purposes. In addition, an incorrect understanding of the potential of the new technical invention might not only hinder the development and improvement of cinema as an art form but might also threaten to destroy all its formal achievements to date.

Contemporary cinema, operating through visual images, has a powerful effect on the individual and rightfully occupies one of the leading positions in the ranks of the arts.

It is well known that the principal (and sole) method which has led cinema to a position of such great influence is *montage*. The confirmation of montage as the principal means of influence has become the indisputable axiom upon which world cinema culture rests.

The success of Soviet pictures on world screens is to a significant extent the result of a number of those concepts of montage which they first revealed and asserted.

And so for the further development of cinema the significant features appear to be those that strengthen and broaden the montage methods of influencing the audience. If we examine every new discovery from this standpoint it is easy to distinguish the insignificance of colour and stereoscopic cinema in comparison with the great significance of *sound*.

Sound is a double-edged invention and its most probable application will be along the line of least resistance, i.e., in the field of the *satisfaction of simple curiosity*.

In the first place there will be commercial exploitation of the most saleable goods, i.e., of *talking pictures*—those in which the sound is recorded in a natural manner, synchronising exactly with the movement on the screen and creating a certain 'illusion' of people talking, objects making a noise, etc.

The first period of sensations will not harm the development of the new art; the danger comes with the second period, accompanied by the loss of innocence and purity of the initial concept of cinema's new textural possibilities can only intensify its unimaginative use for 'dramas of high culture' and other photographed presentations of a theatrical order.

Sound used in this way will destroy the culture of montage, because every mere *addition* of sound to montage fragments increases their inertia as such and their independent significance; this is undoubtedly detrimental to montage which operates above all not with fragments but through the *juxtaposition* of fragments.

Only the contrapuntal use of sound vis-à-vis the visual fragment of montage will open up new possibilities for the development and perfection of montage.

The first experiments in sound must aim at a sharp discord with the visual images. Only such a 'hammer and tongs' approach will produce the necessary sensation that will result consequently in the creation of a new *orchestral counterpoint* of visual and sound images.

The new technical discovery is not a passing moment in the history of cinema but an organic escape for cinema's cultural avant-garde from a whole series of blind alleys which have appeared inescapable.

We must regard as *the first blind alley* the intertitle and all the vain attempts to integrate it into montage composition as a unit of montage (fragmentation of an intertitle, magnification or contraction of the lettering, etc.).

The second blind alley comprises *explanatory* sequences (e.g., long shots) which complicate the composition of the montage and slow down the rhythm.

Every day the problems of theme and plot grow more complex; attempts to solve them by methods of purely 'visual' montage either lead to insoluble problems or involve the director in fantastic montage constructions, provoking a fear of abstruseness and reactionary decadence.

Sound, treated as a new element of montage (as an independent variable combined with the visual image), cannot fail to provide new and enormously powerful means of expressing and resolving the most complex problems, which have been depressing us with their insurmountability using the imperfect methods of a cinema operating only in visual images.

The *contrapuntal method* of structuring a sound film not only does not weaken *the international nature of cinema* but gives to its meaning unparalleled strength and cultural heights.

With this method of construction the sound film will not be imprisoned within national markets, as has happened with the theatrical play and will happen with the 'filmed' play, but will provide an even greater opportunity than before of speeding the idea contained in a film throughout the whole globe, preserving its world-wide viability.

1928

MARY ANN DOANE
THE VOICE IN THE CINEMA: THE ARTICULATION OF BODY AND SPACE

Currently George Hazard Crooker Professor of Modern Culture and Media at Brown University, Mary Ann Doane has written about film theory, feminist theory, cultural studies, and semiotics. *Femmes Fatales: Feminism, Film Theory, Psychoanalysis* (1991) examined the cinematic gaze and the female spectator. In it, she explores the object and subject positions available to the female viewer and the limits of identification and desire when faced with a medium that, she argues, following Laura Mulvey, presupposes a male gaze. In *The Emergence of Cinematic Time: Modernity, Contingency, the Archive* (2002) she explores the impact of film on the understanding and structuring of time in modern culture due to the medium's emergence in an era of changing scientific theory and advancing capitalistic control of time and the human body. Doane's recent work examines photography, digital media, and the phenomenological impact of the close-up on the modern spectator.

SYNCHRONIZATION

The silent film is certainly understood, at least retrospectively and even (it is arguable) in its time, as incomplete, as lacking speech. The stylized gestures of the silent cinema, its heavy pantomime, have been defined as a form of compensation for that lack. Hugo Münsterberg wrote, in 1916, "To the actor of the moving pictures ... the temptation offers itself to overcome the deficiency [the absence of "words and the modulation of the voice"] by a heightening of the gestures and of the facial play, with the result that the emotional expression becomes exaggerated."[1] The absent voice reemerges in gestures and the contortions of the face—it is spread over the body of the actor. The uncanny effect of the silent film in the era of sound is in part linked to the separation, by means of intertitles, of an actor's speech from the image of his/her body.

Consideration of sound in the cinema (in its most historically and institutionally privileged form—that of dialogue or the use of the voice) engenders a network of metaphors whose nodal point appears to be the body. One may readily respond that this is only "natural"—who can conceive of a voice without

---

[1] Hugo Munsterberg, *The Film: A Psychology Study* (New York: Dover, 1970), p. 49.

a body?[2] However, the body reconstituted by the technology and practices of the cinema is a *phantasmatic* body, which offers a support as well as a point of identification for the subject addressed by the film. The purpose of this essay is simply to trace some of the ways in which this phantasmatic body acts as a pivot for certain cinematic practices of representation and authorizes and sustains a limited number of relationships between voice and image.

The attributes of this phantasmatic body are first and foremost unity (through the emphasis on a coherence of the senses) and presence-to-itself. The addition of sound to the cinema introduces the possibility of representing a fuller (and organically unified) body, and of confirming the status of speech as an individual property right. The potential number and kinds of articulations between sound and image are reduced by the very name attached to the new heterogeneous medium—the "talkie." Histories of the cinema ascribe the stress on synchronization to a "public demand"; "the public, fascinated by the novelty, wanting to be sure they were hearing what they saw, would have felt that a trick was being played on them if they were not shown the words coming from the lips of the actors."[3] In Lewis Jacobs' account, this fear on the part of the audience of being "cheated" is one of the factors which initially limits the deployment of sonorous material (as well as the mobility of the camera). From this perspective, the use of voice-off or voice over must be a late acquisition, attempted only after a certain "breaking-in" period during which the novelty of the sound film was allowed to wear itself out. But, whatever the fascination of the new medium (or whatever meaning is attached to it by retrospective readings of its prehistory), there is no doubt that synchronization (in the form of "lip-sync") has played a major role in the dominant narrative cinema. Technology standardizes the relation through the development of the synchronizer, the Moviola, the flatbed editing table. The mixing apparatus allows a greater control over the establishment of relationships between dialogue, music, and sound effects and, in practice, the level of the dialogue generally determines the levels of sound effects and music.[4] Despite a number of experiments with other types of sound/image relationships (those of Clair, Lang, Vigo, and more recently, Godard, Straub, and Duras), synchronous dialogue remains the dominant form of sonorous representation in the cinema.

---

[2] Two kinds of "voices without bodies" immediately suggest themselves—one theological, the other scientific (two poles which, it might be added, are not ideologically unrelated): (1) the voice of God incarnated in the Word; (2) the artificial voice of a computer. Neither seems to be capable of representation outside a certain anthropomorphism, however. God is pictured, in fact, as having a quite specific body—that of a male patriarchal figure. *Star Wars* and *Battlestar Galactica* illustrate the tendencies toward anthropomorphism in the depiction of computers. In the latter, even a computer (named Cora) deprived of mobility and the simulacrum of a human form, is given a voice which is designed to evoke the image of a sensual female body.

[3] Lewis Jacobs, *The Rise of the American Film: A Critical History* (New York: Teachers College Press, 1968), p. 435.

[4] For a more detailed discussion of this hierarchy of sounds and of other relevant techniques in the construction of the sound track, see M. Doane, "Ideology and the Practices of Sound Editing and Mixing," paper delivered at Milwaukee Conference on the Cinematic Apparatus, February, 1978, published in *The Cinematic Apparatus*, ed. Teresa de Lauretis and Stephen Heath (Bloomington: Indiana University Press; London: Macmillan, 1984).

Yet, even when asynchronous or "wild" sound is utilized, the phantasmatic body's attribute of unity is not lost. It is simply displaced—the body *in* the film becomes the body *of* the film. It senses work in tandem, for the combination of sound and image is described in terms of "totality" and the "organic."[5] Sound carries with it the potential risk of exposing the material heterogeneity of the medium; attempts to contain that risk surface in the language of the ideology or organic unity. In the discourse of technicians, sound is "married" to the image and, as one sound engineer puts it in an article on post-synchronization, "one of the basic goals of the motion picture industry is to make the screen look alive in the eyes of the audience. . ."[6]

Concomitant with the demand for a lifelike representation is the desire for "presence," a concept which is not specific to the cinematic sound track but which acts as a standard to measure quality in the sound recording industry as a whole. The term "presence" offers a certain legitimacy to the wish for pure reproduction and becomes a selling point in the construction of sound as a commodity. The television commercial asks whether we can "tell the difference" between the voice of Ella Fitzgerald and that of Memorex (and since our representative in the commercial— the ardent fan—cannot, the only conclusion to be drawn is that owning a Memorex tape is equivalent to having Ella in your living room). Technical advances in sound recording (such as the Dolby system) are aimed at diminishing the noise of the system, concealing the work of the apparatus, and thus reducing the distance perceived between the object and its representation. The maneuvers of the sound recording industry offer evidence which support Walter Benjamin's thesis linking mechanical reproduction as a phenomenon with contemporary society's destruction of the "aura" (which he defines as "the unique phenomenon of a distance, however close it may be").[7] According to Benjamin,

> [the] contemporary decay of the aura . . . rests on two circumstances, both of which are related to the increasing significance of the masses in contemporary life. Namely, the desire of contemporary masses to bring things "closer" spatially and humanly, which is just as ardent as their bent toward overcoming the uniqueness of every reality by accepting its reproduction.[8]

Nevertheless, while the desire to bring things closer is certainly exploited in making sound marketable, the qualities of uniqueness and authenticity are not sacrificed— it is not any voice which the tape brings to the consumer but the voice of Ella Fitzgerald. The voice is not detachable from a body which is quite specific—that of the star. In the cinema, cult value and the "aura" resurface in the star system. In 1930 a writer feels the need to assure audiences that post-synchronization as a technique does not necessarily entail substituting an alien voice for a "real" voice, that the industry does not condone a mismatching of voices and bodies.[9] Thus, the voice

---

[5]Ibid.

[6]W. A. Pozner, "Synchronization Techniques," *Journal of the Society of Motion Picture Engineers* 47, no. 3(September 1946): 191.

[7]Walter Benjamin, "The Work of Art in the Age of Mechanical Reproduction," an *Illuminations*, ed. Hannah Arendt, trans. Harry Zohn (New York: Schocken, 1969), p. 222.

[8]Ibid., p. 223.

[9]George Lewin, "Dubbing and Its Relation to Sound Picture Production," *Journal of the Society of Motion Picture Engineers* 16,no.1(January 1931): 48.

serves as a support for the spectator's recognition and his/her identification of, as well as with, the star.

Just as the voice must be anchored by a given body, the body must be anchored in a given space. The phantasmatic visual space which the film constructs is supplemented by techniques designed to spatialize the voice, to localize it, give it depth, and thus lend to the characters the consistency of the real. A concern for room tone, reverberation characteristics, and sound perspective manifests a desire to recreate, as one sound editor describes it, "the bouquet that surrounds the words, the presence of the voice, the way it fits in with the physical environment."[10] The dangers of post-synchronization and looping stem from the fact that the voice is disengaged from its "proper" space (the space conveyed by the visual image) and the credibility of that voice depends upon the technician's ability to return it to the side of its origin. Failure to do so risks exposure of the fact that looping is "narration masking as dialogue."[11] Dialogue is defined, therefore, not simply in terms of the establishment of an I-you relationship but as the necessary spatializing of that relationship. Techniques of sound recording tend to confirm the cinema's function as a *mise-en-scène* of bodies.

VOICE-OFF AND VOICEOVER

The spatial dimension which monophonic sound is capable of simulating is that of depth—the apparent source of the sound may be moved forward or backward, but the lateral dimension is lacking due to the fact that there is no sideways spread of reverberation or of ambient noise.[12] Nevertheless, sound/image relationships established in the narrative film work to suggest that sound does, indeed, issue from that other dimension. In film theory, this work to provide the effect of a lateral dimension receives recognition in the term "voice-off." "Voice-off" refers to instances in which we hear the voice of a character who is not visible within the frame. Yet the film establishes, by means of previous shots or other contextual determinants, the character's "presence" in the space of the scene, in the diegesis. He/she is "just over there," just beyond the frameline, in a space which "exists" but which the camera does not choose to show. The traditional use of voice-off constitutes a denial of the frame as a limit and an affirmation of the unity and homogeneity of the depicted space.

Because it is defined in terms of what is visible within the rectangular space of the screen, the term "voice-off" has been subject to some dispute. Claude Bailblé, for instance, argues that a voice-off must always be a "voice-in" because the literal source of the sound in the theater is always the speaker placed behind the screen.[13]

---

[10]Walter Murch, "The Art of the Sound Editor: An Interview with Walter Murch," interview by Larry Sturhahn, *Filmmaker's Newsletter* 8, no.2 (December 1974): 23.

[11]Ibid.

[12]Stereo reduces this problem but does not solve it—the range of perspective effects is still limited. Much of the discussion which follows is based on the use of monophonic sound, but also has implications for stereo. In both mono and stereo, for instance, the location of the speakers is designed to ensure that the audience hears sound "which is roughly coincident with the image." See Alec Nisbett, *The Technique of the Sound Studio* (New York: Focal Press Limited, 1972), pp. 530, 532.

[13]C. Bailblé, "Programmation de L'écoute (2)," *Cahiers du cinéma*, no. 293 (October 1978): 9.

Yet, the space to which the term refers is not that of the theater but the fictional space of the diegesis. Nevertheless, the use of the term is based on the requirement that the two spaces coincide, "overlap" to a certain extent. For the screen limits what *can be seen* of the diegesis (there is always "more" of the diegesis than the camera can cover at any one time). The placement of the speaker behind the screen simply confirms the fact that the cinematic apparatus is designed to promote the impression of a homogeneous space—the senses of the phantasmatic body cannot be split. The screen is the space where the image is deployed, while the theater as a whole is the space of the deployment of sound. Yet, the screen is given precedence over the acoustical space of the theater—the screen is posited as the site of the spectacle's unfolding and all sounds must emanate from it. (Bailblé asks, "What would be, in effect, a voice-off which came from the back of the theater? Poor little screen . . ."[14]—in other words, its effect would be precisely to diminish the epistemological power of the image, to reveal its limitations.)

The hierarchical placement of the visible above the audible, according to Christian Metz, is not specific to the cinema but a more general cultural production.[15] And the term voice-off merely acts as a reconfirmation of that hierarchy. For it only appears to describe a sound—what it really refers to is the visibility (or lack of visibility) of the source of the sound. Metz argues that sound is never "off." While a visual element specified as "off" actually lacks visibility, a "sound-off" is always audible.

Despite the fact that Metz's argument is valid and we tend to repeat on the level of theory the industry's subordination of sound to image, the term/"voice-off" does name a particular relationship between sound and image—a relationship which has been extremely important historically in diverse film practices. While it is true that sound is almost always discussed with reference to the image, it does not necessarily follow that this automatically makes sound subordinate. From another perspective, it is doubtful that any image (in the sound film) is uninflected by sound. This is crucially so, give the fact that in the dominant narrative cinema, sound extends from beginning to end of the film—sound is never absent (silence is, at the least, room tone). In fact, the lack of any sound whatsoever is taboo in the editing of the sound track.

The point is not that we need terms with which to describe, honor, and acknowledge the autonomy of a particular sensory material, but that we must attempt to think the heterogeneity of the cinema. This might be done more fruitfully by means of the concept of space than through the unities of sound and image. In the cinematic situation, three types of space are put into play:

(1) The space of the diegesis. This space has no physical limits; it is not contained or measurable. It is a virtual space constructed by the film and is delineated as having both audible and visible traits (as well as implications that its objects can be touched, smelled, and tasted).

(2) The visible space of the screen as receptor of the image. It is measurable and "contains" the visible signifiers of the film. Strictly speaking, the screen is not audible although the placement of the speaker behind the screen constructs that illusion.

---

[14]Ibid. My translation.
[15]C. Metz, "Le Perçu et le nommé," in *Essais sémiotiques* (Paris: Klincksieck, 1977), pp. 153–59.

(3) The acoustical space of the theater or auditorium. It might be argued that this space is also visible, but the film cannot visually activate signifiers in this space unless a second projector is used. Again, despite the fact that the speaker is behind the screen and therefore sound appears to be emanating from a focused point, sound is not "framed" in the same way as the image. In a sense, it *envelops* the spectator.

All these are spaces *for the spectator*, but the first is the only space which the characters of the fiction film can acknowledge (for the characters there are no voices-off). Different cinematic modes—documentary, narrative, avant-garde—establish different relationships between the three spaces. The classical narrative film, for instance, works to deny the existence of the last two spaces in order to buttress the credibility (legitimacy) of the first space. If a character looks at and speaks to the spectator, this constitutes an acknowledgment that the character is seen and heard in a radically different space and is therefore generally read as transgressive.

Nothing unites the three spaces but the signifying practice of the film itself, together with the institutionalization of the theater as a type of metaspace which binds together the three spaces, as the *place* where a unified cinematic discourse unfolds. The cinematic institution's stake in this process of unification is apparent. Instances of voice-off in the classical film are particularly interesting examples of the way in which the three spaces undergo an elaborate imbrication. For the phenomenon of the voice-off cannot be understood outside a consideration of the relationships established between the diegesis, the visible space of the screen, *and* the acoustical space of the theater. The place in which the signifier manifests itself is the acoustical space of the theater, but this is the space with which it is least concerned. The voice-off deepens the diegesis, gives it an extent which exceeds that of the image, and thus supports the claim that there is a space in the fictional world which the camera does not register. In its own way, it *accounts for* lost space. The voice-off is a sound which is first and foremost in the service of the film's construction of space and only indirectly in the service of the image. It validates both what the screen reveals of the diegesis and what it conceals.

Nevertheless, the use of the voice-off always entails a risk—that of exposing the material heterogeneity of the cinema. Synchronous sound masks the problem and this at least partially explains its dominance. But the more interesting question, perhaps, is: how can the classical film allow the representation of a voice whose source is not simultaneously represented? As soon as the sound is detached from its source, no longer anchored by a represented body, its potential work as a signifier is revealed. There is always something uncanny about a voice which emanates from a source outside the frame. However, as Pascal Bonitzer points out, the narrative film exploits the marginal anxiety connected with the voice-offs by incorporating its disturbing effects within the dramatic framework. Thus, the function of the voice-off (as well as that of the voiceover) becomes extremely important in *film noir*. Bonitzer takes as his example *Kiss Me Deadly*, a *film noir* in which the villain remains out of frame until the last sequences of the film. Maintaining him outside of the field of vision "gives to his sententious voice, swollen by mythological comparisons, a greater power of disturbing, the scope of an oracle—dark prophet of the end of the world. And, in spite of that, his voice is submitted to the destiny of the body ... a shot, he falls—and with him in ridicule, his discourse with its prophetic accents."[16]

The voice-off is always "submitted to the destiny of the body" because it *belongs* to a character who is confined to the space of the diegesis, if not to the visible space of the screen. Its efficacy rests on the knowledge that the character can easily be made visible by a slight reframing which would reunite the voice and its source. The body acts as an invisible support for the use of both the voiceover during a flashback and the interior monologue as well. Although the voiceover in a flashback effects a temporal dislocation of the voice with respect to the body, the voice is frequently returned to the body as a form of narrative closure. Furthermore, the voiceover very often simply initiates the story and is subsequently superseded by synchronous dialogue, allowing the diegesis to "speak for itself." In *Sunset Boulevard* the convention is taken to its limits: the voiceover narration is, indeed, linked to a body (that of the hero), but it is the body of a dead man.

In the interior monologue, on the other hand, the voice and the body are represented simultaneously, but the voice, far from being an extension of that body, manifests its inner lining. The voice displays what is inaccessible to the image, what exceeds the visible: the "inner life" of the character. The voice here is the privileged mark of interiority, turning the body "inside out."

The voiceover commentary in the documentary, unlike the voice-off, the voiceover during a flashback, or the interior monologue, is, in effect, a *disembodied* voice. While the latter three voices work to affirm the homogeneity and dominance of diegetic space, the voiceover commentary is necessarily presented as outside that space. It is its radical otherness with respect to the diegesis which endows this voice with a certain authority. As a form of direct address, it speaks without mediation to the audience, bypassing the "characters" and establishing a complicity between itself and the spectator—together they understand and thus *place* the image. It is precisely because the voice is not localizable, because it cannot be yoked to a body, that it is capable of interpreting the image, producing its truth. Disembodied, lacking any specification in space or time, the voiceover is, as Bonitzer points out, beyond criticism—it censors the questions "Who is speaking?" "Where?" "In what time?" and "For whom?"

> This is not, one suspects, without ideological implications. The first of these implications is that the voice-off[17] represents a power, that of disposing of the image and of what it reflects, from a space absolutely *other* with respect to that inscribed in the image-track. *Absolutely other and absolutely indeterminant.* Because it rises from the field of the Other, the voice-off is assumed to know: this is the essence of its power ... The power of the voice is a stolen power, a usurpation.[18]

In the history of the documentary, this voice has been for the most part that of the male, and its power resides in the possession of knowledge and in the privileged,

---

[16]Pascal Bonitzer, "Les Silences de la voix," *Cahiers du cinéma,* (February–March 1975): p. no. 256, 25. My translation.

[17]Bonitzer uses the term "voice-off" in a general sense which includes both voice-off and voiceover, but here he is referring specifically to voiceover commentary.

[18]Bonitzer, "Les Silences," p. 26. My translation.

unquestioned activity of interpretation. This function of the voiceover has been appropriated by the television documentary and television news programs, in which sound carries the burden of "information" while the impoverished image simply fills the screen. Even when the major voice is explicitly linked with a body (that of the anchorman in television news), this body, in its turn, is situated in the nonspace of the studio. In film, on the other hand, the voiceover is quite often dissociated from any specific figure. The guarantee of knowledge, in such a system, lies in its irreducibility to the spatiotemporal limitations of the body.

THE PLEASURE OF HEARING

The means by which sound is deployed in the cinema implicate the spectator in a particular textual problematic—they establish certain conditions for understanding which obtain in the "intersubjective relation" between film and spectator. The voiceover commentary and, differently, the interior monologue and voiceover flash back speak more or less *directly* to the spectator, constituting him/her as an empty space to be "filled" with knowledge about events, character psychology, etc. More frequently, in the fiction film, the use of synchronous dialogue and the voice-off pre suppose a spectator who *overhears* and, overhearing, is unheard and unseen himself. This activity with respect to the sound track is not unlike the voyeurism often exploited by the cinematic image. In any event, the use of the voice in the cinema appeals to the spectator's desire to hear, or what Lacan refers to as the invocatory drive.

In what does the pleasure of hearing consist? Beyond the added effect of "realism" which sound gives to the cinema, beyond its supplement of meaning anchored by intelligible dialogue, what is the specificity of the pleasure of hearing a voice with its elements escaping a strictly verbal codification—volume, rhythm, timbre, pitch? Psychoanalysis situates pleasure in the divergence between the present experience and the memory of satisfaction: "Between a (more or less inaccessible) memory and a very precise (and localizable) immediacy of perception is opened the gap where pleasure is produced."[19] Memories of the first experiences of the voice, of the hallucinatory satisfaction it offered, circumscribe the pleasure of hearing and ground its relation to the phantasmatic body. This is not simply to situate the experiences of infancy as the sole determinant in a system directly linking cause and effect but to acknowledge that the traces of archaic desires are never annihilated. According to Guy Rosolato, it is "the organization of the fantasm itself which implies a permanence, an insistence of the recall to the origin."[20]

Space, for the child, is defined initially in terms of the audible, not the visible: "It is only in a second phase that the organization of visual space insures the perception of the object as *external*" (p. 80). The first differences are traced along the

---

[19] Serge Leclaire, *Démasquer le réel*, p. 64, quoted in C. Bailblé, "Programmation de l'écoute (3)," *Cahiers du cinéma*, no. 297 (February 1979), 46.

[20] Guy Rosolato, "La Voix: entre corps et langage," *Revue française de psychoanalyse* (January 1974), 38:83. My translation. My discussion of the pleasure of hearing relies heavily on the work of Rosolato. Further references to this article will appear in parentheses in the text.

axis of sound: the voice of the mother, the voice of the father. Furthermore, the voice has a greater command over space than the look—one can hear around corners, through walls. Thus, for the child the voice, even before language, is the instrument of demand. In the construction/hallucination of space and the body's relation to that space, the voice plays a major role. In comparison with sight, as Rosolato points out, the voice is reversible: sound is simultaneously emitted and heard, by the subject himself. As opposed to the situation in seeing, it is as if "an 'acoustical' mirror were always in function. Thus, the images of entry and exit relative to the body are intimately articulated. They can therefore be confounded, inverted, favored one over the other" (p. 79). Because one can hear sounds behind oneself as well as those with sources *inside* the body (sounds of digestion, circulation, respiration, etc.), two sets of terms are placed in opposition: exterior/front/sight and interior/back/hearing. And "hallucinations are determined by an imaginary structuration of the body according to these oppositions . . ." (p. 80). The voice appears to lend itself to hallucination, in particular the hallucination of power over space effected by an extension or restructuration of the body. Thus, as Lacan points out, our mass media and our technology, as mechanical extensions of the body, result in "planeterizing" or "even stratospherizing" the voice.[21]

The voice also traces the forms of unity and separation *between* bodies. The mother's soothing voice, in a particular cultural context, is a major component of the "sonorous envelope" which surrounds the child and is the first model of auditory pleasure. An image of corporeal unity is derived from the realization that the production of sound by the voice and its audition coincide. The imaginary fusion of the child with the mother is supported by the recognition of common traits characterizing the different voices and, more particularly, of their potential for harmony. According to Rosolato, the voice in music makes appeal to the nostalgia for such an imaginary cohesion, for a "veritable incantation" of bodies.

> The harmonic and polyphonic unfolding in music can be understood as a succession of tensions and releases, of unifications and divergences between parts which are gradually stacked, opposed in successive chords only to be resolved ultimately into their simplest unity. It is therefore the entire dramatization of separated bodies and their reunion which harmony supports. (p. 82)

Yet, the imaginary unity is associated with the earliest experience of the voice is broken by the premonition of difference, division, effected by the intervention of the father whose voice, engaging the desire of the mother, acts as the agent of separation and constitutes the voice of the mother as the irretrievably lost object of desire. The voice in this instance, far from being the narcissistic measure of harmony, is the voice of interdiction. The voice thus understood is an interface of imaginary and symbolic, pulling at once toward the signifying organization of language and its reduction of the range of vocal sounds to those it binds and codifies, and toward original and imaginary attachments, "representable in the fantasm by the body, or by the corporeal mother, the child at her breast" (p. 86).

---

[21] Jacques Lacan, *The Four Fundamental Concepts of Psycho-Analysis*, ed. Jacques-Alain Miller, trans. Alan Sheridan (London: Hogarth Press and the Institute of Psycho-Analysis, 1977), p. 274.

At the cinema, the sonorous envelope provided by the theatrical space together with techniques employed in the construction of the sound track work to sustain the narcissistic pleasure derived from the image of a certain unity, cohesion, and hence, an identity grounded by the spectator's phantasmatic relation to his/her own body. The aural illusion of position constructed by the approximation of sound perspective and by techniques which spatialize the voice and endow it with "presence" guarantees the singularity and stability of a point of audition, thus holding at bay the potential trauma of dispersal, dismemberment, difference. The subordination of the voice to the screen as the site of the spectacle's unfolding makes vision and hearing work together in manufacturing the "hallucination" of a fully sensory world. Nevertheless, the recorded voice, which presupposes a certain depth, is in contradiction with the flatness of the two-dimensional image. Eisler and Adorno note that the spectator is always aware of this divergence, of the inevitable gap between the represented body and its voice. And for Eisler and Adorno this partially explains the function of film music: first used in the exhibition of silent films to conceal the noise of the projector (to hide from the spectator the "uncanny" fact that his/her pleasure is mediated by a machine), music in the "talkie" takes on the task of closing the gap between voice and body.[22]

If this imaginary harmony is to be maintained, however, the potential aggressivity of the voice (as the instrument of interdiction and the material support of the symptom—hearing voices—in paranoia) must be attenuated. The formal perfection of sound recording in the cinema consists in reducing not only the noise of the apparatus but any "grating" noise which is not "pleasing to the ear." On another level, the aggressivity of the filmic voice can be linked to the fact that sound is directed *at* the spectator—necessitating, in the fiction film, its deflection through dialogue (which the spectator is given only obliquely, to overhear) and, in the documentary, its mediation by the content of the image. In the documentary, however, the voiceover has come to represent an authority and an aggressivity which can no longer be sustained—thus, as Bonitzer points out, the proliferation of new documentaries which reject the absolute of the voiceover and, instead, claim to establish a democratic system, "letting the event speak for itself." Yet, what this type of film actually promotes is the illusion that reality speaks and is not spoken, that the film is not a constructed discourse. In effecting an "impression of knowledge," a knowledge which is given and not produced, the film conceals its own work and posits itself as a voice without a subject.[23] The voice is even more powerful in silence. The solution, then, is not to banish the voice but to construct *another* politics.

THE POLITICS OF THE VOICE

The cinema presents a spectacle composed of disparate elements—images, voices, sound effects, music, writing—which the *mise-en-scène*, in its broadest sense, organizes and aims at the body of the spectator, sensory receptacle of the various stimuli.

---

[22]Hanns Eisler, *Composing for the Films* (New York: Oxford University Press, 1947), pp. 75–77.
[23]Bonitzer, "Les Silences," pp. 23–24.

This is why Lyotard refers to classical *mise-en-scène* (in both the theater and the cinema) as a kind of somatography, or inscription on the body:

> The mise-en-scène turns written signifiers into speech, song, and movements executed by bodies capable of moving, singing, speaking; and this transcription is intended for other living bodies—the spectators—capable of being moved by these songs, movements, and words. It is this transcribing on and for bodies, considered as multi-sensory potentialities, which is the work characteristic of the mise-en-scène. Its elementary unity is polyesthetic like the human body: capacity to see, to hear, to touch, to move. . . . The idea of performance . . . even if it remains vague, seems linked to the idea of inscription on the body.[24]

Classical *mise-en-scène* has a stake in perpetuating the image of unity and identity sustained by this body and in staving off the fear of fragmentation. The different sensory elements work in collusion, and this work denies the material heterogeneity of the "body" of the film. All the signifying strategies for the deployment of the voice discussed earlier are linked with such homogenizing effects: synchronization binds the voice to a body in a unity whose immediacy can only be perceived as a given; the voice-off holds the spectacle to a space—extended but still coherent; and the voiceover commentary places the image by endowing it with a clear intelligibility. In all of this, what must be guarded is a certain "oneness."

The "oneness" is the mark of a mastery and a control and manifests itself most explicitly in the tendency to confine the voiceover commentary in the documentary to a single voice. For, according to Bonitzer, "when one divides that voice or, what amounts to the same things, multiplies it, the system and its effects change. Off-screen space ceases to be that place of reserve and interiority of the voice. . . ."[25] This entails not only or not merely increasing the number of voices but radically changing their relationship to the image, effecting a disjunction between sound and meaning, emphasizing what Barthes refers to as the "grain" of the voice[26] over and against its expressivity or power of representation. In the contemporary cinema, the names which immediately come to mind are those of Godard (who, even in an early film such as *Vivre Sa Vie* which relies heavily upon synchronous sound, resists the homogenizing effects of the traditional use of voice-off by means of a resolute avoidance of the shot/reverse shot structure—the camera quickly panning to keep the person talking *in frame*) and Straub (for whom the voice and sound in general become the marks of a nonprogressive duration). The image of the body thus obtained is not one of imaginary cohesion but of dispersal, division, fragmentation. Lyotard speaks of the "post-modernist" text which escapes the closure of representation by creating its own addressee, "a disconcerted body, invited to stretch its sensory capacities beyond measure."[27] Such an approach, which takes off from a different image of the body, can be understood as an attempt to forge a politics based on an erotics. Bonitzer uses the two terms interchangeably, claiming that the scission of the voice can contribute to the definition of "another politics (or erotics) of the voice-off."[28]

---

[24]Jean-François Lyotard, "The Unconscious as Mise-en-scène," in ed. *Performance in Post-Modern Culture*, Michel Benamou and Charles Caramello (Madison: Coda Press, 1977), p. 88.

[25]Bonitzer, "Les Silences," p. 31.

[26]See Roland Barthes, "The Grain of the Voice," in *Image-Music-Text*, ed. trans. Stephen Heath (New York: Hill and Wang, 1977), pp. 179–89.

[27]Lyotard, "The Unconscious," p. 96.

[28]Bonitzer, "Les Silences," p. 31.

The problem is whether such an erotics, bound to the image of an extended or fragmented body and strongly linked with a particular signifying material, can found a political theory or practice.

There are three major difficulties with the notion of a political erotics of the voice. The first is that, relying as it does on the idea of expanding the range or redefining the power of the senses, and opposing itself to meaning, a political erotics is easily recuperable as a form of romanticism or as a mysticism which effectively skirts problems of epistemology, loading itself firmly in a mind/body dualism. Secondly, the overemphasis upon the isolated effectivity of a single signifying material—the voice—risks a crude materialism wherein the physical properties of the medium have the inherent and final power of determining its reading. As Paul Willemen points out, a concentration upon the specificities of the various "technico-sensorial unities" of the cinema often precludes a recognition that the materiality of the signifier is a "second order factor" (with respect to language understood broadly as symbolic system) and tends to reduce a complex heterogeneity to a mere combination of different materials.[29] Yet, a film is not a simple juxtaposition of sensory elements but a discourse, an enunciation. This is not to imply that the isolation and investigation of a single signifying material such as the voice is a fruitless endeavor but that the establishment of a direct connection between the voice and politics is fraught with difficulties.

Third, the notion of a political erotics of the voice is particularly problematic from a feminist perspective. Over and against the theorization of the look as phallic, as the support of voyeurism and fetishism (a drive and a defense which, in Freud, are linked explicitly with the male),[30] the voice appears to lend itself readily as an alternative to the image, as a potentially viable means whereby the woman can "make herself heard." Luce Irigaray, for instance, claims that patriarchal culture has a heavier investment in seeing than in hearing.[31] Bonitzer, in the context of defining a political erotics, speaks of "returning the voice to women" as a major component. Nevertheless, it must be remembered that, while psychoanalysis delineates a pre-oedipal scenario in which the voice of the mother dominates, the voice, in psychoanalysis, is also the instrument of interdiction, of the patriarchal order. And to mark the voice as an isolated haven within patriarchy, or as having an essential relation to the woman, is to invoke the specter of feminine specificity, always recuperable as another form of "otherness." A political erotics which posits a new phantasmatic, which relies on images of an "extended" sensory body, is inevitably caught in the double bind which feminism always seems to confront: on the one hand, there is a danger in grounding a politics on a conceptualization of the body because the body has always been *the* site of woman's oppression, posted as the final and undeniable

[29]Paul Willemen, "Cinema Thoughts," paper delivered at Milwaukee Conference on Cinema and Language, March 1979, pp. 12 and 3. [A version of this paper has since been published as "Cinematic Discourse: The Problem of Inner Speech" in *Cinema and Language*, ed. S. Heath and P. Mellencamp (Frederick, MD: University Press of America and American Film Institute, 1983).

[30]See Laura Mulvey, "Visual Pleasure and Narrative Cinema," *Screen 16* (Autumn 1975): 6–18 [pp. 711–722 in this volume] and Stephen Heath, "Sexual Difference and Representation," *Screen* (Autumn 1978): 51–112.

[31]For a fuller discussion of the relationship some feminists establish between the voice and the woman see Heath, "Sexual Difference," pp. 83–84.

guarantee of a difference and a lack; but, on the other hand, there is a potential gain as well—it is precisely because the body has been a major site of oppression that perhaps it must be the site of the battle to be waged. The supreme achievement of patriarchal ideology is that it has no outside.

In light of the three difficulties outlined above, however, it would seem unwise to base any politics of the voice *solely* on an erotics. The value of thinking the deployment of the voice in the cinema by means of its relation to the body (that of the character, that of the spectator) lies in an understanding of the cinema, from the perspective of a topology, as a series of spaces including that of the spectator— spaces which are often hierarchized or masked, one by the other, in the service of a representational illusion. Nevertheless, whatever the arrangement or interpenetration of the various spaces, they constitute a *place* where signification intrudes. The various techniques and strategies for the deployment of the voice contribute heavily to the definition of the form that "place" takes.

1980

JOHN BELTON

TECHNOLOGY AND AESTHETICS
OF FILM SOUND

John Belton is the author of *American Cinema/American Culture* (1994), a companion to the PBS series *American Cinema*, which chronicles one hundred years of film history. In addition to *Widescreen Cinema* (1992), where Belton examines the development and rise of the wide-screen film, by drawing on the Twentieth-Century Fox, he has written on the films of Alfred Hitchcock, Kenji Mizoguchi, and Roman Polanski. A founding member of the National Film Preservation Board, Belton's recent work focuses on digital cinema and the impact of changing technologies for the creation and distribution of films. He is currently professor of English and film at Rutgers University.

Contemporary Marxist and psychoanalytic film theory regards technology, the evolution of technology, and the evolution of technique as products of an ideological demand that is, in turn, constituted by socioeconomic determinants.[1] Neither techniques nor technologies are natural, nor do they evolve naturally. Contrary to André Bazin's idealist notions of the history of technology and of cinematic forms, their evolution is not natural but "cultural," responding to the pressures of ideology. These pressures suppress signs of technique and technology. For Jean-Louis Baudry, the technological apparatus of the cinema, for example, the camera, transforms what is set before it but conceals the *work* of that transformation by effacing all traces of it.[2] Thus the basic apparatus reflects the actions of bourgeois ideology in general, which seeks to mask its operations and to present as "natural" that which is a product of ideology.

Recent studies of film sound by Rick Altman and Mary Ann Doane extend this argument to the study of the evolution of sound technology, viewing it as an ideologically determined progression toward self-effacement. For Altman, technological innovations "derive from a felt need to reduce all traces of the sound-work from the soundtrack."[3] And Doane argues that "technical advances in sound recording

---

[1]Jean-Louis Comolli, "Technique et ideologie (part 2: Depth of Field: The Double Scene)," *Cahiers du cinéma*, nos. 229–31 (1971): 2a.2, trans. Chistopher Williams.
[2]Jean-Louis Baudry, "Ideological Effects of the Basic Cinematographic Apparatus," *Film Quarterly* 28 (Winter 1974–75): 40, trans. Alan Williams.
[3]Rick Altman, "Introduction," *Cinema Sound: Yale French Studies*, no. 60 (1980): 4.

(such as the Dolby system) are aimed at diminishing the noise of the system, concealing the work of the apparatus."[4] Even though technological evolution performs an ideological function, I would argue that the work of technology can never quite become invisible. Work, even the work that seeks to efface itself, can never disappear. A fundamental law of physics tells us that energy, though it may change in form, can be neither created nor destroyed. Neither mass nor energy nor work is ever lost. Similarly, technology and the effects of technology—by which I mean the aesthetics and stylistic practices that grow out of it—remain visible, though to varying degrees, in every film. The work of sound technology, through its very efforts to remain inaudible, announces itself and, though concealed, becomes audible for those who choose to listen for it.

Russian formalist notions of the "laying bare" of devices, whereby the work announces itself, are rooted in theories that view art as a perceptual process that derives its effects from a prolongation of the processes of perception. Consideration of the perception of sound and of the prolongation of that process thus constitutes the first step in a study of the "audibility" of the sound track.

The perception of sound is necessarily bound up with perception of the image; the two are apprehended together, though sound is often perceived *through* or *in terms of* the image and, as a result, acquires a "secondary" status. For this reason, the psychology of the image differs from that of the sound track. The viewer perceives and regards the information presented on the sound track differently from that on the image "track," though in both cases the viewer, through his/her response to visual and aural cues, plays a decisive role in the realization of the events seen and heard on the screen.

Sound recording and mixing lack the psychology of the photographic image, which guarantees the authenticity of the reproduction.[5] The camera, recording the visible world set before it, produces images that—"no matter how distorted"—remain directly motivated by that world, the automatic and mechanical nature of the process of their production generating in viewers a "quality of credibility absent from all other picturemaking."[6] At the same time, the image possesses a wholeness that serves as further testimony to its "integrity." The image, as Christian Metz points out, is a unity that cannot be broken down into smaller elements.[7] The microphone, however, records an invisible world—that of the audible—which consists of different categories of sound—dialogue, sound effects, and music—and which is regularly broken down into and experienced as separate elements. Not only does sound in general possess a different psychology from that of the image, but the psychology of each category of sound differs slightly. As Metz argues, sound is experienced not as a concrete object or thing but as an attribute or characteristic of it.[8] The voice (i.e., the dialogue

---

[4]Mary Ann Doane, "The Voice in the Cinema: The Articulation of Body and Space," *Cinema/Sound: Yale French Studies*, no. 60 (1980): 35.

[5]See André Bazin. "The Ontology of the Photographic Image," *What is Cinema?*, vol. 1, trans. Hugh Gray (Berkeley: University of California Press, 1967), pp. 13–14; and Christian Metz, "On the Impression of Reality in the Cinema," *Film Language: A Semiotics of the Cinema*, trans. Michael Taylor (New York: Oxford University Press, 1974), pp. 5–6.

[6]Bazin, "Ontology," p. 13.

[7]Metz, "The Cinema: Language or Language System," *Film Language*, pp. 61–63.

[8]Christian Metz, "Aural Objects." *Cinema/Sound: Yale French Studies*, no. 60 (1980): 26–27.

category) is one of several attributes of the human body, which also produces noises and sounds that fall under the category of sound effects; sound effects, in turn, are the attributes of the world and of the objects within it (and include the body as object).

Sound lacks "objectivity" (thus authenticity) not only because it is invisible but because it is an attribute and is thus incomplete in itself. Sound achieves authenticity only as a consequence of its submission to tests imposed upon it by other senses—primarily by sight. One of the conventions of sound editing confirms this. In order to assure an audience that the dialogue and/or sound effects are genuine, the editor must, as soon as possible in a scene, establish synchronization between sound and image, usually through lip-sync. Once that has been done, the editor is free to do almost anything with the picture and sound, confident that the audience now trust what they hear, since it corresponds to (or is not overtly violated by) what they see.

By the same token, dubbing, and especially the dubbing of foreign films in which one language is seen spoken but another heard, is "read" by audiences as false. As early as 1930, the industry noted "a public reaction against . . . voice doubling," forcing a discontinuation of that practice.[9] More recently, Jean Renoir, an advocate of realistic sound practices, wrote that "if we were living in the twelfth century. . . , the practitioners of dubbing would be burnt in the marketplace for heresy. Dubbing is equivalent to a belief in the duality of the soul."[10] The rather obvious intervention of technology involved with dubbing severely circumscribes our faith in both sound and image, provoking a crisis in their credibility.

This perceptual process of testing or attempting to identify sound can, through a system of delays that postpone the synchronism of sound and source, be manipulated to create suspense, both in the area of voice/dialogue and in that of sound effects, calling attention to sound as a device by playing with our perception of it. The identification of a voice with a body can be delayed, as in the case, say, of *The Wizard of Oz* (1939), in which the Wizard's unmasking occurs at the precise moment that synchronization is established; the achievement of synchronization creates a unity whose completeness spells the end of a hermeneutic chain within which an enigma is introduced, developed, prolonged, and resolved. Or in the more complex case of *Psycho* (1960), in which off-screen sound is employed to create a nonexistent character (Mrs. Bates), the particular revelation of the sound's source carefully avoids synchronism: we never see Bates speak in his mother's voice; even at the end, his/her request for a blanket comes from off-screen and his/her final monologue is interiorized. Image and sound here produce a tenuous, almost schizophrenic "synchronization" of character and voice, which precisely articulates the fragmented nature of the enigma's "resolution" and completes an "incompletable" narrative.

As for sound effects, their separation from their source can produce suspense that ranges from the familiar off-screen footsteps that stalk central characters, such as the helpless L. B. Jeffries trapped in his darkened apartment at the end of *Rear Window* (1954), to the mysterious noises and screeches throughout *The Haunting*

---

[9]Jack Alicoate, ed., *The 1930 Film Daily Year Book of Motion Pictures* (New York: The Film Daily, 1930), p. 857.

[10]Jean Renoir, *My Life and My Films*, trans. Norman Denny (New York: Atheneum, 1974), p. 106.

(1963), whose effects, unlike the earlier example from *The Wizard of Oz*, remain unexplained and unidentified. Though off-screen diegetic sound—whether dialogue or sound effects—will, with few exceptions, ultimately be tied to seen (or unseen) sources and thus be "explained" or "identified," we experience that sound through what we see on the screen. It is an extension or completion (or even denial) of the images, but it operates on a plane that is less concrete than that of the images. One could argue that even our experience of on-screen sound involves, though in a much less extreme form, a recognition of a reality of a different order, a reality one step removed from that of the images. The sound track corresponds not, like the image track, directly to "objective reality" but rather to a secondary representation of it, that is, to the images that, in turn, guarantee the objectivity of the sounds. The sound track, in other words, does not undergo the same tests of verisimilitude to which the images are subjected. Images attain credibility in the conformation to objective reality; sounds, in their conformation to the images of that reality, to a derivative reconstruction of objective reality. The rules the sound track obeys—for the spectator at least—are not those of the visible world or of external reality to which photographic images appear to correspond point by point but those of the audible world, which occupies part of the spectrum of phenomena that remain invisible. Paradoxically, the sound track can only duplicate the invisible by means of the visible. Thus sound defines itself in terms of the temporality and spatiality of the image, observing a synchronism and/or perspective dictated by the visuals. Its mimetic processes take as a model not the pro-filmic event but the recorded image of it. The sound track does not duplicate the world set before it; it realizes an imaginary world, endowing the space and objects within the story space with another dimension that complements their temporal and spatial existence as *representations*.

What the sound track seeks to duplicate is the sound of an image, not that of the world. The evolution of sound technology and, again, that of studio recording, editing, and mixing practice illustrate, to some degree, the quest for a sound track that captures an idealized reality, a world carefully filtered to eliminate sounds that fall outside of understanding or significance; every sound must signify. In other words, the goal of sound technology in reproducing sound is to eliminate any noise that interferes with the transmission of meaningful sound. As Mary Ann Doane points out, technical developments in sound recording, after the creation of the basic technology (which was in place by 1928–29), were inspired, in part, by attempts to improve the system's signal-to-noise ratio, to reduce noise and distortion introduced by recording, developing, printing, and projection or playback practices.[11] During 1929–30, blimps and "bungalows" are developed to encase and thus silence cameras. By 1930, electrical circuits for arc lighting systems are devised to eliminate hum, enabling cinematographers to return from incandescent to arc lighting. Materials used in the construction of sets and the design of costumes are changed to reduce excessive reverberation and rustling. Condenser microphones, which tend to "go noisy" in wet weather, are supplanted (ca. 1931) by the quieter dynamic microphone. By 1939, unidirectional microphones are designed, achieving a 10:1 ratio of "desired to undesired pickup" and effectively reducing "camera noise, floor

---

[11]Mary Ann Doane, "Ideology and the Practice of Sound Editing and Mixing," *The Cinematic Apparatus*, ed. Teresa De Lauretis and Stephen Heath (New York: St. Martin's 1980), p. 55.

squeaks, dolly noises, and sounds reflected from walls and other reflecting surfaces."[12] Biased recording and printing (ca. 1930–31) and push-pull recording (ca. 1935) reduce ground noise and harmonic distortion.[13] Nonslip printers (ca. 1934) further help control noise: by ensuring a more precise registration between negative and print films, they reduce the loss of quality formerly observed in the printing process. And throughout the thirties special fine-grain negative, intermediate, and print film stocks are developed, along with ultraviolet recording and printing lights (ca. 1936), producing a sharper, distortionless image on the sound track. Meanwhile, the frequency characteristics of recording and playback systems are improved from a range of 100 to 4,000 cycles per second in 1928–30 to that of 30 to 10,000 in 1938, expanding the range of the signal while holding the noise level down.[14] The evolutionary process culminates in the Dolby noise reduction and stereo sound system introduced into the cinema in 1975 in such musical films as *Tommy* and *Lisztomania*. By flattening, during recording, the response to low frequencies and boosting the highs and by reversing this process in playback, the Dolby system effectively masks out surface noise, producing a sound that is clean and that permits louder playback in the theater without increasing noise.

Yet the Dolby system also changes the characteristics of whatever sound it records, albeit only slightly. It cuts the very tops and bottoms off the sounds, resulting in a sound that is somewhat "unnatural." At the same time, the nearly total elimination of noise—the goal toward which sound technology has evolved, like that of camera movement "noise" with the perfection of the Steadicam in 1976 (see *Bound for Glory, Marathon Man, Rocky*, etc.)—results in a final product that is too perfect, that is ideal to a fault. In watching Claude Lelouch's Steadicamed opus *Another Man, Another Chance* (1977) or listening to Steven Spielberg's postrecorded and Dolbyized *Raiders of the Lost Ark* (1981), one misses the rough, jittery camera movements, floor squeaks, and unmixed, ambient sound of films like Jean Renoir's *La Chienne* (1931). A certain amount of noise has become necessary to signify realism; its absence betokens a sound that has returned to an ideal state of existence, to a point just before it enters into the world and acquires the imperfections inherent in its own realization. The sound track has become artificially quiet, pushing beyond the realism of the outside world into an inner, psychological realism. The sound track duplicates what sound recordist Mark Dichter and sound designer Walter Murch refer to as the sound one hears in one's head,[15] a sound that has not been

---

[12]G. R. Groves, "The Soundman," *JSMPTE* 48, no. 13 (March 1947): 223.

[13]Biased recording effectively reduces the noise of film grain by reducing the amount of light that reaches the negative. As a result, the sound track on positive prints has a darker exposure. Thus less film grain noise is reproduced during silent or low sound level passages. Push-pull recording involves doubling the width of the track, thereby increasing the useful area of modulated light and decibel output. One variety of push-pull recording splits the track into positive and negative parts of the sound waves. As a result, there is never any transparent or clear area on the track and, thus, ground noise is eliminated.

[14]The frequency range of the human ear extends from 16 to 20,00 cycles per second. Thus evolution in this area might be said to have as its goal the range of the human ear. Unless otherwise noted, technological data in this paragraph derive from material in Groves (see note 12), Edward W. Kellogg, "History of Sound Motion Pictures, Parts I-III," *JSMPTE* 48, nos. 6–8 (June-August 1955); Barry Salt, "Film Style and Technology in the Thirties," *Film Quarterly* 30–31 (Fall 1976).

[15]Mark Dichter, interview with Elisabeth Weis (March 1975). Walter Murch, interview with F. Paine, *University Film Association Journal* 33, no. 4 (1981): 15–20.

marked by any system noise nor by transmission through any medium, such as air, that might alter its fidelity to an ideal.

The technology and practice devoted to the duplication of sound's spatial properties have undergone a similar evolution, becoming unreal in a quest for realism. With the abandonment in 1927–29 of radio-style recording such as that in *The Lights of New York* (1928), in which performers speak into a stationary microphone and depth is "suggested" by changes in volume (e.g., when doors leading onto a dance floor open and close in the background), sound recording strives to model sound the way a cameraman models figures with light. The industry seeks to produce a track that reflects the space of the original scene. Carefully positioning the microphone to blend direct and reflected sound, soundmen record not only the informational "content" of an actor's speech or sound effects but also its spatial presence. The soundman, in effect, duplicates through sound the space seen on the screen: the microphone mimics the angle and distance of the camera, creating a sound perspective that matches the visual perspective of the image. The advent of wide-screen cinematography—whether the Grandeur system (1929–30), Cinerama (1952), CinemaScope (1953), or Todd-AO/70mm (1955)—provides a wider visual field for the sound track to duplicate, necessitating multiple track, stereo sound. In Fox's CinemaScope process, for example, four different tracks play on three separate speakers behind the screen and on one "surround" speaker.[16] The footsteps (or speech) of a character walking across the screen from right to left would originate first from the right horn, then from the center, and finally from the left, the source of the sound matching, point for point, the character's various positions on the screen. The final effect, however, is that of three sound perspectives rather than one. No matter how many speakers or tracks film technology develops, it can never quite duplicate the spatial qualities of the sound of the event seen on the screen. Every square inch of the screen would require a separate speaker and track to reflect the nearly limitless number of potential sources for sounds, while an infinite number of speakers and tracks would be needed to duplicate sounds emanating from off-screen space. Stereo systems that establish two, three, four, or even five sound sources, rather than creating a more perfect illusion of depth on the screen, call attention to the arbitrariness of their choice of sources. Instead of becoming better able to approximate the real and to efface its own presence, stereo sound remains marked by the nature of the system(s) it uses to create the illusion of real space. The infinite supply of original information has been *channeled* into a handful of tracks. We experience stereo soundtracks as a limited (rather than limitless) number of distinct sound sources. No matter how "noiseless" it becomes, the system never quite disappears.

At the same time, perspective undergoes stylistic as well as technological evolution. The careful correlation of aural and visual spaces achieved by Hollywood in the thirties gives way in the postwar period to the violation of perspective. Influenced

---

[16]These tracks are narratively coded. The behind-the-screen tracks contain on-screen sound while the surround track contains off-screen sound and voice-over commentary. The authority of a voice-over track is partly the result of its spatial qualities. It occupies a space that is beyond or outside that of the film, thus it can be either privileged (*Apocalypse Now*) or disadvantaged (*Days of Heaven*) in terms of its knowledge of information on the picture "track."

in part by television sound, which tends to maintain constant close-up levels, ignoring the nuances of perspective, contemporary cinema frequently "mismatches" long shots with close-up sound, as in *The Graduate* (1967) and any number of other films that combine long shots of a car on a highway with close-up sound of its occupants conversing. The current fondness for radio mikes, seen in the work of Robert Altman and others, involves a similar disruption of traditional spatial codes in sound recording. Radio microphones pick up speech (and body tone) *before* it is projected—that is, before it can acquire spatial properties. Though it can be given some perspective during the mixing process, the quality of the sound differs from that recorded by traditional microphones hung just beyond the camera's field of view. Though it permits more freedom in shooting and ensures good sound coverage, recording with radio microphones, like mismatched perspective, lends a surfacy quality to the image, which may suit certain modern stylists such as Altman but which plays havoc with more traditional, illusionistic notions of space. By the same token, contemporary sound editing, in which the sound cut often precedes the picture cut by six to eight frames or more (e.g., *Somebody Up There Likes Me*, 1956; *The Loneliness of the Long Distance Runner*, 1962; *Jaws*, 1975; any number of contemporary Hollywood films; and even recent Robert Bresson films like *L'Argent*, 1983), violates the invisible cutting of the thirties in which the picture cut often precedes the sound cut by a frame or two, the sound bridging and thus concealing the picture cut.

It is perhaps useful to distinguish at some point between technological and stylistic evolution, which do not always share a single goal, and to acknowledge the coexistence of disparate stylistic uses of a single technology. Theories of technological evolution are shaped by Darwinian notions of advancement and self-perfection; the tools that an artist (or culture) uses become more and more perfect, developing from lower into higher forms. But theories of stylistic evolution such as Bazin's are informed, in large part, by the "mimetic fallacy," and are clearly more problematical. As Heinrich Wolfflin argues, "It is a mistake [for art history] to work with the clumsy notion of the imitation of nature, as though it were merely a homogeneous process of increasing perfection."[17] For that matter, can art or even artists themselves be said to possess goals that it/they seek to realize? Is not that notion the height of idealistic thinking? As Jean-Luc Comolli has shown, Bazinian theories of the evolution of cinematic forms are essentially idealistic reconstructions of film history that fail to account for delays, gaps, and contradictions in their development.[18] Given that cinematic forms do not necessarily evolve in the direction of qualities that enable "a recreation of the world in its own image,"[19] can they be said to improve, or to perfect themselves over time? Is the style of a Fassbinder better or even more evolved than that of a Griffith? Is that of Picasso better than that of Rembrandt? No; it is merely *different*, reflecting the different technological, socioeconomic, and cultural systems within which each artist worked. If development

[17]Heinrich Wolfflin, *Principles of Art History* (New York: Dover, n.d.), 13.
[18]Comolli, "Technique et ideologie," 1.7–1.17.
[19]Bazin, "The Myth of Total Cinema," *What Is Cinema?* vol. 1, p. 21.

can be gauged at all, it is not to be found in the comparison of individual artists or works but in that of different schools, groups, or periods, as Wolfflin has demonstrated. It is only in the area of dominant practice—the point of intersection between the timeliness of technology and the timelessness of style, between tools and cultural/individual expression—that change can be charted and given a goal.

At each stage along the axis of technological development, recording, editing, and mixing practices change in response to linear changes in technology and to unpredictable shifts in stylistic concerns of a period, nation, or group of individuals. Thus dominant film practice conforms, more or less, to the direction taken by the technology that informs it, that is, toward self-perfection and invisibility, *and* to the attitudes of those who use that technology, attitudes that color its "invisibility."

Developments in the area of sound recording—especially in the use of radio microphones and Dolby—point, as we have seen, in the direction of the ideal: they culminate in the sounds one hears in one's head. Changes in editing and mixing practice reflect an increase in control over the sound track and in its ability to duplicate the sound not of the pro-filmic event but of that event's photographic image. The initial practice (ca. 1926–29) of mixing sound while it is being recorded and recording it (except for music that was often added later) at the same time that the image is recorded locks the sound indexically into the pro-filmic event of which it is the record, giving it an immediacy and integrity resembling that of the image. The introduction of rerecording and mixing in the early thirties breaks that indexical bond of sound to the pro-filmic event. Mixing now takes place *after* the film has been shot (and often even after it has been edited) during the phase of postproduction. At the same time, the sound track loses its wholeness: it is separated into dialogue, sound effects, and music tracks that are recorded at different times, dialogue and some sound effects being recorded during production, other sound effects, music, and even some dialogue during postproduction. Whereas initially the sound track was "recorded," now it is "built." Sound mixing no longer observes the integrity of any preexistent reality; it builds its own to match earlier recorded visual information. The growth of postproduction departments within the studio system institutionalizes the separation of sound and image that frees the former from its ties to the events that produced the latter. The building of the sound track, using the image rather than the profilmic event as a guide, now becomes a final stage in the "realization" of the image.

During the postwar period, even the recording of dialogue, which is traditionally tied, through concerns for synchronization, to the moment at which the image is recorded, is freed from its bonds to the pro-filmic event. The use of wide-angle lenses (which provide a wide field of view and thus force the microphone further away from its target, resulting in a less acceptable sound) and the practice of shooting on location (where ambient noise cannot be controlled as well as in the studio) result in the use of the "production" sound track as a guide track to cue the actor's dialogue during looping sessions back at the studio. The original track, at times, functions merely as a blueprint for an entirely new track created on the sound stage to match an image that has already been assembled in rough cut form. Again, changing practice reveals that it is the sound of the image that Hollywood strives to recreate.

Neither the cinematic institution, seen in its practices, nor the cinematic apparatus possesses a single identity. Practice seeks to produce a more realistic sound track by "unrealizing" its recording and rerecording methods. Its final product is thus marked as a product. Although Baudry and others argue to the contrary, the cinema never quite succeeds in masking the work that produces it. This is due, in large part, to the very nature of the apparatus itself. The recording aspects of motion picture technology possess dual characteristics: they both transmit and transform. Though the cinematic apparatus becomes, decade by decade, a more perfect transmitter, reducing signs of its own existence by eliminating its system's noise, it inevitably reproduces not only the light and sound waves reflected and emitted by objective reality but also its own presence, which is represented by the perspective from which these waves are seen or heard. In the cinema, there is always present, in the positioning of the camera and the microphone(s), a consciousness that sees and (in the sound film) hears and that coexists with what is seen or heard. Even in the silent cinema, someone is always speaking and something is always spoken. In the sound cinema, we always see and hear events *through* images and sounds of them. The cinema remains the phenomenological art par excellence, wedding, if indeed not collapsing, consciousness with the world.

1985

IV

Film Narrative and the Other Arts

Theorists have often attempted to discover the special characteristics of the film medium by comparing it with other media, principally theater and the novel. In the previous section, Erwin Panofsky contrasts the theater's static use of space and its independence of the principle of coexpressibility with cinema's more dynamic use of space and its rigorous subjection to that principle. For Panofsky, this difference explains why film adaptations of plays are so unlikely to succeed. Any attempt to transfer theater's essentially verbal resources to the cinema violates the principle that no more should be expressed verbally than can be expressed visually. The cinema's business is not the photographing of theatrical decor, a prestylized reality, but the photographing of actual physical reality so that it has style. Panofsky finds cinema the only medium that does justice to the materialistic interpretation of the universe that pervades contemporary civilization.

André Bazin complicates this distinction between what film and theater accomplish by arguing both that many successful films have been adapted from plays and that cinematic effects have been employed successfully in the theater. Cocteau's *Les Parents Terribles* and Olivier's *Henry V*, he believes, are superb films. But he does not feel that one should "cinematify" or simply "open up" the original play by moving the action outdoors, in order to make a successful adaptation. Rather, "a good adaptation should result in a restoration of the essence and spirit" of the original play. Indeed, in films like Cocteau's and Olivier's, one is "no longer adapting, one is staging a play by means of cinema."

Bazin realizes that if the living actor's presence were essential to the effects of theater, the successful staging of a play by means of cinema would be impossible. He therefore argues that there is a sense in which the actor is present on the screen just as a person is "present" in a mirror. Although Bazin's refutation of the importance of presence is not very convincing (Stanley Cavell treats the issue much more systematically in *The World Viewed*), it allows him to assert that the primary difference between stage and screen is not one of living beings but of architecture. Bazin thinks that theatrical speech often fails in a film not because it was written for living speakers but because it was written to be uttered in a particular kind of environment. The problem of filming a play is to find a decor that preserves the closed, microcosmic qualities of theatrical architecture for which the dialogue was written while at the same time preserving the natural realism of the screen. The screen is not a world in itself but a window on the world that consistently dwarfs and dissipates theatrical speech. Bazin believes this problem is worth solving, for even if original scripts are preferable to adaptations, truly distinguished ones are rare. The cinema cannot afford to ignore its theatrical heritage, any more than the drama can afford the loss of the audiences that film can bring it.

Like Bazin, Leo Braudy emphasizes the varying ways that film, theater, and literature have each dealt with the human image and the question of characterization. After broadly distinguishing in *The World in a Frame* between the visual and verbal ways of presenting character, he defines the basic nature of film character as an active omission of all knowledge but what we see immediately in front of us— including the inner life of the character as well as the actor's presence in other films. It is not merely the "presence" of the performer before us in the film that creates the character, but also the palpable absences and implications of that performance, particularly our basic knowledge that the performer is not really there. With a look back at historical styles of stage performance and conceptions of acting, he then explores this elusiveness of the film character in contrast with what he argues are the more patterned ways in which the novel and especially the stage construct character. Directly connected with these differing conceptions of character are very different demands made upon performers in the two visual media.

Similarly aware of the cultural inheritance of cinema, Sergei Eisenstein, as a filmmaker himself, emphasizes the question of the ease and effectiveness of adapting one medium to another. He argues that Griffith learned montage (which Eisenstein considers the essence of film) from the novels of Charles Dickens. Eisenstein plainly sees no theoretical bar to adapting novels successfully to the screen, as proved by his own attempt to adapt Dreiser's *An American Tragedy*. Indeed, it is not implausible to argue, as Bazin has, that the film's deepest affinities are with the novel, not with the play. The novel is "cinematic" in its fluid handling of time and space, in its "focused" narrative control, in its ability to alternate description with dialogue, and even in the privacy and isolation of its audiences. As a result, the film has adapted more fiction than drama.

Because of the polemic commitment of many early writers to defining film in opposition to more traditional art-forms, the question of adaptation still remains a vexed one for most film theorists although in contemporary film criticism it is perhaps the least theoretically considered. This attitude has even been reinforced among later theorists who wish to disentangle not only film but also film study generally from that of literature or theater. Yet there is some reason to think that adaptation might be a way into the processes of creation, since a good number of important filmmakers, like Eisenstein, have not felt the same compunctions about "impurity" that have worried many critics. It may also be a way into understanding the different ways that different media tell stories.

Beginning with some examples drawn from Jean Renoir's *Une Partie de Campagne* (*A Day in the Country*, 1936), Dudley Andrew takes a wide view of the use of any external source material in the making of films. Specifically, Andrew explores the points of contact between two artistic "signifying systems," the literary and the cinematic, that otherwise seem to achieve their effects in exactly reverse ways: film from perception to signification, literature from signification to perception. Rejecting those writers who therefore argue for sharp and unbridgeable distinctions between the media, Andrew moves the question of adaptation from the periphery of film study to its center: "the study of adaptation is logically tantamount to the study of cinema as a whole." What is needed, he concludes, is not a more refined set of medium-specific definitions but an effort to situate the transformations in a historical and sociological context of actual adaptors with their complex motivations.

In one of the most searching book-length considerations of film adaptation, Brian McFarlane begins with a critique of traditional views of cinematic adaptation from literature through the influential lens of Eisenstein's assumptions in "Dickens, Griffith, and the Film Today." He argues that this emphasis has emphasized thematic and narrative parallels rather than more pertinent questions of "possible parallels and disparities between the two different signifying systems." The crucial issue that prevents a thoroughgoing understanding of how adaptation works, he continues, is the issue of fidelity–how faithfully does the film version resemble the original? He suggests instead a distinction between the transferal of elements (plot, character, setting, etc.) from one medium and what must be adapted into other forms.

In recent years, in part because of the interest in issues of film language that are discussed in Section I, questions of adaptation and the particular story-telling resources of the different media have been often rephrased in terms of more general questions of how film narrative works. The backdrop to these discussions is the contrast between classic film narrative, in which things seem to speak transparently for themselves, and a narrative that calls its own procedures into some question. (Compare the discussions of film realism in Section II.) Various theorists have analyzed narrative in various ways, but always in the service of making a primary distinction between a story and its telling, as well as between different aspects of that telling: its language, or discourse; its point-of-view, or enunciation. In a section from his book, *D. W. Griffith and the Origins of American Narrative Film*, Tom Gunning adapts the categories developed by the French literary theorist Gérard Genette and tests them against the body of work created by Griffith, and what Gunning calls the "excess of mimesis over meaning" that is inherent in the photographic and cinematic image. What tells the story in the narrative film as contrasted with the narrative of prose fiction? Gunning answers by focusing on the "profilmic"—what happens in front of the camera and how spectators actively receive and analyze its messages. At the end of this selection, Gunning stresses the role of narration and even a narrator in opposition to their conception of a more depersonalized discourse. In this view even the most detached film still has readable designs on the viewer that can be described as a narrative presence.

Jerrold Levinson takes the issue of narration into the nonverbal narrative form of film music, both that music "appropriated" from pre-existing sources and that composed for a particular film. Levinson argues against those who claim that

nondiegetic sound (sound without a visual source) is "inaudible" and not meant to
be noticed, as well as those who say that there is no necessary narrative presence
in film. In fact, he says, when the various kinds of film music are considered, it
becomes clear that there are actually two narrative presences: one concerned with
"what is fictional *in a film's story*" and the other with "what is fictional *in the world
of a film*."

As Gilles Deleuze argues (see Section II), one of the great narrative innovations
of the period after World War II was the increasing dishevelment of traditional film
narrative, carried on by the Italian neo-realists and the French New Wave that
became a powerful influence on the "New Hollywood" of the 1970s. Peter Wollen,
a film theorist who later would make several independent films himself, discusses
the innovations of Jean-Luc Godard in the 1970s. Wollen shows how what appears
to be the absolute challenge of Godard's films to mainstream narrative traditions
nevertheless itself draws upon formal devices and explorations that were pioneered
by or have intriguing analogies in the novel, theater, and painting. Wollen grants
that films do have resources that the other artistic media may not, but, as Godard's
films of the 1970s illustrate, the traditional critical identification of only classical
film narrative with literary or theatrical sources needs serious revision.

Finally in this section David Bordwell, the influential author of *Narration in the
Fiction Film*, returns to the basic question of how film or any story is understood
by the perceiver, connected to but ultimately apart from its relation to its source
material. Exploring a cognitivist perspective, which postulates a viewer's relation
to "norms" of story-telling, Bordwell takes as his example the classic film noir
Mildred Pierce (1945), based on a 1941 novel by James M. Cain. He argues that in
any medium we recreate the story by drawing upon our knowledge of such elements
as the social roles of characters and our ideas of what is possible for a person to
say, think, and do. Whereas the original novel is told in a straightforward time
sequence, the flashbacks of the film are ways of deceiving and misleading this
process for greater aesthetic pleasure. The emphasis here is less on the process of
adaptation or change than it is on how the spectator makes sense of what he or she
hears and sees–an issue that will be taken up more fully in Section VII.

ANDRÉ BAZIN
FROM WHAT IS CINEMA?

THEATER AND CINEMA

The leitmotiv of those who despise filmed theatre, their final and apparently insuperable argument, continues to be the unparalleled pleasure that accompanies the presence of the actor. "What is specific to theater," writes Henri Gouhier, in *The Essence of Theater*, "is the impossibility of separating off action and actor." Elsewhere he says "the stage welcomes every illusion except that of presence; the actor is there is disguise, with the soul and voice of another, but he is nevertheless there and by the same token space calls out for him and for the solidity of his presence. On the other hand and inversely, the cinema accommodates every form of reality save one—the physical presence of the actor." If it is here that the essence of theater lies then undoubtedly the cinema can in no way pretend to any parallel with it. If the writing, the style, and the dramatic structure are, as they should be, rigorously conceived as the receptacle for the soul and being of the flesh-and-blood actor, any attempt to substitute the shadow and reflection of a man on the screen for the man himself is a completely vain enterprise. There is no answer to this argument. The successes of Laurence Olivier, of Welles, or of Cocteau can only be challenged—here you need to be in bad faith—or considered inexplicable. They are a challenge both to critics and philosophers. Alternatively one can only explain them by casting doubts on that commonplace of theatrical criticism "the irreplaceable presence of the actor."

THE CONCEPT OF PRESENCE

At this point certain comments seem called for concerning the concept of "presence," since it would appear that it is this concept, as understood prior to the appearance of photography, that the cinema challenges.

Can the photographic image, especially the cinematographic image, be likened to other images and in common with them be regarded as having an existence distinct

345

from the object? Presence, naturally, is defined in terms of time and space. "To be in the presence of someone" is to recognize him as existing contemporaneously with us and to note that he comes within the actual range of our senses—in the case of cinema of our sight and in radio of our hearing. Before the arrival of photography and later of cinema, the plastic arts (especially portraiture) were the only interme-diaries between actual physical presence and absence. Their justification was their resemblance which stirs the imagination and helps the memory. But photography is something else again. In no sense is it the image of an object or person, more cor-rectly it is its tracing. Its automatic genesis distinguishes it radically from the other techniques of reproduction. The photograph proceeds by means of the lens to the taking of a veritable luminous impression in light—to a mold. As such it carries with it more than mere resemblance, namely a kind of identity—the card we call by that name being only conceivable in an age of photography. But photography is a feeble technique in the sense that its instantaneity compels it to capture time only piecemeal. The cinema does something strangely paradoxical. It makes a molding of the object as it exists in time and, furthermore, makes an imprint of the duration of the object.

The nineteenth century with its objective techniques of visual and sound repro-duction gave birth to a new category of images, the relation of which to the reality from which they proceed requires very strict definition. Even apart from the fact that the resulting aesthetic problems cannot be satisfactorily raised without this intro-ductory philosophical inquiry, it would not be sound to treat the old aesthetic ques-tions as if the categories with which they deal had in no way been modified by the appearance of completely new phenomena. Common sense—perhaps the best philo-sophical guide in this case—has clearly understood this and has invented an expres-sion for the presence of an actor, by adding to the placards announcing his appearance the phrase "in flesh and blood." This means that for the man in the street the word "presence," today, can be ambiguous, and thus an apparent redundancy is not out of place in this age of cinema. Hence it is no longer as certain as it was that there is no middle stage between presence and absence. It is likewise at the ontological level that the effectiveness of the cinema has its source. It is false to say that the screen is incapable of putting us "in the presence of" the actor. It does so in the same way as a mirror—one must agree that the mirror relays the presence of the person reflected in it—but it is a mirror with a delayed reflection, the tin foil of which retains the image.[1] It is true that in the theater Molière can die on the stage and that we have

---

[1]Television naturally adds a new variant to the "pseudopresences" resulting from the scientific tech-niques for reproduction created by photography. On the little screen during live television the actor is actually present in space and time. But the reciprocal actor-spectator relationship is incomplete in one direction. The spectator sees without being seen. There is no return flow. Televised theater, therefore, seems to share something both of theater and of cinema: of theater because the actor is present to the viewer, of cinema because the spectator is not present to the actor. Nevertheless, this state of not being present is not truly an absence. The television actor has a sense of the millions of ears and eyes virtu-ally present and represented by the electronic camera. This abstract presence is most noticeable when the actor fluffs his lines. Painful enough in the theater, it is intolerable on television since the spectator who can do nothing to help him is aware of the unnatural solitude of the actor. In the theater in similar cir-cumstances a sort of understanding exists with the audience, which is a help to an actor in trouble. This kind of reciprocal relationship is impossible on television.

the privilege of living in the biographical time of the actor. In the film about Manolete however we are present at the actual death of the famous matador and while our emotion may not be as deep as if we were actually present in the arena at that historic moment, its nature is the same. What we lose by way of direct witness do we not recapture thanks to the artificial proximity provided by photographic enlargement? Everything takes place as if in the time-space perimeter which is the definition of presence. The cinema offers us effectively only a measure of duration, reduced but not to zero, while the increase in the space factor reestablishes the equilibrium of the psychological equation.

OPPOSITION AND IDENTIFICATION

An honest appraisal of the respective pleasures derived from theater and cinema, at least as to what is less intellectual and more direct about them, forces us to admit that the delight we experience at the end of a play has a more uplifting, a nobler, one might perhaps say a more moral, effect than the satisfaction which follows a good film. We seem to come away with a better conscience. In a certain sense it is as if for the man in the audience all theater is "Corneillian." From this point of view one could say that in the best films something is missing. It is as if a certain inevitable lowering of the voltage, some mysterious aesthetic short circuit, deprived us in the cinema of a certain tension which is a definite part of theater. No matter how slight this difference it undoubtedly exists, even between the worst charity production in the theater and the most brilliant of Olivier's film adaptations. There is nothing banal about this observation and the survival of the theater after fifty years of cinema, and the prophecies of Marcel Pagnol, is practical proof enough. At the source of the disenchantment which follows the film one could doubtless detect a process of depersonalization of the spectator. As Rosenkrantz wrote in 1937, in *Esprit*, in an article profoundly original for its period, "The characters on the screen are quite naturally objects of identification, while those on the stage are, rather, objects of mental opposition because their real presence gives them an objective reality and to transpose them into beings in an imaginary world the will of the spectator has to intervene actively, that is to say, to will to transform their physical reality into an abstraction. This abstraction being the result of a process of the intelligence that we can only ask of a person who is fully conscious." A member of a film audience tends to identify himself with the film's hero by a psychological process, the result of which is to turn the audience into a "mass" and to render emotion uniform. Just as in algebra if two numbers equal a third, then they are equal to one another, so here we can say, if two individuals identify themselves with a third, they identify themselves with one another. Let us compare chorus girls on the stage and on the screen. On the screen they satisfy an unconscious sexual desire and when the hero joins them he satisfies the desire of the spectator in the proportion to which the latter has identified himself with the hero. On the stage the girls excite the onlooker as they would in real life. The result is that there is no identification with the hero. He becomes instead an object of jealousy and envy. In other words, Tarzan is only possible on the screen. The cinema calms the spectator, the theater excites him. Even when it appeals to the lowest instincts, the theater up to a certain point stands in the way of the creation of a mass mentality.[2] It stands in the way of any collective representation in the psychological sense, since theater calls for an active individual consciousness while the film requires only a passive adhesion.

These views shed a new light on the problem of the actor. They transfer him from the ontological to the psychological level. It is to the extent to which the cinema encourages identification with the hero that it conflicts with the theater. Put this way the problem is no longer basically insoluble, for it is a fact that the cinema has at its disposal means which favor a passive position or on the other hand, means which to a greater or lesser degree stimulate the consciousness of the spectator. Inversely the theater can find ways of lessening the psychological tension between spectator and actor. Thus theater and cinema will no longer be separated off by an unbridgeable aesthetic moat, they would simply tend to give rise to two attitudes of mind over which the director maintains a wide control.

Examined at close quarters, the pleasure derived from the theater not only differs from that of the cinema but also from that of the novel. The reader of a novel, physically alone like the man in the dark movie house, identifies himself with the character. That is why after reading for a long while he also feels the same intoxication of an illusory intimacy with the hero. Incontestably, there is in the pleasure derived from cinema and novel a self-satisfaction, a concession to solitude, a sort of betrayal of action by a refusal of social responsibility.

The analysis of this phenomenon might indeed be undertaken from a psychoanalytic point of view. Is it not significant that the psychiatrists took the term catharsis from Aristotle? Modern pedagogic research on psychodrama seems to have provided fruitful insights into the cathartic process of theater. The ambiguity existing in the child's mind between play and reality is used to get him to free himself by way of improvised theater from the repressions from which he suffers. This technique amounts to creating a kind of vague theater in which the play is of a serious nature and the actor is his own audience. The action that develops on these occasions is not one that is divided off by footlights, which are undoubtedly the architectural symbol of the censor that separates us from the stage. We delegate Oedipus to act in our guise and place him on the other side of a wall of fire—that fiery frontier between fantasy and reality which gives rein to Dionysiac monsters while protecting us from them. These sacred beasts will not cross this barrier of light beyond which they seem out of place and even sacrilegious—witness the disturbing atmosphere of awe which surrounds an actor still made up, like a phosphorescent light, when we visit him in his dressing room. There is no point to the argument that the theater did not always have footlights. These are only a symbol and there were others before them from the cothurnus and mask onwards. In the seventeenth century the fact that young nobles sat up on the stage is no denial of the role of the footlights, on the contrary, it confirms it, by way of a privileged violation so to speak, just as when today Orson Welles scatters actors around the auditorium to fire on the audience with revolvers. He does not do away with the footlights, he just crosses them. The rules of the game are also

---

[2]Crowd and solitude are not antinomies: the audience in a movie house is made up of solitary individuals. Crowd should be taken here to mean the opposite of an organic community freely assembled.

made to be broken. One expects some players to cheat.[3] With regard to the objection based on presence and on that alone, the theater and the cinema are not basically in conflict. What is really in dispute are two psychological modalities of a performance. The theater is indeed based on the reciprocal awareness of the presence of audience and actor, but only as related to a performance. The theater acts on us by virtue of our participation in a theatrical action across the footlights and as it were under the protection of their censorship. The opposite is true in the cinema. Alone, hidden in a dark room, we watch through half-open blinds a spectacle that is unaware of our existence and which is part of the universe. There is nothing to prevent us from identifying ourselves in imagination with the moving world before us, which becomes *the* world. It is no longer on the phenomenon of the actor as a person physically present that we should concentrate our analysis, but rather on the ensemble of conditions that constitute the theatrical play and deprive the spectator of active participation. We shall see that it is much less a question of actor and presence than of man and his relation to the decor.

BEHIND THE DECOR

The human being is all-important in the theater. The drama on the screen can exist without actors. A banging door, a leaf in the wind, waves beating on the shore can heighten the dramatic effect. Some film masterpieces use man only as an accessory, like an extra, or in counterpoint to nature which is the true leading character. Even when, as in *Nanook* and *Man of Aran*, the subject is man's struggle with nature, it cannot be compared to a theatrical action. The mainspring of the action is not in man but nature. As Jean-Paul Sartre, I think it was, said, in the theater the drama proceeds from the actor, in the cinema it goes from the decor to man. This reversal of the dramatic flow is of decisive importance. It is bound up with the very essence of the *mise-en-scène*. One must see here one of the consequences of photographic realism. Obviously, if the cinema makes use of nature it is because it is able to. The camera puts at the disposal of the director all the resources of the telescope and the microscope. The last strand of a rope about to snap or an entire army making an assault on a hill are within our reach. Dramatic causes and effects have no longer any material limits to the eye of the camera. Drama is freed by the camera from all contingencies of time and space. But this freeing of tangible dramatic powers is still only a secondary aesthetic cause, and does not basically explain the reversal of value between the actor and the decor. For sometimes it actually happens

---

[3]Here is a final example proving that presence does not constitute theater except in so far as it is a matter of a performance. Everyone either at his own or someone else's expense has known the embarrassment of being watched without knowing it or in spite of knowing it. Lovers who kiss on public benches offer a spectacle to the passerby, but they do not care. My concierge who has a feeling for the *mot juste* says, when she sees them, that is like being at the movies. Each of us has sometimes found himself forced to his annoyance to do something absurd before other people. On those occasions we experience a sense of angry shame which is the very opposite of theatrical exhibitionism. Someone who looks through a keyhole is not at the theater; Cocteau has rightly demonstrated in *Le sang d'un poète* that he was already at the cinema. And nevertheless there are such things as "shows," when the protagonists are present to us in flesh and blood but one of the two parties is ignorant of the fact or goes through with it reluctantly. This is not "play" in the theatrical sense.

that the cinema deliberately deprives itself of the use of setting and of exterior nature—we have already seen a perfect instance of this in *Les Parents terribles*—while the theater in contrast uses a complex machinery to give a feeling of ubiquity to the audience. Is *La Passion de Jeanne d'Arc* by Carl Dreyer, shot entirely in close-up, in the virtually invisible and in fact theatrical settings by Jean Hugo, less cinematic than *Stagecoach*? It seems to me that quantity has nothing to do with it, nor the resemblance to certain theater techniques. The ideas of an art director for a room in *Les Dames aux camélias* would not noticeably differ whether for a film or a play. It's true that on the screen you would doubtless have some close-ups of the blood-stained handkerchief, but a skillful stage production would also know how to make some play with the cough and the handkerchief. All the close-ups in *Les Parents terribles* are taken directly from the theater where our atten-tion would spontaneously isolate them. If film direction only differed from theater direction because it allows us a closer view of the scenery and makes a more rea-sonable use of it, there would really be no reason to continue with the theater and Pagnol would be a true prophet. For it is obvious that the few square yards of the decor of Vilar's *La Danse de la mort* contributed as much to the drama as the island on which Marcel Cravene shot his excellent film. The fact is that the problem lies not in the decor itself but in its nature and function. We must therefore throw some light on an essentially theatrical notion, that of the dramatic place.

There can be no theater without architecture, whether it be the cathedral square, the arena of Nîmes, the palace of the Popes, the trestle stage on a fairground, the semicircle of the theater of Vicenza that looks as if it were decorated by Bérard in a delirium, or the rococo amphitheaters on the boulevard houses. Whether as a per-formance or a celebration, theater of its very essence must not be confused with nature under penalty of being absorbed by her and ceasing to be. Founded on the reciprocal awareness of those taking part and present to one another, it must be in contrast to the rest of the world in the same way that play and reality are opposed, or concern and indifference, or liturgy and the common use of things. Costume, mask, or make-up, the style of the language, the footlights, all contribute to this dis-tinction, but the clearest sign of all is the stage, the architecture of which has var-ied from time to time without ever ceasing to mark out a privileged spot actually or virtually distinct from nature. It is precisely in virtue of this *locus dramaticus* that decor exists. It serves in greater or less degree to set the place apart, to spec-ify. Whatever it is, the decor constitutes the walls of this three-sided box opening onto the auditorium, which we call the stage. These false perspectives, these façades, these arbors, have another side which is cloth and nails and wood. Everyone knows that when the actor "retires to his apartment" from the yard or from the garden, he is actually going to his dressing room to take off his make-up. These few square feet of light and illusion are surrounded by machinery and flanked by wings, the hidden labyrinths of which do not interfere one bit with the pleasure of the specta-tor who is playing the game of theater. Because it is only part of the architecture of the stage, the decor of the theater is thus an area materially enclosed, limited, cir-cumscribed, the only discoveries of which are those of our collusive imagination.

Its appearances are turned inward facing the public and the footlights. It exists by virtue of its reverse side and of anything beyond, as the painting exists by virtue

of its frame. Just as the picture is not to be confounded with the scene it represents
and is not a window in a wall. The stage and the decor where the action unfolds
constitute an aesthetic microcosm inserted perforce into the universe but essentially
distinct from the Nature which surrounds it.

Above: Jean Marais, Yvonne de Bray, Gabrielle Dorziat, Marcel André, and Josette Day in
Les Parents Terribles (1948). Theater in cinema, "deliberately deprives itself of the use of
setting and of exterior nature" (Bazin, p. 350). *Below*: Anna Magnani onstage in the *commedia
dell'arte* of *The Golden Couch* (1952). Renoir incorporates the artifice of the theater into
the cinema without destroying "that realism of space without which moving pictures do not
constitute cinema" (Bazin, p. 355).

It is not the same with cinema, the basic principle of which is a denial of any frontiers to action.

The idea of a *locus dramaticus* is not only alien to, it is essentially a contradiction of the concept of the screen. The screen is not a frame like that of a picture but a mask which allows only a part of the action to be seen. When a character moves off screen, we accept the fact that he is out of sight, but he continues to exist in his own capacity at some other place in the decor which is hidden from us. There are no wings to the screen. There could not be without destroying its specific illusion, which is to make of a revolver or of a face the very center of the universe. In contrast to the stage the space of the screen is centrifugal. It is because that infinity which the theater demands cannot be spatial that its area can be none other than the human soul. Enclosed in this space the actor is at the focus of a two-fold concave mirror. From the auditorium and from the decor there converge on him the dim lights of conscious human beings and of the footlights themselves. But the fire with which he burns is at once that of his inner passion and of that focal point at which he stands. He lights up in each member of his audience an accomplice flame. Like the ocean in a sea shell the dramatic infinities of the human heart moan and beat between the enclosing walls of the theatrical sphere. This is why this dramaturgy is in its essence human. Man is at once its cause and its subject.

On the screen man is no longer the focus of the drama, but will become eventually the center of the universe. The impact of his action may there set in motion an infinitude of waves. The decor that surrounds him is part of the solidity of the world. For this reason the actor as such can be absent from it, because man in the world enjoys no a priori privilege over animals and things. However there is no reason why he should not be the mainspring of the drama, as in Dreyer's *Jeanne d'Arc*, and in this respect the cinema may very well impose itself upon the theater. As actions *Phèdre* or *King Lear* are no less cinematographic than theatrical, and the visible death of a rabbit in *La Règle du jeu* affects us just as deeply as that of Agnès' little cat about which we are merely told.

But if Racine, Shakespeare, or Molière cannot be brought to the cinema by just placing them before the camera and the microphone, it is because the handling of the action and the style of the dialogue were conceived as echoing through the architecture of the auditorium. What is specifically theatrical about these tragedies is not their action so much as the human, that is to say the verbal, priority given to their dramatic structure. The problem of filmed theater at least where the classics are concerned does not consist so much in transposing an action from the stage to the screen as in transposing a text written for one dramaturgical system into another while at the same time retaining its effectiveness. It is not therefore essentially the action of a play which resists film adaptation, but above and beyond the phases of the intrigue (which it would be easy enough to adapt to the realism of the screen) it is the verbal form which aesthetic contingencies or cultural prejudices oblige us to respect. It is this which refuses to let itself be captured in the window of the screen. "The theater," says Baudelaire, "is a crystal chandelier." If one were called upon to offer in comparison a symbol other than this artificial crystal-like object, brilliant, intricate, and circular, which refracts the light which plays around its center and holds us prisoners of its aureole, we might say of the cinema that it is the little flashlight of the usher, moving like an uncertain comet across the night of our waking dream, the diffuse space without shape or frontiers that surrounds the screen.

The story of the failures and recent successes of theater on film will be found to be that of the ability of directors to retain the dramatic force of the play in a medium that reflects it or, at least, the ability to give this dramatic force enough resonance to permit a film audience to perceive it. In other words, it is a matter of an aesthetic that is not concerned with the actor but with decor and editing. Henceforth it is clear that filmed theater is basically destined to fail whenever it tends in any manner to become simply the photographing of scenic representation even and perhaps most of all when the camera is used to try and make us forget the footlights and the backstage area. The dramatic force of the text, instead of being gathered up in the actor, dissolves without echo into the cinematic ether. This is why a filmed play can show due respect to the text, be well acted in likely settings, and yet be completely worthless. This is what happened, to take a convenient example, to *Le Voyageur sans baggages*. The play lies there before us apparently true to itself yet drained of every ounce of energy, like a battery dead from an unknown short. But over and beyond the aesthetic of the decor we see clearly both on the screen and on the stage that in the last analysis the problem before us is that of realism. This is the problem we always end up with when we are dealing with cinema.

THE SCREEN AND THE REALISM OF SPACE

The realism of the cinema follows directly from its photographic nature. Not only does some marvel or some fantastic thing on the screen not undermine the reality of the image, on the contrary it is its most valid justification. Illusion in the cinema is not based as it is in the theater on convention tacitly accepted by the general public; rather, contrariwise, it is based on the inalienable realism of that which is shown. All trick work must be perfect in all material respects on the screen. The "invisible man" must wear pyjamas and smoke a cigarette.

Must we conclude from this that the cinema is dedicated entirely to the representation if not of natural reality at least of a plausible reality of which the spectator admits the identity with nature as he knows it? The comparative failure of German expressionism would seem to confirm this hypothesis, since it is evident that *Caligari* attempted to depart from realistic decor under the influence of the theater and painting. But this would be to offer an oversimplified explanation for a problem that calls for more subtle answers. We are prepared to admit that the screen opens upon an artificial world provided there exists a common denominator between the cinematographic image and the world we live in. Our experience of space is the structural basis for our concept of the universe. We may say in fact, adapting Henri Gouhier's formula, "The stage welcomes every illusion except the illusion of presence," that "the cinematographic image can be emptied of all reality save one—the reality of space."

It is perhaps an overstatement to say "all reality" because it is difficult to imagine a reconstruction of space devoid of all reference to nature. The world of the screen and our world cannot be juxtaposed. The screen necessarily substitutes for it since the very concept of a universe is spatially exclusive. For a time, a film is the Universe, the world, or if you like, Nature. We will see how the films that have attempted to substitute a fabricated nature and an artificial world for the world of experience have not all equally succeeded. Admitting the failure of *Caligari* and *Die Nibelungen* we then ask ourselves how we explain the undoubted success of *Nosferatu* and *La Passion de Jeanne d'Arc*, the criterion of success being that these films have never aged. Yet it would seem at first sight that the methods of direction belong to the same aesthetic family, and that viewing the varieties of temperament and period, one could group these four films together as expressionist as distinct from realist. However, if we examine them more closely we see that there are certain basic differences between them. It is clear in the case of R. Wiene and Murnau. *Nosferatu* plays, for the greater part of the time, against natural settings whereas the fantastic qualities of *Caligari* are derived from deformities of lighting and decor. The case of Dreyer's *Jeanne d'Arc* is a little more subtle since at first sight nature plays a nonexistent role. To put it more directly, the decor by Jean Hugo is no whit less artificial and theatrical than the settings of *Caligari*; the systematic use of close-ups and unusual angles is well calculated to destroy any sense of space. Regular cinéclub goers know that the film is unfailingly introduced with the famous story of how the hair of Falconetti was actually cut in the interest of the film and likewise, the actors, we are told, wore no make-up. These references to history ordinarily have no more than gossip value. In this case, they seem to me to hold the aesthetic secret of the film; the very thing to which it owes its continued survival. It is precisely because of them that the work of Dreyer ceases to have anything in common with the theater, and indeed one might say, with man. The greater recourse Dreyer has exclusively to the human "expression," the more he has to reconvert it again into Nature. Let there be no mistake, that prodigious fresco of heads is the very opposite of an actor's film. It is a documentary of faces. It is not important how well the actors play, whereas the pockmarks on Bishop Cauchon's face and the red patches of Jean d'Yd are an integral part of the action. In this drama-through-the-microscope the whole of nature palpitates beneath every pore. The movement of a wrinkle, the pursing of a lip are seismic shocks and the flow of tides, the flux and reflux of this human epidermis. But for me Dreyer's brilliant sense of cinema is evidenced in the exterior scene which every other director would assuredly have shot in the studio. The decor as built evoked a Middle Ages of the theater and of miniatures. In one sense, nothing is less realistic than this tribunal in the cemetery or this drawbridge, but the whole is lit by the light of the sun and the gravedigger throws a spadeful of real earth into the hole.[4]

It is these "secondary" details, apparently aesthetically at odds with the rest of the work, which give it its truly cinematic quality.

If the paradox of the cinema is rooted in the dialectic of concrete and abstract, if cinema is committed to communicate only by way of what is real, it becomes all the more important to discern those elements in filming which confirm our sense of natural reality and those which destroy that feeling. On the other hand, it certainly argues

---

[4]This is why I consider the graveyard scene in *Hamlet* and the death of Ophelia bad mistakes on Olivier's part. He had here a chance to introduce sun and soil by way of counterpoint to the setting of Elsinore. Does the actual shot of the sea during the soliloquy of Hamlet show that he had sensed the need for this? The idea, excellent in itself, is not well handled technically.

a lack of perception to derive one's sense of reality from these accumulations of factual detail. It is possible to argue that *Les Dames du Bois de Boulogne* is an eminently realistic film, though everything about it is stylized. Everything, except for
the rarely noticeable sound of a windshield wiper, the murmur of a waterfall, or the
rushing sound of soil escaping from a broken vase. These are the noises, chosen precisely for their "indifference" to the action, that guarantee its reality.

The cinema being of its essence a dramaturgy of Nature, there can be no cinema
without the setting up of an open space in place of the universe rather than as part
of it. The screen cannot give us the illusion of this feeling of space without calling
on certain natural guarantees. But it is less a question of set construction or of architecture or of immensity than of isolating the aesthetic catalyst, which it is sufficient
to introduce in an infinitesimal dose, to have it immediately take on the reality of
nature.

The concrete forest of *Die Nibelungen* may well pretend to be an infinite expanse.
We do not believe it to be so, whereas the trembling of just one branch in the wind,
and the sunlight, would be enough to conjure up all the forests of the world.

If this analysis be well founded, then we see that the basic aesthetic problem of
filmed theater is indeed that of the decor. The trump card that the director must hold
is the reconversion into a window onto the world of a space oriented toward an interior dimension only, namely the closed and conventional area of the theatrical play.

It is not in Laurence Olivier's *Hamlet* that the text seems to be rendered superfluous or its strength diminished by directorial interpretations, still less in Welles'
Macbeth, but paradoxically in the stage productions of Gaston Baty, to the precise
extent that they go out of their way to create a cinematographic space on the stage;
to deny that the settings have a reverse side, thus reducing the sonority of the text
simply to the vibration of the voice of the actor who is left without his "resonance
box" like a violin that is nothing else but strings. One would never deny that the
essential thing in the theater is the text. The latter conceived for the anthropocentric expression proper to the stage and having as its function to bring nature to it
cannot, without losing its raison d'être, be used in a space transparent as glass. The
problem then that faces the filmmaker is to give his decor a dramatic opaqueness
while at the same time reflecting its natural realism. Once this paradox of space has
been dealt with, the director, so far from hesitating to bring theatrical conventions
and faithfulness to the text to the screen will find himself now, on the contrary,
completely free to rely on them. From that point on it is no longer a matter of running away from those things which "make theater" but in the long run to acknowledge their existence by rejecting the resources of the cinema, as Cocteau did in *Les
Parents terribles* and Welles in *Macbeth*, or by putting them in quotation marks as
Laurence Olivier did in *Henry V*. The evidence of a return to filmed theater that we
have had during the last ten years belongs essentially to the history of decor and
editing. It is a conquest of realism—not, certainly, the realism of subject matter or
realism of expression but that realism of space without which moving pictures do
not constitute cinema.

1951

LEO BRAUDY
FROM THE WORLD IN A FRAME

ACTING: STAGE VS. SCREEN

Leo Braudy, the co-editor of this anthology, began his writing about film with an essay on *Psycho* in *Film Quarterly* (1968) that paid special attention to the ways Hitchcock manipulates conventional audience response. After editing an anthology dealing with François Truffaut's *Shoot the Piano Player* (1971) and a book on the films of Jean Renoir (1972), he published *The World in a Frame* (1976), which looked at the effects of film visually in terms of its objects, culturally in terms of its genre myths and structures, and psychologically in terms of the effect of acting and performance. Now primarily working in the area of cultural history, he is also the author of *The Frenzy of Renown: Fame and Its History* (1986) and *From Chivalry to Terrorism: War and the Changing Nature of Masculinity* (2003), as well a book dealing with Elia Kazan's *On the Waterfront* (2005). He is currently University Professor and Bing Professor of English and American literature at the University of Southern California.

(Another selection from Braudy's work appears in Section VII.)

Acting in Europe and America has been historically defined by the varying interplay of the heightened and the normal, the theatrical and the nonchalant, in the conception of the role. Until the Renaissance, there was little attempt to place any special value on the absorption of the rhythm, themes, and gestures of everyday life into drama or acting style. Aristotle had taught that the most intense feelings possible in drama were those in tragedy, when the characters and the acting style were on a much higher plane than the normal life of the audience. Everyday life, where the characters and the way they behave tend to be on the same or lower social levels than the audience, was primarily a source of stylized comedy. The stage was raised above the audience in part because the characters and their impersonators were not to be considered as individually as the audience might assess each other. In Greek, Roman, and medieval society, actors therefore tended to portray beings purer than the audience, the somber figures of myth and the caricatures of comedy—a division of acting labor not unlike that of the silent screen.

Shakespeare helped make an enormous change in this relation between the audience and the actors by elaborating the analogies possible between the world and the stage. He began the European theater's effort to absorb and reflect the life of the audience as much as to bring the audience out of itself into another world. Comedy could therefore become more serious because it was no longer necessary to involve emotions lower than the grand style of tragedy. More intimate theaters and better lighting permitted a more nuanced acting style. By the mid-eighteenth century David Garrick had become the first to attempt historical authenticity in costuming, once again asserting the need to ground the play and the style of acting in some possible and plausible setting rather than a special world of theater. The "fourth wall" theories of the latter nineteenth century further defined theatrical space and dramatic acting as an extension of the world of the audience. Stylized acting did not disappear, of course. The broader styles remained in opera, ballet, and popular comedy, as well as revivals of classics, symbolic and proletarian drama, and the experiments with ritual theater from the end of World War Two to the present.

Acting on stage had necessarily developed a tradition of naturalness as well. In the eighteenth century Diderot had argued that the paradox of acting is that an actor must be cold and tranquil in order to project emotion. Actors who play from the soul, he said, are mediocre and uneven. We are not moved by the man of violence, but by the man who possesses himself. In the early twentieth century, Konstantin Stanislavsky turned Diderot's view of the actor self-possessed in passion into a whole style. He rejected theories of acting based on imitation and emphasized instead an actor's inner life as the source of energy and authenticity for his characterizations. More "mechanical" and expressionist styles of stage acting implicitly attacked Stanislavsky's methods by their emphasis on the intensity of emotion and the visual coherence of the stage ensemble. Minglings of the two traditions produced such hybrids as the Group Theater, in which the interplay between ensemble and individual produced a thematic tension often missing from Eisenstein's productions, whether on stage or in film. Elia Kazan's film style, for example, with its mixture of expressionistic, closed directorial style and open, naturalistic acting, is a direct descendant of this tradition.[1]

Our ability to learn what films can tell us about human character has suffered not only from preconceptions derived from the novel of psychological realism, but also from assumptions about acting that are drawn from the stage. We know much better what our attitude should be toward characters in fiction and drama. Unlike those forms, films emphasize acting and character, often at the expense of forms and language. Films add what is impossible in the group situation of the stage or the omniscient world of the novel: a sense of the mystery inside character, the strange core of connection with the face and body the audience comes to know so well, the sense of an individuality that can never be totally expressed in words or action. The stage cannot have this effect because the audience is constantly aware of the actor's impersonation. Character in film generally is more like character as we perceive it everyday than it is in any other representational art. The heightened style of silent film acting could be considered an extension of stage acting, but the more personal style allowed by sound film paradoxically both increased the appeal of films and lowered their intellectual status. The artistic was the timeless, Garbo not Dietrich, Valentino not Gable.

---

[1] Diderot's *Paradoxe sur le comédien* was not published until 1830, although it was written in the late 1760s. A later printing in 1902 may have had an influence on Stanislavsky's theories.

But character in sound film especially was not so much deficient as it was elusive. Films can be less didactic about character because the film frame is less confining than the fictional narrative or the theatrical proscenium. Sound films especially can explore the tension between the "real person" playing the role and the image projected on the screen. The line between film actor and part is much more difficult to draw than that between stage actor and role, and the social dimension of "role" contrasts appropriately with the personal dimension of "part." Film acting is less impersonation than personation, part of personality but not identifiable with it. "Can Ingrid Bergman commit murder?" ask the advertisements for *Murder on the Orient Express* (Sidney Lumet, 1975); the casual substitution of actress for character crudely makes an assertion that better films explore more subtly. Unlike the stage actor, the film actor cannot get over the footlights. Although this technical necessity may seem to make him less "real" than the stage actor, it makes his relation to the character he plays much more real. Audiences demand to hear more about the private life of the film actor than the stage actor because film creates character by tantalizing the audience with the promise of the secret self, always just out of the grasp of final articulation and meaning. The other life of a stage character is the real life of the person who plays him. But the other life of a film character is the continuity in other films of the career of the actor who plays him. In plays the unrevealed self tends to be a reduced, meaner version of the displayed self; in films it is almost always a complex enhancement. Within the film a character may have a limited meaning. But the actor who plays him can potentially be a presence larger than that one part, at once more intimate and more distant than is ever possible on stage.[2]

Film preserves a performance that is superior to the script, whereas stage performances and plays are separate realities, with the performance often considered second best. The stage actor is performing a role: he may be the best, one of the best, the only, or one of many to play that role. But the role and its potentials will exist long after he has ceased to play it, to be interested in it, to be alive. The film actor does not so much perform a role as he creates a kind of life, playing between his characterization in a particular film and his potential escape from that character, outside the film and perhaps into other films. The stage actor memorizes an entire role in proper order, putting it on like a costume, while the film actor learns his part in pieces, often out of chronological order, using his personality as a kind of armature, or as painters will let canvas show through to become part of the total effect. If the movie is remade and another actor plays the part, there is little sense of the competition between actors that characterizes revivals on stage. "Revival" is a stage word and "remake" is a film word. Hamlet remains beyond Booth's or Olivier's or Gielgud's performance, but Alan Ladd as Gatsby and Robert Redford as Gatsby exist in different worlds.

Filmmaking is a discontinuous process, in which the order of filming is influenced more by economics than by aesthetics. Film actors must therefore either have stronger

---

[2]In these remarks, I am talking not so much about the craft of acting as about the effects of acting on the audience. I would hope, however, that what I say has implications for craft and method as well, at least in terms of a test of effectiveness beyond the pleasures of theory.

personalities than stage actors or draw upon the resources of personality much more than stage actors do. Strong film actors can never do anything out of character. Their presence defines their character and the audience is always ready for them to reveal more. Even though studio heads like Louis Mayer forced actors and actresses to appear "in character" offscreen as well, we sense and accept potential and variety from the greatest movie actors, while we may reject less flamboyant fictional characters as "unreal" or refer to the woodenness of stage characterization. Continuity in stage acting is thematic continuity: "Watch in happiness someone whom you will soon see in sorrow" is one of the fatalistic possibilities. But the discontinuities of film acting allow the actor to concentrate on every moment as if it were the only reality that existed. No matter how conventionalized the plot, the film actor can disregard its clichés and trust instead to the force and continuity of his projected personality to satisfy beyond the more obvious forms of theme and incident. Because he must present his play in straightforward time, a stage director will work with the actor to get a "line" or a "concept" of the character that will permeate every scene. But movie acting, bound

Marlene Dietrich and John Lodge in Josef von Sternberg's *The Scarlet Empress* (1934). "Films add what is impossible in the group situation of the stage or the omniscient world of the novel: a sense of the mystery inside character, the strange core of connection with the face and body the audience comes to know so well, the sense of an individuality that can never be totally expressed in words or action" (Braudy, p. 357).

in time to the shooting schedule and the editing table, must use what is left out as well as what is expressed. The greatest difference between a film and a stage version of the same work is less in the "opening" of space that films usually emphasize than in the different sense of the inner life of the characters we get. . . .

Movies therefore stand between the strongly social emphasis of theater and the strongly individual emphasis of novels, incorporating elements of both. At a play we are always outside the group, at the footlights. But at a film we move between inside and outside, individual and social perspectives. Movie acting can therefore include stage acting better than stage acting can include movie acting. George C. Scott, for example, is essentially a stage actor who also can come across very well in film. When he was making *Patton* (Franklin Schaffner, 1970), he insisted that he repeat his entire first speech eight times to allow for the different camera angles; he refused to repeat only the sections that corresponded to the rephotographing. His sense of the character was therefore what I have been describing as a stage sense of character, in which the continuity is linear and spelled out. The performance is excellent and effective, but Scott's way of doing it tells us nothing of the differences in stage and film acting. It may have a touch of the New York stage actor's almost traditional hostility to films. At best, it is only another example of the way a newer art can more comfortably embrace the methods of an older art than the other way around. In fact, virtuosity in films tends to be a characteristic of second leads or medium minor characters, not stars, and the Academy Awards perpetuate the stage-derived standards by giving so many awards to actors and actresses cast against type, that is, for stage-style "virtuosity."

The film actor emphasizes display, while the stage actor explores disguise. But stage acting is still popularly considered to be superior to film acting. An actor who does a good job disappears into his role, while the bad (read "film") actor is only playing himself. The true actor, the professional craftsman, may use his own experience to strengthen his interpretation. But the audience should always feel that he has properly distanced and understood that experience; it is another tool in his professional workchest. The false actor, the amateur actor, the film actor, on the other hand, works on his self-image, carries it from part to part, constantly projecting the same thing—"himself." Such a belief is rooted in an accurate perception; but it is a false interpretation of that perception. The stage actor does project a sense of holding back, of discipline and understanding, the influence of head over feelings, while the film actor projects effortlessness, nonchalance, immediacy, the seemingly unpremeditated response. Thus, when stage actors attack film actors, they attack in some puritanical way the lack of perceptible hard work, obvious professional craft, in the film actor's performance. Like many nonprofessionals in their audience, such stage actors assume that naïveté, spontaneity, "being yourself," are self-images that anyone in front of a camera can achieve. A frequent Actors Studio exercise, for example, is "Private Moment," in which the student is asked to act out before the group something he or she ordinarily does alone that would be very embarrassing if someone happened to see. Private self-indulgences and private games are thereby mined for their exposable, group potential. But the concentration of film, its ability to isolate the individual, makes every moment that way, and so the problem of the film actor may be to scale down intimacy rather than discover and exaggerate it.

How do we know the "themselves" film actors play except through the residue of their playing? How much do film actors, as opposed to stage actors, model their offscreen selves to continue or contrast with their screen images? To accuse an actor of "playing himself" implies that we have seen and compared the "real" and "false" selves of the actor and reached a conclusion. Film acting deposits a residual self that snowballs from film to film, creating an image with which the actor, the scriptwriter, and the director can play as they wish. Donald Richie has recorded that the Japanese director Yasujiro Ozu said: "I could no more write, not knowing who the actor was to be, than an artist could paint, not knowing what color he was using." Ozu's remark indicates how a director takes advantage of a previously developed image in order to create a better film. But the stage actor in a sense ceases to exist from play to play; we experience only the accumulation of his talent, his versatility. In our minds the stage actor stays within the architectures he has inhabited, while the film actor exists in between as well, forever immediate to our minds and eyes, escaping the momentary enclosures that the individual films have placed around him.

"Playing yourself" involves one's interpretation of what is most successful and appealing in one's own nature and then heightening it. Film actors play their roles the way we play ourselves in the world. Audiences may now get sustenance from films and from film acting because they no longer are so interested in the social possibilities of the self that has been the metaphysic of stage acting since Shakespeare and the Renaissance, the place of role-playing in the life of the audience. The Shakespearean films of Laurence Olivier and Orson Welles clearly express the contrast. The tendency in stage acting is to subordinate oneself to the character, while the great film actor is generally more important than the character he plays. Our sense of Olivier, in his Shakespearean roles is one of distance and disguise: the purified patriotism of Henry V, in which all the play's negative hints about his character have been removed; the blond wig he uses to play Hamlet, so that, as he has said, no one will associate him with the part; the bent back, twisted fingers, and long black hair of Richard III. But Welles assimilates the roles to himself. Costume for Welles is less a disguise than a generation from within and so he presented it in various television appearances of the 1950s, gradually making up for his part while he explained the play to the audience, until he turned full face into the camera and spoke the lines. In theater we experience the gap between actor and role as expertise; in film it may be described as a kind of self-irony. The great stage actor combats the superiority of the text, its preexistence, by choosing his roles: Olivier will play Hamlet; Olivier will play a music-hall comic. The great film actor, assured that his image absorbs and makes real the script, may allow himself to be cast in unpromising roles, if only for visibility. In the audience we feel Welles's character to be part of his role, whereas we perceive not Olivier's character but his intelligence and his ability to immerse himself in a role. Olivier is putting on a great performance, but Welles feels superior enough to the Shakespearean text to cut, reorganize, and invent. Olivier is a great interpreter; Welles is an equal combatant. For both, Shakespeare is like a genre, similar to the western, that offers materials for a contemporary statement. But Olivier sticks closely to the language and form of the play itself. We judge Olivier finally by Shakespeare, but we judge Welles by other films. Both choose those Shakespearean plays that emphasize a central character. But Olivier's willingness to allow Shakespeare the last word frees him for the more assertive political roles, whereas Welles stays with the more domestic or even isolated figures of Macbeth and Othello. Olivier began his Shakespearean film career with the heroic self-confidence of Henry V, while Welles, at least for the moment, has ended his with Falstaff—the choice of the ironic imagination of film over the theatrical assertion of social power.

These distinctions between stage acting and film acting are, of course, not absolute but points on a slippery continuum. Marlon Brando's career, for example, is a constant conflict between his desire to be versatile—to do different kinds of films, use different accents, wear different costumes—and the demand of his audience that he elaborate his residual cinematic personality. Brando tries to get into his roles, and often sinks them in the process, while Cary Grant pumps them up like a balloon and watches them float off into the sky. The main trouble that Chaplin has in *A Countess from Hong Kong* (1967) is taking two actors (Brando and Sophia Loren), whose own sense of their craft emphasizes naturalistic, historically defined character, and placing them within a film world where they would best exist as masks and stereotypes. Their efforts to ground their characters destroys the film. It may be funny if Chaplin or Cary Grant vomited out a porthole, but it's not funny when Brando does it. Brando can be funny in films only as a counterpoint to our sense of "Brando," for example in *Bedtime Story* (Ralph Levy, 1964). When he is acting someone else, the ironic sense of self-image that is natural to a film actor does not exist. We share Cary Grant's sense of distance from his roles, whether they are comic, melodramatic, or whatever, because it corresponds to our sense of personal distance from our daily roles in life. The sense of "putting it on" that we get from Brando's greatest roles—*A Streetcar Named Desire*, *Viva Zapata!*, *The Wild One*, *On the Waterfront*—stands in paradoxical relation to Method theories of submergence in the role. Brando's willingness to cooperate with Bernardo Bertolucci in the commentary on and mockery of his screen image that forms so much of the interest of *Last Tango in Paris* may indicate that he no longer holds to the theatrical definition of great acting. His progenitor role in *The Godfather* seems to have released him to create the paradox of the self-revealed inner life of a screen image elaborated by *Last Tango*. In the films of the 1970s, character, and therefore acting as well, has taken on the central importance in film. And the stage actor in film finds that his virtuosity is more a parlor trick than a technique of emotional and artistic power. Films make us fall in love with, admire, even hate human beings who may actually in the moment we watch them be dead and dust. But that is the grandeur of films as well: the preservation of human transience, the significance not so much of social roles as of fragile, fleeting feelings.

1976

SERGEI EISENSTEIN
DICKENS, GRIFFITH AND OURSELVES
[DICKENS, GRIFFITH AND FILM TODAY]

... Griffith stood out as the most fascinating figure in this field. Because his works did not use cinema as a mere amusement or pastime but contained the rudiments of the art that, in the hands of a constellation of Soviet masters, was destined to cover Soviet film-making with undying glory in the pages of the history of world cinema, thanks to the novelty of the ideas, the unprecedented plots and the perfection of form in equal measure.

The intense curiosity about *construction* and *method* at that time soon identified the source of one of the most powerful influences of Griffith's pictures.

It was in the hitherto unfamiliar field that bears a name that we know of not from art, but from engineering and electronic equipment, and that appeared for the first time in the most progressive art—cinema.

This field, this method, this principle of construction and assembly was *montage*.

Montage, whose principles underlay American film culture, but which owed its full development, definitive interpretation and world recognition to our cinema.

Montage, which played a vital role in Griffith's works, and brought him his most glorious triumphs.

Griffith approached it through the device of parallel action and, essentially, he progressed no further, making it possible for film-makers from the other half of the globe, from another epoch and with a different class structure, to perfect the matter definitively.

But I am getting ahead of myself. Let us look at how montage came to Griffith—or Griffith came to montage.

Griffith came to it through the device of parallel action. But it was none other than Dickens who gave Griffith the idea of parallel action! ...

What were Dickens' novels, for their time?

What were they for his readers?

There is one answer: the same as cinema is now for those same sections of the population.

They made the reader experience the same passions, making the same appeal to the good, the sentimental; like film, they made him shudder at vice, and provided the same escape from the humdrum, prosaic and everyday into something unaccustomed, unusual and fantastic. And at the same time it appears as nothing other than the everyday and prosaic.

And, illuminated by the reflection from the pages of novels to life, this ordinariness came to seem romantic, and the dull people of everyday life were grateful to the author for making them aware of potentially romantic figures.

Hence there was the same fascination for Dickens' novels as there is now for film. . . . And perhaps the secret is that what links Dickens to cinema is the astonishingly plastic quality of his novels. Their astonishing visual and optical quality.

Dickens' characters are just as plastically visible and ever so slightly exaggerated as the screen heroes of today.

These heroes deeply affect the viewers' emotions with their visible image: these villains are remembered for their twisted expressions, these heroes are invariably associated with that special, slightly unnatural shining gleam with which the screen lights them up.

Dickens' characters are just the same—that gallery of Pickwicks, Dombeys, Fagins, Tackletons and others that have been unerringly plastically captured and sketched with pitiless sharpness. . . .

You should not pursue analogies and similarities too far—they lose their conviction and charm and begin to sound contrived or garbled. I would hate it if my comparison between Dickens and Griffith were to lose its persuasiveness, by allowing this abundance of common features to slide into a game of anecdotal semblance between distinguishing features.

The more so as this examination of Dickens no longer concerns Griffith's skill as a film-maker, but has begun to touch on the craft of cinema in general.

But that is precisely why I have to dig more and more deeply into features of Dickens' cinema, using Griffith to show how instructive they were for future cinema.

So I shall expect indulgence if, when leafing through Dickens, I find 'dissolves'. How else can one term this description from *A Tale of Two Cities*?

> Along the Paris streets, the death-cars rumble, hollow and harsh. Six tumbrils carry the day's wine to La Guillotine. . . .
> Six tumbrils roll along the streets. Change these back again to what they were, thou powerful enchanter, Time, and they shall be seen to be the carriages of absolute monarchs, the equipages of feudal nobles, the toilettes of flaring Jezebels, the churches that are not my Father's house but dens of thieves, the huts of millions of starving peasants!

How many such 'cinematic' surprises must be lurking in Dickens' pages!

But I shall gladly restrict myself to the chief constructs of montage which were shown crudely in Dickens' work, and later flourished as elements of film composition in Griffith's.

Let us take a peek under the curtains, at this rich and hitherto useful resource, by opening the first novel that comes to hand.

Oliver Twist, for example.

Let us open it at random. Suppose it is Chapter XXI.

We read the start:

CHAPTER XXI[1]

1.

It was a cheerless morning when they got into the street; blowing and raining hard; and the clouds looking dull and stormy.

The night had been very wet: large pools of water had collected in the road: and the kennels were overflowing.

There was a faint glimmering of the coming day in the sky; but it rather aggravated then relieved the gloom of the scene: the sombre light only serving to pale that which the street lamps afforded, without shedding any warmer or brighter tints upon the wet housetops, and dreary streets.

There appeared to be nobody stirring in that part of the town; the windows of the houses were all closely shut; and the street through which they passed, were noiseless and empty.

2.

By the time they had turned into the Bethnal Green Road, the day had fairly begun to break. Many of the lamps were already extinguished;

a few country waggons were slowly toiling on, towards London;

now and then, a stage-coach, covered with mud, rattled briskly by;

the driver bestowing, as he passed, an admonitory lash upon the heavy waggoner who, by keeping on the wrong side of the road, had endangered his arriving at the office a quarter of a minute after his time.

The public-houses, with gas-lights burning inside, were already open.

By degrees, other shops began to be unclosed, and a few scattered people were met with.

Then, came straggling groups of labourers going to their work;

then, men and women with fish-baskets on their heads;

donkey-carts laden with vegetables;

chaise-carts filled with live-stock or whole carcasses of meat;

milk-women with pails;

an unbroken concourse of people, trudging out with various supplies to the eastern suburbs of the town.

3.

As they approached the City, the noise and traffic gradually increased;

when they threaded the streets between Shoreditch and Smithfield, it had swelled into a roar of sound and bustle.

It was as light as it was likely to be, till night came on again, and the busy morning of half the London population had begun . . .

4.

It was market-morning.

The ground was covered, nearly ankle-deep, with filth and mire;

a thick stream, perpetually rising from the reeking bodies of the cattle,

and mingling with the fog,

which seemed to rest upon the chimney-tops, hung heavily above . . .

---

[1]For purposes of clarity I have broken the beginning of this chapter into smaller fragments than did its author, and numbered them.

Countrymen,
butchers,
drovers,
hawkers,
boys,
thieves,
idlers,
and vagabonds of every low grade,
were mingled together in a mass;

5.
the whistling of drovers,
the barking of dogs,
the bellowing and plunging of oxen,
the bleating of sheep,
the grunting and squeaking of pigs,
the cries of hawkers,
the shouts, oaths, and quarrelling on all sides;
the ringing of bells
and roar of voices, that issued from every public-house;
the crowding, pushing, driving, beating,
whooping, and yelling;
the hideous and discordant din that resounded from every corner of the market;
and the unwashed, unshaven, squalid and dirty figures constantly running to and fro,
and bursting in and out of the throng; rendered it a stunning and bewildering scene,
which quite confounded the senses.

How often have we encountered this construction in Griffith's work!

Using a similarly strict development and acceleration of pace, with the same play of light, from the burning street-lamps to those that are extinguished; from night to dawn and from dawn to the brightness of full daylight ('It was light as it was likely to be, till night came on again'); with its considered succession of purely visual elements interspliced with auditory ones, so that the initial indefinite rumble, echoing from afar the gradual dawn, turns into a full-blooded road, and into constructions that are purely auditory, and already concrete and objective (see section 5 of my breakdown), and with the same vignettes inserted *en passant*—like the coachman dashing for the office before it opens; and finally, with the same amazingly typifying details, such as the reeking bodies of the cattle, from which the steam rises and forms a common cloud with the morning fog, or the close-up of the foot that was 'nearly ankle-deep, with filth and mire', conveying a complete picture of a market better than a dozen pages of description could! . . .

If the examples cited above contain prototypes of the *montage expositions* that are characteristic of Griffith, we have only to read *Oliver Twist* carefully to encounter straight away another montage method typical of Griffith—*the montage progression of parallel scenes, intercut.*

For this let me turn to the set of scenes in the famous episode where Mr Brownlow, to show his faith in Oliver, chooses him to return books to the bookseller; and where Oliver again falls prey to Sikes the burglar, his friend Nancy and old Fagin.

These scenes unfold in a way that is utterly Griffithian, both in their internal emotional content and in the unusual way that the characters stand out—their delineation; in the uncommon richness of their dramatic and comic features; and, finally, in the typically Griffithian montage of parallel splicing of all the links between the separate episodes.

Let us look in particular detail at this last characteristic; it seems so unexpected in Dickens, and so typical of Griffith.

CHAPTER XIV

Comprising further Particulars of Oliver's Stay at Mr Brownlow's, with the remarkable Prediction which one Mr Grimwig uttered concerning him, when he went out on an Errand

'Dear me, I am very sorry for that,' exclaimed Mr Brownlow; 'I particularly wished those books to be returned to-night.'

'Send Oliver with them,' said Mr Grimwig, with an ironical smile; 'he will be sure to deliver them safely, you know.'

'Yes; do let me take them, if you please, sir,' said Oliver. 'I'll run all the way, sir.'

The old gentleman was just going to say that Oliver should not go out on any account; when a most malicious cough from Mr Grimwig determined him that he should; and that, by his prompt discharge of the commission, he should prove to him the injustice of his suspicions: on this head at least: at once.

Oliver is prepared for his errand to the bookseller.

'I won't be ten minutes, sir,' replied Oliver, eagerly.

Mrs Bedwin, Mr Brownlow's housekeeper, gives Oliver directions and sends him off.

'Bless his sweet face!' said the old lady, looking after him. 'I can't bear, somehow, to let him go out of my sight.'

At this moment, Oliver looked gaily round, and nodded before he turned the corner. The old lady smilingly returned his salutation, and, closing the door, went back to her own room.

'Let me see; he'll be back in twenty minutes, at the longest,' said Mr Brownlow, pulling out his watch, and placing it on the table. 'It will be dark by that time.'

'Oh! you really expect him to come back, do you?' inquired Mr Grimwig.

'Don't you?' asked Mr Brownlow, smiling.

The spirit of contradiction was strong in Mr Grimwig's breast, at the moment; and it was rendered stronger by his friend's confident smile.

'No,' he said, smiting the table with his fist, 'I do not. The boy has a new suit of clothes on his back, a set of valuable books under his arm, and a five-pound note in his pocket. He'll join his old friends the thieves, and laugh at you. If ever that boy returns, sir, I'll eat my head.'

With these words he drew his chair closer to the table; and there the two friends sat, in silent expectation, with the watch between them.

This is followed by a short 'insert' in the shape of a digression.

It is worthy of remark, as illustrating the importance we attach to our own judgments, and the pride with which we put forth our most rash and hasty conclusions, that, although Mr Grimwig was not by any means a bad-hearted man, and though he would have been unfeignedly sorry to see his respected friend duped and deceived, he really did most earnestly and strongly hope at that moment, that Oliver Twist might not come back.

And again a return to the two gentlemen:

> It grew so dark, that the figures on the dial-plate were scarcely discernible; but there the two old gentlemen continued to sit, in silence, with the watch between them.

The twilight tells us that a considerable period of time has elapsed; but the *close-up* of the watch, which has already been shown *twice* lying between the old gentlemen, tells us that a great deal of time has passed already. But then, at the same time as not only the two elderly gentlemen but also the kindly reader are drawn into the game of 'will he/won't he return', the worst apprehensions and the vague premonitions of the old lady are justified by the cut to a new scene—Chapter XV: 'Showing how very fond of Oliver Twist the merry old Jew and Miss Nancy were'. (This begins with a short scene in the public house between Sikes the bandit and his dog, old Fagin, and Miss Nancy, who was to spy out Oliver's place of residence.)

> 'You are on the scent, are you, Nancy?' inquired Sikes, proffering the glass.
> 'Yes I am, Bill,' replied the young lady, disposing of its contents; 'and tired enough of it I am, too . . .'

Then comes one of the best scenes in the whole book—at least, the scene which I remember best from childhood, together with the evil figure of Fagin: the scene in which Oliver, walking along with the books under his arm, is suddenly

> startled by a young woman screaming out very loud. 'Oh, my dear brother!' And he had hardly looked up, to see what the matter was, when he was stopped by having a pair of arms thrown tight around his neck.

With this polished manoeuvre, Nancy restores the desperately resisting Oliver—her 'prodigal brother'—to the bosom of Fagin's gang of thieves, while the whole street looks on in sympathy.

The same chapter finished with the now familiar montage phrase:

> The gas-lamps were lighted; Mrs Bedwin was waiting anxiously at the open door; the servant had run up the street twenty times to see if there were any traces of Oliver; and still the two old gentlemen sat, perseveringly, at the dark parlour, with the watch between them.

In Chapter XVI, Oliver has been reinstated in the thieves' den, and subjected to ridicule. Nancy rescues him from a beating:

> 'I won't stand by and see it done, Fagin,' cried the girl. 'You've got the boy and what more would you have?—Let him be—let him be—or I shall put that mark on some of you, that will bring me to the gallows before my time.'

(Incidentally, these sudden bursts of generosity from 'morally degraded' types are typical of both Dickens and Griffith and they unfailingly, if sentimentally, act upon even the most sceptical audiences and readers!)

At the end of the chapter, Oliver is in agonies, exhausted, and falls 'sound asleep'.

Here the physical unity of time is broken up—that evening and night are filled with events; but the montage unity of the episode that binds Oliver to Mr Brownlow, on the other hand, and Fagin's gang on the other, is not broken.

In Chapter XVII there follows the visit of the church beadle, Mr Bumble, responding to the announcement about the missing little boy, and Bumble's appearance at Mr Brownlow's, who is again in Grimwig's company.

The content and sense of their conversation is revealed by the chapter heading: 'Oliver's Destiny continuing unpropitious, brings a Great Man to London to injure His Reputation'.

> 'I fear it is all too true,' said the old gentleman sorrowfully, after looking over the papers. 'This is not much for your intelligence; but I would gladly have given you treble the money, if it had been favourable to the boy.'
>
> It is not improbable that if Mr Bumble had been possessed of this information at an earlier period of the interview, he might have imparted a very different colouring to his little history. It was too late to do it now, however; so he shook his head gravely, and, pocketing the five guineas, withdrew.
>
> Mr Brownlow paced the room to and fro for some minutes; evidently so much disturbed by the beadle's tale, that even Mr Grimwig forbore to vex him further.
>
> At length he stopped, and rang the bell violently.
>
> 'Mrs Bedwin,' said Mr Brownlow, when the housekeeper appeared; 'that boy, Oliver, is an impostor.'
>
> 'It can't be, sir. It cannot be.' said the old lady, energetically.
>
> 'I tell you he is,' retorted the old gentleman. 'What do you mean by can't be? We have just heard a full account of him from his birth; and he has been a thorough-paced little villain, all his life.'
>
> 'I never will believe it, sir,' replied the old lady, firmly. 'Never!'
>
> 'You old women never believe anything but quack-doctors, and lying story-books,' growled Mr Grimwig. 'I knew it all along. Why didn't you take my advice in the beginning; you would, if he hadn't had a fever, I suppose, eh! He was interesting, wasn't he? Interesting! Bah!' And Mr Grimwig poked the fire with a flourish.
>
> 'He was a dear, grateful, gentle child, sir,' retorted Mrs Bedwin, indignantly. 'I know what children are, sir; and have done these forty years; and people who can't say the same, shouldn't say anything about them. That's my opinion!'
>
> This was a hard hit at Mr Grimwig, who was a bachelor. As it extorted nothing from that gentleman but a smile, the old lady tossed her head, and smoothed down her apron preparatory to another speech, when she was stopped by Mr Brownlow.
>
> 'Silence!' said the old gentleman, feigning an anger he was far from feeling. 'Never let me hear the boy's name again. I rang to tell you that. Never. Never, on any pretence, mind! You may leave the room, Mrs Bedwin. Remember! I am in earnest.'

And the whole elaborate montage complex of the entire episode ends with the phrase: 'There were sad hearts at Mr Brownlow's that night.'

It is no accident that I have allowed myself to quote such detailed extracts, concerning not only the composition of the scene but also the delineation of the characters, for, in their very modelling, in their description and conduct, there is much that is typical of Griffith's style. This applies equally to his 'Dickensian' suffering, defenceless beings (think of Lillian Gish and Richard Barthelmess in *Broken Blossoms* or the Gish sisters in *Orphans of the Storm*) and to the characters of the two elderly gentlemen and Mrs Bedwin, who are no less typical of him; and finally to the cronies of Fagin—the merry old Jew—who was entirely characteristic of Griffith.

With respect to our immediate task of analysing how Dickens organises the montage progression of the plot composition, the results may be set out in accordance with the following table:

1. *The elderly gentlemen.*
2. Oliver's departure.
3. *The elderly gentlemen and the watch. It is still light.*

4. Digression about Mr Grimwig's character.
5. *The elderly gentlemen and the watch. Gathering twilight.*
6. Fagin, Sikes, and Nancy in the public house.
7. The street scene.
8. *The elderly gentlemen and the watch. The gas-lamps have been lit.*
9. Oliver is back with Fagin.
10. Digression at the beginning of Chapter XVII.
11. Mr Bumble's journey.
12. *The elderly gentlemen* and Mr Brownlow's instruction that Oliver be forgotten forever.

As we can see, we have before us a typical and, for Griffith, a model of the parallel montage of two storylines; the presence of one (the waiting gentlemen) emotionally heightens the suspense of the other (Oliver's misadventure)—which is dramatic enough as it is.

It is in the 'rescuers' who rush to save the 'damsel in distress' that Griffith earns his greatest laurels in the field of parallel montage!

But what is most curious is another 'insert' at the *very heart* of the episode we have chosen—a whole digression at the beginning of Chapter XVII which I have deliberately kept quiet about. Why is this digression noteworthy?

Because it is an idiosyncratic 'treatment' of the principles of that very same montage plot construction, here executed so beautifully, that has passed from Dickens to Griffith.

Here it is:

It is the custom on the stage, in all good murderous melodramas, to present the tragic and the comic scenes, in as regular alternation, as the layers of red and white in a side of streaky bacon. The hero sinks upon his straw bed, weighed down by fetters and misfortunes; in the next scene, his faithful but unconscious squire regales the audience with a comic song. We behold, with throbbing bosoms, the heroine in the grasp of a proud and ruthless baron: her virtue and her life alike in danger, drawing forth her dagger to preserve the one at the cost of the other; and just as our expectations are wrought up to the highest pitch, a whistle is heard, and we are straightway transported to the great hall of the castle: where a grey-headed seneschal sings a funny chorus with a funnier body of vassals, who are free of all sorts of places, from church vaults to palaces, and roam about in company, carolling perpetually.

Such changes appear absurd; but they are not so unnatural as they would seem at first sight. The transitions in real life from well-spread boards to death-beds, and from mourning weeds to holiday garments, are not a whit less startling; only, there, we are busy actors, instead of passive lookers-on, which makes a vast difference. The actors in the mimic life of the theatre, are blind to violent transitions and abrupt impulses of passion or feeling, which, presented before the eyes of mere spectators, are at once condemned as outrageous and preposterous.

As sudden shiftings of the scene, and rapid changes of time and place, are not only sanctioned in books by long usage, but are by many considered as the greatest art of authorship: an author's skill in his craft being, by such critics, chiefly estimated with relation to the dilemmas in which he leaves his characters at the end of every chapter: this brief introduction to the present one may perhaps be deemed unnecessary.

There is something else of interest in this quoted 'treatment': we have, in his own words, a description of Dickens' direct link with theatrical melodrama.

Dickens hereby seems to establish himself as the connecting link between the future art of cinema, which could not have been guessed at, and the recent (for Dickens) past—the traditions of 'good murderous melodramas'.

The patriarch of American cinema could not have failed to notice this 'treatment', and his works often seem to rehearse the wise advice handed down to the twentieth-century film-maker by the great nineteenth-century novelist. Griffith is right not to conceal this, but to pay Dickens' memory a fitting homage.

Griffith used a similar construction on screen for the first time in the film *After Many Years* (a screen adaptation of Tennyson's *Enoch Arden*, 1908).

This film is also famous because the close-up was applied *meaningfully*, and *utilised*, for the first time.

These were the first close-ups in America since Edwin Porter's celebrated *The Great Train Robbery* [USA, 1903], produced five years earlier, which had one close-up at the most, and that was used for purely sensational effect: the criminal was shown shooting point-blank into the auditorium! . . .

I do not know about the reader, but I have always derived comfort from repeatedly telling myself that our cinema is not entirely without an ancestry and a pedigree, a past and traditions, or a rich cultural heritage from earlier epochs. Only very thoughtless or arrogant people could construct laws and aesthetic for cinema based on the dubious assumptions that this art came out of thin air!

Let Dickens and the whole constellation of ancestors, who go as far back as Shakespeare or the Greeks, serve as superfluous reminders that Griffith and our cinema alike cannot claim originality for themselves, but have a vast cultural heritage; and this causes neither one any difficulty in advancing the great art of cinema, each at their moment of world history. Let this heritage serve as a reproach to these thoughtless people with their excessive arrogance towards literature, which has contributed so much to this apparently unprecedented art, and most important, to the art of viewing—and I mean *viewing*, in both the senses of this term—not *seeing*.

1942

DUDLEY ANDREW
FROM CONCEPTS IN FILM THEORY

ADAPTATION

Dudley Andrew's work approaches film from a historicist, phenomeno-logical, and aesthetic perspective, considering the context of film's dis-semination and reception alongside its content. His early writing includes several works exploring twentieth-century film theory and its repercus-sions, including *The Major Film Theorists* (1976); *Concepts in Film Theory* (1983), which criticized the ahistorical structuralist and post-structuralist schools which had become a mainstay of film theory and analysis by the '80s; and *Film in the Aura of Art* (1984), in which he examines films by D.W. Griffith, F.W. Murnau, Jean Vigo, Frank Capra, Orson Welles, and others, rejecting the idea that their films can be exam-ined outside their historical, collaborative, and artistic milieu. Andrew has also written extensively on French cinema and culture. He is currently the Rose professor of film and comparative literature in the film studies program at Yale.

THE SOURCES OF FILMS

Frequently the most narrow and provincial area of film theory, discourse about adaptation is potentially as far-reaching as you like. Its distinctive feature, the match-ing of the cinematic sign system to prior achievement in some other system, can be shown to be distinctive of all representational cinema.

Let us begin with an example, *A Day in the Country*. Jean Renoir set himself the task of putting his knowledge, his troupe, and his artistry at the service of a tale by Guy de Maupassant. No matter how we judge the process or success of the film, its "being" owes something to the tale that was its inspiration and potentially its mea-sure. That tale, "A Country Excursion," bears a transcendent relation to any and all films that adapt it, for it is itself an artistic sign with a given shape and value, if not a finished meaning. A new artistic sign will then feature this original sign as either its signified or its referent. Adaptations claiming fidelity bear the original as a sig-nified, whereas those inspired by or derived from an earlier text stand in a relation of referring to the original.

The notion of a transcendent order to which the system of the cinema is beholden in its practice goes well beyond this limited case of adaptation.[1] What is a city symphony, for example, if not an adaptation of a concept by the cinema?[2] A definite notion of Berlin preexisted Walter Ruttman's 1927 treatment of that city. What is any documentary for that matter except the signification by the cinema of some prior whole, some concept of person, place, event, or situation. If we take seriously the arguments of Marxist and other social theorists that our consciousness is not open to the world but filters the world according to the shape of its ideology, then every cinematic rendering will exist in relation to some prior whole lodged unquestioned in the personal or public system of experience. In other words, no filmmaker and no film (at least in the representational mode) responds immediately to reality itself, or to its own inner vision. Every representational film *adapts* a prior conception. Indeed the very term "representation" suggests the existence of a model. Adaptation delimits representation by insisting on the cultural status of the model, on its existence in the mode of the text or the already textualized. In the case of those texts explicitly termed "adaptations," the cultural model which the cinema represents is already treasured as a representation in another sign system.

The broader notion of the process of adaptation has much in common with interpretation theory, for in a strong sense adaptation is the appropriation of a meaning from a prior text. The hermeneutic circle, central to interpretation theory, preaches that an explication of a text occurs only after a prior understanding of it, yet that prior understanding is justified by the careful explication it allows.[3] In other words, before we can go about discussing and analyzing a text we must have a global conception of its meaning. Adaptation is similarly both a leap and a process. It can put into play the intricate mechanism of its signifiers only in response to a general understanding of the signified it aspires to have constructed at the end of its process. While all representational films function this way (as interpretations of a person, place, situation, event, and so forth), we reserve a special place for those films which foreground this relation by announcing themselves as versions of some standard whole. A standard whole can only be a text. A version of it is an adaptation in the narrow sense.

Although these speculations may encourage a hopelessly broad view of adaptation, there is no question that the restricted view of adaptation from known texts in other art forms offers a privileged locus for analysis. I do not say that such texts are themselves privileged. Indeed, the thrust of my earlier remarks suggests quite the opposite. Nevertheless, the explicit, foregrounded relation of a cinematic text to a well-constructed original text from which it derives and in some sense strives to reconstruct provides the analyst with a clear and useful "laboratory" condition which should not be neglected.

The making of film out of an earlier text is virtually as old as the machinery of cinema itself. Well over half of all commercial films have come from literary

---

[1] For this idea I am indebted to a paper written by Dana Benelli in a class at the University of Iowa, autumn term 1979.

[2] The "city symphony" is a genre of the 1920s which includes up to fifteen films all built on formal or abstract principles, yet dedicated to the presentation of a single city, be it Berlin, Paris, Nice, Moscow, or the like.

[3] In the theory of interpretation this is generally attributed to Wilhelm Dilthey, although Martin Heidegger has made much of it in our century.

originals—though by no means all of these originals are revered or respected. If we confine ourselves to those cases where the adaptation process is foregrounded, that is, where the original is held up as a worthy source or goal, there are still several possible modes of relation between the film and the text. These modes can, for convenience, be reduced to three: borrowing, intersection, and fidelity of transformation.

BORROWING, INTERSECTING, AND TRANSFORMING SOURCES

In the history of the arts, surely "borrowing" is the most frequent mode of adaptation. Here the artist employs, more or less extensively, the material, idea, or form of an earlier, generally successful text. Medieval paintings featuring biblical iconography and miracle plays based on Bible stories drew on an exceptional text whose power they borrowed. In a later, secular age the artworks of an earlier generation might be used as sacred in their own right. The many types of adaptations from Shakespeare come readily to mind. Doubtless in these cases, the adaptation hopes to win an audience by the prestige of its borrowed title or subject. But at the same time it seeks to gain a certain respectability, if not aesthetic value, as a dividend in the transaction. Adaptations from literature to music, opera, or paintings are of this nature. There is no question of the replication of the original in Strauss's *Don Quixote*. Instead the audience is expected to enjoy basking in a certain pre-established presence and to call up new or especially powerful aspects of a cherished work.

To study this mode of adaptation, the analyst needs to probe the source of power in the original by examining the use made of it in adaptation. Here the main concern is the generality of the original, its potential for wide and varied appeal; in short, its existence as a continuing form or archetype in culture. This is especially true of that adapted material which, because of its frequent reappearance, claims the status of myth: *Tristan and Isolde* for certain, and *A Midsummer Night's Dream* possibly. The success of adaptations of this sort rests on the issue of their fertility not their fidelity. Frank McConnell's ingenious *Storytelling and Mythmaking* catalogues the garden of culture by examining borrowing as the history of grafting and transplantation in the fashion of Northrop Frye or even Carl Jung.[4] This direction of study will always elevate film by demonstrating its participation in a cultural enterprise whose value is outside film and, for Jung and others, outside texts altogether. Adaptation is the name of this cultural venture at its most explicit, though McConnell, Frye, and Jung would all immediately want to extend their theories of artistic fertility to "original" texts which upon inspection show their dependence on the great fructifying symbols and mythic patterns of civilization.

This vast and airy mode of borrowing finds its opposite in that attitude toward adaptation I choose to call "intersecting." Here the uniqueness of the original text is preserved to such an extent that it is intentionally left unassimilated in adaptation. The cinema, as a separate mechanism, records its confrontation with an ultimately intransigent text. Undoubtedly the key film exhibiting this relation is Robert

---

[4]Frank McConnell, *Storytelling and Mythmaking* (New York: Oxford University Press, 1979).

Bresson's *Diary of a Country Priest*. André Bazin, championing this film and this mode,[5] claimed that in this instance we are presented not with an adaptation so much as a refraction of the original. Because Bresson featured the writing of the diary and because he went out of his way to avoid "opening up" or in any other way cinematizing the original, Bazin claims that the film is the novel as seen by cinema. To extend one of his most elaborate metaphors,[6] the original artwork can be likened to a crystal chandelier whose formal beauty is a product of its intricate but fully artificial arrangement of parts while the cinema would be a crude flashlight interesting not for its own shape or the quality of its light but for what it makes appear in this or that dark corner. The intersection of Bresson's flashlight and the chandelier of Bernanos's novel produces an experience of the original modulated by the peculiar beam of the cinema. Naturally a great deal of Bernanos fails to be lit up, but what is lit up is only Bernanos, Bernanos however as seen by the cinema.

The modern cinema is increasingly interested in just this sort of intersecting. Bresson, naturally, has given us his Joan of Arc from court records and his *Mouchette* once again from Bernanos. Straub has filmed Corneille's *Othon* and *The Chronicle of Anna Magdalena Bach*. Pasolini audaciously confronted Matthew's gospel with many later texts (musical, pictorial, and cinematic) which it inspired. His later *Medea*, *Canterbury Tales*, and *Decameron* are also adaptational events in the intersecting mode. All such works fear or refuse to adapt. Instead they present the otherness and distinctiveness of the original text, initiating a dialectical interplay between the aesthetic forms of one period with the cinematic forms of our own period. In direct contrast to the manner scholars have treated the mode of "borrowing," such intersecting insists that the analyst attend to the *specificity* of the original within the *specificity* of the cinema. An original is allowed its life, its own life, in the cinema. The consequences of this method, despite its apparent forthrightness, are neither innocent nor simple. The disjunct experience such intersecting promotes is consonant with the aesthetics of modernism in all the arts. This mode refutes the commonplace that adaptations support only a conservative film aesthetics.

Unquestionably the most frequent and most tiresome discussion of adaptation (and of film and literature relations as well) concerns fidelity and transformation. Here it is assumed that the task of adaptation is the reproduction in cinema of something essential about an original text. Here we have a clear-cut case of film trying to measure up to a literary work, or of an audience expecting to make such a comparison. Fidelity of adaptation is conventionally treated in relation to the "letter" and to the "spirit" of the text, as though adaptation were the rendering of an interpretation of a legal precedent. The letter would appear to be within the reach of cinema for it can be emulated in mechanical fashion. It includes aspects of fiction generally elaborated in any film script: the characters and their inter-relation, the geographical, sociological, and cultural information providing the fiction's context, and the basic narrational aspects that determine the point of view of the narrator (tense, degree of participation, and knowledge of the storyteller, and so on). Ultimately, and this was

---

[5]André Bazin, *What Is Cinema?* (Berkeley: University of California Press, 1968), p. 142.
[6]Bazin, p. 107.

Bazin's complaint about faithful transformations, the literary work can readily become a scenario written in typical scenario form. The skeleton of the original can, more or less thoroughly, become the skeleton of a film.

More difficult is fidelity to the spirit, to the original's tone, values, imagery, and rhythm, since finding stylistic equivalents in film for these intangible aspects is the opposite of a mechanical process. The cinéaste presumably must intuit and reproduce the feeling of the original. It has been argued variously that this is frankly impossible, or that it involves the systematic replacement of verbal signifiers by cinematic signifiers, or that it is the product of artistic intuition, as when Bazin found the pervasive snowy decor in *Symphonie Pastorale* (1946) to reproduce adequately the simple past tense which Gide's verbs all bear in that tale.[7]

It is at this point that the specificity of these two signifying systems is at stake. Generally film is found to work from perception toward signification, from external facts to interior motivations and consequences, from the givenness of a world to the meaning of a story cut out of that world. Literary fiction works oppositely. It begins with signs (graphemes and words) building to propositions which attempt to develop perception. As a product of human language it naturally treats human motivation and values, seeking to throw them out onto the external world, elaborating a world out of a story.

George Bluestone, Jean Mitry, and a host of others find this opposition to be most graphic in adaptation.[8] Therefore they take pleasure in scrutinizing this practice even while ultimately condemning it to the realm of the impossible. Since signs name the inviolate relation of signifier to signified, how is translation of poetic texts conceivable from one language to another (where signifiers belong to diffferent systems); much less how is it possible to transform the signifiers of one material (verbal) to signifiers of another material (images and sounds)? It would appear that one must presume the global signified of the original to be separable from its text if one believes it can be approximated by other sign clusters. Can we attempt to reproduce the meaning of the *Mona Lisa* in a poem, or of a poem in a musical phrase, or even of a musical phrase in an aroma? If one accepts this possibility, at the very least one is forced to discount the primary articulations of the relevant language systems. One would have to hold that while the material of literature (graphemes, words, and sentences) may be of a different nature from the materials of cinema (projected light and shadows, identifiable sounds and forms, and represented actions), both systems may construct in their own way, and at higher levels, scenes and narratives that are indeed commensurable.

The strident and often futile arguments over these issues can be made sharper and more consequential in the language of E. H. Gombrich or the even more systematic language of semiotics. Gombrich finds that all discussion of adaptation introduces the category of "matching."[9] First of all, like Bazin he feels one cannot dismiss adaptation since it is a fact of human practice. We can and do correctly match items from different systems all the time: a tuba sound is more like a rock than like a piece of string; it is more like a bear than like a bird; more like a romanesque church than a baroque one.

---

[7]Bazin, p. 67.

[8]George Bluestone, *Novels into Film* (Berkeley: University of California Press, 1957), and Jean Mitry, "Remarks on the Problem of Cinematic Adaptation," *Bulletin of the Midwest Modern Language Association* 4, no. 1 (Spring 1971): 1–9.

[9]E. H. Gombrich, *Art and Illusion* (Princeton: Princeton University Press, 1960).

We are able to make these distinctions and insist on their public character because we are matching equivalents. In the system of musical instruments the tuba occupies an equivalent position to that enjoyed by the romanesque in its system of architectural styles. Nelson Goodman has treated this issue at length in *Languages of Art* pointing to the equivalence not of elements but of the position elements occupy vis-à-vis their different domains.[10] Names of properties of colors may thus metaphorically, but correctly, describe aspects of the world of sound (a blue note, a somber or bright tone). Adaptation would then become a matter of searching two systems of communication for elements of equivalent position in the systems capable of eliciting a signified at a given level of pertinence, for example, the description of a narrative action. For Gombrich adaptation is possible, though never perfect, because every artwork is a construct of elements built out of a traditional use of a system. Since humans have the general capacity to adapt to new systems with different traditions in achieving a like goal or construct, artistic adaptation poses no insurmountable obstacles. Nevertheless attention to such "proportional consistencies" demands that the study of adaptation include the study of both art forms in their proper *historic* context.

Gombrich and Goodman anticipated the more fashionable vocabulary of semiotics in their clarification of these issues. In *Film and Fiction: The Dynamics of Exchange*, Keith Cohen tries to justify this new, nearly scientific approach to questions of relations between these arts; he writes, citing Metz:

> A basic assumption I make is that both words and images are sets of signs that belong to systems and that, at a certain level of abstraction, these systems bear resemblances to one another. More specifically, within each such system there are many different codes (perceptual, referential, symbolic). What makes possible, then, a study of the relation between two separate sign systems, like novel and film, is the fact that the same codes may reappear in more than one system. . . . The very mechanisms of language systems can thus be seen to carry on diverse and complex interrelations: "one function, among others, of language is to name the units segmented by vision (but also to help segment them), and . . . one function, among others, of vision is to inspire semantic configurations (but also to be inspired by them)."[11]

Cohen, like Metz before him, suggests that despite their very different material character, despite even the different ways we process them at the primary level, verbal and cinematic signs share a common fate: that of being condemned to connotation. This is especially true in their fictional use where every signifier identifies a signified but also elicits a chain reaction of other relations which permits the elaboration of the fictional world. Thus, for example, imagery functions equivalently in films and novels. This mechanism of implication among signs leads Cohen to conclude that "narrativity is the most solid median link between novel and cinema, the most pervasive tendency of both verbal and visual languages. In both novel and cinema, groups of signs, be they literary or visual signs, are apprehended consecutively through time; and this consecutiveness gives rise to an unfolding structure, the diegetic whole that is never fully *present* in any one group yet always *implied* in each such group."[12]

---

[10]Nelson Goodman, *Languages of Art* (Indianapolis, in: Bobbs-Merrill, 1968), esp. pp. 143–48.
   [11]Keith Cohen, *Film and Fiction: The Dynamics of Exchange* (New Haven: Yale University Press, 1979), p. 4. Cohen's citation from Metz comes from Christian Metz, *Langage et cinéma* (Paris: Larçosse, 1971).
   [12]Cohen, p. 92.

Narrative codes, then, always function at the level of implication or connotation. Hence they are potentially comparable in a novel and a film. The story can be the same if the narrative units (characters, events, motivations, consequences, context, viewpoint, imagery, and so on) are produced equally in two works. Now this production is, by definition, a process of connotation and implication. The analysis of adaptation then must point to the achievement of equivalent narrative units in the absolutely different semiotic systems of film and language. Narrative itself is a semiotic system available to both and derivable from both. If a novel's story is judged in some way comparable to its filmic adaptation, then the strictly separate but equivalent processes of implication which produced the narrative units of that story through words and audio-visual signs, respectively, must be studied. Here semiotics coincides with Gombrich's intuition: such a study is not comparative between the arts but is instead intensive within each art. And since the implicative power of literary language and of cinematic signs is a function of its use as well as of its system, adaptation analysis ultimately leads to an investigation of film styles and periods in relation to literary styles of different periods.

We have come round the other side of the argument now to find once more that the study of adaptation is logically tantamount to the study of the cinema as a whole. The system by which film involves us in fictions and the history of that system are ultimately the questions we face even when starting with the simple observation of an equivalent tale told by novel and film. This is not to my mind a discouraging arrival for it drops adaptation and all studies of film and literation out of the realm of eternal principle and airy generalization, and onto the uneven but solid ground of artistic history, practice, and discourse.

THE SOCIOLOGY AND AESTHETICS OF ADAPTATION

It is time for adaptation studies to take a sociological turn. How does adaptation serve the cinema? What conditions exist in film style and film culture to warrant or demand the use of literary prototypes? Although adaptation may be calculated as a relatively constant volume in the history of cinema, its particular function in any moment is far from constant. The choices of the mode of adaptation and of prototypes suggest a great deal about the cinema's sense of its role and aspirations from decade to decade. Moreover, the stylistic strategies developed to achieve the proportional equivalences necessary to construct matching stories not only are symptomatic of a period's style but may crucially alter that style.

Bazin pointed to an important instance of this in the immediate post-war era when adaptations from the stage by Cocteau, Welles, Olivier, Wyler, and others not only developed new ways for the cinema to be adequate to serious theater, but also developed a kind of discipline in *mise-en-scène* whose consequences go far beyond the production of *Macbeth*, *Les Parents terribles*, *The Little Foxes*, and *Henry V*.[13] Cocteau's film, to take one example, derives its style from Welles's use of interior shooting in *Kane* and *Ambersons*, thus responding to a new conception of dramatic

---

[13]Bazin, *What Is Cinema?*, p. 76.

space; but at the same time his film helped solidify a shooting style that would leave its mark on Alexandre Astruc and André Michel among others. Furthermore his particular cinematic *écriture* would allow Truffaut to set him against the cinema of quality in the famous 1954 diatribe.[14] It is instructive to note that while Truffaut railed against the status quo for its literariness and especially for its method of adaptation, the directors he praised were also working with literary originals: Bresson adapting Bernanos, Ophuls adapting Maupassant and Schnitzler, and Cocteau adapting his own theater pieces. Like Bazin, Truffaut looked upon adaptation not as a monolithic practice to be avoided but as an instructive barometer for the age. The cinema *d'auteur* which he advocated was not to be pitted against a cinema of adaptation; rather one method of adaptation would be pitted against another. In this instance adaptation was the battleground even while it prepared the way for a stylistic revolution, the New Wave, which would for the most part avoid famous literary sources.

To take another sort of example, particular literary fashions have at times exercised enormous power over the cinema and, consequently, over the general direction of its stylistic evolution. The Romantic fiction of Hugo, Dickens, Dumas, and countless lesser figures originally set the stylistic requirements of American and mainstream French cinema at the end of the silent era. Similarly Zola and Maupassant, always of interest to French cinéastes, helped Jean Renoir muscularly reorient the style of world cinema in the 1930's. Not only that, through Luchino Visconti this naturalist impulse directly developed one strain of neorealism in his adaptations of Giovanni Verga (*La Terra Trema*) and James M. Cain (*Ossessione*).

This latter case forces us to recall that the "dynamics of exchange," as Cohen calls it, go both ways between film and fiction. Naturalist fiction helped cinema develop its interest in squalid subjects and a hard-hitting style. This in turn affected American hard-boiled novelists like Cain and Hammett, eventually returning to Europe in the film style of Visconti, Carné, Clouzot, and others. This general trading between film and literature in the currency of naturalism had some remarkable individual incidents associated with it. Renoir's adaptation of *The Lower Depths* can serve as an example. In 1881 Zola had cried out for a naturalist theater[15] and had described twenty years before the time precisely the sort of drama Gorki would write in *The Lower Depths*: a collection of real types thrown together without a domineering plot, the drama driven by the natural rhythms of little incidents and facts exposing the general quality of life in an era. Naturalism here coincided with a political need, with Gorki's play preceding the great uprisings in Russia by only a few years.

In another era and in response to a different political need, Renoir leapt at the chance to adapt the Gorki work. This was 1935, the year of the ascendancy of the Popular Front, and Renoir's treatment of the original is clearly marked by the pressures and aspirations of that moment. The film negotiates the mixture of classes

---

[14]François Truffaut, "A Certain Tendency in French Cinema," in Bill Nichols, *Movies and Methods*, I (Berkeley: University of California Press, 1976), pp. 224–36.

[15]Emile Zola, "Naturalism and the Theater," in *The Experimental Novel and Other Essays*, trans. Belle Sherman (New York: Haskell House, 1964).

which the play only hints at. Louis Jouvet as the Baron dominates the film, descending into the social depths and helping organize a collective undoing of Kastylylov, the capitalist landlord. Despite the gloomy theme, the murder, jailing, deaths by sickness and suicide, Renoir's version overflows with a general warmth evident in the airy setting by the Marne and the relaxed direction of actors who breathe languidly between their lines.

Did Gorki mind such an interpretation? We can never know, since he died a few months before its premier. But he did give Renoir his imprimatur and looked forward to seeing the completed version, this despite the fact that in 1932 he declared that the play was useless, out of date, and unperformable in socialist Russia. Perhaps these statements were the insincere self-criticism which that important year elicited from many Russian artists. I prefer, however, to take Gorki at his word. More farsighted than most theorists, let alone most authors, he realized that *The Lower Depths* in 1932 Russia was by no means the same artwork as *The Lower Depths* in the France of the Popular Front. This is why he put no strictures on Renoir assuming that the cinéaste would deal with his play as he felt necessary. Necessity is, among other things, a product of the specific place and epoch of the adaptation, both historically and stylistically. The naturalist attitude of 1902, fleshing out the original plans of Zola, gave way to a new historic and stylistic moment, and fed that style that Renoir had begun elaborating ever since *La Chienne* in 1931, and that despite its alleged looseness and airiness in comparison to the Gorki, would help lead European cinema onto the naturalist path.

This sketch of a few examples from the sociology of adaptation has rapidly taken us into the complex interchange between eras, styles, nations, and subjects. This is as it should be, for adaptation, while a tantalizing keyhole for theorists, nevertheless partakes of the univeral situation of film practice, dependent as it is on the aesthetic system of the cinema in a particular era and on that era's cultural needs and pressures. Filmmaking, in other words, is always an event in which a system is used and altered in discourse. Adaptation is a peculiar form of discourse but not an unthinkable one. Let us use it not to fight battles over the essence of the media or the inviolability of individual art works. Let us use it as we use all cultural practices, to understand the world from which it comes and the one toward which it points. The elaboration of these worlds will demand, therefore, historical labor and critical acumen. The job of theory in all this is to keep the questions clear and in order. It will no longer do to let theorists settle things with a priori arguments. We need to study the films themselves as acts of discourse. We need to be sensitive to that discourse and to the forces that motivate it.

1984

BRIAN MCFARLANE
FROM NOVEL TO FILM

BACKGROUNDS

Brain McFarlane has written extensively on Australian and British film,
including editing many anthologies and encyclopedias devoted to the subject.
An Autobiography of British Cinema (1997) provides a first-hand history of
British film through interviews with key figures in the industry. *Novel to
Film: An Introductiion to the Theory of Adaption* (1996), from which the following is excerpted, examines the alterations to which a literary text is subject during the process of adaption, and locates the sources of such
transformation in narrative constraints, studio requirements, and the filmmaker's vision (or revision) of the book's intent. McFarlane currently teaches
film history at Monash University in Australia.

Everyone who sees films based on novels feels able to comment, at levels ranging from the gossipy to the erudite, on the nature and success of the adaptation
involved. That is, the interest in adaptation, unlike many other matters to do with
film (e.g., questions of authorship), is not a rarefied one. And it ranges backwards
and forwards from those who talk of novels as being 'betrayed' by boorish filmmakers to those who regard the practice of comparing film and novel as a waste
of time.

The filmmakers themselves have been drawing on literary sources, and especially
novels of varying degrees of cultural prestige, since film first established itself as
preeminently a narrative medium. In view of this fact, and given that there has been
a long-running discourse on the nature of the connections between film and literature, it is surprising how little systematic, sustained attention has been given to the
processes of adaptation. This is the more surprising since the issue of adaptation
has attracted critical attention for more than sixty years in a way that few other film-
related issues have. Writers across a wide critical spectrum have found the subject
fascinating: newspaper and journal reviews almost invariably offer comparison
between a film and its literary precursor; from fan magazines to more or less scholarly books, one finds reflections on the incidence of adaptation; works serious and
trivial, complex and simple, early and recent address themselves to various aspects
of this phenomenon almost as old as the institution of the cinema.

I want to [draw] attention to some of the most commonly recurring discussions
of the connections between the film and the novel.

CONRAD, GRIFFITH, AND 'SEEING'

Commentators in the field are fond of quoting Joseph Conrad's famous statement of his novelistic intention: 'My task which I am trying to achieve is, by the powers of the written word, to make you hear, to make you feel—it is, before all, to make to see.'[1] This remark of 1897 is echoed, consciously or otherwise, sixteen years later by D. W. Griffith, whose cinematic-intention is recorded as: 'The task I am trying to achieve is above all to make you see.'[2] George Bluestone's all-but-pioneering work in the film literature field, *Novels into Film*, draws attention to the similarity of the remarks at the start of his study of 'The Two Ways of Seeing,' claiming that 'between the percept of the visual image and the concept of the mental image lies the root difference between the two media.'[3] In this way he acknowledges the connecting link of 'seeing' in his use of the word 'image.' At the same time, he points to the fundamental difference between the way images are produced in the two media and how they are received. Finally, though, he claims that 'conceptual images evoked by verbal stimuli can scarcely be distinguished in the end from those evoked by nonverbal stimuli,'[4] and in this respect, he shares common ground with several other writers concerned to establish links between the two media.

By this, I mean those commentaries that address themselves to crucial changes in the (mainly English) novel toward the end of the nineteenth century; changes that led to a stress on showing rather than on telling and that, as a result, reduced the element of authorial intervention in its more overt manifestations. Two of the most impressive of such accounts, both of them concerned with ongoing processes of transmutation among the arts, notably between literature and film, are Alan Spiegel's *Fiction and the Camera Eye*[5] and Keith Cohen's *Film and Fiction*.[6] Spiegel's avowed purpose is to investigate 'the common body of thought and feeling that unites film form with the modern novel,'[7] taking as his starting point Flaubert, whom he sees as the first great nineteenth-century exemplar of 'concretized form,' a form dependent on supplying a great deal of visual information. His line of enquiry leads him to James Joyce who, like Flaubert, respects 'the integrity of the seen object and . . . gives it palpable presence apart from the presence of the observer.'[8] This line is pursued by way of Henry James who attempts 'a balanced distribution of emphasis in the rendering of what is looked at, who is looking, and what the looker makes of what she [i.e., Maisie in *What Maisie Knew*] sees,'[9] and by way of the Conrad–Griffith comparison. Spiegel presses this comparison harder than Bluestone, stressing that

---

[1]Joseph Conrad, Preface to *The Nigger of the Narcissus* (J. M. Dent and Sons: London, 1945), 5.

[2]Quoted in Lewis Jacobs, *The Rise of the American Film* (New York: Harcourt, Brace, 1939), 119.

[3]George Bluestone, *Novels into Film* (Berkeley and Los Angeles: University of California Press, 1957), 1.

[4]Ibid., 47.

[5]Alan Spiegel, *Fiction and the Camera Eye: Visual Consciousness in Film and the Modern Novel* (Charlottesville: University Press of Virginia, 1976).

[6]Keith Cohen, *Film and Fiction: The Dynamics of Exchange* (New Haven: Yale University Press, 1979).

[7]Spiegel, *Fiction and the Camera Eye*, p. xiii.

[8]Ibid., 63.

[9]Ibid., 55.

though both may have aimed at the same point—a congruence of image and concept—
they did so from opposite directions. Whereas Griffith used his images to tell a story,
as means to understanding, Conrad (Spiegel claims) wanted the reader to " 'see' in
and through and finally past his language and his narrative concept to the hard, clear
bedrock of images.'[10]

One effect of this stress on the physical surfaces and behaviors of objects and
figures is to deemphasize the author's personal narrating voice so that we learn to
read the ostensibly unmediated visual language of the later nineteenth-century novel
in a way that anticipates the viewer's experience of film, which necessarily presents
those physical surfaces. Conrad and James further anticipate the cinema in their
capacity for 'decomposing' a scene, for altering point of view to focus more sharply
on various aspects of an object, for exploring a visual field by fragmenting it rather
than by presenting it scenographically (i.e., as if it were a scene from a stage
presentation).

Cohen, concerned with the 'process of convergence' between art forms, also sees
Conrad and James as significant in a comparison of novels and film. These authors
he sees as breaking with the representational novels of the earlier nineteenth century and ushering in a new emphasis on *showing* how the events unfold dramatically rather than recounting them.'[11] The analogy with film's narrative procedures
will be clear, and there seems no doubt that film, in turn, has been highly influential on the modern novel. Cohen uses passages from Proust and Virginia Woolf to
suggest how the modern novel, influenced by techniques of Eisensteinian montage
cinema, draws attention to its encoding processes in ways that the Victorian novel
tends not to.

DICKENS, GRIFFITH, AND STORYTELLING

The other comparison that trails through the writing about film and literature is
that between Griffith and Dickens, who was said to be the director's favorite novelist. The most famous account is, of course, that of Eisenstein, who compares their
'spontaneous childlike skill for story telling,'[12] a quality he finds in American cinema at large, their capacity for vivifying 'bit' characters, the visual power of each,
their immense popular success, and above all their rendering of parallel action, for
which Griffith cited Dickens as his source. On the face of it, there now seems nothing so remarkable in these formulations to justify their being so frequently paraded
as examples of the ties that bind cinema and the Victorian novel. In fact Eisenstein's
discussion of Dickens's 'cinematic techniques,' including anticipation of such phenomena as frame composition and the close-up, is really not far removed from those
many works that talk about film language, striking similar analogical poses, without giving adequate consideration to the qualitative differences enjoined by the two
media.

---

[10]Ibid., pp. xi–xii.
[11]Cohen, *Film and Fiction,* 5
[12]Sergei Eisenstein, *Film Form,* ed. and trans. Jan Leyda (New York: Harcourt, Brace, 1949); 196.

Later commentators have readily embraced Eisenstein's account:

Bluestone, for instance, states boldly that 'Griffith found in Dickens hints for every one of his major innovations',[13] and Cohen, going further, points to 'the more or less blatant appropriation of the themes and content of the nineteenth-century bourgeois novel.'[14] However, in spite of the frequency of reference to the Dickens–Griffith connection, and apart from the historical importance of parallel editing in the development of film narrative, the influence of Dickens has perhaps been overestimated and under-scrutinized. One gets the impression that critics steeped in a literary culture have fallen on the Dickens–Griffith comparison with a certain relief, perhaps as a way of arguing the cinema's respectability. They have tended to concentrate on the thematic interests and the large, formal narrative patterns and strategies the two great narrative-markers shared, rather than to address themselves, as a film-oriented writer might, to detailed questions of enunciation, of possible parallels and disparities between the two different signifying systems, of the range of 'functional equivalents'[15] available to each within the parameters of the classical style as evinced in each medium.

As film came to replace in popularity the representational novel of the earlier nineteenth century, it did so through the application of techniques practiced by writers at the latter end of the century. Conrad with his insistence on making the reader 'see' and James with his technique of 'restricted consciousness,' both playing down obvious authorial mediation in favor of limiting the point of view from which actions and objects are observed, provide clear examples. In this way they may be said to have broken with the tradition of 'transparency' in relation to the novel's referential world so that the mode and angle of vision were as much a part of the novel's content as what was viewed. The comparisons with cinematic technique are clear, but paradoxically, the modern novel has not shown itself very adaptable to film. However persuasively it may be demonstrated that the likes of Joyce, Faulkner, and Hemingway have drawn on cinematic techniques, the fact is that the cinema has been more at home with novels from—or descended from—an earlier period. Similarly, certain modern plays, such as *Death of a Salesman*, *Equus*, or *M. Butterfly*, which seem to owe something to cinematic techniques, have lost a good deal of their fluid representations of time and space when transferred to the screen.

ADAPTATION: THE PHENOMENON

As soon as the cinema began to see itself as a narrative entertainment, the idea of ransacking the novel—that already established repository of narrative fiction—for source material got underway, and the process has continued more or less unabated for ninety years. Filmmakers' reasons for this continuing phenomenon appear to move between the poles of crass commercialism and high-minded respect for literary works. No doubt there is the lure of a pre-sold title, the expectation that

---

[13]Bluestone, *Novels into Film*, 2.
[14]Cohen, *Film and Fiction*, 4.
[15]David Bordwell's term, in The Classical Hollywood Cinema (London: Routledge and Kegan Paul, 1985), 13.

respectability or popularity achieved in one medium might infect the work created in another. The notion of a potentially lucrative 'property' has clearly been at least one major influence in the filming of novels, and perhaps filmmakers, as Frederic Raphael scathingly claims, 'like known quantities . . . they would sooner buy the rights of an expensive book than develop an original subject.'[16] Nevertheless most of the filmmakers on record profess loftier attitudes than these. DeWitt Bodeen, coauthor of the screenplay for Peter Ustinov's *Billy Budd* (1962), claims, 'Adapting literary works to film is, without a doubt, a creative undertaking, but the task requires a kind of selective interpretation, along with the ability to recreate and sustain an established mood.'[17] That is, the adaptor should see himself as owing allegiance to the source work. Despite Peter Bogdanovich's disclaimer about filming Henry James's *Daisy Miller* ('I don't think it's a great classic story. I don't treat it with that kind of reverence'[18]), for much of the time the film is a conscientious visual transliteration of the original. One does not find filmmakers asserting a bold approach to their source material, any more than announcing crude financial motives.

As to audiences, whatever their complaints about this or that violation of the original, they have continued to want to see what the books 'look like.' Constantly creating their own mental images of the world of a novel and its people, they are interested in comparing their images with those created by the filmmaker. But, as Christian Metz says, the reader 'will not always find *his* film, since what he has before him in the actual film is now somebody else's phantasy.'[19] Despite the uncertainty of gratification, of finding audio-visual images that will coincide with their conceptual images, reader-viewers persist in providing audiences for 'somebody else's phantasy.' There is also a curious sense that the verbal account of the people, places, and ideas that make up much of the appeal of novels is simply *one* rendering of a set of existents that might just as easily be rendered in another. In this regard, one is reminded of Anthony Burgess's cynical view, 'Every best-selling novel *has* to be turned into a film, the assumption being that the book itself whets an appetite for the true fulfilment—the verbal shadow turned into light, the word made flesh.'[20] And perhaps there is a parallel with that late nineteenth-century phenomenon, described by Michael Chanan in *The Dream that Kicks*, of illustrated editions of literary works and illustrated magazines in which great novels first appeared as serials. There is, it seems, an urge to have verbal concepts bodied forth in perceptual concreteness.

Whatever it is that makes film-goers want to see adaptations of novels, and filmmakers to produce them, and whatever hazards lie in the path for both, there is no denying the facts. For instance, Morris Beja reports that, since the inception of the Academy Awards in 1927–28, 'more than three-fourths of the awards for 'best

[16]Frederic Raphael, 'Introduction,' *Two for the Road* (London: Jonathan Cape, 1967).

[17]DeWitt Bodeen, 'The Adapting Art,' *Films in Review* 14, no. 6 (June–July 1963): 349.

[18]Jan Dawson, 'The Continental Divide: Filming Henry James,' *Sight and Sound* 43, no. 1 (Winter 1973–74): 14; repr. in part as 'An Interview with Peter Bogdanovich' in G. Peary and R. Shatzkin (eds.), *The Classic American Novel and the Movies* (New York: Frederick Ungar Publishing, 1977).

[19]Christian Metz, *The Imaginary Signifier* (Bloomingdale: Indiana University Press, 1977), 12.

[20]Anthony Burgess, 'On the Hopelessness of Turning Good Books into Films,' *New York Times,* 20 April 1975, p. 15.

picture' have gone to adaptations . . . [and that] the all-time box-office successes favour novels even more.'[21] Given that the novel and the film have been the most popular narrative modes of the nineteenth and twentieth centuries, respectively, it is perhaps not surprising that filmmakers have sought to exploit the kinds of response excited by the novel and have seen in it a source of ready-made material, in the crude sense of pretested stories and characters, without too much concern for how much of the original's popularity is intransigently tied to its verbal mode.

THE DISCOURSE ON ADAPTATION

On Being Faithful

Is it really 'Jamesian'? Is it 'true to Lawrence'? Does it 'capture the spirit of Dickens'? At every level from newspaper reviews to longer essays in critical anthologies and journals, the adducing of fidelity to the original novel as a major criterion for judging the film adaptation is pervasive. No critical line is in greater need of reexamination—and devaluation.

Discussion of adaptation has been bedevilled by the fidelity issue, no doubt ascribable in part to the novel's coming first, in part to the ingrained sense of literature's greater respectability in traditional critical circles. As long ago as the mid-1940s James Agee complained of a debilitating reverence in even such superior transpositions to the screen as David Lean's *Great Expectations*. It seemed to him that the really serious-minded film-goer's idea of art would be 'a good faithful adaptation of *Adam Bede* in sepia, with the entire text read offscreen by Herbert Marshall.'[22] However, voices such as Agee's, querulously insisting that the cinema make its own art and to hell with tasteful allegiance, have generally cried in the wilderness.

Fidelity criticism depends on a notion of the text as having and rendering up to the (intelligent) reader a single, correct 'meaning' which the filmmaker has either adhered to or in some sense violated or tampered with. There will often be a distinction between being faithful to the 'letter,' an approach that the more sophisticated writer may suggest is no way to ensure a 'successful' adaptation, and to the 'spirit' or 'essence' of the work. The latter is of course very much more difficult to determine since it involves not merely a parallelism between novel and film but between two or more readings of a novel, since any given film version is able only to aim at reproducing the filmmaker's reading of the original and to hope that it will coincide with that of many other readers/viewers. Since such coincidence is unlikely, the fidelity approach seems a doomed enterprise and fidelity criticism unilluminating. That is, the critic who quibbles at failures of fidelity is really saying no more than 'This reading of the original does not tally with mine in these and these ways.'

Few writers on adaptation have specifically questioned the possibility of fidelity; though some have claimed not to embrace it, they still regard it as a viable choice for the filmmaker and a criterion for the critic. Beja is one exception. In asking whether there are 'guiding principles' for filmmakers adapting literature, he asks,

---

[21]Morris Beja, *Film and Literature* (New York: Longman, 1979), 78.
[22]*Agee on Film* (New York: McDowell Oblonsky, 1958), 216.

'What relationship should a film have to the original source? Should it be 'faithful'? Can it be? To what?'[23]

When Beja asks 'To what' should a filmmaker be faithful in adapting a novel, one is led to recall those efforts at fidelity to times and places remote from present-day life. In period films, one often senses exhaustive attempts to create an impression of fidelity to, say, Dickens's London or to Jane Austen's village life, the result of which, so far from ensuring fidelity to the text, is to produce a distracting quaintness. What was a contemporary work for the author, who could take a good deal relating to time and place for granted, as requiring little or no scene-setting for his readers, has become a period piece for the filmmaker. As early as 1928, M. Willson Disher picked up the scent of this misplaced fidelity in writing about a version of *Robinson Crusoe*: 'Mr Wetherell [director, producer, writer and star] went all the way to Tobago to shoot the right kinds of creeks and caves, but he should have travelled not westwards, but backwards, to reach 'the island', and then he would have arrived with the right sort of luggage.'[24] Disher is not speaking against fidelity to the original as such but against a misconstrued notion of how it might be achieved. A more recent example is Peter Bogdanovich's use of the thermal baths sequence in his film of *Daisy Miller*. 'The mixed bathing is authentically of the period', he claims in an interview with Jan Dawson.[25] Authentically of the period, perhaps, but not so of Henry James, so that it is only a tangential, possibly irrelevant fidelity that is arrived at. The issue of fidelity is a complex one, but it is not too gross a simplification to suggest that critics have encouraged filmmakers to see it as a desirable goal in the adaptation of literary works. As Christopher Orr has noted, 'The concern with the fidelity of the adapted film in letter and spirit to its literary source has unquestionably dominated the discourse on adaptation.'[26]

Obscuring Other Issues

The insistence on fidelity has led to a suppression of potentially more rewarding approaches to the phenomenon of adaptation. It tends to ignore the idea of adaptation as an example of convergence among the arts, perhaps a desirable—even inevitable—process in a rich culture; it fails to take into serious account what may be transferred from novel to film as distinct from what will require more complex processes of adaptation; and it marginalizes those production determinants that have nothing to do with the novel but may be powerfully influential upon the film. Awareness of such issues would be more useful than those many accounts of how films 'reduce' great novels.

Modern critical notions of *intertextuality* represent a more sophisticated approach, in relation to adaptation, to the idea of the original novel as a 'resource'. As Christopher Orr remarks, 'Within this critical context [i.e., of intertextuality], the issue is not whether the adapted film is faithful to its source, but rather how the

---

[23]Beja, *Film and Literature*, 80.
[24]M. Willson Disher, 'Classics into Films', *Fortnightly Review*, no. 124 (December 1928), 789.
[25]Dawson, 'The Continental Divide,' 14.
[26]Christopher Orr, 'The Discourse on Adaptation', *Wide Angle* 6, no. 2 (1984): 72.

choice of a specific source and how the approach to that source serve the film's ideology.[27] When, for instance, MGM filmed James Hilton's 1941 bestseller, *Random Harvest*, in the following year, its images of an unchanging England had as much to do with Hollywood anti-isolationism with regard to World War II as with finding visual equivalents for anything in Hilton. The film belongs to a rich context created by notions of Hollywood's England, by MGM's reputation for prestigious literary adaptation and for a glossy 'house style', by the genre of romantic melodrama (cf. *Rebecca*, 1940, *This Above All*, 1942), and by the idea of the star vehicle. Hilton's popular but, in truth, undistinguished romance is but one element of the film's intertextuality.

Some writers have proposed strategies that seek to categorize adaptations so that fidelity to the original loses some of its privileged position. Geoffrey Wagner suggests three possible categories that are open to the filmmaker and to the critic assessing his adaptation: he calls these (*a*) *transposition*, 'in which a novel is given directly on the screen with a minimum of apparent interference';[28] (*b*) *commentary*, 'where an original is taken and either purposely or inadvertently altered in some respect ... when there has been a different intention on the part of the filmmaker, rather than infidelity or outright violation';[29] and (*c*) *analogy*, 'which must represent a fairly considerable departure for the sake of making another work of art.'[30] The critic, he implies, will need to understand which kind of adaptation he is dealing with if his commentary on an individual film is to be valuable. Dudley Andrew also reduces the modes of relation between the film and its source novel to three, which correspond roughly (but in reverse order of adherence to the original) to Wagner's categories; 'Borrowing, intersection, and fidelity of transformation'.[31] And there is a third comparable classification system put forward by Michael Klein and Gillian Parker first, 'fidelity to the main thrust of the narrative'; second, the approach which retains the core of the structure of the narrative while significantly reinterpreting or, in some cases, deconstructing the source text'; and third, regarding 'the source merely as raw material, as simply the occasion for an original work.'[32] The parallel with Wagner's categories is clear.

There is nothing definitive about these attempts at classification, but at least they represent some heartening challenges to the primacy of fidelity as a critical criterion. Further, they imply that, unless the kind of adaptation is identified, critical evaluation may well be wide of the mark. The faithful adaptation (e.g., *Daisy Miller* or James Ivory's *Howard's End*, 1992) can certainly be intelligent and attractive, but is not necessarily to be preferred to the film, which sees the original as 'raw material' to be reworked, as Hitchcock so persistently did, from, say, *Sabotage*

---

[27]Ibid.

[28]Geoffrey Wagner, *The Novel and the Cinema* (Rutherford, NJ: Fairleigh Dickinson University Press, 1975), 222.

[29]Ibid., 224.

[30]Ibid., 226.

[31]Dudley Andrew, 'The Well-Worn Muse: Adaptation in Film History and Theory,' in Syndy Conger and Janice R. Welsch (eds.), *Narrative Strategies* (Macomb, Ill.: West Illinois University Press, 1980), 10.

[32]Michael Klein and Gillian Parker (eds.), *The English Novel and the Movies* (New York: Frederick Ungar Publishing, 1981), 9–10.

(1936) to *The Birds* (1963). Who, indeed, ever thinks of Hitchcock as primarily an adaptor of other people's fictions? At a further extreme, it is possible to think of a film as providing a commentary on a literary text, as Welles does on three Shakespearian plays in *Chimes at Midnight* (1966), or as Gus Van Sant does in *My Own Private Idaho* (1992), drawing on both Shakespeare and Welles. Many kinds of relations may exist between film and literature, and fidelity is only one—and rarely the most exciting.

1996

TOM GUNNING

FROM D.W. GRIFFITH AND THE ORIGINS OF AMERICAN NARRATIVE FILM

NARRATIVE DISCOURSE AND THE NARRATOR SYSTEM

Tom Gunning has written extensively on the emergence of film as a modern technology indebted to its roots within the visual culture and spectacular entertainments of the turn of the twentieth century. In addition to numerous scholarly articles and chapters on early film, he has published monographs on D.W. Griffith and Fritz Lang. *D.W. Griffith and the Origins of American Narrative Film: The Early Years at Biograph* (1991), from which the following article is selected, analyzes the narrative structure and historical context of Griffith's one- and two-reel films for Biograph in 1908 and 1909. Gunning argues that the period marks a shift from spectacle films to a greater emphasis on character and story, highlighting Griffith's role in the development of classic Hollywood narrative cinema. This materialist approach to film theory and history places films and filmmakers, he argues, enables a greater understanding of the distribution and reception of film from its early development through the avant-garde of the 1920s to contemporary cinema and the emergence of digital technologies. He is currently Bergman Distinguished Service professor in the department of art history at the University of Chicago.

(Another selection from Gunning's work appears in Section VII.)

Can film theory and film history interact in a treatment of a specific historical series of films? Because my intention is to deal with Griffith's Biograph films as both esthetic works and industrial products, esthetic forms as well as modes of production, distribution and exhibition are essential to this work. But I am trying to do more than apply two different approaches to these films, critical on the one hand and industrial economic and social on the other. Because I maintain that the change in narrative form that one can trace through the early Biograph films can in part be understood as a response to changes within the film industry and its role in American society, I also want these different approaches to intersect. To demonstrate a change in narrative form, I must define with theoretical precision the way narrative operates in film. To show the relation of this interior change to the broader horizons of the film industry and social discourse about film, I must have a model of how that industry was structured and a concept of how these interior and exterior structures affect each other. . . .

In investigating narrative, we are hardly faced with a chartless wilderness. The nature of narrative has been a theoretical topic since theoretical investigations began and has been particularly scrutinized in recent decades. But we can begin with basic observations. The structure of the word *storytelling* provides a starting point for definition—its essentially double nature involving both a story to be told and the telling of that story.

The work of the literary critic Gérard Genette has focused precisely on narrative discourse, the *telling* of storytelling, and will form my recurrent reference. Genette distinguishes three different meanings for the term *narrative* (*récit* in French). First, narrative can refer to the actual language of a text that tells a story, as Seymour Chatman puts it, "the means by which the [narrative] content is communicated."[1] The second meaning of narrative refers to the content communicated by the discourse, "the succession of events, real or fictitious, that are the subject of this discourse" and which could be studied "without regard to the medium, linguistic or other" in which they are expressed. The third meaning refers to the event of "someone recounting something, the act of narrating in itself."[2] Genette analyzes narrative from these three perspectives: the means of expression, the events conveyed by these means, and the act of enunciation that expresses them.

Genette proposes the term *story* for the content conveyed by a narrative. The term *narrative* he reserves for the first meaning of the term, "the signifier, statement discourse or narrative text itself" which communicates the story. The act of telling a story, producing a narrative, Genette terms *narrating*.[3] I shall use Genette's terms with a slight modification. To avoid the equivocal term *narrative*, I shall call the means of expression of a story *narrative discourse*, a term Gennette often uses for the same concept. Genette's description of narrative discourse in literature provides a model for my treatment of Griffith, although my discussion is tailored to the demands of film rather than literature and to the requirements of a specific body of work.

My work on Griffith will not focus primarily on the analysis of story, but on narrative discourse. However, as Genette points out, the analysis of narrative discourse "implies a study of relationships," and to describe any one of the three aspects of narrative necessarily involves the other.[4] The logic of story can shape narrative discourse, marking how it begins, develops, and ends. Therefore some attention to the basic structure or logic of story is called for. Todorov, revising the Aristotelean beginning, middle, and end, offers the following useful definition of story structure (or in his terms *plot*): "The minimal complete plot consists in the passage from one equilibrium to another. An 'ideal' narrative begins with a stable situation which is disturbed by some power or force. There results a state of disequilibrium: by the action of a force directed in the opposite direction, the equilibrium is re-established; the second equilibrium is similar to the first, but the two are never identical."[5] As David Bordwell has pointed out, this equilibrium model corresponds to the "canonical story format," the story pattern most easily recognized and comprehended within our culture.[6] It also corresponds to the stories found in the majority of Griffith's Biograph films.

---

[1]Seymour Chatman, *Story and Discourse: Narrative Structure in Fiction and Film* (Ithaca, NY: Cornell University Press, 1978), p. 19.

[2]Gérard Genette, *Narrative Discourse: An Essay in Method*, trans. Jane E. Lewin (Ithaca: Cornell University Press, 1980), pp. 25–27.

[3]Genette, *Narrative Discourse*, p. 27.

[4]Ibid., pp. 27, 29.

[5]Todorov, *Introduction to Poetics*, p. 38.

[6]David Bordwell, *Narration in the Fiction Film* (Madison: University of Wisconsin Press, 1985), p. 35.

Narrative discourse is precisely the text itself—the actual arrangement of signifiers that communicate the story—words in literature, moving images and written titles in silent films. It is only through this means of expression that we come in contact with either story or the act of narrating. The story is an imaginary construction that the spectator or reader creates while reading the narrative discourse of the actual text. Likewise, access to the act of narrating (in written literature and in film, at least) is dependent on the traces of telling that exists in the text. The text itself, words, images, or both, is all that we have, and discussions of the other aspects of narrative must begin from the text and refer back to it.[7]

Within narrative discourse Genette defines three functions that relate to either story or the act of narration. The first two relate narrative discourse to story. The first of these is tense, which deals with the temporal relations between narrative discourse and story.[8] Narrative discourse can manipulate the temporal order and form of story events. This temporal patterning shapes and arranges the story, involving the reader or spectator in an often-complex activity of reconstruction. Within tense, Genette describes three principal manipulations of story events. The first, dealing with the succession of events in a narrative, is order. The second, duration, deals with the compression or extension of events within a narrative, while the third, frequency, describes the possibility of multiple retellings of a single event.

The second function of narrative discourse defined by Genette, mood, also relates the discourse to the story it tells. Controlling the reader's access to the events of the story, mood corresponds in many ways to what Anglo-American criticism has called point of view, the narration's perspective of the story told. Genette feels that "one can tell *more* or tell *less* what one tells, and can tell it *according to one point of view or another*." Mood indicates the way the narrative discourse operates as a sort of screen between reader or spectator and the story as it unfolds: "the narrative can furnish the reader with more or fewer details, and in a more or less direct way, and can thus seem (to adopt a common and convenient spatial metaphor, which is not to be taken literally) to keep at a greater or lesser *distance* from what it tells."[9] This perspective on the action may correspond to the viewpoint of a particular character within the story, in which case we say the narrative adopts the character's point of view.

The last of Genette's categories, voice, deals with the relation between narrative discourse and the act of narrating—the traces of telling left in the text through which we sense a storyteller addressing an implied or real audience.[10] In literature this aspect would not only include such determinations as the person of the narrator (the familiar, first-, or third-person narrator), but also a wider range of means to reflect the act of narrating in the text, for example, the temporal relation between the story and the act of telling it, and a variety of ways in which the narrator asserts its presence.

My use of Genette comes from an appreciation of his precision and systematic analysis, rather than a belief that all film theory must be founded in linguistic or

---

[7]Genette, *Narrative Discourse*, pp. 28–29.
[8]Ibid., p. 31.
[9]Ibid., pp. 161–62.
[10]Ibid., p. 31.

literary concepts. But are Genette's concepts applicable to film analysis, and if so, what short of transformations must they undergo? More fundamentally, should the terms *narrative* and *narration* be restricted to literature and verbal language? We speak quite commonly of narrative film, and even narrative dance, painting, and pantomime. What allows this concept to cross between diverse media?

The answer lies in the double nature of storytelling, its division into the story constructed by the reader or viewer and the specific discourse that tells the story. I strongly endorse André Gaudreault's statement, "Any message by means of which any story whatsoever is communicated can rightfully be considered as a narrative."[11] Any communication of a story will be composed of Genette's triad of story, narrative discourse, and act of narrating. Because his narrative functions of tense, mood, and voice describe the interrelations between these universal aspects of narrative, I believe they apply to any narrative media.[12] But the task remains of describing film's specific narrative discourse. Genette clearly states that although story can be studied "without regard to the medium, linguistic or otherwise . . . ,"[13] narrative discourse (because it exists in actual text) cannot be divorced from its specific medium.

Fundamental differences between literature and film rush to meet us. These differences derive from the noncommensurable nature of the types of signs each medium employs. Whereas literature is never directly iconic, film, as a series of photographic representation signs, is. This aspect of the filmic sign gives it a unique narrative status. While in language, as Genette points out (using the vocabulary of the AngloAmerican tradition of Lubbock and Booth), "Showing can only be a *way of telling*,"[14] film in contrast can show more immediately than it can tell.

But across the chasm between showing and telling the two narrative discourses seem to signal each other. Certain literary narratives have sought to give the impression of "showing" in spite of their lack of film's direct access to the visual. In literature the impression (or as Genette would put it, the illusion) of showing is the result of a narrator's consciously chosen and carefully devised strategy. Genette notes that a narrator may seem to abdicate the role of choosing only the most significant elements and instead gather a number of "useless and contingent" details in order to give the impression of showing.[15]

In film, this excess of mimesis over meaning appears automatically with the photographic image. Although a filmmaker can make images relatively abstract, they will still contain a plethora of information compared to a verbal description. For

---

[11] André Gaudreault, *Du Littéraire au filmique: System du récit* (Paris: Meridiens Klincksieck, 1988), p. 84 (my translation).

[12] See letter from Genette quoted in Gaudreault, *Du Littéraire*, p. 29 (footnote), which states in part: "Personally, I favor more and more a narrow definition of narrative, *haplé diégésis*, a statement of actions by a narrator who expresses the actions by verbal means (oral or written) and in this sense a theatrical or filmic narrative does not exist for me" (my translation). I am indebted to Gaudreault's work, including his dissertation, which he was kind enough to make available. Although some of my conclusions differ from his, I am constantly in debt to his thoroughness and clarity in approaching the issue.

[13] Genette, *Narrative Discourse*, p. 25.

[14] Ibid., p. 166.

[15] Ibid.

example, the first films that the Lumière brothers shot in the open air seem much more detailed and realistic than those the Edison Company shot against the dark background of the "Black Maria." But even Edison's films are crowded with the excess of photographic reality. Automatically present are details of posture, costuming, and gesture whose verbal description would overwhelm a written text (e.g., in Edison's kinetoscope film of Annie Oakley, her expression, the way she swings her rifle, the fringe on her costume, the puffs of smoke that seem to issue from the glass balls she shoots, etc.). Film *shows* automatically, recording a world of contingent events and unimportant details.

This dominance of showing over telling is the concealed reef over which the concept of the filmic narrator sails in peril. Does a film "tell" a story? Filmic discourse has an ability to appear nearly neutral. A single shot can seem to show a great deal while telling very little about it. If we approach film as a narrative form which presents stories to an audience, it nonetheless would be foolish to ignore a unique quality of its narrative discourse—its inherent photographic tendency toward mimesis, toward the representation of a world from which the filmic narrator can seem to be absent.

However, this aspect of film does not destroy the concept of the filmic narrator; rather it defines its roles. The primary task of the filmic narrator must be to overcome the initial resistance of the photographic material to telling by creating a hierarchy of narratively important elements within a mass of contingent details. Through filmic discourse, these images of the world become addressed to the spectator, moving from natural phenomenon to cultural products, meanings arranged for a spectator. The filmic narrator shapes and defines visual meanings.

This is partly accomplished by a fourth aspect of narrative discourse that I will add to Genette's triad of story, discourse, and the act of narrating—narrativization. This is less an aspect separate from the other three than a term for the bond among them, and one that takes on particular importance in film. Defined by Stephen Heath, narrativization is precisely what holds Genette's three aspects of narrative together.[16] The process of narrativization binds narrative discourse to story and rules the narrator's address to the spectator. It organizes discourse to tell a story, binding its elements into this single process. In this process the energies of a film are channeled toward the explication of a story, and through this channeling create and define a situation for the spectator.[17]

The concept of narrativization focuses the transformation of showing into telling, film's bending of its excessive realism to narrative purposes. Narrativization, which would be something of a tautology in a literary text where the signs are naturally predisposed to telling, regulates the balance between mimetic and narrative functions in the filmic sign. According to Heath, narrativization "seek[s] to maintain a tight balance between the photographic image as a reproduction of reality and the narrative as the sense, the intelligibility, of that reality." The narrative discourse of a film "picks up—indicating by framing, shot angle, lighting, dialogue mention,

---

[16]See, Stephen Heath, *Questions of Cinema* (Bloomington: Indiana University Press, 1981), pp. 107–8 and *passim*.

[17]Heath, *Questions of Cinema*, p. 109.

musical underscoring, and so on—the notable elements . . . ,"[18] thus carving a story out of a photographed reality.

Film's innate tendency toward mimesis becomes a sign of narrative realism, naturalizing the process of storytelling as the inclusion of apparently useless detail does in verbal narrative. Simultaneously the process of narrativization delivers a sense to this realism, through filmic discourse which "picks up" and selects precisely those meanings necessary for the story to be told. In this way the filmic image, without losing (indeed, using) its capacity for showing, defines its unique way of telling.

The narrative discourse of film involves a unique transaction between showing and telling. The photographic image clearly possesses a unique ability to show. But how do films pick up and indicate the significant elements within this detailed and contingent reality and endow them with a narrative meaning? What is it that tells the story in a narrative film? What are the marks within the film (or to use David Bordwell's more psychological and dynamic term, the cues)[19] by which the film conveys its story to the viewer?

Describing the narrative discourse of film must involve cutting up the filmic text so that its dynamic forces are exposed. Of course a narrative text functions as a whole, and analysis only untangles the synthesis that makes it work. I believe film's narrative discourse can best be described as the interrelation of three different levels that interrelate and express narrative information: the pro-filmic, the enframed image, and the process of editing.[20] I do not claim that they function in isolation, nor do I construct a hierarchy of importance, although I will show that some levels perform some tasks more economically than others. Although I will primarily deal with these levels as they are perceived by viewers, it is not irrelevant that they roughly correspond to the essential stages of film production as well: the periods of before, during, and after shooting.

The pro-filmic refers to everything placed in front of the camera to be filmed. It includes such things as the actors (and therefore casting decisions and performance style), lighting, set design, selection of locations, and selection of props. Strictly speaking, pro-filmic elements do not appear on the screen except through the next level of discourse, their capture on film as enframed images. However film viewers see the images on the screen as images of things, and the selection of the things that make up the image plays an extremely important role in conveying narrative information. Every film makes a selection of elements based on a preexisting set of possibilities (this actor and performance style rather than that one; that sort of set design rather than another). Therefore, as narrative discourse the pro-filmic

---

[18]Ibid., p. 122. Heath's understanding of narrativization is dependent on the Lacanian theory of the constitution of the subject and the Althusserian theory of ideology. If I am bypassing a complete discussion of these issues in relation to Griffith's work, it is because I find the constant circulating of various film texts through this system to be a time-consuming process often undertaken at the expense of other essential issues. For those who would claim that no historical treatment of this material is valid without such an approach, I can only say that I am aware of these methods of analysis, and have certainly, but not exclusively, been influenced by them.

[19]Bordwell, *Narration*, pp. 31–33.

[20]This schema does not deal with the important issue of sound in film, which is not relevant to the films I examine herein, and would have to be approached as a fourth level, itself in need of subdividing.

embodies a series of choices and reveals a narrative intention behind the choices. The viewer receives the results of these choices and makes inferences based on them.

Gaudreault, who in his book *Du Littéraire au filmique* (1988) has largely adopted my schema of filmic discourse, describes the manipulation by the narrator of the profilmic as *mise-en-scène*, referring particularly to the theatrical sense of this term.[21] Too often ignored in narrative theories, the pro-filmic plays an important role in narrative discourse.[22] Many of Griffith's innovations in filmic discourse lay in this area (e.g., the "restraint in expression" in acting style mentioned in his New York *Dramatic Mirror* advertisement).

The second level of filmic discourse is what I call the *enframed image*. At this level of filmic discourse the pro-filmic is transformed from preexistent events and objects into images on celluloid. The process is far from neutral. Placing an image within a frame entails arranging composition and spatial relations. The act of filming transforms the pro-filmic into a two-dimensional image, filmed from a particular point of view, framed within the camera aperture that geometrically defines the borders of the image. The whole host of formal devices that derive from the effects of perspective, selection of camera distance and angle, framing for composition, and the effects of movement within a frame determine specific choices available within this level of discourse. Whether on a conscious or preconscious level the viewer recognizes this construction of the image as a powerful narrative cue. Gaudreault borrows a term from Eisenstein, *mise-en-cadre*, the placement within the frame, to describe the activity responsible for this level of discourse.[23] New approaches in this level of filmic discourse, such as the role of composition in revealing characters's moods, are also seen in Griffith's Biograph work.

The enframed image can also involve a number of other procedures including setting exposure, control of focus, selection of lenses or film stocks with different properties, manipulations of camera speed, and placing devices in front of the lens (such as Bitzer's vignette-masking diaphragms). Camera movement also falls into this category. Putting the frame itself into motion, camera movement can be a powerful device, creating a strong sense of an intervening narrator and strongly marked narrative cues. I also include in this category the processes of filming that involve rephotography and are carried out after the principle photography, such as split screens, superimpositions, and matting processes.

The third level of filmic discourse consists of editing. In most production practices this occurs after the act of filming and involves the cutting and selection of shots as well as their assembly into syntagmas. This process of combination is stressed by Gaudreault's terminology for the activity of editing, the neologism *mise-en-chain*.[24] In Genette's enumeration of the functions of narrative discourse, one seems particularly suited to this level of discourse—that of tense. Tense deals

---

[21]Gaudreault, *Du Littéraire*, p. 199.

[22]However both David Bordwell and George M. Wilson accord the pro-filmic considerable attention in their respective works, *Narration in the Fiction Film*, and *Narration in Light: Studies in Cinematic Point of View* (Baltimore, MD: Johns Hopkins University Press, 1986).

[23]Gaudreault, *Du Litteraire*, p. 199.

[24]Ibid.

with the differences that can arise between the temporality of events as presented in narrative discourse and their time relations within the story being told. The single unedited shot, outside of an edited sequence, allows few differentiations between the time of narrative discourse and that of story.[25] This is evident in temporal order, because it is only through editing that a flashback or flashforward can be clearly signified. There have been attempts to create temporal disjunctions within a single shot, as in *A Love in Germany* (Wadja, 1984) or the opening of *Him and Me* (Benning, 1982), but these remain rarities and involve imitations of editing processes through camera movement. Likewise, the temporal relations between narrative discourse and story that Genette groups under duration, such as summary, ellipsis, or narrative pauses all have clear equivalents in editing processes, with only awkward semi-equivalents within the single shot.[26] Finally to the extent that the temporal relations that Genette groups under frequency can appear in film (e.g., the repetitive account of a single event, as in the multiple presentations of the rape in *Rashomon*), they seem strongly dependent on editing.

The particular suppleness of editing comes from the discontinuity between shots that allows articulation between them, including the temporal differentiations mentioned previously. But spatial articulations are equally important in the process of editing, such as the synthetic space created by continuity editing or the disjunctions of space that occur in other editing styles. Spatial articulations are less defined in literature than in film. They represent an element of the filmic narrator that has no direct equivalent in Genette's treatment of literary narrative discourse. However spatial figures in film tend to be closely interrelated with temporal articulations, and I will generally deal with them together.

In the history of film theory, discussions of the "essential nature" of film have often focused on editing. These have ranged from the proclamation of the supremacy of editing by the early Soviet theorists, through its deemphasis in the work of Bazin, to the reevaluation by theorists such as Marie Ropars-Wuilleumier and Gaudreault.[27] While editing represents a particularly supple level of filmic discourse, I maintain that all three levels must be considered in describing film's narrative discourse. As Bordwell has written, "all film techniques, even those involving the 'profilmic event,' function narrationally, constructing the story world for specific effects."[28]

The emphasis on editing in my analysis of Griffith therefore derives from Griffith's individual and historical situation rather than theoretical privileging. Production during this period favored editing over, for example, an elaborate system

---

[25]See Genette, *Narrative Discourse*, p. 35. There are exceptions to this, however, that do not relate to Griffith's Biograph films but should be included theoretically. Within the level of the enframed image, which corresponds to the production stage of shooting and re-photography, there is the possibility of slow or fast motion, created by shooting or printing, which sets up a differentiation between story time and discourse time. Likewise, the soundtrack can set up a host of temporal relations, most obviously through voice-over, which are not described herein. This seems another indication that sound would operate as a fourth level of filmic discourse, with strong roles in all three of Genette's aspects of narrative discourse.

[26]Ibid., pp. 86–112.

[27]See, Gaudreault, *Du Littéraire*, pp. 105–15, and Marie-Claire Ropars-Wuilleumier, "Function du montage dans la constitution du récit au cinema," *Revue des sciences humaines* 36 (January–March 1971): 51–52.

[28]Bordwell, *Narration*, p. 12.

of camera movement such as appears in some film production after the 1930s. However, historical and technical determinants are not the sole factor. During the same period as Griffith's Biograph career, Louis Feuillade, as well as other directors at Gaumont, such as Léonce Perret and Georges Monca, created a narrative style less dependent on editing, favoring elements such as composition and lighting. The emphatic role of editing in Griffith's filmmaking must partly derive from his own choices. The importance of editing in this work therefore derives from the films I am discussing.

Each of these levels integrates the one before, transforming it as it does so. Their effects on a spectator is generally due to their interrelation, and I separate them for analysis. These three aspects of filmic discourse—the pro-filmic, the enframed image, and editing—almost always work in concert and represent the medication between story and spectator in film. They are how films "tell" stories. Taken together, they constitute the filmic narrator.

Because film's narrative discourse represents the actual text of a film—its existence as a series of filmic images—no narrative film can exist except through its narrative discourse. It logically follows that every narrative film has a filmic narrator embodied by this discourse. The three levels of filmic discourse are not optional ornaments of style. They form the very mode of existence for any narrative film. But within a specific film, the particular stance and tone of its filmic narrator is determined by choices made within the levels of filmic discourse. Therefore the filmic narrator appears in a wide range of forms determined by specific choices within and among the three levels of filmic discourse (e.g., expressionist set design, high angle of camera, and match cutting). Relating these choices to the functions of narrative discourse that Genette lays out allows us to distinguish different types of filmic narrators. However, even if a certain type of narrator has a tendency to give the impression that "events seem to narrate themselves" without the intervention of a narrator (what the linguist Emile Benveniste calls *histoire*),[29] the narrator can never disappear entirely but can only be concealed. As Todorov writes, "Events never 'tell themselves'; the act of verbalization is irreducible."[30]

I would assert that the same is true in film. Although what has been termed "classical film narrative" labors to present the illusion of a direct presentation of events, this is always a labor of concealment, the construction of an illusion. As Paul Ricoeur has said of the ideology of literary transparency from which the classical style of film arises, "the rhetoric of dissimulation, the summit of the rhetoric of fiction, must not fool the critic, even if it may fool the reader."[31] As we shall see, Griffith plays an ambiguous role in the establishment of this classical style.

If the marks of enunciation in filmic discourse (which reveal the hand of the narrator) can only be camouflaged and not eradicated, we can establish a range of filmic narrators stretching from the apparent "invisibility" of the classical Hollywood film to the heavily rhetorical montage of, for example, Eisenstein—and it is significant

[29]Emil Benveniste, *Problems in General Linguistics* (Coral Gables, FL: University of Miami Press, 1970), p. 208.

[30]Todorov, *Introduction*, p. 39.

[31]Paul Ricoeur, *Time and Narrative*, trans. Kathleen Blamey and David Pellauer (Chicago: University of Chicago Press, 1988), vol. 3, p. 161.

that Griffith is often cited as a seminal influence on both extremes. Arranged synchronically, different degrees of assertiveness in the narrative discourse of films could distinguish among the narrative styles of different filmmakers, different cultures, or simply different films. Arranged diachronically, such differences could provide a historical view of the development of film narrative.

While narrative discourse embodies the telling of a story by a filmic narrator, the process of narration involves an interrelation between a narrator and what semioticians call a "narratee."[32] The dynamic aspect of this interaction should be stressed. Although implied by Genette, the role of the narratee has been discussed more explicitly by American film theorists whose concern with the activity of the viewer gives Genette's model a more dynamic twist.[33]

Edward Branigan, in *Point of View in the Cinema*, defines narration as an *activity*. This activity involves more than Genette's act of narrating because it involves the reader or viewer as well as the narrator. As Branigan puts it, narration is "a dialectical process between narrator and reader *through which* is realized a narrative."[34] We have already caught site of this activity in the simple fact that the reader or viewer constructs (or reconstructs) the story from the narrative discourse of the text. Bordwell's attempt to describe film narration through the concepts of Constructivist psychology similarly foregrounds the spectator's activity. According to Bordwell the spectator uses cues within the narrative texts "to make assumptions, draw inferences about current story events, and frame and test hypothesis about prior and upcoming events."[35]

Although my approach differs from Bordwell and Branigan's, I fully agree with their vision of an active spectator who contributes to the construction of the narrative. Their focus on the dynamic interaction between narrative discourse and reader or viewer allows me to specify that film's narrative discourse does not overpower a passive spectator but provides patterns within films that provoke active mental responses and set in motion the range of cognitive processes Bordwell describes. A particular narrative discourse addresses a spectator in a particular way, eliciting specific sorts of activities. The change Griffith brings to the way films are narrated is at the same time a change in the way films are viewed. Along with a new sort of filmic narrator, Griffith's transformation of filmic discourse constructs a new sort of spectator for film. Or to put it in a way that gives the spectator due, the spectator constructs a new sort of film experience as cued by Griffith's narrative discourse.

Both Branigan and Bordwell stress the role of the spectator at the expense of the narrator. In fact, they reject this term, preferring impersonal rubics, Branigan opting for "activity of narration"[36] and Bordwell for "narration." Their discomfort with the term *narrator* is in part understandable and methodologically useful and in part disturbing.

---

[32]Todorov, *Introduction*, p. 40.

[33]And in spite of his own apparent confusion on this matter (see, for example, *Narration*, p. 63), the narratee corresponds precisely to Bordwell's conception of the spectator, "a hypothetical entity executing the operations relevant to constructing a story out of the film's representations" (ibid., p. 30).

[34]Edward R. Branigan, *Point of View in the Cinema: A Theory of Narration and Subjectivity in Classical Film* (Amsterdam: Mouton Publishers, 1984), p. 39.

[35]Bordwell, *Narration*, p. 39.

[36]Branigan, *Point of View*, p. 40.

Both authors stress the impersonal, text-immanent nature of narrative discourse and describe the narrator as an "anthropomorphic fiction."[37] It is theoretically important to avoid identifying a narrator with a biological person such as the author. Narrative discourse is made up of words and images, not flesh and blood. Such theoretical precisions are necessary to maintain the integrity of the esthetic text. I will occasionally use the term *narrative discourse* rather than *narrator* in order to stress that I am dealing with images and their construction rather than a person.

However, the depersonalization of narrative discourse brings its own theoretical blindspot that distorts the way films are received by spectators, and the way they function within history and society. Bordwell particularly seems to set aside the fact that in our perception of films we are aware of them as products, as entities manufactured by human beings with evident purposes and designs upon us. In spite of his emphasis on the spectator's role he distorts the address that films level at audiences. The alert and active spectator proposed by Bordwell's psychological description must realize that these images come from *somewhere*. When Bordwell declares that his theory of narration "presupposes a perceiver, but not a sender, of a message,"[38] one wonders what sort of message this is—and in what universe a receiver can respond to a message without wondering about a sender.

The limits of this depersonalization become particularly clear when Bordwell sets his model of narration in motion. What he has excluded in theory re-emerges in his practice. For Bordwell, narration can be "self conscious," can "voluntarily restrict itself," "refuse to mark," or can "flaunt its ability"[39]—to take only a few examples which indicate that he cannot avoid speaking of this impersonal function as volitional and endowed with something very much like human consciousness. Bordwell grounds some of his objection to the concept of the narrator in the transparency of the classical style, claiming that classical films are not endowed with a perceptible narrator, although certain modernist films do signal that the "spectator should construct a narrator." Only certain exceptional films therefore possess narrators, and even this sort of narrator "does not create the narration" but is constructed by the spectator.[40]

Bordwell's theory is not irrational; the narrative discourse of film with its tendency toward showing does possess a transparent quality that verbal discourse lacks. And certainly the narrator as the embodiment of narrative discourse does not stand outside the text. The narrator communicates to the spectator only through the spectator's engagement with the narrative discourse, so in a sense the spectator does construct the narrator, just as he or she does the story, from the narrative discourse. But storytelling implies a storyteller as surely as it does a story. We must be careful in describing the nature of this teller, this narrator.

In films and literature, the narrator is not a flesh-and-blood entity. The narrator, in my understanding of the term, is a theoretical entity, as divorced from an actual person as Bordwell's spectator is from a particular viewer. But preserving the more

---

[37]Ibid.; Bordwell, *Narration*, p. 62.
[38]Bordwell, *Narration*, p. 62.
[39]Ibid., pp. 58, 65, 89, 146.
[40]Ibid., p. 62.

personal term *narrator* not only avoids academic abstraction but also responds to the experience a reader or spectator has of being addressed by a story. This address can be described by the volitional activities that slip back in Bordwell's window of praxis after being barred at his theoretical door. We receive a text as though it were saying something to us, as though, in the words of my colleague Robert Stein, it has designs on us. We experience it as an intentional object, designed to have certain effects on us.[41] More than a random set of cues, the narrator embodies the design organizing narrative discourse, the intentions which unify its effects. It corresponds to that force in narrative that Peter Brooks calls plot or plotting, "the design and intention of narrative, what shapes a story and gives it a certain direction or intent of meaning."[42] These designs do not exist outside the text but are evident in the rhetorical arrangement of its devices. The more active term *narrator* stresses that this discourse, to paraphrase Brooks, involves force as well as form. It is not only constructed by the reader or spectator, but also addresses and affects him or her through specific devices. Thus in describing film's narrative discourse I have described each level as activities which arrange and organize material in order to address a spectator. No narrative film exists, even the "transparent" films of the classical style, without making such an address.

Another reason for maintaining the term *narrator* is that although it is theoretically separate from the author and processes of production that created the work, it does provide, in the words of Ricoeur, the image of the author within the text. As a series of intentions it recalls the narrative's nature as a unified manufactured object, the product of human labor. As Ricoeur asserts, "the reader does not ascribe this unification to the rules of composition alone but extends it to the choices and to the norms that make the text, precisely, the work of some speaker, hence a work produced by someone and not by nature."[43] Bordwell's theory tends to occult the spectator's perception of a film as something produced. It belongs to the tendency Raymond Williams attacked of dealing with art works solely from the point of view of consumption, ignoring the process of production.[44] Griffith's films address us through their narrative discourse, which creates the sense of an intervening figure who has arranged the images on the screen in a particular manner with specific social consequences. The concept of the filmic narrator helps us relate filmic form to broader contexts.

1991

---

[41]I use the term *intentional* in its phenomenological meaning indicating a product of human consciousness, rather than its psychological meaning. I am not claiming that a particular definable intention lies behind every narrative, or that criticism should reconstruct this intention. This would lead of course to the intentional fallacy. The intention behind a narrative as an intentional object may remain unspecified, its very vagueness drawing a response from the reader or spectator.

[42]Peter Brooks, *Reading for the Plot: Design and Intention in Narrative* (New York: Random House, 1984), p. xi.

[43]Ricoeur, *Time and Narrative*, vol. 3, p. 162.

[44]Bordwell's own historical work pioneered a new serious consideration of the process of production. However I find a contradiction between his theoretical apparatus and his important scholarly work on production modes. Likewise, the brilliance of his analysis of the narrative discourse of films in *Narration in the Fiction Film* seems unencumbered by what I consider his theoretical weak spot, because intentionality actually reemerges in his specific analyses.

JERROLD LEVINSON
FILM MUSIC AND NARRATIVE AGENCY

Jerrold Levinson studied physical chemistry at the Massachusetts Institute of Technology before developing the interest in philosophy that would lead him to a career in aesthetics and the philosophy of mind with books such as *Music, Art, and Metaphysics* (1990) and *Music in the Moment* (1998). Levinson's work deals extensively with the philosophical questions and emotional responses to which music, art, and film give rise. In addition to his contributons to anthologies on philosophy and aesthetics, Levinson has written on erotic art, musical pleasure, flim spectatorship, and creativity. A past president of the American Society for Aesthetics, he is presently Distinguished University professor of philosophy at the University of Maryland.

In this essay I address certain issues about paradigmatic film music, that is, the music that is often heard in the course of a fiction film but that does not originate in or issue from the fictional world revealed on screen. What most interests me is the question that confronts every filmgoer at some level, and to which he or she must, explicitly or implicitly, accord an answer, of who or what is responsible for such music. That is to say, to what agency is film music assigned by a comprehending viewer, and what is this music understood to be doing, in relation either to the film's internal narrative, the viewer's experience of that narrative, or the film as an aesthetic whole? Furthermore, by what principle does a viewer assign, however tacitly, responsibility for the music he or she hears?

It will turn out that different answers to this question of agency are in order from one film to another, and even from one cue to another within a given film. The upshot is a basic division within the realm of film music, one I have not seen marked elsewhere, but which is probably more fundamental than others regularly noted.

I begin with some preliminaries. First, the music I am concerned with is usually designated *nondiegetic* film music, that is, music whose source is not the story (or *diegesis*) being conveyed by the film's sequence of images. It is sometimes also designated *soundtrack* as opposed to *source* music, and sometimes as *extrinsic,* as opposed to *intrinsic,* music.[1] Second, the films I am concerned with are all *narrative fiction* films, both of the "classical" (or "Hollywood") sort, and the "modernist" (or "art film") sort, though not any of the more extreme examples of the latter, in

---

I thank David Bordwell and Noël Carroll for helpful comments on the style and substance of this essay. Needless to say, they do not agree with everything in it.
[1]For more on these categories, see David Bordwell and Kristin Thompson, *Film Art: An Introduction,* 4th ed. (New York: McGraw-Hill, 1993), pp. 295–303.

which the bounds of fictionality or narrative coherence are stretched to their limits.[2] Third, I will consider film music here only as an integral component of a complete film, and not as a genre of music which, in the form of suites or soundtracks, might be enjoyed and evaluated on its own.

Certain kinds of answers to our opening queries can be put aside immediately as not to the point. For instance, the source of nondiegetic film music might in one sense be said to be the composer who composes it, or the producer who commissions it, or the sound editor who integrates it into the finished film, but this does not address the question of where, in relation to the fictional world projected, the music is situated or positioned in comprehending the film. Similarly, the function of nondiegetic film music might be said to be, somewhat vaguely, the aesthetic enhancement of the film, or more specifically, the emotional manipulation of the film viewer, or more crassly, the augmentation of the film's marketability and secondary profits, but none of these answers addresses the question of how such music is understood to function in relation to the central narrative of sight and sound, and thus to contribute ultimately to a film's meaning.

It should be noted straight off that there are two basic sorts of musical score regularly encountered in the domain of the sound film: the first, more traditional sort consists of music composed specifically for the film in question, and generally tailored by the composer to the rough cut, scene by scene; the second sort consists of preexistent music chosen by the filmmaker, often in conjunction with a musical consultant, and applied or affixed to scenes or parts thereof. Call the former sort a *composed* score, and the latter an *appropriated* score.

We can make at least two observations about these two types of score. First, with appropriated scores the issue of specific imported associations, deriving from the original context of composition or performance or distribution, rather than just general associations carried by musical style or conventions, is likely to arise. Second, with appropriated as opposed to composed scores, there will, ironically, generally be more attention drawn to the music, both because it is often recognized as appropriated and located by the viewer in cultural space, and because the impression it gives of chosenness, on the part of the implied filmmaker, is greater. To these two observations I add a third, more contentious one, that later discussion will support: music composed *for* a film (for example, the soundtracks of *Vertigo* or *The Heiress* or *On the Waterfront* or *La Strada*), is more likely to be purely narrative in function than preexisting music appropriated *by* a filmmaker (for example, the sound tracks of *A Clockwork Orange* or *Barry Lyndon* or *Love and Death* or *Death in Venice*).

There are some theoretical claims prevalent in the recent literature on film with which I will be disagreeing, and it is best I signal what they are at the outset. One is that nondiegetic film music is standardly "inaudible," that is, is not, and is not meant to be, consciously heard, attended to, or noticed.[3] This seems to be clearly false, or at any rate, false for a wide range of films in which soundtrack music calls

[2] For example, Snow's *Wavelength* or Resnais's *L'Annee Dernière à Marienbad*.

[3] This is a central thesis in Claudia Gorbman's *Unheard Melodies: Narrative Film Music* (Bloomington: Indiana University Press, 1987), and is echoed by other recent psychoanalytically oriented writers on film.

attention to itself unmistakenly, or requires the viewer to attend to it explicitly if he or she is not to miss something of narrative importance. The "inaudibility" claim seems most true for what is called *underscoring*, music at a low volume that serves as a sort of aural cushion for dialogue that remains the main order of business, or for melodically and rhythmically unmarked music helping to effect transitions between scenes of notably different character. Even here, when the music hovers in the penumbra of consciousness, it is rarely very far from being consciously focused, as is perhaps reflected in the fact of being immediately noticed if stopped. If nondiegetic film music were generally unheard, or not consciously noted by the viewer, then there would not be much of an interpretive issue for the viewer of how to construe such music in relation to the rest of what is going on in the film. But, with respect to many films, there manifestly *is* an issue of some significance. Finally, even if it were the case that casual viewing of films with significant music tracks often goes on without a viewer's explicit awareness of that music, it hardly follows that an aesthetically justified or optimal viewing of such films remains similarly oblivious.

Another idea with some currency is the disavowal of what might be called narration proper—the conveying of a story by an intelligent agent—as actually characterizing the standard fiction film. One variant of this has it that such films are not really narrated by anyone or anything within the film world, but instead narrate themselves. A second variant insists that such films are constituted as narratives only by the viewer, and contain no narration apart from that. A third variant maintains that such films are not only constituted as narratives by viewers, but are in fact narrated by viewers to themselves as well, in the course of viewing.[4]

I reject the first sort of disavowal on grounds of incoherence; if narration means anything, it is the conveying or imparting of a story by means that are distinct both from the story being conveyed and from that which is doing the conveying; if the film, or its processes, are the means of narration, then it, or they, cannot also be conceived to be the agent or source of narration. I reject the second and third sorts of disavowal because they seem based on conflating the viewer's actual task of comprehending a film's story and significance by actively reconstructing or piecing together the narrative on offer, with the viewer's literal creation of that narrative, which would thus not exist apart from the viewer. But this is unnecessarily fanciful; our responsibility as filmgoers is to grasp what the narrative is, so as to further reflect on what it might signify, rather than to create that narrative for ourselves. Furthermore, were we really to create the narrative for ourselves, its significance would not, at any rate, be that of the film we were putatively attempting to understand.

---

[4]Though he argues vigorously against the third form of disavowal in his attack on *enonciation* theorists, there remains something of the first and second in the constructivism about film meaning defended by David Bordwell; see his *Narration in the Fiction Film* (Madison: University of Wisconsin Press, 1985) and *Making Meaning* (Cambridge, MA: Harvard University Press, 1989). For a critique of this aspect of Bordwell's otherwise salutory approach to film, see Berys Gaut, "Making Sense of Films: Neoformalism and Its Limits," *Forum for Modern Language Studies* (January 1995), 8–23. Bordwell's rejection of narrative agents in film as such is also criticized by Seymour Chatman, *Coming to Terms* (Ithaca, NY: Cornell University Press, 1990), chapter 8.

So I am going to assume, following Seymour Chatman,[5] that if there is narration of events in a fiction film, if a comprehensible story comprising them is being conveyed to us, then there is an agency or intelligence we are entitled, and in fact need, to imagine is responsible for doing this narrating—to wit, a narrator, though not necessarily an ordinary human being.

There are, of course, alternatives to this assumption. As noted above, there are those who propose that films or filmic processes are themselves the performers or executants of narration, there not being of necessity any narrator within the film's world on the same plane as the events being displayed. But in addition to the fundamental incoherence remarked above, this proposal, to the extent it can be made out, is simply less interpretively useful than that of a narrator, however minimally characterized, for every successful narration. My response to yet another alternative, that in many cases of filmic narration, we imagine we are presented directly with the events of the story, without imagining there is any agent presenting them to us,[6] is much the same: the postulate of narrative agency in cinema does a better job of accounting for how we, admittedly largely implicitly, make sense of films as conveyors of stories.

For those who yet balk at this postulate, I would offer this. What I want to say about assigning nondiegetic music to narrative agents as opposed to implied filmmakers can, I believe, be translated so as to require instead only the assumption of narrative processes or mere appearances of being narrated. So even if one does not regard the positing of internal narrators or presenters in film as inevitable, the issue will still remain whether soundtrack music is to be thought of as an element in the narrative process or as an appearance of narrative presentation, as opposed to an element, standing outside both the story and its narration, in the construction of the film by a filmmaker. It is that issue I hope to illuminate. . . .

That nondiegetic music standardly serves to advance a film's narrative is something on which theorists of film appear to agree:

> Narrative is not constructed by visual means alone. By this I mean that music works as part of the process that transmits narrative information to the spectator. . . .[7]

> Voice-over is just one of many elements, including musical scoring, sound effects, editing, lighting, and so on, through which the cinematic text is narrated.[8]

> The moment we recognize to what degree film music shapes our perception of a narrative, we can no longer consider it incidental. . . .[9]

---

[5]See his *Coming to Terms*, especially chapters 5, 7, and 8. Another writer who seems to accept the necessity of positing narrative agency in narrative film, though he verges on abstracting this to the point of abandonment, is Edward Branigan, *Point of View in the Cinema* (Berlin: Mouton, 1984).

[6]A position taken, for example, by Gregory Currie, in "Visual Fictions," *Philosophy Quarterly* 41 (April 1991): 129–43. I respond to Currie in "Seeing, Imaginarily, at the Movies," *Philosophy Quarterly* 43 (January 1993): 70–78.

[7]Kathryn Kalinak, *Settling the Score: Music and Classical Hollywood Film* (Madison: University of Wisconsin Press, 1992), p. 30.

[8]Sarah Kozloff, *Invisible Storytellers: Voice-Over in American Fiction Film* (Berkeley: University of California Press, 1988), pp. 43–44.

[9]Gorbman, *Unheard Melodies*, p. 11.

Another point widely agreed upon is that even if the primary purpose of nondiegetic film music is the advancing of the narrative, there may very well be others. Here is a typical admonition concerning film music's multiplicity of ends:

> There is not *one and only one* function that music can perform in relation to movies. Aaron Copland suggested five broad functions: creating atmosphere, underlining the psychological states of characters, providing background filler, building a sense of continuity, sustaining tension and then rounding it off with a sense of closure. These do not seem to be necessarily exclusive categories, nor do they exhaust the range of functions that music can perform in movies.[10]

Not surprisingly, I am happy to join this double consensus: film music often serves narrative in some way, but there is a range of other functions that such music sometimes performs. What I am concerned to demonstrate, however, goes beyond those two pieces of received wisdom. It is that the most fundamental division in the realm of film music concerns the viewer's assignment of responsibility for such music, that is, the agency the viewer posits, usually implicitly, as responsible for the music being heard. It will turn out that there is a rough coincidence between film music to which we intuitively accord narrative significance and film music for which we implicitly hold an internal cinematic narrator accountable, and between film music to which we do not accord narrative significance and film music that we implicitly assign directly to the implied filmmaker.

When, though, can film music be said to have narrative significance? When does nondiegetic music function narratively? In order to answer this question we must have a plausible criterion of narrativity or of actions within the purview of a narrator. In trying to arrive at one, it will be helpful to have before us a survey of the various functions that critics or theorists have observed film music to perform.

These functions include: (1) the indicating or revealing of something about a character's psychological condition, including emotional states, personality traits, or specific cognitions, as when the music informs you that the heroine is happy, or that the hero has just realized who the murderer was; (2) the modifying or qualifying of some psychological attribution to a character independently grounded by other elements of the film, as when the music tells you that a character's grief over a loss is intense; (3) the underlining or corroborating of some psychological attribution to a character independently grounded by other elements of the film, as when music emphasizes something about a situation on screen which is already fully evident; (4) the signifying of some fact or state of affairs in the film world other than the psychological condition of some character, for example, that a certain evil deed has occurred, off-screen; (5) the foreshadowing of a dramatic development in a situation being depicted on screen; (6) the projecting of a story-appropriate mood, attributable to a scene as a whole; (7) the imparting to the viewer of a sense that the happenings in the film are more important than those of ordinary life—the emotions magnified, the stakes higher, the significances deeper; (8) the suggesting to the viewer of how the presenter of the story regards or feels about some aspect of the story, for example, sympathetically; (9) the suggesting to the viewer of how he or

---

[10]Noël Carroll, *Mystifying Movies* (New York: Columbia University Press, 1988), p. 216.

she is to regard or feel about some aspect of the story, for example, compassionately; (10) the imparting of certain formal properties, such as coherence, cogency, continuity, closure, to the film or parts thereof; (11) the direct inducing in viewers of tension, fear, wariness, relaxation, cheerfulness, or other similar cognitive or affective state; (12) the lulling or mesmerizing of the viewer, so as to facilitate emotional involvement in the fictional world to which the viewer would otherwise prove resistant; (13) the distracting of the viewer's attention from the technical features of the film as a constructed artifact, concern with which would prevent immersion in the filmic narrative; (14) the expressing by the filmmaker of an attitude toward, or view on, the fictional story or aspect thereof; (15) the embellishing or enriching of the film as an object of appreciation.

Without deciding, for each of these functions, which are properly considered narrative and which not, it would appear that some of them unequivocally are and some unequivocally are not. What I will do at this point is explore a number of suggestions as to what the criterion of narrativity might be in regard to nondiegetic film music, assessing them against the background of this array of observed functions, some of which, at any rate, would have to come out counting as narrative, some clearly not, and some having a status that might only be settled, clarifyingly, once a given suggestion is adopted.

One possible criterion is this: (C1) does the music seem to issue from, be in service of, the agency one imagines to be bringing one the sights and sounds of the film's world? If so, then it can be reckoned part of the narration proper, and assignable to the cinematic narrator. Perhaps an equivalent formulation would be: (C2) does the intelligence one thinks of as bringing one the music seem to be the same as that charged with conveying the story—as opposed to that charged with constructing the film? If so, then the music can be reckoned part of the narration, and assigned to the cinematic narrator.[11]

Though I think these criteria point in the right direction, there is an evident problem with them, insofar as we hope to look to them for guidance, especially in difficult cases. And that is that they are uncomfortably close to what they purport to analyze or elucidate, namely, whether a use of nondiegetic music is narrative or not. So if we are unsure whether a given cue is functioning narratively, we are likely to be almost equally unsure whether it feels as if it derives from the film's narrative agent. Thus, it would seem desirable to have some other mark, could we discover one, whose conceptual distinctness from the idea of narrative functioning was greater than that of C1 or C2.

Such a mark might be that of *making a difference* in the narrative. Instead of appealing directly to an intuition of a connection of the music to a film's internal narrator, we can appeal instead to the notion of *making fictional,* or generating fictional truths, in a film. A criterion of nondiegetic music having a narrative function, and thus being attributable to a narrative agent, could be thus: (C3) the music makes something fictionally true—true in the story being conveyed—that would not

---

[11]Note that this would apply even when such music is unforegrounded: if it appears to respond to the demands of storytelling, broadly understood, then it can be construed as something like musical musing, *sotto voce,* on the cinematic narrator's part.

otherwise be true, or not to the same degree or with the same definiteness. A counterfactual form of the suggestion is perhaps more transparent: (C4) would deleting the music in a scene change its represented content (that is, what is fictional in it), or only how the scene affects viewers? If the former, then the music is an aspect of narration; if the latter, then not.

We must briefly discuss what it means to make something fictional in a work of fiction such as a narrative film. Something is fictional in a film, according to a well-developed recent account, if it is *to be imagined to be the case* by viewers concerned to experience the film properly.[12] What thus makes something—a proposition about the film's world—something that is to be imagined in the course of viewing is, in short, perceivable features of the film, a public object, taken as a prop for guided imaginings.

When we make believe in accord both with the features of artistic props and the usually tacitly grasped principles for imagining that are in effect in a given art form, we are engaged in tracing out imaginary worlds, ones in which things are *make-believedly*, or *fictionally*, so. The fictional world of a representational art work, unlike that of a daydream or fantasy, is as it is because features of the associated prop—text, canvas, film—properly construed, are the way they are; not all is up to the imaginer. Props, through their existence and nature, generate fictional truths independently of what individual perceivers might choose to imagine.

What does it mean for a proposition to be fictional, or true in a fictional world, in respect of a given work of art? Simply that there is a *prescription to imagine* it, a prescription encoded in the particulars of the artifact that serves as a prop for making believe, and whose force derives from underlying conventions of construing works of the sort in question. Being fictional thus has an ineliminable normative dimension: it is what *is to be* imagined in a given context, rather than merely what *may* be imagined.

For example, in *Citizen Kane*, Orson Welles's image on-screen being that of a large man makes it fictional that Charles Foster Kane is a large man; the opening shots—a series of lap dissolves—having a certain visual content makes it fictional that at the beginning of the story one is shown Kane's estate, Xanadu, from a distance and shrouded in mist, and then at progressively closer range; Ray Collins's voice saying certain things on the soundtrack in the scene at Susan Alexander's apartment makes it fictional that Collins's character, Jim Gettys, has threatened Kane; the way the shot of Kane expiring is sequenced in relation to others which are understood as a flashback to Kane's childhood, makes it fictional that Kane's dying word, "Rosebud," refers to his beloved old sled, and so on. Of course, much of this generation will be indirect, dependent on various conventions of the medium in effect and on other things taken provisionally as fictional, and accordingly, much of our knowledge of such fictional truths will be inferential. And sometimes, what is made fictional by a film's narration is orthogonal to, or even the opposite of, what first appears to be the case, that is, what it initially seems we are to imagine is the

---

[12]See Walton, *Mimesis as Make-Believe*. For an entrée into this important work, see my critical notice, "Making Believe," *Dialogue* 32 (1993): 359–74.

case; unreliable, uninformed, or unforthcoming narrators, though not as common in film as in literature, are still a significant possibility.

Applying this suggestion to the issue of narrativity in film music, then, the question becomes, of a given cue, whether it generates, contributes to generating, or at a minimum, more firmly grounds, a fictional truth in the scene which it accompanies. Thus, film music that, when interpreted in light of prevailing conventions of the medium and the surrounding narrative context, indicated that a character was afraid or was remembering a past incident, or that a man had been executed or an agreement reached, or that a situation was fraught with danger or else full of hope, where these things would not be established, or not so definitely, without the music, would clearly count as narrative.[13]

We should note that nondiegetic music may, indeed, generate fictional truths even if only attended to with half a mind, or not consciously remarked at all while present. It will do this by causing a viewer to, say, perceive a scene as fraught with danger, even if the viewer is not aware of what is making her have that perception. Nevertheless, if such an imaginative perception is reliably produced in attuned viewers, and not undermined by subsequent aspects of the narration, then it may well be fictional that the scene is fraught with danger, even though the rest of the narrative indicators are insufficient to establish that and the viewer never realizes that it is the background music that in fact makes it so.

It is time to look at a range of illustrative examples of film music. I begin with examples whose narrative functioning is obvious, and which conform, expectedly, to the making-fictional criterion proposed above. I then explore another range of examples, ones that exhibit a different sort of narrativity, and show how, on a more encompassing construal of the making-fictional criterion, these can be accommodated as well. Eventually, though, I turn to films containing nondiegetic music that is not, by that criterion or any other, reasonably construed as narrative. The music in such films instead serves other sorts of artistic function, ones attributable directly, I will argue, to implied filmmakers.

One of the least ambiguous narrative uses of soundtrack music in recent film occurs in Steven Spielberg's 1975 blockbuster, *Jaws*. I have in mind the "shark" motto devised by the composer, John Williams. This consists of an ostinato alternation of low staccato notes at the interval of a second—a kind of aural sawing. The motto has an unarguable informational mission, namely, to signal the presence of the shark. It is true that there is another, visual, indicator of the shark's presence when unseen, namely, shots from an offshore point of view, at the water line or slightly below it. But that indicator is not invariant in meaning, since it is sometimes employed when there is no shark about. The musical "shark" motto is the only reliable signifier of the shark, and so has an ineliminable fact-conveying function. Correspondingly, it is clear that it is the presence of that motto on the soundtrack at a given point that makes it fictional that the shark, though as yet unseen, is in the vicinity of what is shown.

---

[13]"Film music . . . often contributes subtly but effectively to the generation of fictional truths—helping to establish, for example, that fictionally a character is nervous or cocky or ecstatic . . ." (*Mimesis as Make-Believe*, p. 172).

David Raksin's ground-breaking score for Otto Preminger's *Laura* provides some further instances of straightforward narrative use of film music. The "Laura" theme, first encountered diegetically on a record player in the apartment of the ostensibly murdered heroine, pervades critic Waldo's (Clifton Webb) represented recollections of the early days of his relationship with Laura (Gene Tierney), and signifies unmistakeably his joy and delight in her companionship. Subsequently we are treated to apprehensive versions of the "Laura" theme as detective McPherson (Dana Andrews), alone in Laura's apartment, studies the portrait of Laura over the fireplace; this cue then climaxes unsettlingly, revealing or underlining McPherson's frustration with his investigation at this point. The most striking cue, one much noted in the film music literature,[14] is a weird version of the theme which is produced by playing it on a piano but only recording the overtones of each note struck. This is heard as McPherson views Laura's portrait on a second occasion, before drinking too much and falling asleep, and it suggests the ghostly influence Laura is beginning to exert over this poor detective's mind. In each of the foregoing cases, the music is plausibly viewed as making, or contributing to making, something fictional in the story: that Waldo delighted in Laura inordinately, that McPherson is (earlier) almost terminally frustrated with Laura's case, that McPherson is (later) succumbing to bewitchment by Laura's spirit.

Another film rich in narrative pointing of a theoretically unproblematic sort is Martin Scorsese's *Taxi Driver*. Regarding a scene in which Travis (Robert De Niro), the film's semipsychotic protagonist, is induced to move his cab away from the Manhattan workplace of a girl he is infatuated with and back into the grime and disorder of the city, one writer affirms that "the music . . . here reveals that Travis's thoughts are not with the street but with Betsy." And of the bluesy, sensual saxophone tune itself, which stands for Betsy (Cybill Shepherd) in Travis's mind, the same writer has this to say: "Travis's vision of idealized womanhood, the music implies, is strongly erotic."[15] Thus, Bernard Herrmann's music does not serve merely to inform us about Travis's mental life, or to second redundantly what other elements of the film establish about his mentality, but rather enters into making it *fictional* in the film that Travis's mental life is a certain way at a certain time. Commenting on the blade-game fight scene in Nicholas Ray's *Rebel without a Cause*, Noël Carroll offers the following: "The uneasy, unstable quality of the music [by Leonard Rosenman] serves to characterize the psychological turmoil—the play of repression and explosive release—with which the scene, and the movie, is concerned."[16] If Carroll is right, the music of this scene, which intuitively seems an aspect of its narration, serves to underwrite as desired a fictional truth about the specific, highly volatile, character of the turmoil afflicting the young protagonists. Another instructive example from *Rebel without a Cause* occurs later in the film, and consists of a montage of two-way phone calls among various adults concerned with the whereabouts of three main youngsters. This montage is covered by tense nondiegetic

---

[14]See Kalinak's informative discussion in *Settling the Score*, p. 178.

[15]Graham Bruce, *Bernard Herrmann: Film Music and Narrative* (Ann Arbor, MI.: UMI Research Press, 1985), p. 68.

[16]*Mystifying Movies*, p. 217.

music, displacing the dialogue that would ordinarily be heard, the music thus signifying that the conversations, whatever their specific contents, are anxious ones.

The opening of Elia Kazan's *On the Waterfront* affords another illuminating example. An establishing shot of city docks, ocean liner in the distance, gives way to a street scene in which longshoreman Terry (Marlon Brando) becomes the focus of attention. Leonard Bernstein's jazz-inflected score at this point involves a persistent drum tattoo overlaid with saxophone insinuations. Terry, in the darkening street, yells up to friend Joey's window, persuading him to go to the roof to recover one of his pet pigeons, where unbeknownst to Joey, two men are waiting for him. After Terry releases the pigeon he's been holding, and promises to join Joey in a moment, the score becomes loud, aggressive, and insistent, its rhythms more syncopated. The music telegraphs us that something bad is in store, that the men glimpsed on the roof are trouble; the music can be said to prefigure Joey's fall, pushed off the roof by thugs of the corrupt union boss, though without defining precisely what is about to happen. The cue is clearly narrative, and just as clearly, makes it fictional that Joey is in danger, even before he leaves the window for his fatal visit to the roof.

Later on, after the boss tells right-hand man Charley (Rod Steiger) to straighten out his brother Terry or else, Charley leaves union headquarters to do something, we know not what. Bernstein's music at this point is very dramatic and tense: a series of rising notes in the brass, leading to a rhythmic explosion, the whole heard twice. The cue arguably conveys Charley's complex state of mind, as he faces the necessity of keeping his errant brother, who is threatening to do the right thing, in line: a mixture of anger, shame, and angst. If it does not single-handedly make it fictional that that is Charley's state of mind, the cue contributes ineliminably to making it so. A dissolve leads directly to the famous conversation between the brothers in the rear of a taxi.

Consider, lastly, the final sequence in Fellini's *La Strada*. Five years ago, Zampano the strongman (Anthony Quinn) has abandoned his assistant, the childlike Gelsomina (Giuletta Masina), after she became too withdrawn and depressed to work. He now discovers, by accident, her fate. That evening he does his act perfunctorily, gets drunk, starts brawling, then goes down to the beach, which reminds us of where he first acquired Gelsomina from her impoverished family. He walks into the water, returns to the beach, looks up at the sky apprehensively, then starts to bawl and grasp at the sand, on which he has flung himself in despair. At this point the "La Strada" theme on the soundtrack removes all doubt as to what it is Zampano is bemoaning—namely, the loss of Gelsomina and her innocent love.

Clearly, making something fictional in a film is a *sufficient* condition of musical narrativity. Is it, however, a necessary one? Though providing the basic fictional truths of a story may be the central activity of a narrator, there are others that are almost equally paradigmatic of narration. One is the evincing of attitudes or feelings on the narrator's part toward the story presented, in virtue of how the story is presented; another is the inviting of the viewer to adopt certain attitudes or feelings toward the story presented. In other words, in addition to giving access, in a particular manner, to the fictional states of affairs that constitute a story, a narrator generally manifests attitudes regarding the states of affairs to which access is afforded, and thereby suggests to the narratee attitudes to be adopted. In literature, for example, the narrator standardly tells us what happened, after his or her fashion, reveals, knowingly or unknowingly, his or her view of these happenings, and also suggests, explicitly or implicitly, how we should view what we are told happened.[17]

Now it seems plain that such narrational effects are often achieved by appropriate nondiegetic music: the music tells you how the presenter of the story regards the events being presented, or else how he would like you to regard them. But on the surface, this does not appear to be a matter of establishing, nuancing, or even confirming a fictional state of affairs in the story. So in light of that, can making fictional be sustained as the effective mark of musical narrativity?

I believe so. We need to make a distinction between what is fictional *in a film's story* and what is fictional *in the world of a film*. The latter is a broader notion than the former. What is fictional in the film's world comprises, in addition to the facts of the story, the facts of its narration by the special, often almost effaced, fictional agent known as the narrator. All that is still within the sphere of the fictional, of propositions to be imagined by a viewer in comprehending the film. The film's story consists of what is fictional about the characters who figure in the action; the film's world includes, as well, what is fictional about the narrator, in relation to either the story narrated or the implied audience of that narration.[18]

Returning to film music, a plausible construal of some nondiegetic cue will often have the implication, not that it makes something fictional in the story, but that it makes it fictional either that the cinematic narrator has a certain attitude or feeling toward some event being presented, or that the narrator encourages viewers to have such an attitude or feeling toward it. In either case, musical narrativity will still correlate with music's making something fictional, only here it is a making fictional in the film's world, as opposed to a making fictional in the embedded story. Some examples will serve to clarify this more encompassing interpretation of musical narration in terms of making-fictional.

Music functions narratively, by any intuitive assessment, in Hitchcock's *Shadow of a Doubt*, particularly at junctures when a scrap of Lehar's "Merry Widow" waltz intrudes itself, suggesting the "Merry Widow Murders" that are central to the plot. Several characters are heard singing or humming the tune in the course of the film, these occurrences being of course diegetic, but the tune is heard, in an altered form, as early as Dmitri Tiomkin's title music, which accompanies a stylized shot of waltzing couples. Two notable nondiegetic occurrences after that are these. First, a few bars of the waltz theme in the cue that accompanies the family's greeting of Uncle Charlie (Joseph Cotten) at the train station, as they walk off to their car to take him home: a tracking shot of the group, heading toward the camera, is eventually reframed so that only Uncle Charlie is in view, and that is when the scrap of tune is heard. Second, a more prominent statement of the theme when Uncle Charlie

---

[17]In some literary fictions, for example, Hemingway's *The Killers* or Robbe-Grillet's *La jalousie*, this latter function may seem to have lapsed. But I would argue that even in such fictions there are attitudes the narrator implicitly invites the reader to adopt, precisely in virtue of so pointedly eschewing normal commentary.

[18]Of course, when a narrator in a film is also a character in the action, as with a homodiegetic voice-over narrator, then certain facts about such a narrator are also facts of the story.

gives young Charlie (Teresa Wright) an emerald ring, and she notices it is already engraved inside with an unknown someone's initials. In both cases, the music arguably serves to communicate something to the viewer about Charlie's identity, connecting him in some as yet unexplained way to the waltzing image presented at the beginning.

But does the music make, or even contribute to making, something true in the film's story as such, something that would not otherwise be the case? It is not clear that it does. To consider just the most obvious candidates, neither cue makes it true—even viewed in retrospect, when a connection to Lehar's tune is understood to import as well a connection to the "Merry Widow" murders—that Uncle Charlie is the murderer, nor does the second make it true, say, that young Charlie suspects that he is. The reason is that those fictional truths are firmly established, and independently, by other elements in the film.[19]

What, then, might they be doing? I suggest that the first cue makes it fictional that the narrator is obliquely hinting to viewers with regard to Uncle Charlie's identity, and the second makes it fictional that the narrator is, even more directly, connecting Uncle Charlie to something sinister in his past, though at that point viewers have no notion of what it might be. The second cue may, in addition, function as the narrator's proposing of a deep psychic link between Uncle Charlie and young Charlie, one that her subsequent moral corner-cutting, in dealing with an uncle she then knows to be an unhinged killer, partially bears out.[20] In any event, the status of these cues as narrative can be recovered in the guise of what is made fictional, not in the story as such, but in the narrator's attitudes or actions with respect to viewers.

But what of the curious musical image of waltzing couples first encountered in the title sequence, which recurs nondiegetically and unchangingly at three crucial points in the story? In each case the image is superimposed over the action already on view, which continues underneath. The first occurrence is after the interaction between Uncle Charlie and young Charlie over the emerald ring, as young Charlie goes off to clear the supper dishes, leaving only Uncle Charlie on screen. The second occurrence is at night in the town library, when young Charlie, after reading the newspaper account of the "Merry Widow" murders, gets up, almost reeling, as the camera tracks upward and away from her. The third and last is just as Uncle Charlie falls to his death beneath the wheels of a hurtling locomotive.

The first and second of these might be interpreted as the narrator's display of the mental contents of the character then in frame, in the one case signifying Uncle

---

[19] For example, that Uncle Charlie is the murderer is underwritten by his unexplained money in the opening hotel room scene, by his evident concern to keep an item in the daily newspaper unread, by his unreasonable aversion to being photographed, by his maniacal utterance at the dinner table about fat, wheezing, useless widows, by the already-inscribed ring itself, and so on. That young Charlie suspects him does not become true until she is informed about the manhunt by one of the two detectives who have been trailing Uncle Charlie—though of course there have been signs, intended for and readable by the viewer, well before that.

[20] Their psychic kinship is adumbrated earlier in the film, in the parallelism of our first views of them both, reclining on beds with their hands behind their heads, in the worried, almost cynical remarks about family values that young Charlie makes when we first hear her speak, and in the coincidence of young Charlie deciding to send her uncle a telegram just hours after he has, unbeknownst to her, sent one in her direction.

Charlie's meditation on his hidden identity, in the other, his niece's realization of that identity. But in addition to being implausible because not reflecting the very different emotional tones with which uncle and niece would have contemplated this identity, this sort of interpretation seems unavailable for the last occurrence, where ascription to the terrified and soon-to-be-obliterated Uncle Charlie of a contemplative thought about his past strains credulity to the breaking point.

This suggests that the recurrent waltzing image should be construed as a form of narrator's commentary: it is employed by the cinematic storyteller at crucial moments to underline in an intentionally jarring manner—because achieved through the elegance and innocence of a waltz—Uncle Charlie's horrific identity. Thus, what is made fictional by these musical cues is *not* that Uncle Charlie is the murderer, but that the *narrator* is adverting to that fact, almost sardonically, both before and after it is narratively established.

Rebel without a Cause provides another example whose analysis helps us to see our way here. The opening scene unfolds at a police station, where three juveniles whose lives will soon importantly intersect find themselves separately in trouble. At one point Jim Stark (James Dean), who has been talking with a sympathetic counselor, bangs and kicks a desk in frustration, at the counselor's explicit invitation. As his outburst concludes, dissonant music surges up briefly on the soundtrack. This undoubtedly adds tension to the scene, but does it contribute to defining the fictional world in any way? That Jim is wildly and angrily frustrated is fully established by what the perceptual enabler of the film has allowed us to see and hear of his outburst. What, then, is the music, which certainly seems to have narrative force, doing there in narrative terms?

Perhaps this: it serves to get across the phenomenology of Jim's feelings, giving viewers access to the quality of his outburst from the inside, supplementing the access afforded from the outside by the ordinary perceptual data of the scene. Suppose that is so. Then on the one hand, this could be construed as a subtle sort of making-fictional in the story, namely, making it fictional that the quality of feeling in Jim's outburst was precisely such and such—the quality the musical cue in question is expressive of. On the other hand, this could equally well be construed as a making-fictional concerning not Jim, whose emotional condition is perhaps overdetermined by other indicators in the scene, but instead the narrator's stance toward the audience. That is, perhaps the cue's cash value is that the narrator is inviting viewers to share in rather than merely observe what Jim was feeling, and as a consequence, encouraging viewers to adopt a sympathetic attitude to him. The cue's narrativity, in other words, may be a matter of its definition of the fictional world of the film, comprising both narrator and story narrated, rather than that of the story per se.

Consider now the common use of background music to create atmosphere in a scene, but without attributing mental states to any character therein. Is there anything that can thus be said to be made fictional in the film world? In cases where an appropriate atmosphere is created, that is, one that seems consonant with the way the story is otherwise told, what is made fictional might be that the narrator wants the viewer to assume a particular mood or frame of mind as certain events are presented for perception. In cases, though, where the atmosphere created does not gibe with the style or tone of narration already established, then even indirect fictional generation of that sort may be absent. The musical creation of mood may then have to be understood not as a narrative action, but rather one of aiming to immediately affect the viewer in a way that has no fictional upshot. Where nondiegetic music adds atmosphere to a scene without plausibly making anything fictional in the film's world, simply producing a mood in viewers, it seems that responsibility for it, as for other nonnarrative, purely compositional elements of a film, must rest directly with the implied filmmaker.

Exploring the interpretive option just broached—of assigning musical cues to the implied filmmaker rather than the film's narrative agent—will be the focus of the remainder of this essay. But before turning to that I conclude this section with a brief look at narrative uses of nondiegetic music in Hitchcock's *Vertigo*. *Vertigo* boasts perhaps the greatest of classical film scores, and its greatness as a film is due, in no small measure, to that score and its masterful integration into the film in almost every respect.

The intrinsic interest and sophistication of Bernard Herrmann's score has been much discussed, but what is most striking about it in the context of the film is how significant a burden it bears for limning the mental states and traits of characters, by comparison with most other films. *Vertigo* abounds in occasions where not only are viewers fictionally *informed* about the inner lives of the characters through sound-track music, but the music is what in large part *makes* it fictional that their inner lives are to be so characterized.

When Scottie (James Stewart) first sees Madeleine/Judy (Kim Novak) at the rear of a restaurant in San Francisco, the music serves significantly to characterize her for us and for him: ". . . if the camera movement toward Madeleine lets us experience the physical nature of Scottie's immediate attraction to her, it is the music that most fully conveys the sensual mystery of the woman."[21] This scene is instructive in other ways as well. Madeleine gets up to leave, comes toward Scottie, pauses momentarily, and is very noticeably framed and lit in profile—shown, in effect, to best advantage. But who is doing that? The cinematic narrator, in order to indicate something about Madeleine and the overwhelming psychic effect she has on Scottie on first encounter. The filmmaker, Hitchcock, cannot do that—though he can do certain parallel things to Kim Novak and the set in order to bring about, on a fictional plane, the narrative result. The cinematic narrator is the one who, fictionally, showcases Madeleine, for our benefit as trackers of the story, and then underscores this showcasing through the musical resources under its control, for example, by crescendoing at the point of held close-up.[22]

After the crisis of the first part of the film, Scottie spends some time in a sanitorium, sunk deep in depression and aimless longing. Soon after his release, we are given a high pan over the front of Madeleine's apartment building, as the "love"

---

[21]Bruce, *Bernard Herrmann*, p. 143.

[22]This scene illustrates nicely a narrative possibility mentioned above (see note 7), whereby a cinematic narrator might be thought of as presenting story events, conceived of as already existing fictionally at a basic level, *in a certain way*, through a partial shaping of the event being viewed.

motif—a four-note Tristan-like descending figure—is sounded romantically by French horns. This foreshadows Scottie's appearance in frame at the end of the camera movement, with Madeleine obviously in mind: he approaches a blonde woman in front of the building, about to get into what was Madeleine's car, only to discover that it isn't her. The exact content of his hope and then disappointment is supplied by the musical cue.

Scottie's vertigo first occurs in the film's opening scene, while he is hanging from a rain gutter, high above the city, having slipped in the course of pursuing a fleeing felon. This is importantly recalled in the plot's pivotal event, occurring halfway through the film, which takes place at the Mission of San Juan Battista, from whose tower the real Madeleine, unwanted wife of Gavin Elster, will appear to have leapt to her death. As Madeleine rushes into the church, and Scottie begins to follow, Herrmann's music foretells the recurrence of Scottie's vertigo: ". . . milder variants of the clash of tonalities which were heard in the [opening] rooftop sequence hint at the probable effect climbing the tower will have upon Scottie. . . ."[23] The musical cue, it seems, generates the fictional truth, at the point it sounds, that Scottie is *going* to experience vertigo when he climbs, though he is not experiencing it *now*. In other words, that Scottie's vertigo is coming becomes something that is to be imagined by viewers at that point in the film. Alternatively, perhaps the truth is generated that *Scottie* knows it is coming, or is concerned that it might.[24] In the film's final scene, also set in this tower, the tremolo trills which are prominent during this, Scottie's second ascent, suddenly cease, suggesting he has at that point overcome his vertigo and will be able to complete his trip to the top.

At the start of the "letter" scene, the moto perpetuo string figures prominent in the opening rooftop scene recur, in an overwrought vein, accompanying Judy's detailed recollection of the tower incident and her role in the deception perpetrated there. This underscores sonically how emotively charged the incident remains for her, and helps us understand why she is ultimately unable to carry through the writing of the letter of confession. In the famous "nightmare" sequence, the habanera music associated with Carlotta—a dead woman with a tragic past with whom Madeleine appears to identify—becomes more discordant, almost parodic, through the addition of stereotypical castanets and tambourine, conveying unmistakeably the intensity of Scottie's oppression by Carlotta/Madeleine. But more specific psychological pointings yet have been laid at the door of the scoring in this film, with some plausibility. According to one writer, the rather banal music that accompanies a walk taken by Scottie and Judy in the park adjacent to the Palace of Fine Arts, soon after he meets her and senses a kinship with the lost Madeleine, "suggests Scottie's feeling of dissatisfaction with this working-class version of the elegant, sophisticated woman of his memory."[25]

---

[23]Bruce, *Bernard Herrmann*, p. 173.

[24]Even more conservatively, perhaps the only fictional truth generated is that the *narrator* is reminding us of the possibility of Scottie's imminent vertigo, without it yet being fictional either that it is imminent, or that Scottie believes it is.

[25]Bruce, *Bernard Herrmann*, p. 163.

I have tried to show, through the varied examples in this section, the viability of a "making-fictional" criterion of narrativity for nondiegetic film music. There is, I submit, an intuitive match between the concepts: any nondiegetic music we would regard as narrative in status is music that can be seen as contributing to making something fictional in the world of the film—and vice versa.

1996

PETER WOLLEN

GODARD AND COUNTER CINEMA: *VENT D'EST*

Peter Wollen first articulated his ideas in *Signs and Meaning in the Cinema* (1969) and in subsequent articles, particularly in the prominent British film journal *Screen*, merging structuralist and semiotic film theory with a focus on directors such as Jean-Luc Godard, Howard Hawks, and John Ford. In 1974 he and his then-wife, Laura Mulvey, began making a series of six avant-garde feature films, the most prominent of which was *Riddles of the Sphinx* (1977). In this period, Wollen also co-wrote the screenplay for Michelangelo Antonioni's *The Passenger* (1975). Wollen and Mulvey's films reflect the theoretical concerns that govern their critical work: feminism, sexuality, the social construction of identity, experimental aesthetics and politics. Broadly interested in visual culture, Wollen has also written on the work of Frida Kahlo and Tina Modotti, the films of Howard Hawks, *Singin' in the Rain*, Andy Warhol, and the significance of dance at the court of Louis XIV. Until retirement he was chair of the department of film, television, and new media studies at the University of California, Los Angeles.

(Another selection from Wollen's work appears in Section V.)

More and more radically Godard has developed a counter-cinema whose values are counterposed to those of orthodox cinema. I want simply to write some notes about the mean features of this counter-cinema. My approach is to take seven of the values of the old cinema, Hollywood–Mosfilm, as Godard would put it, and contrast these with their (revolutionary, materialist) counterparts and contraries. In a sense, the seven deadly sins of the cinema against the seven cardinal virtues. They can be set out schematically as follows:

Narrative transitivity	Narrative intransitivity
Identification	Estrangement
Transparency	Foregrounding
Single diegesis	Multiple diegesis
Closure	Aperture
Pleasure	Unpleasure
Fiction	Reality

Obviously, these somewhat cryptic headings need further commentary. First, however, I should say that my overall argument is that Godard was right to break with Hollywood cinema and to set up his counter-cinema and, for this alone, he

418

is the most important director working today. Nevertheless, I think there are various confusions in his strategy, which blunt its edges and even, at times, tend to nullify it—mainly, these concern his confusion over the series of terms: fiction/mystification/ideology/lies/deception/illusion/representation. At the end of these notes, I shall touch on some of my disagreements. First, some remarks on the main topics.

1. Narrative transivity vs. narrative intransitivity. (One thing following another vs. gaps and interruptions, episodic construction, undigested digression.)

By narrative transivity, I mean a sequence of events in which each unit (each function that changes the course of the narrative) follows the one preceding it according to a chain of causation. In the Hollywood cinema, this chain is usually psychological and is made up, roughly speaking, of a series of coherent motivations. The beginning of the film starts with establishment, which sets up the basic dramatic situation—usually an equilibrium, which is then disturbed. A kind of chain reaction then follows, until at the end a new equilibrium is restored.

Godard began to break with this tradition very early. He did this, at first, in two ways, both drawn from literature. He borrowed the idea of separate chapters, which enabled him to introduce interruptions into the narrative, and he borrowed from the picaresque novel. The picaresque is a pseudo-autobiographical form which for tight plot construction substitutes a random and unconnected series of incidents, supposed to represent the variety and ups-and-downs of real life. (The hero is typically marginal to society, a rogue-errant, often an orphan, in any case without family ties, thrown hither and thither by the twists and turns of fortune.)

By the time he arrives at *Vent d'Est*, Godard has practically destroyed all narrative transitivity. Digressions which, in earlier films, represented interruptions to the narrative have hypertrophied until they dominate the film entirely. The basic story, as much of it as remains, does not have any recognizable sequence, but is more like a series of intermittent flashes. Sometimes it seems to be following a definite order in time, but sometimes not. The constructive principle of the film is rhetorical, rather than narrative, in the sense that it sets out the disposition of an argument, point by point, in a sequence of 1–7, which is then repeated, with a subsidiary sequence of Theories A and B. There are also various figures of amplification and digression within this structure.

There are a number of reasons why Godard has broken with narrative transitivity. Perhaps the most important is that he can disrupt the emotional spell of the narrative and thus force the spectator, by interrupting the narrative flow, to reconcentrate and re-focus his attention. (Of course, his attention may get lost altogether.) Godard's cinema, broadly speaking, is within the modern tradition established by Brecht and Artaud, in their different ways, suspicious of the power of the arts—and the cinema, above all—to 'capture' its audience without apparently making it think, or changing it.

2. Identification vs. estrangement. (Empathy, emotional involvement with a character vs. direct address, multiple and divided characters, commentary.)

Identification is a well-known mechanism though, of course, in the cinema there are various special features which mark cinematic identification off as a distinct phenomenon. In the first place, there is the possibility of double identification with the star and/or with the character. Second, the identification can only take place in a situation of suspended belief. Third, there are spatial and temporal limits either to the identification or, at any rate, to the presence of the imago. (In some respects, cinematic identification is similar to transference in analysis, though this analogy should not be taken too far.)

Again, the breakdown of identification begins early in Godard's films and then develops unevenly after that, until it reaches a new level with *Le Gai Savoir*. Early devices include non-matching of voice to character, introduction of 'real people' into the fiction, characters addressing the audience directly. All these devices are also used in *Vent d'Est*, which takes especially far the device of allowing voices to float off from characters into a discourse of their own on the soundtrack, using the same voice for different characters, different voices for the same character. It also introduces the 'real-life' company into the film itself and, in a rather complicated figure, introduces Gian Maria Volonte, not simply as an actor (Godard shows the actors being made-up) but also as intervening in the process of 'image-building'. As well as this, there is a long and extremely effective direct address sequence in which the audience is described—somewhat pejoratively—from the screen and invited into the world of representation.

It is hardly necessary, after the work of Brecht, to comment on the purpose of estrangement-effects of this kind. Clearly, too, they are closely related to the breakup of narrative transitivity. It is impossible to maintain 'motivational' coherence, when characters themselves are incoherent, fissured, interrupted, multiple and self-critical. Similarly, the ruse of direct address breaks not only the fantasy identification but also the narrative surface. It raises directly the question, 'What is this film for?', superimposed on the orthodox narrative questions, 'Why did that happen?' and 'What is going to happen next?' Any form of cinema which aims to establish a dynamic relationship between film maker and spectator naturally has to consider the problem of what is technically the register of discourse, the content of the enunciation, as well as its designation, the content of the enunciate.

3. Transparency vs. foregrounding. ('Language wants to be overlooked'— Siertsema vs. making the mechanics of the film/text visible and explicit.)

Traditional cinema is in the direct line of descent from the Renaissance discovery of perspective and reformulation of the art of painting, expressed most clearly by Alberti, as providing a window on the world. The camera, of course, is simply the technological means towards achieving a perfect perspective construction. After the Renaissance the painting ceased to be a text which could be 'read,' as the iconographic imagery and ideographic space of pre-Renaissance painting were gradually rejected and replaced by the concept of pure representation. The 'language' of painting became simply the instrument by which representation of the world was achieved. A similar tendency can be seen at work with attitudes to verbal language. From the seventeenth century onwards, language was increasingly seen as an instrument which should efface itself in the performance of its task—the conveyance of meaning. Meaning, in its turn, was regarded as representation of the world.

In his early films Godard introduced the cinema as a topic in his narrative—the 'Lumière' sequence in *Les Carabiniers*, the film within a film in *Le Mépris*. But it was not until his contribution to *Loin du Vietnam* that the decisive step was taken, when he simply showed the camera on screen. In the post-1968 films the process of production is systematically highlighted. In *Vent d'Est* this shows itself not simply in taking the camera behind the scenes, as it were, but also in altering the actual film itself: thus the whole worker's control sequence is shown with the film marked and scratched, the first time that this has happened in Godard's work. In previous films, he had not gone further than using special film stock (*Les Carabiniers*) or printing sequences in negative (*Les Carabiniers, Alphaville*).

At first sight, it looks as if the decision to scratch the surface of the film brings Godard into line with other avant-garde film makers, in the American 'underground' especially. However this is not really the case. In the case of the American film makers, marking the film is best seen alongside developments in painting that have dominated, particularly in the USA, in recent years. Broadly speaking, this involves a reduction of film to its 'optical' substrate. Noise is amplified until, instead of being marginal to the film, it becomes its principal content. It may then be structured according to some calculus or algorithm or submitted to random coding. Just as, in painting, the canvas is foregrounded so, in cinema, the film is foregrounded.

Godard, however, is not interested in this kind of 'de-signification' of the image by foregrounding 'noise' and then introducing a new constructive principle appropriate to this. What he seems to be doing is looking for a way of expressing negation. It is well known that negation is the founding principle of verbal language, which marks it off both from animal signal-systems and from other kinds of human discourse, such as images. However, once the decision is made to consider a film as a process of writing in images, rather than a representation of the world, then it becomes possible to conceive of scratching the film as an erasure, a virtual negation. Evidently the use of marks as erasures, crossing-out an image, is quite different from using them as deliberate noise or to foreground the optical substrate. It presupposes a different concept of 'film-writing' and 'film-reading'.

Some years ago, Astruc, in a famous article, wrote about *le caméra-stylo*. His concept of writing—*écriture*—was closer to the idea of style. Godard, like Eisenstein before him, is more concerned with 'image-building' as a kind of pictography, in which images are liberated from their role as elements of representation and given a semantic function within a genuine iconic code, something like the baroque code of emblems. The sequences in which the image of Stalin is discussed are not simply—or even principally—about Stalin's politics, as much as they are about the problem of finding an image to signify 'repression'. In fact, the whole project of writing in images must involve a high degree of foregrounding, because the construction of an adequate code can only take place if it is glossed and commented upon in the process of construction. Otherwise, it would remain a purely private language.

4. Single diegesis vs. multiple diegesis. (A unitary homogeneous world vs. heterogeneous worlds. Rupture between different codes and different channels.)

In Hollywood films, everything shown belongs to the same world, and complex articulations within that world—such as flashbacks—are carefully signalled and located. The dominant aesthetic is a kind of liberalized classicism. The rigid constraints of the dramatic unities have been relaxed, but mainly because they were overstrict and limiting, whereas the basic principle remains unshaken. The world represented on the cinema must be coherent and integrated, though it need not observe compulsory, statutory constraints. Time and space must follow a consistent order. Traditionally, only one form of multiple diegesis is allowed—the play within a play—whereby the second, discontinuous diegetic space is embedded or bracketed within the first. (It should be added that there are some exemplary cases of transgression of single diegesis within literature, such as Hoffmann's *Life of Tomcat Murr*, which consists of Tomcat Murr's life—the primary diegesis—interleaved at random with pages from another text—the life of Kreisler—supposedly bound into the book by mistake by the bookbinder. The pages from the secondary diegesis begin and end in the middle of sentences and are in the wrong order, with some missing. A novel like Sterne's *Tristram Shandy*, however, simply embeds a number of different diegeses on the play-within-a-play model. Of course, by recursion this principle can be taken to breaking-point, as Borges has often pointed out.)

Godard uses film-within-a-film devices in a number of his early works. At the same time the primary diegesis begins to develop acute fissures and stresses. In *Le Mépris*, for example, there is not only a film-within-a-film, but many of the principal characters speak different languages and can only communicate with each other through an interpreter (an effect entirely lost in some dubbed versions, which have to give the interpreter meaningless remarks to speak). The first radical break with single diegesis, however, comes with *Weekend*, when characters from different epochs and from fiction are interpolated into the main narrative: Saint-Just, Balsamo, Emily Brontë. Instead of a single narrative world, there is an interlocking and interweaving of a plurality of worlds.

At the same time that Godard breaks down the structure of the single diegesis, he also attacks the structure of the single, unitary code that expressed it. Not only do different characters speak different languages, but different parts of the film do too. Most strikingly, there is a rupture between soundtrack and images: indeed, the elaboration of this rupture dominates both *Le Gai Savoir* and *Pravda*. The text becomes a composite structure, like that of a medieval macaronic poem, using different codes and semantic systems. Moreover, these are not simply different, but also often contradictory. *Vent d'Est*, for instance, presents alternative ways of making a film (the Glauber Rocha sequence) only to reject them. It is one of the assumptions of contemporary linguistics that a language has a single, unitary semantic component, just as it has a single syntax. In fact, this is surely not the case. The semantic component of a language is composite and contradictory, permitting understanding on one level, misunderstanding on another. Godard systematically explores the areas of misunderstanding.

   5. *Closure vs. aperture.* (A self-contained object, harmonized within its own bounds, vs. open-endedness, overspill, intertextuality—allusion, quotation and parody.)

It has often been pointed out that in recent years, the cinema has become 'selfconscious', in contrast to the 'innocent' days of Hollywood. In itself, however, 'selfconsciousness' is quite compatible with closure. There is a use of quotation and allusion that simply operates to provide a kind of 'surplus' of meaning, as the scholastics used to say, a bonus for those who catch the allusion. The notorious 'Tell me lies' sequence in *Le Petit Soldat*, borrowed from *Johnny Guitar*, is of this kind: it does not make much difference whether you recognise it or not and, even if you do, it has no effect on the meaning of the sequence. Or else quotation can be simply a sign of eclecticism, primarily a stylistic rather than semantic feature. Or, as with Makavejev's use of quotation, the objective may be to impose a new meaning on material by inserting it into a new context: a form of irony.

Godard, however, uses quotation in a much more radical manner. Indeed, his fondness for quotation has always been one of the distinguishing characteristics of his films. At the beginning of his career, Godard used to give instructions to the cameraman almost entirely in terms of shots from previous films and, at a more explicit level, there are endless direct quotes, both from films and from painting and literature. Whole films contain obvious elements of pastiche and parody: *Une Femme est une Femme* is obviously derivative from the Hollywood musical, *Les Carabiniers* from Rossellini, *Le Mépris* is 'Hawks and Hitchcock shot in the manner of Antonioni' . . . it would be possible to go on endlessly.

However, as Godard's work developed, these quotations and allusions, instead of being a mark of eclecticism, began to take on an autonomy of their own, as structural and significant features within the films. It becomes more and more impossible to understand whole sequences and even whole films without a degree of familiarity with the quotations and allusions which structure them. What seemed at first to be a kind of jackdaw mentality, a personality trait of Godard himself, begins to harden into a genuine polyphony, in which Godard's own voice is drowned out and obliterated behind that of the authors quoted. The film can no longer be seen as a discourse with a single subject, the film maker/auteur. Just as there is multiplicity of narrative worlds, so too there is a multiplicity of speaking voices.

Again, this takes us back to the period before the rise of the novel, the representational painting, to the epoch of the battle of the books, the logomachia. Perhaps the author who comes most to mind is Rabelais, with his endless counterposition of quotations, his parodies, his citation of authorities. The text/film can only be understood as an arena, a meeting-place in which different discourses encounter each other and struggle for supremacy. Moreover these discourses take on an independent life of their own. Instead of each being corked up in its bottle with its author's name on it as a label, the discourses escape, and like genies, are let out to intermingle and quarrel.

In this sense, Godard is like Ezra Pound or James Joyce who, in the same way, no longer insist on speaking to us in their own words, but can be seen more as ventriloquist's dummies, through whom are speaking—or rather being written—palimpsests, multiple *Niederschriften* (Freud's word) in which meaning can no longer be said to express the intention of the author or to be a representation of the world, but must like the discourse of the unconscious be understood by a different kind of decipherment. In orthodox logic and linguistics, context is only important as an arbiter between alternative meanings (amphibologies, as they are called in logic). In Godard's films, the opposite process is at work: the juxtaposition and re-contextualization of discourses leads not to a separating-out of meanings but to a confrontation.

6. Pleasure vs. unpleasure. (Entertainment, aiming to satisfy the spectator vs. provocation, aiming to dissatisfy and hence change the spectator.)

The attack on 'entertainment' cinema is part of a broader attack on the whole of 'consumer society'. Cinema is conceived of as a drug that lulls and mollifies the militancy of the masses, by bribing them with pleasurable dreams, thus distracting them from the stern tasks which are their true destiny. It is hardly necessary to insist on the asceticism and Puritanism—repressiveness—of this conception that unflinchingly seeks to put the reality-principle in command over the pleasure-principle. It is true that the short-term (cinematic) dream is sometimes denounced in the name of a long-term (millenarian) dream, and short-term (false, illusory, deceptive) satisfactions contrasted with long-term (real, genuine, authentic) satisfactions, but this is exactly the kind of argument which is used to explain the accumulation of capital in a capitalist society by the saving principle and postponement of consumption.

Brecht was careful never to turn his back on entertainment and, indeed, he even quotes Horace in favour of pleasure as the purpose of the arts, combined, of course, with instruction. This is not to say that a revolutionary cinema should distract its spectators from realities, but that unless a revolution is desired (which means nothing less than coinciding with and embodying collective fantasies) it will never take place. The reality-principle only works together with the pleasure-principle when survival itself is at stake, and though this may evidently be the case in a revolutionary situation, it is not so in the advanced capitalist countries today. In a situation in which survival is—at least relatively—nonproblematic, the pleasure-principle and the reality-principle are antagonistic and, since the reality-principle is fundamentally adaptive, it is from the pleasure-principle that change must stem. This means that desire, and its representation in fantasy, far from being necessary enemies of revolutionary politics—and its cinematic auxiliary—are necessary conditions.

The problem, of course, concerns the nature of the fantasies on the one hand, and the way in which they are presented in the text/film on the other hand, the way in which fantasy scenarios are related to ideologies and beliefs and to scientific analysis. A revolutionary cinema has to operate at different levels—fantasy, ideology, science—and the articulation of these levels, which involve different modes of discourse and different positions of the subject, is a complicated matter.

In *Vent d'Est* the 'struggle against the bourgeois notion of representation' certainly does not rule out the presence of fantasy: fantasy of shooting the union delegate, fantasies of killing shoppers in a supermarket. Indeed, as long as there are images at all, it is impossible to eliminate fantasy. But the fantasies are almost entirely sado-masochistic in content, and this same fantasy content also seems to govern the relationship between film maker and spectator, rather on the lines of the relationship between the flute-player in the film and his audience. A great many of the devices Godard uses are designed to produce a collective working relationship between film maker and audience, in which the spectator can collaborate in the production/consumption of meaning. But Godard's view of collective work is conceived of in very imprecise terms. 'Criticism' consists of insults and interrogation. The fantasy content of the film is not articulated correctly with the ideology or political theory. This, in turn, seems to spring from a suspicion of the need for fantasy at all, except perhaps in the sado-masochistic form of provocation.

7. Fiction vs. reality. (Actors wearing make-up, acting a story vs. real life, the break-down of representation, truth.)

Godard's dissatisfaction with fiction cinema begins very early. Already in *Vivre sa vie* non-fiction is introduced—the chapter on the economics and sociology of prostitution. There is almost no costume drama in Godard's career, until—ironically enough—*Vent d'Est*. Even within the framework of fiction, he has stuck to contemporary life. His science-fiction films (*Alphaville, Anticipation*) have all been set in a kind of future-in-the-present, without any paraphernalia of special effects or sets.

As with all the features I have described, the retreat from (and eventually attack on) fiction has proceeded unevenly through Godard's career, coming forward strongly in, for instance, *Deux ou trois choses*, then receding again. Especially since May 1968, the attack on fiction has been given a political rationale (fiction = mystification = bourgeois ideology) but, at the beginning, it is much more closely connected with Godard's fascination (Cartesian, rather than Marxist) with the misleading and dissembling nature of appearances, the impossibility of reading an essence from a phenomenal surface, of seeing a soul through and within a body or telling a lie from a truth. At times Godard seems almost to adopt a kind of radical Romanticism, which sees silence (lovers' silence, killers' silence) as the only true communication, when reality and representation, essence and appearance, irreducibly coincide: the moment of truth.

Obviously, too, Godard's attitude to fiction is linked with his attitude to acting. This comes out most clearly in *Une Femme Mariée*, when the actor is interrogated about his true self, his relationship to his roles. Godard is obsessed with the problem of true speech, lying speech and theatrical speech. (In a sense, these three kinds of speech, seen first in purely personal terms, are eventually politicized and given a class content. The bourgeoisie lies, the revisionists lie, though they should speak the truth, the revolutionaries speak the truth, or, rather, stammer an approach to the truth.) Godard has long shown a horror of acting, based originally on a 'logocentric' antipathy to anybody who speaks someone else's words, ironic in the circumstances. Eventually, Godard seems to have reformulated his attitude so that actors are distrusted for speaking other people's words as if they were their own. This accompanies his growing recognition that nobody ever speaks in their own words, hence the impossibility of genuine dialogue and the reduction of dialogue to reciprocal—or often unilateral—interviewing. In *Vent d'Est* there is almost no dialogue at all (only a number of variants of monologue) and this must relate to the caricature of collective work Godard puts forward.

Interviewing is, of course, the purest form of linguistic demand, and the demand Godard makes is for the truth. Yet it never seems to be forthcoming, not surprisingly, since it cannot be produced on demand. It is as if Godard has a lingering hope that if people could find their own words, they might produce it miraculously in our presence, but if not, then it has to be looked for in books, which are the residues of real words. This kind of problematic has been tormenting Godard throughout his cinematic career. In *A Bout de souffle*, for instance, there is the central contrast between Michel Poiccard/Laszlo Kovacs—an honest impostor—and Patricia, whose mania for honesty reveals her in the end as a deceiver.

   The early films tend to explore this kind of problem as one between different levels, but in the post-1968 films, there seems to have been a kind of flattening out, so that fiction = acting = lying = deception = representation = illusion = mystification = ideology. In fact, as anybody reflecting on Godard's earlier films must surely know, these are all very different categories. Ideology, for instance, does not depend primarily on lies. It depends on the acceptance of common values and interests. Similarly mystification is different from deception: a priest does not deceive his congregation about the miracle of the mass in the same way that a conjurer deceives his audience, by hiding something from them. Again, the cinema is a form of representation, but this is not the same as illusion or 'trompe l'oeil'. It is only possible to obliterate these distinctions by defining each of them simply in terms of their departure from truth.

   The cinema cannot show the truth, or reveal it, because the truth is not out there in the real world, waiting to be photographed. What the cinema can do is produce meanings, and meanings can only be plotted, not in relation to some abstract yardstick or criterion of truth, but in relation to other meanings. This is why Godard's objective of producing a counter-cinema is the right objective. But he is mistaken if he thinks that such a counter-cinema can have an absolute existence. It can only exist in relation to the rest of the cinema. Its function is to struggle against the fantasies, ideologies and aesthetic devices of one cinema with its own antagonistic fantasies, ideologies and aesthetic devices. In some respects this may bring it closer—or seem to bring it closer—to the cinema it opposes than *Vent d'Est* would suggest. *Vent d'Est* is a pioneering film, an avant-garde film, an extremely important film. It is the starting-point for work on a revolutionary cinema. But it is not that revolutionary cinema itself.

1972

DAVID BORDWELL
FROM POETICS OF CINEMA

COGNITION AND COMPREHENSION: VIEWING AND FORGETTING IN *MILDRED PIERCE*

David Bordwell's *Film Art* (1979) and *Film History; An Introduction* (1994), co-authored with Kristin Thompson, provide a broad background to the history and aesthetics of film. Together with Noël Carroll, with whom he edited the anthology *Post-Theory: Reconstructing Film Studies* (1996), Bordwell has argued against the theoretical perspectives of semiotic, Marxist, and psychoanalytic theory that emerged in the 1970s and 1980s. His own work takes a cognitive approach, considering both how film achieves its aesthetic and emotional effects and the role of the viewer in constructing those effects. His work on narrative structure includes *Narration in the Fiction Film* (1985), *Making Meaning: Inference and Rhetoric in the Interpretation of Cinema* (1989), and *The Way Hollywood Tells It: Story and Style in Modern Movies* (2006), Bordwell has also written on Dreyer, Eisenstein, and Ozu, as well as discussing Hong Kong action films in *Planet Hong Kong: Popular Cinema and the Art of Entertainment* (2000). He is currently Ledoux professor of film studies emeritus at the University of Wisconsin.

(Another selection from Bordwell's work appears in Section VI.)

By and large, audiences understand the films they see. They can answer questions about a movie's plot, imagine alternative outcomes ("What if the monster hadn't found the couple. . . ?"), and discuss the film with someone else who has seen it. This brute fact of comprehension, Christian Metz asserted in the mid-1960s, could ground semiotic film theory: "The fact that must be understood is that films are understood."[1]

As semiotic research expanded in France, Britain, and the United States, the search for explanations of filmic intelligibility took theorists toward comparisons with language, toward methodological analogies with linguistic inquiry, and across several disciplines. At the same time, though, theorists increasingly abandoned the search for principles governing intelligibility. They turned their attention to understanding the sources of cinematic pleasure, chiefly by defining "spectatorship" within theories of ideology and psychoanalysis. The conceptual weaknesses and empirical shortcomings

---

[1]Christian Metz, "Problems of Denotation in the Fiction Film," in *Film Language*, trans. Michael Taylor (New York: Oxford University Press, 1974), p. 145.

of the latter doctrines have become increasingly evident in recent years.[2] It seems fair to say that interest in them has waned considerably, and most French partisans of psychoanalysis have returned to the "classic" structuralist semiotics of the 1960s and early 1970s, or even to traditional film aesthetics.[3]

The current "cognitivist" trend in film studies has gone back to Metz's point of departure, asking, What enables films—particularly narrative films—to be understood? But the hypotheses that have been proposed recently differ sharply from those involved in semiotic research. The emerging cognitivist paradigm suggests that it's unlikely that spectators apply a set of "codes" to a film in order to make sense of it. Rather, spectators participate in a complex process of actively elaborating what the film sets forth. They "go beyond the information given," in Jerome Bruner's phrase.[4] This doesn't entail that each spectator's understanding of the film becomes utterly unique, for several patterns of elaboration are shared by many spectators.[5]

For example, you are driving down the highway. You spot a car with a flat tire; a man is just opening up the car's trunk. Wholly without conscious deliberation, you expect that he is the driver, and that he will draw out a tool or a spare tire or both. How we're able to grasp such a prosaic action is still largely a mystery, but it seems unlikely that it happens by virtue of a code. In a strict sense, a code is an arbitrary system of alternatives. It's governed by rules of succession or substitution, and it's learned more or less explicitly. The system of traffic lights is a code: Red, green, and amber are correlated with distinct meanings (stop, go, and proceed with caution), and drivers must learn them through a mixture of exposure and tutelage. Yet there's no code for understanding tire-changing behavior. Now imagine a film scene showing our man opening up the trunk of his car. When you see the action onscreen, and in the absence of prior information to the contrary (say, an earlier scene showing the driver depositing a corpse in the trunk), you would conjure up the same expectation as in real life: In opening the trunk, he's looking for a tool or a spare or both. In real life or in a movie, no appeal to a code seems necessary.

This example suggests that the process of understanding many things in films is likely to draw upon ordinary, informal reasoning procedures. Contrary to much film theory of the 1970s and 1980s, we need not ascribe this activity to the Freudian or Lacanian unconscious. Just as you did not learn a code for tire changing, so is there no reason for your expectation to be ascribed to repressed childhood memories purportedly harbored in your unconscious. Presented with a set of circumstances (flat tire, man opening trunk),

---

[2]Apart from the many critiques of poststructuralism in literature and philosophy, see David Bordwell and Noël Carroll, eds. *Post-Theory: Reconstructing Film Studies* (Madison: University of Wisconsin Press, 1996). Interestingly, this remains the only anthology to mount such a critique within film studies, as Carroll's *Mystifying Movies: Fads and Fallacies in Contemporary Film Theory* (New York: Columbia University Press, 1985) is the only monograph to take this position. Film scholars have been remarkably reluctant to criticize the foundations of this paradigm, preferring to quietly switch over to a rival framework, that of cultural studies.

[3]For a discussion, see my essay "Contemporary Film Studies and the Vicissitudes of Grand Theory" in Bordwell and Carroll, *Post-Theory*, 3-36. An example of the return to 1960s Metzian themes is Roger Odin's *Cinéma et production de sens* (Paris: Colin, 1991).

[4]See the collection of Bruner's papers, *Beyond the Information Given: Studies in the Psychology of Knowing* (New York: Norton, 1973).

[5]I outline the emerging paradigm in "A Case for Cognitivism." *Iris* no. 9 (Spring 1989): 11-40. See also "A Case for Cognitivism: Further Reflections," *Iris* no. 11 (Summer 1990): 107-112.

you categorize it (*driver changing flat tire*) and draw an informal, probabilistic conclusion, based on a structured piece of knowledge about what is normally involved in the activity. You aren't aware of doing so—it's a *non*conscious activity—but there seems no need to invoke the drive-and-defense model of the unconscious.

This isn't to say that only real-world knowledge is relevant to understanding films. Obviously in real life it would be unlikely that a space alien would pop out of the car's trunk, but if the film is in a certain genre, and a prior scene had shown said alien creeping around the man's garage, that might be an alternative. Likewise, certain technical choices, such as slow motion or fragmentary editing, require experience of movies in order to be intelligible to viewers. But the point would be that even genre-based or stylistic conventions are learned and applied through processes exercised in ordinary thinking. No special instruction, parallel to that of learning a code like language or even semaphore, is necessary to pick up the conventions of horror films or slow-motion violence.

Looked at from this perspective, understanding narrative films can be seen as largely a matter of "cognizing." Going beyond the information given involves categorizing, drawing on prior knowledge, making informal, provisional inferences, and hypothesizing what is likely to happen next. To be a skilled spectator is to know how to execute these tacit but determining acts. The goal, as story comprehension researchers have indicated, is at least partly the extraction of "gist."[6] When confronted with a narrative, perceivers seek to grasp the crux or fundamental features of the event. Transforming a scene into gist—the basic action that occurs, and its consequences for the characters and the ensuing action—becomes a basis for more complex inferential elaboration.

This perspective has implications for how we look at the films as well. Rather than searching for a "language" of film, we ought to look for the ways in which films are designed to elicit the sorts of cognizing activities that will lead to comprehension (as well as other effects). Put another way: Not all spectators are filmmakers, but all filmmakers are spectators. It's not implausible to posit that they have gained an intuitive, hands-on knowledge of how to elicit the sort of activities that will create the experience they want the spectator to have. True, the design may misfire, or spectators may choose to pursue alternative strategies of sense making. But as a first step in a research program, it makes sense to postulate that filmmakers—scriptwriters, producers, directors, editors, and other artisans of the screen—build their films in ways that will coax most of their spectators to follow the same inferential pathways.

How, then, can a cognitive perspective help us analyze a film's narrative design? Before tackling a particular example, I need to spell out my theoretical frame of reference a little more.

NARRATIVE NORMS

Let's assume that a film displays systematic patterns of narrative, themes, style, and the like. The patterns can be located historically with respect to wider sets of

---

[6]On "gist," see Carol Fleisher Feldman, Jerome Bruner, Bobbi Renderer, and Sally Spitzer, "Narrative Comprehension," in Bruce K. Britton and Anthony D. Pellegrini, eds., *Narrative Thought and Narrative Language* (Hillsdale, New Jersey: Erlbaum, 1990), pp. 1-78.

customary practices, which I'll call *norms*. For example, it's a norm of Hollywood studio filmmaking since the mid-1910s that dramatic action takes place in a coherently unified space—such as a bedroom, a street, or the deck of an ocean liner. That space is portrayed through such means as continuity editing, constancy of items of setting, roughly consistent sound ambience, and so on.

We can think of norm-driven subsystems as supplying *cues* to the spectator. The cues initiate the process of elaboration, resulting eventually in inferences and hypotheses. The spectator brings to the cues various bodies of relevant knowledge, most notably the sort known to cognitive theorists as *schema-based knowledge*. A schema is a knowledge structure that enables the perceiver to extrapolate beyond the information given.[7] Our schema for car breakdowns enables us to fill in what is not immediately evident in the flat-tire situation; we go beyond the immediate picture of a breakdown to extrapolate the driver's plan for getting going again.

Understanding a film calls upon cues and schemas constantly. For example, a series of shots showing characters positioned and framed in particular ways usually cues the viewer to infer that these characters are located in a particular locale. A scene that begins with a detail shot of a table lamp may prompt the spectator to frame hypotheses to the effect that the scene will take place in a living room or parlor. These inferences and hypotheses couldn't get off the ground without schemas. The spectator of a Hollywood film is able to understand that a space is coherent because at some level of mental activity, she or he possesses a schema for typical locales, such as living rooms or pool halls. Similarly, in the spectator's search for gist, she or he must possess some rudimentary notion of narrative structure that permits certain information to be taken for granted and other information to be understood as, say, exposition or an important revelation. When we see a character leave one locale and enter another, we effortlessly assume that the second scene follows the first chronologically and that what happened in the suppressed interval isn't of consequence for the story action. (In some films, such as Fritz Lang's *You Only Live Once* [1937] and Otto Preminger's *Fallen Angel* [1945], such ellipses are later revisited and reveal that the narration skipped over important information.) Finally, I suggest that all these factors vary historically and culturally. We ought to expect that different filmmaking traditions, in various times and places, will develop particular norms, schemas, and cues. Correspondingly, the inferences and hypotheses available to spectators will vary as well.

My outline is very skeletal, so I'll try to put some flesh on the bones by considering a concrete case. My specimen is *Mildred Pierce,* an instantiation of that vast body of norms known as the classical Hollywood cinema.[8] I'll be concentrating on its system of narration, which involves not only its construction of a plot and a diegetic world, but also its use of film technique.

---

[7]The classic source of the concept of schema is F. C. Bartlett, *Remembering: A Study in Experimental and Social* Psychology (Cambridge: Cambridge University Press), 1932. Useful orientations to later conceptions of schemas can be found in Reid Hastie, "Schematic Principles in Human Memory," in E. Tony Higgins, C. Peter Herman, and Mark P. Zanna, eds., *Social Cognition: The Ontario Symposium,* vol. I (Hillsdale, New Jersey: Erlbaum, 1981), pp. 39-88; and Ronald W. Casson, "Schemas in Cognitive Anthropology," *Annual Review of Anthropology* 12 (1983): 429-462.

[8]For information on the film, as well as an edition of the shooting script, see Albert J. LaValley, *Mildred Pierce* (Madison: University of Wisconsin Press, 1980). Production background can be found in Rudy Behlmer, *Inside Warner Bros.* (1935-1951) (New York: Viking, 1985), pp. 254-264.

First, I'll try to show that the film utilizes norms of narration so as to encourage not one but two avenues of inference and hypothesis testing; both of these would seem to have been available to contemporary audiences. Second, I want to show that the film assumes that in the viewer's effort after gist, she or he will ignore or forget certain *stylistic* norms. That is, Hollywood norms posit a hierarchy of importance, with narrative gist at the top and local stylistic manipulations subordinated to that. In *Mildred Pierce*, this hierarchy allows the filmmakers to conceal crucial narrational deceptions.

TWO METHODS OF MURDER

Because *Mildred Pierce* opens with a murder, it's profitable to start our inquiry with a norm-based question. What kinds of options were open to filmmakers in the 1940s who wished to launch their plot with such a scene?

In the early 1940s, the options were essentially two. One is exemplified by the second scene of *The Maltese Falcon* (1941). Here, the murder of Sam Spade's partner, Miles Archer, is rendered in a way that conceals the killer's identity (Figure 36.1). We see the victim from over the killer's shoulder, but a reverse-shot view of the murderer isn't supplied. The film thus poses the question of who killed Archer, and this creates one strand in the overall mystery plot.

A second normative option is exemplified at the very start of *The Letter* (1940). Here the shooting of a colonialist is plainly committed by the Bette Davis character (Figure 36.2). The question posed is now that of why she killed him. What, if any, circumstances justify the crime?

The first two scenes of *Mildred Pierce*, however, offer a more complex case. In a lonely beach house at night, with a car idling outside, a man is shot by an unseen assailant. As he dies, he murmurs, "Mildred." We glimpse a woman driving off in the car. In the next scene, our protagonist, Mildred Pierce, is seen wandering along a deserted pier.

We couldn't ask for a better example of a film that lures us down inferential pathways. In a remarkably brief time—the murder scene lasts only 40 seconds—the spectator has accomplished a great deal. She has perceptually constructed a diegetic world—a beach house at night, peopled by two characters. Further, she infers that a homicide has taken place; that gist is central to understanding this narrative. Only a little less probable is the inference that the killer has fled by car. And the viewer may also have inferred that the murderer is the woman named in the film's title.

Figure 36.1 *The Maltese Falcon* (1941): the unseen killer.   Figure 36.2 *The Letter* (1940): the unseen victim.

Yet such inferences are not one-time-only products. They form the basis of hypotheses, which lead in turn to further inference making. As Meir Sternberg points out, narrative ineluctably leads us to frame hypotheses about the past (what he calls *curiosity hypotheses*) and about the future (*suspense hypotheses*).[9] Here, the spectator will expect that there are prior reasons for the murder of Monte and that the film will reveal them in its progressive unfolding. As a mystery film, *Mildred Pierce* will, so to speak, create suspense hypotheses about how curiosity hypotheses will be confirmed.

We can specify two primary inference chains that this opening prompts. One is that Mildred is the killer. Most critics have assumed that the average spectator comes to this conclusion, and they characteristically take the opening as carefully directing us to form this inference. First, like the *Maltese Falcon* sequence, the scene does not show who fires at Monte; this poses the question of the murderer's identity. Moreover, Mildred is implied to be the killer on the basis of certain cues: the word *Mildred*, which Monte murmurs before he dies; the smooth transition from the murder to Mildred walking along the pier; the next scene, in which she tries to frame Wally for the crime; and the still later scene in which her ex-husband, Bert, steps forward to claim, implausibly, that he committed the murder, presumably to protect Mildred.

But at the film's climax, we'll learn that Mildred is not the killer. The film's opening narration has misdirected us. By suppressing the identity of the killer, and by using tight linkages between scenes, the narration leads the spectator to false curiosity hypotheses. One critic puts the point this way: The film shifts from asking, "Who killed Monte?" to asking, "Why did Mildred kill him?"[10] Indeed, the film couldn't mislead us if we weren't undertaking a process of hypothesis formation and revision.

Still, a second line of inference is available. The blatant suppression of the murderer's identity might lead the viewer to ask, If Mildred did it, why does the film not show her in the act, as the opening of *The Letter* shows its heroine killing her victim? One plausible reason for the film's equivocation was offered by a contemporary critic:

> We are tempted to suspect the murderer is the woman on the bridge, especially when we learn her name is Mildred.
> But naturally, being familiar with the conventions of mystery stories that appearances deceive and circumstantial evidence is not all, we are wary; indeed we feel that somehow we had better not assume that Mildred Pierce Berargon [sic] has just killed the man we duly learn is her second husband.[11]

Under this construal, all the narrative feints I itemized above, the tight scene linkages and the strategic actions taken by Mildred and her ex-husband, will be seen as so many red herrings, tricky but "fair" in the way that misdirection is in, say, an Agatha Christie novel.

We commonly believe that not all spectators make exactly the same inferences, but this film builds such divergences into its structure by creating a pair of alterna-

---

[9]Meir Sternberg, *Expositional Modes and Temporal Ordering in Fiction* (Baltimore: Johns Hopkins University Press, 1978), pp. 45-55. See also Sternberg's trio of essays, "Telling in Time (I): Chronology and Narrative Theory," *Poetics Today* 11: 4 (Winter 1990), 901-948; "Telling in Time (II): Chronology, Teleology, Narrativity," *Poetics Today* 13:3 (Fall 1992), 463-541; and "Telling in Time (III): Chronology, Estrangement, and Stories of Literary History," *Poetics Today* 27, 1 (Spring 2006), 125-235.

[10]Joyce Nelson, "Mildred Pierce Reconsidered," *Film Reader* 2 (1977): 67.

[11]Parker Tyler, *Magic and Myth of the Movies* (New York: Henry Holt, 1947), pp. 214-215.

tive pathways for the viewer. One path is signposted for the trusting spectator, who assumes that Mildred is the killer and who will watch what follows looking for answers to why she did it. There is also a pathway for the skeptical viewer, who will not take her guilt for granted. This spectator will scan the ensuing film for other factors that could plausibly account for the circumstances of the killing. And needless to say, it would be possible for a particular viewer to switch between these alternative hypotheses, or to rank one as more probable than the other. If the goal of the inferential process is that extraction of gist, the ongoing construction of the story, then the filmmakers set for themselves the task of building a system of cues that can be used in both frameworks, the trusting one and the skeptical one.

Across the whole film, hypothesis forming and testing will be guided by cues of various sorts and subordinated to various sorts of schemas. As a first approximation, let's distinguish between two principal varieties of schemas. Some schemas will enable the spectator to assimilate and order cues on the basis of patterns of action; call these *action-based schemas*. The story comprehension research literature offers many particular instances, such as the canonical macrostructure proposed by Jean Mandler and her colleagues. She proposes that a traditional story opens by defining a setting and then presenting a series of episodes. Each episode shows a character responding to an initial condition, and the response is often that of forming a goal to do something about that condition. The result is a goal path that informs future episodes, whereby the character tries to reach the goal and either succeeds or fails.[12] This is a very general account, but that doesn't make it hopelessly vague. In our film, it seems clear that both the trusting and the skeptical spectator will test hypotheses according to the ways that events fill various slots in Mandler's macrostructure. For example, the viewer could take the scene that follows the murder as Mildred's complex reaction to having committed the crime: She attempts suicide. Thwarted in that, she formulates a new goal: to implicate the lubricious Wally in the crime. Luring him to the beach house and locking him in can be seen as serving this larger purpose. Each episode can be seen as springing from a reaction to prior events and leading to a formulation of goals that initiate further action. Each one offers further support for the trusting construal, but none definitively disconfirms the skeptical construal. So the potential uncertainty about the murderer is maintained across the film.

Another general collection of schemas is relevant as well, one that we can label *agent-based schemas*. It is significant, I think, that Mandler's canonical story reduces character identity and activity to plot functions (reaction, goal formation, and so on). In this respect, it resembles structuralist work in narratology, such as the studies by Propp, Greimas, and Barthes. Yet one can recognize that characters are constructs without acknowledging that they are wholly reducible to more fundamental semantic or structural features. This would seem a necessary move to make if you're studying cinema, because here, as opposed to literature, characters are usually embodied. A novel's character may be, as Roland Barthes puts it, no more than a collection of semes, or semantic features, gathered under a proper name.[13] In cinema, however,

---

[12]Jean Mandler, *Stories, Scripts, and Scenes: Aspects of Schema Theory* (Hillsdale, New Jersey: Erlbaum, 1984), 22.

[13]Roland Barthes, *S/z*, trans. Richard Howard (New York: Hill and Wang, 1974), pp. 67, 191.

the character has a palpable body, and actions seem naturally to flow from it. A reaction or a goal is attached to a face and frame. Thus the fact that Monte is not only a victim in the murder scene but also a concrete individual, likely to be important in the narrative to come, must count for a good deal if we are to execute the process of inference and hypothesis casting. Similarly, that Mildred happens to occupy Joan Crawford's body—rather than that of, say, Lucille Ball or even Bette Davis—is not a matter of indifference. More generally, it seems clear that in understanding any film, our hypotheses involve not only courses of action but also the qualities of the characters, not only action-based schemas but also agent-based ones.

Simplifying things, I'd suggest that in any narrative in any medium, characters are built up by the perceiver by virtue of two sorts of agent-based schemas. One sort comprises a set of institutional *roles* (e.g., teacher, father, or boss). Another sort of agent-based schema is that afforded by the concept of the *person*, a prototype possessing a cluster of several default features: a human body, perceptual activity, thoughts, feelings, traits, and a capacity to plan and execute action.[14] Roughly, then, a character consists of some person-like features plus the social roles that she or he fills. This distinction would seem to be constant across cultures, even if the substantive conceptions of agent and role vary.[15]

Aided by role schemas and the person schema, the spectator can build up the narrative's agents to various degrees of individuality. Mildred can be taken as a self-sacrificing mother, as a heedless wife, as a ruthless business owner, and so on. At various points, each of these conceptual constructions is important in making sense of the plot, which in turn reveals new aspects of Mildred's character. (At the climax, we'll learn that she's a *very* self-sacrificing mother.) And each conception of Mildred can coexist with the trusting construal (the reasons why Mildred would kill Monte are rooted in her personality and motives) and with the skeptical construal (even if such characterizations are accurate, they may not actually lead to the murder we more or less witness). And we should note that this construction of Mildred as a character—person plus roles—constitutes no less an effort after gist than does the construal of the action around the murder scene. The viewer plays down or omits concrete details of character action in order to construct a psychic identity and agency of broad import, capable of being integrated into hypotheses about upcoming or past action.

Such hypotheses are, of course, constrained in the overall course of the film. After Mildred has lured Wally into being found at the scene of the murder, she is taken in for questioning. As she tells her story to the police in a series of flashbacks, the film

---

[14]A rich set of reflections along these lines can be found in the essays collected in Michael Carrithers, Steven Collins, and Steven Lukes, eds., *The Category of the Person: Anthropology, Philosophy, History* (Cambridge: Cambridge University Press, 1985). Concrete work supplementing this line of thinking is exemplified by Roy G. D'Andrade, "Character Terms and Cultural Models," in Janet W. D. Dougherty, ed., *Directions in Cognitive Anthropology* (Urbana: University of Illinois Press, 1985), pp. 321-343, and Roy G. D'Andrade, "A Folk Model of the Mind," in Dorothy Holland and Naomi Quinn, eds., *Cultural Models in Language and Thought* (Cambridge: Cambridge University Press, 1987), pp. 112-148. With respect to cinema, see Murray Smith, *Engaging Characters: Fiction, Emotion, and the Cinema* (Cambridge: Cambridge University Press, 1995), 21.

[15]"The existence of an office," writes an anthropologist, "logically entails a distinction between the powers and responsibilities pertaining to it and their exercise by different incumbents. Hence some concept of the individual as distinct from the office is established." J. S. La Fontaine, "Person and Individ~ual: Some Anthropological Reflections," in Carrithers et al., *Category of the Person*, p. 138.

breaks into two large-scale portions, and both action- and agent-based schemas are involved in each. The first part consists of the lengthy flashback showing us Mildred's rise to business success. One purpose of this is to establish that her former husband, Bert, has a motive for killing Monte. This long flashback ends with Bert's granting Mildred a divorce and insultingly knocking the whiskey out of Monte's hand. In the framing story, the police inspector argues that this confirms Bert's guilt. And indeed Bert's willingness to take the blame initially confirms that he is shielding Mildred. Once again, though, this permits two alternative readings of the action. Our trusting viewer takes Bert's confession as confirming that Mildred is guilty. The more suspicious viewer, aware of genre conventions that manipulate this sort of information, is likely to suspect that such an obvious foil for Mildred may conceal more than this. That is, just as Mildred has been a red herring for the real culprit, Bert is a red herring once removed, delaying the revelation of the real killer.

At the end of this framing portion in the police station, Mildred confesses to the crime. This switches attention away from Bert and back to her. But her confession creates a problem in motivation. At the end of the first flashback, Mildred is portrayed as being completely in love with Monte. The task of the next long flashback is to show how she could become capable of murdering him.

The flashback traces her gradual realization that Monte is deeply immoral. He's lazy, evasive, and not above seducing his stepdaughter. The flashback also reveals that Mildred is capable of murder. Here the crucial scene is her high-pitched quarrel with Veda, in which Mildred orders her to leave: "Get out before I kill you." The crisis of this stretch of the film comes when Mildred learns that Monte has destroyed her business on the very night of Veda's birthday. Mildred takes out a revolver and goes to Monte's beach house. This puts her firmly on the scene of the crime.

Confirming that Mildred committed the murder would clinch the trusting viewer's long-range hypothesis, based on action-driven schemas. Killing Monte becomes Mildred's means to the goal of protecting her daughter, a goal she has held throughout her life. The resolution would also invoke person-plus-role schemas: Mildred remains the self-sacrificing mother to the end. But this resolution is invoked only to be dispelled.

Once more we return to the present, and the inspector announces that the police have captured the real murderer. Veda is brought in and, believing that Mildred has implicated her, blurts out a confession. And Mildred's recitation of the events now leads to the final flashback, which we enter with knowledge of the killer's identity. As in *The Letter*, the interest now falls upon what circumstances triggered the murder and how those vary from our initial impression.

The final flashback, recounted by Mildred, shows her arrival at the beach house and her discovery that Monte and Veda are lovers. She pulls the pistol, but Monte dissuades her and she drops it. Mildred walks outside, and Veda learns from Monte that he no longer loves her. As Mildred is about to drive away, Veda shoots Monte. Mildred hurries in and discovers the crime, but through a mixture of lies and cajoling, Veda convinces her not to call the police.

This flashback, the real climax, confirms skepticism about Mildred's culpability, and we learn the reason why the narration withheld the killer's identity. Moreover, all of Mildred's subsequent behavior—trying to frame Wally and later confessing to the crime—is consistent with the fact that Veda killed Monte. Veda's act of fury triggers the same motherly sacrifice that has defined Mildred as agent throughout. Everything that we saw at the start of the film is retrospectively justified by Mildred's acting as Veda's accomplice.

Again, to arrive at this concluding set of inferences is to continue our effort after gist. This ending reminds us that the filmmakers are practical cognitive psychologists. They know, for instance, the importance of default assumptions. One purpose of the murder scene is to make us assume that only one person is in or around the cottage when Monte is killed. This premise is crucial because even if we are not shown who pulls the trigger, the viewer must not suspect Veda at all. If her presence is even hinted at, the redundant and obvious clues pointing to Mildred will be seen immediately for the red herrings they are.

THE PARTIAL REPLAY

Reading, notes Barthes in *S/Z*, involves forgetting.[16] So does viewing. The ending of *Mildred Pierce* is instructive partly because the film is so made as to exploit our likely inability to remember anything but the material made salient by our ongoing inference making and hypothesis testing. As practical psychologists, our filmmakers know that we'll construct a diegetic world chiefly through landmarks, not fine details of setting. They know that we'll move rapidly from items of appearance and behavior to inferences about character beliefs and traits. And they know that under pressure of the clock, we're likely to overlook *stylistic* features. This last aspect is especially critical in *Mildred Pierce*.

I compared the film to a mystery novel in its use of red herrings, but the film compels us to recognize that certain features of cinema as a medium shape our inferential activity too. Although few mystery readers may dutifully page back to check a fact or appreciate how they were misled, they all have the option of doing so. A book is in hand all at once, and you may scan, skim, or skip back at will. This isn't an option for the ordinary film viewer (at least, until the arrival of home video, and even then the exact pairwise comparison of passages is difficult). The classical Hollywood cinema paced its narration for maximum legibility during projection. Accordingly, filmmakers have learned that, for perceivers who can't stop and go back, cues must be highly redundant. But in learning this, filmmakers have also learned how to prompt *mis*remembering. Given our effort after gist and our inability to turn back to check a point (especially one made 90 minutes earlier), the film can introduce both redundant cues and highly nonredundant, even contradictory, ones.

Table 36.1 aligns the two sequences, the opening murder (labeled A) and the climactic replay of the shooting (B).

Many actions are reiterated in the second version, and the redundancies suggest that we are seeing a straight replay. In the opening scene, over the second long shot of the beach house (A2, Figure 36.4), we hear two gunshots. The cut inside to Monte facing the killer (A3, Figure 36.5) comes right on the third pistol shot. In the flashback version, the cut from Mildred in the car (B2, Figure 36.13) comes at exactly the same point. The next shot (B3, Figure 36.14) replaces the image of Monte with that of Veda

---

[16]Barthes, S/Z, p. 11.

Table 36.1   The opening scene and its replay

Opening shots (A)	Replay shots (B)
1. 5 sec: (extreme long shot) Beach house at night, car visible alongside (Fig. 36.3). Dissolve to:	1. 12 sec: (medium shot) Mildred goes (36.12).
2. 4 sec: (long shot) House and car. Two pistol shots heard (36.4).	2. 4 sec: (medium close-up): Mildred slumped over steering wheel. Two shots heard (36.13).
3. 8 sec: (medium long shot) Monte facing camera, looking off left (36.5). Third and fourth pistol shots hit mirror. Monte is hit, staggers forward (36.6) and falls to floor. A pistol is tossed into the frame (36.7).	3. 5 sec: (ms) Veda fires four times (36.14).
4. 13 sec: (ms): Monte wobbles his head, opens his eyes, and says: "Mildred" (36.8).	4. 6 sec: (ms) Monte is staggering forward and falls to floor (36.15). A pistol is tossed into the frame (36.16). Monte wobbles his head, eyes open, and says: "Mildred" (36.17).

Figure 36.3 *Mildred Pierce* (1945): the opening scene, shot 1.

Figure 36.12 *Mildred Pierce*: the final flashback, shot 1.

Figure 36.4 *Mildred Pierce*: the opening scene, shot 3.

Figure 36.13 *Mildred Pierce*: the final flashback, shot 2.

Figure 36.5 *Mildred Pierce*: the opening scene, shot 2.

Figure 36.14 *Mildred Pierce*: the final flashback, shot 3.

Figure 36.6 *Mildred Pierce*: the opening scene, shot 3 (continued).

Figure 36.15 *Mildred Pierce*: the final flashback, shot 4.

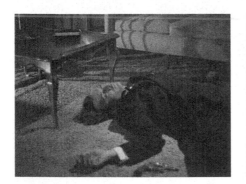

Figure 36.7 *Mildred Pierce*: the opening scene, shot 3 (concluded).

Figure 36.16 *Mildred Pierce*: the final flashback, shot 4 (continued).

firing the revolver. No time can be said to be omitted here. More subtly, the screen time that elapses between the third gunshot and Monte's dying word is virtually identical in both versions (9 seconds and 10 seconds respectively). Finally, the slamming door we hear in the opening scene (A4, over Figure 36.9) is revealed to be not the

Figure 36.8 *Mildred Pierce*: the opening scene, shot 4.

Figure 36.17 *Mildred Pierce*: the final flashback, shot 4 (concluded).

Figure 36.9 *Mildred Pierce*: the opening scene, shot 4 (concluded).

Figure 36.18 *Mildred Pierce*: the final flashback, shot 5.

killer leaving, as we initially inferred, but rather the sound of Mildred entering to find Veda in the living room (B5, Figure 36.18). These are what the mystery novelist might consider fair misdirections of the spectator's attention. They suggest that the second version is identical with the first, except that the former fills in certain details of the latter.

It would seem, however, that the narration profits from so many redundancies in order to introduce some significant disparities. True, some are just minor. In the initial scene (A1 and A2), there is no sound of the car ignition cranking as Mildred tries to start it. (Perhaps Max Steiner's score smothers it.) There is, furthermore, no indication that Mildred is in the car in the first scene (Figures 36.3-36.4). (True, she is slumped over the steering wheel in the later version, but scrutiny of the first scene shows that the driver's seat is empty.)[17] These tiny disparities show again the perceptual saliency of causal, event-centered information, especially as prepared by prior knowledge. On our first view of the first scene, the apparent emptiness of the car suggests that the important action occurs inside the house. If anyone should

---

[17]The odd thing is that in shot 2 of the first scene, a figure can be glimpsed ducking out of sight in the passenger seat. This is a good example of what is not perceivable under normal protocols of viewing.

Figure 36.19 *Mildred Pierce*: the final flashback, shot 5 (concluded).

Figure 36.20 *Mildred Pierce*: the final flashback, shot 10

recall that scene 100 minutes later, the later shot of Mildred bent over the steering wheel (B2, Figure 36.13) suffices as a rough explanation of why the car looked empty. In the absence of a chance to go back and compare, the spectator can easily accept the later scene as consistent with the earlier one.

Other variations in the two scenes reveal that the filmmakers are exploiting the viewer's inability to recall certain details. In the first version, when Monte is shot (A3), he falls to the floor and rolls over on his back as the gun is tossed into the shot (Figures 36.5-36.7). There is a pause. Cut to a closer view of his face (A4, Figure 36.8). As his head wobbles, he opens his eyes, looking left as he murmurs, "Mildred," and expires. The close-up emphasizes his expression and the word he utters, marking the event for us to notice and recall. It may also suggest that he dies looking at his killer and speaking her name.

But in the second version, the event is treated differently; or rather, it is no longer the same event. Monte is shot and tumbles to the floor (B4, Figures 36.15-36.16). But now he utters Mildred's name just as he starts to roll onto his back (Figure 36.17). There is no close-up, and no pause either. He says *nothing* when he is in the position he assumed in the earlier scene (just as earlier, he said nothing when he rolled over). The second version produces a different effect. By speaking when he is not looking toward his killer, he no longer seems to be naming the culprit but rather *recalling* Mildred. In this flashback, she no longer seems guilty. The narration gets two distinct cues out of the two versions, and it is able to do so because it counts on our remembering only that Monte said, "Mildred," not exactly when and how he said it. We recall the salient features marked out for us earlier, but not the details of each situation.[18]

---

[18]It's been suggested to me that the filmmakers were simply sloppy; although they intended both versions of Monte's death to be identical, they were unable to duplicate the details of performance exactly. Even if that were so, when confronted with two versions of Zachary Scott's delivery of the line "Mildred," the filmmakers put the version most likely to throw suspicion on the heroine in the opening and used the non-incriminating version in the revelatory flashback. The published version of the screenplay doesn't call for the reenactment of Monte's final words, so evidently the replay of the murder was devised in the course of shooting and postproduction. See *Mildred Pierce*, ed. LaValley, 233.

Even more striking than the reconstitution of Monte's dying word is the disparity in the handling of the murder's aftermath. In the first scene (A4, Figures 36.8-36.9), a camera movement carries us from Monte's face to the bullet-pocked mirror, which shows a doorway opening onto the hall. We hear footsteps and a slamming door. Cut to a long shot (A5, Figure 36.10) of Monte lying in the empty parlor. Cut outside to the car pulling away, the driver dimly visible (A6, Figure 36.11). But the second version follows Monte's death and the slamming door by Mildred's lengthy and intense confrontation with Veda (B5–B9, Figures 36.18-36.20). And this encounter is played out exactly in the doorway that is shown empty in the first version's fifth shot of the empty parlor (Figure 36.10)! Moreover, because the second version never completes the scene between Mildred and Veda, there is no depiction of either one driving off after their inter-

Figure 36.10 *Mildred Pierce*: the opening scene, shot 5.

Figure 36.11 *Mildred Pierce*: the opening scene, shot 6.

change. (Indeed, we never learn their arrangements about leaving. If Veda took the car, how did Mildred get to the pier?)

If we try to make the two versions compatible, we must posit that in the first version, there is an ellipsis of several minutes between the end of the mirror shot (A4, Figure 36.9) and the beginning of A5 (Figure 36.10), which presumably depicts Monte lying dead in the room after Mildred and Veda have gone their ways. This ellipsis is, of course, not marked at all. Indeed, one overriding default assumption of the classical film is that a cut within a defined locale is taken to convey continuous duration unless there are stylist or contextual indications to the contrary (e.g., a dissolve or some drastic change of costume or furnishings). Alternatively, it is possible in retrospect to construe shot A5, the long-shot framing of Monte's corpse stretched out (Figure 36.10), as simply a false image, provided to mislead us. Either way, the opening scene's narration has concealed the crucial point that two women were present, and it has cued the viewer to infer the gist of the situation—a man was killed, and a woman fled the scene—in such a fashion that the details can't be recalled.

We can be fairly confident that this memory lapse is widespread. First-time spectators seem not to notice the disparities between the two versions, and critics who have written on the film have not mentioned them. Indeed, critics have proven especially vulnerable to remembering gist and forgetting detail. One writer, describing the first scene shot by shot, omits the crucially misleading shot of Monte's corpse by the fire (A5, Figure 36.10).[19] Another critic claims that in the second murder scene, the shot of Veda firing the pistol (Figure 36.14) follows the shot of Monte (Figure 36.15).[20] If critics who have the luxury of reexamining the film can err in such ways, should we be surprised that a writer in 1947, relying on mere memory, fleshed out what he saw in unsupportable ways? He cites "the sequence of camera shots in which we see the outside of the house, the woman's figure (or was it two figures separately?) leaving it, her ride in the auto."[21] And if you feel a need to check my claims to confirm your own recollections, you realize that I'm not condemning these critics. They're doing what we all do, "making sense," and they are making it along the lines laid down by a very powerful system of norms and cues. It's not just that the film encourages us to deceive ourselves. It deceives us blatantly but helps us overlook the deception. It accomplishes this because narrative comprehension demands that we go beyond the data, jump to conclusions—in short, make inferences and frame hypotheses.

SECRETS AND LIES, AND NARRATION

A lone example can't prove a case, but I hope that this examination of *Mildred Pierce* has illustrated how the cognitive perspective might tie together assumptions about comprehension with concrete observations about a film's structure and style. The result is a significantly new picture of a film and its viewer.

Instead of a "pure" text, understandable "in itself," we have a text that gains its effects only in relation to a body of norms, a set of schemas, and the processes that the spectator initiates. Instead of a communication model, which treats meaning as dropped in upstream to be fished out by the spectator, we have a constructive model that treats meaning as an expanding elaboration of cues located in the text. This shift implies as well that, armed with certain schemas and knowledge of certain norms, the spectator could "go beyond the information given" in ways unforeseen by the filmmakers. What makes a film understandable is not necessarily exhausted by what the filmmakers deliberately put in to be understood. But, then, this is true of all human activities; every action has unintended consequences, and so it's hardly surprising that viewers appropriate movies in idiosyncratic ways. But the process of that appropriation, is also a matter of inferential elaboration, based on fresh schemas the spectator brings to bear on the film's discriminable features.

---

[19]Pam Cook, "Duplicity in *Mildred Pierce*," in *Women in Film Noir*, ed. E. Ann Kaplan (London: British Film Institute, 1978), p. 78.

[20]Nelson, "*Mildred Pierce* Reconsidered," p. 65.

[21]Tyler, *Magic and Myth*, p. 214.

In isolating comprehension as a central viewing activity, the cognitive perspective is open to the charge that it ignores other aspects of the experience and of the film itself. What, for instance, about emotion, surely a prime ingredient of the film-going experience? And what about interpretation, which seems to go even farther beyond the information given and involve very high-level constructs?

These are important questions, and the cognitive frame of reference needs to respond to them. Up to a point, setting emotion aside is a useful methodological idealization: in principle, you can understand a film without discernibly having an emotional reaction to it. More positively, studies by Noël Carroll, Murray Smith, Ed Tan, and others suggest that a cognitive perspective can enrich our understanding of emotive qualities.[22] This research boldly proposes that many emotional responses ride upon cognitive judgments.

As for interpretation, elsewhere I've tried to show that, as an intuitive but principled activity, it's highly amenable to a cognitive explanation. When a critic posits Mildred as the Castrating Mother or a symbol of the contradictions of entrepreneurial capitalism, the critic is still seeking out cues, categorizing, applying schemas, and making inferences that carry weight among a particular social group.[23] To interpret is to cognize.

Finally, as a murder mystery, *Mildred Pierce* may play too much into my hands. Not every film poses a mystery at its start; is the cognitive perspective at risk of turning every film into a detective story? It's true that mystery films show the process of hypothesis formation quite clearly, but the cognitive framework doesn't favor them. In *Narration in the Fiction Film*, I try to show that the activity of inferential elaboration is prompted by melodramas (*In This Our Life, Say it with Songs*), Westerns (*Wild and Woolly*), comedies (*His Girl Friday*), and straight dramas (*Heaven Knows, Mr. Allison*). Every narrative of any complexity withholds some story information from both viewers and characters. This creates gaps in our knowledge, disparities among various characters' states of knowledge, and mismatches between a character's knowledge and the viewer's knowledge, all the while generating Meir Sternberg's response-trio of curiosity, suspense, and surprise. Every film's narration depends upon regulating the flow of information, and we don't have perfect information until the end (if then). In this respect, every narrative harbors secrets.

There is much more to understand about how viewers understand films. The line of inquiry sketched here puts a priority on studying particular films in the light of how narrational and stylistic processes are designed to elicit certain spectatorial effects. In this research program, *Mildred Pierce* exemplifies key features of the

---

[22]Noël Carroll, *The Philosophy of Horror; or Paradoxes of the Heart* (New York: Methuen, 1990), pp. 59-96; Murray Smith, *Engaging Characters*, 81-86; Ed Tan, *Emotion and the Structure of Narrative Film: Film as Emotion Machine* (Teaneck, N.J.: Erlbaum, 1996); *Passionate Views: Film, Cognition, and Emotion*, ed. Carl R. Plantinga and Greg R. Smith (Baltimore: Johns Hopkins, 1999); and Greg R. Smith, *Film Structure and the Emotion System* (Cambridge: Cambridge University Press, 2003). See also Joseph Anderson, *The Reality of Illusion: An Ecological Approach to Cognitive Film Theory* (Carbondale: University of Illinois Press, 1997).

[23]*Making Meaning: Inference and Rhetoric in the Interpretation of Cinema* (Cambridge: Harvard University Press, 1989).

classical Hollywood film. There are, of course, other traditions which call on different sorts of narrational cues, schemas, and norms.[24] Comparative inquiry into these traditions can contribute to that research program I've called a film poetics. By avoiding misplaced conceptions of codes or slippery analogies between film and language, the cognitive perspective offers a robust account of the viewer's activity, one that can guide a historical poetics of cinema.

---

[24]See my *Narration in the Fiction Film* (Madison: University of Wisconsin Press, 1985).

V

The Film Artist

The infant American film business grew into a multi-million-dollar industry in the first decade of the twentieth century. By the mid-1910s, in the years during and just after the First World War, that industry organized itself according to what came to be called the Hollywood studio system (although, in fact, the final power of the system resided not in the Hollywood studios where the films were made but in the New York business offices where they were financed and distributed). Consolidated at the same time as Henry Ford's automobile assembly plant, the Hollywood studio also resembled a factory where goods—motion picture entertainments—were manufactured for a mass audience. The films rolled down the assembly line, like one of Henry Ford's Model A's, through story departments, past departments of scenic and costume design, and onto the set where technicians (scenic and make-up craftsmen, camera and lighting crews) and actors united to help shape the final product. Then it continued down the line to the cutting and release departments, until it was shipped to the company's showrooms—whether the small-town Bijous or the big-city Movie Palaces.

From its beginnings, this industrialized studio system provoked a predictable question: how can a work of art result from such varied intentions and collective labors? For years, most American critics argued (or simply assumed) that, whatever the product of this mechanized assembly of disparate talents was, it was not art. They considered it to be, instead, mere commercial entertainment that could not be compared to the "art films" of Europe or the "underground" films of the personal, experimental filmmaker. Ford's assembly line may have made the luxury of automobile ownership possible for a majority of Americans. But when Hollywood similarly brought drama and comedy into the lives of millions, the result, according to such critics, was not the expansion of art but its debasement.

One early reply to this argument was to deny that a purely aesthetic intention or the vision of a single artist is necessary to create a work of art. Erwin Panofsky (see Section III) specifically compares the making of a film to the building of a cathedral, for the cathedral was built for the greater glory of God and was the result of the collective labor of as many specialists as a Hollywood film. François Truffaut, beginning in 1954 with his essay, "On a Certain Tendency of the French Cinema," took the opposite tack and argued instead for a theory of film art that drew upon older ideas of aesthetic creation. His *politique des* auteurs" defended the Hollywood studio film by maintaining that, although unappreciated or even unnoticed, the work of an author, an auteur, could be seen in many Hollywood films. This auteur was not the film's scriptwriter, however, but the film's director whose "signature" could be discerned by the sensitive critic who bothered to look for it. Truffaut's aim in this and succeeding articles was somewhere between a theory of film creation and a theory of film taste. He was reacting against mainstream French film criticism, which had emphasized the "tradition of quality," extolling the polished literary adaptations of such scenarists as Jean Aurenche and Pierre Bost (*La Symphonie Pastorale, The Red and the Black, The Idiot*) at the expense of the genuinely cinematic thinking of Jacques Tati, Jean Renoir, or Robert Bresson.

Truffaut's emphasis on the director as the prime film artist became a critical mainstay of the pioneering French film magazine *Cahiers du Cinéma*, which quickly expanded his focus on the French tradition to encompass the Soviet, German, and especially the American. The essays by Andrew Sarris and Peter Wollen illustrate some of the fierce arguments that subsequently arose over artistic authority. In general, according to what became known as the auteur theory, a director's "style" or "basic motifs," as Wollen calls them, can only be discerned by viewing his work as a whole, because the true marks of an auteur will appear in all of them, despite any differences in writers, cinematographers, or stars. Andrew Sarris, the primary American spokesman for the auteur theory, suggests not only that the distinguishable personality of the director is a criterion of value but also that the "meaning" which he is able to impose on the material with which he must work is the "ultimate" glory of the cinema. This observation raises problems about where exactly the auteur's imprint is most clearly to be found. Is it in style (e.g., the use of deep-focus photography) or in basic motifs (e.g., the elements of a western), or in some undefined combination of the two? A few months after the essay included here, in a special issue of *Film Culture* dedicated to American directors, Sarris published an analysis of the careers of more than one hundred directors (not confined to Americans), including a "pantheon" of twelve—all guaranteed to generate endless argument. Some—such as Charles Chaplin, D. W. Griffith, and Jean Renoir—were already acknowledged masters, but others he praised were, at least in the early 1960s, considered by many writers on film only Hollywood drudges: John Ford, Howard Hawks, and Alfred Hitchcock.

Sarris, like Pauline Kael and others who attacked his views, was a working film critic required to review many films a year. To a great extent, both his desire to categorize films in terms of their directors, as well as the responses by Kael and others, spring from a similar need to find evaluative standards more general than the vagaries of their own taste. Sarris, like those who originally proposed the auteur theory, was not simply arguing that an artist's personality will manifest itself in his works. In the face of a general denigration of American film as an art, he sought to establish that there was, indeed, an artistic force at work where many had refused to believe one existed. In doing so, he unquestionably helped to establish or re-establish the reputations of certain directors who worked within the Hollywood system, directors who did not exert much more control over the total project than many studio hacks, but who managed to make the kind of personal, significant statement that Ford or (as Wollen shows) Hawks did. But Sarris's insistence on the sheer value of an artist's triumphing over the limitations of his materials also raises an intriguing psychological question about the relative importance of limitation and freedom in the creation of a great work. This is certainly a useful strategy for rescuing some Hollywood reputations and rediscovering otherwise forgotten films, but does it also lay the wrong groundwork for demonstrating the merits of directors that Sarris most admires? At important times in their careers, Lubitsch, Renoir, Chaplin, Welles, and Keaton enjoyed a large measure of individual control over scripts, shooting, and cutting—although, at other times, several of them also faced severe limitations. Whether there is any direct relation between the quality of a film and the degree of directorial control thus remains unclear.

Two very different challenges have been offered to the exclusive emphasis on the auteur: first, that other facets of film language and method are more responsible for a film's ultimate success than the will of an individual; and second, that other artists—scriptwriters, cinematographers, stars, producers—better, or at least equally, deserve to be called auteurs. Peter Wollen thus combines the auteur theory's emphasis on the individual creator with a structuralist and semiotic account of film meaning. For Wollen, the auteur theory allows "an operation of decipherment" that distinguishes between auteur films in which the meaning is not just conveyed through style but is "deeply within" and *metteur-en-scène* films in which the meaning is merely cinematically translated from the script or another medium. His prime example is Howard Hawks, who worked in the studio system and yet was able to convey a personal set of attitudes and motifs that permeate his films whatever their ostensible genre or subject matter. In a series of afterthoughts added to a second edition of *Signs and Meaning in the Cinema*, Wollen expands his basic effort to detach the auteur theory from any adulation of the creative personality as such, or any search for the creator behind (rather than in) the work.

As Wollen insists, the essential role of the critic is to show that the film, which appears so directly to us, is not a transparent text, but one that requires interpretive work. But rather than undermine the creator, such an approach may usher in many creators. With film scholarship looking more closely at all the works of the past, rather than the small number of designated classics, critics and historians have been able to describe the special contributions of those in charge of lighting, sound, and set decoration, while more polemical writers have argued the crucial importance of cinematographers and composers for determining the overall effect of a film.

The most serious challenge for any theory that stresses the central importance of one or another of these invisible filmmakers is the visible presence of the star on the screen in front of us. Many stars have made the most decisive contributions to the films in which they appear, and their unique "presence," like that of the director, scriptwriter, and so on, can also be determined by viewing the totality of their works. In *The World Viewed* Stanley Cavell remarks how surprising he found the auteur theory, for it never previously occurred to him that anyone *made* a Hollywood film. For Cavell, the world of film revolved about, and was determined by, the star.

Yet in much film theory, especially that influenced by the montage emphasis of Pudovkin and Eisenstein, the star and the star's performance have been undervalued in favor of the greater expressive meaning of editing (and the greater creative importance of the director and the editor). In Kuleshov's legendary experiment, the same shot of an actor's face was juxtaposed with that of a plate of soup, a coffin, and a little girl playing. The audience response, according to Pudovkin, was to ascribe hunger, sorrow, and joy respectively to what was in fact an unchanging expression. Similarly, in many formalist theories of film, the performer, if mentioned at all, becomes almost indistinguishable from other patterns generated by the film medium. The semiotic perspective of Roland Barthes straddles these two possibilities by implying that Greta Garbo's "face" is both the main object of interest and the main conveyor of meaning in most of the films in which she appears.

An even better candidate for auteur is the film star who not only performs in the scripts of others (like Garbo) but also writes or directs his or her own scripts. Between such a star's onscreen and offscreen characters there is often a symbiotic relation that invites the audience to read one into the other. Mae West is one example of such a star and Clint Eastwood another. But it is pre-eminently the two great silent clowns, Buster Keaton and Charlie Chaplin, who wrote, directed, starred in, and, in Chaplin's case, also composed the music for their films. Gilberto Perez in *The Material Ghost* argues that both particularly conceived of the screen world as a special kind of space—Keaton's more outdoor, Chaplin's more determined by the frame of the studio set—in which the prime continuity was that of the actor's body. From this conception of the space around the actor came as well a view of the social world within the film and the main character's relation to it, Keaton as "a visitor forever having to borrow the world's uniforms, and uncomfortable in any one of them," and Chaplin's Tramp rejected by virtually everyone but the audience.

Another response to arguments against the significance of stars and performance has been first to stress the importance of performance in general to the fabric of film, and then to make a distinction—akin to Wollen's between *metteurs-en-scène* and auteurs—between the cinematic performer and the star who might reasonably be considered a creative force. Richard Dyer takes up these two issues, discussing the nature of film performance and its "recurrent features" in the evolving images of actors like Greta Garbo and John Wayne. He then formulates some of the special characteristics of those stars who might be considered authors, at least of their own images and perhaps of the films in which they appear. Focusing on Katherine Hepburn's effort to recreate her career in the late 1930s after she had been dubbed "box office poison," James Naremore richly details the role both she and her films played in the transition from a disliked image into a "liked" image through such factors as self-conscious play with her more brittle, socially elite image, her frequent erasure of the line between character and star, and the public's awareness of her relation to Spencer Tracy, the rough hewn "man of the people." Discussing *Holiday* (George Cukor, 1938), Naremore shows the vital interaction between the performer, the character, and the many ancillary ways we know stars, through fan magazines, other media appearances, and general gossip about the famous.

In a return from questions of star image to the interplay of forces within a film, Molly Haskell points out the way in which many films of the 1940s, especially those of Howard Hawks, find their shape through the presence of strong female stars. Such actresses often in themselves constitute a "point of view" that their casting brings into the story, even in some contrast or resistance to what the script and perhaps the director demand from them. Unlike Garbo, whose face is a palimpsest of audience projections, Bette Davis, says Haskell, deliberately plays against easy audience sympathy, while Rosalind Russell and Katharine Hepburn similarly upset expectations of pat or traditional distinctions between male and female traits.

Reviving the discussion of the solitary auteur facing the monolith of the studio, Richard B. Jewell, the author of a history of RKO, focuses on that prime example of the auteurist director, Howard Hawks, to show how Hawks's *Bringing Up Baby* (1938) was also the result of choices made within the context of the studio system in reaction to different economic and organizational pressures. Nevertheless, he concludes, knowledge of the external pressures on artistic decision-making does not undermine any estimate of Hawks as an artist but helps only to illustrate again Hawks's central creative power. Jewell explicitly critiques the Ford assembly line metaphor of the movie business with which we began—business and art can be equally served, although in ways neither can predict or anticipate.

Finally, in a more all-out attack on the individual film artist, Thomas Schatz points out that the auteur theory has essentially distorted at least American film history by emphasizing the works and careers of a "few dozen heroic directors." In fact, the studio system makes it impossible to designate any particular individual as the sole creative force. Instead, Schatz argues that it is the producer, who has both the authority and power to make final decisions, whose role ought to be investigated if we are truly to understand the special interplay between individual artistry and collective organization that defines the Hollywood film. Such social issues indicate that the study of film art and the film artist cannot be isolated from the functions of that art and artist in the society as a whole—an issue that will become a direct concern of sections VII and VIII.

ANDREW SARRIS
NOTES ON THE AUTEUR THEORY IN 1962

Andrew Sarris coined the term "auteur theory," which he first used in 1962 in an article in *Film Culture*, introducing the type of criticism (*la politique des auteurs*) already prominent in the *Cahiers du Cinéma* to American film discussion. His *American Cinema: Directors and Directions 1929–1968* (1968) provided a thorough assessment of American sound films, organized by the directors who made them, whose vision (or lack of same) he saw as directly responsible for the success (or failure) of each film. Along with Dwight Macdonald, Stanley Kauffmann, and Pauline Kael (with whom he had a sharp exchange over the auteur theory), Sarris was instrumental in raising the standards of both American film reviewing and American film criticism generally. Sarris has also published books on the work of Josef von Sternberg and John Ford, as well as several collections of interviews with directors. A co-founder of the National Society of Film Critics and member of the New York Film Critics Circle, Sarris continues to write reviews for the *New York Observer* and to teach at Columbia University. Sarris's most recent book is *You Ain't Heard Nothin' Yet: The American Talking Film: History and Memory, 1927–1949* (1998).

... As far as I know, there is no definition of the auteur theory in the English language, that is, by any American or British critic. Truffaut has recently gone to great pains to emphasize that the auteur theory was merely a polemical weapon for a given time and a given place, and I am willing to take him at his word. But, lest I be accused of misappropriating a theory no one wants anymore, I will give the *Cahiers* critics full credit for the original formulation of an idea that reshaped my thinking on the cinema. First of all, how does the auteur theory differ from a straightforward theory of directors. Ian Cameron's article "Films, Directors, and Critics," in *Movie* of September, 1962, makes an interesting comment on this issue: "The assumption that underlies all the writing in *Movie* is that the director is the author of a film, the person who gives it any distinctive quality. There are quite large exceptions, with which I shall deal later." So far, so good, at least for the auteur theory, which even allows for exceptions. However, Cameron continues: "On the whole, we accept the cinema of directors, although without going to the farthest-out extremes of the *la politique des auteurs*, which makes it difficult to think of a bad director making a good film and almost impossible to think of a good director making a bad one." We are back to Bazin again, although Cameron naturally uses different examples. That three otherwise divergent critics like Bazin, Roud, and Cameron make essentially the same point about the auteur theory suggests a common fear of its abuses. I believe there is a misunderstanding here about what the auteur theory actually claims, particularly since the theory itself is so vague at the present time.

First of all, the auteur theory, at least as I understand it and now intend to express it, claims neither the gift of prophecy nor the option of extracinematic perception. Directors, even auteurs, do not always run true to form, and the critic can never assume that a bad director will always make a bad film. No, not always, but almost always, and that is the point. What is a bad director, but a director who has made many bad films? What is the problem then? Simply this: The badness of a director is not necessarily considered the badness of a film. If Joseph Pevney directed Garbo, Cherkassov, Olivier, Belmondo, and Harriet Andersson in *The Cherry Orchard*, the resulting spectacle might not be entirely devoid of merit with so many subsidiary auteurs to cover up for Joe. In fact, with this cast and this literary property, a Lumet might be safer than a Welles. The realities of casting apply to directors as well as to actors, but the auteur theory would demand the gamble with Welles, if he were willing.

Marlon Brando has shown us that a film can be made without a director. Indeed, *One-Eyed Jacks* is more entertaining than many films with directors. A director-conscious critic would find it difficult to say anything good or bad about direction that is nonexistent. One can talk here about photography, editing, acting, but not direction. The film even has personality, but, like *The Longest Day* and *Mutiny on the Bounty*, it is a cipher directorially. Obviously, the auteur theory cannot possibly cover every vagrant charm of the cinema. Nevertheless, the first premise of the auteur theory is the technical competence of a director as a criterion of value. A badly directed or an undirected film has no importance in a critical scale of values, but one can make interesting conversation about the subject, the script, the acting, the color, the photography, the editing, the music, the costumes, the decor, and so forth. That is the nature of the medium. You always get more for your money than mere art. Now, by the auteur theory, if a director has no technical competence, no elementary flair for the cinema, he is automatically cast out from the pantheon of directors. A great director has to be at least a good director. This is true in any art. What constitutes directorial talent is more difficult to define abstractly. There is less disagreement, however, on this first level of the auteur theory than there will be later.

The second premise of the auteur theory is the distinguishable personality of the director as a criterion of value. Over a group of films, a director must exhibit certain recurrent characteristics of style, which serve as his signature. The way a film looks and moves should have some relationship to the way a director thinks and feels. This is an area where American directors are generally superior to foreign directors. Because so much of the American cinema is commissioned, a director is forced to express his personality through the visual treatment of material rather than through the literary content of the material. A Cukor, who works with all sorts of projects, has a more developed abstract style than a Bergman, who is free to develop his own scripts. Not that Bergman lacks personality, but his work has declined with the depletion of his ideas largely because his technique never equaled his sensibility. Joseph L. Mankiewicz and Billy Wilder are other examples of writer-directors without adequate technical mastery. By contrast, Douglas Sirk and Otto Preminger have moved up the scale because their miscellaneous projects reveal a stylistic consistency.

The third and ultimate premise of the auteur theory is concerned with interior meaning, the ultimate glory of the cinema as an art. Interior meaning is extrapolated from the tension between a director's personality and his material. This conception of interior meaning comes close to what Astruc defines as *mise en scène*, but not quite. It is not quite the vision of the world a director projects nor quite his attitude toward life. It is ambiguous, in any literary sense, because part of it is imbedded in the stuff of the cinema and cannot be rendered in noncinematic terms. Truffaut has called it the temperature of the director on the set, and that is a close approximation of its professional aspect. Dare I come out and say what I think it to be is an *élan* of the soul?

Lest I seem unduly mystical, let me hasten to add that all I mean by "soul" is that intangible difference between one personality and another, all other things being equal. Sometimes, this difference is expressed by no more than a beat's hesitation in the rhythm of a film. In one sequence of *La Règle du Jeu*, Renoir gallops up the stairs, turns to his right with a lurching movement, stops in hoplike uncertainty when his name is called by a coquettish maid, and, then, with marvelous postreflex continuity, resumes his bearishly shambling journey to the heroine's boudoir. If I could describe the musical grace note of that momentary suspension, and I can't, I might be able to provide a more precise definition of the auteur theory. As it is, all I can do is point at the specific beauties of interior meaning on the screen and, later, catalogue the moments of recognition.

The three premises of the auteur theory may be visualized as three concentric circles: the outer circle as technique; the middle circle, personal style; and the inner circle, interior meaning. The corresponding roles of the director may be designated as those of a technician, a stylist, and an auteur. There is no prescribed course by which a director passes through the three circles. Godard once remarked that Visconti had evolved from a *metteur en scène* to an auteur, whereas Rossellini had evolved from an auteur to a *metteur en scène*. From opposite directions, they emerged with comparable status. Minnelli began and remained in the second circle as a stylist; Buñuel was an auteur even before he had assembled the technique of the first circle. Technique is simply the ability to put a film together with some clarity and coherence. Nowadays, it is possible to become a director without knowing too much about the technical side, even the crucial functions of photography and editing. An expert production crew could probably cover up for a chimpanzee in the director's chair. How do you tell the genuine director from the quasichimpanzee? After a given number of films, a pattern is established.

In fact, the auteur theory itself is a pattern theory in constant flux. I would never endorse a Ptolemaic constellation of directors in a fixed orbit. At the moment, my list of auteurs runs something like this through the first twenty: Ophuls, Renoir, Mizoguchi, Hitchcock, Chaplin, Ford, Welles, Dreyer, Rossellini, Murnau, Griffith, Sternberg, Eisenstein, von Stroheim, Buñuel, Bresson, Hawks, Lang, Flaherty, Vigo. This list is somewhat weighted toward seniority and established reputations. In time, some of these auteurs will rise, some will fall, and some will be displaced either by new directors or rediscovered ancients. Again, the exact order is less important than the specific definitions of these and as many as two hundred other potential auteurs. I would hardly expect any other critic in the world fully to endorse this list, especially

on faith. Only after thousands of films have been revaluated, will any personal pantheon have a reasonably objective validity. The task of validating the auteur theory
is an enormous one, and the end will never be in sight. Meanwhile, the auteur habit
of collecting random films in directorial bundles will serve posterity with at least a
tentative classification.

Although the auteur theory emphasizes the body of a director's work rather than
isolated masterpieces, it is expected of great directors that they make great films
every so often. The only possible exception to this rule I can think of is Abel Gance,
whose greatness is largely a function of his aspiration. Even with Gance, *La Roue*
is as close to being a great film as any single work of Flaherty's. Not that single
works matter that much. As Renoir has observed, a director spends his life on variations of the same film.

Two recent films—*Boccaccio '70* and *The Seven Capital Sins*—unwittingly reinforced the auteur theory by confirming the relative standing of the many directors
involved. If I had not seen either film, I would have anticipated that the order of
merit in *Boccaccio '70* would be Visconti, Fellini, and De Sica, and in *The Seven
Capital Sins* Godard, Chabrol, Demy, Vadim, De Broca, Molinaro. (Dhomme,
Ionesco's stage director and an unknown quantity in advance, turned out to be the
worst of the lot.) There might be some argument about the relative badness of De
Broca and Molinaro, but, otherwise, the directors ran true to form by almost any
objective criterion of value. However, the main point here is that even in these
frothy, ultracommercial servings of entertainment, the contribution of each director
had less in common stylistically with the work of other directors on the project than
with his own previous work.

Sometimes, a great deal of corn must be husked to yield a few kernels of internal meaning. I recently saw *Every Night at Eight*, one of the many maddeningly
routine films Raoul Walsh has directed in his long career. This 1935 effort featured
George Raft, Alice Faye, Frances Langford, and Patsy Kelly in one of those familiar plots about radio shows of the period. The film keeps moving along in the pleas-
antly unpretentious manner one would expect of Walsh until one incongruously
intense scene with George Raft thrashing about in his sleep, revealing his inner fears
in mumbling dream-talk. The girl he loves comes into the room in the midst of his
unconscious avowals of feeling and listens sympathetically. This unusual scene was
later amplified in *High Sierra* with Humphrey Bogart and Ida Lupino. The point is
that one of the screen's most virile directors employed an essentially feminine narrative device to dramatize the emotional vulnerability of his heroes. If I had not
been aware of Walsh in *Every Night at Eight*, the crucial link to *High Sierra* would
have passed unnoticed. Such are the joys of the auteur theory.

1962

PETER WOLLEN
FROM SIGNS AND MEANING IN THE CINEMA

THE AUTEUR THEORY
[HOWARD HAWKS AND JOHN FORD]

The *politique des* auteur*s*—the auteur theory, as Andrew Sarris calls it—was developed by the loosely knit group of critics who wrote for *Cahiers du Cinéma* and made it the leading film magazine in the world. It sprang from the conviction that the American cinema was worth studying in depth, that masterpieces were made not only by a small upper crust of directors, the cultured gilt on the commercial gingerbread, but by a whole range of authors, whose work had previously been dismissed and consigned to oblivion. There were special conditions in Paris which made this conviction possible. Firstly, there was the fact that American films were banned from France under the Vichy government and the German Occupation. Consequently, when they reappeared after the Liberation they came with a force— and an emotional impact—which was necessarily missing in the Anglo-Saxon countries themselves. And, secondly, there was a thriving ciné-club movement, due in part to the close connections there had always been in France between the cinema and the intelligentsia: witness the example of Jean Cocteau or André Malraux. Connected with this ciné-club movement was the magnificent Paris *Cinémathèque*, the work of Henri Langlois, a great auteur, as Jean-Luc Godard described him. The policy of the *Cinémathèque* was to show the maximum number of films, to plough back the production of the past in order to produce the culture in which the cinema of the future could thrive. It gave French *cinéphiles* an unmatched perception of the historical dimensions of Hollywood and the careers of individual directors.

The auteur theory grew up rather haphazardly; it was never elaborated in programmatic terms, in a manifesto or collective statement. As a result, it could be interpreted and applied on rather broad lines; different critics developed somewhat

A revised and expanded edition of *Signs and Meaning in the Cinema* was published by the British Film Institute in 1997.

different methods within a loose framework of common attitudes. This looseness and diffuseness of the theory has allowed flagrant misunderstandings to take root, particularly among critics in Britain and the United States. Ignorance has been compounded by a vein of hostility to foreign ideas and a taste for travesty and caricature. However, the fruitfulness of the auteur approach has been such that it has made headway even on the most unfavorable terrain. For instance, a recent straw poll of British critics, conducted in conjunction with a Don Siegel Retrospective at the National Film Theatre, revealed that, among American directors most admired, a group consisting of Budd Boetticher, Samuel Fuller and Howard Hawks ran immediately behind Ford, Hitchcock and Welles, who topped the poll, but ahead of Billy Wilder, Josef Von Sternberg and Preston Sturges.

Of course, some individual directors have always been recognised as outstanding: Charles Chaplin, John Ford, Orson Welles. The auteur theory does not limit itself to acclaiming the director as the main author of a film. It implies an operation of decipherment; it reveals authors where none had been seen before. For years, the model of an author in the cinema was that of the European director, with open artistic aspirations and full control over his films. This model still lingers on; it lies behind the existential distinction between art films and popular films. Directors who built their reputations in Europe were dismissed after they crossed the Atlantic, reduced to anonymity. American Hitchcock was contrasted unfavourably with English Hitchcock, American Renoir with French Renoir, American Fritz Lang with German Fritz Lang. The auteur theory has led to the revaluation of the second, Hollywood careers of these and other European directors; without it, masterpieces such as *Scarlet Street* or *Vertigo* would never have been perceived. Conversely, the auteur theory has been sceptical when offered an American director whose salvation has been exile to Europe. It is difficult now to argue that *Brute Force* has ever been excelled by Jules Dassin or that Joseph Losey's recent work is markedly superior to, say, *The Prowler*.

In time, owing to the diffuseness of the original theory, two main schools of auteur critics grew up: those who insisted on revealing a core of meanings, of thematic motifs, and those who stressed style and *mise en scène*. There is an important distinction here, which I shall return to later. The work of the auteur has a semantic dimension, it is not purely formal; the work of the *metteur en scène*, on the other hand, does not go beyond the realm of performance, of transposing into the special complex of cinematic codes and channels a pre-existing text: a scenario, a book or a play. As we shall see, the meaning of the films of an auteur is constructed *a posteriori*; the meaning— semantic, rather than stylistic or expressive—of the films of a *metteur en scène* exists a priori. In concrete cases, of course, this distinction is not always clear-cut. There is controversy over whether some directors should be seen as auteurs or *metteurs en scène*. For example, though it is possible to make intuitive ascriptions, there have been no really persuasive accounts as yet of Raoul Walsh or William Wyler as auteur*s*, to take two very different directors. Opinions might differ about Don Siegel or George Cukor. Because of the difficulty of fixing the distinction in these concrete cases, it has often become blurred; indeed, some French critics have tended to value the *metteur en scène* above the auteur. MacMahonism sprang up, with its cult of Walsh, Lang, Losey and Preminger, its fascination with violence and its notorious text: "Charlton Heston is an axiom of the cinema." What André Bazin called "aesthetic cults of personality" began to be formed. Minor directors were acclaimed before they had, in any real sense, been identified and defined.

Yet the auteur theory has survived despite all the hallucinating critical extravaganzas which it has fathered. It has survived because it is indispensable. Geoffrey Nowell-Smith has summed up the auteur theory as it is normally presented today:

> One essential corollary of the theory as it has been developed is the discovery that the defining characteristics of an author's work are not necessarily those which are most readily apparent. The purpose of criticism thus becomes to uncover behind the superficial contrasts of subject and treatment a hard core of basic and often recondite motifs. The pattern formed by these motifs . . . is what gives an author's work its particular structure, both defining it internally and distinguishing one body of work from another.

It is this "structural approach," as Nowell-Smith calls it, which is indispensable for the critic.

The test case for the auteur theory is provided by the work of Howard Hawks. Why Hawks, rather than, say, Frank Borzage or King Vidor? Firstly, Hawks is a director who has worked for years within the Hollywood system. His first film, *Road to Glory*, was made in 1926. Yet throughout his long career he has only once received general critical acclaim, for his wartime film, *Sergeant York*, which closer inspections reveals to be eccentric and atypical of the main corpus of Hawks' films. Secondly, Hawks has worked in almost every genre. He has made westerns (*Rio Bravo*), gangsters (*Scarface*), war films (*Air Force*), thrillers (*The Big Sleep*), science fiction (*The Thing from Another World*), musicals (*Gentlemen Prefer Blondes*), comedies (*Bringing up Baby*), even a Biblical epic (*Land of the Pharaohs*). Yet all of these films (except perhaps *Land of the Pharaohs*, which he himself was not happy about) exhibit the same thematic preoccupations, the same recurring motifs and incidents, the same visual style and tempo. In the same way that Roland Barthes constructed a species of *homo racinianus*, the critic can construct a *homo hawksianus*, the protagonist of Hawksian values in the problematic Hawksian world.

Hawks achieved this by reducing the genres to two basic types: the adventure drama and the crazy comedy. These two types express inverse views of the world, the positive and negative poles of the Hawksian vision. Hawks stands opposed, on the one hand, to John Ford and, on the other hand, to Budd Boetticher. All these directors are concerned with the problem of heroism. For the hero, as an individual, death is an absolute limit which cannot be transcended: it renders the life which preceded it meaningless, absurd. How then can there be any meaningful individual action during life? How can individual action have any value—be heroic—if it cannot have transcendent value, because of the absolutely devaluing limit of death? John Ford finds the answer to this question by placing and situating the individual within society and within history, specifically within American history. Ford finds transcendent values in the historic vocation of America as a nation, to bring civilisation to a savage land, the garden to the wilderness. At the same time, Ford also sees these values themselves as problematic; he begins to question the movement of American history itself. Boetticher, on the contrary, insists on a radical individualism. "I am not interested in making films about mass feelings. I am for the individual." He looks for values in the encounter with death itself: the underlying metaphor is always that of the bull-fighter in the arena. The hero enters a group of companions, but there is no possibility of group solidarity. Boetticher's hero acts by dissolving groups and collectives of any kind into their constituent individuals, so that he confronts each person face-to-face; the films develop, in Andrew Sarris's words, into "floating poker games, where every character takes turns at bluffing about his hand until the final showdown." Hawks, unlike Boetticher, seeks transcendent values beyond the individual, in solidarity with others. But, unlike Ford, he does not give his heroes any historical dimension, any destiny in time.

For Hawks the highest human emotion is the camaraderie of the exclusive, self-sufficient, all-male group. Hawks' heroes are cattlemen, marlin-fishermen, racing drivers, pilots, big-game hunters, habituated to danger and living apart from society, actually cut off from it physically by dense forest, sea, snow or desert. Their aerodromes are fog-bound; the radio has cracked up; the next mail-coach or packet-boat does not leave for a week. The élite group strictly preserves its exclusivity. It is necessary to pass a test of ability and courage to win admittance. The group's only internal tensions come when one member lets the other down (the drunk deputy in *Rio Bravo*, the panicky pilot in *Only Angels Have Wings*) and must redeem himself by some act of exceptional bravery, or occasionally when too much 'individualism' threatens to disrupt the close-knit circle (the rivalry between drivers in *Red Line 7000*, the fighter pilot among the bomber crew in *Air Force*). The group's security is the first commandment: "You get a stunt team in acrobatics in the air—if one of them is no good, then they're all in trouble. If someone loses his nerve catching animals, then the whole bunch can be in trouble." The group members are bound together by rituals (in *Hatari!* blood is exchanged by transfusion) and express themselves univocally in communal sing-songs. There is a famous example of this in *Rio Bravo*. In *Dawn Patrol* the camaraderie of the pilots stretches even across the enemy lines: a captured German ace is immediately drafted into the group and joins in the sing-song; in *Hatari!* hunters of different nationality and in different places join together in a song over an intercom radio system.

Hawks's heroes pride themselves on their professionalism. They ask: "How good is he? He'd better be good." They expect no praise for doing their job well. Indeed, none is given except: 'The boys did all right'. When they die, they leave behind them only the most meagre personal belongings, perhaps a handful of medals. Hawks himself has summed up this desolate and barren view of life:

> It's just a calm acceptance of a fact. In *Only Angels Have Wings*, after Joe dies, Cary Grant says: "He just wasn't good enough." Well, that's the only thing that keeps people going. They just have to say: "Joe wasn't good enough, and I'm better than Joe, so I go ahead and do it." And they find out they're not any better than Joe, but then it's too late, you see.

In Ford films, death is celebrated by funeral services, an impromptu prayer, a few staves of "Shall we gather at the river?"—it is inserted into an ongoing system of ritual institutions, along with the wedding, the dance, the parade. But for Hawks it is enough that the routine of the group's life goes on, a routine whose only relieving features are "danger" (*Hatari!*) and "fun." Danger gives existence pungency: "Every time you get real action, then you have danger. And the question, 'Are you living or not living?' is probably the biggest drama we have." This nihilism, in which 'living' means no more than being in danger of losing your life—a danger entered into quite gratuitously—is augmented by the Hawksian concept of having "fun." The word "fun" crops up constantly in Hawks's interviews and scripts. It masks his despair.

When one of Hawks's élite is asked, usually by a woman, why he risks his life, he replies: "No reason I can think of makes any sense. I guess we're just crazy." Or Feathers, sardonically, to Colorado in *Rio Bravo*: "You haven't even the excuse I have. We're all fools." By "crazy" Hawks does not mean psychopathic: none of his characters are like Turkey in Peckinpah's *The Deadly Companions* or Billy the Kid in Penn's *The Left-Handed Gun*. Nor is there the sense of the absurdity of life which we sometimes find in Boetticher's films: death, as we have seen, is for Hawks simply a routine occurrence, not a *grotesquerie*, as in *The Tall T* ('Pretty soon that well's going to be chock-a-block') or *The Rise and Fall of Legs Diamond*. For Hawks "craziness" implies difference, a sense of apartness from the ordinary, every-day, social world. At the same time, Hawks sees the ordinary world as being "crazy" in a much more fundamental sense, because devoid of any meaning or values. "I mean crazy reactions—I don't think they're crazy, I think they're normal—but according to bad habits we've fallen into they seemed crazy." Which is the normal, which the abnormal? Hawks recognises, inchoately, that to most people his heroes, far from embodying rational values, are only a dwindling band of eccentrics. Hawks' 'kind of men' have no place in the world.

The Hawksian heroes, who exclude others from their own élite group, are them-selves excluded from society, exiled to the African bush or to the Arctic. Outsiders, other people in general, are perceived by the group as an undifferen-tiated crowd. Their role is to gape at the deeds of the heroes whom, at the same time, they hate. The crowd assembles to watch the showdown in *Rio Bravo*, to see the cars spin off the track in *The Crowd Roars*. The gulf between the out-sider and the heroes transcends enmities among the élite: witness *Dawn Patrol* or Nelse in *El Dorado*. Most dehumanised of all is the crowd in *Land of the Pharaohs*, employed in building the Pyramids. Originally the film was to have been about Chinese labourers building a "magnificent airfield" for the American army, but the victory of the Chinese Revolution forced Hawks to change his plans. ("Then I thought of the building of the Pyramids; I thought it was the same kind of story.") But the presence of the crowd, of external society, is a constant covert threat to the Hawksian élite, who retaliate by having "fun." In the crazy comedies ordinary citizens are turned into comic butts, lampooned and tormented: the most obvious target is the insurance salesman in *His Girl Friday*. Often Hawks's revenge becomes grim and macabre. In *Sergeant York* it is "fun" to shoot Germans "like turkeys"; in *Air Force* it is "fun" to blow up the Japanese fleet. In *Rio Bravo* the geligniting of the badmen "was very funny." It is at these moments that the élite turns against the world outside and takes the opportunity to be brutal and destructive.

Besides the covert pressure of the crowd outside, there is also an overt force which threatens: woman. Man is woman's "prey." Women are admitted to the male group only after much disquiet and a long ritual courtship, phased round the offering, light-ing and exchange of cigarettes, during which they prove themselves worthy of entry. Often they perform minor feats of valour. Even then though they are never really full members. A typical dialogue sums up their position:

Woman: You love him, don't you?
Man (embarrassed): Yes . . . I guess so. . . .
Woman: How can I love him like you?
Man: Just stick around.

The undercurrent of homosexuality in Hawks's films is never crystallised, though in *The Big Sky*, for example, it runs very close to the surface. And he himself described *A Girl in Every Port* as "really a love story between two men." For Hawks men are equals, within the group at least, whereas there is a clear identification between women and the animal world, most explicit in *Bringing Up Baby*, *Gentlemen Prefer Blondes* and *Hatari!* Man must strive to maintain his mastery. It is also worth noting that, in Hawks's adventure dramas and even in many of his comedies, there is no married life. Often the heroes were married or at least intimately committed, to a woman at some time in the distant past but have suffered an unspecified trauma, with the result that they have been suspicious of women ever since. Their attitude is "Once bitten, twice shy." This is in contrast to the films of Ford, which almost always include domestic scenes. Woman is not a threat to Ford's heroes; she falls into her allotted social place as wife and mother, bringing up the children, cooking, sewing, a life of service, drudgery and subordination. She is repaid for this by being sentimentalised. Boetticher, on the other hand, has no obvious place for women at all; they are phantoms, who provoke action, are pretexts for male modes of conduct, but have no authentic significance in themselves. "In herself, the woman has not the slightest importance."

Hawks sees the all-male community as an ultimate; obviously it is very retrograde. His Spartan heroes are, in fact, cruelly stunted. Hawks would be a lesser director if he was unaffected by this, if his adventure dramas were the sum total of his work. His real claim as an author lies in the presence, together with the dramas, of their inverse, the crazy comedies. They are the agonised exposure of the underlying tensions of the heroic dramas. There are two principal themes, zones of tension. The first is the theme of regression: of regression to childhood, infantilism, as in *Monkey Business*, or regression to savagery: witness the repeated scene of the adult about to be scalped by painted children, in *Monkey Business* and in *The Ransom of Red Chief*. With brilliant insight, Robin Wood has shown how *Scarface* should be categorised among the comedies rather than the dramas: Camonte is perceived as savage, child-like, subhuman. The second principal comedy theme is that of sex-reversal and role-reversal. *I Was A Male War Bride* is the most extreme example. Many of Hawks's comedies are centred round domineering women and timid, pliable men: *Bringing Up Baby* and *Man's Favourite Sport*, for example. There are often scenes of male sexual humiliation, such as the trousers being pulled off the hapless private eye in *Gentlemen Prefer Blondes*. In the same film, the Olympic Team of athletes are reduced to passive objects in an extraordinary Jane Russell song number; big-game hunting is lampooned, like fishing in *Man's Favourite Sport*; the theme of infantilism crops up again: "The child was the most mature one on board the ship, and I think he was a lot of fun."

Whereas the dramas show the mastery of man over nature, over woman, over the animal and childish; the comedies show his humiliation, his regression. The heroes become victims; society, instead of being excluded and despised, breaks in with irruptions of monstrous farce. It could well be argued that Hawks's outlook, the alternative world which he constructs in the cinema, the Hawksian heterocosm, is not one imbued with particular intellectual subtlety or sophistication. This does not detract from its force. Hawks first attracted attention because he was regarded naïvely

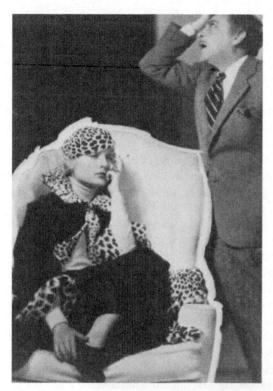

Howard Hawks's battle between the sexes. Carole Lombard and John Barrymore in *Twentieth Century* (1934) (*left*), Cary Grant and Katharine Hepburn in *Bringing Up Baby* (1938) (*below*). "Besides the covert pressure of the crowd outside, there is also an overt force which threatens: woman. Man is woman's prey" (WOLLEN, p. 459).

as an action director. Later, the thematic content which I have outlined was detected and revealed. Beyond the stylemes, semantemes were found to exist; the films were anchored in an objective stratum of meaning, a plerematic stratum, as the Danish linguist Hjelmslev would put it. Thus the stylistic expressiveness of Hawks's films was shown to be not purely contingent, but grounded in significance.

Something further needs to be said about the theoretical basis of the kind of schematic exposition of Hawks's work which I have outlined. The 'structural approach' which underlies it, the definition of a core of repeated motifs, has evident affinities with methods which have been developed for the study of folklore and mythology. In the work of Olrik and others, it was noted that in different folktales the same motifs reappeared time and time again. It became possible to build up a lexicon of these motifs. Eventually Propp showed how a whole cycle of Russian fairy tales could be analysed into variations of a very limited set of basic motifs (or moves, as he called them). Underlying the different, individual tales was an architale, of which they were all variants. One important point needs to be made about this type of structural analysis. There is a danger, as Lévi-Strauss has pointed out, that by simply noting and mapping resemblances, all the texts which are studied (whether Russian fairy tales or American movies) will be reduced to one, abstract and impoverished. There must be a moment of synthesis as well as a moment of analysis: otherwise, the method is formalist, rather than truly structuralist. Structuralist criticism cannot rest at the perception of resemblances or repetitions (redundancies, in fact), but must also comprehend a system of differences and oppositions. In this way, texts can be studied not only in their universality (what they all have in common) but also in their singularity (what differentiates them from each other). This means of course that the test of a structural analysis lies not in the orthodox canon of a director's work, where resemblances are clustered, but in films which at first sight may seem eccentricities.

In the films of Howard Hawks a systematic series of oppositions can be seen very near the surface, in the contrast between the adventure dramas and the crazy comedies. If we take the adventure dramas alone it would seem that Hawks's work is flaccid, lacking in dynamism; it is only when we consider the crazy comedies that it becomes rich, begins to ferment: alongside every dramatic hero we are aware of a phantom, stripped of mastery, humiliated, inverted. With other directors, the system of oppositions is much more complex: instead of there being two broad strata of films there are a whole series of shifting variations. In these cases, we need to analyse the roles of the protagonists themselves, rather than simply the worlds in which they operate. The protagonists of fairy tales or myths, as Lévi-Strauss has pointed out, can be dissolved into bundles of differential elements, pairs of opposites. Thus the difference between the prince and the goose-girl can be reduced to two antinomic pairs: one natural, male versus female, and the other cultural, high versus low. We can proceed with the same kind of operation in the study of films, though, as we shall see, we shall find them more complex than fairy tales. . . .

It is instructive, for example, to consider three films of John Ford and compare their heroes: Wyatt Earp in *My Darling Clementine*, Ethan Edwards in *The Searchers*, and Tom Doniphon in *The Man Who Shot Liberty Valance*. They all act within the recognizable Ford world, governed by a set of oppositions, but their *loci* within that world are very different. The relevant pairs of opposites overlap; different pairs are fore-grounded in different movies. The most relevant are garden versus wilderness, plough-share versus sabre, settler versus nomad, European versus Indian, civilised versus savage, book versus gun, married versus unmarried, East versus West. These anti-monies can often be broken down further. The East, for instance, can be defined either as Boston or Washington and, in *The Last Hurrah*, Boston itself is broken down into the antipodes of Irish immigrants versus Plymouth Club, themselves bundles of such differential elements as Celtic versus Anglo-Saxon, poor versus rich, Catholic versus Protestant, Democrat versus Republican, and so on. At first sight, it might seem that the oppositions listed above overlap to the extent that they become practically syn-onymous, but this is by no means the case. As we shall see, part of the development of Ford's career has been the shift from an identity between civilised versus savage and European versus Indian to their separation and final reversal, so that in *Cheyenne Autumn* it is the Europeans who are savage, the victims who are heroes.

The master antinomy in Ford's films is that between the wilderness and the gar-den. As Henry Nash Smith has demonstrated, in his magisterial book *Virgin Land*, the contrast between the image of America as a desert and as a garden is one which has dominated American thought and literature, recurring in countless novels, tracts, political speeches, and magazine stories. In Ford's films it is crystallised in a number of striking images. *The Man Who Shot Liberty Valance*, for instance, contains the image of the cactus rose, which encapsulates the antinomy between desert and gar-den which pervades the whole film. Compare with this the famous scene in *My Darling Clementine*, after Wyatt Earp has gone to the barber (who civilises the unkempt), where the scent of honeysuckle is twice remarked upon: an artificial perfume, cultural rather than natural. This moment marks the turning point in Wyatt Earp's transition from wandering cowboy, nomadic, savage, bent on personal revenge, unmarried, to married man, settled, civilised, the sheriff who administers the law.

Earp, in *My Darling Clementine*, is structurally the most simple of the three pro-tagonists I have mentioned: his progress is an uncomplicated passage from nature to culture, from the wilderness left in the past to the garden anticipated in the future. Ethan Edwards, in *The Searchers*, is more complex. He must be defined not in terms of past versus future or wilderness versus garden compounded in himself, but in relation to two other protagonists: Scar, the Indian chief, and the family of home-steaders. Ethan Edwards, unlike Earp, remains a nomad throughout the film. At the start, he rides in from the desert to enter the log-house; at the end, with perfect sym-metry, he leaves the house again to return to the desert, to vagrancy. In many respects, he is similar to Scar; he is a wanderer, a savage, outside the law: he scalps his enemy. But, like the homesteaders, of course, he is a European, the mortal foe of the Indian. Thus Edwards is ambiguous; the antinomies invade the personality of the protagonist himself. The oppositions tear Edwards in two; he is a tragic hero. His companion, Martin Pawley, however, is able to resolve the duality; for him, the period of nomadism is only an episode, which has meaning as the restitution of the family, a necessary link between his old home and his new home.

Ethan Edwards's wandering is, like that of many other Ford protagonists, a quest, a search. A number of Ford films are built round the theme of the quest for the

Promised Land, an American re enactment of the biblical exodus, the journey through the desert to the land of milk and honey, the New Jerusalem. This theme is built on the combination of the two pairs: wilderness versus garden and nomad versus settler; the first pair precedes the second in time. Thus, in *Wagonmaster*, the Mormons cross the desert in search of their future home; in *How Green Was My Valley* and *The Informer*, the protagonists want to cross the Atlantic to a future home in the United States. But, during Ford's career, the situation of home is reversed in time. In *Cheyenne Autumn* the Indians journey in search of the home they once had in the past; in *The Quiet Man*, the American Sean Thornton returns to his ancestral home in Ireland. Ethan Edwards's journey is a kind of parody of this theme: his object is not constructive, to found a home, but destructive, to find and scalp Scar. Nevertheless, the weight of the film remains orientated to the future: Scar has burned down the home of the settlers, but it is replaced and we are confident that the homesteader's wife, Mrs Jorgensen, is right when she says: 'Some day this country's going to be a fine place to live.' The wilderness will, in the end, be turned into a garden.

The Man Who Shot Liberty Valance has many similarities with *The Searchers*. We may note three: the wilderness becomes a garden—this is made quite explicit, for Senator Stoddart has wrung from Washington the funds necessary to build a dam which will irrigate the desert and bring real roses, not cactus roses; Tom Doniphon shoots Liberty Valance as Ethan Edwards scalped Scar; a log-home is burned to the ground. But the differences are equally clear: the log-home is burned after the death of Liberty Valance; it is destroyed by Doniphon himself; it is his own home. The burning marks the realisation that he will never enter the Promised Land, that to him it means nothing; that he has doomed himself to be a creature of the past, insignificant in the world of the future. By shooting Liberty Valance he has destroyed the only world in which he himself can exist, the world of the gun rather than the book; it is as though Ethan Edwards has perceived that by scalping Scar, he was in reality committing suicide. It might be mentioned too that, in *The Man Who Shot Liberty Valance*, the woman who loves Doniphon marries Senator Stoddart. Doniphon when he destroys his log-house (his last words before doing so are 'Home, sweet home!') also destroys the possibility of marriage.

The themes of *The Man Who Shot Liberty Valance* can be expressed in another way. Ransom Stoddart represents rational-legal authority, Tom Doniphon represents charismatic authority. Doniphon abandons his charisma and cedes it, under what amounts to false pretences, to Stoddart. In this way charismatic and rational-legal authority are combined in the person of Stoddart and stability thus assured. In *The Searchers* this transfer does not take place; the two kinds of authority remain separated. In *My Darling Clementine* they are combined naturally in Wyatt Earp, without any transfer being necessary. In many of Ford's late films—*The Quiet Man*, *Cheyenne Autumn*, *Donovan's Reef*—the accent is placed on traditional authority. The island of Ailakaowa, in Donovan's Reef, a kind of Valhalla for the homeless heroes of *The Man Who Shot Liberty Valance*, is actually a monarchy, though complete with the Boston girl, wooden church, and saloon made familiar by *My Darling Clementine*. In fact, the character of Chihuahua, Doc Holliday's girl in *My Darling Clementine*, is split into two: Miss Lafleur and Lelani, the native princess. One represents the saloon entertainer, the other the non-American in opposition to the respectable Bostonians,

Amelia Sarah Dedham and Clementine Carter. In a broad sense, this is a part of a general movement which can be detected in Ford's work to equate the Irish, Indians, and Polynesians as traditional communities, set in the past, counterposed to the march forward to the American future, as it has turned out in reality, but assimilating the values of the American future as it was once dreamed.

It would be possible, I have no doubt, to elaborate on Ford's career, as defined by pairs of contrasts and similarities, in very great detail, though—as always with film criticism—the impossibility of quotation is a severe handicap. My own view is that Ford's work is much richer than that of Hawks and that this is revealed by a structural analysis; it is the richness of the shifting relations between antinomies in Ford's work that makes him a great artist, beyond being simply an undoubted auteur. Moreover, the auteur theory enables us to reveal a whole complex of meaning in films such as *Donovan's Reef*, which a recent filmography sums up as just 'a couple of Navy men who have retired to a South Sea island now spend most of their time raising hell.' Similarly, it throws a completely new light on a film like *Wings of Eagles*, which revolves, like *The Searchers*, round the vagrancy versus home antinomy, with the difference that when the hero does come home, after flying round the world, he trips over a child's toy, falls down the stairs and is completely paralysed so that he cannot move at all, not even his toes. This is the macabre *reductio ad absurdum* of the settled.

Perhaps it would be true to say that it is the lesser auteur*s* who can be defined, as Nowell-Smith put it, by a core of basic motifs which remain constant, without variation. The great directors must be defined in terms of shifting relations, in their singularity as well as their uniformity. Renoir once remarked that a director spends his whole life making one film; this film, which it is the task of the critic to construct, consists not only of the typical features of its variants, which are merely its redundancies, but of the principle of variation which governs it, that is its esoteric structure, which can only manifest itself or 'seep to the surface', in Lévi-Strauss's phrase, "through the repetition process". Thus Renoir's 'film' is in reality a 'kind of permutation group, the two variants placed at the far ends being in a symmetrical, though inverted, relationship to each other.' In practice, we will not find perfect symmetry, though as we have seen, in the case of Ford, some antinomies are completely reversed. Instead, there will be a kind of torsion within the permutation group, within the matrix, a kind of exploration of certain possibilities, in which some antinomies are foregrounded, discarded, or even inverted, whereas others remain stable and constant. The important thing to stress, however, is that it is only the analysis of the whole *corpus* which permits the moment of synthesis when the critic returns to the individual film.

Of course, the director does not have full control over his work; this explains why the auteur theory involves a kind of decipherment, decryptment. A great many features of films analysed have to be dismissed as indecipherable because of 'noise' from the producer, the cameraman, or even the actors. This concept of 'noise' needs further elaboration. It is often said that a film is the result of a multiplicity of factors, the sum total of a number of different contributions. The contribution of the director—the 'directorial factor,' as it were—is only one of these, though perhaps the one which carries the most weight. I do not need to emphasize that this view is quite the contrary of the auteur theory and has nothing in common with it at all.

What the auteur theory does is to take a group of films—the work of one director—
and analyse their structure. Everything irrelevant to this, everything non pertinent,
is considered logically secondary, contingent, to be discarded. Of course, it is possible to approach films by studying some other feature; by an effort of critical asce-
sis we could see films, as Von Sternberg sometimes urged, as abstract light-show
or as histrionic feasts. Sometimes these separate texts—those of the cameraman or
the actors—may force themselves into prominence so that the film becomes an indecipherable palimpsest. This does not mean, of course, that it ceases to exist or to
sway us or please us or intrigue us; it simply means that it is inaccessible to criticism. We can merely record our momentary and subjective impressions.

Myths, as Lévi-Strauss has pointed out, exist independently of style, the syntax
of the sentence, or musical sound, euphony or cacophony. The myth functions 'on
an especially high level where meaning succeeds practically in *taking off* from the
linguistic ground on which it keeps rolling.' *Mutatis mutandis*, the same is true of
the auteur film. 'When a mythical schema is transmitted from one population to
another, and there exist differences of language, social organization, or way of life
which make the myth difficult to communicate, it begins to become impoverished
and confused.' The same kind of impoverishment and confusion takes place in the
film studio, where difficulties of communication abound. But none the less the film
can usually be discerned, even if it was a quickie made in a fortnight without the
actors or the crews that the director might have liked, with an intrusive producer
and even, perhaps a censor's scissors cutting away vital sequences. It is as though
a film is a musical composition rather than a musical performance, although, whereas
a musical composition exists a priori (like a scenario), an auteur film is constructed
a posteriori. Imagine the situation if the critic had to construct a musical composition from a number of fragmentary, distorted versions of it, all with improvised passages or passages missing. . . .

What the auteur theory demonstrates is that the director is not simply in command
of a performance of a preexisting text; he is not, or need not be, only a *metteur en
scène*. Don Siegel was asked on television what he took from Hemingway's short
story for his film, *The Killers*; Siegel replied that 'the only thing taken from it was
the catalyst that a man has been killed by somebody and he did not try to run away.'
The word Siegel chose—'catalyst'—could not be bettered. Incidents and episodes in
the original screenplay or novel can act as catalysts; they are the agents which are
introduced into the mind (conscious or unconscious) of the auteur and react there
with the motifs and themes characteristic of his work. The director does not subordinate himself to another author; his source is only a pretext, which provides catalysts, scenes which fuse with his own preoccupations to produce a radically new
work. Thus the manifest process of performance, the treatment of a subject, conceals
the latent production of a quite new text, the production of the director as an auteur.

Of course, it is possible to value performances as such, to agree with André Bazin
that Olivier's *Henry V* was a great film, a great rendering, transposition into the cinema, of Shakespeare's original play. The great *metteurs en scène* should not be dis-
counted simply because they are not auteurs: Vincente Minnelli, perhaps, or Stanley
Donen. And, further than that, the same kind of process can take place that occurred
in painting: the director can deliberately concentrate entirely on the stylistic and

expressive dimensions of the cinema. He can say, as Josef Von Sternberg did about *Morocco*, that he purposely chose a fatuous story so that people would not be distracted from the play of light and shade in the photography. Some of Busby Berkeley's extraordinary sequences are equally detached from any kind of dependence on the screenplay: indeed, more often than not, some other director was entrusted with the job of putting the actors through the plot and dialogue. Moreover, there is no doubt that the greatest films will be not simply auteur films but marvellous expressively and stylistically as well: *Lola Montès, Shinheike Monogatari, La Règle du Jeu, La Signora di Tutti, Sansho Dayu, Le Carrosse d'Or*.

The auteur theory leaves us, as every theory does, with possibilities and questions. We need to develop much further a theory of performance, of the stylistic, of graded rather than coded modes of communication. We need to investigate and define, to construct critically the work of enormous numbers of directors who up to now have only been incompletely comprehended. We need to begin the task of comparing author with author. There are any number of specific problems which stand out: Donen's relationship to Kelly and Arthur Freed, Boetticher's films outside the Ranown cycle. Welles's relationship to Toland (and—perhaps more important—Wyler's), Sirk's films outside the Ross Hunter cycle, the exact identity of Walsh or Wellman, the decipherment of Anthony Mann. Moreover there is no reason why the auteur theory should not be applied to the English cinema, which is still utterly amorphous, unclassified, unperceived. We need not two or three books on Hitchcock and Ford, but many, many more. We need comparisons with authors in the other arts: Ford with Fenimore Cooper, for example, or Hawks with Faulkner. The task which the critics of *Cahiers du Cinéma* embarked on is still far from completed.

1969

. . . At this point, it is necessary to say something about the auteur theory since this has often been seen as a way of introducing the idea of the creative personality into the Hollywood cinema. Indeed, it is true that many protagonists of the auteur theory do argue in this way. However, I do not hold this view and I think it is important to detach the auteur theory from any suspicion that it simply represents a 'cult of personality' or apotheosis of the director. To my mind, the auteur theory actually represents a radical break with the idea of an 'art' cinema, not the transplant of traditional ideas about 'art' into Hollywood. The 'art' cinema is rooted in the idea of creativity and the film as the expression of an individual vision. What the auteur theory argues is that any film, certainly a Hollywood film, is a network of different statements, crossing and contradicting each other, elaborated into a final 'coherent' version. Like a dream, the film the spectator sees is, so to speak, the 'film façade,' the end-product of 'secondary revision', which hides and masks the process which remains latent in the film 'unconscious'. Sometimes this 'façade' is so worked over, so smoothed out, or else so clotted with disparate elements, that it is impossible to see beyond it, or rather to see anything in it except the characters, the dialogue, the plot, and so on. But in other cases, by a process of comparison with other films, it is possible to decipher, not a coherent message or world-view, but a structure which underlies the film and shapes it, gives it a certain pattern of energy cathexis. It is this structure which auteur analysis disengages from the film.

The structure is associated with a single director, an individual, not because he has played the role of artist, expressing himself or his own vision in the film, but because it is through the force of his preoccupations that an unconscious, unintended meaning can be decoded in the film, usually to the surprise of the individual involved. The film is not a communication, but an artefact which is unconsciously structured in a certain way. Auteur analysis does not consist of retracing a film to its origins, to its creative source. It consists of tracing a structure (not a message) within the work, which can then *post factum* be assigned to an individual, the director, on empirical grounds. It is wrong, in the name of a denial of the traditional idea of creative subjectivity, to deny any status to individuals at all. But Fuller or Hawks or Hitchcock, the directors, are quite separate from 'Fuller' or 'Hawks' or 'Hitchcock', the structures named after them, and should not be methodologically confused. There can be no doubt that the presence of a structure in the text can often be connected with the presence of a director on the set, but the situation in the cinema, where the director's primary task is often one of coordination and rationalisation, is very different from that in the other arts, where there is a much more direct relationship between artist and work. It is in this sense that it is possible to speak of a film auteur as an unconscious catalyst.

However, the structures discerned in the text are often attacked in another way. Robin Wood, for example, has argued that the 'auteur' film is something like a Platonic Idea. It posits a 'real' film, of which the actual film is only a flawed transcript, while the archi-film itself exists only in the mind of the critic. This attack rests on a misunderstanding. The main point about the Platonic Idea is that it predates the empirical reality, as an archetype. But the 'auteur' film (or structure) is not an archi-film at all in this sense. It is an explanatory device which specifies partially how any individual film works. Some films it can say nothing or next-to-nothing about at all. Auteur theory cannot simply be applied indiscriminately. Nor does an auteur analysis exhaust what can be said about any single film. It does no more than provide one way of decoding a film, by specifying what its mechanics are at one level. There are other kinds of code which could be proposed, and whether they are of any value or not will have to be settled by reference to the text, to the films in question.

Underlying the anti-Platonic argument, however, there is often a hostility towards any kind of explanation which involves a degree of distancing from the 'lived experience' of watching the film itself. Yet clearly any kind of serious critical work—I would say scientific, though I know this drives some people into transports of rage—must involve a distance, a gap between the film and the criticism, the text and the meta-text. It is as though meteorologists were reproached for getting away from the 'lived experience' of walking in the rain or sunbathing. Once again, we are back with the myth of transparency, the idea that the mark of a good film is that it conveys a rich meaning, an important truth, in a way which can be grasped immediately. If this is the case, then clearly all the critic has to do is to describe the experience of watching the film, reception of a signal, in such a way as to clear up any little confusions or enigmas which still remain. The most that the critic can do is to put the spectator on the right wavelength so that he can see for himself as clearly as the critic, who is already tuned in.

The auteur theory, as I conceive it, insists that the spectator has to work at reading the text. With some films this work is wasted, unproductive. But with others it is not. In these cases, in a certain sense, the film changes, it becomes another film—as far as experience of it is concerned. It is no longer possible to look at it 'with the same eyes'. There is no integral, genuine experience which the critic enjoys and which he tries to guide others towards. Above all, the critic's experience is not essentially grounded in or guaranteed by the essence of the film itself. The critic is not at the heart of the matter. The critic is someone who persists in learning to see the film differently and is able to specify the mechanisms which make this possible. This is not a question of 'reading in' or projecting the critic's own concerns in to the film; any reading of a film has to be justified by an explanation of how the film itself works to make this reading possible. Nor is it the single reading, the one which gives us the true meaning of the film; it is simply a reading which produces more meaning.

Again, it is necessary to insist that since there is no true, essential meaning there can therefore be no exhaustive criticism, which settles the interpretation of a film once and for all. Moreover, since the meaning is not contained integrally in any film, any decoding may not apply over the whole area of it. Traditional criticism is always seeking for the comprehensive code which will give the complete interpretation, covering every detail. This is a wild goose chase, in the cinema, above all, which is a collective form. Both Classical and Romantic aesthetics hold to the belief that every detail should have a meaning—Classical aesthetics because of its belief in a common, universal code; Romantic aesthetics because of its belief in an organic unity in which every detail reflects the essence of the whole. The auteur theory argues that any single decoding has to compete, certainly in the cinema, with noise from signals coded differently. Beyond that, it is an illusion to think of any work as complete in itself, an isolated unity whose intercourse with other films, other texts, is carefully controlled to avoid contamination. Different codes may run across the frontiers of texts at liberty, meet and conflict within them. This is how language itself is structured, and the failure of linguistics, for instance, to deal with the problem of semantics, is exemplified in the idea that to the unitary code of grammar (the syntactic component of language) there must correspond a unitary semantic code, which would give a correct semantic interpretation of any sentence. Thus the idea of 'grammaticality' is wrongly extended to include a quite false notion of 'semanticity'. In fact, no headway can be made in semantics until this myth is dispelled.

The auteur theory has important implications for the problem of evaluation. Orthodox aesthetics sees the problem in predictable terms. The 'good' work is one which has both a rich meaning and a correspondingly complex form, wedded together in a unity (Romantic) or isomorphic with each other (Classical). Thus the critic, to demonstrate the value of a work, must be able to identify the 'content', establish its truth, profundity, and so forth, and then demonstrate how it is expressed with minimum loss or leakage in the signals of the text iself, which are patterned in a way which gives coherence to the work as a whole. 'Truth' of content is not envisaged as being like scientific truth, but more like 'human' truth, a distillation of the world of human experience, particularly interpersonal experience. The world itself is an untidy place, full of loose ends, but the artefact can tie all these loose ends together and thus convey to us a meaningful truth, an insight, which enables us to go back to the real world with a reordered and recycled experience which will enable us to cope better, live more fully, and so on. In this way art is given a humanistic function, which guarantees its value.

All this is overthrown when we begin to see loose ends in works of art, to refuse to acknowledge organic unity or integral content. Moreover, we have to revise our whole idea of criteria, of judgement. The notion behind criteria is that they are timeless and universal. They are then applied to a particular work and it is judged accordingly. This rigid view is varied to the extent that different criteria may apply to different kinds of works or that slightly different criteria may reflect different points of view or kinds of experience, though all are rooted in a common humanity. But almost all current theories of evaluation depend on identifying the work first and then confronting it with criteria. The work is then criticised for falling short on one score or another. It is blemished in some way. Evidently, if we reject the idea of an exhaustive interpretation, we have to reject this kind of evaluation. Instead, we should concentrate on the *productivity* of the work. This is what the 'modern movement' is about. The text, in Octavio Paz's words, is something like a machine for producing meaning. Moreover, its meaning is not neutral, something to be simply absorbed by the consumer.

The meaning of texts can be destructive—of the codes used in other texts, which may be the codes used by the spectator or the reader, who thus finds his own habitual codes threatened, the battle opening up in his own reading. In one sense, everybody knows this. We know that *Ulysses* or *Finnegans Wake* are destructive of the nineteenth-century novel. But it seems difficult to admit this destructiveness into court when judgements are to be made. We have to. To go to the cinema, to read books, or to listen to music is to be a partisan. Evaluation cannot be impartial. We cannot divorce the problem of codes from the problem of criteria. We cannot be passive consumers of films who then stand back to make judgements from above the fray. Judgements are made in the process of looking or reading. There is a sense in which to reject something as unintelligible is to make a judgement. It is to refuse to use a code. This may be right or wrong, but it is not the same thing as decoding a work before applying criteria. A valuable work, a powerful work at least, is one which challenges codes, overthrows established ways of reading or looking, not simply to establish new ones, but to compel an unending dialogue, not at random but productively. . . .

1972

ROLAND BARTHES
THE FACE OF GARBO

After receiving degrees in grammar and philology, Roland Barthes took teaching positions at several colleges and universities, while contributing to journals such as *Combat* and *Les Lettres Nouvelles*, where the essay on Garbo first appeared, collected in *Mythologies* (1957). Later, along with Jean-Louis Baudry and others, he was associated with *Tel Quel*. Throughout his career Barthes remained eclectic in his critical approach, adapting his ideas to the ever-developing field of critical theory. He was influenced early on by Marxist theory, which gave way to structuralism, post-structuralism, semiology, and deconstruction. He wrote on a diverse array of subjects including language, photography, advertising, and celebrity, but above all he was interested in the semiology of daily life and the social "myths" it encodes. In the 1960s, Barthes applied structuralist ideas to topics as diverse as literature and fashion. With *The Empire of Signs* (1970), the result of a trip to Japan, he shifted to a post-structural methodology, positing that signs have no fixed and immutable meaning. Among his other influential works are *Writing Degree Zero* (1953), *S/Z* (1970), and the essay "The Death of the Author" (1967).

Garbo still belongs to that moment in cinema when capturing the human face still plunged audiences into the deepest ecstasy, when one literally lost oneself in a human image as one would in a philtre, when the face represented a kind of absolute state of the flesh, which could be neither reached nor renounced. A few years earlier the face of Valentino was causing suicides; that of Garbo still partakes of the same rule of Courtly Love, where the flesh gives rise to mystical feelings of perdition.

It is indeed an admirable face-object. In *Queen Christina*, a film which has again been shown in Paris in the last few years, the make-up has the snowy thickness of a mask: it is not a painted face, but one set in plaster, protected by the surface of the colour, not by its lineaments. Amid all this snow at once fragile and compact, the eyes alone, black like strange soft flesh, but not in the least expressive, are two faintly tremulous wounds. In spite of its extreme beauty, this face, not drawn but sculpted in something smooth and friable, that is, at once perfect and ephemeral, comes to resemble the flour-white complexion of Charlie Chaplin, the dark vegetation of his eyes, his totem-like countenance.

Now the temptation of the absolute mask (the mask of antiquity, for instance) perhaps implies less the theme of the secret (as is the case with Italian half mask) than that of an archetype of the human face. Garbo offered to one's gaze a sort of Platonic Idea of the human creature, which explains why her face is almost sexually undefined, without however leaving one in doubt. It is true that this film (in which Queen Christina is by turns a woman and a young cavalier) lends itself to this lack of differentiation; but Garbo does not perform in it any feat of transvestism; she is always herself, and carries without pretence, under her crown or her wide-brimmed hats, the same snowy solitary face. The name given to her, *the Divine*, probably aimed to convey less a superlative state of beauty than the essence of her corporeal person, descended from a heaven where all things are formed and per-fected in the clearest light. She herself knew this: how many actresses have con-sented to let the crowd see the ominous maturing of their beauty. Not she, however; the essence was not to be degraded, her face was not to have any reality except that of its perfection, which was intellectual even more than formal. The Essence became gradually obscured, progressively veiled with dark glasses, broad hats and exiles: but it never deteriorated.

And yet, in this deified face, something sharper than a mask is looming: a kind of voluntary and therefore human relation between the curve of the nostrils and the

Greta Garbo in *Love* (1927). "Garbo still belongs to that moment in cinema when capturing the human face still plunged audiences into the deepest ecstasy . . ." (BARTHES, p. 471).

arch of the eyebrows; a rare, individual function relating two regions of the face. A mask is but a sum of lines; a face, on the contrary, is above all their thematic harmony. Garbo's face represents this fragile moment when the cinema is about to draw an existential from an essential beauty, when the archetype leans towards the fascination of mortal faces, when the clarity of the flesh as essence yields its place to a lyricism of Woman.

Viewed as a transition the face of Garbo reconciles two iconographic ages, it assures the passage from awe to charm. As is well known, we are today at the other pole of this evolution: the face of Audrey Hepburn, for instance, is individualized, not only because of its peculiar thematics (woman as child, woman as kitten) but also because of her person, of an almost unique specification of the face, which has nothing of the essence left in it, but is constituted by an infinite complexity of morphological functions. As a language, Garbo's singularity was of the order of the concept, that of Audrey Hepburn is of the order of the substance. The face of Garbo is an Idea, that of Hepburn, an Event.

1957

Greta Garbo in *Anna Christie* (1930), "... where she could ensconce herself, most of the time, in mute or monosyllable sullenness ..." (PANOFSKY, p. 256). "Garbo's face represents this fragile moment when the cinema is about to draw an existential from an essential beauty, when the archetype leans towards the fascination of mortal faces ..." (BARTHES, p. 473).

GILBERTO PEREZ
FROM THE MATERIAL GHOST

[ON KEATON AND CHAPLIN]

Gilberto Perez was close to completing a Ph.D. in theoretical physics at Princeton when he shifted his interest to film studies. Influenced by the work of André Bazin and Guillermo Cabrera Infante, Perez began writing on cinema to express his admiration for film as an artistic medium. His work attempts to balance the rigors of theory with a criticism based in aesthetic and experiential analysis. For Perez, the history of film is the history of an art form. His *Material Ghost: Films and Their Medium* (1997) analyzes the work of a number of directors alongside a consideration of the effects of the medium itself and the tension between its documentary and narrative functions. He currently teaches at Sarah Lawrence in the film history department and is film critic for the *Yale Review*.

Keaton and Chaplin are great actors and great filmmakers, and in their work the actor and the filmmaker are one. Both began in the theater, the popular theater, at a very young age (Keaton at three, in his parents' act in vaudeville). Coming to films after a formative experience acting in that integral space, the stage, where no such thing as a cut is allowed to interrupt a performance, both brought to films a respect for the actor's continuity and a wariness of the editor's scissors: in their craft as film directors both take care to preserve on the screen the integrity of the actor's space.

The actor's discomfort with the disjunctions of film editing is expressed in that wonderful sequence from *Sherlock Junior* (1924) in which Buster, asleep on his job as a movie projectionist, dreams that he walks up to the screen and into the movie being projected. It's as if Keaton had stepped into a movie directed by D. W. Griffith, and didn't like it: the locale keeps shifting on him, by abrupt cutting, while he remains continuously himself, in the same place on the screen from one shot to the next through all the cuts disconcertingly transporting him from one place to another, his performance uninterrupted even as he finds himself now amid city traffic, now up on a mountain, now by a choppy sea, now surrounded by beasts in the jungle. This sequence is a special case of the visitor's situation recurrent with Keaton: here he's a visitor not anywhere on earth but in the world of somebody else's movie, a movie made in a style, foreign to his own, denying him a unified space for his performance.

Such a unified space for the actor to act in is established on the screen by Chaplin and Keaton alike. Chaplin's peerless pantomimes—his mock sermon on David and Goliath in *The Pilgrim* (1923), for example, or his little dance with the buns in *The Gold*

Rush (1925)—unfold in such a *space,* commanding the camera's undivided attention; and in such a space Keaton displays his intricate acrobatics, convincing us that they are actual feats rather than tricks of the cutting room. It is a different kind of space, however, with Chaplin and with Keaton. Chaplin's space recalls the stage not only in its integrity but in its quality of enclosure, in our sense of a demarcated area—the area of a pulpit during the mock sermon, the area of a table during the bun dance—within which each scene is contained. The size of that area may vary, but its boundaries are usually well defined, and the action rarely extends beyond them for the duration of the scene—quite unlike the action in Keaton, which regularly spreads out over a field of indefinite size.

Chaplin's practice of shooting in the studio, and in sets at least slightly stylized, partly accounts for this feeling of confinement; but the studio can be made to yield the illusion of a much larger area, and Chaplin's sets feel nearly as confined as stage sets. Conversely, the use of actual locations by no means ensures the sense of an open space we get in Keaton's films: actual locations can be treated much like a stage back drop—as indeed Chaplin treats them on the occasions in which he uses them—but Keaton is one of the few directors who truly engages an environment and makes us aware that the screen can hardly encompass the dimensions of the actual place. More than in their choice of settings, Chaplin and Keaton differ in the basic conformation of the space they inhabit, a space corresponding, in Chaplin's films, to the stage, and in Keaton's, to the world.

In both cases the actor's space befits the kind of character he plays. "Chaplin's Tramp," wrote Robert Warshow,

> represented the good-hearted and personally cultivated individual in a heartless and vulgar society. The society was concerned only with the pursuit of profit, and often not even with that so much as with the mere preservation of the ugly and impersonal machinery by which the profit was gained; the Tramp was concerned with the practice of personal relations and the social graces. Most of all the Tramp was like an aristocrat fallen on hard times, for what he attempted in all his behavior was to maintain certain standards of refinement and humanity, to keep life dignified and make it emotionally and aesthetically satisfying.

The Tramp, then, is the man who stands apart, the exceptional individual misunderstood and rejected by the society around him, a better grade of human being whose unfitness for the tasks of that society only underscores his personal superiority, his interest in higher things. Although Chaplin's films carry a social protest, an appeal for change, he does not propose his character as any sort of revolutionary, for the Tramp would be as unfit to take any action against the society as he is to work within its constrictions; moreover, he is too insular to show much solidarity with the poor and too singular to be regarded as typical of them. We are to side with the Tramp for his intrinsic human qualities, for what he is in himself, apart from anything he does or could do or anything he stands for beyond himself. His strongest bond is with us, the spectators, rather than with any of the other characters in the film: he communicates with us (to borrow Louise Brooks's phrase) "in a kind of intense isolation," tacitly addressing us with an entreaty for us to recognize his fine qualities and the injustice of a society that does not. Sometimes he gets the girl, but never as a result of his having under-taken any conventional courtship: he gets her because she, like us, is sensitive enough to appreciate his personal worth. (In *The Gold Rush*, the one film in which the Tramp makes good, ending up as a millionaire, the logic of the character demands that he come to his money fortuitously, not through his own efforts, and that the girl, when he runs into her aboard a ship at the end, accepts him *as a tramp*, in a scene arranged so that she thinks he's a stowaway and offers to pay for his passage, before she finds out about his money.)

It would be an exaggeration to say that Chaplin needs no space outside of himself to realize his character: something like a bare stage would not do for the Tramp, who exists in relation to a milieu that Chaplin's sets pithily evoke. In Chaplin's circumscribed space, however, the setting becomes strictly subordinate to the character, and that little fellow scraping through on the outskirts of society assumes on the screen his rightful place at the center of things. That place, due him by virtue of his higher humanity and denied him in a society that has no place for that humanity, must be granted him, Chaplin implies, in a space closed off from the world and constituted for the little fellow's benefit. The man who stands apart from that vulgar milieu deserves, in Chaplin's view, a space set apart for the proper display of his unique attributes. Unlike the Tramp, Keaton's character wants a place in the world, not just in our hearts, and not a special place but one like everybody else's, so Buster accordingly inhabits a space that seems as large as the world and in which he enjoys no primacy over his surroundings.

If the society will not accommodate the Tramp, that is for Chaplin sufficient reason to condemn it, and he concentrates our attention on his character's personal qualities, upholding them against an order that callously discounts them. The world Keaton depicts, though not so inimical to the character, is even more impersonal, even more indifferent to the claims of individuality. Now and again the Tramp comes across a responsive soul—a girl, a kid, men such as the artist who befriends him in *The Immigrant* (1917) or the alcoholic millionaire in *City Lights* (1931), who, when sober, rebuffs him but who at least intermittently takes him to his heart. Nobody in Keaton's world ever departs from the established patterns of behavior; there are no exceptions made in this or that individual case, no exemptions from the rules of courtship granted on account of personal niceness. And Buster has no expectations that things will be otherwise: he accepts the formulistic nature of the world he inhabits and attempts to integrate himself into its formulas, knowing that considerations of personality will have no more effect on the conduct of its inhabitants than on the fall of an apple from a tree.

Even when the Tramp finds himself all alone, rejected by everyone in the film, he still has us, the main recipients of his personal appeal. His directing that appeal to us of course stresses his alienation from his milieu, but it also indicates Chaplin's confidence that the appeal will be heeded, and thus his hope that the established order will be changed. Buster seems to have no thought for us, occupied as he always is with some demanding task at hand—and convinced, we may surmise, that soliciting anybody's sympathy, ours included, is not going to make any difference. (In *The Cameraman* [1928], the first picture Keaton made for MGM after he lost his independence, we can tell that the studio gagmen have tampered with his conception the moment the girl is drawn to Buster because she feels sorry for him.) Keaton's universe is beyond condemnation, and beyond appeal: if it refuses to accommodate personality, there is no point in contesting that, in insisting that things ought not to be so. Whereas the Tramp, above all, projects his personality, Buster suppresses his as much as he can, given that it fits nowhere in a set scheme of things. Personal feelings, which Buster has nonetheless, he might as well not be having, and so tries not to display: hence that famous Keaton face, which is not expressionless at all but on which the expression surfaces as if against his will.

Finding himself in a world of inexorable interlocking systems such as Hawthorne describes in "Wakefield," Buster would not risk stepping aside in his pursuit of a place in the scheme of things; any diversion might lead to his falling hopelessly out of step with the world around him. Other people are nicely adjusted to that world; they play their sports, carry on their feuds, wage their wars, go about their daily business with unruffled expertise in the way things are done: as they belong in the world, so too Buster aspires to belong. But they are natives, and their procedures are to him like an arduous and convoluted foreign language that requires his intent application and that, try as he may, he can never master with their sure fluency. Truly to belong in that immense machine that is Keaton's world, a man must conduct himself with the unthinking proficiency of a machine, and that's not something Buster can manage. The impersonal skills of the acrobat, his best resource in dealing with the scheme of things, he yet fails to make wholly impersonal: the movements of his body remain distinctively his own, unmistakable even in extreme long shot. And on his face his thoughts and feelings are equally unmistakable: they persist in showing through that would-be blank countenance.

It is Keaton's genius as an actor to keep a face so nearly deadpan and yet render it, by subtle inflections, so vividly expressive of inner life. His large deep eyes are the most eloquent feature; with merely a stare he can convey a wide range of emotions, from longing to mistrust, from puzzlement to sorrow. A poignant instance occurs in *Sherlock Junior* during a visit Buster pays to the girl he's courting. He has brought her the conventional present of a box of candies, and she responds with the conventional gesture of putting her hand between them on the couch where they're both sitting. Then, not quite daring to hold her hand but stirred by her offering it, he shuts his eyes in a moment of bashful bliss. She doesn't notice this, nor does the camera come in closer to give it emphasis; it's a private moment, and his eyes, by a very little, betray its subdued intensity.

Keaton rightly avoids close-ups in portraying a character who tries so hard to avoid isolation from his environment. Through other means, however, he brings his character's face into prominence. A strategy he often employs, and one of his invention, is the frontal view taken from some distance, the long shot or sometimes medium shot that, while showing Buster in the midst of things, singles out his face by showing him looking almost straight at the camera. In *The General* (1927) there are many such shots: when Buster looks up to discover the troops around him, for example; or when, inspecting the tracks ahead, he blinks in astonishment at the disappearance of the reappeared car; or when, giving up his initial attempt to enlist in the Confederate army, he addresses the recruiting officer who has turned him down, and says with a hurt expression, "Don't blame me if you lose this war." At the end of *Sherlock Junior*, Buster and the girl are reconciled in the booth where he's at work projecting a movie, and unsure of how to proceed with her, he seeks instruction in the ways of romance from the lovers in the movie, turning periodically to the screen to see what he should do next. Here too he's photographed head-on, through the booth window as he looks out, which points up his inquisitive gaze—and eventually his bewildered stare when the movie to which he looks for guidance skips all the intermediary steps between a kiss and a marriage with children.

Perhaps the most striking of these frontal shots is the one in *Steamboat Bill, Jr.* that shows Buster changing hats. Brought to a haberdashery by his father, who disapproves of the beret he's been wearing and aims to get him a proper hat, he stands before a mirror while variegated hats are tried on him in succession, each making him seem different, as if he were rapidly donning and discarding a succession of identities, all of them imposed on him from the outside, none of them consonant with the inside we perceive through his forlorn eyes. Here his eyes are fixed on the camera for the longest stretch of all, since no cuts are needed to show us what he's looking at: the camera takes the place of the mirror, and Buster stares at it as at his own reflection. In each of these frontal shots, it must be stressed, the object of Buster's gaze is clearly established as something specific in his environment, so that his eyes appear directed not at the camera itself but at some point past it that claims his attention. We never get the feeling that he's looking at us: the effect, instead, is of our looking into him.

Before the mirror in *Steamboat Bill*, (1928) however, the object of his attention happens to be his own image, and that shot has the quality of an introspective monologue, an apprehensive meditation on his own condition. Literally his view of himself, that shot becomes an epitome of Keaton's view of the self as a foreign entity in the world, a visitor forever having to borrow the world's uniforms, and uncomfortable in any of them. The collegiate outfit that Buster affects at the beginning of this film was the fashion in Boston, but in a Southern river town his father is appalled to encounter an arriving son in a beret and a little mustache who is playing a ukelele and singing and dancing to it. (Buster is trying to pacify a baby he accidentally caused to cry, but his father doesn't know about the baby, and concludes that his son is in the habit of breaking into song and dance in the street.) The steamboat captain proceeds to strip away an outfit he finds offensively effeminate: the beret must be replaced, the mustache he has a barber shave off, the ukelele he crushes under his foot. More than these particular items, the principles on which Buster has based his life till now are thrown into question. At the haberdashery, without the trappings of a Boston collegian, he stares into the mirror and sees for the first time the hopeless discrepancy between his inner being and any of the roles he may have to assume in his dealings with the external world.

Such a dawning of self-consciousness usually occurs early on in Keaton's films, as when the rich boy in *The Navigator*, (1924) all dressed up on his first morning on board for a breakfast that nobody is there to serve him, comes to realize that the ocean liner is deserted. In *Sherlock Junior*, the format of a film within the film delays that dawning until the end, when the projectionist is left staring out of the booth window and scratching his head. At that point, in any case, Buster is led to a fearful reappraisal. The unexamined life of the rich boy who expected everything to be done for him, or of the projectionist who looked to the model of fictional detectives, or of the college boy who followed the Bostonian fashion, can no longer continue: Buster comes to the recognition that he must drop his previous assumptions and make a new start, taking nothing for granted in the endeavor, so much more difficult than he thought, of setting up residence in the world. From then on he looks at life with perpetually questioning eyes, knowing he cannot afford to relax his vigilant scrutiny; even amid the urgency of action, while executing some wondrous feat, he retains that perplexed, pondering gaze, which attests to his self-consciousness.

Robert Bresson—another practitioner of the deadpan approach, in a different way from Keaton's but with a similar sense that life is not a matter of personality—once defined originality as the failed attempt to do the same as everybody else, a definition that applies exactly to Buster. For all his efforts to join in, and all his eventual successes in meeting the forces outside, inside he cannot shake off the sense of his singularity. He thinks, therefore he stands alone in a world where no other minds are discernible, only systems of behavior. Ultimately he remains even more isolated than Chaplin's Tramp, since it's not Buster's individual qualities that single him out—these he hardly lets interfere in his transactions with others—but the very fact of his individuality, of his possessing the inner dimension of a self in the realm of the formula.

Buster is not, then, Grierson's "romantic achiever of all things" but a bewildered equilibrist whose mind runs counter to the achievements of his body: a new kind of clown who may not so often trip over physical objects but who, so to speak, keeps tripping over his thoughts. The charming incompetence of the traditional clown was the conception of an earlier time, with more room for eccentricity than has been allowed in our ruthless century. Things were not so good then, of course—things never have been—but at least the clown could thumb his nose at the world and expect the world to let him be. He would puncture our lofty pretensions with his reminder of the claims of the body, of the fact that in our flesh and blood we all fumble our way through life. That conception hasn't lost its validity, and Chaplin can still use it to portray a doughboy in *Shoulder Arms* (1918) or a factory worker in *Modern Times* (1936); but he was looking back to a Victorian humanism that decidedly fails him when portraying a Jew under the Nazis in *The Great Dictator* (1940). Keaton reverses that conception: to our age of increasing mindlessness he offers a comedy of mind. Although he never dealt with contemporary issues as Chaplin did, he accurately depicts the landscape of our time in its vast inhuman organization. He reminds us of the claims of consciousness against a mechanistic order, of the fact that our expert procedures and outward accomplishments take no account of our inner nature. Whereas the old clowns would assert our right to our idiosyncrasies, he asserts our need to live with one another in a community that does justice to our individuality. The sadness that emerges at the end of *College* (1927) underlies all of Keaton's happy endings: it is the sadness of inescapable isolation, of knowing that he does not in the end, any more than he did at the beginning, belong in a world where happiness is available only as a convention. Yet Buster has done his best, and leaves us with the haunting image of his solemn and solitary figure, at once purposeful and detached, bravely attempting the impossible.

1998

RICHARD DYER
FROM STARS

Richard Dyer has written on the culture of celebrity in the books *Stars* (1979) and *Heavenly Bodies: Film Stars and Society* (1987). His later criticism, largely concerned with depictions of race and sexuality in popular media, includes *Now You See It: Historical Studies on Lesbian and Gay Film* (1990), *The Matter of Images: Essays on Representations* (1993), and *White* (1997). His recent work considers film music and pastiche in contemporary art and cinema. He is currently professor of film studies at King's College, London.

PERFORMANCE SIGNS

Performance is what the performer does in addition to the actions/functions she or he performs in the plot and the lines she or he is given to say. Performance is how the action/function is done, how the lines are said.

The signs of performance are: facial expression; voice; gestures (principally of hands and arms, but also of any limb, e.g., neck, leg); body posture (how someone is standing or sitting); body movement (movement of the whole body, including how someone stands up or sits down, how they walk, run, etc.). Of these the first is often held to be the most important, on analogy with its primary importance in interpersonal communication in everyday life. Yet just as its importance may be the greatest, so too is its ambiguity. Shaffer points out that we hold, despite arguments to the contrary, to the illusion that the face is supremely expressive of personality:

> A face that looks 'lived in' is a face that *seems* to comprise (or reprise) its past in any of its momentary expressions. Fredric March's sensibility did not somehow 'inform' his features osmotically . . . And yet that was the illusion.

At the same time, when it comes to deciphering facial expression we are at a considerable loss. Aside from films that use this ambiguity in the service of the notion of the eternal ineffability of the face as the window to the soul, most films do, through the use of codes discussed below, narrow down the range of meanings that a facial expression considered in isolation may have. Nonetheless ambiguity is seldom totally eliminated.

This ambiguity needs to be understood in terms of the relation between the performer and the audience in film. This can be considered by comparing the character of Maurice (Montgomery Clift) in *The Heiress* with the same character in the novel the film is based on, *Washington Square* by Henry James. In the latter, we are clearly told from the word go that Maurice is deceitful. In the film, however, we are in the same position as Catherine (Olivia de Havilland) in this regard; we have to work out from our observation of him whether he is sincere or not. This is further complicated by the particular relation we have to Clift as a star. In these ways, film and especially performance in film fabricates a relationship to, rather than a telling about, the characters. . . . A star will have a particular performance style that through its familiarity will inform the performace she or he gives in any particular film. The specific repertoire of gestures, intonations, and so on that a star establishes over a number of films carries the meaning of her or his image just as much as the 'inert' element of appearance, the particular sound of her/his voice or dress style.

An example is provided by G. Hill who quotes from a reviewer of *The War Wagon*: 'it is worth seeing to watch John Wayne wrap his horse's reins round a hitch post!' It is not only that it happens to be Wayne doing it or that the action is always redolent of meaning, but that the particular way Wayne habitually does it sums up a particular aspect of his image. (The relish with which men tell me of this example suggests that what it sums up above all is Wayne's easy and confident masculinity.)

Part of the business of studying stars is to establish what these recurrent features of performance are and what they signify in terms of the star's image. They will usually only sum up an aspect of that image. The example just given does not remind us of everything about Wayne—in particular its joyous appeal operates because he is in the saddle in the West, not in Vietnam, not with a woman. . . .

One of the few debates about film performance that has recurred in film theory is the degree to which performance may be considered an expressive element of any significance. While everyday critical talking about film tends to concentrate on performance (e.g., 'What was so-and-so like in the film you just saw?'), an important tradition in film theory has tended to deny that performance has any expressive value: what you read into the performer, you read in by virtue of signs *other than* performance signs. . . .

[T]he most famous instance of this is probably the final shot of Garbo in *Queen Christina:* She stands on the prow of the boat taking her away from Sweden and after the death of her lover. She stares ahead and into the wind which ruffles her hair. Much can be read into this shot—of resignation, melancholy, profound feeling. Yet it is well known that the director, Rouben Mamoulian, told Garbo to do nothing for this scene, and she did as she was told. (In itself, one should say, a considerable feat of performance.) The meaning of her face in this shot thus derives entirely from its place in the film's narrative, the way it is shot, and the resonances of Garbo's image carried by her face. . . .

Let us consider John Wayne in relation to the last point. Wayne is a performer commonly credited without acting abilities. The assumption is that he is just there, and just by being there a statement is made. In so far as any other meaning can be attributed to him in a particular film, it has to come from montage, *mise-en-scène*, what is said,—or so runs the argument. This in fact was my view of him. However, an analysis of his performance in the scene in *Fort Apache* where he, as Captain York, and Colonel Thursday (Henry Fonda) go with a cavalry troop to meet Cochise, proved me wrong.

Let it be stressed that this has nothing to do with evaluation (I am not remotely interested in vindicating Wayne as a 'good' actor) nor with (Wayne's) 'authorship'.

Performance is defined as what the performer does, and whether s/he, the director, or some other person is authorially responsible for this is a different question altogether. What is of interest here is whether performance—what Wayne does— contributes to the construction of Wayne/York or whether that construction is achieved purely by other means. (The latter include Wayne as an already-signifying star image, but not Wayne as performing.)

Near the beginning of this scene, there is a single take in which Wayne/York (hereinafter, W/Y), having been summoned from the rear of the cavalry column by Fonda/Thursday (hereinafter F/T), comes up to discuss with the latter where they are to meet Cochise. F/T is placed right (as we look at it); he is rigidly uptight against the sky. W/Y is placed left, lower on the screen than F/T, only partially against the sky; he moves in the saddle. In the course of the conversation, F/T announces his plans to deploy his men. W/Y tells him these are inappropriate to the actual position of the Indians, which he (W/Y) knows because he has been following the dust swirls. He points offscreen. The shot ends here, and there is a cut to a shot of Indians riding up en masse over the brow of a hill (through 'creative geography' where W/Y has pointed) with threatening music over.

Clearly *mise en scène* and montage are important vis-à-vis W/Y here. The placing of him in relation to F/T not only expresses their relative positions in the military hierarchy, but also contrasts F/T's self-styled epic aspirations with W/Y's more down-to-earth/natural (but still in fact 'epic') qualities. (This reading depends of course on knowledge of the elaboration of this contrast throughout the film.) The cut to the Indians confirms the 'truth' of what W/Y has said, and hence stamps him with the mark of authenticity (allied to the fact that he knows this truth through his understanding of 'nature'—the dust swirls).

However, performance *also* signifies. The contrast between F/T's rigidity and W/Y's movement suggests the greater 'relaxedness' of the latter, thus picking up on another aspect of the film's opposition between them, namely, his immediate, intuitive, at-homeness with military life as compared to F/T's bookish approach. (This has class connotations that are explicitly presented in the film in a displaced aristocratic/populist opposition.) When F/T announces that he will be deploying two troops to the North, the placing means that he has only to make a slight turn of his head to the left (of the screen), whereas W/Y has to turn the whole of his body round in the saddle. This he does very swiftly and easily. The placing demands the larger movement, but this performance of the movement both suggests a sense of urgency (F/T is making a disastrous decision) and, because it is so easily done, signifies again W/Y's total at-homeness in the saddle.

Later in this scene, the Spanish interpreter repeats Cochise's extremely derogatory descriptions of the gun-runner Meacham. There is a reaction shot, showing Meacham and F/T seated and the other men standing behind, W/Y to the rear and slightly to the right of F/T. W/Y expresses 'amusement' at Cochise's words by the following performance: his eyes look slightly left, slightly heavenward, there is a faint smile on his face, he moves his right leg and upper body just a little, keeping his arms behind his back. (This performance ends with him casting a contemptuous look at Meacham.) Three points are of interest for our purposes about this: (1) nothing in *mise en scène* or montage constructs for the character the response 'amusement'; it resides in performance alone; (2) it fits with what we know of the character—we can read it in terms of relaxedness, and so on; (3) its more specific signification, beyond 'amusement', is not clear. On the one hand, its subtlety and relative unusualness (i.e., it's not just a grin) suggest 'meaningfulness', yet what that meaning is one would have to select from 'translations' such as 'This proves me right,' 'Cochise is cute,' 'This puts Thursday on the spot', and so forth. (Arguably, it expresses all these fleeting thoughts.)

This sort of exercise is useful not only as part of the business of putting performance signs in their determinate context, but also:

(1) to distinguish between different modes of articulation of character in film (e.g. to test Braudy's distinction between 'closed' and 'open' films);
(2) to distinguish between films in which performance fits with other signs of character (the case, as far as I have gone with it, with Wayne in *Fort Apache*) and those in which the fit is more contradictory;
(3) following from that, to test the possibility of stars resisting their material not only by what they inescapably signify (= miscasting), but also through performance. . . .

STARS AS AUTHORS

The study of stars as themselves authors belongs essentially to the study of the Hollywood production situation. It is certainly possible to establish, as 'auteur theory' enjoins us, continuities, contradictions, and transformations either in the totality of a star's image or in discrete elements such as dress or performance style, roles, publicity, iconography. However, the relationship between these and the star always has to be established by examination of what sources there are concerning the actual making of the image and films. That is to say that a star, in films, publicity, and promotion, is a semiotic construction and the fact that that construction exhibits continuities does not prove that the star as person is responsible for them. S/he may be, but also may not be.

In his study of James Cagney, *Cagney, the Actor as Auteur*, Patrick McGilligan makes this point very clearly:

> The auteur theory can be revised and reproposed with actors in mind: under certain circumstances, an actor may influence a film as much as a writer, director or producer; some actors are more influential than others; and there are certain rare few performers whose acting capabilities and screen personas are so powerful that they embody and define the very essence of their films. If an actor is responsible only for acting but is not involved in any of the artistic decisions of film-making, then it is accurate surely to refer to the actor as a semi-passive icon, a symbol that is manipulated by writers and directors. But actors who not only influence artistic decisions (casting, writing, directing, etc.) but demand certain limitations on the basis of their screen personas, may justly be regarded as 'auteurs.' When the performer becomes so important to a production that he or she changes lines, adlibs, shifts meaning, influences the narrative and style of a film and altogether signifies something clear-cut to audiences despite the intent of writers and directors, then the acting of that person assumes the force, style and integrity of an auteur.

He then proceeds to argue that Cagney does fit the category of actor-auteur, drawing on interviews with him and those he worked with, as well as observing how, for instance, Cagney's films made with directors such as Lloyd Bacon, William Keighley, Roy Del Ruth are all very similar to each other, and more like Cagney's other films than films by those directors with different stars. (Unfortunately this last point lacks the precision of most of McGilligan's study; one needs the specific aspects of performance, characterisation, narrative structure, and so forth, pinpointed in the way that one would expect from auteurist analyses of directors and not the vague references to 'spontaneity' (Bacon), 'a polished emphasis on action and dialogue' (Keighley), and 'urbanity' (Del Ruth).)

McGilligan's aim is to demonstrate that Cagney is *the* author of his films, the classic auteurist position. However, any of the models of authorship outlined above might apply to given stars. In considering this, we must first distinguish between on the one hand authorship of the star image and/or performance, and on the other hand authorship of films.

In the case of images and/or performance, there may be stars who totally controlled this (Fred Astaire, Joan Crawford), or only contributed to it (Marlene Dietrich, Robert Mitchum), as part of a collective team (John Wayne) or just one disparate voice among many (Marilyn Monroe, Marlon Brando); alternatively there will be others who were almost totally the product of the studio/Hollywood machine (Lana Turner). (The names in parentheses are guesses only and require further research to confirm or disprove.) The fact that the person of the star coincides with a text (the star image, the character, the performance) in the construction of which s/he was only a collaborator or even a mere vehicle should warn us not to elide the star-as-person with the star-as-text and assume that the former is the author of the latter. Although I find it hard to conceive of a star having no power in the decisions made about her/his image or performance, just how much power s/he had and how s/he exercised it has to be determined by looking at specific cases.

In the case of stars as authors of the films they starred in, we must begin by excepting those cases where stars directed (or scripted) themselves in films: for instance, Charlie Chaplin, Buster Keaton, Mae West (scripts), Ida Lupino, Jerry Lewis, John Wayne, Clint Eastwood. In these cases, we have to make a theoretical distinction between their role as star and their other role in the production.

The number of cases on which the totality of a film can be laid at the door of the star must be very few indeed. (Candidates include Greta Garbo and *Queen Christina,* Ellen Burstyn and *Alice Doesn't Live Here Any More,* and most persuasively Barbra Streisand and *A Star is Born.*) However, the star as one of the 'voices' in a film (always remembering any voice can only be returned to its author as the point of decision-making in production, not that of unmediated expressivity) is surely very common. This 'voice' is not necessarily confined to matters of performance, dress, etc., but may affect almost any aspect of the film, depending upon how the star exercised his/her power. . . .

This notion of the star and the director mutually bringing something out in each other informs much auteurist criticism. This approach does usually privilege the director over the star in their collaborative interaction, and examples are usually confined to a few paragraphs within broader considerations of a director's work. In *Horizons West,* Jim Kitses notes the Mann-Stewart, Budd Boetticher-Randolph Scott collaborations, while John Baxter in his *The Cinema of John Ford* writes of Ford's different views of the hero according to whether he is using John Wayne, James Stewart, or Henry Fonda. Other less satisfactory examples of this approach include Stanley Solomon's discussion in *The Film Idea* of the use made of Cary Grant by Stanley Donen and Alfred Hitchcock and Gary Carey's article 'The Lady and the Director' dealing with Bette Davis and William Wyler.

One need not, as Perkins, Kitses, and Baxter are, be concerned to find a perfect fit between star image and directorial pattern. Disjunctions between them may be just as interesting, especially from an ideological point of view, since they may correspond to, or at any rate suggest, ideological contradictions. I would cite here Monroe v. Hawks in *Gentlemen Prefer Blondes*. Lorelei, as Anita Loos wrote her, is the hero* of the film, and she is the hero by her deliberate use of her (socially constructed) femininity. In Hawks' films such a character (e.g., Rita Hayworth in *Only Angels Have Wings*) is not so sympathetic, or central. Thus he submits her here to humiliation (trapped in a porthole up to her hips, themselves part of her sexual armoury) and send-up (Jane Russell's impersonation of her in the court scene), while constructing the Russell character as a warm, practical buddy-woman comparable to other Hawksian women (cf. Jean Arthur in *Only Angels Have Wings*). In this context, Monroe's construction of Lorelei as innocently, utterly but not manipulatively, sexual, a construction stemming from the basic pattern of Monroe's image and at variance with Loos' Lorelei, confuses Hawks' division of the female world into manipulative feminine women and likeable masculine (or non-feminine) ones. There is reason for Hawks to deride Loos' Lorelei, but not Monroe's—but this then throws us back to the problem of just what place the 'feminine' has in Hawks' films, and, more importantly, in Hollywood and in patriarchy generally. 'Femininity' is primarily a social construction and, moreover, a construction made by men. Yet it is a construction men often find hard to cope with—it is the category onto which they project more fundamental fears about gender, which one can conceive psychoanalytically in terms of castration or socio-historically in terms of men's power over women and simultaneous dependence on them. Hawks' films, like most films, legitimate this fear. They say, in effect, that women, especially 'feminine' women, really should be feared by men; in other words, they take what is a projection from men and claim that it really emanates from women. Monroe as Lorelei, however, disturbs this pattern, because Lorelei, as Monroe's image has already constructed her and as she plays her, is both extremely feminine and not evil or castrating. Monroe as Lorelei refuses to corroborate this male construction of the female.

1979

---

*I use the term "hero" here, not "heroine", partly to stress that Lorelei for Loos is "heroic", admirable, a winner, and partly because the term "heroine" implies a structural position in narratives in relation to a male protagonist—as the object of his quest or his love.

JAMES NAREMORE
FROM ACTING IN THE CINEMA

KATHARINE HEPBURN IN *HOLIDAY*

James Naremore's scholarly work began with an interest in both modernist literature and popular culture. Also influenced by auteurist criticism, Naremore *In The Magic World of Orson Welles* (1979), considers the psychological links between the director's biography and films, while *More Than Night* (1998) examines film noir as a form of vernacular modernism in which high and low culture mingle. *Acting in the Cinema*, excerpted here, similarly analyzes the psychological and cinematic aspects of film acting. Naremore has also written on Vincente Minnelli, Alfred Hitchcock, John Huston, and Roman Polanski, among others. He is currently professor emeritus of communication and culture at Indian University.

Although the images of players like James Cagney and Marlene Dietrich were eventually adjusted to the demands of the Production Code, stardom for Katharine Hepburn involved a series of subtler, more complex negotiations. Throughout her career, her name connoted not only breeding, intelligence, and "theatah," but also New England austerity, athleticism, and feminine emancipation. Occasionally, she played tomboys or charmingly lost her dignity in screwball comedy, but screenwriters and publicists had trouble making her sufficiently ordinary—a quality successful movie actors need, because they function both as ego ideals and as common folk with whom the audience can identify. Hepburn was badly suited to such ends, at least in terms of the usual formulas. She would have been miscast as a housewife or a dance-hall girl, and she seldom played the suffering women of soap opera. The roles critics have suggested for her include Shakespeare's Rosalind (which she attempted once on stage without much success), Jane Austen's Emma Woodhouse, and Henry James's Isabel Archer. In effect, she was what Andrew Britton has described as a Jamesian "princess"—too privileged and controversial to be well liked—and it was not until her much-publicized relationship with Spencer Tracy that the public truly took her to heart.

On screen Hepburn was alert, idealistic, and active, living in wealthy or professionalized worlds. Rarely flirtatious (except to put comic quotation marks around it), she seemed too witty and willful for the average leading man. Inevitably, her films raised feminist issues, but this inclination, like her upper-class manner, had to be contained or controlled. In fact, her social class could be used as a weapon against her whenever she appeared too progressive. Like Vanessa Redgrave or Jane Fonda—her descendants in some ways—she was frequently described as "spoiled." Her acting technique exacerbated these tensions, because it was clearly associated with "legitimate" theater. Vocally and expressively, she was too lofty for the populist mid-thirties, when John Barrymore (the star of her first film) became a symbol of hammyness, and when Garbo and Dietrich were increasingly regarded as vestiges of an older, elitist sensibility. As a result, the bulk of her films developed strategies to lighten or normalize her highly ostensive, drama-school style, and they usually found ways to tame or chastise the strong-willed, aristocratic characters she played. Moreover, the extended narrative constituted by her various roles tells the story of *a retreat from assertiveness*, a cautious adjustment not unlike the plot resolutions in her individual pictures. Simon Watney has remarked that she "stands for a certain type of `free woman' in her early films, until her persona is eventually overwhelmed by its very longevity, transforming her into an icon of survival, yet another version of the American dream which successfully represses the history which determines it."[1] Andrew Sarris makes a similar point, describing her career in terms of a "premature feminism" and observing that she was complicit in a move toward more conservative roles after 1939.[2]

Like many successful stars, Hepburn selected her own scripts and managed her image to a remarkable degree—abetted by money and a series of friendships with writers. From the beginning, she was regarded as a combative, high-spirited androgyne, and not surprisingly, she achieved her first great theatrical success in *The Warrior's Husband* (1932), a modernized version of *Lysistrata*. Soon afterward, she signed a contract with RKO, where she won an Academy Award in the following year for *Morning Glory* (1933). Throughout the thirties, especially in collaboration with Cukor, Hawks, and Grant, she challenged the dominant modes of Hollywood romance, and partly for that reason, her relationship to the studio system was embattled, involving periodic returns to Broadway. Her most popular film role of the decade was Jo in *Little Women* (1933), which was followed by a disastrous failure on Broadway in *The Lake* (1934), where she provoked Dorothy Parker's famous comment that her performance "ran the gamut of emotions from A to B." Back in California, she acquired a new voice coach and a new co-star, Cary Grant, who appeared with her in *Sylvia Scarlett* (1936) and then in *Bringing Up Baby* (138). But despite the critical praise her films of the late thirties received, only *Stage Door* was popular with audiences.[3] Indeed, the poor showing of *Bringing Up Baby* led Harry Brandt, president of the Independent Theater Owners of America, to pronounce Hepburn "Box Office Poison" (a label he also attached to Garbo, Dietrich,

---

[1] Simon Watney, 61.

[2] Quoted in Watney, 39.

[3] It may be worth noting how *Stage Door*—in some ways the most politically progressive of Hepburn's movies—tends to foreground the "negative" traits of the star in order to defend against them. When the picture was made, Hepburn was known to the public as an aristocratic, feminist type who loved the stage and who often refused to give interviews for fan magazines. Thus, the film depicts Tracy Randall as a New England blue-blood who wants to go on stage (in a play associated with Hepburn herself); the other characters joke about her snooty-sounding accent, Adolph Menjou describes her as a "militant," and at the end, having achieved stardom, she is shown walking out on a crowd of reporters. By way of mitigating against such problems, the picture establishes Randall as a good-hearted, unpretentious democrat; it gives her an excellent reason for skipping out on the interview, and it pairs her with Ginger Rogers, who functions in exactly the same way as she had with Fred Astaire. As Hepburn's "buddy" or displaced love-interest, Rogers provides a "down-to-earth" middle-classness, making Hepburn as Randall seem more ordinary.

Crawford, and Fred Astaire). RKO then began treating Hepburn badly, at one point offering her a project entitled *Mother Carey's Chickens*. In response, she bought out her contract for almost a quarter-million late-Depression dollars and moved to Columbia, where Harry Cohn assembled an attractive package: a remake of Philip Barry's *Holiday*, with Grant as co-star, Cukor as director, and Donald Ogden Stewart as writer. Once again the film was excellent, but it did not arrest Hepburn's declining fortunes. Although Cukor advocated her for Scarlett O'Hara in *Gone With the Wind*, her career in Hollywood seemed virtually ended.[4]

A turning point came soon, however, and it involved Hepburn's active intervention. Her friendship with Philip Barry and her brief romance with Howard Hughes (who became a financial backer) enabled her to commission *The Philadelphia Story*, a play which, as Sarris has observed, "was about Katharine Hepburn *herself*, and what the American people thought about Katharine Hepburn in 1939, and what Katharine Hepburn realized she had to do in order to keep her career going."[5] The result, as everyone knows, was a great stage success and a celebrated MGM adaptation. Although Cary Grant received top billing in the film version, the entire project had obviously been designed to recuperate Hepburn—not so much changing her image as dramatizing her full submission to patriarchal authority and foreshadowing her later attachment to the most conservative of American studios.[6] Grant, in fact, was much less important to *The Philadelphia Story* than James Stewart, who performed the same "service" for Hepburn as he had for Dietrich one year earlier in *Destry Rides Again*. John Kobal's rapt description of a crucial scene in the Hepburn film is a clear, if unwitting, indication of how Stewart functioned ideologically:

> Here the still feverishly overactive spoiled brat is brought down to earth. She is told by a man of the people (James Stewart) that she is not a creature of ice but a real woman. . . . At this moment, her transformation occurs. Stewart woos her on our behalf. Hepburn, dressed by Adrian, incandescently lit and photographed by Joseph Ruttenberg . . . sways, trembles, succumbs, and—with Stewart as our envoy—wins us. Her film career began in earnest.[7]

It was Grant, not Stewart, who "got" Hepburn at the end of the picture. Perhaps significantly, however, it was Stewart who received the Academy Award, and Hepburn and Grant never acted together again. One year later, Hepburn began her remarkable association with Spencer Tracy, an even more plain-spoken "man of the people," who provided a counterbalancing ordinariness for the extraordinary Hepburn persona. Their work together contains some of the finest pieces of comic acting in the history of American cinema, and films such as *State of the Union* (1948) and *Adam's Rib* (1949) still seem "advanced." Nevertheless, the Hepburn

---

[4]David Selznick had been as important to the "discovery" of Hepburn as George Cukor and was the producer of her first film. During the casting of *GWTW*, however, he wrote the following memo to his associate, Daniel T. O'Shea: "I think Hepburn has two strikes against her—first, the unquestionable and very widespread intense public dislike of her at the moment, and second, the fact that she is yet to demonstrate that she possesses the sex qualities which are probably the most important of all the many requisites of Scarlett. . . ."(171).

[5]Quoted in Watney, 39.

[6]L. B. Mayer was fond of Hepburn, although he ordered the sexist conclusion to *Woman of the Year* (1942), in which she dons an apron and tries to cook Spencer Tracy's breakfast (Higham, 103). At MGM, she also worked regularly with her friend Cukor, but scholars make an error when they describe him as an especially sensitive exponent of women's concerns; indeed, some of Cukor's typical films—such as *The Women* (1939) and *Les Girls* (1957)—are profoundly misogynistic.

[7]John Kobal, 32.

and Tracy performances were increasingly predicated on the audience's knowledge of an offscreen relationship, and as various critics have observed, they foster an image of "good old Kate"—a woman who might behave like a liberationist, but who is reassuringly, almost maternally, attached to Tracy and who will, in the last instance, subdue her rebellion for his sake. Increasingly, she became an emblem of safely domesticated feminism, until finally, as if in full payment for all those years of independence, she was cast as a spinster who declared admiration for aging symbols of virility like Humphrey Bogart and John Wayne.

Some of Hepburn's later appearances are outstanding—especially her interpretation of Mary Tyrone in *Long Day's Journey into Night* (1962)—but her most exhilarating work was done in the late thirties, at precisely the moment when her career was foundering. *Holiday* comes from that period (*The Philadelphia Story* might have been written in direct response to it), highlighting her unusual but ravishing beauty and giving full range to the dynamic of her acting. *Holiday* also had an important personal significance. Although Columbia advertised her as "the new Hepburn," she was in fact going back to her earliest theatrical experience. In 1928, just out of college, she had been the understudy for the lead role in Barry's play (written for the stage performer Hope Williams and starring Ann Harding in the 1930 movie version). Later, Hepburn had used one of its scenes as the basis for her original RKO screen test. She seems to have identified with the role, and she certainly knew that it was a good showcase for her technique.

In certain ways, *Holiday* was also an attempt to mollify the more threatening aspects of Hepburn's persona: it allows her to signify patrician manners but at the same time gives her an opportunity to seem unpretentious and even folksy; it lets her challenge the rule of an oppressive father (a typical Republican financier of thirties melodrama), but it also suggests that she will fulfill herself through fond obedience to a husband. As a social commentary, the film is badly compromised—not least because Philip Barry was enamoured of the class he had set out to criticize; nevertheless, in qualified fashion it enables Hepburn to act out an "ideal self," providing a safe outlet for mannerisms the audience may have disliked. In this way, *Holiday* hopes to make viewers love the star.

Holiday belongs to an always problematic and nowadays virtually extinct movie genre—the well-made "comedy of manners" that gently satirizes the *haute bourgeoisie*. Typically, such films are derived from theater pieces set in drawing rooms, and they are composed of neatly rounded, almost epigrammatic speeches. George Cukor has described Barry's language as a form of "singing" dialogue,[8] and Hepburn was attracted to it. She and the other players often try to underplay the evident theatricality of the speeches by overlapping or throwing away lines; stylistically and in most other ways, however, the film remains faithful to the original text, merely rearranging a few scenes, adding some topical references, and "opening out" the action. (The chief screenwriter, Donald Ogden Stewart, was probably as fond of the project as Hepburn, since he had acted in the play when she was an understudy.)

Barry founded his drama on an opposition between two sets of values, visualized quite early in the film by a contrast between the Potter household and the Seton household. On the one hand are Susan and Nick Potter (Jean Dixon and Edward Everett Horton, who repeats the role he played in the first film version), a middle-

---

[8]Higham, 87.

aged, childless pair of academics, representing freedom from possessions, spontaneity, and "life." On the other hand is Edward Seton (Henry Kolker), a widowed patriarch with three children, representing old wealth, capitalism, and joyless acquistion
of power. At first glance, the contrast between these figures seems to be posed in
terms of social class, since the Potters live in a shabby-genteel, almost bohemian
apartment, whereas the Seton mansion looks as large as the Louvre. At bottom, however, the film is offering a choice between two life-styles within bourgeois democracy. The Potters are a distinguished couple with enough income to take a "holiday"
from capitalism. If they were real persons instead of fictional characters, they would
be members of what Marxist theory describes as a social *fraction*—made up in this
case of educated, dissident members of a privileged class who criticize the dominant
ethos (the same fraction, in fact, to which Hepburn, Barry, and Stewart belonged).

Individualists rather than political activists, the Potters see life in terms of friendships and humane, egalitarian relations. They are a distinctly American couple who
sometimes seem more like comics than intellectuals (an effect produced by the casting of Horton and Dixon, who play their roles fairly straight). Nevertheless, they are
also professional educators who in their social position and attitude could be compared with the members of the "Bloomsbury" circle in England during the twenties
and thirties: thus they are sophisticated, disrespectful of unrestrained capitalism, and
vaguely feminist. (The Hepburn character immediately recognizes Susan Eliot Potter
as someone who "once gave a lecture at my school.") In more specific terms, the film
presents them as unpretentious liberals whose chief weapon is wit, as when they give
Nazi salutes to an especially pompous, right-wing couple at a party in the Seton home.

The plot of the picture involves a deepening friendship between Johnny Case
(Grant), a virtual child of the Potters, and Linda Seton (Hepburn), a dissatisfied
daughter of the capitalist. The relationship between these soulmates is complicated
by two factors: first by Johnny's engagement to Linda's sister, Julia (Doris Nolan),
and second, by the conflict between Johnny and Linda's father. The emotional center of the action, however, is Linda, who spends most of her time on the top floor
of the mansion in a children's playroom, which her deceased mother once constructed as a "place to have fun." Not yet a madwoman in the attic, she is a vibrant
character who describes herself as a "black sheep." From the beginning, it is clear
that she must break completely from her father or else become a wasted personality like her brother Ned (Lew Ayres). But she must also cope with an emotional
struggle between her love for Johnny and her love for her sister.

To its credit, *Holiday* does not work out a reconciliation between Linda and her
father; instead, it shows Linda making an intense, heroic denunciation of the Seton
values and going off to live on "holiday" with Johnny. The conclusion is a disappointment nonetheless. Linda's sister has a last-act speech in which she coolly
announces that Johnny's unwillingness to adjust to the Seton way of life has made
him an unworthy partner, thus leaving Linda conveniently free to fly into Johnny's
arms without guilt. Moreover, the impending union between Johnny and Linda
evades the central issues. Johnny Case comes from a wage-earning family, but he
has worked his way through Harvard and acquired all the skills necessary to become
a "young wizard of finance"; his objection to Edward Seton has less to do with capitalism than with the supposedly dreary process of making millions. The major alter-

natives of the plot are therefore posed in terms of a settling/wandering dichotomy typical of American popular fiction. As Andrew Britton has pointed out, the final scenes have a great deal in common with *Stagecoach* (1939), where the ideal couple simply ride off into the sunset, "free of the blessings of civilization."[9] An even deeper evasion can be sensed in Linda's parting speech to her father, in which she declares her independence in terms of her subordination to another man and to another sort of capitalism. She is going to be with Johnny no matter what he wants to do. Even if he decides to sell peanuts, "oh, how I'll love those peanuts!"

Despite these awkward compromises and a few other problems I shall mention, *Holiday* contains a striking performance by Hepburn. In classic fashion, she enters several minutes into the action, creating a mild *coup de théâtre*. The opening sequence shows Johnny Case returning from a vacation and breathlessly announcing to the Potters that he has found his ideal mate. "It's love fellas. I've met the girl!" Given the star system, we know that Hepburn will be his choice, and we assume she is the woman to whom he refers. That assumption is reinforced in the next sequence, when Johnny goes to meet the girl's parents, only to discover that she lives in a mansion. We expect Hepburn to make an appearance when the butler announces Johnny's arrival to "Miss Julia," but Doris Nolan enters instead, and Grant rushes to embrace her. Hepburn shows up later, symbolically intruding on the two lovers as they kiss in the mansion elevator. A door slides open and there she stands, a mink-coated figure casting an ironic glance at the couple: "For shame, Julia!" she says. "Is this the way to spend Sunday morning? Who's your partner, anyone I know?"

Until this point, the film has been relatively disappointing. Grant plays everything with characteristic pep and comic eccentricity, but his dialogue is speechy and somewhat fey. There is an intriguing moment when Lew Ayres appears as Ned—a reserved, rather *triste* drunkard who ignores Grant and asks the butler to have a drink ready at the end of church services; otherwise, however, Hepburn creates all the dramatic tension and interest. She is, in fact, a slightly more dominating presence than Barry had intended. Compare her effect to the stage direction accompanying Linda's entrance in the play, written with Hope Williams in mind: "Linda is twenty-seven, and looks about twenty-two. She is slim, rather boyish, and exceedingly fresh. She is smart, she is pretty, but beside Julia . . . she seems a trifle gauche, and almost plain." Hepburn possesses many of these traits, but clearly she is a glamorous figure, a good deal more attractive than Nolan. When she enters, the acting takes on a discernible pace and heightened energy, partly because of the sexual vitality she brings into the frame; in fact, one of the weaknesses of the film is that it never gives a plausible reason why Johnny should be interested in Julia in the first place. (The 1930 version cast Mary Astor in the Nolan role—a more interesting choice that makes Johnny's behavior plausible. Probably Columbia did not want to set Hepburn against another star, although it did test the young Rita Hayworth for the part.)

Then, too, Hepburn tends to command the screen with her flamboyant theatrical rhetoric. For example, she offers to shake Johnny's hand in a fashion that immediately announces Linda's difference from the rest of the Seton family—a strong move-

---

[9] Andrew Britton, 85.

ment, the spread palm placed exactly at the center of the shared, three-figure composition, connoting a forthright, no-nonsense offer of friendship. She repeats the movement toward the end of the sequence, when she tells Julia "I like this man," and as a signifier of character it is no less vivid than Johnny's repeated somersaults. In conventional terms the gesture is "unladylike," in keeping with the easy way she looks Grant up and down when she requests him to "step out here in the light." It is never "gauche," however, nor does it resemble the aggressive sexual innuendo of a player like Dietrich; instead, it suggests mature, aristocratic self-confidence, together with the unaffected frankness of a woman who expects to meet a man on equal terms.

There is, in other words, a likable sexiness about Hepburn's performance, a quality reminiscent of the leading women in the films of Howard Hawks, who never act coy and who engage in banter like one of the boys. Cukor allows her to exhibit those qualities immediately, and, like Hawks, he gives her plenty of opportunity to walk. One of the chief pleasures of *Bringing Up Baby,* which exerts a subtle influence on this film, comes from watching Hepburn stride confidently across the screen while Grant struggles in her wake, awash in chaos; in *Holiday,* her introductory sequence is photographed in a tracking movement designed to show her wit and physical grace. Leading Grant and Nolan briskly down a hallway, she jokes with Grant, adopting the tone of a family elder—the first of several instances where Linda Seton will parody her father: "This modern generation! Well, young man, I hope you realize what you're getting yourself in for." She pauses briefly to chat, and then as she parts company the camera tilts, watching her jog easily up a long stairway.

Linda's run up the stairs helps establish an affinity with Johnny—a physical exuberance apparent later in the film, when she joins him in a somersault. But it also functions in excess of what the story needs, pointing to Hepburn's own body. She has the flexible, slender build of a tennis player, and she walks or jogs as forthrightly as she shakes hands—legs extended, arms moving in an arc, with no suggestion of a wiggle or sway. This quality, more than any other, led to her "tomboy" roles, and it placed her virtually alone among the glamorous women of her day in suggesting a romantic line and style of movement not based on dance.[10] In certain contexts, her body could evoke a spartan schoolmarm or a willowy fashion model; its composition and musculature, however, were developed from sport, and for a time she resembled what Kenneth Tynan has called an "outdoor Garbo." Several of her films allude to her well-known athletic skill: in *Bringing Up Baby*, she exhibits her golf swing, and in *Pat and Mike* (1952), she plays a character based on Babe Dietrichson. Earlier in her career, her more candid photographs made her look rather like a Wildean youth, especially when she was shown in short hair and slacks or when she was caught in movement. Yet no one who has seen her wearing a skin-tight, silver lamé jumpsuit in *Christopher Strong* (1933) could doubt her potential as an erotic female star.

Whenever *Holiday* wants to give Hepburn a typical glamor, it emphasizes her long hair and exquisite cheekbones—all the while garbing her in a floor-length black

---

[10]In *A Bill of Divorcement* (1932), Hepburn's first film, George Cukor had given her a moment that convinced David Selznick she would become a star: "Not until the preview was the staff convinced that we had a great screen personality. . . . But very early in the picture there was a scene in which Hepburn just walked across the room, stretched her arms, and then lay out on the floor before the fireplace. It sounds very simple, but you could almost feel, and you could definitely hear, the excitement in the audience" (43). The effect of this shot remains electric; the distant framing and the silence allow us to focus on her body, revealing the sex appeal she could give to apparently ordinary movement.

dress, backlighting her face, and photographing her through diffused light. Even at her most "feminine," however, she is unorthodox, and her style has troubled some critics. Charles Higham, for example, has praised Cukor for concealing her "powerful stride" (actually, Cukor does nothing of the kind), meanwhile regretting that her voice is "too harsh and strident," her body insufficiently "soft and yielding."[11] Throughout her career, reviewers and co-stars made similar complaints; often she was regarded as a skinny, rather plain woman who spoke with an odd voice and knew how to create the *illusion* of beauty.[12] The idea that she was not beautiful is, of course, absurd, revealing Hollywood's difficulty in appropriating her manner to conventional norms of femininity. Besides her aristocratic features and fabled "Bryn Mawr accent," she had a lean physique and an energetic, potentially aggressive attitude; in the words of Andrew Britton, she suggested a "too militant beauty whose confidence precisely isn't contingent on male approval."[13]

In spite of all this, Hepburn was a blessing to cameramen, who knew how to accent her remarkable bone structure and who drew out her love of extravagant posing. There was also truth in the theory that she knew how to act like a beautiful woman. "Now that girl there," she once said to John Kobal, pointing to one of her old studio photographs, "liked to show off. . . . I photographed better than I looked, so it was easy for me. . . . I let myself go in front of the camera. I mean you can't photograph a dead cat. . . . it's not how you look that's important but how you come across."[14] Hepburn's way of "coming across," however, could sometimes be as controversial as her appearance. Chaplin had relied on techniques of music hall and mime; Gish had gestured like a heroine of melodrama; Dietrich had stood and posed like a singer in cabaret; and Cagney had evoked a vaudeville dancer. In contrast to these, Hepburn reminded her audience of the legitimate stage—Broadway or West End drama inflected by the older romanticism of Terry, Duse, and Bernhardt. As a result, both theater and movie critics sometimes found her pretentious, like a prima donna who was imitating theatrical conventions rather than genuinely "feeling" the part.

One of Hollywood's solutions to the problem was to cast her as an actor, so that her behavior would be normalized by the role. Thus in *Morning Glory* and *Stage Door* she freely indulges her "actressy" tendencies, projecting her resonant voice as if she were aiming at the back row of an auditorium, gesturing rather grandly, and visibly thinking about the camera. By the same token, her films often contain moments when she amusingly "quotes" old-fashioned performance. In *Desk Set* (1957), for example, she gives readings of "Hiawatha" and "The Curfew Shall Not Toll Tonight," dramatizing the latter piece with elaborate pantomime gestures. In the early thirties, publicists praised her "genius" and directors stressed the theme of theater, allowing her to play characters who adopt visible masks, as in *Sylvia Scarlett* and *Alice Adams* (1935). In such contexts, her technique looked like "fine art" (which may explain why she won three Oscars and was nominated more often than any other actor).

---

[11]Charles Higham, 88.

[12]Hepburn's voice was the chief thing critics complained about, especially in the disastrous production of *The Lake*. Oddly, theater reviewers found her a weak speaker, whereas in movies she seemed just the opposite. In mid career she underwent training with Isaac Van Grove, who tried to make her sound less "affected" (Higham, 95).

[13]Andrew Britton, 13.

[14]John Kobal, 109.

As an instance of Hepburn's rather histrionic effect, notice her vivid changes in posture and voice during the scene in *Holiday* when Linda Seton confronts her father during her sister's engagement party: first she adopts an almost military stance, looking him in the eye and making a ringing declaration: "Listen to me, Father. Tonight means a good deal to me." Trying to explain why she wants time alone with a few friends, she appeals to his feelings, first bending slightly to plead, then turning away, tossing her head back, and gazing along the walls as if she were searching for some remote ideal. "It has something to do with this room, and when I was a child," she says in a tremulous, "singing" voice. When Henry Kolker suggests that she leave ("Why don't you go away? . . . You distress me. You cause nothing but trouble and upset."), she becomes teary and distraught, barely hiding her emotion by turning her back as she promises to go away forever. "I can't bear it here any longer," she says. "It's doing terrible things to me!" Her playing is invested with a good deal of emotional "contagion," but it clearly involves a classy middlebrow variant of melodramatic technique—a series of rather conventional mannerisms well-suited to "coming across" on the proscenium stage.

This style is especially evident in *Holiday* whenever Hepburn is called upon to display expressive incoherence—that is, during scenes when her character tries to mask her deepest feelings. Consider the moment early in the film when she and Doris Nolan are sitting at the bottom of a staircase discussing the forthcoming wedding: Hepburn asks to give an engagement party up in the old "playroom," and she insists that "Father's to have nothing to do with it." As she makes the point, she turns away from Nolan and slightly toward us, as if to conceal emotion from her sister. Holding her head up proudly, she gazes down to the floor in tragic dignity: "No one's to touch my party but me, do you hear?" Suddenly there is a tearful crack in her voice and a hesitation in her speech, covered by an attempt to laugh: "No, if they do I . . . I won't come to it!" In a later scene, Hepburn asks Lew Ayres if her affection for Grant has been showing too much. She stands in profile to the left of the screen, hands resting atop a grand piano. "Ned?" she asks, turning her face as if to hide her expression from him—all the while showing it more clearly to us. She tosses her head up proudly for a moment and then indicates embarrassment by looking down to the floor. "Do you remember when we . . . New Year's Eve?" Raising her handsome shoulders and tucking in her chin, she looks downward even more, as if she were ashamed. Her voice begins to tremble. "Does it stand out all over me?" The answer of course is yes, chiefly because she is behaving so ostentatiously for the camera.

Critics were sometimes distressed by such visible tricks, regarding them as highbrow affectations; nevertheless, the same critics were quite happy when Hepburn played comedy. For instance, the *Time* magazine review of *Bringing Up Baby* in 1938 remarked that "the cinema audience will enjoy . . . seeing stagey Actress Hepburn get a proper mussing up."[15] In fact, she was brilliant in the Hawks film—not only because she had the physical skill for slapstick but also because most forms of comedy are "stagey," relying on heightened expressiveness and crisp theatrical enunciation. For nearly the same reason, Hepburn and Spencer Tracy were a stunning combination whenever they had amusing material; like virtually all the great comic duos, they comprised what Fredric Jameson has called a "tandem" characterization: her slightly over-

---

[15]*Time.*

stated elocution was set off against his dry, conversational tone; her quick, visibly rhetorical movement was played off against his slow, stolid reaction.

Holiday seems particularly well-suited to Hepburn's bravura style, not only because it contains a number of gently comic and even "screwball" scenes but also because it subtly valorizes the art of acting, turning Linda Seton into another variant of the "theatrical character" described by Leo Braudy.[16] A typical film for both Cukor and Hepburn, it uses the idea of performance thematically, contrasting the liberated antics in Linda's upstairs room with the hypocritical playacting elsewhere in the Seton household. During the engagement party, for example, the guests in the "playroom" do acrobatic stunts, stage Punch-and-Judy shows, engage in communal singing, and imitate various funny characters. The dead mother's room becomes a carnivalistic space where acting is a force of personal and social health; paradoxically, it is also the realm of authenticity, where characters regress to pre-Oedipal games or hold heart-to-heart talks that reveal "true" feelings. Meanwhile, in the paternalistic downstairs regions, people become players of a different kind and enact a stifling ritual that they take all too seriously; no joy comes from such behavior, and their staged selves are marked as deceptive or repressive.

This theme is a very old one, common to what C. L. Barber once termed "festive comedy." (Compare Shakespeare's *Henry IV, Part One*, which creates a dialectic between the two forms of playacting, reminding us that "if all the year were playing holidays, / To sport would be as tedious as to work.") An excellent basis for drama, festivity makes us aware of the craft of acting, creating a pretext for "staginess." At the same time, it implicitly justifies theater as a profession, emphasizing the therapeutic value of play and associating the performers' virtuosity with the *joie de vivre* of the most sympathetic characters. Thus the playroom sequences in *Holiday* not only enhance Hepburn's charm, they also suggest that her love of theatrics (like Linda Seton's) is consistent with humane wit and progressive idealism.

Aspects of these scenes are worth considering in detail, both as evidence of Hepburn's mastery of a variety of acting skills and as an indication of how the film merges professional attributes of the star with moral attributes of the character. Consider, for example, the quiet moment early on, when the rest of the Seton family is away at church and Linda invites Johnny upstairs for a chat. Throughout this relatively uncomplicated sequence, Hepburn is very much the center of interest, controlling the changing moods of the conversation. She moves, gestures, and poses more vividly than Grant (who, like most leading men, is reserved and less obviously on display), and as the friendship between Linda and Johnny develops, she becomes increasingly theatrical, dominating the entire space.

When Grant enters, she is munching an apple. "Wanna bite?" she asks, holding it out in a friendly gesture. This ingenious piece of business has no precedent in Barry's text, but it serves to mock the Seton family values: while everyone else is stiffly putting on a front at Sunday services, Johnny and Linda behave with childlike informality, the apple evoking an Eden where women are healthy rather than sinful. Grant

---

[16]Braudy has remarked that such characters in the 1930s are nearly always members of the upper class, "or, better, someone pretending to be upper class.... Whether the aristocrat is Cary Grant, Katharine Hepburn, or Pierre Fresnay's Boeldieu in *La Grande Illusion*, the sense of self as theater, as play, is paramount" (235).

accepts the fruit and walks around, his back to us, while she stands chewing and regarding him. The dramatic pause gives her time to swallow, and because the scene involves polite dialogue and several camera setups, neither character tastes the apple again—Grant merely holds it, preoccupied with the room. After a moment Hepburn picks up a cigarette and thoughtfully taps it against a box, as if considering how to begin. She keeps the cigarette unlit, using the incompleted action to show Linda's pleased response to Johnny's interest in the surroundings. First she explains the significance of the place ("This was Mother's idea . . . she was marvelous."), and as she talks she sits at the right of the screen in a favored position, crossing her legs and propping her elbow on her knee with characteristic angularity.

Answering Grant's questions about various toys, she begins moving about the room, at one point holding a stuffed giraffe named Leopold next to her face, its long neck and equine features echoing her own. "Looks like me," she says, and a medium close-up makes us aware of the actor within the role, joking about herself. When Grant finds a childhood picture of Julia Seton and admires it, Hepburn's amused tone changes, and she makes a frank avowal of how much she loves her sister; squatting on the floor next to him, she adopts the first in a series of overtly theatrical voices, imitating a stereotypical cop in order to ask about his past: "What about these little jaunts to Placid? Come clean, Case!" Grant answers that the skiing vacation where he met Julia was his first holiday and then expresses curiosity about her own background. Rather wistfully she confesses that she once wanted to go on the stage. "Would you care to see me do the sleepwalking scene from *Macbeth*? 'Out, out, damned spot!' " Hepburn flings the line off in her grand Yankee accent, and then turns wryly reminiscent: "The teachers at Miss Porter's school thought it was very promising," she cracks, tapping the still unlit cigarette on her thumbnail.

After Johnny confesses his plans for a "holiday" (not "just to play," but to find out "why I'm working"), the private conversation gives way to frivolous action. Ned and Julia make an entrance, having returned from church. Ned doodles at the piano, reluctantly playing a few bars of a pseudo-Gershwin-esque "Symphony in F Minor" that is supposed to indicate his latent talent as a composer, and Linda becomes gleeful, drawing Johnny into a rehearsal for his upcoming interview with Edward Seton. (Notice once again that the technique bears a resemblance to *Henry IV, Part One*, where characters parody scenes that are later played in earnest.) "Ned," she says to her brother, "I think we can give him some coaching." Lew Ayres picks up a banjo and Hepburn goes into an act, pretending to be a sour patriarch inquiring about his prospective son-in-law. Clearing her throat and folding her arms across her chest, she looks at Grant sternly: "Well, young man?" Grant smiles: "Well, sir, at the moment I have in my pocket exactly thirty-four dollars and a coupon for a bank night."

Julia insists that Johnny ought to take things more seriously, but Hepburn quickly tosses off a whole series of impersonations. "I'm afraid he won't do, Julia," she says in a male drawl. "He's a comely boy, but probably just another of the vast army of clock watchers." When Johnny admits his humble origins, she rears back in the mock astonishment of a society matron: "You mean to say that your mother wasn't even a *whosis*?" Ned interjects that Johnny may have a judge somewhere in the family. "Yes! That might help," she says, and as Ned strums a ditty on the banjo she transforms her act into a minstrel show. "Ol' Jedge Case's boy! Evenin', Massa!" Ned then suggests that a little namedropping would be useful, and Hepburn reverts to her parody of a socialite; standing tall, one hand on her hip, she sashays over to Grant: "Johnny, she says to me (she always calls me Johnny). . . ."[17]

Later in the film during the massive New Year's Eve engagement party Edward Seton arranges for Julia, the behavior in the upstairs room becomes even more theatrical, with everyone joining in the act. Soon after the Potters arrive and introduce themselves to Linda, Ned enters like the pied piper, playing on a whistle and leading a platoon of waiters with champagne. Linda organizes the group into a quartet for a rendition of "Camptown Races," and Nick Potter acts the balcony scene from *Romeo and Juliet* with hand puppets. Johnny, sent upstairs by Julia to persuade everyone to come to the reception below, pretends to be a butler delivering a message. As punishment for his stuffy behavior, the other four make him run the gauntlet. Nick makes a comic public speech, presenting Johnny with the toy giraffe from the earlier scene as a "trophy." Johnny stands on the couch and bows shyly to applause, and then offers to demonstrate his acrobatic skill, teaching Linda how to do a back flip.

Throughout this busy action, the players assume childlike attitudes, putting their feet on the furniture and sprawling on the floor—a device common to many of the thirties screwball comedies, in which wealthy characters are made to seem charmingly irresponsible and "human" by virtue of their posture. Despite the apparent abandon of the party, however, Hepburn is at the center of most of the compositions, and she has a good chance to display the angular grace of her body. A lovely figure in a dark dress, she smiles radiantly and moves with a kind of swashbuckling élan—as when she steps over the back of a couch, plants one foot on the pillowcase, and snatches a champagne bottle off a table. When the festivity is interrupted by the entrance of Seton Cram and his wife (Henry Daniell and Binnie Barnes), she mutters "It's the Witch and Dopey" in a stage whisper and perches atop the backrest of a chair. Crossing her legs, she leans forward and props her elbow on her knee, resting her chin in her hand in a pose that contrasts with the stuffy postures of Daniell and Barnes, making her look as lanky and appealing as the young Stewart or Fonda.

The scene also allows Hepburn to ad-lib an occasional line and behave "amateurishly," as when she harmonizes with the other actors in the singing of "Camptown Races." The result is a sense of the star as "real" person—as if the process of acting silly candidly revealed her nonprofessional attributes, making her seem less like a highbrow. *Bringing Up Baby* is filled with such scenes; for instance, when Hepburn and Grant sing their famous duet of "I Can't Give You Anything But Love, Baby," the humor derives partly from our recognition of two remotely glamorous stars who are behaving a little awkwardly, like people we might encounter at a party. The equivalent moment in *Holiday* comes when Grant teaches Hepburn how to do a somersault—a piece of action devised especially for this film. It hardly matters that the double flip is actually executed by stunt people; the illusion is perfectly maintained, and the action leading up to the trick is both amusing and graceful, clearly alluding to the fact that Grant had begun his show business career as a tumbler.

The stunt begins as Hepburn and Grant step onto the back of a couch, pushing forward with their feet so that it tips and carries them into the air like dancers. They

---

[17]Some of this mockery seems a bit strained, since Grant and Hepburn embody all the traits of sophisticated society. The problem is especially evident in a previous scene, when Grant describes himself as a "plain man of the people." The self-deprecating, ironic twist he gives to his voice cannot save the line from absurdity.

Performance within performance.

acknowledge the applause of the other characters, and Grant lifts Hepburn onto his shoulders, where she stands like a brave, giddy amateur, holding her long skirt in her hand. For a moment, the narrative and characterization become less interesting than the spectacle of the star, who seems relatively unguarded.

"In working with [Hepburn]," John Houseman wrote many years later, "I made a fascinating discovery about star quality in general and hers in particular. Kate had learned . . . that stardom is achieved through beauty, intelligence, courage and energy but, above all, through the bravura that an audience comes to expect from its favorite performers. In every star role there are one or more opportunities for such peaks. If not, they must be created—as they were, in different ways, by Duse, Bernhardt, Terry and all the others."[18] The somersault with Grant is just such a "peak," designed to emphasize Hepburn's beauty and adventurousness, giving the spectators a moment of pure voyeurism, when they seem to glimpse the star enjoying herself.

But if the joyful performance-within-performance in the upstairs room allows Hepburn to show off in a charming way, subsequent developments give her an opportunity to behave like a straightforward dramatic actress. As I have already suggested, the film is filled with calculated displays of expressive incoherence—"actorly" moments that reveal the conflict between Linda Seton's public and private self. Sometimes her technique is localized in a line of dialogue, as when she wishes Johnny "Happy New Year" in a voice that quavers with *chagrin d'amour*. Or it can be seen in her gestures and movement, as in the climactic scene in the Seton drawing room, when Johnny breaks off with Julia and walks out. Hepburn clasps her arm along her stomach and sits down on the arm of a chair as if she had lost her breath. "I'll miss that man," she says, gallantly concealing her love from the family while making it plain to us.

---

[18]John Houseman, 87.

Hepburn and Grant prepare for a double somesault.

An especially dynamic example of what I have described in chapter four as "disclosive compensation" occurs during Julia's engagement party. Deciding to put her sister's happiness first, Linda leaves the playroom and goes downstairs, where she must put on an insincere act for the guests and at the same time try to repair the strained relation between Johnny and Julia. In extreme long shot, Hepburn steps into a hallway, pauses to adjust her hair, and walks to a staircase. Another long shot, photographed from a crane, shows her moving downward in a curve as waltz music wells up from below. She pauses at a landing and glances at the party like a player about to enter a stage; then a second crane shot shows her quick descent of the next staircase. At the bottom, her rather intense expression breaks into a smile and she greets two figures in formal dress who rush up to her. "Isn't it divine?" one of them says. An elderly lady enters the shot to offer congratulations, mistaking Linda for Julia; Hepburn continues to smile, exchanging polite words, and then moves quickly to the left, the camera panning as she weaves through a crowd. During the movement, her expressions alternate systematically between cheerful responses to the guests and anxious little glances around the room in our direction, as if she were looking for Johnny and Julia. Her growing urgency is conveyed not only by the timing and placement of these glances but also by her erect, increasingly rapid walk; as the camera pans along the landing, her stride becomes longer, almost breaking into a run but masking tension as happy excitement.

At last she sees Doris Nolan and rushes to embrace her, making congratulatory remarks in a loud voice for the benefit of the party. Nolan whispers that Grant has disappeared, and Hepburn looks quickly, anxiously around the room. Moving Nolan toward a nearby doorway, she glances back over her shoulder, smiles, and makes a little joke with one of the guests. She and Nolan then enter a darkened, "backstage" area of the house and have a sotto voce conversation, after which Hepburn goes back out into the party once again, fraught with worry about her sister and desperately looking for Grant. A crane shot shows her descending a third staircase toward the ground floor; the waltz music swells and the crowd grows thick. Again the camera pans as she moves neatly across the ballroom, maneuvering past knots of people, her head tossed back in apparent gaiety. "Hello! How's Baltimore?" she says to one of the guests, as she quickens her long steps. Smiling broadly, she opens a doorway into another "backstage" room. A cut shows that she has entered the kitchen, where her smile falls completely away. She dashes across the room toward a servant's entrance, while the kitchen maid tells her that Grant has just left. A close-up shows her arriving at the open back door, where she stands looking out as the maid offers congratulations on the forthcoming marriage. The camera tracks toward her face and the noise of distant traffic flickers on the soundtrack. Wind softly blows her hair and scarf while she gazes out into the night, her expression a commingling of sadness, longing, and admiration for Grant's flight.

Hepburn's elaborate journey through the Seton mansion seems to me to encapsulate most of the issues I have been discussing. It is first of all a considerable technical achievement—a series of lengthy, complex shots in which she skillfully modulates between the character's "private" and "public" expressions, all the while timing her gestures and movements to accommodate the camera and the other players. But in the context of the narrative her technique takes on additional value. By a process of association rather than logic, our appreciation of Hepburn's graceful behavior in difficult circumstances becomes wedded to our admiration for Linda Seton's poise under duress, two forms of theatricality joining to support one another. The synthesis between star and character also functions to control the ideological tensions provoked by Hepburn's style: she walks with athletic, independent energy through a ballroom, acting as the prime agent of the narrative, but at the end of the sequence she expresses yearning for a man in the distance; she crosses the set and speaks her lines with arisocratic panache, but she plays a woman who wants to escape from "one of America's six best families"; her passionate, idealistic, grandly theatrical manner is given full rein, but it is motivated by Linda Seton's need to put on a mask at a formal gathering.

Clearly, *Holiday* has been designed to heighten and glamorize aspects of Hepburn's screen personality even while it guards against the radical or unpopular implications she brought to her performances. Like most star vehicles, it tries to foster a harmonious and undisturbing relationship between the three ways an actor may be regarded by audiences: as subject in the culture, as professional thespian, and as literary character. In Hepburn's case, however, this process was difficult: she was such a strong, unusual actor that she made contradictions or social conflicts beneath the script seem evident. Thus, despite the skill of her work in *Holiday,* and despite the film's attempt to construct her as a popular image, audiences and producers continued to regard her suspiciously as a patrician and a feminist. Perhaps the world of this particular film was too rarefied, even when the heiress character abandoned her father's house; perhaps the male lead was too extraordinary, even when he dressed in a rumpled suit and did circus tricks; perhaps Linda Seton seemed too liberated, even when she sailed off happily ever after with a husband. Whatever the reason, other narrative contexts and other collaborations were necessary before Hepburn could become an appealing object of consumption and a legend of the movies.

1988

MOLLY HASKELL
FROM FROM REVERENCE TO RAPE

FEMALE STARS OF THE 1940s

Molly Haskell's *From Reverence to Rape: The Treatment of Women in the Movies* (1973) examines the roles played by women in film and what these roles tell us about the place of women in society, changing gender dynamics, and shifting definitions of love and family. Haskell argues that women were being increasingly objectified and vilified in the films of the 1960s and 70s. This feminist perspective informs all of Haskell's work, which takes a nuanced view of the complex relation of men and women to film and power. *Holding My Own in No Man's Land: Women and Men, Film and Feminists* (1997) includes essays and interviews on feminist issues surrounding film and literature. Haskell provides analyses and appreciations of proto-feminist films of the thirties, forties, and fifties, celebrating actresses like Mae West and Doris Day for their unique forms of empowerment. She continues to write reviews for *Town and Country* and *The Village Voice*.

The preoccupation of most movies of the forties, particularly the "masculine" genres, is with man's soul and salvation, rather than with woman's. It is man's prerogative to follow the path from blindness to discovery, which is the principal movement of fiction. In the bad-girl films like *Gilda* and *Out of the Past*, it is the man who is being corrupted, his soul which is in jeopardy. Women are not fit to be the battleground for Lucifer and the angels; they are something already decided, simple, of a piece. Donna Reed finally refused to make any more movies with Alan Ladd because he always had a scene (it was in his contract) in which he would leave the little woman in the outer office, or some equivalent, while he went off to deal with the Big Problem that only a man could handle. Even the musicals of the forties—the Donen–Kelly collaborations—concentrate on man's quest, on his rather than her story.

In the penumbral world of the detective story, based on the virile and existentially skeptical work of writers like Hammett, Chandler, Cain, and David Goodis (which found its way into crime films like *Dark Passage*, *The Blue Dahlia*, *Farewell My Lovely*, *Double Indemnity*, *I Wake Up Screaming*, and *The Big Sleep*), the proliferation of women—broads, dames, and ladies in as many shapes and flavors, hard and soft centers as a Whitman's sampler—was a way of not having to concentrate on a single woman, and again, of reducing woman's stature by siphoning her qualities off into separate women.

501

Although Howard Hawks would seem to fall into this tradition with *The Big Sleep*, in which he actually increases the number of women from the Chandler novel, there is something in the women and in Hawks' conception of them that suggests a real, if not entirely articulated, sense of a woman's point of view (or at least an antisexist point of view) that will become increasingly apparent in the work of this supposed "man's director." In contrast to most crime melodramas, where plot and its unraveling are all, the plot of *The Big Sleep* is next to incomprehensible, and the women are what it is all about: Lauren Bacall's sleek feline lead, Martha Vickers' spoiled, strung-out younger sister, Dorothy Malone's deceptively dignified bookstore clerk, Peggy Knudsen's petulant gangster's moll, and an unbilled woman taxi driver. Their lechery is as playful as the plot, and they are not stock figures of good and evil but surprisingly mixed and vivid, some of them in roles lasting only a few moments.

By including women in traditionally male settings (the newspaper office in *His Girl Friday*, the trapping party in *The Big Sky*, the big-game hunters in *Hatari!*), Hawks reveals the tension that other directors conceal or avoid by omitting women or by relegating them to the home. Many of Ford's thirties' and forties' films have no women in them at all, whereas even in Hawks' most rough-and-tumble, male oriented films, the men are generally seen in relation to women, and women are the point of reference and exposition.

Hawks is both a product of sexual puritanism and male supremacy, and, in the evolution of his films and the alternation-compensation between tragedy and comedy, a critic of it. In the group experience of filmmaking, he lives out the homoerotic themes of American life, literature, and his own films. Thus, the John Wayne older-man figure in *Rio Bravo* and its companion westerns seems finally to have developed into a "complete" man, to the point where he is able to go it alone, to find his self-esteem within himself rather than from the admiration of his friends, and to greet a "complete" woman on her own terms. Like most American men, Hawks and Ford and their protagonists become more at ease with women as they grow older. In his early adventure films, in which the women repeatedly break up male friendships and the men do little to resist what filmwriter Robin Wood has called the "lure of irresponsibility," Hawks betrays the sensibility of an arrested adolescent. His fear of woman is twofold: (1) as the emotional and "unmanly" side of human nature, and (2) as its progenitor. He is like the young boy who, in recoiling from his mother's kiss, refuses to acknowledge his debt of birth to her and who simultaneously fears revealing his own feelings of love and dependency.

In *Only Angels Have Wings*, Jean Arthur provides an alternative to the all-male world of stoical camaraderie on the one hand, and to the destructive femininity represented by Rita Hayworth on the other, but what an alternative! A man dies trying to land a plane in a storm in time for a date with her, she breaks down in defiance of the prevailing stiff-upper-lip ethic, and thereafter she hangs around like a puppy dog waiting for Cary Grant to fall in love with her. For female Hawksians, this is the film most difficult to accept, more difficult than the early films in which women figure only as devils *ex machina*. Although the relationship Jean Arthur offers Grant seems to have been conceived as something "different but equal," women feel it (as

Hawks seems to have felt it) as second best. In the all-male community of civil aviators Grant heads up, the central relationship is the tacit, mutual devotion between Grant and Thomas Mitchell. In a milieu of constant, physical danger and sublimated feelings, Arthur's emotionalism is a threat—but it is also, or it is meant to be, a release. The trouble is that Arthur, deprived of the pepperiness and sense of purpose she has in her other thirties' and forties' films (or the sweetly misplaced glamour of *Easy Living*), becomes a sobbing stone around the collective neck of civil aviation; and she doesn't have the easy come–easy go sexual confidence with which Lauren Bacall and Angie Dickinson invest Slim and Feathers, Hawks' most sensually aggressive, European-style heroines. Still, technically, *Only Angels Have Wings* is a transition film. When Mitchell dies, Arthur takes his place, marking the progression of woman from second to first string.

Ball of Fire is a perfect fusion of Hawks' dialectics and those of Brackett and Wilder, who wrote the screenplay. When Barbara Stanwyck as a fast-talking gangster's moll invades the sanctuary of a group of lexicographers headed by Gary Cooper, it is as if Hawks had recognized the sclerotic danger of male camaraderie—and was resisting it. But Sugarpuss O'Shea is as much a Wilder–Brackett creation, a worldly, romantic sensualist who shakes up a group of typically American fuddy-duddies and "regenerates" them. Stanwyck is as emotionally responsive as Jean Arthur, but tougher; she brings her own world of jive and street talk with her, and manages to "corrupt" the ivory-tower purity of the scholars—and expand their vision. Her humanizing influence paves the way for the rapprochement of the sexes that occurs in Hawks' subsequent films, particularly in the Bogart–Bacall melodramas, and in the John Wayne–Angie Dickinson relationship in *Rio Bravo*. If the highest tribute Hawks can pay a woman is to tell her she has performed like a man (Bogey's "You're good, you're awful good"), isn't that, at least partly, what the American woman has always wanted to be told? Hasn't she always wanted to join the action, to be appreciated for her achievements rather than for her sex? But one often seems to have been gained at the expense of the other, the performing excellence at the cost of the "womanly" awareness. Hawks' sensitivity to the American girl's anxiety, to her shame at "being a girl," expresses itself later in such fifties' characters as Charlene Holt in *Red Line 7000*, and Paula Prentiss in *Man's Favorite Sport?* As actresses, and as characters, they lack the usual coordinates of "sex appeal"; both their athletic ability and their anxiety bespeak a lack of sexual confidence that is disturbingly real. In *Man's Favorite Sport?* it is Paula Prentiss who makes Rock Hudson take the plunge into the sport (fishing, or, on an allegorical level, sex) on which he is supposed to be an authority. He has written a "how to" book without ever having gotten his feet wet.

In Hawks' best films, there is a sense of playacting for real, of men and women thrusting themselves ironically at each other, auditioning for acceptance but finding out in the process who they really are. In *To Have and Have Not*, Bacall combines intelligence and sensuality, pride and submission. She holds her own. She is a singer and is as surrounded by her "musical world" as Bogart is by his underground one, and she combines with him to create one of the great perfectly balanced couples, as highly defined by fantasy and wit as Millamant and Mirabell in *The Way of the World*, or as Emma Woodhouse and Mr. Knightley in *Emma*. For the Hawks' heroine, the vocal quality, the facial and bodily gestures are the equivalent of the literary heroine's words, and with these she engages in a thrust-and-parry as highly inflected and intricate as the great love duels of literature.

The fable of *To Have and Have Not*, like so many of the action melodramas during the forties (for example, *Casablanca*) is that of the tough guy who "doesn't believe in" patriotic action or sticking his neck out, and who eventually sticks his neck out farther and more heroically than anyone else. In *To Have and Have Not*, it is Bogart's willingness to risk death, pshawing all the while, to bring a French Resistance fighter into Martinique, under the eyes of the Vichy government. But there is an additional, and even more important, meaning to the idea of involvement in Hawks, the involvement of a man with a woman, a scarier and deeper risk of oneself, perhaps, than death.

Typically, a man (in *Only Angels Have Wings*, *To Have and Have Not*, and *Rio Bravo*) is avoiding women like the plague. He has been badly burned and he doesn't want to get involved. But he, we are entitled to think, doth protest too much. Like the woman's child obsession in the woman's film, which conceals a secret desire to be rid of her offspring, the single man's retreat from marriage conceals a contrary desire. Otherwise, why would he leave so many strings for her to seize upon? (There are very few such "strings," and little sense of heterosexual need, in the action films of the sixties and seventies, which is one of the differences between then and now, and between Hawks and his colleagues and successors.) But it is the woman who has to bring the man around to seeing and claiming the invisible ties (in *To Have and Have Not*, Bacall asks Bogey to walk around her, and then says, "See? No strings," while he is tripping over them without realizing it). The man backs off, using as a pretext or real motive his disapproval of the woman's past. They exchange roles: The woman "proves herself" by playing it his way, by showing her physical courage or competence. And through a respect for her, first on his own terms, then on hers, he is brought around to a more "feminine" point of view.

Because proving themselves to each other is so fundamentally important for the action here, and for Hawks' men, a woman who is (behaves, thinks) like a man is the transitional step to heterosexual love. In some ways this tribute to love means more coming from a "man's director" than if it had come from a "woman's director." *To Have and Have Not* is so far from the machismo mold of the Hemingway original that the Resistance Frenchman's courage is not in being willing to die, but in having brought along the woman whose presence "weakened" him, by making him concerned for her safety. His heroism, for which he will win no medals, is to have accepted the consequences of heterosexual love. And she, as a spoiled, destructive girl, redeems herself when she understands this. *To Have and Have Not* ultimately contradicts the mystique of those forties' films that, in pretending to deprecate heroics, are most infatuated with them as judged by and performed for men themselves. In the end of *Casablanca*, it is with Claude Rains that Bogart walks off into the Moroccan mist, the equivalent of the lovers' sunset; in *To Have and Have Not*, it is with Lauren Bacall. *Casablanca* reaps the conventional glory for an act—rejection—that is easiest; *To Have and Have Not*, opting for the love that is least honored in the virility ethic, is more truly glorious.

Under Hawks' supervision (being forced, the story goes, to yell at the top of her lungs on a mountaintop, to deepen her voice), Lauren Bacall's Slim is one of film's richly superior heroines and a rare example of a woman holding her own in a man's world. Her characters in *The Big Sleep* and *To Have and Have Not* are romantic paragons, women who have been conceived in what remains, essentially, a "man's world." But in the forties, certain movie stars emerged with distinctive, highly intelligent points of view (strong women like Davis, Crawford, Hepburn, and Russell), which they imposed openly or surreptitiously on the films they made. In this, either as stars or in the parts they played, they corresponded to certain kinds of women that literature had abstracted, over the years, from life. Because society dictated the proper, and severely restricted, domain for women, those who didn't "fit"—the "extraordinary women"—were tortured and frustrated; hence, the "neurotic woman." Finding no outlet for her brains or talent except as wife and mother, she dissipates her energies, diverts them, or goes outside society. Of such women, literature gives us two basic types, one European, the other Anglo-Saxon.

The first, and basically European model, is the "superfemale"—a woman who, while exceedingly "feminine" and flirtatious, is too ambitious and intelligent for the docile role society has decreed she play. She is uncomfortable, but not uncomfortable enough to rebel completely; her circumstances are too pleasurable. She remains within traditional society, but having no worthwhile project for her creative energies, turns them onto the only available material—the people around her—with demonic results. Hedda Gabler, Emma Bovary, and Emma Woodhouse are literary superfemales of the first order.

The other type is the "superwoman"—a woman who, like the "superfemale," has a high degree of intelligence or imagination, but instead of exploiting her femininity, adopts male characteristics in order to enjoy male prerogatives, or merely to survive. In this category are the transsexual impersonators (Shakespeare's Rosalind and Viola) who arrogate male freedoms along with their clothes, as well as the Shavian heroines who assume "male logic" and ideology to influence people—and who lose friends and, most triumphantly, make enemies in the process.

Scarlett and Jezebel, Vivien Leigh and Bette Davis, are superfemales. Sylvia Scarlett and Vienna, Joan Crawford and (often) Katharine Hepburn, are superwomen. The southern heroine, because of her conditioning and background, is a natural superfemale. Like the European woman, she is treated by men and her society with something close to veneration, a position she is not entirely willing to abandon for the barricades. Rather than rebel and lose her status, she plays on her assets, becomes a self-exploiter, uses her sex (without ever surrendering it) to gain power over men. Romantically attractive, even magnetic, she is not sexual (though more so than her northern counterpart, hence the incongruity, even neurosis, in the New England Davis' southern belle performances); she is repressed more from Victorianism than puritanism, and instinctively resists any situation in which she might lose her self control. (The distinction between North and South obtains in the literary "superfemales" as well; the "Northern European" types, Hedda Gabler and Emma Woodhouse, suggest respectively sexual frigidity and apathy; Mme Bovary, being more Mediterranean, is more likely to have found sexual satisfaction.)

Bette Davis, superfemale and sometime southern belle, was not born in the South at all, but in Lowell, Massachusetts, of an old, respectable Protestant family. The only clue in her background to the seething polarities of toughness and vulnerability expressed in her roles was the trauma (glossed over in her autobiography) of her father's desertion of the family when she was only a child. She was supported in her theatrical career by her mother, Ruthie, who was also her lifelong friend, even as she progressed (or regressed) from the guardian of her struggling daughter to the spoiled charge of her successful one. All this might or might not explain the conflicting impulses of the Davis persona (in tandem or from film to film): the quicksilver shifts between distrust and loyalty, the darting, fearful eyes, and the bravura, the quick wit of the abruptly terminated sentences, the defensiveness, and the throttled passion.

She was the wicked girl who sometimes was, sometimes wasn't, so bad underneath, while Crawford was the self-made gracious lady with ice water for blood. At some point (Crawford in *Rain* and *A Woman's Face*) each of them was bisected by the puritan ethic into two mutually exclusive extremes of good and evil. But even in her double role in *A Stolen Life*, when she played Katy, the sweet-and-passive sister and her bitch twin, Pat, Davis did not really draw a radical distinction between the two (as de Haviland did in *The Dark Mirror*), thus suggesting the interdependence of the two halves.

In the beginning of her career, Davis was just plain Katy ("the cake," as Glenn Ford describes her, in contrast to Pat, "without the frosting"). In her first picture, *Bad Sister*, reportedly one of the worst films ever made, Davis was not the eponymous hellion (that was Zasu Pitts) but her simpering, virtuous sibling. "Embarrassment always made me have a one-sided smile," she recounts in her autobiography, "and since I was constantly embarrassed in front of a camera, I constantly smiled in a one-sided manner."

She was universally considered unsexy, not to say unusable: still, when her contract expired she managed to hang on until she was taken up by Warners. Her lack of success or star status became an asset, as she was able to take parts—like Mildred in *Of Human Bondage*—that nobody else would touch. This was her first villainess, and her enthusiasm extended to the makeup, which she persuaded director John Cromwell to let her apply herself. In so doing, she thus gained the upper hand, which she would use whenever she could (and not always to her own advantage), and demonstrated that feeling for greasepaint grotesque that only she could get away with, and sometimes even she could not.

She determined to make it very clear "that Mildred was not going to die of a dread disease looking as if a deb had missed her noon nap. The last stages of consumption, poverty and neglect are not pretty and I intended to be convincing-looking. We pulled no punches and Mildred emerged as a reality—as immediate as a newsreel and as starkly real as a pestilence." (Actually, Davis' notions of feminine vanity and excesses, daring as they often are, have led her into those parodies of womanhood that are closer to Grand Guignol than newsreel, and that have surrounded her with camp followers whose image of her obliterates her real strengths.)

From then on, she was one of the few actresses willing—even eager—to play against audience sympathy. In her southern belle phase, she managed to combine the vanity of the "deb" with the venality of Mildred. Even in her superfemale roles, the charm has a cutting edge—the taunting Julie Marsden of *Jezebel* (the consolation role for missing out on Scarlett); the "jinx" actress, Joyce Heath, patterned on Jeanne Eagels, in *Dangerous* (for which she won the consolation Academy Award denied her for *Of Human Bondage*); the mortally ill socialite, Judith Traherne, in *Dark Victory*; and the frivolous Fanny Trellis of *Mr. Skeffington*.

The superfemale is an actress by nature; what is flirtation, after all, but role-playing? Coquetry is an art, and Davis exulted in the artistry. In *Jezebel*, she captivates her beaux but with less natural effervescence than Scarlett. Davis is more neurotic than Vivien Leigh, less cool. When coolness is called for, Davis gives us a cold chill: when warmth, a barely suppressed passion. Her charm, like her beauty, is something willed into being. It is not a question of whether she is inside or outside the part (for curiously she is both) but of the intensity of her conviction, a sense of character in the old-fashioned sense of "moral fiber." Through sheer, driving guts she turns herself into a flower of the Old South, and in that one determined gesture reveals the bedrock toughness of the superfemale that we discover only by degrees in Scarlett.

Davis' reputation is based on a career composed of equal parts art, three-star trash, and garbage, sometimes all in the same film—which makes fine critical distinctions difficult. Warners gave her a hard time, and she reciprocated. (She even brought a lawsuit against them once, which she lost, but in so doing, she paved the way for future action on actors' behalf.) William Wyler was her toughest and best director—on *Jezebel*, *The Letter*, and *The Little Foxes*—but she broke with him over *The Little Foxes*. She was in an invisible competition with Tallulah Bankhead, who had played Regina brilliantly on Broadway, and from whom she also inherited (and probably improved upon) *Jezebel* and *Dark Victory*. Surely none of these films was a "betrayal" of the original stage play, and as to who outshone whom, only those who have witnessed both can decide—and even they, given the fierce, partisan loyalties these two women inspire, are not entirely trustworthy.

For all her enmities, Davis really was a friend to other actresses, content to take the back seat and let them run with the showy parts. (Actually, some of her "backseat" parts—the sweet-tempered but strong girl in *The Great Lie*—are some of her most appealing and underrated roles.) Mary Astor tells the story of how she and Davis built her—Mary's—part in *The Great Lie* into an Academy Award-winning performance. Every day before shooting they added material to the screen play, to make Mary look good as well as to enliven the movie, and between them (and with the sympathetic direction of Edmund Goulding) they created one of the most complex women's relationships in a woman's film. They are cast as stereotypes: Astor, the sophisticated and selfish concert pianist who wants George Brent more than his baby; Davis, Brent's Baltimore bride, who makes a deal with Astor for the baby when they think Brent is dead. Their relationship during Astor's delivery alternates between tenderness and spite, love and hate, as Davis plays the "father" (in jodhpurs, pacing the floor) to Astor's mother.

Part of Davis' greatness lies in the sheer, galvanic force she brought to the most outrageous and unlikely roles, giving an intensity that saved them, usually, from camp. Even when she is "outside" a part (through its, or her, unsuitability), she is dynamic. As the harridan housewife of *Beyond the Forest*, she surveys her despised domestic kingdom and says "What a dump!" and we are with her. By the time Martha in *Who's Afraid of Virginia Woolf?* says the same line, it has already been consecrated as camp. In spite of the fact that the only way we can think of Davis as a femme fatale is if she contemplates murder or literally kills somebody (*The Letter, The Little Foxes*), she makes us accept her as a girl men fight duels over and die for. She is constantly being cast against type as a heartbreaker, and then made to pick up the pieces when foolish hearts shatter. As the actress "witch" (*Dangerous*) whose stage presence has caused suicides and inspired epiphanies, she is made to do penance, for the rest of her life, with her Milquetoast husband. But if we look closely, here and elsewhere, it is not she but others who insist on her supernatural evil, who throw up a smoke screen of illusions, who invoke mystical catchwords to explain her "magic" or her "jinx," why she is "different" from other women.

In her film career, Davis casts a cold eye, and not a few dampening remarks, on sentimentality. When Claude Rains, as the doting Mr. Skeffington, tells her "A woman is beautiful only when she is in love," Davis, miserable over the discovery of her pregnancy, replies, "A woman is beautiful if she has eight hours of sleep and goes to the beauty parlor every day. And bone structure has a lot to do with it."

In King Vidor's *Beyond the Forest*, her wildest and most uncompromising film, one she herself dislikes, she plays the evil Rosa Moline, married to Joseph Cotton's small-town doctor. He is seen as "good" because he goes without, and makes his wife go without, so his impecunious patients won't have to pay their bills—and will "love" the good doctor. His "virtue" succeeds in driving his wife into further malice. One of the earliest discontented housewives on record, Rosa sashays around wearing a long black wig, like her surly housekeeper, Dona Drake, who is a dark-skinned lower-class parody of her. Davis' obsession is to go to Chicago, and to this end she wrecks everyone's lives. In one of the film's most modern, angst-ridden scenes, she wanders the back streets of Chicago, staggering through the rain (having been turned out of a bar where women "without escorts" are not allowed), looking like another star who would later claim her influence—Jeanne Moreau in *La Notte*.

"I don't want people to love me," Rosa says—one of the most difficult things for a woman to bring herself to say, ever, and one of the most important. It is something Davis the actress must have said. Thus, does the superfemale become the superwoman, by taking life into her own hands, her own way.

Davis' performance in *Beyond the Forest*, as a kind of female W. C. Fields, and Vidor's commitment to her, are astonishing. Even though she is contrasted with a "good woman" (Ruth Roman) to show that she is the exception, that all women are not like that (a moralistic pressure that Hollywood is not the only one to exercise— the French government made Godard change the title of *The Married Woman* to *A Married Woman*), the Ruth Roman character has little moral weight or value. As Rosa Moline, Davis creates her own norms, and is driven by motives not likely to appeal to the average audience. She is ready and eager to give up husband, position, security, children (most easily, children), even lover; for what? Not for anything so noble as "independence" in terms of a job, profession, or higher calling, but to be rich and fancy in Chicago! And here is Davis, not beautiful, not sexy, not even young, convincing us that she is all these things—by the vividness of her own self-image, by the vision of herself she projects so fiercely that we have no choice but to accept it. She is smart, though, smarter than everyone around her. She says it for all smart dames when David Brian tells her he no longer loves her, that he's found the "pure" woman of his dreams. "She's a book with none of the pages cut," he says.

"Yeah," Davis replies, "and nothing on them!"

Since she began as a belle and emerged as a tough (in *Beyond the Forest* she is a crack shot and huntress), Davis' evolution from superfemale to superwoman was the most dramatic, but she was by no means the only actress in the forties to undergo such a transformation.[1] Perhaps reflecting the increased number of working women during the war and their heightened career inclinations, other stars made the transition from figurative hoop skirts to functional shoulder pads, and gained authority without necessarily losing their femininity.

The war was *the* major turning point in the pattern and attitudes of (and toward) working women. From 1900 to 1940, women in the labor force had been mostly young, unmarried women in their early twenties who were biding their time until marriage. Suddenly, to fill men's places and aid in the expanded war industries, older, married women were recruited, and from that time to the present (when the typical working woman is forty and married) the median age rose with the percentage of women in the labor force. A poll of working women taken during the war came up with the startling fact that 80 percent wanted to keep their jobs after it was over. After a sharp drop-off following the end of the war—when women were fired with no regard for seniority—married women *did* go back to work, although as late as 1949 it was still frowned upon. This, of course, is the source of the tremendous tension in films of the time, which tried, by ridicule, intimidation, or persuasion, to get women out of the office and back to the home, to get rid of the superwoman and bring back the superfemale.

Rosalind Russell came out of the superfemale closet into superwoman roles fairly early in her career. But in *Craig's Wife*, an adaptation of the George Kelly play, she is not only a superfemale but the definitive superfemale, the housewife who becomes obsessive about her home, the perfectionist housekeeper for whom, finally, nothing else exists. It would be comforting to look upon this film, directed by Dorothy Arzner, as a protest against the mindlessness of housewifery, but, like *The Women*, of which the same claim has been made, it is not so much a satire as an extension, in high relief, of the tics and intellectual tremors of a familiar American type. In *The Women*, as the malicious (and funny and stylish) Mrs. Fowler, Russell is the superfemale par excellence; but in *His Girl Friday*, as the newspaper reporter, in *My Sister Eileen*, as the short-story writer, and in *Take a Letter, Darling*, as the

---

[1] In a characteristically perverse fashion, Ida Lupino went in the opposite direction, from the superwoman matriarch of *The Man I Love* and *The Hard Way* (1942), in which she channels all of her ambitions into promoting her younger sister, to *The Bigamist* (1953), which she herself directed, and in which she plays Edmund O'Brien's mousy, submissive mistress against Joan Fontaine's aggressive career woman. Although Lupino takes the standard anti-career woman position in her treatment of Fontaine, the film presents a positive case for bigamy, or at least suggests that the binary system—one man, one woman, married for life without loopholes—is not the most flexible or realistic arrangement.

business executive, she begins pulling her own weight in a man's world, risks making enemies and losing lovers, becomes, that is, a superwoman.

In *Take a Letter, Darling*, she is the partner in an advertising firm where she began as a secretary. She runs the operation while Robert Benchley, the titular head of the firm, plays miniature golf in his office. He is, to Russell, the kind of benign father figure that Charles Coburn was to Jean Arthur and Irene Dunne. Not in the least bitter at Russell's success, he is quite happy to have been "kicked upstairs" and gives her support and advice whenever she comes to him. At one point, he complains that her competitors—all men, of course—don't understand her:

> "They don't know the difference between a woman and a . . ."
> "A what?" Russell asks.
> "I don't know," Benchley replies, "there's no name for you."

In *My Sister Eileen*, Russell plays the writer-sister trying to sell her stories to a prestigious national magazine. Although the stories concern the escapades of her pretty and popular sister, Russell steals the show as the cerebral one, and gets editor Brian Aherne, too. (The difference in attitudes between the forties and fifties can be seen in the shift of emphasis in the musical remake of *My Sister Eileen* in 1955, in which Betty Garrett retains little dignity as the intellectual sister, but is overshadowed—and shamed—by the popularity of the sister played by Janet Leigh.)[2]

Katharine Hepburn made the transition from superfemale to superwoman most easily and most successfully of all—perhaps because she was already halfway there to begin with. In her second film, Dorothy Arzner's *Christopher Strong*, she played an aviatrix torn between her profession and her man. Flying presents an appropriately extreme metaphor for the freedom of the single woman that has to be surrendered once the idea of a family becomes a concrete reality. Torn apart by these conflicting pulls, Hepburn finally dies in a plane crash—that is, she propels herself, like the dancer in *The Red Shoes*, into the abyss between love and career. In both cases, the ending is not just a cautionary warning to deflect women from careers, but a true reflection of the dynamics of the situation: A woman has only so much energy, so much "self" to give; is there enough for profession (especially if it is a dangerous or demanding one), lover, and children? *Christopher Strong* raises these questions, but doesn't really pursue them, and as a consequence it is a less interesting film than it should be, less interesting than Arzner's more "feminist" film, *Dance, Girl, Dance*. But, for all its weaknesses, *Christopher Strong* leaves us with a blazingly electric image of Katharine Hepburn unlike that of any other film: a woman in a silver lamé body-stocking which covers everything but her face—and suggests the chrysalis of the superwoman of the future.

Hepburn, like most tomboy actresses, played Jo in *Little Women*, and shortly thereafter played the eponymous "transvestite" of *Sylvia Scarlett*, one of George Cukor's most enchanting and least-known films. Disguised as a boy, she accompanies her father, a crook on the lam, through the hills of Cornwall. They join forces

---

[2]If Columbia had used the Bernstein musical, with Rosalind Russell retaining her stage role, the move might have been better but no less sexist, with its rousing point-by-point denunciation of feminism: "100 Ways to Lose a Man."

with a troupe of wandering actors, led by Cary Grant, and embark on a free, magical, oneiric adventure, giving plays in the moonlight. Cukor's feeling for the conventions of theater, where he began his career, leads him into a world halfway between theater and life, a world in which disguises are often worn more easily and more "honestly" than native hues. The milieu and the story of *Sylvia Scarlett* have a Shakespearian feel to them, harking back to an age and a theatrical convention in which sex-exchange was permissible. This is Cukor's first film (and last for a while) in which he dared to challenge, in a lyrical stage whisper, our traditional assumptions about male-female roles.

The delicate equilibrium between a man and a woman and between a woman's need to distinguish herself and the social demands on her become the explicit theme of Cukor's great films of the late forties and early fifties, specifically the Judy Holliday films and Hepburn-Tracy vehicles written by the husband-and-wife team of Ruth Gordon and Garson Kanin. Gordon and Kanin wrote a series of seven screenplays for Cukor, three of which dealt, comically and sublimely, with the problems and the chemistry of individuals.

Almost as a parody of the extraordinary individuals represented by Hepburn and Tracy in *Adam's Rib* and *Pat and Mike*, Aldo Ray and Judy Holliday were a typical, dumb, middle-class, well-meaning, ordinary married couple in Cukor's *The Marrying Kind*. Almost a parody, but not quite. For it is one of the glories of the film that the two characters, without ever being patronized and at the same time without ever being lifted above the class and the cliché in which they are rooted, are intensely moving. Ray and Holliday, on the brink of divorce, have come to a woman judge (who, in her relationship with her male assistant, shows both authority and warmth). Through a series of flashbacks reconstructing their marriage we, and they, come to realize that together they are something they never were apart: a unit, a whole. Two ordinary, less-than-complete individuals who have grown into each other to the point where they can be defined only by the word "couple" have no right to divorce. Separately, they are two more swallowers of the American myth, two more victims of its fraudulence: but together, with their children, they add up to something full and affirmative. In losing their child, they are at first destroyed— their "meaning" evaporates. But in that nothingness, old roles dissolve and they must rediscover themselves. Cukor, Gordon, and Kanin are very much aware of the sexual insecurities that arise from too rigid a concept of male-female roles, and suggest, in the visual and verbal motifs of these "companion" films, that through some kind of "merger" of identities, through a free exchange of traits (as when Holliday, in defiance of the law whereby it is the man who "storms out" of the house in a fight, throws herself into the night), a truer sense of the self may emerge.

In the growing isolation of the New York cultural elite from the rest of America in the sixties, this is the side of marriage and the middle class that has been lost to us. We seem to be able to approach middle-America only through giggles of derision (*The Graduate*, *Sticks and Bones*, "All in the Family"): and; in dismissing the housewife as a lower form of life, women's lib confirms that the real gap is cultural and economic rather than sexual. In the difference between the couples in *The Marrying Kind* and *Adam's Rib*, Cukor and company acknowledge the most fundamental intellectual, spiritual, and economic inequality between the educated elite and the less privileged and less imaginative members of lower-middle-class America; but they never deprive them of their dignity, or deny them joys and sorrows and a capacity to feel as great as the poets of the earth. The true emotional oppression—the oppression of blacks by whites, of housewives by working women, is pity. For in such lessons in life as we get from suffering, degrees are granted without reference to class or sex. Finally, most honestly, Holliday's Florence and Ray's Chet are the sheep of the world rather than its shepherds: They are the victims of emotions they haven't the words to express, the tools of a mechanical-industrial society they haven't the knowledge to resist. Their greatest defense against its monolithic oppressiveness, against being overwhelmed by routine, inhumanity, and their "proletarian" identity, is each other, is their identity as a couple. In the final, quite noble strength we feel in them as a couple, they confirm the theory Cukor, Gordon, and Kanin seem to be endorsing: that marriage is an institution ideally suited to the people at both the bottom and the top—the truly ordinary and the truly extraordinary, those who are preserved and protected by it, and those who can bend it to their will.

Hepburn and Tracy were nothing if not extraordinary. While preserving their individuality, they united to form a whole greater than the sum of its parts. As Tracy says to Hepburn in *Pat and Mike*, in a line that could have been written by Kanin–Gordon, Cukor, or Tracy himself and that finally tapers off into infinity, "What's good for you is good for me is good for you. . . ."

This was true of them professionally. They came together at a time when their careers were foundering: misfits in the Hollywood mold, they were not in any way typical romantic leads. Hepburn had grown older, the face that once blushed in gracious concession to femininity now betrayed in no uncertain terms the recalcitrant New England spirit. And Tracy, too short and dumpy for conventional leading roles, hadn't found the woman who could lure him from the rugged, masculine world he inhabited. Out of their complementary incongruities, they created one of the most romantic couples the cinema has ever known. His virility acts as a buffer to her intelligence: she is tempered by him just as he is sharpened by her, and their self-confidence is increased, rather than eroded, by their need for each other.

Adam's Rib, that rara avis, a commercial "feminist" film, was many years ahead of its time when it appeared in 1949, and, alas, still is. Even the slightly coy happy ending testifies to the fact that the film strikes deeper into the question of sexual roles than its comic surface would indicate and raises more questions than it can possible answer.

Tracy and Hepburn play a couple of married lawyers who find themselves on opposite sides of a case: he is the prosecuting attorney, and she, seizing upon the crime and its implications, takes it upon herself to defend the accused. A dopey young wife—Judy Holliday, in her first major movie role—has shot, but not killed, her husband (Tom Ewell) over another woman. Hepburn, reading an account in the newspaper, is outraged by the certainty that the woman will be dealt with harshly while a man in that position would be acquitted by the courts and vindicated by society. Hepburn goes to visit Holliday at the woman's prison, and, in a long, lovely single-take scene, Holliday spills out her story, revealing, comically and pathetically, her exceptionally low consciousness. One of the constant and most relevant sources of comedy in the film is the lack of rapport between Hepburn's militant lawyer, constructing her case on feminist principles, and Holliday's housewife, contrite and idiotically eager to accept guilt. The film raises the means-and-end dilemma which has long been the philosophical thorn in the side of our thinking about the rights and reparations of minority groups. Hepburn marshals evidence of women's accomplishments to prove their equality with men, even to the point of having a lady wrestler lift Tracy onto her shoulders and make a laughingstock of him. She goes *too* far and humiliates him, while he remains a gentleman. She stoops to unscrupulous methods while he maintains strict honor and decorum. But, then, he can afford to, since the law was created by and for him.

Even down to his animal magnetism, Tracy wears the spoiled complacency of the man, but Hepburn, ambitious and intelligent, scrapes the nerves of male authority. An acute sense of the way male supremacy is institutionalized in the "games people play" occurs in two contrasting situations of one-upmanship: Hepburn, fiery about the case she is about to take, is describing it to Tracy on the telephone: Tracy, in a familiar male (or marital) riposte, effectively cuts her off by teasing, "I love you when you get cause-y." This is greeted with delight by audiences, who usually disapprove of Hepburn's "emasculation" of Tracy in court, a more obvious but perhaps a less damaging tactic of bad faith. Cukor gives Hepburn an ally in the Cole Porter–type composer played by David Wayne, a character who seems to stand, at least partially, for Cukor himself. He identifies with Hepburn and, in marital feuds, takes her side against the virile, meat-and-potatoes "straight" played by Tracy. Thus the neutral or homosexual character, when he is sympathetic, can help to restore some of the balance in the woman's favor. But as soon as the Hepburn–Wayne collusion becomes devious or bitchy, the balance shifts, and our sympathy goes, as it should, to Tracy.

The film brilliantly counterpoints and reconciles two basic assumptions: (1) that there are certain "male" qualities—stability, stoicism, fairness, dullness—possessed by Tracy, and that there are certain "female" qualities—volatility, brilliance, intuition, duplicity—possessed by Hepburn; and (2) that each can, and must, exchange these qualities like trading cards. It is important for Hepburn to be ethical, just as it is important for Tracy to be able to concede defeat gracefully, and if she can be a bastard, he can fake tears. If each can do everything the other can do, just where, we begin to wonder, are the boundaries between male and female? The question mark is established most pointedly and uncomfortably when, during the courtroom session, the faces of Holliday and Ewell are transposed, each becoming the other.

But Hepburn and Tracy are not quite so interchangeable, and the success of their union derives from the preservation of their individuality, not rigidly but through a fluctuating balance of concession and assertion. Tracy can be humiliated and still rebound without (too much) loss of ego. Hepburn occasionally can defer to him and still not lose her identity. A purely political-feminist logic would demand that she be given Tracy's head, in unqualified triumph (an ending that some small part of us would like to see), rather than make an equivocal, "feminine" concession to his masculinity. But marriage and love do not flourish according to such logic. Their love is the admission of their incompleteness, of their need and willingness to listen to each other, and their marriage is the certification—indeed, the celebration—of that compromise.

This finally is the greatness of Hepburn's superwoman, and Davis' and Russell's too—that she is able to achieve her ends in a man's world, to insist on her intelligence, to insist on using it, and yet be able to "dwindle," like Millamant in *The Way of the World*, "into marriage," but only after an equal bargain has been struck of conditions mutually agreed on. It is with just such a bargain, and a contract, that Cukor's great Tracy-Hepburn film of the fifties, *Pat and Mike*, is concerned.

For the most part, the superwoman, with her angular personality and acute, even abrasive, intelligence, begins to disappear in the fifties. The bad-girl is whitewashed, or blown up into some pneumatic technicolor parody of herself. Breast fetishism, a wartime fixation of the G.I.'s, came in in the fifties. (Its screen vogue was possibly retarded by the delay in releasing Howard Hughes' *The Outlaw*, introducing Jane Russell's pair to the world.) But even amidst the mostly vulgar fumblings toward sensuality, Cukor was there—with Ava Gardner in *Bhowani Junction* and Sophia Loren in *Heller in Pink Tights*—to give some dignity to the sex goddesses and, in films like *The Actress* and *Born Yesterday*, to pay tribute to the enterprising woman.

1974

RICHARD B. JEWELL

HOW HOWARD HAWKS BROUGHT *BABY* UP: AN *APOLOGIA* FOR THE STUDIO SYSTEM

Richard Jewell's work places filmmakers within the studio context, revealing the financial, contractual, and practical concerns that helped shape the way movies are made. He writes primarily on the history of American film and frequently contributes commentary to DVDs and documentaries on classic Hollywood flims. *The RKO Story* (1985) chronicles the rise and fall of the studio and provides descriptions of many of the films produced there. Now Hugh M. Hefiner chair for the study of American film at the University of Southern California's School of Cinematic Arts, Jewell's most recent book, *The Golden Age of Cinema: Hollywood, 1929–1945* (2007), provides a detailed history of the forces that helped shape the classical Hollywood film, covering business concerns, teachnological developments, cersorship, the star system, and the demands of narrative and genre.

When the merging of studios, exchanges and theaters into a few large corporations, and the extravagances of the "out-spending" era, had brought an end to the independent production, the inelastic methods of bureaucracy replaced the loose practices of democracy in picture making. Now a new idea, instead of having to win the "O.K." of one autocrat of a little kingdom, had to run the gauntlet of editorial boards, production committees, and conferences of various sorts. A multitude of alleged experts awaited the fellow with the new thought, and when his innovation had completed the circuit of the studio's intricate system there was seldom a trace of originality left in it. The sharp shears and heavy smoothing-irons of the experts had transformed the wild, crazy idea to one of the rigid patterns in favor, at the time, with the studio head and his yes-men and yes-women.

Benjamin B. Bampton, 1931

Production methods under this rigid system became mechanized: the "assembly line" appeared in Hollywood. The resulting standardization of pictures caused the downfall of the most important directors during the late twenties. The various branches of production were divided and specialized so specifically and minutely that directors had a lessening opportunity to contribute to the whole. Most directors became "glorified foremen" under the producer-supervisors.

Lewis Jacobs, 1939

515

Many books and articles dealing with the American cinema have been written since Benjamin Hampton and Lewis Jacobs completed their pioneering studies in the 1930s. Yet the basic descriptions which these two men applied to the studio system, and the general hostility which they expressed toward it, still predominate in contemporary scholarship. No fewer than six recent and major books utilize Jacobs's "factory" and "assembly-line" analogies in their discussions of Hollywood's major studios. Although most qualify their assessments to some extent, the authors of these books tend to agree with Hampton and Jacobs that the studios were bureaucratic, impersonal, conservative, rigidly structured, and antagonistic to technical innovation and artistic achievement. Men and women of taste, intelligence, and imagination are often portrayed as being destroyed by this system—either squandering their talents by producing the formulaic, escapist entertainment demanded by the system, or rebelling against it, only to be crushed (e.g., Von Stroheim) by its steamrolling, assembly-line operations.

The authors often find themselves with a major predicament when they move beyond these general evaluations of the studios to more specific discussions of the filmmakers who worked for them. The writers admire the works of many of these directors, so they are faced with explaining how their favorites could make exemplary films within such a restrictive organizational structure. Here is one representative attempt to reconcile the contradiction:

> These Hollywood directors worked under studio rule, presumably as journeymen employees involved in the mass production of popular entertainment. They were assigned a script rather than choosing one. They were given a cast of performers and told by a producer to shoot the film in so many days. . . . Yet despite all these restrictions and enforced collaborations, somehow these directors, over the years, managed to make films which were stamped with their particular vision.

This type of argument is wonderfully romantic. It conjures up visions of an elite cadre of auteur supermen bending an iron-clad system to their wills or, at the very least, of a slippery band of Houdinis able to wriggle out of their studio straitjackets and "be free." Unfortunately, the explanation does not provide a clue as to how the directors managed these feats of creative hocus-pocus.

The recent availability of studio records—dusty and unmagical though they may be—will help fill in many important gaps in Hollywood scholarship and provide some specific answers to the studio versus auteur dilemma. By studying the production histories of individual films, we gain a more complete understanding of how the studios actually functioned and how auteur directors managed to protect and project their styles and visions while employed by the studios.

My test case is *Bringing Up Baby*, the screwball comedy par excellence, directed by Howard Hawks and released by RKO Radio Pictures in 1938. The story of the making of *Baby* has been pieced together from files in RKO's West Coast archive.

In order to understand how this comedic treasure came to be produced, it is necessary to flash back to late 1935, when Samuel Briskin took charge of production at RKO. Briskin was brought from Columbia to RKO by Leo Spitz, the company's newly appointed corporate president. Although in receivership at the time, RKO was holding its own. *Roberta*, *Alice Adams*, *The Informer*, and *Top Hat* had been released in 1935, and each had received excellent critical notices and performed well at the box office. These films were the product of a unit production system overseen by B. B. Kahane and J. R. McDonough—two executives who allowed their staff producers to handle their pictures with minimal supervision or interference from the front office.

Despite the fine results generated by the system, Spitz followed a well-established principle of corporate management and brought in his "own man" to superintend the studio's filmmaking activities. Sam Briskin had developed a reputation as a tough, stubborn, aggressive executive at Columbia. He was, in the words of Frank Capra, a "hit-first type." Highly ambitious, Briskin must have been delighted to be the top man at RKO after laboring in Harry Cohn's shadow for many years. Briskin's initial move as production chief was to do precisely what Leo Spitz had done— recruit his own staff. By mid-1936, Edward Small, Jesse Lasky, and Howard Hawks were members of the Briskin team, developing projects which he hoped would become hits and strengthen his position at RKO.

Producer-director Hawks was given an exclusive two-year contract that called for a salary of $2500 per week, plus a percentage of the profits from his pictures. The first project to interest him was *Gunga Din*. Staff producer Edward Small had brought the rights to the famous Kipling poem with him to RKO and, after some negotiations, agreed to turn the property over to Hawks for development. Hawks, in turn, interested one of the top writing teams in Hollywood, Ben Hecht and Charles MacArthur, in doing the script, and all three went to New York to work on it. There the writing proceeded at a very leisurely pace; this exasperated Briskin, who periodically informed the threesome of his impatience, but he was powerless to speed them along. Hawks did inform his employer that the story would require three virile male leads, so Briskin began putting out feelers to other studios, hoping to borrow the right stars since RKO had no suitable prospects under contract.

In April 1937, the Hecht-MacArthur script was ready, but Sam Briskin was not. He had failed to convince Louis B. Mayer to lend him Clark Gable, Spencer Tracy, and Franchot Tone, and Ronald Colman had also refused to do the picture. Briskin had no choice but to put *Gunga Din* on the shelf until an appropriate cast could be secured. He, therefore, instructed Hawks to develop something else.

By this time, Howard Hawks had been working for RKO for more than a year without shooting a single frame of film. This reflected negatively on Briskin; a production head's job was to turn out a steady stream of commercially successful pictures, not to pay big salaries to directors who were not making a contribution. Although Briskin might grumble about the length of time required to complete the *Gunga Din* script, he knew that Hawks was not to blame for its postponement. Still, he needed a Hawks film and he needed a good one, for his RKO tenure was not developing as he had hoped. The films made by Briskin's other handpicked producers had, by and large, been an undistinguished and unprofitable lot.

In addition, Sam Briskin had a crucial star problem to solve. Katharine Hepburn had been considered RKO's top female performer when Briskin joined RKO. Beginning with *Sylvia Scarlett*, the studio's first release of 1936, Miss Hepburn had appeared in one flop after another, thereby tarnishing her box office image and diminishing RKO's star roster. This was much more upsetting than the Hawks situation because, compared to its major competitors, RKO was sadly lacking in star power. Since a company sold its product blocks largely by promising to deliver a certain number of films featuring public favorites, it was considered imperative to boost Hepburn back to the lofty position she had once occupied in the show business hierarchy.

Miss Hepburn did not come to mind immediately when Hawks informed Briskin in May that he wished to make a film based on a *Collier's* magazine story entitled "Bringing Up Baby." The RKO story departments had recommended "Baby" for purchase in April, and its head, Robert Sparks, had encouraged Briskin to hire the story's author, Hagar Wilde. Briskin, however, had shown no interest until Hawks made his decision.

Then everything changed. Dudley Nichols, one of RKO's top writers, went to work on the story with Hawks, Miss Wilde was brought out from the East to collaborate with the director and screenwriter, and, in short order, a decision was made to star Katharine Hepburn. The role of daffy socialite Susan Vance would be unlike any part she had played before; perhaps the public would embrace this new Hepburn persona.

The writing continued through the summer of 1937. While Nichols and Wilde developed the script, Briskin and Hawks hunted for the right male lead. Fredric March, Ray Milland, Fred MacMurray, and Leslie Howard were considered before Cary Grant won the job. Grant and Hepburn had worked together before in *Sylvia Scarlett*.

Budget was a matter of special concern to Sam Briskin. Realizing that public hostility to Katharine Hepburn was real enough, at least for the moment, he calculated that *Bringing Up Baby* had little chance of making a profit if it cost much more than a half million dollars. He told Hawks that the script should be prepared so that $600,000 would be the absolute maximum expenditure. Despite this admonition, the director and his writers gave their imaginations free rein. The first estimating script weighed in at a hefty 242 pages, the revised draft at 194 pages, and the final shooting script at 202 pages. Given a certain amount of "overwriting," this still represented a mammoth amount of material. By the time the film was ready to go before the cameras, the budget had been estimated at $767,000 for a fifty-one-day shooting schedule.

Briskin now had three apparent options. He could scrap the film altogether because of the excessive cost; postpone it until script and budget could be brought into line; or allow it to go forward, but instruct Hawks that he must prune the script so that the film would cost no more than $600,000. In reality, the latter was the only viable option. Briskin could not afford to cancel the project for several reasons, including the money that had already been invested in it (Hawks's salary, the writers' salaries, set construction costs, etc.) and the company's need to provide exhibitors with "A" pictures. He could not postpone the film either, because of the nature of the studio commitment system, which, for example, gave RKO the services of Cary Grant for a limited period of time. If Grant were not used during that time, RKO lost him but had to pay his salary anyway.

Therefore, Briskin reluctantly gave Hawks the go-ahead, hoping the director would find a way to whittle down the script and budget. Briskin had become a truly beleaguered executive by this time. His major productions (*The Woman I Love, New Faces of 1937*, and *The Toast of New York*) had proved to be highly disappointing, and he had had more difficulty meeting release schedules than any previous RKO production head. When a company's distribution network promised a film to its most important customers on a certain date and then failed to deliver the picture as promised, it caused shock waves throughout the entire corporate system. Publicity and advertising were disrupted, a mad scramble ensued to find an adequate filler picture, and the film in question often entered the marketplace at a less-than-opportune release time. Most important, the situation damaged the credibility of the studio itself, making exhibitors wary of buying blocks of films from the company in the future.

Briskin definitely needed a breakthrough film to release the pressure that was building against him, and he must have felt that *Bringing Up Baby* could be that film. *Baby* did not even have to be a blockbuster; it would be enough if it returned Katharine Hepburn to public favor, thus breathing life into RKO's moribund star contingent.

Howard Hawks certainly understood all this. He realized that a great deal was riding on *Bringing Up Baby*, and he also realized that, politically speaking, he occupied the true position of power. About six weeks before the film went into production, Briskin's assistant Lou Lusty sent the following memo to his boss. It serves both to confirm the basic auteur contentions about Hawks and to reveal how a cagey director could manipulate the system.

> I know, because the gentleman has said so in so many words that he's only concerned with making a picture that will be a personal credit to Mr. Hawks regardless of its cost—and your [Briskin's] telling him the other day that it would be suicidal to make a Hepburn picture for seven or eight hundred thousand dollars I know made no impression on him at all. . . . Hawks is determined in his own quiet, reserved, soft-spoken manner to have his way about the making of this picture. . . . With the salary he's been getting he's almost indifferent to anything that might come to him on a percentage deal—that's why he doesn't give a damn about how much the picture will cost to make—and you know so well that you couldn't even break even if a Hepburn show cost eight hundred grand. All the directors in Hollywood are developing producer-director complexes and Hawks is going to be particularly difficult.

Shooting commenced on September 27, 1937. In order to protect the studio's interests, Briskin assigned an associate producer to the film. The man chosen was Cliff Reid, a veteran who had worked in the same capacity on John Ford's award-winning RKO film *The Informer*. Reid's job was to "remind" Hawks that the script had to be cut and to make sure the production ran smoothly and efficiently. Reid, however, turned out to be something of a pushover. Disregarding the pressure from both Reid and Briskin, Hawks proceeded at a deliberate pace. Every day the dialogue would be rewritten on the set, causing the company to shoot less than the production department had estimated. Katharine Hepburn had some difficulty learning how to play screwball comedy, so Hawks introduced her to Walter Catlett, who tutored her throughout the rest of the production. Hepburn also missed seven full days due to illness, and Hawks never got around to removing anything from the script. For these and other reasons, the picture quickly fell behind schedule. It soon became obvious that it would go beyond its projected date of completion and exceed its already excessive budget estimate.

These facts did not elude Leo Spitz or the RKO board of directors. A little over one month into the production, Briskin was forced to resign. Although certainly not the sole reason, the chronicle of *Bringing Up Baby* was a factor in Briskin's departure. Production reports indicate that the shooting pace slackened even more after Briskin left. The major question at this point is why RKO did not simply fire Hawks and turn the film over to someone else. One can only speculate, though the reasons seem obvious: the insertion of a new director, who was unfamiliar with both the story and its treatment, would have caused confusion and resentment on the part of cast and crew and, quite probably, have slowed things down even more. It might also have ruined the picture altogether.

Hawks went on working past the November date when the original schedule indicated completion, beyond the holidays and into the new year. Finally, on January 8, 1938, the shooting was completed. The original, fifty-one-day schedule had ballooned to ninety-three days, and the final budget amounted to $1,073,000.

The aftermath was fairly predictable. *Bringing Up Baby* was released to mixed critical notices and average box office business. It did not seem to do much for Katharine Hepburn's career either. Briskin proved to be right in his prediction that a Hepburn film costing more than $700,000 could not make a profit. The final RKO loss on *Baby* amounted to $365,000. It also turned out to be Hepburn's last RKO picture. After a loan-out to Columbia for *Holiday*, she returned to her home studio, refused to appear in *Mother Carey's Chickens*, and was released from her contract. The RKO braintrust were convinced that she was washed up, but she would prove them wrong at MGM, beginning in 1940.

Likewise, Hawks found himself out of a job. *Gunga Din* had been reactivated while *Bringing Up Baby* was shooting. Knowing that it would be a much more ambitious and complicated picture than *Baby*, new executive producer Pandro Berman decided to turn it over to a more reliable director: George Stevens. (Ironically, Stevens developed his own perfectionist qualities on *Gunga Din*, which went $700,000 over budget.) Hawks's brother and agent, William, was called into the studio and informed that Howard would be terminated. The director was upset by this—not because he would be giving up his $2500 weekly salary but because he would not have an opportunity to direct *Gunga Din*, which was precisely the type of male adventure saga he loved best. Nevertheless, his contract was canceled upon payment of $40,000 severance money.

It might seem that the system had prevailed over Hawks after all, since he was now branded as profligate and undependable and was out of a job. But, of course, the system was much larger than RKO Radio Pictures; within a short time, Hawks was back at work at Columbia on *Only Angels Have Wings*. It is important to note that that picture and Hawks's next effort, *His Girl Friday*, both starred Cary Grant. Hawks and Grant had obviously established a solid working relationship on *Bringing Up Baby*, which suggests that Hawks had actually increased his industry clout on *Baby*, rather than decreasing it. In addition to making memorable comedy, he had forged an alliance with a star whose career was rising rapidly. If Cary Grant wanted to work with Howard Hawks, Hawks's pictures would be made by one studio or another.

Now that we have surveyed the making of *Bringing Up Baby*, I would like to offer the following modest proposals:

The time has come to dispense with the assembly-line analogy for studio production. Although the moguls no doubt wished their operations could be as efficient and predictable as those of a Ford plant, their product mitigated against standardization.[*] It is true, of course, that the production history of *Bringing Up Baby* is not typical; the film resulted from a special set of circumstances which enabled its director to control the picture more completely than would normally have been the case. Still, the departmental structures and operating methods of studios never turned filmmaking into a conveyor-belt business. Most pictures presented special problems which could not have been solved by inflexible, factory-inspired methods.

Leo Rosten, who studied the studio system when it was at its peak, has described it very well:

> Movie making is not a systematized process in which ordered routine can prevail, or in which costs can be absolute and controlled. Too many things can and do go awry, every day, every hour, during the manufacture of a movie. Movies are made by ideas and egos, not from blueprints and not with machines. Every story offers fresh and exasperating problems; every actor, director, writer carries within him curious preferences and needs; and the omnipresent hand of a mutable public throws sudden switches in the traffic of ideas through which the making of movies flows. The movie business moves with relentless speed, change is of the essence, and Hollywood must respond to change with short-spanned flexibility.

Unfortunately, most scholars have preferred the depersonalized studio characterizations of Hampton and Jacobs to the somewhat nebulous, but more accurate, depiction of Rosten.

The power and influence of the movie industry's A-level talent during the studio years have been seriously underestimated. The conception of the artist as corporate slave was fueled by periodic tirades against the moguls and their methods. One need only recall Frank Capra's 1939 letter to the *New York Times* in which he claimed that "80% of the directors today shoot scenes exactly as they are told to shoot them without any changes whatsoever, and . . . 90% of them have no voice in the story or in the editing" or Bette Davis's well-publicized battles to prevent Jack Warner from forcing her to appear in mediocre pictures. Nevertheless, studio records contradict the impressions produced by these and other angry outbursts against the system. Most major actors and actresses could and did turn down parts they did not like (even at Warner Brothers), and it was normal for A directors to have considerable freedom in their choice of material, to work with writers on the preparation of the script, to have the strongest voice in casting decisions, and to be left alone when they were directing the film. These basic conventions might be breached if a picture went widely over budget or if the studio executive felt the footage was no

---

[*]Even at the B level, where production elements were more strictly controlled than at the A level, the assembly-line conception is inaccurate. The creative team that worked on the Val Lewton films at RKO, for example, had ample leeway to develop a new strain of psychologically penetrating horror films. Their budgets were limited, but, otherwise, their innovative efforts were unencumbered by studio policies and procedures.

good. Still, as in the case of *Bringing Up Baby*, a studio rarely fired a director or halted production, even if the film did run over in both time and money.

The last proposal is for an open-minded reevaluation of the system itself and of each individual studio. There is more scholarly work to be done if we are to move beyond the one-sided generalizations that prevail in the current literature. We need, first of all, to recognize the complexity of these organizations. It is wrong to lump MGM, Paramount, Warner Brothers, Twentieth Century-Fox, RKO, and, oftentimes, Columbia, Universal, and United Artists together and treat them as if they were carbon copies of one another. Each of these companies had its own special characteristics, and each underwent significant changes during the studio system era. Each was a world unto itself with its own ways of making movies and making money. It is also time that we recognize the intrinsic genius of the system. There were both sound business sense and artistic advantage in the assembling of a diverse group of specialists under one umbrella structure. These talented individuals were able to grow and learn and work together in ways that enriched them all, as well as the capitalistic organizations they served.

A modern systems analyst studying the old Hollywood studios would certainly find them grossly inefficient and honeycombed with flaws. Ironically, these very weaknesses enabled the studios' more imaginative employees to make pictures that are still studied and appreciated today. The studios have taken enough punishment; we should give them a second look, recognizing that they may represent the best system for commercial filmmaking thus far developed in world cinema.

1984

THOMAS SCHATZ
FROM THE GENIUS OF THE SYSTEM

"THE WHOLE EQUATION OF PICTURES"

The Genius of the System (1996), excerpted below, takes its title from a phrase of André Bazin. In it Thomas Schatz argues the central importance of the producer in the Hollywood studio system. In *Hollywood Genres* (1981), excerpted in Section VI, Schatz similarly repudiated auteur theory in favor of an approach to film analysis that considers the broader system of production and consumption within which films are made, especially the genre formulas central to movie making as a commercial enterprise. Also the author of *Boom and Bust: The American Cinema in the 1940s* (1997) and editor of the four-volume anthology *Hollywood: Critical Concepts in Media and Cultural Studies* (2004), Schatz is currently Jones Centennial chair of the Radio-Television-Film department at the University of Texas at Austin.

Walking at dawn in the deserted Hollywood streets in 1951 with David [Selznick], I listened to my favorite movie boss topple the town he had helped to build. The movies, said David, were over and done with. Hollywood was already a ghost town making foolish efforts to seem alive....

But now that the tumult was gone, what had Hollywood been?

Ben Hecht, 1954

... The collapse of the studio system was bound to provoke questions like Ben Hecht's—"What had Hollywood been?"—and the answers have been plentiful but less than adequate. Hecht himself answered as so many of his industry colleagues did, with an anecdotal, self-serving memoir laced with venom for the "system" and for the "Philistines" who controlled it—and who paid Hecht up to $5,000 a week for his services as a screenwriter. Hecht was an essential part of that system, of course, though he hardly saw things that way, and his reminiscence was less revealing of Hollywood filmmaking than of the attitudes of eastern-bred writers toward the priorities and the power structure in the movie industry. Hecht's answer did provide yet another piece of evidence to be factored in, along with countless other interviews and autobiographies, critical studies, and economic analyses. But the accumulated evidence scarcely adds up, and our sense of what Hollywood had been remained a vague impression, fragmented and contradictory, more mythology than history.

Promising to change all that, a cadre of critics and historians in the 1960s and 1970s cultivated a "theory of film history" based on the notion of directorial authorship. As the New Hollywood emerged from the ashes of the studio era, proponents of the auteur theory proclaimed that what the Old Hollywood had been was a director's cinema. They proclaimed, too, that the only film directors worthy of canonization as author-artists were those whose personal style emerged from a certain antagonism toward the studio system at large—the dehumanizing, formulaic, profit-hungry machinery of Hollywood's studio-factories. The auteurist's chief proponent was Andrew Sarris, who in his landmark study, *The American Cinema: Directors and Directions, 1929–1968*, cast the studio boss as the heavy in Hollywood's epic struggle and reduced American film history to the careers of a few dozen heroic directors. Keying on an observation by director George Stevens that as the industry took shape, "the filmmaker became the employee, and the man who had time to attend to the business details became the head of the studio," Sarris developed a simplistic theory of his own, celebrating the director as the sole purveyor of Film Art in an industry overrun with hacks and profitmongers. The closing words of his introduction said it all: "He [the director] would not be worth bothering with if he were not capable now and then of a sublimity of expression almost miraculously extracted from his money-oriented environment."

Auteurism itself would not be worth bothering with if it hadn't been so influential, effectively stalling film history and criticism in a prolonged stage of adolescent romanticism. But the closer we look at Hollywood's relations of power and hierarchy of authority during the studio era, at its division of labor and assembly-line production process, the less sense it makes to assess filmmaking or film style in terms of the individual director—or *any* individual, for that matter. The key issues here are style and authority—creative expression and creative control—and there were indeed a number of Hollywood directors who had an unusual degree of authority and a certain style. John Ford, Howard Hawks, Frank Capra, and Alfred Hitchcock are good examples, but it's worth noting that their privileged status—particularly their control over script development, casting, and editing—was more a function of their role as producers than as directors. Such authority came only with commercial success and was won by filmmakers who proved not just that they had talent but that they could work profitably within the system. These filmmakers were often "difficult" for a studio to handle, perhaps, but no more so than its top stars or writers. And ultimately they got along, doing what Ford called "a job of work" and moving on to the next project. In fact, they did their best and most consistent work on calculated star vehicles for one particular studio, invariably in symbiosis with an authoritative studio boss.

Consider Ford's work with Darryl Zanuck at Twentieth Century-Fox on a succession of Henry Fonda pictures: *Young Mr. Lincoln, Drums Along the Mohawk,* and *The Grapes of Wrath.* Or Alfred Hitchcock doing *Spellbound* and *Notorious,* two psychological dramas scripted by Ben Hecht and prepared by David Selznick for his European discovery, Ingrid Bergman. Or Howard Hawks working for Jack Warner on *To Have and Have Not* and *The Big Sleep,* two hard-boiled thrillers with Bogart and Bacall that were steeped in the Warners' style. These were first-rate Hollywood films, but they were no more distinctive than other star-genre formulations turned out by routine contract directors; Universal's horror films with Boris Karloff directed by James Whale, for instance, or the Paul Muni biopics directed by William Dieterle for Warners. Whale and Dieterle are rarely singled out for their style or artistry, and each would have been lost without the studio's resources and regimented production process. But that doesn't diminish the integrity of films like *Frankenstein, The Old Dark House,* and *The Bride of Frankenstein,* or *The Story of Louis Pasteur* and *The Life of Émile Zola.*

The quality and artistry of all these films were the product not simply of individual human expression, but of a melding of institutional forces. In each case the "style" of a writer, director, star—or even a cinematographer, art director, or costume designer—fused with the studio's production operations and management structure, its resources and talent pool, its narrative traditions and market strategy. And ultimately any individual's style was no more than an inflection on an established studio style. Think of Jimmy Cagney in *Public Enemy,* staggering down that dark, rain-drenched street after a climactic shoot-out with rival gangsters, gazing just past the camera and muttering "I ain't so tough," then falling face-down into the gutter. That was a signature Warner Bros. moment, a narrative-cinematic epiphany when star and genre and technique coalesced into an ideal expression of studio style, vintage 1931. Other studios had equally distinctive styles and signature moments, involving different stars and story types and a different "way of seeing" in both a technical and an ideological sense. On a darkened, rain-drenched street at MGM, for instance, we might expect to find a glossy, upbeat celebration of life and love—Mickey Rooney in another Andy Hardy installment, struggling to get the top up on his old jalopy while his date gets soaked, or Gene Kelly dancing through puddles and singin' in the rain. Over at Universal a late-night storm was likely to signal something more macabre: Count Dracula on the prowl, perhaps, or Dr. Frankenstein harnessing a bolt of lightning for some horrific experiment.

These are isolated glimpses of a larger design, both on screen and off. Each top studio developed a repertoire of contract stars and story formulas that were refined and continually recirculated through the marketplace. Warners in the 1930s, for example, cranked out urban crime films with Cagney and Edward G. Robinson, crusading biopics with Paul Muni, backstage musicals with Dick Powell and Ruby Keeler, epic swashbucklers with Errol Flynn and Olivia de Haviland, and in a curious counter to the studio's male ethos, a succession of "women's pictures" starring Bette Davis. These stars and genres were the key markers in Warners' Depression-era style, the organizing principles for its entire operation from the New York office to the studio-factory across the continent. They were a means of stabilizing marketing and sales, of bringing efficiency and economy into the production of some fifty feature films per year, and of distinguishing Warners' collective output from that of its competitors.

The chief architects of a studio's style were its executives, which any number of Hollywood chroniclers observed at the time. Among the more astute chroniclers was Leo Rosten, who put it this way in *Hollywood: The Movie Colony,* an in-depth study published in 1940:

> Each studio has a personality; each studio's product shows special emphases and values. And, in the final analysis, the sum total of a studio's personality, the aggregate pattern of its choices and its tastes, may be traced to its producers. For it is the producers who establish the preferences, the prejudices, and the predispositions of the organization and, therefore, of the movies which it turns out.

Rosten was not referring to the "supervisors" and "associated producers" who monitored individual productions, nor to the pioneering "movie moguls" who controlled

economic policy from New York. He was referring to studio production executives
like Louis B. Mayer and Irving Thalberg at MGM, Jack Warner and Hal Wallis at
Warner Bros., Darryl Zanuck at Twentieth Century-Fox, Harry Cohn at Columbia,
and major independent producers like David Selznick and Sam Goldwyn. These men—
and they were always men—translated an annual budget handed down by the New
York office into a program of specific pictures. They coordinated the operations of
the entire plant, conducted contract negotiations, developed stories and scripts,
screened "dailies" as pictures were being shot, and supervised editing until a picture
was ready for shipment to New York for release. These were the men Frank Capra
railed against in an open letter to *The New York Times* in April 1939, complaining
that "about six producers today pass on about 90 percent of the scripts and edit 90
percent of the pictures." And these were the men that F. Scott Fitzgerald described
on the opening page of *The Last Tycoon*, the Hollywood novel he was writing at the
time of his death, in 1940. "You can take Hollywood for granted like I did," wrote
Fitzgerald, "or you can dismiss it with the contempt we reserve for what we don't
understand. It can be understood too, but only dimly and in flashes. Not a half dozen
men have been able to keep the whole equation of pictures in their heads."

Fitzgerald was thinking of Irving Thalberg when he wrote that passage, and it would
be difficult to find a more apt description of Thalberg's role at MGM. Nor could we
find a clearer and more concise statement of our objective here: to calculate the whole
equation of pictures, to get down on paper what Thalberg and Zanuck and Selznick
and a very few others carried in their heads. After digging through several tons of
archival materials from various studios and production companies, I have developed
a strong conviction that these producers and studio executives have been the most
misunderstood and undervalued figures in American film history. So in a sense this
is an effort to reconsider their contributions to Hollywood filmmaking; but I don't
want to overstate their case or misstate my own. Hollywood's division of labor
extended well into the executive and management ranks, and isolating the producer
or anyone else as artist or visionary gets us nowhere. We would do well, in fact, to
recall French film critic André Bazin's admonition to the early auteurists, who were
transforming film history into a cult of personality. "The American cinema is a classical art," wrote Bazin in 1957, "so why not then admire in it what is most admirable—
i.e., not only the talent of this or that filmmaker, but the genius of the system."

It's taken us a quarter-century to appreciate that insight, to consider the "classical Hollywood" as precisely that: a period when various social, industrial, technological, economic, and aesthetic forces struck a delicate balance. That balance was
conflicted and ever shifting but stable enough through four decades to provide a
consistent system of production and consumption, a set of formalized creative practices and constraints, and thus a body of work with a uniform style—a standard way
of telling stories, from camera work and cutting to plot structure and thematics.
It was the studio system at large that held those various forces in equilibrium; indeed,
the "studio era" and the classical Hollywood describe the same industrial and historical phenomenon. The sites of convergence for those forces were the studios
themselves, each one a distinct variation on Hollywood's classical style. . . .

The movies were a "vertical" industry in that the ultimate authority belonged to
the owners and top corporate officers in New York. But the New York office

couldn't make movies, nor could it dictate audience interest and public taste. And whatever the efforts to regulate production and marketing, moviemaking remained a competitive and creative enterprise. In the overall scheme of things, the West Coast management team was the key to studio operations, integrating the company's economic and creative resources, translating fiscal policy into filmmaking practice. This demanded close contact with New York and a feel for the company's market skew, but also an acute awareness of the studio's resources and heavy interaction with the top filmmakers on the lot, particularly the directors, writers, and stars.

Because of the different stakes involved for each of these key players, studio filmmaking was less a process of collaboration than of negotiation and struggle—occasionally approaching armed conflict. But somehow it worked, and it worked well. What's most remarkable about the classical Hollywood, finally, is that such varied and contradictory forces were held in equilibrium for so long. The New Hollywood and commercial television indicate all too clearly what happens when that balance is lost, reminding us what a productive, efficient, and creative system was lost back in the 1950s. There was a special genius to the studio system, and perhaps when we understand that we will learn, at long last, what Hollywood had been.

1988

VI

Film Genres

The study of artistic genres is as old as Aristotle, and at least one of his generic terms, "comedy," has been regularly applied to films. (Perhaps significantly, tragedy has not established itself as a film genre.) The generic approach to art has frequently been attacked, however, for its terms are often vague and its methods of categorization unclear. What, precisely, is a documentary film or a screwball comedy? Are films to be classified by their physical properties (silent, color), by their subject matter (gangster, western), or by their purpose or effect (comic, horror)? Further, are these categories legitimate? Of what interest is a category like the "educational" film? In any case, is it even proper to arrange works of art in classes, viewing them as instances of types? Benedetto Croce, the influential Italian philosopher and critic, argued that generic criticism was necessarily incompatible with an aesthetic point of view, which always treats works of art as individual and unique. Croce wrote at the beginning of the twentieth century and, as we have noted in Section V, the privileged position of the single creator and the single work has been severely criticized since then. With a new interest in general issues of language, cultural context, and film history, the concept of genre continues to be employed in film theory and criticism, as it is in art theory and criticism, and with important results.

The most familiar system by which films are generically classified distinguishes between the different kinds of feature films: westerns, gangster films, newspaper pictures, detective dramas, screwball comedies, courtroom dramas, *films noirs*, musicals, war films, spy films, prison films, horror films, science fictions, fantasies, thrillers. An obvious difficulty with such commonly used categories is that they overlap; a film might combine gangsters, detectives, newspapermen, a courtroom, a prison, suspense, and a bleak, *noir* atmosphere; a film might combine screwball comedy, newspapermen, and prisons (as *His Girl Friday* does), or screwball comedy, the western, and the musical (as *Calamity Jane* and *Annie Get Your Gun* do). In classifying such a film one would have to rely on a judgment about what genre is most important. Or one might decide to employ a compound category. But this sort of adjustment does not present genre criticism with an insoluble difficulty, for to be able to speak of a compound genre implies that elemental genres exist in order to be mixed.

Another problem of classifying fictional narrative films in this way arises when we ask if such categories have any impact on either the making of films or our responses to films. Are they critical and commercial conveniences, designed merely to help market a film or to describe a film for those who have not seen it? How conscious are filmmakers of their use of generic conventions? How conscious are audiences of these conventions? How do we recognize that a film does indeed represent a particular genre? How do the conventions of a genre evolve over the history of film? Are such evolutions the result of changing artistic conventions in films, of developing cultural standards in society, or both? Despite these questions, there can be no doubt that treating a film as a representative of a familiar and perceptively formulated genre is often essential to a proper understanding of it.

For Leo Braudy the concept of genre must first be rescued from the presumption that it can only describe a debased and degraded kind of art. "Genre films offend our most common definition of artistic excellence: the uniqueness of the art object, whose value can in part be defined by its desire to be uncaused and unfamiliar, as much as possible unindebted to any tradition, popular or otherwise." After tracing this critical prejudice to its roots in the aesthetic and literary theories of the Romantic era, Braudy explores two of the prime connections that genre films achieve. First, they forge a deliberate connection between each new instance of the genre and its past tradition and manifestations. Second, genre films, because of their popularity and familiarity, have a more powerful—and highly democratic—impact on their audience converting that audience into a unified cultural force: "Genre films strike beneath our intellectual appreciation of high art and make us one with a large mass audience, often despite our more articulate and elitist views." His specific look at musicals of the 1930s and 1940s demonstrates the way that the genre, especially as embodied in the contrast between Fred Astaire and Gene Kelly, sought to interject energy and spontaneity into the repetitiveness of everyday social reality, either by Astaire's escape into the perfect world of dance or by Kelly's effort to make the imperfect world whole by bringing it together in dance.

A frequent preoccupation of genre criticism in both literature and film has been to try to define and enumerate the specific characteristics that distinguish one genre from another. Rick Altman criticizes this prescriptive view as ahistorical, whether it comes from genre purists, from semioticians and structuralists in search of the elements of film language, or from critics (like Robert Warshow) analyzing the social psychology of the audience. Using the western as his model, Altman proposes instead a language-oriented analysis, which distinguishes the semantics of genre (for example, outlaws, deserts, horses) from the syntactics of genre (for example, cattlemen v. farmers, nature v. technology, East v. West). He argues that not only does this distinction clarify questions about individual genres but it also enables an account of how genres change and interrelate historically.

Although Altman emphasizes the spectator as the mediator of semantic and syntactic elements (and in his later work has gone on to emphasize the audience's role even more), his use of linguistic categories also seems to invite the detachment from history that he otherwise criticizes. Thomas Schatz stresses instead the central connection of the Hollywood studio system and the mass audience to genre's cultural position as "a social problem-solving operation." Exploring the genre film's challenge to critical concepts like the *auteur* director, he rejects the internal account of genre history he finds in writers influenced by linguistic models. Instead, he suggests that there is an "evolution" in the history of at least a few major genres (western, musical) "from straightforward storytelling to self-conscious formalism."

Robert Warshow, the influential American analyst of the popular arts in the era just after World War Two, would agree with Braudy's observation that the popular genre film makes connections both with its filmic past and with the temperaments of its contemporary viewers. In the face of those who would dismiss genre films as a lower form of art, Warshow tries to salvage their importance by emphasizing their invariable and almost ritual qualities. Although he would be less willing to grant the general artistic importance to genre films that Braudy does, he does consider the gangster and the westerner as the two most important creations of American movies. The power of both genres, he argues, derives from their concern with the problem of violence and the dark side of American life. Often an immigrant, the gangster in particular is "the man of the city," the striving, ambitious person in a world that is otherwise the opposite of the expansiveness and naturalness of the countryside. We identify with his rise and we detach ourselves from him when he falls, in a parody of the American dream.

In the 1940s and 1950s, the gangster and crime film became absorbed into a difficult-to-define genre style called *film noir*. Paul Schrader, a film critic who later, like Godard and Truffaut, became a filmmaker himself, registers the continuing impact and popularity of such films, often the less prestigious products of Hollywood when they were first made. Beginning with questions about whether *noir* can in fact be called a genre, Schrader explores the social, political, and cultural atmosphere in which these films first appeared, and comments on their particular themes and visual style. Finally, he argues, Robert Warshow's view of the gangster emphasizes the sociological, while the essence of the gangster film and its *noir* descendants is aesthetic, "a moral vision of life based on style."

Thomas Schatz, like Leo Braudy and to a certain extent Rick Altman, roots genre history in the ongoing cultural life of its audience, as a negotiation between seemingly incompatible urges (in the western, for example, to peace or to violence, to communal values or to individual desires). Robin Wood surveys this aspect of the genre question from a Marxist point of view, not the older Marxist aesthetics that assumes a passive and manipulated audience, but a more recent Marxism cultural criticism that stresses the ideological contradictions inherent in genre films, as well as in the audience's response to them. Unlike those who would create a taxonomy that distinguishes and separates individual genres, Wood considers them all to be connected but "different strategies for dealing with the same ideological tensions."

A prime characteristic of the "high" or "classic" art to which genre is so often negatively compared is its creation by a great artist. Genre art, in this account, can never reach the heights of greatness because its creators are too tied to artistic precedents and are therefore not "original." The countervailing argument asserts that genre creativity is defined by exactly that manipulation of past motifs to create a new work. Drawing upon the legacy of the auteur controversy over who should receive the creative "credit" for filmmaking (see Section V, especially the articles by Sarris and Wollen), Wood focuses on the way in which Frank Capra and Alfred Hitchcock embed genre themes and motifs in films that otherwise seem unrelated to genre categories.

Much genre criticism takes one genre—often the western—and tries to derive general principles from analyzing it. The essays by Linda Williams, Tania Modleski, and Cynthia A. Freeland focus on a genre that in the last decade has become one of the prime sites of genre analysis—the horror film—in part because horror, of all the easily identifiable genres, has had the longest and most continuous history. For cultural critics, horror, with its threatening and unsettled landscape, also offers the clearest ground for general social criticism and analysis. Linda Williams connects this "spectacle of a body caught in the grip of intense sensation or emotion" with a general atmosphere of excess that differentiates genre films from "classical" Hollywood narrative. Emphasizing pornography, horror, and melodrama as three prime "body genres," she discusses the lack of distance in such works between the body on the screen and the spectator's body in the audience—as similar emotions course through both. That emotional response is in no way an indication of audience passivity, "but a cultural form of problem solving" or at least problem-formulating of deep-rooted questions of sexual identity.

Many writers who have discussed genre have made a direct equation between its aesthetic use of conventional formulas and what they believe to be its innate political conservatism. Tania Modleski begins her essay on the contemporary horror film by attacking theories of genre (and popular culture in general) that connect aesthetic formulas with a politically passive audience. She emphasizes instead the socially subversive elements of the horror genre, particularly focusing on the ways in which the pleasure that the audience derives from watching such films is not passive or complacent but critically energizing. Contemporary horror films especially, she finds, expose to satire and scrutiny a wide range of conventional values, including the nuclear bourgeois family, consumerism, and technology itself.

Modleski notes that one distinctive focus of the horror film's subversive critique is the violence done to the human body, often male but usually female. Expanding on this basic element in the horror genre, Cynthia A. Freeland situates the discussion of horror films specifically in the context of feminist film theory and criticism. Rejecting the psychodynamic interpretation of the film experience, which emphasizes a reductive view of gender difference (see Mulvey in Section VII), she stresses instead the "real human psychology of actual viewers." Gender is only one element of identity, she argues, and accounts that privilege its importance ignore racial and social difference, as well as the great diversity of horror subgenres that make the attempt to find a univocal "feminist theory of horror" fruitless. Although she too is in search of a "feminist ideological critique" of horror films, she refuses what she considers to be the easy Marxist answers that ascribe overwhelming and determinative power to the forces of production. Once again, as in many more recent critiques, it is the active assimilative power of the audience that is more crucial.

Finally in this section, David Bordwell tests the limits of a genre approach by considering whether the European "art film" can be considered in those terms. Since the directors of such films have generally been treated as consummate film artists and their films as unique products of their genius, the genre terminology of convention and tradition seems totally inappropriate. But Bordwell succinctly demonstrates that there are enough similarities of history and production, as well as formal qualities (for example, the loosening of cause-effect links in narrative), that make it a fruitful way of understanding these films. His analysis might be usefully compared with those of the films of Jean-Luc Godard, by Brian Henderson (Section I) and Peter Wollen (Section IV), as well as the discussions of the *auteur* theory in Section V. For here Bordwell makes "authorial expressivity," the felt presence of the filmmaker in his film, into a genre characteristic.

LEO BRAUDY
FROM THE WORLD IN A FRAME

GENRE: THE CONVENTIONS OF CONNECTION

Actually I do not think that there are any wrong reasons for liking a statue or a picture. . . .
There are wrong reasons for disliking a work of art.

E. H. GOMBRICH,
The Story of Art

No part of the film experience has been more consistently cited as a barrier to serious critical interest than the existence of forms and conventions, whether in such details as the stereotyped character, the familiar setting, and the happy ending, or in those films that share common characteristics—westerns, musicals, detective films, horror films, escape films, spy films—in short, what have been called genre films. Films in general have been criticized for their popular and commercial appeal, seemingly designed primarily for entertainment and escape rather than enlightenment. Genre films especially are criticized because they seem to appeal to a preexisting audience, while the film "classic" creates its own special audience through the unique power of the filmmaking artist's personal creative sensibility. Too often in genre films the creator seems gone and only the audience is present, to be attacked for its bad taste and worse politics for even appreciating this debased art.

The critical understanding of genre films therefore becomes a special case of the problem of understanding films in general. Genre films offend our most common definition of artistic excellence: the uniqueness of the art object, whose value can in part be defined by its desire to be uncaused and unfamiliar, as much as possible unindebted to any tradition, popular or otherwise. The pure image, the clear personal style, the intellectually respectable content are contrasted with the impurities of convention, the repetitions of character and plot. We undervalue their attractions and inner dynamics because there seems to be no critical vocabulary with which to talk about them without condescending, and therefore no aesthetic criteria by which to judge them, no way

535

of understanding why one horror film scares us and another leaves us cold, why one musical is a symphony of style and another a clashing disarray.

Critics have ignored genre films because of their prejudice for the unique. But why should art be restricted only to works of self-contained intensity, while many other kinds of artistic experience are relegated to the closet of aesthetic pleasure, unfit for the daylight? Genre films, in fact, arouse and complicate feelings about the self and society that more serious films, because of their bias toward the unique, may rarely touch. Within film the pleasures of originality and the pleasures of familiarity are at least equally important. Following Marcel Duchamp and Antonin Artaud, Andy Warhol in the early 1960s announced "no more classics." In painting and sculpture this meant an attack on the canonization of museum art and the acceptance of previously unacceptable, often popular, forms. For films, the problem has usually been the other way around. "No more classics" for film might mean no more films defined as separate from the popular forms that are the great energy of film, artistically as well as thematically.

The modern prejudice against genre in art can be traced to the aesthetic theories of the Romantic period. In the later eighteenth century the older idea of poetic inspiration began to be expanded into a major literary theory by works like Edward Young's *Conjectures on Original Composition* (1759). Poetic "imitation," the building of creativity on the achievements of the past, began to fade as the standard of personal vision became more important. Only conventions that could be understood liberally survived, and the eighteenth-century unwillingness to accord imaginative sympathy to convention received its most famous expression in Samuel Johnson's attack on John Milton's *Lycidas*, a poem in the form of a pastoral elegy, which drew upon a tradition of lament that went back to Theocritus and Vergil. The English and German Romantic writers consolidated this trend by establishing originality not only as a criterion of art, but, in their crudest statements, the only criterion of art. Art could owe nothing to tradition or the past because that debt qualified the power and originality of the individual creator. The poet was inspired by what he saw and experienced, and the intervention of any prior categories for that experience doomed the work to secondary value unless the forms that intervened were primitive forms—the folktale or the ballad—that had none of the hated sophistication of the art of the previous age. Any use of genre and convention as such necessarily debarred a work and its author from the status of true art. If poetry were defined as the spontaneous outpouring of strong feelings, how could a work that employed stock characters and stock situations, stock images and stock resolutions, have any art or originality in it? Folk art or popular art could be used because it was generally assumed that serious art was the purity of which popular art was the degeneracy, and that purity necessarily precedes degeneracy.[1] Poetic inspiration and self-sufficiency occupied the

---

[1]Ballad collectors like Bishop Percy or Sir Walter Scott could therefore argue that their rewritings were an effort to restore the ballads to the form in which the "Bard" originally created them, before they were passed on to the fumbling brains of the folk. Pop Art has revived this theory in a somewhat different form. Ostensibly making us look at the common objects of the world with new intensity, Pop Art also conveys the idea that serious art and artists make popular themes and motifs worthy (read "self-conscious") by putting them into museum settings and charging high prices. Warhol may have first done this to satirize the whole elitist-popular division, but the joke seems to have run thin.

higher peaks of art, while hack work and despised formulas inhabited the more populated and bourgeois valleys. Genre and convention were the fare of the multitudes, while originality and storming self-assertion, without a past, without any controls, was the caviar of the truly aware audience.

Until the eighteenth century, artists had generally been distinguished by their class, their education, and their patrons. But, with the growth of a mass society and a mass culture, the hierarchy shifted from distinctions in genealogy to distinctions in sensibility. Almost all of the great eighteenth-century English novelists and essayists had spent some time in Grub Street, that world created to serve the new hunger for the printed word. But the Romantic sensibility turned Grub Street into a synonym for the convention-ridden enemies of art. The true artist was noncommercial, struggling on the fringes of human existence, with neither society nor companions (and hardly any publishers), alone with his indomitable self. Only Byron, the most eighteenth-century of the Romantics, could have said, "I awoke to find myself famous" (on the publication of *Childe Harold*); such an obvious interest in the approval of a book-buying public was disdained in the Romantics' image of their calling. And Byron himself preoccupied much of his writing with the depiction of solitary heroes, striding mountainsides to challenge gloomy fates. The Romantic artist tried to make his work unique to escape from the dead hand of traditional form. The only serious use of the past was the contemplation of vanished greatness, to raise the artist out of what he believed to be an uncultured present and establish for himself a continuity with what has been best before the triumph of modern degeneracy. Like T. S. Eliot in *The Wasteland*, the serious, unpopular artist was the only one in a corrupt age who could summon up the artistic Eden of the past and collect its fragments into some coherence.

Such absolute creativity is finally a fraud because all art must exist in some relation to the forms of the past, whether in contrast or continuation. Both the generic work and the more self-contained work expand our sense of the possibilities of art. But the nineteenth-century stress on literary originality and freedom has inhibited our responses, both intellectual and emotional, to works that try to complicate our appreciation of tradition and form, works that may in fact embody a more radical critique of the past than those which ignore it. More people dislike westerns or musicals because such film genres outrage their inherited and unexamined sense of what art *should* be than because the films are offensive in theme, characterization, style, or other artistic quality. Every lover of musicals, for example, has heard the complaint that musicals are unrealistic and the viewer gets embarrassed when people start singing or dancing. But the relationship between realism and stylization is a central issue in musicals, not an absurd convention. When auteur critics applaud the studio director for triumphing over his material and point to the glimmers of original style shining through the genre assignment, they may awaken us to the merits of an individual artist. But they also fall into the Romantic trap of searching for only what is obviously original and personal in a work. In auteur theory, genre directors with large popular audiences become transformed into embattled Romantic artists trying to establish their personal visions in the face of an assembly-line commercialism. Frank Capra has pointed out the opposite possibility: in the days of big studio monopoly, there was a great deal of freedom to experiment because every film had guaranteed distribution, whereas now, with increased independent production, films have become more uniform and compromised, because each has to justify itself financially. Underground and avant-garde films with their emphasis on the individual creative sensibility above all, are naturally enough the most hostile to genre. But the bulk of films fall between pure personal expression and pure studio exploitation, mingling the demands of art and culture, creativity and talent. By their involvement in collective creativity, film directors have, at least practically, moved away from the image of the isolated Romantic artist, no matter how they may indulge that image in their public statements.

Instead of dismissing genre films from the realm of art, we should therefore examine what they accomplish. Genre in films can be the equivalent of conscious reference to tradition in the other arts—the invocation of past works that has been so important a part of the history of literature, drama, and painting. Miró's use of Vermeer, Picasso's use of Delacroix are efforts to distinguish their view of the proper ends of painting. Eliot's use of Spenser or Pynchon's of Joyce make similar assertions of continuity and difference. The methods of the western, the musical, the detective film, or the science-fiction film are also reminiscent of the way Shakespeare infuses old stories with new characters to express the tension between past and present. All pay homage to past works even while they vary their elements and comment on their meaning.

Perhaps the main difference between genre films and classic films is the way that genre films invoke past forms while classic films spend time denying them. The joy in genre is to see what can be dared in the creation of a new form or the creative destruction and complication of an old one. The ongoing genre subject therefore always involves a complex relation between the compulsions of the past and the freedoms of the present, an essential part of the film experience. The single, unique work tries to be unforgettable by solving the whole world at once. The genre work, because of its commitment to preexisting forms, explores the world more slowly. Its hallmark is less the flash of inspiration than the deep exploration of craft. Like Ford's *Stagecoach* or Aldrich's *Ulzana's Raid* (1972), it can exist both in itself and as the latest in a line of works like it, picking and choosing among possible conventions, refusing one story or motif to indulge another, avoiding one "cliché" in order to show a self-conscious mastery of the cliché that has been avoided. After all, the reason that an artistic element becomes a cliché is that it answers so well to the experience, intelligence, and feelings of the audience. Subsequent artists, perceiving the same aptness, want to exercise its power themselves, even in a potentially hostile new context, to discover if all the possibilities of the form have thoroughly been explored. The only test is its continuing relevance, and a genre will remain vital, as the western has, and the musical has not, so long as its conventions still express themes and conflicts that preoccupy its audience. When either minority or majority art loses contact with its audience, it becomes a mere signpost in history, an aesthetic rather than an art.

Genre films affect their audience especially by their ability to express the warring traditions in society and the social importance of understanding convention. When Irene Dunne, in *The Awful Truth* (Leo McCarey, 1937), disguises herself as Cary Grant's (fictitious) sister and arrives drunk and raucous at a society gathering where Grant is trying to establish himself, we can open a critical trapdoor and say that the other people at the party, who already know her, don't recognize her in her flimsy disguise because of the necessities of plot and comic form. But we must go on to say that this particular convention, used with all its force, allows McCarey, without dropping the general humorous tone, to point out that she is unrecognized because the upper classes base their estimates and knowledge of character on dress, voice, and manners—a theme supported by the rest of the film as well. The conflict between desire and etiquette can define both a social comedy like *The Awful Truth* and even a more obviously stylized genre work like *Dr. Jekyll and Mr. Hyde* (Rouben Mamoulian, 1932); it parallels in the plot the aesthetic contrast between the individual film and the conventions to which it plays a complex homage.

Genre demands that we know the dynamics of proper audience response and may often require a special audience because of the need to refer the latest instance to previous versions. But response is never invariable. Convention isn't only whatever we don't have to pay attention to. Explaining Shakespeare's use of soliloquies by observing that the practice was an Elizabethan dramatic convention tells us as little as saying that Picasso used blue because it was cheap or that Edward Everett Horton appeared in so many Fred Astaire-Ginger Rogers films because comic relief was needed. Why a soliloquy *now*? What does Horton's presence mean *here*? The possibility exists in all art that convention and comment coexist, that overlapping and even contradictory assumptions and conventions may be brought into play to test their power and make the audience reflect on why they were assumed. The genre film lures its audience into a seemingly familiar world, filled with reassuring stereotypes of character, action, and plot. But the world may actually be not so lulling, and, in some cases, acquiescence in convention will turn out to be bad judgment or even a moral flaw—the basic theme of such Hitchcock films as *Blackmail* (1929), *Rear Window* (1954), and *Psycho*. While avant-garde and original works congratulate the audience by implying it has the capacity to understand them, genre films can exploit the automatic conventions of response for the purposes of pulling the rug out from under their viewers. The very relaxing of the critical intelligence of the audience, the relief that we need not make decisions—aesthetic, moral, metaphysical—about the film, allows the genre film to use our expectations against themselves, and, in the process, reveal to us expectations and assumptions that we may never have thought we had. They can potentially criticize the present, because it too automatically *accepts* the standards of the past, to build subversion within received forms and thereby to criticize the forms instead of only setting up an alternate vision.[2]

Through a constant interplay between the latest instance and the history of a particular form, genre films can call upon a potential of aesthetic complexity that would be denied if the art defined itself only in terms of its greatest and most inimitable works. Because of the existence of generic expectations—how a plot "should" work,

---

[2]The three main American critics who appreciated such films before the New Wave popularized them critically—Otis Ferguson, James Agee, and Manny Farber—were less interested in them for their formal qualities than for their action and unpretentiousness, aspects of energy related to their formal self-consciousness. But both Agee and Farber (and Pauline Kael is their true heir in this) wanted to protect at all costs their beloved movies from any charge of art. As far as the definition of art they were attacking goes, they were right. But to continue such attacks now confuses where it once illuminated. One virtue of the French New Wave critics was that they didn't have to defend themselves simultaneously against pompous ideas of high art, the myth of the American tough guy artist, and the specter of Hollywood commercialism.

what a stereotyped character "should" do, what a gesture, a location, an allusion, a line of dialogue "should" mean—the genre film can step beyond the moment of its existence and play against its own aesthetic history. Through genre, movies have drawn upon their own tradition and been able to reflect a rich heritage unavailable to the "high" arts of the twentieth century which are so often intent upon denying the past and creating themselves totally anew each time out. Within the world of genre films one finds battles, equivalent to those in the history of literature, drama, and painting, between artists who are willing to reproduce a tradition through their own vision because they believe it still has the ability to evoke the emotional response that made it a satisfying artistic form to begin with, and those who believe the form has dried up and needs an injection, usually of "realism." Poets, for example, may contrast the city and the country because that opposition answers to some real beliefs in their audience and because the choice of the rural virtues of the country satisfactorily resolves the conflict. Others might question the authenticity of the traditional materials: did shepherds really play their pipes in singing contests? isn't the elaborate language untrue to rural idioms? or, to extend the analogy, did cowboys really respect law and justice so much? do people really break into dances on the street when they're happy, and does the neighborhood automatically join in? The later generations may feel an emotional pull in the form, but they might want to destylize it and make it more real. The directors of the "adult" western of the 1950s accepted the vitality of the western but thought that a more realistic treatment would strengthen its inherent virtues. If controversy were part of film tradition, we might have an argument between John Ford and Fred Zinnemann on the essence of the western like that between Alexander Pope and Ambrose Phillips on the pastoral, Ford and Pope arguing for the value of form and style, while Zinnemann and Phillips press the need to make the characters of art as close as possible to the real persons who live or lived in that place.

Genre films share many of the characteristics of the closed films I have described in the previous chapter. But, instead of being framed visually, genre films are primarily *closed by convention*. Of course, they may be visually enclosed as well, as, for example, are horror films and 1930s musicals; but the more important enclosure is the frame of pre-existing motifs, plot turns, actors, and situations—in short everything that makes the film a special place with its own rules, a respite from the more confusing and complicated worlds outside. The frame of genre, the existence of expectations to be used in whatever way the intelligence of the filmmaker is capable, allows freedoms within the form that more original films cannot have because they are so committed to a parallel between form and content. The typical genre situation is a contrast between form and content. With the expectations of stock characters, situations, or narrative rhythms, the director can choose areas of free aesthetic play within. In genre films the most obvious focus of interest is neither complex characterization nor intricate visual style, but pure story. Think about the novel we can't put down. That rare experience in literature is the common experience in film, where we stay only because we want to, where we often must be intrigued by the first five minutes or not at all, and where we know that once we leave the spell is broken. Like fairy tales or classical myths, genre films concentrate on large contrasts and juxtapositions. Genre plots are usually dismissed with a snide synopsis (a process that is never very kind to drama that employs conventions, like Shakespeare's plays). But, amid the conventions and expectations of plot, other kinds of emphasis can flourish. To the unsympathetic eye, the pleasures of variation are usually invisible, whether they appear in the medieval morality play, the Renaissance sonnet, the Restoration comedy, the eighteenth-century portrait, the Chopinesque étude, the horror film, the romantic comedy, the musical, or the western. When we can perceive the function of vampire film conventions in *Persona* or boxing film conventions in *On the Waterfront* as clearly as we note the debt of Kurosawa's samurai films to American westerns, or that of the New Wave films to American crime films of the 1950s, then we will be able to appreciate more fully the way in which films can break down the old visions between elite and popular art to establish, almost unbeknown to aesthetics and criticism, a vital interplay between them. . . .[3]

The epic sweep of the early westerns could be conveyed by the silent screen, but musicals necessarily begin their real film career with sound (and sound films begin, appropriate enough, with *The Jazz Singer*). The Charleston sequences of the silent *Our Dancing Daughters* (Harry Beaumont, 1928) look oddly impersonal and detached today, hardly more real than the bunny-costumed Rockettes. Sound not only individualizes the performer, but also provides a bridge of music between otherwise separate visual moments, a continuity against which the image can play, potentially freeing the film from a strict adherence to a one-to-one relation between sight and sound. Once sound frees image from the necessity to appear logical and casual, the director can experiment with different kinds of nonlogical, noncausal narrative. But, after the first years of sound and such experiments with the new form as René Clair's *Under the Roofs of Paris* (1929), Lang's *M* (1931), Renoir's *Boudu Saved from Drowning* (1932), and Ernst Lubitsch's *Trouble in Paradise* (1932), primarily musicals explored its possibilities. The western may be self-conscious about its myths, but the musical is self-conscious about its stylization, the heightened reality that is its norm. The games with continuous narrative that Busby Berkeley plays in the musical numbers of *Footlight Parade* (1933), *42nd Street* (1933), or *Gold Diggers of 1935* are hardly attempted by nonmusical directors until the jump-cutting achronicity of the New Wave.

Berkeley's films show how the stylistic self-consciousness of musicals directly concerns the relation of their art to the everyday world outside the confines of the film. His camera presses relentlessly forward, through impossible stages that open up endlessly, expanding the inner space of film and affirming the capacity of the world of style to mock the narrowness of the "real" world outside the theater walls, populated by bland tenors, greedy producers, and harried directors. Ford uses theater in *Liberty Valance* to purify his genre vision. But Berkeley uses theater, the impossible theater available to film artifice, to give a sense of exuberance and potential. Playing

---

[3]The way in which television "cannibalizes" material therefore has less to do with its constant demand than with the speed with which such material becomes outdated. When the audience accepts material as generic and ritualistic—situation comedy, talk shows, sports, news, weather—the form can include an infinite variety of nuance. But when the paradigms are no longer emotionally appealing, formal variety will do no good and there arises a desperate, cannibalizing, attempt to discover the new form of audience solace, whether the subject matter is Dick Cavett or the Vietnam War. Thus the whole process of cultural history is speeded up through successive purgations of used-up subject matter and style.

with space, Berkeley in *Footlight Parade* creates an incredible extravaganza supposedly taking place in miniature within a waterfall, with pyramids of swimming girls, diving cameras, and fifty-foot fountains.

Berkeley's real problem, however, is his concentration on the production number and the spectacle. The sense of play and opulence he brought to the musical, his effort to make its stage artifice a source of strength, was, if we look back upon the direction the musical took, a minor stream in its history. His influence appears in the show business biography (*A Star Is Born*, 1937; *The Jolson Story*, 1946; *Funny Girl*, 1968), the production story (*Summer Stock*, 1950; *The Band Wagon*, 1953), and that great amalgam of realized style and stylized realism, *Singin' in the Rain* (1952). There is also a darker side apparent in a film like *All About Eve* (1950), in which the urge to theater is considered to be manipulative, a reduction of the self rather than an expansion. The dark side may be the truer side of Berkeley's inheritance, because his musicals lack any sense of the individual. The strange melancholy of the "Lullaby of Broadway" number from *Gold Diggers of 1935*, in which, after some elaborately uplifting production numbers, an unsuccessful showgirl commits suicide, combines comedy and the tragedy of sentimental realism in a way that only penetrated serious films in the late 1940s. It presages the urbane tragedies of fatality in a theatrical setting that mark the late films of Julien Duvivier (*Flesh and Fantasy*, 1943) and Max Ophuls (*La Ronde*, 1950; *Lola Montès*, 1955). The showgirl commits suicide in "Lullaby of Broadway" in part because the Berkeley ensemble of faceless dancers holds no place for her at all, perhaps because of her lack of talent, but more clearly because her individuality is contrary to the demands of the uniform musical group. Like Eisenstein or the Lang of *Metropolis*, Berkeley magisterially juxtaposes sequences and articulates crowds with ritual symmetry. Berkeley's attitude toward individuals is that of a silent film director, iconographic and symmetric. The community of the Berkeley girls is cold and anonymous, like Lang's workers, a community created by a nonparticipating choreographer-director. But the kind of musical that had the greatest popular strength, spawned the largest number of descendants, and historically defined the American musical film, is the musical in which the dancer-choreographer himself was a participant, in which an individual man danced with an individual woman, and in which the theme of the individual energy of the dance, the relation of the dancer to his own body, became the main theme of the film. Obviously I am referring to the films of Fred Astaire and Ginger Rogers.[4]

Shall We Dance (1937, songs by George and Ira Gershwin), the last film of the basic Astaire-Rogers series, is a model of their films, perhaps not least because it contains a final sequence that seems to be an implicit attack against the Berkeley emphasis on anonymous spectacle. Astaire plays the Great Petrov, star of the Russian ballet, who is in reality Peter P. Peters, from Philadelphia. The basic conflict of the film is established in the first scene, when Petrov's manager Jeff (Edward Everett Horton) comes into his rehearsal room to find Petrov improvising a dance to a jazz record.

---

[4]Rouben Mamoulian in *Love Me Tonight* (1932, songs by Rodgers and Hart) focuses on individuals (Jeanette MacDonald and Maurice Chevalier), but the style of the film is still one of directional control rather than a performer's energy. The most impressive song settings are those in which parts of the song are sung and played by people in isolated places, visually linked by the director's wit and style (for example, "Isn't It Romantic?").

"The Great Petrov doesn't dance for fun," he tells him, emphasizing that ballet is a serious business to which the artist must devote his full time. "But I do," responds Astaire. "Remember me? Pete Peters from Philadelpha, P.A.?" Horton points to the taps on Astaire's ballet shoes and continues his insistence that whatever Astaire is doing, it's not art. "Maybe it's just the Philadelphia in me," says Astaire, and begins dancing again. The forces have been set in motion: the dancing that Astaire likes to do when he is alone directly expresses his personal emotions as well as his real identity—the American tap dancer under the high-culture disguise of the Russian ballet dancer. Horton, as he usually does in these films, comically combines a commitment to high culture (and high society) with a definite antagonism to emotion and feeling. When Astaire falls in love with Linda Keene (Ginger Rogers), a nightclub dancer, after seeing a series of movie-like flip cards of her dancing, Horton speaks darkly of the danger to Astaire's "serious" career and the need to be personally pure (i.e., nonsexual and nonemotional) for art. Like so many musicals, *Shall We Dance* contrasts the emotionally detached and formal patterns of high art with the involved and spontaneous forms of popular art. (Vincente Minnelli's *Meet Me in St. Louis*, 1944, for example, establishes the same relationship between serious music and popular music, and many musicals include parodies of serious theater by vaudevillians.) The 1930s musical may have its historical roots in the silent-film urge to the respectablity of theater, the importation of theatrical performers both to give the young industry tone and to banish the generally lower-class associations that film had from its vaudeville beginnings. But the sound musical—like so many genres of the 1930s, comedies and horror films included—begins to mock this respect for older forms just as it parodies the upper class in general. Tap dancing is superior to ballet as movies are superior to drama, not merely because they are more popular, but because they contain more life and possibility. The flip-card stills that turn into a sequence of Rogers dancing present her as a creature of the film, not the stage. Like Astaire in the film, Rogers is also an American, but more proudly: she doesn't like the "hand-kissing heel-clickers of Paris" and rejects Peters when he attempts to impress her by coming on as the formal Petrov. Berkeley attacks theater in favor of film and dance by destroying the limits of theatrical space. But Astaire and Rogers (and their directors, especially Mark Sandrich and choreographer Hermes Pan) attack all high art in favor of the new dancing forms of spontaneity, American style. The Berkeleyan world spawns the myth of show-business biography that success on stage buys only unhappiness in one's personal life. But the silvery world of Astaire and Rogers celebrates the ability of individual energy to break away from the dead hand of society, class and art as well. The open space of the western that offers a chance to build becomes in the musical the endless inner energy released in dance.

Shall We Dance is defined by the collision between the forces of inertia and stasis and the forces of vitality, between Astaire as Petrov—the commitment to high art and personal repression—and Astaire as Peters—the commitment to an art that attempts to structure individual energy instead of excluding it. Musical comedy therefore also attacks any theories of acting in which character comes from the past. Character in musical comedy is physiological and external: the ability to dance and the way dancing functions in specific situations becomes a direct expression of the tensions within the self. In the first scene Astaire dances along at the proper speed;

and then, when the machine needs to be wound up again, he slows down as the record itself slows down. On the ship that takes him and Rogers back to America, he descends into the engine room and dances there in time to the pistons while black members of the crew who are taking a musical break play for him. In both sequences the energy of the dance—the personal emphasis in the first, the relation to jazz and black music in the second ("Slap That Bass")—draws upon the analogy between body and machine. But here, unlike literary attacks against the machine, the film, true to its mechanical and technological origins, celebrates the machine as a possible element in the liberation of the individual rather than in his enslavement (similar to the ambivalence about machines that characterizes *Metropolis*). Machines are outside class, purifiers of movement. The real threat to individual energy and exuberance is not the machine, but the forces of society and respectability—the impresario Jeff, the rich suitor Jim with the weak chin (William Brisbane), who wants to take Rogers away from show business, and the punctilious hotel manager Cecil Flintridge (Eric Blore). Here they are comic, but they nevertheless play the same repressive roles as they would in the more melodramatic world of the western.[5]

At the end of *Shall We Dance*, the comically hostile forces (including an outside world of publicity and gossip) are reconciled by Astaire's typical process of self-realization—the search for the perfect partner. The perfect partner is always a dancing partner, since it is within the world of dance that true communication and complementarity can be achieved: the male-female dance duo is a model of male-female relationship in general. Dancing isn't a euphemism for sex; in Astaire-Rogers films at least, dancing is much better. Two sequences in *Shall We Dance* constitute the dance of courtship and they appear after the first dancing sequences, which establish the separate personalities of Astaire and Rogers. In the first, "They All Laughed," Astaire begins with ballet-like steps while Rogers stands still. Then she begins to tap, and he responds, first with a ballet version of the tapping, then a straight tap. In the second such number, "Let's Call the Whole Thing Off," the importance of the dancing situation to their relationship is further underlined. They are taking a walk in a stage-set Central Park and decide to go skating, even though neither of them has skated in a long time. They begin very haltingly, with frequent stumbles. But, as soon as the music starts, they skate perfectly together. Then, at the end of the song, as the music ends, they hit the grass outside the skating rink and fall down. Once the magic world of dance and its ability to idealize personal energy into a model of relationship has vanished, Astaire and Rogers again become separate and even bickering individuals. "Let's Call the Whole Thing Off" memorializes their differences, even while it provides a context for their relationship. The next musical number, "They Can't Take That Away from Me," contains no dancing. It takes place at night on a ferry between New Jersey and New York and emphasizes the problems of their relationship, especially the seeming conflict between their real feelings, which can be expressed at night, and the public and social demands on them that the daylight world of the rest of the film exerts. Like Astaire and Rogers

---

[5]The positive interpretation of the machine analogy to the body is a constant theme in musicals, most recently expressed in the Ken Russell film of *Tommy* (1975, words and music by Peter Townshend and The Who), in which the deaf, dumb, and blind boy first discovers his real nature through his symbiotic relation with pinball machines.

themselves, who feel the pressure to continue their successful film partnership despite their own wishes, Peter Peters and Linda Keene have been forced into marriage primarily so they can get divorced. The publicity generated by their managers is meant to connect them, but it succeeds only in driving them apart, as aesthetic as well as emotional partners.

Astaire solves the conflict and rejoins Rogers in the remarkable final sequence. In a theatrical setting reminiscent of the roof of the Winter Garden, an open space within the city, Astaire stages a show that summarizes the main elements of the film. In the early sequences Astaire plays a Russian ballet dancer; Rogers appears; he loses her. Meanwhile, the real Rogers, the comic Claudius in this mousetrap, sits in a box, part of the audience, but separate from it. Astaire reprises "You Can't Take That Away from Me" to lead into a sequence in which a whole group of dancing partners appear—all wearing a mask with Rogers' face on it. The song then becomes ironic, since the memory of her uniqueness that it celebrates has been confused in the many Rogers of the present. Ruby Keeler is obviously pleased to be multiplied into many images for the adoration of Dick Powell in Berkeley's *Dames* (1934), but the Ginger Rogers in the audience of *Shall We Dance* cannot take this anonymous crowd of Busby Berkeley chorus girls all wearing her face. Astaire's message makes the same plea: deliver me from the life of a single man amid innumerable faceless girls by asserting the perfection of our relationship. Rogers goes backstage and puts on one of the masks. She comes onstage, briefly reveals herself to Astaire, and then glides back into the anonymity of the many Rogers. Which is the real Rogers among the false, the reality and energy of the individual beneath the generalized artifice of the image? Astaire finds her and together they sing and dance the final song, "Shall We Dance," an invitation to let the dancing, emotional energetic self out, to reject depression and the forms of society, and to accept the frame of theater that allows one, through the exuberance of dance, to be free.

The figure of Fred Astaire implies that dance is the perfect form, the articulation of motion that allows the self the most freedom at the same time that it includes the most energy. The figure of Gene Kelly implies that the true end of dance is to destroy excess and attack the pretensions of all forms in order to achieve some new synthesis. Kelly the sailor teaching Jerry the Mouse to dance in *Anchors Aweigh* (George Sidney, 1945) stands next to Bill Robinson teaching Shirley Temple to dance in *The Little Colonel* (David Butler, 1935). Astaire may move dance away from the more formal orders of the ballet, but Kelly emphasizes its appeal to the somewhat recalcitrant, not quite socialized part of the self, where the emotions are hidden. Astaire and Kelly are part of the same continuum of themes and motifs in musicals (an interesting study could be done of the interaction of their images in the 1940s and 1950s). There are many contrasts that can be made between the way they use dance and the way they appear in their films, but the basic fact of their continuity should be remembered. The question of personal energy, which I have characterized as the musical's basic theme, once again appears centrally. The social world against which Astaire defined himself in the 1930s no longer had the same attraction to movie audiences in the 1940s; it was a hangover from the early days of film and their simultaneous fascination with the 1920s high life and the higher seriousness of theater, in a double effort both to imitate and to mock. Astaire is the consummate theatrical dancer, while Kelly is more interested in the life outside the proscenium. The energy that Astaire defines within a theatrical and socially formal framework Kelly takes outside, into a world somewhat more "real" (that is, similar to the world of the audience) and therefore more recalcitrant. Kelly's whole presence is therefore more rugged and less ethereal than Astaire's. Both Astaire and Kelly resemble Buster Keaton, their prime ancestor in dancing's paean to the freedom and confinement of the body. But Astaire is the spiritual Keaton while Kelly is the combative, energetic Keaton, compounded with the glee of Douglas Fairbanks. Kelly has more obvious physical presence than Astaire, who hides his well-trained body in clothes that give the impression he has nothing so disruptive as muscles, so that the form of his dancing is even more an ideal and a mystery. Astaire often wears suits and tuxedos, while Kelly generally wears open-collared shirts, slacks, white socks, and loafers—a studied picture of informality as opposed to Astaire's generally more formal dress. Astaire wears the purified Art Deco makeup of the 1930s, but Kelly keeps the scar on his cheek visible—an emblem of the interplay between formal style and disruptive realism in his definition of the movie musical.[6]

Astaire may mock social forms for their rigidity, but Kelly tries to explode them. Astaire purifies the relation between individual energy and stylized form, whereas Kelly tries to find a new form that will give his energy more play. Astaire dances onstage or in a room, expanding but still maintaining the idea of enclosure and theater; Kelly dances on streets, on the roofs of cars, on tables, in general bringing the power of dance to bear on a world that would ordinarily seem to exclude it. (Astaire absorbs this ability of Kelly's to reorganize normal space and integrates it with his own lighter-than-air quality in the dancing on the walls sequence in *Royal Wedding*, 1951, directed by Kelly's favorite collaborator Stanley Donen.) Astaire usually plays a professional dancer; Kelly sometimes does and sometimes does not, although he is usually an artist of some kind, often, as in *The Pirate*, a popular artist, or, as in *Summer Stock*, a director, associated with the stage but not totally inside it. Kelly therefore merges the director emphasis of Berkeley with the performer emphasis of Astaire. To complement the distance from theatrical form Kelly maintains, his whole style of acting is self-mocking, while Astaire's is almost always serious and heartfelt, at far as comedy will allow. Because the film attitude toward serious art is less defensive in the 1940s than in the 1930s, Kelly can include ballet and modern dance in his films, although always in a specifically theatrical setting (the pirate dream ballet in *The Pirate*, the gangster ballet in *Les Girls*). Theater and style in Astaire's films reconcile the conflict between personal life and social pressures, and allow the self to repair and renovate its energy. Many of his films have more or less autobiographical elements in them, not the autobiography of Astaire's private life, but the autobiography of Astaire's professional life: the effect to get a new partner after Ginger Rogers

---

[6]I have been using Astaire and Kelly to represent the change in the movie musical as much as I have been describing what they do themselves. A full account would also have to include a close consideration of Eleanor Powell, whose fantastic exuberance and bodily freedom often threatened to destroy the generally theatrical plots in which she was encased. The most important film for these purposes might be *Broadway Melody of 1940* (Normal Taurog), in which she and Astaire dance together with an equality of feeling and ability that presages the teaming of Kelly and Judy Garland.

decided to do dramatic films instead (*Easter Parade*, Charles Walters, 1948, with Judy Garland), the celebration of Rogers' return to dance after several "serious" films (*The Barkleys of Broadway*, Charles Walters, 1949). Kelly, however, far from taking refuge in theater, wants to make theater take over daily life. His films are hardly ever autobiographical; unlike Astaire's, they have stories in which Kelly plays a role.

Above: Fred Astaire among the many masks of Ginger Rogers in *Shall We Dance* (1937). "Which is the real Rogers among the false, the reality and energy of the individual beneath the generalized artifice of the image? Astaire finds her and together they sing and dance, 'Shall We Dance', an invitation to let the dancing, emotional energetic self out ..." (BRAUDY, p. 545). *Below*: Gene Kelly and cast at the end of the "Gotta Dance" production number in *Singing' in the Rain* (1952), "another statement of Kelly's belief that dancing is a compulsion from within more authentic than the forms imposed from without" (BRAUDY, p. 551).

Astaire may dance by himself, with a partner, or with a company of dancers. Kelly wants to galvanize a community of nondancers as well. Astaire and his partner are professionals; Kelly and his partner are often amateurs, but everyone they meet knows the steps to their dances and the words to their songs.[7]

A Kelly film that highlights the differences and similarities between the two great definers of the American musical comedy is Vincent Minnelli's *The Pirate* (1948, songs by Cole Porter, story by Frances Goodrich and Albert Hackett). In the beginning of *The Pirate*, Manuela (Judy Garland), the poor niece of a wealthy family on an eighteenth-century Caribbean island, is leafing through a book detailing the highly romanticized adventures of the pirate Macoco. She dreamily desires the embraces of Macoco but is realistically resigned to marrying the unromantic, fat town mayor (Walter Slezak), who courts her with propriety and respect. One of her companions tells her that the life of Macoco is pure fantasy and she responds by expressing the sense of separate worlds she feels within her: "I realize there's a practical world and a dream world. I won't mix them".[8] Enter Serafin (Gene Kelly), the head of a traveling company of players. He flirts with Manuela, and falls in love with her. By accidental hypnosis the reserved Manuela changes into a manic performer, and she and Serafin dance and sing together in a funny scene in which Serafin thinks he's tricked this pretty girl into dancing with him, while the exuberance released in Manuela by the hypnosis threatens to knock him off the stage. Horrified at what she's done, Manuela leaves for her hometown away from the big city to prepare for her marriage to the mayor. Serafin follows her and recognizes the mayor as the real Macoco. He threatens to expose him unless the mayor allows Serafin to pretend that he is Macoco, since Serafin knows of Manuela's hero-worship. The mayor agrees, until he sees that Manuela's attraction to Serafin is increased by the impersonation. The mayor then arrests Serafin and is about to hang him when Serafin, asking for the opportunity to do a last act on stage, plays a scene with Manuela that reveals to the mayor her actual love for Macoco the Pirate. Unaware of the game, the mayor announces that he is the real Macoco and therefore Manuela should love him. He is arrested, and the united Kelly and Garland appear in the last scene as stage partners singing "Be a Clown" to the audience.

Through the personalities of Garland and Kelly, *The Pirate* explores the theme of identity I have discussed in Astaire's films in a very different way. Serafin's courtship of Manuela reveals that her desire for Macoco is a desire for a romantic individualism outside society—a theme made especially strong by setting the film in an eighteenth-century Spanish Roman Catholic country with all its elaborate social forms and ceremonies. Kelly hypnotizes her with a spinning mirror—

---

[7]It is worth mentioning that Astaire and Kelly are appropriately enough the two supreme examples of Hollywood stars who never really gave their private lives in any way over to the fan magazines or the mechanism of offscreen publicity, since their screen presences are personal enough.

[8]Observers of Vincente Minnelli have often pointed out the constant interest in the clash of reality and dream in his films. Here, of course, I am considering these themes in terms of the larger issue of the history of musicals as a genre. The way specific directors, with their own thematic and stylistic preoccupations, interact with pre-existing conventions to change those conventions and clarify their own interests at the same time is a topic that requires much more minute examination than I can give it here.

an image of the many possible selves. The Manuela that is released, the self below the social surface, is a singing, dancing self. Her exuberance indicates that Serafin has in fact released more than he expects or may want. He is a professional artist. But she gets her art directly from her inner life, untamed by society or by learned craft. Garland is perfect for this kind of role because she projects so clearly the image of a restrained, almost mouse-like person until she begins to sing and dance. (Her first important film, *The Wizard of Oz*, Victor Fleming, 1939, solidified this tension in Garland between the acceptance of daily life in a world of drabness and moral boredom, and the possibility of escape to an exuberant singing, dancing world of dream. It appeared as well in *Meet Me in St. Louis*, 1944, another Minnelli film, where the pattern of stability and release is more parallel to that of *The Pirate*.)

Serafin is the alternative to Macoco in more ways than one. The real pirate has changed from an antisocial adventurer to a socially dictatorial mayor, thus rejecting the Macoco side of himself to become almost the opposite. But Kelly instead tries to mediate individuality and community. His first song in the film is "Niña," a typical Kelly dance in a street fair, where he sings and dances with half the surprised people there to weave together a kind of community of otherwise isolated individuals and objects through the catalyst of his own personality and artistic ability. The song relates how he calls every girl he meets "niña," that is, little girl. At the end of the song Garland appears and the amazed Kelly asks her what her name is. Like Rogers at the end of *Shall We Dance*, she stands apart from communal anonymity. Serafin is the articulate adventurer, the popular artist, who sees his art to be part of a creation of community; she is the individual artist, whose art is less craft than a swelling sense of herself from within. We admire and feel friendly to him because he includes us in his dance. But we identify with her, for she, like us, is not professional, even in the loose sense in which Serafin is professional. Serafin realizes this and therefore pretends to be Macoco to win her. In the climactic moment, when he is plotting to get the real Macoco to reveal himself and brings out the mirror to rehypnotize Garland, Slezak breaks the mirror. But it doesn't matter. Manuela is willing to go along with Serafin's plot, as Garland accepts Kelly's choreography and control. Her energy, once released, can be controlled, especially within the context of love and theater. *The Pirate* is therefore a next step from the themes of the Astaire-Rogers films. Kelly makes the perfect couple the center of an ideal community created by dance, a world of harmony where everyone on the street not only sympathizes with the exuberance you feel because you're in love, but also knows all the words and dance steps that express your feelings.

The context of the ideal, the place where the true self can be revealed, is still theatrical space. The final song, "Be a Clown," emphasizes the responsible escape of art, especially popular art, in a way very reminiscent of the title song at the end of *Shall We Dance*. But the inclusion of the Garland figure—the nonprofessional dancer from the heart—indicates the direction that Kelly has taken the musical, as does the fact that Kelly and Garland are not elegant in their world of theater, but clownish and self-mocking, more willing than Astaire and Rogers to include the potential disruptiveness of the world outside them and the world within. Astaire and Rogers dance for us, looking at each other primarily to integrate their dancing. Kelly and

Garland convey a much friendlier and more personal relationship. We may watch Astaire and Rogers. But we empathize with Kelly and Garland.[9]

Kelly in *The Pirate* is an entertainer. But the emphasis of the film is less on his dancing and singing than on the world that dance and theater can create together. The stylization and historical setting of *The Pirate* emphasize the release from the stultifying social self dance allows; the contemporary setting of most other Kelly films further highlights Kelly's effort to bring his dancing out of the enclosed world of theater and make the whole world a theater, responsive to and changed by his energy. Astaire's dances define a world of perfect form, while Kelly's often reach out to include improvisation, spontaneity, and happenstance. The scene that contrasts best with Astaire's imitation of the record player and the machines in *Shall We Dance* is Kelly's marvelous interweaving of a creaky board and a piece of paper left on the stage in *Summer Stock* (1950). Kelly's self-mocking smile reflects the way most of his films continue the attack of Astaire's films against artistic pretension. Embodying the catalytic possibilities of dance to create a new coherence for the nontheatrical world, Kelly journeys through parody and realism, attacking formal excesses on the one hand and transforming everyday reality on the other.

Singin' in the Rain (Kelly and Stanley Donen, 1952) is one aspect of his effort and *On the Town* (Kelly and Stanley Donen, 1949) is the other. The frame of *Singin' in the Rain* is a full-scale parody of the early days of sound film (an appropriate subject for the musical), complete with an attack on artistic high seriousness in favor of the comic exuberance of popular art. The essential scene is Donald O'Connor's incredible acrobatic dance "Make 'Em Laugh" (unfortunately often cut for television), like "Be a Clown" a description of the popular artist's relation to his audience. But this time, instead of being on a stage, the number is done amid a welter of different film sets depicting different worlds, with stagehands moving through the scene. O'Connor's partner for a while is a featureless, uncostumed dummy that he makes seem alive (a reminiscence of the Ginger Rogers dummy in *Shall We Dance*), and for a finale he starts walking up the set walls and finally jumps right through them. In the early scenes of the film, Kelly, the phony silent-screen lover, needs to set up a sound stage and props before he can tell Debbie Reynolds he loves her and sings "You Were Meant for Me." But the declaration becomes acceptable as real emotion only when, in the next scene, he and Donald O'Connor parody the demands of their diction coach in "Moses Supposes." By this time, to parallel his change from form to substance, Kelly has left his suits and tuxedoes behind and dresses in the more familiar open-collared shirt and loafers. Once again, the scar on his cheek is an emblem of the reality that will emerge. In *Singin' in the Rain* silent films are artificial in their stylized actions and hoked-up emotions; only sound is

---

[9]The strength of Minnelli's own vision obviously has its place in understanding *The Pirate* (1948), although the comparative visual stasis and the commitment to the values of stability that characterize *Meet Me in St. Louis* (1944) indicate the importance of Kelly in changing his style and his ideas. Minnelli's musicals may try to celebrate the triumph of the individual through art, but just as often (for example, in *The Band Wagon*, 1953) they catch a tint of gloom from his more melancholic nonmusical films, which often deal with artistic compromise and disintegration, either in the context of the world of film (*The Bad and the Beautiful*, 1952; *Two Weeks in Another Town*, 1962) or the other arts (*Lust for Life*, 1956; *Some Came Running*, 1958). Only in the pure world of the musical can art and individuality succeed without compromise.

real. The discovery of communication with an audience changes clearly from "Shall We Dance" to "Be a Clown" to "Make 'Em Laugh," with an increasing emphasis on the place of informality and personal style. The solution of the plot of *Singin' in the Rain* is to make the bad serious film into the parodic musical; almost all the dances in the film contain parodies of earlier dances and dancers, in the same somewhat mocking homage that characterizes the attitude to Impressionism in *An American in Paris* (Minnelli, 1951). This is the essence of the kind of energy Kelly's film embodies: theater, like the ability to dance, is a manner of inner perspective on the world outside. The reality of sound film that Kelly discovers follows his own curve of increased dancing in the film until the great set piece of "Gotta Dance," another statement of Kelly's belief that dancing is a compulsion from within more authentic than the forms imposed from without. The final scene, in which Debbie Reynolds is revealed as the voice of Jean Hagen from behind the curtain, repeats on still another level the basic theme of outer form and inner reality. Music and dance are the real spirit of film in the same way they are the real soul and energy of New York in *On the Town*, or Paris in *An American in Paris*.

Kelly's dancing tries not to be the aesthetic escape of Astaire's. It is more utopian because it aims to bring the world together. Astaire's films often imply that dance and therefore energy itself can be a refuge from a stuffy world of social forms; Kelly's films imply that dance and the individual can change the world. The three sailors on leave in *On the Town*—Kelly, Frank Sinatra, and Jules Munshin—are searching for the perfect partner and all find their girls, not in a purified world of dance, but in a real New York (the first musical made on location) that embraces both their dancing and their search. The women—Vera-Ellen, Ann Miller, and Betty Garrett—are all at least the equals of the men in exuberance, energy, and wit. They make their own space in a public world, like Kelly in the "Singin' in the Rain" sequence, splashing through puddles of chance and nature. The great pretenders in *On the Town* are Kelly and Vera-Ellen, the small-town kids who come on to each other as sophisticates. The moral is that of almost all Kelly films: don't worry about the true self; it will turn out to be better than the one you're pretending to be. Kelly's kind of musical doesn't retreat from reality. It tries to subvert reality through its new energy, an energy available to everyone in the audience through Kelly's insistence on the nonprofessional character, the musical self that wells from inside instead of being imposed from without, whether by training, tradition, or society. . . .

1976

RICK ALTMAN
A SEMANTIC/SYNTACTIC APPROACH
TO FILM GENRE

Rick Altman's scholarly background is in French and comparative literature.
He has written extensively on film genres, especially the musical, in *The
American Film Musical* (1987), and as editor of the anthology *Genre, the
Musical: A Reader* (1981). *Film/Genre* (1999) provides both a history of genre
theory and a chronicle of the shifting categories by which films have been
classified over the years. In other areas of film study, his *Silent Film Sound*
(2004) offers a thorough history of the techniques and technologies of silent
film accompaniment, and Altman is currently completing a follow-up history
of sound during the studio era. He is currently professor of cinema and comparative literature at the University of Iowa. His most recent book is *A Theory
of Narrative* (2008).

What is a genre? Which films are genre films? How do we know to which genre
they belong? As fundamental as these questions may seem, they are almost never
asked—let alone answered—in the field of cinema studies. Most comfortable in
the seemingly uncomplicated world of Hollywood classics, genre critics have felt
little need to reflect openly on the assumptions underlying their work. Everything
seems so clear. Why bother to theorize, American pragmatism asks, when there
are no problems to solve? We all know a genre when we see one. Scratch only
where it itches. According to this view, genre theory would be called for only in
the unlikely event that knowledgeable genre critics disagreed on basic issues. The
task of the theorist is then to adjudicate among conflicting approaches, not so
much by dismissing unsatisfactory positions but by constructing a model that
reveals the relationship between differing critical claims and their function within
a broader cultural context. Whereas the French clearly view theory as a first principle, we Americans tend to see it as a last resort, something to turn to when all
else fails.

Even in this limited, pragmatic view, whereby theory is to be avoided at all costs,
the time for theory is nevertheless upon us. The clock has struck thirteen; we had
best call in the theoreticians. The more genre criticism I read, the more uncertainty
I note in the choice or extent of essential critical terms. Often what appears as hesitation in the terminology of a single critic will turn into a clear contradiction when
studies by two or more critics are compared. Now, it would be one thing if these
contradictions were simply a matter of fact. On the contrary, however, I suggest that
these are not temporary problems, bound to disappear as soon as we have more

information or better analysts. Instead, these uncertainties reflect constitutive weaknesses of current notions of genre. Three contradictions in particular seem worthy of a good scratch.

When we establish the corpus of a genre we generally tend to do two things at once, and thus establish two alternate groups of texts, each corresponding to a different notion of corpus. On the one hand, we have an unwieldly list of texts corresponding to a simple, tautological definition of the genre (e.g., western = film that takes place in the American West, or musical = film with diegetic music). This *inclusive* list is the kind that gets consecrated by generic encyclopedias or checklists. On the other hand, we find critics, theoreticians, and other arbiters of taste sticking to a familiar canon that has little to do with the broad, tautological definition. Here the same films are mentioned again and again, not only because they are well known or particularly well made, but because they somehow seem to represent the genre more fully and faithfully than other apparently more tangential films. This *exclusive* list of films generally occurs not in a dictionary context, but instead in connection with attempts to arrive at the overall meaning or structure of a genre. The relative status of these alternate approaches to the constitution of a generic corpus may easily be sensed from the following typical conversation:

I mean, what do you do with Elvis Presley films? You can hardly call them musicals.

Why not? They're loaded with songs and they've got a narrative that ties the numbers together, don't they?

Yeah, I suppose. I guess you'd have to call *Fun in Acapulco* a musical, but it's sure no *Singin' in the Rain*. Now there's a real musical.

When is a musical not a musical? When it has Elvis Presley in it. What may at first have seemed no more than an uncertainty on the part of the critical community now clearly appears as a contradiction. Because there are two competing notions of generic corpus on our critical scene, it is perfectly possible for a film to be simultaneously included in a particular generic corpus and excluded from that same corpus.

A second uncertainty is associated with the relative status of theory and history in genre studies. Before semiotics came along, generic titles and definitions were largely borrowed from the industry itself; what little generic theory there was tended therefore to be confused with historical analysis. With the heavy influence of semiotics on generic theory over the last two decades, self-conscious *critical* vocabulary came to be systematically preferred to the now-suspect *user* vocabulary. The contributions of Propp, Lévi-Strauss, Frye, and Todorov to genre studies have not been uniformly productive, however, because of the special place reserved for genre study within the semiotic project. If structuralist critics systematically chose as the object of their analysis large groups of popular texts, it was in order to cover a basic flaw in the semiotic understanding of textual analysis. Now, one of the most striking aspects of Saussure's theory of language is his emphasis on the inability of any single individual to effect change within that language.[1] The fixity of the linguistic community thus serves as justification for Saussure's fundamentally synchronic

[1]Ferdinand de Saussure, *Course in General Linguistics*, edited by Charles Bally and Albert Sechehaye, translated by Wade Baskin (New York: McGraw-Hill, 1959), pp. 14–17.

approach to language. When literary semioticians applied this linguistic model to problems of textual analysis, they never fully addressed the notion of interpretive community implied by Saussure's linguistic community. Preferring narrative to narration, system to process, and *histoire* to *discours*, the first semiotics ran headlong into a set of restrictions and contradictions that eventually spawned the more process-oriented second semiotics. It is in this context that we must see the resolutely synchronic attempts of Propp, Lévi-Strauss, Todorov, and many another influential genre analyst.[2] Unwilling to compromise their systems by the historical notion of linguistic community, these theoreticians instead substituted the generic context for the linguistic community, as if the weight of numerous "similar" texts were sufficient to locate the meaning of a text independently of a specific audience. Far from being sensitive to concerns of history, semiotic genre analysis was by definition and from the start devoted to bypassing history. Treating genres as neutral constructs, semioticians of the sixties and early seventies blinded us to the discursive power of generic formations. Because they treated genres as the interpretive community, they were unable to perceive the important role of genres in exercising influence on the interpretive community. Instead of reflecting openly on the way in which Hollywood uses its genres to short-circuit the normal interpretive process, structuralist critics plunged headlong into the trap, taking Hollywood's ideological effect for a natural ahistorical cause.

Genres were always—and continue to be—treated as if they spring full-blown from the head of Zeus. It is thus not surprising to find that even the most advanced of current genre theories, those that see generic texts as negotiating a relationship between a specific production system and a given audience, still hold to a notion of genre that is fundamentally ahistorical in nature.[3] More and more, however, as scholars come to know the full range of individual Hollywood genres, we are finding that genres are far from exhibiting the homogeneity that this synchronic approach posits. Whereas one Hollywood genre may be borrowed with little change from another medium, a second genre may develop slowly, change constantly, and surge recognizably before settling into a familiar pattern, while a third may go through an extended series of paradigms, none of which may be claimed as dominant. As long as Hollywood genres are conceived as Platonic categories, existing outside the flow of time, it will be impossible to reconcile *genre theory*, which has always accepted as given the timelessness of a characteristic structure, and *genre history*, which has concentrated on chronicling the development, deployment, and disappearance of this same structure.

A third contradiction looms larger still, for it involves the two general directions taken by genre criticism as a whole over the last decade or two. Following Lévi-Strauss, a growing number of critics throughout the seventies dwelled on the mythical

[2]Especially in Vladimir Propp, *Morphology of the Folktale* (Bloomington: Indiana Research Center in Anthropology, 1958); Claude Lévi-Strauss, "The Structural Study of Myths," in *Structural Anthropology*, trans. Claire Jacobson and Brooke Grundfest Schoepf (New York: Basic Books, 1963), pp. 206–31; Tzvetan Todorov, *Grammaire du Décaméron* (The Hague: Mouton, 1969); and Tzvetan Todorov, *The Fantastic*, translated by Richard Howard (Ithaca: Cornell University Press, 1975).

[3]Even Stephen Neale's recent discursively oriented study falls prey to this problem. See *Genre* (London: British Film Institute, 1980).

qualities of Hollywood genres and thus on the audience's ritual relationship to genre film. The film industry's desire to please and its need to attract consumers were viewed as the mechanism whereby spectators were actually able to designate the kind of films they wanted to see. By choosing the films it would patronize, the audience revealed its preferences and its beliefs, thus inducing Hollywood studios to produce films reflecting its desires. Participation in the genre film experience thus reinforces spectator expectations and desires. Far from being limited to mere entertainment, filmgoing offers a satisfaction more akin to that associated with established religion. Most openly championed by John Cawelti, this ritual approach appears as well in books by Leo Braudy, Frank McConnell, Michael Wood, Will Wright, and Tom Schatz.[4] It has the merit not only of accounting for the intensity of identification typical of American genre film audiences, but it also encourages the placing of genre film narratives into an appropriately wider context of narrative analysis.

Curiously, however, while the ritual approach was attributing ultimate authorship to the audience, with the studios simply serving, for a price, the national will, a parallel ideological approach was demonstrating how audiences are manipulated by the business and political interests of Hollywood. Starting with *Cahiers du Cinéma* and moving rapidly to *Screen, Jump Cut*, and a growing number of journals, this view has recently joined hands with a more general critique of the mass media offered by the Frankfurt school.[5] Looked at in this way, genres are simply the generalized, identifiable structures through which Hollywood's rhetoric flows. Far more attentive to discursive concerns than the ritual approach, which remains faithful to Lévi-Strauss in emphasizing narrative systems, the ideological approach stresses questions of representation and identification previously left aside. Simplifying a bit, we might say that it characterizes each individual genre as a specific type of life, an untruth whose most characteristic feature is its ability to masquerade as truth. Whereas the ritual approach sees Hollywood as responding to societal pressure and thus expressing audience desires, the ideological approach claims that Hollywood takes advantage of spectator energy and psychic investment in order to lure the audience into Hollywood's own positions. The two are irreducibly opposed, yet these irreconcilable arguments continue to represent the most interesting and well defended of recent approaches to Hollywood genre film.

---

[4]John Cawelti, *The Six-Gun Mystique* (Bowling Green: Bowling Green University Popular Press, [1970]), and John Cawelti, *Adventure, Mystery and Romance* (Chicago: University of Chicago Press, 1976); Leo Braudy, *The World in a Frame: What We See in Films* (Garden City: Anchor Books, 1977); Frank McConnell, *The Spoken Seen: Films and the Romantic Imagination* (Baltimore: Johns Hopkins University Press, 1975); Michael Wood, *America in the Movies, or Santa Maria, It Had Slipped My Mind* (New York: Delta, 1975); Will Wright, *Sixguns and Society: A Structural Study of the Western* (Berkeley: University of California Press, 1975); Thomas Schatz, *Hollywood Genres: Formulas, Film-making, and the Studio System* (New York: Random House, 1981).

[5]See especially the collective text "*Young Mr. Lincoln* de John Ford," *Cahiers du Cinéma*, no. 223 (August 1970): 29–47, translated in *Screen* 14, no. 3 (Autumn 1973): 29–43; and Jean-Louis Comolli's six-part article "Technique et ideologie," *Cahiers du Cinéma*, nos. 229–41 (1971–1972). The entire *Screen* project has been usefully summarized, with extensive bibliographical notes, by Philip Rosen, "*Screen* and the Marxist Project in Film Criticism," *Quarterly Review of Film Studies* 2, no. 3 (August 1977): 273–87; on *Screen*'s approach to ideology, see also Stephen Heath, "On Screen, in Frame: Film and Ideology," *Quarterly Review of Film Studies* 1, no. 3 (August 1976): 251–65. The most important influence on all these positions is Louis Althusser, "Ideology and Ideological State Apparatuses," in *Lenin and Philosophy and Other Essays*, translated by Ben Brewster (New York: Monthly Review Press, 1971), pp. 127–86.

Here we have three problems that I take to be not limited to a single school of criticism or of a single genre but implicit in every major field of current genre analysis. In nearly every argument about the limits of a generic corpus, the opposition of an inclusive list to an exclusive canon surfaces. Whereever genres are discussed, the divergent concerns of theorists and historians are increasingly obvious. And even when the topic is limited to genre theory alone, no agreement can be found between those who propose a ritual function for film genres and those who champion an ideological purpose. We find ourselves desperately in need of a theory which, without dismissing any of these widely held positions, would explain the circumstances underlying their existence, thus paving the way for a critical methodology that encompasses and indeed thrives on their inherent contradictions. If we have learned anything from poststructuralist criticism, we have learned not to fear logical contradictions but instead to respect the extraordinary energy generated by the play of contradictory forces within a field. What we need now is a new critical strategy enabling us simultaneously to understand and to capitalize on the tensions existing in current generic criticism.

In assessing theories of genre, critics have often labeled them according to a particular theory's most salient features or the type of activity to which it devotes its most concentrated attention. Paul Hernadi, for example, recognizes four general classes of genre theory: expressive, pragmatic, structural, and mimetic.[6] In his extremely influential introduction to *The Fantastic*, Tzvetan Todorov opposes historical to theoretical genres, as well as elementary genres to their complex counterparts.[7] Others, like Frederic Jameson, have followed Todorov and other French semioticians in distinguishing between semantic and syntactic approaches to genre.[8] While there is anything but general agreement on the exact frontier separating semantic from syntactic views, we can as a whole distinguish between generic definitions that depend on a list of common traits, attitudes, characters, shots, locations, sets, and the like—thus stressing the semantic elements that make up the genre—and definitions that play up instead certain constitutive relationships between undesignated and variable placeholders—relationships that might be called the genre's fundamental syntax. The semantic approach thus stresses the genre's building blocks, while the syntactic view privileges the structures into which they are arranged.

The difference between semantic and syntactic definitions is perhaps most apparent in familiar approaches to the western. Jean Mitry provides us with a clear example of the most common definition. The western, Mitry proposes, is a "film whose action, situated in the American West, is consistent with the atmosphere, the values, and the conditions of existence in the Far West between 1840 and 1900."[9] Based on the presence or absence of easily identifiable elements, Mitry's nearly tautological definition implies

---

[6]Paul Hernadi, *Beyond Genre: New Directions in Literary Classification* (Ithaca: Cornell University Press, 1972).

[7]Todorov, *The Fantastic*.

[8]Fredric Jameson, "Magical Narratives: Romance as Genre," *New Literary History* 7 (1975): 135–63. It should be noted here that my use of the term "semantic" differs from Jameson's. Whereas he stresses the overall semantic input of a text, I am dealing with the individual semantic units of the text. His term thus approximates the sense of "global meaning," while mine is closer to "lexical choices."

[9]Jean Mitry, *Dictionnaire du cinéma* (Paris: Larousse, 1963), p. 276.

a broad, undifferentiated generic corpus. Marc Vernet's more detailed list is more sensitive to cinematic concerns, yet overall it follows the same semantic model. Vernet outlines general atmosphere ("emphasis on basic elements, such as earth, dust, water, and leather"), stock characters ("the tough/soft cowboy, the lonely sheriff, the faithful or treacherous Indian, and the strong but tender woman"), as well as technical elements ("use of fast tracking and crane shots").[10] An entirely different solution is suggested by Jim Kitses, who emphasizes not the vocabulary of the western but the relationships linking lexical elements. For Kitses the western grows out of a dialectic between the West as garden and as desert (between culture and nature, community and individual, future and past).[11] The western's vocabulary is thus generated by this syntactic relationship, and not vice versa. John Cawelti attempts to systematize the western in a similar fashion: the western is always set on or near a frontier, where man encounters his uncivilized double. The western thus takes place on the border between two lands, between two eras, and with a hero who remains divided between two value systems (for he combines the town's morals with the outlaw's skills).[12]

In passing we might well note the divergent qualities associated with these two approaches. While the semantic approach has little explanatory power, it is applicable to a larger number of films. Conversely, the syntactic approach surrenders broad applicability in return for the ability to isolate a genre's specific meaning-bearing structures. This alternative seemingly leaves the genre analyst in a quandary: choose the semantic view and you give up *explanatory power*; choose the syntactic approach and you do without *broad applicability*. In terms of the western, the problem of the so-called "Pennsylvania western" is instructive here. To most observers it seems quite clear that films like *High, Wide and Handsome* (Rouben Mamoulian, 1937), *Drums along the Mohawk* (John Ford, 1939), and *Unconquered* (Cecil B. DeMille, 1947) have definite affinities with the western. Employing familiar characters set in relationships similar to their counterparts west of the Mississippi, these films construct plots and develop a frontier structure clearly derived from decades of western novels and films. But they do it in Pennsylvania, and in the wrong century. Are these films westerns because they share the syntax of hundreds of films we call westerns? Or are they not westerns, because they don't fit Mitry's definition?

In fact, the "Pennsylvania western" (like the urban, spaghetti, and sci-fi varieties) represents a quandary only because critics have insisted on dismissing one type of definition and approach in favor of another. As a rule, semantic and syntactic approaches to genre have been proposed, analyzed, evaluated, and disseminated separately, in spite of the complementarity implied by their names. Indeed, many arguments centering on generic problems have arisen only when semantic and syntactic theoreticians have simply talked past each other, each unaware of the other's divergent orientation. I maintain that these two categories of generic analysis are complementary, that they can be combined, and in fact that some of the most important questions of genre study can be asked only when they *are* combined. In short, I propose a semantic/syntactic approach to genre study.

[10]Marc Vernet, *Lectures du film* (Paris: Albatros, 1976), pp. 111–12.
[11]Jim Kitses, *Horizons West* (Bloomington: Indiana University Press, 1969), pp. 10–14.
[12]Cawelti, *The Six-Gun Mystique*.

Now, in order to discover whether the proposed semantic/syntactic approach provides any new understanding, let us return to the three contradictions delineated earlier. First, there is the split corpus that characterizes current genre study—on the one side an inclusive list, on the other an exclusive pantheon. It should now be quite clear that each corpus corresponds to a different approach to generic analysis and definition. Tautological semantic definitions, with their goal of broad applicability, outline a large genre of semantically similar texts, while syntactic definitions, intent as they are on explaining the genre, stress a narrow range of texts that privilege specific syntactic relationships. To insist on one of these approaches to the exclusion of the other is to turn a blind eye on the necessarily dual nature of any generic corpus. For every film that participates actively in the elaboration of a genre's syntax there are numerous others content to deploy in no particular relationship the elements traditionally associated with the genre. We need to recognize that not all genre films relate to their genre in the same way or to the same extent. By simultaneously accepting semantic and syntactic notions of genre we avail ourselves of a possible way to deal critically with differing levels of "genericity." In addition, a dual approach permits a far more accurate description of the numerous intergeneric connections typically suppressed by single-minded approaches. It is simply not possible to describe Hollywood cinema accurately without the ability to account for the numerous films that innovate by combining the syntax of one genre with the semantics of another. In fact, it is only when we begin to take up problems of genre history that the full value of the semantic/syntactic approach becomes obvious.

As I pointed out earlier, most genre theoreticians have followed the semiotic model and steered clear of historical considerations. Even in the relatively few cases where problems of generic history have been addressed, as in the attempts of Metz and Wright to periodize the western, history has been conceptualized as nothing more than a discontinuous succession of discrete moments, each characterized by a different basic version of the genre—that is, by a different syntactic pattern that the genre adopts.[13] In short, genre theory has up to now aimed almost exclusively at the elaboration of a synchronic model approximating the syntactic operation of a specific genre. Now, quite obviously, no major genre remains unchanged over the many decades of its existence. In order to mask the scandal of applying synchronic analysis to an evolving form, critics have been extremely clever in their creation of categories designed to negate the notion of change and to imply the perpetual self-identity of each genre. Westerns and horror films are often referred to as "classic," the musical is defined in terms of the so-called "Platonic ideal" of integration, the critical corpus of the melodrama has largely been restricted to the postwar efforts of Sirk and Minnelli, and so on. Lacking a workable hypothesis regarding the historical dimension of generic syntax, we have insulated that syntax, along with the genre theory that studies it, from the flow of time.

As a working hypothesis, I suggest that genres arise in one of two fundamental ways: either a relatively stable set of semantic givens is developed through syntactic experimentation into a coherent and durable syntax, or an already existing syntax adopts a new set of semantic elements. In the first case, the genre's characteristic semantic configuration is identifiable long before a syntactic pattern has become

---

[13]See, for example, Christian Metz, *Language and Cinema* (The Hague: Mouton, 1974), pp. 148–61; and Wright, *Sixguns and Society, passim.*

stabilized, thus justifying the previously mentioned duality of the generic corpus. In cases of this first type, description of the way in which a set of semantic givens develops into a henceforth relatively stable syntax constitutes the history of the genre while at the same time identifying the structures on which genre theory depends. In dealing with the early development of the musical, for example, we might well follow the attempts during the 1927–1930 period to build a backstage or night-club semantics into a melodramatic syntax, with music regularly reflecting the sorrow of death or parting. After the slack years of 1931–1932, however, the musical began to grow in a new direction; while maintaining substantially the same semantic materials, the genre increasingly related the energy of music-making to the joy of coupling, the strength of the community, and the pleasures of entertainment. Far from being exiled from history, the musical's characteristic syntax can be shown by the generic historian to grow out of the linking of specific semantic elements at identifiable points. A measure of continuity is thus developed between the task of the historian and that of the theoretician, for the tasks of both are now redefined as the study of the interrelationships between semantic elements and syntactic bonds.

This continuity between history and theory is operative as well in the second type of generic development posited earlier. When we analyze the large variety of wartime films that portray the Japanese or Germans as villains, we tend to have recourse to extrafilmic events in order to explain particular characterizations. We thus miss the extent to which films like *All through the Night* (Vincent Sherman, 1942), *Sherlock Holmes and the Voice of Terror* (John Rawlins, 1942), or the serial *The Winslow Boy* (Anthony Asquith, 1948) simply transfer to a new set of semantic elements the righteous cops-punish-criminals syntax that the gangster genre of the early thirties had turned to starting with *G-Men* (William Keighley, 1935). Again, it is the interplay of syntax and semantics that provides grist for both the historical and the theoretical mill. Or take the development of the science fiction film. At first defined only by a relatively stable science fiction semantics, the genre first began borrowing the syntactic relationships previously established by the horror film, only to move in recent years increasingly toward the syntax of the western. By maintaining simultaneous descriptions according to both parameters, we are not likely to fall into the trap of equating *Star Wars* (George Lucas, 1977) with the western (as numerous recent critics have done), even though it shares certain syntactic patterns with that genre. In short, by taking seriously the multiple connections between semantics and syntax, we establish a new continuity, relating film analysis, genre theory, and genre history.

But what is it that energizes the transformation of a borrowed semantics into a uniquely Hollywood syntax? Or what is it that justifies the intrusion of a new semantics into a well-defined syntactic situation? Far from postulating a uniquely internal, formal progression, I would propose that the relationship between the semantic and the syntactic constitutes the very site of negotiation between Hollywood and its audience, and thus between ritual and ideological uses of genre. Often, when critics of opposing persuasions disagree over a major issue, it is because they have established within the same general corpus two separate and opposed canons, each supporting one point of view. Thus, when Catholics and Protestants or liberals and conservatives quote the Bible, they are rarely quoting the same passages. The striking fact about ritual and ideological genre theoreticians, however, is that they regularly stress the same canon, that small group of texts most clearly reflecting a genre's stable syntax. The films of John Ford, for example, have played a major role in the development of ritual and ideological approaches alike. From Sarris and Bogdanovich to Schatz and Wright, champions of Ford's understanding and transparent expression of American values have stressed the communitarian side of his films, while others, starting with the influential *Cahiers du Cinéma* study of *Young Mr. Lincoln* (1939), have shown how a call to community can be used to lure spectators into a carefully chosen, ideologically determined subject position. A similar situation obtains in the musical, where a growing body of ritual analyses of the Astaire-Rogers and postwar MGM Freed unit films is matched by an increasing number of studies demonstrating the ideological investment of those very same films.[14] The corpus of nearly every major genre has developed in the same way, with critics of both camps gravitating toward and eventually basing their arguments on the same narrow range of films. Just as Minnelli and Sirk dominate the criticism of melodrama, Hitchcock has become nearly synonymous with the thriller. Of all major genres, only the film noir has failed to attract critics of both sides to a shared corpus of major texts—no doubt because of the general inability of ritual critics to accommodate the genre's anticommunitarian stance.

This general agreement on a canon stems, I would claim, from the fundamentally bivalent nature of any relatively stable generic syntax. If it takes a long time to establish a generic syntax and if many seemingly promising formulas or successful films never spawn a genre, it is because only certain types of structure, within a particular semantic environment, are suited to the special bilingualism required of a durable genre. The structures of Hollywood cinema, like those of American popular mythology as a whole, serve to mask the very distinction between ritual and ideological functions. Hollywood does not simply lend its voice to the public's desires, nor does it simply manipulate the audience. On the contrary, most genres go through a period of accommodation during which the public's desires are fitted to Hollywood's priorities (and vice versa). Because the public doesn't want to know that it is being manipulated, the successful ritual/ideological "fit" is almost always one that disguises Hollywood's potential for manipulation while playing up its capacity for entertainment.

Whenever a lasting fit is obtained—which it is whenever a semantic genre becomes a syntactic one—it is because a common ground has been found, a region where the audience's ritual values coincide with Hollywood's ideological ones. The development of a specific syntax within a given semantic context thus serves a double function: it binds element to element in a logical order, at the same time accommodating audience desires to studio concerns. The successful genre owes its success not alone to its reflection of an audience ideal, nor solely to its status as apology for the Hollywood enterprise, but to its ability to carry out both functions simulta-

---

[14]This relationship is especially interesting in the work of Richard Dyer and Jane Feuer, both of whom attempt to confront the interdependence of ritual and ideological components. See in particular Richard Dyer, "Entertainment and Utopia," in *Genre: The Musical*, edited by Rick Altman (London and Boston: Routledge and Kegan Paul, 1981), pp. 175–89; and Jane Feuer, *The Hollywood Musical* (Bloomington: Indiana University Press, 1982).

neously. It is this sleight of hand, this strategic overdetermination, that most clearly characterizes American film production during the studio years.

The approach to genre sketched out in this article of course raises some questions of its own. Just where, for example, do we locate the exact border between the semantic and the syntactic? And how are these two categories related? Each of these questions constitutes an essential area of inquiry, one that is far too complex to permit full treatment here. Nevertheless, a few remarks may be in order. A reasonable observer might well ask why my approach attributes such importance to the seemingly banal distinction between a text's materials and the structures into which they are arranged. Why this distinction rather than, for example, the more cinematic division between diegetic elements and the technical means deployed in representing them? The answer to these questions lies in a general theory of textual signification that I have expounded elsewhere.[15] Briefly, that theory distinguishes between the primary, linguistic meaning of a text's component parts and the secondary or textual meaning that those parts acquire through a structuring process internal to the text or to the genre. Within a single text, therefore, the same phenomenon may have more than one meaning depending on whether we consider it at the linguistic or textual level. In the western, for example, the horse is an animal that serves as a method of locomotion. This primary level of meaning, corresponding to the normal extent of the concept "horse" within the language, is matched by a series of other meanings derived from the structures into which the western sets the horse. Opposition of the horse to the automobile or locomotive ("iron horse") reinforces the organic, nonmechanical sense of the term "horse" already implicit in the language, thus transferring that concept from the paradigm "method of locomotion" to the paradigm "soon-to-be-outmoded preindustrial carry-over."

In the same way, horror films borrow from a nineteenth-century literary tradition their dependence on the presence of a monster. In doing so, they clearly perpetuate the linguistic meaning of the monster as "threatening inhuman being," but at the same time, by developing new syntactic ties, they generate an important new set of textual meanings. For the nineteenth century, the appearance of the monster is invariably tied to a romantic overreaching, the attempt of some human scientist to tamper with the divine order. In texts like Mary Shelley's *Frankenstein*, Balzac's *La Recherche de l'absolu*, or Stevenson's *Dr. Jekyll and Mr. Hyde*, a studied syntax equates man and monster, attributing to both the monstrosity of being outside nature as defined by established religion and science. With the horror film, a different syntax rapidly equates monstrosity not with the overactive nineteenth-century mind, but with an equally overactive twentieth-century body. Again and again, the monster is identified with his human counterpart's unsatisfied sexual appetite, thus establishing with the same primary "linguistic" materials (the monster, fear, the chase, death) entirely new textual meanings, phallic rather than scientific in nature.

The distinction between the semantic and the syntactic, in the way I have defined it here, thus corresponds to a distinction between the primary, linguistic elements of which all texts are made and the secondary, textual meanings that are sometimes

---

[15]Charles F. Altman, "Intratextual Rewriting: Textuality as Language Formation," in *The Sign in Music and Literature*, edited by Wendy Steiner (Austin: University of Texas Press, 1981), pp. 39–51.

constructed by virtue of the syntactic bonds established between primary elements. This distinction is stressed in the approach to genre presented here not because it is convenient nor because it corresponds to a modish theory of the relation between language and narrative, but because the semantic/syntactic distinction is fundamental to a theory of how meaning of one kind contributes to and eventually establishes meaning of another. Just as individual texts establish new meanings for familiar terms only by subjecting well-known semantic units to a syntactic redetermination, so generic meaning comes into being only through the repeated deployment of substantially the same syntactic strategies. It is in this way, for example, that making music—at the linguistic level primarily a way of making a living—becomes in the musical a figure for making love—a textual meaning essential to the constitution of that syntactic genre.

We must of course remember that, while each individual text clearly has a syntax of its own, the syntax implied here is that of the genre, which does not appear as *generic* syntax unless it is reinforced numerous times by the syntactic patterns of individual texts. The Hollywood genres that have proven the most durable are precisely those that have established the most coherent syntax (the western, the musical); those that disappear the quickest depend entirely on recurring semantic elements, never developing a stable syntax (reporter, catastrophe, and big-caper films, to name but a few). If I locate the border between the semantic and the syntactic at the dividing line between the linguistic and the textual, it is thus in response not just to the theoretical but also to the historical dimension of generic functioning.

In proposing such a model, however, I may leave too much room for one particular type of misunderstanding. It has been a cliché of the last two decades to insist that structure carries meaning, while the choice of structured elements is largely negligible in the process of signification. This position, most openly championed by Lévi-Strauss in his cross-cultural methodology for studying myth, may seem to be implied by my model, but is in fact not borne out by my research.[16] Spectator response, I believe, is heavily conditioned by the choice of semantic elements and atmosphere, because a given semantics used in a specific cultural situation will recall to an actual interpretive community the particular syntax with which that semantics has traditionally been associated in other texts. This *syntactic expectation*, set up by a *semantic signal*, is matched by a parallel tendency to expect specific syntactic signals to lead to predetermined semantic fields (e.g., in western texts, regular alternation between male and female characters creates expectation of the semantic elements implied by romance, while alternation between two males throughout a text has implied—at least until recently—confrontation and the semantics of the duel). This interpenetration of the semantic and the syntactic through the agency of the spectator clearly deserves further study. Suffice it to say for the present that linguistic meanings (and thus the import of semantic elements) are in large part derived from the textual meanings of previous texts. There is thus a constant circulation in both directions between the semantic and the syntactic, between the linguistic and the textual.

---

[16]The most straightforward statement of Lévi-Strauss's position is in "The Structural Study of Myths." For a useful elucidation of that position, see Edmund Leach, *Claude Lévi-Strauss* (New York: Viking Press, 1970).

Still other questions, such as the general problem of the "evolution" of genres through semantic or syntactic shifts, deserve far more attention than I have given them here. In time, I believe, this new model for the understanding of genre will provide answers for many of the questions traditional to genre study. Perhaps more important still, the semantic/syntactic approach to genre raises numerous questions for which other theories have created no space.

1984

THOMAS SCHATZ
FROM HOLLYWOOD GENRES

FILM GENRE AND THE GENRE FILM

Because it is essentially a narrative system, a film genre can be examined in terms of its fundamental structural components: plot, character, setting, thematics, style, and so on. We should be careful, though, to maintain a distinction between the *film genre* and the *genre film*. Whereas the genre exists as a sort of tacit "contract" between filmmakers and audience, the genre film is an actual event that honors such a contract. To discuss the Western genre is to address neither a single Western film nor even all Westerns, but rather that system of conventions which identifies Western films as such.

There is a sense, then, in which a film genre is both a *static* and a *dynamic* system. On the one hand, it is a familiar formula of interrelated narrative and cinematic components that serves to continually reexamine some basic cultural conflict: one could argue, for example, that all Westerns confront the same fundamental issues (the taming of the frontier, the celebration of the hero's rugged individualism, the hero's conflicts with the frontier community, etc.) in elaborating America's foundation ritual and that slight formal variations do not alter those static thematic characteristics. On the other hand, changes in cultural attitudes, new influential genre films, the economics of the industry, and so forth, continually refine any film genre. As such, its nature is continually evolving. For example, the evolution of Western heroes from agents of law and order to renegade outlaws or professional killers reflect a genuine change in the genre. One could even argue that the term "Western" means something different today from what it did two or three decades ago.

Thus genre experience, like all human experience, is organized according to certain fundamental perceptual processes. As we repeatedly undergo the same type of experience we develop expectations which, as they are continually reinforced, tend to harden into "rules." The clearest example of this process in any culture is in its games. A game is a system of immutable rules (three strikes in baseball) and components determining the nature of play. Yet no two games in a sport are alike, and a theoretically infinite number of variations can be played within the "arena" that the rules provide. Similarly, certain styles of traditional or popular music involve a variations-on-a-theme approach both within and among individual pieces. In folk and blues traditions, for example, most compositions are generated from a very few chord progressions.

The analogies between film genres and other cultural systems are virtually endless. What such examples seem to highlight is the dual nature of any "species" (or "genus," the root for the word "genre"), that is, it can be identified either by its rules, components, and function (by its static deep structure) or conversely by the individual members which comprise the species (by its dynamic surface structure).

Think of a Western movie, or a musical, or a gangster film. Probably you won't think of any individual Western or musical or gangster film, but rather of a vaguely defined amalgam of actions and attitudes, of characters and locales. For as one sees more genre films, one tends to negotiate the genre less by its individual films than by its deep structure, those rules and conventions which render this film a Western and that film a musical. This distinction between deep and surface structures— between a genre and its films—provides the conceptual basis for any genre study. Of all the analogies we might use to better understand this distinction, the most illuminating involves the "deepest" of human structures: language.

THE LANGUAGE ANALOGY

What is natural to mankind is not oral speech but the faculty of constructing a language, i.e. a system of distinct signs corresponding to distinct ideas.

FERDINAND DE SAUSSURE

Among other things, the commercial cinema is a communication system—it structures and delivers meaning. Throughout its history, evocative phrases like "the grammar of film" and "the cinematic language system" have suggested that filmic communication is comparable to verbal communication, although the extent and usefulness of that comparison are limited. Most recently, the film-language analogy has undergone renewed interest within the growing field of *semiology* (or semiotics), a science that proposes to study human interaction as a vast network of social and interpersonal communication systems. Semiology is itself the brain child of Swiss linguist Ferdinand de Saussure, who suggested that language provides the "master pattern" for the study of cultural signification. According to de Saussure, verbal language is the one sign system shared by all cultures; its basic structure informs every system of social communication.

That language study and its jargon are a metaphor for genre study should be obvious. Through the "circuit of exchange" involving box-office "feedback," the studios and the mass audience hold a virtual "conversation" whereby they gradually refine the "grammar" of cinematic "discourse." Thus a genre can be studied, like a language, as a formalized sign system whose rules have been assimilated, consciously or otherwise, through cultural consensus. Our shared knowledge of the rules of any film genre enables us to understand and evaluate individual genre films, just as our shared knowledge of English grammar enables me to write this sentence and you to interpret it. The distinction between *grammar* and *usage*, closely akin to that between deep structure and surface structure, originates in de Saussure's distinction between *langue* and *parole* in verbal language. For de Saussure, the speaker's and listener's shared knowledge of the grammatical rules that make up the language system (*la langue*) enables them to develop and understand a virtually unlimited range of individual utterances (*la parole*). American linguist Noam Chomsky has described this distinction in terms of *competency* and *performance*; he suggests that we should differentiate between our inherent capacity to speak and interpret on the one hand and our actually doing so on the other.

If we extend these ideas into genre study, we might think of the *film genre* as a specific grammar or system of rules of expression and construction and the individual genre films as a manifestation of these rules. Of course, film differs from language in that our verbal competence is relatively consistent from speaker to speaker, whereas our generic competence varies widely. If each of us had the same exposure to Hollywood's thousands of genre films, a critical theory would probably be easier to construct. But obviously not everyone has a minimal understanding of even the most popular and widespread genres, let alone the obscure structural delights of such "subgenres" as the beach-blanket movies of the 1960s or the car-chase movies of the 1970s.

Moreover, although verbal language systems are essentially neutral and meaningless, film genres are not. As a system, English grammar is not meaningful either historically or in socially specific terms. It is manipulated by a speaker to *make* meaning. A film genre, conversely, has come into being precisely because of its cultural significance as a meaningful narrative system. Whereas a verbal statement represents a speaker's organization of neutral components into a meaningful pattern, a genre film represents an effort to *re*organize a familiar, meaningful system in an original way.

Another interesting aspect of the language analogy concerns the tension between grammar and usage. Grammar in language is absolute and static, essentially unchanged by the range and abuses of everyday usage. In the cinema, however, individual genre films seem to have the capacity to affect the genre—an utterance has the potential to change the grammar that governs it. Even in film technology (the impact of widescreen on the Western, for example, or of technicolor on the musical), we can see that individual usage influences both viewers and other filmmakers, and hence encourages them in effect to renegotiate the generic contract. Whether or not some static nuclear deep structure exists, which defines the genre and somehow eludes the effects of time and variation, we cannot overlook the gradual changes (as revealed in individual genre films) in form and substance on the genre's surface. Genres evolve, and they tend to evolve quite rapidly due to the demands of the commercial popular media. But whether this evolution represents mere cosmetic changes in the surface structure (equivalent to fashionable clichés or idioms in verbal language) or whether it reflects substantial changes in the deep structure (the generic system itself) will remain, at least for now, an open question.

Perhaps the ultimate value of the film-language analogy is as a sort of method or methodological model. That is, the similarities between a language and a genre as communication systems should encourage the analyst to approach individual genre films in much the same way that the linguist approaches individual utterances. Like all signifying systems, languages and genres exist essentially within the minds of their users: No single study of English grammar or of a film genre could possibly describe the system completely. In this sense, studying film genre is not unlike going to school as competent six-year-old speakers of English and then being taught English grammar. In each case, we study the system that is the basis for our existing competence.

In all of this, we should not lose sight of the critical, evaluative factor that motivates the genre critic, while it is virtually irrelevant to the linguist. The linguist's concern is the process whereby we verbally communicate meaning; any concern for the *quality* of that communication falls under the domain of rhetoric. As such, the film genre critic must be both linguist and "rhetor"—that is, he or she is concerned with both the process and the quality of any generic communication. The critic develops competence, a familiarity with the system, by watching and interpreting movies and noting similarities. Ultimately, he or she is concerned with recognizing, appreciating, and articulating *differences* among these movies. As critics, we understand genre films because of their similarity with other films, but we appreciate them because of their difference. Therefore an outline of a basic grammar of genre filmmaking should precede any critical analysis of individual films within a genre.

TOWARD A GRAMMAR OF FILM GENRE

At this stage, we are somewhere between the point of departure (watching movies) and the point of arrival (appreciating and articulating difference—i.e., being critical). We can appreciate difference only when we begin to examine films systematically, when we consider the systems whereby an individual film "makes meaning." Thus far, we have considered the commercial and formal systems involved in Hollywood filmmaking from a rather superficial perspective. In narrowing our focus to examine the workings of Hollywood genres, we will begin to understand how commercial and formal systems are realized in actual production. Genre production itself should be addressed on three distinct levels of inquiry: those characteristics shared by virtually all genre films (and thus by all genres), those characteristics shared by all the films within any individual genre, and those characteristics that set one genre film off from all other films.

Our ultimate goal is to discern a genre film's quality, its social and aesthetic value. To do this, we will attempt to see its relation to the various systems that inform it. For example, in examining a film like *The Searchers*, it is not enough simply to isolate the formal characteristics that identify it as belonging to a particular genre. Nor is it enough to isolate the elements that make it superior. Initially we have to discern those traits that make the film—and indeed the Western form itself—generic. To repeat Wood's observation: we are so accustomed to dealing with genres, with familiar filmic narrative types, that we tend to isolate these types from one another, thus overlooking many of their shared social and aesthetic features. Before considering the Western, gangster, musical, and other Hollywood genres as individual narrative systems, then, we will discuss the qualities that identify these forms as genres.

A genre film, like virtually any story, can be examined in terms of its fundamental narrative components: plot, setting, and character. These components have a privileged status for the popular audience, due to their existence within a familiar formula that addresses and reaffirms the audience's values and attitudes. Thus the genre film's narrative components assume a preordained thematic significance that is quite different from non-generic narratives. Each genre film incorporates a specific cultural context—what Warshow termed its "field of reference"—in the guise of a familiar *social community*. This generic context is more than the physical setting, which some genre critics have argued defines the genre as such. The American frontier or the urban underworld is more than a physical locale which identifies the Western or the gangster film; it is a cultural milieu where inherent thematic conflicts are animated, intensified, and resolved by familiar characters and pattern of action. Although all drama establishes a community that is disturbed by conflict, in the genre film both the community and the conflict have been conventionalized. Ultimately, our familiarity with any genre seems to depend less on recognizing a specific setting than on recognizing certain dramatic conflicts that we associate with specific patterns of action and character relationships. There are some genres, in fact, like the musical and the screwball comedy, that we identify primarily through conventions of action and attitude, and whose settings vary widely from one film to the next.

From this observation emerges a preliminary working hypothesis: the determining, identifying feature of a film genre is its cultural context, its community of interrelated character types whose attitudes, values, and actions flesh out dramatic conflicts inherent within that community. The generic community is less a specific place (although it may be, as with the Western and gangster genres) than a network of characters, actions, values, and attitudes. Each genre's status as a distinct cultural community is enhanced by Hollywood's studio production system, in that each generic context is orchestrated by specialized groups of directors, writers, producers, performers, sets, studio lots, and even studios themselves. (Consider Warner Brothers' heavy production of gangster films in the early 1930s and MGM's musicals in the late 1940s.)

A genre, then, represents a *range of expression* for filmmakers and a *range of experience* for viewers. Both filmmakers and viewers are sensitive to a genre's range of expression because of previous experiences with the genre that have coalesced into a system of value-laden narrative conventions. It is this system of conventions— familiar characters performing familiar actions which celebrate familiar values— that represents the genre's narrative context, its meaningful cultural community. . . .

CHARACTER AND SETTING: COMMUNITIES IN CONFLICT

In discussing the grammar (or system of conventions) of any Hollywood film genre, it is important to note that the *material economy*, which motivated the studios to refine story formulas, translated into *narrative economy* for filmmakers and viewers. Each genre incorporates a sort of narrative shorthand whereby significant dramatic conflicts can intensify and then be resolved through established patterns of action and by familiar character types. These dramatic conflicts are themselves the identifying feature of any genre; they represent the transformation of some social, historical, or even geographical (as in the Western) aspect of American culture into one locus of events and characters.

Although the dramatic conflicts are basic to the generic "community," we cannot identify that community solely by its physical setting. If film genres were identified by setting alone, then we would have to deal with an "urban" genre that includes such disparate forms as gangster films, backstage musicals, and detective films. Because the setting provides an *arena* for conflicts, which are themselves determined by the actions and attitudes of the *participants*, we must look to the generic character types and the conflicts they generate in identifying any genre. And we might consider a generic community and its characters in relation to the system of values which both define the problem and eventually are appealed to in solving it.

What emerges as a social problem (or dramatic conflict) in one genre is not necessarily a problem in another. Law and order is a problem in the gangster and detective genres, but not in the musical. Conversely, courtship and marriage are problems in the musical but not in the gangster and detective genres. Individualism is celebrated in the detective genre (through the hero's occupation and world view) and in the gangster film (through the hero's career and eventual death), while the principal characters in the musical compromise their individuality in their eventual romantic embrace and thus demonstrate their willingness to be integrated into the social community. In each of these genres, the characters' identities and narrative roles (or "functions") are determined by their relationship with the community and its value structure. As such, the generic character is psychologically static—he or she is the physical embodiment of an attitude, a style, a world view, of a predetermined and essentially unchanging cultural posture. Cowboy or Indian, gangster or cop, guy or doll, the generic character is identified by his or her function and status within the community.

The static vision of the generic hero—indeed of the entire constellation of familiar character types—helps to define the community and to animate its cultural conflicts. For example, the Western hero, regardless of his social or legal standing, is necessarily an agent of civilization in the savage frontier. He represents both the social order and the threatening savagery that typify the Western milieu. Thus he animates the inherent dynamic qualities of the community, providing a dramatic vehicle through which the audience can confront generic conflicts.

This approach also enables us to distinguish between such seemingly similar urban crime formulas as the gangster and detective genres. Usually, both genres are set in a contemporary urban milieu and address conflicts principally between social order and anarchy and between individual morality and the common good. But because of the characteristic attitudes and values of the genre's principal characters, these conflicts assume a different status in each genre and are resolved accordingly. The detective, like the Westerner, represents the man-in-the-middle, mediating the forces of order and anarchy, yet somehow remaining separate from each. He has opted to construct his own value system and behavioral code, which happens (often, almost accidentally) to coincide with the forces of social order. But the detective's predictable return to his office retreat at film's end and his refusal to assimilate the values and lifestyle of the very society he serves ultimately reaffirm his—and the genre's—ambiguous social stance. The gangster film, conversely, displays little thematic ambiguity. The gangster has aligned himself with the forces of crime and social disorder, so both his societal role and his conflict with the community welfare demand his eventual destruction.

All film genres treat some form of threat—violent or otherwise—to the social order. However, it is the attitudes of the principal characters and the resolutions precipitated by their actions which finally distinguish the various genres from one another. Nevertheless, there is a vital distinction between kinds of generic settings and conflicts. Certain genres (Western, detective, gangster, war, et al.) have conflicts that, indigenous to the environment, reflect the physical and ideological struggle for its control. These conflicts are animated and resolved either by an individual male hero or by a collective (war, science fiction, cavalry, certain recent Westerns). Other genres have conflicts that are not indigenous to the locale but are the result of the conflict between the values, attitudes, and actions of its principal characters and the "civilized" setting they inhabit. Conflicts in these genres (musical, screwball comedy, family melodrama) generally are animated by a "doubled" hero—usually a romantic couple whose courtship is complicated and eventually ideologically resolved. A musical's setting may be a South Pacific island or the backstage of a Broadway theater, but we relate to the film immediately by its treatment of certain sexual and occupational conflicts and also by our familiarity with the type of characters played by its "stars."

Thus, it is *not* the musical numbers themselves which identify these films as musicals. Many Westerns and gangster films, for example, contain musical numbers and still aren't confused with musicals (Westerns like *Dodge City* and *Rio Bravo*, for instance, or gangster films like *The Roaring Twenties* and *The Rise and Fall of Legs Diamond*). The frontier saloon and the gangster's speakeasy may be conventional locales within their respective communities, but their entertainment function clearly is peripheral to the central issue. However, in "musical Westerns" like *Annie Get Your Gun*, *The Harvey Girls*, and *Oklahoma!*, the nature and resolution of the dramatic conflicts as well as the characterization clearly are expressed via the musical formula. In *The Harvey Girls*, for instance, the narrative centers around the exploits of several dozen women—including Judy Garland and Cyd Charisse, which should provide us with a generic cue—who migrate West to work in a restaurant. Certain Western conventions are nodded to initially: the girls are told aboard the train headed West that "You're bringing civilization. . . . You girls are bringing order to the West"; later, there is a comic brawl between these "Harvey Girls" and the local saloon girls. But the Western genre's fundamental traits (the individual male hero responding to the threat of savagery and physical violence within an ideologically unstable milieu) are not basic to the film. Once the characters and conflicts are established, the setting might as well be Paris or New York City or even Oz.

As I hope these examples indicate, the various Hollywood genres manipulate character and social setting quite differently in developing dramatic conflicts. We might consider a broad distinction between genres of *determinate space* and those of *indeterminate space*, between genres of an ideologically contested setting and an ideologically stable setting. In a genre of determinate space (Western, gangster, detective, et al.), we have a symbolic arena of action. It represents a cultural realm in which fundamental values are in a state of sustained conflict. In these genres, then, the contest itself and its necessary arena are "determinate"—a specific social conflict is violently enacted within a familiar locale according to a prescribed system of rules and behavioral codes.

The iconographic arena in determinate genres is entered by an individual or collective hero, at the outset, who acts upon it, and finally leaves. This entrance-exit motif recurs most in genres characterized by an individual hero: for example, the Westerner enters a frontier community, eliminates (or perhaps causes) a threat to its survival, and eventually rides "into the sunset"; the detective takes the case, investigates it, and returns to his office; the gangster, introduced to urban crime, rises to power, and finally is killed or jailed. In these genres, the individual hero incorporates a rigid, essentially static attitude in dealing with his very dynamic, contested world.

In contrast, genres of indeterminate space generally involve a doubled (and thus dynamic) hero in the guise of a romantic couple who inhabit a "civilized" setting, as in the musical, screwball comedy, and social melodrama. The physical and ideological "contest" which determines the arena of action in the Western, gangster, and detective genres is not an issue here. Instead, genres of indeterminate space incorporate a civilized, ideologically stable milieu, which depends less upon a heavily coded place than on a highly conventionalized value system. Here conflicts derive not from a struggle over control of the environment, but rather from the struggle of the principal characters to bring their own views in line either with one another's or, more often, in line with that of the larger community.

Unlike genres of determinate space, these genres rely upon a progression from romantic antagonism to eventual embrace. The kiss or embrace signals the integration of the couple into the larger cultural community. In addition, these genres use iconographic conventions to establish a social setting—the proscenium or theater stage with its familiar performers in some musicals, for example, or the repressive small-town community and the family home in the melodrama. But because the generic conflicts arise from attitudinal (generally male-female) oppositions rather than from a physical conflict, the coding in these films tends to be less visual and more ideological and abstract. This may account for the sparse attention they have received from genre analysts, despite their widespread popularity.

Ultimately, genres of indeterminate, civilized space (musical, screwball comedy, social melodrama) and genres of determinate, contested space (Western, gangster, detective) might be distinguished according to their differing ritual functions. The former tend to celebrate the values of *social integration*, whereas the latter uphold the values of *social order*. The former tend to cast an attitudinally unstable couple or family unit into some representative microcosm of American society, so that their emotional and/or romantic "coupling" reflects their integration into a stable environment. The latter tend to cast an individual, violent, attitudinally static male into a familiar, predetermined milieu to examine the opposing forces vying for control. In making this distinction, though, we should not lose sight of these genres' shared social function. In addressing basic cultural conflicts and celebrating the values and attitudes whereby these conflicts might be resolved, all film genres represent the filmmakers' and audience's cooperative efforts to "tame" those beasts, both actual and imaginary, which threaten the stability of our everyday lives.

PLOT STRUCTURE: FROM CONFLICT TO RESOLUTION

As a popular film audience, our shared needs and expectations draw us into the movie theater. If we are drawn there by a genre film, we are familiar with the ritual. In its animation and resolution of basic cultural conflicts, the genre film celebrates our collective sensibilities, providing an array of ideological strategies for negotiating social conflicts. The conflicts themselves are significant (and dramatic) enough to ensure our repeated attendance. The films within a genre, representing variations on a cultural theme, will employ different means of reaching narrative resolution, but that closure is generally as familiar as the community and its characters. (Think of the general discomfort felt upon realizing, even quite early in seeing a genre film, that Cagney's heroic gangster would "get his" or that Tracy and Hepburn would cease their delightful hostilities and embrace in time for the closing credits.)

Actually, the most significant feature of any generic narrative may be its resolution—that is, its efforts to solve, even if only temporarily, the conflicts that have disturbed the community welfare. The Western, for example, despite its historical and geographical distance from most viewers, confronts real and immediate social conflicts: individual versus community, town versus wilderness, order versus anarchy, and so on. If there is anything escapist about these narratives, it is their repeated assertion that these conflicts can be solved, that seemingly timeless cultural oppositions can be resolved favorably for the larger community.

In a Hollywood Western, as in virtually any Hollywood genre film, plot development is effectively displaced by setting and character: once we recognize the familiar cultural arena and the players, we can be fairly certain how the game will be played and how it will end. Because the characters, conflicts, and resolution of the non-generic narrative are unfamiliar and unpredictable, we negotiate them less by previous filmic experiences than by previous "real-world" (personal and social) experiences. Clearly, both generic and nongeneric narratives must rely to some degree upon real-world and also upon previous narrative-filmic experiences in order to make sense. In the genre film, however, the predictability of conflict and resolution tends to turn our attention away from the linear, cause-and-effect plot, redirecting it to the conflict itself and the opposed value systems it represents. Instead of a linear chain of events, which are organized by the changing perceptions of an individual protagonist, the genre film's plot traces the intensification of some cultural opposition which is eventually resolved in a predictable fashion.

Thus, we might describe the plot structure of a genre film in the following way:

establishment (via various narrative and iconographic cues) of the generic community with its inherent dramatic conflicts;
animation of those conflicts through the actions and attitudes of the genre's constellation of characters;
intensification of the conflict by means of conventional situations and dramatic confrontations until the conflict reaches crisis proportions;
resolution of the crisis in a fashion which eliminates the physical and/or ideological threat and thereby celebrates the (temporarily) well-ordered community.

In this plot structure, linear development is subordinate to and qualified by the *oppositional* narrative strategy. Opposing value systems are either mediated by an individual or a collective, which eliminates one of the opposing systems. Or else these oppositions are actually embodied by a doubled hero whose (usually romantic) coupling signals their synthesis. In either instance, resolution occurs, even if only temporarily, in a way that strokes the collective sensibilities of the mass audience. It is in this context that the genre film's function as cultural ritual is most evident.

In their formulaic narrative process, genre films celebrate the most fundamental ideological precepts—they examine and affirm "Americanism" with all its rampant conflicts, contradictions, and ambiguities. Not only do genre films establish a sense of continuity between our cultural past and present (or between present and future, as with science fiction), but they also attempt to eliminate the distinctions between them. As social ritual, genre films function to stop time, to portray our culture in a stable and invariable ideological position. This attitude is embodied in the generic hero—and in the Hollywood star system itself—and is ritualized in the resolution precipitated by the hero's actions. Whether it is a historical Western or a futuristic fantasy, the genre film celebrates inviolate cultural attributes.

Ultimately, the sustained success of any genre depends upon at least two factors: the thematic appeal and significance of the conflicts it repeatedly addresses and its flexibility in adjusting to the audience's and filmmakers' changing attitudes toward those conflicts. These can be seen, for example, in the Western hero's status as both rugged individualist and also as agent of a civilization that continually resists his individualism. The degree to which that opposition has evolved over the past seventy-five years has accommodated changes in our cultural sensibilities. Or consider science fiction, a literary and cinematic genre that realized widespread popularity in the late '40s and early '50s. This genre articulated the conflicts and anxieties that accompanied the development of atomic power and the prospect of interplanetary travel. Because science fiction deals with so specialized a cultural conflict—essentially with the limits and value of human knowledge and scientific experimentation—it is considerably less flexible, but no less topical, than the Western. Nevertheless, each genre has a static nucleus that manifests its thematic oppositions or recurring cultural conflicts. And each genre has, through the years, dynamically evolved as shown by the ways its individual films manipulate those oppositions. If we see genre as a problem-solving strategy, then, the static nucleus could be conceived as the problem and the variety of solutions (narrative resolutions) as its dynamic surface structure.

In this sense, a genre's basic cultural oppositions or inherent dramatic conflicts represent its most basic determining feature. Also the sustained popularity of any genre indicates the essentially unresolvable, irreconcilable nature of those oppositions. Resolution involves a point of dramatic closure in which a compromise or temporary solution to the conflict is projected into a sort of cultural and historical timelessness. The threatening external force in contested space is violently destroyed and eliminated as an ideological threat; in uncontested space the vital lover's spontaneity and lack of social inhibition are bridled by a domesticating counterpart in the name of romantic love. In each, philosophical or ideological conflicts are "translated" into emotional terms—either violent or sexual, or both—and are resolved accordingly. In the former, the emotive resolution is externalized, in the latter it is internalized. Still, the resolution does not function to *solve* the basic cultural conflict.

The conflict is simply recast into an emotional context where it can be expeditiously, if not always logically, resolved.

As a rule, generic resolution operates by a process of *reduction*: the polar opposition is reduced, either through the elimination of one of the forces (in genres of determinate, contested space) or through the integration of the forces into a single unit (in genres of indeterminate, civilized space). The contest in determinate space generally is physically violent. Frequently, up until the resolution, there is more tension than action. The violent resolution usually helps the community, but only rarely does the hero assimilate its value system. In fact, his insistence that he maintain his individuality emerges as a significant thematic statement. As such, these films often involve a dual celebration: the hero's industrious isolationism offsets the genre's celebration of the ideal social order.

There is a certain logic and symmetry in the gangster's death, the Westerner's fading into the sunset, the detective's return to his office to await another case. Each of these standard epilogues implicitly accepts the contradictory values of its genre, all of which seem to center around the conflict between individualism and the common good. The built-in ambiguity of this dual celebration serves, at least partially, to minimize the *narrative rupture* resulting from the effort to resolve an unresolvable cultural conflict. This violation of narrative logic is itself fundamental to all of Hollywood's story formulas, in that the demand for a "happy ending" resists the complexity and deep-seated nature of the conflict.

Because genres of social order invariably allow the individual hero his formalized flight from social integration and from the compromising of his individuality, the narrative rupture is usually less pronounced than in genres of social integration. The cultural conflicts in genres of integration are revealed through the doubling of the principal characters—that is, through their opposed relationship, usually expressed as romantic antagonism. With the integration of their opposing attitudes into a cohesive unit (the married couple, the family), the conflicts are resolved and basic communal ideals are ritualized. But the cultural contradictions that inhibit integration throughout these films—between spontaneous individual expression and social propriety, for example—cannot be resolved without severely subverting the characters' credibility and motivation.

Are we to assume that the screwball couple's madcap social behavior and mutual antagonism will magically dissolve once they are wed? Or that the conflicts, which have separated the song-and-dance team throughout rehearsals, will somehow vanish after the climactic show? To avoid these questions and to minimize the sense of rupture, these genre films synthesize their oppositions through some formal celebration or social ritual: a Broadway show, a betrothal, a wedding, and so on. In this way, they don't actually resolve their conflicts; they reconstitute them by concluding the narrative at an emotive climax, at precisely the moment when the doubled principals acquiesce to each other's demands. The suggestion of living "happily ever after" tends to mask or gloss over the inevitable loss associated with each character's compromise. What is celebrated is the collective value of their integration into an idealized social unit.

This sense of loss accompanies the resolution of all genre films because of the contradictory, irreconcilable nature of their conflicts. Through violent reduction or romantic coupling, however, the loss is masked. It is, in effect, effectively redressed in the emotional climax. What is to become, we might very well ask ourselves, once the film ends, of the uninhibited music man after he weds the gold-hearted domesticator—and what's to become of her as well? What's to become of the savage frontier lawman once the social order he instills finally arrives? These are questions which, unless initiated by the films themselves, we know better than to ask. Genre films not only project an idealized cultural self-image, but they project it into a realm of historical timelessness. Typically, films produced later in a genre's development tend to challenge the tidy and seemingly naive resolutions of earlier genre films, and we will discuss this tendency in some detail when we examine generic evolution. What we should note here, through, and what is being masked by such a resolution is the fundamental appeal of both sides in a dramatic conflict. Whatever oppositions we examine in genre films—individual versus community, man versus woman, work versus play, order versus anarchy—these do not represent "positive" and "negative" cultural values. For one of the reasons for a genre's popularity is the sustained significance of the "problem" that it repeatedly addresses. Thus, generic conflict and resolution involve opposing systems of values and attitudes, *both of which* are deemed significant by contemporary American culture.

1991

ROBERT WARSHOW
THE GANGSTER AS TRAGIC HERO

A prominent member of the "New York Intellectuals", Robert Warshaw (1917–1955) between 1946 and 1955 published essays in *Partisan Review*, *The Nation*, and *Commentary* (while he edited for eight years). Long before the establishment of cultural studies as an academic field, he wrote on genre films, art films, and comic books collected after his early death in *The Immediate Experience* (1962). Warshow's essays diverged from then-current critical approches that stressed evalution to examine the way films work and what thay tell us about ourselves and our society. He was particularly interested in the way films elicit the responses they do, writing on the archetypal figures of the western hero, the gangster (see below), and the clown. His essays also deal with the films of the Russian revolution, as well as the books and plays of Gertrude Stein, Franz Kafka, Arthur Miller, and Ernest Hemingway, among others.

America, as a social and political organization, is committed to a cheerful view of life. It could not be otherwise. The sense of tragedy is a luxury of aristocratic societies, where the fate of the individual is not conceived of as having a direct and legitimate political importance, being determined by a fixed and supra-political—that is, noncontroversial—moral order or fate. Modern equalitarian societies, however, whether democratic or authoritarian in their political forms, always base themselves on the claim that they are making life happier; the avowed function of the modern state, at least in its ultimate terms, is not only to regulate social relations, but also to determine the quality and the possibilities of human life in general. Happiness thus becomes the chief political issue—in a sense, the only political issue—and for that reason if can never be treated as an issue at all. If an American or a Russian is unhappy, it implies a certain reprobation of his society, and therefore, by a logic of which we can all recognize the necessity, it becomes an obligation of citizenship to be cheerful; if the authorities find it necessary, the citizen may even be compelled to make a public display of his cheerfulness on important occasions, just as he may be conscripted into the army in time of war.

Naturally, this civic responsibility rests most strongly upon the organs of mass culture. The individual citizen may still be permitted his private unhappiness so long as it does not take on political significance, the extent of this tolerance being determined by how large an area of private life the society can accommodate. But every production of mass culture is a public act and must conform with accepted notions of the public good. Nobody seriously questions the principle that it is the function of mass culture to maintain public morale, and certainly nobody in the mass audience objects to having his morale maintained.[1] At a time when the normal condition of the citizen is a state of anxiety, euphoria spreads over our culture like the broad smile of an idiot. In terms of attitudes towards life, there is very little difference between a "happy" movie like *Good News*, which ignores death and suffering, and a "sad" movie like *A Tree Grows in Brooklyn*, which uses death and suffering as incidents in the service of a higher optimism.

But, whatever its effectiveness as a source of consolation and a means of pressure for maintaining "positive" social attitudes, this optimism is fundamentally satisfying to no one, not even to those who would be most disoriented without its support. Even within the area of mass culture, there always exists a current of opposition, seeking to express by whatever means are available to it that sense of desperation and inevitable failure which optimism itself helps to create. Most often, this opposition is confined to rudimentary or semiliterate forms: in mob politics and journalism, for example, or in certain kinds of religious enthusiasm. When it does enter the field of art, it is likely to be disguised or attenuated: in an unspecific form of expression like jazz, in the basically harmless nihilism of the Marx Brothers, in the continually reasserted strain of hopelessness that often seems to be the real meaning of the soap opera. The gangster film is remarkable in that it fills the need for disguise (though not sufficiently to avoid arousing uneasiness) without requiring any serious distortion. From its beginnings, it has been a consistent and astonishingly complete presentation of the modern sense of tragedy.[2]

In its initial character, the gangster film is simply one example of the movies' constant tendency to create fixed dramatic patterns that can be repeated indefinitely with a reasonable expectation of profit. One gangster film follows another as one musical or one Western follows another. But this rigidity is not necessarily opposed to the requirements of art. There have been very successful types of art in the past which developed such specific and detailed conventions as almost to make individual examples of the type interchangeable. This is true, for example, of Elizabethan revenge tragedy and Restoration comedy.

For such a type to be successful means that its conventions have imposed themselves upon the general consciousness and become the accepted vehicles of a particular set of attitudes and a particular aesthetic effect. One goes to any individual example of the type with very definite expectations, and originality is to be welcomed only in the degree that it intensifies the expected experience without fundamentally altering it. Moreover, the relationship between the conventions which go to make up such a type and the real experience of its audience or the real facts of whatever situation it pretends to describe is of only secondary importance and does not determine its aesthetic force. It is only in an ultimate sense that the type appeals

---

[1]In her testimony before the House Committee on Un-American Activities, Mrs. Leila Rogers said that the movie *None But the Lonely Heart* was un-American because it was gloomy. Like so much else that was said during the unhappy investigation of Hollywood, this statement was at once stupid and illuminating. One knew immediately what Mrs. Rogers was talking about; she had simply been insensitive enough to carry her philistinism to its conclusion.

[2]Efforts have been made from time to time to bring the gangster film into line with the prevailing optimism and social constructiveness of our culture; *Kiss of Death* is a recent example. These efforts are usually unsuccessful; the reasons for their lack of success are interesting in themselves, but I shall not be able to discuss them here.

to its audience's experience of reality; much more immediately, it appeals to previous experience of the type itself: it creates its own field of reference.

Thus the importance of the gangster film, and the nature and intensity of its emotional and aesthetic impact, cannot be measured in terms of the place of the gangster himself or the importance of the problem of crime in American life. Those European movie-goers who think there is a gangster on every corner in New York are certainly deceived, but defenders of the "positive" side of American culture are equally deceived if they think it relevant to point out that most Americans have never seen a gangster. What matters is that the experience of the gangster *as an experience of art* is universal to Americans. There is almost nothing we understand better or react to more readily or with quicker intelligence. The Western film, though it seems never to diminish in popularity, is for most of us no more than the folklore of the past, familiar and understandable only because it has been repeated so often. The gangster film comes much closer. In ways that we do not easily or willingly define, the gangster speaks for us, expressing that part of the American psyche which rejects the qualities and the demands of modern life, which rejects "Americanism" itself.

The gangster is the man of the city, with the city's language and knowledge, with its queer and dishonest skills and its terrible daring, carrying his life in his hands like a placard, like a club. For everyone else, there is at least the theoretical possibility of another world—in that happier American culture which the gangster denies, the city does not really exist; it is only a more crowded and more brightly lit country—but for the gangster there is only the city; he must inhabit it in order to personify it: not the real city, but that dangerous and sad city of the imagination which is so much more important, which is the modern world. And the gangster—though there are real gangsters—is also, and primarily, a creature of the imagination. The real city, one might say, produces only criminals; the imaginary city produces the gangster: he is what we want to be and what we are afraid we may become.

Thrown into the crowd without background or advantages, with only those ambiguous skills which the rest of us—the real people of the real city—can only pretend to have, the gangster is required to make his way, to make his life and impose it on others. Usually, when we come upon him, he has already made his choice or the choice has already been made for him, it doesn't matter which: we are not permitted to ask whether at some point he could have chosen to be something else than what he is.

The gangster's activity is actually a form of rational enterprise, involving fairly definite goals and various techniques for achieving them. But this rationality is usually no more than a vague background; we know, perhaps, that the gangster sells liquor or that he operates a numbers racket; often we are not given even that much information. So his activity becomes a kind of pure criminality: he hurts people. Certainly our response to the gangster film is most consistently and most universally a response to sadism; we gain the double satisfaction of participating vicariously in the gangster's sadism and then seeing it turned against the gangster himself.

But on another level the quality of irrational brutality and the quality of rational enterprise become one. Since we do not see the rational and routine aspects of the gangster's behavior, the practice of brutality—the quality of unmixed criminality—becomes the totality of his career. At the same time, we are always conscious that the whole meaning of this career is a drive for success: the typical gangster film presents a steady upward progress followed by a very precipitate fall. Thus brutality itself becomes at once the means to success and the content of success—a success that is defined in its most general terms, not, as accomplishment or specific gain, but simply as the unlimited possibility of aggression. (In the same way, film presentations of businessmen tend to make it appear that they achieve their success by talking on the telephone and holding conferences and that success *is* talking on the telephone and holding conferences.)

From this point of view, the initial contact between the film and its audience is an agreed conception of human life: that man is a being with the possibilities of success or failure. This principle, too, belongs to the city; one must emerge from the crowd or else one is nothing. On that basis the necessity of the action is established, and it progresses by inalterable paths to the point where the gangster lies dead and the principle has been modified: there is really only one possibility— failure. The final meaning of the city is anonymity and death.

In the opening scene of *Scarface,* we are shown a successful man; we know he is successful because he has just given a party of opulent proportions and becaue

Edward G. Robinson as Rico in *Little Caesar* (1931) is toasted as the head of the mob. "Since we do not see the rational and routine aspects of the gangster's behavior, the practice of brutality—the quality of unmixed criminality—becomes the totality of his career. At the same time, we are always conscious that the whole meaning of this career is a drive for success. . ." (WARSHOW, p. 578–579).

he is called Big Louie. Through some monstrous lack of caution, he permits himself to be alone for a few moments. We understand from this immediately that he
is about to be killed. No convention of the gangster film is more strongly established than this: it is dangerous to be alone. And yet the very conditions of success
make it impossible not to be alone, for success is always the establishment of an
individual preeminence that must be imposed on others, in whom it automatically
arouses hatred; the successful man is an outlaw. The gangster's whole life is an
effort to assert himself as an individual, to draw himself out of the crowd, and he
always dies *because* he is an individual; the final bullet thrusts him back, makes
him, after all, a failure. "Mother of God," says the dying Little Caesar, "is this the
end of Rico?"—speaking of himself thus in the third person because what has been
brought low is not the undifferentiated *man*, but the individual with a name, the
gangster, the success; even to himself he is a creature of the imagination. (T. S.
Eliot has pointed out that a number of Shakespeare's tragic heroes have this trick
of looking at themselves dramatically; their true identity, the thing that is destroyed
when they die, is something outside themselves—not a man, but a style of life, a
kind of meaning.)

At bottom, the gangster is doomed because he is under the obligation to succeed,
not because the means he employs are unlawful. In the deeper layers of the modern consciousness, *all* means are unlawful, every attempt to succeed is an act of
aggression, leaving one alone and guilty and defenseless among enemies: one is
punished for success. This is our intolerable dilemma: that failure is a kind of death
and success is evil and dangerous, is—ultimately—impossible. The effect of the
gangster film is to embody this dilemma in the person of the gangster and resolve
it by his death. The dilemma is resolved because it is *his* death, not ours. We are
safe; for the moment, we can acquiesce in our failure, we can choose to fail.

                                                                              1948

PAUL SCHRADER
NOTES ON FILM NOIR

Paul Schrader's first book, *Transcendental Style in Film: Ozu, Bresson, Dreyer* (1972) examined the aesthetics of the directors Yasajiro Ozu, Robert Bresson, and Carl Dreyer. A film school graduate, Schrader became the author of a number of such screenplays as *Taxi Driver* (1976), *Raging Bull (1980)*, *The Mosquito Coast* (1986), and *The Last Temptation of Christ* (1988), as well as directing *Blue Collar* (1978), *Hard Core* (1979), *American Gigolo* (1980), and several other films. A number of his essays and interviews have been collected in *Schrader on Schrader & Other Writings* (1990). He has also written on Japanese gangster movies and representations of the psychopath in film.

In 1946 French critics, seeing the American films they had missed during the war, noticed the new mood of cynicism, pessimism, and darkness that had crept into the American cinema. The darkening stain was most evident in routine crime thrillers, but was also apparent in prestigious melodramas. The French cineastes soon realized they had seen only the tip of the iceberg: as the years went by, Hollywood lighting grew darker, characters more corrupt, themes more fatalistic, and the tone more hopeless. By 1949 American movies were in the throes of their deepest and most creative funk. Never before had films dared to take such a harsh uncomplimentary look at American life, and they would not dare to do so again for twenty years.

Hollywood's film noir has recently become the subject of renewed interest among moviegoers and critics. The fascination that film noir holds for today's young filmgoers and film students reflects recent trends in American cinema: American movies are again taking a look at the underside of the American character, but compared to such relentlessly cynical examples of film noir as *Kiss Me Deadly* (Robert Aldrich, 1955) or *Kiss Tomorrow Goodbye* (Gordon Douglas, 1959), the newer self-hate cinema of *Easy Rider* (Dennis Hopper, 1969) and *Medium Cool* (Haskell Wexler, 1969) seems naive and romantic. As the current political mood hardens, filmgoers and filmmakers will find the film noir of the late forties increasingly attractive. The forties may be to the seventies what the thirties were to the sixties.

Film noir is equally interesting to critics. It offers writers a cache of excellent, little-known films (film noir is oddly both one of Hollywood's best periods and least known) and gives auteur-weary critics an opportunity to apply themselves to the new questions of classification and transdirectorial style. After all, what is a film noir?

Film noir is not a genre, as Raymond Durgnat has helpfully pointed out over the objections of Higham and Greenberg's *Hollywood in the Forties*.[1] It is not defined,

[1]Raymond Durgnat, "Paint It Black: The Family Tree of Film Noir," *Cinema* (U.K.), nos. 6–7 (August 1970): 49–56.

as are the western and gangster genres, by conventions of setting and conflict but rather by the more subtle qualities of tone and mood. It is a film "noir," as opposed to the possible variants of film "gray" or film "off-white." Film noir is also a specific period of film history, like German expressionism or the French New Wave. In general, film noir refers to those Hollywood films of the forties and early fifties that portrayed the world of dark, slick city streets, crime and corruption.

Film noir is an extremely unwieldy period. It harks back to many previous periods: Warner's thirties gangster films, the French "poetic realism" of Carné and Duvivier, Sternbergian melodrama, and ultimately German Expressionist crime films (Lang's Mabuse cycle). Film noir can stretch at its outer limits from *The Maltese Falcon* (John Huston, 1941) to *Touch of Evil* (Orson Welles, 1958), and most every dramatic Hollywood film from 1941 to 1953 contains some noir elements. There are also foreign off-shoots of film noir, such as *The Third Man* (Carol Reed, 1949), *Breathless* (Jean-Luc Godard, 1959), and *Le Doulos* (Jean-Pierre Melville, 1963).

Almost every critic has his or her own definition of film noir, along with a personal list of film titles and dates to back it up. Personal and descriptive definitions, however, can get a bit sticky. A film of urban nightlife is not necessarily a film noir, and a film noir need not necessarily concern crime and corruption. Since film noir is defined by tone rather than genre, it is almost impossible to argue one critic's descriptive definition against another's. How many noir elements does it take to make a film noir? Rather than haggle about definitions, I would rather attempt to reduce film noir to its primary colors (all shades of black), those cultural and stylistic elements to which any definition must return.

INFLUENCES

At the risk of sounding like Arthur Knight, I would suggest that there were four influences in Hollywood in the forties that brought about the film noir. (The danger of Knight's *Liveliest Art* method is that it makes film history less a matter of structural analysis and more a case of artistic and social forces magically interacting and coalescing.) Each of the following four catalytic elements, however, can define the film noir; the distinctly noir tonality draws from each of these elements.

War and Postwar Disillusionment

The acute downer that hit the United States after the Second World War was, in fact, a delayed reaction to the thirties. All through the Depression, movies were needed to keep people's spirits up, and, for the most part, they did. The crime films of this period were Horatio Algerish and socially conscious. Toward the end of the thirties a darker crime film began to appear (*You Only Live Once*, Fritz Lang, 1937; *The Roaring Twenties*, Raoul Walsh, 1939), and were it not for the war, film noir would have been at full steam by the early forties.

The need to produce Allied propaganda abroad and promote patriotism at home blunted the fledgling moves toward a dark cinema, and the film noir thrashed about in the studio system, not quite able to come into full prominence. During the war the first uniquely film noir appeared in *The Maltese Falcon, The Glass Key* (Stuart

Heisler, 1942), *This Gun for Hire* (Frank Tuttle, 1942), and *Laura* (Otto Preminger, 1944), but these films lacked the distinctly noir bite the end of the war would bring.

As soon as the war was over, however, American films became markedly more sardonic—and there was a boom in the crime film. For fifteen years the pressures against America's amelioristic cinema had been building up, and given the freedom, audiences and artists were now eager to take a less optimistic view of things. The disillusionment that many soldiers, small businessmen, and housewife/factory employees felt in returning to a peacetime economy was directly mirrored in the sordidness of the urban crime film.

This immediate postwar disillusionment was directly demonstrated in films like *Cornered* (Edward Dmytryk, 1945), *The Blue Dahlia* (George Marshall, 1946), *Dead Reckoning* (John Cromwell, 1947), and *Ride the Pink Horse* (Robert Montgomery, 1947), in which a serviceman returns from the war to find his sweetheart unfaithful or dead, or his business partner cheating him, or the whole society something less than worth fighting for. The war continues, but now the antagonism turns with a new viciousness toward American society itself.

Postwar Realism

Shortly after the war, every film-producing country had a resurgence of realism. In America it first took the form of films by such producers as Louis de Rochemont (*House on 92nd Street,* Henry Hathaway, 1945; *Call Northside 777,* Hathaway, 1948) and Mark Hellinger (*The Killers,* Robert Siodmak, 1946; *Brute Force,* Jules Dassin, 1947) and directors like Hathaway and Dassin. "Every scene was filmed on the actual location depicted," the publicity for the 1947 de Rochemont-Hathaway *Kiss of Death* proudly proclaimed. Even after de Rochemont's particular "March of Time" authenticity fell from vogue, realistic exteriors remained a permanent fixture of film noir.

The realistic movement also suited America's postwar mood; the public's desire for a more honest and harsh view of America would not be satisfied by the same studio streets they had been watching for a dozen years. The postwar realistic trend succeeded in breaking film noir away from the domain of the high-class melodrama, placing it where it more properly belonged, in the streets with everyday people. In retrospect, the pre–de Rochemont film noir looks definitely tamer than the postwar realistic films. The studio look of films like *The Big Sleep* (Howard Hawks, 1946) and *The Mask of Dimitrios* (Jean Negulesco, 1944) blunts their sting, making them seem polite and conventional in contrast to their later, more realistic counterparts.

The German Expatriates

Hollywood played host to an influx of German expatriates in the twenties and thirties, and these filmmakers and technicians had, for the most part, integrated themselves into the American film establishment. Hollywood never experienced the "Germanization" some civic-minded natives feared, and there is a danger of overemphasizing the German influence in Hollywood.

Jean Wallace is chased by two gangsters through the backstage world of a prize fight in *The Big Combo* (1954). "As in German expressionism, oblique and vertical lines are preferred to horizontal. Obliquity adheres to the choreography of the city, and is direct opposition to the horizontal American tradition of Griffith and Ford" (SCHRADER, p. 586).

But when, in the late forties, Hollywood decided to paint it black, there were no greater masters of chiaroscuro than the Germans. The influence of expressionist lighting has always been just beneath the surface of Hollywood films, and it is not surprising, in film noir, to find it bursting out into full bloom. Neither is it surprising to find a larger number of Germans and East Europeans working in film noir: Fritz Lang, Robert Siodmak, Billy Wilder, Franz Waxman, Otto Preminger, John Brahm, Anatole Litvak, Karl Freund, Max Ophuls, John Alton, Douglas Sirk, Fred Zinnemann, William Dieterle, Max Steiner, Edgar G. Ulmer, Curtis Bernhardt, Rudolph Maté.

On the surface the German expressionist influence, with its reliance on artificial studio lighting, seems incompatible with postwar realism, with its harsh unadorned exteriors; but it is the unique quality of film noir that it was able to weld seemingly contradictory elements into a uniform style. The best noir technicians simply made all the world a sound stage, directing unnatural and expressionistic lighting onto realistic settings. In films like *Union Station* (Maté, 1950), *They Live by Night* (Nicholas Ray, 1948), and *The Killers,* there is an uneasy, exhilarating combination of realism and expressionism.

Perhaps the greatest master of noir was Hungarian-born John Alton, an expressionist cinematographer who could relight Times Square at noon if necessary. No cinematographer better adapted the old expressionist techniques to the new desire for realism, and his black-and-white photography in such gritty examples of film noir as *T-Men* (Anthony Mann, 1948), *Raw Deal* (Mann, 1948); *I, the Jury* (Harry Essex, 1953), and *The Big Combo* (Joseph H. Lewis, 1955) equals that of such German expressionist masters as Fritz Wagner and Karl Freund.

The Hard-Boiled Tradition

Another stylistic influence waiting in the wings was the "hard-boiled" school of writers. In the thirties, authors such as Ernest Hemingway, Dashiell Hammett, Raymond Chandler, James M. Cain, Horace McCoy, and John O'Hara created the "tough," a cynical way of acting and thinking that separated one from the world of everyday emotions—romanticism with a protective shell. The hard-boiled writers had their roots in pulp fiction or journalism, and their protagonists lived out a narcissistic, defeatist code. The hard-boiled hero was, in reality, a soft egg compared to his existential counterpart (Camus is said to have based *The Stranger* on McCoy), but he was a good deal tougher than anything American fiction had seen.

When the movies of the forties turned to the American "tough" moral understrata, the hard-boiled school was waiting with preset conventions of heroes, minor characters, plots, dialogue, and themes. Like the German expatriates, the hard-boiled writers had a style made to order for film noir; and, in turn, they influenced noir screenwriting as much as the Germans influenced noir cinematography.

The most hard-boiled of Hollywood's writers was Raymond Chandler himself, whose script of *Double Indemnity* (from a James M. Cain story) was the best written and most characteristically noir of the period. *Double Indemnity* (Billy Wilder, 1944) was the first film that played film noir for what it essentially was: small-time, unredeemed, unheroic; it made a break from the romantic noir cinema of *Mildred Pierce* (Michael Curtiz, 1945) and *The Big Sleep*. In its final stages, however, film noir adapted and then bypassed the hard-boiled school. Manic, neurotic post-1948 films such as *Kiss Tomorrow Goodbye, D.O.A.* (Maté, 1950), *Where the Sidewalk Ends* (Preminger, 1950), *White Heat* (Raoul Walsh, 1949), and *The Big Heat* (Fritz Lang, 1953) are all post–hard boiled: the air in these regions was even too thin for old-time cynics like Chandler.

STYLISTICS

There is not yet a study of the stylistics of film noir, and the task is certainly too large to be attempted here. Like all film movements, film noir drew upon a reservoir of film techniques, and given the time one could correlate its techniques, themes, and casual elements into a stylistic schema. For the present, however, I'd like to point out some of film noir's recurring techniques.

1. The majority of scenes are lit for night. Gangsters sit in offices at midday with the shades pulled and the lights off. Ceiling lights are hung low and floor lamps are seldom more than five feet high. One always has the suspicion that if the lights were all suddenly flipped on, the characters would shriek and shrink from the scene like Count Dracula at sunrise.

2. As in German expressionism, oblique and vertical lines are preferred to horizontal. Obliquity adheres to the choreography of the city, and is in direct opposition to the horizontal American tradition of Griffith and Ford. Oblique lines tend to splinter a screen, making it restless and unstable. Light enters the dingy rooms of film noir in such odd shapes—jagged trapezoids, obtuse triangles, vertical slits—that one suspects the windows were cut out with a penknife. No character can speak authoritatively from a space that is being continually cut into ribbons of light. Anthony Mann and John Alton's *T-Men* is the most dramatic example, but far from the only one, of oblique noir choreography.

3. The actors and setting are often given equal lighting emphasis. An actor is often hidden in the realistic tableau of the city at night, and, more obviously, his face is often blacked out by shadow as he speaks. These shadow effects are unlike the famous Warner Brothers lighting of the thirties in which the central character was accentuated by a heavy shadow; in film noir, the central character is likely to be standing *in* the shadow. When the environment is given an equal or greater weight than the actor, it, of course, creates a fatalistic, hopeless mood. There is nothing the protagonists can do; the city will outlast and negate even their best efforts.

4. Compositional tension is preferred to physical action. A typical film noir would rather move the scene cinematographically around the actor than have the actor control the scene by physical action. The beating of Robert Ryan in *The Set-Up* (Robert Wise, 1949), the gunning down of Farley Granger in *They Live by Night*, the execution of the taxi driver in *The Enforcer* (Bretaigne Windust, 1951) and of Brian Donlevy in *The Big Combo* are all marked by measured pacing, restrained anger, and oppressive compositions, and seem much closer to the film noir spirit than the rat-tat-tat and screeching tires of *Scarface* (Howard Hawks, 1932) twenty years before or the violent, expressive actions of *Underworld U.S.A.* (Samuel Fuller, 1960) ten years later.

5. There seems to be an almost Freudian attachment to water. The empty noir streets are almost always glistening with fresh evening rain (even in Los Angeles), and the rainfall tends to increase in direct proportion to the drama. Docks and piers are second only to alleyways as the most popular rendezvous points.

6. There is a love of romantic narration. In such films as *The Postman Always Rings Twice* (Tay Garnett, 1946), *Laura, Double Indemnity, The Lady from Shanghai* (Orson Welles, 1949), *Out of the Past* (Jacques Tourneur, 1947), and *Sunset Boulevard* (Billy Wilder, 1950), the narration creates a mood of *temps perdu:* an irretrievable past, a predetermined fate, and an all-enveloping hopelessness. In *Out of the Past* Robert Mitchum relates his history with such pathetic relish that it is obvious there is no hope for any future: one can only take pleasure in reliving a doomed past.

7. A complex chronological order is frequently used to reinforce the feelings of hopelessness and lost time. Such films as *The Enforcer, The Killers, Mildred Pierce, The Dark Past* (Maté, 1948), *Chicago Deadline* (Lewis Allen, 1949), *Out of the Past*, and *The Killing* (Stanley Kubrick, 1956) use a convoluted time sequence to immerse the viewer in a time-disoriented but highly stylized world. The manipulation of time, whether slight or complex, is often used to reinforce a noir principle: the *how* is always more important than the *what*.

THEMES

Raymond Durgnat has delineated the themes of film noir in an excellent article in the British *Cinema* magazine,[2] and it would be foolish for me to attempt to redo his thorough work in this short space. Durgnat divides film noir into eleven thematic categories, and although one might criticize some of his specific groupings, he covers the whole gamut of noir production, thematically categorizing over 300 films. In each of Durgnat's noir themes (whether Black Widow, killers-on-the-run, *doppelgangers*), one finds that the upwardly mobile forces of the thirties have halted; frontierism has turned to paranoia and claustrophobia. The small-time gangster has now made it big and sits in the mayor's chair, the private eye has quit the police force in disgust, and the young heroine, sick of going along for the ride, is taking others for a ride.

Durgnat, however, does not touch upon what is perhaps the overriding noir theme: a passion for the past and present, but also a fear of the future. Noir heroes dread to look ahead, but instead try to survive by the day, and if unsuccessful at that, they retreat to the past. Thus film noir's techniques emphasize loss, nostalgia, lack of clear priorities, and insecurity, then submerge these self-doubts in mannerism and style. In such a world style becomes paramount; it is all that separates one from meaninglessness. Chandler described this fundamental noir theme when he described his own fictional world: "It is not a very fragrant world, but it is the world you live in, and certain writers with tough minds and a cool spirit of detachment can make very interesting patterns out of it."[3]

PHASES

Film noir can be subdivided into three broad phases. The first, the war-time period (1941–1946 approximately), was the phase of the private eye and the lone wolf, of Chandler, Hammett, and Greene, of Bogart and Bacall, Ladd and Lake, classy directors like Curtiz and Garnett, studio sets, and in general, more talk than action. The studio look of this period was reflected in such pictures as *The Maltese Falcon*, *Casablanca* (Michael Cartiz, 1942), *Gaslight* (George Cukor, 1944), *This Gun for Hire*, *The Lodger* (Brahm, 1944), *The Woman in the Window* (Lang, 1945), *Mildred Pierce*, *Spellbound* (Alfred Hitchcock, 1945), *The Big Sleep*, *Laura*, *The Lost Weekend* (Wilder, 1945), *The Strange Love of Martha Ivers* (Lewis Milestone, 1946), *To Have and Have Not* (Howard Hawks, 1944), *Fallen Angel* (Preminger, 1946), *Gilda* (Charles Vidor, 1946), *Murder My Sweet* (Dmytryk, 1944), *The Postman Always Rings Twice*, *Dark Waters* (Andre de Toth, 1944), *Scarlet Street* (Fritz Lang, 1945), *So Dark the Night* (Joseph H. Lewis, 1946), *The Glass Key*, *The Mask of Dimitrios*, and *The Dark Mirror* (Siodmak, 1946).

The Wilder/Chandler *Double Indemnity* provided a bridge to the postwar phase of film noir. The unflinching, noir vision of *Double Indemnity* came as a shock in

---

[2]Ibid.

[3]Raymond Chandler, "The Simple Art of Murder," in *Detective Fiction: Crime and Compromise*, edited by Dick Allen and David Chacko (New York: Harcourt Brace Jovanovich, 1974), p. 398.

1944, and the film was almost blocked by the combined efforts of Paramount, the Hays Office, and star Fred MacMurray. Three years later, however, *Double Indemnitys* were dropping off the studio assembly lines.

The second phase was the postwar realistic period from 1945 to 1949 (the dates overlap and so do the films; these are all approximate phases for which there are exceptions). These films tended more toward the problems of crime in the streets, political corruption, and police routine. Less romantic heroes like Richard Conte, Burt Lancaster, and Charles McGraw were more suited to this period, as were proletarian directors like Hathaway, Dassin, and Kazan. The realistic urban look of this phase is seen in such films as *The House on 92nd Street, The Killers, Raw Deal, Act of Violence* (Zinnemann, 1949), *Union Station, Kiss of Death, Johnny O'clock* (Robert Rossen, 1947), *Force of Evil* (Abraham Polonsky, 1948), *Dead Reckoning, Ride the Pink Horse, Dark Passage* (Delmer Daves, 1947), *Cry of the City* (Siodmak, 1948), *The Set-Up, T-Men, Call Northside 777, Brute Force, The Big Clock* (John Farrow, 1948), *Thieves' Highway* (Dassin, 1949), *Ruthless* (Ulmer, 1948), *The Pitfall* (de Toth, 1948), *Boomerang!* (Elia Kazan, 1947), and *The Naked City* (Dassin, 1948).

The third and final phase of film noir, from 1949 to 1953, was the period of psychotic action and suicidal impulse. The noir hero, seemingly under the weight of ten years of despair, started to go bananas. The psychotic killer, who had in the first period been a subject worthy of study (Olivia de Havilland in *The Dark Mirror*), and in the second a fringe threat (Richard Widmark in *Kiss of Death*), now became the active protagonist (James Cagney in *Kiss Tomorrow Goodbye*). There were no excuses given for the psychopathy in *Gun Crazy* (Joseph H. Lewis, 1949)—it was just "crazy." James Cagney made a neurotic comeback, and his instability was matched by that of younger actors like Robert Ryan and Lee Marvin. This was the phase of the B noir film and of psychoanalytically inclined directors like Ray and Walsh. The forces of personal disintegration are reflected in such films as *White Heat, Gun Crazy, D.O.A., Caught* (Max Ophuls, 1949), *They Live by Night, Where the Sidewalk Ends, Kiss Tomorrow Goodbye, Detective Story* (William Wyler, 1951), *In a Lonely Place* (Ray, 1950), *I, the Jury, Ace in the Hole* (Wilder, 1951), *Panic in the Streets* (Kazan, 1950), *The Big Heat, On Dangerous Ground* (Ray, 1952), and *Sunset Boulevard*.

This third phase is the cream of the film noir period. Some critics may prefer the early "gray" melodramas, others the postwar "street" films, but film noir's final phase was the most aesthetically and sociologically piercing. After ten years of steadily shedding romantic conventions, the later noir films finally got down to the root causes of the period: the loss of public honor, heroic conventions, personal integrity, and finally, psychic stability. The third-phase films were painfully self-aware; they seemed to know they stood at the end of a long tradition based on despair and disintegration and did not shy away from that fact. The best and most characteristically noir films—*Gun Crazy, White Heat, Out of the Past, Kiss Tomorrow Goodbye, D.O.A., They Live by Night,* and *The Big Heat*—stand at the end of the period and are the results of self-awareness. The third phase is rife with end-of-the-line noir heroes: *The Big Heat* and *Where the Sidewalk Ends* are the last stops for the urban cop, *Ace in the Hole* for the newspaper man, the Victor

Saville–produced Spillane series *I, the Jury, The Long Wait* (Victor Saville, 1954), and *Kiss Me Deadly* for the private eye, *Sunset Boulevard* for the Black Widow, *White Heat* and *Kiss Tomorrow Goodbye* for the gangster, *D.O.A.* for the John Doe American.

Appropriately, the masterpiece of film noir was a straggler, *Kiss Me Deadly,* produced in 1955. Its time delay gives it a sense of detachment and thoroughgoing seediness—it stands at the end of a long sleazy tradition. The private eye hero, Mike Hammer, undergoes the final stages of degradation. He is a small-time "bedroom dick," and has no qualms about it because the world around him isn't much better. Ralph Meeker, in his best performance, plays Hammer, a midget among dwarfs. Robert Aldrich's teasing direction carries noir to its sleaziest and most perversely erotic. Hammer overturns the underworld in search of the "great whatsit," and when he finally finds it, it turns out to be—joke of jokes—an exploding atomic bomb. The inhumanity and meaninglessness of the hero are small matters in a world in which the Bomb has the final say.

By the middle fifties film noir had ground to a halt. There were a few notable stragglers—*Kiss Me Deadly,* the Lewis/Alton *The Big Combo,* and film noir's epitaph, *Touch of Evil*—but for the most part a new style of crime film had become popular.

As the rise of McCarthy and Eisenhower demonstrated, Americans were eager to see a more bourgeois view of themselves. Crime had to move to the suburbs. The criminal put on a grey flannel suit, and the foot-sore cop was replaced by the "mobile unit" careening down the expressway. Any attempt at social criticism had to be cloaked in ludicrous affirmations of the American way of life. Technically, television, with its demand for full lighting and close-ups, gradually undercut the German influence, and color cinematography was, of course, the final blow to the noir look.

New directors like Siegel, Fleischer, Karlson, and Fuller, and TV shows like *Dragnet, M-Squad, Lineup,* and *Highway Patrol* stepped in to create the new crime drama. This transition can be seen in Samuel Fuller's 1953 *Pickup on South Street,* a film that blends the black look with the red scare. The waterfront scenes with Richard Widmark and Jean Peters are in the best noir tradition, but a later, dynamic fight in the subway marks Fuller as a director who would be better suited to the crime school of the middle and late fifties.

Film noir was an immensely creative period—probably the most creative in Hollywood's history—at least, if this creativity is measured not by its peaks but by its median level of artistry. Picked at random, a film noir is likely to be a better made film than a randomly selected silent comedy, musical, western, and so on. (A Joseph H. Lewis B film noir is better than a Lewis B western, for example.) Taken as a whole period, film noir achieved an unusually high level of artistry. Film noir seemed to bring out the best in everyone: directors, cameramen, screenwriters, actors. Again and again, a film noir will make the high point on an artist's career graph. Some directors, for example, did their best work in film noir (Stuart Heisler, Robert Siodmak, Gordon Douglas, Edward Dmytryk, John Brahm, John Cromwell, Raoul Walsh, Henry Hathaway); other directors began in film noir and, it seems to me, never regained their original heights (Otto Preminger, Rudolph Maté, Nicholas Ray, Robert Wise, Jules Dassin, Richard Fleischer, John Huston,

André de Toth, and Robert Aldrich); and other directors who made great films in other molds also made great film noir (Orson Welles, Max Ophuls, Fritz Lang, Elia Kazan, Howard Hawks, Robert Rossen, Anthony Mann, Joseph Losey, Alfred Hitchcock, and Stanley Kubrick). Whether or not one agrees with this particular schema, its message is irrefutable: film noir was good for practically every director's career. (Two interesting exceptions to prove the case are King Vidor and Jean Renoir.) Film noir seems to have been a creative release for everyone involved. It gave artists a chance to work with previously forbidden themes, yet had conventions strong enough to protect the mediocre. Cinematographers were allowed to become highly mannered, and actors were sheltered by the cinematographers. It was not until years later that critics were able to distinguish between great directors and great noir directors.

Film noir's remarkable creativity makes its long-time neglect the more baffling. The French, of course, have been students of the period for some time (Borde and Chaumeton's *Panorama du film noir* was published in 1955), but American critics until recently have preferred the western, the musical, or the gangster film to the film noir.

Some of the reasons for this neglect are superficial; others strike to the heart of the noir style. For a long time film noir, with its emphasis on corruption and despair, was considered an aberration of the American character. The western, with its moral primitivism, and the gangster film, with its Horatio Alger values, were considered more American than the film noir.

This prejudice was reinforced by the fact that film noir was ideally suited to the low-budget B film, and many of the best noir films were B films. This odd sort of economic snobbery still lingers on in some critical circles: high-budget trash is considered more worthy of attention than low-budget trash, and to praise a B film is somehow to slight (often intentionally) an A film.

The fundamental reason for film noir's neglect, however, is the fact that it depends more on choreography than sociology, and American critics have always been slow on the uptake when it comes to visual style. Like its protagonists, film noir is more interested in style than theme, whereas American critics have been traditionally more interested in theme than style. American film critics have always been sociologists first and scientists second: film is important as it relates to large masses, and if a film goes awry, it is often because the theme has been somehow "violated" by the style. Film noir operates on opposite principles: the theme is hidden in the style, and bogus themes are often flaunted ("middle-class values are best") that contradict the style. Although, I believe, style determines the theme in every film, it was easier for sociological critics to discuss the themes of the western and gangster film apart from stylistic analysis than it was to do for film noir.

Not surprisingly, it was the gangster film, not the film noir, which was canonized in *The Partisan Review* in 1948 by Robert Warshow's famous essay, "The Gangster as Tragic Hero." Although Warshow could be an aesthetic as well as a sociological critic, in this case he was interested in the western and gangster film as "popular" art rather than as style. This sociological orientation blinded Warshow, as it has many subsequent critics, to an aesthetically more important development in the gangster film—film noir.

The irony of this neglect is that in retrospect the gangster films War-show wrote about are inferior to film noir. The thirties gangster was primarily a reflection of what was happening in the country, and Warshow analyzed this. The film noir, although it was also a sociological reflection, went further than the gangster film. Toward the end film noir was engaged in a life-and-death struggle with the materials it reflected; it tried to make America accept a moral vision of life based on style. That very contradiction—promoting style in a culture that valued themes—forced film noir into artistically invigorating twists and turns. Film noir attacked and interpreted its sociological conditions and, by the close of the noir period, created a new artistic world that went beyond a simple sociological reflection, a nightmarish world of American mannerism that was by far more a creation than a reflection.

Because film noir was first of all a style, because it worked out its conflicts visually rather than thematically, because it was aware of its own identity, it was able to create artistic solutions to sociological problems. And for these reasons films like *Kiss Me Deadly, Kiss Tomorrow Goodbye*, and *Gun Crazy* can be works of art in a way that gangster films like *Scarface, The Public Enemy*, and *Little Caesar* can never be.

1972

ROBIN WOOD
IDEOLOGY, GENRE, AUTEUR

Robin Wood's early film criticism was influenced by the auteurist approach of *Cahiers du Cinéma*, where his first essay, on Hitchcock's *Psycho*, was published. In the 1960s and early 70s, Wood published influential monographs on Alfred Hitchcock, Howard Hawks, Satyajit Ray, Arthur Penn, Michelangelo Antonioni, Ingmar Bergman, and Claude Chabrol. Becoming professor of film studies at York University in 1977 and coming out as a gay man, Wood helped found *CineACTION!*, a journal dedicated not only to film but also to a radical political agenda of socialism, feminism, Marxism, and gay rights, keynoted by his essay "Responsibilities of a Gay Film Critic." His criticism from the 1980s onward is strongly influenced by Freudian, semiotic, and poststructuralist theories, but films and filmmakers remain primary in his analysis. He is currently professor emeritus at York University, where he continues to teach in the graduate film studies program. Among his later books are *Hollywood from Vietnam to Reagan* (1986) and *Sexual Politics and Narrative Film: Hollywood and Beyond* (1998).

The truth lies not in one dream but in many.

Arabian Nights (Pier Paolo Pasolini, 1974)

Each theory of film so far has insisted on its own particular polarization. Montage theory enthrones editing as the essential creative act at the expense of other aspects of film; Bazin's realist theory, seeking to right the balance, merely substitutes its own imbalance, downgrading montage and artifice; the revolutionary theory centered in Britain in *Screen* (but today very widespread) rejects—or at any rate seeks to "deconstruct"—realist art in favor of the so-called open text. Auteur theory, in its heyday, concentrated attention exclusively on the fingerprints, thematic or stylistic, of the individual artist; recent attempts to discuss the complete "filmic text" have tended to throw out ideas of personal authorship altogether. Each theory has, given its underlying position, its own validity—the validity being dependent upon and restricted by the position. Each can offer insights into different areas of cinema and different aspects of a single film.

I have suggested elsewhere[1] the desirability for critics—whose aim should always be to see the work as wholly as possible, as it is—to be able to draw on the discoveries and particular perceptions of each theory, each position, without committing themselves exclusively to any one. The ideal will not be easy to attain, and even the attempt raises all kinds of problems, the chief of which is the validity of evaluative criteria

---

[1] Robin Wood, "Old Wine, New Bottles: Structuralism or Humanism?" *Film Comment* 12, no. 6 (November–December 1976): 22–25.

that are not supported by a particular system. For what, then, *do* they receive support? No critic, obviously, can be free from a structure of values, nor can he or she afford to withdraw from the struggles and tensions of living to some position of "aesthetic" contemplation. Every critic who is worth reading has been, on the contrary, very much caught up in the effort to define values beyond purely aesthetic ones (if indeed such things exist). Yet to "live historically" need not entail commitment to a system or a cause; rather, it can involve being alive to the opposing pulls, the tensions, of one's world.

The past two decades have seen a number of advances in terms of the opening up of critical possibilities, of areas of relevance, especially with regard to Hollywood: the elaboration of auteur theory in its various manifestations; the interest in genre; the interest in ideology. I want here tentatively to explore some of the ways in which these disparate approaches to Hollywood movies might interpenetrate, producing the kind of synthetic criticism I have suggested might now be practicable.

In order to create a context within which to discuss *It's a Wonderful Life* (Frank Capra, 1946) and *Shadow of a Doubt* (Alfred Hitchcock, 1943), I want to attempt (at risk of obviousness) a definition of what we mean by American capitalist ideology— or, more specifically, the values and assumptions so insistently embodied in and reinforced by the classical Hollywood cinema. The following list of components is not intended to be exhaustive or profound, but simply to make conscious, prior to a discussion of the films, concepts with which we are all perfectly familiar:

1. Capitalism, the right of ownership, private enterprise, personal initiative; the settling of the land.

2. The work ethic: the notion that "honest toil" is in itself and for itself morally admirable, this and concept 1 both validating and reinforcing each other. The moral excellence of work is also bound up with the necessary subjugation or sublimation of the libido: "the Devil finds work for idle hands." The relationship is beautifully epitomized in the zoo-cleaner's song in *Cat People* (Jacques Tourneur, 1942):

> Nothing else to do,
> Nothing else to do,
> I strayed, went a-courting
> 'cause I'd nothing else to do.

3. Marriage (legalized heterosexual monogamy) and family—at once the further validation of concepts 1 and 2 (the homestead is built for the woman, whose function is to embody civilized values and guarantee their continuance through her children) and an extension of the ownership principle to personal relationships ("*My* house, *my* wife, *my* children") in a male-dominated society.

4a. Nature as agrarianism; the virgin land as Garden of Eden. A concept into which, in the western, concept 3 tends to become curiously assimilated (ideology's function being to "naturalize" cultural assumptions): for example, the treatment of the family in *Drums along the Mohawk* (John Ford, 1939).

4b. Nature as the wilderness, the Indians, on whose subjugation civilization is built; hence by extension the libido, of which in many westerns the Indians seem an extension or embodiment, as in *The Searchers* (Ford, 1956).

5. Progress, technology, the city ("New York, New York, it's a wonderful town").

6. Success and wealth—a value of which Hollywood ideology is also deeply ashamed, so that, while hundreds of films play on its allure, very few can allow themselves openly to extol it. Thus its ideological "shadow" is produced.

7. The Rosebud syndrome. Money isn't everything; money corrupts; the poor are happier. A very convenient assumption for capitalist ideology; the more oppressed you are, the happier you are, as exemplified by the singing "darkies" of *A Day at the Races* (Sam Wood, 1937).

8. America as the land where everyone is or can be happy; hence the land where all problems are solvable within the existing system (which may need a bit of reform here and there but no *radical* change). Subversive systems are assimilated wherever possible to serve the dominant ideology. Andrew Britton, in a characteristically brilliant article on Hitchcock's *Spellbound* (1945), argues that there even Freudian psychoanalysis becomes an instrument of ideological repression.[2] Above all, this assumption gives us that most striking and persistent of all classical Hollywood phenomena, the happy ending: often a mere "emergency exit" (Sirk's phrase)[3] for the spectator, a barely plausible pretense that the problems the film has raised are now resolved. *Hilda Crane* (Philip Dunne, 1950) offers a suitably blatant example among the hundreds possible.

Out of this list logically emerge two ideal figures:

9. The ideal male: the virile adventurer, the potent, untrammeled man of action.

10. The ideal female: wife and mother, perfect companion, the endlessly dependable mainstay of hearth and home.

Since these combine into an ideal couple of quite staggering incompatibility, each has his or her shadow:

11. The settled husband/father, dependable but dull.

12. The erotic woman (adventuress, gambling lady, saloon "entertainer"), fascinating but dangerous, liable to betray the hero or turn into a black panther.

The most striking fact about this list is that it presents an ideology that, far from being monolithic, is *inherently* riddled with hopeless contradictions and unresolvable tensions. The work that has been done so far on genre has tended to take the various genres as "given" and discrete, defining them in terms of motifs, iconography, conventions, and themes. What we need to ask, if genre theory is ever to be productive, is less *what* than *why*. We are so used to the genres that the peculiarity of the phenomenon itself has been too little noted. The idea I wish to put forward is that the development of the genres is rooted in the sort of ideological contradictions my list of concepts suggests. One impulse may be the attempt to deny such contradiction by eliminating one of the opposed terms, or at least by a process of simplification.

---

[2]Andrew Britton, "Hitchcock's *Spellbound*: Text and Counter-Text," *Cine-Action!* nos 3–4 (January 1986): 72–83.

[3]See *Sirk on Sirk*, edited by Jon Halliday (London: Secker & Warburg/British Film Institute, 1971).

Robert Warshow's seminal essays on the gangster hero and the westerner (still fruitfully suggestive, despite the obvious objection that he took too little into account) might be adduced here. The opposition of gangster film and western is only one of many possibilities. *All* the genres can be profitably examined in terms of ideological oppositions, forming a complex interlocking pattern: small-town family comedy/sophisticated city comedy; city comedy/film noir; film noir/small-town comedy, and so on. It is probable that a genre is ideologically "pure" (i.e., safe) only in its simplest, most archetypal, most aesthetically deprived and intellectually contemptible form—such as the Hopalong Cassidy films or Andy Hardy comedies.

The Hopalong Cassidy films (in which Indians, always a potentially disruptive force in ideological as well as dramatic terms, are, in general, significantly absent), for example, seem to depend on two strategies for their perfect ideological security: the strict division of characters into good and evil, with no "grays"; and Hoppy's sexlessness (he never becomes emotionally entangled). Hence the possibility of evading all the wandering/settling tensions on which aesthetically interesting westerns are generally structured. (An intriguing alternative: the ideal American family of Roy Rogers/Dale Evans/Trigger.) *Shane* (George Stevens, 1953) is especially interesting in this connection. A deliberate attempt to create an "archetypal" western, it also represents an effort to resolve the major ideological tensions harmoniously.

One of the greatest obstacles to any fruitful theory of genre has been the tendency to treat the genres as discrete. An ideological approach might suggest why they can't be, however hard they may appear to try: at best, they represent different strategies for dealing with the same ideological tensions. For example, the small-town movie with a contemporary setting should never be divorced from its historical correlative, the western. In the classical Hollywood cinema motifs cross repeatedly from genre to genre, as can be made clear by a few examples. The home/wandering opposition that Peter Wollen rightly sees as central to Ford[4] is not central only to Ford or even to the western; it structures a remarkably large number of American films covering all genres, from *Out of the Past* (Tourneur, 1947) to *There's No Business Like Show Business* (Walter Lang, 1954). The explicit comparison of women to cats connects screwball comedy (*Bringing Up Baby*, Howard Hawks, 1938), horror film (*Cat People*), melodrama (*Rampage*, Phil Karlson, 1963), and psychological thriller (*Marnie*, Hitchcock, 1964). Another example brings us to this essay's specific topic: notice the way in which the potent male adventurer, when he enters the family circle, immediately displaces his "shadow," the settled husband/father, in both *The Searchers* and *Shadow of a Doubt*.

Before we attempt to apply these ideas to specific films, however, one more point needs to be especially emphasized: the presence of ideological tensions in a movie, though it may give it an interest beyond Hopalong Cassidy, is not in itself a reliable evaluative criterion. It seems probable that artistic value has always been dependent on the presence—somewhere, at some stage—of an individual artist, whatever the function of art in the particular society and even when (as with the Chartres cathedral) one no longer knows who the individual artists were. It is only through the medium of the individual that ideological tensions come into particular focus, hence become of

---

[4]Peter Wollen, *Signs and Meaning in the Cinema*, 3d ed. (Bloomington and London: Indiana University Press, 1972), pp. 94–101.

aesthetic as well as sociological interest. It can perhaps be argued that works are of especial interest when the defined particularities of an auteur interact with specific ideological tensions and when the film is fed from more than one generic source.

The same basic ideological tensions operate in both *It's a Wonderful Life* and *Shadow of a Doubt*. They furnish further reminders that the home/wandering antinomy is by no means the exclusive preserve of the western. Bedford Falls and Santa Rosa can be seen as the frontier town seventy or so years on; they embody the development of the civilization whose establishment was celebrated around the same time by Ford in *My Darling Clementine* (1946). With this relationship to the western in the background (but in Capra's film made succinctly explicit), the central tension in both films can be described in terms of genre: the disturbing influx of film noir into the world of small-town domestic comedy. (It is a tension clearly present in *Clementine* as well: the opposition between the daytime and nighttime Tombstones.)

The strong contrast presented by the two films testifies to the decisive effect of the intervention of a clearly defined artistic personality in an ideological-generic structure. Both films have as a central ideological project the reaffirmation of family and small-town values that the action has called into question. In Capra's film this reaffirmation is magnificently convincing (but with full acknowledgment of the suppressions on which it depends and, consequently, of its precariousness); in Hitchcock's it is completely hollow. The very different emotional effects of the films—the satisfying catharsis and emotional fullness of Capra's, the "bitter taste" (on which so many have commented) of Hitchcock's—are very deeply rooted not only in our response to two opposed directorial personalities but in our own ideological structuring.

One of the main ideological and thematic tensions of *It's a Wonderful Life* is beautifully encapsulated in the scene in which George Bailey (James Stewart) and Mary (Donna Reed) smash windows in a derelict house as a preface to making wishes. George's wish is to get the money to leave Bedford Falls, which he sees as humdrum and constricting, and travel about the world; Mary's wish (not expressed in words, but in its subsequent fulfillment—confirming her belief that wishes don't come true if you speak them) is that she and George will marry, settle down, and raise a family in the same derelict house, a ruined shell that marriage-and-family restores to life.

This tension is developed through the extended sequence in which George is manipulated into marrying Mary. His brother's return home with a wife and a new job traps George into staying in Bedford Falls to take over the family business. With the homecoming celebrations continuing inside the house in the background, George sits disconsolately on the front porch; we hear an off-screen train whistle, to which he reacts. His mother (the indispensable Beulah Bondi) comes out and begins "suggesting" that he visit Mary; he appears to go off in her direction, physically pointed that way by his mother, then reappears and walks away past the mother—in the opposite direction.

This leads him, with perfect ideological/generic logic, to Violet (Gloria Grahame). The Violet/Mary opposition is an archetypally clear rending of that central Hollywood female opposition that crosses all generic boundaries—as with Susan (Katherine Hepburn) and Alice (Virginia Walker) in *Bringing Up Baby*, Irene (Simone Simon) and Alice (Jane Randolph) in *Cat People*, Chihuahua (Linda Darnell) and Clementine (Cathy Downs) in *My Darling Clementine*, Debby (Gloria

Grahame) and Katie (Jocelyn Brando) in *The Big Heat* (Fritz Lang, 1953). But Violet (in front of an amused audience) rejects his poetic invitation to a barefoot ramble over the hills in the moonlight; the good-time gal offers no more solution to the hero's wanderlust than the wife-mother figure.

So back to Mary, whom he brings to the window by beating a stick aggressively against the fence of the neat, enclosed front garden—a beautifully precise expression of his ambivalent state of mind: desire to attract Mary's attention warring with bitter resentment of his growing entrapment in domesticity. Mary is expecting him; his mother has phoned her, knowing that George would end up at her house. Two ideological premises combine here: the notion that the "good" mother always knows, precisely and with absolute certitude, the workings of her son's mind; and the notion that the female principle is central to the continuity of civilization, that the "weaker sex" is compensated with a sacred rightness.

Indoors, Mary shows George a cartoon she has drawn of George, in cowboy denims, lassoing the moon. The moment is rich in contradictory connotations. It explicitly evokes the western and the figure of the adventurer-hero to which George aspires. Earlier, it was for Mary that George wanted to "lasso the moon," the adventurer's exploits motivated by a desire to make happy the woman who will finally entrap him in domesticity. From Mary's point of view, the picture is at once affectionate (acknowledging the hero's aspirations), mocking (reducing them to caricature), and possessive (reducing George to an image she creates and holds within her hands).

The most overtly presented of the film's structural oppositions is that between the two faces of capitalism, benign and malignant. On the one hand, there are the Baileys (father and son) and their building and loan company, its business practice based on a sense of human needs and a belief in human goodness; on the other, there is Potter (Lionel Barrymore), described explicitly as a spider, motivated by greed, egotism, and miserliness, with no faith in human nature. Potter belongs to a very deeply rooted tradition. He derives most obviously from Dickens's Scrooge (the film is set at Christmas)—a Scrooge disturbingly unrepentant and irredeemable—but his more distant antecedents are in the ogres of fairy tales.

The opposition gives us not only two attitudes to money and property but two father images (Bailey, Sr., and Potter), each of whom gives his name to the land (Bailey Park, in small-town Bedford Falls, and Pottersville, the town's dark alternative). Most interestingly, the two figures (representing American choices, American tendencies) find their vivid ideological extensions in Hollywood genres: the happy, sunny world of small-town comedy (Bedford Falls is seen mostly in the daytime) and the world of film noir, the dark underside of Hollywood ideology.

Pottersville—the vision of the town as it would have been if George had never existed, shown him by his guardian angel (Henry Travers)—is just as "real" as (or no more stylized than) Bedford Falls. The iconography of small-town comedy is exchanged, unmistakably, for that of film noir, with police sirens, shooting in the streets, darkness, vicious dives, alcoholism, burlesque shows, strip clubs, and the glitter and shadows of noir lighting. George's mother, embittered and malevolent, runs a seedy boardinghouse; the good-time gal/wife-mother opposition, translated into noir terms, becomes an opposition of prostitute and repressed spinster-librarian. The towns emerge as equally valid images of America—validated by their generic familiarity.

Beside *Shadow of a Doubt*, *It's a Wonderful Life* manages a convincing and moving affirmation of the values (and value) of bourgeois family life. Yet what is revealed, when disaster releases George's suppressed tensions, is the intensity of his resentment of the family and desire to destroy it—and with it, in significant relationship, his work (his culminating action is furiously to overthrow the drawing board with his plans for more small-town houses). The film recognizes explicitly that behind every Bedford Falls lurks a Pottersville, and implicitly that within every George Bailey lurks an Ethan Edwards of *The Searchers*. Potter, tempting George, is given the devil's insights into his suppressed desires. His remark, "You once called me a warped, frustrated old man—now you're a warped, frustrated *young* man," is amply supported by the evidence the film supplies. What is finally striking about the film's affirmation is the extreme precariousness of its basis; and Potter survives without remorse, his crime unexposed and unpunished. It may well be Capra's masterpiece, but it is more than that. Like all the greatest American films—fed by a complex generic tradition and, beyond that, by the fears and aspirations of a whole culture—it at once transcends its director and would be inconceivable without him.

Shadow of a Doubt has always been among the most popular of Hitchcock's middle-period films, with critics and public alike, but it has been perceived in very different, almost diametrically opposed ways. On its appearance it was greeted by British critics as the film marking Hitchcock's coming to terms with America; his British films were praised for their humor and "social criticism" as much as for their suspense, and the early American films, notably *Rebecca* (1940) and *Suspicion* (1941), seemed like attempts artificially to reconstruct England in Hollywood. In *Shadow of a Doubt* Hitchcock (with the aid of Thornton Wilder and Sally Benson) at last brought to American middle-class society the shrewd, satirical, affectionate gaze previously bestowed on the British. A later generation of French critics (notably Rohmer and Chabrol in their Hitchcock book) praised the film for very different reasons, establishing its strict formalism (Truffaut's "un film fondé sur le chiffre 2") and seeing it as one of the keys to a consistent Catholic interpretation of Hitchcock, a rigorous working out of themes of original sin, the loss of innocence, the fallen world, the exchange (or interchangeability) of guilt.[5] The French noted the family comedy beloved of British critics, if at all, as a mildly annoying distraction.

That both these views correspond to important elements in the film and throw light on certain aspects of it is beyond doubt; both, however, now appear false and partial, dependent upon the abstracting of elements from the whole. If the film is, in a sense, completely dominated by Hitchcock (nothing in it is unmarked by his artistic personality), a complete reading would need to see the small-town-family elements and the Catholic elements are threads weaving through a complex fabric in which, again, ideological and generic determinants are crucial.

The kind of "synthetic" analysis I have suggested (going beyond an interest in the individual auteur) reveals *It's a Wonderful Life* as a far more potentially subversive film than has been generally recognized, but its subversive elements are, in the end, successfully contained. In *Shadow of a Doubt* the Hollywood ideology

---

[5]See Eric Rohmer and Claude Chabrol, *Hitchcock: The First Forty-Four Films*, trans. Stanley Hochman (New York: Ungar, 1979), p. 72.

I have sketched is shattered beyond convincing recuperation. One can, however, trace through the film its attempts to impose itself and render things "safe." What is in jeopardy is above all the family—but, given the family's central ideological significance, once that is in jeopardy, everything is. The small town (still rooted in the agrarian dream, in ideals of the virgin land as a garden of innocence) and the united happy family are regarded as the real sound heart of American civilization; the ideological project is to acknowledge the existence of sickness and evil but preserve the family from their contamination.

A number of strategies can be discerned here: the attempt to insist on a separation of Uncle Charlie from Santa Rosa; his death at the end of the film as the definitive purging of evil; the production of the young detective (the healthy, wholesome, small-town male) as a marriage partner for Young Charlie so that the family may be perpetuated; above all, the attribution of Uncle Charlie's sexual pathology to a childhood accident as a means of exonerating the family of the charge of producing a monster, a possibility the American popular cinema, with the contemporary overturning of traditional values, can now envisage—for example, *It's Alive* (Larry Cohen, 1974).

The famous opening, with its parallel introductions of Uncle Charlie and Young Charlie, insists on the city and the small town as *opposed*, sickness and evil being of the city. As with Bedford Falls/Pottersville, the film draws lavishly on the iconography of usually discrete genres. Six shots (with all movement and direction—the bridges, the panning, the editing—consistently rightward) leading up to the first interior of Uncle Charlie's room give us urban technology, wreckage both human (the down-and-outs) and material (the dumped cars by the sign "No Dumping Allowed"), children playing in the street, the number 13 on the lodging-house door. Six shots (movement and direction consistently left) leading to the first interior of Young Charlie's room give us sunny streets with no street games (Santa Rosa evidently has parks), an orderly town with a smiling, paternal policeman presiding over traffic and pedestrians.

In Catholic terms, this is the fallen world against a world of apparent prelapsarian innocence; but it is just as valid to interpret the images, as in *It's a Wonderful Life*, in terms of the two faces of American capitalism. Uncle Charlie has money (the fruits of his crimes and his aberrant sexuality) littered in disorder over table and floor; the Santa Rosa policeman has behind him the Bank of America. The detailed paralleling of uncle and niece can of course be read as comparison as much as contrast, and the opposition that of two sides of the same coin. The point is clearest in that crucial, profoundly disturbing scene where film noir erupts into Santa Rosa itself: the visit to the Til Two bar, where Young Charlie is confronted with her alter ego Louise the waitress, her former classmate. The scene equally invites Catholic and Marxist commentaries; its force arises from the revelation of the fallen world/capitalist-corruption-and-deprivation at the heart of the American small town. The close juxtaposition of genres has implications that reach throughout the whole generic structure of the classical Hollywood cinema.

The subversion of ideology within the film is everywhere traceable to Hitchcock's presence, to the skepticism and nihilism that lurk just behind the jocular facade of his public image. His Catholicism is in reality the lingering on in his work of the darker aspects of Catholic mythology: hell without heaven. The traces are clear enough. Young Charlie wants a "miracle"; she thinks of her uncle as "the one who can save us" (and her mother immediately asks, "What do you mean, save us?"); when she finds his telegram, in the very act of sending hers, her reaction is an ecstatic "He heard me, he heard me!" Hitchcock cuts at once to a low-angle shot of Uncle Charlie's train rushing toward Santa Rosa, underlining the effect with an ominous crashing chord on the sound track.

Uncle Charlie is one of the supreme embodiments of the key Hitchcock figure: ambiguously devil and lost soul. When he reaches Santa Rosa, the image is blackened by its smoke. From his first appearance, Charlie is associated consistently with a cigar (its phallic connotations evident from the outset, in the scene with the landlady) and repeatedly shown with a wreath of smoke curling around his head (no one else in the film smokes except Joe, the displaced father, who has a paternal pipe, usually unlit). Several incidents (the escape from the policemen at the beginning, the garage door slammed as by remote control) invest him with a quasi-supernatural power. Rather than restrict the film to a Catholic reading, it seems logical to connect these marks with others: the thread of superstition that runs through the film (the number 13; the hat on the bed; "Sing at table and you'll marry a crazy husband"; the irrational dread of the utterance, however innocent, of the forbidden words "Merry Widow") and the telepathy motif (the telegrams, the tune "jumping from head to head")—the whole Hitchcockian sense of life at the mercy of terrible, unpredictable forces that have to be kept down.

The Hitchcockian dread of repressed forces is characteristically accompanied by a sense of the emptiness of the surface world that represses them, and this crucially affects the presentation of the American small-town family in *Shadow of a Doubt*. The warmth and togetherness, the mutual responsiveness and affection that Capra so beautifully creates in the Bailey families, senior and junior, of *It's a Wonderful Life* are here almost entirely lacking—and this despite the fact, in itself of great ideological interest, that the treatment of the family in *Shadow of a Doubt* has generally been perceived (even, one guesses, by Hitchcock himself) as affectionate.

The most striking characteristic of the Spencers is the separateness of each member; the recurring point of the celebrated overlapping dialogue is that no one ever listens to what anyone else is saying. Each is locked in a separate fantasy world: Emmy in the past, Joe in crime, Anne in books that are read apparently less for pleasure than as a means of amassing knowledge with which she has little emotional contact (though she also believes that everything she reads is "true"). The parents are trapped in a petty materialism (both respond to Young Charlie's dissatisfaction with the assumption that she's talking about money) and reliance on "honest toil" as the means of using up energies. In *Shadow of a Doubt* the ideological image of the small-town happy family becomes the flimsiest facade. That so many are nonetheless deceived by it testifies only to the strength of the ideology—one of whose functions is of course to inhibit the imagining of radical alternatives.

I have argued elsewhere that the key to Hitchcock's films is less suspense than sexuality (or, alternatively, that his "suspense" always carries a sexual charge in ways sometimes obvious, sometimes esoteric); and that sexual relationships in his work are inevitably based on power, the obsession with power and dread of impotence being as central to his method as to his thematic. In *Shadow of a Doubt* it is above all sexuality that cracks apart the family facade. As far as the Hays Code permitted, a double incest theme runs through the film: Uncle Charlie and Emmy, Uncle Charlie and Young Charlie. Necessarily, this is expressed through images and motifs, never becoming verbally explicit; certain of the images depend on a suppressed verbal play for their significance.

For the reunion of brother and sister, Hitchcock gives us an image (Emmy poised left of screen, arrested in mid-movement, Charlie right, under trees and sunshine) that iconographically evokes the reunion of lovers (Charlie wants to see Emmy again as she was when she was "the prettiest girl on the block"). And Emmy's breakdown, in front of her embarrassed friends and neighbors, at the news of Charlie's imminent departure is eloquent. As for uncle and niece, they are introduced symmetrically lying on beds, Uncle Charlie fondling his phallic cigar, Young Charlie, prone, hands behind head. When Uncle Charlie gets off the train he is bent over a stick, pretending to be ill; as soon as he sees Young Charlie, he "comes erect," flourishing the stick. One of his first actions on taking over her bedroom is to pluck a rose for his buttonhole ("deflowering"). More obviously, there is the business with the ring, which, as a symbolic token of engagement, not only links Charlie sexually with her uncle, but also links her, through its previous ownership, to his succession of merry widows. The film shows sexual pathology at the heart of the American family, the necessary product of its repressions and sublimations.

As for the "accident"—that old critical stumbling block—it presents no problem at all, provided one is ready to acknowledge the validity of a psychoanalytical reading of movies. Indeed, it provides a rather beautiful example of the way in which ideology, in seeking to impose itself, succeeds merely in confirming its own subversion. The "accident" (Charlie was "riding a bicycle" for the first time, which results in a "collision") can be read as an elementary Freudian metaphor for the trauma of premature sexual awakening (after which Charlie was "never the same again"). The smothering sexual/possessive devotion of a doting older sister may be left to provide a clue to the sexual motivation behind the merry-widow murders; Charlie isn't interested in money. Indeed, Emmy is connected to the merry widows by an associative chain in which important links are her own practical widowhood (her ineffectual husband is largely ignored), her ladies' club, and its leading light, Mrs. Potter, Uncle Charlie's potential next-in-line.

A fuller analysis would need to dwell on the limitations of Hitchcock's vision, nearer the nihilistic than the tragic; on his inability to conceive of repressed energies as other than evil and the surface world that represses them as other than shallow and unfulfilling. This explains why there can be no heaven corresponding to Hitchcock's hell, for every vision of heaven that is not merely negative is rooted in a concept of the liberation of the instincts, the resurrection of the body, which Hitchcock must always deny. But my final stress is less on the evaluation of a particular film or director than on the implications for a criticism of the Hollywood cinema of the notions of interaction and multiple determinacy I have been employing. Its roots in the Hollywood genres, and in the very ideological structure it so disturbingly subverts, make *Shadow of a Doubt* so much more suggestive and significant a work than Hitchcock the bourgeois entertainer could ever have guessed.

1977

LINDA WILLIAMS
FILM BODIES:
GENDER, GENRE, AND EXCESS

Linda Williams brings together genre study and feminist theory to explore the permutations of gender and sexuality in popular "body genres" including pornography, melodrama, and horror in such books as *Hard Core: Power, Pleasure, and the "Frenzy of the Visible" (1989), and Playing the Race Card: Melodramas of Black and White from Uncle Tom to O. J. Simpson* (2001). Her current project, *Screening Sex*, continues the work she began in the 1980s, analyzing the portrayal of sex in film and new media since the 1960s. She currently directs the film studies program at University of California, Berkeley, where she is a professor of film studies and rhetoric.

When my seven-year-old son and I go to the movies, we often select from among categories of films that promise to be sensational, to give our bodies an actual physical jolt. He calls these movies "gross." My son and I agree that the fun of "gross" movies is in their display of sensations that are on the edge of respectable. Where we disagree—and where we as a culture often disagree, along lines of gender, age, or sexual orientation—is in which movies are over the edge, too "gross." To my son the good "gross" movies are those with scary monsters like Freddy Krueger (of the *Nightmare on Elm Street* series) who rip apart teenagers, especially teenage girls. These movies both fascinate and scare him; he is actually more interested in talking about than seeing them.

A second category, one that I like and my son doesn't, are sad movies that make you cry. These are gross in their focus on unseemly emotions that may remind him too acutely of his own powerlessness as a child. A third category, of both intense interest and disgust to my son (he makes the puke sign when speaking of it), he can only describe euphemistically as "the 'K' word." K is for kissing. To a seven-year-old boy it is kissing precisely which is obscene.

There is no accounting for taste, especially in the realm of the "gross." As a culture we most often invoke the term to designate excesses we wish to exclude; to say, for example, which of the Robert Mapplethorpe photos we draw the line at, but not to say what form and structure and function operate within the representations deemed excessive. Because so much attention goes to determining where to draw the line, discussions of the gross are often a highly confused hodgepodge of different cate-

I owe thanks to Rhona Berenstein, Leo Braudy, Ernest Callenbach, Paul Fitzgerald, Jane Gains, Mandy Harris, Brian Henderson, Marsha Kinder, Eric Rentschler, and Pauline Yu for generous advice on drafts of this essay.

gories of excess. For example, pornography is today more often deemed excessive for its violence than for its sex, while horror films are excessive in their displacement of sex onto violence. In contrast, melodramas are deemed excessive for their gender- and sex-linked pathos, for their naked displays of emotion; Ann Douglas once referred to the genre of romance fiction as "soft-core emotional porn for women."[1]

Alone or in combination, heavy doses of sex, violence, and emotion are dismissed by one faction or another as having no logic or reason for existence beyond their power to excite. Gratuitous sex, gratuitous violence and terror, gratuitous emotion are frequent epithets hurled at the phenomenon of the "sensational" in pornography, horror, and melodrama. This essay explores the notion that there may be some value in thinking about the form, function, and system of seemingly gratuitous excesses in these three genres. For if, as it seems, sex, violence, and emotion are fundamental elements of the sensational effects of these three types of films, the designation "gratuitous" is itself gratuitous. My hope, therefore, is that by thinking comparatively about all three "gross" and sensational film body genres we might be able to get beyond the mere fact of sensation to explore its system and structure as well as its effect on the bodies of spectators.

BODY GENRES

The repetitive formulas and spectacles of film genres are often defined by their differences from the classical realist style of narrative cinema. These classical films have been characterized as efficient action-centered, goal-oriented linear narratives driven by the desire of a single protagonist, involving one or two lines of action, and leading to definitive closure. In their influential study of the Classical Hollywood Cinema, Bordwell, Thompson, and Staiger call this the Classical Hollywood style.[2]

As Rick Altman has noted in a recent article, both genre study and the study of the somewhat more nebulous category of melodrama has long been hampered by assumptions about the classical nature of the dominant narrative to which melodrama and some individual genres have been opposed. Altman argues that Bordwell, Thompson, and Staiger, who locate the Classical Hollywood Style in the linear, progressive form of the Hollywood narrative, cannot accommodate "melodramatic" attributes like spectacle, episodic presentation, or dependence on coincidence except as limited exceptions or "play" within the dominant linear causality of the classical (346).[3]

Altman writes: "Unmotivated events, rhythmic montage, highlighted parallelism, overlong spectacles—these are the excesses in the classical narrative system that alert us to the existence of a competing logic, a second voice" (345–46). Altman, whose own work on the movie musical has necessarily relied upon analyses of seemingly "excessive" spectacles and parallel constructions, thus makes a strong

---

[1] Ann Douglas, "Soft-Porn Culture," *The New Republic*, 30 August 1980.

[2] David Bordwell, Janet Staiger, and Kristin Thompson, *The Classical Hollywood Cinema: Film Style and Mode of Production to 1960.* (New York: Columbia University Press, 1985).

[3] Rick Altman, "Dickens, Griffith, and Film Theory Today," *South Atlantic Quarterly* 88 (1989): 321–59.

case for the need to recognize the possibility that excess may itself be organized as a system (347). Yet analyses of systems of excess have been much slower to emerge in the genres whose nonlinear spectacles have centered more directly upon the gross display of the human body. Pornography and horror films are two such systems of excess. Pornography is the lowest in cultural esteem, gross-out horror is next to lowest.

Melodrama, however, refers to a much broader category of films and a much larger system of excess. It would not be unreasonable, in fact, to consider all three of these genres under the extended rubric of melodrama, considered as a filmic mode of stylistic and/or emotional excess that stands in contrast to more "dominant" modes of realistic, goal-oriented narrative. In this extended sense melodrama can encompass a broad range of films marked by "lapses" in realism, by "excesses" of spectacle and displays of primal, even infantile emotions, and by narratives that seem circular and repetitive. Much of the interest of melodrama to film scholars over the last fifteen years originates in the sense that the form exceeds the normative system of much narrative cinema. I shall limit my focus here, however, to a more narrow sense of melodrama, leaving the broader category of the sensational to encompass the three genres I wish to consider. Thus, partly for purposes of contrast with pornography, the melodrama I will consider here will consist of the form that has most interested feminist critics—that of "the woman's film" or "weepie." These are films addressed to women in their traditional status under patriarchy— as wives, mothers, abandoned lovers, or in their traditional status as bodily hysteria or excess, as in the frequent case of the woman "afflicted" with a deadly or debilitating disease.[4]

What are the pertinent features of bodily excess shared by these three "gross" genres? First, there is the spectacle of a body caught in the grip of intense sensation or emotion. Carol Clover, speaking primarily of horror films and pornography, has called films which privilege the sensational "body" genres (189).[5] I am expanding Clover's notion of low body genres to include the sensation of overwhelming pathos in the "weepie." The body spectacle is featured more sensationally in pornography's portrayal of orgasm, in horror's portrayal of violence and terror, and in melodrama's portrayal of weeping. I propose that an investigation of the visual and narrative pleasures found in the portrayal of these three types of excess could be important to a new direction in genre criticism that would take as its point of departure—rather than as an unexamined assumption—questions of gender construction, and gender addresses in relation to basic sexual fantasies.

Another pertinent feature shared by these body genres is the focus on what could probably best be called a form of ecstasy. While the classical meaning of the original

---

[4]For an excellent summary of many of the issues involved with both film melodrama and the "women's film," see Christine Gledhill's introduction to the anthology *Home is Where the Heart Is: Studies in Melodrama and the Woman's Film* (Gledhill, 1987). For a more general inquiry into the theatrical origins of melodrama, see Peter Brooks's (1976) *The Melodramatic Imagination*. And for an extended theoretical inquiry and analysis of a body of melodramatic women's films, see Mary Ann Doane (1987), *The Desire to Desire*.

[5]Carol J. Clover, "Her Body, Himself: Gender in the Slasher Film," *Representations* 20 (Fall 1987): 187–228.

Greek word is insanity and bewilderment, more contemporary meanings suggest components of direct or indirect sexual excitement and rapture, a rapture which informs even the pathos of melodrama.

Visually, each of these ecstatic excesses could be said to share a quality of uncontrollable convulsion or spasm—of the body "beside itself" with sexual pleasure, fear and terror, or overpowering sadness. Aurally, excess is marked by recourse not to the coded articulations of language but to inarticulate cries of pleasure in porn, screams of fear in horror, sobs of anguish in melodrama.

Looking at, and listening to, these bodily ecstasies, we can also notice something else that these genres seem to share: though quite differently gendered with respect to their targeted audiences, with pornography aimed, presumably, at active men and melodramatic weepies aimed, presumably, as passive women, and with contemporary gross-out horror aimed at adolescents careening wildly between the two masculine and feminine poles, in each of these genres the bodies of women figured on the screen have functioned traditionally as the primary *embodiments* of pleasure, fear, and pain.

In other words, even when the pleasure of viewing has traditionally been constructed for masculine spectators, as is the case in most traditional heterosexual pornography, it is the female body in the grips of an out-of-control ecstasy that has offered the most sensational sight. So the bodies of women have tended to function, ever since the eighteenth-century origins of these genres in the Marquis de Sade, Gothic fiction, and the novels of Richardson, as both the *moved* and the *moving*. It is thus through what Foucault has called the sexual saturation of the female body that audiences of all sorts have received some of their most powerful sensations.[6]

There are, of course, other film genres which both portray and affect the sensational body—e.g., thrillers, musicals, comedies. I suggest, however, that the film genres that have had especially low cultural status—which have seemed to exist as excesses to the system of even the popular genres—are not simply those which sensationally display bodies on the screen and register effects in the bodies of spectators. Rather, what may especially mark these body genres as low is the perception that the body of the spectator is caught up in an almost involuntary mimicry of the emotion or sensation of the body on the screen along with the fact that the body displayed is female. Physical clown comedy is another "body" genre concerned with all manner of gross activities and body functions—eating shoes, slipping on banana peels. Nonetheless, it has not been deemed gratuitously excessive, probably because the reaction of the audience does not mimic the sensations experienced by the central clown. Indeed, it is almost a rule that the audience's physical reaction of laughter does not coincide with the often dead-pan reactions of the clown.

In the body genres I am isolating here, however, it seems to be the case that the success of these genres is often measured by the degree to which the audience sensation mimics what is seen on the screen. Whether this mimicry is exact, e.g., whether the spectator at the porn film actually orgasms, whether the spectator at the horror

---

[6]Michel Foucault, *The History of Sexuality*, Vol. 1, *An Introduction*, trans. Robert Hurley (New York: Pantheon Books, 1978).

film actual shudders in fear, whether the spectator of the melodrama actually dis-solves in tears, the success of these genres seems a self-evident matter of measur-ing bodily response. Examples of such measurement can be readily observed: in the "peter meter" capsule reviews in *Hustler* magazine, which measure the power of a porn film in degrees of erection of little cartoon penises; in horror films which mea-sure success in terms of screams, fainting, and heart attacks in the audience (horror producer William Castle specialized in this kind of thing with such films as *The Tingler*, 1959); and in the long-standing tradition of women's films measuring their success in terms of one-, two-, or three-handkerchief movies.

What seems to bracket these particular genres from others is an apparent lack of proper esthetic distance, a sense of over-involvement in sensation and emotion. We feel manipulated by these texts—an impression that the very colloquialisms of "tear jerker" and "fear jerker" express—and to which we could add pornography's even cruder sense as texts to which some people might be inclined to "jerk off." The rhetoric of violence of the jerk suggests the extension to which viewers feel too directly, too viscerally manipulated by the text in specifically gendered ways. Mary Ann Doane, for example, writing about the most genteel of these jerkers—the mater-nal melodrama—equates the violence of this emotion to a kind of "textual rape" of the targeted female viewer, who is "feminized through pathos" (95).[7]

Feminist critics of pornography often evoke similar figures of sexual/textual vio-lence when describing the operating of this genre. Robin Morgan's slogan "pornog-raphy is the theory, and rape is the practice" is well known (139).[8] Implicit in this slogan is the notion that women are the objectified victims of pornographic repre-sentations, that the image of the sexually ecstatic woman so important to the genre is a celebration of female victimization and a prelude to female victimization in real life.

Less well known, but related, is the observation of the critic of horror films, James Twitchell, who notices that the Latin *horrere* means to bristle. He describes the way the nape hair stands on end during moments of shivering excitement. The aptly named Twitchell thus describes a kind of erection of the hair founded in the con-flict between reactions of "fight and flight" (10).[9] While male victims in horror films may shudder and scream as well, it has long been a dictum of the genre that women make the best victims. "Torture the women!" was the famous advice given by Alfred Hitchcock.[10]

In the classic horror film the terror of the female victim shares the spectacle along with the monster. Fay Wary and the mechanized monster that made her scream in *King Kong* is a familiar example of the classic form. Janet Leigh in the shower in *Psycho* is a familiar example of a transition to a more sexually explicit form of the tortured and terrorized woman. And her daughter, Jamie Lee Curtis in *Halloween*, can serve as the more contemporary version of the terrorized woman victim. In both of these later films the spectacle of the monster seems to take second billing to the increasingly numerous victims slashed by the sexually disturbed but entirely human monsters.

---

[7]Mary Ann Doane, *The Desire to Desire: The Woman's Film of the 1940s* (Bloomington: Indiana University Press, 1987).

[8]Robin Morgan, "Theory and Practice: Pornography and Rape," in *Take Back the Night*, ed. Laura Lederer (New York: Morrow, 1980).

[9]James Twitchell, *Dreadful Pleasures: An Anatomy of Modern Horror* (New York: Oxford, 1985).

[10]Carol J. Clover discusses the meanings of this famous quote in her essay, "Her Body/Himself."

In the woman's film a well-known classic is the long-suffering mother of the two early versions of *Stella Dallas* who sacrifices herself for her daughter's upward mobility. Contemporary film goers could recently see Bette Midler going through the same sacrifice and loss in the film *Stella*. Debra Winger in *Terms of Endearment* is another familiar example of this maternal pathos.

With the above genre stereotypes in mind we should now ask about the status of bodily excess in each of these genres. Is it simply the unseemly, "gratuitous" presence of the sexually ecstatic woman, the tortured woman, the weeping woman—and the accompanying presence of the sexual fluids, the blood and the tears that flow from her body and which are presumably mimicked by spectators—that mark the excess of each type of film? How shall we think of these bodily displays in relation to one another, as a system of excess in the popular film? And finally, how excessive are they really?

The psychoanalytic system of analysis that has been so influential in film study in general and in feminist film theory and criticism has been remarkably ambivalent about the status of excess in its major tools of analysis. The categories of fetishism, voyeurism, sadism, and masochism frequently invoked to describe the pleasures of film spectatorship are by definition perversions. Perversions are usually defined as sexual excesses, specifically as excesses which are deflected away from "proper" end goals onto substitute goals or objects—fetishes instead of genitals, looking instead of touching, etc.—which seems excessive or gratuitous. Yet the perverse pleasures of film viewing are hardly gratuitous. They have been considered so basic that they have often been presented as norms. What is a film, after all, without voyeurism? Yet, at the same time, feminist critics have asked, what is the position of women within this pleasure geared to a presumably sadistic "male gaze"?[11] To what extent is she its victim? Are the orgasmic woman of pornography and the tortured woman of horror merely in the service of the sadistic male gaze? And is the weeping woman of melodrama appealing to the abnormal perversions of masochism in female viewers?

These questions point to the ambiguity of the terms of perversion used to describe the normal pleasures of film viewing. Without attempting to go into any of the complexities of this discussion here—a discussion which must ultimately relate to the status of the term perversion in theories of sexuality themselves—let me simply suggest the value of not invoking the perversions as terms of condemnation. As even the most cursory reading of Freud shows, sexuality is by definition perverse. The "aims" and "objects" of sexual desire are often obscure and inherently substitutive. Unless we are willing to see reproduction as the common goal of the sexual drive, we have to admit, as Jonathan Dollimore has put it, that we are all perverts. Dollimore's goal of retrieving the "concept of perversion as a category of cultural analysis"—as a structure intrinsic to all sexuality rather than extrinsic to it—is crucial to any attempt to understand cultural forms—such as our three body genres—in which fantasy predominates.[12]

---

[11]Laura Mulvey, "Visual Pleasure and Narrative Cinema," *Screen* 16, no. 3 (1975): 6–18.

[12]Jonathan Dollimore, "The Cultural Politics of Perversion: Augustine, Shakespeare, Freud, Foucault," *Genders* 8 (1990). Dollimore's project, along with Teresa de Lauretis's more detailed examination of the term "perversion" in Freudian psychoanalysis is central to any more detailed attempts to understand the perverse pleasures of these gross body genres. See *The Practice of Love: Lesbian Sexuality and Perverse Desire* (Bloomington: Indiana University Press, 1994).

STRUCTURES OF PERVERSION IN THE
"FEMALE BODY GENRES"

Each of the three body genres I have isolated hingers on the spectacle of a "sexually saturated" female body, and each offers what many feminist critics would agree to be spectacles of feminine victimization. But this victimization is very different in each type of film and cannot be accounted for simply by pointing to the sadistic power and pleasure of masculine subject positions punishing or dominating feminine objects.

Many feminists have pointed to the victimization of the woman performers of pornography who must actually do the acts depicted in the film, as well as to the victimization of characters within the films.[13] Pornography, in this view, is fundamentally sadistic. In women's weepies, on the other hand, feminists have pointed to the spectacles of intense suffering and loss as masochistic.

Stella Dallas (1937). Stella (Barbara Stanwyck), after sacrificing herself for her daughter, stands in the rain with a crowd of curious passersby to watch the wedding. "But even in the most extreme displays of feminine masochistic suffering, there is always a component of either power or pleasure for the woman victims. . . . In melodramatic woman's weepies, feminine subject positions appear to be constructed which achieve a modicum of power and pleasure within the given limits of patriarchal constraints on women" (WILLIAMS, p. 610).

---

[13]See Andrea Dworkin, *Pornography: Men Possessing Women* (New York: Perigee Books, 1979); and MacKinnon, *Feminism Unmodified: Discourses on Life and Law* (Cambridge, MA: Harvard University Press, 1987).

In horror films, while feminists have often pointed to the women victims who suffer simulated torture and mutilation as victims of sadism,[14] more recent feminist work has suggested that the horror film may present an interesting, and perhaps instructive, case of oscillation between masochistic and sadistic poles. This more recent argument, advanced by Carol J. Clover, has suggested that pleasure, for a masculine-identified viewer, oscillates between identifying with the initial passive powerlessness of the abject and terrorized girl-victim of horror and her later, active empowerment.[15]

This argument holds that when the girl-victim of a film like *Halloween* finally grabs the phallic knife, or ax, or chain saw to turn the tables on the monster-killer, that viewer identification shifts from an "abject terror gendered feminine" to an active power with bisexual components. A gender-confused monster is foiled, often symbolically castrated by an "androgynous" "final girl" (206–209).[16] In slasher films, identification with victimization is a roller-coaster ride of sadomasochistic thrills.

We could thus initially schematize the perverse pleasures of these genres in the following way: pornography's appeal to its presumed male viewers would be characterized as sadistic, horror films' appeal to the emerging sexual identities of its (frequently adolescent) spectators would be sadomasochistic and women's films appeal to presumed female viewers would be masochistic.

The masochistic component of viewing pleasure for women has been the most problematic term of perversion for feminist critics. It is interesting, for example, that most of our important studies of masochism—whether by Deleuze,[17] Silverman,[18] or Studlar[19]—have all focused on the exoticism of masculine masochism rather than the familiarity of female masochism. Masochistic pleasure for women has paradoxically seemed either too normal—too much the normal yet intolerable condition of women—or too perverse to be taken seriously as pleasure.

There is thus a real need to be clearer than we have been about what is in masochism for women—how power and pleasure operate in fantasies of domination which appeal to women. There is an equal need to be clearer than we have about what is in sadism for men. Here the initial opposition between these two most gendered genres—women's weepies and male heterosexual pornography—needs to be complicated. I have argued elsewhere, for example, that pornography has too simplistically been allied with a purely sadistic fantasy structure. Indeed, those troubling films and videos which deploy instruments of torture on the bodies of women have been allied so completely with masculine viewing pleasures that we have not paid enough attention to their appeal to women except to condemn such appeal as false consciousness (184–228).[20]

---

[14]Linda Williams, "When the Woman Looks," in *Re-Vision: Essays in Feminist Film Criticism*, Mary Ann Doane, Patricia Mellencamp, and Linda Williams, eds., American Film Institute Monograph Series, vol. 3 (Frederick, MD: University Publications of America, 1983).

[15]Clover, "Her Body, Himself."

[16]Ibid.

[17]Gilles Deleuze, *Masochism: An Interpretation of Coldness and Cruelty*, trans. Jean McNeil (New York, Braziller, 1971).

[18]Kaja Silverman, "Masochism and Subjectivity," *Framework* 12 (1980): 2–9; and "Masochism and Male Subjectivity," *Camera Obscura* 17 (1988): 31–66.

[19]Gaylyn Studlar, *In the Realm of Pleasure: Von Sternberg, Dietrich and the Masochistic Aesthetic* (Urbana: University of Illinois Press, 1985).

[20]Linda Williams, *Hard Core: Power, Pleasure and the "Frenzy of the Visible"* (Berkeley: University of California Press, 1989).

One important complication of the initial schema I have outlined would thus be to take a lesson from Clover's more bisexual model of viewer identification in horror film and stress the sadomasochistic component of each of these body genres through their various appropriations of melodramatic fantasies that are, in fact, basic to each. All of these genres could, for example, be said to offer highly melodramatic enactments of sexually charged, if not sexually explicit, relations. This subgenre of sadomasochistic pornography, with its suspension of pleasure over the course of prolonged sessions of dramatic suffering, offers a particularly intense, almost parodic, enactment of the classic melodramatic scenario of the passive and innocent female victim suffering at the hands of a leering villain. We can also see in horror films of tortured women a similar melodramatization of the innocent victim. An important difference, of course, lies in the component of the victim's overt sexual pleasure in the scenario of domination.

But even in the most extreme displays of feminine masochistic suffering, there is always a component of either power or pleasure for the woman victim. In slasher horror films we have seen how identification seems to oscillate between powerlessness and power. In sadomasochistic pornography and in melodramatic woman's weepies, feminine subject positions appear to be constructed which achieve a modicum of power and pleasure within the given limits of patriarchal constraints on women. It is worth noting as well that *non*-sadomasochistic pornography has historically been one of the few types of popular film that has not punished women for actively pursuing their sexual pleasure.

In the subgenre of sadomasochistic pornography, however, the female masochist in the scenario must be devious in her pursuit of pleasure. She plays the part of passive sufferer in order to obtain pleasure. Under a patriarchal double standard that has rigorously separated the sexually passive "good" girl from the sexually active "bad" girl, masochistic role-playing offers a way out of this dichotomy by combining the good girl with the bad: the passive "good girl" can prove to her witnesses (the superego who is her torturer) that she does not will the pleasure that she receives. Yet the sexually active "bad" girl enjoys this pleasure and has knowingly arranged to endure the pain that earns it. The cultural law which decides that some girls are good and others are bad is not defeated but within its terms pleasure has been negotiated and "paid for" with a pain that conditions it. The "bad" girl is punished, but in return she receives pleasure.[21]

In contrast, the sadomasochistic teen horror films kill off the sexually active "bad" girls, allowing only the nonsexual "good" girls to survive. But these good girls become, as if in compensation, remarkably active, to the point of appropriating phallic power to themselves. It is as if this phallic power is granted so long as it is rigorously separated from phallic or any other sort of pleasure. For these pleasures spell sure death in this genre.

In the melodramatic woman's film we might think to encounter a purer form of masochism on the part of female viewers. Yet even here the female viewer does not seem to be invited to identify wholly with the sacrificing good woman, but rather with a variety of different positions, including those which empathically look on at

---

[21]I discuss these issues at length in a chapter on sadomasochistic pornography in my book *Hard Core*.

her own suffering. While I would not argue that there is a very strong sadistic component to these films, I do argue that there is a strong mixture of passivity and activity, and a bisexual oscillation between the poles of each, in even this genre.

For example, the woman viewer of a maternal melodrama such as *Terms of Endearment* or *Steel Magnolias* does not simply identify with the suffering and dying heroines of each. She may equally identify with the powerful matriarchs, the surviving mothers who preside over the deaths of their daughters, experiencing the exhilaration and triumph of survival. The point is simply that identification is neither fixed nor entirely passive.

While there are certainly masculine and feminine, active and passive, poles to the left and right of the chart on which we might position these three genres (see below), the subject positions that appear to be constructed by each of the genres are not as gender-linked and as gender-fixed as has often been supposed. This is especially true today as hard-core pornography is gaining appeal with women viewers. Perhaps the most recent proof in this genre of the breakdown of rigid dichotomies of masculine and feminine, active and passive is the creation of an alternative, oscillating category of address to viewers. Although heterosexual hard core once addressed itself exclusively to heterosexual men, it has now begun to address itself to heterosexual couples and women as well; and in addition to homosexual hard core, which has addressed itself to gay and (to a lesser extent) lesbian viewers, there is now a new category of video called bisexual. In these videos men do it with women, women do it with women, men do it with men and then all do it with one another, in the process breaking down a fundamental taboo against male-to-male sex.[22]

A related interpenetration of once more separate categories of masculine and feminine is what has come to be known in some quarters as the "male weepie." These are mainstream melodramas engaged in the activation of the previously repressed emotions of men and in breaking the taboos against male-to-male hugs and embraces. The father-son embrace that concludes *Ordinary People* (1980) is exemplary. More recently, paternal weepies have begun to compete with the maternal—as in the conventional *Dad* (1989) or the less conventional, wild paternal displays of *Twin Peaks*.

The point is certainly not to admire the "sexual freedom" of this new fluidity and oscillation—the new femininity of men who hug and the new masculinity of women who leer—as if it represented any ultimate defeat of phallic power. Rather, the more useful lesson might be to see what this new fluidity and oscillation permits in the construction of feminine viewing pleasures once thought not to exist at all. (It is instructive, for example, that in the new bisexual pornography women characters are shown verbally articulating their visual pleasure as they watch men perform sex with men.)

The deployment of sex, violence, and emotion would thus seem to have very precise functions in these body genres. Like all popular genres, they address persistent problems in our culture, in our sensualities, in our very identities. The deployment

---

[22]Titles of these relatively new (post-1986) hard-core videos include: *Bisexual Fantasies*; *Bi-Mistake*; *Karen's Bi-Line*; *Bi-Dacious*; *Bi-Night*; *Bi and Beyond*; *The Ultimate Fantasy*; *Bi and Beyond II*; *Bi and Beyond III: Hermaphrodites*.

of sex, violence, and emotion is thus in no way gratuitous and in no way strictly limited to each of these genres; it is instead a cultural form of problem solving. As I have argued in *Hard Core*, pornographic films now tend to present sex as a problem, to which the performance of more, different, or better sex is posed as the solution.[23] In horror a violence related to sexual difference is the problem, more violence related to sexual difference is also the solution. In women's films the pathos of loss is the problem, repetitions and variations of this loss are the generic solution.

STRUCTURES OF FANTASY

All of these problems are linked to gender identity and might be usefully explored as genres of gender fantasy. It is appropriate to ask, then, not only about the structures of perversion, but also about the structures of fantasy in each of these genres. In doing so, we need to be clear about the nature of fantasy itself. For fantasies are not, as is sometimes thought, wish-fulfilling linear narratives of mastery and control leading to closure and the attainment of desire. They are marked, rather, by the prolongation of desire, and by the lack of fixed position with respect to the objects and events fantasized.

In their classic essay "Fantasy and the Origins of Sexuality," Jean Laplanche and J. B. Pontalis argue that fantasy is not so much a narrative that enacts the quest for an object of desire as it is a setting for desire, a place where conscious and unconscious, self and other, part and whole meet. Fantasy is the place where "desubjectified" subjectivities oscillate between self and other occupying no fixed place in the scenario (16).[24]

In the three body genres discussed here, this fantasy component has probably been better understood as belonging to the "fantastic." However, it has been less well understood in pornography and women's film melodrama. Because these genres display fewer fantastic special effects and because they rely on certain conventions of realism—the activation of social problems in melodrama, the representation of real sexual acts in pornography—they seem less obviously fantastic. Yet the usual criticisms that these forms are improbable, that they lack psychological complexity and narrative closure, and that they are repetitious, become moot as evaluation if such features are intrinsic to their engagement with fantasy.

There is a link, in other words, between the appeal of these forms and their ability to address, if never *really* to "solve," basic problems related to sexual identity. Here, I would like to forge a connection between Laplanche and Pontalis's structural understanding of fantasies as myths of origins which try to cover the discrepancy between two moments in time and the distinctive temporal structure of these particular genres. Laplanche and Pontalis argue that fantasies which are myths of origins address the insoluble problem of the discrepancy between an irrecoverable original experience presumed to have actually taken place—as in the case, for example, of the historical primal scene—and the uncertainty of its

---

[23]Williams, *Hard Core*.

[24]Jean Laplanche and J. B. Pontalis, "Fantasy and the Origins of Sexuality," *The International Journal of Psycho-Analysis* 49, no. 1 (1968): 1–18.

An Anatomy of Film Bodies

Genre	Pornography	Horror	Melodrama
Bodily excess	sex	violence	emotion
Ecstasy shown by:	ecstatic sex orgasm ejaculation	ecstatic violence shudder blood	ecstatic woe sob tears
Presumed audience:	men (active)	adolescent boys (active/passive)	girls, women (passive)
Perversion:	sadism	sadomasochism	masochism
Originary fantasy:	seduction	castration	origin
Temporality of fantasy:	on time!	too early!	too late!
Genre cycles: "classic"	stag films (20s–40s) *The Casting Couch*	"classic" horror: *Dracula* *Frankenstein* *Dr. Jekyll/Mr. Hyde* *King Kong*	"classic" women's films: maternal melodrama: *Stella Dallas* *Mildred Pierce* romance: *Back Street* *Letter from an* *Unknown Woman*
Contemporary:	feature-length hard core porn: *Deep Throat*, etc. *The Punishment of Anne* Femme Productions Bi-sexual Tri-sexual	post-*Psycho*: *Texas Chainsaw* *Massacre* *Halloween* *Dressed to Kill* *Videodrome*	male and female "weepies" *Steel Magnolias* *Stella* *Dad*

hallucinatory revival. The discrepancy exists, in other words, between the actual existence of the lost object and the sign which evokes both this existence and its absence.

Laplanche and Pontalis maintain that the most basic fantasies are located at the juncture of an irrecoverable real event that took place somewhere in the past and a totally imaginary event that never took place. The "event" whose temporal and spatial existence can never be fixed is thus ultimately, according to Laplanche and Pontalis, that of "the origin of the subject"—an origin which psychoanalysts tell us cannot be separated from the discovery of sexual difference.[25]

---

[25]Ibid., p. 11.

It is this contradictory temporal structure of being situated somewhere between the "too early" and the "too late" of the knowledge of difference that generates desire that is most characteristic of fantasy. Freud introduced the concept of "original fantasy" to explain the mythic function of fantasies which seem to offer repetitions of and "solutions" to major enigmas confronting the child.[26] These enigmas are located in three areas: the enigma of the origin of sexual desire, an enigma that is "solved," so the speak, by the fantasy of seduction; the enigma of sexual difference, "solved" by the fantasy of castration; and finally the enigma of the origin of self, "solved" by the fantasy of family romance or return to origins.[27]

Each of the three body genres I have been describing could be seen to correspond in important ways to one of these original fantasies: pornography, for example, is the genre that has seemed to endlessly repeat the fantasies of primal seduction, of meeting the other, seducing or being seduced by the other in an ideal "pornotopia" where, as Steven Marcus has noted, it is always bedtime[28]. Horror is the genre that seems to endlessly repeat the trauma of castration as if to "explain," by repetitious mastery, the originary problem of sexual difference. And melodramatic weepie is the genre that seems to endlessly repeat our melancholic sense of the loss of origins—impossibly hoping to return to an earlier state which is perhaps most fundamentally represented by the body of the mother.

Of course each of these genres has a history and does not simply "endlessly repeat." The fantasies activated by these genres are repetitious, but not fixed and eternal. If traced back to origins each could probably be shown to have emerged with the formation of the bourgeois subject and the intensifying importance to this subject of specified sexualities. But the importance of repetition in each genre should not blind us to the very different temporal structure of repetition in each fantasy. It could be, in fact, that these different temporal structures constitute the different utopian component of problem-solving in each form. Thus the typical (non-sadomasochistic) pornographic fantasies of seduction operate to "solve" the problem of the origin of desire. Attempting to answer the insoluble question of whether desire is imposed from without through the seduction of the parent or whether it originates within the self, pornography answers this question by typically positing a fantasy of desire coming from within the subject *and* from without. Non-sado-masochistic pornography attempts to posit the utopian fantasy of perfect temporal coincidence: a subject and object (or seducer and seduced) who meet one another "on time!" and "now!" in shared moments of mutual pleasure that it is the special challenge of the genre to portray.

In contrast to pornography, the fantasy of recent teen horror corresponds to a temporal structure which raises the anxiety of not being ready, the problem, in effect, of "too early!" Some of the most violent and terrifying moments of the horror film genre occur in moments when the female victim meets the psycho-killer-monster unexpectedly, before she is ready. The female victims who are not ready for the attack die.

---

[26]Sigmund Freud, "Instincts and Their Vicissitudes," vol. 14 of *The Standard Edition of The Complete Psychological Works of Sigmund Freud* (London: Hogarth, 1915), p. 14.

[27]Laplanche and Pontalis, "Fantasy and the Origins of Sexuality," 11.

[28]Steven Marcus, *The Other Victorians: A Study of Sexuality and Pornography in Mid-Nineteenth Century England* (New York: New American Library, 1964, 1974).

This surprise encounter, too early, often takes place at a moment of sexual anticipation when the female victim thinks she is about to meet her boyfriend or lover. The monster's violent attack on the female victims vividly enacts a symbolic castration which often functions as a kind of punishment for an ill-time exhibition of sexual desire. These victims are taken by surprise in the violent attacks which are then deeply felt by spectators (especially the adolescent male spectators drawn to the slasher subgenre) as linked to the knowledge of sexual difference. Again the key to the fantasy is timing—the way the knowledge of sexual difference too suddenly overtakes both characters and viewers, offering a knowledge for which we are never prepared.

Finally, contrast to pornography's meeting "on time!" and horror's unexpected meeting "too early!," we can identify melodrama's pathos of the "too late!" In these fantasies the quest to return to and discover the origin of the self is manifest in the form of the child's fantasy of possessing ideal parents in the Freudian family romance, in the parental fantasy of possessing the child in maternal or paternal melodrama, and even in the lovers' fantasy of possessing one another in romantic weepies. In these fantasies the quest for connection is always tinged with the melancholy of loss. Origins are already lost, the encounters always take place too late, on death beds or over coffins.[29]

Italian critic Franco Moretti has argued, for example, that literature that makes us cry operates via a special manipulation of temporality: what triggers our crying is not just the sadness or suffering of the character in the story but a very precise moment when characters in the story catch up with and realize what the audience already knows. We cry, Moretti argues, not just because the characters do, but at the precise moment when desire is finally recognized as futile. The release of tension produces tears—which become of kind of homage to a happiness that is kissed goodbye. Pathos is thus a surrender to reality but it is a surrender that pays homage to the ideal that tried to wage war on it.[30] Moretti thus stresses a subversive, utopian component in what has often been considered a form of passive powerlessness. The fantasy of the meeting with the other that is always too late can thus be seen as based upon the utopian desire that it not be too late to remerge with the other who was once part of the self.

Obviously there is a great deal of work to be done to understand the form and function of these three body genres in relation to one another and in relation to the fundamental appeal as "original fantasies." Obviously also the most difficult work of understanding this relation between gender, genre, fantasy, and structures of perversion will come in the attempt to relate original fantasies to historical context and specific generic history. However, there is one thing that already seems clear: these "gross" body genres which may seem so violent and inimical to women cannot be dismissed as evidence of a monolithic and unchanging misogyny, as either pure sadism for male viewers or masochism for females. Their very existence and popularity hinges upon rapid changes taking place in relations between the "sexes" and by rapidly changing notions of gender—of what it means to be a man or a woman.

---

[29]Steve Neale, "Melodrama and Tears," *Screen* 27 (November–December 1986): 6–22.
[30]Franco Moretti, "Kindergarten," in *Signs Taken for Wonders* (London: Verso, 1983).

To dismiss them as bad excess whether of explicit sex, violence, or emotion, or as bad perversions, whether of masochism or sadism, is not to address their function as cultural problem-solving. Genres thrive, after all, on the persistence of the problems they address; but genres thrive also in their ability to recast the nature of these problems.

Finally, as I hope this most recent example of the melodrama of tears suggests, we may be wrong in our assumption that the bodies of spectators simply reproduce the sensations exhibited by bodies on the screen. Even those masochistic pleasures associated with the powerlessness of the "too late!" are not absolutely abject. Even tear jerkers do not operate to force a simple mimicry of the sensation exhibited on the screen. Powerful as the sensations of the jerk might be, we may only be beginning to understand how they are deployed in generic and gendered cultural forms.

1991

TANIA MODLESKI

THE TERROR OF PLEASURE:
THE CONTEMPORARY HORROR FILM
AND POSTMODERN THEORY

Tania Modleski's work is centrally concerned with the relation of women to the mass media they consume and the gender and power relations encoded within such media. Her early book *Loving with a Vengeance: Mass Produced Fantasies for Women* (1982) argues that romance novels offer women an outlet for the fears and frustrations engendered by their status within patriarchal society. *The Women Who Knew Too Much: Hitchcock and Feminist Theory* (1988), from which the following essay is drawn, focuses on the heroines in several Hitchcock films, examining the trials to which the director submits his female characters and the misogynistic undertone of these works. Modleski has written on race and queer theory, the language of patriarchy, and feminist revisions of the highly masculinized genres like the western and war film. Her essays are collected in *Old Wives' Tales, and Other Women's Stories* (1998). Modleski is currently Scott professor of English at the University of Southern California.

(Another selection from Modleski's work appears in Section VII.)

In the *Grundrisse*, Karl Marx's description of the capitalist as a werewolf turns into an enthusiastic endorsement of that creature's activities. Marx tells us that the capitalist's "werewolf hunger," which drives him continually to replace "living labor" with "dead labor" (that is, human beings with machines), will lead to a mode of production in which "labour time is no longer the sole measure and source of wealth."[1] Thus, in the words of one commentator, "capitalism furnishes the material basis for the eventual realization of an age-old dream of humankind: the liberation from burdensome toil."[2] Marx's critics have tended to place him in the role of mad scientist, with his vision of the miracles to be wrought by feeding the werewolf's insatiable appetite. Writers from Jacques Ellul to Isaac Balbus have argued (to mix narratives here) that allowing the capitalist his unhindered experimentation in the "workshops of filthy creation"—his accumulation of more and more specimens of dead labor—cannot possibly provide a blessing to humankind.

---

[1] Karl Marx, *Grundrisse: Foundations of the Critique of Political Economy* (Middlesex, England: Penguin, 1973), p. 706.

[2] Isaac Bulbus, *Marxism and Domination* (Princeton, NJ: Princeton University Press, 1982), p. 41.

These critics claim that rather than truly liberating humanity by freeing it from burdensome toil, the proliferation of dead labor—of technology—has resulted in the invasion of people's mental, moral, and emotional lives, and thus has rendered them incapable of desiring social change. To quote Jacques Ellul, who has traced the intrusion of technique into all aspects of human existence, "as big city life became for the most part intolerable, techniques of amusement were developed. It became indispensable to make urban suffering acceptable by furnishing amusements, a necessity which was to assure the rise, for example, of a monstrous motion picture industry."[3] In advanced capitalism, the narrative shifts, though the genre remains the same: physical freedom—that is, increased leisure time—is bought at the price of spiritual zombieism. The masses, it is said, are offered various forms of easy, false pleasure as a way of keeping them unaware of their own desperate vacuity. And so, apparently, we are caught in the toils of the great monster, mass culture, which certain critics, including some of the members of the Frankfurt School and their followers, have equated with ideology. For the Frankfurt School, in fact, mass culture effected a major transformation in the nature of ideology from Marx's time: once "socially necessary illusion," it has now become "manipulative contrivance," and its power is such that, in the sinister view of T. W. Adorno, "conformity has replaced consciousness."[4]

Today many people tend to believe that other, more sophisticated approaches to the issue have superseded the Frankfurt School's conception of mass culture as a monstrous and monolithic ideological machine. The work of Roland Barthes is often cited as an example of such an advance. But when Barthes offers the converse of the proposition that mass culture (for example, the cinema) is ideology and contends rather that "ideology is the Cinema of society," we are entitled, I think, to question just how far this removes us from many of the premises we think we have rejected.[5] Isn't Barthes here implying that both cinema and ideology, being seamless and without gaps or contradictions, create what the Frankfurt School called the "spurious harmony" of a conformist mass society?

According to many of the members of the Frankfurt School, high art was a subversive force capable of opposing spurious harmony. On this point especially, certain contemporary theorists have disagreed. In *The Anti-Aesthetic*, a recent collection of essays on postmodern culture, the editor, Hal Foster, suggests the need to go beyond the idea of the aesthetic as a negative category, claiming that the critical importance of the notion of the aesthetic as subversive is now "largely illusory."[6] However, despite such pronouncements, which are common enough in the literature of postmodernism, I believe it can be shown that many postmodernists do in fact engage in the same kind of oppositional thinking about mass culture that characterized the work of the Frankfurt School. Take, for example, Barthes' writings on

---

[3]Jacques Ellul, *The Technological Society*, trans. John Wilkinson (New York: Vintage, 1964), pp. 113–14.

[4]Theodor W. Adorno, "Culture Industry Reconsidered," trans. Anson G. Rabinbach, *New German Critique* 6 (Fall 1975): 17.

[5]Roland Barthes, "Upon Leaving the Movie Theater," trans. Bertrand Augst and Susan White, *University Publishing* 6 (Winter 1979): 3.

[6]Hal Foster, "Postmodernism: A Preface," *The Anti-Aesthetic: Essays on Postmodern Culture*, ed. Hal Foster (Port Townsend, WA: Bay Press, 1983), p. xv.

pleasure. Although it is inaccurate to maintain, as critics sometimes do, that Barthes always draws a sharp distinction between pleasure and jouissance (since in *The Pleasure of the Text* Barthes straightaway denies any such strenuous opposition), whenever Barthes touches on the subject of mass culture, he is apt to draw a fairly strict line—placing pleasure on the side of the consumer, and jouissance in contrast to pleasure. Here is a remarkable passage from *The Pleasure of the Text*, in which Barthes begins by discussing the superiority of a textual reading based on disavowal and ends by casually condemning mass culture:

> Many readings are perverse, implying a split, a cleavage. Just as the child knows its mother has no penis and simultaneously believes she has one . . . so the reader can keep saying: *I know these are only words, but all the same.* . . . Of all readings that of tragedy is the most perverse: I take pleasure in hearing myself tell a story *whose end I know*: I know and I don't know, I act toward myself as though I did not know: I know perfectly well Oedipus will be unmasked, that Danton will be guillotined, *but all the same*. . . . Compared to a dramatic story, which is one whose outcome is unknown, there is here an effacement of pleasure and a progression of *jouissance* (today, in mass culture, there is an enormous consumption of "dramatics" and little *jouissance*).[7]

Anyone who has read Christian Metz's persuasive argument that disavowal is *constitutive* of the spectator's pleasure at the cinema will find it difficult to give ready assent to Barthes' contention that mass culture deprives the consumer of this "perverse" experience.[8] And anyone who is acquainted with the standardized art products—the genre and formula stories—which proliferate in a mass society will have to admit that their import depends precisely upon our suspending our certain knowledge of their outcome—for example, the knowledge that, as the critics say, the gangster "will eventually lie dead in the streets." Barthes' remarks are illuminating, then, not for any direct light they shed on the high/mass culture debate, but because they vividly exemplify the tendency of critics and theorists to make mass culture into the "other" of whatever, at any given moment, they happen to be championing—and, moreover, to denigrate that other primarily because it allegedly provides pleasure to the consumer.

While Barthes' *The Pleasure of the Text* has become one of the canonical works of postmodernism, in this respect it remains caught up in older modernist ideas about art. In an essay entitled "The Fate of Pleasure," written in 1963, the modernist critic Lionel Trilling speculated that high art had dedicated itself to an attack on pleasure in part because pleasure was the province of mass art: "we are repelled by the idea of an art that is consumer-oriented and comfortable, let alone luxurious."[9] He went on to argue that, for the modernist, pleasure is associated with the "specious good"—with bourgeois habits, manners, and morals—and he noted, "the destruction of what is considered to be specious good is surely one of the chief literary enterprises of our age."[10] Hence, Trilling has famously declared, aesthetic modernity is primarily adversarial in impulse.

---

[7] Roland Barthes, *The Pleasure of the Text*, trans. Richard Miller (New York: Hill and Wang, 1975), pp. 47–48. Earlier Barthes remarks that "no significance (no *jouissance*) can occur, I am convinced, in a mass culture . . . for the model of this culture is petit bourgeois" (p. 38).

[8] Christian Metz, *The Imaginary Signifier: Psychoanalysis and the Cinema*, trans. Celia Britton, Annwyl Williams, Ben Brewster, and Alfred Guzzetti (Bloomington: Indiana University Press, 1982), pp. 99–148.

[9] Lionel Trilling, "The Fate of Pleasure: Wordsworth to Dostoevsky," *Partisan Review* (Summer 1963): 178.

[10] Ibid., p. 182.

The "specious good," or "bourgeois taste," remains an important target of contemporary thinkers, and postmodernism continues to be theorized as its adversary.
Indeed, it might be argued that post-modernism is valued by many of its proponents
insofar as it is considered *more* adversarial than modernism, and is seen to wage
war on a greatly expanded category of the "specious good," which presently includes
meaning (Barthes speaks of the "regime of meaning") and even form.[11] For example, in an essay entitled "Answering the Question: What is Postmodernism?" Jean-
François Lyotard explicitly contrasts postmodernism to modernism in terms of their
relation to "pleasure." For Lyotard, modernism's preoccupation with form meant
that it was still capable of affording the reader or viewer "matter for solace and pleasure, [whereas the postmodern is] that which denies itself the solace of good forms,
the consensus of a taste which would make it possible to share collectively the nostalgia for the unattainable."[12] It is important to recognize the extent to which Lyotard
shares the same animus as the Frankfurt School, although his concern is not merely
to denounce *spurious* harmony, but to attack *all* harmony—consensus, collectivity—as spurious, that is, on the side of "cultural policy," the aim of which is to offer
the public "well-made" and "comforting" walks of art.[13]

Although Lyotard has elsewhere informed us that "thinking by means of oppositions does not correspond to the liveliest modes of postmodern knowledge," he does
not seem to have extricated himself entirely from this mode.[14] Pleasure (or "comfort" or "solace") remains the enemy for the postmodernist thinker because it is
judged to be the means by which the consumer is reconciled to the prevailing cultural policy, or the "dominant ideology." While this view may well provide the critic
with "matter for solace and pleasure," it is at least debatable that mass culture today
is on the side of the specious good, that it offers, in the words of Matei Calinescu,
"an ideologically manipulated illusion of taste," that it lures its audience to a false
complaceny with the promise of equally false and insipid pleasures.[15] Indeed, the
contemporary horror film—the so-called exploitation film or slasher film—provides
an interesting counterexample to such theses. Many of these films are engaged in
an unprecedented assault on all that bourgeois culture is supposed to cherish—like
the ideological apparatuses of the family and the school. Consider Leonard Maltin's
capsule summary of an exemplary film in the genre, *The Brood*, directed by David
Cronenberg and starring Samantha Eggar: "Eggar eats her own afterbirth while
midget clones beat grandparents and lovely young school teachers to death with
mallets."[16] A few of the films, like *The Texas Chainsaw Massacre*, have actually
been celebrated for their adversarial relation to contemporary culture and society.
In this film, a family of men, driven out of the slaughterhouse business by advanced
technology, turns to cannibalism. The film deals with the slaughter of a group of

---

[11]Roland Barthes, *Image, Music, Text*, trans. Stephen Heath (New York: Hill and Wang, 1977), p. 167.
   [12]Jean-François Lyotard, "Answering the Question: What is Postmodernism?" trans. Régis Durand,
Innovation/Renovation: New Perspectives on the Humanities, ed. Ihab Hassan and Sally Hassan (Madison:
The University of Wisconsin Press, 1983), p. 340.
   [13]Ibid., p. 335.
   [14]Jean-François Lyotard, *La Condition postmoderne* (Paris: Minuit, 1979), p. 29.
   [15]Matei Calinescu, *Faces of Modernity: Avant-Garde, Decadence, Kitsch* (Bloomington: Indiana
University Press, 1977), p. 240.
   [16]Leonard Maltin, *T.V. Movies*, revised edition (New York: Signet, 1981–82), p. 95.

young people travelling in a van and dwells at great length on the pursuit of the last survivor of the group, Sally, by the man named Leatherface, who hacks his victims to death with a chainsaw. Robin Wood has analyzed the film as embodying a critique of capitalism, since the film shows the horror both of people quite literally living off other people, and of the institution of the family, since it implies that the monster is the family.[17]

In some of the films the attack on contemporary life strikingly recapitulates the very terms adopted by many culture critics. In George Romero's *Dawn of the Dead*, the plot involves zombies taking over a shopping center, a scenario depicting the worst fears of the culture critics who have long envisioned the will-less, soul-less masses as zombie-like beings possessed by the alienating imperative to consume. And in David Cronenberg's *Videodrome*, video itself becomes the monster. The film concerns a plot, emanating from Pittsburgh, to subject human beings to massive doses of a video signal which renders its victims incapable of distinguishing hallucination from reality. One of the effects of this signal on the film's hero is to cause a gaping, vagina-like wound to open in the middle of his stomach, so that the villains can program him by inserting a video cassette into his body. The hero's situation becomes that of the new schizophrenic described by Jean Baudrillard in his discussion of the effects of mass communication:

> No more hysteria, no more projective paranoia, properly speaking, but this state of terror proper to the schizophrenic: too great a proximity of everything, the unclean promiscuity of everything which touches, invests, and penetrates without resistance, with no halo of private protection, not even his own body, to protect him anymore.... The schizo is bereft of every scene, open to everything in spite of himself, living in the greatest confusion.[18]

"You must open yourself completely to us," says one of *Videodrome*'s villains, as he plunges the cassette into the gaping wound. It would seem that we are here very far from the realm of what is traditionally called "pleasure" and much nearer to so-called *jouissance*, discussions of which privilege terms like "gaps," "wounds," "fissures," "splits," "cleavages," and so forth.

Moreover, if the text is "an anagram for our body," as Roland Barthes maintains, the contemporary text of horror could aptly be considered an anagram for the schizophrenic's body, which is so vividly imaged in Cronenberg's film.[19] It is a ruptured body, lacking the kind of integrity commonly attributed to popular narrative cinema. For just as Baudrillard makes us aware that terms like "paranoia" and "hysteria," which film critics have used to analyze both film characters and textual mechanisms, are no longer as applicable in mass culture today as they once were, so the much more global term "narrative pleasure" is similarly becoming outmoded.

What is always at stake in discussions of "narrative pleasure" is what many think of as the ultimate "spurious harmony," the supreme ideological construct—the "bourgeois ego." Contemporary film theorists insist that pleasure is "ego-reinforcing" and

---

[17]Robin Wood, *American Nightmare: Essays on the Horror Film* (Toronto: Festival of Festivals, 1979), pp. 20–22.

[18]Jean Baudrillard, "The Ecstasy of Communication," trans. John Johnston, *The Anti-Aesthetic*, pp. 132–33.

[19]Barthes, *The Pleasure of the Text*, p. 17. Barthes, however, specifies the "erotic body."

that narrative is the primary means by which mass culture supplies and regulates this pleasure. For Stephen Heath, Hollywood narratives are versions of the nineteenth-century "novelistic," or "family romance," and their function is to "remember the history of the individual subject" through processes of identification, through narrative continuity, and through the mechanism of closure.[20] Julia Kristeva condemns popular cinema in similar terms in her essay on terror in film, "Ellipsis on Dread and the Specular Seduction":

> [The] terror/seduction node . . . becomes, through cinematic commerce, a kind of cut-rate seduction. One quickly pulls the veil over the terror, and only the cathartic relief remains; in mediocre potboilers, for example, in order to remain within the range of petty bourgeois taste, film plays up to narcissistic identification, and the viewer is satisfied with "three-buck seduction."[21]

But just as the individual and the family are *dis*-membered in the most gruesomely literal way in many of these films, so the novelistic as family romance is also in the process of being dismantled.

First, not only do the films tend to be increasingly open-ended in order to allow for the possibility of countless sequels, but they also often delight in thwarting the audiences' expectations of closure. The most famous examples of this tendency are the surprise codas of Brian de Palma's films—for instance, the hand reaching out from the grave in *Carrie*. And in *The Evil Dead*, *Halloween*, and *Friday the Thirteenth*, the monsters and slashers rise and attempt to kill over and over again each time they are presumed dead. At the end of *The Evil Dead*, the monsters, after defying myriad attempts to destroy them, appear finally to be annihilated as they are burned to death in an amazing lengthy sequence. But in the last shot of the film, when the hero steps outside into the light of day, the camera rushes toward him, and he turns and faces it with an expression of horror. In the final sequence of *Halloween*, the babysitter looks at the spot where the killer was apparently slain and, finding it vacant, says, "It really was the bogey man."

Secondly—and this is the aspect most commonly discussed and deplored by popular journalists—these films tend to dispense with or drastically minimize the plot and character development that is thought to be essential to the construction of the novelistic. In Cronenberg's *Rabid*, the porn star Marilyn Chambers plays a woman who receives a skin transplant and begins to infect everyone around her with a kind of rabies. The symptom of her disease is a vagina-like wound in her armpit out of which a phallic-shaped weapon springs to slash and mutilate its victims. While the film does have some semblance of a plot, most of it comprises disparate scenes showing Marilyn, or her victims, or her victims' victims, on the attack. Interestingly, although metonymy has been considered to be the principle by which narrative is constructed, metonymy in this film (the contagion signified by the title) becomes the means by which narrative is *disordered*, revealing a view of a world in which the center no longer holds. Films like *Maniac* and *Friday the Thirteenth* and its sequels go even further in the reduction of plot and character. In *Friday the*

---

[20]Stephen Heath, *Questions of Cinema* (Bloomington: Indiana University Press, 1981), p. 157.
[21]Julia Kristeva, "Ellipsis on Dread and the Specular Seduction," trans. Dolores Burdick, *Wide Angle* 3, no. 3 (1979): 46.

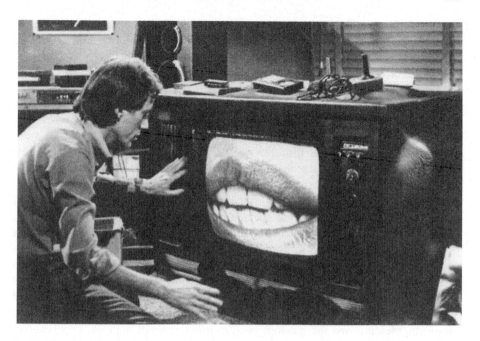

James Woods hypnotized by a television image in *Videodrome* (1983). "In some of the films the attack on contemporary life strikingly recapitulates the very terms adopted by many culture critics. . . . In David Cronenberg's *Videodrome*, video itself becomes the monster" (Modleski, p. 621).

Thirteenth, a group of young people are brought together to staff a summer camp and are randomly murdered whenever they go off to make love. The people in the film are practically interchangeable, since we learn nothing about them as individuals, and there is virtually no building of a climax—only variations on the theme of slashing, creating a pattern that is more or less reversible.

Finally, it should scarcely need pointing out that when villains and victims are such shadowy, undeveloped characters and are portrayed equally unsympathetically, narcissistic identification on the part of the audience becomes increasingly difficult. Indeed, it could be said that some of the films elicit a kind of *anti*-narcissistic identification, which the audience delights in indulging just as it delights in having its expectations of closure frustrated. Of *The Texas Chainsaw Massacre*, Robin Wood writes, "Watching it recently with a large, half-stoned youth audience who cheered and applauded every one of Leatherface's outrages against their representatives on the screen was a terrifying experience."[22] The same might be said of films like *Halloween* and *Friday the Thirteenth*, which adopt the point of view of the slasher, placing the spectator in the position of an unseen nameless presence which, to the audiences' great glee, annihilates one by one their screen surrogates. This kind of joyful self-destructiveness on the part of the masses has been discussed by Jean

---

[22]Wood, p. 22.

Baudrillard in another context—in his analysis of the Georges Pompidou Center in Paris to which tourists flock by the millions, ostensibly to consume culture, but also to hasten the collapse of the structurally flawed building.[23] There is a similar paradox in the fact that *Dawn of the Dead*, the film about zombies taking over a shopping center, has become a midnight favorite at shopping malls all over the United States. In both cases the masses are revelling in the demise of the very culture they appear most enthusiastically to support. Here, it would seem, we have another variant of the split, "perverse" response favored by Roland Barthes.

The contemporary horror film thus comes very close to being "the other film" that Thierry Kuntzel says the classic narrative film must always work to conceal: "a film in which the initial figure would not find a place in the flow of a narrative, in which the configuration of events contained in the formal matrix would not form a progressive order, in which the spectator/subject would never be reassured . . . within the dominant system of production and consumption, this would be a film of sustained *terror*."[24] Both in form and in content, the genre confounds the theories of those critics who adopt an adversarial attitude toward mass culture. The type of mass art I have been discussing—the kind of films which play at drive-ins and shabby downtown theaters, and are discussed on the pages of newsletters named *Trashola*, and *Sleazoid Express*—is as apocalyptic and nihilistic, as hostile to meaning, form, pleasure, and the specious good as many types of high art. This is surely not accidental. Since Jean-François Lyotard insists that postmodernism is an "aesthetic of the sublime," as Immanuel Kant theorized the concept, it is interesting to note that Kant saw an intimate connection between the literature of the sublime and the literature of terror, and moreover saw the difference as in part a matter of audience education: "In fact, without the development of moral ideas, that which, thanks to preparatory culture, we call sublime, merely strikes the untutored man as terrifying."[25] And there is certainly evidence to suggest that the converse of Kant's statement has some truth as well, since a film like *The Texas Chainsaw Massacre*, which might seem designed principally to terrify the untutored man, strikes a critic like Robin Wood as sublime—or at least as "authentic art." Wood writes, "*The Texas Chainsaw Massacre* . . . achieves the force of authentic art. . . . As a 'collective nightmare,' it brings to a focus a spirit of negativity, an undifferentiated lust for destruction that seems to lie not far below the surface of the modern collective consciousness."[26] It is indeed possible for the tutored critic versed in preparatory film culture to make a convincing case for the artistic merit of a film like *The Texas Chainsaw Massacre*, as long as art continues to be theorized in terms of negation, as long as we demand that it be uncompromisingly oppositional.

However, instead of endorsing Wood's view, we might wish to consider what these films have to teach us about the *limits* of an adversarial position which makes a virtue of "sustained terror." Certainly women have important reasons for doing

---

[23]Jean Baudrillard, *L'Effet beaubourg: implosion et dissuasion* (Paris: Galilée, 1977), pp. 23–25.

[24]Thierry Kuntzel, "The Film Work 2," trans. Nancy Huston, *Camera Obscura* 5 (1980): 24–25.

[25]Immanuel Kant, *Critique of Judgment*, trans. James Creed (Oxford: Clarendon, 1952), p. 115, quoted in Franco Moretti, *Signs Taken for Wonders* (London: Verso, 1983), p. 253 n. See his chapter on "The Dialectic of Fear" for a very different reading of the vampire image in Marx.

[26]Wood, p. 22.

so. In Trilling's essay, "The Fate of Pleasure," he notes almost parenthetically that, according to the *Oxford English Dictionary*, "Pleasure in the pejorative sense is sometimes personified as a female deity."[27] Now, when pleasure has become an almost wholly pejorative term, we might expect to see an increasing tendency to incarnate it as a woman. And, indeed, in the contemporary horror film it is personified as a lovely young school teacher beaten to death by midget clones (*The Brood*), as a pretty blond teenager threatened by a maniac wielding a chainsaw (*The Texas Chainsaw Massacre*), or as a pleasant and attractive babysitter terrorized throughout the film *Halloween* by a grown-up version of the little boy killer revealed in the opening sequence. Importantly, in many of the films the female is attacked not only because, as has often been claimed, she embodies sexual pleasure, but also because she represents a great many aspects of the specious good—just as the babysitter, for example, quite literally represents familial authority. The point needs to be stressed, since feminism has occasionally made common cause with the adversarial critics on the grounds that we too have been oppressed by the specious good. But this is to overlook the fact that in some profound sense we have also been historically and psychically identified with it.

Further, just as Linda Williams has argued that in the horror film woman is usually placed on the side of the monster even when she is its pre-eminent victim, so too in the scenario I outlined at the beginning woman is frequently associated with the monster mass culture.[28] This is hardly surprising since, as we have seen, mass culture has typically been theorized as the realm of cheap and easy pleasure—"pleasure in the pejorative sense." Thus, in Ann Douglas's account, the "feminization of American culture" is synonymous with the rise of mass culture.[29] And in David Cronenberg's view, mass culture—at least the video portion of it—is terrifying because of the way it feminizes its audience. In *Videodrome*, the openness and vulnerability of the media recipient are made to seem loathsome and fearful through the use of feminine imagery (the vaginal wound in the stomach) and feminine positioning: the hero is raped with a video cassette. As Baudrillard puts it, "no halo of private protection, not even his own body . . . protect[s] him anymore." Baudrillard himself describes mass-mediated experience in terms of rape, as when he speaks of "the unclean promiscuity of everything which touches, invests and penetrates without resistance." No resistance, no protection, no mastery. Or so it might seem. And yet the mastery that these popular texts no longer permit through effecting closure or eliciting narcissistic identification is often reasserted through projecting the experience of submission and defenselessness onto the female body. In this way the texts enable the male spectator to distance himself somewhat from the terror. And, as usual, it is the female spectator who is *truly* deprived of "solace and pleasure." Having been denied access to pleasure, while simultaneously being scapegoated for seeming to represent it, women are perhaps in the best position to call into ques-

---

[27]Trilling, p. 22.

[28]Linda Williams, "When the Woman Looks," *Re-vision: Essays in Feminist Film Criticism*, ed. Mary Ann Doane, Patricia Mellencamp, and Linda Williams, The American Film Institute Monograph Series, Vol. III (Frederick, MD: University Publications of America, 1984), pp. 85–88.

[29]Ann Douglas, *The Feminization of American Culture* (New York: Avon, 1977).

tion an aesthetic wholly opposed to it. At the very least, we might like to experience more of it before deciding to denounce it.

Beyond this, it remains for the postmodernist to ponder the irony of the fact that when critics condemn a "monstrous motion picture industry" they are to a certain extent repeating the gestures of texts they repudiate. And the question then becomes: How can an adversarial attitude be maintained toward an art that is itself increasingly adversarial? In *The Anti-Aesthetic*, Hal Foster considers modernism to be postmodernism's other, and he pointedly asks, "how can we exceed the modern? How can we break with a program that makes a value of crisis . . . or progress beyond the era of Progress . . . or *transgress the ideology of the transgressive?*"[30] Foster does not acknowledge the extent to which mass culture has also served as postmodernism's other, but his question is pertinent here too.

Part of the answer may lie in the fact that for many artists, transgression is not as important a value as it is for many theorists. A host of contemporary artistic endeavors may be cited as proof of this, despite the efforts of some critics to make these works conform to an oppositional practice. In literature, the most famous and current example of the changed, friendly attitude toward popular art is Umberto Eco's *The Name of the Rose*, which draws on the Sherlock Holmes mystery tale. Manual Puig's novels (his *Kiss of the Spider Woman*, for example) have consistently explored the pleasures of popular movies. In the visual arts, Cindy Sherman's self-portraiture involves the artist's masquerading as figures from old Hollywood films. The "Still Life" exhibition organized by Marvin Heiferman and Diane Keaton consists of publicity stills from the files of Hollywood movie studios. In film, Rainer Werner Fassbinder continually paid homage to Hollywood melodramas; Wim Wenders and Betty Gordon return to film noir; Mulvey and Wollen to the fantastic; Valie Export to science fiction; and so on.

A few theorists have begun to acknowledge these developments, but usually only to denounce them. In a recent article entitled "Post-modernism and Consumer Society," Fredric Jameson concludes by deploring the fact that art is no longer "explosive and subversive," no longer "critical, negative, contestatory, . . . oppositional, and the like."[31] Instead, says Jameson, much recent art appears to incorporate images and stereotypes garnered from our pop cultural past. However, instead of sharing Jameson's pessimistic view of this tendency, I would like to end on a small note of comfort and solace. Perhaps the contemporary artist continues to be subversive by being nonadversarial in the modernist sense, and has returned to our pop cultural past partly in order to explore the site where pleasure was last observed, before it was stoned by the gentry and the mob alike, and recreated as a monster.

1986

[30]Foster, p. ix. My emphasis.
[31]Fredric Jameson, "Postmodernism and Consumer Society," *The Anti-Aesthetic*, p. 125.

CYNTHIA A. FREELAND

FEMINIST FRAMEWORKS FOR HORROR FILMS

Cynthia A. Freeland writes from a feminist perspective on philosophy, ethics, and aesthetics. in addition to her work on Aristole, Plato, and the history of ancient and modern philosophy, her books include *But Is it Art?* (2001), an introduction to art theory. *The Naked and the Undead: Evil and the Appeal of Horror* (1999) argues that films like *Alien, The Brood*, and *The Texas Chainsaw Massacre* reflect cultural anxieties about shifting gendor roles in the late 1970s, at the crest of the second wave of the feminist movement. With Thomas E. Wartenberg she edited *Philosophy and Film* (1995), a collection of essays that spans a diverse array of theoretical approaches to film including Marxist, feminist, postmodern, and classical theory. She is currently professor of philosophy at the University of Houston.

The horizon for feminists studying horror films appears bleak. Since *Psycho*'s infamous shower scene, the big screen has treated us to Freddie's long razor-nails emerging between Nancy's legs in the bathtub (*A Nightmare on Elm Street I*), De Palma's exhibitionist heroine being power-drilled into the floor (*Body Double*), and Leatherface hanging women from meat hooks (*The Texas Chain Saw Massacre*). Even in a film with a strong heroine like *Alien*, any feminist point is qualified by the monstrousness of the alien mother, the objectification of Sigourney Weaver in her underwear, and her character Ripley's forced assumption of a maternal role.

Despite all this, there has been some feminist work on horror, and I believe there is room for more. In the first part of this paper I shall survey and criticize currently dominant psychodynamic feminist approaches to horror. In the second part, I propose an alternative framework for constructing feminist interpretations of horror films by critically interrogating their gender ideologies. My proposal focuses less on the psychology of viewers than on the nature of films as artifacts with particular structures and functions. In the third part I illustrate my recommended framework by sketching readings of *Jurassic Park* (Spielberg 1993), *The Fly* (Cronenberg 1986), and *Repulsion* (Polanski 1965).

PART I: PSYCHOANALYTIC FEMINIST APPROACHES TO HORROR

Most current feminist studies of horror films are psychodynamic. That is, though they may consider films as artifacts, recognizing such aspects as plot, narrative, or point of view, their chief emphasis is on viewers' motives and interests in watching horror films, and on the psychological effects such films have. Typically this sort of feminist film theory relies upon a psychoanalytic framework in which women are described as castrated or as representing threats evoking male castration anxiety. These theories also standardly presume some connection between gazing, violent aggression, and masculinity, and they suggest that there are particularly "male" motivations for making, watching, and enjoying horror films.

Feminist psychodynamic approaches to film in general were launched by Laura Mulvey's influential essay "Visual Pleasure and Narrative Cinema" (1975).[1] Mulvey's model presupposes a Lacanian psychoanalytic perspective and draws upon key Lacanian conceptions of castration anxiety and visual fetishism, and the association of the "Law of the Father" or patriarchy with such traditional film features as narrative order. Mulvey argued that narrative forms characteristic of mainstream Hollywood cinema differentially use women and serve men. There is a dual analogy between the woman and the screen (the object of the look), and between the man and the viewer (the possessor of the look). A tension arises in the viewer between libido and ego needs, and this tension is resolved by a process of identification, whereby the [male] viewer identifies with the [male] protagonist in the film. Thus possessing the film character of the woman by proxy, the viewer can proceed to focus energy on achieving a satisfactory narrative resolution.

Mulvey's view has come in for a number of persuasive criticisms by other feminist film theorists, and she has even revised it herself.[2] Nevertheless, it will be instructive to begin by extrapolating from her basic model so as to generate a simple feminist, psychoanalytic account of horror, as follows: The tension between the viewer's desire to look and the ongoing narrative of a film is especially acute in the horror film. Typically in horror, the woman or visual object is also the chief victim sacrificed to the narrative desire to know about the monster. Horror flirts directly with the threat of castration underlying the fetish or visual appearance of the woman, and this means that looking (visual pleasure) is even more immediately at odds with narrative in horror films than in other mainstream Hollywood movies. The woman's

---

[1]Laura Mulvey, "Visual Pleasure and Narrative Cinema," originally published in *Screen* 16 (1975); reprinted in Mulvey, *Visual and Other Pleasures* (Bloomington: Indiana University Press, 1990); my page references are to the reprinted version in *Issues in Feminist Film Criticism*, ed. Patricia Erens (Bloomington: Indiana University Press, 1990), pp. 28–40.

[2]Feminist critics have argued against Mulvey on various grounds, particularly that she ignores the social and historical conditions of gendered subjects and oversimplifies the role of the viewer/director/camera (so that, for example, a subtler view may be necessary to account for the ambivalence of certain film directors like Hitchcock). See, for example, Mary Ann Doane, "Film and the Masquerade, Theorizing the Female Spectator," in *Issues in Feminist Film Criticism*, pp. 41–57; Jane Gaines, "Women and Representation: Can We Enjoy Alternative Pleasure?" also in *Issues in Feminist Film Criticism*, pp. 75–92; Marian Keane, "A Closer Look at Scophilia: Mulvey, Hitchcock, and Vertigo," in *The Hitchcock Reader*, ed. Marshall Deutelbaum and Leland Poague (Ames: Iowa State University Press, 1986), pp. 231–48; and Naomi Scheman, "Missing Mothers/Desiring Daughters: Framing the Sight of Women," *Critical Inquiry* 15 (Autumn 1988): 62–89. Mulvey's revisions of her view may be found in "Afterthoughts on Visual Pleasure and Narrative Cinema," in *Visual and Other Pleasures*. But for limitations that seem to persist in this volume, see my critical review of *Visual and Other Pleasures* in the *APA Newsletter on Feminism and Philosophy* 89, 2 (Winter 1990): 52–55.

flesh, the reality behind the surface appearance, *is* made visible, and horror shows the "wound" that we are revolted to look upon. To make up for this horror, this account continues, the viewer must turn attention to the narrative thrust of the investigator, typically a male, who will complete the story for us.

For example, in *Psycho*, we, like Janet Leigh, see the vague blurred and threatening shape of the attacker behind the shower curtain. But after this central murder scene, the audience and camera look into the blind eye of the victim. Since the woman herself can no longer see, and her beautiful body no longer be looked upon, we viewers are forced to proceed beyond her vision. And once our identification with the woman/victim has been disrupted, it shifts to the male investigators who will solve the crime and identify the murderer, and ultimately to the male psychiatrist who, in the film's words, "has all the answers."

A modified version of the simple Mulveyan schema I have just sketched is offered by Linda Williams, who scrutinizes one of the more vulnerable aspects of Mulvey's theory, her straitjacketed association between males and the pleasures of looking or spectatorship.[3] Williams points out that often in horror, contrary to mainstream cinema, women do possess "the gaze." That is, they are typically the first to get to see, inquire about, and know the monster. Similarly, although monsters may threaten the bodies of women in horror, even so, the fates of women and monsters are often linked. Both may somehow seem to stand outside the patriarchal order. (Think of vampire stories, for example, where a fascinating foreign Dracula seduces women away from their husbands and fathers, undermining the patriarchal institutions of law, marriage, motherhood, medicine, and religion.) Despite these observations about the shortcomings of a Mulveyan account, Williams's account remains consistent in its outlines with the sort of Mulveyan view I have just sketched. Williams argues that women who possess the gaze in horror, and who become aligned with monsters, are typically shown themselves to represent threats to patriarchy and hence to require punishment. In the end Williams seems to accept the basic idea that horror films reinforce conceptions of the active (sadistic) male viewer and the passive (suffering) female object. Women are punished for their appropriation of "the gaze," and a sort of masculine narrative order (what Lacan would call the Law of the Father) is restored.

More recently, feminist film theorists have turned to the work of one of Lacan's successors, the French feminist psychoanalyst Julia Kristeva. Kristeva's book *Powers of Horror: An Essay on Abjection*[4] focuses on literature and not film, but her views have been adapted to the study of visual horror by Barbara Creed, in a 1986 *Screen* article about *Alien*, and in her more recent book *The Monstrous-Feminine: Film, Feminism, Psychoanalysis.*[5] Kristeva locates the sources and origins of horror

---

[3]Linda Williams, "When the Woman Looks," in *Re-Vision: Essays in Feminist Film Criticism*, ed. Mary Ann Doane, Patricia Mellencamp, and Linda Williams (American Film Institute, 1984), pp. 83–99, and "Film Bodies: Gender, Genre, and Excess," *Film Quarterly* 44 (Summer 1991): 2–13.

[4]Julia Kristeva, *Powers of Horror: An Essay on Abjection*, trans. Leon Roudiez (New York: Columbia University Press, 1982).

[5]Barbara Creed, "Horror and the Monstrous-Feminine: An Imaginary Abjection," *Screen* 27, 1 (1986): 45–70, and *The Monstrous-Feminine: Film, Feminism, Psychoanalysis* (London: Routledge, 1993).

not in castration anxiety, but in the preoedipal stage of the infant's ambivalence toward the mother as it struggles to create boundaries and forge its own ego identity. The mother is "horrific" in the sense of being all-engulfing, primitive, and impure or defiled by bodily fluids—particularly breast milk and flowing menstrual blood. Kristeva uses the term "abjection" to designate the psychic condition inspired by this image of the horrific mother. For Kristeva, horror is fundamentally about boundaries—about the threat of transgressing them, and about the need to do so. Hence she emphasizes the duality of our attraction/repulsion to the horrific.

In applying this theory to *Alien*, Creed stresses the film's repeated birth scenarios and numerous versions of the engulfing, threatening, voracious, horrific Alien mother, "a toothed vagina, the monstrous-feminine as the cannibalistic mother." Creed also offers an explanation of why, in the final scenes of *Alien* (notoriously), Sigourney Weaver undresses before the camera, strolls around in her thin undershirt, and eventually returns to her sleeping pod with the small orange cat she has rescued: "Ripley's body is pleasurable and reassuring to look at. She signifies the 'acceptable' form and shape of woman."

Creed departs in certain important respects from the simplistic Mulveyan model I sketched. She emphasizes, contra the Mulveyan-Lacanian position, that horror importantly concerns not just women as victims—women who are attacked because they present a horrific vision of a castrated body—but also monstrous women who threaten to castrate men. "Virtually all horror texts represent the monstrous-feminine in relation to Kristeva's notion of maternal authority and the mapping of the self's clean and proper body."[6] More specifically, Creed thinks that horror texts all serve to illustrate "the work of abjection."[7] They do so in three basic ways. First, horror depicts images of abjection, such as corpses and bodily wastes; second, horror is concerned with borders, with things that threaten the stability of the symbolic order; and third, horror constructs the maternal figure as abject.

Let me pause now for some assessment. As I have noted, both the Mulvey-Lacanian and Creed-Kristevan frameworks for feminist film theory build upon a psychoanalytic foundation. Despite all the details of their different pictures, each view construes the familiar tensions of horror in terms of an opposition between "female" and "male" aspects, where these are understood or defined within the terms of depth psychology. There is, in other words, a tension between spectacle or the horrific feminine (associated with the castrated woman, preoedipal mother, or castrating woman), and plot or narrative resolution (associated with the patriarchal order that the child achieves after resolving the Oedipal complex). In broader ways that go beyond psychoanalysis, in all these theories (Mulvey's, Creed's, and Williams's) the focus is also psychodynamic—that is, there is some presumed general or universal psychological theory that grounds their analysis. To back up speculations of this sort Creed, for example, begins her book by appealing to both universal cultural practices and classical mythology. Psychodynamic feminist theorists speculate about why "we" are interested in horror and more basically about why certain things are

---

[6]Creed, *The Monstrous-Feminine*, p. 13.
[7]Ibid., p. 10.

horrifying. These kinds of question are seen to require an answer within a psychological theory, which remains the chief concern even when the theorist speaks about how to "interpret" such films or about what various aspects of these films "represent." The "deep" explanations offered are (putative) psychological explanations. For instance, here is Creed on *The Exorcist*:

> Regan's carnivalesque display of her body reminds us quite clearly of the immense appeal of the abject. Horror emerges from the fact that woman has broken with her proper feminine role—she has "made a spectacle of herself"—put her unsocialized body on display. And to make matters worse, she has done all of this before the shocked eyes of two male clerics.[8]

The theoretical approaches of feminist film analysts like Creed, Mulvey, and Williams are significantly constrained by their psychodynamic framing, and more particularly (and significantly) by the theoretical apparatus of psychoanalysis. I here present six objections to such approaches.

First, psychoanalysis is itself a very problematic enterprise that is far from achieving anything like general acceptance as a psychological theory. Feminists adapting the views of Lacan or Kristeva do so either in ignorance of or indifference to forceful philosophical critiques of psychoanalysis offered by Crews, Grünbaum, Deleuze and Guattari, and others.[9] Attempts to defend psychoanalysis by reconceiving it as hermeneutic explanation are also problematic, because they loosen the theory from its crucial underpinnings in causal hypothesizing, leaving key theses, about, say, abject preoedipal mothers, castration anxiety, and so on, as, at best, hermeneutical aids to reading film "texts." Such hermeneutical aids should be taken seriously only insofar as they produce valid readings. But typically in film studies, psychoanalytic interpretations are advanced a priori, rather than in an open-minded spirit of testing how well they actually work. Though a Kristevan reading may seem illuminating for *Alien*, with its many birth scenarios and theme of monstrous mothering, why should we believe in advance that it will work equally for all kinds of examples of horror? The notion of abjection expands in Creed's theory so as to be almost vacuous, because we are to understand in advance that all the varieties of horrific monstrousness we can think of really just are "illustrations" of the "work" of abjection. This includes an astonishing variety, ranging from *Alien*'s monstrous mother to the disintegrating cannibalistic zombies in *Night of the Living Dead*, or from Seth Brundle's hideously gooey and amoral fly to the *Texas Chain Saw Massacre*'s cannibalistic family. In what sense is a psychological theory of abjection "explanatory" when it becomes so broad? And in any case, why can't it be the case that there are unique, distinctive, sui generis human fears of a variety of things? Keep in mind that abjection in a Kristevan framework always refers at bottom to the necessity of separation from the primal mother. Why must all other fears somehow equal or be reduced to fear of the primal mother?

---

[8]Ibid., p. 42.

[9]See Frederick Crews, "The Unknown Freud," *The New York Review of Books* 11, 19 (November 18, 1993): 55–66; Adolf Grönbaum, *The Philosophical Foundations of Psychoanalysis* (Berkeley: University of California Press, 1984); Gilles Deleuze and Félix Guattari, *Anti-Oedipus*, trans. by Robert Hurley et al. (New York: Viking, 1977).

Second, even supposing one were to grant that psychoanalysis is a worthy psychological theory, this is not an argument for the particular psychoanalytic views of Lacan or Kristeva. There are many alternatives; so why settle on these? Lacan makes problematic and philosophically disputable metaphysical assertions about the self, the nature of desire, and so on.[10] Kristeva makes equally problematic quasi-empirical claims about, say, the infant's acquisition of language. Her views are quite controversial even within feminism; she has been criticized for, variously, essentialist theorizing, promoting anarchy, idealizing maternity, or adopting views that are fascistic, apolitical, or ahistorical.[11] Luce Irigaray offers both scathing critiques of Lacan and intriguing alternatives to some of Kristeva's most basic claims.[12]

Clearly, within psychoanalysis, we can identify many alternatives to Lacanian or Kristevan frameworks that might also be fruitful for film studies. Stanley Cavell, for example, borrows from traditional Freudian psychoanalysis to offer quite subtle and complex accounts of viewers' desires and interests in relation to both male and female actors' embodiments of film characters' roles.[13] He seems to provide a promising framework for the analysis of certain types of films, such as melodrama or the genre he calls the "comedy of remarriage." Alternatively, for all we know, Jungian or Reichian psychoanalytic theories might be intriguing psychological theories to put to the test in film studies. Jungians, with their theory of universal unconscious archetypal structures, might pay more attention to cross-cultural considerations in films, or to films' links with various kinds of fairy tales and myths. Reichians have the virtue of emphasizing concrete external sociomaterial factors in identity formation and repression. Perhaps Horney's notion of womb envy or Klein's of the bad mother would enable us to offer better interpretations of certain films, like *Frankenstein* or *The Brood*.

Third, moving away from the particular restrictions of psychoanalysis, I find that psychodynamic theories often tend to be weak as film readings because they are too reductive. They tend to utilize a one-dimensional system of symbolic interpretation. For example, even when a Kristevan interpretation seems illuminating for certain aspects of a film, as for example it does when Creed uses it to comment on horrific aspects of the climactic birth scene in *The Brood*, her focus on this aspect of the film alone seems to lead her to neglect many other important features of the film.[14] In my view this film offers a critique of several concrete contemporary social problems: the evils of charismatic psychotherapists, and the ways in which child abuse gets perpetuated from one generation to the next. It is limiting to translate a social critique into a depth-psychological thesis about how we all (allegedly) have deep

---

[10]See my "Woman, Revealed or Reveiled? An Approach to Lacan via the *Blithedale Romance* of Nathaniel Hawthorne," *Hypatia, a Journal for Feminist Philosophy* (Fall 1986): 49–70.

[11]See Kelly Oliver, *Reading Kristeva: Unraveling the Double-Bind* (Bloomington: Indiana University Press, 1993), introduction, "Oscillation Strategies," and chapter 1, "The Prodigal Child."

[12]See ibid., chapter 7, for discussion of Irigaray's differences with Kristeva.

[13]Stanley Cavell, *Pursuits of Happiness: The Hollywood Comedy of Remarriage* (Cambridge: Harvard University Press, 1981); for feminist departures that build upon Cavell's work, see Naomi Scheman, "Missing Mothers/Desiring Daughters: Framing the Sight of Women," *Critical Inquiry* 15 (Autumn 1988): 62–89.

[14]Creed, *The Monstrous-Feminine*, pp. 43–58.

ambivalences about our abjected mothers. Even more of a problem is the fact that Creed's framework locates the film's chief source of horror in the freakish mother (Samantha Eggar), setting aside the film's apparent depiction of the megalomaniac psychiatrist, Dr. Hal Raglan (Oliver Reed), as its central villain. Creed's account thereby becomes insensitive to historical allusions the film makes (and that Cronenberg quite typically makes) to the tradition of mad scientist horror films. She also misrepresents the structure of the film's plot, which depicts an appropriate punishment that Dr. Raglan suffers for his hubris—as he is destroyed by the monstrous children he has so freakishly "fathered."

Fourth, psychodynamic film theories that depend upon very basic distinctions between males and females—whether as viewers, objects of the gaze, or pursuers of distinct sorts of pleasures—rely upon certain notions of gender that are themselves problematic and under question by feminists. Many feminist and other critics have pointed out that assertions about fears of castration, or about the masculinity of logic and language, may be radically culture- and era-bound. To make very broad generalizations about "male" or "female" viewers blocks the recognition of significant individual differences among viewers that surely affect how they experience films. These include significant differences of social class, sexual orientation, age, race, and so on. For example, given that racial identity seems an important factor in some horror movies, such as *Night of the Living Dead* and its sequel *Dawn of the Dead*, it seems unreasonable to presume that white and black female viewers will experience the film, its "gazes" and its "visual objects" in just the same ways. These films seem explicitly to pair white females and black males as sharing a certain "victim" status.[15]

Even the most basic assumption of psychodynamic feminist film theorists, that it is conceptually useful and appropriate to distinguish between male and female viewers, and even between heterosexual and homosexual men or women, have been placed under attack in recent theoretical work in queer and performance theory by writers like Judith Butler and Eve Sedgwick. A focused awareness of issues in queer theory could lead, for example, to intriguing re-visions of a movie like *The Silence of the Lambs*. I have in mind not the obvious problems with the film's homophobic depiction of the "Buffalo Bill" character, but critical textures that may be added to readings of the film when we focus on its strange pairing of Jodie Foster, who was at the time of the film's release controversially "outed" by ActUp, with the villainous yet charming "Hannibal Lecter" character whose fussy mannerisms allow him to be read as "an old queen."[16]

Fifth, another difficulty with a psychodynamic, especially a psychoanalytic, framework for feminist film studies is that this view has mysteriously acquired a predominance within feminist film theory that is completely disproportionate to its status within contemporary feminist theorizing in general. British, American, and

---

[15]For a particularly acute critique of feminist film theory's neglect of race issues, see Jane Gaines, "White Privilege and Looking Relations: Race and Gender in Feminist Film Theory," in Erens, ed. *Issues in Feminist Film Criticism*, pp. 197–214.

[16]This observation was made by Douglas Crimp in a lecture he delivered at the University of Houston in the fall of 1991.

French feminists differ from one another and among themselves, not to mention from Third World anticolonialist feminists, and major books in both popular and academic feminism in the United States have adopted widely divergent theoretical bases—but these are typically not psychoanalytic. Instead, they range from a rather vague and standard liberalism grounded in the tradition of John Stuart Mill, to more radical forms of Marxist socialism; and from Foucauldian emphases on disciplinary techniques of knowledge and bodily control to new, visionary feminist work on ecosystems and the possibly liberating role of technology. Surely these diverse and flourishing forms of feminist theory also have something to offer to film studies. Many of them focus, for example, on subjectivity and desire, on visual objectification and equality, or on technologies of representation in ways that would seem readily adaptable to film studies.

Sixth and last, I doubt that whatever insights are produced by psychodynamic readings of horror films require a grounding in some particular psychogenetic theory that allegedly explains viewers' interests and responses in general filmic narratives and representations. As I have noted, psychoanalytic feminists construct genderized accounts of the tensions in horror between key features of spectacle and plot. But it is entirely possible to construct a theory of horror that emphasizes these same tensions without genderizing them. As far back as the ancient world, Aristotle's account of tragedy in the *Poetics* recognized a tension between the aesthetic effects evoked by tragedy and its narrative structures.[17] Noël Carroll's *The Philosophy of Horror* follows Aristotle and similarly pays central attention to the dichotomy horror typically depends upon between the cognitive pleasures of following out the narrative and the emotional pain of art-horror associated with monsters and spectacles.[18] If an account like Carroll's grasps these same tensions and offers reasonable explanations of them without alluding to either gender or depth psychology, it is hard to see why as feminists thinking about horror we need to resort to such theorizing. To my own mind, if there is any particular merit in the sort of comment that Creed makes about *The Exorcist* in the passage I quoted above, we can make this judgment by looking at the movie, without any special devotion to or even knowledge of the intricate theoretical grounding (and jargon) of Kristevan psychoanalysis.

Some of the general problems I have just enumerated will likely arise for other psychodynamic feminist approaches to horror, even ones that do not begin from a strictly psychoanalytic framework, such as Carol Clover's "gender rezoning" proposal in her recent book *Men, Women, and Chain Saws: Gender in the Modern Horror Film*.[19] Clover's approach does have much to recommend it: she discusses subgenres of horror rather than trying to create a wholly uniform theory; she attempts to locate horror films within their sociocultural context; and she recognizes and

---

[17]Of course, certain of Aristotle's sexist assumptions may have had an impact on his evaluational schema for tragedies; for more on this, see my "Plot Imitates Action: Aesthetic Evaluation and Moral Realism in Aristotle's *Poetics*," in *Essays on Aristotle's Poetics*, ed. Amelie Rorty (Princeton: Princeton University Press, 1992), esp. pp. 126–28.

[18]Noël Carroll, *The Philosophy of Horror: Paradoxes of the Heart* (New York: Routledge, 1990).

[19]Carol J. Clover, *Men, Women, and Chain Saws: Gender in the Modern Horror Film* (Princeton: Princeton University Press, 1992). See also my review in *Afterimage* (March 1993).

indeed focuses on some of the elusiveness of gender categories. Her theory is much less subject, then, to my fourth objection listed above.[20]

Yet even so, Clover's account is problematic because, in the place of psychoanalysis, she assumes the validity of an alternative theory of gender and of our psychological conceptualizations of it—Thomas Laqueur's "one sex" model. According to Laqueur, sex is primitively conceived as involving one norm, masculinity, of which femininity is a defective version. Clover thinks this model is somehow operative both in the construction and in the experience of works in the horror genre. There are several distinct questions to raise here. First, one might ask on what basis we should be persuaded to adopt this particular theory of gender. Laqueur is a historian of science whose views are by no means universally accepted, and so relying on his theory is a rather strange and arbitrary choice. It seems doubtful to me that any book of film theory can argue convincingly for the truth of a particular psychological theory of gender. Next, we might ask Clover to argue for the applicability of this theory of gender to the horror genre. She does make a stab at this, but only vaguely, by asserting that horror originated in the time of the rather primitive science that Laqueur is analyzing. This claim itself needs more detailed defense. Does it even hold of the early works *Frankenstein* and *Dracula* for instance? I doubt it. Finally, even granted that her historical claim about the psychological theories prevalent during the creation of early works of horror were correct, Clover ought to recognize that such a theory is hardly predominant any longer. Accordingly, it would seem reasonable for us to expect more recent forms of horror to reflect the current state of public knowledge and scientific theorizing about sex. My doubts about all the gaps in Clover's exposition lead me to question her particular observations about individual films. Again, where I find such observations insightful, I am inclined to think that their value stems more from how acutely they "read" film texts than from how accurately they reflect the real human psychology of actual viewers.

PART 2: A PROPOSED FEMINIST FRAMEWORK FOR READING HORROR FILMS

In Part 1 I described various approaches to horror within contemporary feminist film studies and identified problems in these approaches, some involving specific psychoanalytic tenets, others, more general problems about psychodynamic approaches. But the feminist theorists I have examined are limited by more than their problematic universalizing views about human psychosexual development.

---

[20]Despite her attention to "rezoning" of gender distinctions and to social factors in horror film plots. Clover still seems at times to fall prey to reductive generalizations or rather simplistic dichotomies and associations between viewer characteristics and stereotyped gender notions. By her own admission, she is mainly interested in why the predominantly male viewers of horror subject themselves to being "hurt" (= "feminized") by the genre. Her fourth chapter, "The Eye of Horror," examines the role of eyes, watching, and gazing in horror films like *Peeping Tom* (1960). On the one hand, Clover argues that this film depicts what she calls the "assaultive gaze" of the camera, which is "figured as masculine" ("A hard look and a hard penis mean the same thing"); but on the other hand, it also critiques that gaze and showcases the "reactive gaze," "figured as feminine, of the spectator" (p. 181).

They also lack a deep and well-grounded historical awareness of horror's roots and varieties. Clover's book does focus on a range of horror plots and on their social and cultural contexts, but only on horror films of the past two decades. Horror has a much longer, more complex history. It originated from the gothic novel, a fact in itself important for feminists to note because of the unusual prevalence of women as both writers and readers in this genre.[21] Much good feminist work has been done in recent years concerning gothic romance and the origins of horror in works like those of Mary Shelley.[22] Ideally, feminist readings of horror films would benefit from awareness of this research and of related work in cultural studies that examines the history of horror in relation to specific sociocultural contexts.[23]

Further, feminist psychodynamic accounts do not seem sensitive to the dazzling diversity of horror's subgenres: gothic, mad scientist, alien invader, slasher-psycho, rape revenge, B-movie, cult film, science fiction, monster, possession film, zombie, comedy, Japanese horror (Godzilla), and so on—even music video horror (Michael Jackson's *Thriller*)! In light of all this genre diversity, I doubt there can be any one "feminist theory of horror." Reflecting on the astounding variety of styles, nuances, and tones within this genre would also lead me to doubt any particular theory that associates gender with the kind of looking, or monstrousness, or victimization that is typical of horror, or with some "work" of abjection that horror films necessarily "illustrate." Films within a single subgenre like the vampire film may present male monsters as distinctive as the emaciated Kinski Nosferatu, the campy Bela Lugosi, the languid Frank Langella, the sinister Christopher Lee, and the macabre ball-goers of Polanski. A quite horrific and gory movie can also be wildly funny (*Texas Chain Saw Massacre II, An American Werewolf in London*). Horror films can be very eerie and subtly creepy (*The Dead Zone*), or they can revel in over-the-top, hair-raising, outrageous effects (*Evil Dead II*). They can be depth-psychological "family romances" (*Repulsion*) or virtual cartoons (*Predator 2*). They can be historical costume dramas (Herzog's *Nosferatu*, Coppola's *Bram Stoker's Dracula*) or technophilic futuristic visions (*Alien*). They can be vividly realistic (*Jurassic Park*) or ridiculously fake (*Godzilla*). They can be incredibly original (*Scanners, Brain Dead*), mindlessly imitative (*Silent Madness, Orca*), or a little of both (*Body Double*).

I assume, then, that a promising feminist approach to cinematic horror should be historically aware and also broad and open enough to work for all of these varieties of horror. In light of these observations, as well as the list of six criticisms I made in Part 1, the task of building a "feminist theory of horror" may seem monumental. And in fact, this is not exactly what I aim at here. My proposal is perhaps best understood not as a "theory" of horror, but as an attempt to begin making good on some of the deficiencies and positive requirements I have outlined. I suggest a

---

[21]Eugenia de la Motte. *Perils of the Night: A Feminist Study of Nineteenth-Century Gothic* (New York: Oxford University Press, 1990).

[22]See Anne K. Mellor, *Mary Shelley: Her Life, Her Fiction, Her Monsters* (New York: Methuen, 1988); and Susan Gilbert and Susan Gubar, *The Madwoman in the Attic*) (New Haven: Yale University Press, 1979), especially chapter 7, pp. 213–47.

[23]See James Twitchell, *Dreadful Pleasures: An Anatomy of Modern Horror* (Oxford: Oxford University Press, 1985); and Andrew Tudor, *Monsters and Mad Scientists: A Cultural History of the Horror Movie* (London: Basil Blackwell, 1989).

strategy or framework for constructing feminist readings of horror films. My strategy would emphasize the structure of horror films and place special weight on their gender ideologies, in a sense I shall explain further below.

First, it is useful to distinguish various roles that feminism can play in film studies. For convenience I shall label these roles, somewhat pretentiously, the "extra-filmic" and "intra-filmic." By the "extra-filmic" role, I mean to refer to feminist investigations, in a sociological, anthropological, or historical vein, into actual concrete issues concerning the historical context, production, and reception of horror films. In this role, feminist critics would ask questions, for example, about women's motives and experiences in producing, writing, directing, editing, and acting in horror films. Alternatively, they might explore reception theory, looking at actual examples of how various kinds of periodicals and audiences, such as feminist and lesbian audiences, review and read horror films—perhaps in unusually creative and non-standard ways.[24] Another type of extra-filmic exploration would be that of the cultural historian who aims to locate specific periods or varieties of horror movies within the sort of historical and social context that I find absent in most current feminist theorizing. In this role, feminist critics could examine the links between horror films and related works of literature.

Though I consider all the types of extra-filmic exploration that I have just mentioned very important, my own focus, stemming in part from my own perspective in philosophy—a notoriously nonempirical discipline—will instead be on what I call the intra-filmic questions about horror. My proposal for producing feminist readings or interpretations of horror films is that we should focus on their representational contents and on the nature of their representational practices, so as to scrutinize how the films represent gender, sexuality, and power relations between the sexes. I suggest that feminist readings of a horror film proceed by looking at various crucial sorts of film elements. Some of these elements concern the representation of women and monsters within films. Others explore how the film is structured and how it works. Within my recommended framework, we must shift attention away from the psychodynamics of viewing movies, and onto the nature of films as artifacts that may be studied by examining both their construction and their role in culture. To study their construction we look at such standard features as plot, characters, and point of view. To study their role in culture—that is, to inquire about this as feminists—we examine their gender ideology. This is my chief goal in producing feminist readings of horror films.

Let me offer some clarifying comments here about my proposal. The label "ideology" I borrow from Marxist theory, supposing that an ideology is a distorted representation of existing relations of power and domination. In the particular project I am interested in, obviously, these would be relations of patriarchy or male domination (together with any relevant associated relations of class or race dominance). Feminist ideology critique is a deep interpretive reading that criticizes or analyzes a film's presentation of certain naturalized messages about gender—messages that the film takes for granted and expects its audience to agree with and accept. These

---

[24]As a parallel, see "Illicit Pleasures: Feminist Spectators and *Personal Best*," by Elizabeth Ellsworth, in *Issues in Feminist Film Criticism*, pp. 183–96.

will typically be messages that perpetuate the subordination and exploitation of women; they present gender hierarchy or genderized roles and relations that are somehow portrayed as normal in the discourse of the film.[25] Or, occasionally and more interestingly, an analysis of the film's ideology might show that the film itself is raising questions about "normal" relations of gender dominance.

It might be thought that the strategy I favor resembles a somewhat old-fashioned feminist approach to film studies, the "images of women" approach.[26] On this approach, one would analyze a genre of horror like the slasher film, say, by observing how images of women are presented in these films. Thus, typically, young women are shown either as tomboys or as teenaged sex fiends who somehow deserve their dismemberment at the hands of a Jason or Michael Myers. I do recommend that to explore a film's gender ideology, we ask various questions that would also be asked on this approach, such as, How does the film depict/represent women— as agents, patients, knowers, sufferers? or, What role do women play vis-a-vis men in the film? However, I take feminist ideology critique to go beyond this rather simple set of questions in two main ways.

First, I want to emphasize films as complex functioning artifacts composed of a wide variety of elements, including more than simply the representation of characters. Obviously, films also include technical and formal filmic features such as editing, visual point of view, lighting, sound, and costuming, as well as features shared with literary works such as plots, dialogue, audience point of view, and narrative structure. Feminist ideology critique will explore any or all of these features that seem relevant to understanding a film's presentation of gender ideology. This may include focusing on what Noël Carroll has called rhetorical strategies, such as the elicitation of audience presumptions in completing gaps in the story.[27] So on my approach we would ask questions like these: How do the film's structures of narrative, point of view, and plot construction operate in effecting a depiction of gender roles and relations? Does the film offer a "heroic modernist" narrative of mastery, centered upon a male character, offering up either a clear resolution or a noble tragedy? Or, is there a nonstandard narrative centered upon female characters, offering, perhaps, a more open-ended and ambiguous con-

---

[25]For another example of an ideological examination of horror films that takes a different approach from mine, see Tania Modleski's "The Terror of Pleasure: The Contemporary Horror Film and Postmodern Theory," in *Studies in Entertainment: Critical Approaches to Mass Culture*, Tania Modleski, ed. (Bloomington: University of Indiana Press, 1986), pp. 155–66. Modleski advances a complicated set of reasons for rejecting the ways in which certain postmodern theorists have championed some horror films for allegedly deconstructing the self, revealing the primacy of spectacle, and so on. She sees these films as attacking the feminine through their attacks on representatives of the family or consumer culture; examples she discusses are *Halloween* and *Dawn of the Dead*). [See pp. 617–26 this volume.]

[26]For discussion of this approach, see Noël Carroll, "The Image of Women in Film. A Defense of a Paradigm," *The Journal of Aesthetics and Art Criticism* 48, 4 (Fall 1990): 349–60.

[27]Noël Carroll has discussed a somewhat different notion of the ideological effects of cinema. The particular conception Carroll criticizes, the "Althusserian Model," rather narrowly alleges that films' contents and formal structures function to present a certain distorted picture of the viewing subject. Carroll offers persuasive objections to this approach and considers an alternative rhetorical analysis that draws upon Aristotle's, to show how "rhetorical strategies may be implemented in narrative film" (p. 223). Noël Carroll, "Film, Rhetoric, and Ideology," in *Explanation and Value in the Arts*, ed. Salim Kemal and Ivan Gaskell (Cambridge: Cambridge University Press, 1973), pp. 215–37.

clusion? Does the film reference historical or genre precedents—say, a particular earlier vampire film, or the mad scientist genre in general—and if so, how does it comment upon, replicate, parody, or revise the gender thematics of its predecessors? What are the film's implicit rhetorical presuppositions about natural gender roles and relations? Does the film present possibilities of questioning or challenging these presumptions?

Second, I do mean something by calling feminist ideological critique of horror a "deep" interpretive reading. An interesting and creative feminist reading of a film may look "below" its surface representations of male or female characters to consider gaps, presumptions, and even what is "repressed," by which I mean simply blocked, omitted, or avoided, in these representations. My strategy accords with advice laid out by the French feminist Luce Irigaray in her discussions of how to construct disruptive feminist readings of the discourse of the male western philosophical tradition: "The issue is not one of elaborating a new theory of which woman would be the subject or the object, but of jamming the theoretical machinery itself, of suspending its pretension to the production of a truth and of a meaning that are excessively univocal."[28] Referencing Irigaray may seem inconsistent on my part, given that she operates within the Lacanian psychoanalytic tradition. However, Irigaray has in fact written some of the strongest feminist critiques I have read of the most basic assumptions of Freudian and Lacanian psychoanalytic theory. Further, I do not believe that a use of her recommended strategies of reading—for philosophy, literature, or film—must rely on any specific psychosexual assumptions. That is, as strategies of *reading* they work much like deconstructive textual strategies that are logically separable from those psychological assumptions. A brief example may help show this.

Irigaray has written critically about Plato's and Aristotle's treatment of form and matter in their metaphysics. She shows how they regard form as more valuable because they associate it with masculinity and order. Now, it could well be said that Irigaray proceeds by offering some sort of depth psychological reading of how these philosophers treat matter: Plato, as the "womb," Cave, or receptacle; Aristotle as the "envelope" or penis sheath. This sort of reading could be regarded as an analysis of their motives or of the ongoing appeal of Greek philosophical frameworks to subsequent, mostly male philosophers. However, it strikes me that Irigaray's critique functions equally as a deconstructive reading that enables one to question some of the most basic assumptions of the discourse she is examining, in this case, ancient metaphysics. One can find actual passages in which these philosophers associated form with masculinity. So, Irigaray's "deep" reading conforms with my conception of ideology critique, in that she questions the most basic ways in which an apparently neutral and objective field, metaphysics, conceals and contains hierarchized gender notions. One need not accept any psychoanalytic tenets to use this style of reading so as to query the particular discourse at issue, asking in this case, not only why form was associated with masculinity and considered by the ancient Greeks as

---

[28]Luce Irigaray, "The Power of Discourse," in Irigaray, *This Sex Which Is Not One*, trans. Catherine Porter (Ithaca, NY: Cornell University Press, 1985), p. 78.

more valuable than matter, but also what an alternative metaphysical schema would look like.[29]

Similarly, to try to transfer the point of this last paragraph to film studies, Carol Clover, in her examination of the depiction of the feminine in slasher films, has provided something like an Irigarayan "deep reading" that criticizes an existing form of discourse. She points out first, the obvious, that these films typically show young women as somehow bad—too sexy and alluring—before they are attacked by a male. Beyond this, she offers a "deeper" reading by arguing that slashers also reinforce cultural messages about the virtues of masculinity by presenting a villain who is defectively masculine—often someone pudgy, awkward, shy, or seemingly impotent—and a heroine (the "Final Girl") who is more masculine than feminine. I would call this a "deep" reading because it shows that the apparently male villains are actually bad because they are culturally coded as feminine. Where I part ways with Clover is that I reject her assumptions about the need for grounding this sort of reading in the truth of a given psychosexual model (Laqueur's), or about the processes through which slasher audience's psychological investment (and hence pleasure) in these movies alleged reflects certain standard, universal, gender-associated psychological interests.

My recommended approach is continuous with previous approaches to artworks in the Western aesthetic tradition, ranging from Aristotle's account of tragedy in the *Poetics* and Kant's *Critique of Judgment* to more contemporary works like Kendall Walton's *Mimesis as Make-Believe*. Philosophers have typically supposed that it is appropriate in aesthetic theory to discuss aspects of the psychology of our response to artworks, but they have done so without presuming any particularly detailed theory of the psyche. They emphasize that paintings, tragedies, or even landscape gardens are a particular kind of phenomenon, intentionally created and structured to produce a certain kind of effect—catharsis, aesthetic distance, the free play of the imagination, and so on. It is enough for purposes of philosophical aesthetics to employ commonsense, everyday notions of human psychology, to assume that we are capable of being frightened, excited, horrified, and so on, by artistic representations, and then proceed to try to analyze how this occurs.

Adopting my proposed framework means simply that a feminist critic will construct a reading that focuses on gender representation within a film, beginning with a list of specific questions that can vary as appropriate—according to the film's own period, style, and tone. Distinct feminist readings of the same horror film could easily be constructed. It is indeed always possible that a film may not have much to say that is particularly exciting or illuminating on the subject of gender. Also, and

---

[29]For more thoughts about the usefulness of Irigaray's approach for a nonpsychoanalytic feminist analytic philosophical reading of historical texts, see my "Nourishing Speculation: A Feminist Reading of Aristotelian Science," in *Engendering Origins: Critical Feminist Essays on Plato and Aristotle*, ed. Bat-Ami Bar On (Albany, NY: SUNY Press, 1994), pp. 145–87; and "Reading Irigaray Reading Aristotle," in *Re-Reading the Canon: Feminist Essays on Aristotle*, ed. Cynthia Freeland (Pennsylvania University Press: forthcoming), pp. 126–42. Kelly Oliver offers a somewhat similar approach, which she also calls ideology critique in drawing upon both Irigaray and Kristeva's theories, in her article "The Politics of Interpretation: The Case of Bergman's *Persona*," in *Philosophy and Film*, ed. Cynthia A. Freeland and Thomas E. Wartenberg (New York: Routledge, 1995), pp. 233–48. However, I believe that Oliver shows much more sympathy to psychoanalytic accounts of, say, "the maternal" than I do.

importantly, a feminist reading need not be a "complete" reading of the movie that purports to attend to all its many elements.

I believe that my proposal to use a basic set of questions about gender ideology as a broad strategy for feminist film readings helps overcome some of the defects of current feminist film theorizing I enumerated in Part 1, and I want to explain more here how I see it as an improvement. Recall that my first two objections concerned the problematic assumptions of a particular psychoanalytic theory or of psychoanalysis generally. Obviously, my proposed strategy does not encounter these problems. It does not adopt any particular psychodynamic theory or theory of sexual or gender difference. My third objection queried currently dominant presumptions about gender dichotomies between, for example, the aggressive masculine gaze and the passive female spectacular body. I avoid these sorts of assumptions about gender precisely by foregrounding as my first question the issue of *how* a film depicts gender. My fourth objection was a challenge to the theoretical reductivism of dominant feminist film criticism; on this point, I would hope that my strategy opens out to connected issues concerning race, class, and so on.

My fifth objection concerned the narrowness of psychodynamic feminism in comparison to other important forms of feminist theorizing. One could use the map I propose in combination with many types of feminism. For example, to diagnose the gender ideology of a film, one could adopt the viewpoint of a Marxist or liberal feminist; in either case I would suppose one could be critical, though of different aspects of the film, and to different ends. Similarly, a feminist theorist steeped in Foucault or Donna Haraway might ask about some of my questions by looking at very different features of a film—at, for instance, how it portrays disciplines of the female body, or how it depicts women in relation to technology.

My sixth objection stated that one might equally well achieve the insights of feminist psychoanalytic film theory without its propping in a psychodynamic theory. I think that some of the questions I have listed above actually do this, that is, would work to take the place of others posed on the more problematic basis of, for instance, depth psychoanalysis. Questions about "the gaze," the sadistic male viewer, the masculine narrative order, and so forth, are replaced here by questions about whether the film presents women as primarily suffering and tortured physical beings, or whether they are also shown to be alert, curious, intelligent, capable of independent investigation, and so on, and also by questions about whether the women characters help move the narrative along, or are simply targets of the horrific spectacle. I would hope that a careful consideration of these questions would avert reductivism and allow flexibility in recognizing that horror movies often have very complex, mixed representations of women.

PART 3: ILLUSTRATIONS

It is time to illustrate how I would use my own recommended strategy to generate critical feminist readings of horror films and their gender ideologies. I will first discuss *Jurassic Park* and *The Fly*, films I choose specifically because, on the surface at least, they seem to present positive images of strong, intelligent, and active women. This makes them especially interesting to read for underlying ideologies.

Next I shall compare these films to *Repulsion*, a film that on the surface seems problematic because it features a horrific female slasher/murderer, but which I find to present a surprisingly radical questioning of existing gender ideology.

I begin with *Jurassic Park*. First, how does the film represent women? Superficially at least, it displays a contemporary, 1990s feminist vision of women and girls. The female paleobotanist Dr. Ellie Sattler (Laura Dern) is presumably well-educated and authoritative in her own field; she shows enthusiasm and expertise in classifying the ancient plants in the park. She is courageous and physically active, and she makes cracks about the other characters' sexism. And the young girl is said to be a computer hacker.

Nevertheless, we can hardly call the movie an unmitigated feminist achievement. The paleobotanist's own scientific expertise is never treated as especially deep or relevant. It is rather the male scientist Dr. Alan Grant (Sam Neill) who espouses a controversial theory (about dinosaurs' close relation to birds) that will get tested and confirmed in the park. Ellie is shown enthusiastically identifying plant species in the park but, importantly, the plants themselves are not intrinsically interesting here but function only as fodder for the dinosaurs. Thus, even in her scientific role, the woman could be said to be chiefly concerned with nourishment and caregiving. Amazingly, she has never heard of chaos theory, and the male mathematician Ian Malcolm (Jeff Goldblum) explains it to her in the context of a teasing sex scene that treats her like a silly teenage bimbo. This sort of depiction is further enforced by the fact that she is blonde, pretty, slender, and at least ten years younger than her male scientist colleague and lover. Further, through most of the film she, unlike any of the male characters, consistently wears little shorts that show off her long coltish legs.

Similarly, the young girl (Ariana Richards) spends most of the film in abject fear of the T-rex. She is even afraid of the large gentle brontosaurus, who sneezes all over her and makes her look ridiculous. The fact that she is a computer hacker is introduced rather casually and coincidentally toward the end of the film and does not seem especially well integrated into her character. When she manages to get into the computer system, her task is the relatively minor one of figuring out how to get a door to close properly.

Next, how is monstrousness in the film related to femininity? All the monsters (dinosaurs) in the movie are female, but initially it seems that not much is made of this—nothing particularly horrific about primal mothers on the scale of *Alien*, at least. It is not easy to read the femininity of the monsters here, since it is not uniform, but seems to permit a great range of difference: some varieties are huge and voracious; others (the raptors) are smaller, clever, and vicious; yet others are large, gentle, cow-like beings vulnerable to indigestion or colds. I would suggest that the film presents a standard array of culturally coded, negative messages about females through its depiction of these various dinosaurs. Some dinosaurs, like some women, are fat, sweet, and gentle; and others are thin, vicious, and scheming. (There can be, in other words, no sweet, smart dinosaurs!) One could go further in noting that from the perspective of the male scientists who create and study the park, all female dinosaurs have a mysterious sexuality that is "other": their peculiar threat lies in their frog-derived ability to convert their sex so as to be able to reproduce independently. Thus on a deep reading, the female dinosaurs represent a culturally coded threat centering upon a kind of uncontrolled, rampant female sexuality, as well as awesome reproductive abilities.

Another question to ask about in assessing a film's gender ideology concerns who moves the narrative along, who its chief agents are; here, clearly in *Jurassic Park* it is not the woman or girl. There are no women involved in the creation or operation of the park itself. The key human agents of the movie who initiate the chain of events presenting the movie's central problem—the park mogul, the shark lawyer, and the computer wizard—are all men. Men are thus shown in the film as running the show in all the relevant senses: setting up the problematic situations, making them worse, and then resolving them. True, girls can be hackers and scientists, but this seems peripheral to their chief roles, since during most of the action sequences of the movie they are relegated to functions of nurturing the ill or taking care of men. Ellie is not at the center of the key scenes that depict the children's being threatened, then escaping, the tyrannosaurus. Instead, the male scientist/father figure does this, while she is confined mainly to nursing, first the sick triceratops, then the wounded mathematician. Her sudden interest in the sick triceratops seems poorly explained by her alleged scientific expertise in the plants it eats, but it furthers a general depiction of her as caring and nurturing. She has, literally, the ideal human mother's ability to deal with mounds of shit!

On the whole, then, the gender ideology of *Jurassic Park* seems to be to confirm that women, even when they are brave and scientific, must remain pretty, flirtatious, and nurturing. From the very start the film represents it as a central aim in Ellie's life to convince her lover to have children. Thus in the film's trajectory, Grant fulfills his chief aim, demonstrating his scientific hypothesis about dinosaurs, while she fulfills hers in parallel, as one of the film's closing scenes shows her smiling happily (in a view we share) at Alan, now appropriately fatherly, sleeping with the two children he has saved cuddled in his arms. The film's ending thus depicts a resolution that produces a happy, relieved, and idealized nuclear family. It includes none of the foreigners who are lowly park laborers, no computer nerds, no greedy lawyers, and no black members—just the white surrogate parents and grandfather whose regret signifies that he is to be exonerated for his mistakes in the otherwise "innocent" desire to entertain people. Even more significantly, the very last scene of the film is a vision of flying birds—pelicans who, seen in silhouette over the water, resemble pterodactyls. Thus the film concludes with a subtle message that reinforces the "heroic" male scientist's creative vision and theoretical achievement in hypothesizing correctly about the bird-like nature of dinosaurs.

I move now to my second example, David Cronenberg's remake of *The Fly*. In this film, the heroine, Veronica Quaife (Geena Davis), is represented as an ambitious, intelligent, pragmatic, and successful career woman, a science writer. She is also charming, funny, beautiful, and sexually forward—either a fantasy woman who falls straight into bed with men, or the confident new woman assertive about her own sexual desires. True, she could be said to behave in unprofessional ways (having first slept with one of her college professors, who is now her editor, and later with the subject of her current research article)—but so do the men in the movie. More problematic is the fact that she only seems to exist in the film in relations of subordination to men. As a science writer her position is more lowly than that of the creative scientists whose genius she will simply record and report on to the world. Similarly as a writer, she is subordinate to her editor at the science magazine.

These relations of subordination parallel Veronica's position in the film's plot and narrative structure. She exists in the movie primarily in a dependent relationship to the male scientist Dr. Seth Brundle (Jeff Goldblum). The film is a variant on the mad scientist genre, and Brundle is the mad scientist at the center of its narrative trajectory. If this film reaches greater tragic heights than many other mad scientist movies, that may be because it fulfills some of Aristotle's criteria for a tragic plot: the hero is a great man, sympathetic, deserving of our pity, who engages in action that involves some sort of fatal mistake and hubris bringing about his downfall.[30] This film is a narrative about *the man's* activities, his heroism, and tragic downfall. Veronica functions in it as an aspect of his tragedy and loss, and also as a modern variant on the ancient Greek chorus guiding our responses of pity and fear (or in this case, horror). The film often puts viewers into her viewpoint, forcing us to observe from closer up, so to speak, the hideous transformations that occur as the fly takes him over.[31]

The particular horrific threat of this movie is an invasion by the other species of *both* the male and female body. It does take a specific turn against women when the scientist seeks his own rescue by demanding to use, and corrupt, her reproductive abilities (showcased in a disgusting nightmare she has of giving birth to a giant maggot). Yet ultimately it is he and not she who suffers; he is punished for his scientific hubris, as she fights for survival (with some male assistance, but nevertheless she is very courageous) and resists his final appeals to sacrifice herself for him. It is difficult to force a reading of the monstrousness here as a feminization of his body; what makes more sense is to see these transformations as metaphors for aging or for ravaging illnesses like cancer or AIDS.

The Fly's narrative has a very traditional, male-centered and male-driven form: the male scientist exceeds his role and must pay for it. The male acts, the woman feels. She occupies a traditional role in the sense that her emotions and perceptions are clues to guide us, the film viewer, to regard the man, despite his hubris, with love, pity, and sympathy. In *The Fly* as in *Jurassic Park*, the mad scientist who creates the crux of the story is a man, and the woman has to deal with the man's problem; love and empathy are the key female traits. There is no real challenge to this gendered division of labor or to the idea that stories are primarily about men, only secondarily about the women who love them. Consider, for example, the fact that

---

[30]For some thoughts about the sexism implicit in Aristotle's basic articulation of the nature of tragic plot, see my "Plot Imitates Action: Aesthetic Evaluation and Moral Realism in the *Poetics*," in *Essays on Aristotle's Poetics,* ed. Amelie Rorty (Princeton, NJ: Princeton University Press, 1992), pp. 111–32.

[31]David Bordwell has suggested that a "reading against the grain" approach might take this film to be a subversive exposé of the mad scientist's "hypermasculinity" ("Nerd becomes barroom thug and rapacious seducer"). While this is an intriguing line of interpretation, I do not think it can work, mainly because of the film's continued sympathy for Brundle. Here again, as I suggest, the fact that Veronica's love and pity persist despite his ugly behavior and transformation is meant to be our guide as to how to react. I think my interpretation of the movie as a high-end horror mad scientist tragedy is more in accord with the plot and its ultimate conclusion when the creature mutely asks to be put out of its misery.

Veronica's own tragedy in this movie is in itself a subordinate tragedy brought about by Brundle's mistake, and one centered in the realm of her body and her emotional life: the loss of a lover, together with a forced abortion. The movie makes absolutely nothing of the fact that she loses out on what could easily be the biggest scientific scoop of her journalistic career! (Indeed, wouldn't the savvy and competitive woman journalist she seemed to be at the start immediately begin writing up the whole thing, complete with video illustrations?) In other words, just as in *Jurassic Park*, beneath the surface depiction of an independent career woman in *The Fly* lies the ideological message that women are primarily creatures of their emotions who exist first and foremost in their love relations to men and potential offspring.

These are two examples of films I have chosen because they seem to offer positive depictions of independent women characters which I believe are undermined by deeper ideological messages. Further, they are interesting to examine in contrast with typical feminist psychoanalytic views because their depictions of the horrific monsters are not the typical ones of castrating woman or primal mother. Instead I would locate the most problematic aspects in their gender ideology at the level of their narrative, which is in each case predominantly a narrative focused on male energies, activities, triumphs, or tragedies.

Now let me shift and describe a very different example of a horror movie with a quite different logic, *Repulsion*. Again I want to argue that surface appearances can be deceiving. On the surface this is a horror story in which a very beautiful and sexy woman, Carol Ledoux (Catherine Deneuve) becomes a mad slasher and villain who attacks and destroys men. One might initially suppose then that this is a sort of film noir anticipating the recent genre of *Fatal Attraction*-style villainess females. Carol seems to be depicted as the alluring yet shy and inhibited femme fatale whose repressed sexuality must unleash itself ultimately in horrific acts of violence against the men she desires. This view of her as repressed and even voyeuristic might seem to be confirmed by various aspects of the plot and the filmic depiction of her; she dresses demurely, speaks in a low voice, hides behind her hair, constantly peers out the windows of her flat, listens in on her sister's sexual moans and cries, inspects and throws away the shaving glass used by her sister's lover, and so on.

However, I think that this surface reading does not capture much that is going on in this film. Many of the point-of-view shots in the movie identify the audience members with leering men, from her erstwhile boyfriend to the construction workers who jeer and whistle at Carol as she walks past them on the sidewalk. On the other hand the film also switches to adopt the young woman's own viewpoint as she is chased and visually assaulted by these men. In doing so, it shows her to be a victim who merits our sympathy and empathy. Thus the feeling of the scene where she overhears her sister's lovemaking is less one of voyeurism than one of tormented embarrassment and the desire to escape. Clearly she feels threatened by her sister's involvement with the man and by her departure with him for vacation. Once she is alone in the flat, Carol becomes increasingly psychotic and delusional. As she goes mad, the audience shares her heightened perceptions, nightmares, and hallucinations. Polanski shocks and frightens us in parallel with her by showing faces that suddenly materialize in mirrors, hands that reach out from rubbery walls, or menacing shadows creeping from above on the bedroom ceiling, accompanied by weird and threatening grunting noises. Given this increasingly deranged system of perceptions, we can actually be persuaded that Carol's reaction as she reacts and kills men who enter her apartment is a reasonable one. This is particularly true when she repulses the advances of her lecherous landlord, who has offered to accept something other than money for his rental payments.

This means that what is really horrific in this movie is not the female killer (as it is, say, in *Basic Instinct* or *Fatal Attraction*); it is instead lechery, male attitudes of lust toward such a beautiful woman. The film highlights Carol's victimization by men and strongly hints that her psychosis and sexual repression stem from a history of child sexual abuse. She cannot escape the pursuit of men who wolf-whistle at her on the street, press her for dates, or attack her in her own apartment. Her sister's lover has carelessly scattered his personal hygiene items all around in the bathroom. She is even trapped in her job as a manicurist in the industry of making women beautiful so as to please men. By repeated shots linking Carol to the naked, stripped rabbit that rots uncooked on an empty plate in her flat, she is represented as childlike, vulnerable, and psychically decaying.

The overall narrative structure of *Repulsion* reflects a logic of disruption and fragmentation rather than resolution; of suffering and reacting, rather than action. The story could not be said to be a tragedy in the classic sense, even one like that of *The Fly*. That is, *Repulsion* does not offer a narrative of a deed and its consequences, or a heroine whose action is somehow flawed, precipitating her tragic downfall. Instead this is a sort of antinarrative that presents an inability to act, a continual waiting, passivity, and suffering. Even Carol's final acts of killing the two men seem to be reactions rather than genuinely intended deeds. Surely Carol does not "deserve" her suffering, nor is she an evil *Fatal Attraction*-style femme fatale. To be sure, this film is not visionary in the sense of offering up an alternative model of gender roles. Nevertheless, it certainly does call existing roles and attitudes into question in a particularly interesting way, by implicating the audience in watching this woman—who is indeed very beautiful—by following her as she walks down the street, by extreme close-ups of her face and appearance—so much so that she begins to seem to want to hide from the camera itself behind her long pale hair.

In *The Fly* too the heroine's story revolves around her emotional suffering, but as I interpreted that film's gender ideology, it represented such suffering as appropriate for a woman character whose fate is basically subordinated to that of the male hero. Her suffering functions as a cue for us in the audience, guiding us to react "appropriately" to Brundle with sympathy and pity. By contrast, in my view *Repulsion* presents a certain gender ideology in such a way as to raise a number of serious questions about it. It constructs a surprisingly critical representation of male sexual desire and the accompanying objectification of women, and it even links this kind of visual objectification to acts of violence and sexual abuse like incest. Moreover, and finally, it suggests that when women fight back against such violence and abuse, their actions may be reasonable and warranted. But it does *not* suggest, as do many movies in the recent "rape revenge" genre, that women who fight back against such abuse will achieve psychological satisfaction or be backed by a powerful judicial system.[32] It would be a less good movie, in my mind, if it did so—more problematically ideological—because it would misrepresent and gloss over existing power and dominance relations within patriarchy.

CONCLUSION

In closing, I would like to make one cautionary point about my recommended framework for producing readings of horror films that focus on their gender ideologies. One reason I distinguish my recommended feminist ideological critique from an ordinary Marxist sort is that I want to resist a certain sort of Marxist line that places great power within the hands of the productive apparatuses of Hollywood, and correspondingly little power in the hands of audience members, treated generically as members of one social class. I believe that audience members have the power to create individual, often subversive readings of films. To speak of a film's ideology suggests that some powerful agent is distorting a message for sinister purposes of domination and control. This is misleading, I think, both because the nature of the agency in question in filmic representation is actually very diffuse, and also because it makes viewers into powerless Pavlovian dogs. Horror movie viewers are in fact often highly sophisticated and critical; horror movie screenings, in my experience, may be much more participatory than other forms of films. If the dominance relations distorted by ideology in my approach are those of patriarchy, I believe that individual viewers, in particular female viewers, may either see through such relations or reread intended ones in subversive ways.

This means that even when a film presents a problematic image of women, the audience reaction may subvert or undercut it. For example, the audience may react so as to bring out the potential dark humor of a scene. Let me offer an example here. Douglas Kellner and Michael Ryan, in their book *Camera Politica*, adopted a more standardly Marxist view of film ideology than my own. Ryan and Kellner discuss, among other topics, sexist ideologies of horror films in the early 1980s, which they interpret as expressing male backlash against feminist advances of the time.[33] They are highly critical, for instance, of the bondage scenes in *Cat People*; their discussion seems to assume that the filmmakers had an agenda that would determine audience responses by buying into their assumed agreement, that is, a shared resistance to new feminist values. Yet when I saw the film in a crowded theater in New York at the time of its release, the audience hooted derisively at just these scenes. That is, they seemed to see through this maneuver of the filmmakers so as to resist the film's surface ideology. Horror films seem often to solicit just such cynical, subversive audience responses.

In this paper I have presented not so much a feminist *theory* of horror films as a framework that I hope will prove useful for producing readings of horror films. I would like to emphasize that in my view, for any given film, a number of feminist

---

[32]On the rape revenge genre, see Carol J. Clover, *Men, Women, and Chain Saws*, chapter 3, "Getting Even," pp. 114–65.

[33]Michael Ryan and Douglas Kellner, *Camera Politica: The Politics and Ideology of Contemporary Hollywood Film* (Bloomington: Indiana University Press, 1988), pp. 136–67.

readings might be possible. Feminist film readings interpret how films function as artifacts, and to do this they may successfully explore such diverse aspects of a film as its plot, editing, sound track, point of view, dialogue, character representations, use of rhetoric, or narrative structures. But film artifacts function within a context, and the context is constantly changing. I do not contend, for example, that the sort of reading of *Repulsion* I have offered here would have been possible or even appropriate in 1965 when the movie was released. We may see this film differently in retrospect, for example, against the contemporary background of *Fatal Attraction* and *Basic Instinct*, as well as by comparison with the recently emerging genre of the rape revenge movie. Further, there is much greater social awareness in 1995 than in 1965 of problems of incest and child sexual abuse, and these might significantly affect how a feminist of today sees certain slight allusions in the film.

My quick sketch here of film readings of *Jurassic Park*, *The Fly*, and *Repulsion*, is only that, a sketch. I have mainly intended to suggest how such critical feminist readings can be engaged in, and prove potentially fruitful, without psychodynamic underpinnings. Again, I emphasize films as functioning complex artistic artifacts, and I emphasize audience's critical readings rather than purportedly universal or totalizing psychological responses. My readings ask a set of central questions about films' representations of gender roles and relations, the horrific monster, and the type of resolution presented. I believe that my proposal offers a more flexible, potentially illuminating framework than psychodynamic approaches for constructing creative feminist readings of horror films.[34]

1996

---

[34]For a more extended illustration, see my discussion of *Henry: Portrait of a Serial Killer* in "Realist Horror," in *Philosophy and Film* (New York: Routledge, 1995).

DAVID BORDWELL
THE ART CINEMA AS A MODE
OF FILM PRACTICE

La Strada, 8½, Wild Strawberries, The Seventh Seal, Persona, Ashes and Diamonds, Jules et Jim, Knife in the Water, Vivre sa vie, Muriel: whatever else one can say about these films, cultural fiat gives them a role altogether different from *Rio Bravo* on the one hand and *Mothlight* on the other. They are "art films," and, ignoring the tang of snobbishness about the phrase, we can say that these and many other films constitute a distinct branch of the cinematic institution. My purpose in this essay is to argue that we can usefully consider the "art cinema" as a distinct mode of film practice, possessing a definite historical existence, a set of formal conventions, and implicit viewing procedures. Given the compass of this paper, I can only suggest some lines of work, but I hope to show that constructing the category of the art cinema is both feasible and illuminating.

It may seem perverse to propose that films produced in such various cultural contexts might share fundamentally similar features. Yet I think there are good reasons for believing this, reasons which come from the films' place in history. In the long run, the art cinema descends from the early *film d'art* and such silent national cinema schools as German Expressionism and Neue Sachlichkeit and French Impressionism.[1] (A thorough account of its sources would also have to include literary modernism, from Proust and James to Faulkner and Camus.) More specifically, the art cinema as a distinct mode appears after World War II when the dominance

---

I am grateful to Edward Branigan, Noel Carroll, Bruce Jenkins, Bob Self, Janet Staiger, and Kristin Thompson for their helpful criticism of this essay.

[1]More radical avant-garde movements, such as Soviet montage filmmaking, Surrealism, and *cinéma pur* seem to have been relatively without effect upon the art cinema's style. I suspect that those experimental styles which did not fundamentally change narrative coherence were the most assimilable to the postwar art cinema.

of the Hollywood cinema was beginning to wane. In the United States, the courts' divorcement decrees created a shortage of films for exhibition. Production films needed overseas markets and exhibitors needed to compete with television. In Europe, the end of the war reestablished international commerce and facilitated film export and coproductions. Thomas Guback has shown how, after 1954, films began to be made for international audiences.[2] American films sponsored foreign production, and foreign films helped American exhibitors fill screen time. The later Neorealist films may be considered the first postwar instances of the international art cinema, and subsequent examples would include most works of the New Wave, Fellini, Resnais, Bergman, De Sica, Kurosawa, Pasolini, et al. While the art cinema is of little economic importance in the United States today, it evidently continues, as such international productions as *The Serpent's Egg* or *Stroszek* show.

Identifying a mode of production/consumption does not exhaustively characterize the art cinema, since the cinema also consists of formal traits and viewing conventions. To say this, however, is to invite the criticism that the creators of such films are too inherently different to be lumped together. Yet I shall try to show that whereas stylistic devices and thematic motifs may differ from director to director, the overall *functions* of style and theme remain remarkably constant in the art cinema as a whole. The narrative and stylistic principles of the film constitute a logically coherent mode of cinematic discourse.

REALISM, AUTHORSHIP, AMBIGUITY

The classical narrative cinema—paradigmatically, studio feature filmmaking in Hollywood since 1920—rests upon particular assumptions about narrative structure, cinematic style, and spectatorial activity. While detailing those assumptions is a task far from complete,[3] we can say that in the classical cinema, narrative form motivates cinematic representation. Specifically, cause-effect logic and narrative parallelism generate a narrative which projects its action through psychologically defined, goal oriented characters. Narrative time and space are constructed to represent the cause-effect chain. To this end, cinematic representation has recourse to fixed figures of cutting (e.g., 180° continuity, crosscutting, "montage sequences"), *mise-en-scene* (e.g., three-point lighting, perspective sets), cinematography (e.g., a particular range of camera distances and lens lengths), and sound (e.g., modulation, voice-over narration). More important than these devices themselves are their functions in advancing the narrative. The viewer makes sense of the classical film through criteria of verisimilitude (is X plausible?), of generic appropriateness (is X characteristic of this sort of film?) and of compositional unity (does X advance the story?). Given this background set, we can start to mark off same salient features of the art cinema.

First, the art cinema defines itself explicitly against the classical narrative mode, and especially against the cause-effect linkage of events. These linkages become looser, more tenuous in the art film. In *L'Avventura*, for example, Anna is lost and

---

[2]See Thomas Guback, *The International Motion Picture Industry* (Bloomington: Indiana University Press, 1969), *passim*.

[3]See, for example, Philip Rosen, "Difference and Displacement in *Seventh Heaven*," *Screen* XVIII, 2 (Summer 1977): 89–104.

never found; in *A bout de souffle*, the reasons for Patricia's betrayal of Michel remain unknown; in *Bicycle Thieves*, the future of Antonio and his son is not revealed. It will not do, however, to characterize the art film solely by its loosening of causal relations. We must ask what motivates that loosening, what particular modes of unity follow from these motivations, what reading strategies the film demands, and what contradictions exist in this order of cinematic discourse.

The art cinema motivates its narratives by two principles: realism and authorial expressivity. On the one hand, the art cinema defines itself as a realistic cinema. It will show us real locations (Neorealism, the New Wave) and real problems (contemporary "alienation," "lack of communication," etc.). Part of this reality is sexual; the aesthetics and commerce of the art cinema often depend upon an eroticism that violates the production code of pre-1950 Hollywood. *A Stranger Knocks* and *And God Created Woman* are no more typical of this than, say *Jules et Jim* and *Persona* (whereas one can see *Le Mépris* as consciously working upon the very problem of erotic spectacle in the art cinema). Most important, the art cinema uses "realistic"—that is, psychologically complex—characters.

The art cinema is classical in its reliance upon psychological causation; characters and their effects on one another remain central. But whereas the characters of the classical narrative have clear-cut traits and objectives, the characters of the art cinema lack defined desires and goals. Characters may act for inconsistent reasons (Marcello in *La Dolce Vita*) or may question themselves about their goals (Borg in *Wild Strawberries* and the Knight in *The Seventh Seal*). Choices are vague or nonexistent. Hence a certain drifting episodic quality to the art film's narrative. Characters may wander out and never reappear; events may lead to nothing. The Hollywood protagonist speeds directly toward the target; lacking a goal, the art-film character slides passively from one situation to another.

The protagonist's itinerary is not completely random; it has a rough shape: a trip (*Wild Strawberries, The Silence, La Strada*), an idyll (*Jules et Jim, Elvira Madigan, Pierrot le fou*), a search (*L'Avventura, Blow-up, High and Low*), even the making of a film (*8½, The Clowns, Fellini Roma, Day for Night, The Last Movie, Le Mépris*). Especially apt for the broken teleology of the art film is the biography of the individual, in which events become pared down toward a picaresque successivity (*La Dolce Vita, The Apu Trilogy, Alfie*). If the classical protagonist struggles, the drifting protagonist traces an itinerary, an encyclopedic survey of the film's world. Certain occupations (stockbroking in *L'Eclisse*, journalism in *La Dolce Vita* and *The Passenger*, prostitution in *Vivre sa vie* and *Nights of Cabiria*) favor a survey form of narrative. Thus the art film's thematic of *la condition humaine*, its attempt to pronounce judgements on "modern life" as a whole, proceeds from its formal needs: had the characters a goal, life would no longer seem so meaningless.

What is essential to any such organizational scheme is that it be sufficiently loose in its causation as to permit characters to express and explain their psychological states. Slow to act, these characters tell all. The art cinema is less concerned with action than reaction; it is a cinema of psychological effects in search of their causes. The dissection of feeling is often represented explicitly as therapy and cure (e.g., *Through a Glass Darkly, Persona*), but even when it is not, the forward flow of causation is braked and characters pause to seek the aetiology of their feelings. Characters often tell one another stories: autobiographical events (especially from childhood), fantasies, and dreams. (A recurring line: "I had a strange dream last night.") The hero becomes a supersensitive individual, one of those people on whom nothing is lost. During the film's survey of its world, the hero often shudders on the edge of breakdown. There recurs the realization of the anguish of ordinary living, the discovery of unrelieved misery: compare the heroines of *Europa 51*, *L'Avventura*, *Deserto rosso*, and *Une femme mariée*. In some circumstances the characters must attribute their feelings to social situations (as in *Ikiru*, *I Live in Fear*, and *Shame*). In *Europe 51*, a communist tells Irene that individuals are not at fault; "If you must blame something, blame our postwar society." Yet there is seldom analysis at the level of groups or institutions; in the art cinema, social forces become significant insofar as they impinge upon the psychologically sensitive individual.

A conception of realism also affects the film's spatial and temporal construction, but the art cinema's realism here encompasses a spectrum of possibilities. The options range from a documentary factuality (e.g., *Il posto*) to intense psychological subjectivity (*Hiroshima mon amour*). (When the two impulses meet in the same film, the familiar "illusion/reality" dichotomy of the art cinema results.) Thus room is left for two reading strategies. Violations of classical conceptions of time and space are justified as the intrusion of an unpredictable and contingent daily reality or as the subjective reality of complex characters. Plot manipulations of story order (especially flashbacks) remain anchored to character subjectivity as in *8½* and *Hiroshima mon amour*. Manipulations of duration are justified realistically (e.g., the *temps morts* of early New Wave films) or psychologically (the jump cuts of *A bout de souffle* signaling a jittery lifestyle). By the same token, spatial representation will be motivated as documentary realism (e.g., location shooting, available light), as character revelation, or in extreme cases as character subjectivity. Andre Bazin may be considered the first major critic of the art cinema, not only because he praised a loose, accidental narrative structure that resembled life but also because he pinpointed privileged stylistic devices for representing a realistic continuum of space and time (deep-focus, deep space, the moving camera, and the long take). In brief, a commitment to both objective and subjective verisimilitude distinguished the art cinema from the classical narrative mode.[4]

Yet at the same time, the art cinema foregrounds the *author* as a structure in the film's system. Not that the author is represented as a biographical individual (although some art films, e.g., Fellini's, Truffaut's, and Pasolini's, solicit confessional readings), but rather the author becomes a formal component, the overriding intelligence organizing the film for our comprehension. Over this hovers a notion that the art-film director has a creative freedom denied to her/his Hollywood counterpart.[5] Within this frame of reference, the author is the textual force "who" communicates

[4]This point is taken up in Christian Metz, "The Modern Cinema and Narrativity," *Film Language*, tr. by Michael Taylor (New York: Oxford University Press, 1974), 185–227.

[5]Arthur Knight compares the Hollywood film to a commodity and the foreign film to an art work: "Art is not manufactured by committees. Art comes from an individual who has something that he must express. . . . This is the reason why we hear so often that foreign films are 'more artistic' than our own. There is in them the urgency of individual expression, an independence of vision, the coherence of a single-minded statement." In Michael F. Mayer, *Foreign Films on American Screens* (New York: Arco, 1965), vii.

(what is the film *saying*?) and "who" expresses (what is the artist's *personal vision*?). Lacking identifiable stars and familiar genres, the art cinema uses a concept of authorship to unify the text.

Several conventions operate here. The competent viewer watches the film expecting not order in the narrative but stylistic signatures in the narration: technical touches (Truffaut's freeze frames, Antonioni's pans) and obsessive motifs (Buñuel's anticlericalism, Fellini's shows, Bergman's character names). The film also offers itself as a chapter in an *oeuvre*. This strategy becomes especially apparent in the convention of the multi-film work (*The Apu Trilogy*, Bergman's two trilogies, Rohmer's "Moral Tales," and Truffaut's Doinel series). The initiated catch citations: references to previous films by the director or to works by others (e.g., the New Wave homages).

A small industry is devoted to informing viewers of such authorial marks. International film festivals, reviews and essays in the press, published scripts, film series, career retrospectives, and film education all introduce viewers to authorial codes. What is essential is that the art film be read as the work of an expressive individual. It is no accident, then, that the *politique de auteurs* arose in the wake of the art cinema, that *Cahiers du cinéma* admired Bergman and Antonioni as much as Hawks and Minnelli, that Robin Wood could esteem both Preminger and Satayajit Ray. As a critical enterprise, auteur analysis of the 1950s and 1960s consisted of applying art-cinema reading strategies to the classical Hollywood cinema.[6]

How does the author come forward in the film? Recent work in *Screen* has shown how narrational marks can betray the authorial code in the classical text, chiefly through gaps in motivation.[7] In the art-cinema text, the authorial code manifests itself as recurrent violations of the classical norm. Deviations from the classical canon—an unusual angle, a stressed bit of cutting, a prohibited camera movement, an unrealistic shift in lighting or setting—in short any breakdown of the motivation of cinematic space and time by cause-effect logic—can be read as "authorial commentary." The credits for the film, as in *Persona* or *Blow-up*, can announce the power of the author to control what we see. Across the entire film, we must recognize and engage with the shaping narrative intelligence. For example, in what Norman Holland calls the "puzzling film,"[8] the art cinema foregrounds the narrational act by posing enigmas. In the classic detective tale, however, the puzzle is one of *story*: who did it? how? why? In the art cinema, the puzzle is one of *plot*: Who is telling this story? How is this story being told? Why is this story

---

[6]"The strategy was to talk about Hawks, Preminger, etc. as artists like Buñuel and Resnais" (Jim Hillier, "The Return of *Movie*," *Movie* no. 20 [Spring 1975], 17). I do not mean to imply that auteur criticism did not at times distinguish between the classical narrative cinema and the art cinema. A book like V. G. Perkins's *Film as Film* (Baltimore: Penguin, 1978) insists not only upon authorial presence but also upon the causal motivation and the stylistic economy characteristic of the classical cinema. Thus Perkins finds the labored directorial touches of Antonioni and Bergman insufficiently motivated by story action. Nevertheless, Perkins' interpretation of the jeep sequence in *Carmen Jones* in terms of characters' confinement and liberation (pp. 80–82) is a good example of how Hollywood cutting and camera placement can be invested with symbolic traces of the author.

[7]See, for instance, Mark Nash, "*Vampyr* and the Fantastic," *Screen* XVII, 3 (Autumn 1976): 29–67; and Paul Willemen, "The Fugitive Subject," *Raoul Walsh*, ed. by Phil Hardy (London: Edinburgh Film Festival, 1974), 63–89.

[8]Norman Holland, "The Puzzling Movies: Three Analyses and a Guess at Their Appeal," *Journal of Social Issues* XX, 1 (January 1964): 71–96.

being told this way? Another example of such marking of narration is the device of the flashforward—the plot's representation of a future story action. The flashforward is unthinkable in the classical narrative cinema, which seeks to retard the ending and efface the mode of narration. But in the art cinema, the flashforward functions perfectly to stress authorial presence: we must notice how the narrator teases us with knowledge that no character can have. Far from being isolated or idiosyncratic, such instances typify the tendency of the art film to throw its weight onto plot, not story; we play a game with the narrator.

Realism and authorial expressivity, then, will be the means whereby the art film unifies itself. Yet these means now seem contradictory. Verisimilitude, objective or subjective, is inconsistent with an intrusive author. The surest signs of authorial intelligibility—the flashforward, the doubled scene in *Persona*, the color filters at the start of *Le Mépris*—are the least capable of realistic justification. Contrariwise, to push the realism of psychological uncertainty to its limit is to invite a haphazard text in which the author's shaping hand would not be visible. In short, a realist aesthetic and an expressionist aesthetic are hard to merge.

The art cinema seeks to solve the problem in a sophisticated way: by the device of *ambiguity*. The art film is nonclassical in that it foregrounds deviations from the classical norm—there are certain gaps and problems. But these very deviations are *placed*, resituated as realism (in life things happen this way) or authorial commentary (the ambiguity is symbolic). Thus the art film solicits a particular reading procedure: Whenever confronted with a problem in causation, temporality, or spatiality, we first seek realistic motivation. (Is a character's mental state causing the uncertainty? Is life just leaving loose ends?) If we're thwarted, we next seek authorial motivation. (What is being "said" here? What significance justifies the violation of the norm?) Ideally, the film hesitates, suggesting character subjectivity, life's untidiness, and author's vision. Whatever is excessive in one category must belong to another. Uncertainties persist but are understood as such, as *obvious* uncertainties, so to speak. Put crudely, the slogan of the art cinema might be, "When in doubt, read for maximum ambiguity."

The drama of these tendencies can play across an entire film, as *Giulietta degli spiriti* and *Deserto rosso* illustrate. Fellini's film shows how the foregrounding of authorial narration can collapse before the attempt to represent character subjectivity. In the hallucinations of Giulietta, the film surrenders to expressionism. *Deserto rosso* keeps the elements in better balance. Putting aside the island fantasy, we can read any scene's color scheme in two registers simultaneously: as psychological verisimilitude (Giulietta sees her life as a desert) or as authorial commentary (Antonioni-as-narrator says that this industrial landscape is a desert.)

If the organizational scheme of the art film creates the occasion for maximizing ambiguity, how to conclude the film? The solution is the open-ended narrative. Given the film's episodic structure and the minimization of character goals, the story will often lack a clear-cut resolution. Not only is Anna never found, but the ending of *L'Avventura* refuses to specify the fate of the couple. At the close of *Les 400 coups*, the freeze-frame becomes the very figure of narrative irresolution, as does the car halted before the two roads at the end of *Knife in the Water*. At its limit, the art cinema creates an *8½* or a *Persona*, a film which, lacking a causally adequate ending, seems to conclude several distinct times. A banal remark of the 1960s, that such films make you leave the theatre thinking, is not far from the mark: the ambiguity, the play of thematic interpretation, must not be halted at the film's close. Furthermore, the pensive ending acknowledges the author as a peculiarly humble intelligence; s/he knows that life is more complex than art can ever be, and the only way to respect this complexity is to leave causes dangling, questions unanswered. With the open and arbitrary ending, the art film reasserts that ambiguity is the dominant principle of intelligibility, that we are to watch less for the tale than the telling, that life lacks the neatness of art and *this art knows it.*

THE ART CINEMA IN HISTORY

The foregoing sketch of one mode of cinema needs more detailed examination, but in conclusion it may be enough to suggest some avenues for future work.

We cannot construct the art cinema in isolation from other cinematic practices. The art cinema has neighbors on each side, adjacent modes which define it. One such mode is the classical narrative cinema (historically, the dominant mode). There also exists a modernist cinema—that set of formal properties and viewing protocols that presents, above all, the radical split of narrative structure from cinematic style, so that the film constantly strains between the coherence of the fiction and the per-

Vacationers on an island look for a missing friend they will never find in Antonioni's *L'Avventura* (1960). ". . . [T]he art cinema defines itself explicitly against the classical narrative mode, and especially against the cause-effect linkage of events. . . . Whereas the characters of the classical narrative have clear-cut traits and objectives, the characters of the art cinema lack defined desires and goals" (BORDWELL, pp. 650, 651).

ceptual disjunctions of cinematic representation. It is worth mentioning that the modernist cinema is not ambiguous in the sense that the art cinema is; perceptual play, not thematic ambivalence, is the chief viewing strategy. The modernist cinema seems to me manifested (under various circumstances) in films like *October, La Passion de Jeanne d'Arc, Lancelot du lac, Playtime*, and *An Autumn Afternoon*. The art cinema can then be located in relation to such adjacent modes.

We must examine the complex historical relation of the art cinema to the classical narrative cinema. The art film requires the classical background set because deviations from the norm must be registered as such to be placed as realism or authorial expression. Thus the art film acknowledges the classical cinema in many ways, ranging from Antonioni's use of the detective story to explicit citations in New Wave films. Conversely, the art cinema has had an impact on the classical cinema. Just as the Hollywood silent cinema borrowed avant-garde devices but assimilated them to narrative ends, so recent American filmmaking has appropriated art-film devices. Yet such devices are bent to causally motivated functions—the jumpcut for violence or comedy, the sound bridge for continuity or shock effect, the elimination of the dissolve, and the freeze frame for finality. (Compare the narrative resolution of the freeze frame in *Les 400 coups* with its powerful closure in *Butch Cassidy and the Sundance Kid*). More interestingly, we have seen an art cinema emerge in Hollywood. The open endings of *2001* and *Five Easy Pieces* and the psychological ambiguity of *The Conversation, Klute*, and *Three Women* testify to an assimilation of the conventions of the art film. (Simplifying brusquely, we might consider *The Godfather I* as a classical narrative film and *The Godfather II* as more of an art film) Yet if Hollywood is adopting traits of the art cinema, that process must be seen as not simple copying but complex transformation. In particular, American film genres intervene to warp art-cinema conventions in new directions (as the work of Altman and Coppola shows).[9]

It is also possible to see that certain classical filmmakers have had something of the art cinema about them. Sirk, Ford, and Lang all come to mind here, but the preeminent instance is Alfred Hitchcock. Hitchcock has created a textual persona that is in every way equal to that of the art-cinema author's; of all classical films, I would argue, Hitchcock's foreground the narrational process most strikingly. A film like *Psycho* demonstrates how the classical text, with its psychological causality, its protagonist/antagonist struggle, its detective story, and its continuous time and homogeneous space, can under pressure exhibit the very negation of the classical system: psychology as inadequate explanation (the psychiatrist's account); character as only a position, an empty space (the protagonist is successively three characters, the antagonist is initially two, then two-as-one); and crucially stressed shifts in point-of-view which raise the art-film problem of narrational attitude. It may be that the attraction of Hitchcock's cinema for both mass audience and English literature professor lies in its successful merger of classical narrative and art-film narration.

---

[9]See Steve Neale, "New Hollywood Cinema," *Screen* 17, 2 (Summer 1976): 117–22; and Paul Willemen, "Notes on Subjectivity: On Reading Edward Branigan's 'Subjectivity Under Siege,' " *Screen* XIX, 1 (Spring 1978): 59–64; cf. Robin Wood, "Smart-Ass and Cutie Pie: Notes toward an Evaluation of Altman," *Movie*, no. 21 (Autumn 1975): 1–17.

Seen from the other side, the art cinema represents the domestication of modernist filmmaking. The art cinema softened modernism's attack on narrative causality by creating mediating structures—"reality," character subjectivity, authorial vision—that allowed a fresh coherence of meaning. Works of Rossellini, Eisenstein, Renoir, Dreyer, and Ozu have proven assimilable to art-cinema reading strategies: each director has been assigned a distinct authorial world-view. Yet modernist cinema has responded in ways that make the art cinema in its turn, an important point of departure. By the 1960s, the art cinema enabled certain filmmakers to define new possibilities. In *Gertrud*, Dreyer created a perceptual surface so attenuated that all ambiguity drains away, leaving a narrative vacuum.[10] In *L'Année dernière à Marienbad*, Resnais dissolved causality altogether and used the very conventions of art cinema to shatter the premise of character subjectivity. In *Nicht Versöhnt*, Straub and Huillet took the flashback structure and *temps morts* of the art cinema and orchestrated empty intervals into a system irreducible to character psychology or authorial commentary. Nagisha Oshima turned the fantasy-structures and the narrational marks of the New Wave to political-analytical ends in *The Ceremony* and *Death by Hanging*. Most apparently, Godard, one of the figureheads of the 1960s art cinema, had by 1968 begun to question it. (*Deux ou trois choses que je sais d'elle* can be seen as a critique of *Deserto rosso*, or even of *Une femme mariée*). Godard also reintroduced the issue of montage, a process which enabled *Tout va bien* and subsequent works to use Brechtian principles to analyze art-film assumptions about the unity of ideology. If, as some claim, a historical-materialist order of cinema is now appearing, the art cinema must be seen as its necessary background, and its adversary.

1979

---

[10]See David Bordwell, *The Films of Carl Theodor Dreyer* (Berkeley: University of California Press, 1981).

VII
Spectator and Audience

What are the nature and sources of film's psychological and political power? Is there something special about the film medium that confers this power? Is this power repressive or liberating? Can it be criticized and controlled? Questions of this sort have always been asked about cinema, but in recent years film studies have focused on them with unusual intensity. Many of these studies have relied on the Marxist notions of superstructure and ideology and on Freudian ideas about the development and constitution of the self. Writers in this tradition have been committed to exposing the ideological biases of classic narrative film and, in the writings of feminist critics, to revealing its sexist procedures and assumptions. Earlier sections have included essays that apply these perspectives to such perennial issues as the nature of film reality, the film medium, and film genre. In this section the reader will find some of the most arresting writing on the psychological, political, and social bases of film.

In his classic 1936 essay, the Marxist critic Walter Benjamin reflects on alterations in the artistic superstructure that the capitalist mode of production produces. In the past, art works have been unique objects, possessing "aura" and traditional "authority." They played a ritual role, contemplated by men who kept a "natural" distance from them. But contemporary audiences want to see things closer, spatially and humanly. They overcome the uniqueness of the work of art by accepting a mechanical reproduction of it as equivalent. In Benjamin's view, the film and the audience's relation to it are so different from all that has gone before that he is inclined to think that photography has transformed the very nature of art. These reproductions are no longer hallowed cult objects but consumer goods sold on the market; instead of absorbing their beholders, they are absorbed by them. Reactions to these "works of art" are rarely personal and are almost completely determined by the mass audience to which the individual is subordinated. Indeed, films have become one of the most powerful agents of mass political movements—in them the mass has for the first time come face to face with itself.

In the period subsequent to the student uprisings in Paris in 1968, Jean-Luc Comolli and Jean Narboni, then editors of *Cahiers du Cinéma* became central to the discussions represented in this section. They argued that film produced in the West today has two aspects. On the one hand, it is a commodity produced by labor and exchanged according to the laws of the market. On the other hand, it is part of the ideological superstructure determined by the capitalist economic system. One assumption of the prevailing ideological system is that cinema "reproduces" reality but, in fact, it only reproduces the world of the dominant ideology. As Louis Althusser formulates it, ideologies express not the actual relation of human beings to the conditions of their existence, but how they react to those conditions. The film-maker's primary task is, therefore, to expose the cinema's alleged "depiction of reality." If this can be done, there is some chance that we will be able to disrupt and sever the connection between cinema and its ideological function.

Some filmmakers are simply imbued with the dominant ideology and reflect it in both the form and content of their works. The task of the film critic, in these cases, is to exhibit the film's blindness to the ideology it presents. Other films attack their ideological assimilation on two levels. On the level of the signified (plot, context) they engage in direct political action while on the level of the signifier (visual expression, style) they try to break down the traditional way of depicting reality. These levels, which it is the critic's task to display, are indissolubly linked.

Another category of film appears to be completely within the dominant ideology yet can be shown to be ambiguous. John Ford's *Young Mr. Lincoln* is a film of this type and is the subject of a famous analysis by the editors of *Cahiers*. They contend that the film attempts to suppress the realities of politics by presenting Lincoln's career as one based on an idealist morality superior to mere politics. Yet Ford, who is consciously sympathetic to that ideology, nevertheless shows us a Lincoln characterized by a violence that displays his truly repressive character. According to J. P. Oudart this shows the distance Ford, in his "writing," keeps between himself and the idealist propositions he deploys.

If Comolli and Narboni draw on the theories of Marx and Althusser in analysing the situation of the film spectator, Christian Metz, in his later work, extends the investigations of Freud and Lacan. In particular, he appeals to Lacan's conceptions of the imaginary, the symbolic, and the real in understanding the child's changing perception of the world. For Metz the uniqueness of the cinema lies in the duality of its signifier. As a machine of the visible, films give us an unprecedented range of perceptions. Yet at the same time those perceptions are "stamped with unreality to an unusual degree" because we perceive on screen no actual object—because it is really not there—but rather its absence, "its phantom, its double, its *replica* in a new kind of mirror." In the primordial mirror postulated by Lacan, which the mother holds before the child, the child perceives its own image, and its ego is formed by its identification with this likeness. But in the mirror of cinema, from which the spectator is absent, the identification is with perception itself, that is, with the camera.

These passions of cinematic perception—to see and to hear—differ, says Metz, from other sexual drives because they are defined not by a distant but by an absent object. This phenomenon grounds desire in lack and results in an unending pursuit of the imaginary. The voyeurism or scopophilia of the cinematic spectator exists therefore without the direct consent of the object of desire. It more properly resembles the Oedipal situation of the Freudian primal scene, in which the child sees but cannot participate, than it does the exhibitionist and potentially interactive art of theater. The lure of cinema is thus similar to that of the taboo perception of the primal scene, now institutionalized and made socially permissible, but still a peephole opening onto something more crazy and less acceptable than what one does in "normal" life.

One result of this connection to the buried psychology of the cinematic spectator is the fetishizing of the cinematic experience and the disavowal of the actual object of perception in preference for what is associated with it. But because, as Freud argued, fetishism was linked to the fear of castration and the child's belief that the mother has been castrated, the fetish simultaneously attempts to make up for the lack, even as it also affirms the lack—mirroring the dual feeling of presence and absence, belief and disavowal, instilled by the objects seen on film. The concept of the fetish may thus be expanded to cinema itself, and the attraction of its apparatus, its effects, and the exploits of its technical performance, as an expression of the viewer's ability to forget the actual absence and replace it with love.

Metz's psychoanalytic conception of the film viewer emphasizes general human traits, influenced but not crucially determined by gender. (He never, for example, addresses the issue of the relevance of his Oedipal model for women in the audience.) Laura Mulvey, working from similar Freudian and Lacanian assumptions, specifically differentiates the male and the female perspectives in an effort to help explain the pleasure and "unpleasure" offered by narrative film. She argues that narrative film provides what Freud calls "scopophilic" pleasure, the pleasure of viewing another, characteristically a woman, as an erotic object. But narrative film, echoing the experience of the child at Lacan's mirror, also provides the contrasting narcissistic pleasure of identification with the projected images, in particular with that of the male character, who makes things happen and controls them. Woman is, however, also a source of unpleasure since she represents the threat of castration and, in so being, motivates the voyeuristic and fetishistic mechanisms that attempt to circumvent her threat.

Studying these mechanisms in the films of Sternberg and Hitchcock, Mulvey argues that none is intrinsic to film. The male-oriented pleasures of mainstream film can be challenged by breaking down the cinematic codes and the formative external structures that support them. Indeed, radical filmmakers have already begun to undermine the ideologically inspired illusion of three-dimensional space in which the spectator's surrogate performs and in which the look of the spectator is denied intrinsic force. This deconstruction is accomplished by freeing the camera and transforming the scopophilic gaze of the audience into a detached and dialectical one. These changes destroy the pleasures and privilege of the "invisible guest" and highlight the ways film has depended on voyeuristic mechanisms. Women, whose images have continually been stolen and used for this purpose, cannot view the decline of traditional film with anything more than sentimental regret.

Tania Modleski questions Mulvey's claim that Hitchcock's *Rear Window* is cut to the measure of male desire. To be sure, the film seems to confine us to the hero's vision of events and to insist on that vision by stressing his point of view through-out. The film spectator apparently has no choice but to identify with the male pro-tagonist, who exerts an active, controlling gaze over a passive female object. But a closer look at the film calls these assumptions into doubt. The impotence of the immobilized Jeff is suggested by the enormous cast on his leg. By contrast Lisa is anything but helpless and incapable despite Mulvey's characterization of her a "pas-sive image of perfection." Indeed our first view of her is of an overwhelmingly pow-erful, self-assured presence. She is continually shown to be physically superior to the hero, not only in her physical movements but also in her dominance within the frame: she towers over Jeff in nearly every shot in which they both appear. In view of all this, and of Lisa's aggressive sexuality, it seems odd that Mulvey sees in the image of Lisa only a passive object of the male gaze.

For Modleski, the film increasingly stresses a dual point of view. Both Jeff and Lisa intently stare out of the window but from different points of view. Lisa is less interested in spying and relates to characters through empathy and identification. Lisa is able to provide the missing evidence because she claims a special knowl-edge of women that men lack. And at the climatic moment in the film, the scene in which Lisa is flung around the room by Thorwald, Jeff himself—and, by extension the male film viewer—is forced to identify with Lisa. Jeff becomes aware of his own passivity and helplessness in relation to the events unfolding before his eyes. When Thorwald finally attacks Jeff, the "feminization" process is complete and Jeff finds himself in the role previously played by Mrs. Thorwald and then by Lisa—a victim of male violence. Jeff ends up with two broken legs while Lisa has become the mirror image of the man—dressed in masculine clothes and reading a book of male adventure while Jeff sleeps. The film gives her the last look. And we are left with the suspicion that while men sleep and dream their dreams of omnipotence over a safely reduced world, women are hardly locked into the male "view" of them, imprisoned in their master's dollhouse.

Tom Gunning adds a historical perspective to this discussion of film spectator-ship. Referring to, among others, Metz's description of the first silent film audi-ences as terrorized and overcome by its experience of the illusion of film, Gunning criticizes this distinction between the credulous and incredulous aspects of specta-torship along with the "legend" of the naive spectator of early film. He argues instead for an aware audience for whom film was an extension of illusionistic theater. It is an informed amazement at film's power rather than a child's incomprehension that is at work in what Gunning calls this "cinema of attractions," characteristic of the first decade of early film—"an encounter with modernity" in all its fragmentation. The moment of spectacle, then, which Mulvey defines more narrowly as the stop-ping of narrative in order to gaze at the image of woman, thus goes back to the beginning of film's preoccupation with spectacle of many kinds, including today's action films with their grandiose special effects.

Robert Stam and Louise Spence believe that studies of racism and anti-colonial-ism need to make the kind of methodological leap made by feminist criticism when journals like *Screen* and *Camera Obscura* transcended the usefully angry, but methodologically flawed, "image" analysis practiced by such critics as Molly Haskell and Marjorie Rosen. They wish to pose questions concerning the apparatus, the position of the spectator, and the specifically cinematic codes. These studies should apply, as well, to the understanding of other oppressions including sexism, class subordination, and anti-Semitism, indeed, to all situations in which difference is transformed into "other"-ness and exploited or penalized by and for power. The approaches that Stam and Spence wish to supersede tend to focus on issues of social portrayal, plot, and character. While making an invaluable contribution by alerting us to the hostile distortion and affectionate condescension with which the colonized have been treated, these approaches have often been marred by a certain naïveté. They pose legitimate questions concerning narrative plausibility and mimetic accuracy, negative stereotypes and positive images, but their emphasis on realism had often betrayed an exaggerated faith in the possibilities of verisimilitude in art in general and cinema in particular, avoiding the fact that films are inevitably constructs, fabrications, representations. It is important, therefore, that we pay attention to the mediations which intervene between "reality" and representation. The emphasis should be on narrative structure, genre convention, and cinematic style rather than on perfect correctness of representation or fidelity to an original "real" model or prototype.

One important mediation specific to cinema is spectator positioning. Stam and Spence cite Tom Engelhardt's point that the paradigmatic filmic encounters between whites and Indians in the western typically involve images of encirclement. The attitude toward the Indian is premised on exteriority. The besieged wagon train or fort is the focus of our attention and sympathy, and from this center our familiars sally out against unknown attackers characterized by inexplicable customs and irrational hostility. The possibility of sympathetic identifications with the Indians is simply ruled out by the point-of-view conventions. The spectator is unwittingly sutured into a colonialist perspective. But such techniques are not inevitably colonialist in their operation. One of the innovations of Gillo Pontocorvo's *Battle of Algiers* (1966) is to invert the imagery of encirclement and exploit the identificatory mechanisms of cinema on behalf of the colonized rather than the colonizer. It is from within the casbah that we see and hear the French troops and helicopters. This time it is the colonized who are encircled and menaced and with whom we identify. The sequence in which three Algerian women dress in European style in order to pass the French checkpoints is particularly effective in controverting traditional patterns through the mechanisms of cinematic identification: scale (close shots individualize the three women); off-screen sound (we hear the sexist comments as if from the women's aural perspective); and especially point-of-view editing. By the time the women plant the bombs, our identification is so complete that we are less disturbed by a series of close shots of the bombs' potential victims.

Stam and Spence argue that we must allow, therefore, for the possibility of aberrant readings, readings that go against the grain of the discourse. Although fiction films are agents of persuasion designed to produce specific impressions and emotions, they are not all-powerful, and they may be read differently by different audiences. Hollywood's ill-informed portrayals of Latin American life were often laughed off the screen within Latin America itself, and black Americans, presumably, never took Stepin Fetchit to be an accurate representation of their race as a whole. We must be aware, too, of the institutionalized expectations, the mental machinery, that serve as the subjective support to the film industry and that lead us to prize films with high production values. But many Third World filmmakers find such a model, if not repugnant, at least inappropriate—not only because of their critique of dominant cinema, but also because the Third World, with its scarcer capital and higher costs, simply cannot afford it. To expect to find First World production values in Third World films is to be both naive and ethnocentric. The objective of the study of filmic colonialism and racism is, finally, not to hurl charges of racism at individual filmmakers or critics. Rather, is to learn how to decode and deconstruct racist images and sounds. Racism is not permanently inscribed in celluloid or in the human mind; it forms part of a constantly changing dialectical process within which, we must never forget, we are far from powerless.

Manthia Diawara focuses the discussion of film spectatorship on black spectatorship in particular. As Mulvey argued that the classical Hollywood film is made for the pleasure of the male spectator, Diawara argues that the dominant cinema situates black characters primarily for the pleasure of white spectators (male or female). In response, and using examples from *The Birth of a Nation* and *The Color Purple*, Diawara develops the concept of what he calls "resisting" spectatorship. On this approach the film's presentation of characters and events can be read by its audience in a way that complicates and even contradicts what seem to be its basic intentions. Thus, the resisting spectator rejects the representation of the Little Colonel in *The Birth of a Nation* as an authoritative figure as well as the narrative proposition that lynching is a means of restoring the racial and symbolic order of the South. Yet the question of how some black spectators identify with the representation of blacks in dominant cinema remains to be explored. However that may be, resisting spectators are transforming the problem of passive identification into active criticism that both informs and interrelates with contemporary oppositional filmmaking. Black directors like Charles Barnett practice a "cinema of the real" in which there is no manipulation of the look to bring the spectator to a passive state of uncritical identification. This type of film constructs a critical position for the spectator in relation to the "real" and its representation. Other directors use a mixed form of fiction and documentary in which the documentary element serves to deconstruct the illusion created by the fiction and makes the spectator question the representation of "reality" through the contrast of the different modes. As more audiences discover such independent black films, spectator resistance to Hollywood's figuration of blacks will become increasingly focused and sharpened.

WALTER BENJAMIN
THE WORK OF ART IN THE AGE OF MECHANICAL REPRODUCTION

Born in Berlin, Walter Benjamin earned a degree in philosophy but was unable to obtain a university position and began writing for newspapers, translating and publishing both fiction and literary criticism until fleeing to Paris in 1933 when the Nazis took over the German government. Over the years he was a friend of, and influenced by, such disparate writers and thinkers as Georg Lukács, Bertholt Brecht, Theodor Adorno, and Gershon Scholem, the scholar of Jewish mysticism. In Paris, he wrote radio scripts and essays on art, culture, literature, and film for a number of journals including the *Zeitschrift für Sozialforschung* of the Institute for Social Research, headed by Theodor Adorno and Max Horkheimer, in which "The Work of Art in the Age of Mechanical Reproduction" appeared in 1936. Just before Paris was occupied by the Germans, Benjamin escaped to Spain with a small group of refugees. Detained at the border, Benjamin took his own life with an overdose of morphine. The rest of the group was able to cross the following day. His massive work, *The Arcades Project*, an assemblage in his "mosaic technique" of found language and socio-cultural analysis of the walking arcades of Paris, remained unfinished at his death.

Our fine arts were developed, their types and uses were established, in times very different from the present, by men whose power of action upon things was insignificant in comparison with ours. But the amazing growth of our techniques, the adaptability and precision they have attained, the ideas and habits they are creating, make it a certainty that profound changes are impending in the ancient craft of the Beautiful. In all the arts there is a physical component which can no longer be considered or treated as it used to be, which cannot remain unaffected by our modern knowledge and power. For the last twenty years neither matter nor space nor time has been what it was from time immemorial. We must expect great innovations to transform the entire technique of the arts, thereby affecting artistic invention itself and perhaps even bringing about an amazing change in our very notion of art.

PAUL VALÉRY, *Pièces sur l'art*,
"La Conquète de l'ubiquité," Paris

PREFACE

When Marx undertook his critique of the capitalistic mode of production, this mode was in its infancy. Marx directed his efforts in such a way as to give them prognostic value. He went back to the basic conditions underlying capitalistic production and through his presentation showed what could be expected of capitalism in the future. The result was that one could expect it not only to exploit the proletariat with increasing intensity, but ultimately to create conditions which would make it possible to abolish capitalism itself.

The transformation of the superstructure, which takes place far more slowly than that of the substructure, has taken more than half a century to manifest in all areas of culture the change in the conditions of production. Only today can it be indicated what form this has taken. Certain prognostic requirements should be met by these statements. However, theses about the art of the proletariat after its assumption of power or about the art of a classless society would have less bearing on these demands than theses about the developmental tendencies of art under present conditions of production. Their dialectic is no less noticeable in the superstructure than in the economy. It would therefore be wrong to underestimate the value of such theses as a weapon. They brush aside a number of outmoded concepts, such as creativity and genius, eternal value and mystery—concepts whose uncontrolled (and at present almost uncontrollable) application would lead to a processing of data in the Fascist sense. The concepts which are introduced into the theory of art in what follows differ from the more familiar terms in that they are completely useless for the purposes of Fascism. They are, on the other hand, useful for the formulation of revolutionary demands in the politics of art.

I

In principle a work of art has always been reproducible. Man-made artifacts could always be imitated by men. Replicas were made by pupils in practice of their craft, by masters for diffusing their works, and, finally, by third parties in the pursuit of gain. Mechanical reproduction of a work of art, however, represents something new. Historically, it advanced intermittently and in leaps at long intervals, but with accelerated intensity. The Greeks knew only two procedures of technically reproducing works of art: founding and stamping. Bronzes, terra cottas, and coins were the only art works which they could produce in quantity. All others were unique and could not be mechanically reproduced. With the woodcut graphic art became mechanically reproducible for the first time, long before script became reproducible by print. The enormous changes which printing, the mechanical reproduction of writing, has brought about in literature are a familiar story. However, within the phenomenon which we are here examining from the perspective of world history, print is merely a special, though particularly important, case. During the Middle Ages engraving and etching were added to the woodcut; at the beginning of the nineteenth century lithography made its appearance.

With lithography the technique of reproduction reached an essentially new stage. This much more direct process was distinguished by the tracing of the design on a stone rather than its incision on a block of wood or its etching on a copperplate and permitted graphic art for the first time to put its products on the market, not only in large numbers as hitherto, but also in daily changing forms. Lithography enabled graphic art to illustrate everyday life, and it began to keep pace with printing. But only a few decades after its invention, lithography was surpassed by photography. For the first time in the process of pictorial reproduction, photography freed the hand of the most important artistic functions which henceforth devolved only upon the eye looking into a lens. Since the eye perceives more swiftly than the hand can draw, the process of pictorial reproduction was accelerated so enormously that it could keep pace with speech. A film operator shooting a scene in the studio captures the images at the speed of an actor's speech. Just as lithography virtually implied the illustrated newspaper, so did photography foreshadow the sound film. The technical reproduction of sound was tackled at the end of the last century. These convergent endeavors made predictable a situation which Paul Valéry pointed up in this sentence: "Just as water, gas, and electricity are brought into our houses from far off to satisfy our needs in response to a minimal effort, so we shall be supplied with visual or auditory images, which will appear and disappear at a simple movement of the hand, hardly more than a sign." Around 1900 technical reproduction had reached a standard that not only permitted it to reproduce all transmitted works of art and thus to cause the most profound change in their impact upon the public; it also had captured a place of its own among the artistic processes. For the study of this standard nothing is more revealing than the nature of the repercussions that these two different manifestations—the reproduction of works of art and the art of the film—have had on art in its traditional form.

II

Even the most perfect reproduction of a work of art is lacking in one element: its presence in time and space, its unique existence at the place where it happens to be. This unique existence of the work of art determined the history to which it was subject throughout the time of its existence. This includes the changes which it may have suffered in physical condition over the years as well as the various changes in its ownership.[1] The traces of the first can be revealed only by chemical or physical analyses which it is impossible to perform on a reproduction; changes of ownership are subject to a tradition which must be traced from the situation of the original.

The presence of the original is the prerequisite to the concept of authenticity. Chemical analyses of the patina of a bronze can help to establish this, as does the proof that a given manuscript of the Middle Ages stems from an archive of the fifteenth century. The whole sphere of authenticity is outside technical—and, of course, not only technical—reproducibility.[2] Confronted with its manual reproduction, which was usually branded as a forgery, the original preserved all its authority; not so vis-à-vis technical reproduction. The reason is twofold. First, process reproduction is more independent of the original than manual reproduction. For example, in photography, process reproduction can bring out those aspects of the original that are unattainable

---

[1]Of course, the history of a work of art encompasses more than this. The history of the "Mona Lisa," for instance, encompasses the kind and number of its copies made in the seventeenth, eighteenth, and nineteenth centuries.

[2]Precisely because authenticity is not reproducible, the intensive penetration of certain (mechanical) processes of reproduction was instrumental in differentiating and grading authenticity. To develop such differentiations was an important function of the trade in works of art. The invention of the woodcut may be said to have struck at the root of the quality of authenticity even before its late flowering. To be sure, at the time of its origin a medieval picture of the Madonna could not yet be said to be "authentic." It became "authentic" only during the succeeding centuries and perhaps most strikingly so during the last one.

to the naked eye yet accessible to the lens, which is adjustable and chooses its angle at will. And photographic reproduction, with the aid of certain processes, such as enlargement or slow motion, can capture images which escape natural vision. Secondly, technical reproduction can put the copy of the original into situations which would be out of reach for the original itself. Above all, it enables the original to meet the beholder halfway, be it in the form of a photograph or a phonograph record. The cathedral leaves its locale to be received in the studio of a lover of art; the choral production, performed in an auditorium or in the open air, resounds in the drawing room.

The situations into which the product of mechanical reproduction can be brought may not touch the actual work of art, yet the quality of its presence is always depreciated. This holds not only for the art work but also, for instance, for a landscape which passes in review before the spectator in a movie. In the case of the art object, a most sensitive nucleus—namely, its authenticity—is interfered with whereas no natural object is vulnerable on that score. The authenticity of a thing is the essence of all that is transmissible from its beginning, ranging from its substantive duration to its testimony to the history which it has experienced. Since the historical testimony rests on the authenticity, the former, too, is jeopardized by reproduction when substantive duration ceases to matter. And what is really jeopardized when the historical testimony is affected is the authority of the object.[3]

One might subsume the eliminated element in the term "aura" and go on to say: that which withers in the age of mechanical reproduction is the aura of the work of art. This is a symptomatic process whose significance points beyond the realm of art. One might generalize by saying: the technique of reproduction detaches the reproduced object from the domain of tradition. By making many reproductions it substitutes a plurality of copies for a unique existence. And in permitting the reproduction to meet the beholder or listener in his own particular situation, it reactivates the object reproduced. These two processes lead to a tremendous shattering of tradition which is the obverse of the contemporary crisis and renewal of mankind. Both processes are intimately connected with the contemporary mass movements. Their most powerful agent is the film. Its social significance, particularly in its most positive form, is inconceivable without its destructive, cathartic aspect, that is, the liquidation of the traditional value of the cultural heritage. This phenomenon is most palpable in the great historical films. It extends to ever new positions. In 1927 Abel Gance exclaimed enthusiastically: "Shakespeare, Rembrandt, Beethoven will make films . . . all legends, all mythologies and all myths, all founders of religion, and the very religions . . . await their exposed resurrection, and the heroes crowd each other at the gate." Presumably without intending it, he issued an invitation to a far-reaching liquidation.

III

During long periods of history, the mode of human sense perception changes with humanity's entire mode of existence. The manner in which human sense perception is

---

[3]The poorest provincial staging of *Faust* is superior to a Faust film in that, ideally, it competes with the first performance at Weimar. Before the screen it is unprofitable to remember traditional contents which might come to mind before the stage—for instance, that Goethe's friend Johann Heinrich Merck is hidden in Mephisto, and the like.

organized, the medium in which it is accomplished, is determined not only by nature but by historical circumstances as well. The fifth century, with its great shifts of population, saw the birth of the late Roman art industry and the Vienna Genesis, and there developed not only an art different from that of antiquity but also a new kind of perception. The scholars of the Viennese school, Riegl and Wickhoff, who resisted the weight of classical tradition under which these later art forms had been buried, were the first to draw conclusions from them concerning the organization of perception at the time. However far-reaching their insight, these scholars limited themselves to showing the significant, formal hallmark which characterized perception in late Roman times. They did not attempt—and, perhaps, saw no way—to show the social transformations expressed by these changes of perception. The conditions for an analogous insight are more favorable in the present. And if changes in the medium of contemporary perception can be comprehended as decay of the aura, it is possible to show its social causes.

The concept of aura which was proposed above with reference to historical objects may usefully be illustrated with reference to the aura of natural ones. We define the aura as the unique appearance of a distance, however close it may be. If, while resting on a summer afternoon, you follow with your eyes a mountain range on the horizon or a branch which casts its shadow over you, you experience the aura of those mountains, of that branch. This image makes it easy to comprehend the social bases of the contemporary decay of the aura. It rests on two circumstances, both of which are related to the increasing significance of the masses in contemporary life. Namely, the desire of contemporary masses to bring things "closer" spatially and humanly, which is just as ardent as their bent toward overcoming the uniqueness of every reality by accepting its reproduction. Every day the urge grows stronger to get hold of an object at very close range by way of its image, or, rather, its copy.[4] Unmistakably, reproduction as offered by picture magazines and newsreels differs from the image seen by the unarmed eye. Uniqueness and permanence are as closely linked in the latter as are transitoriness and reproducibility in the former. To pry an object from its shell, to destroy its aura, is the mark of a perception whose "sense of the universal equality of things" has increased to such a degree that it extracts it even from a unique object by means of reproduction. Thus is manifested in the field of perception what in the theoretical sphere is noticeable in the increasing importance of statistics. The adjustment of reality to the masses and of the masses to reality is a process of unlimited scope, as much for thinking as for perception.

IV

The uniqueness of a work of art is inseparable from its being imbedded in the fabric of tradition. This tradition itself is thoroughly alive and extremely changeable. An ancient statue of Venus, for example, stood in a different traditional context with the Greeks, who made it an object of veneration, than with the clerics of the Middle Ages,

---

[4]To satisfy the human interest of the masses may mean to have one's social function removed from the field of vision. Nothing guarantees that a portraitist of today, when painting a famous surgeon at the breakfast table in the midst of his family, depicts his social function more precisely than a painter of the seventeenth century who portrayed his medical doctors as representing this profession, like Rembrandt in his "Anatomy Lesson."

who viewed it as an ominous idol. Both of them, however, were equally confronted with its uniqueness, that is, its aura. Originally the contextual integration of art in tradition found its expression in the cult. We know that the earliest art works originated in the service of a ritual—first the magical, then the religious kind. It is significant that the existence of the work of art with reference to its aura is never entirely separated from its ritual function.[5] In other words, the unique value of the "authentic" work of art has its basis in ritual, the location of its original use value. This ritualistic basis, however remote, is still recognizable as secularized ritual even in the most profane forms of the cult of beauty.[6] The secular cult of beauty, developed during the Renaissance and prevailing for three centuries, clearly showed that ritualistic basis in its decline and the first deep crisis which befell it. With the advent of the first truly revolutionary means of reproduction, photography, simultaneously with the rise of socialism, art sensed the approaching crisis which has become evident a century later. At the time, art reacted with the doctrine of *l'art pour l'art*, that is, with a theology of art. This gave rise to what might be called a negative theology in the form of the idea of "pure" art, which not only denied any social function of art but also any categorizing by subject matter. (In poetry, Mallarmé was the first to take this position.)

An analysis of art in the age of mechanical reproduction must do justice to these relationships, for they lead us to an all-important insight: for the first time in world history, mechanical reproduction emancipates the work of art from its parasitical dependence on ritual. To an ever greater degree the work of art reproduced becomes the work of art designed for reproducibility.[7] From a photographic negative, for

---

[5]The definition of the aura as a "unique phenomenon of a distance however close it may be" represents nothing but the formulation of the cult value of the work of art in categories of space and time perception. Distance is the opposite of closeness. The essentially distant object is the unapproachable one. Unapproachability is indeed a major quality of the cult image. True to its nature, it remains "distant, however close it may be." The closeness which one may gain from its subject matter does not impair the distance which it retains in its appearance.

[6]To the extent to which the cult value of the painting is secularized the ideas of its fundamental uniqueness lose distinctness. In the imagination of the beholder the uniqueness of the phenomena which hold sway in the cult image is more and more displaced by the empirical uniqueness of the creator or of his creative achievement. To be sure, never completely so; the concept of authenticity always transcends mere genuineness. (This is particularly apparent in the collector who always retains some traces of the fetishist and who, by owning the work of art, shares in its ritual power.) Nevertheless, the function of the concept of authenticity remains determinate in the evaluation of art; with the secularization of art, authenticity displaces the cult value of the work.

[7]In the case of films, mechanical reproduction is not, as with literature and painting, an external condition for mass distribution. Mechanical reproduction is inherent in the very technique of film production. This technique not only permits in the most direct way but virtually causes mass distribution. It enforces distribution because the production of a film is so expensive that an individual who, for instance, might afford to buy a painting no longer can afford to buy a film. In 1927 it was calculated that a major film, in order to pay its way, had to reach an audience of nine million. With the sound film, to be sure, a setback in its international distribution occurred at first: audiences became limited by language barriers. This coincided with the Fascist emphasis on national interests. It is more important to focus on this connection with Fascism than on this setback, which was soon minimized by synchronization. The simultaneity of both phenomena is attributable to the Depression. The same disturbances which, on a larger scale, led to an attempt to maintain the existing property structure by sheer force led the endangered film capital to speed up the development of the sound film. The introduction of the sound film brought about a temporary relief, not only because it again brought the masses into the theaters but also because it merged new capital from the electrical industry with that of the film industry. Thus, viewed from the outside, the sound film promoted national interests, but seen from the inside it helped to internationalize film production even more than previously.

example, one can make any number of prints; to ask for the "authentic" print makes no sense. But the instant the criterion of authenticity ceases to be applicable to artistic production, the total function of art is reversed. Instead of being based on ritual, it begins to be based on another practice—politics.

V

Works of art are received and valued on different planes. Two polar types stand out: with one, the accent is on the cult value; with the other, on the exhibition value of the work.[8] Artistic production begins with ceremonial objects destined to serve in a cult. One may assume that what mattered was their existence, not their being on view. The elk portrayed by the man of the Stone Age on the walls of his cave was an instrument of magic. He did expose it to his fellow men, but in the main it was meant for the spirits. Today the cult value would seem to demand that the work of art remain hidden. Certain statues of gods are accessible only to the priest in the cella; certain Madonnas remain covered nearly all year round; certain sculptures on medieval cathedrals are invisible to the spectator on ground level. With the emancipation of the various art practices from ritual go increasing opportunities for the exhibition of their products. It is easier to exhibit a portrait bust that can be sent here and there than to exhibit the statue of a divinity that has its fixed place in the interior of a temple. The same holds for the painting as against the mosaic or fresco

---

[8]This polarity cannot come into its own in the aesthetics of Idealism. Its idea of beauty comprises these polar opposites without differentiating between them and consequently excludes their polarity. Yet in Hegel this polarity announces itself as clearly as possible within the limits of Idealism. We quote from his *Philosophy of History*:

Images were known of old. Piety at an early time required them for worship, but it could do without *beautiful* images. These might even be disturbing. In every beautiful painting there is also something nonspiritual, merely external, but its spirit speaks to man through its beauty. Worshipping, conversely, is concerned with the work as an object, for it is but a spiritless stupor of the soul.... Fine art has arisen ... in the church ..., although it has already gone beyond its principle as art.

Likewise, the following passage from *The Philosophy of Fine Art* indicates that Hegel sensed a problem here.

We are beyond the stage of reverence for works of art as divine and objects deserving our worship. The impression they produce is one of a more reflective kind, and the emotions they arouse require a higher test.....—G. W. F. Hegel, *The Philosophy of Fine Art*, trans., with notes, by F. P. B. Osmaston, Vol. 1, p. 12, London, 1920.

The transition from the first kind of artistic reception to the second characterizes the history of artistic reception in general. Apart from that, a certain oscillation between these two polar modes of reception can be demonstrated for each work of art. Take the Sistine Madonna. Since Hubert Grimme's research it has been known that the Madonna originally was painted for the purpose of exhibition. Grimme's research was inspired by the question: What is the purpose of the molding in the foreground of the painting which the two cupids lean upon? How, Grimme asked further, did Raphael come to furnish the sky with two draperies? Research proved that the Madonna had been commissioned for the public lying-in-state of Pope Sixtus. The Popes lay in state in a certain side chapel of St. Peter's. On that occasion Raphael's picture had been fastened in a nichelike background of the chapel, supported by the coffin. In this picture Raphael portrays the Madonna approaching the papal coffin in clouds from the background of the niche, which was demarcated by green drapes. At the obsequies of Sixtus a preeminent exhibition value of Raphael's picture was taken advantage of. Some time later it was placed on the high altar in the church of the Black Friars at Piacenza. The reason for this exile is to be found in the Roman rites which forbid the use of paintings exhibited at obsequies as cult objects on the high altar. This regulation devalued Raphael's picture to some degree. In order to obtain an adequate price nevertheless, the Papal See resolved to add to the bargain the tacit toleration of the picture above the high altar. To avoid attention the picture was given to the monks of the far-off provincial town.

that preceded it. And even though the public presentability of a mass originally may have been just as great as that of a symphony, the latter originated at the moment when its public presentability promised to surpass that of the mass.

With the different methods of technical reproduction of a work of art, its fitness for exhibition increased to such an extent that the quantitative shift between its two poles turned into a qualitative transformation of its nature. This is comparable to the situation of the work of art in prehistoric times when, by the absolute emphasis on its cult value, it was, first and foremost, an instrument of magic. Only later did it come to be recognized as a work of art. In the same way today, by the absolute emphasis on its exhibition value the work of art becomes a creation with entirely new functions, among which the one we are conscious of, the artistic function, later may be recognized as incidental.[9] This much is certain: today photography and the film are the most serviceable exemplifications of this new function.

VI

In photography, exhibition value begins to displace cult value all along the line. But cult value does not give way without resistance. It retires into an ultimate retrenchment: the human countenance. It is no accident that the portrait was the focal point of early photography. The cult of remembrance of loved ones, absent or dead, offers a last refuse for the cult value of the picture. For the last time the aura emanates from the early photographs in the fleeting expression of a human face. This is what constitutes their melancholy, incomparable beauty. But as man withdraws from the photographic image, the exhibition value for the first time shows its superiority to the ritual value. To have pinpointed this new stage constitutes the incomparable significance of Atget, who, around 1900, took photographs of deserted Paris streets. It has quite justly been said of him that he photographed them like scenes of crime. The scene of a crime, too, is deserted; it is photographed for the purpose of establishing evidence. With Atget, photographs become standard evidence for historical occurrences, and acquire a hidden political significance. They demand a specific kind of approach; free-floating contemplation is not appropriate to them. They stir the viewer; he feels challenged by them in a new way. At the same time picture magazines begin to put up signposts for him, right ones or wrong ones, no matter. For the first time, captions have become obligatory. And it is clear that they have an altogether different character than the title of a painting. The directives which the captions give to those looking at pictures in illustrated magazines soon become even more explicit and more imperative in the film where the meaning of each single picture appears to be prescribed by the sequence of all preceding ones.

---

[9]Bertolt Brecht, on a different level, engaged in analogous reflections: "If the concept of 'work of art' can no longer be applied to the thing that emerges once the work is transformed into a commodity, we have to eliminate this concept with cautious care but without fear, lest we liquidate the function of the very thing as well. For it has to go through this phase without mental reservation, and not as noncommittal deviation from the straight path; rather, what happens here with the work of art will change it fundamentally and erase its past to such an extent that should the old concept be taken up again—and it will, why not?—it will no longer stir any memory of the thing it once designated."

VII

The nineteenth-century dispute as to the artistic value of painting versus photography today seems devious and confused. This does not diminish its importance, however; if anything, it underlines it. The dispute was in fact the symptom of a historical transformation the universal impact of which was not realized by either of the rivals. When the age of mechanical reproduction separated art from its basis in cult, the semblance of its autonomy disappeared forever. The resulting change in the function of art transcended the perspective of the century; for a long time it even escaped that of the twentieth century, which experienced the development of the film.

Earlier much futile thought had been devoted to the question of whether photography is an art. The primary question—whether the very invention of photography had not transformed the entire nature of art—was not raised. Soon the film theoreticians asked the same ill-considered question with regard to the film. But the difficulties which photography caused traditional aesthetics were mere child's play as compared to those raised by the film. Whence the insensitive and forced character of early theories of the film. Abel Gance, for instance, compares the film with hieroglyphs: "Here, by a remarkable regression, we have come back to the level of expression of the Egyptians. . . . Pictorial language has not yet matured because our eyes have not yet adjusted to it. There is as yet insufficient respect for, insufficient cult of, what it expresses." Or, in the words of Séverin-Mars: "What art has been granted a dream more poetical and more real at the same time! Approached in this fashion the film might represent an incomparable means of expression. Only the most high-minded persons, in the most perfect and mysterious moments of their lives, should be allowed to enter its ambience." Alexandre Arnoux concludes his fantasy about the silent film with the question: "Do not all the bold descriptions we have given amount to the definition of prayer?" It is instructive to note how their desire to class the film among the "arts" forces these theoreticians to read ritual elements into it—with a striking lack of discretion. Yet when these speculations were published, films like *L'Opinion publique* and *The Gold Rush* had already appeared. This, however, did not keep Abel Gance from adducing hieroglyphs for purposes of comparison, nor Séverin-Mars from speaking of the film as one might speak of paintings by Fra Angelico. Characteristically, even today ultrareactionary authors give the film a similar contextual significance—if not an outright sacred one, then at least a supernatural one. Commenting on Max Reinhardt's film version of *A Midsummer Night's Dream*, Werfel states that undoubtedly it was the sterile copying of the exterior world with its streets, interiors, railroad stations, restaurants, motorcars, and beaches which until now had obstructed the elevation of the film to the realm of art. "The film has not yet realized its true meaning, its real possibilities . . . these consist in its unique faculty to express by natural means and with incomparable persuasiveness all that is fairylike, marvelous, supernatural."

VIII

The artistic performance of a stage actor is definitely presented to the public by the actor in person; that of the screen actor, however, is presented by a camera, with a twofold consequence. The camera that presents the performance of the film actor to the public need not respect the performance as an integral whole. Guided by the cameraman, the camera continually changes its position with respect to the performance. The sequence of positional views which the editor composes from the material supplied him constitutes the completed film. It comprises certain factors of movement which are in reality those of the camera, not to mention special camera angles, close-ups, etc. Hence, the performance of the actor is subjected to a series of optical tests. This is the first consequence of the fact that the actor's performance is presented by means of a camera. Also, the film actor lacks the opportunity of the stage actor to adjust to the audience during his performance, since he does not present his performance to the audience in person. This permits the audience to take the position of a critic, without experiencing any personal contact with the actor. The audience's identification with the actor is really an identification with the camera. Consequently the audience takes the position of the camera; its approach is that of testing.[10] This is not the approach to which cult values may be exposed.

IX

For the film, what matters primarily is that the actor represents himself to the public before the camera, rather than representing someone else. One of the first to sense the actor's metamorphosis by this form of testing was Pirandello. Though his remarks on the subject in his novel *Si Gira* were limited to the negative aspects of the question and to the silent film only, this hardly impairs their validity. For in this respect, the sound film did not change anything essential. What matters is that the part is acted not for an audience but for a mechanical contrivance—in the case of the sound film, for two of them. "The film actor," wrote Pirandello, "feels as if in exile—exiled not only from the stage but also from himself. With a vague sense of discomfort he feels inexplicable emptiness: his body loses its corporeality, it evaporates, it is deprived of reality, life, voice, and the noises caused by his moving about, in order to be changed into a mute image, flickering an instant on the screen, then vanishing into silence. . . . The projector will play with his shadow before the public, and he himself must be content to play before the camera." This situation might also be characterized as follows: for the first time—and this is the effect of the film—man has to operate with his whole living person, yet forgoing its aura. For aura is tied to his presence; there can be no replica of it. The aura which, on the stage, emanates from Macbeth, cannot be separated for the spectators from that of the actor. However, the singularity of the shot in the studio is that the camera is substituted for the public. Consequently, the aura that envelops the actor vanishes, and with it the aura of the figure he portrays.

---

[10]"The film . . . provides—or could provide—useful insight into the details of human actions. . . . Character is never used as a source of motivation; the inner life of the persons never supplies the principal cause of the plot and seldom is its main result." (Bertolt Brecht, *Versuche*, "Der Dreigroschenprozess," p. 268.) The expansion of the field of the testable which mechanical equipment brings about for the actor corresponds to the extraordinary expansion of the field of the testable brought about for the individual through economic conditions. Thus, vocational aptitude tests become constantly more important. What matters in these tests are segmental performances of the individual. The film shot and the vocational aptitude test are taken before a committee of experts. The camera director in the studio occupies a place identical with that of the examiner during aptitude tests.

It is not surprising that it should be a dramatist such as Pirandello who, in characterizing the film, inadvertently touches on the very crisis in which we see the theater. Any thorough study proves that there is indeed no greater contrast than that of the stage play to a work of art that is completely subject to or, like the film, founded in, mechanical reproduction. Experts have long recognized that in the film "the greatest effects are almost always obtained by 'acting' as little as possible. . . ." In 1932 Rudolf Arnheim saw "the latest trend . . . in treating the actor as a stage prop chosen for its characteristics and . . . inserted at the proper place."[11] With this idea something else is closely connected. The stage actor identifies himself with the character of his role. The film actor very often is denied this opportunity. His creation is by no means all of a piece; it is composed of many separate performances. Besides certain fortuitous considerations, such as cost of studio, availability of fellow players, décor, etc., there are elementary necessities of equipment that split the actor's work into a series of mountable episodes. In particular, lighting and its installation require the presentation of an event that, on the screen, unfolds as a rapid and unified scene, in a sequence of separate shootings which may take hours at the studio; not to mention more obvious montage. Thus a jump from the window can be shot in the studio as a jump from a scaffold, and the ensuing flight, if need be, can be shot weeks later when outdoor scenes are taken. Far more paradoxical cases can easily be construed. Let us assume that an actor is supposed to be startled by a knock at the door. If his reaction is not satisfactory, the director can resort to an expedient: when the actor happens to be at the studio again he has a shot fired behind him without his being forewarned of it. The frightened reaction can be shot now and be cut into the screen version. Nothing more strikingly shows that art has left the realm of the "beautiful semblance" which, so far, had been taken to be the only sphere where art could thrive.

X

The feeling of strangeness that overcomes the actor before the camera, as Pirandello describes it, is basically of the same kind as the estrangement felt before one's own image in the mirror. But now the reflected image has become separable, transportable.

---

[11]Rudolf Arnheim, *Film als Kunst*, Berlin, 1932, pp. 176 f. In this context certain seemingly unimportant details in which the film director deviates from stage practices gain in interest. Such is the attempt to let the actor play without make-up, as made among others by Dreyer in his *Jeanne d'Arc*. Dreyer spent months seeking the forty actors who constitute the Inquisitors' tribunal. The search for these actors resembled that for stage properties that are hard to come by. Dreyer made every effort to avoid resemblances of age, build, and physiognomy. If the actor thus becomes a stage property, this latter, on the other hand, frequently functions as actor. At least it is not unusual for the film to assign a role to the stage property. Instead of choosing at random from a great wealth of examples, let us concentrate on a particularly convincing one. A clock that is working will always be a disturbance on the stage. There it cannot be permitted its function of measuring time. Even in a naturalistic play, astronomical time would clash with theatrical time. Under these circumstances it is highly revealing that the film can, whenever appropriate, use time as measured by a clock. From this more than from many other touches it may clearly be recognized that under certain circumstances each and every prop in a film may assume important functions. From here it is but one step to Pudovkin's statement that "the playing of an actor which is connected with an object and is built around it . . . is always one of the strongest methods of cinematic construction." (W. Pudovkin, *Filmregie und Filmmanuskript*, Berlin, 1928, p. 126.) The film is the first art form capable of demonstrating how matter plays tricks on man. Hence, films can be an excellent means of materialistic representation.

And where is it transported? Before the public.[12] Never for a moment does the screen actor cease to be conscious of this fact. While facing the camera he knows that ultimately he will face the public, the consumers who constitute the market. This market, where he offers not only his labor but also his whole self, his heart and soul, is beyond his reach. During the shooting he has as little contact with it as any article made in a factory. This may contribute to that oppression, that new anxiety which, according to Pirandello, grips the actor before the camera. The film responds to the shriveling of the aura with an artificial build-up of the "personality" outside the studio. The cult of the movie star, fostered by the money of the film industry, preserves not the unique aura of the person but the "spell of the personality," the phony spell of a commodity. So long as the movie-makers' capital sets the fashion, as a rule no other revolutionary merit can be accredited to today's film than the promotion of a revolutionary criticism of traditional concepts of art. We do not deny that in some cases today's films can also promote revolutionary criticism of social conditions, even of the distribution of property. However, our present study is no more specifically concerned with this than is the film production of Western Europe.

It is inherent in the technique of the film as well as that of sports that everybody who witnesses its accomplishments is somewhat of an expert. This is obvious to anyone listening to a group of newspaper boys leaning on their bicycles and discussing the outcome of a bicycle race. It is not for nothing that newspaper publishers arrange races for their delivery boys. These arouse great interest among the participants, for the victor has an opportunity to rise from delivery boy to professional racer. Similarly, the newsreel offers everyone the opportunity to rise from passer-by to movie extra. In this way any man might even find himself part of a work of art, as witness Vertoff's *Three Songs About Lenin* or Ivens' *Borinage*. Any man today can lay claim to being filmed. This claim can best be elucidated by a comparative look at the historical situation of contemporary literature.

For centuries a small number of writers were confronted by many thousands of readers. This changed toward the end of the last century. With the increasing extension of the press, which kept placing new political, religious, scientific, professional, and local organs before the readers, an increasing number of readers became writers—at first, occasional ones. It began with the daily press opening to its readers space for "letters to the editor." And today there is hardly a gainfully employed European who could not, in principle, find an opportunity to publish somewhere or other comments on his work, grievances, documentary reports, or that sort of thing.

---

[12]The change noted here in the method of exhibition caused by mechanical reproduction applies to politics as well. The present crisis of the bourgeois democracies comprises a crisis of the conditions which determine the public presentation of the rulers. Democracies exhibit a member of government directly and personally before the nation's representatives. Parliament is his public. Since the innovations of camera and recording equipment make it possible for the orator to become audible and visible to an unlimited number of persons, the presentation of the man of politics before camera and recording equipment becomes paramount. Parliaments, as much as theaters, are deserted. Radio and film not only affect the function of the professional actor but likewise the function of those who also exhibit themselves before this mechanical equipment, those who govern. Though their tasks may be different, the change affects equally the actor and the ruler. The trend is toward establishing controllable and transferrable skills under certain social conditions. This results in a new selection, a selection before the equipment from which the star and the dictator emerge victorious.

Thus, the distinction between author and public is about to lose its basic character. The difference becomes merely functional; it may vary from case to case. At any moment the reader is ready to turn into a writer. As expert, which he had to become willy-nilly in an extremely specialized work process, even if only in some minor respect, the reader gains access to authorship. In the Soviet Union work itself is given a voice. To present it verbally is part of a man's ability to perform the work. Literary license is now founded on polytechnic rather than specialized training and thus becomes common property.[13]

All this can easily be applied to the film, where transitions that in literature took centuries have come about in a decade. In cinematic practice, particularly in Russia, this change-over has partially become established reality. Some of the players whom we meet in Russian films are not actors in our sense but people who portray *themselves*— and primarily in their own work process. In Western Europe the capitalistic exploitation of the film denies consideration to modern man's legitimate claim to being reproduced. Under these circumstances the film industry is trying hard to spur the interest of the masses through illusion-promoting spectacles and dubious speculations.

XI

The shooting of a film, especially of a sound film, affords a spectacle unimaginable anywhere at any time before this. It presents a process in which it is impossible to assign to a spectator a viewpoint which would exclude from the actual scene such extraneous accessories as camera equipment, lighting machinery, staff assistants, etc.—unless his eye were on a line parallel with the lens. This circumstance, more than any other, renders superficial and insignificant any possible similarity between a

---

[13]The privileged character of the respective techniques is lost. Aldous Huxley writes:
Advances in technology have led . . . to vulgarity. . . . Process reproduction and the rotary press have made possible the indefinite multiplication of writing and pictures. Universal education and relatively high wages have created an enormous public who know how to read and can afford to buy reading and pictorial matter. A great industry has been called into existence in order to supply these commodities. Now, artistic talent is a very rare phenomenon; whence it follows . . . that, at every epoch and in all countries, most art has been bad. But the proportion of trash in the total artistic output is greater now than at any other period. That it must be so is a matter of simple arithmetic. The population of Western Europe has a little more than doubled during the last century. But the amount of reading—and seeing—matter has increased, I should imagine, at least twenty and possibly fifty or even a hundred times. If there were n men of talent in a population of x millions, there will presumably be 2n men of talent among 2x millions. The situation may be summed up thus. For every page of print and pictures published a century ago, twenty or perhaps even a hundred pages are published today. But for every man of talent then living, there are now only two men of talent. It may be of course that, thanks to universal education, many potential talents which in the past would have been stillborn are now enabled to realize themselves. Let us assume, then, that there are now three or even four men of talent to every one of earlier times. It still remains true to say that the consumption of reading—and seeing—matter has far outstripped the natural production of gifted writers and draughtsmen. It is the same with hearing-matter. Prosperity, the gramophone and the radio have created an audience of hearers who consume an amount of hearing-matter that has increased out of all proportion to the increase of population and the consequent natural increase of talented musicians. It follows from all this that in all the arts the output of trash is both absolutely and relatively greater than it was in the past; and that it must remain greater for just so long as the world continues to consume the present inordinate quantities of reading-matter, seeing-matter, and hearing-matter.—Aldous Huxley, *Beyond the Mexique Bay: A Traveller's Journal*, London, 1949, pp. 274 ff. First published in 1934.
This mode of observation is obviously not progressive.

scene in the studio and one on the stage. In the theater one is well aware of the place from which the play cannot immediately be detected as illusionary. There is no such place for the movie scene that is being shot. Its illusionary nature is that of the second degree, the result of editing. That is to say, in the studio the mechanical equipment has penetrated so deeply into reality that its pure aspect, freed from the foreign substance of equipment, is the result of a special procedure, namely, shooting from a particular camera angle and linking the shot with other similar ones. The equipment-free aspect of reality here has become the height of artifice; the sight of immediate reality has become the [unattainable] blue flower in the land of technology.

Even more revealing is the comparison of these circumstances, which differ so much from those of the theater, with the situation in painting. Here the question is: How does the cameraman compare with the painter? To answer this we take recourse to an analogy with a surgical operation. The surgeon represents the polar opposite of the magician. The magician heals a sick person by the laying on of hands; the surgeon cuts into the patient's body. The magician maintains the natural distance between the patient and himself; though he reduces it very slightly by the laying on of hands, he greatly increases it by virtue of his authority. The surgeon does exactly the reverse; he greatly diminishes the distance between himself and the patient by penetrating into the patient's body, and increases it but little by the caution with which his hand moves among the organs. In short, in contrast to the magician—who is still hidden in the medical practitioner—the surgeon at the decisive moment abstains from facing the patient man to man; rather, it is through the operation that he penetrates into him.

Magician and surgeon compare to painter and cameraman. The painter maintains in his work a natural distance from reality, the cameraman penetrates deeply into its web.[14] There is a tremendous difference between the pictures they obtain. That of the painter is a total one, that of the cameraman consists of multiple fragments which are assembled under a new law. Thus, for contemporary man the representation of reality by the film is incomparably more significant than that of the painter, since it offers, precisely because of the thoroughgoing permeation of reality with mechanical equipment, an aspect of reality which is free of all equipment. And that is what one is entitled to ask from a work of art.

XII

Mechanical reproduction of art changes the reaction of the masses toward art. The reactionary attitude toward a Picasso painting changes into the progressive reaction toward a Chaplin movie. The progressive reaction is characterized by the direct, intimate fusion of visual and emotional enjoyment with the orientation of the expert.

---

[14]The boldness of the cameraman is indeed comparable to that of the surgeon. Luc Durtain lists among specific technical sleights of hand those "which are required in surgery in the case of certain difficult operations. I choose as an example a case from oto-rhinolaryngology; . . . the so-called endonasal perspective procedure; or I refer to the acrobatic tricks of larynx surgery which have to be performed following the reversed picture in the laryngoscope. I might also speak of ear surgery which suggests the precision work of watchmakers. What range of the most subtle muscular acrobatics is required from the man who wants to repair or save the human body! We have only to think of the couching of a cataract where there is virtually a debate of steel with nearly fluid tissue, or of the major abdominal operations (laparotomy)."—Luc Durtain, *op. cit.*

Such fusion is of great social significance. The greater the decrease in the social significance of an art form, the sharper the distinction between criticism and enjoyment by the public. The conventional is uncritically enjoyed, and the truly new is criticized with aversion. With regard to the screen, the critical and the receptive attitudes of the public coincide. The decisive reason for this is that individual reactions are predetermined by the mass audience response they are about to produce, and this is nowhere more pronounced than in the film. The moment these responses become manifest they control each other. Again, the comparison with painting is fruitful. A painting has always had an excellent chance to be viewed by one person or by a few. The simultaneous contemplation of paintings by a large public, such as developed in the nineteenth century, is an early symptom of the crisis of painting, a crisis which was by no means occasioned exclusively by photography but rather in a relatively independent manner by the appeal of art works to the masses.

Painting simply is in no position to present an object for simultaneous collective experience, as it was possible for architecture at all times, for the epic poem in the past, and for the movie today. Although this circumstance in itself should not lead one to conclusions about the social role of painting, it does constitute a serious threat as soon as painting, under special conditions and, as it were, against its nature, is confronted directly by the masses. In the churches and monasteries of the Middle Ages and at the princely courts up to the end of the eighteenth century, a collective reception of paintings did not occur simultaneously, but by graduated and hierarchized mediation. The change that has come about is an expression of the particular conflict in which painting was implicated by the mechanical reproducibility of paintings. Although paintings began to be publicly exhibited in galleries and salons, there was no way for the masses to organize and control themselves in their reception.[15] Thus the same public which responds in a progressive manner toward a grotesque film is bound to respond in a reactionary manner to surrealism.

XIII

The characteristics of the film lie not only in the manner in which man presents himself to mechanical equipment but also in the manner in which, by means of this apparatus, man can represent his environment. A glance at occupational psychology illustrates the testing capacity of the equipment. Psychoanalysis illustrates it in a different perspective. The film has enriched our field of perception with methods which can be illustrated by those of Freudian theory. Fifty years ago, a slip of the tongue passed more or less unnoticed. Only exceptionally may such a slip have revealed dimensions of depth in a conversation which had seemed to be taking its course on the surface. Since the *Psychopathology of Everyday Life* things have changed. This book isolated and made analyzable things which had heretofore floated along unnoticed in the broad stream of perception. For the entire spectrum of optical, and now

---

[15]This mode of observation may seem crude, but as the great theoretician Leonardo has shown, crude modes of observation may at times be usefully adduced. Leonardo compares painting and music as follows: "Painting is superior to music because, unlike unfortunate music, it does not have to die as soon as it is born. . . . Music which is consumed in the very act of its birth is inferior to painting which the use of varnish has rendered eternal." (*Trattato* I, 29.)

also acoustical, perception the film has brought about a similar deepening of apperception. It is only an obverse of this fact that behavior items shown in a movie can be analyzed much more precisely and from more points of view than those presented on paintings or on the stage. As compared with painting, filmed behavior lends itself more readily to analysis because of its incomparably more precise statements of the situation. In comparison with the stage scene, the filmed behavior item lends itself more readily to analysis because it can be isolated more easily. This circumstance derives its chief importance from its tendency to promote the mutual penetration of art and science. Actually, of a screened behavior item which is neatly brought out in a certain situation, like a muscle of a body, it is difficult to say which is more fascinating, its artistic value or its value for science To demonstrate the identity of the artistic and scientific uses of photography which heretofore usually were separated will be one of the revolutionary functions of the film.[16]

By close-ups of the things around us, by focusing on hidden details of familiar objects, by exploring common place milieus under the ingenious guidance of the camera, the film, on the one hand, extends our comprehension of the necessities which rule our lives; on the other hand, it manages to assure us of an immense and unexpected field of action. Our taverns and city streets, our offices and furnished rooms, our railroad stations and our factories appeared to have us locked up beyond hope. Then came film and burst this prison-world asunder by the dynamite of the tenth of a second, so that now, in the midst of its far-flung ruins and debris, we calmly and adventurously go traveling. With the close-up, space expands; with slow motion, movement is extended. The enlargement of a snapshot does not simply render more precise what in any case was visible, though unclear: it reveals entirely new structural formations of the subject. So, too, slow motion not only presents familiar qualities of movement but reveals in them entirely unknown ones "which, far from looking like retarded rapid movements, give the effect of singularly gliding, floating, supernatural motions." Evidently a different nature speaks to the camera than opens to the naked eye—if only because an unconsciously penetrated space is substituted for a space consciously explored by man. Even if one has a general knowledge of the way people walk, one knows nothing of a person's posture during the fractional second of a stride. The act of reaching for a lighter or a spoon is familiar routine, yet we hardly know what really goes on between hand and metal, not to mention how this fluctuates with our moods. Here the camera intervenes with the resources of its lowerings and liftings, its interruptions and isolations, it extensions and accelerations, its enlargements and reductions. The camera introduces us to unconscious optics as does psychoanalysis to unconscious impulses.

---

[16]Renaissance painting offers a revealing analogy to this situation. The incomparable development of this art and its significance rested not least on the integration of a number of new sciences, or at least of new scientific data. Renaissance painting made use of anatomy and perspective, of mathematics, meteorology, and chromatology. Valéry writes: "What could be further from us than the strange claim of a Leonardo to whom painting was a supreme goal and the ultimate demonstration of knowledge? Leonardo was convinced that painting demanded universal knowledge, and he did not even shrink from a theoretical analysis which to us is stunning because of its very depth and precision. . . ."—Paul Valéry, *Pièces sur l'art*, "Autour de Corot," Paris, p. 191.

XIV

One of the foremost tasks of art has always been the creation of a demand which could be fully satisfied only later.[17] The history of every art form shows critical epochs in which a certain art form aspires to effects which could be fully obtained only with a changed technical standard, that is to say, in a new art form. The extravagances and crudities of art which thus appear, particularly in the so-called decadent epochs, actually arise from the nucleus of its richest historical energies. In recent years, such barbarisms were abundant in Dadaism. It is only now that its impulse becomes discernible: Dadaism attempted to create by pictorial—and literary—means the effects which the public today seeks in the film.

Every fundamentally new, pioneering creation of demands will carry beyond its goal. Dadaism did so to the extent that it sacrificed the market values which are so characteristic of the film in favor of higher ambitions—though of course it was not conscious of such intentions as here described. The Dadaists attached much less importance to the sales value of their work than to its usefulness for contemplative immersion. The studied degradation of their material was not the least of their means to achieve this uselessness. Their poems are "word salad" containing obscenities and every imaginable waste product of language. The same is true of their paintings, on which they mounted buttons and tickets. What they intended and achieved was a relentless destruction of the aura of their creations, which they branded as reproductions with the very means of production. Before a painting of Arp's or a poem by August Stramm it is impossible to take time for contemplation and evaluation as one would before a canvas of Derain's or a poem by Rilke. In the decline of middle-class society, contemplation became a school for asocial behavior; it was countered by distraction as a variant of social

---

[17]"The work of art," says André Breton, "is valuable only in so far as it is vibrated by the reflexes of the future." Indeed, every developed art form intersects three lines of development. Technology works toward a certain form of art. Before the advent of the film there were photo booklets with pictures which flitted by the onlooker upon pressure of the thumb, thus portraying a boxing bout or a tennis match. Then there were the slot machines in bazaars; their picture sequences were produced by the turning of a crank.

Secondly, the traditional art forms in certain phases of their development strenuously work toward effects which later are effortlessly attained by the new ones. Before the rise of the movie the Dadaists' performances tried to create an audience reaction which Chaplin later evoked in a more natural way.

Thirdly, unspectacular social changes often promote a change in receptivity which will benefit the new art form. Before the movie had begun to create its public, pictures that were no longer immobile captivated an assembled audience in the so-called *Kaiserpanorama*. Here the public assembled before a screen into which stereoscopes were mounted, one to each beholder. By a mechanical process individual pictures appeared briefly before the stereoscopes, then made way for others. Edison still had to use similar devices in presenting the first movie strip before the film screen and projection were known. This strip was presented to a small public which stared into the apparatus in which the succession of pictures was reeling off. Incidentally, the institution of the *Kaiserpanorama* shows very clearly a dialectic of the development. Shortly before the movie turned the reception of pictures into a collective one, the individual viewing of pictures in these swiftly outmoded establishments came into play once more with an intensity comparable to that of the ancient priest beholding the statue of a divinity in the cella.

conduct.[18] Dadaistic activities actually assured a rather vehement distraction by making works of art the center of scandal. One requirement was foremost: to outrage the public.

From an alluring appearance or persuasive structure of sound the work of art of the Dadaists became an instrument of ballistics. It hit the spectator like a bullet, it happened to him, thus acquiring a tactile quality. It promoted a demand for the film, the distracting element of which is also primarily tactile, being based on changes of place and focus which periodically assail the spectator. Let us compare the screen on which a film unfolds with the canvas of a painting. The painting invites the spectator to contemplation; before it the spectator can abandon himself to his associations. Before the movie frame he cannot do so. No sooner has his eye grasped a scene than it is already changed. It cannot be arrested. Duhamel, who detests the film and knows nothing of its significance, though something of its structure, notes this circumstance as follows: "I can no longer think what I want to think. My thoughts have been replaced by moving images." The spectator's process of association in view of these images is indeed interrupted by their constant, sudden change. This constitutes the shock effect of the film, which, like all shocks, should be cushioned by heightened presence of mind.[19] By means of its technical structure, the film has taken the physical shock effect out of the wrappers in which Dadaism had, as it were, kept it inside the moral shock effect.[20]

XV

The mass is a matrix from which all traditional behavior toward works of art issues today in a new form. Quantity has been transmuted into quality. The greatly increased mass of participants has produced a change in the mode of participation. The fact that the new mode of participation first appeared in a disreputable form must not confuse the spectator. Yet some people have launched spirited attacks against precisely this superficial aspect. Among these, Duhamel has expressed himself in the most radical manner. What he objects to most is the kind of participation which the movie elicits from the masses. Duhamel calls the movie "a pastime for helots, a diversion for uneducated, wretched, worn-out creatures

---

[18]The theological archetype of this contemplation is the awareness of being alone with one's God. Such awareness, in the heyday of the bourgeoisie, went to strengthen the freedom to shake off clerical tutelage. During the decline of the bourgeoisie this awareness had to take into account the hidden tendency to withdraw from public affairs those forces which the individual draws upon in his communion with God.

[19]The film is the art form that is in keeping with the increased threat to his life which modern man has to face. Man's need to expose himself to shock effects is his adjustment to the dangers threatening him. The film corresponds to profound changes in the apperceptive apparatus—changes that are experienced on an individual scale by the man in the street in big-city traffic, on a historical scale by every present-day citizen.

[20]As for Dadaism, insights important for Cubism and Futurism are to be gained from the movie. Both appear as deficient attempts of art to accommodate the pervasion of reality by the apparatus. In contrast to the film, these schools did not try to use the apparatus as such for the artistic presentation of reality, but aimed at some sort of alloy in the joint presentation of reality and apparatus. In Cubism, the premonition that this apparatus will be structurally based on optics play a dominant part; in Futurism, it is the premonition of the effects of this apparatus which are brought out by the rapid sequence of the film strip.

who are consumed by their worries . . . , a spectacle which requires no concentration and presupposes no intelligence . . . , which kindles no light in the heart and awakens no hope other than the ridiculous one of someday becoming a 'star' in Los Angeles." Clearly, this is at bottom the same ancient lament that the masses seek distraction whereas art demands concentration from the spectator. That is a commonplace. The question remains whether it provides a platform for the analysis of the film. A closer look is needed here. Distraction and concentration form polar opposites which may be stated as follows: A man who concentrates before a work of art is absorbed by it. He enters into this work of art the way legend tells of the Chinese painter when he viewed his finished painting. In contrast, the distracted mass absorbs the work of art. This is most obvious with regard to buildings. Architecture has always represented the prototype of a work of art the reception of which is consummated by a collectivity in a state of distraction. The laws of its reception are most instructive.

Buildings have been man's companions since primeval times. Many art forms have developed and perished. Tragedy begins with the Greeks, is extinguished with them, and after centuries its "rules" only are revived. The epic poem, which had its origin in the youth of nations, expires in Europe at the end of the Renaissance. Panel painting is a creation of the Middle Ages, and nothing guarantees its uninterrupted existence. But the human need for shelter is lasting. Architecture has never been idle. Its history is more ancient than that of any other art, and its claim to being a living force has significance in every attempt to comprehend the relationship of the masses to art. Buildings are appropriated in a twofold manner: by use and by perception—or rather, by touch and sight. Such appropriation cannot be understood in terms of the attentive concentration of a tourist before a famous building. On the tactile side there is no counterpart to contemplation on the optical side. Tactile appropriation is accomplished not so much by attention as by habit. As regards architecture, habit determines to a large extent even optical reception. The latter, too, occurs much less through rapt attention than by noticing the object in incidental fashion. This mode of appropriation, developed with reference to architecture, in certain circumstances acquires canonical value. For the tasks which face the human apparatus of perception at the turning points of history cannot be solved by optical means, that is, by contemplation, alone. They are mastered gradually by habit, under the guidance of tactile appropriation.

The distracted person, too, can form habits. More, the ability to master certain tasks in a state of distraction proves that their solution has become a matter of habit. Distraction as provided by art presents a covert control of the extent to which new tasks have become soluble by apperception. Since, moreover, individuals are tempted to avoid such tasks, art will tackle the most difficult and most important ones where it is able to mobilize the masses. Today it does so in the film. Reception in a state of distraction, which is increasing noticeably in all fields of art and is symptomatic of profound changes in apperception, finds in the film its true means of exercise. The film with its shock effect meets this mode of reception halfway. The film makes the cult value recede into the background not only by putting the public in the position of the critic, but also by the fact that at the movies this position requires no attention. The public is an examiner, but an absent-minded one.

EPILOGUE

The growing proletarianization of modern man and the increasing formation of masses are two aspects of the same process. Fascism attempts to organize the newly created proletarian masses without affecting the property structure which the masses strive to eliminate. Fascism sees its salvation in giving these masses not their right, but instead a chance to express themselves.[21] The masses have a right to change property relations; Fascism seeks to give them an expression while preserving property. The logical result of Fascism is the introduction of aesthetics into political life. The violation of the masses, whom Fascism, with its *Führer* cult, forces to their knees, has its counterpart in the violation of an apparatus which is pressed into the production of ritual values.

All efforts to render politics aesthetic culminate in one thing: war. War and war only can set a goal for mass movements on the largest scale while respecting the traditional property system. This is the political formula for the situation. The technological formula may be stated as follows: Only war makes it possible to mobilize all of today's technical resources while maintaining the property system. It goes without saying that the Fascist apotheosis of war does not employ such arguments. Still, Marinetti says in his manifesto on the Ethiopian colonial war: "For twenty-seven years we Futurists have rebelled against the branding of war as antiaesthetic. . . . Accordingly we state: . . . War is beautiful because it establishes man's dominion over the subjugated machinery by means of gas masks, terrifying megaphones, flame throwers, and small tanks. War is beautiful because it initiates the dreamt-of metalization of the human body. War is beautiful because it enriches a flowering meadow with the fiery orchids of machine guns. War is beautiful because it combines the gunfire, the cannonades, the cease-fire, the scents, and the stench of putrefaction into a symphony. War is beautiful because it creates new architecture, like that of the big tanks, the geometrical formation flights, the smoke spirals from burning villages, and many others. . . . Poets and artists of Futurism! . . . remember these principles of an aesthetics of war so that your struggle for a new literature and a new graphic art . . . may be illumined by them!"

This manifesto has the virtue of clarity. Its formulations deserve to be accepted by dialecticians. To the latter, the aesthetics of today's war appears as follows: If the natural utilization of productive forces is impeded by the property system, the increase in technical devices, in speed, and in the sources of energy will press for an unnatural utilization, and this is found in war. The destructiveness of war furnishes proof that society has not been mature enough to incorporate technology as

---

[21]One technical feature is significant here, especially with regard to newsreels, the propagandist importance of which can hardly be overestimated. Mass reproduction is aided especially by the reproduction of masses. In big parades and monster rallies, in sports events, and in war, all of which nowadays are captured by camera and sound recording, the masses are brought face to face with themselves. This process, whose significance need not be stressed, is intimately connected with the development of the techniques of reproduction and photography. Mass movements are usually discerned more clearly by a camera than by the naked eye. A bird's-eye view best captures gatherings of hundreds of thousands. And even though such a view may be as accessible to the human eye as it is to the camera, the image received by the eye cannot be enlarged the way a negative is enlarged. This means that mass movements, including war, constitute a form of human behavior which particularly favors mechanical equipment.

its organ, that technology has not been sufficiently developed to cope with the elemental forces of society. The horrible features of imperialistic warfare are attributable to the discrepancy between the tremendous means of production and their inadequate utilization in the process of production—in other words, to unemployment and the lack of markets. Imperialistic war is a rebellion of technology which collects, in the form of "human material," the claims to which society has denied its natural material. Instead of draining rivers, society directs a human stream into a bed of trenches; instead of dropping seeds from airplanes, it drops incendiary bombs over cities; and through gas warfare the aura is abolished in a new way.

"Fiat ars—pereat mundus," says Fascism, and, as Marinetti admits, expects war to supply the artistic gratification of a sense perception that has been changed by technology. This is evidently the consummation of *l'art pour l'art.* Mankind, which in Homer's time was an object of contemplation for the Olympian gods, now is one for itself. Its self-alienation has reached such a degree that it can experience its own destruction as an aesthetic pleasure of the first order. This is the situation of politics which Fascism is rendering aesthetic. Communism responds by politicizing art.

1936

JEAN-LUC COMOLLI AND
JEAN NARBONI
CINEMA/IDEOLOGY/CRITICISM

Jean-Louis Comolli was one of the key members of the editorial board of
Cahiers du Cinéma between 1966 and 1971. In response to the 1968 student uprisings in Paris, he and Jean Narboni called for a critique of the
underlying ideologies that help create films. Comolli has published extensively in *Cahiers* and other film journals, both during and since his time
there. Comolli's recent work focuses on documentary film and the politics
of jazz music. He has produced films for the Ateliers Varan documentary
film group since 1996 and teaches at the Haute École d'Art et Design in
Geneva.

Jean Narboni and Jean-Louis Comolli met as medical students in Algeria
in the 1950s, where they developed a passion for film that led them to
move to Paris in 1961. As an editor at *Cahiers du Cinéma* in the 1960s
and 1970s, Narboni wrote extensively on films and filmmakers, including
Jean-Luc Godard, Alfred Hitchcock, John Ford, and Samuel Fuller. In the
1980s, he compiled and introduced a number of essay collections by
Cahiers contributors. His recent book (2006) deals with the Japanese director Mikio Naruse. Narboni has also taught film at the University of Paris,
Saint Denis.

Scientific criticism has an obligation to define its field and methods. This implies
awareness of its own historical and social situation, a rigorous analysis of the proposed field of study, the conditions which make the work necessary and those which
make it possible, and the special function it intends to fulfill.

It is essential that we at *Cahiers du Cinéma* should now undertake just such a
global analysis of our position and aims. Not that we are starting entirely from zero.
Fragments of such an analysis have been coming out of material we have published
recently (articles, editorials, debates, answers to readers' letters) but in an imprecise
form and as if by accident. They are an indication that our readers, just as much as
we ourselves, feel the need for a clear theoretical base to which to relate our critical practice and its field, taking the two to be indivisible. 'Programmes' and 'revolutionary' plans and declarations tend to become an end in themselves. This is a trap
we intend to avoid. Our objective is not to reflect upon what we 'want' (would like)
to do, but upon what we *are* doing and what we *can* do, and this is impossible without an analysis of the present situation.

WHERE?

(a) First, our situation. *Cahiers* is a group of people working together; one of the results of our work appearing as a magazine.[1] A magazine, that is to say, a particular product, involving a particular amount of work (on the part of those who write it, those who produce it and, indeed, those who read it). We do not close our eyes to the fact that a product of this nature is situated fairly and squarely inside the economic system of capitalist publishing (modes of production, spheres of circulation, etc.). In any case it is difficult to see how it could be otherwise today, unless one is led astray by Utopian ideas of working 'parallel' to the system. The first step in the latter approach is always the paradoxical one of setting up a false front, a 'neo-system' alongside the system from which one is attempting to escape, in the fond belief that it will be able to negate the system. In fact all it can do is reject it (idealist purism) and consequently it is very soon jeopardized by the enemy upon which it modelled itself.[2] This parallelism works from one direction only. It touches only one side of the wound, whereas we believe that both sides have to be worked upon. And the danger of the parallels meeting all too speedily in infinity seems to us sufficient to argue that we had better stay in the finite and allow them to remain apart.

This assumed, the question is: what is our attitude to our situation? In France the majority of films, like the majority of books and magazines, are produced and distributed by the capitalist economic system and within the dominant ideology. Indeed, strictly speaking all are, whatever expedient they adopt to try and get around it. This being so, the question we have to ask is: which films, books, and magazines allow the ideology a free, unhampered passage, transmit it with crystal clarity, serve as its chosen language? And which attempt to make it turn back and reflect itself, intercept it, make it visible by revealing its mechanisms, by blocking them?

(b) For the situation in which we are *acting* is the field of cinema (*Cahiers* is a film magazine),[3] and the precise object of our study is the history of a film: how it is produced, manufactured, distributed,[4] understood.

What is the film today? This is the relevant question; not, as it possibly once was: what is the cinema? We shall not be able to ask that again until a body of knowledge, of theory, has been evolved (a process to which we certainly intend to contribute) to inform what is at present an empty term, with a concept. For a film magazine the question is also: what work is to be done in the field constituted by films? And for Cahiers in particular: what is our specific function in this field? What is to distinguish us from other film magazines?

---

[1]Others include distribution, screening, and discussion of films in the provinces and the suburbs, sessions of theoretical work.

[2]Or tolerated, and jeopardized by this very toleration. Is there any need to stress that it is the tried tactic of covertly repressive systems not to harass the protesting fringe? They go out of their way to take no notice of them, with the double effect of making one half of the opposition careful not to try their patience too far and the other half complacent in the knowledge that their activities are unobserved.

[3]We do not intend to suggest by this that we want to erect a corporatist fence round our own field, and neglect the infinitely larger field where so much is obviously at stake politically. Simply, we are concentrating on that precise point of the spectrum of social activity in this article, in response to precise operational needs.

[4]A more and more pressing problem. It would be inviting confusion to allow it to be tackled in bits and pieces and obviously we have to make a unified attempt to pose it theoretically later on. For the moment we leave it aside.

THE FILMS

What is a film? On the one hand it is a particular product, manufactured within a given system of economic relations, and involving labour (which appears to the capitalist as money) to produce—a condition to which even 'independent' filmmakers and the 'new cinema' are subject—assembling a certain number of workers for this purpose (even the director, whether he is Moullet or Oury, is in the last analysis only a film worker). It becomes transformed into a commodity, possessing exchange value, which is realized by the sale of tickets and contracts, and governed by the laws of the market. On the other hand, as a result of being a material product of the system, it is also an ideological product of the system, which in France means capitalism.[5]

No filmmaker can, by his own individual efforts, change the economic relations governing the manufacture and distribution of his films. (It cannot be pointed out too often that even filmmakers who set out to be 'revolutionary' on the level of message and form cannot effect any swift or radical change in the economic system—deform it, yes, deflect it, but not negate it or seriously upset its structure. Godard's recent statement to the effect that he wants to stop working in the 'system' takes no account of the fact that any other system is bound to be a reflection of the one he wishes to avoid. The money no longer comes from the Champs-Elysées but from London, Rome, or New York. The film may not be marketed by the distribution monopolies but it is shot on film stock from another monopoly—Kodak.) Because every film is part of the economic system it is also a part of the ideological system, for 'cinema' and 'art' are branches of ideology. None can escape, somewhere, like pieces in a jigsaw, all have their own allotted place. The system is blind to its own nature, but in spite of that, indeed because of that, when all the pieces are fitted together they give a very clear picture. But this does not mean that every filmmaker plays a similar role. Reactions differ.

It is the job of criticism to see where they differ, and slowly, patiently, not expecting any magical transformations to take place at the wave of a slogan, to help change the ideology which conditions them.

A few points, which we shall return to in greater detail later: *every film is political*, inasmuch as it is determined by the ideology which produces it (or within which it is produced, which stems from the same thing). The cinema is all the more thoroughly and completely determined because unlike other arts or ideological systems its very manufacture mobilizes powerful economic forces in a way that the production of literature (which becomes the commodity 'books', does not—though once we reach the level of distribution, publicity, and sale, the two are in rather the same position).

---

[5]Capitalist ideology. This term expresses our meaning perfectly, but as we are going to use it without further definition in this article, we should point out that we are not under any illusion that it has some kind of 'abstract essence'. We know that it is historically and socially determined, and that it has multiple forms at any given place and time, and varies from historical period to historical period. Like the whole category of 'militant' cinema, which is totally vague and undefined at present. We must (a) rigorously define the function attributed to it, its aims, its side effects (information, arousal, critical reflection, provocation 'which always has *some* effect' . . .); (b) define the exact political line governing the making and screening of these films—'revolutionary' is too much of a blanket term to serve any useful purpose here; and (c) state whether the supporters of militant cinema are in fact proposing a line of action in which the cinema would become the poor relation, in the illusion that the less the cinematic aspect is worked on, the greater the strength and clarity of the 'militant' effect will be. This would be a way of avoiding the contradictions of 'parallel' cinema and getting embroiled in the problem of deciding whether 'underground' films should be included in the category, on the pretext that their relationship to drugs and sex, their preoccupation with form, might possibly establish new relationships between film and audience.

Clearly, the cinema 'reproduces' reality: this is what a camera and film stock are for—so says the ideology. But the tools and techniques of filmmaking are a part of 'reality' themselves, and furthermore 'reality' is nothing but an expression of the prevailing ideology. Seen in this light, the classic theory of cinema that the camera is an impartial instrument which grasps, or rather is impregnated by, the world in its 'concrete reality' is an eminently reactionary one. What the camera in fact registers is the vague, unformulated, untheorized, unthought-out world of the dominant ideology. Cinema is one of the languages through which the world communicates itself to itself. They constitute its ideology for they reproduce the world as it is experienced when filtered through the ideology. (As Althusser defines it, more precisely: 'Ideologies are perceived-accepted-suffered cultural objects, which work fundamentally on men by a process they do not understand. What men express in their ideologies is not their true relation to their conditions of existence, but how they react to their conditions of existence; which presupposes a real relationship and an imaginary relationship.') So, when we set out to make a film, from the very first shot, we are encumbered by the necessity of reproducing things not as they really are but as they appear when refracted through the ideology. This includes every stage in the process of production: subjects, styles, forms, meanings, narrative traditions; all underline the general ideological discourse. The film is ideology presenting itself to itself, talking to itself, learning about itself. Once we realize that it is the nature of the system to turn the cinema into an instrument of ideology, we can see that the filmmaker's first task is to show up the cinema's so-called depiction of reality. If he can do so there is a chance that we will be able to disrupt or possibly even sever the connection between the cinema and its ideological function.

The vital distinction between films today is whether they do this or whether they do not.

(a) The first and largest category comprises those films which are imbued through and through with the dominant ideology in pure and unadulterated form, and give no indication that their makers were even aware of the fact. We are not just talking about so-called commercial films. The *majority* of films in all categories are the unconscious instruments of the ideology which produces them. Whether the film is commercial or 'ambitious', 'modern' or 'traditional', whether it is the type that gets shown in art houses, or in smart cinemas, whether it belongs to the 'old' cinema or the 'young' cinema, it is most likely to be a rehash of the same old ideology. For all films are commodities and therefore objects of trade, even those whose discourse is explicitly political—which is why a rigorous definition of what constitutes 'political' cinema is called for at this moment when it is being widely promoted. This merging of ideology and film is reflected in the first instance by the fact that audience demand and economic response have also been reduced to one and the same thing. In direct continuity with political practice, ideological practice reformulates the social need and backs it up with a discourse. This is not a hypothesis, but a scientifically established fact. The ideology is talking to itself; it has all the answers ready before it asks the questions. Certainly there is such a thing as public demand, but 'what the public wants' means 'what the dominant ideology wants'. The notion of a public and its tastes was created by the ideology to justify and perpetuate itself. And this public can only express itself via the thought-patterns of the ideology. The whole thing is a closed circuit, endlessly repeating the same illusion.

The situation is the same at the level of artistic form. These films totally accept the established system of depicting reality: 'bourgeois realism' and the whole conservative box of tricks: blind faith in 'life', 'humanism', 'common sense', etc. A blissful ignorance that there might be something wrong with this whole concept of 'depiction' appears to have reigned at every stage in their production, so much so, that to us it appears a more accurate gauge of pictures in the 'commercial' category than box-office returns. Nothing in these films jars against the ideology or the audience's mystification by it. They are very reassuring for audiences for there is no difference between the ideology they meet every day and the ideology on the screen. It would be a useful complementary task for film critics to look into the way the ideological system and its products merge at all levels: to study the phenomenon whereby a film being shown to an audience becomes a monologue, in which the ideology talks to itself, by examining the success of films by, for instance, Melville, Oury, and Lelouch.

(b) A second category is that of films which attack their ideological assimilation on two fronts. Firstly, by direct political action, on the level of the 'signified', that is, they deal with a directly political subject. 'Deal with' is here intended in an active sense: they do not just discuss an issue, reiterate it, paraphrase it, but use it to attack the ideology (this presupposes a theoretical activity which is the direct opposite of the ideological one). This act only becomes politically effective if it is linked with a breaking down of the traditional way of depicting reality. On the level of form, *Unreconciled*, *The Edge,* and *Earth in Revolt* all challenge the concept of 'depiction' and mark a break with the tradition embodying it.

We would stress that only action on both fronts, 'signified' and 'signifiers'[6] has any hope of operating against the prevailing ideology. Economic/political and formal action have to be indissolubly wedded.

(c) There is another category in which the same double action operates, but 'against the grain'. The content is not explicitly political, but in some way becomes so through the criticism practised on it through its form.[7] To this category belong

---

[6]We are not shutting our eyes to the fact that it is an oversimplification (employed here because operationally easier) to make such a sharp distinction between the two terms. This is particularly so in the case of the cinema, where the signified is more often than not a product of the permutations of the signifiers, and the sign has dominance over the meaning.

[7]This is not a magical doorway out of the system of 'depiction' (which is particularly dominant in the cinema) but rather a rigorous, detailed, large-scale work on this system—what conditions make it possible, what mechanisms render it innocuous. The method is to draw attention to the system so that it can be seen for what it is, to make it serve one's own ends, condemn itself out of its own mouth. Tactics employed may include 'turning cinematic syntax upside-down' but it cannot be just that. Any old film nowadays can upset the normal chronological order in the interests of looking vaguely 'modern'. But *The Exterminating Angel* and *The Diary of Anna Magdalena Bach* (though we would not wish to set them up as a model) are rigorously chronological without ceasing to be subversive in the way we have been describing, whereas in many a film the mixed-up time sequence simply covers up a basically naturalistic conception. In the same way, perceptual confusion (avowed intent to act on the unconscious mind, changes in the texture of the film, etc.) are not sufficient in themselves to get beyond the traditional way of depicting 'reality'. To realize this, one has only to remember the unsuccessful attempts there have been of the '*lettriste*' or '*zacum*' type to give back its infinity to language by using nonsense words or new kinds of onomatopoeia. In the one and the other case only the most superficial level of language is touched. They create a new code, which operates on the level of the impossible, and has to be rejected on any other, and is therefore not in a position to transgress the normal.

Méditerranée, The Bellboy, Persona. . . . For *Cahiers* these films (b and c) constitute the essential in the cinema, and should be the chief subject of the magazine.

(d) Fourth case: those films, increasingly numerous today, which have an explicitly political content (Z is not the best example as its presentation of politics is unremittingly ideological from first to last; a better example would be *Le Temps de Vivre*) but which do not effectively criticize the ideological system in which they are embedded because they unquestioningly adopt its language and its imagery.

This makes it important for critics to examine the effectiveness of the political criticism intended by these films. Do they express, reinforce, strengthen the very thing they set out to denounce? Are they caught in the system they wish to break down . . . ? (See a.)

(e) Five: films which seem at first sight to belong firmly within the ideology and to be completely under its sway, but which turn out to be so only in an ambiguous manner. For though they start from a nonprogressive standpoint, ranging from the frankly reactionary through the conciliatory to the mildly critical, they have been worked upon, and work, in such a real way that there is a noticeable gap, a dislocation, between the starting point and the finished product. We disregard here the inconsistent—and unimportant—sector of films in which the director makes a *conscious* use of the prevailing ideology, but leaves it absolutely straight. The films we are talking about throw up obstacles in the way of the ideology, causing it to swerve and get off course. The cinematic framework lets us see it, but also shows it up and denounces it. Looking at the framework one can see two moments in it: one holding it back within certain limits, one transgressing them. An internal criticism is taking place which cracks the film apart at the seams. If one reads the film obliquely, looking for symptoms; if one looks beyond its apparent formal coherence, one can see that it is riddled with cracks: it is splitting under an internal tension which is simply not there in an ideologically innocuous film. The ideology thus becomes subordinate to the text. It no longer has an independent existence: It is *presented* by the film. This is the case in many Hollywood films, for example, which while being completely integrated in the system and the ideology end up by partially dismantling the system from within. We must find out what makes it possible for a filmmaker to corrode the ideology by restating it in the terms of his film: if he sees his film simply as a blow in favour of liberalism, it will be recuperated instantly by the ideology; if on the other hand, he conceives and realizes it on the deeper level of imagery, there is a chance that it will turn out to be more disruptive. Not, of course, that he will be able to break the ideology itself, but simply its reflection in his film. (The films of Ford, Dreyer, Rossellini, for example.)

Our position with regard to this category of films is: that we have absolutely no intention of joining the current witch-hunt against them. They are the mythology of their own myths. They criticize themselves, even if no such intention is written into the script, and it is irrelevant and impertinent to do so for them. All we want to do is to show the process in action.

(f) Films of the 'live cinema' (*cinéma direct*) variety, group one (the larger of the two groups). These are films arising out of political (or, it would probably be more exact to say: social) events or reflections, but which make no clear differentiation between themselves and the nonpolitical cinema because they do not challenge the cinema's traditional, ideologically conditioned method of depiction. For instance a miner's strike will be filmed in the same style as *Les Grandes Familles*. The makers of these films suffer under the primary and fundamental illusion that if they once break off the ideological filter of narrative traditions (dramaturgy, construction, domination of the component parts by a central idea, emphasis on formal beauty) reality will then yield itself up in its true form. The fact is that by doing so they only break off one filter, and not the most important one at that. For reality holds within itself no hidden kernel of self-understanding, of theory, of truth, like a stone inside a fruit. We have to manufacture those. (Marxism is very clear on this point, in its distinction between real and perceived objects.) Compare *Chiefs* (Leacock) and a good number of the May films.

This is why supporters of *cinéma direct* resort to the same idealist terminology to express its role and justify its successes as others use about products of the greatest artifice: 'accuracy', 'a sense of lived experience', 'flashes of intense truth', 'moments caught live', 'abolition of all sense that we are watching a film' and finally: fascination. It is that magical notion of 'seeing is understanding': ideology goes on display to prevent itself from being shown up for what it really is, contemplates itself but does not criticize itself.

(g) The other kind of 'live cinema'. Here the director is not satisfied with the idea of the camera 'seeing through appearances', but attacks the basic problem of depiction by giving an active role to the concrete stuff of his film. It then becomes productive of meaning and is not just a passive receptacle for meaning produced outside it (in the ideology): *La Règne du Jour, La Rentrée des Usines Wonder.*

CRITICAL FUNCTION

Such, then, is the field of our critical activity: these films, within the ideology, and their different relations to it. From this precisely defined field spring four functions: (1) in the case of the films in category (a): show what they are blind to; how they are totally determined, moulded, by the ideology; (2) in the case of those in categories (b), (c) and (g), read them on two levels, showing how the films operate critically on the level of signified and signifiers; (3) in the case of those of types (d) and (f), show how the signified (political subject matter) is always weakened, rendered harmless, by the absence of technical/theoretical work on the signifiers; (4) in the case of those in group (e) point out the gap produced between film and ideology by the way the films work, and show how they work.

There can be no room in our critical practice either for speculation (commentary, interpretation, de-coding even) or for specious raving (of the film-columnist variety). It must be a rigidly factual analysis of what governs the production of a film (economic circumstances, ideology, demand, and response) and the meanings and forms appearing in it, which are equally tangible.

The tradition of frivolous and evanescent writing on the cinema is as tenacious as it is prolific, and film analysis today is still massively predetermined by idealistic presuppositions. It wanders farther abroad today, but its method is still basically empirical. It has been through a necessary stage of going back to the material elements of a film, its signifying structures, its formal organization. The first steps here were undeniably taken by André Bazin, despite the contradictions that can be picked out in his articles. Then followed the approach based on structural linguistics (in which there are two basic traps, which we fell into—phenomenological positivism and mechanistic materialism). As surely as criticism had to go through this stage, it has to go beyond. To us, the only possible line of advance seems to be to use the theoretical writing of the Russian filmmakers of the twenties (Eisenstein above all) to elaborate and apply a critical theory of the cinema, a specific method of apprehending rigorously defined objects, in direct reference to the method of dialectical materialism.

It is hardly necessary to point out that we know that the policy of a magazine cannot—indeed, should not—be corrected by magic overnight. We have to do it patiently, month by month, being careful in our own field to avoid the general error of putting faith in spontaneous change, or attempting to rush into a 'revolution' without the preparation to support it. To start proclaiming at this stage that the truth has been revealed to us would be like talking about 'miracles' or 'conversion'. All we should do is to state what work is already in progress and publish articles which relate to it, either explicitly or implicitly.

We should indicate briefly how the various elements in the magazine fit into this perspective. The essential part of the work obviously takes place in the theoretical articles and the criticisms. There is coming to be less and less of a difference between the two, because it is not our concern to add up the merits and defects of current films in the interests of topicality, nor, as one humorous article put it 'to crack up the product'. The interviews, on the other hand, and also the diary columns and the list of films, with the dossiers and supplementary material for possible discussion later, are often stronger on information than theory. It is up to the reader to decide whether these pieces take up any critical stance, and if so, what.

1969

CHRISTIAN METZ
FROM THE IMAGINARY SIGNIFIER

IDENTIFICATION, MIRROR

. . . Among the specific features of the cinematic signifier that distinguish the cinema from literature, painting, etc. which ones by nature call most directly on the type of knowledge that psychoanalysis alone can provide?

PERCEPTION, IMAGINARY

The cinema's signifier is *perceptual* (visual and auditory). So is that of literature, since the written chain has to be *read*, but it involves a more restricted perceptual register: only graphemes, writing. So too are those of painting, sculpture, architecture, photography, but still within limits, and different ones: absence of auditory perception, absence in the visual itself of certain important dimensions such as time and movement (obviously there is the time of the look, but the object looked at is not inscribed in a precise and ordered time sequence forced on the spectator from outside). Music's signifier is perceptual as well, but, like the others, less "extensive" than that of the cinema: here it is vision which is absent, and even in the auditory, extended speech (except in song). What first strikes one then is that the cinema is *more perceptual*, if the phrase is allowable, than many other means of expression; it mobilises a larger number of the axes of perception. (That is why the cinema has sometimes been presented as a "synthesis of all the arts"; which does not mean very much, but if we restrict ourselves to the quantitative tally of the registers of perception, it is true that the cinema contains within itself the signifiers of other arts: it can present pictures to us, make us hear music, it is made of photographs, etc.)

Nevertheless, this as it were numerical "superiority" disappears if the cinema is compared with the theatre, the opera and other spectacles of the same type. The latter too involve sight and hearing simultaneously, linguistic audition and nonlinguistic audition, movement, real temporal progression. Their difference from the cinema lies elsewhere: they do not consist of *images*, the perceptions they offer to the eye and the ear are inscribed in a true space (not a photographed one), the same one as that occupied by the public during the performance; everything the audience hear and see is actively produced in their presence, by human beings or props which are themselves present. This is not the problem of fiction but that of the definitional characteristics of the signifier: whether or not the theatrical play mimes a fable, its *action*, if need be mimetic, is still managed by real persons evolving in real time and space, *on the same stage or "scene" as the public*. The "other scene," which is precisely not so called, is the cinematic screen (closer to phantasy from the outset): what unfolds there may, as before, be more or less fictional, but the unfolding itself is fictive: the actor, the "décor," the words one hears are all absent, everything is *recorded* (as a memory trace which is immediately so, without having been something else before), and this is still true if what is recorded is not a "story" and does not aim for the fictional illusion proper. For it is the signifier itself, and as a whole, that is recorded, that is absence: a little rolled up perforated strip which "contains" vast landscapes, fixed battles, the melting of the ice on the River Neva, and whole lifetimes, and yet can be enclosed in the familiar round metal tin, of modest dimensions, clear proof that it does not "really" contain all that.

At the theatre, Sarah Bernhardt may tell me she is Phèdre or, if the play were from another period and rejected the figurative regime, she might say, as in a type of modern theatre, that she is Sarah Bernhardt. But at any rate, I should see Sarah Bernhardt. At the cinema, she could make the same two kinds of speeches too, but it would be her shadow that would be offering them to me (or she would be offering them in her own absence). Every film is a fiction film.

What is at issue is not just the actor. Today there are a theatre and a cinema without actors, or in which they have at least ceased to take on the full and exclusive function which characterises them in classical spectacles. But what is true of Sarah Bernhardt is just as true of an object, a prop, a chair for example. On the theatre stage, this chair may, as in Chekhov, pretend to be the chair in which the melancholy Russian nobleman sits every evening; on the contrary (in Ionesco), it can explain to me that it is a theatre chair. But when all is said and done it is a chair. In the cinema, it will similarly have to choose between two attitudes (and many other intermediate or more tricky ones), but it will not be there when the spectators see it, when they have to recognise the choice; it will have delegated its reflection to them.

What is characteristic of the cinema is not the imaginary that it may happen to represent, but the imaginary that it *is* from the start, the imaginary that constitutes it as a signifier (the two are not unrelated; it is so well able to represent it because it is it; however it is it even when it no longer represents it). The (possible) reduplication inaugurating the intention of fiction is preceded in the cinema by a first reduplication, always-already achieved, which inaugurates the signifier. The imaginary, by definition, combines within it a certain presence and a certain absence. In the cinema it is not just the fictional signified, if there is one, that is thus made present in the mode of absence, it is from the outset the signifier.

Thus the cinema, "more perceptual" than certain arts according to the list of its sensory registers, is also "less perceptual" than others once the status of these perceptions is envisaged rather than their number or diversity; for its perceptions are all in a sense "false." Or rather, the activity of perception which it involves is real (the cinema is not a phantasy), but the perceived is not really the object, it is its shade, its phantom, its double, its *replica* in a new kind of mirror. It will be said that literature, after all, is itself only made of replicas (written words, presenting absent objects). But at least it does not present them to us with all the really perceived detail that the screen does (giving more and taking as much, i.e., taking more). The unique position of the cinema lies in this dual character of its signifier: unaccustomed perceptual wealth, but at the same time stamped with unreality to an unusual degree, and from the very outset. More than the other arts, or in a more unique way, the cinema involves us in the imaginary: it drums up all perception, but to switch it immediately over into its own absence, which is nonetheless the only signifier present.

THE ALL-PERCEIVING SUBJECT

Thus film is like the mirror. But it differs from the primordial mirror in one essential point: although, as in the latter, everything may come to be projected, there is one thing and one thing only that is never reflected in it: the spectator's own body. In a certain emplacement, the mirror suddenly becomes clear glass.

In the mirror the child perceives the familiar household objects, and also its object par excellence, its mother, who holds it up in her arms to the glass. But above all it perceives its own image. This is where primary identification (the formation of the ego) gets certain of its main characteristics: the child sees itself as an other, and beside another. This other other is its guarantee that the first is really it: by her authority, her sanction, in the register of the symbolic, subsequently by the resemblance between her mirror image and the child's (both have a human form). Thus the child's ego is formed by identification with its like, and this in two senses simultaneously, metonymically and metaphorically: the other human being who is in the glass, the own reflection which is and is not the body, which is like it. The child identifies with itself as an object.

In the cinema, the object remains: fiction or no, there is always something on the screen. But the reflection of the own body has disappeared. The cinema spectator is not a child and the child really at the mirror stage (from around six to around eighteen months) would certainly be incapable of "following" the simplest of films. Thus, what *makes possible* the spectator's absence from the screen—or rather the intelligible unfolding of the film despite that absence—is the fact that the spectator has already known the experience of the mirror (of the true mirror), and is thus able to constitute a world of objects without having first to recognise himself within it. In this respect, the cinema is already on the side of the symbolic (which is only to be expected): the spectator knows that objects exist, that he himself exists as a subject, that he becomes an object for others: he knows himself and he knows his like: it is no longer necessary that this similarity be literally *depicted* for him on the screen, as it was in the mirror of his childhood. Like every other broadly "secondary" activity, the practice of the cinema presupposes that the primitive undifferentiation of the ego and the non-ego has been overcome.

But *with what*, then, does the spectator identify during the projection of the film? . . .

The spectator is absent from the screen: contrary to the child in the mirror, he cannot identify with himself as an object, but only with objects which are there without him. In this sense the screen is not a mirror. The perceived, this time, is entirely on the side of the object, and there is no longer any equivalent of the own image, of that unique mix of perceived and subject (of other and I) which was precisely the figure necessary to disengage the one from the other. At the cinema, it is always the other who is on the screen; as for me, I am there to look at him. I take no part in the perceived, on the contrary, I am *all-perceiving*. All-perceiving as one says all-powerful (this is the famous gift of "ubiquity" the film makes its spectator); all-perceiving, too, because I am entirely on the side of the perceiving instance: absent from the screen, but certainly present in the auditorium, a great eye and ear without which the perceived would have no one to perceive it, the instance, in other words, which *constitutes* the cinema signifier (it is I who make the film). If the most extravagant spectacles and sounds or the most unlikely combination of them, the combination furthest removed from any real experience, do not prevent the constitution of meaning (and to begin with do not *astonish* the spectator, do not really astonish him, not intellectually: he simply judges the film as strange), that is because he knows he is at the cinema.

In the cinema the *subject's knowledge* takes a very precise form without which no film would be possible. This knowledge is dual (but unique). I know I am perceiving something imaginary (and that is why its absurdities, even if they are extreme, do not seriously disturb me), and I know that it is I who am perceiving it. This second knowledge divides in turn: I know that I am really perceiving, that my sense organs are physically affected, that I am not phantasising, that the fourth wall of the auditorium (the screen) is really different form the other three, that there is a projector facing it (and thus it is not I who am projecting, or at least not all alone), and I also know that it is I who am perceiving all this, that this perceived-imaginary material is deposited in me as if on a second screen, that it is in me that it forms up into an organised sequence, that therefore I am myself the place where this really perceived imaginary accedes to the symbolic by its inauguration as the signifier of a certain type of institutionalised social activity called the "cinema."

In other words, the spectator *identifies with himself*, with himself as a pure act of perception (as wakefulness, alertness): as the condition of possibility of the perceived and hence as a kind of transcendental subject, which comes before every *there is*.

A strange mirror, then, very like that of childhood, and very different. Very like, as Jean-Louis Baudry has emphasized, because during the showing we are, like the child, in a sub-motor and hyper-perceptive state; because, like the child again, we are prey to the imaginary, the double, and are so paradoxically through a real perception. Very different, because this mirror returns us everything but ourselves, because we are wholly outside it, whereas the child is both in it and in front of it. As an *arrangement* (and in a very topographical sense of the word), the cinema is more involved on the flank of the symbolic, and hence of secondariness, than is the mirror of childhood. This is not surprising, since it comes long after it, but what is more important to me is the fact that it is inscribed in its wake with an incidence at once so direct and so oblique, which has no precise equivalent in other apparatuses of signification.

IDENTIFICATION WITH THE CAMERA

The preceding analysis coincides in places with others which have already been proposed and which I shall not repeat: analyses of *quattrocento* painting or of the cinema itself which insist on the role of monocular perspective (hence of the *camera*) and the "vanishing point" that inscribes an empty emplacement for the spectator-subject, an all-powerful position which is that of God himself, or more broadly of some ultimate signified. And it is true that as he identifies with himself as look, the spectator can do no other than identify with the camera, too, which has looked before him at what he is now looking at and whose stationing (= framing) determines the vanishing point. During the projection this camera is absent, but it has a representative consisting of another apparatus, called precisely a "projector." An apparatus the spectator has behind him, *at the back of his head*, that is, precisely where phantasy locates the "focus" of all vision. All of us have experienced our own look, even outside the so-called *salles obscures* [= cinemas], as a kind of searchlight turning on the axis of our own necks (like a pan) and shifting when we shift (a tracking shot now): as a cone of light (without the microscopic dust scattered through it and streaking it in the cinema) whose vicariousness draws successive and variable slices of obscurity from nothingness wherever and whenever it comes to rest. (And in a sense that is what perception and consciousness are, a *light*, as Freud put it, in the double sense of an illumination and an opening, as in the arrangement of the cinema, which contains both, a limited and wandering light that only attains a small part of the real, but on the other hand possesses the gift of casting light on it.) Without this identification with the camera certain facts could not be understood, though they are constant ones: the fact, for example, that the spectator is not amazed when the image "rotates" (= a pan) and yet he knows he has not turned his head. The explanation is that he has no need to turn it really, he has turned it in his all-seeing capacity, his identification with the movement of the camera being that of a transcendental, not an empirical subject.

All vision consists of a double movement: projective (the "sweeping" searchlight) and introjective: consciousness as a sensitive recording surface (as a screen). I have the impression at once that, to use a common expression, I am "casting" my eyes on things, and that the latter, thus illuminated, come to be deposited within me (we then declared that it is these things that have been "projected," on to my retina, say). A sort of stream called the look, and explaining all the myths of magnetism, must be sent out over the world, so that objects can come back up this stream in the opposite direction (but using it to find their way), arriving at last at our perception, which is now soft wax and no longer an emitting source.

The technology of photography carefully conforms to this (banal) phantasy accompanying perception. The camera is "trained" on the object like a fire-arm (= projection) and the object arrives to make an imprint, a trace, on the receptive surface of the film-strip (= introjection). The spectator himself does not escape these pincers, for he is part of the apparatus, and also because pincers, on the imaginary plane (Melanie Klein), mark our relation to the world as a whole and are rooted in the primary figures of orality. During the performance the spectator is the searchlight I have described, duplicating the projector, which itself duplicates the camera, and he is also the sensitive surface duplicating the screen, which itself duplicates the film-strip. There are two cones in the auditorium: one ending on the screen and starting both in the projection box and in the spectator's vision insofar as it is projective, and one starting from the screen and "deposited" in the spectator's perception insofar as it is introjective (on the retina, a second screen). When I say that "I see" the film, I mean thereby a unique mixture of two contrary currents; the film is what I receive, and it is also what I release, since it does not preexist my entering the auditorium and I only need close my eyes to suppress it. Releasing it, I am the projector, receiving it, I am the screen; in both these figures together, I am the camera, which points and yet which records.

Thus the constitution of the signifier in the cinema depends on a series of mirror-effects organised in a chain, and not on a single reduplication. In this the cinema as a topography resembles that other "space," the technical equipment (camera, projector, film-strip, screen, etc.), the objective precondition of the whole institution: as we know, the apparatuses too contain a series of mirrors, lenses, apertures and shutters, ground glasses, through which the cone of light passes: a further reduplication in which the equipment becomes a metaphor (as well as the real source) for the mental process instituted. Further on we shall see that it is also its fetish.

In the cinema, as elsewhere, the constitution of the symbolic is only achieved through and above the play of the imaginary: projection-introjection, presence-absence, phantasies accompanying perception, etc. Even when acquired, the ego still depends in its underside on the fabulous figures thanks to which it has been acquired and which have marked it lastingly with the stamp of the lure. The secondary process does no more than "cover" (and not always hermetically) the primary process which is still constantly present and conditions the very possibility of what covers it.

Chain of many mirrors, the cinema is at once a weak and a robust mechanism: like the human body, like a precision tool, like a social institution. And the fact is that it is really all of these at the same time.

And I, at this moment, what am I doing if not to add to all these reduplications one more whereby theory is attempting to set itself up? Am I not looking at myself looking at the film? This *passion for seeing* (and also hearing), the foundation of the whole edifice, am I not turning it, too, on (against) that edifice? Am I not still the voyeur I was in front of the screen, now that it is this voyeur who is being seen, thus postulating a second voyeur, the one writing at present, myself again? . . .

There are various sorts of subjective image and I have tried elsewhere (following Jean Mitry) to distinguish between them. Only one of them will detain me for the moment, the one which "expresses the viewpoint of the filmmaker" in the standard formula (and not the viewpoint of a character, another traditional sub-case of the subjective image): unusual framings, uncommon shot-angles, etc. as for example in one of the sketches which make up Julien Duvivier's film *Carnet de bal* (the sketch with Pierre Blanchar, shot continuously in tilted framings). In the standard definitions one thing strikes me: I do not see why these uncommon angles should express the viewpoint of the film maker any more than perfectly ordinary angles, closer to the horizontal. However, the definition is comprehensible even in its inaccuracy: precisely because it is uncommon, the uncommon angle makes us more aware of what we had merely forgotten to some extent in its absence: an identification with the camera (with "the author's viewpoint"). The ordinary framings are finally felt to be nonframings: I espouse the film maker's look (without which no cinema would be possible), but my consciousness is not too aware of it. The uncommon angle reawakens me and (like the cure) teaches me what I already knew. And then, it obliges my look to stop wandering freely over the screen for the moment and to scan it along more precise lines of force which are imposed on me. Thus for a moment I became directly aware of the *emplacement* of my own presence-absence in the film simply because it has changed.

Now for looks. In a fiction film, the characters look at one another. It can happen (and this is already another "notch" in the chain of identifications) that a character looks at another who is momentarily out-of-frame, or else is looked at by him. If we have gone one notch further, this is because everything out-of-frame *brings us closer to the spectator*, since it is the peculiarity of the latter to be out-of-frame (the out-of-frame character thus has a point in common with him: he is looking at the screen). In certain cases the out-of-frame character's look is "reinforced" by recourse to another variant of the subjective image, generally christened the "character's point of view": the framing of the scene corresponds precisely to the angle from which the out-of-frame character looks at the screen. (The two figures are dissociable moreover: we often know that the scene is being looked at by someone other than ourselves, by a character, but it is the logic of the plot, or an element of the dialogue, or a previous image that tells us so, not the position of the camera, which may be far from the presumed emplacement of the out-of-frame onlooker.)

In all sequences of this kind, the identification that founds the signifier is *twice relayed*, doubly duplicated in a circuit that leads it to the heart of the film along a line which is no longer hovering, which follows the inclination of the looks and is therefore governed by the film itself: the spectator's look (= the basic identification), before dispersing all over the surface of the screen in a variety of intersecting lines (= looks of the characters in the frame = second duplication), must first "go through"—as one goes through a town on a journey, or a mountain pass—the look of the character out-of-frame (= first duplication), himself a spectator and hence the first delegate of the true spectator, but not to be confused with the latter since he is inside, if not the frame, then at least the fiction. This invisible character, supposed (like the spectator) to be seeing, will collide obliquely with the latter's look and play the part of an obligatory intermediary. By offering himself as a crossing for the spectator, he inflects the circuit followed by the sequence of identifications and it is only in this sense that he is himself seen: as we see through him, we see ourselves not seeing him.

Examples of this kind are much more numerous and each of them is much more complex than I have suggested here. At this point textual analysis of precise film sequences is an indispensable instrument of knowledge. I just wished to show that in the end there is no break in continuity between the child's game with the mirror and, at the other extreme, certain localised figures of the cinematic codes. The mirror is the site of primary identification. Identification with one's own look is secondary with respect to the mirror, i.e. for a general theory of adult activities, but it is the foundation of the cinema and hence primary when the latter is under discussion: it is *primary cinematic identification* proper ("primary identification" would be inaccurate from the psychoanalytic point of view; "secondary identification," more accurate in this respect, would be ambiguous for a cinematic psychoanalysis). As for identifications with characters, with their own different levels (out-of-frame character, etc.), they are secondary, tertiary cinematic identifications, etc.; taken as a whole in opposition to the identification of the spectator with his own look, they constitute secondary cinematic identification in the singular.

"SEEING A FILM"

Freud noted, vis-à-vis the sexual act, that the most ordinary practices depend on a large number of psychical functions which are distinct but work consecutively, so that all of them must be intact if what is regarded as a normal performance is to be possible (it is because neurosis and psychosis dissociate them and put some of them out of court that a kind of commutation is made possible whereby they can be listed retrospectively by the analyst). The apparently very simple act of *seeing a film* is no exception to this rule. As soon as it is subjected to analysis it reveals to us a complex, multiply interconnected imbrication of the functions of the imaginary, the real and the symbolic, which is also required in one form or another for every procedure of social life, but whose cinematic manifestation is especially impressive since it is played out on a small surface. (To this extent the theory of the cinema may some day contribute something to psychoanalysis, even if, through force of circumstances, this "reciprocation" remains very limited at the moment, the two disciplines being very unevenly developed.)

In order to understand the fiction film, I must both "take myself" for the character (= an imaginary procedure) so that he benefits, by analogical projection, from all the schemata of intelligibility that I have within me, and not take myself for him (= the return to the real) so that the fiction can be established as such (= as symbolic): this is *seeming-real*. Similarly, in order to understand the film (at all), I must perceive the photographed object as absent, its photograph as present, and the presence of this absence as signifying. The imaginary of the cinema presupposes the symbolic, for the spectator must first of all have known the primordial mirror. But as the latter instituted the ego very largely in the imaginary, the second mirror of the screen, a symbolic apparatus, itself in turn depends on reflection and lack. However, it is not phantasy, a "purely" symbolic-imaginary site, for the absence of the object and the codes of that absence are really produced in it by the *physis* of an equipment: the cinema is a body (a *corpus* for the semiologist), a fetish that can be loved.

THE PASSION FOR PERCEIVING

The practice of the cinema is only possible through the perceptual passions: the desire to see (= scopic drive, scopophilia, voyeurism), which was alone engaged in the art of the silent film, the desire to hear which has been added to it in the sound cinema (this is the *pulsion invocante*, the invocatory drive, one of the four main sexual drives for Lacan; it is well known that Freud isolated it less clearly and hardly deals with it as such).

These two sexual drives are distinguished from the others in that they are more dependent on a lack, or at least dependent on it in a more precise, more unique manner, which marks them from the outset, even more than the others, as being on the side of the imaginary.

However, this characteristic is to a greater or lesser degree proper to all the sexual drives insofar as they differ from purely organic instincts or needs (Lacan), or in Freud from the self-preservation drives (the "ego drives" which he tended subsequently to annex to narcissism, a tendency he could never quite bring himself to pursue to its conclusion). The sexual drive does not have so stable and strong a relationship with its "object" as do for example hunger and thirst. Hunger can only be satisfied by food, but food is quite certain to satisfy it; thus instincts are simultaneously more and less difficult to satisfy than drives; they depend on a perfectly real object for which there is no substitute, but they depend on nothing else. Drives, on the contrary, can be satisfied up to a point outside their objects (this is sublimation, or else, in another way, masturbation) and are initially capable of doing without them without putting the organism into immediate danger (hence repression). The needs of self-preservation can neither be repressed nor sublimated; the sexual drives are more labile and more accommodating, as Freud insisted (more radically perverse, says Lacan). Inversely, they always remain more or less unsatisfied, even when their object has been attained; desire is very quickly reborn after the brief vertigo of its apparent extinction, it is largely sustained by itself as desire, it has its own rhythms, often quite independent of those of the pleasure obtained (which seemed nonetheless its specific aim); the lack is what it wishes to fill, and at the same time what it is always careful to leave gaping, in order to survive as desire. In the end it has no object, at any rate no real object; through real objects which are all substitutes (and all the more numerous and interchangeable for that), it pursues an imaginary object (a "lost object") which is its truest object, an object that has always been lost and is always desired as such.

How, then, can one say that the visual and auditory drives have a stronger or more special relationship with the absence of their object, with the infinite pursuit of the imaginary? Because, as opposed to other sexual drives, the "perceiving drive"—combining into one the scopic drive and the invocatory drive—*concretely represents the absence of its object* in the distance at which it maintains it and which is part of its very definition: distance of the look, distance of listening. Psychophysiology makes a classic distinction between the "senses at a distance" (sight and hearing) and the others all which involve immediate proximity and which it calls the "senses of contact" (Pradines): touch, taste, smell, coenaesthetic sense, etc. Freud notes that voyeurism, like sadism in this respect, always keeps apart the *object*. (Here the object looked at) and the *source* of the drive, i.e. the generating organ (the eye); the voyeur does not look at his eye. With orality and anality, on the contrary, the exercise of the drive inaugurates a certain degree of partial fusion, a coincidence (= contact, tendential abolition of distance) of source and aim, for the aim is to obtain pleasure at the level of the source organ (= "organ pleasure"): e.g. what is called "pleasure of the mouth."

It is no accident that the main socially acceptable arts are based on the senses at a distance, and that those which depend on the senses of contact are often regarded as minor arts (e.g., the culinary arts, the art of perfumes, etc.). Nor is it an accident that the visual or auditory imaginaries have played a much more important part in the histories of societies than the tactile or olfactory imaginaries.

The voyeur is very careful to maintain a gulf, an empty space, between the object and the eye, the object and his own body: his look fastens the object at the right distance, as with those cinema spectators who take care to avoid being too close to or too far from the screen. The voyeur represents in space the fracture which forever separates him from the object; he represents his very dissatisfaction (which is precisely what he needs as a voyeur), and thus also his "satisfaction" insofar as it is of a specifically voyeuristic type. To fill in this distance would threaten to overwhelm the subject, to lead him to consume the object (the object which is now too close so that he cannot see it any more), to bring him to orgasm and the pleasure of his own body, hence to the exercise of other drives, mobilising the senses of contact and putting an end to the scopic arrangement. *Retention* is fully part of perceptual pleasure, which is thereby often coloured with anality. Orgasm is the object rediscoverd in a state of momentary illusion; it is the phantasy suppression of the gap between object and subject (hence the amorous myths of "fusion"). The looking drive, except when it is exceptionally well developed, is less directly related to orgasm than are the other component drives; it favours it by its excitatory action, but it is not generally sufficient to produce it by its figures alone, which thus belong to the realm of "preparatives." In it we do not find that illusion, however brief, of a lack filled, of a non-imaginary, of a full relation to the object, better established in other drives. If it is true of all desire that it depends on the infinite pursuit of its absent object, voyeuristic desire, along with certain forms of sadism, is the only desire whose principle of distance symbolically and spatially evokes this fundamental rent. . . .

THE SCOPIC REGIME OF THE CINEMA

However, although this set of features seems to me to be important, it does not yet characterise the signifier of the cinema proper, but rather that of all means of expression based on sight or hearing, and hence, among other "languages," that of practically all the arts (painting, sculpture, architecture, music, opera, theatre, etc.). What distinguishes the cinema is an extra reduplication, a supplementary and specific turn of the screw bolting desire to the lack. . . .

What defines the specifically cinematic *scopic regime* is not so much the distance kept, the "keeping" itself (first figure of the lack, common to all voyeurism), as the absence of the object seen. Here the cinema is profoundly different from the theatre as also from more intimate voyeuristic activities with a specifically erotic aim (there are intermediate genres, moreover: certain cabaret acts, strip-tease, etc.): cases where voyeurism remains linked to exhibitionism, where the two faces, active and passive, of the component drive are by no means so dissociated; where the object seen is present and hence presumably complicit; where the perverse activity—aided if need be by a certain dose of bad faith and happy illusion, varying from case to case, moreover, and sometimes reducible to very little, as in true perverse couples— is rehabilitated and reconciled with itself by being as it were undividedly taken in charge by two actors assuming its constitutive poles (the corresponding phantasies, in the absence of the actions, thus becoming interchangeable and shared by the play of reciprocal identification). In the theatre, as in domestic voyeurism, the passive actor (the one seen), simply because he is bodily present, because he does not go away, is presumed to consent, to cooperate deliberately. It may be that he really does, as exhibitionists in the clinical sense do, or as, in a sublimated fashion, does that oft noted triumphant exhibitionism characteristic of theatrical acting, counter- posed even by Bazin to cinematic representation. It may also be that the object seen has only accepted this condition (thus becoming an "object" in the ordinary sense of the word, and no longer only in the Freudian sense) under the pressure of more or less powerful external constraints, economic ones for example with certain poor strippers. (However, they must have consented at some point; rarely is the degree of acceptance zero, except in the case of *victimisation*, e.g. when a fascist militia strips its prisoners; the specific characteristics of the scopic arrangement are then distorted by the overpowerful intervention of another element, sadism.) Voyeurism which is not too sadistic (there is none which is not so at all) rests on a kind of *fic- tion*, more or less justified in the order of the real, sometimes institutionalised as in the theatre or striptease, a fiction that stipulates that the object "agrees," that it is therefore exhibitionist. Or more precisely, what is necessary in this fiction for the establishment of potency and desire is presumed to be sufficiently guaranteed by the physical presence of the object: "Since it is there, it must like it," such, hypo- critical or no, deluded or no, is the retrenchment needed by the voyeur so long as sadistic infiltrations are insufficient to make the object's refusal and constraint nece- sary to him. Thus, despite the distance instituted by the look—which transforms the object into a *picture* (a *tableau vivant*) and thus tips it over into the imaginary, even in its real presence—that presence, which persists, and the active consent which is its real or mythical correlate (but always real as myth) reestablish in the scopic space, momentarily at least, the illusion of a fullness of the object relation, of a state of desire which is not just imaginary.

It is this last recess that is attacked by the cinema signifier, it is in its precise emplacement (*in its place*, in both senses of the word) that it installs a new figure of the lack, the physical absence of the object seen. In the theatre, actors and spec- tators are present at the same time and in the same location, hence present one to another, as the two protagonists of an authentic perverse couple. But in the cinema, the actor was present when the spectator was not (= shooting), and the spectator is present when the actor is no longer (= projection): a failure to meet of the voyeur and the exhibitionist whose approaches no longer coincide (they have "missed" one another). The cinema's voyeurism must (of necessity) do without any very clear mark of consent on the part of the object. There is no equivalent here of the theatre actors' final "bow." And then the latter could see their voyeurs, the game was less unilateral, slightly better distributed. In the darkened hall, the voyeur is rally left alone (or with other voyeurs, which is worse), deprived of his other half in the myth-ical hermaphrodite (a hermaphrodite not necessarily constituted by the distribution of the sexes but rather by that of the active and passive poles in the exercise of the drive). Yet still a voyeur, since there is something to see, called the film, but some-thing in whose definition there is a great deal of "flight": not precisely something that hides, rather something that *lets* itself be seen without *presenting* itself to be seen, which has gone out of the room before leaving only its trace visible there. This is the origin in particular of that recipe of the classical cinema which said that the actor should never look directly at the audience (= the camera).

Thus deprived of rehabilitatory agreement, of a real or supposed consensus with the other (which was also the Other, for it had the status of a sanction on the plane of the symbolic), cinematic voyeurism, *unauthorised* scopophilia, is from the out-set more strongly established than that of the theater in direct line from the primal scene. Certain precise features of the institution contribute to this affinity: the obscu-rity surrounding the onlooker, the aperture of the screen with its inevitable keyhole effect. But the affinity is more profound. It lies first in the spectator's solitude in the cinema: those attending a cinematic projection do not, as in the theatre, consti-tute a true "audience," a temporary collectivity; they are an accumulation of indi-viduals who, despite appearances, more closely resemble the fragmented group of readers of a novel. It lies on the other hand in the fact that the filmic spectacle, the object seen, is more radically ignorant of its spectator, since he is not there, than the theatrical spectacle can ever be. A third factor, closely linked to the other two, also plays a part: the *segregation of spaces* that characterises a cinema performance and not a theatrical one. The "stage" and the auditorium are no longer two areas set up in opposition to each other within a single space; the space of the film, repre-sented by the screen, is utterly heterogeneous, it no longer communicates with that of the auditorium: one is real, the other perspective: a stronger break than any line of footlights. For its spectator the film unfolds in that simultaneously very close and definitively inaccessible "elsewhere" in which the child *sees* the amorous play of the parental couple, who are similarly ignorant of it and leave it alone, a pure onlooker whose participation is inconceivable. In this respect the cinematic signifier is not only "psychoanalytic"; it is more precisely Oedipal in type.

DISAVOWAL, FETISHISM

As can be seen, the cinema has a number of roots in the unconscious and in the great movements illuminated by psychoanalysis, but they can all be traced back to the specific characteristics of the institutionalised signifier. I have gone a little way in tracing some of these roots, that of mirror identification, that of voyeurism and exhibitionism. There is also a third, that of fetishism.

Since the famous article by Freud that inaugurated the problem, psychoanalysis has linked fetish and fetishism closely with castration and the fear it inspires. Castration, for Freud, and even more clearly for Lacan, is first of all the mother's castration, and that is why the main figures it inspires are to a certain degree com-mon to children of both sexes. The child who sees its mother's body is constrained by way of perception, by the "evidence of the senses," to accept that there are human beings deprived of a penis. But for a long time—and somewhere in it for ever—it will not interpret this inevitable observation in terms of an anatomical difference between the sexes (= penis/vagina). It believes that all human beings originally have a penis and it therefore understands what it has seen as the effect of a mutilation which redoubles its fear that it will be subjected to a similar fate (or else, in the case of the little girl after a certain age, the fear that she has already been subjected to it). Inversely, it is this very terror that is projected on to the spectacle of the mother's body, and invites the reading of an absence where anatomy sees a different conformation. The scenario of castration, in its broad lines, does not differ whether one understands it, like Lacan, as an essentially symbolic drama in which castration takes over in a decisive metaphor all the losses, both real and imaginary, that the child has already suffered (birth trauma, maternal breast, excrement, etc.), or whether on the contrary one tends, like Freud, to take that scenario slightly more literally. Before this *unveiling of a lack* (we are already close to the cinema signifier), the child, in order to avoid too strong an anxiety, will have to double up its belief (another cinematic characteristic) and from then on forever hold two contradictory opinions (proof that in spite of everything the real perception has not been without effect): 'All human beings are endowed with a penis' (primal belief) and 'Some human beings do not have a penis' (evidence of the senses). In other words, it will, perhaps definitively, retain its former belief *beneath* the new one, but it will also hold to its new perceptual observation while *disavowing* it on another level (= denial of perception, disavowal, Freud's *Verleugnung*). Thus is established the lasting matrix, the affective prototype of all the splittings of belief which man will henceforth be capable of in the most varied domains, of all the infinitely complex unconscious and occasionally conscious interactions which he will allow himself between 'believing' and 'not believing' and which will on more than one occasion be of great assistance to him in resolving (or denying) delicate problems. (If we were all a little honest with ourselves, we would realise that a truly integral belief, without any 'underside' in which the opposite is believed, would make even the most ordinary everyday life almost impossible.)

At the same time, the child, terrified by what it has seen or glimpsed, will have tried more or less successfully in different cases, to *arrest* its look, for all its life, at what will subsequently become the fetish: at a piece of clothing, for example, which masks the frightening discovery, or else precedes it (underwear, stockings, boots, etc.). The fixation on this 'just before' is thus another form of disavowal, of retreat from the perceived, although its very existence is dialectical evidence of the fact that the perceived has been perceived. The fetishistic prop will become a precondition for the establishment of potency and access to orgasm [*jouissance*], sometimes an indispensable precondition (true fetishism); in other developments it will only be a favourable condition, and one whose weight will vary with respect to the other features of the erotogenic situation as a whole. (It can be observed once again that the defence against desire itself becomes erotic, as the defence against anxiety itself becomes anxiogenic; for an analogous reason: what arises 'against' an affect also arises 'in' it and is not easily separated from it, even if that is its aim.) Fetishism is generally regarded as the 'perversion' par excellence, for it intervenes itself in the 'tabulation' of the others, and above all because they, like it (and this is what makes it their model), are based on the avoidance of castration. The fetish always represents the penis, it is always a substitute for it, whether metaphorically (= it masks its absence) or metonymically (= it is contiguous with its empty place). To sum up, the fetish signifies the penis as absent, it is its negative signifier; supplementing it, it puts a 'fullness' in place of a lack, but in doing so it also affirms that lack. It resumes within itself the structure of disavowal and multiple belief.

These few reminders are intended above all to emphasise the fact that the dossier of fetishism, before any examination of its cinematic extensions, contains two broad aspects which coincide in their depths (in childhood and by virtue of structure) but are relatively distinct in their concrete manifestations, i.e. the problems of belief (= disavowal) and that of the fetish itself, the latter more immediately linked to erotogenicity, whether direct or sublimated.

STRUCTURES OF BELIEF

I shall say very little about the problems of belief in the cinema because I have already discussed them in this part apropos of identification and the mirror: I have tried to describe, outside the special case of fiction, a few of the many and successive twists, the reversals (reduplications) that occur in the cinema to articulate together the imaginary, the symbolic and the real; each of these twists presupposes a division of belief; in order to work, the film does not only require a splitting, but a whole series of stages of belief, imbricated together into a chain by a remarkable machinery. In the third place, because the subject has already been largely dealt with by Octave Mannoni in his remarkable studies of the theatrical illusion, with reference to the fictional theatre. Of course, I have said above that theatrical fiction and cinematic fiction are not fictional in the same way; but this deviation concerned the representation, the signifying material and not the represented, i.e. the fiction-fact as such, in which the deviation is much smaller (at any rate so long as one is dealing with *spectacles* such as theatre and cinema—written fiction obviously presents somewhat different problems). Mannoni's analyses are just as valid for the fiction film, with the single reservation that the divergences in representation that I have already discussed are borne in mind.

I shall rest content to adapt these analyses to a cinematic perspective, and not feel obliged to repeat them (not so well) in detail. It is understood that the audience is not duped by the diegetic illusion, it knows that the screen presents no more than a fiction. And yet, it is of vital importance for the correct unfolding of the spectacle that this make-believe be scrupulously respected (or else the fiction film is declared poorly made), that everything is set to work to make the deception effective and to give it an air of truth (this is the problem of *verisimilitude*). Any spectator will tell you that he doesn't believe it, but everything happens as if there were nonetheless someone to be deceived, someone who really would believe in it. (I shall say that behind any fiction there is a second fiction: the diegetic events are fictional, that is the first; but everyone pretends to believe that they are true, and that is the second; there is even a third: the general refusal to admit that somewhere in oneself one believes they are genuinely true.) In other words, asks Mannoni, since it is accepted that the audience is incredulous, *who is it who is credulous* and must be maintained in his credulousness by the perfect organisation of the machinery (of the machination)?

This credulous person is, of course, another part of ourselves, he is still seated *beneath* the incredulous one, or in his heart, it is he who continues to believe, who disavows what he knows (he for whom all human beings are still endowed with a penis). But by a symmetrical and simultaneous movement, the incredulous person disavows the credulous one; no one will admit that he is duped by the plot. That is why the instance of credulousness is often projected into the outer world and constituted as a separate person, a person completely abused by the diegesis: thus, in Corneille's *L'Illusion comique*, a play with a significant title, the character Pridamant, the *naif*, who does not know what theatre is, and *for whom*, by a reversal foreseen in Corneille's plot itself, the representation of the play is given. By a partial identification with this character, the spectators can sustain their credulousness in all incredulousness.

This instance which believes and also its personified projection have fairly precise equivalents in the cinema: for example, the credulous spectators at the *Grand Café* in 1895, frequently and complacently evoked by the incredulous spectators who have come *later* (and are no longer children), those spectators of 1895 who fled their seats in terror when the train entered La Ciotat station (in Lumière's famous film), because they were afraid it would run them down. Or else, in so many films, the character of the dreamer—the sleeping dreamer—who during the film believed (as we did!) that it was true, whereas it was he who saw it all in a dream and who wakes up at the end of the film (as we do again). Octave Mannoni compares these switches of belief with those the ethnologist observes in certain populations in which his informers regularly declare that 'long ago we used to believe in the masks' (these masks are used to deceive children, like our Father Christmas, and adolescents learn at their initiation ceremonies that the 'masks' were in fact adults in disguise); in other words, these societies have always 'believed' in the masks, but have always relegated this belief to a 'long ago': they still believe in them, but always in the aorist tense (like everyone). This 'long ago' is childhood, when one really was duped by masks; among adults, the beliefs of 'long ago' irrigate the unbelief of today, but irrigate it by denegation (one could also say: *by delegation*, by attributing credulity to the child and to former times).

Certain cinematic subcodes inscribe disavowal into the film in the form of less permanent and more localised figures. They should be studied separately in this perspective. I am not thinking only of films which have been dreamt in their entirety by one of their characters, but also of all the sequences accompanied by a voice-off commentary, spoken sometimes by a character, sometimes by a kind of anonymous speaker. This voice, precisely a voice off, beyond jurisdiction, represents the rampart of unbelief (hence it is the opposite of the Pridamant character, yet has the same effect in the last analysis). The distance it establishes between the action and ourselves comforts our feeling that we are not duped by that action: thus reassured (behind the rampart), we can allow ourselves to be duped by it a bit longer (it is the speciality of naive distanciations to resolve themselves into alibis). There are also all those films within a film which downgear the mechanism of our belief-unbelief and anchor it in several stages, hence more strongly: the included film was an illusion, so the including film (the film as such) was not, or was somewhat less so.

THE CINEMA AS TECHNIQUE

As for the fetish itself, in its cinematic manifestations, who could fail to see that it consists fundamentally of the equipment of the cinema (= its technique), or of the cinema as a whole as equipment and as technique, for fiction films and others? It is no accident that in the cinema some cameramen, some directors, some critics, some spectators demonstrate a real fetishism of technique, often noted or denounced as such ("fetishism" is taken here in its ordinary sense, which is rather loose but does contain within it the analytical sense that I shall attempt to disengage). As strictly defined, the fetish, like the apparatus of the cinema, is a *prop*, the prop that disavows a lack and in doing so affirms it without wishing to. A prop, too, which is as it were placed on the body of the object; a prop which is the penis, since it negates its absence, and hence a partial object that makes the whole object lovable and desirable. The fetish is also the point of departure for specialised practices, and as is well known, desire in its modalities is all the more technical the more perverse it is.

Thus with respect to the desired body—to the body of desire rather—the fetish is in the same position as the technical equipment of the cinema with respect to the cinema as a whole. A fetish, the cinema as a technical performance, as prowess, as an *exploit*, an exploit that underlines and denounces the lack on which the whole arrangement is based (the absence of the object, replaced by its reflection), an exploit which consists at the same time of making this absence forgotten. The cinema fetishist is the person who is enchanted at what the machine is capable of, at the *theatre of shadows* as such. For the establishment of his full potency for cinematic enjoyment [*jouissance*] he must think at every moment (and above all *simultaneously*) of the force of presence the film has and of the absence on which this force is constructed. He must constantly compare the result with the means deployed (and hence pay attention to the technique), for his pleasure lodges in the gap between the two. Of course, this attitude appears most clearly in the connoisseur, the cinephile, but it also occurs, as a partial component of cinematic pleasure, in those who just go to the cinema: if they do go it is partly in order to be carried away by the film (or the fiction, if there is one), but also in order to *appreciate* as such the machinery that is carrying them away: they will say, precisely when they have been carried away, that the film was a good one, that it was well made (the same thing is said in French of a harmonious body).

It is clear that fetishism, in the cinema as elsewhere, is closely linked to the good object. The function of the fetish is to restore the latter, threatened in its "goodness" (in Melanie Klein's sense) by the terrifying discovery of the lack. Thanks to the fetish, which covers the wound and itself becomes erotogenic, the object as a whole can become desirable again without excessive fear. In a similar way, the whole cinematic institution is as it were *covered* by a thin and omnipresent garment, a stimulating prop through which it is consumed: the ensemble of its equipment and its tricks—and not just the celluloid strip, the *pellicule* or "little skin" which has been rightly mentioned in this connection—of the equipment which *needs* the lack in order to stand out in it by contrast, but which only affirms it insofar as it ensures that it is forgotten, and which lastly (its third twist) needs it also not to be forgotten, for fear that at the same stroke the fact that *it* caused it to be forgotten will be forgotten.

The fetish is the cinema in its *physical* state. A fetish is always material: insofar as one can make up for it by the power of the symbolic alone one is precisely no longer a fetishist. At this point it is important to recall that of all the arts the cinema is the one that involves the most extensive and complex equipment; the technical dimension is more obtrusive here than elsewhere. Along with television, it is the only art that is also an industry, or at least is so from the outset (the others become industries subsequently: music through the gramophone record or the cassette, books by mass printings and publishing trusts, etc.). In this respect only architecture is a little like it; there are "languages" that are *heavier* than others, more dependent on "hardware."

At the same time as it localises the penis, the fetish represents by synecdoche the whole body of the object as desirable. Similarly, interest in the equipment and technique is the privileged representative of *love for the cinema*. . . .

FETISH AND FRAME

Just like the other psychical structures that constitute the foundation of the cinema, fetishism does not intervene only in the constitution of the signifier, but also in certain of its more particular configurations. Here we have *framings* and also certain *camera movements* (the latter can anyway be defined as progressive changes in framing).

Cinema with directly erotic subject matter deliberately plays on the edges of the frame and the progressive, if need be incomplete revelations allowed by the camera as it moves, and this is no accident. Censorship is involved here: censorship of films and censorship in Freud's sense. Whether the form is static (framing) or dynamic (camera movements), the principle is the same; the point is to gamble simultaneously on the excitation of desire and its nonfulfilment (which is its opposite and yet favours it), by the infinite variations made possible precisely by the studios' technique on the exact emplacement of the *boundary* that bars the look, that puts an end to the seen, that inaugurates the downward (or upward) tilt into the dark, towards the unseen, the guessed-at. The framing and its displacements (that determine the *emplacement*) are in themselves forms of suspense and are extensively used in suspense films, though they retain this function in other cases. They have an inner affinity with the mechanisms of desire, its postponements, its new impetus, and they retain this affinity in other places than erotic sequences (the only difference lies in the *quantum* which is sublimated and the *quantum* which is not). The way the cinema, with its wandering framings (wandering like the look, like the caress), finds the means to reveal space has something to do with a kind of permanent undressing, a generalised striptease, a less direct but more perfected striptease, since it also makes it possible to dress space again, to remove from view what it has previously shown, to *take back* as well as to retain (like the child at the moment of the birth of the fetish, the child who has already seen, but whose look beats a rapid retreat): a striptease pierced with flash-backs, inverted sequences that then give new impetus to the forward movement. These veiling-unveiling procedures can also be compared with certain cinematic punctuations, especially slow ones strongly marked by a concern for control and expectation (slow fade-ins and fade-outs, irises, drawn-out lap-dissolves like those of Sternberg).

1975

LAURA MULVEY
VISUAL PLEASURE AND NARRATIVE CINEMA

Laura Mulvey came to film theory with a background in history. Her early essays, like the frequently cited "Visual Pleasure and Narrative Cinema," included here, consider the connections between film spectatorship and gender. Between 1974 and 1983, Mulvey collaborated on a number of avant-garde films with her then-husband, film theorist Peter Wollen, that grapple with issues central to her critical work: mythology and fantasy, the potential of film as a feminist medium, and the search for identity and subjectivity in patriarchal culture. Her recent work considers the digital technologies that are changing film, spectatorship, and bodily perception. Mulvey is currently a professor in the history of art, film, and visual media at Birkbeck College, University of London.

I. INTRODUCTION

A. A Political Use of Psychoanalysis

This paper intends to use psychoanalysis to discover where and how the fascination of film is reinforced by preexisting patterns of fascination already at work within the individual subject and the social formations that have moulded him. It takes as starting point the way film reflects, reveals and even plays on the straight, socially established interpretation of sexual difference which controls images, erotic ways of looking and spectacle. It is helpful to understand what the cinema has been, how its magic has worked in the past, while attempting a theory and a practice which will challenge this cinema of the past. Psychoanalytic theory is thus appropriate here as a political weapon, demonstrating the way the unconscious of patriarchal society has structured film form.

The paradox of phallocentrism in all its manifestations is that it depends on the image of the castrated woman to give order and meaning to its world. An idea of woman stands as lynch pin to the system: it is her lack that produces the phallus as a symbolic presence, it is her desire to make good the lack that the phallus signifies. Recent writing in *Screen* about psychoanalysis and the cinema has not sufficiently brought out the importance of the representation of the female form in a symbolic order in which, in the last resort, it speaks castration and nothing else. To summarise briefly: the function of woman in forming the patriarchal unconscious is two-fold, she first symbolises the castration threat by her real absence of a penis and second thereby raises her child into the symbolic. Once this has been achieved, her meaning in the process is at an end, it does not last into the world of law and language except as a memory which oscillates between memory of maternal plenitude and memory of lack. Both are posited on nature (or on anatomy in Freud's famous phrase). Woman's desire is subjected to her image as bearer of the bleeding wound, she can exist only in relation to castration and cannot transcend it. She turns her child into the signifier of her own desire to possess a penis (the condition, she imagines, of entry into the symbolic). Either she must gracefully give way to the word, the Name of the Father and the Law, or else struggle to keep her child down with her in the half-light of the imaginary. Woman then stands in patriarchal culture as signifier for the male other, bound by a symbolic order in which man can live out his phantasies and obsessions through linguistic command by imposing them on the silent image of woman still tied to her place as bearer of meaning, not maker of meaning.

There is an obvious interest in this analysis for feminists, a beauty in its exact rendering of the frustration experienced under the phallocentric order. It gets us nearer to the roots of our oppression, it brings an articulation of the problem closer, it faces us with the ultimate challenge: how to fight the unconscious structured like a language (formed critically at the moment of arrival of language) while still caught within the language of the patriarchy. There is no way in which we an produce an alternative out of the blue, but we can begin to make a break by examining patriarchy with the tools it provides, of which psychoanalysis is not the only but an important one. We are still separated by a great gap from important issues for the female unconscious which are scarcely relevant to phallocentric theory: the sexing of the female infant and her relationship to the symbolic, the sexually mature woman as nonmother, maternity outside the signification of the phallus, the vagina. . . . But, at this point, psychoanalytic theory as it now stands can at least advance our understanding of the status quo, of the patriarchal order in which we are caught.

B. Destruction of Pleasure is a Radical Weapon

As an advanced representation system, the cinema poses questions of the ways the unconscious (formed by the dominant order) structure ways of seeing and pleasure in looking. Cinema has changed over the last few decades. It is no longer the monolithic system based on large capital investment exemplified at its best by Hollywood in the 1930s, 1940s, and 1950s. Technological advances (16mm, etc.) have changed the economic conditions of cinematic production, which can now be artisanal as well as capitalist. Thus it has been possible for an alternative cinema to develop. However self-conscious and ironic Hollywood managed to be, it always restricted itself to a formal *mise-en-scène* reflecting the dominant ideological concept of the cinema. The alternative cinema provides a space for a cinema to be born which is radical in both a political and an aesthetic sense and challenges the basic assumptions of the mainstream film. This is not to reject the latter moralistically, but to highlight the ways in which its formal preoccupations reflect the psychical obsessions of the society which produced it, and, further, to stress that the alternative cinema must start specifically by reacting against these obsessions and assumptions. A politically and aesthetically avant-garde cinema is now possible, but it can still only exist as a counterpoint.

The magic of the Hollywood style at its best (and of all the cinema which fell within its sphere of influence) arose, not exclusively, but in one important aspect, from its skilled and satisfying manipulation of visual pleasure. Unchallenged, mainstream film coded the erotic into the language of the dominant patriarchal order. In the highly developed Hollywood cinema it was only through these codes that the alienated subject, torn in his imaginary memory by a sense of loss, by the terror of potential lack in phantasy, came near to finding a glimpse of satisfaction: through its formal beauty and its play on his own formative obsessions. This article will discuss the interweaving of that erotic pleasure in film, its meaning, and in particular the central place of the image of woman. It is said that analysing pleasure, or beauty, destroys it. That is the intention of this article. The satisfaction and reinforcement of the ego that represent the high point of film history hitherto must be attacked. Not in favour of a reconstructed new pleasure, which cannot exist in the abstract, nor of intellectualised unpleasure, but to make way for a total negation of the ease and plenitude of the narrative fiction film. The alternative is the thrill that comes from leaving the past behind without rejecting it, transcending outworn or oppressive forms, or daring to break with normal pleasurable expectations in order to conceive a new language of desire.

II. PLEASURE IN LOOKING, FASCINATION WITH THE HUMAN FORM

A. The cinema offers a number of possible pleasures. One is scopophilia. There are circumstances in which looking itself is a source of pleasure, just as, in the reverse formation, there is pleasure in being looked at. Originally, in his *Three Essays on Sexuality*, Freud isolated scopophilia as one of the component instincts of sexuality which exist as drives quite independently of the erotogenic zones. At this point he associated scopophilia with taking other people as objects, subjecting them to a controlling and curious gaze. His particular examples centre around the voyeuristic activities of children, their desire to see and make sure of the private and the forbidden (curiosity about other people's genital and bodily functions, about the presence or absence of the penis and, retrospectively, about the primal scene). In this analysis scopophilia is essentially active. (Later, in *Instincts and their Vicissitudes*, Freud developed his theory of scopophilia further, attaching it initially to pregenital autoeroticism, after which the pleasure of the look is transferred to others by analogy. There is a close working here of the relationship between the active instinct and its further development in a narcissistic form.) Although the instinct is modified by other factors, in particular the constitution of the ego, it continues to exist as the erotic basis for pleasure in looking at another person as object. At the extreme, it can become fixated into a perversion, producing obsessive voyeurs and Peeping Toms, whose only sexual satisfaction can come from watching, in an active controlling sense, an objectified other.

At first glance, the cinema would seem to be remote from the undercover world of the surreptitious observation of an unknowing and unwilling victim. What is seen of the screen is so manifestly shown. But the mass of mainstream film, and the conventions within which it has consciously evolved, portray a hermetically sealed world which unwinds magically, indifferent to the presence of the audience, producing for them a sense of separation and playing on their voyeuristic phantasy. Moreover, the extreme contrast between the darkness in the auditorium (which also isolates the spectators from one another) and the brilliance of the shifting patterns of light and shade on the screen helps to promote the illusion of voyeuristic separation. Although the film is really being shown, is there to be seen, conditions of screening and narrative conventions give the spectator an illusion of looking in on a private world. Among other things, the position of the spectators in the cinema is blatantly one of repression of their exhibitionism and projection of the repressed desire on to the performer.

B. The cinema satisfies a primordial wish for pleasurable looking, but it also goes further, developing scopophilia in its narcissistic aspect. The conventions of mainstream film focus attention on the human form. Scale, space, stories are all anthropomorphic. Here, curiosity and the wish to look intermingle with a fascination with likeness and recognition: the human face, the human body, the relationship between the human form and its surroundings, the visible presence of the person in the world. Jacques Lacan has described how the moment when a child recognises its own image in the mirror is crucial for the constitution of the ego. Several aspects of this analysis are relevant here. The mirror phase occurs at a time when the child's physical ambitions outstrip his motor capacity, with the result that his recognition of himself is joyous in that he imagines his mirror image to be more complete, more perfect than he experiences his own body. Recognition is thus overlaid with misrecognition: the image recognised is conceived as the reflected body of the self, but its misrecognition as superior projects this body outside itself as an ideal ego, the alienated subject, which, reintrojected as an ego ideal, gives rise to the future generation of identification with others. This mirror-moment predates language for the child.

Important for this article is the fact that it is an image that constitutes the matrix of the imaginary, of recognition/misrecognition and identification, and hence of the first articulation of the "I," of subjectivity. This is a moment when an older fascination with looking (at the mother's face, for an obvious example) collides with the initial inklings of self-awareness. Hence it is the birth of the long love affair/despair between image and self-image which has found such intensity of expression in film and such joyous recognition in the cinema audience. Quite apart from the extraneous similarities between screen and mirror (the framing of the human form in its surroundings, for instance), the cinema has structures of fascination strong enough to allow temporary loss of ego while simultaneously reinforcing the ego. The sense of forgetting the world as the ego has subsequently come to perceive it (I forgot who I am and where I was) is nostalgically reminiscent of that presubjective moment of image recognition. At the same time the cinema has distinguished itself in the production of ego ideals as expressed in particular in the star system, the stars centering both screen presence and screen story as they act out a complex proccess of likeness and difference (the glamorous impersonates the ordinary).

C. Sections II. A and B have set out two contradictory aspects of the pleasurable structures of looking in the conventional cinematic situation. The first, scopophilic, arises from pleasure in using another person as an object of sexual stimulation through sight. The second, developed through narcissism and the constitution of the ego, comes from identification with the image seen. Thus, in film terms, one implies a separation of the erotic identity of the subject from the object on the screen (active scopophilia), the other demands identification of the ego with the object on the screen through the spectator's fascination with and recognition of his like. The first is a function of the sexual instincts, the second of ego libido. This dichotomy was crucial for Freud. Although he saw the two as interacting and overlaying each other, the tension between instinctual drives and self-preservation continues to be a dramatic polarisation in terms of pleasure. Both are formative structures, mechanisms not meaning. In themselves they have no signification, they have to be attached to an idealisation. Both pursue aims in indifference to perceptual reality, creating the imagised, eroticised concept of the world that forms the perception of the subject and makes a mockery of empirical objectivity.

During its history, the cinema seems to have evolved a particular illusion of reality in which this contradiction between libido and ego has found a beautifully complementary phantasy world. In *reality* the phantasy world of the screen is subject to the law which produces it. Sexual instincts and identification processes have a meaning within the symbolic order which articulates desire. Desire, born with language, allows the possibility of transcending the instinctual and the imaginary, but its point of reference continually returns to the traumatic moment of its birth: the castration complex. Hence the look, pleasurable in form, can be threatening in content, and it is woman as representation/image that crystallises this paradox.

III. WOMAN AS IMAGE, MAN AS BEARER OF THE LOOK

A. In a world ordered by sexual imbalance, pleasure in looking has been split between active/male and passive/female. The determining male gaze projects its phantasy on to the female figure which is styled accordingly. In their traditional exhibitionist role women are simultaneously looked at and displayed, with their appearance coded for strong visual and erotic impact so that they can be said to connote *to-be-looked-at-ness*. Women displayed as sexual object is the leit-motif of erotic spectacle: from pin-ups to striptease, from Ziegfeld to Busby Berkeley, she holds the look, plays to and signifies male desire. Mainstream film neatly combined spectacle and narrative. (Note, however, how in the musical song-and-dance numbers break the flow of the diegesis.) The presence of woman is an indispensible element of spectacle in normal narrative film, yet her visual presence tends to work against the development of a story line, to freeze the flow of action in moments of erotic contemplation. This alien presence then has to be integrated into cohesion with the narrative. As Budd Boetticher has put it:

> What counts is what the heroine provokes, or rather what she represents. She is the one, or rather the love or fear she inspires in the hero, or else the concern he feels for her, who makes him act the way he does. In herself the woman has not the slightest importance.

(A recent tendency in narrative film has been to dispense with this problem alto-gether; hence the development of what Molly Haskell has called the "buddy movie," in which the active homosexual eroticism of the central male figures can carry the story without distraction.) Traditionally, the woman displayed has functioned on two levels: as erotic object for the characters within the screen story, and as erotic object for the spectator within the auditorium, with a shifting tension between the looks on either side of the screen. For instance, the device of the show-girl allows the two looks to be unified technically without any apparent break in the diegesis. A woman performs within the narrative, the gaze of the spectator and that of the male charac-ters in the film are neatly combined without breaking narrative verisimilitude. For a moment the sexual impact of the performing woman takes the film into a no-man's-land outside its own time and space. Thus Marilyn Monroe's first appearance in *The River of No Return* and Lauren Bacall's songs in *To Have or Have Not*. Similarly, conventional close-ups of legs (Dietrich, for instance) or a face (Garbo) integrate into the narrative a different mode of eroticism. One part of a fragmented body destroys the Renaissance space, the illusion of depth demanded by the narrative, it gives flat-ness, the quality of a cut-out or icon rather than verisimilitude to the screen.

B. An active/passive heterosexual division of labour has similarly controlled nar-rative structure. According to the principles of the ruling ideology and the psychi-cal structures that back it up, the male figure cannot bear the burden of sexual objectification. Man is reluctant to gaze at his exhibitionist like. Hence the split between spectacle and narrative supports the man's role as the active one of for-warding the story, making things happen. The man controls the film phantasy and also emerges as the representative of power in a further sense: as the bearer of the look of the spectator, transferring it behind the screen to neutralise the extra-diegetic tendencies represented by woman as spectacle. This is made possible through the processes set in motion by structuring the film around a main controlling figure with whom the spectator can identify. As the spectator identifies with the main male* protagonist, he projects his look on to that of his like, his screen surrogate, so that the power of the male protagonist as he controls events coincides with the active power of the erotic look, both giving a satisfying sense of omnipotence. A male movie star's glamourous characteristics are thus not those of the erotic object of the gaze, but those of the more perfect, more complete, more powerful ideal ego con-ceived in the original moment of recognition in front of the mirror. The character in the story can make things happen and control events better than the subject/spec-tator, just as the image in the mirror was more in control of motor coordination. In contrast to woman as icon, the active male figure (the ego ideal of the identifica-tion process) demands a three-dimensional space corresponding to that of the mir-ror-recognition in which the alienated subject internalised his own representation of this imaginary existence. He is a figure in a landscape. Here the function of film is

---

*There are films with a woman as main protagonist, of course. To analyse this phenomenon seriously here would take me too far afield. Pam Cook and Claire Johnston's study of *The Revolt of Mamie Stover* in Phil Hardy, ed., *Raoul Walsh* (Edinburgh 1974), shows in a striking case how the strength of this female protagonist is more apparent than real.

to reproduce as accurately as possible the so-called natural conditions of human perception. Camera technology (as exemplified by deep focus in particular) and camera movements (determined by the action of the protagonist), combined with invisible editing (demanded by realism) all tend to blur the limits of screen space. The male protagonist is free to command the stage, a stage of spatial illusion in which he articulates the look and creates the action.

C.1 Sections III. A and B have set out a tension between a mode of representation of woman in film and conventions surrounding the diegesis. Each is associated with a look: that of the spectator in direct scopophilic contact with the female form displayed for his enjoyment (connoting male phantasy) and that of the spectator fascinated with the image of his like set in an illusion of natural space, and through him gaining control and possession of the woman within the diegesis. (This tension and

Marilyn Monroe and Robert Mitchum in a publicity shot from *River of No Return* (1954). "As the spectator identifies with the main male protagonist, he projects his look on to that of his like, his screen surrogate, so that the power of the male protagonist as he controls events coincides with the active power of the erotic look, both giving a satisfying sense of omnipotence" (MULVEY, p. 716).

the shift from one pole to the other can structure a single text. Thus both in *Only Angels Have Wings* and in *To Have and Have Not*, the film opens with the woman as object of the combined gaze of spectator and all the male protagonists in the film. She is isolated, glamourous, on display, sexualised. But as the narrative progresses she falls in love with the main male protagonist and becomes his property, losing her outward glamorous characteristics, her generalised sexuality, her show-girl connotations; her eroticism is subjected to the male star alone. By means of identification with him, through participation in his power, the spectator can indirectly possess her too.)

But in psychoanalytic terms, the female figure poses a deeper problem. She also connotes something that the look continually circles around but disavows: her lack of penis, implying a threat of castration and hence unpleasure. Ultimately, the meaning of woman is sexual difference, the absence of the penis as visually ascertainable, the material evidence on which is based the castration complex essential for the organisation of entrance to the symbolic order and the law of the father. Thus the woman as icon, displayed for the gaze and enjoyment of men, the active controllers of the look, always threatens to evoke the anxiety it originally signified. The male unconscious has two avenues of escape from this castration anxiety: preoccupation with the reenactment of the original trauma (investigating the woman, demystifying her mystery), counterbalanced by the devaluation, punishment or saving of the guilty object (an avenue typified by the concerns of the film noir); or else complete disavowal of castration by the substitution of a fetish object or turning the represented figure itself into a fetish so that it becomes reassuring rather than dangerous (hence over-valuation, the cult of the female star). This second avenue, fetishistic scopophilia, builds up the physical beauty of the object, transforming it into something satisfying in itself. The first avenue, voyeurism, on the contrary, has associations with sadism: pleasure lies in ascertaining guilt (immediately associated with castration), asserting control and subjecting the guilty person through punishment or forgiveness. This sadistic side fits in well with narrative. Sadism demands a story, depends on making something happen, forcing a change in another person, a battle of will and strength, victory/defeat, all occurring in a linear time with a beginning and an end. Fetishistic scopophilia, on the other hand, can exist outside linear time as the erotic instinct is focussed on the look alone. These contradictions and ambiguities can be illustrated more simply by using works by Hitchcock and Sternberg, both of whom take the look almost as the content or subject matter of many of their films. Hitchcock is the more complex, as he uses both mechanisms. Sternberg's work, on the other hand, provides many pure examples of fetishistic scopophilia.

C.2 It is well known that Sternberg once said he would welcome his films being projected upside down so that story and character involvement would not interfere with the spectator's undiluted appreciation of the screen image. This statement is revealing but ingenuous. Ingenuous in that his films do demand that the figure of the woman (Dietrich, in the cycle of films with her, as the ultimate example) should be identifiable. But revealing in that it emphasises the fact that for him the pictorial space enclosed by the frame is paramount rather than narrative or identification processes. While Hitchcock goes into the investigative side of voyeurism, Sternberg produces the ultimate fetish, taking it to the point where the powerful look of the male protagonist (characteristic of traditional narrative film) is broken in favour of the image in direct erotic rapport with the spectator. The beauty of the woman as object and the screen space coalesce; she is no longer the bearer of guilt but a perfect product, whose body, stylised and fragmented by close-ups, is the content of the film, and the direct recipient of the spectator's look. Sternberg plays down the illusion of screen depth; his screen tends to be one-dimensional, as light and shade, lace, steam, foliage, net, streamers, etc, reduce the visual field. There is little or no mediation of the look through the eyes of the main male protagonist. On the contrary, shadowy presences like La Bessière in *Morocco* act as surrogates for the director, detached as they are from audience identification. Despite Sternberg's insistence that his stories are irrelevant, it is significant that they are concerned with situation, not suspense, and cyclical rather than linear time, while plot complications revolve around misunderstanding rather than conflict. The most important absence is that of the controlling male gaze within the screen scene. The high point of emotional drama in the most typical Dietrich films, her supreme moments of erotic meaning, take place in the absence of the man she loves in the fiction. There are other witnesses, other spectators watching her on the screen, their gaze is one with, not standing in for, that of the audience. At the end of *Morocco*, Tom Brown has already disappeared into the desert when Amy Jolly kicks off her gold sandals and walks after him. At the end of *Dishonoured*, Kranau is indifferent to the fate of Magda. In both cases, the erotic impact, sanctified by death, is displayed as a spectacle for the audience. The male hero misunderstands and, above all, does not see.

In Hitchcock, by contrast, the male hero does see precisely what the audience sees. However, in the films I shall discuss here, he takes fascination with an image through scopophilic eroticism as the subject of the film. Moreover, in these cases the hero portrays the contradictions and tensions experienced by the spectator. In *Vertigo* in particular, but also in *Marnie* and *Rear Window*, the look is central to the plot, oscillating between voyeurism and fetishistic fascination. As a twist, a further manipulation of the normal viewing process which in some sense reveals it, Hitchcock uses the process of identification normally associated with ideological correctness and the recognition of established morality and shows up its perverted side. Hitchcock has never concealed his interest in voyeurism, cinematic and non-cinematic. His heroes are exemplary of the symbolic order and the law— a policeman (*Vertigo*), a dominant male possessing money and power (*Marnie*)— but their erotic drives lead them into compromised situations. The power to subject another person to the will sadistically or to the gaze voyeuristically is turned on to the woman as the object of both. Power is backed by a certainty of legal right and the established guilt of the woman (evoking castration, psychoanalytically speaking). True perversion is barely concealed under a shallow mask of ideological correctness—the man is on the right side of the law, the woman on the wrong. Hitchcock's skilful use of identification processes and liberal use of subjective camera from the point of view of the male protagonist draw the spectators deeply into his position, making them share his uneasy gaze. The audience is absorbed into a voyeuristic situation within the screen scene and diegesis which parodies his own in the cinema. In his analysis of *Rear Window*, Douchet takes the film as a metaphor for the cinema. Jeffries is the audience, the events in the apartment block opposite correspond to the screen. As he watches, an erotic dimension is added to his look, a central image to the drama. His girlfriend Lisa had been of little sexual interest to him, more or less a drag, so long as she remained on the spectator side. When she crosses the barrier between his room and the block opposite, their relationship is reborn erotically. He does not merely watch her through his lens, as a distant meaningful image, he also sees her as a guilty intruder exposed by a dangerous man threatening her with punishment, and thus finally saves her. Lisa's exhibitionism has already been established by her obsessive interest in dress and style, in being a passive image of visual perfection: Jeffries' voyeurism and activity have also been established through his work as a photo-journalist, a maker of stories and captor of images. However, his enforced inactivity, binding him to his seat as a spectator, puts him squarely in the phantasy position of the cinema audience.

In *Vertigo*, subjective camera predominates. apart from one flash-back from Judy's point of view, the narrative is woven around what Scottie sees or fails to see. The audience follows the growth of his erotic obsession and subsequent despair precisely from his point of view. Scottie's voyeurism is blatant: he falls in love with a woman he follows and spies on without speaking to. Its sadistic side is equally blatant: he has chosen (and freely chosen, for he had been a successful lawyer) to be a policeman, with all the attendant possibilities of pursuit and investigation. As a result, he follows, watches and falls in love with a perfect image of female beauty and mystery. Once he actually confronts her, his erotic drive is to break her down and force her to tell by persistent cross-questioning. Then, in the second part of the film, he reenacts his obsessive involvement with the image he loved to watch secretly. He reconstructs Judy as Madeleine, forces her to conform in every detail to the actual physical appearance of his fetish. Her exhibitionism, her masochism, make her an ideal passive counterpart to Scottie's active sadistic voyeurism. She knows her part is to perform, and only by playing it through and then replaying it can she keep Scottie's erotic interest. But in the repetition he does break her down and succeeds in exposing her guilt. His curiosity wins through and she is punished. In *Vertigo*, erotic involvement with the look is disorientating: the spectator's fascination is turned against him as the narrative carries him through and entwines him with the processes that he is himself exercising. The Hitchcock hero here is firmly placed within the symbolic order, in narrative terms. He has all the attributes of the patriarchal superego. Hence the spectator, lulled into a false sense of security by the apparent legality of his surrogate, sees through his look and finds himself exposed as complicit, caught in the moral ambiguity of looking. Far from being simply an aside on the perversion of the police, *Vertigo* focuses on the implications of the active/looking, passive/looked-at split in terms of sexual difference and the power of the male symbolic encapsulated in the hero. Marnie, too, performs for Mark Rutland's gaze and masquerades as the perfect to-be-looked-at image. He, too, is on the side of the law until, drawn in by obsession with her guilt, her secret, he longs to see her in the act of committing a crime, make her confess and thus save her. So he, too, becomes complicit as he acts out the implications of his power. He controls money and words, he can have his cake and eat it.

IV. SUMMARY

The psychoanalytic background that has been discussed in this article is relevant to the pleasure and unpleasure offered by traditional narrative film. The scopophilic instinct (pleasure in looking at another person as an erotic object), and, in contradistinction, ego libido (forming identification processes) act as formations, mechanisms, which this cinema has played on. The image of woman as (passive) raw material for the (active) gaze of man takes the argument a step further into the structure of representation, adding a further layer demanded by the ideology of the patriarchal order as it is worked out in its favourite cinematic form—illusionistic narrative film. The argument turns again to the psychoanalytic background in that woman as representation signifies castration, inducing voyeuristic or fetishistic mechanisms to circumvent her threat. None of these interacting layers is intrinsic to film, but it is only in the film form that they can reach a perfect and beautiful contradiction, thanks to the possibility in the cinema of shifting the emphasis of the look. It is the place of the look that defines cinema, the possibility of varying it and exposing it. This is what makes cinema quite different in its voyeuristic potential from, say, strip-tease, theatre, shows, etc. Going far beyond highlighting a woman's to-be-looked-at-ness, cinema builds the way she is to be looked at into the spectacle itself. Playing on the tension between film as controlling the dimension of time (editing, narrative) and film as controlling the dimension of space (changes in distance, editing), cinematic codes create a gaze, a world, and an object, thereby producing an illusion cut to the measure of desire. It is these cinematic codes and their relationship to formative external structures that must be broken down before mainstream film and the pleasure it provides can be challenged.

To begin with (as an ending), the voyeuristic-scopophilic look that is a crucial part of traditional filmic pleasure can itself be broken down. There are three different looks associated with cinema: that of the camera as it records the profilmic event, that of the audience as it watches the final product, and that of the characters at each other within the screen illusion. The conventions of narrative film deny the first two and subordinate them to the third, the conscious aim being always to eliminate intrusive camera presence and prevent a distancing awareness in the audience. Without these two absences (the material existence of the recording process, the critical reading of the spectator), fictional drama cannot achieve reality, obviousness and truth. Nevertheless, as this article has argued, the structure of looking in narrative fiction film contains a contradiction in its own premises: the female image as a castration threat constantly endangers the unity of the diegesis and bursts through the world of illusion as an intrusive, static, one-dimensional fetish. Thus the two looks materially present in time and space are obsessively subordinated to the neurotic needs of the male ego. The camera becomes the mechanism for producing an illusion of Renaissance space, flowing movements compatible with the human eye, an ideology of representation that revolves round the perception of the subject; the camera's look is disavowed in order to create a convincing world in which the spectator's surrogate can perform with verisimilitude. Simultaneously, the look of the audience is denied an intrinsic force: as soon as fetishistic representation of the female image threatens to break the spell of illusion, and the erotic image on the screen appears directly (wthout mediation) to the spectator, the fact of fetishisation, concealing as it does castration fear, freezes the look, fixates the spectator and prevents him from acheiving any distance from the image in front of him.

This complex interaction of looks is specific to film. The first blow against the monolithic accumulation of traditional film conventions (already undertaken by radical filmmakers) is to free the look of the camera into its materiality in time and space and the look of the audience into dialectics, passionate detachment. There is no doubt that this destroys the satisfaction, pleasure and privilege of the 'invisible guest', and highlights how film has depended on voyeuristic active/passive mechanisms. Women, whose image has continually been stolen and used for this end, cannot view the decline of the traditional film form with anything much more than sentimental regret.

1975

TANIA MODLESKI

FROM THE WOMEN WHO KNEW TOO MUCH: HITCHCOCK AND FEMINIST THEORY

THE MASTER'S DOLLHOUSE: *REAR WINDOW*

In "Visual Pleasure and Narrative Cinema," Laura Mulvey uses two Hitchcock films to exemplify her theory. According to Mulvey, both *Rear Window* (1954) and *Vertigo* (1958) are films "cut to the measure of male desire"—tailored, that is, to the fears and fantasies of the male spectator, who, because of the threat of castration posed by the woman's image, needs to see her fetishized and controlled in the course of the narrative.[1] Certainly, these two films appear perfectly to support Mulvey's thesis that classic narrative film negates woman's view, since each of them seems to confine us to the hero's vision of events and to insist on that vision by literally stressing the man's point of view throughout. The film spectator apparently has no choice *but* to identify with the male protagonist, who exerts an active, controlling gaze over a passive female object. Of *Rear Window*, Mulvey writes, "Lisa's exhibitionism [is] established by her obsessive interest in dress and style, in being a passive image of visual perfection; Jeffries's voyeurism and activity [are] established through his work as a photojournalist, a maker of stories and captor of images. However, his enforced inactivity, binding him to his seat as a spectator, puts him squarely in the phantasy position of the cinema audience."[2]

This last observation connects Mulvey to a tradition of criticism of the film that begins with the work of the French critic Jean Douchet and that sees the film as a metacinematic commentary: spectators identifying with the chair-bound, voyeuristic protagonist find themselves in complicity with his guilty desires.[3] Because of

---

[1]Laura Mulvey, "Visual Pleasure and Narrative Cinema," *Screen* 16, no. 3 (1975): 17.
[2]Mulvey, "Visual Pleasure," p. 16.
[3]Jean Douchet, "Hitch et son Public," *Cahiers du Cinéma*, no. 113 (November 1960): 10. For the most recent discussion of the film in relation to questions of spectatorship, see R. Barton Palmer, "The Metafictional Hitchcock: The Experience of Viewing and the Viewing of Experience in *Rear Window* and *Psycho*," *Cinema Journal* 26, no. 2 (Winter 1986): 4–29.

Hitchcock's relentless insistence on the male gaze, even critics like Robin Wood, who are anxious to save the film for feminism, restrict themselves to discussing the film's critique of the position of the hero and, by extension, of the *male* spectator whose "phantasy position the hero occupies."[4] But what happens, in the words of a recent relevant article by Linda Williams, "when the woman looks"?[5] I shall argue, against the grain of critical consensus, that the film actually has something to say about this question.[6]

Rear Window is the story of photojournalist, L. B. Jeffries (James Stewart), who, as a result of an accident on the job, is confined to a wheel chair in his apartment, where he whiles away the time spying on his neighbors. These include a middle-aged, alcoholic musician with composer's block; a newlywed couple who spend all their time in bed behind closed shades; a childless couple who sleep on the balcony at night and own a little dog; a voluptuous dancer, "Miss Torso," who practices her suggestive dance routines as she goes about her daily chores; "Miss Lonelyhearts," who fantasizes about gentlemen callers; and Lars Thorwald, a costume jewelry salesman with a nagging, invalid wife.

The film opens with the camera panning the courtyard of a lower east side housing development and then moving back through a window where we see L. B. Jeffries asleep, his chair turned away from the window, beads of sweat on his face. There is a cut to a thermometer, which registers over ninety degrees, and then the camera tilts down Jeffries's body to reveal that his leg is in a cast. The camera proceeds to explore the apartment, calling our attention to some smashed camera equipment, a photograph of a car accident, some other photographs Jeff has taken in his travels, and, finally, a negative of a blonde woman's face followed by a "positive" photograph of her on the cover of *Life* magazine. When Jeff wakes up, he begins to observe his neighbors and then complains on the phone to his editor that if he doesn't get back to the job soon, he's going to do "something drastic like get married." While he speaks of the horrors of marriage, we watch from his point of view as Thorwald (Raymond Burr) returns home to be greeted by a nagging wife.

Soon after, Stella (Thelma Ritter), the insurance company nurse, comes in to give Jeff a massage. She immediately begins to scold him for being a Peeping Tom, and tries to persuade him to marry Lisa Freemont, claiming that his lukewarm attitude to the woman he claims is "too perfect" is abnormal. Later that evening, Lisa (Grace Kelly) comes to visit, dressed in an $1100 gown and accompanied by a waiter from the Twenty One Club, who is delivering their dinner. Lisa and Jeff have an argument as he tells her that marriage to him, given his grueling lifestyle and her pampered one, is out of the question. When she goes home, Jeff begins to watch the neighbors again and observes some strange movements on the part of Lars Thorwald. Eventually Jeff falls asleep, and we see Thorwald and a woman leaving Thorwald's

[4]Robin Wood, "Fear of Spying," *American Film* (November 1982): 31–32.

[5]Linda Williams, "When the Woman Looks," in *Revision: Essays in Feminist Film Criticism*, eds. Mary Ann Doane, Patricia Mellencamp, and Williams. The American Film Institute Monograph Series, Vol. 3 (Frederick, MD: University Publications of America, 1984).

[6]"Robert Stam and Roberta Pearson do, however, devote one brief paragraph to this issue in their article, "Hitchcock's *Rear Window:* Reflexivity and the Critique of Voyeurism," *Enclitic* 7, no. 1 (Spring 1983): 143.

apartment. The next day Jeff notices that Mrs. Thorwald has gone, and he becomes convinced that Thorwald has murdered his wife—a conviction that becomes more and more obsessive as the film progresses—to the point where he uses first binoculars and then a huge telephoto lens to see more closely. He attempts to persuade Lisa, Stella, and his friend, policeman Tom Doyle (Wendell Corey), of his interpretation of the events across the way. Though Doyle remains skeptical, the women eventually come to accept Jeff's view and actually go looking for clues.

Lisa is caught by Thorwald as she searches his apartment for the wedding ring that will prove Jeff's theory, and Jeff is forced to look helplessly on as Thorwald pushes her around. Jeff warns the police, whom he has just contacted on the phone to alert them that Miss Lonelyhearts is about to take an overdose of pills. The police arrive in time to prevent any harm from befalling Lisa, and they take her to jail. After Jeff sends Stella off with the bail money, he finds himself face to face with the guilty Thorwald, who asks, "What is it you want of me?" and steps forward menacingly. Jeff tries to keep him at bay by popping off flashbulbs in his face, but Thorwald manages to grab him and, during a struggle, Jeff falls to the ground from a window ledge.

The film ends with another pan around the courtyard. The various plots featuring the neighbors have been resolved: workmen are repainting the bathroom of Thorwald's apartment, where blood had splattered when Thorwald murdered his wife and cut her up in pieces; Miss Lonelyhearts, whose suicide was prevented when she heard the musician's beautiful song, has formed a relationship with the musician; Miss Torso's little soldier boyfriend Stanley arrives and asks what's in the refrigerator; the childless couple, whose dog was murdered by Thorwald because it was digging in the flower garden where evidence was buried (the dog who "knew too much," as Lisa puts it), have gotten another dog; and the newlywed wife is nagging her husband because he has lost his job. The camera tracks back into the window to show L.B. asleep, as before, only this time both his legs are in casts. The camera movement ends on a medium shot of Lisa lying on Jeff's bed, in pants and shirt, and reading a book entitled *Beyond the High Himalayas*. She steals a glance at Jeff to make sure he is still asleep, puts down the book, and picks up a copy of Harper's *Bazaar*. On the sound-track is the musician's song, "Lisa," finally completed, like the narrative itself.

A number of critics, most of whom center their analyses around the film's critique of voyeurism, have pointed out that the film's protagonist is fixated at an infantile level of sexual development and must in the course of the narrative grow into "mature sexuality": "Jeffries's voyeurism goes hand in hand with an absorbing fear of mature sexuality. Indeed, the film begins by hinting at a serious case of psychosexual pathology. The first image of Jeffries, asleep with hand on thigh is quietly masturbatory, as if he were an invalid who had just abused himself in the dark."[7] By the end of the film Jeff has supposedly learned his lesson and "has realized the corollary psychic costs of both voyeurism and solitude": he is now ready for the marriage he has all along resisted and for the "mature" sexual relation that this implies. Yet there is a sense in which the image of Lisa in masculine clothes,

[7] Stam and Pearson, "Hitchcock's *Rear Window*: Reflexivity," p. 140.

absorbed in "masculine" interests only places Jeff—and the audience—more squarely than ever in the Imaginary. For as the narrative proceeds, the sexuality of the woman, which is all along presented as threatening, is first combated by the fantasy of female dismemberment and then, finally, by a re-membering of the woman according to the little boy's fantasy that the female is no different from himself.[8]

Jeff claims that Lisa is "too perfect." On the face of it, of course, this reason for resisting marriage is patently absurd, as Stella does not fail to point out. (This absurdity leads one critic to argue that the project of the film is to stimulate the audience's desire for the couple's union by inducing frustration at "Jeff's indifference to her allure."[9]) But, while it may indeed be "unrealistic" that any red-blooded man would reject Grace Kelly, there is a certain psychological plausibility in Jeff's fear of Lisa's "perfection"—a fear that is related to man's fear of women's difference and his suspicion that they may not, after all, be mutilated (imperfect) men, may not be what, as Susan Lurie puts it, *men* would be if they lacked penises— "bereft of sexuality, helpless, incapable."[10] Lurie's words certainly describe the situation of Jeff, whose impotence is suggested by the enormous cast on his leg and his consequent inability to move about, so that ultimately he is unable to rescue the woman he loves from danger. By contrast, Lisa Freemont is anything but helpless and incapable, despite Mulvey's characterization of her as a "passive image of visual perfection"—and this is where the "problem" lies.

In our very first view of her, Lisa is experienced as an overwhelmingly powerful presence. Jeff is asleep in his chair, the camera positioned over him, when suddenly an ominous shadow crosses his face. There is a cut to a closeup of Grace Kelly, a vision of loveliness, bending down toward him and us: the princess-to-be waking Sleeping Beauty with a kiss. These two shots—shadow and vibrant image— suggest the underlying threat posed by the desirable woman and recall the negative and positive images of the woman on the cover of *Life*. When Jeff jokingly inquires, "Who are you?" Lisa turns on three lamps, replies, "Reading from top to bottom, Lisa . . . Carol . . . Freemont," and strikes a pose. While the pose confirms the view of her as exhibitionist, her confident nomination of herself reveals her to be extremely self-possessed—in contrast to the man who is known by only one of *his* three names. The two engage in small talk as Lisa sets about preparing the dinner brought in from the Twenty One Club, and Jeff makes continual jibes about married life. Lisa ends the conversation by claiming, "At least you can't say the dinner's not alright," and over a shot of a very appetizing meal, Jeff replies, exasperated, "Lisa, it's perfect, as *always*." In the meantime we have witnessed Thorwald taking dinner in to his wife, who pushes it from her in disgust and flings away the rose he has placed on the tray.

---

[8]A constant theme in the writings of Stephen Heath is the way cinema works to "remember" the (male) spectator: e.g., "the historical reality it encounters [is] a permanent crisis of identity that must be permanently resolved by remembering the history of the individual subject." "Film Performance," *Questions of Cinema* (Bloomington: Indiana University Press, 1981), p. 125.

[9]Ruth Perlmutter, "*Rear Window*: A Construction Story," *Journal of Film and Video* 37 (Spring 1985): 59.

[10]Susan Lurie, "Pornography and the Dread of Women: The Male Sexual Dilemma," *Take Back the Night: Women on Pornography*, ed. Laure Lederer (New York: William Morrow, 1980), p. 166.

Important parallels are thus set up between Lisa and Thorwald, on the one hand, and Jeff and the wife, on the other. Critics have seldom picked up on this parallelism, preferring instead to stress a symmetry along sexual lines—that is, Jeff's similarity to Thorwald and Lisa's resemblance to the blonde wife. Interestingly, Hitchcock himself was quite explicit about the gender reversal: "The symmetry is the same as in *Shadow of a Doubt.* On one side of the yard you have the Stewart–Kelly couple, with him immobilized by his leg in a cast, while she can move about freely. And on the other side there is a sick woman who's confined to her bed, while the husband comes and goes."[11] Raymond Bellour has shown how in classic cinema a binary opposition between movement and stasis generally works to establish male superiority in classical narrative cinema.[12] In *Rear Window*, however, the *woman* is continually shown to be physically superior to the hero, not only in her physical movements but also in her dominance within the frame: she towers over Jeff in nearly every shot in which they both appear.

Given this emphasis on the woman's mobility, freedom, and power, it seems odd that an astute critic like Mulvey sees in the image of Lisa Freemont only a passive object of the male gaze. Mulvey bases her judgment on the fact that Lisa appears to be "obsessed with dress and style," continually putting herself on visual display for Jeff so that he will notice her and turn his gaze away from the neighbors.[13] (In this respect, the "project" of the film resembles that of *Rebecca*, which also deals with a woman's efforts to get the man she loves to look at her.) It is important, however, not to dismiss out of hand Lisa's professional and personal involvement with fashion but to consider all the ways this involvement *functions* in the narrative. This is no simple matter. For if, on the one hand, woman's concern with fashion quite obviously serves patriarchal interests, on the other hand, this very concern is often denigrated and ridiculed by men (as it is by Jeff throughout the film)—thus putting women in a familiar double bind by which they are first assigned a restricted place in patriarchy and then condemned for occupying it. For feminist criticism to ignore the full complexity of woman's contradictory situation is to risk acquiescing in masculine contempt for female activities. In *A Room of One's Own*, Virginia Woolf suggested that a necessary, if not sufficient, feminist strategy must be to reclaim and revalue women's actual experience under patriarchy. The example Woolf gives of the double literary standard operating against this experience is telling, and relevant to our discussion here: "Speaking crudely, football and sport are important, the worship of fashion, the buying of clothes trivial, and these values are inevitably transferred from life to fiction."[14] Certainly these two sets of values are counterpoised in the fiction of *Rear Window* (Jeff has, after all, broken his leg at a *sporting* event, where he stepped in front of an oncoming race car to get a spectacular

---

[11]François Truffaut, *Hitchcock* (New York: Simon and Schuster, 1983), p. 166.

[12]This point is developed at great length in Raymond Bellour, "*The Birds*: Analysis of a Sequence," Mimeograph, The British Film Institute Advisory Service, n.d.

[13]That he is so reluctant to do so provides an interesting confirmation of Christian Metz's thesis that in narrative cinema, it is the story, rather than any particular character, that "exhibits itself." "History/discourse: a note on two voyeurisms," *Theories of Authorship,* ed. John Caughie (London: Routledge & Kegan Paul, 1981), p. 231.

[14]Virginia Woolf, *A Room of One's Own* (New York: Harbinger, 1957), p. 77.

photograph) and are the source of the couple's quarrels. Jeff dwells on the hard-ships of his manly life style and belittles Lisa's work when she enthusiastically describes her day to him. In the film, then, "fashion" is far from representing woman's unproblematic assimilation to the patriarchal system, but functions to some extent as a signifier of feminine desire and female sexual difference.

Throughout the film, Lisa's exquisite costumes give her the appearance of an alien presence in Jeff's milieu, more strange and marvelous than the various exotic wonders he has encountered in his travels—a strangeness that is fascinating and threatening at the same time. The threat becomes especially evident in the sequence in which Lisa boldly acts on her desire for Jeff and comes to spend the night with him. Significantly, this is the night when she becomes convinced of the truth of Thorwald's guilt. Jeff has just observed Thorwald talking on the phone and sort-ing through some jewelry, which includes a wedding ring, in his wife's purse. In Hitchcock's films, women's purses (and their jewelry) take on a vulgar Freudian significance relating to female sexuality and to men's attempts to investigate it. One might think, for example, of the purse in the opening closeup shot of *Marnie* (1964) that contains Marnie's "identity" cards and the booty of her theft from patriarchy. In *Rear Window*, Lisa concludes that Mrs. Thorwald *must* have been murdered rather than, as Tom Doyle believes, sent on a trip because no woman would leave behind her favorite purse (to say nothing of her wedding ring). As she muses, Lisa picks up her own designer purse, which we discover is a kind of "trick" purse; it is really a tiny suitcase, and in one of her many lines that sound like sexual double entendres (this one unwittingly echoing the Freudian notion of male and female sexuality, but reversing their values since it takes the latter as the standard), she says, "I'll bet *yours* isn't this small." When she opens the case, an elaborate and expensive negligee comes tumbling out, along with a pair of lovely slippers. The purse connects Lisa to the victimized woman, as does the negligee, since the invalid Mrs. Thorwald was always seen wearing a nightgown; but it also, importantly, connects her to the criminal, Lars Thorwald, and so is an overdetermined image like the images in the Freudian dreamwork. Thus when Tom Doyle comes to Jeff's apartment later in the evening, he keeps casting mean-ingful glances at the nightgown as if it were an incriminating object; when Jeff asks why Thorwald didn't tell his landlord where he was going, Doyle looks at the suitcase and asks pointedly, "Do you tell *your* landlord everything?" After Doyle has gone, Lisa picks up the suitcase, offering Jeff a "preview of coming attractions," and as she goes into the bathroom to change, she asks, "Do you think Mr. Doyle thought I stole this case?"

Lisa's aggressive sexuality, which is thus humorously labelled "criminal," would seem to provoke in Jeff and the male spectator a retaliatory aggression that finds an outlet in Thorwald's acts of murder and dismemberment. The interpretation of *Rear Window* which critics like Robin Wood take to be primary—that Lars Thorwald's murder of his wife enacts a wish on the part of Jeff to be rid of Lisa—is persuasive as far as it goes, but this wish may further be analyzed as a response to the male fear of impotence and lack. Jeff's impairment—his helplessness, passivity, and invalidism—impel him to construct a story that, in the words of Kaja Silverman (describing the male's psychic trajectory), attempts to "resituate . . . loss at the level of the female anatomy, thereby restoring to the [male] an imaginary wholeness."[15] Hence the fantasy of female dismemberment that pervades the film: not only are there many gruesome jokes about Lars Thorwald's cutting up his wife's body, but Jeff also names the women across the way according to body parts: Miss Lonelyhearts and Miss Torso—yet another decapitated woman.[16]

This response is a psychic consequence of Jeff's placement at the mirror stage of development, a placement that, as critics like to point out, makes him very much like Christian Metz's cinematic spectator, who occupies a transcendent, god-like position in relation to the screen.[17] To some extent, however, this analogy between the windows across the way and the cinema screen is misleading, since it is the very *difference* between the world observed by Jeff and the larger-than-life-world of most films that accounts for the strong effect of transcendence evoked by *Rear Window*. For Jeff's world is a miniature one, like a dollhouse—a world, as Susan Stewart writes, "of inversion [wherein] contamination and crudeness are controlled . . . by an absolute manipulation of space and time."[18] Resembling other fantasy structures, . . . even sleep," the miniature, according to Stewart, "tends toward tableau rather than narrative" and "is against speech, particularly as speech reveals an inner dialectical, or dialogic, nature. . . . All senses are reduced to the visual, a sense which in its transcendence remains ironically and tragically remote" (pp. 66–67).[19] It is significant that in *Rear Window* only little snatches of conversation may be heard across the way; generally the events proceed mutely, with diegetic noises and music filling the soundtrack (one song even proclaims the primacy of the visual: Bing Crosby's "To See You is to Love You," playing, ironically, while Miss Lonelyhearts entertains a phantom lover). Moreover, the tableau-like spaces of the microscreens across the way find their temporal equivalent in the device of the fade which punctuates the film, likewise creating a sense of a sealed-off fantasy world impervious to the dialogic, "contaminated" world of lived experience.

Just as the cinema, in its resemblance to the mirror at the mirror stage, offers the viewer an image of wholeness and plenitude, so too does the dollhouse world of the

---

[15]Kaja Silverman, "Lost Objects and Mistaken Subjects: Film Theory's Structuring Lack," *Wide Angle* 7, nos. 1–2 (1985): 24. In many respects, Silverman's position is close to Lurie's. However, Lurie, in common with many "American" feminists (as opposed to French or French-influenced feminists), seems to share to some extent the little boy's fantasy, which he comes to deny, of woman's "wholeness," whereas for Silverman all subjects are inevitably divided, but in patriarchal culture men are able to project division on to women, thus maintaining the illusion of their own completeness.

[16]On this point see Perlmutter, "*Rear Window*: A Construction Story," p. 58.

[17]Metz speaks of "that *other mirror*, the cinema screen, in this respect a veritable psychical substitute, a prosthesis for our primally dislocated limbs." Quoted in Stam and Pearson, "Hitchcock's *Rear Window*: Reflexivity," p. 138.

[18]Susan Stewart, *On Longing: Narratives of the Miniature, the Gigantic, the Souvenir, the Collection* (Baltimore: Johns Hopkins University Press, 1984), p. 63. It is important to recognize, as John Belton has pointed out, that Jeff does not merely watch, but actively manipulates his neighbors, "writing a blackmail letter ('What have you done with her?') which keeps the suspected killer from leaving town and later luring him out of his apartment with a phone call so that it can be searched." *Cinema Stylists* (Metuchen, NJ: Scarecrow, 1983), p. 15. Hereafter cited in the text.

[19]In his meditation on the miniature in *The Poetics of Space*, Gaston Bachelard makes a similar point. However, unlike Stewart, Bachelard celebrates the tendency of the miniature to place us in a position of transcendence. See *The Poetics of Space*, trans. Maria Jolas (Boston: Beacon, 1964), pp. 148–82.

apartment buildings Jeff watches. In fact, one of the reasons the miniature is so appealing is that it suggests completeness and "perfection," as in the description of Tom Thumb quoted by Stewart: "No mis-shapen limbs, no contorted features were there, but all was sweet and beautiful" (p. 46; unlike, say, Gulliver's ugly Brobdingnags, whose every imperfection is magnified a hundredfold). But just as this passage must raise the spectre of physical mutilation in order to banish it, the mirror phase—the phase at which the child first "anticipates . . . the apprehension and mastery of its bodily unity"—evokes retroactively in the child a phantasy of "the-body-in-pieces."[20] This fantasy, according to Lacan, corresponds to the auto-erotic stage preceding the formation of the ego (precisely the stage evoked by the "quietly masturbatory" image of the "mutilated" Jeff at the film's opening).[21] On the one hand, then, there is the anticipation of bodily "perfection" and unity which is, importantly, first promised by the body of the woman; on the other hand, the fantasy of dismemberment, a fantasy that gets disavowed by projecting it onto the body of the woman, who, in an interpretation which reverses the state of affairs the male child most fears, eventually comes to be perceived as castrated, mutilated, "imperfect."

Similarly, Jeff's interpretation of the events he sees across the way—his piecing together the fragments of evidence he observes in the Thorwald apartment into a coherent narrative—is designed to reverse the situation in his own apartment, to invalid-ate the female and assure his own control and dominance. It is not enough, however, for him to construct an interpretation that victimizes woman; for patriar-chal interpretations to work, they require her assent: man's conviction must become woman's conviction—in a double sense. Those critics who emphasize the film's restriction of point of view to the male character neglect the fact that it increasingly stresses a *dual* point of view, with the reverse shots finding *both* Jeff and Lisa intently staring out the window at the neighbors across the way. It seems possible, then, to consider Lisa as a representative of the *female* spectator at the cinema. And through her, we can ask if it is true that the female spectator simply acquiesces in the male's view or, if, on the contrary, her relationship to the spectacle and the narrative is different from his?

From the outset, Lisa is less interested than Jeff in spying on the neighbors and adopting a transcendent and controlling relation to the texts of their lives; rather, she relates to the "characters" through empathy and identification. Early in the film, Jeff jokingly points out a similarity between her apartment and that of Miss Torso, who at the time is seen entertaining several men. Jeff says, "she's like a queen bee with her pick of the drones," to which Lisa responds, "I'd say she's doing a woman's hardest job—juggling wolves." Miss Torso accompanies one of the men onto the balcony where she kisses him briefly and tries to go back inside while he attempts to restrain her. Jeff says, "she sure picked the most prosperous looking one," and Lisa disparages this notion, claiming, "she's not in love with *him*—or with any of them for that matter." When Jeff asks her how she can be so certain, she replies,

---

[20]Jean Laplanche and J.-B. Pontalis, *The Language of Psychoanalysis,* Trans. Donald Nicholson Smith (London: Hogarth, 1973), p. 251.

[21]Jacques Lacan, *Ecrits: A Selection,* trans. Alan Sheridan (New York: Norton, 1977), pp. 1–7.

"you *said* it resembled my apartment didn't you?" Later the same man forces himself on Miss Torso, who has to fight him off, and still later—at the end of the film—Miss Torso's true love, Stanley, will come to visit her. Thus despite critics' emphasis on the film's limited point of view, Lisa and Jeff have very *different* interpretations about the woman's desire in this scene fraught with erotic and violent potential, and it is *Lisa's* interpretation, arrived at through identification, that is ultimately validated.

Whereas Jeff sees Miss Torso as "queen bee," Lisa significantly changes the metaphor: Miss Torso is prey to "wolves." In fact, Lisa's increasing absorption in Jeff's story, her fascination with his murderous, misogynist tale, is accompanied by a corresponding discovery of women's victimization at the hands of men. At one point in the film, Lisa can be seen staring even more intently than Jeff: that is, when Miss Lonelyhearts picks up a young man at a bar and brings him home, only to be assaulted by him. As Lisa stares and Jeff looks away in some embarrassment, the song "Mona Lisa" is heard, sung by drunken revellers at the musician's party. The title of the song suggests an important link between the two women ("is it only cause you're *lonely,* Mona *Lisa*"), and between the male fantasies that are projected onto woman ("Mona Lisa, Mona Lisa, men have named you"; and "many dreams have been brought to your doorstep") and the brutal reality of male violence to which women are frequently subjected.

Of course, the most brutal act of all is Thorwald's butchering of his wife's body—an act devoutly desired by Jeff—and later, by Lisa herself. At one level, *Rear Window* may be seen as a parable of the dangers involved for women of becoming invested in male stories and male interpretations. Or perhaps we should say "overinvested"—unable, as Mary Ann Doane maintains, to adopt, as men do, the appropriate, voyeuristic distance from the text.[22] Rather, women supposedly "enter into" films so thoroughly that they tend to confuse the very boundary between fantasy and reality—like Lisa crossing over and merging into the "screen" opposite Jeff's window. This merger is a logical extension of her ready identification with the victimized woman, an identification that actually leads to the solution of the crime. Lisa is able to provide the missing evidence because she claims a special knowledge of women that men lack: the knowledge, in this case, that no woman would go on a trip and leave behind her purse and her wedding ring. Lisa appeals to the authority of Stella, asking her if she would ever go somewhere without her ring, and Stella replies, "They'd have to cut off my finger."

Embarking on a search for this incriminating ring, Lisa becomes trapped in Thorwald's apartment when he returns unobserved by Stella and Jeff, who have been preoccupied by the sight of Miss Lonelyhearts about to kill herself. Jeff alerts the police and then watches in agonized helplessness as Lisa is flung about the room by Thorwald. The police arrive in time to prevent another woman from being cut up, and as Lisa stands with her back to the screen—caught, like so many Hitchcock

---

[22] I again refer the reader to the opening pages of Mary Ann Doane's *The Desire to Desire: The Woman's Film of the 1940's* (Bloomington: Indiana University Press, 1987).

heroines, between the criminal and the legal authorities—she points to the wedding ring on her finger. François Truffaut has admired this touch:

> One of the things I enjoyed in the film was the dual significance of that wedding ring. Grace Kelly wants to get married but James Stewart doesn't see it that way. She breaks into the killer's apartment to search for evidence and she finds the wedding ring. She puts it on her finger and waves her hand behind her back so that James Stewart, looking over from the other side of the yard with his spyglasses, can see it. To Grace Kelly, that ring is a double victory; not only is it the evidence she was looking for, but who knows, it may inspire Stewart to propose to her. After all, she's already got the ring.[23]

Thus speaks the male critic, who has habitually considered the film to be a reflection on marriage from the man's point of view. A female spectator of *Rear Window* may, however, use her special knowledge of women and their position in patriarchy to see another kind of significance in the ring; to the woman identifying, like Lisa herself, with the female protagonist of the story, the episode may be read as pointing up the victimization of women by men. Just as Miss Lonelyhearts, pictured right below Lisa in a kind of split-screen effect, has gone looking for a little companionship and romance and ended up nearly being raped, so Lisa's ardent desire for marriage leads straight to a symbolic wedding with a wife-murderer. For so many women in Hitchcock—and this is the point of his continual reworking of the "female Gothic"—"wedlock is deadlock" indeed.[24]

But it is not only the female spectator who is bound to identify with Lisa at this climactic moment in the story—the moment which seems actually to be the point of the film. Jeff himself—and, by extension, the male film viewer—is forced to identify with the woman and to become aware of his *own* passivity and helplessness in relation to the events unfolding before his eyes. Thus, all Jeff's efforts to repudiate the feminine identification the film originally sets up (Jeff and Anna Thorwald as mirror images) end in resounding failure, and he is forced to be, in turn, the victim of *Hitchcock's* cinematic manipulations of space and time. In a discussion with Truffaut about his theory of suspense, Hitchcock uses this scene with Grace Kelly as his chief example of how to create "the public's identification" with an endangered person, even when that person is an unlikable "snooper." "Of course," he explains, "when the character is attractive, as for instance Grace Kelly in *Rear Window,* the public's emotion is greatly intensified" (p. 73). The implication here is that in scenes of suspense, which in Hitchcock films, as in other thrillers, usually take woman as their object as well as their subject, our identification is generally with the imperiled woman. In this respect, we do in fact all become masochists at the cinema—and it is extremely interesting to note that Theodor Reik considered suspense to be a major factor in masochistic fantasies.[25]

---

[23]Truffaut, *Hitchcock,* p. 223. Hereafter cited in the text.

[24]The phrase is taken from James B. McLaughlin's excellent discussion of Hitchcock's *Shadow of a Doubt,* "All in the Family: Alfred Hitchcock's *Shadow of a Doubt,*" *Wide Angle* 4, no. 1 (1980): 18.

[25]Theodor Reik, *Masochism and Modern Man,* trans. Margaret H. Biegel and Gertrud M. Kurth (New York: Farrar, Straus, 1941), pp. 59–71. On the primacy of masochism in human development, see Jean Laplanche, *Life and Death in Psychoanlysis,* trans. Jeffrey Mehlman (Baltimore: Johns Hopkins University Press, 1976), p. 89.

Suspense, Truffaut has claimed, "is simply the dramatization of a film's narrative material, or, if you will, the most intense presentation possible of dramatic situations"; suspense is not "a minor form of the spectacle," but "*the* spectacle in itself" (p. 15). Granted this equivalence between suspense and "*the* spectacle," *the* narrative, might we not then say that spectatorship and "narrativity" are themselves "feminine" (to the male psyche) in that they place the spectator in a passive position and in a submissive relation to the text? Robert Scholes has observed that "narrativity"—the "process by which a perceiver actively constructs a story from the fictional data provided by any narrative medium,"[26] (the process, that is, which is inscribed in *Rear Window* through the character of Jeff)—is a situation of "licensed and benign paranoia" in that "it assumes a purposefulness in the activities of narration which, if it existed in the world, would be truly destructive of individuality and personality as we know them" (p. 396).[27] Narrativity involves, in Scholes's words, a "quality of submission and abandon" (we may recall the paranoid Dr. Schreber's attitude of "voluptuousness" toward God's grand narrative which featured a plot to impregnate the feminized doctor). This quality once noted by Scholes leads him to call for stories which reward the "most energetic and rigorous kinds of narrativity" as a means of exercising control over the text that seeks to manipulate and seduce its audience (p. 397). Of course, it is precisely Jeff's suspicion that there is a "purposefulness" to the activities across the way that impels him to adopt an "energetic and rigorous"—i.e., controlling, transcendent, and, above all, "masculine"—narrativity.

At this moment in the film the camera traces a triangular trajectory from Jeff's gaze at the ring to Thorwald, who sees the ring and then looks up at Jeff, returning the gaze for the first time. And then Thorwald proceeds to complete the "feminization" process by crossing over to Jeff's apartment and placing Jeff in the role previously played by Mrs. Thorwald and then by Lisa—that of victim to male violence. Jeff's "distancing" techniques, of course, no longer work, and the flashing bulbs only manage to slow Thorwald down a bit. Like Lisa, Jeff finally becomes a participant in his story, though *his* identification with the female character is involuntary, imposed on him by Thorwald, whose visit comes like the return of the repressed.

Although Jeff's interpretation of the Thorwald story has been validated by the end of the film, Jeff himself remains *invalided*, ending up with *two* broken legs, the body less "perfect" than ever, while Lisa, lounging on the bed, has become the mirror image of the man—dressed in masculine clothes and reading a book of male adventure. No longer representing sexual difference, nominating herself and speaking her own desire, Lisa is now spoken *by* the male artist—by the musician, whose completed song "Lisa" plays on the soundtrack ("men have named you," indeed),

---

[26]Robert Scholes, "Narration and Narrativity in Film," in *Film Theory and Criticism*, ed. Gerald Mast and Marshall Cohen (New York: Oxford University Press, 1985), p. 393. Hereafter cited in the text.

[27]Peter Brooks speaks of the same activity in similar terms, terms recalling the way in which "femininity" is perceived and constructed under patriarchy: "The assumption of another's story, the entry into narratives not one's own, runs the risk of an alienation from self that in Balzac's work repeatedly evokes the threat of madness and aphasia." See his *Reading for the Plot: Design and Intention in Narrative* (New York: Vintage, 1985), p. 219.

and ultimately by Hitchcock himself, who earlier made his appearance in the musician's apartment. More clearly than most, the film's ending and its "narrative image" of Lisa in masculine drag[28] reveals the way in which acceptable femininity is a construct of male narcissistic desire; despite Freud's claim that women tend to be more narcissistic than men, who supposedly possess a greater capacity for object love.[29] The film has consistently shown the opposite state of affairs to be the case, and in particular has revealed Jeff to be unable to care for Lisa except insofar as she affirms and mirrors him: significantly, he becomes erotically attracted to her only when she begins to corroborate his interpretation of the world around him (the first time he looks at her with real desire is not, as Mulvey claims, when she goes into the Thorwald apartment and becomes the object of his voyeurism, but when she begins to supply arguments in favor of his version of events).

One of the most highly reflexive of films, *Rear Window* indicates that what Jean-Louis Baudry has argued to be characteristic of the cinematic apparatus as a whole—and in particular of *projection*—is also true at the level of narrative, which functions as masculine fantasy *projected* onto the body of woman. Baudry maintains that because film projection depends on negation of the individual image as such "we could say that film . . . lives on the denial of difference: the difference is necessary for it to live, but it lives on its negation."[30] Similarly, much narrative cinema negates the *sexual* difference that nevertheless sustains it—negates it in the dual sense of transforming women into Woman and Woman into man's mirror. (Thus Baudry's analogy between cinema and woman is more revealing than he seems to know: speaking of our tendency to "go to movies before deciding which film we want to see," Baudry writes that cinéphiles "seem just as blind in their passion as those lovers who imagine they love a woman because of her qualities or because of her beauty. They need good movies, but most of all, to rationalize their need for cinema."[31] Any woman, like any movie, will do to fulfill man's "need." Put a paper bag over their heads and all women are like Miss Torso or the headless "Hunger" sculpture of the female artist in Jeff's courtyard, both of whom function, like the - cinematic apparatus itself, to displace male fears of fragmentation. "What might one say," Baudry asks, "of the function of the head in this captivation [of the spectator at the movies]: it suffices to recall that for Bataille materialism makes itself headless—like a wound that bleeds and thus transfuses."[32])

---

[28]Teresa de Lauretis borrows this term, "narrative image," from Stephen Heath: "In cinema . . . woman properly represents the fulfillment of the narrative promise (made, as we know, to the little boy), and that representation works to support the male status of the mythical subject. The female position, produced as the end result of narrativization, is the figure of narrative closure, the narrative image in which the film, as Heath says, 'comes together.'" *Alice Doesn't: Feminism, Semiotics, Cinema* (Bloomington: Indiana University Press, 1984), p. 140.

[29]Sigmund Freud, "On Narcissism: An Introduction," *The Standard Edition of the Complete Psychological Works of Sigmund Freud*, Vol. 14, trans. James Strachey (London: Hogarth, 1974), pp. 88–89.

[30]Jean-Louis Baudry, "Ideological Effects of the Basic Cinematographic Apparatus," trans. Alan Williams, *Apparatus: Cinematographic Apparatus: Selected Writings*, ed. Theresa Hak Kyung Cha (New York: Tanam, 1980), p. 29.

[31]Jean-Louis Baudry, "Author and Analyzable Subject," in *Apparatus*, p. 68.

[32]Baudry, "Ideological Effects," p. 32. In light of the "headless woman" motif in Hitchcock, consider the following remark by Joan Copjec, "We know that the dreamer dreams of himself when he dreams of a person whose head he cannot see." "The Anxiety of the Influencing Machine," *October* 23 (Winter 1982): 44.

That "difference is necessary" for cinema to live and therefore can never be destroyed, but only continually negated, is implied by the ending of *Rear Window*. Jeff is once again asleep, in the same position as he was at the film's opening, and Lisa, after assuring herself that he is *not* watching her (in contrast to former times when she had worked so hard to attract his gaze), puts away his book and picks up her own magazine. As important as this gesture is, even more important is the fact that the film gives her the last look. This is, after all, the conclusion of a movie that all critics agree is about the power the man attempts to wield through exercising the gaze. We are left with the suspicion (a preview, perhaps, of coming attractions) that while men sleep and dream their dreams of omnipotence over a safely reduced world, women are not where they appear to be, locked into male "views" of them, imprisoned in their master's dollhouse.

1988

TOM GUNNING

AN AESTHETIC OF ASTONISHMENT: EARLY FILM AND THE (IN)CREDULOUS SPECTATOR

TERROR IN THE AISLES

The damming of the stream of real life, the moment when its flow comes to a standstill, makes itself felt as reflux: this reflux is astonishment.

WALTER BENJAMIN, "What Is Epic Theatre?" (first version)

In traditional accounts of the cinema's first audiences, one image stands out: the terrified reaction of spectators to Lumière's *Arrival of a Train at the Station*. According to a variety of historians, spectators reared back in their seats, or screamed, or got up and ran from the auditorium (or all three in succession). As with most myths of origin, the source for these accounts remains elusive. It does not figure in any report of the first screening at the Salon Indien of the Grand Café that I have located.[1] And as with such myths, its ideological uses demand probing

---

[1] Accounts of the first exhibitions can be read in most standard film histories. Georges Sadoul, in *Histoire générale du cinéma*, t. I. *L'Invention du cinéma 1832–1897* (Paris: Denoël, 1948), p. 288, describes the panic of the crowds before *The Arrival of a Train*, but, curiously, the testimony he cites refers to a Lumière street scene, rather than the train film. Other testimonies sometimes cited, such as Maxim Gorky's article discussed below, or the article Lynne Kirby quotes from *L'Illustration* (30 May 1896), describe the threat inscribed in the image itself, but do not indicate actual panic in the audience (see Lynne Kirby, "Male Hysteria and Early Cinema," *Camera Obscura* 17 (May 1988): 130. Recent histories are content to cite Sadoul, or simply repeat the legend. However, Charles Musser tells me that his research on early travelling exhibitor Lyman H. Howe has uncovered a number of references to spectators screaming during early projections of train films, although not at the first Lumière screenings.

I would like to indicate here the inspiration provided by Kirby's article and her ongoing work on early cinema and trains. I feel few writers have so well grasped the importance of shock in early cinema, even if I view its implications for early spectatorship somewhat differently than she does. I would also like to acknowledge the conversations with NYU graduate student Richard Decroix, which stimulated my thinking about this essay.

as much as its veracity. This panicked and hysterical audience has provided the basis for further myths about the nature of film history and the power of the film image.

The first audiences, according to this myth, were naive, encountering this threatening and rampant image with no defenses, with no tradition by which to understand it. The absolute novelty of the moving image therefore reduced them to a state usually attributed to savages in their primal encounter with the advanced technology of Western colonialists, howling and fleeing in impotent terror before the power of the machine. This audience of the first exhibitions exists outside of the willing suspension of disbelief, the immediacy of their terror short-circuiting even disavowal's detour of "I know very well . . . but all the same." Credulity overwhelms all else, the physical reflex signaling a visual trauma. Thus conceived, the myth of initial terror defines film's power as its unprecedented realism, its ability to convince spectators that the moving image was, in fact, palpable and dangerous, bearing towards them with physical impact. The image had taken life, swallowing, in its relentless force, any consideration of representation—the imaginary perceived as real.

Furthermore, this primal scene at the cinema underpins certain contemporary theorisations of spectatorship. The terrorised spectator of the Grand Café still stalks the imagination of film theorists who envision audiences submitting passively to an all-dominating apparatus, hypnotised and transfixed by its illusionist power. Contemporary film theorists have made careers out of underestimating the basic intelligence and reality-testing abilities of the average film viewer and have no trouble treating previous audiences with similar disdain. The most subtle reading of this initial terror comes from Metz. But Metz's admirable subtlety tenders his analysis all the more deficient from a historical point of view. Metz describes this panicked reaction on the part of the Grand Café audience as a displacement of the contemporary viewer's credulity onto a mythical childhood of the medium. Like the childhood when one still believed in Santa Claus, like the dawn of time when myths were still believed literally, belief in this legendary audience, Metz claims, allows us to disavow our own belief in the face of the cinema. We don't believe in the screen image in the manner that *they* did. Our credulity is displaced onto an audience from the infancy of cinema.[2]

---

[2]Christian Metz, *The Imaginary Signifier: Psychoanalysis and the Cinema*, trans. Celia Britton, Annwyl Williams, Ben Brewster, and Alfred Guzzetti (Bloomington: Indiana University Press, 1982), pp. 72–73. Ben Singer has pointed out the limitations of Metz's application of Freud's concept of the fetish to cinema in his article, "Film, Photography and Fetish: The Analyses of Christian Metz," *Cinema Journal* 27/4 (Summer 1988). However, my main problem with Metz's always stimulating discussion lies in its a historical nature, which leads to an oversimplified view of cinema spectatorship. At the same time, I find that the lack Metz finds at the centre of the cinematic image is a profound insight, worthy of more than a metapsychological treatment.

Charles Musser (in his volume in the History of American Film Series, vol. I, *The Emergence of Cinema in America*) points out that in *Ars magna lucis et umbrae* of 1671—the first full treatment of the catoptric lamp, a forerunner of the magic lantern—Athanasius Kircher declared that demystifying illusion is essential to any display of the apparatus, absolutely forbidding any understanding of the spectacle as magic. The religious and social motivations (Kircher was a Jesuit) for such a demystification are obvious. Musser makes the provocative claim that this moment "suggests a decisive turning point for screen practice when the observer of projected/reflected images became the historically constituted subject we now call the spectator" (p. 31). In other words, Musser would see demystification as essential to the existence of the spectator, and points out that a tradition of screen spectatorship preceded Lumière by centuries.

Metz's penetrating analysis of the mythical role of this first audience does not lead to demythologisation. He instead introjects this primal audience, removing it from historical analysis by internalising it as an aspect of a presumably timeless cinema viewer. No longer a historical spectator in the Grand Café in 1895, the naive spectator "is still seated *beneath* the incredulous one, or in his heart."[3] Thus removed from place and time, this inner credulous viewer supplies the motive power for Metz's understanding of the fetishistic viewer, wavering between the credulous position of believing the image and the repressed, anxiety-causing knowledge of its illusion. The historical panic at the Grand Café would be, according to Metz, simply a projection of an inner deception onto the mythical site of cinema's "once upon a time."

Although I have my doubts whether actual panic took place in the Grand Café's Salon Indien, there is no question that a reaction of astonishment and even a type of terror accompanied many early projections. I therefore don't intend to simply deny this founding myth of the cinema's spectator, but rather to approach it historically. We cannot simply swallow whole the image of the naive spectator, whose reaction to the image is one of simple belief and panic; it needs digesting. The impact of the first film projections cannot be explained by a mechanistic model of a naive spectator who, in a temporary psychotic state, confuses the image for its reality. But what context does account for the well-attested fact that the first projections caused shock and astonishment, an excitement pushed to the point of terror, if we exclude childlike credulity? And, equally important, how could this agitating experience be understood as part of the *attraction* of the new invention, rather than a disturbing element that needed to be removed? And what roles does an illusion of reality play in this terrified reception?

Only a careful consideration of the historical context of these earliest images can restore an understanding of the uncanny and agitating power they exerted on audiences. This context includes the first modes of exhibition, the tradition of turn-of-the-century visual entertainments, and a basic aesthetic of early cinema I have called the cinema of attractions, which envisioned cinema as a series of visual shocks. Restored to its proper historical context, the projection of the first moving images stands at the climax of a period of intense development in visual entertainments, a tradition in which realism was valued largely for its uncanny effects. We need to recognise this tradition and speculate on its role at the turn of the century.

As I have shown elsewhere, many early spectators recognised the first projection of films as a crowning achievement in the extremely sophisticated developments in the magic theatre, as practiced by Méliès at the Théâtre Robert Houdin and his English mentor Maskelyne at London's Egyptian Hall.[4] At the turn of the century, this tradition used the latest technology (such as focused electric light

---

[3]Metz, op. cit., p. 72.

[4]See my article "Primitive Cinema: A Frame Up? or The Trick's On Us," in *Cinema Journal* 29, no. 2 (Winter 1988–89). Accounts of Méliès's theatrical illusions can be found in Madeliene Maltete-Méliès, ed., *Méliès et la naissance du spectacle cinématographique* (Paris: Klincksieck, 1984), esp. pp. 53–58, and in Pierre Jenn, *Méliès, Cinéaste* (Paris: Albatros, 1984), pp. 139–68. Paul Hammond's *Marvellous Méliès* (London: Gordon Fraser, 1974, pp. 15–26) also includes a discussion of Méliès's stage work and an indication of his debt to Maskelyne.

and elaborate stage machinery) to produce apparent miracles. The seeming transcendence of the laws of the material universe by the magical theatre defines the dialectical nature of its illusions. The craft of late nineteenth-century stage illusions consisted of making visible something which could not exist, of managing the play of appearances in order to confound the expectations of logic and experience. The audience this theatre addressed was not primarily gullible country bumpkins, but sophisticated urban pleasure seekers, well aware that they were seeing the most modern techniques in stage craft. Méliès's theatre is inconceivable without a widespread decline in belief in the marvellous, providing a fundamental rationalist context. The magic theatre laboured to make visual that which it was impossible to believe. Its visual power consisted of a trompe l'oeil play of give-and-take, an obsessive desire to test the limits of an intellectual disavowal— I know, but yet I see.

Trompe l'oeil as a genre of aesthetic illusion underscores the problematic role perfect illusion plays within traditional aesthetic reception. As Martin Battersby puts it, trompe l'oeil aims not simply at accuracy of representation, but at causing "a feeling of disgust in the mind of the beholder." This disquiet arises from "a conflict of messages": on the one hand, the knowledge that one is seeing a painting, and on the other, a visual experience sufficiently convincing as "to warrant a closer examination and even the involvement of the sense of touch."[5] The realism of the image is at the service of a dramatically unfolding spectator experience, vacillating between belief and incredulity. Although trompe l'oeil shares with *The Arrival of a Train* and the magic theatre a pleasurable vacillation between belief and doubt, it also displays important differences from them. The usually small scale of trompe l'oeil paintings and the desire to reach out and touch them contrast sharply with the "grandeur naturale"[6] of the Lumière train film and the viewer's impulse to rear back before it, as well as with the spectator's physical distance from the illusions of the magic theatre. But all three forms show that, rather than being a simple reality effect, the illusionistic arts of the nineteenth century cannily exploited their unbelievable nature, keeping a conscious focus on the fact that they were only illusions.

In fact, in the most detailed and articulate account we have of an early Lumière projection, Maxim Gorky (reporting on a showing at the Nizhny-Novgorod Fair in July of 1896) stresses the uncanny effect of the new attraction's mix of realistic and nonrealistic qualities. For Gorky, the cinématographe presents a world whose vividness and vitality have been drained away: "before you a life is surging, a life deprived of words and shorn of the living spectrum of colours—the grey, the soundless, the bleak and dismal life." The cinématographe, Gorky explains, presents not life but

---

[5]Martin Battersby, *Trompe l'Oeil: The Eye Deceived* (London: Academy Editions, 1974), p. 19. I must signal here that my essay has been both inspired and provoked by Mary Ann Doane's fascinating essay "When the Direction of the Force Acting on the Body Is Changed: The Moving Image," *Wide Angle* 7, nos. 2–3. There is a great deal of convergence in the topics covered by my essay and hers, as well as a great deal of divergence in method and conclusion.

[6]The importance of the large scale of the original Lumière projections, particularly in competition with the Edison kinetoscope, has been pointed out by Jacques and Marie André in their volume *Une Saison Lumière à Montpellier* (Perpignan, France: Institut Jean Vigo, 1987), pp. 64–75.

its shadow, and he allows no possibility of mistaking this cinematic shade for substance. Describing *The Arrival of a Train*, Gorky senses its impending threat: "It speeds right at you—watch out! It seems as though it will plunge into the darkness in which you sit, turning you into a ripped sack full of lacerated flesh and splintered bones." But, he adds, "this too is but a train of shadows." Belief and terror are larded with an awareness of illusion and even, to Gorky's sophisticated palate, the ennui of the insubstantial, the bleak disappointment of the ungraspable phantom of life.[7]

One might dismiss Gorky's reaction as the sophisticated disdain of a cultured intellectual, deliberately counter to the more common reception of early film images. Gorky's negative assessment of the cinema *was* unusual in a period when new advances in the technology of entertainment were generally hailed with excitement and satisfaction. But his recognition that the film image combined realistic effects with a conscious awareness of artifice may correspond more closely to general audience reaction than the screaming dupes of traditional accounts. While contemporary accounts of audience responses, particularly unsophisticated viewers, are hard to come by, the very mode of presentation of the Lumière screenings (and of other early filmmakers as well) contains an important element which served to undermine a naive experience of realism. It is too infrequently pointed out that in the earliest Lumière exhibitions the films were initially presented as frozen unmoving images, projections of still photographs. Then, flaunting a mastery of visual showmanship, the projector began cranking and the image moved. Or as Gorky described it, "suddenly a strange flicker passes through the screen and the picture stirs to life."[8]

While such a presentation would seem to forbid any reading of the image as reality—a real physical train—it strongly heightened the impact of the moment of movement. Rather than mistaking the image for reality, the spectator is astonished by its transformation through the new illusion of projected motion. Far from credulity, it is the incredible nature of the illusion itself that renders the viewer speechless. What is displayed before the audience is less the impending speed of the train than the force of the cinematic apparatus. Or to put it better, the one demonstrates the other. The astonishment derives from a magical metamorphosis rather than a seamless reproduction of reality. The initial impact of this transformation at the Lumière premiere is described by an expert in such effects, Georges Méliès:

> a *still* photograph showing the place Bellecour in Lyon was projected. A little surprise, I just had time to say to my neighbor: "They got us all stirred up for projections like this? I've been doing them for over ten years."
> I had hardly finished speaking when a horse pulling a wagon began to walk towards us, followed by other vehicles and then pedestrians, in short all the animation of the

---

[7]Gorky's account is included as an appendix in Jay Leyda, *Kino: A History of the Russian and Soviet Film* (London: Allen & Unwin, 1960), pp. 407–409. The translation is by "Leda Swan."

[8]Ibid., p. 407. I must add that it was Annette Michelson who first pointed out this fact to me when I was a graduate student years ago. Her discussion of the *frisson* of this instance of motion was a generative point for this essay. One might point out that a possibly equally rich projection trope can be found in Lumière's *Destruction of a Wall*, which was projected first forwards and then in reverse, creating the magical effect of the wall reassembling and rising to its original height. A Montpellier journalist noted that this film "has always drawn applause from its admirers" (André, *Une Sasion Lumière*, p. 84, my translation).

street. Before this spectacle we sat with gaping mouths, struck with amazement, astonished beyond all expression.[9]

This coup de théâtre, the sudden transformation from still image to moving illusion, startled audiences and displayed the novelty and fascination of the cinématographe. Far from being placed outside a suspension of disbelief, the presentation acts out the contradictory stages of involvement with the image, unfolding, like other nineteenth-century visual entertainments, a vacillation between belief and incredulity. The moving image reverses and complicates the trajectory of experience solicited by a trompe l'oeil still life. The film first presents itself as merely an image, rather than appearing to be the actual butterflies, postcards, or cameos which the initial apperception of a trompe l'oeil canvas seems to reveal. Instead of a gradual disquiet arising from the divergence of what we know and what we see, the shock of the film image comes from a sudden transformation while the hardly novel projected photograph (Gorky also stressed his initial disappointment at this "all too familiar scene"[10]) gives way to the astonishing moment of movement. The audience's sense of shock comes less from a naive belief that they are threatened by an actual locomotive than from an unbelievable visual transformation occurring before their eyes, parallel to the greatest wonders of the magic theatre.

As in the magic theatre the apparent realism of the image makes it a successful illusion, but one understood as an illusion nonetheless. While such a transformation would be quite capable of causing a physical or verbal reflex in the viewer, one remains aware that the film is merely a projection. The initial still image demonstrated that irrefutably. But this still projection takes on motion, becomes endowed with animation, and it is this unbelievable moving image that so astounds. The initial projection of a still image, withholding briefly the illusion of motion which is the apparatus's raison d'être, brought an effect of suspense to the first film shows. The audience knew that motion was precisely what the cinématographe promised (hence Méliès's restlessness). By delaying its appearance. the Lumière's exhibitor not only highlights the device but signals his allegiance to an aesthetic of astonishment which goes beyond a scientific interest in the reproduction of motion.

Another account of early projections, this time from the other side of the Atlantic, further demonstrates the theatricality of this device and clearly aligns the terror of early spectators with a conscious delectation of shocks and thrills. The memoirs of Albert E. Smith, one of the founders of the Vitagraph company, describe his early years as a travelling exhibitor with Vitagraph cofounder J. Stuart Blackton. Smith had toured earlier with quick-sketch artist Blackton as an illusionist combining "sleight of hand and invisible mechanical appliances of his own invention."[11] But like a large number of stage illusionists, they had turned to the exhibition of

---

[9]Quoted in Georges Sadoul, *Histoire Général du Cinéma*, p. 271 (my translation).

[10]Erik Barnouw, *The Magician and the Cinema* (New York: Oxford University Press, 1981), p. 75. The phrase is quoted from an 1899 article in the magical trade periodical *Mahatma*.

[11]Albert E. Smith, in collaboration with Phil A. Koury, *Two Reels and a Crank* (Garden City, NY: Doubleday, 1952), p. 39. Smith's book is notoriously inaccurate, as Charles Musser has shown. However, most of these errors seem to be misleading claims of fanciful achievements (e.g., filming in Cuba during the Spanish American War) and don't necessarily lessen the value of the description of his film shows.

moving pictures as the most technologically advanced form of visual entertainments. Smith contributed a mechanical improvement to the Edison projecting kinetoscope— a water cell between the film and the light source that absorbed heat and allowed the film to be projected as a still image a bit longer without danger of the celluloid bursting into flames.

The most popular item on Smith and Blackton's exhibition tours was *The Black Diamond Express*, a one-shot film of a locomotive rushing towards the camera. As in most early film shows, a patter spoken by Blackton accompanied the projection, preparing the audience for the film and providing dramatic atmosphere. Smith describes Blackton's role in presenting *The Black Diamond Express* as that of a "terrorist mood setter." As he recalled it, Blackton's lecture (delivered over the frozen image of the locomotive) went like this:

> Ladies and gentlemen you are now gazing upon a photograph of the famous Black Diamond Express. In just a moment, a cataclysmic moment, my friends, a moment without equal in the history of our times, you will see this train take life in a marvellous and most astounding manner. It will rush towards you, belching smoke and fire from its monstrous iron throat.

Although Smith's memory of Blackton's oration decades later may not be entirely reliable, it captures the address of the first film shows and places the audience's terror in a new light. Blackton directly addresses the audience, mediating between it and the film and stressing the actual act of display. Like a fairground barker, he builds an atmosphere of expectation, a pronounced curiosity leavened with anxiety as he stresses the novelty and astonishing properties which the attraction about to be revealed will possess. This sense of expectation, sharpened to an intense focus on a single instant of transformation, heightened the startling impact of the first projections. Far from being a simple reality effect, the impact derives from a moment of crisis, prepared for and delayed, then bursting upon the audience. This suspenseful presentation of an impossible transformation, Smith reports, caused women to scream and men to sit aghast.[12]

THE AESTHETIC OF ATTRACTIONS

There came a day when a new and urgent need for stimuli was met by the film. In a film, perception in the form of shocks was established as a formal principle.

WALTER BENJAMIN, "Some Motifs in Baudelaire"

While these early films of on-coming locomotives present the shock of cinema in an exaggerated form, they also express an essential element of early cinema as a whole. I have called the cinema that precedes the dominance of narrative (and this period lasts for nearly a decade, until 1903 or 1904) The cinema of attractions.[13] The aesthetic of

---

[12]Ibid., pp. 39–40.

[13]See Tom Gunning, "The Cinema of Attraction: Early Film, Its Spectator and the Avant-Garde," *Wide Angle* 8, nos. 3–4. This term was first introduced by myself and André Gaudreault in a paper delivered to the colloquium Nouvelles approches de l'histoire du cinéma at Cerisy in 1985, called "Cinéma des premiers temps: un défi à l'histoire du cinéma?" Conversations with Adam Simon, a teaching assistant at the Carpenter Center of Visual and Environmental Studies of Harvard University, 1984–85, were also

attraction addresses the audience directly, sometimes, as in these early train films, exaggerating this confrontation in an experience of assault. Rather than being an involvement with narrative action or empathy with character psychology, the cinema of attractions solicits a highly conscious awareness of the film image engaging the viewer's curiosity. The spectator does not get lost in a fictional world and its drama, but remains aware of the act of looking, the excitement of curiosity and its fulfilment. Through a variety of formal means, the images of the cinema of attractions rush forward to meet their viewers. These devices range from the implied collision of the early railroad films to the performance style of the same period, when actors nodded and gestured at the camera (e.g., Méliès on screen directing attention to the transformations he causes) or when a showman lecturer presented the views to the audience. This cinema addresses and holds the spectator, emphasising the act of display. In fulfilling this curiosity, it delivers a generally brief dose of scopic pleasure.

And pleasure is the issue here, even if pleasure of a particularly complicated sort. When a Montpellier journalist in 1896 described the Lumière projections as provoking "an excitement bordering on terror," he was praising the new spectacle and explaining its success.[14] If the first spectators screamed, it was to acknowledge the power of the apparatus to sweep away a prior and firmly entrenched sense of reality. This vertiginous experience of the frailty of our knowledge of the world before the power of visual illusion produced that mixture of pleasure and anxiety which the purveyors of popular art had labelled sensations and thrills and on which they founded a new aesthetic of attractions. The on-rushing train did not simply produce the negative experience of fear but the particularly modern entertainment form of the thrill, embodied elsewhere in the recently appearing attractions of the amusement parks (such as the roller coaster), which combined sensations of acceleration and falling with a security guaranteed by modern industrial technology. One Coney Island attraction, the Leap Frog Railway, literalised the thrill of *The Arrival of a Train*. Two electric cars containing as many as forty people were set towards each other at great speed on a collision course. Just before impact one car was lifted up on curved rails and skimmed over the top of the other. Lynne Kirby has also noted the popularity of staged collisions between railroad locomotives at the turn of the century, both at county fairs and in such films as Edison's 1904 *The Railroad Smash-Up*.[15]

Confrontation rules the cinema of attractions in both the form of its films and their mode of exhibition. The directness of this act of display allows an emphasis

---

influential in developing these ideas. The term "attractions" refers backwards to a popular tradition and forwards to an avant-garde subversion. The tradition is that of the fairground and carnival, and particularly its development during the turn of the century in such modern amusement parks as Coney Island. The avant-garde radicalisation of this term comes in the theoretical and practical work in theatre and film of Sergei Eisenstein, whose theory of the montage of attractions intensified this popular energy into an aesthetic subversion, through a radical theoreticisation of the power of attractions to undermine the conventions of bourgeois realism. For a clear account of this theory and a discussion of its roots in popular culture, see Jacques Aumont's *Montage Eisenstein*, trans. Lee Hildreth, Constance Penley, and Andrew Ross (Bloomington: Indiana University Press, 1987), pp. 41–48, as well as Eisenstein's own essays "The Montage of Attractions" and "The Montage of Film Attractions," in Eisenstein, *Writings*, vol. I, 1922–34, ed. and trans. Richard Taylor (Bloomington: University of Indiana Press, 1988).

[14]Quoted in Jacques and Marie André, *Une Saison Lumière*, p. 66.

[15]John F. Kasson, *Amusing the Millions: Coney Island at the Turn of the Century* (New York: Hill & Wang, 1978), pp. 77–78. Lynne Kirby, from *L'Illustration*, pp. 119–20.

on the thrill itself—the immediate reaction of the viewer. The film lecturer focuses attention on the attraction, sharpening viewer curiosity. The film then performs its act of display and fades away. Unlike psychological narrative, the cinema of attractions does not allow for elaborate development; only a limited amount of delay is really possible. But such a film program consists of a series of attractions, a concatenation of short films all of which offer the viewer a moment of revelation. The succession of thrills is potentially limited only by viewer exhaustion. This concatenation may have some thematic structuring and builds toward a climactic moment, a final *clou* (such as Smith and Blackton's *Black Diamond Express*). The showman rather than the films themselves gives the program an overarching structure, and the key role of exhibitor showman underscores the act of monstration that founds the cinema of attractions.[16]

A film like Edison's *Electrocuting an Elephant* from 1903 shows the temporal logic of this scenography of display. The elephant is led onto an electrified plate, and secured. Smoke rises from its feet and after a moment the elephant falls on its side. The moment of technologically advanced death is neither further explained nor dramatised. Likewise a fictional film produced by the Biograph Company in 1904, *Photographing a Female Crook*, presents a single shot of a woman held between two uniformed policemen who try to steady her for a mug shot. The camera tracks in on this group, ending by framing the woman in medium close-up. Attempting to sabotage the photographing of her face for identification purposes, the female crook mugs outrageously, contorting her face. The inward movement by the movie camera and the progressive enlargement of the woman's face emphasise the act of display which underlies the film. While both these films show considerable formal differences from *The Arrival of a Train*, they all three demonstrate the solicitation of viewer curiosity and its fulfilment by the brief moment of revelation typical of the cinema of attractions. This is a cinema of instants, rather than developing situations.

As I have stated elsewhere,[17] the scenography of the cinema of attractions is an exhibitionist one, opposed to the cinema of the unacknowledged voyeur that later narrative cinema ushers in. This display of unique view belongs most obviously to the period before the dominance of editing, when films consisting of a single shot—both actualities and fictions—made up the bulk of film production. However, even with the introduction of editing and more complex narratives, the aesthetic of attraction can still be sensed in periodic doses of non-narrative spectacle given to audiences (musicals and slapstick comedy provide clear examples). The cinema of attractions persists in later cinema, even if it rarely dominates the form of a feature film as a whole. It provides an underground current flowing beneath narrative logic and diegetic realism, producing those moments of cinematic *dépaysement* beloved by the surrealists.[18]

---

[16]The role of the exhibitor showman in early American cinema has been brilliantly demonstrated in the work of Charles Musser, particularly in his article "The Nickelodeon Era Begins, Establishing the Framework for Hollywood's Mode of Representation" (*Framework*, Autumn 1983), as well as in *Before the Nickelodeon: Edwin S. Porter and the Edison Manufacturing Company* (Berkeley: University of California Press, 1991.

[17]Gunning, "Cinema of Attraction," p. 64. This issue is also discussed in my book *D.W. Griffith and the Origins of American Narrative Cinema* (Urbana: University of Illinois Press, 1991).

[18]On the surrealist love of disorienting images in the cinema, see Paul Hammond, ed., *The Shadow and Its Shadow: Surrealist Writings on the Cinema* (London: British Film Institute, 1978), particularly Breton's essay "As in a Wood" (p. 14).

This aesthetic so contrasts with prevailing turn-of-the-century norms of artistic reception—the ideals of detached contemplation—that it nearly constitutes an anti-aesthetic. The cinema of attractions stands at the antipode to the experience Michael Fried, in his discussion of eighteenth-century painting, calls absorption.[19] For Fried, the painting of Greuze and others created a new relation to the viewer through a self-contained hermetic world which makes no acknowledgement of the beholder's presence. Early cinema totally ignores this construction of the beholder. These early films explicitly acknowledge their spectator, seeming to reach outwards and confront. Contemplative absorption is impossible here. The viewer's curiosity is aroused and fulfilled through a marked encounter, a direct stimulus, a succession of shocks.

By tapping into a visual curiosity and desire for novelty, attractions draw upon what Augustine, at the beginning of the fifth century, called *curiositas* in his catalogue of "the lust of the eyes." In contrast to visual *voluptas* (pleasure), *curiositas* avoids the beautiful and goes after its exact opposite "simply because of the lust to find out and to know." *Curiositas* draws the viewer towards unbeautiful sights, such as a mangled corpse, and "because of this disease of curiosity monsters and anything out of the ordinary are put on show in our theatres." For Augustine, *curiositas* led not only to a fascination with seeing, but a desire for knowledge for its own sake, ending in the perversions of magic and science.[20] While beauty in Augustine's Platonic schema may form the first rung of an ascent to the ideal, *curiositas* possesses only the power to lead astray. Attractions imply the danger of distraction, a cardinal sin in Augustine's contemplative and vigilant model of Christian life.

The aesthetic of attractions developed in fairly conscious opposition to an orthodox identification of viewing pleasure with the contemplation of beauty. A nineteenth-century satirical engraving shows London's Egyptian Hall (which existed as a home for natural curiosities—freaks and artifacts of natural history—before it became the home of Maskelyne's magic theatre) proclaiming itself "the Hall of Ugliness" and advertising the "Ne Plus Ultra of Hideousness."[21] This attraction to

---

[19]Michael Fried, *Absorption and Theatricality: Painting and Beholder in the Age of Diderot* (Berkeley and Los Angeles: University of California Press, 1980). See, for example, pp. 64, 104. A similar exclusion of the spectator is evident in the scenography and style of the nineteenth-century naturalist theatre, embodied in the idea of the fourth wall.

[20]St. Augustine, *The Confessions*, trans. Rex Warner (New York: New American Library, 1963), pp. 245–47.

[21]This satirical drawing is reproduced in Richard D. Altick, *The Shows of London* (Cambridge, MA: Harvard University Press, 1978), p. 254. As Miriam Hansen has pointed out to me, Michael Fried's discussion of Thomas Eakins' painting "Gross Clinic" raises issues relevant to the aesthetic of attractions and its relation to repulsion. Although Fried convincingly places the painting within a tradition of absorption, the foci of Gross' bloodstained fingers and scalpel and the patient's open wound seem to provide another experience, which "mixes pain and pleasure, violence and voluptuousness, repulsion and fascination" (Fried, "Realism, Writing and Disfiguration in Thomas Eakins' Gross Clinic," *Representations*: 9, Winter 1985, 71). As Fried says, "It is above all the conflictedness of that situation that grips and excruciates and in the end stupefies us before the picture" (p. 73). This seems to me to describe the essential experience of the aesthetic of attractions; however, it is somewhat unclear to me how Fried sees this in relation to the experience of absorption. Fried does not relate this conflict to the tradition of the sublime, which clearly represents the acceptable form of the aesthetic of attractions (recall that Burke defines astonishment as the effect of the sublime in the highest degree). The relation of popular entertainment to the sublime is a basically unexplored and potentially fascinating topic, beyond the confines of this essay. But it is not irrelevant to point out that Fried follows Thomas Weiskel in associating the effect of the sublime with a Freudian understanding of the terror of castration. Although I am not inclined at the moment to pursue it, speculation in this direction about the trauma produced by the

the repulsive was frequently rationalised by appealing to that impulse which Augustine found equally dubious, intellectual curiosity. Like the early film exhibitions, freak shows and other displays of curiosities were described as instructive and informing. Similarly, a popular and longlasting genre of the cinema of attractions consisted of educational actualities (such as Charles Urban's *Unseen World* series beginning in 1903), which presented magnified images of cheese mites, spiders and water fleas.[22] As late as 1914 a proponent of the reform movement in cinema objected to the vulgarity of films displaying such "slimy and unbeautiful abominations," which he claimed repulsed spectators with more refined sensibilities.[23] But showmen were well aware that a thrill needed an element of repulsion or a controlled threat of danger. Louis Lumière understood that his films, which directed physical action out at the audience, added a vital energy alongside the scientific curiosity addressed by his reproduction of motion and daily life.

DISTRACTION AND THE AMBIVALENCE OF SHOCK

The film corresponds to profound changes in the apperceptive apparatus—changes that are experienced on an individual scale by the man in the street in big city traffic, on a historical scale by every present day individual.

WALTER BENJAMIN, "The Work of Art in the Age of Mechanical Reproduction"

While the impulse to *curiositas* may be as old as Augustine, there is no question that the nineteenth century sharpened this form of "lust of the eyes" and its commercial exploitation. Expanding urbanisation with its kaleidoscopic succession of city sights, the growth of consumer society with its new emphasis on stimulating spending through visual display, and the escalating horizons of colonial exploration with new peoples and territories to be categorised and exploited all provoked the desire for images and attractions. It is not surprising that city street scenes, advertising films, and foreign views all formed important genres of early cinema. The enormous popularity of foreign views (already developed and exploited by the stereoscope and magic lantern) expresses an almost unquenchable desire to consume the world through images. The cinema was, as the slogan of one early film company put it, an invention which put the world within your grasp. Early cinema categorised the visible world as a series of discrete attractions, and the catalogues of the first production companies present a nearly encyclopoedic survey of this new hypervisible topology, from landscape panoramas to microphotography, from domestic scenes to the beheading of prisoners and the electrocution of elephants.

If not all the attractions of early cinema express the violence of an on-rushing train, some sense of wonder or surprise nonetheless underlies all these films, if only

---

first projections could provide a new way of approaching the issue of fetishism in early cinema, locating the trauma that Metz did little to isolate. The interest of this speculation could be considerable if approached from a historical point of view, as in Benjamin's and Schivelbusch's understanding (which I will discuss later in this essay) of the Freudian concept of the stimulus shield as a response to modern experience, rather than a biological principle.

[22]Urban's series of films is described in Rachel Low and Roger Manvell, *The History of the British Film, Vol. I 1896–1906*, (London: Allen & Unwin, 1948), p. 60.

[23]Harry Furniss, *Our Lady Cinema*, reprint of 1914 ed. (New York: Garland Publishing, 1978), p. 41.

wonder at the illusion of motion. Even a filmed landscape panorama does not lend itself to pure aesthetic contemplation. One is fully aware of the machine which mediates the view, the camera pivoting on its tripod. The most common form of landscape panorama—films show from the front or back of trains—doubled this effect, invoking not only the motion picture machine but the locomotive which pulls the seated viewer through space. These train films provide an even more technologically mediated example of what Wolfgang Schivelbusch, in his description of the transformation of perception occasioned by the railway journey, calls panoramic perception. In contrast to the traditional traveller's experience of a landscape, the train passenger "no longer belongs to the same space as the perceived objects; the traveller sees the objects, landscapes, etc., *through* the apparatus which moves him through the world."[24] A film taken from the front of a train, an "unseen energy swallowing space" (as one journalist described the experience of such a train panorama[25]), doubled this effect imposed by industrial apparatuses, intensifying the alienation *and* the dynamic sensation of train travel. Such train films might turn the on-rushing Black Diamond Express inside out, but still provoked viewer amazement through a technologically mediated experience of space and movement.

Ultimately the encyclopedic ambition of this impulse of early cinema, transforming all of reality into cinematographical views, recalls Gorky's vague discomfort and depression before the cinématographe. While the cinema of attractions fulfills the curiosity it excites, it is in the nature of curiosity, as the lust of the eye, never to be satisfied completely. Thus the obsessional nature of early film production and the early film show the potentially endless succession of separate attractions. But beyond the unlimited metonymy of curiosity, Gorky's unease derived from the abstraction and alienation of this new pursuit of thrills.

Gorky also found a pervasive ennui in the dreamworld home of attractions, Coney Island (which he visited in 1906), calling it "a slavery to a varied boredom." For Gorky, Coney Island purveyed "an amazement in which there is neither transport nor joy."[26] While the tone of a European intellectual's distaste for the mass pleasures of a capitalist society is unmistakable, Gorky also provides insight into the need for thrills in an industrialised and consumer-oriented society. The peculiar pleasure of screaming before the suddenly animated image of a locomotive indicates less an audience willing to take the image for reality than a spectator whose daily experience has lost the coherence and immediacy traditionally attributed to reality. This loss of experience creates a consumer hungry for thrills.

The cinema of attractions not only exemplifies a particularly modern form of aesthetics but also responds to the specifics of modern and especially urban life, what Benjamin and Kracauer understood as the drying up of experience and its replacement by a culture of distraction. While Benjamin's writing provides the most brilliantly dialectical (and ambivalent) description of the modern transformation of

---

[24]Wolfgang Schivelbusch, *The Railway Journey* (New York: Urizen Press, 1979), p. 66.

[25]From the *New York Mail and Express* (25 September 1897), reprinted in Kemp R. Niver, *The Biograph Bulletins 1896–1908* (Los Angeles: Locare Research Group, 1971), p. 27. The journalist was commenting on a Biograph film shot from a locomotive going through the Haverstraw Tunnel.

[26]Maxim Gorky, "Boredom," *The Independent* (8 August 1907): 311–12.

perception and experience,[27] Kracauer's essay "The Cult of Distraction: On Berlin's Picture Palaces" provides a specific focus on the role of cinema and particularly that element foregrounded by the cinema of attractions—exhibition.[28]

Lost sight of now after decades of text-obsessed film analysis, the exhibition situation transforms and structures a film's mode of address to an audience. In early cinema, the act of presentation was stressed by both exhibition context and the direct address of the films themselves. By the 1920s, when Kracauer wrote, the architecture of the picture palace and the variety format of the evening's program played a major role in defining movie-going as a succession of attractions, what Kracauer describes as the "fragmented sequence of splendid sense impressions."[29] The opulence and design of the Berlin movie theatres served to offset the coherence that classical narrative cinema had brought to film. As Kracauer described it:

> The interior design of the movie theatres served one sole purpose: to rivet the audience's attention to the peripheral so that they will not sink into the abyss. The stimulations of the senses succeed each other with such rapidity that there is no room left for even the slightest contemplation to squeeze in between them.[30]

The spectacular design of the theatre itself (accented and temporalised by elaborate manipulations of light) interacted with the growing tendency to embed the film in a larger program, a revue which included music and live performance. The film was only one element in an experience that Kracauer describes as a "total artwork of effects" which "assaults every one of the senses using every possible means."[31] For Kracauer, the discontinuity and variety of this form of cinema program (juxtaposing a two-dimensional film with three-dimensional live performances) strongly undermined film's illusionistic power. The projected film "recedes into the flat surface and the deception is exposed."[32] As in the first projections, the very aesthetic of attraction runs counter to an illusionistic absorption, the variety format of the picture palace program continually reminding the spectator of the act of watching by a succession of sensual assaults. As if in defiance of the increased length and the

---

[27]The key essays are, of course, "The Work of Art in the Age of Mechanical Reproduction" (in *Illuminations*, ed. Hannah Arendt, trans. Harry Zohn: New York: Schocken Books, 1969) and the two drafts of the essay on Baudelaire (in *Charles Baudelaire: A Lyric Poet in the Era of High Capitalism*, trans. Harry Zohn: London: NLB, 1973). My understanding of Benjamin's work has been shaped by Miriam Hansen's masterful essay "Benjamin, Cinema and Experience: The Blue Flower in the Land of Technology," *New German Critique* 40 (Winter 1987). This essay and Hansen's forthcoming work on the spectator of American silent film, *Babel and Babylon*, provide an essential background to my own essay. Her influence has been pervasive, and I see my ideas as developing out of a dialogue with her, without in any way implicating her in their final formulation. I also wish to thank her for her comments on a draft of this essay. [For Benjamin, see pp. xxx–xx in this volume.]

[28]Siegfried Kracauer, "The Cult of Distraction," *New German Critique* 40 (Winter 1987). I would also like to indicate my debt to Heide Schlüpmann's penetrating essay on Kracauer's early film theory, "Phenomenology of Film: On Siegfried Kracauer's Writings of the 1920s" (in the same issue), as well as the valuable discussions of Kracauer contained in the essays by Thomas Elsaesser, Patrice Petro, and Sabine Hake in this extraordinary issue on Weimar Film Theory.

[29]Kracauer, ibid., p. 94.

[30]Ibid.

[31]Ibid., p. 92.

[32]Ibid., p. 96.

voyeuristic fictional address of the featured films, the effect of a discontinuous suite of attractions still dominates the evening.

But in spite of (or rather motivating) this smorgasboard of sensual thrills, Kracauer discerns an experience of lack not unrelated (even if differently interpreted) to Gorky's malaise. The unifying element of the cult of distraction lies in what Kracauer calls pure externality. And this celebration of the external responds to a central lack in the life of its audience, particularly that of the working masses:

> an essentially formal tension which fills their day without making it fulfilling. Such a lack demands to be compensated, but this need can only be articulated in terms of the same surface which imposed the lack in the first place. The form of entertainment necessarily corresponds to that of enterprise.[33]

The sudden, intense, and external satisfaction supplied by the succession of attractions was recognised by Kracauer as revealing the fragmentation of modern experience. The taste for thrills and spectacle, the particularly modern form of *curiositas* that defines the aesthetic of attractions, is moulded by a modern loss of fulfilling experience. Once again, Wolfgang Schivelbusch's understanding of the changes in modern perception brought about by railway travel provides a theoretical tool. Crossbreeding Freud's metapsychological formulations with the urban sociology of Simmel (and thus following a trajectory traced by Benjamin), Schivelbusch describes a stimulus shield, which inhabitants of the overstimulated environments of the modern world develop in order to ward off its constant assaults.[34] But one could also point out that this stimulus shield dulls the edge of experience, and more intense aesthetic energies are required to penetrate it. As Miriam Hansen points out in her reading of Benjamin, the modern experience of shock corresponds to "[t]he adaptation of human perception of industrial modes of production and transportation, especially the radical restructuration of spatial and temporal relations."[35] Shock becomes not only a mode of modern experience, but a strategy of a modern aesthetic of astonishment. Hence the exploitation of new technological thrills that flirt with disaster.

Attractions are a response to an experience of alienation, and for Kracauer (as for Benjamin) cinema's value lay in exposing a fundamental loss of coherence and authenticity. Cinema's deadly temptation lay in trying to attain the aesthetic coherence of traditional art and culture. The radical aspiration of film must lie along the path of consciously heightening its use of discontinuous shocks, or as Kracauer puts it, "must aim radically towards a kind of distraction which exposes disintegration rather than masking it."[36] As Hansen has indicated, Benjamin's analysis of shock has a fundamental ambivalence, moulded certainly by the impoverishment of

---

[33]Ibid., p. 93.

[34]Schivelbusch, *The Railway Journey*, pp. 156–57.

[35]Miriam Hansen, *Benjamin, Cinema*, p. 184. Lynne Kirby observes about the popularity of staged railroad smash-ups: "As a spectacularisation of technological destruction based on an equation of pleasure with terror, the 'imagination of disaster' says volumes about the kinds of violent spectacle demanded by a modern public, and the transformation of 'shock' into eagerly expected, digestible spectacle" (Kirby, from *L'Illustration*, p. 120).

[36]Kracauer, "Cult of Distraction," p. 96.

experience in modern life, but also capable of assuming "a strategic significance—as an artificial means of propelling the human body into moments of recognition."[37]

The panic before the image on the screen exceeds a simple physical reflex, similar to those one experiences in a daily encounter with urban traffic or industrial production. In its double nature, its transformation of still image into moving illusion, it expresses an attitude in which astonishment and knowledge perform a vertiginous dance, and pleasure derives from the energy released by the play between the shock caused by this illusion of danger and delight in its pure illusion. The jolt experienced becomes a shock of recognition. Far from fulfilling a dream of total replication of reality—the *apophantis* of the myth of total cinema—the experience of the first projections exposes the hollow centre of the cinematic illusion. The thrill of transformation into motion depended on its presentation as a contrived illusion under the control of the projectionist showman. The movement from still to moving image accented the unbelievable and extraordinary nature of the apparatus itself. But in doing so, it also undid any naive belief in the reality of the image.

Cinema's first audiences can no longer serve as a founding myth for the theoreticalisation of the enthralled spectator. History reveals fissures along with continuities, and we must recognise that the experience of these audiences was profoundly different from the classical spectator's absorption into an empathetic narrative. Placed within a historical context and tradition, the first spectators' experience reveals not a childlike belief, but an undisguised awareness (and delight in) film's illusionistic capabilities. I have attempted to reverse the traditional understanding of this first onslaught of moving images. Like a demystifying showman, I have frozen the image of crowds scattered before the projection of an on-rushing train and read it allegorically rather than mythically. This arrest should astonish us with the realisation that these screams of terror and delight were well prepared for by both showmen and audience. The audience's reaction was the antipode to the primitive one: it was an encounter with modernity. From the start, the terror of that image uncovered a lack, and promised only a phantom embrace. The train collided with no one. It was, as Gorky said, a train of shadows, and the threat that it bore was freighted with emptiness.

1989

---

[37]Hansen, *Benjamin, Cinema*, pp. 210–11.

ROBERT STAM AND LOUISE SPENCE
COLONIALISM, RACISM, AND
REPRESENTATION: AN INTRODUCTION

Much of Robert Stam's work deals with the intersection of race, class, gender, and nationality in international cinema, all of which, he argues, are necessary in the multicultural and postcolonial analysis of film. His point of view has been influenced by that of Mikhail Bakhtin, on whom he has written several books, and by Christian Metz, whose semiotic theory Stam elaborated in *New Vocabularies of Film Semiotics; Structuralism, Post-structuralism and Beyond* (1992), co-authored with Robert Burgoyne and Sandy Flitterman-Lewis. He has written extensively on Brazilian film and devlops his multicultural perspective in *Unthinking Eurocentrism; Multiculturalism and the Media* (1994), and *Multiculturalism, Postcoloniality, and Transnational Media* (2003), both written with Ella Shohat. Stam is professor of cinema studies at New York University.

Louise Spence has written about western, critical methodologies in film study, and international soap opera. Her *Watching Daytime Soap Operas: The Power of Pleasure* (2005) uses reception data to consider the role of soap opera in women's daily lives and provides an overview of the history and development of the genre and its audience. With Pearl Bowser, she has also written *Writing Himself into History: Oscar Micheaux, His Silent Films, and his Audiences* (2000). She is currently professor of media studies at Sacred Heart University.

Racism and colonialism in the cinema have been the subject of many books and essays. The stereotyping of black Americans has been explored by Thomas Cripps in *Slow Fade to Black*,[1] by Daniel Leab in *From Sambo to Superspade*,[2] and by Donald Bogle in *Toms, Coons, Mulattoes, Mammies and Bucks*.[3] The pernicious distortion of African history and culture has been denounced by Richard Maynard

---

We would like to express our appreciation to the members of the study group in racism, all graduate students in the Cinema Studies Program at New York University, for their suggestions and insights: Pat Keeton, Charles Musser, Richard Porton, Susan Ryan, Ella Shochat, and Ed Simmons.
[1]Oxford, 1977.
[2]Houghton Mifflin, 1976.
[3]Bantam, 1974.

in *African on Film: Myth and Reality*.[4] Ralph Friar and Natasha Friar's *The Only Good Indian*[5] chronicles the imagistic mistreatment dealt out to the Native American. Lester Friedman's *Hollywood's Image of the Jew*[6] documents the process by which most screen Jews have had to sacrifice all ethnic specificity in order to conform to a WASP-dominated assimilationist creed. Allen Woll's *The Latin Image in American Film*[7] focuses on the stereotypical 'bandidos' and 'greasers' common in Hollywood films about Latin America, while Pierre Boulanger's *Le Cinéma colonial*[8] exposes the caricatural vision of North Africa and the Near East displayed in such films as *Pépé le Moko* and *Lawrence of Arabia*. And Tom Engelhardt's essay 'Ambush at Kamakazi Pass'[9] places screen anti-Asiatic racism within the context of the war in Vietnam.

Our purpose here is not to review the research or criticise the conclusions of the aforementioned texts. Rather, we would like to sketch out the background of the questions raised in them, offer some preliminary definitions of key terms, and propose the outlines of a methodology in the form of a series of concerns addressable to specific texts and their representations. We would like both to build on and go beyond the methodologies implicit in existing studies. These studies of filmic colonialism and racism tend to focus on certain dimensions of film—social portrayal, plot, and character. While such studies have made an invaluable contribution by alerting us to the hostile distortion and affectionate condescension with which the colonised have been treated in the cinema, they have often been marred by a certain methodological naiveté. While posing legitimate questions concerning narrative plausibility and mimetic accuracy, negative stereotypes and positive images, the emphasis on realism has often betrayed an exaggerated faith in the possibilities of verisimilitude in art in general and the cinema in particular, avoiding the fact that films are inevitably constructs, fabrications, representations. The privileging of social portrayal, plot and character meanwhile, has led to the slighting of the specifically cinematic dimensions of the film; the analyses might easily have been of novels or plays rather than films. The insistence on 'positive images', finally, obscures the fact that 'nice' images might at times be as pernicious as overtly degrading ones, providing a bourgeois facade for paternalism, a more pervasive racism.

Although we are quite aware of the crucial importance of the *contextual*, that is, of those questions bearing on the cinematic industry, its processes of production, distribution and exhibition, those social institutions and production practices which construct colonialism and racism in the cinema, our emphasis here will be *textual and intertextual*.[10] An anticolonialist analysis, in our view, must make the same kind

---

[4]Hayden, 1974.

[5]Drama, 1972.

[6]Ungar, 1982.

[7]UCLA Publications, 1980.

[8]Seghers, 1974.

[9]*Bulletin of Concerned Asian Scholars* 3, no. 1 (Winter–Spring 1971).

[10]For a discussion of the contextual dimension of racism in cinema, see "Racism in the Cinema: Proposal for a Methodological Model of Investigation," by Louise Spence and Robert Stam, with the collaboration of Pat Keeton, Charles Musser, Richard Porton, Susan Ryan, Ella Shochat, and Ed Simmons *Critical Arts: A Journal for Media Studies*, vol. 2, no. 4, 6–12.

of methodological leap effected by feminist criticism when journals like *Screen* and *Camera Obscura* critically transcended the usefully angry but methodologically flawed 'image' analysis of such critics as Molly Haskell and Marjorie Rosen in order to pose questions concerning the apparatus, the position of the spectator, and the specifically cinematic codes.[11] Our discussion draws from, and hopefully applies by extension to, the analysis of other oppressions, such as sexism, class subordination and anti-Semitism, to all situations, that is, in which difference is transformed into 'other'-ness and exploited or penalised by and for power.

SOME DEFINITIONS

We should begin, however, with some preliminary definitions. What do we mean by 'colonialism', 'the Third World' and 'racism'? By colonialism, we refer to the process by which the European powers (including the United States) reached a position of economic, military, political and cultural domination in much of Asia, Africa and Latin America. This process, which can be traced at least as far back as the 'voyages of discovery' and which had as its corollary the institution of the slave trade, reached its apogee between 1900 and the end of World War I (at which point Europe had colonised roughly 85 percent of the earth) and began to be reversed only with the disintegration of the European colonial empires after World War II.

The definition of the 'Third World' flows logically out of this prior definition of colonialism, for the 'Third World' refers to the historical victims of this process— to the colonised, neocolonised or decolonised nations of the world whose economic and political structures have been shaped and deformed within the colonial process. The colonial relation has to do with *structural* domination rather than with crude economic ('the poor'), racial ('the nonwhite'), cultural ('the backward'), or geographical categories.[12]

Racism, finally, although not limited to the colonial situation (anti-Semitism being a case in point), has historically been both an ally and a product of the colonisation process. It is hardly accidental that the most obvious victims of racism are those whose identity was forged within the colonial process: blacks in the United States, Asians and West Indians in Great Britain, Arab workers in France, all of whom share an oppressive situation and the status of second-class citizens. We will define racism, borrowing from Albert Memmi, as 'the generalized and final assigning of values to real or imaginary differences, to the accuser's benefit and at his victim's expense, in order to justify the former's own privilege or aggression'.[13] Memmi's definition has the advantage of calling attention to the *uses* to which racism is put. Just as the logic of sexism leads to rape, so the logic of racism leads to violence and exploitation. Racism, for Memmi, is almost always a rationale for an already

---

[11]See, for example, Molly Haskell, *From Reverence to Rape* (New York: Holt, Rinehart and Winston, 1974), and Marjorie Rosen, *Popcorn Venus* (New York: Avon, 1974).

[12]These notions of the Third World are imprecise because the Third World nations are not necessarily poor in resources (Mexico, Venezuela and Kuwait are rich in petroleum), nor culturally backward (as witnessed by the brilliance of contemporary Latin American literature), nor nonindustrialised (Brazil is highly industrialised) nor nonwhite (Argentina is predominantly white).

[13]Albert Memmi, *Dominated Man* (Boston: Beacon Press, 1968), p. 186.

existing or contemplated oppression. Without ignoring the accumulated prejudices and cultural attitudes which prepared the way for racism, there is a sense in which it can be argued that racism comes in the wake of concrete oppressions. Amerindians were called beasts and cannibals *because* white Europeans were slaughtering them and expropriating their land; blacks were slandered as lazy *because* they were being exploited as slaves; Mexicans were caricatured as greasers and bandidos *because* the United States had seized half of their territory; and the colonised were ridiculed as lacking in culture and history *because* colonialism, in the name of profit, was destroying the basis of that culture and the memory of that history.

The same Renaissance humanism which gave birth to the code of perspective—subsequently incorporated, as Baudry points out, into the camera itself—also gave birth to the 'rights of man'. Europe constructed its self-image on the backs of its equally constructed Other—the 'savage', the 'cannibal'—much as phallocentrism sees its self-flattering image in the mirror of woman defined as lack. And just as the camera might therefore be said to inscribe certain features of bourgeois humanism, so the cinematic and televisual apparatuses, taken in their most inclusive sense, might be said to inscribe certain features of European colonialism. The magic carpet provided by these apparatuses flies us around the globe and makes us, by virtue of our subject position, its audiovisual masters. It produces us as subjects, transforming us into armchair conquistadores, affirming our sense of power while making the inhabitants of the Third World objects of spectacle for the First World's voyeuristic gaze.

Colonialist representation did not begin with the cinema: it is rooted in a vast colonial intertext, a widely disseminated set of discursive practices. Long before the first racist images appeared on the film screens of Europe and North America, the process of colonialist image-making, and resistance to that process, resonated through Western literature. Colonialist historians, speaking for the 'winners' of history, exalted the colonial enterprise, at bottom little more than a gigantic act of pillage whereby whole continents were bled of their human and material resources, as a philanthropic 'civilising mission' motivated by a desire to push back the frontiers of ignorance, disease and tyranny, Daniel Defoe glorified colonialism in *Robinson Crusoe* (1719), a novel whose 'hero becomes wealthy through the slave trade and through Brazilian sugar mills, and whose first thought, upon seeing human footprints after years of solitude, is to 'get (him) a servant'.[14]

Other European writers responded in more complex and ambiguous ways. The French philosopher Montaigne, writing at the end of the sixteenth century, suggested in 'Des Cannibales' that the Amerindian cannibalising of dead enemy warriors paled in horror when compared to the internecine warfare and torture practiced by European Christians in the name of a religion of love. Shakespeare has Caliban in *The Tempest*, whose name forms an annagram of 'cannibal', curse the European Prospero for having

---

[14]Buñuel's film version of the novel mocks Defoe's protagonist by haunting him with surrealist dreams, turning him into a transvestite, and making it singularly difficult for him to make rational sense out of the tenets of Christianity to an inquisitive Friday. The film *Man Friday*, which we have not seen, reportedly tells the story from Friday's point of view. And in a recent Brazilian adaptation of the novel, black actor Grande Otelo subverts Defoe's classic by playing a Friday who refuses the coloniser's power to name, repeatedly telling the Englishman: 'Me Crusoe, *You* Friday!'

robbed him of his island: 'for I am all the subjects that you have/which first was mine own king'. (Aimé Césaire had to alter Shakespeare's character but slightly, in his 1969 version, to turn him into the anti-colonialist militant Caliban X.[15]) And Jonathan Swift, a century later in *Gulliver's Travels* (1726), portrays colonialism in satirical images that in some ways anticipate Herzog's *Aguirre*:

> A crew of pyrates are driven by a storm they know not whither; at length a Boy discovers Land from the Topmast; they go on shore to rob and plunder; they see an harmless people, are entertained with kindness, they give the country a new name, they take formal possession of it for the king, they set up a rotten plank or a stone for a memorial, they murder two or three dozen of the natives, bring away a couple more by force for a sample, return home and get their Pardon. . . . And this execrable crew of butchers employed in so pious an expedition, is a modern colony sent to convert and civilise an idolatrous and barbarous people.[16]

The struggle over images continues, within literature, into the period of the beginnings of the cinema. Conrad's *Heart of Darkness* (1902), published but a few years after the first Lumière screenings, describes colonialism in Africa as 'just robbery with violence, aggravated murder on a grand scale' and emphasises its racist underpinnings. 'The conquest of the earth, which mostly means the taking it away from those who have a different complexion or slightly flatter noses than ourselves,' Conrad has his narrator say, 'is not a pretty thing when you look into it too much.'[17] 'The settler,' Fanon writes, 'makes history; his life is an epoch, an Odyssey,' while against him 'torpic creatures, wasted by fevers, obsessed by ancestral customs, form an almost inorganic background for the innovating dynamism of colonial mercantilism.'[18] Since the beginnings of the cinema coincided with the height of European imperialism, it is hardly surprising that European cinema portrayed the colonised in an unflattering light. Indeed, many of the misconceptions concerning Third World people derive from the long parade of lazy Mexicans, shifty Arabs, savage Africans and exotic Asiatics that have disgraced our movie screens. Africa was portrayed as a land inhabited by cannibals in the Lubin comedy *Rastus in Zululand* (1910), Mexicans were reduced to 'greasers' in films like *Tony the Greaser* (1911) and *The Greaser's Revenge* (1914), and slavery was idealised, and the slaves degraded, in *The Birth of a Nation* (1915). Hundreds of Hollywood westerns turned history on its head by making the Native Americans appear to be intruders on what was originally their land, and provided a paradigmatic perspective through which to view the whole of the nonwhite world.

The colonialist inheritance helps account for what might be called the tendentiously flawed mimesis of many films dealing with the Third World. The innumerable ethnographic, linguistic and even topographical blunders in Hollywood films are illuminating in this regard. Countless safari films present Africa as the land of 'lions in the jungle' when in fact only a tiny proportion of the African land mass could be called 'jungle' and when lions do not live in jungle but in grasslands.

[15]See Aimé Césaire, *Une Tempête* (Paris: Seuil, 1969).
[16]Jonathan Swift, *Gulliver's Travels* (New York: Random House, 1958), p. 241.
[17]Joseph Conrad, *Heart of Darkness* (New York: New American Library, 1950), p. 69.
[18]Frantz Fanon, *The Wretched of the Earth* (New York: Grove Press, 1968), p. 51.

Hollywood films, in any case, show disproportionate interest in the animal, as opposed to the human life of Africa. And as regards human beings, the Western world has been oddly fascinated by Idi Amin, in many ways an atypical leader in the continent of Nyerere, Mugabe and Machel.

At times the 'flaw' in the mimesis derives not from the *presence* of distorting stereotypes but from the *absence* of representations of an oppressed group. *King of Jazz* (1930), for example, paid tribute to the origins of jazz by pouring (through superimposition) a series of musical ensembles, representing diverse European ethnic groups, into a gigantic melting pot, completely bypassing both Africa and Afro-Americans. Black Brazilians, similarly, formed a structuring absence within Brazilian cinema during the first few decades of this century, as filmmakers exalted the already annihilated and mythically connoted 'Indian warrior' in preference to the more problematically present black, victim of a slavery abolished just ten years before the founding of Brazilian cinema. Many American films in the fifties gave the impression that there were no black people in America. The documentary-like *The Wrong Man* (Hitchcock, 1957), for example, shows the subways and even the prisons of New York City as totally devoid of blacks.

At other times the structuring absence has to do not with the people themselves but with a dimension of that people's history or institutions. A whole realm of Afro-American history, the slave revolts, is rarely depicted in film or is represented (as in the television series *Roots*) as a man, already dead, in a ditch. The revolutionary dimension of the black church, similarly, is ignored in favour of a portrayal which favours charismatic leaders and ecstatic songs and dancers.[19] The exclusion of whites from a film, we might add paradoxically, can also be the result of white racism. The all-black Hollywood musicals of the twenties and thirties, like present-day South African films made by whites for black audiences, tend to exclude whites because their mere presence would destroy the elaborate fabric of fantasy constructed by such films.

The absence of the language of the colonised is also symptomatic of colonialist attitudes. The languages spoken by Third World peoples are often reduced to an incomprehensible jumble of background murmurs, while major 'native' characters are consistently obliged to meet the coloniser on the coloniser's linguistic turn (here westerns, with their Indian-pidgin English, again provide the paradigm). Anna, in *The King and I*, teachers the Siamese natives 'civilised' manners along with English. Even *Cuba* (directed by Richard Lester, 1980), a generally sympathetic portrait of the Cuban revolution, perpetuates a kind of linguistic colonialism by having the Cubans speak English in a variety of accents (many of which have nothing Hispanic about them beyond an occasional rolled *r*) not only to English-speaking characters, but also to one another. In other films, major nations are mistakenly attributed the wrong language. In *Latin Lovers* (directed by Mervyn Leroy, 1953), for example, Portuguese-speaking Brazilians, when they are not speaking English, are made to speak Spanish.[20]

---

[19]A recent example of this tendency is the ecstatic song led by James Brown in *The Blues Brothers* (directed by John Landis, 1980).

[20]For a discussion of Hollywood's view of Brazil, see Sergio Augusto, 'Hollywood Looks at Brazil: From Carmen Miranda to Moonraker', in Randal Johnson and Robert Stam, *Brazilian Cinema* (East Brunswick, NJ: Associated University Presses, 1982).

In response to such distortions, the Third World has attempted to write its own history, take control of its own cinematic image, speak in its own voice. The colonialist wrote the colonised *out* of history, teaching Vietnamese and Senegalese children, for example, that their 'ancestors' were the Gauls. A central impulse animating many Third World films is precisely the effort to reclaim the past. Thus *Ganga Zumba* (directed by Carlos Diegues, 1963) memorialises the proud history of black rebellion in Brazil by focusing on the seventeenth-century fugitive slave republic called Palmares. *Emitai* (directed by Ousmane Sembene, 1972) deals with French colonialism and Senegalese resistance during the period of the Second World War. *Chronicle of the Years of Embers* (directed by Lakdar Hamina, 1975) recounts the Algerian revolution, and *The Promised Land* (directed by Miguel Littin, 1973) renders homage to the short-lived 'socialist republic' of Marmaduke Grove as a way to examine both the contradictions and the revolutionary potential of the Chile of the Allende period.

Many oppressed groups have used 'progressive realism' to unmask and combat hegemonic images. Women and Third World filmmakers have attempted to counterpose the objectifying discourse of patriarchy and colonialism with a vision of themselves and their reality as seen 'from within'. But this laudable intention is not always unproblematic. 'Reality' is not self-evidently given, and 'truth' cannot be immediately captured by the camera. We must distinguish, furthermore, between realism as a goal—Brecht's 'laying bare the causal network'—and realism as a style or constellation of strategies aimed at producing an illusionistic reality effect. Realism as a goal is quite compatible with a style which is reflexive and deconstructive, as is eloquently demonstrated by *El Otro Francisco* (directed by Sergio Giral, 1974), a Cuban film which deconstructs a romantic abolitionist novel by highlighting the historical realities (economic motivations on the part of the whites, armed resistance on the part of the blacks) elided by it, while at the same time underlining its own processes of construction as a filmic text.

POSITIVE IMAGES?

Much of the work on racism in the cinema, like early work on the representation of women, has stressed the issue of the 'positive image'. This reductionism, though not wrong, is inadequate and fraught with methodological dangers. The exact nature of 'positive', first of all, is somewhat relative: black incarnations of patience and gradualism, for example, have always been more pleasing to whites than to blacks. A cinema dominated by positive images, characterised by a bending-over-backwards-not-to-be-racist attitude, might ultimately betray a lack of confidence in the group portrayed, which usually itself has no illusions concerning its own perfection. ('Just because you're black don't make you right,' one black brother tells another in *Ashes and Embers*, directed by Haile Gerima.) A cinema in which all black actors resembled Sidney Poitier might be as serious a cause for alarm as one in which they all resembled Stepin Fetchit.

We should be equally suspicious of a naive integrationism which simply inserts new heroes and heroines, this time drawn from the ranks of the oppressed, into the old functional roles that were themselves oppressive, much as colonialism invited a few assimilated 'natives' to join the club of the 'elite'. A film like *Shaft* (1971) simply sub-stitutes black heroes into the actantial slot normally filled by white ones, in order to flatter the fantasies of a certain (largely male) sector of the black audience. *Guess Who's Coming to Dinner* (directed by Stanley Kramer, 1967), as its title suggests, invites an elite black into the club of the truly human, but always on white terms. Other films, such as *In the Heat of the Night* (1967), *Pressure Point* (1962), or the television series *Mod Squad*, place black characters in the role of law-enforcers. The ideological func-tion of such images is not dissimilar to that pointed out in Barthes's famous analysis of the *Paris Match* cover which shows a black soldier in French uniform, eyes upraised, saluting what we presume to be the French flag. All citizens, regardless of their colour, can serve law and order, and the black soldier's zeal in serving the established law is the best answer to critics, black and white, of that society. The television series *Roots*, finally, exploited positive images in what was ultimately a cooptive version of Afro-American history. The series's subtitle, 'the saga of an American family', reflects an emphasis on the European-style nuclear family (retrospectively projected onto Kunta's life in Africa) in a film which casts blacks as just another immigrant group making its way toward freedom and prosperity in democratic America.

The complementary preoccupation to the search for positive images, the expo-sure of negative images or stereotypes, entails similar methodological problems. The positing and recognition of these stereotypes has been immensely useful, enabling us to detect structural patterns of prejudice in what had formerly seemed random phenomena. The exclusive preoccupation with images, however, whether positive or negative, can lead both to the privileging of characterological concerns (to the detriment of other important considerations) and also to a kind of essen-tialism, as the critic reduces a complex diversity of portrayals to a limited set of reified stereotypes. Behind every black child performer, from Farina to Gary Coleman, the critic discerns a 'pickaninny', behind every sexually attractive black actor a 'buck' and behind every attractive black actress a 'whore'. Such reduc-tionist simplifications run the risk of reproducing the very racism they were ini-tially designed to combat.

The analysis of stereotypes must also take cultural specificity into account. Many North American black stereotypes are not entirely congruent with those of Brazil, also a multiethnic New World society with a large black population. While there are analogies in the stereotypical images thrown up by the two cultures—the 'mammy' is certainly a close relation to the *mae preta* (black Mother), there are disparities as well. Brazilian historian Emilia Viotti da Costa argues, for instance, that the 'sambo' figure never existed, as reality or stereotype, in Brazilian colonial society.[21] The themes of the 'tragic mulatto' and 'passing for white', similarly, find little echo in the Brazilian context. Since the Brazilian racial spectrum is not binary (black *or* white) but nuances its shades across a wide variety of racial descriptive terms, and since Brazil, while in many ways oppressive to blacks, has never been a rigidly *segregated* society, no figure exactly corresponds to the North American 'tragic mulatto', schizophrenically torn between two radically separate social worlds.

---

[21]See Emilia Viotti da Costa, "Slave Images and Realities", in *Comparative Perspectives on Slavery in New World Plantation Societies* (New York: New York Academy of Sciences, 1977).

An ethnocentric vision rooted in North American cultural patterns can lead, similarly, to the 'racialising', or the introjection of racial themes into, filmic situations which Brazilians themselves would not perceive as racially connoted. *Deus e Diabo na Terra do Sol* (*God and the Devil in the Land of the Sun*, directed by Glauber Rocha, 1964) was mistranslated into English as *Black God, White Devil*, suggesting a racial dichotomy not emphasized either in the original title or in the film itself. The humour of *Macunaíma* (1969), similarly, depends on an awareness of Brazilian cultural codes. Two sequences in which the title character turns from black to white, for example, occasionally misread as racist by North Americans, are in fact sardonic comments on Brazil's putative 'racial democracy'.

A comprehensive methodology must pay attention to the *mediations* which intervene between 'reality' and representation. Its emphasis should be on narrative structure, genre conventions, and cinematic style rather than on perfect correctness of representation or fidelity to an original 'real' model or prototype. We must beware of mistakes in which the criteria appropriate to one genre are applied to another. A search for positive images in *Macunaíma*, for example, would be fundamentally misguided, for that film belongs to a carnivalesque genre favouring what Mikhail Bakhtin calls 'grotesque realism'. Virtually all the film's characters are two-dimensional grotesques rather than rounded three-dimensional characters, and the grotesquerie is democratically distributed among all the races, while the most archly grotesque characters are the white industrialist cannibal and his ghoulish spouse. Satirical or parodic films, in the same way, may be less concerned with constructing positive images than with challenging the stereotypical expectations an audience may bring to a film. *Blazing Saddles* lampoons a whole range of ethnic prejudices, mocking audience expectations by having the whites sing 'Ole Man River' while the blacks sing 'I Get No Kick from Champagne'.

POLITICAL POSITIONING

One mediation specific to cinema is spectator positioning. The paradigmatic filmic encounters of whites and Indians in the western, as Tom Engelhardt points out, typically involve images of encirclement. The attitude toward the Indian is premised on exteriority. The besieged wagon train or fort is the focus of our attention and sympathy, and from this centre our familiars sally out against unknown attackers characterised by inexplicable customs and irrational hostility: 'In essence, the viewer is forced behind the barrel of a repeating rifle and it is from that position, through its gun sights, that he [*sic*] receives a picture history of western colonialism and imperialism.'[22] The possibility of sympathetic identifications with the Indians is simply ruled out by the point-of-view conventions. The spectator is unwittingly sutured into a colonialist perspective.

A film like *The Wild Geese* (directed by Andrew McLaglen, 1978) inherits the conventions of anti-Indian westerns and extends them to Africa. This glorification of the role of white mercenaries in Africa makes the mercenaries, played by popular

---

[22]Engelhardt, op. cit.

heroic actors Richard Burton, Richard Harris, and Roger Moore, the central focus of our sympathy. Even the gamblers and opportunists among them, recruited from the flotsam and jetsam of British society, are rendered as sympathetic, lively and humorous. Killing Africans en masse, the film implies, fosters camaraderie and somehow brings out their latent humanity. White Europe's right to determine Africa's political destiny, like the white American right to Indian land in the western, is simply assumed throughout the film.[23]

In *The Wild Geese,* the imagery of encirclement is used against black Africans, as the spectator, positioned behind the sight of mercenary machine guns, sees them fall in their hundreds. One of the crucial innovations of *Battle of Algiers* (directed by Gillo Pontecorvo, 1966) was to invert this imagery of encirclement and exploit the identificatory mechanisms of cinema on behalf of the colonised rather than the coloniser. Algerians, traditionally represented in cinema as shadowy figures, picturesquely backward at best and hostile and menacing at worst, are here treated with respect, dignified by close-ups, shown as speaking subjects rather than as manipulable objects. While never caricaturing the French, the film exposes the oppressive logic of colonialism and consistently fosters our complicity with the Algerians. It is through Algerian eyes, for example, that we witness a condemned Algerian's walk to his execution. It is from *within* the casbah that we see and hear the French troops and helicopters. This time it is the colonised who are encircled and menaced and with whom we identify.

One sequence, in which three Algerian women dress in European style in order to pass the French checkpoints and plant bombs in the European sector, is particularly effective in controverting traditional patterns of identification. Many critics, impressed with the film-makers' honesty in showing that the FLN committed terrorist acts against civilians, lauded this sequence for its 'objectivity'. (Objectivity, as Fanon pointed out, almost always works against the colonised.) But that *Battle of Algiers* shows such acts is ultimately less important than *how* it shows them; the signified of the diegesis (terrorist actions) is less important than the mode of address and the positioning of the spectator. The film makes us want the women to complete their task, not necessarily out of political sympathy but through the mechanisms of cinematic identification: scale (close shots individualise the three women); off-screen sound (we hear the sexist comments as if from the women's aural perspective); and especially point-of-view editing. By the time the women plant the bombs, our identification is so complete that we are not terribly disturbed by a series of close shots of the bombs' potential victims. Close-ups of one of the women alternate with close-ups of French people in a cafe, the eyeline matches suggesting

---

[23]In the racist hierarchies of *The Wild Geese*, white males stand at the apex, while women are treated as comically dispensable and blacks are relegated to the bottom. The film camouflages its racism, however, by two plot devices involving positive images: first, by including a token black (a positive image?) as a member of the mercenary force (genocide rendered palatable by 'integrating' its perpetrators) and second, by having the entire operation be undertaken on behalf of a black leader characterised as 'the best there is'. The African 'best', however, is embodied by a sick, helpless, dying 'good Negro' who must be literally carried on the backs of whites. In this white rescue fantasy, the black leader of the 70s speaks the Sidney Poitier dialogue of the 50s; he pleads for racial understanding. The blacks, he says, must forgive the white past, and whites must forgive the black present. Thus centuries of colonialism are cancelled out in the misleading symmetry of an aphorism.

that she is contemplating the suffering her bomb will cause. But while we might think her cruel for taking innocent life, we are placed within her perspective and admire her for having the courage to perform what has been presented as a dangerous and noble mission.

Other narrative and cinematic strategies are deployed in this sequence to solicit support for the three women. The narrative placement of the sequence itself presents their action as the fulfilment of the FLN promise, made in the previous sequence, to respond to the French terror bombing of the casbah. Everything here contributes to the impression that the bombing will be an expression of the rage of an entire people rather than the will of a fanatical minority. It is constructed, therefore, not as an individual emotional explosion but as a considered political task undertaken with reluctance by an organised group. The sequence consequently challenges the image of anti-colonialist guerrillas as terrorist fanatics lacking respect for human life. Unlike the Western mass media, which usually restrict their definition of 'terror' to anti-establishment violence—state repression and government-sanctioned aerial bombings are not included in the definition—*Battle of Algiers* presents anti-colonialist terror as a response to colonialist violence. We are dealing here with what might be called the political dimension of syntagmatic organisation; while the First World media usually present colonial repression as a response to 'leftist subversion', *Battle of Algiers* inverts the sequencing. Indeed, examining the film as a whole, we might say that Pontecorvo 'highjacks' the techniques of mass-media reportage—hand-held cameras, frequent zooms, long lenses—to express a political point of view rarely encountered in establishment-controlled media.

The *mise-en-scène*, too, creates a nonsexist and anticolonialist variant on the classic cinematic *topos*: women dressing in front of a mirror. The lighting highlights the powerful dignity of the women's faces as they remove their veils, cut their hair and apply make-up so as to look European. The mirror here is not the instrument of *vanitas*, but a revolutionary tool. The women regard themselves, without coyness, as if they were putting on a new identity with which they do not feel entirely comfortable. They perform their task in a disciplined manner and without vindictive remarks about their future victims.

The film also highlights the larger social dimension of the drama in which the women are involved. The colonial world, writes Fanon, is a world cut in two: 'In the colonies it is the policeman and the soldier who are the official instituted go-betweens, the spokesmen of the settler and his rule of oppression.'[24] The background imagery, readable thanks to the depth of field, shows that the French have imposed their regime by what amounts to military occupation. The French are in uniform, the Algerians in civilian dress. The casbah is the Algerian's home; for the French it is an outpost on a frontier. The barbed wire and checkpoints remind us of other occupations, thus eliciting our sympathy for a struggle against a foreign occupant. The proairetic 'code of actions', meanwhile, shows the soldiers treating the Algerians with racist scorn and suspicion, while they greet the Europeans with a friendly *bonjour*. They misperceive the three women as French and flirtatious when in fact

---

[24]Frantz Fanon. op. cit., p. 38.

they are Algerian and revolutionary. Their sexism, furthermore, prevents them from seeing women, generally, as potential revolutionaries. In the negative dialectic of oppression, the slave (the colonised, the black, the woman) knows the mind of the master better than the master knows the mind of the slave.

Western attitudes toward non-Western peoples are also played on here. Hassiba is first seen in traditional Arab costume, her face covered by a veil. So dressed, she is a reminder of Arab women in other films who function as a sign of the exotic. But as the sequence progresses, we become increasingly close to the three women, though paradoxically, we become close to them only as they strip themselves of their safsaris, their veils, and their hair. They transform themselves into Europeans, people with whom the cinema more conventionally allows the audience to identify. At the same time, we are made aware of the absurdity of a system in which people warrant respect only if they look and act like Europeans. The French colonialist myth of assimilation, the idea that select Algerians could be first-class French citizens, is demystified. Algerians can assimilate, it is suggested, but only at the price of shedding everything that is characteristically Algerian about them—their religion, their clothes, their language.[25]

If *Battle of Algiers* exploits conventional identification mechanisms on behalf of a group traditionally denied them, other films critique colonialism and colonialist point-of-view conventions in a more ironic mode.[26] *Petit à Petit* (directed by Jean Rouch, 1969) inverts the hierarchy often assumed within the discipline of anthropology, the academic offspring of colonialism, by having the African protagonist Damouré 'do anthropology' among the strange tribe known as the Parisians, interrogating them about their folkways. Europe, usually the bearer of the anthropological gaze, is here subjected to the questioning regard of the other. *How Tasty Was My Little Frenchman* (directed by Nelson Pereira dos Santos, 1971), meanwhile, updates Montaigne by persuading us to sympathise with Tupinamba cannibals.[27] The film plays ironically on the traditional identification with European heroes by placing the camera, initially, on American shores, so that the Amerindian discovers the European rather than the reverse. By the final shot, which shows the Frenchman's Tupinamba lover dining on him while manifesting no emotion beyond ordinary culinary pleasure, our 'natural' identification with the coloniser has been so completely subverted that we are quite indifferent to his fate.

---

[25]For a fuller discussion of this film, see Joan Mellen, *Filmguide to the Battle of Algiers* (Bloomington: Indiana University Press, 1973), and Robert Stam, *The Battle of Algiers: Three Women, Three Bombs*, Macmillan Films Study Extract, 1975.

[26]Some Left critics dismissed *The Battle of Algiers* as a Hollywooden Z-style exercise in political melodrama. Such critiques run the dangers of being (1) *ahistorical* (we must situate the film in the context of 1966); (2) politically *counter-productive* (the Left deprives itself of a powerful instrument of anticolonialist persuasion); and (3) *ethnocentric* (offering an example of a kind of Left colonialism). While the Right asks all pro–Third World films to display high production values and be entertaining, a certain Left asks all pro–Third World films to be disconstructive, reflexive, and to display the precise variant of Marxism that the particular First World critic finds most sympathetic.

[27]Montaigne's essay "Des Cannibales" was, ironically, based on interviews with Brazilian Indians then on display in Europe. The Indians, according to Montaigne, asked him three questions, only two of which he could remember: (1) Why were some people rich and others poor? (2) Why did Europeans worship kings who were no bigger than other people? Lévi-Strauss, more than three centuries later, claims to have been asked the same questions by Brazilian Indians.

The question of point of view is crucial then, but it is also more complex than might at first appear. The granting of point-of-view shots to the oppressed does not guarantee a noncolonialist perspective, any more than Hitchcock's granting of subjective shots to the female protagonist of *Marnie* inoculates that film from what is ultimately a patriarchal and infantilising discourse. The arch-racist *The Birth of a Nation* grants Gus, the sexually aggressive black man, a number of subjective shots as he admires little Flora. The racism in such a case may be said to be displaced from the code of editing onto the code of character construction, here inflected by the projection of white sexual paranoia onto the black male, in the case of Gus, and of patriarchal chivalry (tinged perhaps with authorial desire), in the case of Flora. The Brazilian film *João Negrinho* (directed by Oswaldo Censoni, 1954) is entirely structured around the perspective of its focal character, an elderly ex-slave. The film apparently presents all events from João's point of view so as to elicit total sympathy, yet what the film elicits sympathy *for* is in fact a paternalistic vision in which 'good' blacks are to leave their destiny in the hands of well-intentioned whites.

CODES AND COUNTER STRATEGIES

A more comprehensive analysis of character status as speaking subject as against spoken object would attend to cinematic and extra-cinematic codes, and to their interweaving within textual systems. In short, it must address the instances through which film speaks—composition, framing, scale, off- and on-screen sound, music— as well as questions of plot and character. Questions of image scale and duration, for example, are intricately related to the respect afforded a character and the potential for audience sympathy, understanding and identification. Which characters are afforded close-ups and which are relegated to the background? Does a character look and act, or merely appear, to be looked at and acted upon? With whom is the audience permitted intimacy? If there is off-screen commentary or dialogue, what is its relation to the image? *Black Girl* (directed by Ousmane Sembene, 1966) uses off-screen dialogue to foster intimacy with the title character, a Senegalese maid working in France. Shots of the maid working in the kitchen coincide with overhead slurs from her employers about her 'laziness'. Not only do the images point up the absurdity of the slurs—indeed, she is the *only* person working—but also the coincidence of the off-screen dialogue with close shots of her face makes us hear the comments as if through her ears.

An emphasis on identification, however, while appropriate to fiction films in the realist mode, fails to allow for films which might *also* show sensitivity to the point of view, in a more inconclusive sense, of the colonised or the oppressed, but in a rigorously distanced manner. A film like *Der Leone Have Sept Cabeças* (directed by Glauber Rocha, 1970), whose multilingual title already subverts the cultural positioning of the spectator by mingling the languages of five of Africa's colonisers, allows identification with none of its characters, because it is essentially a Brechtian 'tricontinental' fable which animates emblematic figures representing the diverse incarnations of coloniser and colonised in the Third World. Zumbi, named after the founder of the Brazilian fugitive slave republic Palmares, encapsulates the revolution in Africa and among the black diaspora; Samba embodies the power of Afroculture; and Xobu figures in caricatural form the corruption of the black puppets of colonialism. To condemn such a film for not creating identification with the oppressed is to reduce the broad question of the articulation of narrative, cinematic and cultural codes to the single question of the presence or absence of a particular subcode of editing.

The music track can also play a crucial role in the establishment of a political point of view and the cultural positioning of the spectator. Film music has an emotional dimension: it can regulate our sympathies, extract our tears or trigger our fears. The Ray Budd score in *The Wild Geese* consistently supports the mercenaries, waxing martial and heroic when they are on the attack, and maudlin when they emote. At one point, the Borodin air 'This Is My Beloved' musically eulogises one of the slain mercenaries. In many classical Hollywood films, African polyrhythms became aural signifiers of encircling savagery, a kind of synecdochic acoustic shorthand for the atmosphere of menace implicit in the phrase 'the natives are restless'. *Der Leone Have Sept Cabeças*, in contrast, treats African polyrhythms with respect, as music, while ironically associating the puppets of colonialism with 'La Marseillaise'. *Black and White in Color* employs music satirically by having the African colonised carry their colonial masters, while singing—in their own language—satirical songs about them ('My master is so fat, how can I carry him? . . . Yes, but mine is so ugly. . . .').

In many consciously anticolonialist films, a kind of textual uneven development makes the film politically progressive in some of its codes but regressive in others. *Burn!* (directed by Gillo Pontecorvo, 1970), for example, a didactic assault on neocolonialism, partially vitiates its message by imposing highly Europeanised choral music on its Third World setting.[28] *Compasso de Espera* (*Marking Time*, directed by Antunes Filho, 1973), a denunciation of Brazilian-style racism, subverts its pro-black position with a music track that mixes Erik Satie and Blood Sweat and Tears while ignoring the rich Afro-Brazilian musical heritage. On the other hand *Land in Anguish* (directed by Glauber Rocha, 1967) uses music to the opposite effect. Here, in a film dealing with Brazil's white political elite, Afro-Brazilian music serves as a constant reminder of the existence of the marginalised majority of blacks and mulattoes absent from the screen and not represented by that elite. Brazilian films in general, perhaps because of the ethnically polyphonic nature of that society, are particularly rich in intercodic contradiction, at times instituting a veritable battle of the codes on the music tracks. *The Given Word* (directed by Anselmo Duarte, 1962) sets in motion a cultural conflict between the Afro-Brazilian *berimbau* instrument and the bells of the Catholic Church, while *Tent of Miracles* (directed by Nelson Pereira dos Santos, 1976) counterpoints opera and samba to represent a larger conflict between Bahia's white elite and its subjugated *mestizos*.

---

[28]The film also made the mistake of pitting one of the First World's most charismatic actors (Marlon Brando), as the coloniser, against a former peasant non-actor (Evaristo Marques), as the colonised, thus disastrously tipping the scales of interest, if not sympathy, in favour of the coloniser.

ABERRANT READINGS

The filmic experience must inevitably be infected by the cultural awareness of the audience itself, constituted outside the text and traversed by sets of social relations such as race, class and gender. We must allow, therefore, for the possibility of aberrant readings, reading which go against the grain of the discourse. Although fiction films are persuasive machines designed to produce specific impressions and emotions, they are not all-powerful; they may be read differently by different audiences. Hollywood's ill-informed portrayals of Latin-American life were sometimes laughed off the screen within Latin America itself. The Spanish version of *Dracula*, for example, made concurrently with the 1931 Bela Lugosi film, mingles Cuban, Argentine, Chilean, Mexican and peninsular Spanish in a linguistic hodge-podge that struck Latin-American audiences as quite ludicrous.

A particular audience's knowledge or experience can also generate a counter-pressure to colonialist representations. Black Americans, presumably, never took Stepin Fetchit to be an accurate representation of their race as a whole. *One Potato Two Potato* (directed by Larry Peerce, 1964), a film about interracial marriage, provides a poignant narrative example, in which the experience of oppression inflects a character's reading of the film-within-the-film. The black husband, enraged by a series of racially motivated slights, attends a western in a drive-in movie theatre. Projecting his anger, he screams his support for the Indians, whom he sees as his analogues in suffering, and his hatred for the whites. His reading goes against the grain of the colonialist discourse.

The movement of an aberrant reading can also proceed in the opposite direction; an antiracist film, when subjected to the ethnocentric prejudices of a particular critic or interpretative community, can be read in a racist fashion. A sequence in *Masculine, Feminine*, a quotation from LeRoi Jones's play *The Dutchman*, shows a blonde white woman in the metro accompanied by two black men. At the conclusion of the sequence, a shot of the woman's hand holding a revolver gives way, shortly thereafter, to the sound of gunfire and a title 'Nothing but a Woman / and a Man / And a Sea of Blood.' Andrew Sarris, in his account of the sequence, ignores the visual and written evidence that it is the woman who wields the gun: '. . . a Negro nationalist draws out a gun with phallic fury in the metro.'[29] Here, cultural expectations inform the very perceptions of the viewer, who projects his own racial and sexual expectations onto the film.[30]

---

[29]From Sarris' review in the *Village Voice*, September 29–October 6, 1966, included in *Masculine, Feminine* (New York: Grove Press, 1969), pp. 275–79.

[30]In the case of Cuban films, ethnocentrism merges with anticommunism to distort the perception of First World critics. Many American critics, for example, identified very strongly with the alienated artist-intellectual protagonist of Alea's *Memories of Underdevelopment* (1968) and with his disabused view of the Cuban people. Seeing the film as an auteurist lament concerning the low level of cultural life in Cuba and the repressive nature of the Cuban regime, Andrew Sarris spoke for these critics (in his explanation of the award given the film by the National Society of Film Critics) when he claimed that what struck them most favourably was the film's 'personal and very courageous confrontation of the artist's doubts and ambivalences regarding the Cuban revolution'. Such critics completely missed the film's critique both of the protagonist and of prerevolutionary Cuba.

We must be aware, then, of the cultural and ideological assumptions spectators bring to the cinema. We must be conscious, too, of the institutionalised expectations, the mental machinery that serves as the subjective support to the film industry, and which leads us to consume films in a certain way. This apparatus has adapted most of us to the consumption of films which display high production values. But many Third World filmmakers find such a model, if not repugnant, at least inappropriate—not only because of their critique of dominant cinema, but also because the Third World, with its scarcer capital and higher costs, simply cannot *afford* it. Significantly, such film-makers and critics argue for a model rooted in the actual circumstances of the Third World: a 'third cinema' (Solanas-Gettino), 'an aesthetic of hunger' (Rocha), and 'an imperfect cinema' (Espinosa). To expect to find First World production values in Third World films is to be both naive and ethnocentric. To prospect for Third World auteurs, similarly, is to apply a regressive analytical model which implicitly valorises dominant cinema and promises only to invite a few elite members of the Third World into an already established pantheon.

The objective of this study of filmic colonialism and racism, finally, is not to hurl charges of racism at individual filmmakers or critics—in a systematically racist society few escape the effects of racism—but rather to learn how to decode and deconstruct racist images and sounds. Racism is not permanently inscribed in celluloid or in the human mind; it forms part of a constantly changing dialectical process within which, we must never forget, we are far from powerless.

1983

MANTHIA DIAWARA
BLACK SPECTATORSHIP: PROBLEMS OF IDENTIFICATION AND RESISTANCE

Mathina Diawara grew up in Mali and Guinea during the decolonization period of the late '50s and early '60s. His work on race, ethnicity and gendor has been influenced by Stuart Hall and Paul Gilroy. Diawara rejects "Afrocentric" theories that glamorize African history and instead focuses on analyzing and reclaiming contemporary African experiences around the world. He has also worked in documentary films as a writer and director, most recently writing and directing *Conakry Kas* (2003), and *Who's Afraid of Ngugi?* (2006). He is currently professor of comparative literature and director of African studies and the Institute of African American Affairs at New York University,

Whenever blacks are represented in Hollywood, and sometimes when Hollywood omits blacks from its films altogether, there are spectators who denounce the result and refuse to suspend their disbelief. The manner in which black spectators may circumvent identification and resist the persuasive elements of Hollywood narrative and spectacle informs both a challenge to certain theories of spectatorship and the aesthetics of Afro-American independent cinema. In this article I posit the interchangeability of the terms 'black spectator' and 'resisting spectator' as a heuristic device to imply that just as some blacks identify with Hollywood's images of blacks, some white spectators, too, resist the racial representations of dominant cinema. Furthermore, by exploring the notion of the resisting spectator my aim is to reassess some of the claims of certain theories of spectatorship which have not so far accounted for the experiences of black spectators.

Since the mid-1970s much has been written on the subject of spectatorship. Early landmarks in the debate, such as articles like Christian Metz's on the Imaginary Signifier[1], Laura Mulvey's on 'Visual Pleasure and Narrative Cinema'[2] and Stephen Heath's on 'Difference'[3] with their recourse to Freud and Lacan, tended to concentrate the argument around gendered spectatorship. More recently, debates have begun to focus on issues of sexuality as well as gender, yet with one or two exceptions[4], the prevailing approach has remained colour-blind. The position of the spectator in the

---

[1]Christian Metz, 'The Imaginary Signifier', *Screen* 16, no. 2 (Summer 1975): 14–76.
[2]Laura Mulvey, 'Visual Pleasure and Narrative Cinema', *Screen* 16, no. 3 (Autumn 1975): 6–18.
[3]Stephen Heath, 'Difference', *Screen* 19, no. 3 (Autumn 1978): 51–112.
[4]Homi K Bhabha, 'The Other Question', *Screen* 24, no. 6 (November–December 1983): 18–36.

cinematic apparatus has been described by recourse to the psychoanalytic account of the mirror phase, suggesting that the metapsychology of identification (with the camera or point of enunciation) entails a narcissistic form of regression which leads to a state similar to the infant's illusion of a unified ego. But since spectators are socially and historically as well as psychically constituted, it is not clear whether the experiences of black spectators are included in this analysis. Indeed, there are instances of film consumption which reveal the inadequacies of this approach and which implicitly question certain aspects of the prevailing problematic around spectatorship. To examine these instances, from the specific perspective of my own position as a black male spectator, I want to suggest that the components of 'difference' among elements of race, gender and sexuality give rise to different readings of the same material. Specifically, as an African film scholar based in the North American context, I am interested in the way that Afro-American spectators may, at times, constitute a particular case of what I call resisting spectatorship. From the specificity and limitations of my own position as a black male spectator the aim is to consider what insights this particular formation of spectatorship can bring to the analysis of Hollywood films.

To illustrate my argument I have chosen to begin with a sequence from *The Birth of a Nation* (directed by D W Griffith, 1915) to demonstrate how aspects of a dominant film can be read differently once the alternative readings of Afro-American spectators are taken into account, as the black spectator's reluctance to identify with the dominant reading of this archetypical Hollywood text also underpins the protest elicited by a film as recent as *The Color Purple* (directed by Steven Spielberg, 1986). The five-minute sequence from *The Birth of a Nation* involves the pursuit of a young white girl by a black man, often referred to as the 'Gus chase' sequence. It takes place in the second part of the film, set in the period of Reconstruction in the South. Prior to this sequence, Senator Stoneman, one of the leading Northern white liberals, sends Silas Lynch, his mulatto protegé, to run for the seat of Lieutenant Governor in a Southern state. Silas conspires with 'carpetbaggers' to deny whites the right to vote and wins the election by means of the new black vote. Soon, the new leaders of the South lift the ban on interracial marriages and the whites, in response, form the Ku Klux Klan to protect themselves from what they call 'the new tyrants'.

The 'Gus chase' sequence begins with 'Little Sister', from the plantocrat Confederate Cameron family, going to a secluded stream in the woods and ends with her death in her brother's arms. The sequence contains about 105 shots in six narrational units: (1) Little Sister on her way to the stream / Gus, the black man, following her unseen. (2) Little Sister playing with a squirrel / Gus watching her unseen. (3) Gus confronting Little Sister and proposing to her / Little Colonel looking for Little Sister. (4) Gus chasing Little Sister / Little Colonel coming towards the stream to look for his sister. (5) Gus pursuing Little Sister to the top of the cliff where she jumps off / Little Colonel approaching the scene. (5) Gus, seeing Little Colonel, fleeing / Little Colonel taking his dying sister in his arms. The sequence is situated between two intertitles, one stating that Little Sister went into the woods despite her brother's warning, and the other that the gates of heaven will welcome her. Each alternated section is made up of several shots, some of which are repeated within the sequence. The rhythm of the editing is faster when Gus chases Little Sister and slower when Little Colonel takes her in his arms. Bright lights are cast on Little Sister and her brother while Gus is cast in dark shadows. Where Little Colonel wears a suit befitting his title and his sister wears a modest dress, Gus does not wear his captain's uniform and his broken English confirms his 'inferiority' and otherness.

The dominant reading of this sequence supports a Manichean world view of race in which Gus represents absolute evil and Little Colonel and his sister embody absolute good. Editing, *mise-en-scène*, narrative content all combine to compel the spectator to regard Gus as the representation of danger and chaos: he is the alien, that which does not resemble oneself, that from which one needs protection. Whether black or white, male or female, the spectator is supposed to identify with the Camerons and encouraged to hate Gus. Similarly, the popular Tarzan movies position all spectators, white and black, to identify with the white hero; likewise, the Blaxploitation genre is intelligible to white spectators only if they suspend their critical judgement and identify with the black heroes like Shaft in the film of that name (1971). What is at issue in this fragment from *The Birth of a Nation* is the contradiction between the rhetorical force of the story—the dominant reading compels the black spectator to identify with the racist inscription of the black character—and the resistance, on the part of Afro-American spectators, to this version of US history, on account of its Manichean dualism.

In discussing the structure of myths, A J Griemas argues that at the basis of every story is a confrontation between *desire* and *law*.[5] The Oedipus myth provides a point of reference for certain theories of spectatorship which argue that each story fascinates the spectator to the extent that it retells the primordial Oedipus narrative, with its confrontation of desire and patriarchal order. But does this account for the positioning of the black spectator of *The Birth of a Nation*? At the beginning of the story Gus enters the scene as the wrong-doer, and his punishment starts with the arrival of Little Colonel as part of a process to restore order and harmony in the South. Such an endeavour entails the resolution of the narrative fragment through Gus' punishment. The narrative thus proposes Little Colonel as the representative of the symbolic *white/Father* who will restore the law of patriarchal order by castrating the rebellious black, Gus. It is Little Colonel who persuades the other whites to form a Klan to terrorise and discipline the blacks who threaten to destroy the social and symbolic order of the South. Thus Gus's desire for Little Sister is a transgression: the narrative of miscegenation links isomorphically with the Oedipal narrative of incestuous desire, an assault on the symbolic order of the Father which merits the most serious punishment—lynching. At the level of spectator identification, the narrative function summarised by the narrational sequence—'death of Little Sister'—is organised to position the spectator as the subject who desires to see, in the words of the intertitle, the 'punishment and discipline of Gus and the black race he symbolises'.

The resisting spectator, however, refutes the representation of Little Colonel as an authoritative father figure and the narrative proposition that lynching is a means of restoring the racial and symbolic order of the South. By the time the film was made, the Civil War was understood by most Afro-Americans as a revolutionary war which emancipated the slaves and united the nation. The father figures and heroes of the story should, therefore, have come from the side of the victors, not

---

[5]A.J. Greimas, *Sémantique Structurale* (Paris: Larousse, 1966), p. 213.

that of the Klan which symbolised resistance to the ideals of democracy. *The Birth of a Nation* appears to misread history for ideological reasons: Not only is Little Colonel a fake father and hero, but the black experience is rendered absent in the text. The argument that blacks in the South were docile and happy with their condition as slaves and that black Northerners were only rebellious mulattos aspiring to be white is totally unconvincing once it is compared to historical accounts of the black American experience.[6]

It would be worthwhile to note how spectatorial resistance to the racist ideology encoded in *The Birth of a Nation* is expressed, often in 'realist' terms, by invoking an alternative account based on Afro-American historical experience. This response has been recently echoed in certain reactions to *The Color Purple*. Pointing to the many racial stereotypes that it features, Rita Dandridge argues that, 'Spielberg's credentials for producing *The Color Purple* are minimal. He is not a Southerner. He has no background in the black experience, and he seems to know little about feminism'.[7] Bearing this point in mind I want to consider the image of the punished and disciplined black man in contemporary films such as *Rocky II* (1979), *A Soldier's Story* (1984), and *Forty-Eight Hours* (1982), as well as *The Color Purple* itself.

It seems to me that the re-inscription of the image of the 'castrated' black male in these contemporary Hollywood films can be illuminated by a perspective similar to that advanced by feminist criticism. Laura Mulvey argues that the classical Hollywood film is made for the pleasure of the male spectator. However, as a *black* male spectator, I wish to argue, in addition, that the dominant cinema situates black characters primarily for the pleasure of white spectators (male or female). To illustrate this point, one may note how black male characters in contemporary Hollywood films are made less threatening to whites either by white domestication of black customs and culture—a process of deracination and isolation—or by stories in which blacks are depicted playing by the rules of white society and losing.

In considering recent mainstream films, Eddie Murphy presents an interesting case for the analysis of the problematic 'identification' between the black (male) spectator and the image of the black (male) character. Throughout the films in which Murphy has starred—*Trading Places* (1983), *Forty-Eight Hours*, and *Beverley Hills Cop I* and *II* (1984 and 1987)—his persona is that of the street-wise Afro-American dude, which might appear somewhat threatening. Yet in each narrative Murphy's character is deterritorialised from a black milieu and transferred to a predominantly white world. As the *Beverley Hills Cop* he leaves Detroit for an assignment in Los Angeles, and in *Forty-Eight Hours* he leaves the prison (scene of punishment) to team up with the white policeman played by Nick Nolte. In this story, Murphy's character, Reggie Hammond, is a convict enlisted by the police to help track down two fellow prisoners who have escaped. Murphy's persona invokes the image of the criminalised black male, and yet he is called upon to protect and

---

[6]Reactions to *Birth of a Nation* and its place in Hollywood's history of racial representation are discussed in Donald Bogle, *Toms, Coons, Mulattos and Bucks* (New York Bantam, 1974): Daniel Leab, *From Sambo to Superspade* (New York, Houghton Mifflin, 1976): Thomas Cripps, *Slow Fade to Black*: (New York, Oxford University Press), 1977.

[7]Rita Dandridge, 'The Little Book (and Film) that Started the Big War', *Black Film Review* 2, no. 2 1986), p 28.

enforce the law, given a gun, a police badge and handcuffs, all of which symbolise the same order that has punished and disciplined him. The two male protagonists are presented as antagonistic, but in the eyes of the black/resisting spectator it is clear that he is only there to complement the white character as an authority figure. Nolte's character, Jack Cates, is tough, persevering and just, whereas Murphy's is exhibitionistic, inconsistent (swaying between good and evil) and inauthentic (he is to Nolte's character what Gus is to Little Colonel): Reggie Hammond transgresses the boundaries of the law established by Jack Cates as the representative of white authority. In one scene, which takes place in a redneck bar, Hammond asks Cates, the white policeman, to give him his gun and the badge temporarily, so that he can use them to obtain information from people in the bar. But Hammond cannot even get their attention until he starts an exhibition, shouting and screaming and throwing a glass which breaks on a mirror. It is interesting to compare this exhibitionist act to an earlier shot of a partially naked (white) female go-go dancer, the image of which frames the beginning and ending of this barroom sequence. Hammond takes the place of the woman as he becomes the object of the look of the men in the bar—and figure of the white spectator's fascination. In the fight between the two protagonists played by Nolte and Murphy, which takes place after the bar scene, Cates cannot get the desired information from Hammond, but on the other hand the fight is also motivated by the way that Hollywood requires that the black character must be punished after he has behaved like a hero (albeit a comic one) and humiliated the white people in the bar. *Forty-Eight Hours* mixes genres (the police story and the comedy, the serious and the fake authority figures) and achieves a balance whereby the black character is only good at subverting order, while the white character restores narrative order—in the end Hammond returns to jail. For the Afro-American audience, however, this racial tension and balance preempts any sense of direct identification with Murphy's character because ultimately his 'transgressions' are subject to the same process of discipline and punishment—he is not the hero of the story, although he may be the star of the show. Black protagonists, such as Apollo Creed in *Rocky II*, receive a similar narrative treatment in which their defeat is necessary to establish the white male character, Rocky, as the hero. In both cases, the Afro-American spectator is denied the possibility of identification with black characters as credible or plausible personalities. Thus, it cannot be assumed that black (male or female) spectators share in the 'pleasures' which such films are able to offer to white audiences.

Alongside the textual deracination or isolation of blacks, the narrative pattern of blacks playing by hegemonic rules and *losing* also denies the pleasure afforded by spectatorial identification. In terms of the Oedipal analogy in the structure of such narrative patterns, the black male subject always appears to lose in the competition for the symbolic position of the father or authority figure. And at the level of spectatorship, the black spectator, regardless of gender or sexuality, fails to enjoy the pleasures which are at least available to the white male heterosexual spectator positioned as the subject of the films' discourse. Moreover, the pleasures of narrative resolution—the final tying-up of loose ends in the hermeneutic code of detection—is also an ambiguous experience for black spectators. In *A Soldier's Story*, for example, Captain Davenport (Howard E Rollins), a black lawyer from Washington, comes to an army base in a small Southern town to investigate the murder of a black sergeant. The dead sergeant had been hated by the enlisted blacks because he blamed them for the problems caused by racism in the army. He was opposed to any expression of black culture by the soldiers and is revealed at the end of the story of have been responsible for the death of Private CJ, who sang the blues, told folktales and played sports, thus asserting elements of black culture. The black soldiers resented the conflation of standard army behaviour with white culture and accused the sergeant of wanting to pass for white. Captain Davenport also represses his racial identity and idealises the U.S. army, yet while the sergeant displays his weakness through tears, uncontrollable laughter and alcoholism, the captain is cold, austere and businesslike. He rejects the probable but easy solution that the murder of the black soldier was committed by the Klan, and embarks instead on a search for 'the truth'. The complex psychology of the two characters is not explored; the film simply idealises the army as a homogenous and just institution and ends with the arrest and punishment of a *black* suspect, Pete (Denzel Washington). This surprise twist at the end of the narrative, which sacrifices one more black man in order to show

The Birth of a Nation (1915). Silas Lynch (George Siegmann), the mulatto protege of her father, proposes marriage to a horrified Elsie Stoneman (Lillian Gish). "What is at issue in ... *The Birth of a Nation* is the contradiction between the rhetorical force of the story—the dominant reading compels the black spectator to identify with the racist inscription of the black character—and the resistance, on the part of Afro-American spectators, to this version of U.S. history, on account of its Manichean dualism" (DIAWARA, p. 769).

that justice exists, fails to satisfy the expectation, on the part of the black spectator, to find the Klan or a white soldier responsible for the crime. The plot of *Soldier's Story*, with its predominantly black cast, suggests a liberal reading of race in the American South; but by implicitly transferring villainy from the Klan to the blacks, it denies the pleasure of resolution to the Afro-American spectator.

If we return to the sequence from *The Birth of a Nation* it is possible to see the interaction of race and gender in two narrative situations which position the black spectator in a similarly problematic relation to the film's ideological standpoint. The first is voyeuristic: Gus watches Little Sister as she innocently plays with a squirrel. Knowing that Gus has been following her, the spectator begins to fear for her safety. As the opening intertitle states, her brother warned her about the danger of being alone in the woods. Being watched unawares here connotes not the lures of voyeurism and exhibitionism, but danger, and equates Gus, intertextually, with the unseen danger that stalks the innocent in many thrillers and horror movies. The other situation concerns the chase itself. As Gus begins pursuing Little Sister, the parallel montage accelerates, encouraging the spectator to identify with the helpless condition of Little Sister. Only when Little Colonel appears does the spectator feel a moment of release, as she or he is repositioned to identify with the rescue of Little

Reggie Hammond (Eddie Murphy) and Jack Cates (Nick Nolte) in *48HRS* (1982). "The two male protagonists are presented as antagonistic, but in the eyes of the black/resisting spectator it is clear that [Murphy] is only there to complement the white character as an authority figure. . . . Reggie Hammond transgresses the boundaries of the law established by Jack Cates as the representative of white authority" (DIAWARA, p. 771).

Sister. The long take of Little Colonel slowly raising his sister in his arms, and its subsequent repetition, is organised to make the spectator feel grief and desire vengeance against Gus. As I have argued, the black spectator is placed in an impossible position—drawn by the narrative to identify with the white woman, yet resisting the racist reading of the black man as a dangerous threat. It seems to me that a parallel dilemma is created in some scenes from *The Color Purple*, especially where Mister (Danny Glover) chases Netti (Akosua Busia) on her way to school. This chase scenario is similar to that of the Gus chase sequence in many respects.

Both take place in the woods, outside 'civilisation' and, in each case, a tall, menacing black man chases an innocent girl with the intention of raping her. In each the girl epitomises innocence while the black male connotes evil. The girls' activities—Little Sister playing with a squirrel, Nettie on her way to school to get a much needed education—encourage the sympathy of the spectator, while Gus and Mister symbolise a danger and brutality that solicits only antipathy on the part of the viewer. In *The Birth of a Nation*, evil and lust are attributed to the black man and the black woman alike, but in *The Color Purple* they are attributed to the black male alone. Close-ups of Gus' nose and eyes appear to make him deformed and telephoto lenses are used in *The Color Purple* to exaggerate Mister's features, as if to emphasise his inhumanity or bestial nature. Both films use parallel montage and fast rhythm to encourage the spectator to identify with the victims of the danger represented by Gus/Mister, and to desire lynching for Gus and punishment by death for Mister.

The pairing of these two 'chase' sequences suggests another reading of the rhetoric of punishment. When Netti hits Mister in the genitals her action can be seen as castrating, signifying the removal of the penis from an undeserving man; but in terms of narrative structure this can be read as a replay of the Gus chase sequence. The Manichean figuration of Mister as evil (with its implicit judgement of black males in general) is the main reason why some spectators—and black men in particular—have resisted the dominant reading of *The Color Purple*. Its simplistic portrayal of the black man as quintessentially evil prevents the film from dealing adequately with such complex issues as black female and black male relationships, white racism, sex and religion that Alice Walker's original text addressed.

The treatment of the two shaving scenes also illustrates the film's denigration of the black male. Here Celie replaces Little Colonel as the punishing agent or the father figure, just as Nettie does in the scene of the chase. Must the spectator adopt the dominant reading of these scenes, and be implicated thereby in the vengeance of black women against black men, or should this reading be resisted because it attempts to ally black women with the symbolic white father in the castration of black men? While the former reading is obvious in the first shaving scene, the latter reading is made possible through the montage of the second scene and the ideological positions of race and gender which it narrativises. Because the first scene is preceded by a heart-rending separation of the sisters imposed by Mister's cruelty, Celie's wish to kill him may be seen as a justified end to black male tyranny and the liberation of the black woman. But in repeating the same scene (note that *The Birth of a Nation* also repeats the vengeance-denoting shot of Little Colonel holding his sister), its message is unmistakable. The black man's place of origin, Africa, it is implied, is the source of his essential evil and cruelty. By intercutting violent shots of ritualistic scarring and other initiation ceremonies with shots of Celie and Mister, the film might be read as suggesting that sexism is fundamental to black male and female relationships and that its locus is Africa. For the resisting spectator, the problem with this interpretation is that such juxtapositions might equally be read by a white male spectator as not only exonerating 'the white man' from sexism, but more importantly, calling for the punishment of the black man as the inevitable resolution to the conflict.

Throughout this article I have argued for an analysis of resistant spectatorship, but the question of how some black spectators identify with the representation of blacks in dominant cinema—through an act of disavowal?—remains to be explored. On a more positive note, however, resisting spectators are transforming the problem of passive identification into active criticism which both informs and interrelates with contemporary oppositional film-making. The development of black independent productions has sharpened the Afro-American spectator's critical attitude towards Hollywood films. Black directors such as Charles Burnett, Billie Woodberry and Warington Hudlin practice a 'cinema of the real' in which there is no manipulation of the look to bring the spectator to a passive state of uncritical identification. The films show a world which does not position the spectator for cathartic purposes, but one which constructs a critical position for him or her in relation to the 'real' and its representation. Other directors such as Larry Clarke, Julie Dash, Haile Gerima, and Alile Sharon Larkin use a mixed form of fiction and documentary in which the documentary element serves to deconstruct the illusion created by the fiction and makes the spectator question the representation of 'reality' through the different modes. Clyde Taylor describes Clarke's *Passing Through* (1977) as an attempt to 'subvert the Hollywood action genre, riffing its search, confrontation, chase and vengeance formulas with unruly notes from the underground'.[8] Women filmmakers like Larkin and Dash practice the mixed form, to counter dominant sexist and racist perceptions of black women.

As more audiences discover such independent black films, spectatorial resistance to Hollywood's figuration of blacks will become increasingly focused and sharpened. In the influential 'Third Cinema' film, *The Hour of the Furnaces* (1968), Frantz Fanon is quoted as saying that 'every spectator is a coward or traitor', a comment which resonates in independent film practices that question the passive role of the spectator in the dominant film culture. One of the roles of black independent cinema, therefore, must be to increase spectator awareness of the impossibility of an uncritical acceptance of Hollywood products.

1988

---

[8]Clyde Taylor, 'The L A Rebellion: New Spirit in American Film', *Black Film Review* 2, no. 2 (1986): 11.

VIII
Digitization and Globalization

The recent development of digital technologies and the growing force of globalization have powerfully affected the production, distribution, and reception of film and raised or transformed many questions about its nature. Does the advent of computed generated imagery (CGI) radically transform the nature of cinema, bringing it closer to painting than to photography? Has CGI dissolved the media-specific differences among movies, television and computers? How has the incorporation of special effects altered the aesthetic strategies of filmmakers and the aesthetic experiences of audiences? It is clear that digital technologies have transformed the nature, range and rapidity of international communication and contributed to a more cosmopolitan awareness of foreign cultures. But knowledge of foreign film cultures is still highly parochial and calls for a more global awareness. How does the economic and aesthetic dominance of Hollywood affect national and ethnic cinemas as well as the formation of critical canons? To what extent is it possible for scholars and audiences to understand and appropriately experience films expressing other cultures and sensibilities?

For Lev Manovich the advent of computer media redefines the privileged indexical relation of the photographic to a profilmic reality. Manovich sketches the theoretical and practical development of cinematic realism offered by such writers as Bazin (idealist), Comolli (materialist) and Bordwell and Staiger (industrial), then decenters the realistic tradition they all assume. He contends that from the perspective of a future historian of visual culture the differences among classical Hollywood film, European art films, and most avant-garde ones may appear less significant than a common feature–their reliance on lens-based recordings of reality. When it becomes possible to generate photorealistic scenes entirely on a computer using 3-D computer animation, there is a fundamental change. In the digital era it becomes possible to cut, bend, stretch, and stitch digitized film images into something with perfect photographic credibility, even though they were never actually filmed. Seen from this perspective, Manovich argues, the manual construction of images in digital cinema represents a return to the precinematic practices of the nineteenth century, when images were hand-painted and hand-animated. Digital cinema in his view uses live-action footage as only one of it many raw materials to be manipulated. Born of animation, cinema pushed animation to its periphery, only in the end to become based on animation yet again.

Anne Friedberg also argues that the cinema has been dramatically transformed, now embedded in—or perhaps lost in—the new technologies that surround it. The differences among the media of movies, television, and computers are rapidly diminishing. This is true both for the technologies of production and for the technologies of reception and display. The movie screen, the home television screen, and the computer screen retain their separate locations, yet the types of image seen on each of them are losing their medium-based specificity. Marshall McLuhan famously claimed that the medium is the message, but more recently, as she points out, Nicholas Negroponte argued, "The medium is not the message in the digital world. It is the embodiment of it. A message might have several embodiments automatically derivable from the same data." Digital imaging, delivery, and display effectively erase the "messages" implicit in the source "medium." In the 1970s and 1980s a number of technologies began to erode the historical differences between television and film. The video cassette recorder, the television remote control, and the growth of cable television significantly altered the terms of both televisual and cinematic viewing. These developments led to a convergence of film and television technologies that began before fiber-optic cable, the digitalization of imagery, and the advent of the home computer.

As a result of these initial reconfigurations and as our visual field has been transformed by newer technologies, argues Friedberg, the field of "film studies" finds itself at a transitional moment. The history of "film studies" in its own way parallels the history of film itself, with a lag of perhaps forty years. In what has been called the "classical" Hollywood period of film history there was a consensus not only as to what constituted narrative "content" but also as to the size, shape, color, and scope of the screen. Similarly, during the "classical" period of film studies there has been a general agreement as to what constitutes the size, shape, and scope of the discipline's objects. Now, a variety of screens—long and wide and square, large and small, composed of grains, composed of pixels—compete for our attention without any arguments about hegemony. Our concept of "film history" needs to be reconceptualized in light of these changes in technology because assumptions about "spectatorship" have lost their theoretical validity. As screens have changed, so have our relations to them. The apparatus we came to know as "the cinema" is being displaced by systems of circulation and transmission that abolish the projection screen and begin to link the video screens of the computer and television with the dialogic interactivity of the telephone. Multimedia home stations combining telephone, television, and computer will further reduce the technical differentiation of film, television, and the computer. Once thought to be the province of "information science" and not part of the study of "visual culture," histories of the telephone and the computer become significant tributaries in the converging multimedia stream.

In contrast to Manovich and Friedberg, Philip Rosen criticizes the notion that there is a radical historical break between the old and the new found in many discussions of the digital. On the plane of imagery this break manifests itself in the distinction between the indexical and the digital. But Rosen finds overlaps between them and a variety of admixtures and hybrid cases, which imply temporal or historical conflations. What he calls "utopians of the digital" try to avoid acknowledging these cases by employing the language of the forecast and viewing the break as a thing of the future, the consequence of an irrevocable linear temporality already in operation. In its strongest forms, the utopians assert that digital imaging does not just introduce a new element into representational cultures and practices, but causes those cultures and practices to take a radically transformative turn. But, Rosen points out, the claim of the infinite malleability of the digital image ignores that it was possible to fake photographs long before digitization. The absolute difference from photography and film claimed by the digital utopia cannot therefore be the simple presence or absence of manipulability per se or, as the example of painting on film shows, even of indexicality per se. The newness of image manipulability in the digital is a matter of degree rather than kind.

Another theme of the digital utopians Rosen criticizes is conquest: digital imaging is unprecedented not because it produces original kinds of images but because it encompasses older images, subordinating them to the digital regime. The digital is not simply a more efficient supplement to older regimes of image making, but a radical obliteration of the categories by which they have gained their authority. The digital utopia is dependent on no specific technology, but on incorporeal computation itself–Peter Binkley's incorporeal metamedium. But, in Rosen's view, this historiography of conquest does not actually dispose of its predecessors. The digital utopia is shaped by the very genres and regimes of imaging that it defines as passé. The ideal of infinite manipulability demands a hybridity of old and new.

Michael Allen looks in detail at the ways in which digitally produced images have changed the formal parameters of the modern film text. Like Rosen, he finds that the reality is a combination of change and continuity over time. The assumed historical trajectory of CGI for many observers has always been towards the perfecting of a photo-realistic quality. Digital technologies and techniques thus strive to replicate what already exists. In Allen's view it is only since James Cameron's *The Abyss* (1989) that CGI has become a significant element in modern film-making. Since that time its role in the creation of spectacular images in big-budget films has grown considerably. But the success or failure of any digital image lies in the degree to which it persuades its spectator that it is not digital, but photographic. The difficulty of combining photographic and digital imaging to create a coherent and seamless filmic world lies at the heart of the matter. Allen, therefore, examines how shot length, framing, camera movement, the combination of CGI and live action, and the placing and timing of CGI sequences have worked to achieve this coherence in some of the most significant films produced between *Star Wars* (1977) and *Godzilla* (1998), including *The Abyss* (1989), *Terminator 2: Judgment Day* (1991), and *Jurassic Park* (1993).

Allen concludes that there have been no radical changes in shot length, or in framing or camera movement. A series of computer-generated shots will often begin with shorter length shots intercut with live-action equivalents, before a later, longer shot spectacularly presents the climatic computer-generated image. The flow of images is thus slightly different from ordinary scene construction and shows one way in which CGI demands a privileged space for a final display of itself as spectacular image, and thereby subtly modifies the rules of film grammar. In using and manipulating the formal parameters of mainstream film-making in this way CGI sequences construct themselves as simultaneously ordinary *and* extraordinary, as photo-realistic elements of transparent film-making and as non-real, spectacular images designed to be noticed, to be separated from the flow of the rest of the film's images, and appreciated for their non-photographic visual qualities. The tension between these two states, between the two kinds of film form, has come to typify the experience of watching any film with a significant degree of CGI in it.

Kristen Whissel argues that following the release of *The Matrix* (1999, 2003) and *The Lord of the Rings* (2001, 2002, 2003) trilogies, *X-Men* and *X-2* (2000, 2003), *Crouching Tiger, Hidden Dragon* (2000) and *Hero* (2002) CGI technologies have given rise to a new generation of films that make increasing use of the screen's vertical axis. Recent blockbusters deploy a broad range of digital special effects to create composite film bodies that effortlessly defy gravity or tragically succumb to its pull. They create breathtaking imaginary worlds defined by extreme heights and plunging depths whose stark verticality becomes the referential axis of many narrative conflicts. Whissel explicitly connects this stylistic effect with the themes of these films: Because verticality automatically implies the intersection of two opposed forces–gravity and the force required to overcome it–it is an ideal technique for visualizing power and the individual's relationship to powerful historical forces. Horizontality in this context stands for temporal and historical continuity ruptured by some abrupt change or crisis in the course of personal and public events. Whereas the upward vertical movement of a protagonist's gravity-defying body frequently symbolizes a leap towards a new future, downward verticality is inseparable from the rapid approach of an inevitable end. Because verticality lends itself so well to the dynamic elaboration of conflict between opposed (historical, ideological, and natural) forces it also seems remarkably suitable for an era defined by economic polarization and new forms of political, religious and military extremism.

That films defined by their spectacular use of CGI should be so concerned with historical thresholds is not surprising, particularly if we keep in mind the centrality of powerful new (and sometimes alien) technologies to the plots of so many recent blockbusters in which verticality is notable. For, as theorists and historians (such as Manovich and Rosen) note, CGI synthesizes "old" and "new" media and frequently provokes speculations about the relation of the cinema's (digital) future to its (celluloid) past. Indeed, the vertical bodies under consideration here are composites of old and new, of film and digital media–and visibly so. Through flying and falling bodies, the new verticality makes visible the position occupied by computer generated images within the recent past of commercial film history–poised at an historical threshold, between continuity with past tradition and a future defined by aesthetic and technological change. While the popularity of the blockbusters Whissel considers can be explained in part by their presentation of astonishing digitally rendered spectacles, the "structure of feeling" invoked by verticality also causes them to resonate with the blockbuster's broad global audience. Precisely by defying verisimilitude, the new verticality lends these films a different sort of truth–a symbolic or emotional one that mediates present geopolitical reality.

The concept of national cinema has long played an important role in the discourse of cinema. But Stephen Crofts argues that a reconceptualization of national cinema is urgent not only in view of the general fraying of nation states as organizers of populations but more specifically in view of major changes that have recently affected world cinema: the global spread of corporate markets, the consolidation of global markets, the speed and range of electronic communications. He proposes to theorize the global range of national cinemas in terms of the multiple politics of their production, distribution, and reception, their textuality, their relations with the state and with multiculturalism.

Especially in the West, national cinema is usually defined against Hollywood. Hollywood is hardly ever spoken of as a national cinema, perhaps indicating its transnational reach. In the context of such unequal cultural and economic exchange, most national cinema producers have to operate in terms of an agenda set by Hollywood (although some Asian cinemas significantly maintain their own terrain). Crofts wants in particular to consider national cinemas in non-First World terms. The mental maps of film scholars and historians must become more global. This is especially pertinent given that Third World production–for that is the prime excluded category–is more plentiful than European and North American by a factor of 2 to 1. The ongoing critical tendency to hypostatize the "national" of national cinema must also be questioned in non-First World terms. Not only do regional and diasporic cinema productions challenge notions of national cinemas as would-be autonomous cultural businesses. So, too, Hollywood domination of world film markets renders most national cinemas profoundly unstable market entities, marginalized in most domestic and all export markets, and thus readily susceptible to projected appropriations of their indigenous cultural meanings. The cultural hybridity of the nation-state also must be recognized. In the context of the unequal economic and cultural relations between Hollywood and (other) national cinemas, the generation and/or survival of indigenous genres is a gauge of the strength and dynamism of a national cinema (the Hong Kong martial arts film, the French "stylish" thriller, the Ealing comedy). The production category that most obviously confounds any attempts at a neat parceling of "national" cinemas is, of course, the international co-production. This amalgamation more likely than not–especially at the upper end of the budget range–encourages culturally bland films.

Finally, argues Crofts, we must notice that underpinning First World approaches to national cinemas is the antinomy of self/other. This dualist model is inappropriate and must be overcome, for it authorizes only two political stances: imperial aggression and defiant national chauvinism. With the recognition of ethnic-cultural hybridity, as Homi Bhabha notes, "the threat of cultural difference is no longer a problem of other people." It becomes a question of "the otherness of the people-as-one."

Mitsuhiro Yoshimoto is concerned with the epistemological, cultural and political issues inherent in the study of national cinemas with particular attention to Japanese film. He notes that the theoretical mode of Japanese film studies derives its impetus from the rigorous theorization of the narrational mode of Hollywood cinema and a renewed interest in possible radical alternatives of which the critic, Noël Burch, believes Japanese cinema to be a prime example. But, Yoshimoto asks: What does traditional Japanese art subvert? Is it, as Burch argues, the representational mode of the classical Hollywood cinema? What does traditional Japanese art have to do with the Hollywood cinema? Nobody can question the dominance of Hollywood cinema in the world film market. However, this does not automatically mean that the Hollywood cinema has been dominant trans-historically or trans-culturally. Another question concerns the special position accorded to Japanese cinema in non-Western national cinema scholarship. Why has the Japanese cinema become so important in the battle against Hollywood's institutional mode of representation? Yoshimoto approaches these questions by recalling the debate in which David Bordwell and Kristin Thompson maintain that Ozu is a modernist filmmaker in a class with Dreyer, Bresson, and Godard, while Noël Burch asserts that prewar Japanese cinema as a unified whole is comparable to European avant-garde cinemas. Despite the difference in their claims, argues Yoshimoto, Burch and Bordwell/Thompson participate in the same critical project. They find not simply an affinity, but an identity, between the Western avant-garde and the Japanese cinema, or between Ozu and Western modernist filmmakers. Japan fulfills their utopian dreams. On the one hand it is exotic, on the other similar enough to the West to create illuminating if problematic affinities.

Yoshimoto insists that film critics and theoreticians need to reexamine carefully whether, by engaging themselves in national cinema studies, they are mechanically reproducing, instead of analyzing, the ideological picture of a postcolonial world situation constructed by Western postindustrial nations. The problem cannot be solved by going back to the epistemological question, "Can we ever know the Other as the truly Other?" The problem is not in the impossibility of an answer but in the formulation of the question itself. By construing the Other as the sole bearer of difference, this seemingly sincere question does nothing but conceal the fundamentally problematic nature of the identity of the self. The Other cannot be misrepresented, since it is always already a misrepresentation. Imperialism starts to show its effect not when it domesticates the Other but the moment it posits the difference of the Other against the identity of the self. This fundamental imperialism of the self/Other dichotomy can never be corrected by the hermeneutics of the Other or cross-cultural exchange; on the contrary, the latter reinforces the imperialist logic under the guise of liberal humanism, or what Gayatri Spivak calls "neocolonial anticolonialism."

According to Wimal Dissanayake a series of binaries underpin the discourse of cinema in Asia, Latin America and Africa: binaries of Westernization and indigenization, tradition and modernity, the local and the global. Any discussion of these cinemas must necessarily address these crucial issues. How a nation tells the unifying and legitimizing story about itself to its citizens is crucial in the understanding of nationhood. What is of interest in terms of the relationship between the nation-state and cinema is that, in general, while popular cinema upholds notions of a unified nation-state, the artistic cinema tends to offer critiques, while the experimental cinema calls into question its very existence.

Cinema was an imported art form that quickly became indigenized in the non-Western world. From the very beginning, cinemas in South America, Africa and

Asia asked important questions about tradition, Westernization, democracy, the caste system, and cultural identity. Similarly, European-American theories of cinema encroach powerfully on the thought and sensibility of both filmmakers and film critics in Asian, African, and Latin American countries. Is it possible, Dissanayake asks, to broaden the European-American referents that guide Western film theories so as to accommodate the cinematic experiences of the non-Western world? Do those African, Asian. Middle Eastern, and Latin American intellectuals and film scholars who are vigorously antipathetic to those Western theories subscribe to a merely spurious notion of cultural authenticity and purity? What is the nature of the theoretical space from which Asian, Latin American, and African film scholars and theorists speak?

It is clear that Eurocentric paradigms are not universal and can hamper a deeper understanding and appreciation of cinemas in the non-Western world. In recent years, for example, the genre of melodrama has been critically rehabilitated in Western film studies. However, melodramas produced in Latin America, Africa, and Asia–and the majority of films made in these regions have been melodramas–cannot be judged in terms of Western conceptualizations of melodrama. Melodrama functions differently in different cultural contexts. In India, for example, film melodramas bear the cultural inscriptions of folk theater as well as the Parsee theater of the nineteenth century. Other analytical tools developed by Western film scholars–such as point of view, the gaze, and textual subjectivity–may also be seen to have limited application. In Ozu's films, stillness and emptiness play a crucial role in the production of meaning. On the surface, if seen through Western eyes, nothing happens. But at a deeper level of emotional and cultural apprehension, says Dissanayake, much is going on that connects with traditional Japanese aesthetics. Japanese manuals of painting, for instance, stress that emptiness does not occur until the first ink mark is inscribed on the paper, calling attention to the vital interplay between emptiness and inscriptions as co-producers of meaning. However, these are not only questions of aesthetics; there are also ideological and political aspects to them. In *Yellow Earth* (Chen Kaige, 1988), the extreme long shots, the absence of depth, and the empty spaces that fill the frame can be read as a critique of the Cultural Revolution and its excesses. Any meaningful discussion of the cinemas of the non-Western world thus compels us to confront issues of economics, politics, aesthetics, institutions, technology, and cultural discourse in general. What the outstanding filmmakers from Asia, Africa, and Latin America have done begins with a recognition of the multilayeredness of their own cultural-historical formations, with each layer being shaped by intricate linkages between local as well as international forces. As a consequence, these filmmakers suggest a way of inhabiting one's culture that is neither myopically nationalist nor evasively cosmopolitan.

LEV MANOVICH
FROM THE LANGUAGE OF NEW MEDIA

SYNTHETIC REALISM AND ITS DISCONTENTS

Lev Manovich studied fine arts and architecture in Moscow before moving to New York, where he worked briefly as an animator. He has continued to work as a new media artist and animator, showing his work in several international exhibitions, including Future Cinema (2002–2004), for which the ZKM Center for Art and Media commissioned his project *Soft Cinema* (DVD, 2005), a series of database films that have the potential to be combined differently on each viewing. As a new media theorist, Manovich considers contemporary visual and digital culture alongside the histories of film and art with which they are allied, focusing particularly on the relation of contemporary artistic and technological developments to the avant-gardes of the 1920s. He has also written on motion graphics, the history of user interfaces, remix culture, and the aesthetics of interactivity. Manovich is currently professor in the visual arts department at the University of California, San Diego.

Realism is the concept that inevitably accompanies the development and assimilation of 3-D computer graphics. In media, trade publications, and research papers, the history of technological innovation and research is presented as a progression toward realism—the ability to simulate any object in such a way that its computer image is indistinguishable from a photograph. At the same time, it is constantly pointed out that this realism is qualitatively different from the realism of optically based image technologies (photography, film), for the simulated reality is not indexically related to the existing world.

Despite this difference, the ability to generate three-dimensional stills does not represent a radical break in the history of the visual representation of the multitude comparable to the achievements of Giotto. A Renaissance painting and a computer image employ the same technique (a set of consistent depth cues) to create an illusion of space—existent or imaginary. The real break is the introduction of a moving synthetic image—interactive 3-D computer graphics and computer animation. With these technologies, a viewer has the experience of moving around a simulated 3-D space—something one cannot do with an illusionistic painting.

To better understand the nature of the "realism" of the synthetic moving image, it is relevant to consider a contiguous practice of the moving image—the cinema.

I will approach the problem of "realism" in 3-D computer animation starting from the arguments advanced in film theory in regard to cinematic realism.

This section considers finished 3-D computer animations created before hand and then incorporated in a film, television program, Web site, or computer game. In the case of animations generated by a computer in real time, and thus dependent not only on available software but also on hardware capabilities, a somewhat different logic applies. An example of a new media object from the 1990s that uses both types of animation is a typical computer game. The interactive parts of the game are animated in real time. Periodically, the game switches to a "full motion video" mode. "Full motion video" is either a digital video sequence or a 3-D animation that has been prerendered and therefore has a higher level of detail—and thus "realism"—than the animations done in real time. . . .

TECHNOLOGY AND STYLE IN CINEMA

The idea of cinematic realism is associated first and foremost with André Bazin, for whom cinematic technology and style move toward a "total and complete representation of reality."[1] In "The Myth of Total Cinema," Bazin claims that the idea of cinema existed long before the medium actually appeared and that the development of cinema technology "little by little made a reality out of original 'myth'" (21). In this account, the modern technology of cinema is a realization of the ancient myth of mimesis, just as the development of aviation is a realization of the myth of Icarus. In another influential essay, "The Evolution of the Language of Cinema," Bazin reads the history of film style in similar teleological terms: The introduction of depth of field at the end of the 1930s and the subsequent innovations of Italian neorealists in the 1940s gradually allow the spectator to have a more intimate relation with the image than is possible in reality. The essays differ not only in that the first interprets film technology whereas the second concentrates on film style, but also in their distinct approaches to the problem of realism. In the first essay realism stands for the approximation of phenomenological qualities of reality, "the reconstruction of a perfect illusion of the outside world in sound, color and relief"(20). In the second essay, Bazin emphasizes that a realistic representation should also approximate the perceptual and cognitive dynamics of natural vision. For Bazin, this dynamic involves active exploration of visual reality. Consequently, he interprets the introduction of depth of field as a step toward realism because now the viewer can freely explore the space of film image (36–37).

Against Bazin's "idealist" and evolutionary account, Jean-Louis Comolli proposes a "materialist" and fundamentally nonlinear reading of the history of cinematic technology and style. The cinema, Comolli tells us, "is born immediately as a social machine . . . from the anticipation and confirmation of its social profitability; economic, ideological and symbolic."[2] Comolli thus proposes to read the history of cinema techniques as an intersection of technical, aesthetic, social, and ideological

---

[1]Bazin, *What Is Cinema?* 20.
[2]Comolli, "Machines of the Visible," 122.

determinations; however, his analyses clearly privilege the ideological function of the cinema. For Comolli, this function is " 'objective' duplication of the 'real' itself conceived as specular reflection" (133). Along with other representational cultural practices, cinema works endlessly to reduplicate the visible, thus sustaining the illusion that it is the phenomenal forms that constitute the social "real"—rather than the "invisible" relations of productions. To fulfill its function, cinema must maintain and constantly update its "realism." Comolli sketches this process using two alternative figures—addition and substitution.

In terms of technological developments, the history of realism in the cinema is one of addition. First, additions are necessary to maintain the process of disavowal that for Comolli defines the nature of cinematic spectatorship (132). Each new technological development (sound, panchromatic stock, color) points out to viewers just how "unrealistic" the previous image was and also reminds them that the present image, even though more realistic, will also be superseded in the future—thus constantly sustaining the state of disavowal. Second, because cinema functions in a structure with other visual media, it has to keep up with their changing level of realism. For instance, by the 1920s the spread of photographic images that offered richer gradations of tones made the cinematic image seem harsh by comparison, and the film industry was forced to change to panchromatic stock to keep up with the standard of photographic realism (131). This example is a good illustration of Comolli's reliance on Althusserian structuralist Marxism. Unprofitable economically for the film industry, this change is "profitable" in more abstract terms for the social structure as a whole, helping to sustain the ideology of the real/visible.

In terms of cinematic style, the history of realism in cinema is one of substitution of cinematic techniques. For instance, while the change to panchromatic stock adds to image quality, it leads to other losses. If earlier cinematic realism was maintained through the effects of depth, now "depth (perspective) loses its importance in the production of 'reality effects' in favor of shade, range, color" (131). So theorized, realistic effect in the cinema appears as a constant sum in an equation with a few variables that change historically and have equal weight: If more shading or color is "put in," perspective can be "taken out." Comolli follows the same logic of substitution/substraction in sketching the development of cinematic style in its first two decades: The early cinematographic image announces its realism through an abundance of moving figures and the use of deep focus; later, these devices fade away and others, such as fictional logic, psychological characters, coherent space-time of narration, take over (130).

While for Bazin realism functions as an Idea (in a Hegelian sense), for Comolli it plays an ideological role (in a Marxist sense); for David Bordwell and Janet Staiger, realism in film is connected first and foremost with the industrial organization of cinema. Put differently, Bazin draws the idea of realism from mythological, utopian thinking. For him, realism is found in the space between reality and a transcendental spectator. Comolli sees realism as an effect produced between the image and the historical viewer and continuously sustained through the ideologically determined additions and substitutions of cinematic technologies and techniques. Bordwell and Staiger locate realism within the institutional discourses of film industries, implying that it is a rational and pragmatic tool in industrial competition.[3] Emphasizing that cinema is an industry like any other, Bordwell and Staiger attribute the changes in cinematic technology to factors shared by all modern industries—efficiency, product differentiation, maintenance of a standard of quality (247). One of the advantages of adopting an industrial model is that it allows the authors to look at specific agents—manufacturing and supplying firms and professional associations (250). The latter are particularly important, since it is in their discourses (conferences, trade meetings, and publications) that the standards and goals of stylistic and technical innovations are articulated.

Bordwell and Staiger agree with Comolli that the development of cinematic technology is not linear; however, they claim that it is not random either, as the professional discourses articulate goals of the research and set the limits for permissible innovations (260). According to Bordwell and Staiger, realism is one of these goals. They believe that such a definition of a realism is specific to Hollywood:

> "Showmanship," realism, invisibility: such canons guided the SMPE [Society of Motion Picture Engineers] members toward understanding the acceptable and unacceptable choices in technical innovations, and these too became telelogical. In another industry, the engineer's goal might be an unbreakable glass or a lighter alloy. In the film industry, the goals were not only increased efficiency, economy, and flexibility but also spectacle, concealment of artifice, and what Goldsmith [1934 president of SMPE] called "the production of an acceptance semblance of reality." (258)

Bordwell and Staiger are satisfied with Goldsmith's definition of realism as "the production of an acceptance semblance of reality." However, such a general and transhistorical definition does not seem to have any specificity for Hollywood and thus cannot really account for the direction of technological innovation. Moreover, although they claim to have successfully reduced realism to a rational and functional notion, in fact they have not managed to eliminate Bazin's idealism. It reappears in the comparison between the goals of innovation in film and other industries. If the aviation industry expends effort developing "lighter alloy," does this not remind us of the myth of Icarus; and is there not something mythical and fairytale-like about "unbreakable glass"?

TECHNOLOGY AND STYLE IN COMPUTER ANIMATION

How can these three influential accounts of cinematic realism be used to approach the problem of realism in 3-D computer animation? Bazin, Comolli, and Bordwell and Staiger offer us three different strategies, three different starting points. Bazin builds his argument by comparing the changing quality of the cinematic image with the phenomenological impression of visual reality. Comolli's analysis suggests a different strategy—to think of the history of computer graphics technologies and changing stylistic conventions as a chain of substitutions that function to sustain the reality effect for audiences. Finally, to follow Bordwell and Staiger's approach is to analyze the relationship between the character of realism in computer animation

---

[3]Bordwell and Staiger, "Technology, Style, and Mode of Production," 243–61.

and the particular industrial organization of the computer graphics industry. (For instance, we can ask how this character is affected by the cost difference between hardware and software development.) Further, we should pay attention to professional organizations in the field and their discourses that articulate the goals of research including "admonitions about the range and nature of permissible innovations" (Bordwell and Staiger, 260). I will try the three strategies in turn.

If we follow Bazin's approach and compare images drawn from the history of 3-D computer graphics with the visual perception of natural reality, his evolutionary narrative appears to be confirmed. During the 1970s and the 1980s, computer images progressed towards a fuller and fuller illusion of reality—from wireframe displays to smooth shadows, detailed textures, and aerial perspective; from geometric shapes to moving animal and human figures; from Cimabue to Giotto to Leonardo and beyond. Bazin's idea that deep focus cinematography allowed the spectator a more active position in relation to the film image, thus bringing cinematic perception closer to real life perception, also finds a recent equivalent in interactive computer graphics, where the user can freely explore the virtual space of the display from different points of view. And with such extensions of computer graphics technology as virtual reality, the promise of Bazin's "total realism" appears to be closer than ever, literally within arm's reach of the VR user.

The history of the style and technology of computer animation can also be seen in a different way. Comolli reads the history of realistic media as a constant trade-off of codes, a chain of substitutions producing the reality effect for audiences, rather than as an asymptotic movement toward the axis labeled "reality." His interpretation of the history of film style is first of all supported by the shift he observes between the cinematic style of the 1900s and the 1920s, the example I have already mentioned. Early film announces its realism by excessive representations of deep space achieved through every possible means: deep focus, moving figures, frame compositions which emphasize the effect of linear perspective. In the 1920s, with the adaptation of panchromatic film stock, "depth (perspective) loses its importance in the production of 'reality effects' in favor of shade, range, color" (Comolli, 131). A similar trade-off of codes can be observed during the short history of commercial 3-D computer animation, which begins around 1980. Initially, the animations were schematic and cartoon-like because the objects could only be rendered in wireframe or facet-shaded form. Illusionism was limited to the indication of an object's volume. To compensate for this limited illusionism in the representation of objects, computer animations of the early 1980s ubiquitously showed deep space. This was done by emphasizing linear perspective (mostly, through the excessive use of grids) and by building animations around rapid movement in depth in the direction perpendicular to the screen. These strategies are exemplified by the computer sequences of the Disney movie *Tron*, released in 1982. Toward the end of the 1980s, with commercial availability of such techniques as smooth shading, texture mapping, and cast shadows, the representation of objects in animations approached more closely the ideal of photorealism. At this time, the codes by which early animation signaled deep space started to disappear. In place of rapid in-depth movements and grids, animations began to feature lateral movements in shallow space.

The observed substitution of realistic codes in the history of 3-D computer animation seems to confirm Comolli's argument. The introduction of new illusionistic techniques dislodges old ones. Comolli explains this process of sustaining the reality effect from the point of view of audiences. Following Bordwell and Staiger's approach, we can consider the same phenomenon from the producer's point of view. For the production companies, the constant substitution of codes is necessary to stay competitive. As in every industry, the producers of computer animation stay competitive by differentiating their products. To attract clients, a company has to be able to offer some novel effects and techniques. But why do the old techniques disappear? The specificity of the industrial organization of the computer animation field is that it is driven by software innovation. (In this respect, the field is closer to the computer industry as a whole than it is to the film industry or to graphic design.) New algorithms to produce new effects are constantly developed. To stay competitive, a company has to incorporate quickly the new software into their offerings. Animations are designed to show off the latest algorithm. Correspondingly, the effects possible with older algorithms are featured less often—available to everybody else in the field, they no longer signal "state of the art." Thus, the trade-off of codes in the history of computer animation can be related to the competitive pressure to utilize quickly the latest achievements of software research.

THE SYNTHETIC IMAGE AND ITS SUBJECT

. . . [T]he achievement of photorealism is the main goal of research in the field of computer graphics. The field defines photorealism as the ability to simulate any object in such a way that its computer image is indistinguishable from its photograph. Since this goal was first articulated at the end of the 1970s, significant progress has been made toward getting closer to this goal: Compare, for instance, the computer images of *Tron* (1982) with those of *Star Wars: Episode 1* (1999). Yet common opinion still holds that synthetic 3-D images generated by computer graphics are not yet (or perhaps will never be) as "realistic" in rendering visual reality as images obtained through a photographic lens. In this section, I will suggest that this common opinion is mistaken. Such synthetic photographs are already more "realistic" than traditional photographs. In fact, they are too real.

This seemingly paradoxical argument will become less strange once we place the current preoccupation with photorealism in a larger historical framework, considering not only the present and recent past (computer imaging and analog film, respectively) but also the more distant past and the future of visual illusionism. For although the computer graphics field tries desperately to replicate the particular kind of images created by twentieth-century film technology, these images represent only one episode in a longer history of visual culture. We should not assume that the history of illusion ends with 35mm frames projected on the screen across the movie hall—even if a film camera is replaced with computer software, a film projector is replaced with a digital projector, and the film reel itself is replaced with data transmitted over a computer network.

GEORGES MÉLIÈS, THE FATHER OF COMPUTER GRAPHICS

When a future historian writes about the computerization of cinema in the 1990s, she will highlight such movies as *Terminator 2* and *Jurassic Park*. Along with a few others, these films by James Cameron and Steven Spielberg were responsible for turning Hollywood around: from extreme skepticism about computer animation in the early 1990s to a full embrace by the middle of the decade. These two movies, along with the host of others that followed in their wake, dramatically demonstrated that total synthetic realism seemed to be in sight. Yet they also exemplified the triviality of what at first may appear to be an outstanding technical achievement—the ability to fake visual reality. For what is faked is, of course, not reality but photographic reality, reality as seen by the camera lens. In other words, what computer graphics have (almost) achieved is not realism, but rather only *photorealism*—the ability to fake not our perceptual and bodily experience of reality but only its photographic image.[1] This image exists outside our consciousness, on a screen—a window of limited size that presents a still imprint of a small part of outer reality, filtered through a lens with limited depth of field, and then filtered through the film's grain and limited tonal range. It is only this film-based image that computer graphics technology has learned to simulate. And the reason we may think that computer graphics has succeeded in faking reality is that, over the course of the last hundred and fifty years, we have come to accept the image of photography and film as reality.

What is faked is only a film-based image. Once we came to accept the photographic image as reality, the way to its future simulation was open. What remained were small details—the development of digital computers (1940s) followed by a perspective-generating algorithm (early 1960s), and then working out how to make a simulated object solid with shadow, reflection, and texture (1970s), and finally simulating artifacts of the lens such as motion blur and depth of field (1980s). So, while the distance from the first computer graphics images, circa 1960, to the synthetic dinosaurs of *Jurassic Park* in the 1990s is tremendous, we should not be too impressed. Conceptually, photorealistic computer graphics had already appeared with Félix Nadar's photographs in the 1840s and certainly with the first films of Georges Méliès in the 1890s. Conceptually, they are the inventors of 3-D photorealistic computer graphics.

In saying this, I do not want to negate the human ingenuity and the tremendous amount of labor that today goes into creating computer-generated special effects. Indeed, if our civilization has any equivalent to medieval cathedrals, it is special effects Hollywood films. They are truly epic both in their scale and attention to detail. Assembled by thousands of highly skilled craftsmen over the course of years, each such movie is the ultimate display of collective craftsmanship that we have today. But if medieval masters left after themselves material wonders of stone and glass inspired by religious faith, today our craftsmen leave only pixel sets to be projected on movie theater screens or played on computer monitors. These are immaterial cathedrals made of light; and appropriately, they often still have religious

---

[1]Research in VR aims to go beyond the screen image to simulate both the perceptual and bodily experience of reality.

referents, both in the stories (consider, for example, the Christian references in *Star Wars: Episode 1*: Skywalker was conceived without a father, etc.) and in the grandeur and transcendence of their virtual sets.

JURASSIC PARK AND SOCIALIST REALISM

Consider one of these immaterial cathedrals: *Jurassic Park*. This triumph of computer simulation took more than two years of work by dozens of designers, animators, and programmers at Industrial Light and Magic (ILM), one of the premier companies specializing in the production of computer animation for feature films in the world today. Because a few seconds of computer animation often requires months and months of work, only the huge budget of a Hollywood blockbuster could pay for such extensive and highly detailed computer-generated scenes as those of *Jurassic Park*. Most of the 3-D computer animation produced today has a much lower degree of photorealism, and this photorealism … is uneven, higher for some kinds of objects and lower for others. And even for ILM, the photorealistic simulation of human beings, the ultimate goal of computer animation, still remains impossible. (Some scenes in the 1997 *Titanic* feature hundreds of synthetic human figures, yet they appear for a few seconds and are quite small, being far away from the camera.)

Typical images produced with 3-D computer graphics still appear unnaturally clean, sharp, and geometric looking. Their limitations especially stand out when juxtaposed with a normal photograph. Thus one of the landmark achievements of *Jurassic Park* was the seamless integration of film footage of real scenes with computer-simulated objects. To achieve this integration, computer-generated images had to be degraded; their perfection had to be diluted to match the imperfection of film's graininess.

First, the animators needed to figure out the resolution at which to render computer graphics elements. If the resolution were too high, the computer image would have more detail than the film image, and its artificiality would become apparent. Just as medieval masters guarded their painting secrets, leading computer graphics companies used to carefully guard the resolution of images they simulate.

Once computer-generated images are combined with film images, additional tricks are used to diminish their perfection. With the help of special algorithms, the straight edges of computer-generated objects are softened. Barely visible noise is added to the overall image to blend computer and film elements. Sometimes, as in the final battle between the two protagonists in *Terminator 2*, the scene is staged in a particular location (in this example, a smoky factory), which justifies the addition of smoke or fog to blend further the film and synthetic elements.

So, although we normally think that synthetic photographs produced with computer graphics are inferior to real photographs, in fact, they are *too perfect*. But beyond that we can also say that, paradoxically, they are also *too real*.

The synthetic image is free of the limitations of both human and camera vision. It can have unlimited resolution and an unlimited level of detail. It is free of the depth-of-field effect, this inevitable consequence of the lens, so everything is in focus. It is also free of grain—the layer of noise created by film stock and by human perception. Its colors are more saturated, and its sharp lines follow the economy of geometry. From the point of view of human vision, it is hyperreal. And yet, it is completely realistic. The synthetic image is the result of a different, more perfect than human, vision.

Whose vision is it? It is the vision of a computer, a cyborg, an automatic missile. It is a realistic representation of human vision in the future when it will be augmented by computer graphics and cleansed of noise. It is the vision of a digital grid. *Synthetic computer-generated imagery is not an inferior representation of our reality, but a realistic representation of a different reality.*

By the same logic, we should not consider clean, skinless, too flexible, and at the same time too jerky, human figures in 3-D computer animation as unrealistic, as imperfect approximations to the real thing—our bodies. They are perfectly realistic representations of a cyborg body yet to come, of a world reduced to geometry, where efficient representation via a geometric model becomes the basis of reality. The synthetic image simply represents the future. In other words, *if a traditional photograph always points to a past event, a synthetic photograph points to a future event.*

Is this a totally new situation? Was there already an aesthetic that consistently pointed to the future? In order to help us locate this aesthetic hisotrically, I will invoke a painting by the Russian-born conceptual artists Komar and Melamid. Called *Bolsheviks Returning Home after a Demonstration* (1981–82), it depicts two workers, one carrying a red flag, who come across a tiny dinosaur, smaller than a human hand, standing in the snow. Part of the "Nostalgic Socialist Realism" series, this painting was created a few years after the painters had arrived in the United States, well before Hollywood embraced computer-generated visuals. Yet it seems to comment on such movies as *Jurassic Park* and on Hollywood as a whole, connecting its fictions with the fictions of Soviet history as depicted by Socialist Realism, the official style of Soviet art from the early 1930s until the late 1950s.

Taking the hint from this painting, we are now in a position to characterize the aesthetics of *Jurassic Park*. This aesthetic is one of Soviet Socialist Realism. Socialist realism wanted to show the future in the present by projecting the perfect world of future socialist society onto a visual reality familiar to the viewer—the streets, interiors, and faces of Russia in the middle of the twentieth century—tired and underfed, scared and exhausted from fear, unkempt and gray. Socialist realism had to retain enough of then-everyday reality while showing how that reality would look in the future when everyone's body would be healthy and muscular, every street modern, every face transformed by the spirituality of communist ideology. This is how socialist realism differs from pure science fiction, which does not have to carry any feature of today's reality into the future. In contrast, Socialist Realism had to superimpose the future on the present, projecting the Communist ideal onto the very different reality familiar to viewers. Importantly, Socialist realism never depicted this future directly: There is not a single Socialist Realist work of art set in the future. Science fiction as a genre did not exist in Russia from the early 1930s until Stalin's death. The idea was not to make the workers dream about the perfect future while closing their eyes to imperfect reality, but rather to make them see the signs of this future in the reality around them. This is one of the meanings behind

Vertov's notion of the "communist decoding of the world." To decode the world in such a way means to recognize the future all around you.

The same superimposition of the future onto the present happens in *Jurassic Park*. It tries to show the future of sight itself—the perfect cyborg vision, free of noise and capable of grasping infinite details. This vision is exemplified by the original computer-graphics images before they were blended with film images. But just as Socialist Realist paintings blended the perfect future with the imperfect reality, *Jurassic Park* blends the future supervision of computer graphics with the familiar vision of the film image. In *Jurassic Park*, the computer image bends down before the film image; its perfection is undermined by every possible means and is also masked by the film's content. As already discussed, computer-generated images, originally clean and sharp, free of focus and grain, are degraded in a variety of ways: Resolution is reduced; edges are softened; depth of field and grain effect artificially added. Additionally, the very content of the film—prehistoric dinosaurs that come to life—can be interpreted as another way to mask the potentially disturbing reference to our cyborg future. The dinosaurs are present to tell us that computer images belong safely to a past long gone—even though we have every reason to believe that they are messengers from a future still to come.

In that respect *Jurassic Park* and *Terminator 2* are opposites. If in *Jurassic Park* the dinosaurs function to convince us that computer imagery belongs to the past, the Terminator in *Terminator 2* is more "honest." He himself is a messenger from the future—a cyborg who can take on human appearance. His true form is that of a futuristic alloy. In perfect correspondence with this logic, this form is represented with computer graphics. While his true body perfectly reflects its surrounding reality, the very nature of these reflections shows us the future of human and machine sight. The reflections are extrasharp and clean, without any blur. This is indeed the look produced by the reflection mapping algorithm, one of the standard techniques to achieve photorealism. Thus to represent the Terminator who comes from the future, designers used the standard computer graphics techniques without degrading them; in contrast, in *Jurassic Park* the dinosaurs that come from the past were created by systematically degrading computer images. What of course is the past in this movie is the film medium itself—its grain, its depth of focus, its motion blur, its low resolution.

This, then, is the paradox of 3-D photorealistic computer animation. Its images are not inferior to those of traditional photography. They are perfectly real—all too real.

DIGITAL CINEMA AND THE HISTORY OF A MOVING IMAGE

CINEMA, THE ART OF THE INDEX

Most discussions of cinema in the computer age have focused on the possibilities of interactive narrative. It is not hard to understand why: Since the majority of viewers and critics equate cinema with storytelling, computer media is understood as something that will let cinema tell its stories in a new way. Yet as exciting as the idea of a viewer participating in a story, choosing different paths through the narrative space, and interacting with characters may be, it addresses only one aspect of cinema that is neither unique nor, as many will argue, essential to it—narrative.

The challenge that computer media pose to cinema extends far beyond the issue of narrative. Computer media redefine the very identity of cinema. In a symposium that took place in Hollywood in the spring of 1996, one of the participants provocatively referred to movies as "flatties" and to human actors as "organics" and "soft fuzzies."[1] As these terms accurately suggest, what used to be cinema's defining characteristics are now just default options, with many others available. Now that one can "enter" a virtual three-dimensional space, viewing flat images projected on a screen is no longer the only option. Given enough time and money, almost everything can be simulated on a computer; filming physical reality is but one possibility.

This "crisis" of cinema's identity also affects the terms and categories used to theorize cinema's past. French film theorist Christian Metz wrote in the 1970s that "most films shot today, good or bad, original or not, 'commercial' or not, have as a common characteristic that they tell a story; in this measure they all belong to one and the same genre, which is, rather, a sort of 'super-genre' [sur-genre]."[2] In identifying fictional film as a "super-genre" of twentieth-century cinema, Metz did not bother to mention another characteristic of this genre because at that time it was too obvious: Fictional films are live-action films; that is, they largely consist of unmodified photographic recordings of real events that took place in real, physical space. Today, in the age of photorealistic 3-D computer animation and digital compositing, invoking this characteristic becomes crucial in defining the specificity of twentieth-century cinema. From the perspective of a future historian of visual culture, the differences between classical Hollywood films, European art films, and avant-garde films (apart from abstract ones) may appear less significant than this common feature—their reliance on lens-based recordings of reality. This [essay] is concerned with the effect of computerization on cinema as defined by its "super-genre," fictional live-action film.[3]

During cinema's history, a whole repertoire of techniques (lighting, art direction, the use of different film stocks and lenses, etc.) was developed to modify the basic record obtained by a film apparatus. Yet behind even the most stylized cinematic

[1]Scott Billups, presentation during the "Casting from Forest Lawn (Future of Performers)" panel at "The Artists Rights Digital Technology Symposium '96," Los Angeles, Directors Guild of America, 16 February 1996. Billups was a major figure in bringing together Hollywood and Silicon Valley by way of the American Film Institute's Apple Laboratory and Advanced Technologies Programs in the late 1980s and early 1990s. See Paula Parisi, "The New Hollywood Silicon Stars," *Wired* 3.12 (December 1995): 142–45, 202–10.

[2]Christian Metz, "The Fiction Film and Its Spectator," 402.

[3]Cinema as defined by its "super-genre" of fictional live-action film belongs to the media arts, which in contrast to traditional arts, rely on recordings of reality as their basis. Another term not as popular as "media arts" but perhaps more precise is "recording arts." For the use of this term, see James Monaco, *How to Read a Film*, rev. ed. (New York: Oxford University Press, 1981), 7.

images, we can discern the bluntness, sterility, and banality of early nineteenth-century photographs. No matter how complex its stylistic innovations, the cinema has found its base in these deposits of reality, these samples obtained by a methodical and prosaic process. Cinema emerged out of the same impulse that engendered naturalism, court stenography, and wax museums. Cinema is the art of the index; it is an attempt to make art out of a footprint.

Even for director Andrey Tarkovsky, film-painter par excellence, cinema's identity lies in its ability to record reality. Once, during a public discussion in Moscow sometime in the 1970s, he was asked whether he was interested in making abstract films. He replied that there can be no such thing. Cinema's most basic gesture is to open the shutter and to start the film rolling, recording whatever happens to be in front of the lens. For Tarkovsky, an abstract cinema is thus impossible.

But what happens to cinema's indexical identity if it is now possible to generate photorealistic scenes entirely on a computer using 3-D computer animation; modify individual frames or whole scenes with the help a digital paint program; cut, bend, stretch, and stitch digitized film images into something with perfect photographic credibility, even though it was never actually filmed?

This section will address the meaning of these changes in the filmmaking process from the point of view of the larger cultural history of the moving image. Seen in this context, the manual construction of images in digital cinema represents a return to the procinematic practices of the nineteenth century, when images were hand-painted and hand-animated. At the turn of the twentieth century, cinema was to delegate these manual techniques to animation and define itself as a recording medium. As cinema enters the digital age, these techniques are again becoming common-place in the filmmaking process. Consequently, cinema can no longer be clearly distinguished from animation. It is no longer an indexical media technology but, rather, a subgenre of painting.

This argument will be developed in two stages. I will first follow a historical trajectory from nineteenth-century techniques for creating moving images to twentieth-century cinema and animation. Next I will arrive at a definition of digital cinema by abstracting the common features and interface metaphors of a variety of computer software and hardware that are currently replacing traditional film technology. Seen together, these features and metaphors suggest the distinct logic of a digital moving image. This logic subordinates the photographic and the cinematic to the painterly and the graphic, destroying cinema's identity as a media art. . . .

A BRIEF ARCHEOLOGY OF MOVING PICTURES

As testified by its original names (kinetoscope, cinematograph, moving pictures), cinema was understood from its birth as the art of motion, the art that finally succeeded in creating a convincing illusion of dynamic reality. If we approach cinema in this way (rather than as the art of audio-visual narrative, or the art of the projected image, or the art of collective spectatorship, etc.), we can see how it superseded earlier techniques for creating and displaying moving images.

These earlier techniques share a number of common characteristics. First, they all relied on hand-painted or hand-drawn images. Magic-lantern slides were painted at least until the 1850s, as were the images used in the Phenakistiscope, the Thaumatrope, the Zootrope, the Praxinoscope, the Choreutoscope, and numerous other nineteenth-century procinematic devices. Even Muybridge's celebrated Zoopraxiscope lectures of the 1880s featured not actual photographs but colored drawings painted from photographs.[4]

Not only were the images created manually, they were also manually animated. In Robertson's *Phantasmagoria*, which premiered in 1799, magic-lantern operators moved behind the screen to make projected images appear to advance and withdraw (25). More often an exhibitor used only his hands, rather than his whole body, to put the images in motion. One animation technique involved using mechanical slides consisting of a number of layers. An exhibitor would slide the layers to animate the image.[5] Another technique was to move a long slide containing separate images slowly in front of a magic lantern lens. Nineteenth-century optical toys enjoyed in private homes also required manual action to create movement—twirling the strings of the Thaumatrope, rotating the Zootrope's cylinder, turning the Viviscope's handle.

It was not until the last decade of the nineteenth century that the automatic generation of images and automatic projection were finally combined. A mechanical eye was coupled with a mechanical heart; photography met the motor. As a result, cinema—a very particular regime of the visible—was born. Irregularity, nonuniformity, the accident, and other traces of the human body that previously had inevitably accompanied moving-image exhibitions, were replaced by the uniformity of machine vision.[6] A machine, like a conveyer belt, now spat out images, all sharing the same appearance and the same size, all moving at the same speed, like a line of marching soldiers.

Cinema also eliminated the discrete character of both space and movement in moving images. Before cinema, the moving element was visually separated from the static background, as with a mechanical slide show or Reynaud's Praxinoscope Theater (1892) (Robinson, 12). The movement itself was limited in range and affected only a clearly defined figure rather than the whole image. Thus, typical actions would include a bouncing ball, a raised hand or raised eyes, a butterfly moving back and forth over the heads of fascinated children—simple vectors charted across still fields.

Cinema's most immediate predecessors share something else. As the nineteenth-century obsession with movement intensified, devices that could animate more than just a few images became increasingly popular. All of them—the Zootrope, Phonoscope, Tachyscope, and Kinetoscope—were based on loops, sequences of images featuring complete actions that can be played repeatedly. Throughout the nineteenth-century, the loops grew progressively longer. The Thaumatrope (1825),

---

[4]Musser, *The Emergence of Cinema*, 49–50.

[5]C. W. Ceram, *Archeology of the Cinema*, 44–45.

[6]The birth of cinema in the 1890s is accompanied by an interesting transformation: While the body as the generator of moving pictures disappears, it simultaneously becomes their new subject. Indeed, one of the key themes of early films produced by Edison is a human body in motion—a man sneezing, the famous bodybuilder Sandow flexing his muscles, an athlete performing a somersault, a woman dancing. Films of boxing matches play a key role in the commercial development of Kinetoscope. See Musser, *The Emergence of Cinema*, 72–79; and David Robinson, *From Peep Show to Palace: The Birth of American Film* (New York: Columbia University Press, 1996), 44–48.

in which a disk with two different images painted on each face was rapidly rotated by twirling strings attached to it, was, in essence, a loop in its most minimal form—two elements replacing one another in succession. In the Zootrope (1867) and its numerous variations, approximately a dozen images were arranged around the perimeter of a circle.[7] The Mutoscope, popular in America throughout the 1890s, increased the duration of the loop by placing a larger number of images radially on an axle (Ceram, 140). Even Edison's Kinetoscope (1892–96), the first modern cinematic machine to employ film, continued to arrange images in a loop (Musser, 78). Fifty feet of film translated to an approximately twenty-second-long presentation—a genre whose potential development was cut short when cinema adopted a much longer narrative form.

FROM ANIMATION TO CINEMA

Once the cinema was stabilized as a technology, it cut all references to its origins in artifice. Everything that characterized moving pictures before the twentieth century—the manual construction of images, loop actions, the discrete nature of space and movement—was delegated to cinema's bastard relative, its supplement and shadow—animation. Twentieth-century animation became a depository for nineteenth-century moving-image techniques left behind by cinema.

The opposition between the styles of animation and cinema defined the culture of the moving image in the twentieth century. Animation foregrounds its artificial character, openly admitting that its images are mere representations. Its visual language is more aligned to the graphic than to the photographic. It is discrete and self-consciously discontinuous—crudely rendered characters moving against a stationary and detailed background, sparsely and irregularly sampled motion (in contrast to the uniform sampling of motion by a film camera—recall Jean-Luc Godard's definition of cinema as "truth 24 frames per second"), and finally space constructed from separate image layers.

In contrast, cinema works hard to erase any traces of its own production process, including any indication that the images that we see could have been constructed rather than simply recorded. It denies that the reality it shows often does not exist outside the film image, an image arrived at by photographing an already impossible space, itself put together with the use of models, mirrors, and matte paintings, and then combined with other images through optical printing. It pretends to be a simple recording of an already existing reality—both to the viewer and to itself.[8] Cinema's public image stressed the aura of reality "captured" on film, thus implying that cinema was about photographing what existed before the camera rather than creating the "never-was" of special effects.[9] Rear-projection and blue-screen photography, matte paintings and glass shots, mirrors and miniatures, push development, optical effects, and other

---

[7]This arrangement was previously used in magic lantern projections; it is described in the second edition of Althanasius Kircher's *Ars magna* (1671). See Musser, *The Emergence of Cinema*, 21–22.

[8]The extent of this lie is made clear by the films of Andy Warhol from the early 1960s—perhaps the only real attempt to create cinema without language.

[9]I have borrowed this definition of special effects from David Samuelson, *Motion Picture Camera Techniques* (London: Focal Press, 1978).

techniques that allowed filmmakers to construct and alter moving images, and thus could reveal that cinema was not really different from animation, were pushed to cinema's periphery by its practitioners, historians, and critics.[10]

In the 1990s, with the shift to computer media, these marginalized techniques moved to the center.

CINEMA REDEFINED

A visible sign of this shift is the new role that computer-generated special effects have come to play in the Hollywood industry in the 1990s. Many blockbusters have been driven by special effects; feeding on their popularity, Hollywood has even created a new minigenre of "The Making of . . . ," videos and books that reveal how special effects are created.

I will use special effects from 1990s' Hollywood films as illustrations of some of the possibilities of digital filmmaking. Until recently, Hollywood studios were the only ones who had the money to pay for digital tools and for the labor involved in producing digital effects. However, the shift to digital media affects not just Hollywood, but filmmaking as a whole. As traditional film technology is universally being replaced by digital technology, the logic of the filmmaking process is being redefined. What I describe below are the new principles of digital filmmaking that are equally valid for individual or collective film productions, regardless of whether they are using the most expensive professional hardware and software or amateur equivalents.

Consider, the following principles of digital filmmaking:

1. Rather than filming physical reality, it is now possible to generate film-like scenes directly on a computer with the help of 3-D computer animation. As a result, live-action footage is displaced from its role as the only possible material from which a film can be constructed.

---

[10]The following examples illustrate this disavowal of special effects; other examples can be easily found. The first example is from popular discourse on cinema. A section entitled "Making the Movies" in Kenneth W. Leish's *Cinema* (New York: Newsweek Books, 1974) contains short stories from the history of the movie industry. The heroes of these stories are actors, directors, and producers; special effects artists are mentioned only once. The second example is from an academic source: The authors of the authoritative *Aesthetics of Film* state, "The goal of our book is to summarize from a synthetic and didactic perspective the diverse theoretical attempts at examining these empirical notions [terms from the lexicon of film technicians], including ideas like frame vs. shot, terms from production crews' vocabularies, the notion of identification produced by critical vocabulary, etc." The fact that the text never mentions special effects techniques reflects the general lack of any historical or theoretical interest in the topic by film scholars. Bordwell and Thompson's *Film Art: An Introduction*, which is used as a standard textbook in undergraduate film classes, is a little better as it devotes three of its five hundred pages to special effects. Finally, a relevant statistic: A library of the University of California, San Diego, contains 4,273 titles catalogued under the subject "motion pictures" and only sixteen titles under "special effects cinematography." For the few important works addressing the larger cultural significance of special effects by film theoreticians, see Vivian Sobchack and Scott Bukatman. Norman Klein is currently working on a history of special effects environments. Kenneth W. Leish, *Cinema* (New York: Newsweek Books, 1974); Jacques Aumont, Alain Bergala, Michel Marie, and Marc Vernet, *Aesthetics of Film,* trans. Richard Neupert (Austin: University of Texas Press, 1992), 7; Bordwell and Thompson, *Film Art*; Vivian Sobchack, *Screening Space: The American Science Fiction Film*, 2d ed. (New York: Ungar, 1987); Scott Bukatman, "The Artificial Infinite," in *Visual Display*, eds. Lynne Cooke and Peter Wollen (Seattle: Bay Press, 1995).

2. Once live-action footage is digitized (or directly recorded in a digital format), it loses its privileged indexical relationship to prefilmic reality. The computer does not distinguish between an image obtained through a photographic lens, an image created in a paint program, or an image synthesized in a 3-D graphics package, since they are all made from the same material—pixels. And pixels, regardless of their origin, can be easily altered, substituted one for another, and so on. Live-action footage is thus reduced to just another graphic, no different than images created manually.[11]

3. If live-action footage were left intact in traditional filmmaking, now it functions as raw material for further compositing, animating, and morphing. As a result, while retaining the visual realism unique to the photographic process, film obtains a plasticity that was previously only possible in painting or animation. To use the suggestive title of a popular morphing software, digital filmmakers work with "elastic reality." For example, the opening shot of *Forrest Gump* (Zemeckis, Paramount Pictures, 1994; special effects by Industrial Light and Magic) tracks an unusually long and extremely intricate flight of a feather. To create the shot, the real feather was filmed against a blue background in different positions; this material was then animated and composited against shots of a landscape.[12] The result: a new kind of realism, which can be described as "something which looks exactly as if it could have happened, although it really could not."

4. In traditional filmmaking, editing and special effects were strictly separate activities. An editor worked on ordering sequences of images; any intervention within an image was handled by special-effects specialists. The computer collapses this distinction. The manipulation of individual images via a paint program or algorithmic image-processing becomes as easy as arranging sequences of images in time. Both simply involve "cut and paste." As this basic computer command exemplifies, modification of digital images (or other digitized data) is not sensitive to distinctions of time and space or to differences in scale. So, reordering sequences of images in time, compositing them together in space, modifying parts of an individual image, and changing individual pixels become the same operation, conceptually and practically.

Given the preceding principles, we can define digital film in this way:

digital film = live action material + painting + image processing + compositing + 2-D computer animation + 3-D computer animation

Live-action material can either be recorded on film or video or directly in a digital format.[13] Painting, image processing, and computer animation refer to the processes of modifying already existent images as well as creating new ones. In

---

[11]For a discussion of the subsumption of the photographic by the graphic, see Peter Lunenfeld, "Art Post-History: Digital Photography and Electronic Semiotics," *Photography after Photography*, eds. Hubertus von Amelunxen, Stefan Iglhaut, and Florian Rötzer, 58–66 (Munich: Verlag der Kunst, 1995).

[12]For a complete list of people at ILM who worked on this film, see SIGGRAPH '94 Visual Proceedings (New York: ACM SIGGRAPH, 1994), 19.

[13]In this respect, 1995 can be called the last year of digital media. At the 1995 National Association of Broadcasters convention, Avid showed a working model of a digital video camera that records not on a videocassette but directly onto a hard drive. Once digital cameras become widely used, we will no longer have any reason to talk about digital media since the process of digitization will have been eliminated.

fact, the very distinction between creation and modification, so clear in film-based media (shooting versus darkroom processes in photography, production versus post-production in cinema), no longer applies to digital cinema, given that each image, regardless of its origin, goes through a number of programs before making it into the final film.[14]

Let us summarize these principles. Live-action footage is now only raw material to be manipulated by hand—animated, combined with 3-D computer-generated scenes, and painted over. The final images are constructed manually from different elements, and all the elements are either created entirely from scratch or modified by hand. Now we can finally answer the question "What is digital cinema?" *Digital cinema is a particular case of animation that uses live-action footage as one of its many elements.*

This can be reread in view of the history of the moving image sketched earlier. Manual construction and animation of images gave birth to cinema and slipped into the margins . . . only to reappear as the foundation of digital cinema. The history of the moving image thus makes a full circle. *Born from animation, cinema pushed animation to its periphery, only in the end to become one particular case of animation.*

2001

---

[14]Here is another, even more radical definition: Digital film = $f(x, y, t)$. This definition would be greeted with joy by the proponents of abstract animation. Since a computer breaks down every frame into pixels, a complete film can be defined as a function that, given the horizontal, vertical, and time location of each pixel, returns its color. This is actually how a computer represents a film, a representation that has a surprising affinity with a certain well-known avant-garde vision of cinema! For a computer, a film is an abstract arrangement of colors changing in time, rather than something structured by "shots," "narrative," "actors," and so on.

ANNE FRIEDBERG

THE END OF CINEMA: MULTIMEDIA AND TECHNOLOGICAL CHANGE

The work of Anne Friedberg deals with both the historiography of film and emerging digital technologies, and modern visual culture from the nineteenth century to the present. Her *Window Shopping: Cinema and the Postmodern* (1993) considers the way nineteenth-century technologies and visual culture anticipate the contemporary experience of mass culture. Her recent book, *The Virtual Window: From Alberti to Microsoft* (2006), explores the history and aesthetics of the windows and screens that mediate our experience of art, architecture, film, and digital media. She is professor of critical studies in the School of Cinematic Arts at the University of Southern California.

As this millennium draws to an end, the cinema—a popular form of entertainment for almost a century—has been dramatically transformed. It has become embedded in—or perhaps lost in—the new technologies that surround it. One thing is clear: we can note it in the symptomatic discourse, inflected with the atomic terms of 'media fusion' or 'convergence' or the pluralist inclusiveness of 'multimedia'—the differences between the media of movies, television, and computers are rapidly diminishing. This is true both for technologies of production (that is, film is commonly edited on video; video is transferred to film; computer graphics and computer-generated animation are used routinely in both film and television production) and for technologies of reception and display (that is, we can watch movies in digitized formats on our computer screens or in video formats on our television screens). The movie screen, the home television screen, and the computer screen retain their separate locations, yet the types of images you see on each of them are losing their medium-based specificity.

When Marshall McLuhan proclaimed 'the medium is the message' in 1964, this sound-bite aphorism drew attention not only to the *media*tion that the media incurred but also to the specificity of each separate medium. McLuhan inveighed against content-based studies: 'The "content" of any medium,' McLuhan wrote, 'blinds us to the characteristics of the medium.' Instead, he prescribed an account of the effects—'the change of scale or pace or pattern'—that each particular medium might produce. McLuhan analysed the interrelatedness of media in an evolutionary scheme ('The content of any medium is always another medium'), and he insisted that each new medium would 'institute new ratios, not only among our private senses, but among themselves, when they interact among themselves'.[1] In the new media environment of the 1990s, the media of radio, telephone, television, movies, computer not only interact among themselves, but their cross-purposed interactions pose new questions about their technological specificities. German media theorist Friedrich Kittler anticipated this convergence of media when he wrote: 'The general digitalization of information and channels erases the difference between individual media' (102).[2] Yet Kittler predicted that the installation of fiber-optic cable was the technology that would turn film, music and phone calls into a 'single medium'. We must now ask: how have the material differences between cinematic, televisual, and computer media been altered as *digital* technologies transform them?

Nicholas Negroponte answers this question with a counter-polemical aphorism, turning McLuhan's 'the medium is the message' on its head. 'The medium is not the message in the digital world,' declares Negroponte, 'It is an embodiment of it. A message might have several embodiments automatically derivable from the same data'.[3] Digital imaging, delivery, and display effectively erase the 'messages' implicit in the source 'medium'. The digitized *Metropolis* illustrates how almost all of our assumptions about the cinema have changed: its image is digital, not photographically based, its screen format is small and not projection-based, its implied interactivity turns the spectator into a 'user'.

The first part of this essay examines a number of technologies introduced in the 1970s and 1980s which began to erode the historical differences between television and film. The video cassette recorder, the television remote control, and the growth of cable television significantly altered the terms of both televisual and cinematic viewing. As I will argue, these technologies led to a convergence of film and television technology that began without fiber-optic cable, occurred before the digitalization of imagery, and preceded the advent of the home computer.

Secondly, as a result of these initial reconfigurations and as our visual field has been transformed by newer technologies, the field of 'film studies' finds itself at a transitional moment. We must add computer screens (and digital technologies), television screens (and interactive video formats) to our conceptualization (both historical and theoretical) of the cinema and its screens. *Screens* are now 'display and delivery' formats—variable in versions of projection screen, television screen, computer screen, or headset device. *Film* is a 'storage' medium—variable in versions of video, computer disks, compact discs (CDs), high-density compact video-disc players (DVDs), databanks, on-line servers. *Spectators* are 'users' with an 'interface'— variable in versions of remotes, mice, keyboards, touch screens, joysticks, goggles and gloves and body suits. Just as the chemically based 'analog' images of photography have been displaced by computer-enhanced digital images; the apparatus we came to know as 'the cinema' is being displaced by systems of circulation and transmission which abolish the projection screen and begin to link the video screens of the computer

---

[1]Marshall McLuhan, *Understanding Media* (Cambridge, MA: MIT Press, 1964, 1994), pp. 8–9, 53.
[2]Friedrich Kittler, *Grammophon, film, typewriter* (Berlin: Brinkmann and Bose, 1986). Trans. Dorthea Von Mücke with Philippe L. Similon as "Gramophone, film, typewriter," *October* 41 (1986): 101–18.
[3]Nicolas Negroponte, *Being Digital* (New York: Alfred Knopf, 1995), p. 71.

and television with the dialogic interactivity of the telephone. Multimedia home stations combining telephone, television, and computer (what will we call these: teleputers? image-phones?) will further reduce the technical differentiation of film, television, and the computer.

It now seems that a singular history of 'the film' without its dovetailing conspirators—the telephone, the radio, the television, the computer—provides a too narrowly constructed geneology. Once thought to be the province of 'information science' and not part of the study of 'visual culture', histories of the telephone and the computer become significant tributaries in the converging multimedia stream.[4] In this way, perhaps, Charles Babbage's 1832 'analytical engine' could be measured as significant in the contemporary remaking of visual imagery as Joseph Plateau's 1832 phenakistiscope. Babbage's 'analytical engine'—a mechanical precursor to modern digital computing—could store a number, retrieve it, modify it, and then store it in another location. Plateau's phenakistiscope—an optical toy now considered a key pre-cinematic apparatus—demonstrated how movements analyzed into their static components could be perceived as moving images when perceived through the slits of a spinning disc. The 'analytical engine' turned information into discrete, manipulable units; the phenakistiscope turned images into discrete and manipulable units. The historical coincidence between these two devices only emerges as significant in light of recent technologies of digital imaging and display.

THE NEW MEDIA ENVIRONMENT

But there were a number of predigital technologies that significantly changed our concept of film-going and television-viewing before the digital 'revolution'. The video cassette recorder (VCR), cable television, and the television remote control have prepared us for the advent of computer screens with wired (Internet) connections—for interactive 'usage' instead of passive spectatorship—and continue to produce profound changes to our sense of temporality.[5] If television's innate 'liveness'—its ability to collapse the time of an event with the time of its transmission—was one of its key apparatical distinctions from the movies, the VCR collapsed these separations. Television's mode of absolute presence, as Jane Feuer has eloquently argued, became a key determinant of televisual aesthetics.[6] The VCR demolished the aura of live television and the broadcast event, freeing the television screen from its servitude to the metaphysics of presence. Whereas the cinematic apparatus had the potential for re-seeing a film built into its means of mechanical reproduction, television had to await the advent of

---

[4]In the United States, the 1995 Telecommunications Bill introduced procompetitive deregulatory policies which encouraged the merging of technology industries, thus erasing many of the historical bases for their separation.

[5]These three technologies fit as examples of Raymond Williams's tripartite typology of communication technologies as: *amplificatory* (distributing messages), *durative* (storing messages), and *alternative* (altering the form of messages). In this way, the VCR is durative, cable television is amplificatory, and the television remote is alternative. Williams, "Means of communication as means of production," in *Problems of Materialism and Culture* (London: New Left Books, 1980).

[6]Jane Feuer, "The concept of Live Television: Ontology as Ideology," in *Regarding Television*, ed. E. Ann Kaplan (Los Angeles: American Film Institute Monographs, 1983), pp. 12–22.

videotape recording and playback features of the VCR. The VCR introduced the potential to 'time-shift' (to view what you want, when you want), to 'zip' [to fast-forward and/or reverse the video cassette, effectively skipping portions of the taped program (with televised programming, this usually meant commercials)], and also made it easier to re-see a film or program over (and over) again. With the VCR, both the cinematic and the televisual past became more easily accessible and interminably recyclable.

Cable television not only changed the quality of and criteria for television reception, but expanded its offerings with increased channel choice, effectively breaking the monopolies of network broadcasting. In turn, the television remote control allowed the viewer instantaneously to change televised channels (to 'zap'), to fast-forward and/or reverse the video cassette (to 'zip'), to switch between live and taped programming, and to eliminate the lure or distraction of television's sound (to 'mute'). As a result of these technologies, the premises of cinema spectatorship and televisual viewing changed radically.[7]

THE VCR

The Time-Shift Machine

As the VCR became widely available in the mid-1980s, the number of VCR households grew in a parallel 'penetration' of the American home to the growth of television in the 1950s. In 1952 fewer than 250,000 sets were owned by American households; by 1960, 80 per cent of American homes had television; by 1993 there were 93.1 million television households, with a near total saturation, in the high 90 per cent. The marketing of the VCR followed this curve. While there were a variety of video cassette systems marketed in the 1970s, it was not until the early 1980s that the VCR became a common household appliance. In 1985, only 20 per cent of American households had VCRs; in 1989 the figure was 65.5 per cent. But by 1993 the total reached 80 per cent and by 1997, 88 per cent of American homes had VCRs.[8]

A videotape machine with the capacity for recording and playback on video cassettes, the VCR not only solved broadcast television's reception difficulties, but also freed the television viewer from its programming limitations and rigid timetable. In 1970, there were six competing 'cassette TV' systems in development, set for target marketing dates in mid-1971 or early 1972. (Five of these—Avco, Sony, Ampex. Magnavox, Norelco—relied on videotape. CBS' EVR—Electronic Video Recording—used a photographic film which was scanned and converted to a television signal.)[9] The Sony Betamax, introduced in 1975, used 1/2 inch videotape in a cassette format that could record for an hour; and a competing 1/2 inch format VHS (Video Home System) was introduced in 1976. The VHS format initially had

---

[7]Hence, the schoolyard epithet: `Your folks are so old, they get up to change the channels'. More recently, as `picture in picture' television sets allow for the simultaneous viewing of multiple channels, the sequential tide of television `flow' no longer applies.

[8]See Lauren Lipton, "VCR: very cool revolt," *Los Angeles Times,* TV Times cover story, "How we tape," 4 August 1991; and A. C. Nielsen, *The Home Technology Report* (A.C. Nielsen Company, July 1996).

[9]Edward Kern, "Cassette TV: the good revolution," *Life* 69, no. 16 (16 October 1970): 46–55.

the advantage of recording for up to two hours. Since cassette recorders were first used primarily for recording broadcast feature films, the two-hour cassette made a difference in the competitive market.[10]

VCRs were first used for recording off the air, but through the 1980s as more and more pre-recorded video cassettes became available, a rental market (an entirely new industry) developed for movies, exercise videos, educational, and self-help material. Hence, the VCR—originally intended by its marketers to be used as a recording and 'time-shifting' device—became essentially a playback device. Both formats—Betamax and VHS—quickly adopted 1) pause buttons so that the viewer could eliminate commercials while recording; 2) timers that allowed the viewer to record while not at home; 3) devices that allowed the viewer to view one program while taping another; and 4) still frame and variable-speed playback features. The sales of VCRs soared beyond expectations.[11] As the major film studios sold video rights to their archives, slowly, through the 1980s, most films—even foreign—were transferred to video.

There was only a small cloud over the steamrolling success of the VCR in the marketplace: the issue of copyright. In 1976, Universal and Disney sued the Sony Corporation claiming that any machine that could record, hence 'copy', copyrighted material was in violation of basic copyright laws and should not be manufactured. In 1979, a federal judge sided with Sony, declaring that recording and viewing television program material in the home were 'fair use'. An appeals court reversed this decision, and it was not until a 1984 Supreme Court decision ruled that home taping does not violate copyright laws that the machine itself was in the clear.[12]

As the VCR became a fixture in American living rooms, its penetration of the global market also proceeded apace. A 1983 study showed that VCR penetration of the Third World exceeded television growth. VCRs were used for viewing videotapes, especially of banned material: Indian films in Pakistan and Bangladesh, Western films in Eastern Europe, pornography everywhere. VCRs became an easy 'open door' for cultural contraband—material kept out of cinemas and off television but available for viewing on this playback box. Video cassettes and VCRs also penetrated countries bereft of television; offering uncensored mass entertainment by supplying the immediacy of television without its political impediments. (Statistics from 1982 demonstrated some interesting things about cross-cultural usage: 92 per cent of television homes in Kuwait had VCRs; 82 per cent in Panama, 70 per cent in Oman, 43 per cent in Bahrain, whereas in 1984, in France the figure was 10 per cent, Japan 26 per cent, Singapore 62 per cent, United Arab Emirates 75 per cent, UK 30 per cent.)[13]

---

[10]James Lardner, *Fast Forward: Hollywood, the Japanese, and the VCR Wars* (New York: New American Library, 1987).

[11]The VCR became a basic household appliance, but the puzzle of programming a VCR became a running national gag. President George H. W. Bush joked at a commencement speech at Caltech in 1991: 'The seventh goal of education should be that by the turn of the century, Americans must be able to get their VCRs to stop flashing 12:00.' From Andrew Ferguson, "Charge of the Couch Brigade," *National Review* 45, no. 19 (4 October 1993), p. 72.

[12]Soon after Sony won the copyright battle it lost the format battle. Betamax was a format that—although it offered better picture quality—lost its market share as the majority of new VCR buyers bought VHS.

[13]Gladys D. Ganley and Oswald H. Ganley, *Global Political Fallout: The VCR's First Decade* (Cambridge, MA: Harvard University, Program on Information and Resources Policy, 1987).

Despite the initial fear of theater owners and film producers that VCRs would detract from their box-office receipts, the statistical evidence from the 1980s did not support this fear: movie-goers attended in record numbers and still rented videos. While 40 per cent of feature-film viewing is done on VCRs, movie attendance is still strong; as if the use of VCRs actually stimulates movie-orientated activity. Nielsen reports that movie rentals cut into only a small percentage of total television use.[14] So, if the statisticians have it right, television use has not decreased, movie attendance has not decreased while VCR usage has increased. This would lead us to conclude that in the past 15 years we have spent more time watching television and films and videotapes of both.

A New Temporality: When Will Then Be Now? Soon!

Now that 'time' is so easily electronically 'deferred' or 'shifted' one can ask: has the VCR produced a new temporality, one that has dramatically affected our concept of history and our access to the past? The VCR treats films or videotapes as objects of knowledge to be explored, investigated, deconstructed as if they were events of the past to be studied.[15] The 1987 film *Spaceballs* (Mel Brooks, 1987) parodies some of the changes in movie reception produced by the VCR and the rental marketing of video cassettes. In the film, Dark Helmet (Rick Moranis) and his commander, Colonel Sanders, chase an intergalactic 'winnebago' driven by a space-bum-for-hire Lone Star (Bill Pullman) and his canine sidekick, Barf (John Candy). Dark Helmet and Colonel Sanders stand by the spaceship's video scanner screen when Sanders introduces a 'new breakthrough in video marketing—instant cassettes'. The riff between Helmet and Sanders toys with the new temporality produced by the video cassette: 'Prepare to fast forward . . . go past this part . . . the part on ridiculous speed'. When they suddenly stop the tape at a frame that matches the moment they are in, they do a double take between the screen and each other:

'When does this happen? Then?'
'Now.'
'When will then be now?'
'Soon!'

The jumbled tenses of present and past here form a parody on the very paradoxes of televisual presence ('Now') and the VCR's deeper challenges to time and memory ('When will then be now? Soon!').

---

[14]A. C. Nielsen, *The Home Technology Report*.
[15]The Mia Farrow character, Cecilia, in *The Purple Rose of Cairo* (Woody Allen, 1985) was a pre-VCR viewer who had a viewing repetition compulsion made possible by the cinematic potential to for re-seeing/re-experiencing the identical film over and over.
There seems to be little statistical evidence on how often films were re-viewed by the same viewer, or how often the same viewer re-viewed a film over time—in its original release and then again in its re-release, or its release in repertory. Television viewing was always thought of as more transient. The pleasures of re-viewing television programs, once only available on the cycle of summer re-runs, have been more fully discovered since cable networks become repertories for revisiting the televisual past and since the VCR has made it technologically possible to capture and replay them on videotape. In this regard, it is worth considering how we commonly listen to an audio recording repeatedly, while visual media are thought to be more disposable and, in fact, is often constructed as such.

Paul Virilio has described the new temporality made possible by the VCR:

> The machine, the VCR, allows man [*sic*] to organize a time which is not his own, *a deferred time,* a time which is somewhere else—and to capture it. . . . The VCR . . . creates two days: a reserve day which can replace the ordinary day, the lived day.[16]

For Virilio, the VCR produces a time that is shifted, borrowed, made asynchronous. The VCR is like an electronic melatonin, resetting the viewer's internal clock to a chosen moment from the past.

While these new attributes of televisual time often lead to liberatory rhetoric about the VCR—freeing its viewers from the tyranny of standard time and broadcast choices with button-pushing empowerment—there remain limits to the choices available. Richard Dienst forecloses any emancipatory potential of this new temporality, reminding us that the privilege of individual prerogative ultimately profits 'paranational . . . conglomerates':

> VCRs do nothing but extend the range of still and automatic time, offering an additional loop of flexibility in the circulation of images, bringing new speeds and greater turnover.... video allows people to operate another series of switches, a privilege bought with more time, money and subjective attachment.... who profits from this new and immense expansion in the volume of overall televisual time? ... paranational electronic manufacturers and entertainment conglomerates.[17]

And now that the VCR has become a well-entrenched consumer durable, electronics companies are trying to supplant it with laser disc technology, hoping that the DVD player will become the next VCR, just as audio CD machines have supplanted record players in the past decade.[18] DVD technology offers some advantages: as with the larger laser disc formats, one can access a different section of the disc in a near instant; there is no fast-forwarding or rewinding required. But owing to more sophisticated image compression algorithms, a DVD, unlike larger laser discs and CD-ROM technology, can hold an entire feature film on a single disc. CD-ROM technology promised to bring 'movies' to your computer, with new playback possibilities, but the DVD may be the format that succeeds in doing so.

CABLE TELEVISION

Cable television is almost as old as commercial broadcast television. Because broadcast television required a clear 'line of sight' between the transmitter and the receiving set for adequate 'reception', cable television developed in areas where broadcast television was not easily received, where antennae could not 'see' each other, and where alternative methods were needed for transmitting broadcast signals. But cable television also offered some additional advantages: because it delivered television signals on coaxial cable it could carry more than one channel on the

---

[16]Paul Virilio, "The third window: An interview with Paul Virilio," in *Cahiers du Cinéma*, trans. Yvonne Shafir, in *Global Television*, eds. Cynthia Schneider and Brian Wallis (Cambridge, MA: MIT Press, 1988), pp. 185–97.

[17]Richard Dienst, *Still Life in Real Time: Theory after Television* (Durham, NC: Duke University Press, 1994), pp. 165–66.

[18]Adam S. Bauman and Amy Harmon, "Rival systems of VCR 'Replacement' could spark standards war," *Los Angeles Times*, 14 September 1994, pp. 1, D1, D4.

coaxial cable and import distant signals which were received by one master antenna (or, later, by one master satellite dish) and retransmit them.

In 1975—the year that began the Betamax/VHS format wars—a dramatic change in cable programming occurred: Home Box Office (HBO) began distributing special events (beginning with the Ali-Frazier 'Thriller in Manila' fight) and movies via satellite. Shortly after HBO launched its service, Viacom launched a competing pay television service (Showtime) in 1976, and Warner Communication followed with The Movie Channel (which showed movies 24 hours a day) in 1979. These 'pay' or 'premium' cable channels relied heavily on the programming of feature films.

And not long after HBO began using satellite transmission, the owner of a low-rated UHF station in Atlanta put his station's signal on satellite to be seen nationwide. This station, WTBS, owned by Ted Turner, became known as a 'superstation' because of its national availability. Turner's 'superstation' was a 'cable network' which made economic sense both to subscribers and to local cable companies. Cable subscribers were not charged for an extra station, the local cable company was only charged a dime a month per subscriber, and the extra service increased subscribers. And even though the revenues from the local cable companies did not cover the superstation's costs, the superstation could charge higher advertisement fees because it could boast a bigger audience. The core programming on WTBS consisted of Hollywood's movie past. (In 1986 Turner bought MGM and its film library; in 1987 Turner bought rights to an additional 800 RKO films.)[19]

In the late 1970s and early 1980s cable television grew phenomenally. Most of what we know now as 'basic cable'—CNN, MTV, Nickelodeon, C-Span, the superstations TBS, WOR, USA Network—were born within a timespan of a few years. In 1993, 64 per cent of television owners subscribed to cable; by 1996, the figure was 68.5 per cent.[20] While studies on the movie-going habits of basic and pay cable subscribers have shown mixed results, indicating both a decrease and increase in movie-going,[21] one thing is certain: the increase in VCR users and cable subscribers meant that the cinematic spectator became a televisual viewer.

The Television Remote Control

A third technology that transformed televisual viewing (and exacerbated its differences from film spectatorship) is the television remote control. The television remote control penetrated the American household as rapidly as VCRs and cable: in 1976, 9.5 per cent of televisions were sold with remote controls; by 1990, 90 per cent of them were;[22] in 1985, only 29 per cent of households had remote controls, in 1996, 90 per cent of US household had at least one.[23] Versions of the television

---

[19]Douglas Gomery, *Shared Pleasures: A History of Movie Presentation in the United States* (Madison: University of Wisconsin Press, 1992), pp. 263–75.

[20]A. C. Nielsen, *The Home Technology Report.*

[21]Bruce Austin, "Video Cassettes as an Ancillary Market," in Tina Balio, ed., *Hollywood in the Age of Television* (Madison: University of Wisconsin Press, 1990), pp. 93–94.

[22]Lisa Napoli, "A gadget that taught a nation to surf: the TV remote control," *New York Times*, 11 February 1999, p. D10.

[23]A. C. Nielsen, *The Home Technology Report.*

'remote' control device were marketed in the 1950s—first tethered to a wire and later as a wireless light-sensor remote—but these offered fewer options to the couch-bound viewer of 1950s' broadcast television than the same device did for the later VCR or cable subscriber. With a television remote control, the viewer becomes a *montagiste,* editing at will with the punch of a fingertip, 'zipping', 'zapping', and 'muting'. Television programmers have noted that to capture the armchair channel-surfer requires more and more 'visual' programming—relying less on plot and characterization and more on fast rhythmic editing. Some studies have shown that this form of viewing even changes the ability to follow linear arguments.[24] And, as if to demonstrate its teleological relation to computer usage, the television remote control is now—retronymically—referred to as an 'air mouse'.

The Film Screen, the Television Screen, the Computer Screen

Certainly, much of the early competition between film and television centered around screen size and format; the television providing a 10- to 12-inch screen tailored to the domestic scale of the home, the movie screen differentiating its offerings with color, three-dimensional, and wider screen formats, compensating for what the black-and-white flat screens of television could not supply. Television 'viewing' altered some of the protocols of cinema 'spectatorship': unlike the cinema spectator, the television viewer watches a light-emanating cathode ray box in a partially darkened room. The optics of television do not rely on persistence of vision and projection but on scanning and transmission. [Our eyes have grown accustomed to NTSC 525 lines per image at 30 frames per second; or phase alteration line (PAL) at 624 lines at 25 frames per second; high definition television (HDTV) has 1125 lines per image.] And, as television scholars are quick to note, the placement of televisions in the home significantly alters the function of such spectatorship. Lynn Spigel, for example, likens the television's screen—a form of 'home theater'—to the 1950s' architectural use of the picture window, a 'window-wall' designed to bring the outside in.[25]

Although both the content and the form of television competed with the film industry for viewers, television also became a delivery system for motion pictures—first in broadcast and syndicated format and later in basic and premium cable movie channels.[26] As films were shown on television, changes in cinema screen aspect ratios meant that films were either panned and scanned or—more appropriately—'letterboxed' to fit in the 4:3 rectangular format of the television screen. The television 'viewer' could now view films in a space that was, as Roland Barthes described it, 'familiar, organized, tamed'.[27] In 1974, Raymond Williams predicted: 'The major development of the late seventies may well be the large screen receiver:

---

[24]Joshua Meyerowitz, *No Sense of Place: The Impact of Electronic Media on Social Behavior* (New York: Oxford University Press, 1985).

[25]Lynn Spigel, *Make Room for TV: Television and the Family Ideal in Postwar America* (Chicago: University of Chicago Press, 1992), p. 102.

[26]Gomery, *Shared Pleasures*, pp. 247–75.

[27]Roland Barthes, "En Sortant du cinéma," *Communications* 23, trans. Bertrand Augst and Susan White, 1975; in *Apparatus*, ed. Theresa Hak Kyung Cha (New York: Tanam Press, 1980), 1–4.

first the screen of four by six feet which is already in development; then the flat-wall receiver'.[28] As HDTV flat screen technology improves and screens replace real windows with a kind of 'inhabited television', a 'windows environment' may come to mean a virtual 'window-wall'.

The scale and domestic place of the television have prepared us for the screens of the 'personal' computer. Computer 'users' are not spectators, not viewers. Immobile with focused attention on a cathode ray screen, the computer 'user' inter-acts directly with the framed image on a small flat screen, 'using' a device—keyboard, mouse, or, in the case of touch screens, the finger—to manipulate what is contained within the parameter of the screen.[29] While computers have been designed to 'interface' with humans in ways that emulate the associative patterns of human thought,[30] to become dyadic partners in a metaphysical relationship,[31] complaints about the awkwardness of this relationship are surfacing. As one critic has proclaimed: 'Using computers is like going to the movie theater and having to watch the projector instead of the film'.[32]

REINVENTING 'FILM STUDIES'

As the field of 'film studies' has been redefining itself, both revising its internal historical accounts and opening up its field to the emerging multiplicities of 'cultural studies' and 'visual studies', much of this work has been coincident with the campaign for the academic legitimacy of film studies as a republic separate from its former disciplinary overlords. But as new technologies trouble the futures of cinematic production and reception, 'film' as a discrete object becomes more and more of an endangered species, itself in need of asserting its own historicity. In the past decade or so, first with the VCR and more recently with on-line and digital technologies, the methods and source material for film and television scholarship have been radically transformed.[33]

---

[28]Raymond Williams, *Television: Technology as Cultural Form* (New York: Schocken, 1974), p. 136.

[29]When Microsoft trademarked its second-generation software as Windows™ they emphasized the metaphoric nature of much of our computer usage—'mice' which scurry under our fingers at the fluid command of wrist and palm; 'desktops' which defy gravity and transform the horizontal desk into a vertical surface with an array of possible colors and digital textures. The computer 'window' is only a portion of the computer screen, scalable in size. Windows can overlap, stack, or abut each other. The windows 'environment' makes the screen smaller and allows for simultaneous applications. As an 'interface', Windows™ extends screen space by overlapping screens of various sizes; each 'window' can run a different application; you can scroll through a text within a 'window', arrange windows on your screen in stacked or overlapping formations, decorate your windows (with wallpapers, textured patterns). A paradox begins to emerge: the more the image becomes digital, the more the interface tries to compensate for its departure from reality-based representation by adopting the metaphors of familiar objects in space.

[30]Vannevar Bush, "As we may think," *Atlantic Monthly*, July 1945.

[31]Sherry Turkle, *Life on the Screen: Identity in the Age of the Internet* (New York: Simon and Schuster, 1995).

[32]David Kline, "The Embedded Internet," *Wired* 5, no. 2 (February 1997).

[33]For example: as part of an on-line collection deemed 'American Memory' the Library of Congress has made films in their 'Early Motion Picture Collection' available for downloading off the World Wide Web along with hyperlinked texts detailing the historical context of 'America at the turn of the century', complete with a selected bibliography. (Although conclusions drawn from these films have to take into account that in their digitized format, 5 to 10 per cent of the original film frames are lost in the transfer.)

Here it seems necessary to describe the following historiographical conundrum: David Bordwell and Kristin Thompson, arbiters of film history-as-text (and as textbook) have marked the history of film as a field of academic research 'no more than thirty years old'.[34] Yet in the past several decades, while film scholars have been reworking the histories of cinema's past—adjusting or refuting its teleologies, challenging its grand narratives—our concept of and access to not just the cinema's past but to the past itself have also radically been transformed and this due in no small part to the cinema. Hence, there is a troubling paradox in the way in which the ascendency of film historical discourse in the past several decades may have worked to mask the very *loss* of history that the film itself inflicted. What I am invoking here are a familiar set of historiographic questions about the ways in which we can know the past, the truth claims of histories, and the nature of historical knowledge. As the field of 'film history' has flourished in its vitality, the concomitant changes to our concept of the past produce a reflexive problematic. Cinema spectatorship, as one of its essential features, has always produced experiences that are not temporally fixed, has freed the spectator to engage in the fluid temporalities of cinematic construction—flash-backs, ellipses, achronologies—or to engage in other time frames (other than the spectator's moment in historical time, whether watching the diegetic fiction of a period drama or simply a film from an earlier period).

Without the discourse of film history, films would lose their historical identity, would slip into the fog of uncertain temporality. (As an exercise in my undergraduate film history classes, I ask them to turn on TNT in the middle of the night, without their television guides in hand, and to try to identify a rough production date for the films they are watching.) But even with the discourse of film history, films continue to reconstitute our sense of historical past. Recent films which have digitally 'revised' film footage from the 1960s—*Nixon, JFK, Forrest Gump*—illustrate the compelling urge to reprogram popular memory. And as the past is dissolved as a real referent and reconstituted by cinematic images which displace it, Charles Baudelaire's 1859 cynical prophesy about photography's 'loathing for history'[35] meets Fredric Jameson's 1983 dystopic symptomology of history's 'disappearance'.[36]

And just as soon as film scholars have undone the set of teleologies which read film history backward from the classical Hollywood model, a newly constructed tele-

---

[34]David Bordwell and Kristin Thompson, *Film History: An Introduction* (New York: McGraw-Hill, 1994), p. xxvi.

[35]In 1859, Charles Baudelaire indicted photography as being a 'cheap method of disseminating a loathing for history'. Baudelaire was an early declaimer of the dangerous transformations of history and memory that the photographic image would produce. Despite photography's 'loathing for history', Baudelaire also recognized it as a technique that could preserve 'precious things whose form is dissolving and which demand a place in the archives of our memory'. Baudelaire, "The salon of 1859," in *Art in Paris 1845–1862: Salons and Other Exhibitions*, trans. and ed. Jonathan Mayne (Oxford: Phaidon Press, 1962, 1965), 144–216.

[36]In a 1983 essay, Fredric Jameson, one of the key diagnosticians of postmodernity, catalogued some of its symptoms as '*the disappearance of history*, the way in which our entire contemporary social system has little by little begun to *lose its capacity to retain its own past*, and has begun to live in a perpetual present and in a perpetual change that obliterates traditions' (emphasis added). From Jameson, "Postmodernism and consumer society," in *The Anti-Aesthetic*, ed. Hal Foster (Port Townsend, WA: Bay Press, 1983), pp. 111–25.

ology seems to be in the making. If a 1995 *New York Times* front-page story, 'If the medium is the message, the message is the Web', is any indication, a new *telos* is beginning to appear.[37] In a feature-spread headlined, 'How the earlier media achieved critical mass', separate articles on the printing press, the motion picture, radio, and television were juxtaposed, suggesting a synergy of the mythic moments that have transformed each medium from one with technological potential into one with 'critical mass', that is, into a medium of mass reception. In this article, Molly Haskell's account of 'the defining moment for motion pictures as a mass medium' formulaically replays *Birth of a Nation*'s New York premiere as the event 'that catapulted the medium from its 19th-century peep-show origins into its status as the great new popular art form of the 20th century'.[38] While *The New York Times* did not directly assert the World Wide Web as *the* heir to the cultural centrality of the motion pictures and television ('there will be no certainty that this medium will achieve the critical mass that capitalism demands of its mass media'), the Web was positioned as a challenging successor which, unlike 'each previous mass medium . . . does not require its audience to be merely passive recipients of information'. Certainly, as the World Wide Web has become the *modem* (*modus*) *operandi* of everyday life, media savants have had to change their predictions about the electronic future of the 500-channel information highway and adjust for a much more computer-based key to the electronic future.[39]

And now as the cynical futurologists prophesy the future of each new technology, it is worth recalling that in 1895, Louis Lumière boasted 'the cinema is an invention with no future'. While we have some indications of where new technologies might take us, we still have no clear sense of what will be a 'sustainable' technology in market terms. Even the current storage and display media—CD-ROMs and video cassettes—may be seen as transitional technologies as films and other visual material move online. And yet it is more than apparent that with the speed of such rapid and radical transformations, our technological environments cannot be conclusively theorized.

The history of 'film studies' in its own way parallels the history of film itself, with a lag of perhaps 40 years. In what has been called the 'classical' Hollywood period of film history there was a consensus not only as to what constituted narrative 'content' but also as to the size, shape, color, and scope of the screen. Similarly, during the 'classical' period of film studies there has been a general agreement as to what constitutes the size, shape, and scope of the discipline's objects. Now, a variety of screens—long and wide and square, large and small, composed of grains, composed of pixels—compete for our attention without any arguments about hegemony. Not only does our concept of 'film history' need to be reconceptualized in light of these changes in technology, but our assumptions about 'spectatorship' have lost their theoretical pinions as screens have changed, as have our relations to them.

2000

[37]"If the medium is the message, the message is the Web," *New York Times*, 20 November 1995, pp. A1, C5.

[38]Molly Haskell, " 'The Birth of a Nation,' the birth of serious film," *New York Times*, 20 November 1995, p. C5.

[39]Steven Levy, "How the Propeller Heads Stole the Electronic Future," *The New York Times Magazine*, 24 September 1995, p. 458.

PHILIP ROSEN
FROM CHANGE MUMMIFIED

Philip Rosen has written on historiography, national cinemas, documentary film, television, and digital media. His work focuses on historiography and ideology in national cinemas, which he considers in detail in *Change Mummified: Cinema, Historicity, Theory* (2001). In it Rosen argues for the role film plays in the construction of a national history, pervaded as it is by historical modes and attempts to recapture the past in both narrative and documentary film. He is currently a professor of modern culture and media at Brown University, where he is working on a collection of essays on nationality and globalization in cinema.

A UTOPIA OF THE DIGITAL

Discourses characterizing the digital are produced by a wide range of social agents, including artists, aesthetic theorists, and sociocultural theorists and critics, as well as journalists, corporate researchers, and publicists. Discourses of the digital include various tendencies, of course, but one strain that pervades many of them is that of the radical historical break between old and new. This is why the digital insistently seems to propose the question of its own history.

On the plane of imaging, this history is commonly located in the opposition between indexical and digital: the indexical is the old, the digital the new. But at some point such accounts will encounter the kinds of overlaps between the categories indicated above. These overlaps may take on the appearance of a variety of admixtures or hybrid cases, which imply, among other things, temporal or historiographic conflations. (Digital mimicry is always an indicator of such hybridity.) If I see a photograph on the computer screen, this means that the digital images has the ability to assume the exact compositional form of the conventional photograph. This is not only implict in the digital camera, but also in the digital capacity to transform or fake photographs. The compositional flexibility of this imaging teachnology, which is supposed to be non- or even anti-photographic, includes initating photographic form. My term for the capacity of the digital to imitate such preexisting compositional forms of imagery is *digital mimicry*. Digital mimicry is not limited to photography or the indexical, for the digital possesses the capacity to mime any kind of nondigital image. However, given the importance of the opposition to indexicality in theories of digital imaging, it may be that the mimicry of camera images holds special interest. Such hybridities may be obvious or implicit and covert, but they go to the heart of definitions of the digital. On the one hand, they make it difficult to define the digital by means of absolute categorization; on the other hand, it may turn out that these hybridities themselves characterize the digital as much as any "pure" nonindexicality.

In that case, the historiography of old and new, which is so often at the heart of conceptions of the digital, threatens to dissolve into a complex, "impure" historicity and a complex, "impure" historiographic temporality. The digital would have to be referred to a radical historicity without stable points of source and end, old and new. Historical sequencing would have to become provisional, and the categories enabling such sequencing would themselves have to be temporalized (historicized), de-idealized, returned to the complexity that characterizes the concrete rather than the conceptual, the nondigital as much as the digital. My point here is not that ideals should never be articulated or presented as purities, or that it is possible to completely avoid sequenciation; however, that said, one would have to seek the digital in the contradictory junctures of idealized purities and impure hybridities.

But discourses of the digital have strategies to counter hybridities and restore a historiographic temporality that can maintain the radical novelty of the digital against the indexical image. One of the most significant is a rhetoric of the forecast. With it the account of the digital locates itself in a moment of directional change. Hybridizations of old and new—as when the computer becomes a virtual camera, thus realizing the digital on the model of the indexical—are made into transitional phenomena on the way to an era of "purer" digitalization.

Examples are plentiful. When Binkley remarks that "the computer is initially made to emulate familiar genres for want of knowing off-hand what else to do with it," the term *initially* is crucial. In the future, things will be different, and emulation—the digital mimicry that manifests hybridity—will eventually be minimized. Definitions of the digital and its capabilities are repeatedly made into a matter of the future. "With digitised photo-imagery," proclaims Anne-Marie Willis, "the index will be erased as the photo becomes pure iconicity." Opposing the view that the digital realm is "simply a set of rather complicated tools extending the range of painting and sculpture, performed music, or published literature," Roy Ascott predicts, "the further development of this field will clearly mean an interdependence of artistic, scientific and technological competencies and aspirations." Thus, Dan Slater points to something that goes well beyond his specific example when he complains that if one avoids "engaging in ungrounded prediction, it is not at all clear that domestic photography—in the sense of snapshooting—has been transformed in the slightest by digital technology." He hits upon one of the most typical—and perhaps *the* typical—mode for defining the digital, the forecast.[1]

The strategy of the forecast has a crucial function in freeing an account of the digital from having to deal with hybridities as constitutive. It delineates the characteristics of the digital as existing through pure ideals rather than impure actuali-

---

[1]Timothy Binkley, "The Quickening of Galatea: Virtual Creation without Tools or Media," *Art Journal* 49, no. 3 (fall 1990): 234. Anne-Marie Willis, "Digitisation and the Living Death of Photography," in Philip Hayward, ed., *Culture, Technology, and Creativity in the Late Twentieth Century* (London: John Libbey, 1990), 201–2. Roy Ascott, "Is There Love in the Telematic Embrace?" *Art Journal* 49, no. 3 (fall 1990): 247. Dan Slater, "Domestic Photography and Digital Culture," in *The Photographic Image in Digital Culture*, ed. Martin Lister (New York: Routledge, 1995), 133. Slater argues the contemporary increase in the flow of images is intimately tied to consumerist culture as it intersects with modified domestic contexts. See also the sketch of the close relations between accounts of the digital and science-fiction narratives in Philip Hayward, "Situating Cyberspace: The Popularization of Virtual Reality," in Philip Hayward and Tana Wollen, *Future Visions: New Technologies of the Screen* (London: British Film Institute 1993). This affinity for science fiction is undoubtedly linked to the prevalence of the forecast in the digital. Incidentally, Binkley has a more interesting way to deal with hybridity, and he sometimes acknowledges the irreducibility of some analog element in the digital. See "Transparent Technology: The Swan Song of Electronics," *Leonardo* 28, no. 5 (1995): 427.

ties, things that will eventually be achieved, rather than an achieved state of things. Extrapolating from contemporary impurities, such accounts are written from a position "just before" an era of pure digitalization. In that sense, the forecast puts in place a temporal structure that suggests that such accounts are implicated not just in fetishizing digital technology, but in a kind of *historiographic* fetishization. Purely digital practices become something like an inevitability that is nevertheless "not yet." This fetish structure has a wide ambit. It can, for example, serve as the rationale for technical and profit-seeking practices and goals, just as it can conceivably ground an effect/affect for an individual computer operator. It also legitimates describing a technical and cultural phenomenon as if it existed outside socioeconomic determinations and functions.

The structure of the forecast constitutes the digital on the basis of a modern form of historical temporality. Reinhart Koselleck argues that the forecast, or rational extrapolation, is one of the progenitors of modern historicity.[2] In its assumption of an irrevocable linear temporality already in operation, the disavowal of hybridity through the forecast characterizes a mode of historicity underlying a certain theorization of the digital. On this level, what is disavowed is temporal complexity and historical overlap. Like a symptom, the "not yet" of the forecast simultaneously conceals and yet suggests the extent to which historicity is not a contingent, but a necessary element of any account of the digital, and furthermore the extent to which that historicity exceeds temporal linearity and categorical purity in spite of itself.

This is not to say that such forecasts will always turn out to be wrong. For Koselleck, the rational forecast was developed as a pragmatic tool. It provided a method of feasible means-ends calculation that came into its own in the balance-of-power politics of the European Absolute State during the seventeenth and eighteenth centuries. Since then capitalism itself has generated a forecasting industry, and forecasts today sustain similar functions in everything from weather prediction to marketing research. But, of course, as they shade into utopian projections with a futurological bent, they will not necessarily turn out to be right either.

Within the discourse of the digital utopia, the rhetoric of the forecast unveils the extent to which definitions of the digital rely on ideals, much as Bazin's account of the history of film textuality posited perfect "realism" as an ideal. But Bazin made his ideal both subject to a variety of cinematic approximations and also asymptotic, ultimately unreachable. This is not always the case in accounts of the digital, where a state of transition and change is commonly invoked only in order to mummify the digital by means of a realization of the new that is, nevertheless, projected into a future never quite here and now.

Suppose we attempt to name some of the most important ideals that recur in accounts of digital imaging as radically new. Insofar as the writers are genuinely knowledgeable about existing digital imaging practices and goals, we will undoubtedly end up with categories of some descriptive and analytic value; and yet we will not necessarily end up with a map of the terrain of actually existing digital imagery. Rather, we will produce a kind of utopia of the digital heavily penetrated by the stratagem of the forecast, which disavows hybridity and temporal complexity. The

---

[2]Reinhart Koselleck, *Futures Past: On the Semantics of Historical Time*, trans. Keith Tribe (Cambridge, Mass.: MIT Press, 1985), 13ff.

digital utopia may be explicit or implicit in a given text aimed at conceptualizing digital imaging, and it may dominate that text or appear in it only implicitly, partially and/or contradictorily. In its strongest forms, it asserts that digital imaging does not just introduce a new element into representational cultures and practices, but it causes those cultures and practices to take a radically transformative turn.[3]

The digital utopia seems to call on the interplay of three fundamental characterizations of the novelty of digital imaging, which one repeatedly finds in discourses of theorists and practitioners. These three ideals taken together provide a provisional sketch for a utopia of the digital. They are (1) the *practically infinite manipulability* of digital images; (2) *convergence* among diverse image media; and (3) *interactivity*. It will quickly become clear that the three are mutually interdependent, but they can be separated for purposes of exposition. Each of them will be defined in opposition to older indexical (camera/photochemical) imaging practices. Speaking roughly, each may be predominantly associated with one phase of the orthodox breakdown of mainstream film production practices: production (practically infinite manipulability), distribution (convergence), and exhibition/reception (interactivity). Full implementation of these digital ideals would mean the realization of the claim for radical novelty.[4]

PRODUCTION: PRACTICALLY INFINITE MANIPULABILITY

By practically infinite manipulability, I mean the unprecedented capability the digital is supposed to provide for an operator to implement his or her own conceptions of an image. Now, there are clearly constant pressures that channel the bulk of actual digital imaging practices in more or less disciplined ways. This is evident in the uses to which digital imaging is put by many kinds of professionals and their institutions, including fine artists and advertising graphic designers, computer programmers and cognitive scientists, and theme park designers and filmmakers, to name a few.

But the theoretical point typically made is that since digital imaging is split off from physical causality to an unprecedented degree, it is liberated from previously operative constraints on image making. Even a critic of the digital utopia like Kevin Robins can write, "The essence of digital information is that it is inherently malleable." As Binkley puts it:

> One of the most important features of digital media is that they can be manipulated with all the resources of a digital computer to create, filter, augment, refine, or alter the information they contain. . . . A creative imagination roams through digital domains unencumbered by the constraints of corporeal existence that are a way of life for analogue artists.[5]

---

[3]Several variations of the digital utopia are recognized and subject to significant critique in *Fractal Dreams: New Media in Social Context*, ed. Jon Dovey (London: Lawrence and Wishart, 1996); see especially Kevin Robins, "Cyberspace and the World We Live In," 1–30, and Sean Cubitt, "It's Life Jim, But Not as We Know It," 31–58. One example of an informative account not limited to imaging, but with a strong utopian component is Richard Lanham, *The Electronic Word: Democracy, Technology, and the Arts* (Chicago: University of Chicago Press, 1993).

[4]To put it like this suggests an elegantly exhaustive schema of underlying claims for the novelty of the digital, but I am neutral as to whether additional defining characteristics of the digital utopia could be adduced. And there may also be a wide range of digital utopias, some of which may begin from more intensive sociopolitical considerations rather than claiming to begin from a technological given.

[5]Kevin Robins, "The Virtual Unconscious in Postphotography," in Timothy Druckrey, ed., *Electronic Culture: Technology and Visual Representation* (New York: Aperture, 1996), 156. Timothy Binkley, "Refiguring Culture," in Hayward and Wollen, *Future Visions*, 100.

The logic is clear. From a first principle that the underlying constitution of digital images is numerical, he establishes an opposition between conceptuality and physicality. The next step is to argue that the digital consists in subordinating the physical constraints of image production to the conceptual to an unprecedented degree; and conceptuality is identified with creativity. This logic underlies many accounts of the digital, and it is not only demonstrated but given substance by the opposition between the digital and the indexical.

The two great physical determinants on image making overcome by the digital are concrete reference and the physical characteristics of a medium. We have already seen that a fundamental difference between the digital and normalized photography or film is that the digital does not require the existence of a profilmic object for the apparatus to make an image of it. But also, as Gene Youngblood puts it, "the computer . . . has no meaning, no intrinsic nature, identity, or use value until we talk it into becoming something by programming it."[6] The processes of high-speed computation are indifferent to the medium as well as the product in a way indexical cameras cannot be, for cameras are dedicated to the task of physio-chemical contact with the profilmic. The digital is not even dependent on the electronic computer, if more efficient means of high-speed computation can be devised. It has been forecast, for example, that electronic computers may some day be replaced by computing/storage entities made up of biological molecules.[7]

For the theoretically rigorous Binkley, these two positive lacks—lack of authority of the referent and of determination by the physics of the apparatus—follow from the abstract, conceptual nature of numbers: "The abstract structure [of digital encoding] precedes the source and stays independent of it, communicating only through an interface, and never brought into direct contact with an image or its referent."[8] They mean that the operator can instantiate any image conception she or he is able to dream up. They make the indexical image seem the appropriate opposing term for the digital ideal of practically infinite manipulability. But they also suggest something important about the very notion of manipulability.

It is true, as Philip Hayward and Tana Wollen remark, that "[d]igitisation has made the malleability of sounds and images seem like something new," but the reasons for their implicit skepticism are obvious to anyone with any knowledge of the histories of photography and cinema.[9] It was, after all, possible to fake photographs before digitization. Despite the sociocultural pressures that make these media repositories of referentiality, their histories are replete with examples of "manipulating" image configurations. A detailed rehearsal of means of such manipulation in photography and film—some of which fall within the range of the indexical and some outside it—is too extensive to undertake here. But it might be useful to remind

---

[6]Gene Youngblood, "The New Renaissance: Art, Science, and the Universal Machine," in Richard L. Loveless, ed., *The Computer Revolution and the Arts* (Tampa: University of South Florida Press, 1989); p. 11.

[7]"We are witnessing a dramatic shift in the physical basis of computing from electrons to light to DNA." Timothy Binkley, "Transparent Technology," 427–28. For related, even more visionary remarks, see Paul Brown, "Metamedia in Cyberspace: Advanced Computers and the Future of Art," in Hayward, *Culture, Technology, Creativity*, 231 ff.

[8]Binkley, "Camera Fantasia," 18.

[9]Hayward and Wollen, "Introduction: Surpassing the Real," in *Future Visions*, 7.

ourselves of a few examples. These could include affecting tonality and hue by lens filters and film stock characteristics, painting on the image (as in some Indian domestic photography), stencil painting or tinting (as in silent films), fabricating cinema images by painting frames (as in some avant-garde films), unconventional lenses, such as prisms, which modify referential status by distorting compositional norms, and so forth. Postfilmic laboratory processes have sometimes included combinations of distinct images that may have differing referential statuses (composite printing, "Hollywood montage sequences," matting painted sets, animation, or other filmed actions into a standard film shot—which has also been much done for illusionistic effects in the history of filmic textuality). The list could go on, but the point is that the difference from photography and film claimed by the digital utopia cannot be the simple presence or absence of manipulability *per se*, or, as the example of painting on film shows, even of indexicality *per se*.

Given the possibility of manipulability in the stipulated realm of the indexical, then, it is more precise to try to describe the newness of image manipulability in the digital as a matter of degree rather than kind. There is an *increase* in the ease and hence the "quantity" of manipulability. But then we must ask, quantities of what? Time is as good an answer as any. Just as theories of the indexical image tend to presuppose the film-developing process, theories of the digital presuppose the technological capacity for high-speed computation. If the flexibility of digital image-formation and transformation does have limitations, these consist only in the speed with which numerical operations can be processed. And in that case, as they say, speed is of the essence.[10]

In that sense, the sector of the digital utopia I call practically infinite manipulability is about the rapidity with which compositional choices can be implemented and made visible. If it seems to the digital artist that a new level of creative freedom is being breached, it is because the intention (imaginative or otherwise) of an operating subject can become more speedily determinant. So grounds for asserting practically infinite manipulability lie in the relation of the operating speed of the digital to the phenemonological temporality of the operating subject. This unprecedented temporality of image composition and production leads directly to claims for a new level of subjective freedom with respect to the construction of the space of the image. Restrictions of compositional manipulation and production time that have always impregnated imaging practices are overcome.

Of course, the rhetoric of the digital utopia may absolutize its difference from what preceded it, and this is registered in my adjective, "infinite". But since it means "more instantaneous," the digital ideal of practically infinite manipulability is relative rather than absolute. And it is not only relative, but *historically* relative. That is, the claims of the digital utopia implicitly rest on assertions about a certain relation in historical time, a historical sequence; for in it, "more instantaneity" functions

---

[10]"Computers don't do anything you couldn't do," remarks Binkley. "They are just faster at it" ("The Quickening of Galatea," 239). However, he elsewhere notes, "Although computers are fast, they are not instantaneous and never will be" ("Transparent Technology," 431). Cf. Michael Benedikt, "Cyberspace: Some Proposals," in *Cyberspace: First Steps*, ed. Michael Benedikt (Cambridge, Mass.: MIT Press, 1991), 170–71, where he intimates that because of temporal restrictions, access to computer time bears exchange value.

to mark a historical break to the unprecedented. The physical characteristics and restraints the digital overcomes are those imposed by older imaging technologies, that is, older media. The opposition between indexical and digital becomes one between a past and a present or, more typically given the prevalence of the forecast, a present-future. Here we come to the historicity definitive of all the digital ideals, which require a before and an after to constitute themselves.

Like all historicities, this one generates historiographies, whether explicit or implicit. One especially pertinent in comparisons of the digital and the indexical is what can be called a historiography of conquest. The digital ideal of practically infinite manipulability ultimately envisions technologies that can enable technically unfettered image production. But the ultimate demonstration of the unprecedented characteristics of digital imaging is arguably not in producing original kinds of images; it is in the fact that the ideal of infinite manipulability also applies to *preexisting* images. The full power of the digital regime is evidenced not simply by replacing other kinds of images, but by encompassing them.

As already noted, any kind of preexisting image—digital or not, technically produced or not—can be digitized and consequently be subject to a huge range of modifications: recompositions, combinations with other images, or any other imaginable transformations. This is also part of practically infinite manipulability. Practically infinite manipulability therefore implies that no image is necessarily stable, for any preexistent image is susceptible to an unending series of transformations with all the speed implied by infinite manipulability. In combination with the next digital ideal, convergence, this has given rise to a widespread notion summarized by Peter Wollen as "a vast image bank, an archive from which images can be taken and recontextualized at will."[11]

In a fully realized digital utopia, such an electronic archive would presumably consist of all previously made images, now digitized and permanently available for such later reuses. "In principle," writes Anne-Marie Willis, "every photograph that still remains in existence could become nothing more than raw material for image banks whose manipulators are free to do what they want" with them. Willis here seems to be discussing current applications, but her account is typical in being infiltrated by a rhetoric of the forecast. Hence she moves rapidly to complete unrestrictedness: "The new technologies make possible the storage of an endless range of imagery and . . . the idea of the archive is transformed into a limitless decentered mirror-maze of images available to be used and transformed in countless ways."[12] In fact, the ideal of infinite manipulability entails an infinity of raw materials to be manipulated without limitation, including already existing images. The ideal terrain of digital imaging necessarily includes the capacity to incorporate other kinds of images—not just for reproduction, but to make them susceptible to practically infinite manipulability, *thereby subordinating them to the digital regime.*

In the historiography of conquest that is definitive of the digital utopia, digital imaging drives to overcome the authority of anything that it determines is old, that

---

[11]Peter Wollen, "Modern Times: Cinema/Americanism/The Robot," in *Raiding the Icebox: Reflections on Twentieth-Century Culture* (Bloomington: Indiana University Press, 1993), 65.
[12]Anne-Marie Willis, "Digitisation and the Living Death of Photography," 206, 205.

is, that preexists its own operations. There are at least three levels of preexistent authority that, in different ways, are to be invaded, occupied, and superceded by the digital. The first is the profilmic event itself. As I have noted, theorists of indexicality have often treated the profilmic event as possessing a certain recalcitrance based on the priority of its existence. For many theorists of indexicality, the recalcitrant pregivenness of the profilmic, its preexistent facticity in space and time, imposes necessary limits on image production and implies certain peculiarities about image reception. Bazin promoted this limitation as engendering an attitude of "respect," and for the Barthes of *Camera Lucida* it could provoke a special kind of subjective engagement. But in the discourse of the digital, the resistances that concrete space and time might offer to the abstractions of compositional manipulability become an object of assault. Any postulated profilmic event—of traditional as well as digital photography—is definitionally vulnerable to almost instantaneous, practically infinite, "postfilmic" manipulations of the image.

The second preexistent whose authority is to be overturned is that of any specific, preexisting image, digitally produced or not. In fact, as we have just seen, it is crucial that nondigital images can be digitized and stored electronically, thus becoming susceptible to a potentially unending chain of digital manipulation and transformation. This leads directly to the third preexistent, whose authority is overrun in the digital utopia: not just specific images, but all genres and regimes of image making that historically preceded digitalization, such as drawing, painting, engraving, photography, cinema, and analog video, to name a few. In the digital utopia, images are being perpetually recoded into numbers. Historically precedent regimes of media and signification are thereby perpetually appropriated and subjected to a unique capacity of the digital, practically infinite manipulablity. Thus the digital spreads, infiltrates, overwhelms, conquers all other media—but, like many modern conquerors, does so in the name of liberation, liberation from constraint.

If practically infinite manipulability entails overcoming the authority of the preexistent—as the profilmic, as preexisting images, and especially as historically precedent regimes of image making—it follows that the digital is not simply a more efficient supplement to older modes of image making, but a radical obliteration of the categories by which they have been delimited. This is one reason why it becomes important to assert that the digital utopia is dependent on no specific technology, only computation itself. "There are many fundamental differences between photography and computer media," writes artist Richard Wright, "the most important being that the computer is a nonspecific technology." According to Binkley, the digital incorporates the techniques of other image-making tools and thereby "transcends them," thus constituting itself as "an incorporeal metamedium."[13] In its practices of incorporation that make it incorporeal, the digital manifests an imperializing historiography of conquest, imposed by the winner—itself.

---

[13]Richard Wright, "Technology as the People's Friend: Computers, Class, and the New Cultural Politics," in Penny, *Critical Issues*, 89. Binkley, "The Quickening of Galatea," 235, 234. A few years later, he modified his terminology: "[T]he computer is not a transcendent technology. It is a *transparent* technology" (Binkley, "Transparent Technology," 431).

And yet, the vocation of the digital to appropriate nondigital images has a major implication that tends to get overlooked within the digital's own historicity. As we have seen, this historiography of conquest does not actually dispose of its others. This is registered at all levels by the prevalence of digital mimicry. It is not just that the digital requires an other against which to define itself and its radical novelty, nor just that it sometimes reduplicates the very capacities of those differential others, as with digital photography. It is that discourses of the digital utopia are simultaneously compelled to indicate that the digital interpenetrates and is interpenetrated by the very genres and regimes of imaging that it defines as the old. If the digital ideal of practically infinite manipulability obliterates the prior representational ideals connected to medium-specificities, then the digital can never be described through its own properties, can never claim to be just itself. The digital demonstrates its radically new capabilities and superior representational powers through its capacity to appropriate the old. But in that case, it is as if the digital is not able to allow the old regime to disappear. The ideal of practically infinite manipulability demands a hybridity of old and new.[14]

But this implies the persistence of all the preexistents attacked in the digital utopia: specific images, previous media, and, ultimately, the concrete itself. This persistence is embedded in the ideal of practically infinite manipulability itself. Simply beginning from the digitization of indexical images at the very least, the digital utopia involves a constitutive mixture of old and new—something it does not always acknowledge. As we will see when we come to interactivity, the new of the digital utopia may well remain caught in the dialectic of subjectivity and objectivity envisioned by theorists of "older" media. One wonders to what extent a master-slave dialectic is implicit in the historiography of digital conquest. This suggests that representational hybridity in general and digital mimicry in particular are necessary and permanent consequences of the digital utopia—not merely pragmatic, temporary necessities that can therefore be bypassed or repressed in accounts of the digital. Ron Burnett gets at this when he writes with respect to imaging:

> This is, I believe, a crucial historical interregnum. Older imaging technologies like the cinema and broadcast television remain in place while the newer technologies adapt and adopt both substance and form of those media which preceded them. The combination carries traces of the past, present and future within a cultural and social context which is being recreated even at this moment.[15]

---

[14]In recent articles, Binkley notes a similar problem with respect to the conceptuality at the heart of the digital ideal. "A mathematical equation can still be lucid when modeled in a physical system, but its pristine state must be compromised at least a little to the contingencies of real space and time in order for it to have any efficacy in our lives" ("Transparent Technology," 431). That is, the digital has to presume the physical need to appeal to a preexisting body. Thus Binkley moves toward acknowledging that a basic hybridity of analog and digital is unavoidable: "As a result of this dependence on interfaces, digital media augment rather than undermine their analog forebears" ("The Vitality of Digital Creation," *Journal of Aesthetics and Art Criticism* 55, no. 2 (spring 1997): 112.

[15]Ron Burnett, "A Torn Page, Ghosts in the Computer Screen, Words, Images, Labyrinths: Exploring the Frontiers of Cyberspace," in *Connected: Engagements with Media,* ed. George E. Marcus (Chicago: University of Chicago Press, 1996), 91.

Only perhaps the "interregnum" should be conceived as being oxymoronically permanent. In that case even Burnett's stance includes elements of the digital utopia. With its insistence on a sharp break between old and new, the digital utopia seems to embrace the principle of perpetual transformation of *images*; and yet, it simultaneously tries to avoid the state of transition and consequent impurity, which is actually fundamental to its definitional *historicity*. The state of transition, instability, change bypassed unenthusiastic forecasts, may well have to be posited as a constant.

2001

MICHAEL ALLEN

THE IMPACT OF DIGITAL TECHNOLOGIES ON FILM AESTHETICS

With a background in software development Michael Allen has designed programs for use in editing film clips and in teaching media studies. After a book on the films of D. W. Grriffith, he has focused on the interrelation between film history and technological developments, as well as television and interactive media. He has written on the role of the blockbuster film in showcasing new technologies, sound in early British cinema, the history of film technologies and their impact on Hollywood, and the epistemological shift in film studies due to changing modes of production and distribution. He is currently a lecturer in film, television and electronic media in Birkbeck College at the University of London.

Computer-based digital imaging technologies and techniques have had a substantial impact on contemporary film-making over the past ten to fifteen years. From hesitant beginnings, these technologies and techniques, and the particular kind of images they have helped create, have become increasingly central to many films of the period. This chapter will look at the effect of the digital on previous media technologies – namely, celluloid film – and examine the ways in which digitally produced images have changed the formal parameters of the modern film text. It will also look closely at specific instances of this development across the past decade or more, in order to determine in which ways these effects and changes are historically specific. As I hope to demonstrate, the reality is a combination of change and continuity over time.

Although computer-generated imaging (CGI) technologies have been around for some time, even before what is commonly seen as their landmark arrival in the film *Tron* (1982), it is really only since 1989, in James Cameron's *The Abyss*, that CGI has become a significant element in modern filmmaking. Since that time, its role in the creation of spectacular images in big-budget films has grown considerably. While certainly this has often been the result of hype and expectation as much as actual reality, CGI has now become the focal point around which the promotion of a major new release might be organised. Indeed, it could be said that the dominant identity of mainstream big-budget filmmaking of the past decade is one framed by such images and such image-making technologies.

This growing dominance is testimony to a certain sense of historical development both of the hardware and software programs and of the techniques they facilitate and make possible. The failure of *Tron* was at least partly perceived to have been the result of the much-heralded CGI effects falling some way short of expectations, of a palpable sense of disappointment about the capability of such effects to produce convincing images. The success of *Jurassic Park* (1993) a decade later, conversely, was due to an acknowledgment of the quantum leap such effects work had taken in the intervening years. I mention these two seminal moments in order to stress, at the outset, the need to keep in mind the several specific, historical moments when the films under discussion were created. This is important because it is only by doing so that the true effect of CGI on the formal level of these films can be adequately and accurately analysed.

Within this general historical framework, the assumed trajectory of CGI, for many observers, has always been toward the perfecting of a photo-realistic quality for the images, an endeavor encapsulated in the following comment by Phil Tippett, the stop-motion supervisor on *Jurassic Park*:

> Artistic realism was the goal on all of the animation. We worked to get rid of all anthropomorphic actions. We wanted the dinosaurs to be as naturalistic as possible. It was the subtlety and all the refinements to the animation that allowed us to make those creatures look like real animals and not like movie monsters.[1]

In this sense, digital imaging technologies and techniques are striving to replicate what already exists: the photographic representation of reality. The success or failure of any digital image lies in the degree to which it persuades its spectator that it is not digital, but *is* photographic. The difference between the two, as has been widely analyzed, is that whereas the photographic record automatically assumes a referent, an original object whose image has been captured by light passing through a camera lens and altering the chemical make-up of a strip of celluloid, a digital image need have no such referent. This difference, seemingly impossible to reconcile, lies at the heart of the matter in hand: how to combine photographic and digital imaging to create a coherent and seamless filmic world. This chapter aims to examine how this process has been formally achieved in some of the most significant films that have employed computer-generated imagery in recent history.

SHOT LENGTH

One of my working hypotheses going into the researching and writing of this chapter was that the advent and development of computer-generated images has led to changes in editing patterns and scene construction in some films of the past decade or so. My basic supposition was that the visual 'fragility' of the computer-generated image made it difficult for it to be scrutinised for very long before its essential artificiality became obvious to the observer. Consequently, it might be assumed such images had to be given short, fleeting appearances on screen, so that the spectator's eye could not settle upon them, could not 'see through' them.

---

[1] Mark Cotta Vaz and Patricia Rose Duignan, *Industrial Light and Magic: Into the Digital Realm* (London: Virgin, 1996), p. 218.

There would be little new in this. Effects sequences created before the digital revolution, such as the mining car ride at the end of *Indiana Jones and the Temple of Doom* (1984), rapidly edited together live action with more traditional models and animation. While this was partly because of the narrative demands of speed and action, it was also designed to mask the potentially disruptive shots of model-work, the artificiality of which, if allowed to remain on screen long enough, would have become obvious to the audience.

A close examination of several seminal CGI films from the past decade or so shows an historical specificity to the use of such effects works in constructing sequences and scenes in the films. This historical perspective also complicates the simple hypothesis suggested above concerning the brevity of CGI images. In *The Abyss,* for example, the only sequence to use CGI comes halfway through the film and consists of 53 shots, from the first point of view of the creature as it approaches the submarine bay of the underwater rig, through to its final retreat back into the water as it flees from attack by the film's chief villain. The sequence runs five minutes in total. Of the 53 shots, some 20 contain CGI work and 33 are traditionally photographed shots of the actors only. The CGI shots make up a total of 67 seconds of the 300 seconds that the sequence lasts; that is to say, while the ratio of CGI to traditional shots is roughly 1:1.5, the ratio of total lengths of the two types of shot is 1:5. The CGI shots are on screen far shorter amounts of time than the photographed shots: an average of three seconds per shot, as opposed to around seven for the photographed shots. The screen time for each CGI shot is enough to register each effect, but not usually long enough to scrutinise it fully. The creature's first emergence out of the water is in a shot lasting around four seconds, but it only begins to form its shape in the latter half of the shot. The next few appearances each last around two to three seconds and establish the creature's presence within the space of the scene. Longer duration shots are then used to allow the creature to form the facial features of the two main characters, Bud and Ace.

Contrast this with the first explicit appearance of CGI effects in *Jurassic Park*: the scene in which Alan Grant (Sam Neill) and Ellie Sattler (Laura Dern) are shown the brachiosaurs. From the jeeps coming to a halt through to the end of the scene, where Richard Attenborough offers to show them how he made the creatures, there are 25 shots, six of them CGI, ten non-CGI. The scene lasts three minutes. The six CGI shots run a total of one minute, the non-CGI shots the remaining two; an average shot length of ten and 6.3 seconds, respectively. Now the CGI shots run longer, on average twice as long, as the non-CGI shots.

Why the difference? It is partly to do with the narrative purpose of the two scenes. While in some ways similar – the first contact of the main characters with, respectively, alien and extinct creatures – in other ways the two scenes differ significantly. In *The Abyss*, the scene depicts a tentative and nervous meeting in which the two parties are cautious about full contact. The tension then increases with the appearance, and aggressive behaviour, of the film's villain, who scares the water creature away. In *Jurassic Park*, the purpose of the scene is to stun the two main characters, to impress them overwhelmingly by allowing them to gaze long and closely at the dinosaurs. Hence they, and we as fellow gazers, are given lengthy views of the creatures.

Partly, it also has to do with sophistication of the CGI software itself. In *The Abyss*, the uncertainty surrounding the programs, and the images produced by them, meant that the film-makers felt comfortable in using them only in short bursts. In *Jurassic Park*, the creators had far more faith in the software and were far more confident in allowing the images to remain on screen for far longer. They *wanted* the audience to stare at them and still be amazed. Talking about this scene, the film's effects supervisor, Dennis Muren, commented that: "In the sequence, the graceful animals are revealed in long, lingering shots that are in marked contrast to the quick, flaw-concealing cuts typical of 'creature' films."[2] The scene is really an announcement of the arrival of a state-of-the-art image-creating process, especially explicit coming so near to the beginning of the film. If this is the first display of their image-making capabilities, what more is to come?

Finally, in *Godzilla* (1998), the length of shot is carefully controlled for dramatic rather than for technical reasons, in spite of the fact that the makers admit that the imaging software programs they used improved as production went on. The computer-generated images are overwhelmingly brief in the first scene in which Godzilla appears to the people of New York. But this fleetingness is not the result of the fragility of the technology so much as a means of teasingly suggesting the huge size of the creature and the panic induced by it in the people on the streets. But when much longer shots of the creature are needed, such as the one that comically ends the sequence, in which the news anchorman with his back to the window does not see Godzilla passing by, the shot is held for a noticeable length of time (around ten seconds).

Therefore, far from limiting their screen time, the gradual lengthening of shots featuring ever more photo-realistic computer-generated images, made possible by advances in the imaging software programs, can be said to present the images overtly for the gaze of the spectator. They become moments of sheer spectacle, their length intended to announce their importance as new kinds of image.

FRAMING

The scene in *Godzilla* mentioned above indicates another element of film form that has come under scrutiny in terms of CGI. In a production in which all objects and figures are physically real and inhabit the same real space, the combining of some or all of them within one shot, one framing, is not particularly problematic. The determinant is one of artistic choice, rather than technical constraint. In early CGI work, conversely, the latter rationale applied. Michele Pierson has observed the tendency of computer-generated objects in these early films to be separated from the flesh-and-blood figures in a scene: "Beginning with *The Abyss,* the arts-and-effects direction for films produced in the first half of this decade [1990s] emphasised the alterity of the computer-generated special effect by formally bracketing the presentation of it off from the action."[3] The problem of combining CGI with

---

[2]Jody Duncan, "Jurassic Park: The Beauty in the Beasts," *Cinefex*, no. 55 (August 1993); p. 64.

[3]Michele Pierson, "GI Effects in Hollywood Science-Fiction Cinema 1989–95: The Wonder Years," *Screen* 40, no. 2 (Summer 1999); 172.

real objects within the same shot was sufficiently difficult, technically, to result in a separation of the two, resulting in an alternation between CGI image and non-CGI image. As Pierson notes, this can be seen in the CGI scene in *The Abyss,* where, although a few of the framings show the CGI creature and the human actors in the same shot, most show the CGI creature alone.

By 1991, with *Terminator 2: Judgment Day,* this tendency was still in place. Most of the CGI effects in the film take place either in a separate shot or in the empty half of a shot containing humans or other real objects. For example, take the scene in which the T-800 has just rescued John Connor from the T-1000, who has been chasing him through the storm drains in a truck. After the truck has crashed and burst into flames, the T-800 and the boy stare back at the flaming wreck to check that the terminator has been destroyed. When they feel assured that he has, they ride away from the scene. A cut to a shot framing the wreckage is held for several seconds before the T-1000 appears, morphing back to the cop as he walks through the flames. This shot, explicitly separated from the preceding sequence of shots, presents a spectacular moment of CGI; a moment in which, while there is narrative content (the T-1000 is alive and still in pursuit), the foregrounded element is of the image being computer-generated; of having a particular visual quality which is unreal, but also situated in ostensibly 'real' space.

Again, this particular formal parameter altered over time as the software programs became more sophisticated and allowed computer-generated images to be seamlessly combined with real objects and people. *Jurassic Park* does this throughout its first scene involving the digital dinosaurs, as does *Godzilla,* in which the fragmented body of the huge creature is continually obscured by objects in front of it in the frame. Shot length and framing combine together to present the CGI object in a particular way that also has developed across time. In 1989, in *The Abyss,* the creature is generally framed in short, separate shots. By 1993, the dinosaurs are composited with the humans and the shots showing the two together are held for far longer. By 1998, CGI creature and real objects and humans are composited together in short shots, for dramatic rather than technical reasons.

CAMERA MOVEMENT

Until the appearance of motion-control camerawork in *Star Wars* (1977), there was a tendency in model-based effects work for the camera to have to remain stationary. The blocking out of specific areas of the image into which the animated models would later be optically inserted worked against the possibility of moving the camera and tended to implement instead a regime in which scenes were constructed of separate static shots. Motion-control, as the name suggests, freed the camera again and allowed it to follow models as they moved through space, in a kind of continuous frame-by-frame animation process whereby camera and model moved incrementally as single frames were photographed, sometimes in operations lasting several hours.

Early digital effects tended to immobilise the camera once again. In the scene in *The Abyss,* almost all of the CGI shots have a static framing and stand in stark contrast to both the fluid tracking shots from the creature's optical point of view as it enters the crew's quarters and the hand-held camerawork as the team chase after the creature later in the scene. There are two exceptions to this: first, when the creature moves toward Bud and Ace in the second shot of their encounter, there is a very slight track in toward the actors as the creature itself moves forward; second, in the very last shot, when the creature, having been scared off by the film's villain, whips back into the water, an upward tilt and then a rapid pan down right follows the creature as it disappears. However the latter's position at the very end of the scene, together with its speed and brevity, however, make it a coda more than an integral stylistic feature of the scene. The governing formal parameter of the scene is to have static framing for the CGI shots to simplify the image-creating process.

Once again, contrast this with the scene of the first dinosaur sighting in *Jurassic Park,* in which the camera movements are explicit and made obvious to us, and work to confirm the authenticity of what we are witnessing, essentially by suggesting that only real objects can be tracked by the camera in such a complex way. The registers of the real world (perspective, depth cues, light, and shade) work with the camera movement to overwhelm our means of analysing the effect.

However, the camera movements in this scene from *Jurassic Park* are kept frontal to the action; both dinosaurs and humans are kept to one side of the laterally moving camera. Even the extravagant low-angle shot that tracks as it tilts up steeply to frame Alan and Ellie in the foreground and the brachiosaur rising up behind them maintains this frontality. Later scenes, however, such as the herd of gallimuses that run past the characters, present a more complex spatial situation, the camera tracking backwards as the creatures run past on either side. A reverse angle then shows them running away from camera as it tracks forward. But the presentation of space is somehow discontinuous; separate spaces each allowing the CGI creatures to be repositioned anew.

It is only in the past couple of years that the presentation of continuous 3D space containing CGI objects and spaces has been achieved. In the scene in *Godzilla* in which the creature first appears in New York, there is a sweeping shot in which the camera tracks backward as a cabdriver begins to run from Godzilla, whose giant feet and lower legs are just visible in the background. As Godzilla approaches the foreground, the camera swings around 180 degrees, temporarily losing sight of the creature before it reappears in frame, its foot smashing down onto the street. The presentation of continuous space achieved by the 180-degree camera movement serves to reinforce our belief in the reality of the scene we are witnessing. The same effect is achieved in *Gladiator* (2000), when, as the gladiators enter the arena of the Coliseum, the camera swirls around them, showing computer-generated walls and tiers of spectators present continuously behind them. CGI space appears to be really there, behind and around the live actors.

An important point must be made here. These camera movements try to mimic as precisely as possible identical camera movements that might be used in a wholly live-action film. In one sense, they try to become invisible, to hide the role they play in persuading the spectator that the image they present is a computer-generated illusion. In another, however, their very extravagance, their overt sweep and style, are intended to be noticed by the spectator. They are in some sense pulled out of the constant and invisible flow of images that go to make up the scene and allowed to stand apart as moments for awed appreciation. Therefore, they both confirm the spatial reality of the scenes in which they appear and simultaneously announce their amazing presence as illusion. This tension between the real and the illusory lies at the heart of the impact computer-generated images often have for their spectators.

LIVE AND VIRTUAL

More generally speaking, a specific formal structure has developed that establishes the rules by which CGI and live action are combined. While CGI shots, in themselves, might be lengthy, allowing the spectator to gaze at and to scrutinise them, it is rare that several CGI shots are run together in a sequence at any one time. More normally, a CGI shot will be bracketed by live-action shots before and/or after it. The moment of "artificiality", therefore, is both set up as coming out of, perhaps extending, the real and is also retrospectively reconfirmed by the real. This interaction can occur with non-CGI effects work using models and/or animatronics instead, as evidenced by the comment made by Mark Goldblatt, the picture editor on *Terminator 2*, on the commentary track of the DVD edition of the film: "You have to use the stuff [model effects and animatronics] judiciously and keep referencing it with the real actors so that you never get the impression that you're looking at a puppet." But it could be argued that the necessity for such strategies of confirmation is heightened with CGI, in that the models at least have a physical reality, whereas the CGI is pure immaterial illusion. The need to refer back to real objects, in order to continually convince the viewer that the computer-generated object really exists, is thereby greater and becomes a determining formal strategy in the construction of sequences containing CGI work.

To take an example: in *Deep Impact* (1998), the complex, digitally composited shot of the large number of helicopters taking off across Washington is framed before and after by shots of, one assumes (perhaps dangerously), hundreds of real cars jamming a highway upon which another of the main characters is trying to find his new wife. The large number of cars and trucks in the framing shots echoes, and somehow confirms by association, the unfeasibly large number of helicopters all flying in the same air space during the middle CGI shot. Furthermore, the reality of 'helicopters' is verified by having one land on the rooftop helipad at the beginning of the CGI sequence while another flies past in the background (an entirely feasible production logistic). Finally, at the end of the sequence, Tea Leoni's character is shown clutching two photographs of her father, to whom she will now return so they can face death together, as confirmation of the notion of the existence of originating referents. The potentially 'fragile' CGI moment, lasting at most four or five seconds in an otherwise live and photographed event, but still capable of being 'seen through' by the vigilant spectator, therefore has considerable, one might say overwhelming, real-world, live confirmation. This relationship between real and photographed, and simulated and computer-generated images, in which the latter is carefully framed by the former in order to boost its chances of establishing and maintaining a weight of authenticity, will inevitably change as CGI systems and techniques become ever more sophisticated.

This interaction between real and simulated images can be placed within the framework of Stephen Prince's theory of correspondence.[4] Prince argues that with objects and beings that are outside our actual real-life experience, such as the dinosaurs in *Jurassic Park*, we bring to our assessment of the believability of such beings a set of prior knowledges. So, generally, we refer to the scientific laws of gravity, weight, mass, and so on. Specifically, we draw upon our knowledge of the texture of the thick skin of a large mammal, such as an elephant or rhino, light as it falls on such a skin, and so forth.

This theory of referencing allows us to understand the dynamic interaction between CGI effects and shots of live action, in which the live-action shots explicitly give us the information to which we will refer as the simulated equivalent in the following CGI shot appears on screen. While it might be thought that this could work to undermine the integrity of the diegetic world, especially if the CGI version fares poorly when directly juxtaposed with the 'real thing,' generally the shift into the 'virtual world' and back out to the real repairs any momentary viewer scepticism about the believability of the former.

It is perhaps significant in this respect that many of the substantial CGI sequences are prefaced, and thereby mediated, by already known audiovisual systems within the diegetic world of the films themselves. In *Godzilla*, the creature is initially represented as a physical reality by a radar display on the Japanese fish-processing ship. In *The Abyss*, characters communicate via videophone monitor, fixing in place a known set of images that lay the groundwork for the later, further step to take place in representing the water creature. In *Jurassic Park*, we are given an audiovisual presentation that sets out the scientific and technical premise of the film. Though this context is constructed retrospectively, we have already seen the CGI dinosaurs for the first time. The ultimate effect, however, is the same: the known and believable audiovisual form provides a link and bridge from the real world to the virtual CGI one.

THE PLACING AND TIMING OF CGI SEQUENCES

I would now like to move on to consider whether there is anything significant about how CGI sequences are positioned in terms of their film's shape and flow as a whole. Essentially, it is a question of the timing of the initial presentation of computer-generated imagery in any of the films in question. What is revealed is a range of strategies, rather than a standard template. Once again, this range is partly, but by no means wholly, historically conditioned. In *The Abyss*, the CGI images are withheld for over an hour (exactly halfway through the film) before the water creature is revealed to us. In *Jurassic Park*, as just indicated, the first sustained sight of the CGI dinosaurs comes after only 19 minutes and is not preceded by any suggestion or foretaste to whet the audience's expectations. In *Godzilla*, several brief but violent events introduce us to the presence and potential of the eponymous creature; scenes largely created using models as well as the mystery of the unseen. All fleeting sightings of the lizard are fragmentary and intentionally confusing.

---

[4] Stephen Prince, "True Lies: Perceptual Realism, Digital Images and Film Theory," *Film Quarterly* 49, no. 3 (Spring 1996).

The contrast between these films is the result both of narrative and historical pressures. In *The Abyss* and *Godzilla,* the rationale is certainly one of building narrative suspense, of positing the presence of a massive and/or fantastic creature, then delaying the moment when that creature is finally revealed to the viewer. However, it is also a question of the sophistication of the technology and software programs available at the time when each film was produced. In *The Abyss,* the imaging software was so new and untested that director James Cameron both protected his production by arranging traditional processes for producing the same images and allowed the film to spend an hour establishing the physical reality of its world. Indeed, the extreme and real physicality of the film's production was hyped in all promotion and word on the film.

In *Godzilla,* the software capability has less of an uncertainty. Indeed, proof of concept could be said to have passed the test several years earlier in *Jurassic Park.* The moment of revealing the full image of the creature has therefore become far more one of dramatic necessity than technical protectionism.

The case of *Jurassic Park* represents a perfect balance between these two points. Coming 19 minutes into the film, the first viewing has narrative logic; it is imperative that the two main characters see the dinosaurs as soon as possible so that they sign up to support the park. It also has industrial logic, spectacularly and almost arrogantly announcing the arrival of a significant advance in the field of CGI effects. The two logics, effectively, map onto one another—a mapping illustrated by the stunned, open-jawed reaction of the two characters. This is also a representation of the reaction the filmmakers hope the audience would be having as they first see the CGI creatures.

The presence and incorporation of computer-generated images within feature films involving traditionally photographed actors, objects and spaces, therefore, has resulted in a number of changes to the parameters of conventional film form, as well as a number of continuities. Except, perhaps, in the very early attempts, there have been no radical changes in shot length, or in framing or camera movement either. Each of these elements has continued to be varied and determined according to the dramatic requirements of the scenes in which they are used. Shots get shorter as action sequences build. Framings change with the dramatic content of a scene. Camera movement is still used to follow moving objects or to reveal new spaces in which new actions take place. In these senses, at least, CGI has fitted into existing formal properties of feature films. The conventional two-shot, for example, is now used to provide a space within the framed image where a computer-generated object can later be added. The framing, unbalanced in the original filming, becomes balanced and conforms to conventional aesthetic rules, due to the later computer-generated additions.

If there have been few major changes to film form, there have been modifications to some of the existing parameters. A series of computer-generated shots will often begin with shorter length shots intercut with live-action equivalents, before a later, longer shot spectacularly presents the climactic computer-generated image. This flow of images is slightly different from ordinary scene construction and shows one way in which CGI, in demanding a privileged space for a final display of itself as spectacular image, is subtly modifying the rules of film grammar. Similarly, the

sweeping 180-degree or circular, space-to-reverse-space camera movements operate not so much to follow live, on-screen action as to convince their spectators that
the non-real action being seen on screen is actually happening.

Repeatedly, therefore, we see CGI sequences taking the accepted rules of film
form and scene construction and either using them, unaltered, to confirm the reality of the digital images by editing them together with images of real objects to persuade us they exist in the same world or to present them as images which are
spectacularly apart. In this latter case, it is the minor abuse of conventional film
form that opens up a space for this display: the slightly "too-long" contrasting with
the series of "just-long-enough" shots, or the too perfectly executed camera movement. In using and manipulating the formal parameters of mainstream film-making
in this way, CGI sequences construct themselves as simultaneously ordinary *and*
extraordinary, as photo-realistic elements of transparent filmmaking and as non-real,
spectacular images designed to be noticed, to be separated from the flow of the rest
of the film's images, and appreciated for their nonphotographic visual qualities. The
tension between these two states, between these two kinds of film form, has come
to typify the experience of watching any film with a significant degree of CGI in
it. Whether this relationship will change again, as CGI processes continue to develop,
remains to be seen.

2002

KRISTEN WHISSEL

TALES OF UPWARD MOBILITY: THE NEW VERTICALITY AND DIGITAL SPECIAL EFFECTS

Kristen Whissel frequently writes on the technologies surrounding film, from the inventions and changes that characterize modernity to the developments that are changing contemporary filmmaking. She has also written on imperialism in early cinema, the spectacle of turn of the twentieth-century battle re-enactments, and the presentation of new technologies at the World's Fairs. Her essays have appeared in *A Feminist Reader in Early Cinema* (2002) and *Queer Screen: A Screen Reader* (2007). In 2007 she guest-edited an issue of *Film Criticism* on digital visual effects in contemporary films. She is currently an associate professor of film studies at the University of California, Berkeley.

So neither the horizontal nor the vertical proportion of the screen *alone* is ideal for it. *In actual fact, as we saw, in the forms of nature as in the forms of industry, and in the mutual encounter between these forms, we find the struggle, the conflict between both tendencies. And the screen, as a faithful mirror, not only of conflicts emotional and tragic, but equally of conflicts psychological and optically spatial, must be an appropriate battleground for the skirmishes of both these optical-by-view, but profoundly psychological-by-meaning, spatial tendencies on the part of the spectator.*

—Sergei Eisenstein, "The Dynamic Square"[1]

Following the release of *The Matrix* (1999, 2003) and *The Lord of the Rings* (2001, 2002, 2003) trilogies, *X-Men* and *X2* (2000, 2003), *Crouching Tiger, Hidden Dragon* (2000), and *Hero* (2002), it is safe to say that CGI technologies have given rise to a new generation of films that make increasing use of the screen's vertical axis. Drawing from cultural sources ranging from comic books and fantasy novels to the visual logics of video games and virtual reality, recent blockbusters deploy a

---

[1]Sergei Eisenstein, "The Dynamic Square," in *S. M. Eisenstein: Selected Writings 1922–1934*, ed. Richard Taylor (Bloomington: Indiana University Press, 1988), 208. My thanks to Tom Gunning for this reference and for a productive conversation about an earlier version of this article at the 2003 Film and Literature Conference at Florida State University. I am also grateful to Linda Williams and Isaac Hager for their advice on revisions.

broad range of digital special effects to create composite film bodies that effortlessly defy gravity or tragically succumb to its pull. In keeping with this tendency, these same films create breathtaking imaginary worlds defined by extreme heights and plunging depths whose stark verticality becomes the referential axis of many narrative conflicts. Such verticality is now pervasive enough to have become an important feature of popular cinema of the early twenty-first century and as such demands critical attention.

The following investigates what might be thought of as the spatial dialectics of contemporary cinema's vertical imagination—its tendency to map the violent collision of opposed forces onto a vertical axis marked by extreme highs and lows. Specifically, it approaches digitally enhanced verticality as a mode of cinematic representation designed to exploit to an unprecedented degree the visual pleasures of power and powerlessness.[2] Precisely because verticality automatically implies the intersection of two opposed forces—gravity and the force required to overcome it—it is an ideal technique for visualizing power. Verticality thereby facilitates a rather literal naturalization of culture in which the operation and effects of (social, economic, military) power are mapped onto the laws of space and time. Hence, in recent blockbuster films, vertically oriented bodies and objects imply a relation not just to the laws of physics but also to the spaces and times that define a fictional world's prevailing order. Vertical movement thereby gives dynamic, hyperkinetic expression to power and the individual's relation to it—defiant, transcendent, or subordinate.

This article will explore what recent (post-1996) blockbusters reveal about cinematic verticality and, in turn, what verticality can tell us about contemporary global cinema. While I will make reference to a number of popular films along the way, I will focus on *Titanic* (1997), *Hero*, *X-Men*, *The Matrix*, and *Crouching Tiger, Hidden Dragon*. Though the films under investigation here span a number of genres—including martial arts films, disaster films, comic book adaptations, science fiction films, action-adventure films, and fantasy films—and are produced in the United States, Hong Kong, China, and Taiwan, they all share a number of characteristics linked to their insistent deployment of verticality.

To be sure, film history is replete with breathtaking falls and astonishing ascents enabled by historically available special effects, from Harold Lloyd's precarious climb up the side of a department store in *Safety Last!* (1923) to James Stewart's defenestration at the end of *Rear Window* (1954), and Slim Pickens' descent through the atmosphere astride a bomb in *Dr. Strangelove* (1964). However, the blockbusters of the 1970s marked a turning point in the history of cinematic verticality; they deployed big-budget special effects to exploit the screen's vertical axis to a degree not seen before. While *The Poseidon Adventure* (1972) capsized an ocean liner and forced its protagonists to ascend through a series of inverted sets to find a way out through the ship's upended hull, *The Towering Inferno* (1974) turned the skyscraper into an upright labyrinth difficult to exit alive, and *King Kong* (1976) staged a battle between Kong and the NYPD on the top of the World Trade Center. Films like *Star Wars* (1977), *Superman* (1978), *Close Encounters of the Third Kind* (1979),

---

[2] In *The Vatican to Vegas: A History of Special Effects* (New York: The New Press, 2004), Norman M. Klein persuasively argues that all special effects are, in one way or another, an articulation of power.

and *E.T.* (1982) increasingly used models, miniatures, blue screens, and mattes to animate their characters' movements and desires along the screen's vertical axis, while *High Anxiety* (1977) parodied the use of the fall as a device for creating suspense in classical film.

The increasing exploitation of the screen's vertical axis continued through the 1980s and became significantly more pronounced with the development of digital special effects. In 1989, *The Abyss* used digital special effects to stage a deep-sea encounter with alien life forms: much of the film takes place on the edge of an underwater chasm plunging two-and-a-half miles to the ocean floor. In 1990, wire removal software created convincing images of bodies and matter in flight in *Back to the Future III*, while in 1993 Industrial Light and Magic's Digital Input Device animated the screen's vertical axis with towering photorealistic dinosaurs in *Jurassic Park*. In 1994, the infant protagonist of *Baby's Day Out* scaled the heights of Chicago's skyline thanks to composites that synthesized the baby's blue screen image with digitized photos of the cityscape.[3] Such developments reached a watershed in 1996, when the three top-grossing films of the year—*Independence Day*, *Twister* (both of which used new particle animation software), and *Mission: Impossible* (for which The Computer Film Company did digital compositing, paintwork, wire removal, and tracking)— suggested that digital technology's ability to polarize action along extreme spatial coordinates would continue to develop into the new millennium.

At its most basic level, the new digital verticality is a technique for activating polarized extremes. Its abstract spatial coordinates are those of the zenith and the nadir, and its favorite location is the precipice, regardless of setting. Since the early 1990s, skyscrapers, national monuments, elevator shafts, upended ocean liners, high towers, tall (and sometimes ambulatory) trees, mountaintops, hilltop cities, and chasms all function with equal efficiency to polarize conflict, to frame possible outcomes in terms of a devastating fall and/or a willfully insurgent rise. Even when action returns to terra firma and ordinary horizontality, digitally enhanced *mises-en-scène* activate the screen's vertical axis: pillared interiors, banners streaming down from high ceilings, drops of water falling in slow motion, and showers of brightly colored petals and bullet casings all indicate that actions and events will inevitably follow lines of ascent and descent, thereby compounding the thematic significance of vertical movement in these films.

In the process, verticality mobilizes various connotative meanings and feelings attached to ascent and descent. Upward mobility gives dynamic expression to feelings of soaring hope, joy, unbridled desire, and aspiration; it implies lightness, vitality, freedom, transcendence, defiance, and lofty ideals. In turn, falling and sinking give expression to dread, doom, and terror and are linked to heavy burdens, inertia, subordination, loss, and the void.[4] As a dynamic device for conveying the heightened emotions to which violent conflict gives rise, the new verticality draws heavily from

---

[3]David Cook, *A History of Narrative Film*, 4th ed. (London: W.W. Norton & Company, 2004), 881–927.

[4]For phenomenological analyses of verticality and horizontality, see Gaston Bachelard, *Air and Dreams: An Essay on the Imagination of Movement* (Dallas, TX: The Dallas Institute Publications, 2002) and Bernd Jaeger, "Horizontality and Verticality: A Phenomenological Exploration into Lived Space," *Duquesne Studies in Phenomenological Psychology*, vol. 1 (Pittsburgh, PA: Duquesne University Press, 1971), 212–35.

1950s Hollywood melodrama's use of expressionistic *mise-en-scène*, and takes the genre's association of staircases with rising and falling emotions to new extremes.[5] Not only has the scale of the vertical setting expanded exponentially with the development of CGI (to, say, elevator shafts spanning more than 100 floors, or the steep incline of a volcano), but so have the stakes: frequently a struggle for the survival of an entire city (*Spider-Man, X-Men, Godzilla* [1998]) or humanity itself (*The Matrix, The Lord of the Rings, The Day After Tomorrow* [2004], *Armageddon* [1998], *Independence Day, Sky Captain and the World of Tomorrow* [2004], *The War of the Worlds* [2005]) is played out along spatial coordinates of extreme highs and lows. Because the new verticality vastly expands the terrain upon which (and with which) the cinema compels its protagonists to struggle, it logically favors the epic.

As the above suggests, verticality's link to gravity and the laws of space and time makes it an ideal aesthetic for dramatizing the individual's relationship to powerful historical forces. Horizontality, in this context, stands for temporal and historical continuity which, when ruptured by the upsurge or fall of a vertically articulated mass, creates a dynamized moment, a temporal–historical break that radically changes the course of events. In *Jurassic Park* the sudden and astonishing appearance of the massive T-Rex signals the violent resurrection of the evolutionary past and the foolhardiness of the park owner's plan, as Constance Balides describes it, to appropriate "historical time for profit on a grand scale."[6] In *The Day after Tomorrow*, a wall of water crashes into and submerges Manhattan to signal an irreversible shift in the international balance of power: the United States' economic and military supremacy comes to an end, initiating a new era in which it is dependent upon Mexico. In *Reign of Fire* (2002), *Deep Impact* (1998), *Armageddon*, and *Pearl Harbor* (2001), digitally rendered danger descends from above and threatens to bring human time itself to an end. Most recently, *The War of the Worlds* imagines the end of humanity through the apocalyptic arrival of alien forces from above and below: in an astonishing special-effects sequence, towering alien tripods erupt from deep beneath the earth's surface. The machines are themselves operated by creatures driven below ground by bolts of lightning that spike down violently from stormy skies above.

When verticality finds expression through the gravity-defying body of a protagonist, it often implies a crisis inseparable from his or her problematic relation to the historical, familial, and traditional past. Whereas a protagonist's upward vertical movement is frequently symbolic of a leap towards a new future, downward verticality is inseparable from the rapid approach of an inevitable end. In some of these films, the past is represented as a burden that constrains the protagonist's freedom precisely so that powerful social and political formations may carry on, unchanged, into the future (*Titanic, Crouching Tiger, Hidden Dragon*). In some cases, the past repeats itself and revives dark forces that promise to annihilate the protagonist in the not-so-distant future (*X-Men, The Fifth Element* [1997], *The Lord of the Rings* trilogy, *Minority Report* [2002], *Van Helsing*, and *Hellboy* [2004]). Conversely, in yet

---

[5]On the use of the staircase in melodramas, see Thomas Elsaesser, "Tales of Sound and Fury: Observations on the Family Melodrama," in *Home Is Where the Heart Is: Studies in Melodrama and the Woman's Film,* ed. Christine Gledhill (London: BFI, 1987), 43–68.

[6]Constance Balides, "Jurassic Post-Fordism: Tall Tales of Economics in the Theme Park," *Screen* 41, no. 2 (Summer 2000): 135.

another group, historical continuity and a tangible relation to the past provide the conditions of possibility for an historical agency able to overcome forces whose power stems precisely from an ability to manipulate space and time at will (*The Matrix* trilogy, *Dark City* [1998]). Since extreme forms of vertical movement inevitably involve a violation of physical laws (which then often reassert themselves), vertically oriented bodies and narratives provide the ideal form for abstracting power and representing the struggles of the emergent against the dominant—a concept neatly conveyed by the title *Sky Captain and the World of Tomorrow.*

While the popularity of the blockbusters under consideration here can be explained in part by their presentation of astonishing digitally rendered spectacles, I would add that the "structure of feeling" invoked by verticality also causes them to resonate with contemporary audiences. Because verticality lends itself so well to the dynamic elaboration of conflict between opposed (historical, ideological, and natural) forces, it seems remarkably suitable for an era defined by economic polarization and new forms of political, religious, and military extremism, all of which seem to have had the effect (or so we are regularly told) of evacuating previously available middle grounds.[7] (The way that such global conflicts played out at the World Trade Center on September 11, 2001, only reinforced the link between verticality and the struggle for power in the popular imaginary.) Indeed, verticality allows these films simultaneously to acknowledge extremism, economic polarization, and thwarted upward mobility as significant aspects of their global audience's condition of existence, and to charge these crises with new visual pleasures. Even when they purport to represent actual historical events, these blockbusters feature mythological characters, breathtaking vertical terrains, and forms of embodiment—all of them more or less detached from any referent in the real world—onto which international audiences can map their conflicting identifications and emotional affiliations.[8] Precisely by defying verisimilitude, the new verticality lends these films a different sort of truth— a symbolic or emotional one that mediates present geopolitical reality.

This is not to say that previous eras have been free of either extremism or cinematic verticality. Indeed, verticality has been used to dramatize violent conflict since Flora Cameron was chased to the cliff's edge by Gus in *The Birth of a Nation* [1915]).[9]

---

[7] I have in mind here a number of mass-mediated conflicts taking placed in the past decade or so, including the Balkan wars of the 1990s, the suppression of student protests and the Tiananmen Square uprising in Beijing in 1989, the ongoing conflict between China and Taiwan, the rise of religious fundamentalism throughout the world, the recent unilateralism in U.S. foreign policy and George W. Bush's now-notorious declaration "Either you are with us or you are against us," the polarization of electoral politics in the U.S. (red states vs. blue), the hyper-violent discourse on terror, and the increasing disparity between wealthy and poor nations and populations, thanks in part to the increasing power of multinational corporations.

[8] Film scholars argue that this is a general tendency of the blockbuster. See especially Geoff King, *Spectacular Narratives: Hollywood in the Age of the Blockbuster* (New York: I.B. Tauris, 2000); Charles Acland, *Screen Traffic Movies, Multiplexes, and Global Culture* (Durham, NC: Duke University Press, 2003).

[9] Two notable works link verticality to historical change and conflict in previous eras. Zhang Zhen argues that 1930s martial arts films used "flying bodies" to express anxiety toward social and cultural changes precipitated by the emergence of technological modernity in China in "Bodies in the Air: The Magic of Science and the Fate of Early 'Martial Arts' Film in China," *Post Script* 20 (2001): 43–60. Ed Dimendberg argues that film noir represents the alienating effects of the American city's postwar verticality to express "longing for older horizontal forms and a reminder of the discomforts of the elevated city of capitalist commerce" in *Film Noir and the Spaces of Modernity* (Cambridge, MA: Harvard University Press, 2004), 96.

However, prior to the special-effects advances of the early 1990s, cinematic being-in-the-world remained for the most part anchored on a horizontal axis and terrestrial plane of existence, and verticality was used primarily to punctuate action and accent narrative climaxes and dramatic conflict. Recent blockbuster films exponentially extend and expand upon the cinema's ongoing exploitation of gravity's dramatic potential. Digital technologies have helped liberate many aspects of production from the laws of physics, allowing for much more pronounced and sustained exploitation of the screen's vertical axis. Hence, it seems that just as widescreen processes "created the functional grounds for a new film aesthetic based upon composition in width and depth" in the 1950s,[10] digital processes are currently giving rise to a new film aesthetic based on height and depth. As a result, verticality is no longer confined to hair-raising stunts and dramatic camera angles, but has become a cinematic mode that structures and coordinates setting, action, dialogue, and characterization along radical lines of ascent and descent. Now characters such as Gandalf in *The Lord of the Rings* plunge (followed by the "camera") thousands of feet without bodily injury, displacing the long fall's dramatic effect away from the body and onto narrative. Struggles between protagonists and antagonists hinge upon the degree to which each is able to defy or master the laws of physics, making extreme vertical settings—skyscrapers, deep chasms, mountain peaks—pervasive and imperative. The resulting spatialization of power and time allows the new verticality to map spatial transience onto historical transition and radical forms of mobility onto the possibilities and perils of change.

GRAVITY, HISTORICAL INERTIA, AND INEVITABILITY

I want to begin with two extremely profitable films—*Titanic* and *Hero*[11]—that use verticality's spatial dialectics to represent mythologized historical pasts defined by the violent opposition of polarized (political, economic) extremes. By mapping complex struggles for power onto the laws of physics, verticality can make historical change a matter of inertia or inevitability. While *Titanic*'s verticality represents history as a body or force that will remain in motion along a specific trajectory unless displaced by another force, *Hero* uses verticality to make the outcome of imperial history as predictable as the operation of gravity itself. And while verticality loans some support to the "official" histories that these films appear to confirm (i.e., class conflict lies submerged in America's distant past; national greatness demands the violent suppression of internal dissent), its dual movement also accommodates contradictory interpretations.

We can begin with *Titanic*, which links its ship's forward propulsion to historical inertia and a sense that the early twentieth century was drifting blindly toward disaster. As many scholars have argued, *Titanic* depicts 1914 as a moment in American history defined by a rigid and punitive class–gender system in which a corrupt and decadent industrial patriarchy (modeled after European aristocracy)

---

[10]Cook, 389.

[11]*Titanic* made over $600 million and is the top-grossing film of all time. *Hero* made more than $217 million in China and more than $53 million in the USA.

greedily pursued wealth and fame at the expense of others.[12] This world is remarkably polarized: there is no middle class (the ship offers only first- and third-class passage), and proper Victorian femininity (contrasted only by the French prostitutes in Jack's sketchbook) remains unchallenged by the New Woman. The ship's rigid segregation of classes by deck emphasizes two-tiered hierarchy and subordination from above. Aside from some minor grumblings about the tendency of first-class passengers to walk their dogs on the third-class deck, and the hushed explanation that women's choices are always difficult, acquiescence to a corrupt industrial patriarchy prevails among female and third-class passengers. Described as "a steamer so grand in scale and so luxurious in its appointments that its supremacy would never be challenged," the ship materializes both the decadent excesses of the industrial class and the arrogant presumption that it, like the *Titanic*, is unsinkable. Computer-generated tracking shots emphasize the ship's considerable length while wide shots display its smooth passage along the ocean's flat, expansive surface, linking the prevailing order with a seemingly endless horizontality. The film thereby turns the *Titanic* into an emblem of historical inertia: unless acted upon by another force, history will move in the direction of increasing imbalance of power between classes and genders.

Historical inertia is doubled by the inertia that seems to govern the fate of Rose Dewitt Bukater (Kate Winslet), whose impending marriage has been arranged purely for the profit of others: it will both enable her fiancé to come into his inheritance, and her mother to retain the upper-class lifestyle threatened by her late husband's debts. Marriage seems to reduce Rose to a mute object, incapable of action. A panning shot of the dining room at teatime shows other women gossiping animatedly about the wedding as Rose sits paralyzed, staring blankly ahead. Rose's voiceover explains: "I felt like I was standing at a great precipice with no one to pull me back, no one who cared or even noticed." Her later suicide attempt links her plight to a descent into a dark void. When asked why she tried to jump over board, she explains: "It was everything: my whole world and the people in it. And the inertia of my life plunging ahead and me powerless to stop it." To extend the association of the bride with falling matter and social constraints with the force of gravity, Rose shows Jack (Leonardo DiCaprio) her engagement ring and he comments: "God, look at that thing: you would have gone straight to the bottom."

Verticality intervenes as a spectacular figure for temporal rupture and violent historical "break." Looming high above the ship's upper decks, an iceberg's sudden appearance reconfigures the ocean's topography by activating vertical space high above and deep below its surface: it punctures the ship's hull, rushing water into it from below, and showers chunks of ice onto the deck from above. This reorganization of linear space prepares the way for the astonishing special-effects shots of the ship's stern catapulting high up into the air, converting the *Titanic*'s unprecedented length into a terrifying precipice that spurs the fall of an unjust era. Gravity

[12]See especially, Laurie Ouellette, "Ship of Dreams: Cross-Class Romance and the Cultural Fantasy of *Titanic*," and Adrienne Munich and Maura Spiegel, "Heart of the Ocean: Diamonds and Desire in *Titanic*," both in *Titanic: Anatomy of a Blockbuster*, ed. Kevin S. Sandler and Gaylyn Studlar (New Brunswick, NJ: Rutgers University Press, 1999), 169–88 and 155–68, respectively.

therefore acts as an historical corrective in this film: it violently undoes the flattened hierarchy of the ship's two-tiered class configuration by turning the first- and third-class decks into equivalent parallel lines aligned upright, side by side. Computer-generated long shots and point-of-view shots from the top of the upended stern show hundreds of (digital) passengers—transformed into mere objects by gravity—tumbling the length of ship to the icy waters far below. All fall to their deaths at the same speed regardless of class or rank as the ship's bow points to its new destination at the bottom of the ocean. Social determinism gives way to "mathematical certainties," and the indifferent laws of physics take control of the *Titanic*'s fate, emphasizing the idea that: "In the act of falling, history relentlessly marches on to its foregone conclusion."[13] Verticality further materializes the notion of an historical break as the ship cleaves in two before upending again and then plummeting down to the depths of the ocean floor.

That Rose's struggle for survival takes place at the stern is significant, for this site is associated with her earlier desire to give herself over to gravity and dissolution. The ship's sinking ultimately provokes her resistance to the force to which she earlier wished to succumb: she refuses to stay in the lifeboat (reserved for first-class passengers) that would preserve her identity and ends up quite literally on a new precipice where, with Jack's help, she resists gravity's (previously alluring) pull. Verticality repeats and inverts the logic of Rose's attempted suicide: rather than escape an oppressive regime by jumping overboard, the oppressive regime is instead sent plunging into the depths of the ocean. Rose's temporary submersion ultimately dissolves oppressive social–familial ties and consigns Victorian femininity to an obscure past: kicking to the surface, she emerges from disaster as Rose Dawson, New Woman. By simultaneously resisting gravity and succumbing to its corrective forces, Rose bridges verticality's historical break to become the subject of a new history defined not by polarizations and inertia, but by middle grounds and hyperkinetic motion. While the frame narrative reveals that Rose went on to get married in the mid-West and has grown into old age as part of California's comfortable middle class, old photographs show a young Rose Dawson standing in front of a bi-plane and riding a horse in front of a roller coaster.

Critics have argued that Rose's transformation into a penniless third-class passenger who eventually rises to the middle class upholds the American ideology of upward economic mobility.[14] I agree, but would add that *Titanic* is equally concerned (as its special effects suggest) with downward mobility and that its focus upon descent simultaneously addresses a global audience for whom such myths of prosperity are untenable. Verticality is masterfully and profitably deployed in. *Titanic* to charge downward mobility with unprecedented visual pleasure: not only are the most astonishing digital special effects reserved for the ship's near 90-degree inversion, but the latter facilitates a decline in Rose's social status that the film implies has only liberating consequences. Fantasies of potential and possibility are ultimately tied to a protagonist who wins by losing. Her ongoing determination to cast off the burdens of the society life she left behind is signaled when the elderly

---

[13] Jaeger, 225.
[14] See Oullette, 169–88.

Rose tosses the Heart of the Ocean diamond into the sea—a moment that should remind us that she never was, in fact, lower-class. In contrast, Jack, who is the film's primary figure for irrepressible upward mobility, heroically slips beneath the ocean's surface. Even as the frame narrative makes the myth of upward mobility available to some audiences, the film's tendency to map mobility along a downward trajectory acknowledges that the middle class may indeed only be accessible from above. As *Titanic* suggests, verticality's spatial dialectics and dual movement allow it to mobilize extremes, elaborate struggles for and imbalances in power, and accommodate contradictory interpretations of each. In this way, verticality dramatizes and makes pleasurable the (spectatorial) position of being caught in the middle of violent conflict between polarized extremes, whatever its outcome.

Like *Titanic*, *Hero* represents historical shift through verticality in order to dramatize the spectacular end of an era. In this film, verticality finds its most stunning elaboration through the four assassins who attempt to end the bloody conquest of the region's warring kingdoms by the King of Qin (Daoming Chen). Digitally enhanced wire fighting mobilizes their bodies along an expanded vertical axis and works in tandem with a highly stylized *mise-en-scène* to map complex historical forces onto (spatially) polarized oppositions.

Hero is organized around three narratives that provide competing versions of the events that have brought the assassin Nameless (Jet Li) within ten paces, and hence striking distance, of the King. Within them, the assassins defy gravity in settings defined by high bookshelves, tall trees, mountains, desert rock formations, and cascading waterfalls, linking verticality to their obstruction of the King's plans for conquest. From the beginning, *mise-en-scène* supplements vertical motion to materialize the idea that history proceeds dialectically from the intersection of directionally opposed forces. When Nameless arrives at the King's court, horizontal and vertical lines clash to create a form of graphic montage within the frame. As he mounts the stairs to the palace, his upright figure cuts sharply against the lines of the broad staircase that span the entire width of the screen. Once inside, the interior of the Great Hall is even more starkly defined by linear conflict: in one shot taken from the King's point of view, Nameless's upright figure and the palace's pillars are dwarfed by horizontally aligned ceiling beams and rows of candles that dominate the frame and appear to exert pressure upon vertical elements from above and below. The visual dominance of horizontality in the opening scene is important, for *Hero* concludes with a funeral procession that celebrates the willing demise of forces of resistance. As the narrative unfolds, increasingly graceful images of downward mobility invest the assassins' surrender of power with elegiac beauty. In this respect, verticality aids in the aestheticization of acquiescence, and gravity's inescapable pull lends a sense of inevitability to past (and future) history and to the protagonist's heroic willingness to be leveled by the forward thrust of imperial "progress."

In the first, most fictional narrative, Nameless impersonates a prefect who defeats the King's enemies—Sky (Donnie Yen), Broken Sword (Tony Leung), and Flying Snow (Maggie Cheung)—by taking advantage of a love triangle that has bitterly divided the assassins. Here gravity-defiant insurgency is linked to heightened emotions and feuds fueled by jealousy and disloyalty. These connotations are most pronounced in the scene when Moon (Zhang Ziyi) fights Flying Snow to avenge her master's murder. Throughout the scene, rage fuels vertical mobility as the combatants whirl through the air like tornados, give chase over treetops, and dive from high up in the air towards grounded targets below. Throughout the fight, bright yellow leaves rain down upon the combatants, suggesting that the unbridled passions that propel them upwards will ultimately lead to their downfall. Indeed, when Flying Snow fatally wounds Moon, the trees and the falling leaves turn blood red. *Mise-en-scène* appears to mourn the futility of Moon's death, giving the impression that the natural world bleeds with her. At the end of the tale none but Nameless—the King's loyal prefect—is left standing. Though the King ultimately disproves this story, it serves the broader ideological function of allowing vertically articulated bodies to stand for the warring kingdoms that suffer needlessly by fighting amongst themselves, making unity through empire appear natural and necessary.

In the second tale, the King narrates events as he imagines they must have transpired, given his knowledge of the assassins' honorable character. The King correctly surmises that Nameless, too, is an assassin and assumes that unity of purpose among the assassins has allowed him to come within striking distance of the King's throne. In this version, verticality allows the King's admiration for the assassins' willingness to sacrifice themselves for their cause to be expressed through stunning images of descent. After picturing Flying Snow's heroic death during her staged battle with Nameless (as they fight, she exclaims: "I die willingly for our cause! Please make your move!"), the King imagines a subsequent, more spectacular fight between Nameless and Broken Sword. However, this one unfolds only in their minds as a tribute to Flying Snow, whose body lies nearby on a bier. The fight takes place on a lake, the surface of which mirrors the tree-covered mountains in the background, inverting the treetops and peaks so they point to the bottom of the frame. In some shots, only the reflection is visible in the frame, orienting *mise-en-scène* along a downward trajectory, while in others the frame is divided between the landscape and its mirror image, between competing images of ascent and descent that match the rising and falling action. The camera cuts between images of the fighters skipping across the surface of the water like birds taking flight and wide shots of them plunging headlong toward the lake, using the tips of their swords to rebound off the water's smooth surface. Here, ascent (and with it, insurgent power) is most beautiful when followed by images of descent that aestheticize the surrender to gravity and the loss of power. Not surprisingly, then, the King's imagination privileges and aestheticizes self-sacrifice and points towards the film's conclusion in which Nameless is given a hero's funeral after he sacrifices himself and his cause to the King's ostensibly higher goals of empire.

The third and final tale combines elements of the first two: the assassins are divided not by desire and jealousy but by conflicting political ideals. While Snow and Nameless still oppose the King (their families were killed by his army), Broken Sword embraces the vision of "Our Land" and the unification of the warring kingdoms through bloody conquest. Predictably, Broken Sword's decision to succumb to the forward march of progress follows the line of descent. In a flashback within the tale, he describes the fight in which he passed up the opportunity to assassinate the King. The fight unfolds in the Great Hall among long green banners that hang from the high ceiling and match the color of Broken Sword's clothing. Here, vertically articulated *mise-en-scène* aids wire fighting to give outward expression to Broken Sword's desire to relinquish his part in the struggle, and thereby helps map a shift in power. At a crucial moment, Broken Sword has the chance to cut the King's throat but ultimately pulls back. After the King realizes his life has been spared, a long shot shows the massive banners streaming gently to the floor on either side of the combatants. Opposed spatial coordinates of high and low are flattened as opposition gives way to acquiescence, allowing gravity to double for the inexorable force of China's (future) imperial history.

This force finds expression through the arrows that slice across the court when the King gives the order to execute Nameless, sacrificing him to the ideology of "Our Land." Having taken to heart Broken Sword's argument that only the King has the power to end suffering and "bring peace by uniting our land," Nameless also declines to assassinate the future Emperor and therefore forfeits his life. His execution concludes with an image that simultaneously documents the fall of oppositional power and aestheticizes its absence. The camera tracks along the Court Wall—now transformed by thousands of black arrows that protrude from a thick horizontal mass on its surface—until it reaches the empty, blank space where Nameless once stood. The negative space that gives shape to the assassin's absent upright figure perfectly emblematizes the ideology that national history always demands the noble self-erasure of insurgent forces which resist its forward movement and idealizes (self-)subordination to an oppressive regime.[15]

WALLED CITIES, MOUNTAINTOPS, AND THE FORCE OF TRADITION

Crouching Tiger, Hidden Dragon, a *wu xia* film that undoubtedly helped prime *Hero*'s enthusiastic reception by Western audiences, uses digitally enhanced special effects to melodramatize a dynamic struggle for power by protagonists whose upward verticality is linked to insurgency against ongoing traditions and the past. As in *Hero*, resistance has deadly consequences and the film ends with a willing fall. At the opening of *Crouching Tiger*, each of the main characters is poised to break from the customs and institutions that define their lives. However, the past thwarts each attempt and asserts itself primarily through the obligations of duty and revenge, both of which preserve lines of power and maintain the past in the present.

Jen (Zhang Ziyi) is about to enter into an arranged marriage certain to advance her father's career and increase her family's power. Though she appears to be an obedient daughter, she is in fact, secretly, a powerful fighter trained by the notorious Jade Fox (Pei-Pei Cheng) and is in love with Lo (Chen Chang), an outlaw bandit. Jen wishes to lead a warrior's life, which she mistakenly believes is defined by

---

[15]This aesthetic beauty of the film's images of self-sacrifice has led most reviewers to describe the film as an homage to pacifism. However, J. Hoberman argues: "*Hero*'s vast imperial sets and symmetrical tumult, its decorative dialectical montage and sanctimonious traditionalism, its glorification of ruthless leadership and self-sacrifice on the altar of national greatness, not to mention the sense that this might stoke the engine of political regeneration, are all redolent of fascinatin' fascism." "Man With No Name Tells Story of Heroics, Color Coordination," *The Village Voice* (August 23, 2004), http://www.villagevoice.com/film/0434,hoberman2,56140,20.html.

Jen (Zhang Ziyi) rises into the air to defeat her foes in *Crouching Tiger, Hidden Dragon* (2003). "Upward mobility gives dynamic expression to feelings of soaring hope, joy, unbridled desire, and aspiration; it implies lightness, vitality, freedom, transcendence, defiance, and lofty ideals. In turn, falling and sinking give expression to dread, doom, and terror and are linked to heavy burdens, inertia, subordination, loss, and the void." (WHISSEL, p. 836)

freedom from duty to others. Li Mu Bai (Chow Yun Fat) wishes to quit his life as a warrior in order to spend it instead with Shu Lien (Michelle Yeoh), and she, too, contemplates forgetting her duty to honor the memory of her dead fiancé to be with Li Mu Bai. However, loyalty to his dead master (Yi) binds Li Mu Bai to the past. At the beginning of the film, he gives away the Green Destiny sword to escape the Giang Hu underworld, but, as he notes, "the cycle of bloodshed continues" as Jade Fox's arrival in Peking forces him to avenge his master's murder. In *Crouching Tiger*, vengeance maintains the past in the present by keeping one murder alive, so to speak, until another one consigns it to the past. Though Li Mu Bai kills Jade Fox, she slays him with the same poison she used to kill his master. Rather than free Li Mu Bai to pursue a new future, the act of vengeance gives the past the power to repeat itself and foreclose upon the future altogether. As in *Titanic* and *Hero*, the struggle for power between polarized forces takes place on an historical threshold, a moment of potential transition whose upheaval is figured through vertical movement.

Li Mu Bai and Jen are defined in part by their desire to jettison traditional duties to fathers and masters in favor of satisfying individual desire. They also imagine and long for a future that departs from the traditional order of things. In the first half of the film, Li Mu Bai plans to abandon his training altogether to be with Shu Lien, but in the second half, decides to return to Wudan to train a female disciple. In turn, Jen leaves behind the obligations of aristocratic femininity to roam freely as a rogue warrior unbound by any duty to others—even the consideration of others (Qing) that Shu Lien points out is necessary for survival. Indeed, Jen rejects the traditional female virtues of both Xie and Zhen (sexual purity), gives way to Yin (excessive sexual feeling), and fails to exhibit Li (propriety or conformity to accepted standards of social behavior).[16] Not surprisingly, Jen and Li Mu Bai are the film's primary and secondary agents of verticality. Ultimately, the film is ambivalent about any complete rejection of or acquiescence to the demands of the past, for both the fulfillment of traditional duties and rejection of them have disastrous consequences.

The first vertically oriented fight scene occurs immediately after Jen indicates to Shu Lien her desire to evade the confinement and subordination of her approaching arranged marriage. In an act of rebellion that will give her a material connection to the warrior life she desires, Jen steals the Green Destiny sword. Hearing the raised alarm, Shu Lien pursues Jen over peaked rooftops, giving the chase an undulating effect that choreographs their contrasting relation to the traditions and duties that bind present and future behavior to the past. As Christina Klein notes, whereas the dutiful Shu Lien acts as with the force of gravity throughout the scene, Jen defies gravity much as she desires to defy duty and tradition. Hence throughout the fight scene, Shu Lien counters each of Jen's vertical ascents: she knocks Jen out of the air by throwing bales of hay and pieces of brick at her; she steps on Jen's feet as Jen pushes off the ground to fly away; grabs her clothes before she soars out of reach; and scrambles up a wall to cut off Jen's ascent, demanding that she "Get down here!"[17]

Indeed, given her function as an anchor that works to keep the fight on solid ground, it is significant that throughout much of the film Shu Lien chooses to remain bound by tradition: she exemplifies filial piety to her dead father by successfully operating the security business he passed on to her (one client declares her an honor to her father's memory); she protects the interests and reputation of Sir Te (who regards her as a daughter) at all costs; and she explains that she and Li Mu Bai have forsaken their desire for one another to remain faithful to the memory of Meng Si Zhao, her fiancé and Li Mu Bai's blood brother. Rather than challenge patriarchy, her role as a warrior and security agent fulfills the principle of filial piety: she carries on her father's work in his absence.[18] If the digitally rendered walled city of Peking is an architectural manifestation of Jen's confinement by ongoing traditions and family histories far more powerful than she, then Shu Lien embodies the structural support of dutiful femininity on which tradition's continuity depends. Hence, throughout their first fight, tradition and duty—figured as the earth's gravitational pull—exercise themselves through Shu Lien, who acts as a counterweight to Jen's vertical flight.

We can compare the vertical action of this scene with the fight between Li Mu Bai and Jen atop the bamboo forest. In contrast with the rigid up-or-down verticality

---

[16]For a discussion and application of these Confucian principles to Chinese film, see Jenny Kowk Wah Lau, "*Ju Dou*: A Hermeneutical Reading of Cross-Cultural Cinema," *Film Quarterly* 25, no. 2 (Winter 1991–92): 2–10.

[17]Christina Klein, "*Crouching Tiger, Hidden Dragon*: A Diasporic Reading," *Cinema Journal* 43, no. 4 (Summer 2002): 34.

[18]For a discussion of unmarried daughters, female warriors, and their relation to tradition and modernity in Chinese cinema, see especially Chris Berry and Mary Farquhar, *China on Screen: Cinema and Nation* (New York: Columbia University Press, 2006).

of the first fight (materialized in the walls and buildings of the city), the choreography of the fight in the forest is defined by the swaying flux of the bamboo trees that yield to the lightness and weight of the fighters' bodies. This pliant, bending verticality is a visual manifestation of Jen's wavering position, her suspension between courses of action: she may return to her parents and subordinate herself to tradition, become Li Mu Bai's disciple and subordinate herself to another tradition, or roam free as a masterless warrior. Whereas in the first fight scene Jen seems far more weightless than Shu Lien, in this scene Li Mu Bai floats and balances with far greater ease. Here the forest is an important element of verticality's *mise-en-scène*, for the trees provide a structural support for the weightless body that demands the masterful use of gravity as much as a transcendence or defiance of it. If gravity represents the force of tradition and the past, then Li Mu Bai's more powerful verticality derives in part from his connection to the traditions, training, and duties of Wudan. Hence he uses the rise and fall of the branches with far greater skill than Jen, who plunges halfway below the tree line when he shakes her from a branch. His greater utilization of gravity's force thereby implies that without some structural support from past tradition, without any master, the future is characterized by a perilous free-fall. Yet as an agent of verticality, he is also at odds with tradition. Indeed, at this point in the narrative, Li Mu Bai chases Jen into the treetops because he wishes simultaneously to carry on tradition and transform it by bringing a female disciple to Wudan Mountain.

In keeping with its ambivalence toward the new future each of the characters longs for, the film ends by suspending its protagonists between old worlds and new. As mentioned above, the past repeats itself in the present when Li Mu Bai is poisoned by Jade Fox (who thus kills off the future). Rather than using his last moments to meditate and enter heaven, Li Mu Bai chooses instead to remain a ghost, walking the earth by Shu Lien's side. This figurative suspension between two worlds, between heaven and earth, past life and future life, is visually expressed through the film's final image, as Jen jumps off Wudan Mountain. On the one hand, Jen's fall may be read as an elegiac image of an insurgent figure's fatal acquiescence to the laws of physics and hence to the laws that govern the social order she has so violently resisted. On the other, her fall might fulfill Lo's wish for them to return to the desert and a life unrestrained by family duty and class identity. Though the path has been cleared for Jen to live a life of freedom and autonomy, the film holds the future at bay, suspending the narrative and the spectator between opposing outcomes. Jen's descent through space emblematizes verticality's more general ability to accommodate ambivalence and the film's specific negotiation of—and refusal to resolve—the complicated relations between the past and the future, the desire for change and the insistent pull of tradition, and the struggle of emergent power against the dominant. *Crouching Tiger*'s concluding fall foregrounds the blockbuster's predictable refusal to pursue the outcome of verticality's spatial dialectics: rather than using its dynamic conflict between opposing powers to envision a radically new outcome, verticality ultimately remains suspended between potential outcomes or follows a downward trajectory towards an already-past, familiar future that confirms the present. In this way, verticality ultimately works not only to mobilize but also to accommodate the conflicting desires and demands of the blockbuster's broadly heterogeneous global audience.

MONUMENTAL HEIGHTS: LEAPING FORWARD, AND LOOPING BACK

Like the *wu xia* film, comic book films have provided an ideal outlet for the new verticality precisely because their source materials have always located their polarized struggles for power in bodies that effortlessly transcend the laws of physics.[19] Similar to the other films discussed here, *X-Men* locates violent conflict between polarized extremes on an historical threshold. Set in the not-too-distant future after radical genetic mutation has precipitated a break with the evolutionary past, the film opens with a voiceover that explains: "Mutation: it is the key to our evolution. It has enabled us to evolve from a single-celled organism into the dominant species on the planet. This process is slow, normally taking thousands and thousands of years. But every few hundred millennia, evolution leaps forward." This evolutionary leap is bodied forth by genetic mutants endowed with a broad variety of powers, ranging from omniscience and telekinesis, to control over magnetic fields and the weather. Radical mutation's rupture of evolutionary time is countered by the cyclical return of a horrifying historical past via the Mutant Registration Act, a piece of legislation that echoes both the Nazi propaganda of the past century and contemporary anti-homosexual propaganda (when Senator Kelly [Bruce Davison] debates the Registration Act, he insists that all mutants be outed, arguing: "I think the American people have the right to decided whether they want their children to be in school with mutants, to be taught by mutants").

X-Men begins with a prologue set in a Nazi concentration camp in Poland, positing a cyclical continuity between the dreadful past and the to-be-dreaded future. In the opening scene, the mutant powers of Eric/Magneto (Ian McKellan) emerge as a form of resistance to the violent and broad-scale fragmentation and annihilation of the Jewish family. Demonstrated in greater detail throughout the rest of the film, Magneto's powers make him the film's primary agent of verticality. When he kidnaps Rogue (Anna Paquin), he floats down the aisle of a passenger train and then suspends Wolverine (Hugh Jackman) several feet above the ground. When ordered to surrender by police, he instead levitates patrol cars high into the air and sends them crashing down onto other vehicles below. The expectation of fascism's return in the near future (he warns Charles Xavier [Patrick Stewart]—"Let them pass that law and they'll have you in chains with a number burned into your forehead") propels Magneto upward to monumental heights. Like the vertical chase sequences in *Dark City* and *Minority Report*, the X-Men's pursuit of Magneto follows an upward trajectory that maps conflict onto spatial extremes, and shifts in power onto bodies that rise and fall: they track him to the top of the Statue of Liberty, where he plans to turn the world's leaders, positioned vulnerably below on Ellis Island, into mutants. Magneto is thereby an extreme version of a figure whose power—defined as the mastery of space, time and matter and made visible through gravity-defiance—is the expression of a desire to transcend constraints placed upon the freedom of a demonized minority. However, Magneto's antifascism has become so extreme that it threatens humanity's survival.

---

[19]On comic book characters and flight, see Scott Bukatman, *Matters of Gravity: Special Effects and Supermen in the 20th Century* (Durham, NC: Duke University Press, 2003).

And so *X-Men* intensifies the spectatorial pleasure of being caught between violently opposed extremes by triangulating its power struggle and aligning audience identification with the X-Men, who struggle to thwart the efforts of both sides.

Magneto's ascent to the top of the Statue of Liberty is an attempt to prevent not just the return of the historical past in the shape of a second Holocaust, but to escape the weight of past family history as well. By Magneto's perverse logic, forcing an evolutionary leap forward in the bodies of the world's most powerful leaders will result in a new *mutant* family unity and continuity that will compensate for the annihilation of the Jewish family. When asked why he pursues his plans even though doing so requires the sacrifice of another mutant, he explains:

> Because there is no land of tolerance, there is no peace—not here or anywhere else. Women and children—whole families—destroyed simply because they were born different from those in power. Well after tonight, the world's powerful will be just like us. They will return home as brothers, as mutants. Our cause will be theirs. Your sacrifice will mean our survival.

Here, the "returning home" of the powerful as "brother mutants" promises to break the cyclical return of fascism. Magneto seems to be driven by the idea that once he manufactures another evolutionary leap forward, the scene of family fragmentation with which the film begins may never return again (from atop the Statue of Liberty he reasons: "Those people down there control our fate and the fate of every other mutant. Soon our fate will be their fate"). However, unknown to Magneto, his plan will first transport the powerful (and much of New York) into the genetic future but will then slowly liquefy them and return them all to a primordial ooze. Hence, rather than effecting a break from the past, his plan will instead result in a looping back, a return of humanity to its prehistorical origins. This evolutionary reversion is first represented by Senator Kelly's long fall from his clifftop prison following his transformation by Magneto. After plunging to the ocean far below, the mutant Senator Kelly that emerges from the ocean resembles a jellyfish. Eventually, he is reduced to an entirely liquid state and splatters to the floor in a cascade of water.

When the X-Men ultimately thwart his plan, Magneto is captured and rendered powerless within a plastic prison. If within the film verticality maps the longing for a future unbound from the horrors of the past, then it also maps the inverse outcome of a return to the past. Gravity reasserts itself in direct proportion to the intensity of the desire to escape the historical and political constraints for which it stands. Verticality is not just a spatial or directional figure; rather, it is a figure for elaborating a flight from, or a return to, a former state—whether of the body, history, or narrative. Though Magneto drives towards a new future through upward verticality, such motion ultimately brings him full circle: in the end, he is imprisoned much as he was at the beginning of the film. Rather than provide clear resolution of its polarized conflict, the prison cell is a figure of narrative suspension: while it quite literally suspends Magneto over a dark void and forces a momentary cessation of hostilities, it also leaves the spectator poised between the narrative past of the trilogy's first installment and the narrative future toward which its concluding dialogue points (Magneto warns Xavier: "You know this plastic prison won't hold me for long").

SEVERED PASTS, AND SKYSCRAPERS

Science fiction's focus on the nature of time and its tendency to imagine worlds, technologies, and forms of embodiment that defy the laws of physics has made it another genre ideally suited to exploit the new verticality (prime examples include *Sky Captain and the World of Tomorrow*, *Dark City*, *The Fifth Element*, *I, Robot*, and *The War of the Worlds*). *The Matrix* is undoubtedly the film that most insistently ties vertically oriented action to the struggle for control over the laws of space and time. In it, humanity has been enslaved by a race of machines and exists in a state of suspended animation, as nothing more than a power source for artificially intelligent computers. Implicit and explicit in *The Matrix* is the idea that history operates according to horrifying cycles and ironic inversions: while images of the shackled Morpheus (Laurence Fishburne) link the current enslavement of mankind to the trans-Atlantic slave trade, humanity's mechanical subordination perverts modernity's equation of historical progress with technological development. Once freed from the matrix, Neo (Keanu Reeves) struggles to rescue humanity from machine-made, simulated space and time. In turn, this struggle has evolutionary overtones: while Agent Smith (Hugo Weaving) compares humans to dinosaurs and viruses, Neo (like Murdoch) will become the One precisely because he has somehow acquired the characteristics of his captors (Tank [Marcus Chong] refers to him as "a machine"). In turn, the film borrows and expands upon the vertically oriented action of the martial arts film to spatialize its protagonist's relation to time and power. Whereas Neo's powerlessness is emphasized through his fear of heights at the beginning of the film (he is first captured by Agent Smith when too frightened to climb the scaffolding to the top of the Metacortex building), his ascension to his position as the One is marked by his increasing ability to bend the laws of physics.

As in the other films discussed here, *The Matrix* does not use verticality simply for the sake of spectacle. Rather, verticality is the dynamic articulation of a desire to change the course of history, to precipitate a new future. Nearly all violent conflict with the Agents takes place along a vertical axis, from the opening scene when bullet-time sequences first display the spectacle of Trinity suspended in the air as she kicks her way out of a trap, to a later scene in which the rebels flee the hotel by sliding down through its interior walls. The spatialization of power is most evident in the scenes organized around Morpheus' rescue from the Agents, which begins with Neo and Trinity storming the lobby of a skyscraper and engaging in a shootout with security guards. The pillars that line the lobby materialize the film's broader theme of imprisonment and structure the vertical *mise-en-scène* and action of the fight sequence. As agents of verticality, Neo and Trinity create a downpour of falling shrapnel, objects, and bodies even as they defy gravity themselves. Fragments of marble and concrete, spent bullet casings, shards of glass, and water from a sprinkler system create a constant stream of downward motion that mimics the descent of binary codes seen falling across computer screens throughout the film. As other bodies drop, Neo and Trinity rise: in one of the rescue scene's many high-angle shots, they propel themselves to the top of the skyscraper by means of the cables of an elevator car they have sent plunging to the lobby, packed with explosives.

The bidirectional movement of this shot foregrounds the link between vertical-ity and narratives of emergence. Neo's repeated defiance and bending of the matrix's machine-made gravity (he dodges bullets, runs up walls, dangles over a digitized bluescreen cityscape, and rescues Trinity as she falls from a downed heli-copter) ultimately demonstrate that he is the One who will bring about the poten-tial liberation of humanity. Importantly, the film exploits the skyscraper to do so. While the jagged, burnt-out spikes of the real world's city skyline represent the end of human progress, the mirrored postmodern skyscrapers in the matrix repre-sent an inversion of the principles according to which modern progress was mea-sured. If the upward reach of the twentieth-century skyscraper implied the limitless potential of human endeavor, the simulated skyscrapers of the matrix imply human-ity's backward slide, its reduction to nothing more than the energy given off by its biological processes. Hence the simulated skyscraper filled with workers lodged in tiny cubicles simply cloaks the real-world skyscrapers of the film's twenty-second century—the massive energy towers that reduce human history to the ahistorical temporality of thermodynamics. Like some of the other films discussed here, *The Matrix* has a somewhat inconclusive resolution. While *Crouching Tiger* ends with its protagonist's downward fall, *X-Men* with a figure of suspension, *The Matrix* ends with Neo promising a future revolution in voiceover, and soaring above the city skyline of the matrix. While we might link this open-endedness with the film's position as the first installment of a trilogy, it is worth noting that the trilogy itself ends not with a triumphant victory of human over machine, but with a truce between polarized forces.

MYTHOLOGICAL AND TECHNOLOGICAL THRESHOLDS

That films defined by their spectacular use of CGI should be so concerned with historical thresholds is not surprising, particularly if we keep in mind the centrality of powerful new (and sometimes alien) technologies to the plots of so many recent blockbusters in which verticality is notable. For, as theorists and historians note, CGI synthesizes "old" and "new" media and frequently provokes critical specula-tions about the relation of the cinema's (digital) future to its (celluloid) past.[20] Indeed, the vertical bodies under consideration here are composites of old and new, of film and digital media—and visibly so. Though the harnesses and wires that keep the actors airborne can be erased from the digitized image, the visual effects of the actual force of gravity sometimes cannot. Unless compensated for by some other dynamic motion (kicking, running up a wall) occasionally these vertical bodies retain visible traces of their true condition in space: they, too, exist in a state of suspen-sion between the upward pull of an invisible apparatus and the downward force of gravity. In such instances, gravity's visible trace corresponds, roughly, to the state of suspension in which these characters exist within their fictional worlds *as well*

[20]See especially Lev Manovich, *The Language of New Media* (Cambridge, MA: MIT Press, 2002); Michelle Pierson, *Special Effects: Still in Search of Wonder* (New York: Columbia University Press, 2002); and Philip Rosen, *Change Mummified: Cinema, Historicity, Theory* (Minneapolis: University of Minnesota Press, 2001), 301–50.

as within film history. Put differently, digital verticality's occasional lack of transparency foregrounds its association with the emergent.

Through flying and falling bodies, the new verticality makes visible the position occupied by computer-generated images within the recent past of commercial film history—poised at an historical threshold, between continuity with past tradition and a future defined by aesthetic and technological change.[21]

2006

---

[21]In his article "The Impact of Digital Technologies on Film Aesthetics," Michael Allen argues that the impact of digital technologies on celluloid film form has been "a combination of change and continuity over time." *The New Media Book,* ed. Dan Harries (London: BFI, 2002), 109.

STEPHEN CROFTS

RECONCEPTUALIZING NATIONAL CINEMA(S)

Stephen Crofts's recent work deals with post-colonial theory, cosmopolitanism, and cross-cultural reception, particularly of films and television shows that feature or are made in Australia. He has also written on socialist realist cinema, psychoanalytic film theory, and the ideology of montage in Sergei Eisenstein's *Strike*. His books include *Identification, Gender and Genre: The Case of Shame* (1993), and *Programmed Politics: A Study of Australian Television* (with Philip Bell and Kathe Boehringer). He is currently honorary research associate at the University of Queensland.

VARIETIES OF NATIONAL CINEMA PRODUCTION

Especially in the West, national cinema production is usually defined against Hollywood. This extends to such a point that in Western discussions, Hollywood is hardly ever spoken of as a national cinema, perhaps indicating its transnational reach. That Hollywood has dominated most world film markets since as early as 1919 is well known.[1] Whereas in 1914 90 percent of films shown worldwide were French, by 1928, 85 percent were American.[2] And for all the formal disinvestiture secured domestically by the 1948 Paramount Decree, transnationally Hollywood still operates effectively as a vertically integrated business organization.

Throughout most film-viewing countries outside South and Southeast Asia, Hollywood has successfully exported and naturalized its construction of the cinema as fictional entertainment customarily requiring narrative closure and assuming a strong individual—usually male—hero as the necessary agent of that closure. In anglophone markets especially, Hollywood interests have often substantially taken control of the distribution and exhibition arms of the domestic industry. Elsaesser can thus comment: "Hollywood can hardly be conceived. . . as totally other, since so much of any nation's film culture is implicitly 'Hollywood' ".[3]

In the context of such unequal cultural and economic exchange, most national cinema producers have to operate in terms of an agenda set by Hollywood—though, as indicated by the fourth variety of national cinema listed below, some

---

[1]Thompson 1985. Guback 1976. Sklar 1975.
[2]Moussinac 1967 [1925], p. 238.
[3]Elsaesser 1987, p. 166.

Asian cinemas significantly maintain their own terrain. The political, economic and cultural regimes of different nation-states license some seven varieties of "national cinema" sequenced in rough order of decreasing familiarity to the present readership: (1) cinemas that differ from Hollywood, but do not compete directly, by targeting a distinct, specialist market sector; (2) those that differ, do not compete directly, *but* do directly *critique* Hollywood; (3) European and Third World entertainment cinemas struggle against Hollywood with limited or no success; (4) cinemas which ignore Hollywood, an accomplishment managed by few; (5) anglophone cinemas try to beat Hollywood at its own game; (6) cinemas work within a wholly state-controlled and often substantially state-subsidized industry; and (7) regional or national cinemas whose culture and/or language take their distance from the nation-states which enclose them.

It should be noted at the outset that, as in most taxonomies, these categories are highly permeable. Not only do individual films cross-breed from between different groups, but a given national cinema, operating different production sectors, will often straddle these groupings. Thus French cinema operates in the first and third fields, with exceptional forays into the second, and Australian in the fifth and first with yet rarer excursions into the second, while Indian produces in the fourth, the first and the second. Moreover, the export of a given text may shift its category, most commonly recycling films of the second and sixth groupings as the first, as art cinema. In such cases, distribution and reception criteria supplant production and textual criteria. . . .

1. European-Model Art Cinemas

This is, to most of the present readership, the best-known form of national cinema. Indeed, it constitutes the limits of some accounts of national cinema, which collapse national cinema into the European art film flourishing in the 1960s and 1970s.[4] This model aims to differentiate itself textually from Hollywood, to assert explicitly or implicitly an indigenous product, and to reach domestic and export markets through those specialist distribution channels and exhibition venues usually called "arthouse." Outside Europe, the model includes, for example, the art cinema of India exemplified by Satyajit Ray as well as the Australian period film.

Insofar as the discourses supporting such a model of national cinema are typically bourgeois-nationalist, they also subtend the European popular cinemas considered below. Those of the former are more elitist and more targeted at export markets for financial and cultural reasons. (This is not to say, of course, that popular cinemas do not seek out foreign markets.) National pride and the assertion at home and abroad of national cultural identity have been vital in arguing for art cinemas. Central, too, have been arguments about national cultural and literary traditions and quality as well as their consolidation and extension through a national cinema; hence the frequent literary sources and tendencies in this European model of national cinema.[5]

---

[4]Neale 1981.
[5]Elsaesser 1989, pp. 108, 333.

Such arguments have issued in and maintained legislation for European cinemas of quality as well as European popular cinemas. The most meaningful legislation has been that for state subvention, directly via grants, loans, prizes and awards, or indirectly through taxation (the state in the post–World War Two period replaces the private patronage, which outside Russia substantially supported the art/avant-garde cinema of the 1920s). State legislation has also been used to govern quotas and tariffs on imported films. These various legislative and financial arrangements allow for the establishment of what Elsaesser calls a "cultural mode of production"[6] as distinct from the industrial mode of Hollywood. Though it depends on state subsidies—increasingly via television—this production mode is successful because of a meshing, often developed over decades, between economic and cultural interests in the country concerned. Such a mesh is less common in other modes of national cinemas considered below. Significantly, as elucidated by Colin Crisp, the French cinema—that most successfully nationalist of national cinemas—became so in the post-1945 era by virtue of its cinema workers' vigorous campaign against the post-Vichy influx of Hollywood films that obliged the government to impose a quota on Hollywood imports as well as box-office taxes to subsidize indigenous feature film production.[7] A key variant affecting the success of an art cinema is the cultural status of cinema relative to other artistic practices in the country concerned. France rates cinema more highly than West Germany, for instance, with Britain in between, and Australia, adopting a European funding model, hovers near the bottom.

Textually, European-model art cinema has been typified by features such as the psychologized characterization, narrational ambiguity, and objective verisimilitude noted by David Bordwell.[8] And in defiance of claims that art cinema died with Tarkovsky, such textual features survive, with the metaphysics and the high-cultural address, in the work of Resnais, Rivette, Rohmer, and newcomers like Kieslowski and Greenaway. But Bordwell's schema is modified by two factors. The supersession of early 1960s existentialism by later 1960s political radicalism and subsequent apoliticisms is one, pursued later. The other is Hollywood's development of its own art cinema. This has contributed to a blurring of boundaries between specialist and entertainment market sectors in its own market and abroad, and has weakened the assertions of independence made by other art cinemas. The generic mixing of Hollywood from, say, the early 1960s has been complicated by its interchange with European art cinema developments. Hollywood has developed its own art cinema after and alongside the spaghetti Western, Nouvelle Vague *hommages* to Hollywood genres and directors, Fassbinder's recasting of Hollywood melodrama and gangster genres, and the adoption by such directors as Schlondorff, Hauff, and Jodrell of Hollywood genres and modes of character identification to deal with nationally specific, West German and Australian issues. Penn, Altman, Schrader, and Allen in the first wave all had their own favorite European influences, whereas a later star such as Lynch arrives with a more postmodernist pedigree, and Soderberg, Hartley, and Stillman have more modest projects. A principal upshot has been a blurring of

[6]Ibid., pp. 41–43.
[7]Colin Crisp,1993
[8]David Bordwell, 1979, 1985. 884

national cinema differences. Coupled with the aging market demographics of the European art film—the babyboomers forsake the cinema for their families—this blurring leaves these production sectors less able to differentiate their product from Hollywood's. Such insecurity is compounded by substantial American successes at recent Cannes festivals, long the preserve of European films.

Although a politicized art cinema diverges from the metaphysical orientation of the textual norms cited above, state subsidy does impose limitations. Elsaesser neatly pinpoints the contradictions ensuing from state subsidy of a cultural mode of film production: it encourages aesthetic difference from the dominant (Hollywood) product, but discourages biting the hand that feeds it.[9] In the West German instance, this tension explains the adoption of political allegory as a mode of self-censorship, as variously seen in *Artists at the Top of the Big Top: Disoriented* (as regards state funding of film), *The American Friend* (American cultural influences in West Germany), and *Germany, Pale Mother* (recent German history and feminist readings of it). Left political films found their way through the liberal pluralist interstices of such cultural funding arrangements: for example, the critical realism of a Rosi or a Rossellini and the critical antirealism of Kluge and Straub-Huillet. Godard, in the heady affluent days of turn-of-the-70s New Leftism, constituted a limit-case: on the basis of his cultural prestige as renowned art film director, he persuaded four television stations to finance ultra-leftist films, only one of which was then screened.[10] Such explicit leftism partly borrows its discourses from, and marks a border zone between, a European art cinema and the second mode of national cinema.

2. Third Cinema

Third Cinema 1960s–1970s opposed the United States and Europe in its anti-imperialist insistence on national liberation, and in its insistence on the development of aesthetic models distinct from those of Hollywood and European art cinema. As Getino and Solanas proclaimed in their famous 1969 manifesto, "Towards a Third Cinema":

> While, during the early history . . . of the cinema, it was possible to speak of a German, an Italian or a Swedish cinema clearly differentiated from, and corresponding to, specific national characteristics, today such differences have disappeared. The borders were wiped out along with the expansion of US imperialism and the film model that it imposed: Hollywood movies . . . The first alternative to this type of cinema . . . arose with the so-called "author's cinema" . . . the second cinema. This alternative signified a step forward inasmuch as it demanded that the film-maker be free to express him/herself in non-standard language . . . But such attempts have already reached, or are about to reach, the outer limits of what the system permits . . . In our times it is hard to find a film within the field of commercial cinema . . . in both the capitalist and socialist countries, that manages to avoid the models of Hollywood pictures.[11]

From the perspective of revolutionary, national liberation movements in Latin American, African, and Asian nations, such an identification of "first" with "second"

---

[9] Elsaesser 1989, p. 44.
[10] Crofts 1972, p. 37.
[11] Getino and Solanas, 1969, pp. 20–21.

cinemas has an understandable basis in a critique of bourgeois individualism. For the existentialist-influenced "universal" humanism of much 1960s art cinema (canonically Bergman, Antonioni, Resnais) shares a Western individualism with the achieving heroes of Hollywood who resolve plots within the global-capitalist terms of a U.S. world view.

Third Cinema has proven to be one of the more elastic signifiers in the cinematic lexicon. Some writers have tried to homogenize the enormously diverse range of Third World film production under its rubric,[12] whereas others have sought to build on the 1960s liberationist political moment of Getino and Solanas's manifesto, a moment extending well into the 1980s in ex-Portuguese colonies in Africa. Insofar as Third Cinema distinguishes itself politically and largely aesthetically from Hollywood and European art cinema models, its history has been a fitful one. In its concern with "a historically analytic yet culturally specific mode of cinematic discourse,"[13] its radical edge distinguished it also from the bulk of Third World production, primarily devoted to comedies, action genres, musicals, and varieties of melodrama/romance/titillation. Especially in the 1960s, such radicalism rendered Third Cinema liable to ferocious censorship. More recently, Third Cinema abuts and overlaps with art film's textual norms and, its militant underground audience lost, seeks out art cinema's international distribution-exhibition channels. Names such as those of Solanas, Mrinal Sen, Tahimik, Sembene, and Cissé serve notice of the ongoing importance of Third Cinema as a cinema of political and aesthetic opposition.

It follows from its political oppositionality and Third World "national [cultural] powerlessness"[14] that funding for such cinema is highly unreliable. In the instance of films from impoverished, black African one-party states with few cinemas and minimal film culture, film subsidy is easier found in France, in Switzerland, or from the UK's Channel 4 and BBC2. Such production conditions give Third Cinema a more urgent intensity than the political allegories of West German cinema and raise vital questions about the cultural role played by First World financing of Third World cinemas. Rod Stoneman of Channel 4 sounds an appropriate warning note on international coproductions: "Vital though the input of hard currency from European television may be, it is important that it does not distort the direction of African cinema."[15]

Discourses on Third Cinema undo many First World notions of national cinema, perhaps most strikingly the notion of national cultural sovereignty. As polemically adopted by the 1986 Edinburgh Film Festival Special Event on the topic, Third Cinema offered a particular reconceptualization of national cinema. It became a means of disaggregating the congealed stolidity of a British film culture unwilling to recognize in its midst a plethora of ethnic, gender, class, and regional differences.[16] The Event extended the definition of Third Cinema to take in, for instance, black British

---

[12]Burton 1985, pp. 6–10. Willemen 1987, pp. 21–23. On Gabriel 1982.
[13]Willemen 1987, p. 8.
[14]Stam 1991, p. 227.
[15]Quoted in Leahy 1991, p. 65.
[16]Pines and Willemen 1989.

cinema. Another conceptual dividend of Third Cinema is its decisive refutation of the easy Western assumption of the coincidence of ethnic background and home. Pinochet's military dictatorship in Chile, for example, produced a diasporic cinema. As Zuzana Pick notes: "The dispersal of filmmakers . . . made problematic their identification within the Chilean national and cultural formation."[17] Similarly exiled have been such erstwhile Fifth Generation Chinese filmmakers as Wu Tianming, Chen Kaige, Huang Jianxin, and Zhang Yimou, whose *Ju Dou,* coproduced with a Japanese company, is still banned in China, probably for its allegorical resonances of the 1960s–1989 period as well as for the expressed concern that it is a "foreign exposé" of a "backward China." And within their "own" countries filmmakers such as Paradjanov and Yilmaz Guney have been exiled and/or imprisoned . . .

3. Third World and European Commercial Cinemas

Art cinema and Third Cinema, the two best known reactions to Hollywood, do not exhaust the field. Both Europe and the Third World produce commercial cinemas that compete, with varying degrees of success, with Hollywood product in domestic markets. These cinemas, and all those considered henceforth, are less well known than the first two because they are less exported to the European and anglophone film cultures, which largely define the critical terms of national cinemas.

Much Third World production, as distinct from Third Cinema, aims, like European art cinema, to compete with Hollywood in indigenous markets—or, in Africa, with Indian cinema too—but it differs from European art cinema in being populist. This may be explained, in part, by lesser degrees of American cultural influence (that is, there is more screen space) and by the fact that local cultural elites outside Latin America are weaker and little concerned with cinema, thus encouraging lesser art cinemas. (Third World cinema here excludes China and Russia, considered later.)

European commercial cinema, however, should be treated here. It targets a market sector somewhat distinct from European-model art cinema, and thus vies more directly with Hollywood for box office. Its most successful country has been France, where until 1986 indigenous cinema won out over Hollywood at the local box office. French production, it might be noted, has partly dissolved the industrial/cultural distinction by successfully promoting auteurs within an industrial context. Other European commercial/art cinemas such as Holland's and Ireland's, based on small language communities, have a much more parlous existence, with production levels often tailing off to zero per year and with few exports. Typical genres of a European commercial cinema include the thriller, comedy and, especially in the 1960s, soft-core.

Excluding the booming economies of East Asia, the dependent capitalist status of most Third World countries, with stop-go economies and vulnerability to military dictatorships with short cultural briefs, rarely provides the continuous infrastructural support that nurtures indigenous cinemas. Economic dependency and hesitant cultural commitment typically promote private over public forms of invest-

---

[17]Pick 1987, p. 41.

ment, which further weakens indigenous film production. John King notes the common failure in Latin America to bite the bullet for import quotas:

> [I]n general the state has been more successful in stimulating production than in altering distribution and exhibition circuits. The transnational and local monopolies have strongly resisted any measures to restrict the free entry of foreign films and have grudgingly obeyed, or even ignored, laws which purport to guarantee screen time to national products. . . . [T]he logic of state investment was largely economic: to protect the profits of dominantly private investors. There are fewer examples of what Thomas Elsaesser calls a "cultural mode of production."[18]

Throughout the Third World, with exceptions noted below, foreign (mainly Hollywood) films dominate local screens. Even in Turkey, where "film production was . . . neither dominated by foreign companies nor supported or tightly controlled by the state . . . the market was still dominated by the four or five hundred imported films (mostly Hollywood movies)."[19] Uruguay represents an extreme instance, insofar as it has a dynamic film culture and almost no local production.[20] Yet that same film culture afforded more admissions to Solanas's *Tangos: El Exilio de Gardel* than to *Rambo*.[21] Slightly differently, Tunisia has since 1966 hosted the significant Carthage Film Festival while having only some seventy film theaters, insufficient to sustain regular local production. In francophone black Africa, only recently has the French distribution duopoly been displaced, allowing the screening of more African films on African screens.[22]

Countries of the East Asian economic boom clearly differ. Although Japan is Hollywood's largest overseas market, in 1988 domestic product retained 49.7 percent of box office,[23] specializing largely in softcore and adolescent melodramas.[24] And South Korea in the same year battled the Motion Picture Export Association of America (MPEAA) to reduce Hollywood imports to roughly five per year.[25] As such, it broaches the category of "Ignoring Hollywood."

4. Ignoring Hollywood

In Paul Willemen's gloss, "some countries (especially in Asia) have managed to prevent Hollywood from destroying their local film industry."[26] This option is open only to nation-states with large domestic markets and/or effective trade barriers, such as India and Hong Kong (there are some similarities between these countries and the totalitarian cinemas considered below). In these Asian countries, culturally specific cinemas can arise and flourish. In Hong Kong, the national cinema outsells Hollywood by a factor of four to one. And in India the national cinema sells four

---

[18]John King 1990, pp. 248–49.
[19]Armes 1987, pp. 195–96.
[20]King 1990, p. 97.
[21]Solanas 1990, p. 115.
[22]Armes 1987, pp. 212, 223.
[23]Lent 1990, p. 47.
[24]Yoichi 1990, p. 110.
[25]Lent 1990, pp. 122–23.
[26]Willemen 1987, p. 25.

times as many tickets per year as does Hollywood in the United States. In 1988, a typical year, the Indian industry produced 773 films, 262 more than Hollywood. That Indian features are produced in some twenty languages for local consumption protects Indian films very ably from foreign competition.[27] And in the Hollywood vein—if less expansively—Bombay exports its product to Indian communities worldwide, just as Hong Kong exports through East Asia, dominating the Taiwan market, for instance, and to Chinatowns throughout the Western world. Furthermore, Indian cinema long colonized Ceylon (now Sri Lanka). All Sinhalese films prior to 1956 were made in South India, and "local actors were decked out as Indian heroes and heroines who mouthed Sinhalese."[28]

5. Imitating Hollywood

Some sectors of some national cinemas have sought to beat Hollywood at its own game—and overwhelmingly failed. Such aspirations have emanated largely from anglophone countries: Britain, Canada, Australia. In the memorable dictum of British producer, Leon Clore, "If the United States spoke Spanish, we would have a film industry."[29] State investment in the countries' film industries has secured relatively stable production levels but has not guaranteed a culturally nationalist product. Anglophony has encouraged these nations to target the West's largest, most lucrative—and well-protected—market, that of the United States. But these national cinemas have already had their indigenous cultural bases modified, if not undercut, by the substantial inroads made into domestic distribution and exhibition by Hollywood interests and product. Geoffrey Nowell-Smith's provocative remarks on British cinema are yet more pertinent to Canada and Australia: "British cinema is in the invidious position of having to compete with an American cinema which, paradoxical as this may seem, is by now far more deeply rooted in British cultural life than is the native product."[30] Already weaker than those of major European countries, the local film cultures of these anglophone nations have been further weakened through the 1980s by the unequal economic exchanges that have locked British, Canadian, and Australian film production increasingly into dependence on the U.S. market through pre-sales and distribution guarantees. For each success story like *A Fish Called Wanda* and *Crocodile Dundee*, which have drawn on some local cultural values, there have been hundreds of films made in these lesser-player countries that, in trying to second-guess the desires of the U.S. market, have produced pallid imitations. An index of the price exacted for the American/world distribution of *Crocodile Dundee* can be seen in the reediting required by Paramount, which quickened the narrative pace and made the film look more like a wholesome family entertainment.[31] A fantasy of a foreign market can, then, exercise an inordinate influence over "national" product.

---

[27]Lent 1991, p. 230–31.
[28]Coorey and Jayatilaka 1974, p. 303.
[29]Quoted in Roddick 1985, p. 5.
[30]Nowell-Smith 1985, p. 152.
[31]Crofts 1990.

The logic of such blithe bleaching-out of domestic cultural specificity can have two further consequences: the country may become an offshore production base for Hollywood—witness Britain, Canada, and Australia's branch of Warner Brothers' "Hollywood on the Gold Coast"—or Hollywood may exercise its longstanding vampirism of foreign talent.[32] In the Australian case, all the major name directors of the 1980s have now moved to Hollywood, most without returning to Australia: the two George Millers, Peter Weir, Gillian Armstrong, Fred Schepisi, Bruce Beresford, Phil Noyce, Carl Schultz, Simon Wincer. Four leading Australian actors have now made the Hollywood grade: Mel Gibson, Judy Davis, Bryan Brown, Colin Freils. Even that stalwart of Australian cultural nationalism, playwright and scriptwriter David Williamson, has been writing a script in Hollywood. Similarly Bangladeshi & Indian.

6. Totalitarian Cinemas

Sixthly, there is the national cinema of the totalitarian state: Fascist Germany and Italy, Chinese cinema between 1949 and the mid-1980s, and of course, the Stalinist regimes of the Soviet bloc. By far the predominant mode of the Communist brand of such national cinemas has been socialist realism, which sought to convince viewers of the virtues of the existing political order.[33] Peripheral to this core production has been the often political art cinema of Tarkovsky, Jancsó, Makaveyev, Wajda, various proponents of the Cuban and Czech New Waves, and Chinese Fifth Generation cinema. Such peripheral production has been conditional upon the liberalism or otherwise of national policies at the time, both as regards cultural production and the cultural diplomacy of products exported. A further aspect of any analysis of this mode of national cinema might seek to disentangle cultural specificities from the homogenizing fictions of nationalism. As Chris Berry notes in surveying Fifth Generation departures from the Han Chinese norm, there are "56 races in the People's Republic."[34] The undoubted popularity of such Communist and also fascist cinemas might need to be mapped against the discursive regimes and the range of other entertainment, within and outside the home, offered by such nation-states.

7. Regional/Ethnic Cinemas

Given the historical recency of the disintegration of the nation-state and its forcefully homogenizing discourses and political sanctions, it is not surprising that ethnic and linguistic minorities have generally lacked the funds and infrastructure to support regional cinemas or national cinemas distinct from the nation-states that enclose them. Marvin D'Lugo has written of Catalan cinema as "something like a national cinema,"[35] but perhaps the best-known regional cinema, the Québecois, has benefitted from cultural and political support strong enough to propel its major name director, Denys Arcand, into international fame. Cinemas such as the Welsh have

---

[32]Prédal 1990.
[33]Crofts 1976.
[34]Berry 1992, p. 47.
[35]D'Lugo 1991, p. 131.

not achieved such prominence nor, within settler societies, have Aboriginal, Maori, or Native American cinemas, nor indeed, within an immigrant society, has Chicano cinema, though Afro-American cinema reaches back to Oscar Micheaux and has broken into the mainstream with Spike Lee and others. . . .

CONCLUSIONS

. . . In general, this essay seeks to enable a consideration of national cinemas in non–First World terms. This firstly requires acknowledging a wider range of national cinemas than is regularly treated under that rubric. Film scholars' mental maps of world film production are often less than global. Even as assiduously encyclopedic an historian as George Sadoul devotes more pages of his *Histoire du Cinéma* to the Brighton School and the beginnings of Pathé than he does to the whole of Latin American cinema between 1900 and 1962.[36] As Edward Said magisterially demonstrates with reference to "Orientalism" as academic discipline and world-view, so the world-views of different national film cultures are substantially informed by their country's relations—military, economic, diplomatic, cultural, ethnic—with other parts of the globe.[37] Thus Sadoul, informed by French colonialism, knows more of African cinema than of Latin American, while an American scholar, informed by the U.S. imperium and substantial Hispanic immigration, knows more of Latin American than African cinema, and a British scholar, informed by European and American cultural influences, may not see much outside that transatlantic axis. At the other end of the East-West axis, a hybrid, non-Eurocentric film culture such as the Thai—even if it does not as yet support substantial film scholarship—draws substantially on both Hong Kong and Hollywood sources as well as local production. Annette Hamilton thus remarks that "the average viewer in Thailand or Singapore has been exposed to a much wider range of visual material in style, genre, and cultural code that is the case for any 'average Western viewer.' "[38]

Such skewed world views will demonstrably influence canon formation in the country concerned. And given that Third World production—for that is the prime excluded category—is more plentiful than European and North American by a factor of more than 2 to 1[39], Luis Buñuel's trenchant comments on the canon of world literature could justly apply to that of world cinema:

It seems clear to me that without the enormous influence of the canon of American culture, Steinbeck would be an unknown, as would Dos Passos and Hemingway. If they'd been born in Paraguay or Turkey, no one would ever have read them, which suggests the alarming fact that the greatness of a writer is in direct proportion to the power of his/her country. Galdós, for instance, is often as remarkable as Dostoevski, but who outside Spain ever reads him?[40]

1993

---

[36]George Sadoul, *Histoire du Cinéma*, 1962, pp. 43–64, 421–37.
[37]Said 1985.
[38]Hamilton 1992, p. 91.
[39]Sadoul 1962, pp. 530–31.
[40]Buñuel 1984[1982], p. 222.

Armes, Roy
1987 *Third World Film Making and the West,* Berkeley and London: University of
    California Press.
Berry, Chris
1992 "Race, Chinese Film and the Politics of Nationalism," *Cinema Journal* vol 31, no. 2,
    Winter.
Bordwell, David
1979 "Art Film as a Mode of Film Practice," *Film Criticism* vol 4, no 1.
1985 *Narration in the Fiction Film,* London: Methuen.
Buñuel, Luis
1984 [1982] *My Last Sigh,* London: Jonathan Cape.
Burton, Julianne
1985 "Marginal Cinemas and Mainstream Critical Theory," *Screen* vol 26, no. 3–4,
    May–August.
Coorey, Philip and Amarnath Jayatilaka
1974 "Sri Lanka (Ceylon)," in Peter Cowie, ed., *International Film Guide*, London:
    Tantivy Press.
Crisp, Colin
Classic French Cinema, 1930–1960, Bloomington: Indiana University Press, 1993.
Crofts, Stephen
1972 *Jean-Luc Godard,* London: British Film Institute.
1976 "Ideology and Form: Soviet Socialist Realism and Chapayev," *Film Form* no 1.
1990 "Crocodile Dundee Overseas," *Cinema Papers* no 77, January.
D'Lugo, Marvin
1991 "Catalan Cinema: Historical Experience and Cinematic Practice," *Quarterly Review
    of Film and Video* vol 13, no. 1–3.
Elsaesser, Thomas
1987 "Chronicle of a Death Retold," *Monthly Film Bulletin* vol 54, no. 641, June.
1989 *New German Cinema: A History,* London: Macmillan.
Getino, Octavio and Fernando Solanas
1969 "Towards a Third Cinema," *Afterimage* no 3.
Guback, Thomas
1976 "Hollywood's International Market," in Tino Balio, ed., *The American Film Industry*,
    University of Wisconsin Press.
Hamilton, Annette
1992 "The Mediascape of Modern Southeast Asia," *Screen* vol 33, no. 1, Spring.
King, John
1990 *Magical Reels: A History of Cinema in Latin America*, London: Verso.
Leahy, James
1991 "Beyond the Frontiers," *Monthly Film Bulletin* vol 58, no. 686, March.
Lent, John
1990 *The Asian Film Industry*, Austin, Texas: University of Texas Press.
Moussinac, Leon
1967 [1925] *L'Age Ingrat du Cinéma*, Paris: EFR.
Neale, Steve
1981 "Art Cinema as Institution," *Screen* vol 22, no 1, Spring.
Nowell-Smith, Geoffrey
1985 "But Do We Need It?", in Martin Auty and Nick Roddick, eds., *British Cinema Now*,
    London: British Film Institute.

Pick, Zuzana
1987 "Chilean Cinema in Exile," *Framework* no 34.
Pines, Jim and Paul Willemen
1989 *Questions of Third Cinema*, London: British Film Institute.
Prédal, René
1990 "Un rassemblement mondial de talents," in Francis Bordat, ed., *L'amour du cinéma américain*, Paris: Cinémaction/Corlet/Télérama.
Rentschler, Eric
1982 "American Friends and the New German Cinema," *New German Critique* nos 24–5, Fall-Winter.
1984 *New German Cinema in the Course of Time*, Bedford Hills, New York: Redgrave.
Roddick, Nick
1985 "If the United States Spoke Spanish We Would Have a Film Industry," in Martin Auty and Nick Roddick, eds., *British Cinema Now*, London: British Film Institute.
Sadoul, Georges
1962 *Histoire du Cinéma*, Paris: Flammarion.
Said, Edward
1985 [1978] *Orientalism*, London: Penguin.
Sklar, Robert
1975 *Movie-Made America*, New York: Random House.
Solanas, Fernando
1990 "Amérique Latine: le point de vue d'un cinéaste," in Francis Bordat, ed., *L'amour du cinéma américain,* Paris: Cinémaction/Corlet/Télérama.
Stam, Robert
1991 "Eurocentrism, Afrocentrism, Polycentrism," *Quarterly Review of Film and Video* vol 13, nos. 1–3.
Thompson, Kristin
1985 *Exporting Entertainment: America in the World Film Market 1907–34*, London: British Film Institute.
Willemen, Paul
1987 "The Third Cinema Question: Notes and Reflections," *Framework* no 34.
Yoïchi, Umemoto
1990 "Quelles images pour le Japan?" in Francis Bordat, ed., *L'amour du cinéma américain*, Paris: Cinémaction/Corlet/Télérama.

MITSUHIRO YOSHIMOTO

THE DIFFICULTY OF BEING RADICAL: THE DISCIPLINE OF FILM STUDIES AND THE POSTCOLONIAL WORLD ORDER

Mitsuhiro Yoshimoto's first book *Kurosawa: Film Studies and Japanese Cinema* (2000) analyzes the shifting place of Japanese cinema within American film studies, Japanese studies, and comparative literature, arguing for an anti-essentialist, post-colonial, historically and culturally specific examination of Japanese films. He has advanced this project in *Empire of Images and the End of Cinema* (2007) and *Site of Resistance* (2007), co-written with Masao Miyoshi. Yoshimoto is currently professor of East Asian studies at New York University.

DISCOURSE ON THE OTHER

Dilemmas of Western Film Scholars?

Writing about national cinemas used to be an easy task: Film critics believed all they had to do was to construct a linear historical narrative describing a development of a cinema within a particular national boundary whose unity and coherence seemed to be beyond all doubt. Yet, this apparent obviousness of national cinema scholarship is now in great danger, since, on the one hand, we are no longer so sure about the coherence of the nation-state and, on the other hand, the idea of history has also become far from self-evident. As the question of authorship in the cinema was reproblematized by poststructuralist film theory, the notion of national cinema has been similarly put to an intense, critical scrutiny.

The problematic of national cinema scholarship becomes further complicated when we deal with non-Western national cinemas; these pose an additional problem with regard to the production of knowledge. It is often argued that any attempt to write about non-Western national cinemas should be accountable for all the complicated questions concerning the discourse on the Other. Writing about non-Western national cinemas has been situated in such a way that it is inescapable from the question, "Can we ever know the Other as the truly Other?"[1] What is required by

---

[1]Zhang Longxi, "The Myth of the Other: China in the Eyes of the West," *Critical Inquiry* 15, no. 1 (Autumn 1988): 127.

the hermeneutics of the Other sought out in non-Western national cinema scholarship is neither a simple identification with the Other nor an easy assimilation of the Other into the self. Instead, it is a construction of a new position of knowledge through a careful negotiation between the self and the Other.

To explore further this problematic of non-Western film scholarship, let us focus on the study of Japanese cinema. Not surprisingly, the axiomatics of the discursive mode of Japanese film scholarship has also been constructed on the opposition between the self and the Other or between Western theory and Japanese culture. This opposition in Japanese film studies creates a certain epistemological difficulty, which Peter Lehman summarizes as follows:

> Japan raises unique problems for Western film scholars. The situation can be summarized, perhaps a little too cynically, as follows: Western film scholars are accusing each other of being Western film scholars. Or to put it a bit more accurately, Western film scholars are accusing each other of being Western in their approach to Japanese film. Is this a genuine dilemma with possible solutions or is it a pseudo-issue which obscures the real issues? Is it productive for us as modern Western film scholars to pursue this quest for the proper Japanese response?[2]

As this passage suggests, there are many writings or metadiscourses on how to study the Japanese cinema properly, and by problematizing dilemmas of Western scholars of Japanese film, Lehman himself contributes to this thriving metadiscourse industry. More specifically, Lehman intervenes in critical exchanges between David Bordwell / Kristin Thompson, and Joseph Anderson / Paul Willemen.

One of the points of dispute in this controversy is whether we should call Ozu Yasujiro a modernist filmmaker. It starts with Bordwell and Thompson's claim that since the narrative mode of Ozu's films systematically defies the rules established by the classical Hollywood cinema, Ozu should be regarded as a modernist director. Paul Willemen criticizes Bordwell and Thompson by saying that to call Ozu a modernist is not so much different from European modernist artists' questionable appropriation of African tribal sculpture in the early twentieth century. Bordwell responds that Willemen's critique does not hold, since African sculptors never saw modernists' art work, but Ozu was thoroughly familiar with the Hollywood cinema. Lehman intervenes in this skirmish and takes side with Willemen. According to Lehman, Bordwell dismisses too easily the similarities between traditional Japanese art and Ozu's films, both of which, as Joseph Anderson points out, construct discontinuous, non-narrative space. Furthermore, Lehman quotes Willemen to claim that Bordwell has completely misunderstood the meaning of modernism:

> Ozu's films cannot be claimed as modernist, since the point about modernism is precisely that it is a *critique* of, not a neutral alternative to, dominant aesthetic practices.[3]

Lehman's critique of Bordwell and Thompson is well taken. We should all join Lehman and be "baffled as to why Bordwell and Thompson ever characterized Ozu

[2]Peter Lehman, "The Mysterious Orient, the Crystal Clear Orient, the Non-Existent Orient: Dilemmas of Western Scholars of Japanese Film," *Journal of Film and Video* 39, no. 1 (Winter 1987): 5.

[3]Lehman, "The Mysterious Orient," 8. Lehman quotes this passage from Paul Willemen, "Notes on Subjectivity: On Reading Edward Branigan's `Subjectivity under Siege,' " *Screen* 18, no. 1 (1978): 56.

as a modernist in the first place."[4] At the same time, we should also be appalled by Willemen's and Lehman's Eurocentric view of modernism, which does not consider what modernism possibly means for the non-West. A seemingly innocent question of Ozu's modernity, in fact, cannot be answered unless we carefully take into account the specificities of Japanese cinema, social formations, and history. Such a problematic in Japanese or non-Western cinema scholarship will finally lead to many more fundamental questions concerning the definitions of a nation and of a cinema.

The Subject of Cross-Cultural Analysis

The possibility of studying a non-Western national cinema without erasing its own specificities has been recently attempted in the emerging field of Chinese film studies. E. Ann Kaplan's essay on the Chinese cinema shows great sensitivity toward the issue of cultural specificities and the difficulty of what she calls "cross-cultural analysis."[5] As Kaplan points out, "Cross-cultural analysis . . . is difficult—fraught with danger," since "[w]e are forced to read works produced by the Other through the constraints of our own frameworks/theories/ideologies" (CCA, 42). Yet, despite its inherent danger, according to Kaplan, it is still worth attempting cross-cultural analysis, because "theorists outside the producing culture might uncover different strands of the multiple meanings than critics of the originating culture just because they bring different frameworks/theories/ideologies to the texts" (CCA, 42). The question is whether cross-cultural analysis can really contribute to a cultural exchange between two different cultures on an equal basis, to the understanding of the Other without making it fit to the underlying assumptions of the analyst's own culture, or simply, to a nondominating way of knowing and understanding the Other.

The major feature of Kaplan's essay is its nonlinearity. It contains so many questions, self-reflexive remarks, and qualifications; that is, the tone of the essay is, as Kaplan says, "tentative":

> So, on the one hand, we have Chinese film scholars turning to American and European film theories to see what might be useful for them, in their writing on both American film and their own cinema; on the other hand, we have some American scholars writing tentative essays on Chinese films. (Those scholars, like Chris Berry, who have lived in China and know the culture and the language are obviously no longer "tentative.") We have, then, a sort of informal film-culture exchange of a rather unusual kind, precisely because of its relative informality. (CCA, 40)

Kaplan's essay on the Chinese cinema is tentative because she has not lived in China and does not know the Chinese language and culture. Yet, according to Kaplan, this tentativeness of informal discourse can become formal knowledge if one goes to and lives in China and becomes an expert in things Chinese. Thus, there is nothing *unusual* about this "informal film-culture exchange"; on the contrary, the model of cross-cultural exchange presented here is a classic example of what Gayatri Spivak calls the "arrogance of the radical European humanist conscience, which will

---

[4]Lehman, "The Mysterious Orient," 8.

[5]E. Ann Kaplan, "Problematizing Cross-Cultural Analysis: The Case of Women in the Recent Chinese Cinema," *Wide Angle* 11, no. 2 (1989): 40–50; hereafter cited in my text as CCA.

consolidate it*self* by imagining the other, or, as Sartre puts it, 'redo in himself the other's project,' through the collection of information."[6]

As we will see in a moment, the mapping of critical discourses on the Chinese cinema by Kaplan is remarkably similar to the polarized scholarship on the Japanese cinema. While either the Western or native expert on a national cinema provides specific information about the cultural background of that cinema, the Western theorist constructs a theoretical framework that gives rise to new insight on the aspects of the national cinema never noticed by area studies experts before. The only difference is that the position of the theorist has become less certain vis-à-vis the non-Western culture, so that any theoretical analysis of the Other can no longer escape a certain sense of hesitation that is hard to find in actual writings on the Japanese cinema.

This sense of hesitation about Western intellectuals' own critical position on and distance from the non-Western culture is widespread in the postmodern West, and compared to the extreme logical consequences reached by postmodern critical ethnography, Kaplan's self-reflexive essay does not go far enough. By pushing to the limit the self-examination of knowledge production in relation to the Other, postmodern critical ethnography has radically put into question not only the position of the analyzing subject, equipped with the latest knowledge of theory and critical methodologies, but also those of the expert subject and the "radical European [or American] humanist conscience" that claim to know the Other based on the authenticity of experience and self-claimed deep understanding of the Other's culture.

In his essay on the Japanese cinema, Scott Nygren attempts to re-articulate the terms of cross-cultural exchange between Japan and the West from a "postmodern perspective." Nygren argues that postmodernism puts into question a linear, evolutionary model of history constructed by a paradigm of modernism, so that "a discontinuous and reversible model of history now seems more productive in conceptualizing cross-cultural relationships."[7] Instead of accepting the traditional view that modern Japanese history is a history of mere imitation and assimilation of the West, Nygren proposes an alternative relation between the West and Japan, characterized by a mutual cross-cultural exchange: Traditional Japanese culture gave inspiration to Western modernists as much as Western humanism had a deconstructive impact on feudal aspects of Japanese society. Nygren thus posits a chiasmatic correspondence between Japan and the West on the one hand and between tradition and modernism on the other:

> This paper will argue that classical Hollywood conventions often valorized (although misleadingly) under the name "realism" served to reinforce dominant cultural ideology in the West, while functioning to deconstruct dominant values in Japan. . . . Although the influence of Japanese traditional culture on the formation of Western modernism is

---

[6]Gayatri Chakravorty Spivak, "Theory in the Margin: Coetzee's *Foe* Reading Defoe's *Crusoe/Roxana*," in *Consequences of Theory*, ed. Jonathan Arac and Barbara Johnson (Baltimore: Johns Hopkins University Press, 1991), 155. The passage quoted continues as follows: "Much of our literary critical globalism or Third Worldism cannot even qualify to the conscientiousness of this arrogance."

[7]Scott Nygren, "Reconsidering Modernism: Japanese Film and the Postmodernist Context," *Wide Angle* 11, no. 3 (1989): 7.

well known, in many respects the situation in Japan was the reverse: it was Western tradition, not Western modernism, that played a key role in the formation of what we call "Japanese modernism."[8]

What Nygren attempts to find in this reversed specularity is an "alternative access to a postmodern situation":

> If postmodernism is conceived in the West as a non-progressivist freeplay of traditionalist and modernist signification without progressivist determinism, is it possible to discuss a postmodernist reconfiguration of Japanese culture where Western values of humanism and anti-humanism seem reversed in their relation to tradition and the modern? Can Asian societies in general be theorized in terms of an alternative access to a postmodernist situation?[9]

Yet, this particular model of cross-cultural exchange between the West and Japan, in light of the postmodernism articulated in the passages above, begs the basic facts of West/non-West relations.

There is no need for us to remind ourselves that the West and the non-West do not voluntarily engage in cross-cultural exchange. The relation between the two has always taken the form of political, economic, and cultural domination of the non-West by the West. Not surprisingly, the emergence of modern Japanese literature and film more or less coincides with the age of high imperialism and nationalism. Yet, nowhere in the text do we find questions concerning the ineluctable relations existing among modernism, imperialism, and nationalism (or nativism). Is it the case that by providing Japan with Western tradition, which is said "to deconstruct dominant values in Japan," Western imperialism had some empowering effect on Japan? I don't think this is what is argued in the essay; yet at the same time, it is hard not to deduce this disturbing conclusion from the essay's logic.[10]

The notions of cross-cultural analysis and cross-cultural exchange are ideologically dubious for the following reasons. First, as we will see in a moment, it contributes to the concealment of the questionable, complicit division of national cinema scholarship between history and theory. Second, it also contributes to the myth of a specular relation between Western theory and non-Western practice. In film studies, there are many examples of arguments perpetuating this myth. We have just discussed two examples above. Another powerful instance can also be found in the field of Japanese film studies. In *To the Distant Observer: Form and Meaning in the Japanese Cinema*, which still remains the most provocative study on the Japanese cinema in any language, Noel Burch calls for the "possibility of an immense productive relationship which could and should be developed between contemporary

---

[8]Nygren, "Reconsidering Modernism," 8.

[9]Nygren, "Reconsidering Modernism," 7.

[10]In her essay on the writing of history, Janet Abu-Lughod cautions us that "with each higher level of generality, there are reduced options for reconceptualization. That is why I believe it is absolutely essential, if we are to get away from Eurocentric views of the universe, to 'pick our respondents' carefully and broadly." See "On the Remaking of History: How to Reinvent the Past," in *Remaking History*, ed. Barbara Kruger and Phil Mariani (Seattle: Bay Press, 1989), 118. Those who write on Japan as nonspecialists necessarily have to depend on the works by specialists, which are already interpretations of the primary materials. There is nothing wrong with this dependency itself; the problem is that they often choose wrong authorities to support their argument.

European theory and Japanese practice." "And," continues Burch, "Marxism had always regarded such mutually informative relationships between theory and practice as essential to its growth."[11] Inspired by Roland Barthes's "study" of "Japan," *Empire of Signs*, Burch constructs a utopia called "Japan," in which Western critical theory materializes its critical insight in concrete artistic practices. Japan as the Other is then conceived as mere supplement, safety contained within the epistemological limit of the West.

Examples of this discursive mode are not confined within Japanese film scholarship. Julianne Burton presents a similar view in her article on Third World cinema and First World theory, "Marginal Cinemas and Mainstream Critical Theory."[12] While Burch tries to establish a complementary relation between Western theory and Japanese practice, Burton attempts to appropriate Third World cinema within the sphere of Western critical discourse by designating the former "marginal" and the latter "mainstream." In Burton's scheme, critics of Third World cinema should be enlightened by the insights of Western critical theory, particularly by the "theory of mediation," and Western critical theory in turn should be modified so that it can accommodate and appropriate Third World films and the specific contexts surrounding them. This sounds good as far as it goes. But who in the end benefits by this cross-cultural exchange? Who dictates the terms of this transaction between the West and the Third World?[13] Burton's critique of Third World filmmakers and critics is dependent on her misuse of the concept of mediation. She does not use this crucial concept to articulate the relation between Third World film practices and various subtexts of film production and consumption. Rather, Burton has recourse to the concept of mediation to insert Western theorists into the position of subject, which, by criticizing the naïveté of Third World practitioners who believe in "unmediated" transparency of meaning, plays the role of "mediator" between Western high theory and Third World practice not only for the First World audience of Third World film but also for Third World people as the uninitiated.

In his essay on the Third Cinema debate, Homi Bhabha argues that critical theory's appropriation of the Other as a good object of knowledge is an epistemological colonization of the non-West:

> Montesquieu's Turkish Despot, Barthes' Japan, Kristeva's China, Derrida's Nambikwara Indians, Lyotard's Cashinahua "pagans" are part of this strategy of containment where the Other text is forever the exegetical horizon of difference, never the active agent of articulation. The Other is cited, quoted, framed, illuminated, encased in the shot/reverse-shot strategy of a serial enlightenment. Narrative and the *cultural* politics of difference become the closed circle of interpretation. The Other loses its power to signify, to negate, to initiate its "desire," to split its "sign" of identity, to establish

---

[11]Noel Burch, *To the Distant Observer: From and Meaning in the Japanese Cinema* (Berkeley: University of California Press, 1979), 13; hereafter cited in my text as *JC*.

[12]Julianne Burton, "Marginal Cinemas and Mainstream Critical Theory," *Screen* 26, nos. 3–4 (May–August 1985): 2–21.

[13]For an extensive critique of Julianne Burton's argument, see Teshome H. Gabriel, "Colonialism and 'Law and Order' Criticism," *Screen* 27, nos. 3–4 (May–August 1986): 140–47. See also Scott Cooper, "The Study of Third Cinema in the United States: A Reaffirmation," in *Questions of Third Cinema*, ed. Jim Pines and Paul Willemen (London: BFI, 1989): 218–22.

its own institutional and oppositional discourse. However impeccably the content of an "other" culture may be known, however anti-ethnocentrically it is represented, it is its *location* as the "closure" of grand theories, the demand that, in analytic terms, it be always the "good" object of knowledge, the docile body of difference, that reproduces a relation of domination and is the most serious indictment of the institutional powers of critical theory.[14]

Interestingly, the title of Bhabha's essay is "The Commitment to Theory," not "The Indictment of Theory," although what Bhabha argues is diametrically opposite to Burton's project. This false resemblance between the two, or the double nature of theory in relation to the Other, is precisely a sign of the complexity of the problem we must deal with. What is to be done is neither a simple celebration nor condemnation of critical theory; instead, what is at stake is the precise location of theory in critical discourse on/of/by the non-West. This problematic of theory will be discussed more fully in the following sections, but for a moment, I would like to come back to my third point about the notion of cross-cultural exchange (or analysis). By designating only one direction of subject-object relation, this popular notion elides the issue of power/knowledge. While Western critics as subject can analyze a non-Western text as object, non-Western critics are not allowed to occupy the position of subject to analyze a Western text as object. When non-Western critics study English literature or French cinema, it is not called cross-cultural analysis. Whatever they say is interpreted and judged only within the context of Western discourses. The cross-cultural analysis, which is predicated on the masking of power relations in the production of knowledge, is a newer version of legitimating cultural colonization of the non-West by the West.

A binarism of self/Other, which underlies the project of cross-cultural analysis, is a trap. It abstracts the role of power in the production of knowledge, and depoliticizes the structure of domination found in West/non-West opposition. The studies of non-Western national cinemas based on the axiomatics of self/Other opposition cannot but reproduce the hegemonic ideology of Western neocolonialism. It can produce knowledge on non-Western national cinemas only for those who can put themselves into the position of the subject (i.e., Western theorists). Discourse on the Other and its corollary, cross-cultural analysis, not only fix the non-West as the object to be appropriated but also transform serious political issues into bad philosophical questions. For instance, as we have already observed, Peter Lehman's critique of Bordwell, Thompson, Heath, and so forth is right on target; however, the dilemmas of Western scholars of Japanese film on which he speculates are also false dilemmas created by the mistaken assumptions and premises of meta-discourses on Japanese film criticism. Being dependent on the framework of self/Other dichotomy, Lehman misses what is fundamentally at stake: The structural dilemma created by discourse on the Other is in fact only a disguise for a legitimation of Western subjectivity supported by another fundamental opposition underlying Japanese film scholarship.

[14.] Homi K. Bhabha, "The Commitment to Theory," in *Questions of Third Cinema*, 124.

HISTORY AND THEORY

Two Types of Japanese Film Scholarship

In *Cinema: A Critical Dictionary*, edited by Richard Roud, there are seven entries on Japanese directors; of these seven, three essays (on Mizoguchi, Naruse, and Ozu) are written by Donald Richie, while Noel Burch contributes two essays (on Kurosawa and Oshima).[15] This division of labor in Roud's volume mirrors the two different types of Japanese film scholarship: On the one hand, the Japanese film and area studies specialists tend to take up the historical study of Japanese cinema, since they possess a good command of the Japanese language and are familiar with Japanese culture but not with the theoretical advancement made in film studies; on the other hand, film critics well versed in theory but not in the Japanese language write on Japanese cinema from "theoretical perspectives."

The critic who represents area studies specialists is Donald Richie, whose *Japanese Film: Art and Industry*,[16] cowritten with Joseph Anderson, is a combination of conventional, linear narrative sketching the development of the Japanese film industry and a compilation of chronologically arranged, short commentaries on hundreds of films. If, as the blurb by David Bordwell on the back cover of the book says, *The Japanese Film* is really "the definitive study in any Western language of the Japanese cinema," it is presumably because Richie and Anderson know the language and culture, or simply Japan. The fact that Richie freely draws on his firsthand knowledge of directors like Ozu and Kurosawa also seemingly gives a sense of authenticity to his other important books on those directors and secures his position as the authority of the Japanese cinema. What Richie embodies in Japanese film scholarship is the figure of cultural expert. What is appreciated and valued is the authenticity of the personal experience of the (anthropologist) expert "who was actually there."

In contrast to the empiricism of Donald Richie, the strength of a theoretical study is said to lie in the analyst's mediated detachment from the object of study. The importance of Noel Burch's work on the Japanese cinema is derived precisely from this sense of detachment as a result of his unfamiliarity with the mass of native Japanese discourses. By radically decontextualizing the Japanese cinema, Burch has succeeded in displacing the Japanese cinema from the margin to the forefront of contemporary film scholarship and, however indirectly, has contributed to the critique of ethnocentrism in the institution of film studies.

Thus, the real division in Japanese film scholarship is created not by the West/Japan dichotomy but by the opposition between theory and history. What is at stake is not simply the shortcomings of either theoretical work (Burch) or historical study (Richie) but the unproblematic division between history and theory itself. Generally speaking, both sides are quite respectful of each other and do not meddle in the affairs of the other group. Far from creating antagonism, the split

---

[15]Richard Roud, ed., *Cinema: A Critical Dictionary*, 2 vols. (London: Martin Secker and Warburg, 1980).
[16]Joseph L. Anderson and Donald Richie, *The Japanese Film: Art and Industry*, expanded ed. (Princeton: Princeton University Press, 1982).

within Japanese film studies has reached a curious equilibrium, a peaceful coexistence of theorists with area studies specialists. It is this mutually complicit relation between theory and history that should be questioned and re-articulated. Put another way, we need to reexamine how the differentiation of empirical history from abstract theory creates an illusion that different critical approaches could democratically coexist side by side without any interference. What is at stake in the end is not a specific problem debated in the field of Japanese film studies but the question of how Japanese film studies is constructed as an academic subdiscipline.[17]

The Classical Hollywood Cinema and a New Tribal Art

The theoretical mode of Japanese film studies derives its impetus from the rigorous theorization of the narrational mode of Hollywood cinema and a renewed interest in possible radical alternatives. One of the major accomplishments of film studies is the deconstruction of the sense of continuity and the impression of reality created by the Hollywood cinema. It has been shown that that sense of continuity becomes possible precisely because of, for instance, numerous discontinuities whose existence is concealed by a series of alternations and repetitions constructing symmetrical structures. In theoretical studies of the Japanese cinema, the indigenous mode of Japanese film practice, based on structural principles of traditional art—privileging of surface over depth, presentation instead of representation, organization of nonlinear, non-narrative signifiers, and so on—is said to be inherently radical and thus puts into question the representational mode of the classical Hollywood cinema. From this particular theoretical perspective, Burch rewrites the history of the Japanese cinema in order to present the Japanese cinema as a prime example of an alternative to the institutional mode of representation.

Understandably, this theoretical tyranny of Burch's argument is not unchallenged. David Desser is one of those who question Burch's formalist position; however, by accepting formalist reification of a form/content division, he presents a confused counterproposal. According to Desser, "since traditional Japanese art is already formally subversive, a genuinely radical, political Japanese art must move beyond the merely formally subversive; it must also move beyond the kind of radical content apparent in the prewar tendency films or the postwar humanistic, left-wing cinema of the 1950s."[18] To the extent that he asserts the formal subversiveness of traditional Japanese art, Desser writes within the framework constructed by Noel Burch, and his criticism is not really a criticism but a revision within a formalist framework. The questions I would like to ask are much more simple and fundamental: What does traditional Japanese art subvert? Is it, as Burch argues, the representational mode of the

---

[17]For instance, see David Desser, *Eros Plus Massacre: An Introduction to the Japanese New Wave Cinema* (Bloomington: Indiana University Press, 1988), 2–3. Desser argues that his purpose is to "situate the New Wave within a particular historical, political, and cultural context" without challenging the already existing other modes of critical discourse. Yet contextualization should not be mere supplement to theoretical abstraction or formalism. If it is merely supplemental, then, that mode of contextualization is nothing more than vulgar historicism. When it takes the form of a radical questioning, contextualization becomes a critical practice of *mediation*, which demolishes the edifice of democratic pluralism.

[18]Desser, *Eros Plus Massacre*, 24.

classical Hollywood cinema? What does traditional Japanese art have to do with the Hollywood cinema?

The classical Hollywood cinema has certainly played a crucial role in the formation of any national cinema that had access to it, yet it can never have complete control over how a particular national cinema is constructed. A national cinema as the culture industry exists in a complex web of economic, ideological, and social relations, and the classical Hollywood cinema constitutes only one element of those relations. As Judith Mayne correctly points out, the excessive emphasis on the classical Hollywood cinema as the norm has a constrictive effect on the attempt to study and/or search for an "alternative" cinema:

> The classical Hollywood cinema has become the norm against which all other alternative practices are measured. Films which do not engage the classical Hollywood cinema are by and large relegated to irrelevance. Frequently, the very notion of an "alternative" is posed in the narrow terms of an either-or: either one is within classical discourse and therefore complicit, or one is critical of and/or resistant to it and therefore outside of it.[19]

Nobody can question the dominance of the Hollywood cinema in the world film market. However, this does not automatically mean that the Hollywood cinema has been dominant trans-historically or trans-culturally. We need to put the Hollywood cinema in specific historical contexts; instead of talking about the Hollywood cinema as the norm, we must examine the specific and historically changing relations between the Hollywood cinema and other national cinemas.[20]

Other questions concern a special position accorded to the Japanese cinema in non-Western national cinema scholarship. Why has the Japanese cinema become so important in the battle against the institutional mode of representation? Why can the Japanese cinema be so easily incorporated into theoretical discourses of Anglo-American film studies, while theory seems to become problematic in the analysis of, say, the Chinese cinema? Why suddenly has the possibility of cross-cultural analysis become an issue in the analysis of the Chinese cinema, while it has never been an issue in studies of the Japanese cinema, except in various metadiscourses that appeared mostly in the form of review essays?

One way of approaching these questions is to go back to the issues of modernism, the avant-garde, and the Japanese cinema to which I briefly refer in the beginning of this essay. For Bordwell and Thompson, Ozu is a modernist filmmaker in a class with Dreyer, Bresson, Godard, and the like. For Burch, the prewar Japanese cinema as a unified whole is comparable to European avant-garde cinemas. Despite the difference in their claim and the register of concepts used in their argument, Burch and Bordwell/Thompson participate in the same critical project. In both cases, the logic used to legitimate their claims is dependent on the observable formal features commonly found in two groups of objects that are drastically different in other aspects. To this extent, Burch, Bordwell, and Thompson's argument seems to be a variation

---

[19]Judith Mayne, *Kino and the Woman Question* (Columbus: Ohio State University Press, 1989), 3.

[20]For the specific place of Hollywood in the postwar Japanese cultural system, see my forthcoming "The Aporia of Modernity: The Japanese Cinema and the 1960s," (Ph.D. diss., University of California, San Diego).

of the discourse of art history claiming the existence of affinity between modern and tribal artifacts. This formalist logic is criticized by James Clifford as wishful thinking by Western critics:

> Actually the tribal and modern artifacts are similar only in that they do not feature the pictorial illusionism or sculptural naturalism that came to dominate Western European art after the Renaissance. Abstraction and conceptualism are, of course, pervasive in the arts of the non-Western World. To say that they share with modernism a rejection of certain naturalist projects is not to show anything like an affinity. . . .

> The affinity of the tribal and the modern is, in this logic, an important optical illusion—the measure of a *common differentness* from artistic modes that dominated in the West from the Renaissance to the late nineteenth century.[21]

But what Burch and Bordwell/Thompson argue is more "radical" than a kind of colonial discourse questioned by Clifford. For what they find is not just affinity but identity between the Western avant-garde and the Japanese cinema or Ozu and Western modernist filmmakers. For their projects, a mere affinity or optical illusion is not enough, so that, for instance, according to Burch, instead of merely resembling avant-garde practices, the Japanese cinema should be an avant-garde art. Burch's purpose is to find an autonomous group of film practices that is not analogous to but identical with what he calls avant-garde.

By the recent Japanese film scholarship, the Japanese cinema is construed as a new tribal art. At the same time, the emphasis on identity instead of affinity also makes it the avant-garde in the guise of a tribal art. For this reason, Burch and others choose to study Japanese but not Chinese, Indian, or any other non-Western national cinemas. The double identity of the cinema—tribal *and* avant-garde—requires them to choose the cinema of a nation that is perceived to be sufficiently different from, but have some common elements with, Western capitalist nations. Japan fulfills their utopian dream. On the one hand, Japan is exotic; according to Burch, "Japan offer[s] traits which seem even more remote from our own, Western ways of thinking and doing, more remote than comparable traits of other Far-Eastern societies" (*JC*, 89). On the other hand, an exotic Japan is similar enough to the West, since "these traits also lend themselves to *a Marxist critique of modern Western history in many of its aspects*" (*JC*, 89). Burch sublates the contradiction of Japan and the Japanese cinema by situating them "with regard both to the dominant ideological profile of Western Europe and the Americas, and to those practices, scientific, literary and artistic, which instantiate the Marxist critique of that dominance" (*JC*, 89). What makes Burch's sublation possible is Japan's ambivalent geopolitical position: economically part of the First World but culturally part of the Third World. The dialectic of the traditional art form and Western influences that Burch finds in the history of the Japanese cinema is homologous with the schizophrenic division of Japan's relations to other nations.

---

[21]James Clifford, *The Predicament of Culture: Twentieth-Century Ethnography, Literature, and Art* (Cambridge: Harvard University Press, 1988), 192.

CONCLUSION

The genealogy of film studies shows that it started as a contestation against the academicism in the 1960s and remained in the forefront of the changing humanities and a redrawing of disciplinary boundaries. In the name of the avant-garde and subversion, however, film studies has consolidated itself as a respectable academic discipline whose discursive organization is not very different from such a traditional discipline as literary studies. One of the concrete examples of this irony can be observed in the division of labor in national cinema studies, which uncannily mirrors the geopolitical configuration and division of a contemporary postcolonial world order. The opposition between the classical Hollywood cinema and the alternative modes of film practices is created with a good intention of avant-garde radicalism; however, the kind of politics articulated in this binarism is a different matter entirely. In the peculiar division of national cinema studies, American, European, Japanese, and other non-Western cinemas are studied to promote distinctively different critical and political agendas. Therefore, we need to carefully reexamine whether, by engaging ourselves in national cinema studies, we are mechanically reproducing, instead of analyzing, the ideological picture of a postcolonial world situation constructed by Western postindustrial nations. More precisely, we must question whether, in the name of critical opposition to Hollywood, we are, on the contrary, contributing to the hegemony of and the accumulation of cultural capital by the United States.

How can we stop fashioning the discipline of film studies into a mirror of postcolonial world geopolitics? Can the neocolonial logic of film studies be corrected by going back to that perennial epistemological question, "Can we ever know the Other as the truly Other?" The problem here is not that this question is too complicated to be sufficiently answered by any response; that is, the problem is not the impossibility of the answer but the formulation of this particular question itself. By construing the Other as the sole bearer of difference, this seemingly sincere question does nothing but conceal the fundamentally problematic nature of the identity of the self.

The so-called imperialist misrepresentation or appropriation of the Other is an oxymoron. The Other cannot be misrepresented, since it is always already a misrepresentation. Imperialism starts to show its effect not when it domesticates the Other but the moment it posits the difference of the Other against the identity of the self. This fundamental imperialism of the self/Other dichotomy can never be corrected by the hermeneutics of the Other or cross-cultural exchange; on the contrary, the latter reinforces the imperialist logic under the guise of liberal humanism, or what Spivak calls "neocolonial anticolonialism."

Let us debunk once and for all the imperialist logic of questions based on the self/Other dichotomy. Let us go back to that spirit of true radicalism that once made film studies such an exciting space for critical thinking.

1991

WIMAL DISSANAYAKE
ISSUES IN WORLD CINEMA

Born in Sri Lanka, Wimal Dissanayake has written extensively on Asian cinema and literature, particularly the construction of national identity within Southeast Asian film, with special attention to the work of Wong Kar-wai, Satyajit Ray, and Raj Kapoor. He has also co-edited several texts on communication theory and cultural studies, focusing on the construction of self in East Asian culture. A poet who writes in both Sinhalese and English, Dissanayake has also edited a number of anthologies, including *Melodrama and Asian Cinema* (1993), *Colonialism and Nationalism in Asian Cinema* (1994), and *Sights of Contestation: Localism, Globalism and Cultural Production in Asia* (2004). Founder of the *East-West Film Journal*, he is currently a lecturer in the Academy for Creative Media at the University of Hawaii at Manoa.

Dadasaheb Phalke, who is generally regarded by Indian film historians as the father of Indian cinema, relates an interesting anecdote. His *Raja Harishchandra*, released on 3 May 1913, is highlighted by scholars as the first Indian feature film. Phalke tells us that he was inspired to make this film after seeing the movie *The Life of Christ* (USA, 1906) in the America–India Picture Palace in Bombay in 1910. As he was watching the film, he was overwhelmed by both a deep religiosity and an awareness of the potentialities of the art of cinematography. As he watched the life of Christ unfold before his eyes, he thought of the gods Krishna and Ramachandra and wondered how long it would be before Indians would be able to see Indian images of their divinities on screen. In fact, it was not long: three years later Phalke made the first Indian feature film based on the celebrated Indian epic the *Ramayana*. However, what this anecdote—and many similar ones by the early filmmakers in Asia, Latin America, and Africa—points to is a series of binaries that underpin the discourse of cinema in those continents: binaries of Westernization and indigenization, tradition and modernity, the local and the global. Any discussion of these cinemas, and the trajectories of their development, must necessarily address these crucial issues.

However, it is important that we do not lump these cinemas together indiscriminately as non-Western. It is, of course; true that, geographically, they are from the non-Western world (with "Western" here referring to North America and Europe), and that they share many interests and preoccupations. However, . . . although they may display commonalities of interest, each of the countries, because of its specific

877

social formations and historical conjunctures, has its own distinctive trajectories of cinematic development and concerns.

In the same way, we must also avoid treating non-Western cinemas as expressive of some unchanging "essence." Instead, we must see them as sites of discursive contestations, or representational spaces, in which changing social and cultural meanings are generated and fought over. The discursive boundaries of the various societies that constitute the non-Western world are constantly expanding and cannot be accounted for in essentialist terms. Moreover, the filmmakers and film commentators (critics as well as scholars) who are at the leading edge of development of the film cultures of their respective societies have been exposed to, and in many cases trained in, Western countries so that their self-positioning in relation to the contours of their specific cultures is understandably complex and multifaceted.

The concept of Third Cinema, originally formulated by the Argentinian film directors Fernando Solanas and Octavio Getino[1] and later expanded by film scholars such as Teshome H. Gabriel[2], addresses a number of issues related to non-Western cinemas. Put simply, one can say that First Cinema refers to mainstream Hollywood cinema, and Second Cinema to European "art" cinema. In distinguishing it from First and Second Cinemas, proponents of Third Cinema see it as the articulation of a new culture and a vehicle of social transformation. Paul Willemen,[3] however, suggests how the manifestos laying out the guiding ideas of Third Cinema give the impression that it was developed by Latin Americans for Latin America and that its wider applicability was added as an afterthought. He also argues that there is a danger in the concept of Third Cinema of homogenizing non-Western cinema and not grappling sufficiently with questions of ethnic and gender divisions as well as the vexed relationship between cinema and nationhood. It is this complicated relationship between nationhood and cinema with which we shall begin.

NATIONHOOD AND CINEMA

Nationhood, as with all other forms of identity, revolves around the question of difference, with how the uniqueness of one nation differs from the uniqueness of other comparable nations. Benedict Anderson[4] suggests that nationhood may be understood as an "imagined community," and indicates how nationhood is a cultural artiefact of a particular kind. It is imagined, because the members of even the smallest nation can never get to know, or even meet, most of their fellow members; yet in the imagination of each the notion of the nation persists. The nation is also imagined as a community because, regardless of the very real inequities and injustices that exist in society, it is always perceived as deep and horizontal comradeship. It is important, however, to note that Anderson employed the term "imagined" and not "imaginary." "Imaginary" signifies absence, or nothingness, while "Imagined" foregrounds a nice

[1]Fernando E. Solanas and Octavio Getino, *Cine: cultura y descolonizacion* (Buenos Aires: Siglo XXI Argentino Editores, 1973).

[2]Teshome K. Gabriel, *Third Cinema in the Third World* (Ann Arbor, MI: UMI Research Press, 1982).

[3]Paul Willemen, *Questions of Third Cinema* (London: British Film Institute, 1989).

[4]Benedict Anderson, *Imagined Communities: Reflections on the Origin and Spread of Nationalism* (London: Verso, 1983).

balance between the real and not the real. The critical weakness of Benedict Anderson's formulation, however, is that it pays scant attention to materialities and underplays the discontinuities of history. It also minimizes the salience of the political character of nationhood and the role that ethnicity and religion have played in the construction of the nation. Any investigation into the ways in which cinema constructs nationhood, therefore, has to consider these thorny issues of ethnic loyalties, religious affinities, and local patriotism. It must also recognize that the nation also contains within itself diverse local narratives of resistance and memory and therefore take into account the full force of these local and dissenting narratives, which are embedded in the larger narrative of the nation.

It is evident that cinema is a very powerful cultural practice and institution that both reflects and inflects the discourse of nationhood. As a result, the concept of national cinema is at the base of many discussions of popular culture in Africa, Asia, the Middle East, and Latin America. It is generally analyzed at two interrelated levels: the textual and the industrial.... The textual level involves a focus upon the distinctiveness of a given cinema—whether it be Indonesian or Nigerian, Mexican or Senegalese—in terms of content, style, and indigenous aesthetics. The industrial level involves a focus upon the relationship between cinema and industry, the nature of film production, distribution, and consumption, and the ways in which the ever-present threats from Hollywood are met. However, it should also be noted that the concept of national cinema serves to privilege notions of coherence and unity and to stabilize cultural meanings linked to the perceived uniqueness of a given nation. As I have pointed out,[5] it is implicated in national myth-making and ideological production and serves to delineate both otherness and legitimate selfhood.

How a nation tells its unifying and legitimizing story about itself to its citizens is crucial in the understanding of nationhood, and after the popularization of cinema as a medium of mass entertainment in Latin America, Asia, the Middle East, and Africa, the role of cinema in this endeavor has come to occupy a significant place.... Benedict Anderson[6] focused attention on the centrality of print capitalism in giving rise to the idea of the nation and the deep horizontal comradeship it promoted. He observed that newspapers and nationalistic novels were primarily responsible for the creation of a national consciousness. In social circumstances that were antecedent to the establishment of nation-states, newspapers, journals, and fiction served to coordinate time and space in a way that enabled the formation of the imagined community that is the nation. In the contemporary world, cinema has assumed the status of a dominant medium of communication, and its role in conjuring up the imagined community among both the literate and illiterate strata of society is both profound and far-reaching. David Harvey[7] suggests that the way in which cinema works to capture the complex and dynamic relationship between temporality and spatiality is not available to other media, and this becomes a significant issue for non-Western cinemas.

---

[5]Wimal Dissanayake, *Colonialism and Nationalism in Asian Cinema* (Bloomington: Indiana University Press, 1994).

[6]Anderson, *Imagined Communities*.

[7]David Harvey, *The Condition of Postmodernity: An Enquiry into the Origins of Cultural Change* (Oxford: Blackwell, 1989).

The *topos* of nationhood becomes significant for another reason as well. Cinema in most countries in Africa, the Middle East, Asia, and Latin America is closely linked to the concept and functioning of the nation-state. Questions of economics—production, distribution, and exhibition—and control of content through overt and covert censorship have much to do with this. For most film producers in Latin American, African, and Asian countries that depend on the patronage of local audiences for returns on their investments, the assistance, intervention, and coordination of governments become extremely important (in the form of film corporations, training institutes, script boards, censorship panels, national festivals, and the honoring of filmmakers). It is evident, therefore, that the demands of the economics of film industries and the imperatives of the nation-state are interlinked in complex, and at times disconcertingly intrusive, ways.

Speaking in very broad terms, we can divide films made in Asia, Africa, and South America into three main groups: the popular, the artistic, and the experimental.... The popular films are commercial by nature and are designed to appeal to the vast mass of moviegoers and to secure the largest profit. The artistic films, although not immune to commercial pressures, are nonetheless driven by "high art" concerns and tend to be showcased at international film festivals. The experimental films are much smaller in number and much less visible in the filmic landscape; they are committed to the creation of an oppositional cinema characterized by an audacious attempt to interrogate the Establishment and its values. Thus, if we take India as an example, filmmakers such as Raj Kapoor, Manmohan Desai, and Ramesh Sippy represent the popular tradition; directors such as Satyajit Ray and Adoor Gopalakrishnan belong to the "art" tradition; while some of the work of Kumar Sahani and Mani Kaul may be categorized as experimental.... What is of interest in terms of the relationship between the nation-state and cinema is that—again in general terms—whereas popular cinema generally upholds notions of a unified nation, the artistic cinema tends to offer critiques of the nation-state (and its associated economic, social, political, and cultural discourses and institutions) and the experimental cinema characteristically calls into question the hegemonic project of the nation-state and the privileged vocabularies of national narration. Thus, in a large country like India with its numerous languages and religions, films produced in regional languages like Bengali or Malayalam tend to valorize, directly or obliquely, the regional at the expense of the national, thereby revealing certain fissures and fault lines in the national discourse. The artistic and experimental filmmakers seek to draw attention to the ambiguous unities, silenced voices, emergent and oppositional discourses, that occupy the national space, and thereby instigate a de-totalizing project.

For filmmakers in Asia, Africa, and Latin America, the cinematic representation of minorities presents a challenging problem, and this issue is inseparable from the dictates of the nation-state. The putatively homogeneous nature of the nation-state and its legitimizing meta-narratives begin to come under scrutiny as filmmakers attempt to articulate the experiences and life-worlds of the minorities, whether they be ethnic, religious, linguistic, or caste, who inhabit the national space. Films that thematize the hardships of minorities create a representational space from where the hegemonic discourse of the state can be usefully subverted, and the idea of social and cultural difference emphasized. Indeed, one can see a wholly understandable tension between the idea of the unitary nation and cultural difference in many works of cinema produced in Asian, Latin American, and African countries. This tension is discernible in some of the works of internationally celebrated film directors like Nagisa Oshima of Japan, as well as in the creations of less well-known filmmakers such as Ji Qingchun (China), Park (Korea), and Euthana Mukdasnit (Thailand).

Film commentators in Latin America and Africa also display such propensities to rethink issues and repose questions. For example, if we take Mexican cinema, we find that in the past the concept of *mexicanidad* (Mexicanness) was privileged in intellectual and aesthetic discussions, and was perceived as a leading *topos* guiding Mexican cinema. Distinguished writers, such as the Nobel laureate Octavio Paz, underlined its significance, and both filmmakers and film critics positively valorized it. However, modern commentators of Mexican cinema now highlight how *mexicanidad,* as it was formulated, was élitist, sexist, and class-bound, and privileged the *criollo* over the *mestizo* and the Indians. Through the interrogation of such concepts as "Japaneseness" and "Mexicanness" associated with filmic discourse, scholars are emphasizing the need for the reacquisition of subaltern agency and the repossessing of history. The discursive spaces that they are opening up can have profound consequences in examining afresh the cinemas of the non-West.

THE PUBLIC SPHERE

This discussion of the interconnections between cinema and nationhood leads to the importance of cinema in the public sphere. From the very beginning, cinemas in South America, Africa, and Asia were involved in the public sphere, addressing important questions related to tradition, Westernization, democracy, the caste system, and cultural identity. The pioneering work of the German social philosopher Jürgen Habermas[8] has resulted in the widespread interest in the concept of the public sphere, which has helped to foreground issues of democratization, public participation, and oppositionality. Others such as Oskar Negt and Alexander Kluge[9] have built upon Habermas's work and discussed the ability of cinema to provide a site for the contestation of meaning in an increasingly technologically saturated public sphere, where democratic self-realization and community participation have become much more problematic. The question of the public sphere is particularly important in the case of the nations of Asia, Africa, and Latin America. In many of these countries, cinema has always been perceived as playing a social role and continues to be a significant form of mass communication, even in the face of the censorship which many countries—whether Indonesia or the Philippines or Nigeria—impose.

Many examples of the mutual animation of cinema and the public sphere may be provided. In the 1930s Indian filmmakers addressed the issue of untouchability, which continues to be extremely sensitive. In 1946 Akira Kurosawa made *No Regrets for*

---

[8]Jürgen Habermas, *The Structural Transformation of the Public Sphere: An Inquiry into a Category of Bourgeois Society,* trans. Thomas Burger and Frederick Lawrence (Cambridge, MA: MIT Press, 1991).
[9]Oskar Negt and Alexander Kluge, *Public Sphere and Experience: Towards an Analysis of the Bourgeois and Proletarian Public Sphere* (Minneapolis: University of Minnesota Press, 1993).

Youth, which had a profound impact on Japanese society, raising the whole issue of the democratization of society and leaving an indelible mark on later filmmakers such as Oshima, Kei Kumai, and Kazuo Kuroki. Oshima, in his earlier films, made cinema a vital part of the public sphere by raising issues related to the plight of Korean minorities in Japan, capital punishment, and sexuality. The Indian film director Ritwik Ghatak, in his works, sought to focus on important issues related to the Indian public sphere such as the partitioning of India, the plight of the poor, the predicament of the artists, and the nature of mechanization. Many of the most interesting films made in Argentina after 1983, when the country returned to constitutional democracy, textualize the nature, significance, and urgency of re-democratization and the sweeping aside of fascistic tendencies. African filmmakers like Idrissa Ouedraogo have sought to make cinema a vital adjunct of the public sphere by raising questions concerning tradition, cultural identity, stereotypes, and misleading Western representations of African society.

However, it is in China where this relationship between cinema and the public sphere can be seen in its most vivid form. The work of the post-1980 group of filmmakers, generally referred to as the Fifth Generation of filmmakers, stirred up a great deal of interest both inside and ouside China.... Many of these films deal with the Cultural Revolution and seek to textualize directly or indirectly the phenomenon of the Cultural Revolution and its effects on the rural population, in particular, through an innovative filmmaking approach characterized by minimal narration, striking camera movements, a stress on spatiality, and disruptive montage. Films such as Chen Kaige's *Yellow Earth* (1984), *King of the Children* (1985), *The Big Parade* (1986), and *Farewell, my Concubine* (1993), Zhang Yimou's *Red Sorghum* (1988) and *To Live* (1994), Tian Zhuangzhuang's *The Horse Thief* (1986) and *The Blue Kite* (1991), to mention but a few titles, all bear testimony to a desire to make cinema an indispensable facet of the public sphere.

INTERTEXTUALITY

As indicated at the start of this chapter, cinema was an imported art form that quickly became indigenized in the non-Western world. In a similar manner, European–American theories of cinema are impinging ever more strongly on the thought and sensibility of both filmmakers and film critics in Asian, African, and Latin American countries. The impact of European–American film scholarship on the non-Western world raises some fundamental issues related to comparative film study.

Is it possible to broaden the European-American referents that guide Western film theories so as to accommodate the cinematic experiences of the non-Western world? Do those African, Asian, Middle Eastern, and Latin American intellectuals and film scholars who are vigorously antipathetic to these Western theories subscribe to a merely spurious notion of cultural authenticity and purity? What is the nature of the theoretical space from which Asian, Latin American, and African film scholars and theorists speak? Writing in the context of literature, African-born

Harvard professor Kwarne Anthony Appiah[10] argues against both the pseudo-universalism of Eurocentric theorizations that pose as universal and a "nativism" that nostalgically appeals to an apparently "pure" and "authentic" indigeneous culture. As Appiah points out, while "nativism" may challenge Western norms, the way in which the contest is framed remains unchanged. "The Western emperor has ordered the natives to exchange their robes for trousers: their act of defiance is to insist on tailoring them from homespun material. Given their arguments, plainly, the cultural nationalists do not go far enough; they are blind to the fact that their nativist demands inhabit a Western architecture."[11] These remarks also have a relevance for film theory.

It is clear that Eurocentric paradigms cannot take on the mantle of universal templates or they will hamper a deeper understanding and appreciation of cinemas in the non-Western world.... During the last fifteen years or so, following a retheorization of such issues as the nature of cinematic representation, the role of ideology in cultural production, and the importance of female subjectivity in cinema, the genre of melodrama, for example, has been critically rehabilitated in Western film studies. However, melodramas produced in Latin America, Africa, and Asia—and the majority of films made in these regions have been melodramas—cannot be judged in terms of Western conceptualizations of melodrama. Melodrama functions differently in different cultural contexts, and the melodramatic traditions evolved in these countries, especially in the theater, have acquired highly distinctive characteristics. For example, in India, film melodramas bear the cultural inscriptions of folk theater as well as the Parsee theater of the nineteenth century. Other analytical tools developed by Western film scholars—such as those relating to point of view, the gaze, and textual subjectivity—may also be seen to have limited application. Paul Willemen,[12] for example, has perceptively demonstrated, in relation to the work of the Israeli filmmaker Amos Gitai, how in his cinema it is most decidedly not through point-of-view shots that we are mobilized, but through the differences between one point of view and another even within the one shot. The role of the aesthetic intertexts and cultural contexts, in this respect, are crucial to the understanding of the various non-Western cinemas.

Film is not an isolated art form; it inhabits a common expressive culture fed by tradition, cultural memory, and indigenous modes of symbolic representation. Therefore, films and other arts are mutually implicated in the production of meaning and pleasure, and this deserves to be examined more closely. In most African, Latin American, and Asian countries cinema, from the very beginning, has had a symbiotic relationship with the theater, and continues to do so. Similarly with painting. The complex ways in which traditional arts inspire modern filmmaking would reward further exploration and are vitally, connected to what Paul Willemen refers to as the "orchestration of meaning" in cinema.

---

[10]Kwame Anthony Appiah, *In My Father's House: Africa in the Philosophy of Culture* (Oxford: Oxford University Press, 1992).

[11]Appiah, *In My Father's House*, p. 60.

[12]Paul Willemen, *Looks and Frictions: Essays in Cultural Studies and Film Theory* (Bloomington: Indiana University Press, 1994).

Let us, for example, consider the filmmaker Yasujiro Ozu. In his films, stillness and emptiness play a crucial role in the production of meaning. On the surface, if seen through Western eyes, nothing happens. But at a deeper level of emotional and cultural apprehension, much is going on in those stillnesses and emptinesses. This is, of course, connected with traditional Japanese aesthetics. For example, in Japanese manuals of painting it is remarked that emptiness does not occur until the first ink mark is inscribed on the paper, thereby calling attention to the vital interplay between emptiness and inscriptions as coproducers of meaning. In the same way, African filmmakers have made a conscious attempt to draw on the traditional African arts in filmmaking, especially the art of oral storytelling, and the use of dreams, fantasies, narrative detours, and parallelisms in the films of Ousmane Sembene, Haile Gerima, Souleymane Cissé, and Idrissa Ouedraogo demonstrate this link....

The interconnections between cinema and painting in most Asian countries is a fascinating one. Japanese, Chinese, and Korean filmmakers in the past have tapped the rich resources of painting in framing their shots, creating *mise-en-scène*, and organizing their visual material, and they continue to do so. For example, in the visual style of films such as Chen Kaige's *Yellow Earth*, one can see the impact of Taoism and traditional Chinese paintings of nature. The towering presence of hills and mountains and the diminutive human beings etched against them, the use of a limited range of colors, natural lighting, and the non-perspectival deployment of space, bear testimony to this fact. Similarly, in the work of Ritwik Ghatak, one perceives an attempt to use creatively and innovatively traditional Indian iconography associated with painting to communicate a cinematic experience that is anchored in the past but reaching out to the present.

However, we also need to bear in mind that this is not only a question of aesthetics; there is also an ideological and political aspect to it. For example, in *Yellow Earth*, the extreme long shots, the absence of depth, and the empty spaces that fill the frame can be read as a critique of the Cultural Revolution and its excesses. The supposedly apolitical visuals inscribed in the massive presence of nature therefore make a political statement. Going beyond this reading, as Rey Chow[13] points out, we need to examine the film in terms of its material makings and rethink the cognitive value of emptiness and blankness. As she rightly observes, to make sense of "space," the viewer would have to "view" space from a position whose locality would "see" non-signifying blankness in relation to the representational presence itself. Hence, to grasp the complexities of the enunciative positions and spectatorships that characterize non-Western cinemas, texts—and their intertexts—must be analyzed in terms of ideology and politics as well as artistic apprehension.

Any meaningful discussion of the cinemas of the non-Western world would compel us to confront issues of economics, politics, aesthetics, institutions, technology, and cultural discourse in general. What is the nature of the national film industry? What role do governments play, both positive and negative? How are the cinema industries located at the local and the global? How are they dealing with the hege-

---

[13]Rey Chow, *Primitive Passions: Visibility, Ethnography, and Contemporary Chinese Cinema* (New York: Columbia University Press, 1995).

mony of Hollywood? How do filmmakers seek to construct alternative histories and cultural identities? These and similar issues that merit closer anlaysis. . . . What I have sought to do in this [essay] is to raise some salient issues related to the cinemas of the non-Western world. As Paul Willemen[14] observes, what the outstanding filmmakers from Asia, Africa, and Latin America have done is to start from a recognition of the multilayeredness of their own cultural-historical formations, with each layer being shaped by intricate linkages between local as well as international forces. As a consequence, these filmmakers suggest a way of inhabiting one's culture that is neither myopically nationalist nor evasively cosmopolitan. This is the ideal that stands before the filmmakers of the non-Western world.

2000

---

[14]Willemen, *Questions of Third Cinema.*

INDEX

We have designed this index to help the reader find discussions of directors, individual films, film critics, and theorists that cut across the otherwise topical organization of *Film Theory and Criticism*. However, those references are indexed only when they are multiple or when there is an extended discussion. Single references within only one article are therefore, for the most part, not included unless they are otherwise significant. Any essays included by a given author are listed by page number under that author's name, along with any references to his or her work in other essays. Films are listed under the heading of their director and in their most commonly used title. When authors have cited slightly different film titles (for reasons of translation or British versus American spelling), and when they have transliterated names with slight differences (Vertov/Vertoff, Gorki/Gorky), we have not altered their texts but grouped the references in the index under the most familiar spelling.

CPSIA information can be obtained at www.ICGtesting.com
Printed in the USA
BVOW09s1940070115

382261BV00002B/2/P